The Oxford Dictionary of American Quotations

The Oxford Dictionary of American Quotations

Selected and Annotated by

Hugh Rawson and Margaret Miner

OXFORD
UNIVERSITY PRESS

OXFORD
UNIVERSITY PRESS

Oxford University Press, Inc., publishes works that furthers
Oxford University's objective of excellence in research, scholarship, and education.

Oxford New York
Auckland Cape Town Dar es Salaam Hong Kong Karachi
Kuala Lumpur Madrid Melbourne Mexico City Nairobi
New Delhi Shanghai Taipei Toronto

With offices in
Argentina Austria Brazil Chile Czech Republic France Greece
Guatemala Hungary Italy Japan Poland Portugal Singapore
South Korea Switzerland Thailand Turkey Ukraine Vietnam

Published by Oxford University Press, Inc.
198 Madison Avenue, New York, New York, 10016
http://www.oup.com/us

The first edition of this book was published as *The American Heritage Dictionary of American Quotations* by Penguin Reference in 1997.

Library of Congress Cataloging-in-Publication Data

The Oxford dictionary of American quotations / selected and annotated
by Hugh Rawson & Margaret Miner.
p. cm.
Rev. ed. of: American heritage dictionary of American quotations.
1997.
ISBN-13: 978-0-19-516823-5 ISBN-10: 0-19-516823-2
1. Quotations, American—Dictionaries. I. Rawson, Hugh. II. Miner,
Margaret. III. American heritage dictionary of American quotations.
PN6081.A623 2006
081.03—dc22

2005027725

Printing number: 9 8 7 6 5 4 3 2 1

Printed in the United States of America on acid-free paper

For our nieces and nephews
Peter, Caroline, Robert, James, Rachel
Laura, Jennifer, Zoë, Peter
and of the rising generation
Sunday *and* Jackson

Introduction

Who is this American, this new man?
—J. Hector St. John de Crèvecoeur

A morsel of genuine history is so rare a thing as to be always valuable.
—Thomas Jefferson

By necessity, by proclivity, and by delight, we all quote.
—Ralph Waldo Emerson

The Oxford Dictionary of American Quotations weaves together the three strands picked out by de Crèvecoeur, Jefferson, and Emerson: It is a collection, organized along historical lines, of nearly six thousand memorable quotations on more than five hundred some aspects of American life and culture. As a new millennium begins, this book offers a unique way of looking back to see how far we have traveled.

From "Advertising" to "Massachusetts" to "Zeal," from the "American Revolution" to "Marriage" to "the West," *The Oxford Dictionary of American Quotations* records our national experience as viewed by Americans from all walks of life—presidents and generals, pioneers and poets, entertainers and lawyers, athletes and Native American chiefs. John and Abigail Adams, Thomas Jefferson, and Abraham Lincoln are here, of course—and so are Yogi Berra, Bill Gates, John Kerry, Grover Norquist, and Paul Newman, along with Madonna, the Roosevelts (Teddy, F.D.R., and Eleanor), Gertrude Stein, John Updike, Oprah Winfrey, the Wachowski brothers (of *Matrix* fame), and Brigham Young. And so are such foreign observers of the American scene as Alexis de Tocqueville, Harriett Martineau, Charles Dickens, and Rudyard Kipling. We also have counted as Americans a few foreigners who spent significant parts of their working lives in this country, such as W. H. Auden, while retaining our claim on Americans who spent most of their alives abroad, such as T. S. Eliot.

This new second edition is a revision of the first as well as a substantial expansion of it. Hundreds of new quotations have been added. At the same time, every quotation in the first edition has been re-examined, with the result that many improvements have been made in annotations and sourcing details. Thus, we have benefited from the recent discovery that one of the more famous quotes in American history, "Go west, young man," has been attributed wrongly for many years to John B. L. Soule, editor of the

Terre Haute (Ind.) *Express*. (Credit more properly belongs to *New York Tribune* editor Horace Greeley, previously thought to have been merely the popularizer of the idea.)

For this edition some completely new categories have been added (on the current Iraq war, for instance), while existing topical categories have been brought up to date. For example, the section on "Insults" now includes Arnold Schwarzenegger's dismissal of his political opponents as "girlie-men" (along with a note that tracks this particular epithet as far back as 1894); "Politics and Politicians" now ends with Jack Rosenthal's pithy insight of 2004 that "Spin pays," and "Foreign Policy" concludes with Secretary of Defense Donald Rumsfeld's declaration that "We don't do empire," followed by President George W. Bush's insistence that "America will never seek a permission slip to defend the security of our people."

Still other categories have been enlarged with older quotations that seem to resonate more than they did originally, such as the line (also in "Politics and Politicians") from the 1997 film *Wag the Dog*: "You want to win this election, you better change the subject. You wanna change the subject, you better have a war. It's show business," and E. B. White's uncannily prescient warning (from 1949) of New York's vulnerability: "The city, for the first time in its long history is destructible. A single flight of planes no bigger than a wedge of geese can quickly end this island fantasy, burn the towers, crumble the bridges, turn the underground passages into lethal chambers, cremate the millions. The intimation of mortality is part of New York now: in the sound of jets overhead, in the black headlines of the latest edition."

As in the first edition, quotations have been chosen not only for their historical significance but with an eye to their future utility. A great many of the entries in this book convey insights that transcend the immediate situations—often moments of stress and conflict—in which the words were written or spoken. They range from the brave reply of John Paul Jones, "I have not yet begun to fight," when asked to surrender his ship, to Jefferson's warning, "Our liberty depends on the freedom of the press, and that cannot be limited without being lost," to Thoreau's perception that "A man more right than his neighbors constitutes a majority of one," to Lincoln's "A house divided against itself cannot stand," to Mae West's admission that "I used to be Snow White—but I drifted," to Jim Henson's witty admonition (wearing his Miss Piggy mask), "Never eat more than you can lift," to President George W. Bush's reaffirmation in the course of a eulogy for the seven astronauts killed when the space shuttle *Columbia* disintegrated that "The cause of exploration and discovery is not an option we choose; it is a desire written in the human heart."

The Oxford Dictionary of American Quotations is arranged to give readers at least three chances to find the quotations they want—through the main text, which is organized by subject; through the keyword index at the back of the book; and through the author index. Thus, Emerson's famous quote about building a better mousetrap—"If a man can make a better book, preach a better sermon, or make a better mousetrap than his neighbor, the world will make a beaten path to his door"—is filed in the main text under "Excellence." But the reader may also find the quote in the keyword index under "mousetrap." Finally, by consulting the author index under Emerson, the reader also will be led back to the right quote in the "Excellence" category. Birth and death dates also are given in the author index, as well as pseudonyms and titles.

The subject categories are listed alphabetically in the main text, with the principal topics printed in boldface letters along the left-hand margin of the page. Thus:

Abolition
Action & Doing
Adventure

and so on, through to

Wyoming
Youth
Zeal

Most subject categories also include references to related topics. These are printed in small-cap letters beneath the main heads. For example:

Action & Doing

See also ADVENTURE; BOLDNESS & INITIATIVE; BUSINESS; DANGER & DANGEROUS PEOPLE; ROOSEVELT, THEODORE; WORK & WORKERS.

Within the subject categories, quotations are arranged in chronological order. They also are numbered, with a new sequence beginning on each page. Thus, Emerson's mousetrap quote, the fourth quote on page 240, is listed in the keyword and author indexes as 240:4. Following each quotation is the name of the author in boldface (**Anonymous**, if unknown), the title and date of the source. In instances where quotations are drawn from later works, the year of publication is enclosed in brackets—[1998], for example. Many of the quotations are also are accompanied by notes. These are indicated with a star icon: ★.

The extensive annotations, together with the chronological method of arranging quotations within subject categories, constitute the chief features that distinguish *The Oxford Dictionary of American Quotations* from other collections of quotations. The notes—approximately thirty percent of the entries are annotated—set the quotations in historical context, provide additional information about the writer or speaker, and give earlier and later examples of similar turns of phrase. Many of the notes also cite other sources for attributions and refer the reader to related topics.

In addition, the notes assess questions of authenticity and originality in the case of quotations that have been commonly attributed to the wrong person, "improved" in some way over the years, or simply made up out of whole cloth. An example of the first sort is "Put all your eggs in one basket—and watch that basket," commonly credited to Mark Twain, who included the line in *Pudd'nhead Wilson*. But did he originate it? Actually, as noted in "Wisdom, Words of," Twain was given this advice, and in these very words, at dinner on the night of April 6, 1893, by a canny Scotsman: Andrew Carnegie.

Other quotations have become famous because they sound as though they *should* have been said or because they support patriotic interpretations of the past. Thus, Patrick Henry's ringing "give me liberty or give me death" has been repeated in schoolbooks for generations. Strangely, however, neither Washington nor Jefferson, who were present in the Virginia House of Burgess when Henry made this presumably memorable declaration, mentioned it in their own writings. Their silence is suspicious. The quotation, it turns out, comes from a biography of Henry that was published more than forty years after the event. The same biographer also added considerable sheen to Henry's "If this be treason, make the most of it," neglecting to mention that the orator went on to beg the pardon of the House if in the heat of moment he had said more than he had intended.

Spurious quotes are just as useful as real ones for making points, of course, and may be repeated unknowingly over and over again. The authority of "Lincoln," in particular, as noted in the entry on the sixteenth president, often is invoked by citing him as the source for words he never said. Thus, Ronald Reagan quoted Lincoln at the 1992 Republic national convention as having said, "You cannot strengthen the weak by weakening the strong. You cannot help the wage earner by pulling down the wage payer. You cannot help men permanently by doing for them what they could and should do for themselves." But these solid, conservative sentiments actually came from the pen of a Rev. William John Henry Boetcker in 1916.

This dictionary's second distinctive feature, the chronological method of organization within subjects, helps show how Americans' understanding and views have developed over time on such diverse topics as "Education" and the "Environment," the "Media" and "Military Strategy," the "Presidency" and "George Washington." Thus, under "Freedom," Patrick Henry precedes Davy Crockett, who precedes Thoreau, who precedes, among others—and moving forward in time—Lincoln, Harriet Tubman, Oliver Wendell Holmes, Jr., Franklin D. Roosevelt, and Martin Luther King, Jr. The section on the "West" begins optimistically with Thoreau in 1836 ("Eastward I go only by force; but westward I go free") and concludes with Wallace Stegner in 1991 ("Ghost towns and dust bowls, like motels, are western inventions"). That on "Women" ranges forward from Abigail Adams, writing to her husband in 1776 ("Men of sense of all ages abhor those customs which treat us only as vassals of your sex"), to Gloria Steinem, addressing Yale students more than two hundred years later ("Some of us are becoming the men we wanted to marry").

The chronological arrangement also allows one to follow the progress of the "American Revolution," the "Civil War," "World War I," "World War II," and other events and related sequences, such as "Foreign Policy," national elections (see "Political Slogans"), and "Watergate." Thus, the section on the Civil War begins with William Seward's prewar warning (1858) of an "irrepressible conflict," then encapsulates key moments in the conflict, from Confederate General Barnard Bee's rallying cry at the first Battle of Bull Run in 1861, "See, there is Jackson, standing like a stone wall," to Lincoln's complaint in 1862, "If McClellan is not using the army, I should like to borrow it for a while," to Sherman's 1864 signal "Hold out, Relief is coming" (often erroneously reported as "Hold the fort. I am coming"). And this section concludes with the postwar observation of Mark Twain, "In the South, the war is what A.D. is elsewhere; they date from it" (1883), and Gertrude Stein's summation (1937): "There will never be anything in America more interesting than the Civil War, never."

This dictionary's notes and method of organization suit it for browsing as well as for reference. Both readers with an interest in history and those searching for apt quotations are likely to make many happy discoveries here. Anyone who is disappointed by not finding a favorite quotation is invited to submit it, along with the necessary source details, to the editors in care of the publisher so that it can be considered for inclusion when the next edition is prepared.

Acknowledgments

While this collection is the product of wide reading in books, newspapers, and magazines, as well as tuning in to radio and television, watching movies, and following up the suggestions of friends, it nevertheless is true that no collection of this sort can be assembled without also consulting other dictionaries of quotations both to ensure comprehensive coverage and to verify our own findings.

General works that we found to be particularly valuable, aside from our own *The New International Dictionary of Quotations* (Signet, 3rd edition, 2000), which served as a starting point for this book, included *Bartlett's Familiar Quotations* (17th edition, Justin Kaplan, ed., Little, Brown and Co., 2002), *A New Dictionary of Quotations on Historical Principles from Ancient and Modern Sources* (H. L. Mencken, Knopf, 1942), *Respectfully Quoted* (Suzy Platt, ed., Library of Congress, 1989), the *International Thesaurus of Quotations* (Rhoda Thomas Tripp, ed., Thomas Y. Crowell Co., 1970), *The Penguin Thesaurus of Quotations* (M. J. Cohen, Penguin Books, 1998), the *Quotationary* (Leonard Roy Frank, Random House, 2001), and the *Oxford Dictionary of Quotations* (6th edition, Elizabeth Knowles, ed., Oxford University Press, 2004).

Dictionaries dealing specifically with American quotations that we used included *American Quotations* (Gorton Carruth and Eugene Ehrlich, Wings Books, 1992), *The New York Public Library Book of 20th-Century Quotations* (ed. by Stephen Donadio et al., Warner Books, 1992), *A Dictionary of American Proverbs* (Wolfgang Mieder, editor in chief, Oxford University Press, 1992), *Words to Make My Children Live: A Book of African American Quotations* (Deirdre Mullane, Anchor Books, 1995), *The Oxford Dictionary of American Legal Quotations* (Fred R. Shapiro, Oxford University Press, 1993), and *American Sayings* (Henry F. Woods, Duell, Sloan and Pearce, 1945).

Other specialized dictionaries of help to us included *A Dictionary of Military and Naval Quotations* (Robert Debs Heinl, Jr., United States Naval Institute, 1966), *The Mystery Lovers' Book of Quotations* (Jane E. Horning, Mysterious Press, 1988), *The New Quotable Woman* (Elaine Partnow, Facts on File, 1992), *Nobody Said It Better!* (Miriam Ringo, Rand McNally, 1980), *The Travellers' Dictionary of Quotations* (Peter Yapp, Routledge & Kegan Paul, 1983), the *Macmillan Dictionary of Political Quotations* (Lewis D. Eigen and Jonathan P. Siegel, Macmillan Publishing Co., 1993), and the *Oxford Dictionary of Political Quotations* (Anthony Jay, ed., 1996).

For checking attributions for quotations, we frequently consulted *They Never Said It* (Paul F. Boller, Jr. and John George, Oxford University Press, 1989) and *Nice Guys Finish Seventh* (Ralph Keyes, HarperCollins Publishers, 1992).

Fertile sources of quotations, aside from back issues (into the 1950s) of *American Heritage* magazine, included *Looking Far West* (ed. by Frank Bergon and Zeese Papanikolas, Meridian, 1978), *The Heritage of America* (ed. by Henry Steele Commager and Allan Nevins, Little, Brown and Co., 1939), *A Documentary History of the United States* (5th ed., Richard D. Heffner, Mentor, 1991), and *The Faber Book of America* (ed. By Christopher Ricks and William L. Vance, Faber and Faber, 1992).

Collections of twentieth-century quotations that we consulted included *The Oxford Dictionary of Modern Quotations* (Tony Augarde, ed., Oxford University Press, 1991), *Simpson's Contempory Quotations* (James B. Simpson, HarperCollins, 1997), and the *New Penguin Dictionary of Modern Quotations* (Robert Andrews, Penguin Books, 2001).

Other references that were kept close at hand when preparing notes for quotations included *The Reader's Encyclopedia* (William Rose Benét, Thomas Y. Crowell Co., 2nd edition, 1965), *Benét's Encyclopedia of American Literature* (ed. by George Perkins, Barbara Perkins, and Philip Leininger, HarperCollins, 1991), *A Dictionary of Contemporary American History* (Stanley Hochman and Eleanor Hochman, Signet, 1993), *The Reader's Encyclopedia of the American West* (Howard R. Lamar, ed., Thomas Y. Crowell Co., 1977), *Folk Song USA* (John A. and Alan Lomax, Plume, 1975), *The Oxford History of the American People* (Samuel Eliot Morison, Oxford University Press, 1965), and *Safire's New Political Dictionary* (William Safire, Random House, 1978). For dating of quotations from films, we consider the annually published Leonard Maltin's *Movie & Video Guide* (Signet) to be authoritative.

Many individuals also helped us in preparing both editions in various ways, including Kerry Acker; Cathleen Anderson; Valerie G. Annis, librarian at Minor Memorial Library, Roxbury, Connecticut, her predecessor, Tim Beard, and staff members Betty Synnestvedt, Silky Berger, and Peter Titchner; Anonymous, editor at *Soap Opera Digest*; Bredna Bailey at the Mark Twain Project, the University of California at Berkeley; David Barrett at *Golf* magazine; Douglas Brinkley; Jesse Cohen; Robert Creamer; Harold Davis at the Brownsville Mills health store in Brownsville, Nebraska; Stuart Davis at The Nature Conservancy; Elizabeth Dunn, librarian at the Hartman Center, Duke University; Christopher A. Fuchs, research physicist at Lucent Technologies' Bell Labs; Abigail Fuller; Peter Galison, historian of science and physics at Harvard University; Jody Goggins at Wendy's International; Spencer Howard at the Herbert Hoover Presidential Library; Shaughan Lavine; Barbara Livesey (for lightning-fast research); Andrew Lytle; Arthur Maisel; Leonard Maltin; Martin Marty and Micah Marty; Joyce Melito, librarian at Saatchi & Saatchi Advertising in New York City; Dr. Albert Meloni at the Institute for American Indian Studies in Washington, Connecticut; Mary Elizabeth Miner and Claire Wescott, for assistance on the indexes; Henry Price; Noel Rae; Emily Robinson at The National Archives; Virginia Rodriguez at the *Washington Post*; Jeff Rovin; physicist John A. Wheeler of Princeton University; Robert Spencer Wilson, literary editor of *Civilization* magazine; Catherine Rawson for help in indexing; Byron Preiss, president, and Michael Sagalyn, executive editor, at Byron Preiss Visual Publications, Inc.; and extra thanks, for duty far and beyond the normal call of family obligations, to William Fuller and, on this new edition, Nathaniel Rawson.

We also are indebted to our agent, the late Jane Jordan Browne; her successor as head of the firm, Danielle Egan-Miller; our editor at Oxford University Press, Erin McKean; our index copyeditor, Stephen Dodson; and to Oxford's director of editorial development and production, Timothy DeWerff.

Hugh Rawson, Margaret Miner
Roxbury, Conn.
August 2005

The Oxford Dictionary of American Quotations

Abolition

See RACES & PEOPLES; SLAVERY.

Action & Doing

See also ADVENTURE; BOLDNESS & INITIATIVE; BUSINESS; DANGER & DANGEROUS PEOPLE; DECISION; ROOSEVELT, THEODORE; WORK & WORKERS.

All great and honorable actions are accompanied with great difficulties. 1
—**William Bradford,** *History of Plymouth Plantation*, written 1630–1651

★ Bradford, longtime governor of the colony—he was reelected thirty times—referred here to the dangers that the Pilgrims foresaw in leaving Holland in 1620 for a new land. His history (to 1646) disappeared during the American Revolution, but was discovered in a library in London in 1855 and returned to Massachusetts.

It is wonderful how much may be done if we are always doing. 2
—**Thomas Jefferson,** letter to Martha Jefferson, May 5, 1787

I leave this rule for others when I'm dead, 3
Be always sure you're right—then go ahead.
—**David Crockett,** his motto from the War of 1812, in his *Narrative of the Life of David Crockett*, 1834

Always do what you are afraid to do. 4
—**Mary Moody Emerson,** motto

★ She was the aunt of Ralph Waldo Emerson, and a famous eccentric: just four feet, three inches tall, she slept in a coffin-shaped bed. She had, however, a large spirit, and was an expansive, sophisticated religious thinker. She inspired her nephew to trust his own ideas, enthusiasms, and perceptions.

In this country . . . men seem to live for action as long as they can and sink into apathy when they retire. 5
—**Charles Francis Adams,** diary, April 15, 1836

Let us, then, be up and doing, 6
With a heart for any fate;
Still achieving, still pursuing,
Learn to labor and to wait.
—**Henry Wadsworth Longfellow,** *A Psalm of Life*, 1839

★ See also Longfellow at HUMANS & HUMAN NATURE.

But do your thing, and I shall know you. 7
—**Ralph Waldo Emerson,** *Self-Reliance*, in *Essays: First Series*, 1841

★ The hippies of the 1960s may have stumbled independently upon the motto "do your own thing," since the phrase here was changed by an editor to "do your own work" in the 1903 edition of Emerson's writings; it has appeared that way in all subsequent collections. Or possibly young people in the 1960s were influenced by Chaucer, who used the expression a number of times in *The Canterbury Tales*, e.g., from "The Clerk's Tale": "Ye been oure lord; dooth with youre owene thyng."

1 Something attempted, something done
Has earned a night's repose.
—**Henry Wadsworth Longfellow,** *The Village Blacksmith*, 1842

2 The reward of a thing well done, is to have done it.
—**Ralph Waldo Emerson,** *Nominalist and Realist*, in *Essays: Second Series*, 1844

3 It is not light that is needed but fire.
—**Frederick Douglass**, *The Hypocrisy of American Slavery*, July 4, 1852

★ Douglass continued, "Not the gentle shower, but thunder. We need the storm, the whirlwind, and the earthquake." See also James Baldwin at RACES & PEOPLE.

4 What the Puritans gave the world was not thought but action.
—**Wendell Phillips,** *The Pilgrims*, speech, Dec. 21, 1855

5 I find the great thing in this world is not so much where we stand, as in what direction we are moving: to reach the port of heaven, we must sail sometimes with the wind and sometimes against it—but we must sail, and not drift, nor lie at anchor.
—**Oliver Wendell Holmes, Sr.,** *The Autocrat of the Breakfast-Table*, 1858

6 As we are, so we do; and as we do, so is it done to us; we are the builders of our fortunes.
—**Ralph Waldo Emerson,** *Worship*, in *The Conduct of Life*, 1860

★ See also Emerson on when "duty whispers" at YOUTH.

7 I am only one,
But still I am one.
I cannot do everything,
But still I can do something;
And because I cannot do everything
I will not refuse to do the something that I can do.
—**Edward Everett Hale,** *Lend a Hand*, c. 1871

★ Hale founded the first Lend a Hand Club, see CHARITY & PHILANTHROPY.

8 I am a verb.
—**Ulysses S. Grant,** letter to his physician, John H. Douglas, July 1885

★ For God as a verb, see R. Buckminster Fuller at GOD.

9 'Tis the motive exalts the action;
'Tis the doing, and not the deed.
—**Margaret Junkin Preston,** *The Proclamation of Miles Standish*, c. 1875

10 It is better to light one candle than to curse the darkness.
—**Christopher Society,** motto

★ Adlai Stevenson praised Eleanor Roosevelt for lighting a candle; see VIRTUE.

Carry a message to Garcia. 1

—**Elbert Hubbard,** *A Message to Garcia*, March 1899

★ Similar to "Just do it." Hubbard's article, which appeared in his magazine, *The Philistine*, called on young men "to be loyal to a trust, to act promptly, concentrate their energies, do a thing—'carry a message to Garcia.' " He was referring to the exploits of Lt. Andrew Summers Rowan of the U.S. Army Bureau of Intelligence, who, under orders from Pres. William McKinley, made his way into Cuba in 1898 to deliver a message to Gen. Calixto García y Iñiguez, the leader of a revolt against Spanish rule. See also SPANISH-AMERICAN WAR. Rowan received the Distinguished Service Cross for this achievement. Hubbard, a strange mixture of reformer, huckster, and businessman, died in 1915 on the *Lusitania*, which was torpedoed off the coast of Ireland. He and Alfred Vanderbilt were the most famous victims.

Get action. Seize the moment. Man was never intended to become an oyster. 2

—**Theodore Roosevelt,** to his children, quoted in David McCullough, *Mornings on Horseback* [1981] "Seize the day," or *carpe diem*, dates back at least to Horace, *Odes* I, xi.

It is not the critic who counts, not the man who points out how the strong man stum- 3
bles, or where the doer of deeds could have done better. The credit belongs to the man who is actually in the arena; whose face is marred by dust and sweat and blood; who strives valiantly; who errs and comes short again and again, because there is no effort without error and shortcoming; but who does actually strive to do the deeds; who knows the great enthusiasms, the great devotions; who spends himself in a worthy cause; who, at the best, knows in the end the triumph of high achievement; and who, at the worst, if he fails, at least fails while daring greatly, so that his place shall never be with those cold and timid souls who know neither victory nor defeat.

—**Theodore Roosevelt,** speech, the Sorbonne, Paris, France, April 23, 1910

★ Included in Roosevelt's *The Strenuous Life*, 1926, with the title *Citizenship in a Republic.*

Life is action and passion. 4

—**Oliver Wendell Holmes, Jr.,** speech, to Harvard Law School alumni, New York City, Feb. 1916

★ More at LIFE.

5

There are times when words seem empty and only actions seem great.

—**Woodrow Wilson**, Memorial Day address, May 30, 1917

To act is to affirm the value of an end. 6

—**Oliver Wendell Holmes, Jr.,** Harvard College reunion, June 28, 1911

The country needs and, unless I mistake its temper, the country demands bold, per- 7
sistent experimentation. It is common sense to take a method and try it. If it fails, admit it frankly and try another. But above all, try something.

—**Franklin D. Roosevelt,** Oglethorpe University, Atlanta, Ga., May 22, 1932

1 By acting now we will assuredly make mistakes. But if we don't act now, I'm afraid we will not have even the opportunity to make mistakes a little later.

—**Franklin D. Roosevelt**, remark, March 28, 1933, in *The New York Times* [May 9, 1998]

★ The comment was made in the White House living quarters to a group of lawmakers, some of whom were urging the recently inaugurated president to move deliberately in grappling with the nation's economic problems. It was remembered by Jennings Randolph, then a young representative and later a senator, and included in his obituary.

2 The difficult we do immediately. The impossible takes a little longer.

—**U.S. Army Service Forces,** motto, World War II

★ A number of military groups have used a variant of this motto. One early source is Anthony Trollope, "The difficult is done at once; the impossible takes a little longer," *Phineas Redux*, 1873. Even earlier, French finance minister Charles-Alexandre de Calonne is said to have replied to a request from Marie-Antoinette, which she acknowledged would be "difficult," "If it is only difficult, it is done; if it is impossible, we shall see."

3 He started to sing as he tackled the thing
That couldn't be done, and he did it.

—**Edgar A. Guest,** *It Couldn't Be Done*, in *The Collected Works of Edgar A. Guest*, 1934

4 How do you know what you're going to do until you do it? The answer is, you don't. It's a stupid question.

—**J.D. Salinger,** *The Catcher in the Rye*, 1951

5 Watch what we do, not what we say.

—**John Mitchell,** remark reported in the press, July 1969

★ This is the usual rendering; but in *Respectfully Quoted*, published by the Library of Congress, the remark is given as, "You will be better advised to watch what we do instead of what we say." Attorney General Mitchell was talking to civil rights workers protesting the Nixon administration's policies.

6 It can be done!

—**Colin Powell,** *My American Journey*, 1995

★ Gen. Powell listed this as one of his guiding maxims (the fourth), leading many to wonder if he was referring to a run for the presidency. Later in the year, he declined the opportunity, and in 1997 he became Secretary of State under George W. Bush. For another maxim from his list, see OPTIMISM & PESSIMISM.

7 We're history's actors ... and you, all of you, will be left to just study what we do.

—**Anonymous,** senior White House advisor, summer 2002, quoted by Ron Suskind, *The New York Times Magazine* [Oct. 17, 2004]

★ More at FOREIGN POLICY.

Adventure, Exploration & Discovery

See also DANGER & DANGEROUS PEOPLE; BOLDNESS & INITIATIVE.

For premature adventure one pays an atrocious price. 1

—F. Scott Fitzgerald, letter to his daughter, Scottie, quoted in *The New Yorker* [July 3, 2000]

★ The quote continues "It's the logic of life that no young person ever gets away with anything."

I live only in the moment in this strange unmortal space, crowded with beauty, pierced with danger. 2

—Charles Lindbergh, *Spirit of St. Louis*, 1954

★ His transatlantic flight was in 1927. A saying of his, recorded in Carl Sandburg's *The Proverbs of a People*, in *Good Morning, America*, 1928, was: "There must be pioneers, and some of them get killed." See also Amelia Earhart at COURAGE.

To boldly go where no man has gone before. 3

—Gene Roddenberry, *Star Trek* lead-in, 1966–69

★ More fully, "Space—the final frontier. . . . These are the voyages of the starship *Enterprise*. Its five-year mission: to explore strange new worlds, to seek out new life and new civilizations, to boldly go where no man has gone before."

The cause of exploration and discovery is not an option we choose; it is a desire written in the human heart. 4

—**George W. Bush,** memorial speech for the seven crew members of the space craft Columbia, which had broken to pieces three days earlier, Feb. 4, 2003

Adversity

See ANXIETY & WORRY; BAD TIMES; TROUBLE.

Advertising, Advertising Slogans, & Publicity

Secure the shadow ere the substance fade. 5

—Anonymous, advertising slogan from the 1840s promoting photography

★ The reference is to the widespread custom of taking daguerreotype portraits of dead people, children especially. Requests for such portraits became an important source of income for many of the itinerant "professors" of photography who fanned out across the nation in the mid 1840s. By the next decade, photographic supply houses offered framing mats in black and daguerreotype cases with sentimental designs for deathbed portraits, according to William Welling's *Photography in America: The Formative Years, 1839–1900*.

Only a woman can understand a woman's ills. 6

—Lydia E. Pinkham, slogan for her Vegetable Compound, c. 1875

★ The tonic was patented in 1876. The "sure cure" contained almost 18 percent alcohol, as well as some herbal extracts, according to Gerald Carson, *American Heritage*, June 1971. For another appeal to women, *see* Shirley Polykoff's copy for Miss Clairol at QUESTIONS & ANSWERS.

1 Satisfaction Guaranteed or Your Money Back!

—**Aaron Montgomery Ward, motto,** *Montgomery Ward Catalogue,* 1875

★ The Montgomery Ward mail order catalogue transformed rural life in America. The store existed from 1872 to 2001.

2 The advertisements in a newspaper are more full of knowledge in respect to what is going on in a state or community than the editorial columns are.

—**Henry Ward Beecher,** *Proverbs from Plymouth Pulpit*, 1887

3 You press the button, we do the rest.

—**George Eastman,** c. 1889

★ Eastman wrote this copy for his fabulously successful Kodak camera, which he patented in September 1888. He coined the name *Kodak*, too; it was catchy, he thought. Starting in 1889, when the camera went on the market, Kodak campaigned to have shutterbugs send their film to its plant in Rochester, N.Y., for developing and printing. Within a year, the company was processing 6,000 to 7,000 negatives a day. The Kodak rapidly became known the world round, as witness this verse from the 1893 Gilbert and Sullivan operetta *Utopia, Limited*. Two demure English girls are singing: "To diagnose / Our modest pose / The Kodaks do their best: / If evidence you would possess / Of what is maiden bashfulness, / You only need a button press— / And we do all the rest."

4 Half the money I spend on advertising is wasted, and the trouble is, I don't know which half.

—**John Wanamaker,** quoted in David Ogilvy, *Confessions of an Advertising Man* [1963]

★ Ogilvy gave equal credit for this observation to William Lever, the founder of Lever Brothers, who died in 1925. Mr. Lever became Lord Leverhulme and Lever Brothers became the cornerstone of Unilever. The anxiety concerning wasted money faded in the next century. See Douglas Rushkoff below.

★ See also a similar, anonymous quote from the 1980s at DOCTORS & MEDICINE.

5 99 44/100 per cent pure.

—**Harley Procter,** slogan for Ivory soap, 1904

★ Procter & Gamble's most famous claim for its most famous product was based on the theory that pure soap consists of nothing but fatty acids and alkali. Chemical analysis of Ivory showed that it contained 0.11 percent uncombined alkali, 0.28 percent carbonates, and 0.17 percent mineral matter, a total of 0.56 percent of impurities, or, stated positively, that it was 99 44/100 percent pure. Mr. Procter also was responsible for dreaming up the Ivory name (trademarked July 18, 1879) while attending church in Cincinnati. His inspiration was the reading of the 45th psalm, eighth verse: "All thy garments smell of myrrh, and aloes, and cassia, out of the ivory palaces, whereby they have made thee glad."

6 They all laughed when I sat down at the piano, But oh!, when I began to play.

—**John Caples,** legendary ad copy for mail-order piano lessons, 1925

★ Zelda Fitzgerald followed her famous comment on the power of advertising (see below) with a specific reference to Caples's copy: "I *still* believe," she wrote, "that one can learn to play the piano by mail and that mud will give you a perfect complexion."

Quick, Henry, the Flit! 1

—**Dr. Seuss (Theodor Seuss Geisel),** ad copy for the Flit account of Standard Oil of New Jersey, 1928

★ The wife of advertising executive H. K. McCann happened to see a cartoon in which freelancer Geisel used this line. This led to his being hired as the artist for the account. Flit, by the way, was a spray to kill flying insects.

The pause that refreshes. 2

—**Anonymous,** Coca-Cola Company; slogan, 1929

We are living in an age of publicity. It used to be only saloons and circuses that 3
wanted their name in the paper, but now it's corporations, churches, preachers, scientists, colleges, and cemeteries.

—**Will Rogers,** *Daily Telegrams*, June 23, 1931

We grew up founding our dreams on the infinite promise of American advertising. 4

—**Zelda Fitzgerald,** *Save Me the Waltz*, 1932

★ True, too true, despite a few naysayers, like Judge William Jay Gaynor, who while campaigning for mayor of New York City in 1909, gave a speech to the Advertising Men's League, in which he undiplomatically quoted *The Merchant of Venice*: "Oh what a goodly outside falsehood hath!" In a rare triumph for plain speaking, Judge Gaynor won the election. Unfortunately, a year later, he was shot and seriously wounded by a disgruntled city employee. See also Gaynor under LANGUAGE & WORDS.

I think that I shall never see 5
A billboard lovely as a tree.
Indeed, unless the billboards fall,
I'll never see a tree at all.

—**Ogden Nash,** *Song of the Open Road*, in *Happy Days*, 1933

Within This Vale 6
Of Toil and Sin
Your Head Grows Bald
But Not Your Chin
Burma-Shave

—**Allan G. Odell,** advertising jingle, c. 1940

★ Starting in 1925, and peaking in the early 1950s, Burma-Shave jingles amused American motorists. Each line in a jingle appeared on a small sign, with the signs set about one hundred feet apart. Burma Vita Inc. was an Odell family business, and the copy was produced first by the Odells and later by the public in nation-wide contests. The jingle above was Mr. Odell's favorite. Another popular one was "Henry the Eighth / Sure Had Trouble / Short-Term Wives / Long-Term Stubble / Burma-Shave." And again mining the distant past: "Pity All / The Mighty Caesars / They Pulled / Each Whisker Out / With Tweezers / Burma-Shave."

Hey, quit kicking sand in my face. 7

—**Charles Roman,** ad for the Charles Atlas Company, from c. 1930

★ In this ad, which in various versions appeared in comic books and magazines for years, a "ninety-seven pound weakling" is bullied by a big fellow at the beach, but, after a course of muscle building, he defeats the bad guy. The story is based on a true event: In 1909, Angelo Siciliano, age 15, took his girl to the beach at Coney Island, and a lifeguard kicked sand in his face. The young man developed a course of "dynamic tension" exercises that worked wonders, and he changed his name to Charles Atlas. His fortune was made when he teamed up with advertiser Charles Roman, and in 1929 opened a mail-order body-building business. In 1991, Pres. George H. Bush described Iraqi dictator Saddam Hussein as "a classic bully who thinks he can get away with kicking sand in the face of the world." See also Atlas at HEALTH.

1 The art of publicity is a black art; but it has come to stay, and every year adds to its potency.

—**Learned Hand,** speech at the Elizabethan Club, May 1951

★ For another, more lighthearted quote on deception through publicity, see Joseph Levine at THE PEOPLE, in the note to Lincoln's remark on fooling the people.

2 The trouble with us in America isn't that the poetry of life has turned to prose, but that it has turned to advertising copy.

—**Louis Kronenberger,** *The Spirit of the Age*, in *Company Manners*, 1954

3 Doing business without advertising is like winking at a girl in the dark. You know what you are doing, but nobody else does.

—**Steuart Henderson Britt,** quoted in the *New York Herald Tribune*, Oct. 30, 1956

4 Does she or doesn't she?—

—**Shirley Polykoff,** ad for Miss Clairol hair dye, 1956

★ The men who ran *Life* magazine were so troubled by this provocative line that they rejected the ad when it was originally submitted by Foote, Cone & Belding. Polykoff got them to accept it by suggesting that they poll women staffers, who saw no problem. The prospective Clairol customer, Miss Polykoff contended, would never admit "that a nice girl ever got an off-color meaning about anything." See also the Anonymous entry at REPUTATION.

5 Do you sincerely want to be rich?

—**Bernard Cornfeld,** saying, c. 1956

★ Cornfeld used this tag line to recruit sales people and investors for his vast and shaky Investors Overseas Services. His mutual-fund empire collapsed in 1970.

6 The deeper problems connected with advertising come less from the unscrupulousness of our "deceivers" than from our pleasure in being deceived, less from the desire to seduce than from the desire to be seduced.

—**Daniel J. Boorstin,** *The Image*, 1962

7 A pseudo event . . . comes about because someone has planned, planted, or incited it. Typically, it is not a train wreck or an earthquake, but an interview.

—**Daniel J. Boorstin,** *The Image*, 1962

The consumer is not a moron. She is your wife. Try not to insult her intelligence. 1

—**David Ogilvy,** *Confessions of An Advertising Man,* 1964

You've come a long way, baby. 2

—**Philip Morris Co.,** *ad slogan for Virginia Slim cigarettes*

★ The campaign targeted women.

As advertising blather becomes the nation's normal idiom, language becomes printed noise. 3

—**George Will,** *Personality Against Character*, July 1, 1976, in *The Pursuit of Happiness and Other Sobering Thoughts* [1978]

Where's the beef? 4

—**Cliff Freeman,** Dancer Fitzgerald Sample agency, slogan for Wendy's, Jan. 1984

★ Television commercials for Wendy's hamburger chain featured 82-year-old actress Clara Peller with a small burger, presumably from a Wendy's competitor. After lifting the top of the bun, she incredulously poses this question to two friends, who appear amazed at the beeflessness of non-Wendy's hamburgers. The query was soon applied in all sorts of contexts, most famously by Democratic presidential candidate Walter Mondale with respect to his opponent in the Democratic primaries, Gary Hart.

[A press agent:] A man of a few thousand well-chosen words. 5

—**Irving Rudd,** *The Sporting Life*, 1990

★ Rudd, a veteran sports press agent, is absolutely not a PR person. He explains that in the sports world in the 1930s and 1940s, "You were a press agent or a publicity man. Period." His view of PR people: "They're posturing phonies." For other unminced words from Rudd, see under INSULTS.

It keeps going, and going, and going. 6

—**Chiat/Day advertising agency,** slogan for Energizer batteries, 1989

★ "It" is the Energizer pink bunny.

Anxiety is giving away to a confidence that they [advertisers] will soon have access to the core emotional needs of nearly every American shopper and voter. 7

Douglas Rushkoff, *The Persuaders* on *Frontline,* Nov. 9, 2004

★ Rushkoff was speaking of the traditional anxiety among advertisers and persuaders of all sorts that their messages may not hit their targets; see John Wanamaker above. But sophisticated research and subtle message-delivery have diminished that worry. The advertizing catch phrase to describe the result is "loyalty beyond reason," coined by Kevin Roberts, CEO of Saatchi & Saatchi. The brands that evoke this loyalty are "love-brands" or "Lovemarks."

Advice

See also WISDOM, WORDS OF.

The advice of the elders to young men is very apt to be as unreal as a list of the hundred best books. 8

—**Oliver Wendell Holmes, Jr.,** speech, Boston, Jan. 8, 1897

1 He had only one vanity; he thought he could give advice better than any other person.
—**Mark Twain,** *The Man That Corrupted Hadleyburg*, 1899

2 *Advice, n.* The smallest current coin.
—**Ambrose Bierce,** *The Devil's Dictionary*, 1906

3 A good scare is worth more to a man than good advice.
—**Edgar Watson Howe,** *Country Sayings*, 1911

4 The Miss Lonelyhearts are the priests of twentieth-century America.
—**Nathanael West,** *Miss Lonelyhearts*, 1933

★ In this brilliant novel, Miss Lonelyhearts, putative author of a newspaper advice column, is in reality a troubled male writer.

5 Pay attention to what they tell you to forget.
—**Muriel Rukeyser,** *Double Ode for Bill and Alison,* in *The Gates*, 1976

6 Advice is what we ask for when we already know the answer but wish we didn't.
—**Erica Jong**, *How to Save Your Own Life*, 1977

Africa

See NATIONS.

African Americans

See RACES & PEOPLES.

Ages

See also CHILDREN; GENERATIONS; MIDDLE AGE & MIDLIFE CRISIS; OLD AGE; YOUTH.

7 Youth is the time of getting, middle age of improving, and old age of spending.
—**Anne Bradstreet,** *Meditations Divine and Moral*, 1644

8 Consider well the proportions of things. It is better to be a young June-bug than an old bird of paradise.
—**Mark Twain,** *Pudd'nhead Wilson's Calendar*, in *Pudd'nhead Wilson*, 1894

9 The first half of life consists of the capacity to enjoy without the chance; the last half consists of the chance without the capacity.
—**Mark Twain,** letter to Edward L. Dimmit, July 19, 1901

10 Youth condemns; maturity condones.
—**Amy Lowell,** *Tendencies in Modern American Poetry*, 1917

11 The young man who has not wept is a savage, and the old man who will not laugh is a fool.
—**George Santayana,** *Dialogues in Limbo*, 1925

From birth to age eighteen, a girl needs good parents. From eighteen to thirty-five, she needs good looks. From thirty-five to fifty-five, she needs a good personality. From fifty-five on, she needs good cash. 1

—**Sophie Tucker,** attributed, 1953

★ *Bartlett's* reports that Tucker said this at age sixty-nine. Ralph Keyes in *Nice Guys Finish Seventh* notes that the passage has also been attributed to novelist Kathleen Norris. Tucker, however, was a nationally recognized expert on aging; she was known as "The Last of the Red Hot Mamas," from the title of a Jack Yellen song that she introduced in 1928. Mary Kay Ash, who founded beauty-products empire at age forty-five, gave a similar definition of a woman's needs: "From fourteen to forty she needs good looks; forty to sixty she needs personality; and I'm here to tell you that after sixty, she needs cash," in the *The New York Times* [Nov. 24, 2001]. See also Lena Horne at OLD AGE and, for Tucker's prescription for longevity, HEALTH.

I will not make age an issue. . . . I am not going to exploit for political purposes my opponent's youth and inexperience. 2

—**Ronald Reagan**, TV campaign debate with Walter F. Mondale, Oct. 21, 1984

★ Mr. Reagan was 73 at the time; Mr Mondale, 56.

A man has every season, while a woman only has the right to spring. 3

—**Jane Fonda**, quoted in the London *Daily Mail*, Sept. 13, 1989

Age is nothing but experience, and some of us are more experienced than others. 4

—**Andy Rooney**, NBC-TV commentary, Feb. 2, 1995

★ Mr. Rooney was then an experienced 76.

Alabama

See also CITIES (BIRMINGHAM; MOBILE).

There is no one here but carries arms under his clothes. It is a semi-barbarous state of society. 5

—**Anonymous,** quoted in *Democracy in America,* by Alexis de Tocqueville, 1835

Alabama . . . seems to have a bad name even among those who reside in it. 6

—**J. S. Buckingham,** *The Slave States of America*, 1839

★ Buckingham was an English traveler and writer.

I came from Alabama with my banjo on my knee. 7

—**Stephen Foster,** *Oh! Susanna*, 1848

As I have walked in Alabama my morning walk, 8
I have seen where the she-bird the mocking bird sat on her nest in the briers hatching her brood.
I have seen the he-bird also,
I have paused to hear him near at hand inflating his throat and joyfully singing.

—**Walt Whitman,** *Starting from Paumanok*, in *Leaves of Grass*, 1881

1 Once upon a time, stars fell on Alabama, changing the land's destiny.
—**Carl Carmer,** *Stars Fell on Alabama*, 1934

★ The reference is to a memorable, pre-Civil War meteor shower.

2 When I get to be a composer
I'm gonna write me some music about
Daybreak in Alabama.
And I'm gonna put the purtiest songs in it
Rising out of the ground like a swamp mist
And falling out of heaven like soft dew.
—**Langston Hughes,** *Daybreak in Alabama*, 1940

3 *Audemus iura nostra defendere.*
We dare defend our rights.
—Motto, Alabama

Alaska

See also CITIES (NOME).

4 Seward's folly.
—**Anonymous,** popular name for Alaska, 1867

★ Also, "Seward's icebox." Secretary of State William H. Seward was the leading advocate for acquisition of Alaska. He signed the agreement with Russia by which the U.S. took over the vast territory for $7.2 million—about two cents an acre.

5 It is proposed to pay $7,200,000 for a country where none but malefactors will ever live, and where we are likely to be at constant war with the savages.
—**Cadwallader C. Washburn**, debate on whether to appropriate funds for the acquisition of Alaska, U.S. House of Representatives, 1867

6 A practical race of intrepid navigators will swarm the coast, ready for any enterprise. . . . Commerce will find new arms, the country new defenders, the national flag new hands to bear it aloft.
—**Charles Sumner,** speech in favor of ratifying treaty with Russia to acquire Alaska, U.S. Senate, 1867

7 This is the law of the Yukon, that only the strong shall thrive;
That surely the weak shall perish, and only the fit survive.
Dissolute, damned and despairful, crippled and palsied and slain,
This is the Will of the Yukon—Lo, how she makes it plain!
—**Robert W. Service** *The Law of the Yukon*, in *Songs of a Sourdough*, 1907

★ Reprinted as *The Spell of the Yukon*, 1915.

8 Some say God was tired when he made it [the land of Alaska];
Some say it's a fine land to shun;
Maybe; but there's some as would trade it
For no land on earth—and I'm one.
—**Robert W. Service,** *Songs of a Sourdough*, 1907

And those who have undergone [life in Alaska] claim that in the making of the world God grew tired, and when He came to the last barrowload, "just dumped it anyhow," and that was how Alaska happened to be. 1

—**Jack London,** *Gold Hunters of the North*, in *Revolution and Other Essays*, 1910

This Alaska is a great country. If they can just keep from being taken over by the U.S., they got a great future. 2

—**Will Rogers,** *Daily Telegrams*, August 13, 1935

★ Rogers and aviator Wiley Post died two days later in a plane crash near Point Barrow, Alaska.

The forty-ninth star twinkles. The Senate can make it shine. 3

—**Houston Press,** editorial on statehood for Alaska, 1958

You are no longer an Arctic frontier. You constitute a bridge to the continent of Asia and all its people. 4

—**Dwight D. Eisenhower,** speech, Anchorage, Alaska, June 12, 1960

A handful of people clinging to a subcontinent. 5

—**John McPhee,** *Coming into the Country*, 1977

Alaska's forests are the most welcoming I know. There are no ticks, no snakes, no poison ivy in Alaska. 6

—**Charles Kuralt,** *Charles Kuralt's America*, 1995

North to the future. 7

—Motto, state of Alaska

Alcohol & Drinking

See also Food, Wine, & Eating; Last Words (Dylan Thomas).

I am sure the Americans can fix nothing without a drink. If you meet, you drink; if you part, you drink; if you make acquaintance, you drink. . . . They drink because it is hot; they drink because it is cold. If successful in elections, they drink and rejoice; if not, they drink and swear; they begin to drink early in the morning; they leave off late at night; they commence it early in life, and they continue it, until they drop down into the grave. 8

—**Frederick Marryat,** *A Diary in America*, 1839

It's a long time between drinks. 9

—**John Motley Morehead,** c. 1843

★ The remark was immortalized by Robert Louis Stevenson, who, in his comic story *The Wrong Box*, attributed it to a governor of South Carolina in conversation with a governor of North Carolina. But Stevenson mixed up his states. Morehead was governor of North Carolina from 1841 to 1845. Tradition has it that the remark was made to James H. Hammond, governor of South Carolina, who had come to Raleigh to demand the surrender of a North Carolinian who was wanted for a crime in South Carolina.

When Morehead declined, Hammond became furious, threatening to call up his militia and to take the fugitive by force of arms. "Governor, what do you say?" demanded Hammond. To which Morehead replied, "I say, Governor, that it is a long time between drinks." The discussion continued, cordially so to speak, and Hammond and Morehead eventually parted on good terms. The fugitive was never returned.

1 Better sleep with a sober cannibal than a drunken Christian.
—Herman Melville, *Moby-Dick*, 1851

2 A slave to the demon rum.
—Timothy Shay Arthur, *Ten Nights in a Barroom and What I Saw There*, 1854

★ This phrase, which may have originated with Arthur, was commonly used in the 19th-century temperance movement, with "rum" standing for all alcoholic drinks. Arthur, an editor, was not a teetotaler or prohibitionist; temperance was his message. This popular story was made into a play, which enjoyed success both as a serious drama and, later, as a comic offering.

3 Let me know what brand of whiskey Grant uses. For if it makes fighting generals like Grant, I should like to get some of it for distribution.
—Abraham Lincoln, to a Congressional delegation, 1863

★ Grant's enemies in Congress had approached Lincoln, saying that Grant was a drunk and should be demoted. Grand had trouble with the bottle before the war but apparently stayed sober during it, despite rumors to the contrary, and Lincoln stuck with him, though perhaps not in such witty terms. The remark was recorded by Chaplain John Eaton, who was told about the meeting with the congressmen by Lincoln, but the president himself denied making it. According to Ralph Keyes's *Nice Guys Finish Seventh*, Lincoln thought the story might have been inspired by an anecdote about King George II who, when told that Gen. James Wolfe was mad, is said to have retorted, "If General Wolfe is mad, I hope he bites some of my other generals." In any case, Lincoln was by nature forgiving toward drinkers. In 1842, in a speech on February 22 to the Springfield (Ill.) Washingtonian Temperance Society, he said: "I believe, if we take habitual drinkers as a class, their heads and their hearts will bear an advantageous comparison with those of any other class."

4 Father, dear father, come home with me now;
The clock in the steeple strikes one;
You promised, dear father, that you would come home
As soon as your day's work was done.
—Henry Clay Work, *Come Home, Father*, temperance song, 1864

5 The first course was whiskey, the second whiskey, the third whiskey, all the courses were whiskey, but still they called it supper.
—Oscar Wilde, letter describing a dinner with miners in Leadville, Colo., April 13, 1882

★ On the same evening, Wilde spotted a sign calling for restraint toward the piano player; see ART: MUSIC.

6 The cocktail is a pleasant drink;
It's mild and harmless—I don't think.

When you've had one, you call for two,
And then you don't care what you do.
—George Ade, *The Sultan of Sulu*, 1902

They got between the people and its beer. 1
—Alfred Henry Lewis, *The Boss*, 1903

★ A character in Lewis's novel pinpoints the fatal error of turn-of-the-century reformers. In an article on political machines in *American Heritage*, June 1969, William Shannon notes that while Theodore Roosevelt, head of the New York City police board, was prowling the streets at night searching for saloon violations, the populace was singing that great vaudeville hit, *I Want What I Want When I Want It!*.

There are two things that will be believed of any man whatsoever, and one of them 2
is that he has taken to drink.
—Booth Tarkington, *Penrod*, 1914

Gimme a whiskey—ginger ale on the side. And don't be stingy, baby. 3
—Eugene O'Neill, *Anna Christie*, 1921

★ This is Anna's opening line, and in 1930, when the play was made into a movie, Garbo had the lead, and it was her first appearance in a film with sound. "Garbo Talks!" the publicity posters boasted. She talked in German, too—in a version of the film that was shot at the same time and released abroad. The German line was, *"Whiskey, aber nicht zu knapp!"* ("Whiskey, but not too stingy.")

[Prohibition:] A noble experiment. 4
—Herbert Hoover, attributed

★ This is the popular short form of comments by Hoover on the prohibition of alcohol enacted in the Eighteenth Amendment. In a letter to Sen. William E. Borah of Idaho, dated February 28, 1928, Hoover wrote, "Our country has deliberately undertaken a great social and economic experiment, noble in motive and far-reaching in purpose." He repeated the thought in accepting the Republican presidential nomination on August 11.

The wine had such ill effects on Noah's health that it was all he could do to live 950 5
years.
—Will Rogers, in Alex Ayres, ed., *The Wit and Wisdom of Will Rogers* [1993]

Three highballs, and I think I'm St. Francis of Assisi. 6
—Dorothy Parker, *Just a Little One*, in *Laments for the Living*, 1930

★ See also Parker at SIN, VICE, & NAUGHTINESS.

Candy 7
Is dandy
But liquor
Is quicker.
—Ogden Nash, *Reflections on Ice-Breaking*, in *Hard Lines*, 1931

1 There is something about a Martini,
Ere the dining and dancing begin.
And to tell you the truth,
It's not the vermouth—
I think that perhaps it's the gin.
—Ogden Nash, *A Drink with Something in It*, in *The Primrose Path*, 1935

2 You ought to get out of those wet clothes and into a dry martini.
—Mae West, *Every Day's a Holiday*, 1937

★ Tony Augarde, editor of *The Oxford Dictionary of Modern Quotations*, came up with this early citation for a quip usually associated with Robert Benchley. Benchley himself attributed the line to his friend Charles Butterworth, who spoke it in this Mae West movie, addressing Charles Winninger. In the 1942 movie *The Major and the Minor*, written by Billy Wilder and Charles Brackett, Benchley says to Ginger Rogers, "Why don't you get out of that wet coat and into a dry martini?" Alexander Woollcott has also been credited with the thought.

3 There is no cure for the hangover, save death.
—Robert Benchley, quoted in *The New York Times* [Dec. 28, 1997]

4 God created alcohol.
—William Carlos Williams, *Io Baccho!*, 1950

★ See also Williams at PLEASURE & HEDONISM.

5 You're not drunk if you can lie on the floor without holding on.
—Dean Martin, in Paul Dickson, *The Official Rules* [1978]

6 There is nothing more dangerous than a lengthy cocktail hour.
—A. R. Gurney, *The Cocktail Hour*, 1988

Alienation

See also MADNESS; SOLITUDE & LONELINESS.

7 From childhood's hour I have not been
As others were—I have not seen
As others saw.
—Edgar Allan Poe, *Alone*, 1829 [published 1875]

8 Call me Ishmael.
—Herman Melville, *Moby-Dick*, 1851

★ The opening line of the novel, spoken by the hero. The name *Ishmael* stands for *outcast*, from the biblical Ishmael, who was the bastard son of Abraham and the bondservant Hagar, and the older brother of Isaac. Ishmael was disinherited and, with his mother, exiled to the wilderness.

9 I would prefer not to.
—Herman Melville, *Bartleby the Scrivener*, 1856

★ With these words, Bartleby repeatedly rejects—everything.

Miniver Cheevy, child of scorn, **1**
Grew lean while he assailed the seasons;
He wept that he was ever born,
And he had reasons.

—Edwin Arlington Robinson, *Miniver Cheevy*, 1910

Which of us is not forever a stranger and alone? **2**

—Thomas Wolfe, *Look Homeward, Angel*, foreword, 1929

I'm less than two months old and I'm tired of living. **3**

—E. B. White, *Charlotte's Web*, 1952

There is no alienation that a little power will not cure. **4**

—Eric Hoffer, *Reflections on the Human Condition*, 1973

Ambition & Aspiration

In the long run, men hit only what they aim at. **5**

—Henry David Thoreau, "Economy," *Walden*, 1854

Most people would succeed in small things, if they were not so troubled by great ambitions. **6**

—Henry Wadsworth Longfellow, *Drift-Wood,*1857

Nothing is so commonplace as the wish to be remarkable. **7**

—Oliver Wendell Holmes, Sr., *The Autocrat of the Breakfast-Table,*1860

Hitch your wagon to a star. **8**

—Ralph Waldo Emerson, *Civilization*, in *Society and Solitude*, 1870

★ A Yankee version of the Latin proverb: *Ad astra per ardua*—"To the stars through difficulties."

The ripest peach is highest on the tree. **9**

—James Whitcomb Riley, *The Ripest Peach*

Aim High—Then Shoot. **10**

—Anonymous, "work-incentive" poster, 1920s

★ These inspirational posters were intended to evoke greater effort and company loyalty.

What Makes Sammy Run? **11**

—Bud Schulberg, novel title, 1941

★ The story of Sammy Glick, a self-made, ruthlessly ambitious Hollywood success. For Sammy's credo, see WINNING & LOSING, VICTORY & DEFEAT.

Men are more often bribed by their loyalties and ambitions than by money. **12**

—Robert H. Jackson, *United States v. Wunderlich*, dissent, 1951

The amphetamine of ambition. **13**

—Edward O. Wilson, describing what roused him to write *Sociobiology*, 1975

1 Ambition, if it feeds at all, does so on the ambition of others.
—**Susan Sontag**, *The Benefactor*, 1983

2 The requirement for great success is great ambition ... for triumph over other men, not merely over nature.
—**Richard C. Lewontin,** quoted in Jane S. Smith, *Patenting the Sun: Polio and the Salk Vaccine,* 1990

★ Lewontin, Alexander Agassiz Professor of Biology at Harvard, specializes in evolutionary biology.

3 I have the same goal I've had ever since I was a girl. I want to rule the world.
—**Madonna**, quoted in *People*, July 27, 1992

Ambivalence

See INDECISION.

America & Americans

See also AMERICAN HISTORY: MEMORABLE MOMENTS; CONSTITUTION, THE; DECLARATION OF INDEPENDENCE; DEMOCRACY; FOREIGN POLICY; MILITARY, THE; PATRIOTISM & THE FLAG; RACES & PEOPLES; SERVING ONE'S COUNTRY; UNION, THE.

4 O my America! my new-found-land.
—**John Donne,** *To His Mistris Going to Bed,* c. 1595

★ The quote is famous. The undiscovered "new-found-land" is metaphorical, as the title suggests.

5 Columbus did not find out America by chance, but God directed him at that time to discover it; it was contingent to him, but necessary to God.
—**Robert Burton,** *The Anatomy of Melancholy*, 1621

6 They knew they were pilgrims.
—**William Bradford,** *History of Plymouth Plantation*, written 1630–1651

★ Bradford came to America on the *Mayflower* and was governor of the colony at Plymouth for most of his adult life. His history, covering years 1620–46, led to the use of the term *pilgrims* for the colonists. See also Bradford at ACTION & DOING.

7 We shall be as a city upon a hill.
—**John Winthrop,** *A Model of Christian Charity*, sermon on board the *Arbella*, 1630

★ Winthrop, leader of the Puritan group that founded the Massachusetts Bay Colony, borrowed here from *Matthew* 5:14: "Ye are the light of the world. A city that is set on a hill cannot be hid." His full statement reads: "For we must consider that we shall be as a city upon a hill. The eyes of all people are upon us, so if we shall deal falsely with our God in this work we have undertaken, and so cause him to withdraw his present help from us, we shall be made a story and a byword through the world."

In the beginning all the world was America. 1
—**John Locke,** *Two Treatises of Government*, 1690

Westward the course of empire takes its way; 2
The four first acts already past,
A fifth shall close the drama with the day:
Time's noblest offspring is the last.
—**George Berkeley,** *On the Prospect of Planting Arts and Learning in America*, 1726 [published 1752]

★ Bishop Berkeley's thought was echoed in 1862 by Arthur Hugh Clough in *Say Not the Struggle Nought Availeth*: "In front the sun climbs slow, how slowly, / But westward, look, the land is bright." See also Horace Walpole below.

People are far more sincere and generous than in Germany; therefore our Americans 3
live more quietly and peacefully together than the Europeans; and all this is the result of the liberty which they enjoy and which makes them all equal.
—**Gottlieb Mittelberger,** *Journey to Pennsylvania,* 1754

★ For more from Mittelberger's report on his trip, see PENNSYLVANIA.

Yankee Doodle came to town 4
Riding on a pony,
He stuck a feather in his hat
And called it Macaroni.
Yankee Doodle keep it up,
Yankee Doodle dandy,
Mind the music and the step,
And with the girls be handy.
—**Anonymous,** c. 1755

★ Calling the hat and feather "Macaroni" is a reference to Italian leadership in fashion. English dandies of the period were called "macaronies." See under CONNECTICUT for the origin of *Yankee*, and under PATRIOTISM & THE FLAG for George M. Cohan's Yankee Doodle. The song, with verses set to an old English tune, was originally aimed derisively by British troops at colonial would-be soldiers. A British army surgeon, Dr. Richard Shuckburgh, gave the old tune its title and possibly wrote down some verses, which apparently were being improvised, often bawdily. The American militiamen turned the tables militarily and musically, triumphantly adopted the Yankee Doodle label, and sang the song for dispirited British forces as they retreated from Concord in 1775, and later on numerous occasions. The most familiar version of the words apparently was composed in 1776 by Edward Bangs, a Harvard sophomore and Minute Man.

America is more wild and absurd than ever. 5
—**Edmund Burke,** letter to Lord Rockingham, Sept. 9, 1769

★ Nevertheless, Burke's sympathies were with the American colonists in their protests against the Stamp Act and other intrusions upon their traditional liberties.

1 The next Augustan age will dawn on the other side of the Atlantic.
—Horace Walpole, letter to Horace Mann, Nov. 24, 1774

2 Don't tread on me.
—Anonymous, American motto

★ The motto appeared on the first official flag of the North American colonists—the "Rattlesnake Flag"—raised by Lt. John Paul Jones on the flagship *Alfred*, December 3, 1775.

3 The cause of America is in a great measure the cause of all mankind.
—Thomas Paine, *Common Sense*, 1776

4 We have it in our power to begin the world over again.
—Ibid.

★ Often cited by Ronald Reagan.

5 *E Pluribus Unum.*
Out of many, one.
—Anonymous, motto for the national seal, selected by committee, 1776

★ The committee, which consisted of Thomas Jefferson, John Adams, and Benjamin Franklin, was appointed on July 4, 1776. The members may have had in mind the classical history of the phrase; it was used by Virgil in the form *E pluribus unus*. But more immediately, it was the motto of *Gentleman's Magazine*, which was published in England, but was popular in the U.S., too. This periodical reprinted selected newspaper articles, and was the first such publication to describe itself as a magazine; the term originally meant "storehouse." A Swiss artist, Pierre Eugene du Simitière, who was employed by the committee, has been credited with suggesting the motto in a design for the seal that the committee did not, in fact, accept. See also Rev. Jesse Jackson below (1984).

6 You cannot conquer America.
—William Pitt, speech, House of Lords, Nov. 18, 1777

★ More at AMERICAN REVOLUTION.

7 They [Americans] are the hope of this world. They may become its model.
—A. R. J. Turgot, letter to Dr. Richard Price, March 22, 1778

★ Turgot, French economist and finance minister, foresaw that the choice for his nation was reform or revolution.

8 I am willing to love all mankind, *except an American.*
—Samuel Johnson, April 15, 1778, quoted in James Boswell, *Life of Johnson*

9 What then is the American, this new man?
—Michel Guillaume Jean de Crèvecoeur (pen name, J. Hector St. John), *Letters from an American Farmer*, 1782

10 Here individuals of all nations are melted into a new race of men, whose labors and posterity will one day cause great changes in the world.
—Ibid.

★ Israel Zangwill made famous the melting pot metaphor. See below.

Indeed, I tremble for my country when I reflect that God is just. **1**

—Thomas Jefferson, *Notes on the State of Virginia*, 1781–85

★ Jefferson was speaking of the injustice in slavery. More at FREEDOM.

I wish the bald eagle had not been chosen as the representative of our country. . . . **2**
The turkey . . . is a much more respectable bird.

—Benjamin Franklin, letter to Sarah Bache, Jan. 26, 1784

★ More at NATURE: ANIMALS.

A republic if you can keep it. **3**

—Benjamin Franklin, answer to the question, "Well, doctor, what have we got, a republic or a monarchy?" Sept. 18, 1787

★ The dialogue was recorded by James McHenry, an aide to George Washington. The conversation took place in Philadelphia. A Mrs. Powel posed the question.

No human power can now stop the march of a nation destined to exert its influence **4**
all over the world, and perhaps to dominate it.

—Dominique Dufour de Pradt, *Des Colonies et de la Révolution actuelle de l'Amérique*, 1817

★ The Abbé de Pradt had been Napoleon's chaplain.

Who reads an American book, or goes to an American play, or looks at an American **5**
picture or statue?

—Sydney Smith, *Edinburgh Review*, 1820

★ Rev. Smith's famous taunt dated rapidly, as Longfellow became a best-seller in England, Poe was taken up by the French, and so on to the situation today, in which American culture more than holds its own.

Wherever the standard of freedom and independence has been unfurled, there will **6**
[America's] heart, her benedictions, and her prayers be. But she goes not abroad in search of monsters to destroy.

—John Quincy Adams, *speech,* July 4, 1821

★ Adams explained that if America enlisted in foreign conflicts, "She would involve herself ... in all the wars of interest and intrigue, of individual avarice, envy, and ambition." He concluded, "She might become dictatress of the world; she would no longer be the ruler of her own spirit."

The happy union of these states is a wonder; their Constitution a miracle; their **7**
example the hope of liberty throughout the world.

—James Madison, "Outline" notes, Sept. 1829

★ Inscribed in Madison Memorial Hall of the Library of Congress.

The whole [American] people appear to be divided into an almost endless variety of **8**
religious factions.

—Frances Trollope, *Domestic Manners of the Americans*, 1832

★ She made this observation in 1828, according to *American Heritage*, June 1976.

1 I know of no country, indeed, where the love of money has taken a stronger hold on the affections of men.

—Alexis de Tocqueville, *Democracy in America*, 1835

★ See also Tocqueville at MONEY & THE RICH.

2 America is a land of wonders, in which everything is in constant motion and every change seems an improvement. . . . No natural boundary seems to be set to the efforts of man; and in his eyes, what is not yet done is only what he has not yet attempted to do.

—Ibid.

3 Although the travelers who have visted North America differ on many points, they all agree in remarking that the morals are far more strict there than elsewhere.

—Ibid.

4 If destruction be our lot, we must ourselves be its author and finisher. As a nation of freemen, we must live through all time or die by suicide.

—Abraham Lincoln, speech, Young Men's Lyceum, Springfield, Ill., Jan. 27, 1838

★ On the suicide of democracies, see also John Adams at DEMOCRACY. Lincoln prefaced the comments above with the questions: "At what point shall we expect the approach of danger? . . . Shall we expect some trans-Atlantic military giant to step the ocean and crush us at a blow?" He answered, "Never! All the armies of Europe, Asia, and Africa combined with all the treasure of the earth . . . could not by force take a drink from the Ohio, or make a track on the Blue Ridge, in a trial of a thousand years."

5 We are the nation of human progress, and who will, what can, set limits to our onward march?

—John L. O'Sullivan, *The Great Nation of Futurity*, in the *Democratic Review*, Nov. 1839

★ O'Sullivan, one of the most influential journalists of his time, later summarized this imperialist vision in the phrase "manifest destiny"; see below. The "nation of human progress" quote is usually ascribed to him, although the piece was unsigned and some scholars have had doubts on the point. Incidentally, this essay also referred to America's mission to spread four freedoms through the world, later used by Franklin D. Roosevelt; see FREEDOM.

6 Our manifest destiny to overspread and to possess the whole of the continent, which Providence has given us for the great experiment of liberty.

—John L. O'Sullivan, editorial, *Morning News*, New York City, Dec. 27, 1845

★ O'Sullivan was writing in support of incorporating Oregon into the U.S. This editorial made the phrase "manifest destiny" famous. O'Sullivan had, however, used it earlier in the year: "Our manifest destiny is to overspread the continent allotted by Providence for the free development of our yearly multiplying millions," *Democratic Review*, July-August, 1845. And a year earlier, George Bancroft referred to "the manifest purpose of Providence, that the light of democratic freedom should be borne from our fires to the domain beyond the Rocky Mountains," in a letter of August 15, 1844, accepting the nomination as Democratic candidate for governor of Massachusetts. See also Walt Whitman at MEXICAN WAR, and THE FRONTIER; and William McKinley at HAWAII.

Sail on, O Ship of State! 1
Sail on, O Union, strong and great!
Humanity with all its fears,
With all the hopes of future years,
Is hanging breathless on thy fate!

—**Henry Wadsworth Longfellow,** *The Building of the Ship*, 1849

We Americans are the peculiar, chosen people—the Israel of our time; we bear the ark of the liberties of the world. 2

—**Herman Melville,** *White-Jacket*, 1850

We are the pioneers of the world; . . . In our youth is our strength; in our inexperience, our wisdom. 3

—**Ibid.**

★ These energetic and optimistic comments came two years before the devastating reviews of *Moby-Dick*, which essentially brought Melville's writing to an end—forty years before his death. *Billy Budd*, which we regard as a classic, was found in manuscript form in an old suitcase and published in the 1920s.

The United States themselves are essentially the greatest poem. 4

—**Walt Whitman,** Preface, *Leaves of Grass*, 1st ed., 1855

America has not yet settled down. She is an unfinished edifice. 5

—**Alexander Herzen,** *My Past and Thoughts*, 1855

★ Herzen, a philosopher and revolutionary, had contradictory feelings about America, but on balance did not favor emigrating there. He wrote, "America, as Garibaldi said, is the 'land for forgetting one's own'; let those who have no faith in their fatherland go there."

The United States is . . . a warning rather than an example to the world. 6

—**Lydia Maria Child,** speech at the 25th anniversary of the Massachusetts Anti-Slavery Society, 1857

This country, with its institutions, belongs to the people who inhabit it. Whenever they shall grow weary of the existing government, they can exercise their constitutional right of amending it, or their revolutionary right to dismember or overthrow it. 7

—**Abraham Lincoln,** First Inaugural Address, March 4, 1861

America means opportunity, freedom, power. 8

—**Ralph Waldo Emerson,** *Public and Private Education*, Nov. 1864, in *Uncollected Lectures* [1932]

I hear America singing, the varied carols I hear. 9

—**Walt Whitman,** *I Hear America Singing*, 1867

★ For a parody of Whitman, see Peter De Vries at SEX.

1 America is a country of young men.
—**Ralph Waldo Emerson,** *Old Age*, in *Society and Solitude*, 1870

2 I hate this shallow Americanism which hopes to get rich by credit, to get knowledge by raps on midnight tables, to learn the economy of the mind by phrenology, or skill without study, or mastery without apprenticeship.
—**Ralph Waldo Emerson,** *Success*, in *Society and Solitude*, 1870

3 I shall use the word America and democracy as convertible terms.
—**Walt Whitman,** *Democratic Vistas*, 1871

4 And at this day, though I have kind invitations enough to visit America, I could not, even for a couple of months, live in a country so miserable as to possess no castles.
—**John Ruskin,** *Fors Clavigera*, Vol. I, letter 10, 1871

5 No sovereign, no court, no aristocracy, no church, no clergy, no army, no diplomatic service, no country gentlemen, no palaces, no castles, nor manors nor old country houses, nor parsonages nor thatched cottages nor ivied ruins.
—**Henry James,** on "the absent things in American life," *Hawthorne*, 1879

6 Among the rank and file, [in] both armies [in the Civil War], it was very general to speak of the different States they came from by their slang names. Those from Maine were call'd Foxes; New Hampshire, Granite Boys; Massachusetts, Bay Staters; Vermont, Green Mountain Boys; Rhode Island, Gun Flints; Connecticut, Wooden Nutmegs; New York, Knickerbockers; New Jersey, Clam Catchers; Pennsylvania, Logher Heads; Delaware, Muskrats; Maryland, Claw Thumpers; Virginia, Beagles; North Carolina, Tar Boilers; South Carolina, Weasels; Georgia, Buzzards; Louisiana, Creoles; Alabama, Lizards; Kentucky, Corn Crackers; Ohio, Buckeyes; Michigan, Wolverines; Indiana, Hoosiers; Illinois, Suckers; Missouri, Pukes; Mississippi, Tad Poles; Florida, Fly Up the Creeks; Wisconsin, Badgers; Iowa, Hawkeyes; Oregon, Hard Cases.
—**Walt Whitman,** *Slang in America*, in *North American Review*, Nov. 1885

★ Whitman certainly heard many of these names while serving as a volunteer nurse in army hospitals, but, as reported by Howard Birss in *American Speech* (June 1932), his list was drawn from an unsigned article in the *Broadway Journal* of May 3, 1845.

7 O beautiful for spacious skies,
For amber waves of grain,
For purple mountain majesties
Above the fruited plain!
America! America!
God shed his grace on thee
And crown thy good with brotherhood
From sea to shining sea!
—**Katharine Lee Bates,** *America the Beautiful*, 1893

★ The music was by Samuel Ward. See PATRIOTISM & THE FLAG for *The Star-Spangled Banner* and *My Country 'Tis of Thee.*

Whether they will or no, Americans must now begin to look outward. 1

—**Alfred T. Mahan,** *The United States Looking Outward*, 1890, included in *The Interest of America in Sea Power*, 1897

★ Capt. Mahan's writings on the importance of sea power strongly influenced Theodore Roosevelt, who was assistant secretary of the navy before becoming president. Mahan was a frank imperialist. See also Roosevelt at THE MILITARY and SPANISH-AMERICAN WAR.

This is a billion-dollar country. 2

—**Thomas Brackett Reed,** remark in defense of the national deficit, c. 1890

★ The administration of Republican president Benjamin Harrison, elected in 1889, ran up an unprecedented deficit of $1 billion. When the Democrats expressed alarm at this "raid on the Treasury," Speaker of the House Reed silenced them with this comment.

[America] is a very great country, my dear Jack, not pretty or romantic but great and 3
utilitarian.

—**Winston Churchill,** letter to his brother, 1895

To the frontier the American intellect owes its striking characteristics: that coarse- 4
ness and strength combined with acuteness and inquisitiveness; that practical, inventive turn of mind, quick to find expedients; that masterful grasp of material things, lacking in the artistic but powerful to effect great ends; that restless, nervous energy; that dominant individualism, working for good and for evil, and withal that buoyancy and exuberance which comes with freedom.

—**Frederick J. Turner,** *The Significance of the Frontier in American History*, 1893

★ For more on this great historical essay, see THE FRONTIER.

America has been another name for opportunity. 5

—**Ibid.**

The youth of America is their oldest tradition. It has been going on now for three 6
hundred years.

—**Oscar Wilde,** *A Woman of No Importance*, 1893

It was wonderful to find America, but it would have been more wonderful to miss it. 7

—**Mark Twain,** *Pudd'nhead Wilson's Calendar*, in *Pudd'nhead Wilson*, 1894

It is by the goodness of God that in our country we have those three unspeakably 8
precious things: freedom of speech, freedom of conscience, and the prudence never to practice either of them.

—**Mark Twain,** *Pudd'nhead Wilson's New Calendar*, in *Following the Equator*, 1897

The political and social morals of America are not only food for laughter, they are an 9
entire banquet.

—**Mark Twain,** *Mark Twain in Eruption*, edited by Bernard DeVoto from Twain's unpublished memoirs [1940]

1 Don't sell America short.

—John Pierpont Morgan, popularized version of favorite saying, 1890s

★ Morgan's aphorism ran on the lines of "Don't be a bear [as opposed to a stockmarket bull] on America." This was abbreviated to the version given here. The aphorism may have originated with J. P. Morgan's father, Junius Spenser Morgan.

2 From the old-world point of view, the American had no mind; he had an economic thinking-machine which could work only on a fixed line. The American mind exasperated the Europeans as a buzz-saw might exasperate a pine forest.

—Henry Adams, *The Education of Henry Adams*, 1907

3 America is God's crucible, the great melting pot, where all the races of Europe are melting and re-forming. . . . Germans and Frenchmen, Irishmen and Englishmen, Jews and Russians—into the crucible with you all! God is making the American!

—Israel Zangwill, *The Melting Pot*, 1908

★ The quote is from Act One of Zangwill's play. The image may have come from Michel Guillaume Jean de Crèvecoeur's *Letters from an American Farmer*, 1782; see above. See also RACES & PEOPLES; for boiling rather than melting, Thomas Dewey on New York City under CITIES, and for sizzling, Barbara Mikulski under FOREIGNERS.

4 Our country—this great republic—means nothing unless it means the triumph of a real democracy, the triumph of popular government, and, in the long run, of an economic system under which each man shall be guaranteed the opportunity to show the best that there is in him.

—Theodore Roosevelt, *The New Nationalism*, 1910

5 America first.

—Woodrow Wilson, speech, April 20, 1915

★ Pres. Wilson was defending not entering the war in Europe. He said, "Our whole duty, for the present, at any rate, is summed up in the motto, 'America first.' Let us think of America before we think of Europe, in order that America may be fit to be Europe's friend when the day of tested friendship comes." See also WORLD WAR I.

6 I believe in the United States of America as a government of the people, by the people, for the people.

—William Tyler Page, *The American Creed*, adopted by the U.S. House of Representatives, April 3, 1918

★ See GETTYSBURG ADDRESS and GOVERNMENT for more on "government of the people."

7 There can be no fifty-fifty Americanism in this country. There is room here for only one hundred percent Americanism.

—Theodore Roosevelt, speech, July 19, 1918

★ See also Roosevelt on "hyphenated Americans" at FOREIGNERS. The influence of the World War made this sort of chauvinistic rhetoric widely acceptable. See also Roosevelt at PATRIOTISM & THE FLAG.

Sooner or later, the American people are going to wake up. 1

—**Emma Goldman,** Detroit, Michigan, Nov. 26, 1919, *Emma Goldman Papers Project*, University of California, Berkeley

[The] ordinary American crowd, the best-natured, best-dressed, best-behaving, and best-smelling crowd in the world. 2

—**Edwin Slosson,** 1920, quoted in David Nasaw, *The Rise and Fall of Public Amusements*, Basic Books, 1994

The essential American soul is hard, isolate, stoic, a killer. 3

—**D. H. Lawrence,** *Cooper's Leatherstocking Novels*, in *Studies in Classic American Literature*, 1922

Oh, America, 4
The sun sets in you.
Are you the grave of our day?

—**D. H. Lawrence,** *The Evening Land*, in *Birds, Beasts, and Flowers*, 1923

The pure products of America go crazy 5

—**William Carlos Williams,** *Spring and All*, XVIII, 1923

The discovery of America was the occasion of the greatest outburst of cruelty and reckless greed known to history. 6

—**Joseph Conrad,** *Geography and Some Explorers*, 1924, in *Last Essays* [1926]

America must be kept American. 7

—**Calvin Coolidge,** May 26, 1924

★ Coolidge made this comment while signing the exclusionary Immigration Act of 1924. The Act particularly discriminated against Japanese and others from Asia. See Emmanuel Celler at FOREIGNERS.

The chief business of the American people is business. 8

—**Calvin Coolidge,** speech, The American Society of Newspaper Editors, Jan. 17, 1925

★ See also Charles F. Wilson on General Motors and the U.S. at BUSINESS.

The men the American people admire most extravagantly are the most daring liars; the men they detest the most violently are those who try to tell the truth. 9

—**H. L. Mencken,** from Alistair Cooke, ed., *The Vintage Mencken* [1955]

★ For Mencken on the questionable intelligence of the American people, see THE PEOPLE.

The American system of rugged individualism. 10

—**Herbert Hoover,** campaign speech, Oct. 22, 1928

★ Hoover, campaigning in New York, said, "We were challenged with a peace-time choice between the American system of rugged individualism and a European philosophy of diametrically opposed doctrines—doctrines of paternalism and state socialism." Hoover wrote later, in *The Challenge to Liberty*, 1934, that the phrase "rugged individualism" had been used by American leaders for at least fifty years, but he added,

1 "I should be proud to have invented it." The phrase referred, he wrote, to "those God-fearing men and women of honesty whose stamina and character and fearless assertion of rights led them to make their own way in life."

2 While we [the English] have shadows that stalk behind us, they [Americans] have a light that dances in front of them. That is what makes them the most interesting people in the world—they face the future, not the past.

—Virginia Woolf, c. 1938

3 There is nothing wrong with Americans except their ideals. The real American is all right; it is the ideal American who is all wrong.

—G. K. Chesterton, in *The New York Times*, Feb. 1, 1931

In America, public opinion is the leader.

—Frances Perkins, *People at Work*, 1934

4 America . . . it is the only place where miracles not only happen, but where they happen all the time.

—Thomas Wolfe, *Of Time and the River,* 1935

★ Cited by Sen. Tom Daschle (D., South Dakota) on January 3, 2001, upon becoming majority leader for 17 days, pending the inauguration of George W. Bush as president and Dick Cheney as Vice President. At that time, Cheney took over from Al Gore as President of the Senate, and, since the Senate was divided 50-50, Republicans and Democrats, the former took control under majority leader Trent Lott of Mississippi. But six months later, in another miracle, Sen. Jim Jeffords of Vermont resigned from the Republican party and became an Independent. Thus Daschle became once again majority leader. (In 2004, Republicans won both houses of Congress, and Daschle was not re-elected senator.)

5 If we ever pass out as a great nation, we ought to put on our tombstone, "America died of the delusion that she had moral leadership."

—Will Rogers, *The Autobiography of Will Rogers* [1949]

★ Rogers died in 1935 in a plane crash. The *Autobiography* was published posthumously.

6 A continent ages quickly once we come.

—Ernest Hemingway, *The Green Hills of Africa,* 1935

★ This book, part fact, part fiction, describes a safari to East Africa in 1933. This sentence, however, refers to America and to the countryside in Illinois where Hemingway grew up. The country is no longer wild but filled with people, a fate he foresees for Africa. Compare the view of the outdooors man Hemingway with that of the indoors woman Gertrude Stein, below.

7 In the United States there is more space where nobody is than where anybody is. That is what makes America what is.

—Gertrude Stein, *The Geographical History of America*, 1936

8 Let America be America again.
Let it be the dream it used to be . . .
O, let America be America again—

The land that has never been yet—
And yet must be—
The land where every man is free.
. . .
America never was America to me.
And yet, I swear this oath—
America will be!
—Langston Hughes, *Let America Be America*, 1938

There are no second acts in American lives. **1**
—F. Scott Fitzgerald, *The Last Tycoon*, notes [1941]

★ The unfinished book was published posthumously. Fitzgerald died in 1940. In a letter to *American Heritage*, November 1998, Ronald Semone said that the quote is usually misunderstood. In the theater, the first act traditionally presents the problem; the second act, the complications and alternatives; and the third act, the resolution. Americans prefer to jump over the second act.

I believe that we are lost here in America, but I believe that we shall be found. **2**
—Thomas Wolfe, *You Can't Go Home Again*, 1940

The land was ours before we were the land's. **3**
She was our land more than a hundred years
Before we were her people.
—Robert Frost, *The Gift Outright*, 1941

★ The poet read this verse at the inauguration of Pres. John F. Kennedy, Jan. 20, 1961. He had presented it first, twenty years earlier, to the Phi Beta Kappa Society at William and Mary College. Commenting on these lines, Wallace Stegner wrote that to become healthy as a people, we must "learn to be quiet part of the time, and acquire the sense not of ownership but of belonging. . . . Only in the act of submission is the sense of place realized and a sustainable relationship between people and earth established," *The Sense of Place*, 1986. For similar thoughts see Aldo Leopold at ENVIRONMENT.

God bless the USA, so large **4**
So friendly, and so rich.
—W. H. Auden, *On the Circuit*, 1941

I don't see much future for the Americans. In my view, it's a decayed country. **5**
—Adolf Hitler, remark, Jan. 7, 1942, cited in *Hitler's Table Talk, 1941–1944: His Private Conversations* [1953]

Of nothing [in the U.S.] are you allowed to get the real odor or savor. Everything is **6**
sterilized and wrapped in cellophane.
—Henry Miller, *The Air-Conditioned Nightmare*, 1945

★ In the same essay, Miller described America as "prematurely old . . . a fruit which rotted before it had a chance to ripen."

The national vice is waste. **7**
—Henry Miller, *Dr. Souchon: Surgeon-Painter*, in *The Air-Conditioned Nightmare*, 1945

1 All races and religions: that's America to me.
—**Earl Robinson,** quoted in *The New York Times*, obituary [July 23, 1991]

★ Robinson wrote the music for the Alfred Hayes poem *Joe Hill*, honoring the labor organizer who was executed in 1915; see under CAPITALISM & CAPITAL V. LABOR.

2 The United States always does the right thing, after exploring every other possible course of action.
—**Winston Churchill,** quoted by President Bill Clinton in Santiago, Chile [April 1998]

3 I, in my own mind, have always thought of America as a place in the divine scheme of things that was set aside as a promised land.
—**Ronald Reagan**, commencement address, William Woods College, Fulton, Mo., June, 1952

4 America is a large, friendly dog in a very small room. Every time it wags its tail it knocks over a chair.
—**Arnold Toynbee,** BBC news summary, July 14, 1954

5 This land is your land, this land is my land,
From California to the New York island,
From the redwood forest to the Gulf Stream waters,
This land was made for you and me.
—**Woody Guthrie,** *This Land Is Your Land*, 1956

6 Americans are suckers for good news.
—**Adlai Stevenson,** speech, June 8, 1958

7 You Americans, to you time implies hope.
—**W. H. Auden,** quoted by Thekla Clark, *Wystan and Chester* [1996]

8 Our national flower is the concrete cloverleaf.
—**Lewis Mumford,** cited in *Quote* magazine, Oct. 8, 1961

9 We started from scratch, every American an immigrant who came because he wanted change. *Why are we now afraid to change?*
—**Eleanor Roosevelt,** *Tomorrow Is Now*, 1963

★ The book was published a year after her death.

10 Americans—like omelettes:
there is no such thing
as a pretty good one.
—**W. H. Auden,** *Marginalia*, 1965–1968

11 Solitude is un-American.
—**Erica Jong,** *Fear of Flying*, 1973

12 America is a vast conspiracy to make you happy.
—**John Updike,** *How to Love America and Leave It at the Same Time* in *Problems*, 1980

We are a nation that has a government—not the other way around. And this makes us special among the nations of the earth. 1

—**Ronald Reagan,** First Inaugural Address, 1981

Our flag is red, white, and blue, but our nation is a rainbow—red, yellow, brown, black, and white—and we're all precious in God's sight. 2

—**Jesse Jackson,** Democratic National Convention, San Francisco, July 17, 1984

★ Rev. Jackson later named his political organization the National Rainbow Coalition. And in the same speech, he suggested another metaphor: "America is not like a blanket—one piece of unbroken cloth, the same color, the same texture, the same size. America is more like a quilt, many pieces, many colors, many sizes, all woven and held together by a common thread."

The genius of America is that out of the many, we become one. 3

—**Jesse Jackson,** Democratic National Convention, Atlanta, Ga., July 20, 1988

We are a nation of communities . . . a brilliant diversity spread like stars, like a thousand points of light in a broad and peaceful sky. 4

—**George H. W. Bush,** presidential nomination acceptance speech, Republican National Convention, New Orleans, August 18, 1988.

★ The thousand points of light may come from Thomas Wolfe's *The Web and The Rock* (1939), as suggested by *Bartlett's:* "Instantly he could see the town below now, coiling in a thousand fumes of homely smoke, now winking into a thousand points of friendly light its glorious small design, its aching passionate assurances of walls, warmth, comfort, food, and love." Stanley and Eleanor Hochman in *The Penguin Dictionary of Contemporary American History* point to another passage that might have been familiar to Bush's speechwriter, Peggy Noonan—C. S. Lewis's description of the birth of Narnia, the magic kingdom in his classic trilogy for children, *The Chronicles of Narnia:* "One moment there was nothing but darkness; next moment a thousand points of light leaped out." Noonan herself, in her book *What I Saw at the Revolution*, did not acknowledge either source, however. "I don't know," she wrote, "a thousand clowns [a movie], a thousand days [the administration of Pres. John Kennedy]—a hundred wasn't enough and a million is too many."

There is nothing wrong with America that cannot be cured by what is right with America. 5

—**Bill Clinton,** Inaugural Address, Jan. 20, 1993

There are no angels in America. 6

—**Tony Kushner,** *Angels in America,* 1993

Americans are impatient with memory. 7

—**Jamaica Kincaid,** *Alien Soil,* in *The New Yorker,* June 21, 1993

Americans are funny people. First you shock them, and then they put you in a museum. 8

—**Mick Jagger,** Channel 13, documentary on the Rolling Stones, Aug. 10, 1994

America must be described in romantic terms. . . . America is a romance in which we all partake. 9

—**Newt Gingrich,** *To Renew America,* 1995

1 We respect, here in America,
what is concrete, visible. We ask
What is it for? What does it lead to?
—**Louise Glück**, U.S. Poet Laureate, *The Seven Ages,* 2001

2 America has, and intends to keep, military strengths beyond challenge.
—**George W. Bush,** speech at West Point, June 2002

★ More at FOREIGN POLICY.

3 The United States is the empire that dare not speak its name. It is an empire in denial.
—**Niall Ferguson,** *Empire: How Britain Made the Modern World,* 2002

★ Ferguson continues, "US denial of this poses a real danger to the world. An empire that doesn't recognize its own power is a dangerous one." Charles Maier of Harvard addressed the same issue in his article *An American Empire*, also referring to "an empire that dared not speak its name" (*Harvard Magazine,* Nov.-Dec. 2002). He maintained that now, however, we do dare. For more on empire, see Donald Rumsfeld at FOREIGN POLICY.

American Cities

See CITIES.

American History: Memorable Moments

See also AMERICA & AMERICANS; CONSTITUTION, THE; DECLARATION OF INDEPENDENCE; DEPRESSION, THE; FOREIGN POLICY; GETTYSBURG ADDRESS; HEROES (INGERSOLL AND ROOSEVELT); PATRIOTISM & THE FLAG; POLITICAL SLOGANS; PRESIDENCY, THE; SERVING ONE'S COUNTRY; UNION, THE; entries for specific wars; WATERGATE.

4 *Lumbre! Tierra!*
Light! Land!
—**Pedro Yzquierdo,** midnight, Oct. 11, 1492

★ Yzquierdo, a seaman on the *Santa María*, probably saw a shaft of moonlight on a Bahamian beach. Neither Yzquierdo nor the seaman on the *Pinta* who spotted the island at 2:00 A.M., October 12, received the royal annuity offered to the first member of the expedition to sight land. Columbus reported that he had seen light about two hours before Yzqeuierdo did, and collected the reward.

5 I went into the ocean where many islands inhabited by innumerable people I found.
—**Christopher Columbus,** letter to King Ferdinand and Queen Isabella of Spain, 1493

★ On his first voyage, he landed on San Salvador Island. The next year he arrived at Puerto Rico, Jamaica, and other islands.

6 Being thus arrived in a good harbor, and brought safe to land, they fell upon their knees and blessed the God of Heaven, who had brought them over the vast and

furious ocean, and delivered them from all the perils and miseries thereof, again to set their feet on the firm and stable earth, their proper element.

—William Bradford, *Of Plymouth Plantation*, covering years 1620–46, written 1630-51

No taxation without representation. **1**

—Anonymous, slogan, 1765

★ From early on, taxes have been one of the most emotional subjects in American political life; see TAXES. The issue in 1765 was the Stamp Act, by which the English Parliament required that government stamps be used on newspapers and legal documents.

If this be treason, make the most of it. **2**

—Patrick Henry, speech, Virginia House of Burgesses, May 29, 1765

★ Henry, in protesting the Stamp Act, reminded the burgesses that "Tarquin and Caesar each had his Brutus, Charles I his Cromwell, and George III"—the Speaker of the House interrupted, calling out "Treason!"—"may profit by their example," Henry continued. "If this be treason, make the most of it." This, at least, is how the speech was reconstructed a half century later by Henry's biographer William Wirt. Notes made by a French visitor to Williamsburg at the time, but not discovered until 1921, suggest that Henry actually backed down when interrupted by the Speaker, begging pardon of the House if "the heat of passin [as the anonymous Frenchman spelled it] might have lead (*sic*) him to have said something more than he intended." See also Henry at FREEDOM and PATRIOTISM & THE FLAG.

Let every man do his duty, and be true to his country. **3**

—Anonymous, rallying cry, Boston Tea Party, Dec. 16, 1773

★ The words were recorded by George Hewes in *A Retrospect of the Boston Tea Party*, 1834. Hewes participated in the tax protest, in which colonists boarded three merchant vessels in Boston harbor on the night of December 16, 1773, and dumped their cargoes of tea overboard. Hewes dressed as a Mohawk and carried a hatchet. Among the leaders of the protest were Samuel Adams and Paul Revere.

The country shall be independent, and we will be satisfied with nothing short of it. **4**

—Samuel Adams, March 1774

★ For Adams's reaction upon hearing the exchange of gunfire at Lexington, see AMERICAN REVOLUTION. See also DECLARATION OF INDEPENDENCE.

Give me liberty or give me death! **5**

—Patrick Henry, speech, Virginia Convention, March 23, 1775

★ More at FREEDOM. For the words of Nathan Hale, who met death in the fight for liberty, see AMERICAN REVOLUTION.

With a heart full of love and gratitude, I now take my leave of you. I most devoutly **6**
wish that your latter days may be as prosperous and happy as your former ones have been glorious and honorable.

—George Washington, farewell to his officers, Fraunces Tavern, New York City, Dec. 4, 1783

★ This was an emotional scene—Washington, Henry Knox, and others wept freely.

1 Millions for defense, but not one cent for tribute.

—Robert Goodloe Harper, toast at Congressional dinner for John Marshall, June 18, 1798, quoted in the *American Daily Advertiser*, June 20, 1798

★ Pres. John Adams in 1797 had sent John Marshall and Elbridge Gerry to assist Pinckney in what became known as the X Y Z Affair, because the officials were not named. Robert Goodloe Harper, incidentally, was from South Carolina, as was Pinckney. Often attributed to Charles C. Pinckney, this quote is an elaboration of Pinckney's refusal to bribe three French officials to obtain French acceptance of his ambassadorship and a pledge to cease attacks on American shipping. Pinckney actually said, "Not a penny! Not a penny!" or possibly "No, no, not a six pence" (sources vary).

2 We are all Republicans—we are all Federalists.

—Thomas Jefferson, First Inaugural Address, 1801

★ More at THE UNION.

3 Entangling alliances with none.

—Thomas Jefferson, First Inaugural Address, 1801

★ More at FOREIGN POLICY.

4 We have lived long, but this is the noblest work of our lives.

—Robert R. Livingston, on the signing of the Louisiana Purchase, May 1803

★ The agreement was an extraordinary bargain. For $15 million, the U.S. acquired from France the entire watershed of the Mississippi, including the present states of Louisiana, Arkansas, Oklahoma, Missouri, North and South Dakota, Iowa, Nebraska, Kansas, Minnesota, Colorado, Wyoming, and Montana. Livingston was Pres. Thomas Jefferson's minister to France, and he worked together with U.S. special envoy James Monroe. The French foreign minister, Charles Maurice de Talleyrand, negotiated on behalf of the emperor Napoleon. A revolt in Haiti and impending war with Great Britain had inspired France to propose the deal.

5 Ocian in view! O! The joy!

—William Clark, *Journal,* Nov. 7, 1805

★ Exclamation, in Clark's original spelling, upon sighting the Pacific Ocean. Lewis and Clark may have mistaken the bay at the mouth of the Columbia River for the ocean. Still, they were close to their destination, having traveled some 18 months and 4,000 miles from St. Louis to reach this point.

6 Oh, say, can you see by the dawn's early light,
What so proudly we hailed at the twilight's last gleaming?

—Francis Scott Key, *The Star-Spangled Banner*, Sept. 14, 1814

★ More at PATRIOTISM & THE FLAG.

7 I shall never surrender nor retreat.

—William Barrett Travis, commander of the Alamo, letter, Feb. 24, 1836

★ In this letter requesting reinforcements, Lt. Col. Travis announced that he would not surrender to the Mexican army under Gen. Antonio López Santa Anna. He concluded, "VICTORY OR DEATH." The Mexican army of several thousand had beseiged the Alamo, a fortified mission in San Antonio; some 183 men were trapped inside. But as Col. David Crockett noted in his *Alamo Journal* on February 23, 1836, "They'll find that they have to do with men who will never lay down their arms as long as they can stand on their legs." (The supposedly autobiographical journal was written after Crockett's death by Richard Penn Smith, but it became a best-seller and was long believed to have portrayed the siege accurately.) On March 6, the Alamo was captured and all the defenders killed. For more, see Crockett at FREEDOM. See also Crockett at BOASTS.

Thermopylae had her messenger of defeat—the Alamo had none. **1**

—Thomas Jefferson Green, attributed

★ Green apparently wrote this thought for a speech by Edward Burleson. The sentence was engraved on the first monument to the Alamo in Austin, as well as on the rebuilt monument.

Remember the Alamo! **2**

—Sidney Sherman, battle cry, April 21, 1836

★ The saying is traditionally attributed to Col. Sherman, whose troops advanced at San Jacinto chanting this battle cry. One month earlier, Gen. Santa Anna, the president of Mexico, had conquered the Alamo, leaving no survivors. In the battle at San Jacinto, Texans led by Commander in Chief Sam Houston, captured Santa Anna. In the Treaty of Velasco, which Santa Anna was forced to sign, Mexico recognized the independence of Texas. See also MEXICAN WAR.

Your petitioner therefore prays your Honorable Court to grant him leave to sue as a **3**
poor person, in order to establish his right to freedom.

—Dred Scott, petition, July 1, 1847

★ With this petition, Scott, a slave, initiated litigation that led to one of the all-time decisions ever in a major case before a high court. Scott was seeking his freedom on the grounds that his owner had taken him from Missouri to Wisconsin territory, where slavery was illegal and where Scott had married and started a family; subsequently Scott was taken back to Missouri. When the case reached the Supreme Court, Chief Justice Roger B. Taney, ruled: "They [slaves and their descendants] are not included and were not intended to be included under the word 'citizens' in the Constitution." He referred to slaves as "beings of an inferior order" and found that the court's duty was for all time to protect the rights of the property owner, i.e., slaveholder (*Dred Scott v. Sandford*, 1857). The ruling further inflamed the violent passions of the time, and brought civil war yet closer.

A house divided against itself cannot stand. I believe this government cannot endure **4**
permanently half slave and half free.

—Abraham Lincoln, speech, Republican State Convention, Springfield, Ill., June 16, 1858

★ More at THE UNION.

I believe that to have interfered as I have done—as I have always freely admitted **5**
I have done—in behalf of His despised poor, was not wrong but right.

—John Brown, Oct. 31, 1859, in James Redpath, *The Public Life of John Brown*, 1860

★ This was part of Brown's eloquent statement to the court on being sentenced to death for his raid on the arsenal at Harpers Ferry on October 16. He willingly took on the martyr's role, saying, "If it is deemed necessary that I should forfeit my life for the furtherance of the ends of justice and mingle my blood further with the blood of my children and with the blood of millions in this slave country whose rights are disregarded by wicked, cruel, and unjust enactments—I submit; so let it be done." Southerners were greatly relieved by the failure of Brown's raid; no slaves had come to join him, as he had hoped. Meanwhile, many Northerners looked upon him as a saint. Church bells tolled in the North on December 2 when he was hanged, and Henry Wadsworth Longfellow predicted in his diary: "This will be a great day in our history, the date of a new revolution—quite as much needed as the old one. . . . As I write, they are leading old John Brown to execution. . . . This is sowing the wind to reap the whirlwind, which will soon come." See also Brown at CIVIL WAR and LAST WORDS.

1 We must not be enemies. Though passion may have strained, it must not break our bonds of affection.

—Abraham Lincoln, First Inaugural Address, March 4, 1861

★ More at PEACE.

2 Thenceforward, and forever, free.

—Abraham Lincoln, Preliminary Emancipation Proclamation, Sept. 22, 1862

★ For the context, see SLAVERY.

3 Fourscore and seven years ago, our fathers brought forth on this continent a new nation, conceived in liberty, and dedicated to the proposition that all men are created equal.

—Abraham Lincoln, Gettysburg Address, Nov. 19, 1863

★ More at GETTYSBURG ADDRESS.

4 With malice toward none, with charity for all, with firmness in the right, as God gives us to see the right, let us strive on to finish the work we are in.

—Abraham Lincoln, Second Inaugural Address, March 4, 1865

★ More at THE CIVIL WAR.

5 *Sic semper tyrannis!* The South is avenged!

—John Wilkes Booth, after shooting Pres. Abraham Lincoln, April 14, 1865

★ The Latin saying used by Booth means "Thus always to tyrants," and is also the Virginia motto.

6 God reigns and the government at Washington still lives.

—James A. Garfield, speech, New York City, April 15, 1865

★ Rep. Garfield of Ohio was in New York on the day of Lincoln's death, and addressed the public from a balcony at the U.S. Customs house on Wall Street. He later became president, and he, too, was assassinated.

7 Let us have peace.

—Ulysses S. Grant, presidential nomination acceptance speech, May 29, 1868

8 Dr. Livingstone, I presume?

—Henry Morton Stanley, remark to David Livingstone, Nov. 10, 1871

★ Stanley fled to America from Wales when he was fifteen, and took his surname from the man who adopted him, Henry Stanley. He became a citizen and a correspondent for the *New York Herald*, which assigned him to find Livingstone, the famed Scottish missionary and explorer in Africa, who had been searching for the source of the Nile. After a dreadful journey, Stanley reached the ailing Livingstone at Ujiji on Lake Tanganyika, scoring a journalistic coup for the U.S. His query, which quickly became a catch phrase, was cited in his book, *How I Found Livingstone.*

Give me your tired, your poor, **1**
Your huddled masses yearning to breathe free,
The wretched refuse of your teeming shore,
Send these, the homeless, tempest-tost to me:
I lift my lamp beside the golden door.
—Emma Lazarus, *The New Colossus: Inscription for the Statue of Liberty*, 1883

You shall not crucify mankind upon a cross of gold. **2**
—William Jennings Bryan, speech, Democratic National Convention, Chicago, July 8, 1896

★ This "Cross of Gold" speech won Bryan the presidential nomination at age thirty-six. He had developed the metaphor some years earlier, and used it to great effect. More at ECONOMICS.

Success. Four flights Thursday morning all against twenty-one mile wind. **3**
—Wilbur Wright & Orville Wright, telegram to their father, from Kitty Hawk, N.C., Dec. 17, 1903

★ More at SCIENCE: TECHNOLOGY.

Perdicaris alive, or Raisuli dead. **4**
—John Hay, cablegram to the Sultan of Morocco, 1904

★ An early hostage crisis. Perdicaris, a Greek-American, was kidnapped by a Moroccan outlaw, Achmed Ben Mohammed Raisuli, and held for $70,000 ransom. Secretary of State Hay's ultimatum became a national rallying cry in the summer of 1904, when his cable was read at the Republican National Convention in Chicago in June. "We want Perdicaris alive, or Raisuli dead," Hay had cabled. The sultan, despite being in a semi-war with Raisuli, paid the ransom, and the hostage was freed.

We stand at Armageddon, and we battle for the Lord. **5**
—Theodore Roosevelt, speech, Republican National Convention, June 18, 1912

★ Despite this ringing declaration, Pres. William Howard Taft won the nomination of the convention, after unseating seventy-two Roosevelt delegates. Roosevelt formed the Progressive Party and challenged Taft. Woodrow Wilson benefited from the split Republican vote and won the election.

It must be a peace without victory. . . . Only a peace between equals can last. **6**
—Woodrow Wilson, speech, U.S. Senate, Jan. 22, 1917

★ Pres. Wilson was describing to the Senate his understanding of the kind of peace that would be acceptable to the warring European powers. His assessment proved prescient, as the eventual peace, a peace based on victory and defeat, lasted only twenty years—until the Nazi invasion of Poland. See also World War I and World War

II. On the other hand, some historians argue that the peace failed because the victory was not sufficiently complete; Germany had not been totally destroyed.

1 The world must be made safe for democracy.

—**Woodrow Wilson,** speech to the U.S. Congress asking for a declaration of war, April 2, 1917

★ More at WORLD WAR I.

2 A general association of nations must be formed under specific covenants for the purpose of affording mutual guarantees of political independence and territorial integrity to great and small states alike.

—**Woodrow Wilson,** "Fourteen Points" speech to Congress, Jan. 8, 1918

★ The reference here is to the League of Nations, established after World War I. It became moribund in the 1930s, unable to cope with German and Japanese military aggression. After World War II, the League was succeeded by the United Nations. See also FOREIGN POLICY and PEACE.

3 We must stabilize and strive for normalcy.

—**Warren G. Harding,** presidential nomination acceptance speech, July 22, 1920

★ Use of the rare term *normalcy* instead of the more normal *normality* was one of the few memorable aspects of Harding's campaign. The call for a return to normalcy was a rejection of the idealism and internationalism of the Wilson years. Earlier in the year, on May 20, in a speech in Boston, Harding summed up his message in these words: "America's present need is not heroics, but healing; not nostrums, but normalcy; not revolution, but restoration; not experimentation, but equipoise."

4 An opportunity as does seldom come to mortal man to free seventeen million from political slavery was mine.

—**Henry Thomas Burn,** speech, Tennessee House of Representatives, August 1920

★ On August 18, 1920, Rep. Burn, age twenty-three, broke a tie in the Tennessee legislature by casting a vote in favor of the Nineteenth Amendment, granting suffrage to women. See also Burn at PARENTS and TENNESSEE; and his mother, Febb Ensminger Burn, at WOMEN.

5 We in America today are nearer to the final triumph over poverty than ever before in the history of a land.

—**Herbert Hoover,** presidential nomination acceptance speech, Republican National Convention, 1928

★ The great Wall Street crash was a year away.

6 We offer one who has the will to win—who not only deserves success but commands it. Victory is his habit—the happy warrior, Alfred Smith.

—**Franklin Delano Roosevelt,** nominating New York governor Al Smith as president, Democratic National Convention, Houston, Texas, 1928

★ The happy warrior, as he was known thereafter, lost to Herbert Hoover. The epithet comes from the Wordsworth poem *The Character of the Happy Warrior.* According to Henry F. Woods, in *American Sayings* (1945), Roosevelt had previously used the phrase in a eulogy for Grover Cleveland in 1908. See also Roosevelt at HEROES.

Wall St. Lays an Egg. 1

—**Sime Silverman,** headline, *Variety*, Oct. 30, 1929

★ More at THE DEPRESSION.

I pledge you, I pledge myself, to a new deal for the American people. 2

—**Franklin D. Roosevelt,** presidential nomination acceptance speech, Democratic National Convention, Chicago, July 2, 1932

★ "The New Deal" became a popular label for Roosevelt's administration and policies in the 1930s. The phrase had been used earlier in British as well as American politics, but neither F.D.R. nor the men who worked on his acceptance speech, Samuel Rosenman and Raymond Moley, attached particular importance to the words. The press latched onto them right away, however. What first made the Democrats realize that they had tumbled onto an exciting catch phrase, according to *Safire's New Political Dictionary*, was a cartoon drawn by Rollin Kirby on the day of the speech of a bewildered but hopeful man, leaning on a hoe, and watching an airplane labeled "New Deal" flying overhead. A rather different view was expressed in 1940 by Joseph Pew, whose money came from Sun Oil. He called the New Deal a "gigantic scheme to raze U.S. businesses to a dead level and debase the citizenry into a mass of ballot-casting serfs," quoted in *The Wall Street Journal* (April 1, 2005). See also POLITICAL SLOGANS.

The only thing we have to fear is fear itself, nameless, unreasoning, unjustified terror which paralyzes needed efforts to convert retreat into advance. 3

—**Franklin D. Roosevelt,** First Inaugural Address, March 4, 1933

★ The heartening effect of these words on a worried people cannot be exaggerated. Many, perhaps most, who heard this speech feared that the nation was on the brink of chaos and possibly revolution; see THE DEPRESSION. For the occasion, Roosevelt turned to rhetoric already proved effective. His predecessors include Henry David Thoreau—see under FEAR—and the duke of Wellington, "The only thing I am afraid of is fear." Going back further, similar comments were made by Francis Bacon and Montaigne. Another moving passage in this inaugural speech drew on the Bible: In 1964, Lyndon Johnson recalled that when Roosevelt "quoted from Proverbs: 'Where there is no vision, the people perish,' it gave me an inspiration that has carried me all through the years since."

This generation of Americans has a rendezvous with destiny. 4

—**Franklin D. Roosevelt,** presidential nomination acceptance speech, Democratic National Convention, June 27, 1936

★ More at GENERATIONS.

I see one-third of a nation ill-housed, ill-clad, ill-nourished. 5

—**Franklin D. Roosevelt,** Second Inaugural Address, Jan. 20, 1937

We must be the great arsenal of democracy. 6

—**Franklin D. Roosevelt,** fireside radio talk, Dec. 29, 1940

★ This speech marked the beginning of the end of U.S. neutrality in World War II. The president called upon Americans to support Great Britain with "the same resolution, the same sense of urgency, the same spirit of patriotism and sacrifice as we would show were we at war." A week later, he recommended to Congress a lend-lease act that would give him the authority to send war materials to those nations fighting fascism. The talk recalls Woodrow Wilson's appeal to Congress in 1917 to make the world safe for democracy; see DEMOCRACY. Gorton Carruth and Eugene Ehrlich, in *American Quotations*, credit French statesman Jean Monnet with the first use of the "arsenal of democracy" metaphor, in conversation with Felix Frankfurter. Writing in *The New Yorker*, August 15, 1994, Doris Kearns Goodwin credited presidential aide Harry Hopkins with suggesting the phrase to Roosevelt.

1 We look forward to a world founded upon four essential human freedoms.
—Franklin D. Roosevelt, the "Four Freedoms" speech, a State of the Union message, Jan. 6, 1941

★ More at FREEDOM.

2 Yesterday, December 7, 1941—a date which will live in infamy.
—Franklin D. Roosevelt, message to Congress, Dec. 8, 1941

★ More at WORLD WAR II.

3 Boys, if you ever pray, pray for me now.
—Harry S. Truman, remark to the White House press corps, April 13, 1945

★ Truman had been sworn in as president the day before, just ninety minutes after Eleanor Roosevelt told him that her husband was dead. "I felt like the moon, the stars, and all the planets had fallen on me," Truman told the press.

4 Let us not be deceived—we are today in the midst of a cold war.
—Bernard Baruch, speech, Columbia, S.C., April 16, 1947

★ A year earlier, Winston Churchill had announced gloomily, "From Stettin in the Baltic to Trieste in the Adriatic, an iron curtain has descended across the Continent," speech, April 5, 1946. According to William Safire in *Safire's New Political Dictionary* (1993), "cold war" was coined in 1946 in a draft for a speech for Baruch by journalist and political consultant Herbert Bayard Swope but not used by Baruch until the following year. The phrase was popularized by (and sometimes is mistakenly credited to) columnist Walter Lippmann, who used *The Cold War* as a book title in 1947. For the end of the Cold War, see George H. W. Bush and Paul Tsongas below. See also COMMUNISM.

5 The time has come for the Democratic party of America to get out of the shadow of states' rights and walk forthrightly into the bright sunshine of human rights.
—Hubert H. Humphrey, speech, Democratic national convention, Philadelphia, July 14, 1948

★ The future senator and vice president was then mayor of Minneapolis. The convention's stand on civil rights ruptured the party. The break-away Dixiecrats supported Strom Thurmond for president that year, heralding the end of what had been for seventy-five years the Democratic party's "solid South." States rights were typically invoked to defend racist laws and policies in the South.

6 I'm going to fight hard, and I'm going to give them hell.
—Harry S. Truman, campaign pledge, 1948

★ See also POLITICAL SLOGANS.

Dewey Defeats Truman. 1

—**Chicago Tribune,** banner headline, Nov. 3, 1948

★ Bad guess.

While I cannot take the time to name all the men in the State Department who have 2
been named as members of the Communist Party and members of a spy ring, I have here in my hand a list of 205 that were known to the Secretary of State [Dean Acheson] as being members of the Communist Party and are still working and shaping the policy of the State Department.

—**Joseph R. McCarthy,** speech, Wheeling, W. Va., Feb. 9, 1950

★ This accusation established the junior senator from Wisconsin as the chief Communist hunter in the U.S., but McCarthy seemed not to sense its importance, judging by the odd forum in which the charge was first aired—The Women's Republican Club of Ohio County, West Virginia. The speech derived in part from remarks on January 26, 1950, by fellow Republican Richard M. Nixon, a member of the House Committee on Un-American Activities. The paper in McCarthy's hand apparently was a letter, more than three years old, from former Secretary of State James F. Byrnes to a member of the House that gave figures on security risks in general, not just Communists. McCarthy never actually came up with a single name from his list, and the number changed from 205 to 57 to 81, 10, 116, then 1, 121, and 106. It was four years before McCarthy's authority was challenged; see Edward R. Murrow and Joseph N. Welch below. See also COMMUNISM.

When I joined the Army, even before the turn of the century, it was the fulfillment 3
of all my hopes and dreams. The hopes and dreams have long since vanished. But I still remember the refrain of one of the most popular barracks ballads of that day, which proclaimed proudly that, "Old soldiers never die. They just fade away." And like the old soldier of the ballad, I now close my military career and just fade away—an old soldier who tried to do his duty as God gave him the light to see that duty.

—**Douglas MacArthur,** speech, joint session of Congress, April 19, 1951

★ The general had just been relieved of duty by Pres. Truman for insubordination. The hugely popular MacArthur believed that to win the Korean War the U.S. would have to move against Communist China, using nuclear weapons and the Nationalist forces under Chiang Kai-shek. This undermined the president's international initiatives; moreover, MacArthur had posted mixed results as commander of the Korean action. Nevertheless, Truman's decision was risky, and MacArthur's speech inspired such a wave of emotion nationwide that there was fear of a popular uprising in favor of the general that would force his reinstatement and the impeachment or censure of the president. But within a month, MacArthur did indeed begin to fade. See also Gen. Omar Bradley at WAR. For more on the song, see under MacArthur at THE MILITARY.

Pat doesn't have a mink coat. But she does have a good respectable Republican cloth 4
coat.

—**Richard M. Nixon,** "Checkers" speech, Sept. 23, 1952

★ Nixon was the vice-presidential candidate on the ticket headed by Gen. Dwight D. Eisenhower, when it was disclosed in the press that a group of California businessmen had quietly given him more than $18,000 for campaign expenses. It had appeared that

Eisenhower might drop his running mate until Nixon scored a public relations coup with a televised speech to the nation stressing that his family was scratching along with little money. "Pat [his wife] and I have the satisfaction that every dime that we've got is honestly ours," he said. He did admit accepting a spotted spaniel from a man in Texas, adding emotionally—see below.

1 And our little girl, Tricia, the six-year-old, named it Checkers. And you know, the kids love the dog, and I just want to say this right now, that regardless of what they do about it, we're going to keep it.

—Ibid.

★ Checkers was not the only famous dog in American politics. Fala, short for Murray of Fallahill, Franklin D. Roosevelt's Scottie, was frequently in the news, and Pres. George H. W. Bush's dog Millie allegedly wrote a book with First Lady Barbara Bush. F.D.R. memorably defended his pet in 1944, when Republican newspapers spread a rumor that the dog had been left by mistake on an Aleutian island and then retrieved at great expense to taxpayers. F.D.R. bested his critics with humor. "I don't resent attacks," he said, "and my family doesn't resent attacks, but Fala does resent them. You know, Fala is Scotch, and being a Scottie, as soon as he learned that the Republican fiction writers . . . had concocted a story that I . . . had sent a destroyer back to find him . . . his Scotch soul was furious. He has not been the same dog since." Then there was Speaker of the House Champ Clark of Missouri, who used a hillbilly-dog song in his 1912 campaign for the Democratic presidential nomination. The idea was to project a down-home image in contrast to Woodrow Wilson's elitist mien. Clark's song went in part: "Ev'ry time I come to town, / The boys keep kickin' my dawg aroun'; / Makes no dif'rence if he is a houn', / They've gotta quit kickin' my dawg aroun'." For another sample of Clark's populist politics, see his epitaph for himself at EPITAPHS & GRAVESTONES.

2 We must not confuse dissent with disloyalty.

—Edward R. Murrow, *Report on Sen. Joseph R. McCarthy*, in Murrow's documentary television series *See It Now*, March 7, 1954

★ This was the first major assault on McCarthyism. Even the popular and influential Murrow felt that he had to bide his time until McCarthy's excesses began to worry the American public. The program was considered risky, but Murrow told his audience, "Remember that we are not descended from fearful men, not from men who feared to write, to speak, to associate, and to defend causes which were, for the moment, unpopular." The fatal blow to McCarthy was struck three months later; see Joseph N. Welch below.

3 We conclude that in the field of public education "separate but equal" has no place. Separate educational facilities are inherently unequal.

—Earl Warren, *Brown v. Board of Education of Topeka*, May 17, 1954

★ This Supreme Court decision marked the end of state-sanctioned segregation in the U.S. Reflecting on the fortieth anniversary of *Brown*, U. S. Rep. John Lewis of Georgia, said, "This country is a different country now. It is a better country. We have witnessed a nonviolent revolution," speech at the John F. Kennedy Library, Washington, D.C., April 1994. The attorney for the plaintiffs was Thurgood Marshall, who was appointed to the Supreme Court himself in 1967. The victory was also a vindication of Justice John Marshall Harlan, who in a dissenting opinion in the case of *Plessy v. Ferguson*,

1894, said that segregation was "the badge of slavery." In 1992, a federal appeals court found that the Topeka Board of Education still was not in compliance with the Constitutional requirement to integrate its schools. See also THE CONSTITUTION; RACES & PEOPLES.

Have you no sense of decency, sir, at long last? Have you no sense of decency? 1

—Joseph N. Welch, Army-McCarthy hearings, June 9, 1954

★ Attorney Welch, representing the U.S. Army, addressed this remark to Sen. Joseph McCarthy in televised hearings conducted by the senator to ferret out alleged Communist subversives in the military. People in the hearing room cheered. From this moment, McCarthy's power, and McCarthyism itself, began to wane.

Ask not what your country can do for you—ask what you can do for your country. 2

—John F. Kennedy, inaugural address, Jan. 20, 1961

★ More at SERVING ONE'S COUNTRY.

We're eyeball to eyeball, and I think the other fellow just blinked. 3

—Dean Rusk, conversation, Oct. 24, 1962

★ Secretary of State Rusk was speaking of Premier Nikita Khrushchev. This was in the midst of the Cuban missile crisis. Pres. John F. Kennedy had demanded that Russia remove its ballistic missiles from Cuba. The blink was scarcely perceptible on October 24. The nation seemed to be on the brink of nuclear war, and it was another four days before Khrushchev backed down, and everyone breathed easier. This quote is in *Bartlett's*.

You won't have Nixon to kick around any more, because, gentlemen, this is my last 4
press conference.

—Richard M. Nixon, Nov. 5, 1962, after losing to incumbent Pat Brown in the California gubernatorial race

★ It wasn't.

Ich bin ein Berliner. 5

—John F. Kennedy, speech, West Berlin, June 26, 1963

★ Delivered to a large crowd at city hall in West Berlin, this speech affirmed U.S. commitment to the embattled democracy. The full passage was: "All free men wherever they may live, are citizens of Berlin. And therefore, as a free man, I take pride in the words, 'Ich bin ein Berliner [I am a Berliner].' " It is sometimes said—in *Bartlett's* sixteenth edition and elsewhere—that JFK made a linguistic faux pas in referring to himself as a "Berliner" because a "Berliner" also is a sort of jelly doughnut. But Reinhold Aman, a native speaker of German as well as an authority on the language of aggression, debunked this theory in *Maledicta XI*, maintaining that Kennedy's words were perfectly intelligible. And in fact, the declaration was greeted with overwhelming, almost riotous cheering, not puzzlement or snickers.

Now is the time to make real the promises of democracy. *Now* is the time to rise 6
from the dark and desolate valley of segregation to the sunlit path of racial justice. *Now* is the time to open the doors of opportunity to all of God's children. *Now* is the

time to lift our nation from the quicksands of racial injustice to the solid rock of brotherhood.

—**Martin Luther King, Jr.,** speech at the Lincoln Memorial in Washington, D.C., to 200,000 civil rights marchers, August 28, 1963

★ For the incident that led to King's emergence as a civil rights leader, see Rosa Parks at RACES & PEOPLES.

1 Let us not seek to satisfy our thirst for freedom by drinking from the cup of bitterness and hatred. . . . Again and again we must rise to the majestic heights of meeting physical force with soul force.

—**Ibid.**

2 No, no, we are not satisfied, and we will not be satisfied until justice rolls down like waters and righteousness like a mighty stream.

—**Ibid.**

★ Here Dr. King drew on the Old Testament, *Amos*, 5:24: "Let judgment run down as waters, and righteousness as a mighty stream."

3 I say to you today, my friends, that in spite of the difficulties and frustrations of the moment, I still have a dream. It is a dream deeply rooted in the American dream.

4 I have a dream that one day on the red hills of Georgia, the sons of former slaves and the sons of former slaveowners will be able to sit down together at the table of brotherhood.

—**Ibid.**

★ The "I have a dream" passages were the highpoint of this great address. Not since the wartime talks of Winston Churchill and Franklin D. Roosevelt had a speech reached so many so memorably.

5 I have a dream that my four little children will one day live in a nation where they will not be judged by the color of their skin but by the content of their character.

I have a dream that one day this nation will rise up and live out the true meaning of its creed: "We hold these truths to be self-evident; that all men are created equal."

I have a dream today.

—**Ibid.**

6 When we let freedom ring, when we let it ring from every village and every hamlet, from every state and every city, we will be able to speed up that day when all of God's children, black men and white men, Jews and Gentiles, Protestants and Catholics, will be able to join hands and sing in the words of the old Negro spiritual, "Free at last! Free at last! Thank God Almighty, we are free at last!"

—**Ibid.**

★ The finale of the speech.

7 This administration today, here and now, declares unconditional war on poverty in America. . . . It will not be a short or easy struggle, no single weapon or strategy will suffice, but we shall not rest until that war is won.

—**Lyndon B. Johnson,** State of the Union speech, Jan. 8, 1964

★ The war went quite well, a key initiative being passage of the Economic Opportunity Act later that year. But Johnson became ever more deeply engaged in a second war, in Vietnam. And as it turned out, the nation could not afford both guns and butter.

For in your time we have the opportunity to move not only toward the rich society and the powerful society, but upward to the Great Society. **1**

—**Lyndon B. Johnson,** speech, University of Michigan, Ann Arbor, May 22, 1964

★ See also Johnson at POLITICAL SLOGANS.

I would remind you that extremism in the defense of liberty is no vice. And let me remind you also that moderation in the pursuit of justice is no virtue. **2**

—**Barry Goldwater,** presidential nomination acceptance speech, Republican National Convention, July 16, 1964

★ Reminiscent of Thomas Paine's "Moderation in temper is always a virtue, but moderation in principle is always a vice," *The Rights of Man*, 1791. Possibly borrowed from the Roman politican and orator Cicero, who defended his execution of five followers of his enemy Catiline in 63 B.C. thus: "I must remind you, Lords, Senators, that extreme patriotism in the defense of freedom is no crime, and let me respectfully remind you that pusillanimity in the pursuit of justice is no virtue in a Roman." Goldwater's speech writer was probably Karl Hess.

That's one small step for [a] man, one giant leap for mankind. **3**

—**Neil A. Armstrong,** disembarking from the Apollo 11 Eagle lunar lander, July 20, 1969

★ More at SCIENCE: TECHNOLOGY.

Houston, we've had a problem here. Houston, we've had a problem. **4**

—**James A. Lovell, Jr.,** from Apollo 13, April 1970

★ The problem was that an exploding oxygen tank on the space ship had knocked out one engine and the main supply of electric power. The command module was essentially incapacitated, and the three astronauts had to use the lunar landing module for power and air.

We, therefore, conclude that the right of personal privacy includes the abortion decision, but that this right is not unqualified and must be considered against important state interests in regulation. **5**

—**Harry A. Blackmun,** *Roe v. Wade*, 1973

Mr. Gorbachev, tear down this wall! **6**

—**Ronald Reagan,** speech at the Brandenburg Gate, Berlin Wall, West Berlin, June 12, 1987

★ The fortified Wall was built under Soviet orders in 1961 to stop the flow of residents of Communist East Germany into the Western sector of Berlin. Pres. Reagan's challenge to the Russian leader was exceptionally bold, and some government diplomats advised against using it. The president knew better, and the moment exemplified his determination to bring down Communist rule. Two years later, the East German regime lifted travel restrictions, and dismantled the Wall. In 1990, the two Germanys were reunited.

1 Read my lips: No new taxes.

—George H. W. Bush, presidential nomination acceptance speech, Republican National Convention, Aug. 18, 1988

★ More at TAXES. Two other phrases stand out from this speech: "a thousand points of light"—see AMERICA & AMERICANS; and "a kinder, gentler, nation"—see POLITICAL SLOGANS.

2 It is a high-tech lynching for uppity blacks.

—Clarence Thomas, testimony before the U.S. Senate Judiciary Committee, Oct. 11, 1991

★ Thomas was referring to the tough questioning directed at him during the hearing on his nomination to the Supreme Court. He had been accused of sexual harassment by former colleague Anita Hill.

3 By the grace of God, America won the cold war.

—George H. W. Bush, Jan. 28, 1992

4 The cold war is over, and Japan won.

—Paul E. Tsongas, 1992

★ The former senator from Massachusetts used this line to press his campaign for the Democratic presidential nomination. He lost to Bill Clinton.

5 It depends what the meaning of "is" is.

—Bill Clinton, grand jury testimony, August 17, 1998

★ The president gave this reply when asked whether he should have corrected his lawyer during a deposition on Jan. 17, 1998, when the lawyer said, "There is absolutely no sex of any kind, in any manner, shape or form." This denial of a sexual relationship between Clinton and White House Intern Monica Lewinsky had to be retracted, and the affair led to impeachment proceedings that did not succeed. Here, the president was making the point that the lawyer was technically correct in that there was no current affair in January. The sentence became instantly famous as emblematic of Mr. Clinton's evasive use of language.

6 Let's roll.

—Todd Beamer, Sept. 11, 2001

★ Reported rallying cry to fellow passengers on Flight 93, hijacked by terrorists. As passengers tried to storm the cockpit, the pilot crashed the plane, killing all aboard. Evidently this plane, which went down in rural Pennsylvania, was to be flown into the White House. Subsequent study of the audio tapes indicated that the shout may have been, "Roll it!" with reference to using a food cart in the charge.

7 *Nous sommes tous des américains.* [We Are All Americans.]

—Jean-Marie Colombani, headline, *Le Monde,* Sept. 12, 2001

★ Colombani, editor-in-chief of this leading French newspaper was expressing the near universal shock at the attacks on the World Trade Center. The second sentence was, "We are all New Yorkers," with reference to Kennedy's, "Ich bin ein Berliner" (see above). Incidentally, while the paper appeared on Sept. 12, the issue is actually dated Sept. 13.

States like these, and their terrorist allies, constitute an axis of evil, arming to threaten the peace of the world. 1

—**George W. Bush,** State of the Union address, Jan. 29, 2002

★ The president was speaking of states that he said were developing weapons of mass destruction. The three states specifically included in the axis were Iran, Iraq and North Korea. Discussion of the unexpected "axis of evil" dominated news reports of the speech. Subsequently, White House speechwriter David Frum resigned after his wife sent an email to friends and family saying that he was the author of the famous passage. Actually, according to Bob Woodward in *Plan of Attack,* Frum wrote of an "axis of hatred," changed later by speechwriter Michael Gerson to "axis of evil."

Your government failed you, those entrusted with with protecting you failed you, and I failed you. 2

—**Richard Clarke,** former national counter-terrorism director, testifying before the 9/11 commission, March 24, 2004

YES!!! Red Sox Complete Sweep, Win First Series Since 1918 3

—**headline,** *The Boston Globe*, Oct. 28, 2004

★ It was the greatest comeback in sports history. The ill-fated Red Sox were down three games to none against the mythic Yankees in the American League Championship Series. But they won four straight games to beat the Yankees, and swept the formidable St. Louis Cardinals in the World Series.

American Revolution (1775–1783)

See also AMERICAN HISTORY: MEMORABLE MOMENTS; DECLARATION OF INDEPENDENCE; INDEPENDENCE DAY; TAXES.

United we stand, divided we fall. 4

—**Anonymous,** watchword of the American revolutionaries

★ See also John Dickinson's *Liberty Song* at UNITY.

In the name of the Great Jehovah and the Continental Congress. 5

—**Ethan Allen,** Fort Ticonderoga, May 10, 1775

★ Allen's reply, so he said several years later, to the British officer at Fort Ticonderoga who asked by what authority he demanded the post's surrender. Other Green Mountain boys had differing recollections. One said that Allen shouted, "Come out of here, you damned old rat"; another that he threatened, "Come out of there, you sons of British whores, or I'll smoke you out." Pioneer sociologist William Graham Sumner asserted in a lecture at Yale in the 1890s on the expurgation of American history that Allen used the even stronger "Open up here, you goddamned son of a bitch." If Allen did make some sort of reference to Jehovah and the Continental Congress, he certainly exaggerated, as neither had authorized his mission.

There [in Charlestown] I agreed with a Colonel Conant and some other gentlemen 6
that if the British went out by water, we [in Boston] would show two lanterns in the North Church steeple; and if by land, one as a signal; for we were apprehensive it

would be difficult [for a messenger] to cross the Charles River or get over Boston Neck.

—Paul Revere, letter to Dr. Jeremy Belknap

★ This describes the arrangement made on Sunday, April 16, 1775, with Col. Conant of the Charlestown Committee of Safety for a signal if and when British troops moved out of Boston. Revere feared that when the moment came, the British might post guards to prevent American couriers from leaving Boston and spreading the word. The colonists had learned that the British hoped to arrest Samuel Adams and John Hancock, who were in hiding in Lexington, and to seize ammunition and other supplies hidden at Concord. Their informer may have been the American-born wife of Gen. Thomas Gage, the commander of British troops in North America. As the troops prepared to go on active duty on the night of April 18, the revolutionary leader Dr. Joseph Warren dispatched Revere and another courier, William Dawes, to Lexington. See below for Longfellow's version of events.

1 Stand your ground. Don't fire unless fired upon, but if they mean to have a war, let it begin here!

—John Parker, order to his militiamen, Lexington, Mass., April 19, 1775

★ This is as recounted by Capt. Parker's grandson, and is probably a well-polished rendition. Lexington's company of militia had gathered on the town green. Parker's order came just before the British opened fire.

2 What a glorious morning for America!

—Samuel Adams, hearing the sound of gunfire at Lexington, April 19, 1775

★ This exclamation, traditionally attributed to Adams, is on Lexington's town seal. Emerson called the gunfire "the shot heard 'round the world"; see below.

3 Don't fire until you see the whites of their eyes.

—William Prescott, battle of Bunker Hill, June 17, 1775

★ Also attributed to Israel Putnam, but he was probably relaying the order from Prescott, commander of the 1,500 colonial troops at Breeds Hill, where the battle actually took place. (Bunker Hill is nearby.) The British, with twice the manpower, needed three tries to dislodge the Americans. The order has European precedents, including Prince Charles of Prussia at Jägerndorf, May 23, 1745: "Silent till you see the whites of their eyes"; and Frederick the Great at Prague, May 6, 1757: "No firing till you see the whites of their eyes." Historian Robert M. Ketchum has described the order as a "time-honored admonition," *American Heritage*, June 1973.

4 I wish this cursed place was burned!

—Thomas Gage, June 17, 1775

★ Lt. Gen. Gage, at this early date, foresaw the disaster that would eventually overtake British forces. He made this bitter exclamation after the battle of Bunker Hill.

5 The period of debate is closed. Arms, as a last resource, must decide the contest.

—Tom Paine, *Common Sense*, 1776

6 Rebellion to tyrants is obedience to God.

—Anonymous, motto on Thomas Jefferson's seal, c. 1776

★ In a letter to Edward Everett written on February 24, 1823, Jefferson said that he believed that this was the motto of one of the regicides of Charles I. That probably would have been John Bradshaw.

The time is now near at hand which must probably determine whether Americans are to be freemen or slaves . . . . The fate of unborn millions will now depend, under God, on the courage and conduct of this army. Our cruel and unrelenting enemy leaves us no choice but a brave resistance or the most abject submission. We have therefore to resolve to conquer or die. 1

—**George Washington,** general orders, July 2, 1776

I only regret that I have but one life to lose for my country. 2

—**Nathan Hale,** at the gallows in Artillery Park, New York City (near Third Avenue and 66th Street), Sept. 22, 1776

★ Capt. Hale, age twenty-one, was a graduate of Yale College, known as an excellent orator with liberal views—his graduation speech addressed the importance of educating women. When urged not to be a spy, Hale replied with a classic defense of cloak-and-dagger work: "Every kind of service necessary to the public good becomes honorable by being necessary," letter to William Hull, September 10, 1776. Hale's famous pronouncement prior to his execution was probably part of a fairly long and spirited statement. Hale adapted a line from Joseph Addison's *Cato:* "What a pity is it / That we can die but once to serve our country." See also under Joseph Addison at FREEDOM. In the end, the British paid dearly for their treatment of Hale; see under Maj. John André below.

These are the times that try men's souls. The summer soldier and the sunshine patriot will, in this crisis, shrink from the services of their country; but he that stands it NOW deserves the love and thanks of man and woman. 3

—**Tom Paine,** *The American Crisis*, Dec. 23, 1776

★ Paine, an English immigrant but an ardent supporter of independence, had joined George Washington's beaten and discouraged army. With winter closing in, Paine exhorted the downcast troops to stand fast.

Necessity, dire necessity, will, nay must, justify my attack. 4

—**George Washington,** attributed, Dec. 25, 1776

★ Washington was preparing to attack Trenton the next day. The Americans were truly desperate for a victory, and they got one, surprising the Hessians posted at Trenton. These German mercenaries did not think that the Continental army would attack in the foul winter weather—and they were under the weather themselves, having celebrated Christmas with too much cheer. As the American countersign—the phrase that the Continentals would use to identify themselves to each other—Washington selected "Victory or Die."

It is a common observation here [Paris] that our cause is *the cause of all mankind*, and that we are fighting for their liberty in defending our own. 5

—**Benjamin Franklin,** letter to Samuel Cooper, 1777

I desired as many as could to join together in fasting and prayer, that God would restore the spirit of love and of a sound mind to the poor deluded rebels in America. 6

—**John Wesley,** *Journal*, August 1, 1777

1 We beat them tonight or Molly Stark's a widow.

—John Stark, August 16, 1777

★ Another version is, "There, my lads, are the Hessians! Tonight our flag floats over yonder hill, or Molly Stark sleeps a widow." Gen. Stark was addressing his New Hampshire militiamen men before the Battle of Bennington. His force, aided by Lt. Col. Seth Warner's Green Mountain Boys, who arrived at a crucial moment, just before sunset, shattered a column of Hessians sent by British general John Burgoyne to raid an American supply depot at Bennington. The action was one of numerous setbacks in the British Saratoga campaign, which was aimed at dividing the colonies along the line of the Hudson River. Burgoyne was marching south from Canada. His counterparts to the south never made it up to Albany as planned. Burgoyne's surrender at Saratoga on October 17 marked a turning point in the Revolution.

2 If I were an American, as I am an Englishman, while a foreign troop was landed in my country, I would never lay down my arms—never, never, never! You cannot conquer America.

—William Pitt, speech, House of Lords, Nov. 18, 1777

3 I wish to have no connection with any ship that does not sail *fast*; for I intend to go *in harm's way*.

—John Paul Jones, letter, Nov. 16, 1778

4 I have not yet begun to fight.

—John Paul Jones, reply from the *Bonhomme Richard* to the *Serapis*, Sept. 23, 1779

★ Reports of Captain Jones's exact words vary but the sense is the same. The savage battle took place on a moonlit night off Flamborough Head on the east coast of England. Seeing that the *Richard* had been badly damaged in the opening salvos, the British called for its surrender. Jones, his decks awash in blood, replied that he would fight on. He managed to cross in front of the *Serapis*, causing it to collide with his vessel, then lashed the two ships together, and continued the fight with cannon and small arms at point-blank range. In the end, the *Serapis* struck its colors. The *Richard* was sinking, so the Americans returned to their home base in France in the *Serapis*. This is the only naval battle in which the winning captain has lost his ship and returned in a captured vessel. When Jones heard that the British captain had been knighted for his valor, he is said to have observed: "Should I have the good fortune to fall in with him again, I'll make a Lord of him."

5 It will be but a moment's pang. I pray you bear witness that I met my fate like a brave man.

—John André, Oct. 2, 1780

★ André, an attractive and talented young major in the British army, was hanged as a spy. The Americans were saddened, but his death seemed necessary as a response to the British execution of Nathan Hale; see above.

6 We fight, get beat, rise and fight again.

—Nathanael Greene, letter to Chevalier de la Luzerne, June 22, 1781

★ The chevalier was the French ambassador to the American colonies, and Greene was writing about the campaign in the Carolinas, which weakened the British even as they seemed to be winning. On July 18, 1781, Greene described his strategy in a letter to

Henry Knox: "There are few generals that have run oftener, or more lustily than I have done. But I have taken care not to run too far, and commonly have run as fast forward as backward, to convince the enemy that we were like a crab, that could run either way."

The World Turned Upside Down. **1**

—**Anonymous,** song, traditionally said to have been played by the British when surrendering to the Americans and French at Yorktown, Oct. 19, 1781

★ Contemporary accounts do not mention this particular tune; the tradition seems to date to the 19th century. Music was an important part of the surrender ceremony, however. Ordinarily, a besieged army would be permitted to march out with colors flying and playing one of the victor's marching tunes when it surrendered. But the British had not allowed these honors of war to Americans in 1780, when Gen. Benjamin Lincoln surrendered at Charleston, S.C., following a six-week siege. Now, Washington insisted that the British march out of Yorktown with colors encased and playing their own or German music. This humiliating requirement probably explains the "indisposition" that kept Earl Cornwallis from participating in the ceremony. When Gen. Charles O'Hara, the British second-in-command, offered his sword to the American commander, Washington directed O'Hara to his own second, who on this occasion happened to be—proving, if there were any doubt, how the world had been turned upside down—Gen. Benjamin Lincoln.

The old spirit of '76. **2**

—**Thomas Jefferson,** letter to James Monroe, 1793

★ Archibald Willard's famous painting for the 1876 Centennial Exhibition in Philadelphia, *The Spirit of '76*, shows three generations of military musicians, playing drums and fife. Actually the first title was *Yankee Doodle*, but Willard subsequently came up with the more sentimental tag.

The Revolution was effected before the war commenced. The Revolution was in the hearts and minds of the people. . . . This radical change in the principles, opinions, sentiments, and affections of the people was the real American Revolution. **3**

—**John Adams,** letter to Hezekiah Niles, Feb. 13, 1818

★ Adams favored this view of the revolution. For example, in an earlier letter to Thomas Jefferson, he wrote: "The revolution was in the minds of the people," August 24, 1815. The phrase "hearts and minds" has had a long life. For example, in 1906, Pres. Theodore Roosevelt told his young aide Lt. Douglas MacArthur that the secret of popularity with the people is "to put into words what is in their hearts and minds but not in their mouths"; cited by William Safire in his *New Political Dictionary*. More recently the Vietnam War was frequently described as a battle for the hearts and minds of the Vietnamese people; see Nixon at VIETNAM WAR, below (note).

By the rude bridge that arched the flood, **4**
Their flag to April's breeze unfurled,
Here once the embattled farmers stood,
And fired the shot heard round the world.

—**Ralph Waldo Emerson,** *Concord Hymn*, 1837

★ Emerson wrote the hymn for the dedication of the monument at the battle-ground in Concord. Here, on April 19, 1775, at the bridge entering Concord, Minutemen stood up against 800 British troops and forced them to retreat to Charlestown.

1 Listen, my children, and you shall hear,
Of the midnight ride of Paul Revere,
On the eighteenth of April, in Seventy-five,
Hardly a man is now alive
Who remembers that famous day and year.

—**Henry Wadsworth Longfellow,** *The Landlord's Tale: Paul Revere's Ride*, in *Tales of a Wayside Inn*, 1863–1874

2 One if by land and two if by sea;
And I on the opposite shore will be,
Ready to ride and spread the alarm
Through every Middlesex village and farm.

—**Ibid.**

3 The fate of a nation was riding that night.

—**Ibid.**

★ See Paul Revere above. Thanks to this poem, he has become one of our most enduring heroes.

Anger

See also ARGUMENTS.

4 Anger is never without a reason, but seldom with a good one.

—**Benjamin Franklin,** *Poor Richard's Almanack*, 1753

5 We boil at different degrees.

—**Ralph Waldo Emerson,** *Eloquence*, in *Society and Solitude*, 1870

6 When angry, count four; when very angry, swear.

—**Mark Twain,** *Pudd'nhead Wilson's Calendar*, in *Pudd'nhead Wilson*, 1894

★ A takeoff from the proverbial, "When angry, count ten before you speak; if very angry, an hundred." This was one of ten rules included by Thomas Jefferson in a letter to Thomas Jefferson Smith, February 21, 1825. Re Twain's recommendation to swear, he also pointed out that "In certain trying circumstances, urgent circumstances, desperate circumstances, profanity furnishes a relief denied even to prayer," quoted by his friend and biographer, Albert Bigelow Paine, in *Mark Twain, A Biography*, 1912.

7 Speak when you are angry, and you will make the best speech you will ever regret.

—**Ambrose Bierce,** *The Devil's Dictionary*, 1906

★ Bierce, a newspaperman, mixed aphorisms with cynical definitions. In 1906, his publisher insisted upon calling this collection of sayings *The Cynic's Word Book*, but since then, Bierce's own title has been used. The advice here is prudent, but Bierce was not a cautious person himself. He disappeared in Mexico during the revolution of 1913–14.

8 Don't get mad, get even.

—**Joseph Patrick Kennedy,** saying, attributed

★ A variant is "Don't Get Mad; Don't Get Even; Get Ahead," used as a chapter title by Christopher Matthews in *Hardball: How Politics Is Played—Told by One Who Knows the Game* (1988). And going a step further is "Don't get mad, get everything," uttered by Ivana Trump, former wife of The Donald and others, in a cameo appearance in the 1996 film *First Wives Club* (screenplay by Robert Herling from Olivia Goldsmith's novel).

Never go to bed mad. Stay up and fight. **1**
—**Phyllis Diller,** *Phyllis Diller's Housekeeping Hints*, 1966

We are surrounded by the enraged. **2**
—**Diane Johnson,** *The Shadow Knows*, 1974

I'm mad as hell, and I'm not going to take it any more. **3**
—**Paddy Chayevsky,** *Network* screenplay, 1976

★ London-born actor Peter Finch spoke this line, in the role of an anchorman driven over the edge by the television industry. The line is repeated several times in the film, sometimes in the form "I'm not going to take this any more." Ultimately, crowds join him in shouting, "I'm mad as hell (etc.)," and the statement has become a sort of rallying cry for a populist, antigovernment political trend, particularly among white males. Finch died a year after the movie was released.

What I've learned about being angry with people is that it generally hurts you more **4**
than it hurts them.
—**Oprah Winfrey**, quoted in Robert Waldron, *Oprah!*, 1987

Don't lose your temper, use it. **5**
—**Dolly Parton**, TV interview with Joan Rivers, Nov. 26, 1993

Animals

See NATURE: ANIMALS; AMERICAN HISTORY: MEMORABLE MOMENTS (Richard Nixon's "Checkers" speech).

Answers

See QUESTIONS & ANSWERS.

Anxiety & Worry

See also CALMNESS; EMOTIONS

How much pain have cost us the evils which have never happened! **6**
—**Thomas Jefferson,** "A Decalogue of Canons for observation in practical life," letter to Thomas Jefferson Smith, Feb. 21, 1825

The cares, that infest the day, **7**
Shall fold their tents, like the Arabs,
And as silently steal away.
—**Henry Wadsworth Longfellow,** *The Day Is Done*, 1845

★ More at ART: MUSIC.

1 Never hurry and never worry!
—E. B. White, *Charlotte's Web*, 1952

★ Charlotte the spider to Wilbur, an endangered pig.

2 What, Me Worry?
—Mad Magazine, motto of signature character, Alfred E. Newman, 1955, from an advertising slogan c. 1900

3 There is no such thing as inner peace. There is only nervousness or death.
—Fran Lebowitz, *Metropolitan Life*, 1978

4 We are, perhaps uniquely among the earth's creatures, the worrying animal. We worry away our lives, fearing the future, discontent with the present, unable to take in the idea of dying, unable to sit still.
—Lewis Thomas, *The Medusa and the Snail*, 1979

★ Dr. Thomas, described in his *New York Times* obituary as a "poet-philosopher of medicine," headed the Memorial Sloan-Kettering Cancer Center. He was best known for brilliant essays on biology, music, and life in general.

5 Economic man has given way to the psychological man of our times—the final product of bourgeois individualism. The new narcissist is haunted not by guilt but by anxiety.
—Christopher Lasch, *The Culture of Narcissism,* 1979

Appearances

See also Beauty; Body & Looks; Fashion & Clothes; Reality, Illusions, & Images.

6 All visible objects, man, are but as pasteboard masks. . . . Strike, strike through the mask!
—Herman Melville, *Moby-Dick*, 1851

7 Let be be finale of seem.
—Wallace Stevens, *The Emperor of Ice-Cream,* 1923

8 You can't expect men not to judge by appearances.
—Ellen Glasgow, *The Sheltered Life*, 1932

★ Glasgow, a Pulitzer Prize-winner "was a major historian of our times," wrote Henry Seidel Canby, "who, almost single-handedly, rescued Southern fiction from the glamorous sentimentality of the Lost Cause."

9 Don't be misled. Beneath that cold, austere, severe exterior, there beats a heart of stone.
—Rudolf Bing, on himself, attributed, in *The New York Times* [Sept. 3, 1997]

10 It's better to look good than to feel good.
—Anonymous, Public Television, Channel 12, Dec. 7, 2003

★ The saying was described as a "mantra on television" during a broadcast of a

University of Connecticut's women's basketball game. The women seemed to both look good and feel good in the midst of another record-breaking season.

Argentina

See NATIONS.

Arguments

See also ANGER; CONFLICT; CONVERSATION; DIFFERENCES.

'Tis by our quarrels that we spoil our prayers. **1**
—Cotton Mather, *The Wonders of the Invisible World*, 1693

It were endless to dispute upon everything that is disputable. **2**
—William Penn, *Some Fruits of Solitude*, 1693

I never saw an instance of one of two disputants convincing the other by argument. **3**
—Thomas Jefferson, letter to John Taylor, June 1, 1798

I am not arguing with you—I am telling you. **4**
—James Abbott McNeill Whistler, *The Gentle Art of Making Enemies*, 1890

Arguments only confirm people in their own opinions. **5**
—Booth Tarkington, *Looking Forward to the Great Adventure,* 1926

All right, have it your own way—you heard a seal bark! **6**
—James Thurber, cartoon caption, in *The New Yorker*, Jan. 30, 1932

★ A large, alert seal is leaning over the headboard of a double bed in which a middle-aged couple are at odds. The woman evidently heard a seal bark, and has said so. The man declines to dispute such a ridiculous claim.

Arizona

It is my land, my home, my father's land, to which I now ask to be allowed to return. **7**
I want to spend my last days there, and be buried among those mountains.
—Geronimo, letter to Pres. Ulysses S. Grant from the reservation at Fort Sill, Okla., 1875

Come to Arizona where summer spends the winter. **8**
—Anonymous, booster slogan, c. 1935

★ H. L. Mencken in his dictionary of quotations notes that local wits added, "And hell spends the summer." In *Roughing It* (1872), Mark Twain passes along a story he heard from humorist George Horatio Derby about a wicked soldier from Yuma, who dies and goes "to the hottest corner of perdition—and the next day he *telegraphed back for his blankets!*"

The Grand Canyon is carven deep by the master hand; it is the gulf of silence, **9**
widened in the desert; it is all time inscribing the naked rock; it is the book of earth.
—Donald Culross Peattie, *The Road of a Naturalist*, 1941

1 Land of extremes. Land of contrasts. Land of surprises. Land of contradictions.
—Federal Writers' Project, *Arizona: The Grand Canyon State*, 1956

2 Across the Colorado River from Needles, the dark and jagged ramparts of Arizona stood up against the sky, and behind them the huge tilted plain rising toward the backbone of the continent again.
—John Steinbeck, *Travels with Charley*, 1962

3 It's a tough country.
—Charles Kuralt, *Dateline America*, 1979

4 *Ditat Deus.*
God enriches.
—Motto, Arizona

Arkansas

See also CITIES (ARKANSAS CITY).

5 All the trees, the year round, were as green as if they stood in orchards, and the woods were open.
—A Knight of Elvas, *Narratives of the Career of Hernando de Soto in the Conquest of Florida* [1557]

★ The anonymous author, who signed himself "A Gentleman of Elvas," accompanied De Soto on his expedition in 1539 to North America. This is a description from 1541 of what is now Arkansas.

6 If I could rest anywhere, it would be in Arkansaw, where the men are of the real half-horse, half-alligator breed such as grows nowhere else on the face of the earth.
—David Crockett, *Narrative of the Life of David Crockett*, 1834

★ This alternate spelling of ARKANSAS was used in the title of *The Arkansaw Traveler*, a popular comedy disrespectful of the great state. Poor Arkansas suffered such abuse that some considered giving it a new name. This proposal was rejected in a famous apocryphal speech supposedly delivered in the Arkansas legislature about 1875. The hyperbolic speech has been passed down in a number of versions, some extremely raunchy. The speaker, sometimes identified as Sen. Cassius M. Johnson, concludes, "Change the name of Arkansaw? Hell, No!"

7 [Re Arkansas:] Its airs—just breathe them, and they will make you snort like a horse.
—Thomas B. Thorpe, *The Big Bear of Arkansas*, 1841

8 I've met with ups and downs in life, and better days I've saw;
But I never knew what mis'ry were, till I came to Arkansas.
—Anonymous, *The State of Arkansas*, 19th century, in John A. and Alan Lomax, *Folk Song U.S.A.* [1947]

★ This song, probably dating from before the Civil War, is an early example of the humorous but unflattering treatment of Arkansas in popular culture. The speaker was a migrant worker, perhaps Irish, who couldn't wait to get out of the state and write this verse.

Biggest fool I ever saw 1
Came from the state of Arkansas;
Put his shirt on over his coat,
Button his britches up round his throat.
—Anonymous, folk song, in Howard W. Odum, *Wings on My Feet* [1929]

If I die in Arkansas, 2
Jes' ship my body to my mother-in-law.
—Anonymous, folk song

So the duke said these Arkansaw lunkheads couldn't come up to Shakespeare; what they wanted was low comedy—any maybe something rather worse than low comedy, he reckoned. 3

—Mark Twain, *The Adventures of Huckleberry Finn*, 1885

★ The duke made up some handbills for his show, with one line in capital letters: "*ladies and children not admitted*. 'There,' says he, 'if that line don't fetch them, I don't know Arkansaw!' "

I've never seen nothin; I don't know nothin; I haint got nothin; and I don't want nothin! 4

—Anonymous, Arkansas saying, c. 1930s

There is pretty strong characters down there [in Arkansas]. You can't redeem 'em, you just join 'em. 5

—Will Rogers, Alex Ayres, ed., *The Wit and Wisdom of Will Rogers* [1993]

★ Rogers's wife was from Arkansas.

Any time you tangle with an Arkansaw hillbilly or hillbillyess, you are going to run second. 6

—Will Rogers, Alex Ayres, ed., *The Wit and Wisdom of Will Rogers* [1993]

Regnat populus. 7
The people rule.
—Motto, Arkansas

Army

See MILITARY, THE; VIOLENCE.

Art

Art is long, and Time is fleeting. 8

—Henry Wadsworth Longfellow, *A Psalm of Life*, 1839

★ An ancient saying expressed in a variety of ways, including the anonymous traditional *Ars longa, vita brevis*—"Art is long, life is short." Hippocrates, with reference to the difficulty of mastering the art of medicine in a short lifetime, wrote: "Life is short, art long, opportunity fleeting, experience treacherous, judgment difficult," *Aphorisms*.

1 Art is power.
—**Henry Wadsworth Longfellow,** *Hyperion*, 1839

2 Art is the gift of God, and must be used unto his glory.
—**Henry Wadsworth Longfellow,** *Michael Angelo*, 1872–1882, published, 1886

3 Art is a jealous mistress.
—**Ralph Waldo Emerson,** *Wealth*, in *The Conduct of Life*, 1860

4 Art without life is a poor affair.
—**Henry James,** *The Art of Fiction*, 1888

5 There is truth and that should form the basis of all art.
—**Alfred Stieglitz,** *American Amateur Photographer,* 1893

6 It is art that *makes* life, makes interest, makes importance.
—**Henry James,** letter to H. G. Wells, July 10, 1915

7 Mrs. Ballinger is one of the ladies who pursue Culture in bands, as though it were dangerous to meet it alone.
—**Edith Wharton,** *Xingu*, 1916

★ For Dorothy Parker on horticulture, see EDUCATION.

8 Art is the stored honey of the human soul, gathered on wings of misery and travail.
—**Theodore Dreiser,** *Life, Art, and America*, 1917

9 Authors and actors and artists and such
Never know nothing, and never know much.
Sculptors and singers and those of their kidney
Tell their affairs from Seattle to Sydney.
Playwrights and poets and such horses' necks
Start off from anywhere, end up at sex.
Diarists, critics, and similar roe
Never say nothing and never say no.
People Who Do Things exceed my endurance;
God, for a man who solicits insurance!
—**Dorothy Parker,** *Bohemia*, 1927

10 The cultural influences in this country are like the floo floo bird. I am referring to the peculiar and especial bird who always flew backward. . . . because it didn't give a darn where it was going, but just had to see where it had been.
—**Frank Lloyd Wright,** speech, 1938, included in William Safire, *Lend Me Your Ears: Great Speeches in History*, rev. edition [2004]

11 The work of art is invariably the creation of a new world.
—**Vladimir Nabokov**, *Good Reader and Good Writers*, 1948

12 In everything that can be called art there is a quality of redemption.
—**Raymond Chandler,** *The Simple Art of Murder*, 1950

Music and art and poetry attune the soul to God. 1

—**Thomas Merton,** *No Man Is an Island*, 1955

This [the arts] is an area where we have lagged far behind other countries. We have been so preoccupied with our industrial growth that we have thought of little else. The culture of a nation is, after all, as important as its economy. 2

—**Eleanor Roosevelt,** *My Day*, Feb. 27, 1957

This nation cannot afford to be materially rich and spiritually poor. 3

—**John F. Kennedy,** State of the Union address, 1963

★ This is the inscription on the Kennedy Center for the Performing Arts in Washington, D.C.

The man who insists on high and serious pleasures is depriving himself of pleasure; he continually restricts what he can enjoy; in the constant excercise of his good taste he will eventually price himself out of the market, so to speak. 4

—**Susan Sontag,** *Notes on Camp* in *Partisan Review*, 1964

★ This instantly famous essay introduced the uninitiated to Camp, then the province primarily of gay culture. "Camp taste supervenes upon good taste as a daring and witty hedonism," Sontag wrote. Since then Camp has become mainstream, with numerous television shows featuring gay humor and sensibility.

Art is the objectification of feeling and the subjectification of nature. 5

—**Suzanne K. Langer,** *Mind: An Essay on Human Feeling*, 1967

No artist is ahead of his time. He *is* his time; it is just that others are behind the times. 6

—**Martha Graham**, quoted in the London *Observer*, July 9, 1979

Art is the affirmation of life. 7

—**Ansel Adams,** in *Playboy*, May 1983

★ Adams attributed this saying to his great predecessor Alfred Stieglitz.

Brave art . . . the best sense we can make of our times. 8

—**Tony Kushner,** quoted in John Lahr, *After Angels* in *The New Yorker*, Jan. 3, 2005

Art: Aesthetics

See also ART: CRITICISM; ART: STYLE IN WRITING & EXPRESSION; ART: WRITING; BEAUTY; SIMPLICITY.

The art of art . . . is simplicity. 9

—**Walt Whitman,** Preface, *Leaves of Grass*, 1855–92

★ More at ART: STYLE IN WRITING & EXPRESSION.

In art, economy is always beautiful. 10

—**Henry James,** in *Prefaces (The Altar of the Dead)*, 1907–1909

★ See also architect Mies Van der Rohe's motto under ART: ARCHITECTURE.

1 The only way of expressing emotion in the form of art is by finding an "objective correlative"; in other words, a set of objects, a situation, a chain of events which shall be the formula of that *particular* emotion.

—**T. S. Eliot,** *Hamlet and His Problems*, 1919

2 Whatever is felt upon the page without being specifically named there—that, one might say, is created. It is the inexplicable presence of the thing not named, of the overtone divined by the ear but not heard by it, the verbal mood, the emotional aura of the fact or the thing or the deed, that gives high quality to the novel or the drama, as well as to poetry itself.

—**Willa Cather,** *The Novel Démeublé*, c. 1925

★ For her title—"the novel de-furnished"—Cather drew on the elder Alexandre Dumas. She credits him with the observation that "to make a drama, a man needed one passion, and four walls."

3 Our American professors like their literature clear and cold and pure and very dead.

—**Sinclair Lewis,** *The American Fear of Literature*, Nobel Prize acceptance speech, Dec. 12, 1930

4 Art strives for form, and hopes for beauty.

—**George Bellows,** quoted in Stanley Walker, *City Editor*, 1934

★ Bellows is best known for his paintings of boxing matches and other scenes of city life.

5 Can you draw sweet water from a foul well?

—**Brooks Atkinson,** review of *Pal Joey*, *The New York Times*, 1940

★ Atkinson, the most influential theater reviewer in the U.S., penned this often-quoted question as he wrestled with a classic critic's dilemma: what to say about a well-done work of which one disapproves. *Pal Joey*, based on a John O'Hara story, featured a sleazy hero and great songs by Richard Rodgers and Lorenz Hart.

Atkinson could have consulted a senior colleague, George Jean Nathan, who said, "There is no such thing as a dirty theme. There are only dirty writers," *Testament of a Critic*, 1931.

6 Less is more.

—**Ludwig Mies van der Rohe,** motto

★ German-born architect Mies van der Rohe borrowed the aphorism from the 19th-century poet Robert Browning, who used it in *Andrea del Sarto*. Cellist Mstislav Rostropovich totally disagrees. His motto is, "More is more" (quoted in the television program *Kennedy Center Honors Performance*, Dec. 30, 1992). Bandleader Artie Shaw remarked, "I did all you can do with a clarinet, any more would have been less."

See also Mae West at EXCESS. For another favorite Mies van der Rohe aphorism, see DETAILS & OTHER SMALL THINGS, note under Anonymous. Nobel Prize winner Philip W. Anderson had something to say about more; see SCIENCE: PHYSICS & COSMOLOGY.

7 True originality refocuses the attentive eye.

—**Lincoln Kirstein,** *What Ballet Is All About*, 1959

Art: Architecture

See also SCIENCE: TECHNOLOGY (for bridges).

Form ever follows function. 1

—Louis Henri Sullivan, *The Tall Office Building Artistically Considered*, in *Lippincott's Magazine*, March 1896

★ "Form follows function" was the motto of the Bauhaus school of architecture and art. For a related principle, see Ludwig Mies van der Rohe at ART: AESTHETICS above.

The architect should always live better than his clients. 2

—Stanford White, saying, c. 1900, quoted in American Experience, Public Broadcasting Station [July 21, 2003]

The physician can bury his mistakes, but the architect can only advise his client to 3
plant vines.

—Frank Lloyd Wright, in *The New York Times Magazine*, Oct. 4, 1953

Architecture begins where engineering ends. 4

—Walter Gropius, speech, Harvard University, quoted in Paul Heyer, ed., *Architects on Architecture* [1978]

Architecture is . . . life itself taking form. 5

—Frank Lloyd Wright, *An Organic Architecture*, 1970

Preservation is not just about preserving brick and mortar, lintel and beam. It is 6
about the quality of life and the possibility of a bright future.

—Sen. John H. Chaffee, remarks, 50th anniversary celebration of the National Trust for Historic Preservation, Washington National Cathedral, Oct. 26, 1999

★ This was the Rhode Island senator's last public appearance. He died three days later.

Art: Criticism

See also ART: AESTHETICS; CRITICISM; INSULTS.

Nature fits all her children with something to do: He who would write and can't 7
write can surely review.

—James Russell Lowell, *A Fable for Critics*, 1848

The public is the only critic whose opinion is worth anything at all. 8

—Mark Twain, "A General Reply," *The Galaxy* magazine, Nov. 1870

Persons attempting to find a motive in this narrative will be prosecuted; persons 9
attempting to find a moral in it will be banished; persons attempting to find a plot in it will be shot.

—Mark Twain, "Notice," *Adventures of Huckleberry Finn*, 1885

★ In 1990, the first half of the handwritten manuscript turned up, with new material and changes. Originally, this "Notice," had not included the reference to a moral. Twain scholar Victor Doyno speculated in *The New York Times* (May 16, 1995) that the reference was added after the narrative came to focus more than first planned on the liberation of the slave Jim and Huck's hard lessons in empathy and integrity.

1 The practice of "reviewing" . . . in general has nothing in common with the art of criticism.

—**Henry James,** *Criticism*, 1893

★ In *Prefaces*, 1907–1909, writing of his *Portrait of a Lady*, James elaborated: "To criticize is to appreciate, to appropriate, to take intellectual possession, to establish in fine a relation with the criticized thing and to make it one's own."

2 I don't know anything about music, really, but I know what I like.

—**Gelett Burgess,** "Bromide no. 1," in *Are You a Bromide?*, 1906

★ Burgess was making fun of this cliché, so useful to the uninformed. He coined this sense of *bromide*; see Burgess under DIFFERENCES.

3 I have read your lousy review of Margaret's concert. I've come to the conclusion that you are an eight-ulcer man on a four-ulcer job. . . . Someday, I hope to meet you. When that happens, you'll need a new nose, a lot of beefsteak for black eyes, and perhaps a supporter below.

—**Harry S. Truman,** to critic Paul Hume, quoted in *Time* magazine, Dec. 18, 1950

★ The president's hotheaded defense of his daughter's singing seemed to some undignified, but others found it human and refreshing.

4 [Critics are] essential to the theater: as ants to a picnic, as boll weevils in a cotton field.

—**Joseph L. Mankiewicz,** *All About Eve*, 1950

5 Be kind and considerate with your criticism. . . . It's just as hard to write a bad book as a good book.

—**Malcolm Cowley,** quoted by Ken Kesey, *The New York Times* [Dec. 31, 1989]

6 Pleasure is by no means an infallible guide, but it is the least fallible.

—**W. H. Auden,** *The Dyer's Hand*, 1962

7 One cannot review a bad book without showing off.

—**Ibid.**

8 Interpretation is the revenge of the intellect upon art.

—**Susan Sontag,** *Against Interpretation*, title essay, 1966

★ She explained, "A work of art is a thing *in* the world, not just a text or commentary *on* the world." Don't "translate" it.

9 [Response to negative reviews:] I cried all the way to the bank.

—**Liberace,** *Liberace, An Autobiography*, 1973

10 Don't read the review, just measure it.

—**Sidney Janis,** attributed, *The New York Times*, "Week in Review," Oct. 23, 1994

★ Janis was an influential Manhattan gallery owner.

Critics ought now and then to hesitate. 1
—Irving Howe, *A Critic's Notebook* [1995]

Art: Dance

One becomes . . . an athlete of God. 2
—Martha Graham, May 15, 1945

★ More at GRACE. See also later Graham quotes below.

When in doubt, twirl. 3
—Ted Shawn, saying, quoted by Edward Gorey in *The New Yorker* [Nov. 9, 1992]

Dance is motion, not emotion. 4
—Alwin Nikolais, saying, quoted in *The New York Times* [Jan. 24, 1993]

I just put my feet in the air and move them around. 5
—Fred Astaire, attributed in the quotation game *Daring "Passages,"* cited in *The New York Times*, August 21, 1994

Dancing is just discovery, discovery, discovery. 6
—Martha Graham, interview, *New York Times*, March 31, 1985

Dance is the hidden language of the soul. 7
—Ibid.

Movement never lies. 8
—Martha Graham, *Blood Memory*, 1991

★ Graham wrote in her posthumously published autobiography, *Blood Memory* (1991), that this was a favorite saying of her father, a specialist in mental disorders, who felt that his patients' movements revealed their mental condition.

Art: Drama, Magic & Movies

See ART: THEATER, DRAMA, MOVIES & MAGIC

Art: Music

Music is the universal language of mankind—poetry their universal pastime and delight. 9
—Henry Wadsworth Longfellow, *Outre-Mer; a Pilgrimage Beyond the Sea*, originally, *The Schoolmaster*, c. 1832

And the night shall be filled with music, 10
And the cares that infest the day,
Shall fold their tents like the Arabs,
And as silently steal away.
—Henry Wadsworth Longfellow, *The Day Is Done*, 1844

1 God sent his Singers upon earth
With songs of sadness and of mirth.
—Henry Wadsworth Longfellow, *The Singers*, 1849

2 So is music an asylum. It takes us out of the actual and whispers to us dim secrets that startle our wonder as to who we are, and for what, whence and whereto.
—Ralph Waldo Emerson, attributed

3 I known only two tunes: one is *Yankee Doodle*, and the other isn't.
—Ulysses S. Grant, attributed

4 The banging and slamming and booming and crashing were beyond belief.
—Mark Twain, describing a production of *Lohengrin*, in *A Tramp Abroad*, 1879

★ The states were rich in opera companies in the 19th century. But the quality evidently fluctuated. In the same period, Josh Billings remarked, "I have seen wimmin in opera, and also have seen them in fits, and I prefer the fits, for then I know what tew do for them."

5 Over the piano was printed a notice: Please do not shoot the pianist. He is doing his best.
—Oscar Wilde, *Leadville* (Colo.), in *Personal Impressions of America*, 1883

★ For an understanding of why the piano player—and everyone else—was at risk, see ALCOHOL & DRINKING for Wilde's description of the dinner menu.

6 I have been told that Wagner's music is better than it sounds.
—Bill Nye, attributed, in *Mark Twain's Autobiography* [1924]

7 Lift Ev'ry Voice and Sing.
—James Weldon Johnson, song title, 1900

★ The first lines of the lyric run, "Lift evr'y voice and sing,/ Till earth and heaven ring./ Ring with the harmonies of Liberty." With music by Johnson's brother, John Rosamond Johnson, this song became known as "the Negro National Anthem."

8 Opera's no business, it's a disease.
—Oscar Hammerstein I, remark to a reporter, c. 1906

★ Theater magnate Hammerstein built the Manhattan Opera House in 1906 to compete with the Met. His opera house in Philadelphia went up two years later. Alas, his wonderful Manhattan Opera Company lasted just four seasons.

9 When people hear good music, it makes them homesick for something they never had, and never will have.
—Edgar Watson Howe, *Country Town Sayings*, 1911

10 If you don't like the blues, you've got a hole in your soul.
—Anonymous, saying

11 Drum on your drums, batter on your banjos, sob on the long cool winding saxophones.
Go to it, O jazzmen.
—Carl Sandburg, *Jazz Fantasia*, 1920

Classic music is th' kind that we keep thinkin'll turn into a tune. 1

—Frank McKinney "Kin" Hubbard, *Comments of Abe Martin and His Neighbors*, 1923

I care not who writes the laws of a country so long as I may listen to its songs. 2

—George Jean Nathan, *The World in Falseface*, 1923

When we hear the Ninth Symphony, *we are listening to the voice of God.* 3

—William Lyon Phelps, *Music* 1930

★ Phelps was a fine professor of literature at Yale, and was a teacher and friend of the composer Charles Ives. One of many stories about Phelps was offered in commencement speech on May 20, 2000, at North Carolina State University by Donna E. Shalala, then Secretary of Health and Human Services. "Phelps . . . once gave an examination in English literature just before Christmas break. He asked his students to discuss Gerard Manley Hopkins 'sprung rhythm' technique. One young man handed in his exam, reading, 'Only God knows the answer to your question. Merry Christmas.' Professor Phelps returned the paper after Christmas with the note, 'God gets an A. You get an F. Happy New Year.' "

It Don't Mean a Thing If It Ain't Got That Swing. 4

—Duke Ellington, song title, 1932

They said, "You have a blue guitar, 5
You do not play things as they are."
The man replied, "Things as they are
Are changed upon the blue guitar."

—Wallace Stevens, *The Man with the Blue Guitar,* 1937

Lady, if you got to ask, you ain't got it. 6

—Thomas "Fats" Waller, supposed response when asked to explain rhythm, attributed

★ Similarly, Louis Armstrong is said to have replied, "Man, if you gotta ask, you'll never know," when asked what jazz is.

If, as is nearly always the case, music appears to express something, this is only an 7
illusion and not a reality.

—Igor Stravinsky, *An Autobiography*, 1936

★ "Music, is by its very nature, essentially powerless to *express* anything at all," Stravinsky notoriously asserted in this autobiography.

Music heard so deeply 8
That it is not heard at all, but you are the music
While the music lasts.

—T. S. Eliot, *Four Quartets: The Dry Salvages*, 1941

Play it, Sam. Play "As Time Goes By." 9

—Julius Epstein, Philip Epstein, & Howard Koch, *Casablanca*, screenplay, 1942

★ For the lyric, see Herman Hupfield at SEASONS & TIMES.

1 You play Bach your way, I'll play Bach his way.
—**Wanda Landowska,** getting the last word in an argument with Pablo Casals, c. 1945

★ A quip often said to have been directed at pianist Rosalyn Turck. The correction comes from Denise Restout, assistant and companion of Mme. Landowska, interviewed in *The Litchfield County Times,* Jan. 6, 1995.

2 Songs are the pulse of a nation's heart. A fever chart of its health. Are we at peace? Are we in trouble? Are we floundering? Do we feel beautiful? Do we feel ugly? . . . Listen to our songs.
—**E. Y. "Yip" Harburg,** in Harold Myerson and Ernie Harburg, *Who Put the Rainbow in the Wizard of Oz?* [1995]

★ Ernie Harburg is Yip's son. The father registered the nation's pulse with songs as diverse as *Brother Can You Spare a Dime?* and *Somewhere Over the Rainbow.*

3 Composers shouldn't think too much—it interferes with their plagiarism.
—**Howard Dietz,** news reports, Dec. 31, 1974

4 There's no addiction like the eight o'clock curtain at the opera.
—**Rudolf Bing,** quoted in *The New York Times* [March 7, 1995]

★ Bing was general manager of the Metropolitan Opera in New York from 1950 to 1972.

5 Talking about music is like singing about architecture.
—**Elliott Carter,** attributed, *NPR Radio, MarketPlace,* Nov. 17, 2003

★ Widely attributed in various forms, with the best citation found by Alan P. Scott: Elvis Costello, *Musician* magazine, Oct., 1983, in the form: "Writing about music is like dancing about architecture—it's a really stupid thing to want to do."

6 Form is rhythm on a larger scale.
—**Tom Harrell,** quoted by Whitney Balliett, *The New Yorker*, April 15, 1996

★ Music critic Balliett ranks Harrell, a trumpeter, flugelhornist, and composer, among the best contemporary jazz artists. Harrell has overcome diagnosed schizophrenia with the help of medicine and musical genius.

Art: Painting

See ART: VISUAL.

Art: Poetry

7 You will never be alone with a poet in your pocket.
—**John Adams,** letter to his son John Quincy Adams, May 14, 1781

8 Poetry their universal pastime and delight.
—**Henry Wadsworth Longfellow,** *Outre-Mer*, c. 1832

★ More at ART: MUSIC.

I would define, in brief, the poetry of words as the rhythmical creation of beauty. Its sole arbiter is taste. . . . Unless incidentally, it has no concern whatever with duty or with truth. **1**

—Edgar Allan Poe, review of Henry Wadsworth Longfellow's *Ballads and Other Poems*, in *Graham's Magazine*, April 1842, incorporated into *The Poetic Principle* [1850]

The experience of each new age requires a new confession, and the world seems always waiting for its poet. **2**

—Ralph Waldo Emerson, *The Poet*, in *Essays: Second Series*, 1844

Poetry must be as new as foam, and as old as the rock. **3**

—Ralph Waldo Emerson, *Journal*, March 1845

To have great poets, there must be great audiences, too. **4**

—Walt Whitman, *Ventures on an Old Theme*, in *Notes Left Over*, 1882

Publishing a volume of poetry is like dropping a rose petal down the Grand Canyon and waiting for the echo. **5**

—Don Marquis, *The Sun Dial*, New York *Sun* column, started 1912

Immature poets imitate; mature poets steal. **6**

—T. S. Eliot, *Philip Massinger*, 1920

The courage of the poet is to keep ajar the door that leads to madness. **7**

—Christopher Morley, *Inward Ho*, 1923

Poetry is the opening and closing of a door, leaving those who look through to guess about what is seen during a moment. **8**

—Carl Sandburg, *Poetry Considered* in *The Atlantic Monthly*, March 1923

★ From the same work, "Poetry is the journal of the sea animal living on land, wanting to fly in the air. Poetry is a search for syllables to shoot at the barriers of the unknown and the unknowable. Poetry is a phantom script telling how rainbows are made and why they go away."

A poem should not mean / but be. **9**

—Archibald MacLeish, *Ars Poetica*, 1926

Genuine poetry can communicate before it is understood. **10**

—T. S. Eliot, *Dante*, 1929

Poetry atrophies when it gets too far from music. **11**

—Ezra Pound, *How to Read*, 1931

Writing free verse is like playing tennis with the net down. **12**

—Robert Frost, speech at Milton Academy in Massachusetts, May 17, 1935

Poetry is the subject of the poem. **13**

—Wallace Stevens, *The Man with the Blue Guitar*, 1937

★ In *A High-toned Old Christian Woman*, 1923, Stevens described poetry as "the supreme fiction." In *Notes Toward a Supreme Fiction*, 1947, he wrote, "You must become an ignorant man again / And see the sun again with an ignorant eye / And see it clearly in the idea of it." In accepting the National Book Award in 1955, he said, "We can never have great poetry unless we believe that poetry serves great ends." Also, "The poem is a nature created by the poet [and should contain] the full flower of the actual, not the California fruit of the ideal," Milton J. Bates, ed., expanded *Opus Posthumous.*

1 A poem is a meteor.
—Wallace Stevens, *Adagia*, in *Opus Posthumous* [1957]

2 Poetry is a search for the inexplicable.
—Ibid.

3 The poet is the priest of the invisible.
—Ibid.

4 The figure a poem makes. It begins in delight and ends in wisdom. The figure is the same as for love.
—Robert Frost, Preface, *Collected Poems*, 1939

5 Poetry is a way of taking life by the throat.
—Robert Frost, comment, quoted in *Bartlett's Familiar Quotations*, 16th edition [1992]

6 All poets' wives have rotten lives.
—Delmore Schwartz, quoted in obituary of Eileen Simpson, wife of John Berryman, *The New York Times* [Oct. 24, 2002]

7 There are so many ways to ruin a poem it's quite amazing good ones ever get written.
—John Berryman, remark to Philip Levine, 1954

8 It is difficult to get the news from poems, yet men die miserably every day for lack of what is found there.
—William Carlos Williams, *Asphodel, That Greeny Flower*, in *A Journey to Love*, 1955

9 When power narrows the areas of man's concern, poetry reminds him of the richness and diversity of his existence. When power corrupts, poetry cleanses.
—John F. Kennedy, speech, Oct. 26, 1963

★ For more on this speech, see the note to Fulbright at POWER.

10 The only thing that can save the world is the reclaiming of the awareness of the world. That's what poetry does.
—Allen Ginsberg, quoted in Helen Weaver, review of Ginsberg's *Collected Poems, Litchfield County Times* [May 31, 1985]

11 Poetry . . . is always unexpected, and always as faithful and honest as dreams.
—Alice Walker, *We Have a Beautiful Mother*, 1991

12 All poetry is political. It either maintains the status quo or it talks about change.
—Sonia Sanchez, interview, *The New York Times,* Jan. 29, 2005

★ Poet Sanchez is inspiration and support for spoken-word, hip-hop performers.

"Poetry [will] take you places you don't want to go," she told the interviewer. "It's saying to the audience, 'Come, take this journey with us. It's possible for a poem and musical voice to come together.'"

Art: Style in Writing & Expression

See also ART: AESTHETICS; ART: WRITING; LANGUAGE & WORDS; SIMPLICITY; STYLE.

The art of art, the glory of expression, and the sunshine of the light of letters, is simplicity. **1**

—**Walt Whitman,** Preface, *Leaves of Grass*, 1855–92

Spartans, stoics, heroes, saints, and gods use a short and positive speech. **2**

—**Ralph Waldo Emerson,** *The Superlative*, in *Lectures and Biographical Sketches*, 1883

As to the Adjective: when in doubt, strike it out. **3**

—**Mark Twain,** *Pudd'nhead Wilson's Calendar*, in *Pudd'nhead Wilson*, 1894

A successful book is not made of what is in it, but what is left out of it. **4**

—**Mark Twain,** letter to William Dean Howells, Feb. 23, 1897

He has lived heroic poetry, and he can, therefore, afford to talk simple prose. **5**

—**William Dean Howells,** referring to a speech by Booker T. Washington at Madison Square Garden Concert Hall, in New York City, on Dec. 4, 1899

Use no superfluous word, no adjective which doesn't reveal something . . . Go in fear of abstractions. **6**

—**Ezra Pound,** *A Retrospect [including] A Few Don'ts*, in *Pavannes and Divagations*1918

Omit needless words. Vigorous writing is concise. A sentence should contain no unnecessary words, a paragraph no unnecessary sentences, for the same reason that a drawing should have no unnecessary lines and a machine no unnecessary parts. **7**

—**William Strunk, Jr.,** *The Elements of Style*, 1918

It is the beginning of the end when you discover you have style. **8**

—**Dashiell Hammett**, quoted in *Smithsonian* [May 1994]

His [Warren Harding's] speeches left the impression of an army of pompous phrases moving over the landscape in search of an idea. **9**

—**William G. McAdoo,** quoted in Leon A. Harris, *The Fine Art of Political Wit* [1964]

★ More at WARREN G. HARDING, where there is also H. L. Mencken's characterization of Harding's writing as "rumble and bumble, flap and doodle, balder and dash."

Give a footnote an inch, and it'll take a foot. **10**

—**Frank Sullivan,** comment on scholarly writing, quoted in *The New York Times* [Aug. 14, 1996]

1 A happy heart loves a cliché.
—**Lenore J. Coffee,** screenplay *Sudden Fear,* 1952, based on an Edna Sherry novel

2 Verbal felicity is the result of art and diligence and refusing to be false.
—**Marianne Moore,** quoted by Louise Bogan, *College English*, Feb. 1953

3 Style and Structure are the essence of a book; great ideas are hogwash.
—**Vladimir Nabokov**, interview, in George Plimpton, ed., *Writers at Work*, fourth series, 1976

4 Good style . . . is unseen style. It is style that is felt.
—**Sidney Lumet,** *Making Movies*, 1995

Art: Theater, Drama, Movies & Magic

See also Cities: Los Angeles; Laughter & Mirth (Preston Sturges)

5 Behind the curtain's mystic fold
The glowing future lies unrolled.
—**Bret Harte,** speech, opening of the California Theatre, San Francisco, Jan. 19, 1870

6 A man in the theatrical business is allowed more liberties than his business brothers. His business demands it.
—**Oscar Hammerstein I,** explanation of his relationship with an opera singer known as the Texas Patti, quoted in *American Heritage* [Feb. 1973]

7 The Great Actor always must act. . . . Every last second of his life must be pose and posture.
—**Lionel Barrymore,** 1904, quoted in Gene Fowler, *Good Night, Sweet Prince* [1943]

8 If you have ever been an actor . . . why it just about ruins you for any useful employment for the rest of your life.
—**Will Rogers,** in Alex Ayres, ed., *The Wit and Wisdom of Will Rogers* [1993]

★ Rogers noticed that the same is true of politics: "Once a man wants to hold a public office, he is absolutely no good for honest work," *Weekly Articles*, March 22, 1925.

9 The theater should be an instrument for giving, not a machinery for taking.
—**Eva Le Gallienne,** motto of the Civic Repertory Theater, the first classical repertory theater in the U.S., 1926–1935

10 Satire is what closes on Saturday night.
—**George S. Kaufman,** saying, c. 1930, attributed in Howard Teichmann, *George S. Kaufman* [1972]

★ See also James Thurber at Humor.

I'd rather play a maid than be one. 1

—**Hattie McDaniel,** response when criticized for playing the role of Mammy in the 1939 movie *Gone With the Wind*, quoted in *The New York Times*, "Editorial Notebook" [Oct. 19, 1994]

★ McDaniel was the first African American to win an Academy Award.

Dying is easy. Comedy is difficult. 2

—**Edmund Gwenn,** attributed

★ Actor Gwenn is probably most remembered for his role as Santa Claus in the movie *Miracle on 34th Street*, 1947. This attribution, said to be Gwenn's last words, comes from the *Yale Alumni Magazine* [May 2002]

There's No Business Like Show Business. 3

—**Irving Berlin,** song title, *Annie Get Your Gun*, 1946

There isn't anything on earth so obstinate and perverse as an audience. 4

—**Al Jolson,** quoted in the documentary *Vaudeville,* PBS [Nov. 26, 1997]

[Actor:] What is my motivation? 5

[Director George Abbott:] Your job.

—**George Abbott,** quoted in *The New York Times*, obituary [Feb. 2, 1995]

★ Abbott, a legend in his time—he worked until his death at age 107—was making fun of the then fashionable Method school of acting, which encourages actors to find motivation for their onstage performance in their offstage experience.

Speak low and speak slow. 6

—**John Wayne,** advice to young actors

★ Cited by attorney Robert L. Shapiro in *The Champion*, magazine of the National Association of Criminal Defense Lawyers, Jan.–Feb. 1993. Shapiro recommended that lawyers use the same technique when talking to the press.

Know your lines and don't bump into the furniture. 7

—**Spencer Tracy,** advice to actors

★ Widely attributed, sometimes beginning with, "Come to work on time, know your lines," etc. Noel Coward also has been credited with giving this advice to young actors.

We want a story that starts with an earthquake and builds to a climax. 8

—**Samuel Goldwyn,** attributed

★ Goldwyn was famous for his malapropisms but this one, like many others that went the rounds in Hollywood, may well have been pinned on him by one of the many gag writers in his employ. See the note on Goldwyn at LANGUAGE & WORDS.

Nobody can really *like* an actor. 9

—**Alfred Hitchcock,** quoted in Donald Spoto, *The Dark Side of Genius: The Life of Alfred Hitchcock* [1983]

You can make a killing in the theater, but not a living. 10

—**Robert Anderson,** c. 1954

1 [A play:] a snare for the truth of human experience.
—**Tennessee Williams,** stage direction, *Cat on a Hot Tin Roof*, 1955

2 An actor's a guy who, if you ain't talking about him, ain't listening.
—**George Glass**, "Sayings of the Year," London *Observer*, Jan. 1, 1956

★ Glass was a Hollywood producer. Marlon Brando agreed, and repeated the observation often enough, that it is sometimes credited to him.

3 What if the world is some kind of—of *show!* . . . What if we are only talent assembled by the Great Talent Scout Up Above! The Great Show of Life! Starring Everybody! Suppose entertainment is the Purpose of Life!
—**Philip Roth,** *On the Air*, short story

★ For a similar notion, see Ishmael Reed at UNIVERSE, THE.

4 The movie actor, like the sacred king of primitive tribes, is a god in captivity.
—**Alexander Chase,** *Perspective*, 1966

5 The words "Kiss Kiss Bang Bang," which I saw on an Italian movie poster, are perhaps the briefest statement imaginable of the basic appeal of the movies.
—**Pauline Kael,** *Kiss Kiss Bang Bang,* 1968

6 If an actor has a message, he should call Western Union. An actor's job is to act, nothing more.
—**Humphrey Bogart,** quoted in Stephen Humphrey Bogart, *In Search of My Father* [1995]

★ Often attributed to Samuel Goldwyn with reference to movies in general: "If you want to send a message, call Western Union." But the attribution is apocryphal according to biographer A. Scott Berg in *Goldwyn* (1990).

7 In Europe, they think you're as good as the best you've ever been. In Hollywood, it's "What have you done lately?"
—**Billy Wilder,** quoted in Charlotte Chandler, *Nobody's Perfect: Billy Wilder, A Personal Biography*, 2002

★ Near the end of his brilliant career, Wilder could not get work. His movies included *Sunset Boulevard* and *Some Like It Hot.* Spencer Tracy, in a 1960 interview in the *Sunday Express,* said, "In Hollywood sometimes you're dead before you're dead."

8 The trouble with the theater is that it's no longer a way of life for an audience. It's just a way to kill an evening.
—**Jessica Tandy,** comment, 1986, quoted in *The New York Times*, obituary [Sept. 12, 1994]

9 Theater was a verb before it was a noun.
—**Martha Graham,** *Blood Memory*, 1991

★ For other verbs see Buckminster Fuller at GOD, and Ulysses S. Grant at ACTION & DOING.

You can't be boring. Life is boring. The weather is boring. Actors must not be boring. 1

—Stella Adler, *The New York Times*, obituary [Dec. 22, 1992]

The mind is led on, step by step, to defeat its own logic. 2

—Dai Vernon, definition of magic, *The New York Times*, Feb. 19, 1994

★ For another magician on reality and perception, see Jerry Andrus at REALITY, ILLUSIONS, & IMAGES.

The actor does not need to "become" the character. There is no character. There are only lines on a page. 3

—David Mamet, *True and False: Heresy and Common Sense for the Actor,* 1997

Hollwood was a central place in the history of art in the 20th century; it was human idealism preserved. And then, like any great place, it collapsed, and it collapsed into the most awful machinery in the world. 4

—Emir Kusturica, quoted in *The New York Times Magazine*, May 8, 2005

Art: Visual

See also KNOWLEDGE (Walker Evans).

In a big picture you can see what o'clock it is, afternoon or morning, if it's hot or cold, winter or summer, and what kind of people are there, and what they are doing, and why they are doing it. 5

—Thomas Eakins, letter from Paris, c. 1866, cited in *The New Yorker* [Dec. 26, 1995/Jan. 2, 1996]

You don't take a photograph, you make it. 6

—Ansel Adams, attributed

The supreme gift, after light, is scale. 7

—Helen Frankenthaler, in Frank O'Hara, *Robert Motherwell*, 1965

I really believe there are things nobody would see if I didn't photograph them. 8

—Diane Arbus, in *Diane Arbus*, edited by Doon Arbus and Marvin Israel, 1972

A photograph is a secret about a secret. The more it tells you, the less you know. 9

—Diane Arbus, *Notebook,* 1960, quoted in Patricia Bosworth, *Diane Arbus* [1983]

Content is a glimpse of something, an encounter like a flash. It's very tiny—very tiny, content. 10

—Willem de Kooning, quoted in memorial article, *The New York Times* [March 23, 1997]

In America the photographer is not simply the person who records the past, but the one who invents it. 11

—Susan Sontag, *On Photography,* 1977

A painting [is] a symbol for the universe. 12

—Corita Kent, in *Newsweek*, Dec. 17, 1984

1 A portrait is not a likeness. The moment an emotion or fact is transformed into a photograph, it is an opinion. There is no such thing as inaccuracy in a photograph. All photographs are accurate. None of them is the truth.
—**Richard Avedon,** commenting on his 1985 book, *In The American West,* quoted in *The New York Times* obituary [Oct. 2, 2004]

2 When we claim to "remember" our pasts, we are surely remembering our favorite snapshots, in which the long-faded past is given a distinct visual immortality.
—**Joyce Carol Oates** in *Civilization* magazine, Feb./Mar. 1997

Art: Writing

See also ART: STYLE IN WRITING & EXPRESSION; BOOKS & READING.

3 All writing comes by the grace of God.
—**Ralph Waldo Emerson,** *Experience* in *Essays: Second Series*, 1844

4 Writing may be either the record of a deed or a deed. It is nobler when it is a deed.
—**Henry David Thoreau,** *Journal*, Jan. 7, 1844

5 In his [the writer's] eyes, a man is the faculty of reporting, and the universe is the possibility of being reported.
—**Ralph Waldo Emerson,** *Goethe; or the Writer* in *Representative Men* 1850

6 To produce a mighty book, you must choose a mighty theme.
—**Herman Melville,** *Moby-Dick,* 1851

7 It is the business of the novel to picture daily life in the most exact terms possible.
—**William Dean Howells,** interview with Stephen Crane, 1894

★ Howells was a leader in the realist movement in fiction, a movement that inspired extensive controversy. Ambrose Bierce called realism "the art of depicting nature as seen by toads." Realist Henry James said that realism in fiction meant being "bravely and richly, and continuously psychological." His brother William pointed out that without the work of minds, reality lacks meaning: "Our minds are not here simply to copy a reality that is already complete. They are here to complete it, to add to its importance by their own remodeling of it." The subject is treated in David E. Shi's *Realism in American Thought and Culture*, 1994. See also REALITY, ILLUSIONS, & IMAGES.

8 If you steal from one author, it's plagiarism; if you steal from many, it's research.
—**Wilson Mizner,** attributed

9 Literature is news that stays news.
—**Ezra Pound,** *How to Read*, 1931

10 What I like in a good author is not what he says, but what he whispers.
—**Logan Pearsall Smith,** *Afterthoughts*, 1931

11 I always say, keep a diary and some day it'll keep you.
—**Mae West,** *Every Day's a Holiday*, 1937

No tears in the writer, no tears in the reader. **1**

—Robert Frost, Preface, *Collected Poems*, 1939

Compose. (No ideas **2**
but in things) Invent!

—William Carlos Williams, *A Sort of a Song*

The art of fiction is dead. Reality has strangled invention. Only the utterly impossi- **3**
ble, the inexpressibly fantastic can ever be plausible again.

—Walter "Red" Smith, report on the final game of baseball's National League playoff, 1951

★ Bobby Thomson, at bat for the Giants in the bottom of the ninth, his team down 4-2, with one out and two on, hit a home run—the "shot heard round the world"—to beat the Dodgers.

One must be ruthless with one's own writing or someone else will be. **4**

—John Berryman, 1954

★ Poet Philip Levine, who studied with Berryman, reported this remark in *The New York Times Book Review*, Dec. 26, 1993.

For a true writer, each book should be a new beginning where he tries again for **5**
something that is beyond attainment.

—Ernest Hemingway, speech in acceptance of the Nobel Prize for literature, 1954

The writer's only responsibility is to his art. **6**

—William Faulkner, interview, *The Paris Review*, spring 1956

If a writer has to rob his mother, he will not hesitate; the *Ode on a Grecian Urn* is **7**
worth any number of old ladies.

—Ibid.

The most essential gift for a good writer is a built-in, shockproof shit detector. This **8**
is the writer's radar, and all great writers have had it.

—Ernest Hemingway, in *The Paris Review*, spring 1958

Literary genius is not an equal opportunity employer. **9**

—Susan Sontag, speech, 1968 International PEN Congress

Writers are always selling somebody out. **10**

—Joan Didion, *Slouching Toward Bethlehem,* 1968

★ For Didion on telling ourselves stories, see STORIES.

Science fiction writers foresee the inevitable, and although problems and catastro- **11**
phes may be inevitable, solutions are not.

—Isaac Asimov, *How Easy to See the Future* in *Natural History,* April 1975

★ Asimov was an extraordinarily prolific writer of fiction, science, and criticism. He told a *Life* magazine reporter in 1981, "If my doctor told me I only had six months to live, I wouldn't brood. I'd type a little faster."

1 Let's face it. Writing is hell.
—**William Styron,** 1979, quoted in *Civilization* magazine [Dec. 1996–Jan. 1997]

2 There's nothing to writing. All you do is sit down at a typewriter and open a vein.
—**Walter "Red" Smith,** in *Reader's Digest*, July 1982

3 Being a great writer is not the same as writing great.
—**John Updike,** in *The New Yorker*, May 20, 1985

4 If there is a book you really want to read but it hasn't been written yet, then you must write it.
—**Toni Morrison**

★ This has been attributed to Morrison in a number of sources, including *The New York Times*. She told this book's editors that she remembers only that she said it in a speech.

5 Be aware that your reader is at least as bright as you are.
—**William Maxwell,** maxim, quoted by Larry Woiwode, in *The New York Times Book Review*, August 14, 1988

★ Maxwell, a novelist, edited fiction at *The New Yorker* magazine for forty years.

6 At this weak, pale, tabescent moment in the history of American literature, we need a battalion, a brigade of Zolas to head out into this wild, bizarre unpredictable, hog-stomping country of ours and reclaim its literary property.
—**Tom Wolfe,** *Stalking the Billion-footed Beast: A Literary Manifesto for the New Social Novel,* in *Harper's,* 1989

7 Writers legislate the interior world.
—**E. L. Doctorow,** speech, 1990, quoted in *The Wall Street Journal* [Sept. 16, 1992]

8 There is no writer's block in a newsroom. There's only unemployment block.
—**Carl Hiaasen,** interview, *The New York Times Magazine,* July 25, 2004

Aspiration

See AMBITION & ASPIRATION; DREAMS & DREAMERS; IDEAS & IDEALS.

Atheism

See also GOD.

9 [The Bible] has noble poetry in it; and some clever fables; and some blood-drenched history; and a wealth of obscenity; and upwards of a thousand lies.
—**Mark Twain,** *Letters from Earth* [1962]

10 My atheism, like that of Spinoza, is true piety towards the universe, and denies only gods fashioned by men in their own image, to be servants of their human interests.
—**George Santayana,** *On My Friendly Critics*, in *Soliloquies in England and Later Soliloquies*, 1922

In spite of all the yearnings of men, no one can produce a single fact or reason to support the belief in God and in personal immortality. 1
—**Clarence Darrow,** *Sign* magazine, May 1938

There are no atheists in the foxholes. 2
—**William Thomas Cummings,** field sermon, Bataan, 1942

★ Father Cummings, a Maryknoll missionary and commissioned first lieutenant, courageously provided solace to the doomed American and Filipino troops on the Bataan peninsula. He refused to leave when he had the chance, and was taken prisoner when Bataan surrendered to the Japanese. He lived through the sixty-mile Death March that killed 14,000 of the 70,000 prisoners only to die when the unmarked ship transporting him and other prisoners to Japan was torpedoed by a U.S. submarine. See also WORLD WAR II.

The day that this country ceases to be free for irreligion, it will cease to be free for religion—except for the sect that can win political power. 3
—**Robert H. Jackson,** Supreme Court, dissent, *Zorach v. Clauson*, 1952

An atheist is a man who has no invisible means of support. 4
—**Fulton J. Sheen,** *Look* magazine, Dec. 14, 1955

Atheism is a non-prophet religion. 5
—**Anonymous**, saying and bumper sticker, from c. 2000

★ The line often is attributed in collections of jokes on the Internet to comedian George Carlin, but on his own website he denies responsibility for it.

Australia

See NATIONS.

Automobiles

See SCIENCE: TECHNOLOGY.

Autumn

See NATURE: SEASONS.

Bad Times

See also DEPRESSION, THE; MODERN TIMES; TROUBLE.

Lost is our old simplicity of times, 6
The world abounds with laws, and teems with crimes.
—**Anonymous,** from the *Pennsylvania Gazette*, Feb. 8, 1775, borrowed from an earlier, unidentified London magazine

These are the times that try men's souls. 7
—**Thomas Paine,** *The American Crisis*, Dec. 1776

★ More at AMERICAN REVOLUTION.

1 Society seems everywhere unhinged, and the demon of blood and slaughter has been let loose upon us.

—**Hezekiah Niles,** in *Niles' Weekly Register*, 1835

★ The *Niles' Register* was a popular newsweekly. In the age of Jackson, the conflict between the privileged and the laboring classes was intense, and people feared that a revolution might erupt. See also below and under CAPITALISM & CAPITAL V. LABOR.

2 In society as it is now constituted, monotony, uniformity, intellectual inaction, and torpor reign: distrust, isolation, separation, conflict, and antagonism are almost universal: very little expansion of the generous affections and feelings obtain . . . Society is spiritually a desert.

—**Albert Brisbane,** article in *The Bay State Democrat*, Jan. 15, 1844

★ Brisbane was the nation's leading Fourierite, a perceptive anti-capitalist but not strong on solutions.

3 This is an age of the world where nations are trembling and convulsed.

—**Harriet Beecher Stowe,** *Uncle Tom's Cabin*, 1852

★ More at INJUSTICE.

4 The age is dull and mean. Men creep,
Not walk.

—**John Greenleaf Whittier,** *Line Inscribed to Friends Under Arrest for Treason Against the Slave Power*, 1856

5 Can anybody remember when the times were not hard, and money not scarce?

—**Ralph Waldo Emerson,** *Works and Days*, in *Society and Solitude*, 1870

6 Never was there, perhaps, more hollowness at heart than at present, and here in the United States.

—**Walt Whitman,** *Democratic Vistas*, 1871

7 [There] is looming up a new and dark power . . . the enterprises of the country are aggregating vast corporate combinations of unexampled capitalism, boldly marching, not for economical conquests only, but for political power.

—**Edward G. Ryan,** graduation address, University of Wisconsin Law School, 1873

★ Ryan was chief justice of the Wisconsin Supreme Court.

8 The grass will grow in the streets of a hundred cities.

—**Herbert Hoover,** speech, Oct. 31, 1936

★ More at ECONOMICS.

9 The epidemic of world lawlessness is spreading.

—**Franklin D. Roosevelt,** "Quarantine the Aggressors" speech, Chicago, Oct. 5, 1937

10 I saw the best minds of my generation destroyed by madness, starving hysterical naked.

—**Allen Ginsberg,** *Howl*, 1956

★ More at MADNESS.

The prairies were dust. Day after day, summer after summer, the scorching winds blew the dust and the sun was brassy in a yellow sky. Crop after crop failed. Again and again the barren land must be mortgaged for taxes and food and next year's seed. The agony of hope ended when there was no harvest and no more credit, no money to pay interest and taxes. The banker took the land. Then the bank failed. 1

—**Rose Wilder Lane & Laura Ingalls Wilder,** *On the Way Home,* 1962

★ Rose Wilder Lane, journalist and writer, was the daughter of Laura Ingalls Wilder, author of the "Little House" series. This passage, based on Laura's diary from 1894, describes dreadful conditions in Dakota Territory that forced the family to retreat to a farm in the Ozarks. Drought combined with the financial Panic of 1893 had brought ruin to the West. The term "depression" was not used at that time, but the financial crises of the 1890s and the drought parallel the Depression and the Dust Bowl of the 1930s.

In a dark time, the eye begins to see. 2

—**Theodore Roethke,** *In a Dark Time,* 1964

No matter how cynical we become, it's never enough to keep up. 3

—**Lily Tomlin** as herself in *The Search for Intelligent Life in the Universe* by Jane Wagner, 1992

Americans . . . need to watch what they say, watch what they do. 4

—**Ari Fleischer,** White House press conference, Sept. 26, 2001

★ Presidential spokesman Fleischer's warning was a reaction to comments by Bill Maher, host of a late-night talk show, *Politically Incorrrect*, to the effect that terrorists who flew airplanes into building were not cowards while Americans who launched cruise missiles at their enemies from two thousand miles away were. The phrase, "watch what they say," was initially omitted from the briefing transcript on the White House website. This did not keep Mr. Maher from quickly losing advertisers and then his show.

The delusional is no longer marginal. 5

—**Bill Moyers,** acceptance speech for Harvard Medical School's Global Environment Citizen Award, Dec. 6, 2004

Barriers

See DIVISIONS & BARRIERS.

Beauty

See also APPEARANCES; ART: AESTHETICS; BODY & LOOKS.

With beauty before me, I walk 6
With beauty behind me, I walk
With beauty above and about me, I walk.

—**Anonymous,** Navaho night chant, in Frank Bergon & Zeese Papaniklas, *Looking Far West* [1978]

★ More at NATURE.

1 The perception of beauty is a moral test.
—Henry David Thoreau, *Journal*, June 21, 1852

2 We must have beauty around us to make us good.
—M. E. W. Sherwood, c. 1855

★ Mrs. Sherwood pontificated on style in the 1850s.

3 A beautiful woman is a practical poet.
—Ralph Waldo Emerson, *Beauty*, in *The Conduct of Life*, 1860

4 Beauty as we feel it is something indescribable: what it is or what it means can never be said.
—George Santayana, *The Sense of Beauty*, 1896

5 The superior gratification derived from the use and contemplation of costly and supposedly beautiful products is, commonly, in great measure, a gratification of our sense of costliness masquerading under the name of beauty.
—Thorstein Veblen, *The Theory of the Leisure Class*, 1899

6 A Pretty Girl Is Like a Melody.
—Irving Berlin, song title, *Ziegfeld Follies*, 1919

7 Beauty is momentary in the mind—
The fitful tracing of a portal;
But in the flesh it is immortal;
The body dies; the body's beauty lives.
—Wallace Stevens, *Peter Quince at the Clavier*, 1923

8 Oh, no, it wasn't the aviators, it was beauty that killed the beast.
—James Creelman and Ruth Rose, *King Kong*, 1933

★ Said by the hero, Carl Denham, played by Robert Armstrong. The movie was based on a story by Merian C. Cooper, the director, and Edgar Wallace.

9 Beauty is everlasting
And dust is for a time.
—Marianne Moore, *In Distrust of Merits*, 1941

10 There are no ugly women, only lazy ones.
—Helena Rubinstein, saying, quoted in Lindy Woodhead, *War Paint* [2004]

11 I'm tired of all this business about beauty being only skin-deep. That's deep enough. What do you want—an adorable pancreas?
—Jean Kerr, *Mirror, Mirror on the Wall I Don't Want to Hear One Word Out of You*, in *The Snake Has All the Lines*, 1960

12 Beauty is now underfoot wherever we take the trouble to look.
—John Cage, quoted in *The New York Times* [Sept. 19, 1997]

★ Said in praise of his friend Robert Rauschenberg, whose art found beauty in the litter of urban life.

Beginnings & Endings

That's all there is, there isn't any more. 1

—**Ethel Barrymore,** signature curtain line, written in by her to Thomas Raceward's play *Sunday*, 1904

What we call the beginning is often the end 2
And to make an end is to make a beginning.
The end is where we start from.

—**T. S. Eliot,** *Little Gidding*, in *Four Quartets*, 1943

★ See also Eliot at FATE & DESTINY.

The happy ending is our national belief. 3

—**Mary McCarthy,** *America the Beautiful: The Humanist in the Bathtub*, in *Commentary*, Sept. 1947

The opera ain't over till the fat lady sings. 4

—**Anonymous**

★ A folk saying with numerous variations, including "It ain't over until the fat lady sings," and, "Church ain't out until the fat lady sings," *Southern Words and Sayings*, 1976, Fabia R. Smith and Charles R. Smith, eds. It was used with reference to sports by commentator Dan Cook and Chicago Bulls' coach Dick Motta in the 1970s. See also Yogi Berra below.

It ain't over till it's over. 5

—**Yogi Berra,** saying, attributed

★ *Bartlett's* says that he was referring to the 1973 National League pennant race. The saying has taken a variety of forms; see also SPORTS.

There will come a time when you believe everything is finished. That will be the 6
beginning.

—**Louis L'Amour,** *Lonely on the Mountain*, 1980

Bigness

See also SMALLNESS; STRENGTH & TOUGHNESS.

I think no virtue goes with size. 7

—**Ralph Waldo Emerson,** *The Titmouse*, in *Poems*, 1847

The bigger they come, the harder they fall. 8

—**John L. Sullivan,** saying, c. 1900

★ More at SPORTS.

This [the RKO movie studio] is the biggest electric train set any boy ever had! 9

—**Orson Welles,** in Roy Fowler, *Orson Welles* [1946]

★ RKO promised the twenty-five-year old "boy wonder" complete freedom, including right of "final cut," and he responded with *Citizen Kane* (1941), one of the greatest movies ever made. But *Kane* was not a box-office hit, and no studio ever gave Welles such freedom again.

1 We must develop huge demonstrations, because the world is used to big, dramatic affairs. They think in terms of hundreds of thousands and millions and billions . . . Nothing little counts.

—**A. Philip Randolph,** speech, policy conference, March on Washington Movement, Detroit, Sept. 26, 1942

★ Randolph was the most influential African American labor leader of his time—and it was a time in which labor gained great power. As president of the Brotherhood of Sleeping Car Workers (BSCW), who were usually called Pullman porters, he brought this successful black trade union into the American Federation of Labor. When the AFL failed to fight discrimination vigorously, Randolph moved the BSCW to rival labor alliance, the Congress of Industrial Organizations. As the quote indicates, he was thinking of a massive civil-rights march as early as the 1940s (prompting Pres. Franklin D. Roosevelt to bar discrimination in defense industries and federal bureaus). A generation later, he was one of the core organizers of the 1963 March on Washington, which attracted upward of 250,000 people, and is most often remembered for Rev. Martin Luther King's "I Have a Dream" speech. See AMERICA HISTORY: MEMORABLE MOMENTS.

2 The horror of the Twentieth Century was the size of each event, and the paucity of its reverberation.

—**Norman Mailer**, *A Fire on the Moon*, 1970

The Bill of Rights

See also CONSTITUTION.

3 **The Bill of Rights: Amendment 1**
Congress shall make no law respecting an establishment of religion, or prohibiting the free exercise thereof; or abridging the freedom of speech, or of the press; or the right of the people peaceably to assemble, and to petition the Government for a redress of grievances.

4 **The Bill of Rights: Amendment 2**
A well regulated militia, being necessary to the security of a free state, the right of the people to keep and bear arms, shall not be infringed.

5 **The Bill of Rights: Amendment 3**
No soldier shall, in time of peace be quartered in any house, without the consent of the owner, nor in time of war, but in a manner to be prescribed by law.

6 **The Bill of Rights: Amendment 4**
The right of the people to be secure in their persons, houses, papers, and effects against unreasonable searches and seizures, shall not be violated, and no warrants shall issue, but upon probable cause, supported by oath or affirmation, and particularly describing the place to be searched, and the persons or things to be seized.

7 **The Bill of Rights: Amendment 5**
No person shall be held to answer for a capital, or otherwise infamous crime, unless on a presentment or indictment of a grand jury, except in cases arising in the land or naval forces, or in the militia, when in actual service in time of war or public danger; nor shall any person be subject for the same offence to be twice put in jeopardy of

life or limb; nor shall be compelled in any criminal case to be a witness against himself, nor be deprived of life, liberty, or property, without due process of law; nor shall private property be taken for public use, without just compensation.

The Bill of Rights: Amendment 6 1
In all criminal prosecutions, the accused shall enjoy the right to a speedy and public trial, by an impartial jury of the state and district wherein the crime shall have been committed, which district shall have been previously ascertained by law, and to be informed of the nature and cause of the accusation; to be confronted with the witnesses against him; to have compulsory process for obtaining witnesses in his favor, and to have the assistance of counsel for his defense.

The Bill of Rights: Amendment 7 2
In suits at common law, where the value in controversy shall exceed twenty dollars, the right of a trial by jury shall be preserved, and no fact tried by a jury, shall be otherwise re-examined in any court of the United States, than according to the rules of the common law.

The Bill of Rights: Amendment 8 3
Excessive bail shall not be required, nor excessive fines imposed, nor cruel and unusual punishments inflicted.

The Bill of Rights: Amendment 9 4
The enumeration in the Constitution, of certain rights, shall not be construed to deny or disparage others retained by the people.

The Bill of Rights: Amendment 10 5
The powers not delegated to the United States by the Constitution, nor prohibited by it to the states, are reserved to the states respectively, or to the people.

Biology

See SCIENCE: BIOLOGY & PHYSIOLOGY.

Blacks

See RACES & PEOPLES.

Boasting

I'm that same David Crockett, fresh from the backwoods, half-horse, half-alligator, a 6
little touched with the snapping-turtle; can wade the Mississippi, leap the Ohio, ride upon a streak of lightning, and slip without a scratch down a honey-locust; can whip my weight in wild cats—and if any gentleman pleases, for a ten dollar bill, he may throw in a panther—hug a bear too close for comfort, and eat any man opposed to Jackson.

—David Crockett, in *Sketches and Eccentricities of Col. David Crockett, of West Tennessee*, 1833

★ Crockett served three terms in the House, 1827–31 and 1833–35, representing a district in western Tennessee. His image as a backwoods hero was largely self-created.

He was so ugly, he said, that his grin would bring a coon down from a tree—and once, mistaking a tree knot for a coon, he grinned the bark right off the tree. He also had "the roughest racking horse, the prettiest sister, the surest rifle, and the ugliest dog in the district" (speech, House of Representatives, cited in *Davy Crockett's Almanac*, 1837). Campaigning in 1827, and short of funds to treat voters in the manner to which they were accustomed, he bagged a coon and traded its skin to a Yankee vendor for a quart of rum. While the voters drank up, Crockett snuck the skin from beneath the bar, then traded it back for another quart. In this way, he obtained ten quarts of rum for the same skin, won the election, and earned his nickname as "the coonskin congressman." After his death at the Alamo in 1836, Crockett quickly became a mythic figure; tall tales about him were popularized in a series of "Crockett" almanacs published through 1856.

1 I'm a Salt River roarer! I'm a ring-tailed squealer! I'm a reg'lar screamer from the ol' Massassip'! WHOOP! I'm the very infant that refused his milk before his eyes were open, and called out for a bottle of old rye! I love the women, and I'm chockful of fight! I'm half wild horse and half cock-eyed alligator, and the rest of me is crooked snags an' red-hot snappin' turkle. I can hit like fourth-proof lightnin' an' every lick I make in the woods lets in an acre o' sunshine. I can out-run, out-jump, out-shoot, out-brag, out-drink, an' out-fight, rough-an'-tumble, no holts barred, ary man on both sides of the river from Pittsburgh to New Orleans an' back ag'in to St. Louiee. Come on, you flatters, you bargers, you milk-white mechanics, an' see how tough I am to chaw! I ain't had a fight for two days an' I'm spilein' for exercise. Cock-a-doodle-do!

—**Mike Fink,** his brag, in Walter Blair and Franklin J. Meine, *Mike Fink, King of the Mississippi Keelboatmen* [1933]

★ Legends collected around Fink, who was a deadly shot, a diabolical practical joker, and "King of the Keelboatmen." These men floated cargos down the Mississippi River to New Orleans and laboriously poled and towed their way back, a round-trip that could take nine months. The notoriously rough, coarse, riotous keelboatmen gradually were displaced by steamboats. By 1823, Fink had left the river and was working for a fur company in Montana. While engaging in the frontier sport of shooting a tin whisky cup off another man's head, he killed the fellow, perhaps not accidentally. He then was shot to death himself by a friend of the man he had slain.

2 Whoo-oop! I'm the original iron-jawed, brass-mounted, copper-bellied corpse-maker from the wilds of Arkansas! Look at me! I'm the man they call Sudden Death and General Desolation! Sired by a hurricane, dam'd by an earthquake, half-brother to the cholera, nearly related to the smallpox on my mother's side. Look at me! I take nineteen alligators and a bar'l of whiskey for breakfast when I'm in robust health, and a bushel of rattlesnakes and a dead body when I'm ailing. I split the everlasting rocks with my glance, and I squench the thunder when I speak! Whoo-oop! Stand back and give me room according to my strength! Blood's my natural drink, and the wails of the dying is music to my ear. Cast your eye on me gentlemen! and lay low and hold your breath, for I'm 'bout to turn myself loose!

—**Anonymous,** keelboatman's boast in Mark Twain, *Life on the Mississippi*, 1883

★ Twain apprenticed as a steamboat pilot before the Civil War. By Twain's time, the keelboats were gone, and the men had become hands on steamboats or else tended the huge coal- and timber-carrying rafts that the steamboats shepherded downriver. The rough-talking tradition of Mike Fink remained very much alive, however.

I come to this country riding a lion, whipping him over the head with a .45 and picking my teeth with a .38 and wearing a .45 on each hip, using a cactus for a piller, whe-ee-e! I'm a two-gun man and very bad man and won't do to monkey with. Whe-ee-o, I'm a bad man! Whoopee! 1

—**Anonymous,** cowboy yell, from B. A. Botkin, *Tall Talk and Tall Tales of the Southwest*, in *The New Mexico Candle* [June 18, 1933]

I'm wild and woolly 2
And full of fleas;
Ain't never been curried
Below the knees.
I'm a wild she wolf
From Bitter Creek,
And it's my time
To h-o-w-l, whoop-i-e-e-ee.

—**Anonymous,** cowboy boast, in *American Ballads and Folk Songs* [1934], collected and compiled by John A. Lomax and Alan Lomax

It ain't braggin' if you can do it. 3

—**Dizzy Dean,** attributed

★ Mr. Dean could do it. In his glory years as a pitcher for the St. Louis Cardinals (1932–37), he won 133 games and lost only 75.

I'm the greatest. 4

—**Muhammad Ali,** brag, from June, 1961

★ Mr. Ali said in his 1975 autobiography, aptly entitled *The Greatest*, that prior to a bout on June 26 in Las Vegas he talked openly for the first time about beating another boxer, calling out "I'm the Greatest! I can't be beat!" He won the match in ten rounds.

You know what I knew—that my God was bigger than his. I knew that my God was a real God, and his was an idol. 5

—**Lt. Gen. William G. Boykin**, remark, 2003, cited in *The New York Times* [Oct. 17, 2003]

★ Gen. Boykin's was referring to a Somalian warlord. He made this and similar observations during a series of twenty-three appearances before evangelical groups. The general received considerable criticism after NBC televised tapes of some of his talks but kept his job as deputy undersecretary of defense for intelligence.

Underpromise. Overperform. 6

—**Michael Eisner**, saying, quoted on National Public Radio, Morning Edition, Mar. 2, 2004

Body & Looks

See also Beauty; Health; Mind, Thought, & Understanding (Dickinson); Physical Fitness.

1 If anything is sacred, the human body is sacred.
—**Walt Whitman,** *I Sing the Body Electric* in *Leaves of Grass*, 1855

2 The Lord prefers common-looking people. That is the reason he makes so many of them.
—**Abraham Lincoln,** Dec. 23, 1863, quoted by John Hay, *Letters of John Hay and Extracts from His Diary*, C. L. Hay, ed. [1908, reprint 1969]

★ As Hay tells it, Lincoln reported that he'd had a dream in which he was in a crowd, and someone, recognizing him, had said, "He is a very common-looking man." The president responded with the above remark.

3 Now the body is an instrument, the mind its function, the witness and reward of its operation.
—**George Santayana,** *Life of Reason: Reason in Commons Sense*, 1905

4 My face, I don't mind it,
Because I'm behind it;
It's the people out front that I jar.
—**Woodrow Wilson,** saying

★ Surely not original with Wilson, but since he was unaffected enough to use it, he deserves credit.

5 The body dies; the body's beauty lives.
—**Wallace Stevens,** *Peter Quince at the Clavier*, 1923

★ More at Beauty.

6 The strongest, surest way to the soul is through the flesh.
—**Mabel Dodge,** *Lorenzo in Taos*, 1932

★ The Lorenzo of the title is D. H. Lawrence.

7 The human body is an instrument for the production of art in the human soul.
—**Alfred North Whitehead,** *Adventures of Ideas*, 1933

8 The body says what words cannot.
—**Martha Graham,** interview, *The New York Times*, March 31, 1985

Boldness & Initiative

See also Action & Doing; Decision; Military Strategy; Speed.

9 Offense is the best defense.
—**Anonymous**

★ Traced to the 1700s in Bartlett Jere Whiting, ed., *Early American Proverbs and Proverbial Phrases*, 1977.

Take calculated risks. That is quite different from being rash. 1
—**George S. Patton,** letter to his son, June 6, 1944 [D-day]

★ See also Patton on boldness in war at MILITARY STRATEGY.

Always run from a knife but charge a gun. 2
—**Jimmy Hoffa,** advice, 1964, in *The New York Times* [May 18, 1998]

★ Hoffa offered this bit of advice about self-preservation to his lawyer, Frank Ragano, who had been at the Teamster president's side when a man burst into a courtroom in Nashville, Tenn., and started shooting with an air pistol. Hoffa was hit three times but managed to punch the man with the gun.

If you're not living on the edge, you're taking up too much space. 3
—**Tommy G. Thompson,** speech, National Advisory Committee on Violence Against Women, April 24, 2003

★ Thompson, U.S. Secretary of Health and Human Service, was using here a contemporaneous saying that appears in a variety of forms, "If you're not on the edge, you're taking up too much room."

Books & Reading

See also ART: WRITING; CENSORSHIP; MEDIA.

I cannot live without books. 4
—**Thomas Jefferson,** letter to John Adams, June 10, 1815

Books are for nothing but to inspire. 5
—**Ralph Waldo Emerson,** *The American Scholar*, 1837

There is then creative reading as well as creative writing. 6
—**Ralph Waldo Emerson,** *The American Scholar*, 1837

Read the best books first, or you may not have a chance to read them at all. 7
—**Henry David Thoreau,** *A Week on the Concord and Merrimack Rivers*, 1849

How many a man has dated a new era in his life from the reading of a book. 8
—**Henry David Thoreau,** "Reading," *Walden*, 1854

Books must be read as deliberately and reservedly as they were written. 9
—**Ibid.**

Books are the treasured wealth of the world and the fit inheritance of generations 10
and nations.
—**Ibid.**

Never read any book that is not a year old. 11
—**Ralph Waldo Emerson,** *In Praise of Books*, in *The Conduct of Life*, 1860

Old books . . . are books of the world's youth, and new books are fruits of its age. 12
—**Oliver Wendell Holmes, Sr.,** *The Professor at the Breakfast Table, 1860*

Some books are so familiar that reading them is like being home again. 13
—**Louisa May Alcott,** *Little Women*, 1868

1 There are books . . . which take rank in your life with parents and lovers and passionate experiences.
—Ralph Waldo Emerson, *Society and Solitude,* 1870

2 There is no Frigate like a Book
To take us Lands away,
Nor any Coursers like a Page
Of prancing poetry—
—Emily Dickinson, poem no. 1263, c. 1873

3 The love of learning, the sequestered nooks,
And all the sweet serenity of books.
—Henry Wadsworth Longfellow, *Morituri Salutamus*, 1875

4 Wear the old coat and buy the new book.
—Austin Phelps, *The Theory of Preaching; Lectures on Homilectics*, 1881

5 Wisdom is wealth, and every good book is equivalent to a wise head—the head may die, but the book may live forever.
—Joseph Wheeler, speech, U.S. House of Representatives, debate on constructing the Library of Congress, Feb. 1883

★ Rep. Wheeler was a well-known Confederate cavalry commander.

6 Camerado, this is no book,
Whoso touches this touches a man.
—Walt Whitman, *So Long!*, in *Leaves of Grass*, 1891–1892

7 "Classic." A book which people praise and don't read.
—Mark Twain, *Pudd'nhead Wilson's New Calendar*, in *Following the Equator*, 1897

8 Literature is my utopia.
—Helen Keller, *The Story of My Life*, 1902

9 The mortality of all inanimate things is terrible to me, but that of books most of all.
—William Dean Howells, letter to Charles Eliot Norton, April 6, 1903

10 No girl was ever ruined by a book.
—James J. "Jimmy" Walker, attributed

★ Walker, a ladies' man, was mayor of New York City from 1925 to 1932. See also Herman Melville at CENSORSHIP.

11 People say that life is the thing, but I prefer reading.
—Logan Pearsall Smith, *Afterthoughts*, 1931

12 All good books are alike in that they are truer than if they really happened and after you have finished reading one you will feel that it all happened to you, and afterwards it all belongs to you.
—Ernest Hemingway, *An Old Newsman Writes*, in *Esquire*, Dec. 1934

All modern American literature comes from one book by Mark Twain called *Huckleberry Finn.* 1
—**Ernest Hemingway,** *Green Hills of Africa*, 1935

People die, but books never die. 2
—**Franklin D. Roosevelt,** speech to the American Booksellers Association, April 23, 1942

★ He was speaking with reference to book burning in Nazi Germany.

There are some people who read too much: bibliobibuli. 3
—**H. L. Mencken,** *Minority Report: H. L. Mencken's Notebooks* [1956]

In reading, one should notice and fondle details. 4
—**Vladmir Nabokov,** *Good Readers and Good Writers*, 1948

What really knocks me out is a book that, when you're all done reading it, you wish that the author that wrote it was a terrific friend of yours and you could call him up on the phone whenever you felt like it. That doesn't happen much, though. 5
—**J. D. Salinger,** *The Catcher in the Rye*, 1951

We shouldn't teach great books; we should teach a love of reading. 6
—**B. F. Skinner,** quoted in Richard I. Evans, *B. F. Skinner: The Man and His Ideas*

Some books are undeservedly forgotten; none are undeservedly remembered. 7
—**W. H. Auden,** *The Dyer's Hand*, 1962

Human beings can lose their lives in libraries. They ought to be warned. 8
—**Saul Bellow,** *Him With His Foot in His Mouth*, 1984

Libraries . . . house our dreams. 9
—**Nikki Giovanni** in *American Libraries*, May 1996

Good books don't give up all their secrets at once. 10
—**Stephen King,** *Hearts in Atlantis*, 1999

Bores & Dullness

Speeches measured by the hour die with the hour. 11
—**Thomas Jefferson,** letter to David Harding, April 20, 1824

It is the peculiarity of the bore that he is the last person to find himself out. 12
—**Oliver Wendell Holmes, Sr.**, *Over the Teacups*, 1891

Bore, n. A person who talks when you wish him to listen. 13
—**Ambrose Bierce,** *The Devil's Dictionary*, 1906

The godless are the dull and the dull are the damned. 14
—**E. E. Cummings,** *Proud of his scientific attitude*, in *Poems*, 1940

1 [Comment following a tedious speech]: Gentlemen, you have just been listening to that Chinese sage, On Tu Long.

—**Will Rogers,** in Alex Ayres, ed., *The Wit and Wisdom of Will Rogers* [1993]

2 The capacity of human beings to bore one another seems to be vastly greater than that of any other animals. Some of their most esteemed inventions have no other apparent purpose, for example, the dinner party of more than two, the epic poem, and the science of metaphysics.

—**H. L. Mencken,** *Minority Report: H. L. Mencken's Notebooks* [1956]

★ See also Mencken at WORK.

3 A healthy male adult bore consumes each year one and a half times his weight in other people's patience.

—**John Updike,** *Confessions of a Wild Bore,* in *Assorted Prose,* 1965

Bravery

See COURAGE; HEROES.

Brazil

See NATIONS.

Bureaucracy

See GOVERNMENT; MANAGEMENT TECHNIQUES.

Business

See also CAPITALISM & CAPITAL V. LABOR; ECONOMICS; MANAGEMENT TECHNIQUES; MONEY & THE RICH; SECURITY & SAFETY (Iacocca).

4 Method goes far to prevent trouble in business: for it makes the task easy, hinders confusion, saves abundance of time, and instructs those that have business depending, both what to do and what to hope.

—**William Penn,** *Some Fruits of Solitude,* 1693

5 The creditors are a superstitious sect, great observers of set days and times.

—**Benjamin Franklin,** *Poor Richard's Almanack,* 1737

6 No nation was ever ruined by trade.

—**Benjamin Franklin,** *Thoughts on Commercial Subjects*

7 How impure are the channels through which trade hath a conveyance. How great is that danger to which poor lads are now exposed, when placed on shipboard to learn the art of sailing.

—**John Woolman,** *Journal* [1774]

8 Merchants love nobody.

—**Thomas Jefferson,** letter to John Langdon, 1785

The selfish spirit of commerce knows no country, and feels no passion or principle but that of gain. 1

—**Thomas Jefferson**, letter to Larkin Smith, 1809

Banking establishments are more dangerous than standing armies. 2

—**Thomas Jefferson,** letter to John Taylor, May 28, 1816

Corporations have neither bodies to be kicked nor souls to be damned. 3

—**Anonymous**

★ This aphorism, cited by Arthur Schlesinger, Jr., in *The Age of Jackson* (1945) is similar to Sir Edward Coke's pronouncement in the 17th century, "They [corporations] cannot commit treason, nor be outlawed nor excommunicated, for they have no souls," *Case of Sutton's Hospital*. See also Henry Demarest Lloyd below.

Every monopoly and all exclusive privileges are granted at the expense of the public, which ought to receive a fair equivalent. 4

—**Andrew Jackson,** veto of the bill to renew the charter of the Bank of the United States, 1832

★ The battle over whether to continue the bank pitted the populist westerner Jackson against the privileged easterners who ran the bank for the benefit of the moneyed class—or at least Jackson was able to present the issue this way, and his veto propelled him to reelection. See also Daniel Webster below.

As directors of a company, men will sanction actions of which they would scorn to be guilty in their private capacity. A crime which would press heavily on the conscience of one man, becomes quite endurable when divided among many. 5

—**William M. Gouge,** *A Short History of Money and Banking in the United States*, 1833

Credit is the vital air of the system of modern commerce. 6

—**Daniel Webster,** speech in the U.S. Senate, March 18, 1834

★ Webster was speaking in support of the Bank of the United States. See also Herbert Hoover under ECONOMICS.

A power has risen up in the government greater than the people themselves, consisting of many and various and powerful interests, combined into one mass, and held together by the cohesive power of the vast surplus in the banks. 7

—**John C. Calhoun,** speech, May 27, 1836

★ *Bartlett's* comments that this passage is the origin of the phrase, "cohesive power of public plunder."

Corporations will do what individuals would not dare to do. 8

—**Peter C. Brooks,** remark to Edward Everett, July 15, 1845

★ Arthur Schlesinger, Jr., in *The Age of Jackson* (1945), describes Brooks as the wealthiest man in Boston.

Well, I've got just as much conscience as any man in business can afford to keep—just a little, you know, to swear by, as 't were. 9

—**Harriet Beecher Stowe,** *Uncle Tom's Cabin*, 1852

1 Trade curses everything it handles, and though you trade in messages from heaven, the whole curse of trade attaches to the business.

—Henry David Thoreau, "Economy," *Walden*, 1854

2 Through want of enterprise and faith men are where they are, buying and selling, and spending their lives like serfs.

—Henry David Thoreau, "Baker Farm," *Walden*, 1854

3 I *don't* believe in princerple,
But oh I *du* in interest.

—James Russell Lowell, *The Biglow Papers*, "The Courtin' " in Series II, 1866

4 The dealers in money have always, since the days of Moses, been the dangerous class.

—Peter Cooper, c. 1875, quoted in Peter Lyon, *The Honest Man*, in *American Heritage* [Feb. 1959]

★ Cooper, the founder of Cooper Union in New York City, used to say that his life fell into three parts: thirty years to get started, thirty years to gain a fortune, and thirty years to dispose of it wisely. In old age, he ran for president as a radical protest candidate, heading the National Independent party, usually called the Greenback party. See also under MONEY & THE RICH.

5 The public be damned! I'm working for my stockholders.

—William H. Vanderbilt, comment to a news reporter, Oct. 2, 1882

★ This impatient remark by the railroad tycoon was seized on immediately as a summation of the attitude of the captains of industry toward the common people.

6 When a man sells eleven ounces for twelve, he makes a compact with the devil, and sells himself for the value of an ounce.

—Henry Ward Beecher, *Proverbs from Plymouth Pulpit*, 1887

7 Buying and selling is essentially antisocial.

—Edward Bellamy, *Looking Backward, 2000–1887*,1888

8 Monopoly is business at the end of its journey.

—Henry Demarest Lloyd, *Wealth Against Commonwealth*, 1894

9 Corporations have no souls, but they can love each other.

—Ibid.

★ Lloyd was an influential economist, journalist, reformer, and wit. For more on the famous aphorism on corporations and souls, see under Anonymous above.

10 There are two times in a man's life when he should not speculate: when he can't afford it and when he can.

—Mark Twain, *Pudd'nhead Wilson's New Calendar*, in *Following the Equator*, 1897

★ Twain didn't heed his own advice. He repeatedly invested in new ventures, and repeatedly lost money, most notably in the case of a typesetting machine that never quite worked. In *Pudd'nhead Wilson's Calendar (Pudd'nhead Wilson*, 1894), Twain wrote: "October. This is one of the peculiarly dangerous months to speculate in stocks in. The others are July, January, September . . . " and so on through the rest of the months.

We demand that big business give people a square deal. **1**

—Theodore Roosevelt, 1901

★ More at POLITICAL SLOGANS. At the turn of the century, politicians had to address the concentration of power and money in the hands of a few men and corporations, such as J. P. Morgan's U.S. Steel. Roosevelt lost the 1912 presidential election to Woodrow Wilson, whose "New Freedom" program was tougher on big business.

Corporation: An ingenious device for obtaining individual profit without individual **2**
responsibility.

—Ambrose Bierce, *The Devil's Dictionary*, 1906

Most men are the servants of corporations. **3**

—Woodrow Wilson, *The Old Order Changeth*, in *The New Freedom*, 1913

★ The whole sentence reads: "There was a time when corporations played a very minor part in our business affairs, but now they play the chief part, and most men are the servants of corporations." See also below.

The present organization of business was meant for the big fellows and was not **4**
meant for the little fellows; it was meant for those who are at the top and was meant to exclude those who are at the bottom; it was meant to shut out beginners, to prevent new entries in the race, to prevent the building up of competitive enterprises that would interfere with the monopolies which the great trusts have built up.

—Ibid.

All business sagacity reduces itself in the last analysis to judicious use of sabotage. **5**

—Thorstein Veblen, *An Inquiry into the Nature of Peace and the Terms of Its Perpetuation*, 1917

Smoke and blood is the mix of steel. **6**

—Carl Sandburg, *Smoke and Steel*, 1920

The chief business of the American people is business. **7**

—Calvin Coolidge, speech, The American Society of Newspaper Editors, Washington, D.C., Jan. 17, 1925

No man's credit is as good as his money. **8**

—Edgar Watson Howe, *Sinner Sermons*, 1926

The customer is always right. **9**

—Carl Sandburg, *Good Morning, America*, 1928

★ The saying quoted here by Sandburg was also the motto of the London department store Selfridge's, founded by H. Gordon Selfridge.

If it don't go up, don't buy it. **10**

—Will Rogers, advice on selecting a stock, *Daily Telegrams*, Oct. 31, 1929

1 [Wall Street:] A thoroughfare that begins in a graveyard and ends in a river.
—**Anonymous,** traditional saying

★ The street begins at Trinity Church and graveyard; it ends at the East River. One ex-stockbroker contended, however, that the saying " is striking, but incomplete," because "it omits the kindergarten in the middle" (Fred Schwed, Jr., *Where Are the Customer's Yachts?*, 1940). As it happens, Schwed's title also derives from an old Wall St. joke, this one about a client being given a tour of the area. "Over there are the yachts of the powerful Wall St. brokers," says the guide, pointing to the East River. "And where," asks the client, "are the customers' yachts?"

2 You can't mine coal without machine guns.
—**Richard B. Mellon,** testimony, U.S. Congress, quoted in *Time*, June 14, 1937

3 [The insurer] insures all people against all happenings of everyday life, even the worm in the apple or the piano out of tune.
—**Wallace Stevens,** article on insurance, in Milton J. Bates, ed., expanded *Opus Posthumous*

★ Stevens, one of our great poets, was also a lawyer for Hartford Accident and Indemnity Company.

4 For years I thought what was good for our country was good for General Motors and vice versa. The difference did not exist.
—**Charles E. Wilson,** testimony, U.S. Senate Armed Services Committee, Jan. 15, 1953

★ Often quoted, perhaps somewhat unfairly, in the vice versa form: "What is good for General Motors is good for the country." GM President Wilson made the remark in hearings on his nomination to be Secretary of Defense. See also Calvin Coolidge on the business of the American people at AMERICA & AMERICANS, and for another peek into auto-industry thought, see Lee Iacocca at SECURITY & SAFETY.

5 Ben, I just want to say one word to you—just one word—plastics.
—**Buck Henry & Calder Willingham,** *The Graduate*, screenplay, 1967

★ Based on Charles Webb's novel.

6 He's a businessman. I'll make him an offer he can't refuse.
—**Mario Puzo,** *The Godfather*, 1969

★ The Godfather, Don Corleone, devising a strategy to deal with a Hollywood producer.

7 This administration is not sympathetic to corporations, it is indentured to corporations.
—**Ralph Nader,** news conference, Oct. 3, 1972

★ He was speaking of the Nixon administration. The remark was quoted the next day in the *Washington Post*.

8 Just remember this: If bankers were as smart as you are, you would starve to death.
—**Henry Harfield,** quoted in Martin Mayer, *The Bankers*, 1975

★ Attorney Harfield, senior partner of Shearman & Sterling, said this in a tape-recorded talk to a group of lawyers. Mayer used the comment as the epigraph for his book on the banking business, which hardly was a favor to Mr. Harfield, as Shearman & Sterling were the lead counsel for Citicorp bank.

The bottom line is in heaven. **1**

—**Edwin Herbert Land,** shareholders' meeting, Polaroid Corp., April 26, 1977

There is no limit to what a man can do or where he can go, if he doesn't mind who **2**
gets the credit.

—**Anonymous,** business aphorism

★ The saying derives from the 19th-century classics scholar Benjamin Jowett of Oxford University. He said, "The way to get things done is not to mind who gets the credit of doing them." The quote is included in *Handbook of Business Quotations*, Charles Robert Lightfoot, ed., 1991.

No one on his deathbed ever said, "I wish I had spent more time on my business." **3**

—**Paul E. Tsongas,** quoting a letter from a friend, 1983

★ This thought, which made the rounds in the famously materialistic 1980s, was passed on to Sen. Tsongas after he announced on Jan. 12, 1983, that on account of illness he would not complete his 1979–85 term as junior senator from Massachusetts. In 1992, he ran for the Democratic nomination for president in 1992, losing to Bill Clinton. In May 1993, Clinton's deputy legal counsel and personal attorney, Vincent Foster, used the same theme in addressing the graduating class of the University of Arkansas: "No one was ever heard to say on their deathbed, 'I wish I had spent more time at the office.' . . . The office can wait. . . . If you find yourself getting burned out or unfulfilled, unappreciated . . . then have the courage to make a change." On July 20, Foster shot himself. Tsongas died of cancer in 1997.

When a person with experience meets a person with money, the person with experi- **4**
ence will get the money. And the person with the money will get some experience.

—**Leonard Lauder,** speech, Woman's Economic Development Corporation, Feb. 1985

★ Lauder was speaking of the early years of the Estée Lauder Company, founded by his mother.

It is better to lose opportunity than capital. **5**

—**Susan M. Byrne,** *Wall Street Week in Review* television show, Feb. 15, 1985

Shopping is the chief cultural activity in the United States. **6**

—**Anonymous,** museum curator, on why a museum had to be combined with a shopping mall, quoted in Juliet B. Shor, *The Overworked American; The Unexpected Decline of Leisure,* 1992

An infectious greed seemed to grip much of our business community. **7**

—**Alan Greenspan,** testimony to the Senate Banking Committee, July 16, 2002

★ The Federal Reserve Chairman's reference to "infectious greed" was a harsher comment on the business climate of the 1990s than his earlier reference to "irrational exuberance," see ECONOMICS.

[Business Rule No. 1] If you don't tell people about your success, they probably **8**
won't know about it.

—**Donald J. Trump,** *How to Get Rich,* 2004.

California

See also CITIES (LOS ANGELES, OAKLAND, SAN FRANCISCO).

1 There is no part of earth to be taken up, wherein there is not some special likelihood of gold or silver.

—**Richard Hakluyt,** *The Famous Voyage of Sir Francis Drake*, 1589, in *Principal Navigations . . . of the English Nation*, 1598–1600

2 The men [of California] are thriftless, proud, and extravagant, and very much given to gaming; and the women have but little education, and a good deal of beauty, and their morality, of course, is none of the best.

—**Richard Henry Dana, Jr.,** *Two Years Before the Mast*, 1840

3 This valley [the San Joaquin] is a paradise. Grass, flowers, trees, beautiful clear rivers, thousands of deer, elk, wild horses, wonderful salmon . . . thousands of different kinds of ducks here; geese standing around as if tame.

—**Charles Preuss,** diary, March 27, 1844, in *Exploring with Fremont* [1958]

★ Preuss was the cartographer on Fremont's first, second, and fourth expeditions.

4 Satan, from one of his elevations, showed mankind the kingdom of California, and they entered into a compact with him at once.

—**Henry David Thoreau,** *Journal*, Feb. 2, 1852

★ Thoreau was writing specifically of the discovery of gold in California.

5 California can and does furnish the best bad things that are obtainable in America.

—**Hinton R. Helper,** *Land of Gold: Reality versus Fiction*, 1855

★ More at CITIES (SAN FRANCISCO).

6 California annexes the United States.

—**Anonymous,** May 1869

★ This message was carried on a banner in the streets of San Francisco in celebration of the completion of the transcontinental railroad.

7 The attraction and superiority of California are in its days. It has better days, and more of them, than any other country.

—**Ralph Waldo Emerson,** *Journal*, April-May 1871

8 These Californian scoundrels are invariably lighthearted; crime cannot overshadow the exhilaration of the outdoor life; remorse and gloom are banished like clouds before this perennially sunny climate. They make amusement out of killing you.

—**Clarence King,** *Mountaineering in the Sierra Nevada*, 1872

9 All scenery in California requires distance to give it charm.

—**Mark Twain,** *Roughing It*, 1872

10 An enthusiastic writer declared the climate of California to be "eminently favourable to the cure of gunshot wounds."

—**G. A. Sala,** *America Revisited*, 1882

When a tree takes a notion to grow in California nothing in heaven or on earth will stop it. **1**

—**Lilian Leland,** *Travelling Alone, A Woman's Journey Round the World*, 1890

East is East, and West is San Francisco, according to Californians. Californians are a race of people; they are not merely inhabitants of a state. **2**

—**O. Henry,** *A Municipal Report*, in *Strictly Business*, 1910

It is a shame to take this country away from the rattlesnakes. **3**

—**D. W. Griffith,** attributed

Yes, I have walked in California, **4**
And the rivers there are blue and white.
Thunderclouds of grapes hang on the mountains.
Bears in the meadows pitch and fight.

—**Vachel Lindsay,** *The Golden Whales of California, I: A Short Walk along the Coast*, 1920

I met a Californian who would **5**
Talk California—a state so blessed,
He said, in climate, none had ever died there
A natural death.

—**Robert Frost,** *New Hampshire*, 1923

California, Here I come. **6**

—**Buddy De Sylva,** song title, 1924

California's a wonderful place to live—if you happen to be an orange. **7**

—**Fred Allen** in *American Magazine*, Dec. 1945

California is a tragic country—like Palestine, like every Promised Land. **8**

—**Christopher Isherwood,** *Los Angeles* 1947, in *Exhumations* [1966]

★ For more from this essay see SECURITY & SAFETY.

The land around San Juan Capistrano is the pocket where the Creator keeps all his treasures. Anything will grow there. **9**

—**Frances Marion,** *Westward the Dream*, 1948

Nothing wrong with southern California that a rise in the ocean wouldn't cure. **10**

—**Ross MacDonald,** *The Drowning Pool*, 1950

It was the end of a continent. They didn't give a damn. **11**

—**Jack Kerouac,** *On the Road*, 1957

It's a scientific fact that for every year you live in California, you lose two points off your I.Q. It's redundant to die in L.A. **12**

—**Truman Capote,** remark, 1975, quoted in Jay Presson Allen's play, *Tru* [1989]

1 Whatever starts in California unfortunately has a tendency to spread.
—**Jimmy Carter,** remark, cabinet meeting, March 21, 1977, quoted in Robert Shogun, *Promises to Keep: Carter's First 100 Days* [1977]

2 *Eureka.*
I have found it.
—Motto, state of California

Calmness

See also ANXIETY & WORRY.

3 Calmness is always godlike.
—**Ralph Waldo Emerson,** *Journal*, 1840

4 Keep cool: it will be all one a hundred years hence.
—**Ralph Waldo Emerson,** *Representative Men*, 1850

★ A proverbial saying having many variations, including: It will be all the same a hundred years hence.

5 It's the still hog that eats the most.
—**Daniel Drew,** saying quoted in Peter Lyon, *The Honest Man*, in *American Heritage* [Feb. 1959]

★ A variant on the proverbial expression, "The stillest hog gets the most swill," or, "The quiet hog drinks the most swill." Drew, dubbed ironically "Uncle Dan," knew his livestock. This nonavuncular sharpie made his first bundle by feeding his steers salt on the night before a sale. The next morning, the desperately thirsty animals would drink so much water that each might gain up to fifty pounds in weight. From this trick comes the phrase "watered stock." Drew was also called "the Great Bear." In the 1860s, with aides Jim Fisk and Jay Gould, he embarked on a marginally legal selling-short spree (starting with shares of the Erie Railroad, a company of which he was treasurer). Before his luck and fortune collapsed in 1870, he had ruined thousands and was almost universally hated.

6 A relaxed man is not necessarily a better man.
—**Jenny Holzer,** aphorism in exhibit at the Solomon R. Guggenheim Museum, New York City, 1989

7 Never let them see you sweat.
—**Anonymous,** actors' axiom

Campaign Slogans

See POLITICAL SLOGANS.

Canada

See NATIONS.

Capitalism & Capital v. Labor

See also BUSINESS; ECONOMICS; MONEY & THE RICH; PROPERTY; RICH & POOR, WEALTH & POVERTY; WORK & WORKERS.

The feud between the capitalist and laborer, the house of Have and the house of Want, is as old as social union, and can never be entirely quieted; but he who will act with moderation, prefer fact to theory, and remember that everything in this world is relative and not absolute, will see that the violence of the contest may be stilled. 1

—**George Bancroft,** *To the Workingmen of Northampton*, in the *Boston Courier*, Oct. 22, 1834

Those who produce all wealth are themselves left poor. They see principalities extending and palaces built around them, without being aware that the entire expense is a tax upon themselves. 2

—**Amos Kendall,** in the *Washington Globe*, Nov. 7, 1834

★ The early quotations in this section reflect Marxist insights prior to the *Communist Manifesto*, 1848. In a letter dated March 5, 1852, Marx wrote: "The honor does not belong to me for having discovered the existence either of classes in modern society or of the struggle between the classes. Bourgeois historians a long time before me expounded the historical development of this class struggle, and bourgeois economists, the economic anatomy of classes."

These capitalists generally act harmoniously and in concert to fleece the people. 3

—**Abraham Lincoln,** speech, Illinois legislature, Jan. 1837

What we object to is the division of society into two classes, of which one class owns the capital, and the other performs the labor. 4

—**Orestes Brownson,** *The Laboring Classes*, in the *Boston Quarterly Review*, July 1840

I am glad to see that a system of labor prevails in New England under which laborers can strike when they want to . . . I like the system that lets a man quit when he wants to, and wish it might prevail everywhere. 5

—**Abraham Lincoln,** speech, New Haven, Conn., March 6, 1860

Labor is prior to, and independent of, capital. Capital is only the fruit of labor, and could never have existed if labor had not first existed. Labor is the superior of capital, and deserves much the higher consideration. Capital has its rights, which are as worthy of protection as any other rights. 6

—**Abraham Lincoln,** first annual message to Congress, Dec. 3, 1861

★ The "party of Lincoln" tends to quote the last sentence. Supporter of labor focus on the prior sections.

Join the union, girls, and together say, "Equal pay for equal work." 7

—**Susan B. Anthony,** in *The Revolution* newspaper, March 18, 1869

Labor disgraces no man; unfortunately, you occasionally find men disgrace labor. 8

—**Ulysses S. Grant,** speech, Midland International Arbitration Union, Birmingham, England, 1877

1 Capital is a result of labor, and is used by labor to assist it in further production. Labor is the active and initial force, and labor is therefore the employer of capital.
—**Henry George,** *Progress and Poverty*, 1879

2 *Labor, n.*, One of the processes by which A acquires property for B.
—**Ambrose Bierce,** *The Devil's Dictionary*, 1906

3 With all their faults, trade-unions have done more for humanity than any other organization of men that ever existed.
—**Clarence Darrow,** in *The Railroad Trainman*, Nov. 1909

4 Solidarity forever, for the Union makes us strong.
—**Ralph Chaplin,** International Workers of the World song, 1915

★ This was sung to the tune of *The Battle Hymn of the Republic*. Ralph Chaplin, a Chicago commercial artist, who had joined the International Workers of the World (IWW, popularly called "the Wobblies") in 1913, wrote the verse. The Wobblies proselytized through music, and this song was taken over by the entire labor movement. Chaplin went on to edit and illustrate the IWW publications *Solidarity* and *Industrial Worker*. He also was one of 101 Wobblies tried in 1918 for opposing the draft in World War I; he was convicted and served four years in jail. Along with Joe Hill (see below), Chaplin was the most popular of the bards included in *I.W.W. Songs to Fan the Flames of Discontent*, known generally as "The Little Red Song Book" (first edition, 1909). Other Wobbly songs were *Halleluja, I'm a Bum*, sung to the tune of *Revive Us Again*, and *I Dreamed I Saw Joe Hill Last Night*; see below.

5 We want more.
—**Samuel Gompers,** slogan for labor movement

★ Note Gompers, founder of the American Federation of Labor, was the leading voice of labor from the 1880s until his death in 1926. "More" was his byword, and is quoted in different formulations and contexts, such as "More, more, more now," quoted in *Editor & Publisher* [1952]

6 After God had finished the rattlesnake, the toad, the vampire, he had some awful substance left with which he made a scab.
—**Jack London,** *A Scab*, in *C.I.O. News* [Sept. 13, 1946]

★ See also INSULTS.

7 Don't waste any time mourning—organize!
—**Joe Hill,** telegram to William Dudley "Big Bill" Haywood, Nov. 18, 1915

★ Hill had been convicted of murdering two policemen in Salt Lake City, Utah, while robbing a grocery store. He was executed by firing squad the day after sending this message to Haywood, who was one of the founders of the International Workers of the World. Scholars still argue over whether Hill was framed. Thirty thousand people attended his funeral. He was an activist and a musician and had written many of the IWW's favorite songs, including *The Preacher and the Slave*, in which he popularized (and possibly coined) the phrase "pie in the sky" in the ironic refrain, "You will eat, bye and bye, / In that glorious land above the sky; / Work and pray, live on hay / You'll get pie in the sky when you die." (The verse parodied a Salvation Army hymn that begins "In the sweet bye and bye.") Today, Hill is remembered best for the song about him by Alfred Hayes and Earl Robinson; see below.

There is no right to strike against the public safety by anybody, anywhere, any time. **1**

—Calvin Coolidge, telegram to Samuel Gompers, Sept. 14, 1919

★ This was a reply to a protest telegram sent by American Federation of Labor president Gompers. Coolidge, who was governor of Massachusetts, had called in troops to restore order during a strike by the Boston police, who were AFL union members. Coolidge's position was widely applauded and he won the Republican nomination for the vice presidency the next year. He succeeded to the presidency upon the death of Warren G. Harding in 1923.

The only trouble with capitalism is capitalists; they're too damn greedy. **2**

—Herbert Hoover, remark to columnist Mark Sullivan, c. 1929

★ Just when Hoover first offered this analysis is not known, but Spencer Howard, an archivist at the Hoover Presidential Library, reports that Sullivan's son recalled overhearing Hoover say this to his father at least once in the early 1930s. Another quotation, commonly attributed to Hoover at the start of his presidency, "Excessive fortunes are a menace to true liberty," may be mythical. The Library has no evidence that he ever said it.

I dreamed I saw Joe Hill last night **3**
Alive as you and me.
Says I "But Joe, you're ten years dead."
"I never died," says he.

—Alfred Hayes, *The Daily Worker*, Sept. 4, 1936

★ The music was by Earl Robinson. Labor leader Joe Hill was executed in 1915; see Hill above.

Private enterprise is ceasing to be free enterprise. **4**

—Franklin D. Roosevelt, message to Congress proposing investigation of monopolies, 1938

The trouble with the profit system has always been that it is highly unprofitable to **5**
most people.

—E. B. White, *One Man's Meat*, 1944

The object of liberalism has never been to destroy capitalism . . . only to keep the **6**
capitalists from destroying it.

—Arthur M. Schlesinger, Jr. *The Age of Jackson*, 1945

Heroic materialism. **7**

—Kenneth Clark, *Civilization,* television series, closing comments, 1969

★ Clark was referring to commercial culture at its best, illustrated with a shot of the skyline of lower Manhattan. Adam Gopnik, writing in *The New Yorker,* Dec. 15, 2003, observed that W. H. Auden, commenting on the same city, asked, "Why are the public buildings so high?" and answered, "Why, that's because the spirits of the public are so low."

Reflecting the values of the larger capitalistic society, there is no prestige whatsoever **8**
attached to actually working. Workers are invisible.

—Marge Piercy, *The Grand Coolie Damn*, in Robin Morgan, ed., *Sisterhood Is Powerful*, 1970

1 Companies come and go. It's part of the genius of capitalism.
—Paul H. O'Neill, Fox News, Jan. 14, 2002

★ Thus, the Secretary of the Treasury dismissed the collapse of Enron, the seventh largest corporation in the United States—on paper, at least—and the largest ever to declare bankruptcy.

Cards

See GAMES.

Censorship

See also BOOKS & READING; FREE SPEECH; PRESS, THE.

2 Subject opinion to coercion: whom will you make your inquisitors? Fallible men; governed by bad passions, by private as well as public reasons.
—Thomas Jefferson, *Notes on the State of Virginia*, 1781–85

3 It is error alone which needs the support of government. Truth can stand by itself.
—Ibid.

4 Every suppressed or expunged word reverberates through the earth from side to side
—Ralph Waldo Emerson, *Compensation*, in *Essays: First Series*, 1841

5 Those whom books will hurt will not be proof against events. Events, not books, should be forbid.
—Herman Melville, *The Encantadas*, in *The Piazza Tales*, 1856

★ See also Jimmy Walker at BOOKS & READING.

6 We write frankly and freely, but then we "modify" before we print.
—Mark Twain, *Life on the Mississippi*, 1883

★ This is what we now call "self-censorship." Twain did much of his "modifying" at the behest of his beloved wife, Libby. Sometimes he put things in just for the fun of seeing her strike them out.

7 The mind that becomes soiled in youth can never again be washed clean; I know this by my own experience, and to this day I cherish an unappeasable bitterness against the unfaithful guardians of my young life, who not only permitted but compelled me to read an unexpurgated Bible through before I was fifteen years old.
—Mark Twain, letter to Asa Don Dickinson, Nov. 21, 1905

★ The letter to Mr. Dickinson, a Brooklyn Public Library staffer, was occasioned by news that the head of the children's department at the BPL had banished *Tom Sawyer* and *Huckleberry Finn* to the adult stacks because they were too unrefined for younger readers. Twain claimed to be disturbed that children had been permitted to read the books in the first place, asserting that he had written them "for adults exclusively" and that it always distressed him to hear "that boys and girls had been allowed access" to works that might soil their youthful minds, etc.

Scenes of passion should not be introduced when not essential to the plot. In general, passion should be so treated that these scenes do not stimulate the lower and baser element. 1

—**The Motion Picture Producers and Distributors of America, Inc.,** *Code for the Industry*, 1930

Sex perversion or any inference of it is forbidden. White slavery shall not be treated. 2
Miscegenation is forbidden. . . . Scenes of actual childbirth, in fact or in silhouette, are never to be represented.

—**Ibid.**

★ See also MARRIAGE for more from the *Code*.

Did you ever hear anyone say "that work had better be banned, because I might read 3
it and it might be very damaging to me"?

—**Joseph Henry Jackson,** saying

★ Jackson was the editor of the *San Francisco Chronicle*.

I know it when I see it. 4

—**Potter Stewart,** concurring opinion, *Jacobellis v. Ohio*, 1964

★ This is the closest that Supreme Court Justice Stewart could come to defining "hard-core pornography"—the sentence runs in full "I know it when I see it; and the motion picture in this case is not that." The motion picture was Louis Malle's comparatively tame *The Lovers*. As Justice Arthur Goldberg opined, "The love scene deemed objectionable is so fragmentary and fleeting that only a censor's alert would make an audience conscious that something 'questionable' is being portrayed. Except for this rapid sequence, the film concerns itself with the history of an ill-matched and unhappy marriage—a familiar subject in old and new novels and in current television soap operas." The court, since then, has not done much better in its search for a definition of obscenity. The currently reigning test, from *Miller v. California*, 1973, hinges on such nebulous notions as "contemporary community standards," and whether a work "taken as a whole" is "patently offensive" or lacks "serious literary, artistic, political, or scientific value." Justice William J. Brennan finally threw up his hands, telling Nat Hentoff: "I put sixteen years into that damn obscenity thing. I tried and I tried, and I waffled back and forth, and I finally gave up. If you can't define it, you can't prosecute people for it" (*The New Yorker*, March 12, 1990).

One man's vulgarity is another man's lyric. 5

—**John M. Harlan,** *Cohen v. California,* 1971

Whatever the individual motives of censors may be, censorship is a form of social 6
control.

—**Carey McWilliams,** *Censorship: For and Against,* 1971

Without censorship, things can get terribly confused in the public mind. 7

—**William C. Westmoreland,** 1982, quoted in Stanley Hochman & Eleanor Hochman, eds., *The Penguin Dictionary of Contemporary American History* [1997]

★ More at VIETNAM WAR.

1 Not everything's for children. Not everything's for everyone.
—Robert Crumb, in the documentary *Crumb* by Terry Zwigoff, 1995

★ Counterculture cartoonist Robert Crumb commenting on the political incorrectness of his work.

Chance

See LUCK.

Change

See also AMERICA & AMERICANS (Eleanor Roosevelt); NEW THINGS; TRUTH (Robert Frost).

2 Things do not change; we change.
—Henry David Thoreau, *Journal*, 1850

3 I shall try to correct errors when shown to be errors and I shall adopt new views as fast as they shall appear to be true views.
—Abraham Lincoln, reply to Horace Greeley, August 19, 1862

★ Greeley had asked Lincoln to make emancipation a government goal. Lincoln was still inching toward that decision. See SLAVERY.

4 It is not best to swap horses while crossing the river.
—Abraham Lincoln, comment, June 9, 1864

★ The president addressed this proverbial remark to a delegation from the National Union League. He told the League members, "I do not allow myself to suppose that either the convention or the League have concluded to decide that I am either the greatest or best man in America, but rather that they have decided it is not best to swap horses while crossing the river, and have further concluded that I am not so poor a horse that they might not make a botch of it in trying to swap." The metaphor apparently stems from a joke, popular in the 1840s, about an Irishman (or Dutchman) who was crossing a river with a mare and a colt. Falling off the mare, he grabbed the colt's tail. Observers on the riverbank shouted that he should take hold of the mare's tail as she was the stronger swimmer. The man declined the advice, yelling back that this was not a good time for him to swap horses. "Don't change horses" made a good campaign slogan; see POLITICAL SLOGANS. Democrats later recycled this bit of folk wisdom in F.D.R.'s reelection campaigns of 1940 and 1944. They also gave it an ironic twist in 1932: with the nation's economy in shambles and Herbert Hoover running for reelection, the Dems maintained that the Republican motto must be, "Don't swap barrels while going over Niagara."

5 There is one great basic fact which underlies all the questions that are discussed on the political platforms at the present moment. That singular fact is that nothing is done in this country as it was done twenty years ago.
—Woodrow Wilson, *The Old Order Changeth*, in *The New Freedom*, 1913

★ The essay took its title from this sentence: "The old order changeth—changeth under our very eyes, not quietly and equably, but swiftly and with the noise and heat and tumult of reconstruction." Wilson was alluding to Lord Tennyson's, "The old order changeth, yielding place to new; / And God fulfills himself in many ways, / Lest one good custom should corrupt the world," *Idylls of the King*, "The Passing of Arthur." And see Wilson below.

Most of the change we think we see in life 1
Is due to truths being in and out of favor.
—**Robert Frost,** *The Black Cottage* in *North of Boston*, 1914

If you want to make enemies, try to change something. 2
—**Woodrow Wilson,** speech, July 10, 1916

People change and forget to tell each other. 3
—**Lillian Hellman,** *Toys in the Attic*, 1960

For the times they are a-changin'. 4
—**Bob Dylan,** *'The Times They Are A-changin'*, 1963

Change is the law of life. And those who look only to the past or the present are certain to miss the future. 5
—**John F. Kennedy,** speech, Frankfurt, West Germany, June 25, 1963

It is change, continuing change, inevitable change, that is the dominant factor in society today. 6
—**Isaac Asimov,** *My Own View* in Robert Holdstock, ed., *The Encyclopedia of Science Fiction*, 1978

Never underestimate your power to change yourself; never overestimate your power to change others. 7
—**H. Jackson Brown, Jr.,** *Life's Little Instruction Book*, 1991

The people who are crazy enough to think they can change the world are the ones who do. 8
—**Apple Computer, Inc.,** TV ad, 1997

If we don't change directions, we might just end up where we're heading. 9
—**Kenny Ausubel,** Bioneers Conference, Oct. 17, 2003

★ A similar remark is attributed to the comedian Professor Irwin Corey.

Character

See also ENEMIES (Newman); GRACE; VIRTUE.

Character, not circumstance, makes the person. 10
—**Booker T. Washington,** *Democracy and Education*, speech, Insitutute of Arts and Sciences, Brooklyn, N.Y., Sept. 30, 1896

Character, in the long run, is the decisive factor in the life of an individual and of nations alike. 11
—**Theodore Roosevelt,** *American Ideals*, 1897

1 Character is the basis of happiness, and happiness the sanction of character.
—**George Santayana,** *Life of Reason: Reason in Common Sense,* 1905

2 If you will think about what you ought to do for other people, your character will take care of itself. Character is a by-product, and any man who devotes himself to its cultivation in his own case will become a selfish prig.
—**Woodrow Wilson,** attributed in George Seldes, *The Great Quotations,* 1966

3 Character is what you are in the dark.
—**Anonymous**

★ Attributed to a sermon by Dwight L. Moody in a 1930 biography by his son. The quote has not been found, however.

4 You can tell a lot about a fellow's character by the way he eats jelly beans.
—**Ronald Reagan,** in *The New York Times,* Jan. 15, 1981

★ Mr. Reagan was very fond of jelly beans.

5 But rules cannot substitute for character.
—**Alan Greenspan,** *Capitalizing Reputation,* 2004 Financial Markets Conference of the Federal Reserve Bank of Georgia, April 16, 2004

Charity & Philanthropy

6 We do not quite forgive a giver. The hand that feeds us is in some danger of being bitten.
—**Ralph Waldo Emerson,** *Gifts*, in *Essays: Second Series*, 1844

7 Philanthropy is almost the only virtue which is sufficiently appreciated by mankind.
—**Henry David Thoreau,** "Economy," *Walden*, 1854

8 Look up and not down;
Look forward and not back;
Look out and not in;
Lend a hand.
—**Edward Everett Hale,** motto of the Lend a Hand Society, formed 1891

★ Hale founded the first Lend a Hand Club in Boston in 1871, and the society, or league, of clubs formed twenty years later. Hale later became chaplain to the U.S. Senate, and is remembered for a remark on prayer and senators; see CONGRESS.

9 The heart hath its own memory, like the mind,
And in it are enshrined
The precious keepsakes, into which are wrought
The giver's loving thought.
—**Henry Wadsworth Longfellow,** *From My Arm-chair*, 1879

10 Charity has in it sometimes, perhaps often, a savor of superiority.
—**James Russell Lowell,** speech, Westminster Abbey, London, England, Dec. 13, 1881

Do not give, as many rich men do, like a hen that lays her egg and then cackles. 1
—**Henry Ward Beecher,** *Proverbs from Plymouth Pulpit*, 1887

★ A Yankee version of the biblical, "Therefore when thou doest thine alms, do not sound a trumpet before thee, as the hypocrites do," *Matthew* 6:2.

Private beneficence is totally inadequate to deal with the vast numbers of the city's 2
disinherited.
—**Jane Addams,** *Twenty Years at Hull House*, 1910

★ Addams founded Hull House in Chicago, the first social settlement house in the U.S. She was co-winner of the Nobel Peace Prize in 1931.

Better to go down dignified 3
With boughten friendship at your side
Than none at all. Provide, provide!
—**Robert Frost,** *Provide, Provide*, 1936

Don't deprive yourself of the joy of giving. 4
—**Michael Greenberg,** motto, 1963

★ Greenberg put this motto into practice by giving gloves to the derelicts in and around the Bowery in New York City. He began doing this in 1963, between Thanksgiving and Christmas, in memory of his father, from whom he had learned the motto. Upon his death in 1995, a cousin said he intended to continue "Gloves" Greenberg's work.

Philanthropy is commendable, but it must not cause the philanthropist to overlook 5
the circumstances of economic injustice which make philanthropy necessary.
—**Martin Luther King, Jr.,** *Strength to Love*, 1963

One thing I had in my mind, I'm never going to be the richest person in the ceme- 6
tery.
—**Frances L. Loeb,** announcing a gift of $7.5 million to Vassar College, 1990

★ This was just one of numerous gifts by a woman who devoted her life to philanthropy and good works.

There is no greater joy in life than giving to worthy causes. 7
—**Ted Turner,** announcing a gift of $1 billion to the United Nations, Sept. 1997

Children

See also YOUTH.

Childhood knows the human heart. 8
—**Edgar Allan Poe,** *Tamerlane*, 1827

There was never a child so lovely but his mother was glad to get asleep. 9
—**Ralph Waldo Emerson,** *Journal*, 1836

★ Three years later in his journal, Emerson similarly noted, "As soon as a child has left the room his strewn toys become affecting."

Children are all foreigners. 10
—**Ralph Waldo Emerson,** *Journal*, 1839

1 What a difference it makes to come home to a child!
—**Margaret Fuller,** letter to friends, 1849

2 "Do you know who made you?" "Nobody as I knows on," said the child, with a short laugh . . . "I 'spect I growed. Don't think nobody never made me."
—**Harriet Beecher Stowe,** *Uncle Tom's Cabin*, 1852

★ Topsy is speaking.

3 Blessings on thee, little man,
Barefoot boy, with cheek of tan! . . .
From my heart I give thee joy—
I was once a barefoot boy!
—**John Greenleaf Whittier,** *The Barefoot Boy*, 1856

4 A torn jacket is soon mended; but hard words bruise the heart of a child.
—**Henry Wadsworth Longfellow,** "Table-Talk," in *Driftwood*, 1857

5 We find delight in the beauty and happiness of children that makes the heart too big for the body.
—**Ralph Waldo Emerson,** *Illusions*, in *The Conduct of Life*, 1860

6 Between the dark and the daylight,
When the night is beginning to lower,
Comes a pause in the day's occupations,
That is known as the Children's Hour.
—**Henry Wadsworth Longfellow,** *The Children's Hour*, 1860

7 I hear in the chamber above me
The patter of little feet.
There was a little girl
Who had a little curl
Right in the middle of her forehead;
And when she was good
She was very, very good,
But when she was bad she was horrid.
—**Henry Wadsworth Longfellow,** *There Was a Little Girl* c. 1850 in B. R. Tucker-Macchetta, *The Home Life of Henry W. Longfellow* [1882]

★ The verse refers to the poet's second daughter, then a babe in arms.

8 A baby is an inestimable blessing and bother.
—**Mark Twain,** letter to Annie Webster, Sept. 1, 1876

9 Children troop down from heaven because God wills it.
—**Patrick Hayes,** 1921

★ Archbishop Hayes of New York City was doing battle with birth-control pioneer Margaret Sanger.

10 Childhood Is the Kingdom Where Nobody Dies.
—**Edna St. Vincent Millay,** title of poem in *Wine from These Grapes*, 1934

There's no such thing in the world as a bad boy, I'm sure of that. 1
—**Eleanore Griffin & Dore Schary,** *Boys Town*, 1938

★ The line is spoken by Spencer Tracy playing Father Flanagan.

2

We seem hell-bent on eliminating much of childhood.
—**Eda L. Shan** *The Conspiracy Against Childhood*, 1967

★ The author was writing about "the busiest, most competitive, highly pressured and over-organized generation of youngsters in our history—and possibly the unhappiest."

It Takes A Village [To Raise A Child]. 3
—**Hillary Rodham Clinton,** book title, 1995

★ The title derives from an African proverb widely quoted in support of funding for education and child care. Louis Menand writing in *The New Yorker* (Nov. 8, 2004), commented that like many political books, this one may have been created by more than one author: "It has been said that it took a village to make *It Takes a Village.*"

There is no such thing as other peoples' children. 4
—**Hillary Rodham Clinton,** *Newsweek,* Jan. 15, 1996

The happy childhood is hardly worth your while. 5
—**Frank McCourt,** *Angela's Ashes*, 1996

China

See NATIONS.

Christmas

How many observe Christ's birthday! How few, his precepts! O! 'tis easier to keep 6
holidays than commandments.
—**Benjamin Franklin,** *Poor Richard's Almanack*, 1732–1757

'Twas the night before Christmas, when all through the house 7
Not a creature was stirring—not even a mouse;
The stockings were hung by the chimney with care,
In hopes that St. Nicholas soon would be there.
The children were nestled all snug in their beds,
While visions of sugar plums danced in their heads.
—**Clement C. Moore,** *A Visit from St. Nicholas*, in the *Troy Sentinel*, Dec. 23, 1823

★ This poem, written by Moore in 1822 as a Christmas present for his seriously ill daughter, was first published anonymously as *A Visit from St. Nicholas*. Some 20 years later, in 1844, authorship was claimed by Dr. Moore, a major landholder in the Chelsea region of Manhattan and a distinguished classical scholar—his works include the comprehensive *Hebrew and English Lexicon*. But in 2000, Vassar Callege professor Don Foster made a strong case in his book *Author Unknown* that the real author was Henry Livingston, Jr., a little known gentleman-poet. Whoever the author, he created the best Father Christmas, a combination of St. Nicholas and the Norwegian Kriss Kringle, who helped St. Nicholas by driving a sleigh pulled by reindeer. Children's book writer X. J.

Kennedy observed in *The New York Times Book Review*, December 5, 1993, that this St. Nicholas was a great improvement over other contenders for top Christmas billing, such as Washington Irving's St. Nick, who went around in a wagon, "riding jollily among the treetops."

1 Now, *Dasher*! now, *Dancer*! now, *Prancer* and *Vixen*!
On, *Comet*! on, *Cupid!* on, *Donner* and *Blitzen*!
—Clement C. Moore, *The Night Before Christmas*, in the *Troy Sentinel*, Dec. 23, 1823

2 He had a broad face and a little round belly,
That shook when he laughed, like a bowlful of jelly.
—Ibid.

3 But I heard him exclaim, ere he drove out of sight,
"Happy Christmas to all and to all a good night."
—Ibid.

4 It came upon the midnight clear,
That glorious song of old,
From angels bending near the earth
To touch their harps of gold;
"Peace on the earth, good will to men
From Heaven's all-gracious King"—
The world in solemn stillness lay
To hear the angels sing.
—Edmund Hamilton Sears, *Christmas Carol*, 1850

5 I heard the bells on Christmas Day
Their old, familiar carols play,
And wild and sweet
The words repeat
Of peace on earth, good-will to men!
—Henry Wadsworth Longfellow, *Christmas Bells*, in *Flower-de-Luce*, 1867

6 Christmas won't be Christmas without any presents.
—Louisa May Alcott, *Little Women*, 1868

7 O little town of Bethlehem,
How still we see thee lie!
Above thy deep and dreamless sleep
The silent stars go by.
—Phillips Brooks, *O Little Town of Bethlehem*, 1868

8 Yes, Virginia, there is a Santa Claus. . . . Thank God! he lives, and he lives forever. A thousand years from now, Virginia, nay ten times ten thousand years from now, he will continue to make glad the heart of childhood.
—Francis Pharcellus Church, *The Sun*, editorial, New York City, Sept. 21, 1897

★ Virginia O'Hanlon of 115 West Ninety-fifth Street had written: "Dear Editor, I am eight years old. Some of my little friends say there is no Santa Claus. Papa says, 'If you see it in *The Sun* it's so.' Please tell me the truth; is there a Santa Claus?" Church, formerly a Civil War correspondent with *The New York Times*, wrote a long, anonymous editorial reply of five paragraphs. After his death in 1906, the paper made an exception to its rule of editorial anonymity to reveal that he was the author of what is probably the most famous editorial in journalistic history.

Angels come down, with Christmas in their hearts, 1
Gentle, whimsical, laughing, heaven-sent;
And, for a day, fair Peace have given me.
—Vachel Lindsay, *Springfield Magical*, in *The Sangamon County Peace Advocate*, Christmas, 1909

★ More at CITIES (SPRINGFIELD).

A cold coming we had of it, 2
Just the worst time of the year.
—T. S. Eliot, *Journey of the Magi*, 1927

I'm Dreaming of a White Christmas. 3
—Irving Berlin, *White Christmas*, song in *Holiday Inn*, 1942

★ The song, one of the greatest hits of all time, made Bing Crosby a superstar.

To perceive Christmas through its wrapping becomes more difficult every year. 4
—E. B. White, *Time Present* in *The Second Tree from the Corner*, 1953

I grew up in a gentler, slower time . . . Christmases were years apart, and now it's 5
about five months from one to the next.
—Garrison Keillor, Introduction, *We Are Still Married: Stories & Letters*, 1989

Cities

When we get piled upon one another in large cities as in Europe, we shall become 6
corrupt as in Europe, and go to eating one another as they do there.
—Thomas Jefferson, letter to James Madison, Dec. 20, 1787

★ Similarly, in 1800, Jefferson wrote to Benjamin Rush, "I view great cities as pestilential to the morals, the health, and the liberties of mankind" (Memorial Edition, 10:173).

Cities degrade us by magnifying trifles. 7
—Ralph Waldo Emerson, *Culture*, in *The Conduct of Life*, 1860

The thing generally raised on city land is taxes. 8
—Charles Dudley Warner, *My Summer in a Garden*, 1870

The government of cities is the one conspicuous failure of the United States. 9
—James Bryce, *The American Commonwealth*, 1888

★ Bryce served as ambassador from England to the U.S., and this book was probably the most influential study of America by a foreigner since Tocqueville's *Democracy in*

America. The first edition was suppressed here after the author included a supplementary chapter on New York City's Tweed Ring.

1 Thine alabaster cities gleam.

—Katharine Lee Bates, *America the Beautiful*, 1893

★ This is from the fourth verse. The first verse is given at AMERICA & AMERICANS.

2 In Boston they ask, How much does he know? In New York, How much is he worth? In Philadelphia, Who were his parents?

—Mark Twain, *What Paul Bourget Thinks of Us*, 1895

★ Twain identifies this as a familiar joke.

3 The Shame of the Cities.

—Lincoln Steffens, book title, 1904

4 In the Big City a man will disappear with the suddenness and completeness of the flame of a candle that is blown out.

—O. Henry, *The Sleuths*, in *Sixes and Sevens*, 1911

5 But look what we have built . . . This is not the rebuilding of cities. This is the sacking of cities.

—Jane Jacobs, Introduction, *The Death and Life of Great American Cities*, 1961

★ In this passage from her classic analysis of how a generation of city planners and architects went wrong, Ms. Jacobs refers to low-income housing projects more dangerous than the slums they replace, "cultural centers that are unable to support a good bookstore," "civic centers that are avoided by everyone but bums, empty promenades that go nowhere," and "expressways that eviscerate cities."

6 We will neglect our cities to our peril, for in neglecting them we neglect the nation.

—John F. Kennedy, speech to Congress, Jan. 30, 1962

7 The more intelligent the people of a city, the worse its government.

—John Kenneth Galbraith, c. 1962

★ Quoted in *Plain Tales from the Embassy*, excerpts from letters and quotes dating from Mr. Galbraith's tenure as ambassador to India, *American Heritage*, October 1969.

8 A city on hills has it over flat-land places.

—John Steinbeck, *Travels with Charley*, 1962

★ He had in mind San Francisco, but the thought holds true worldwide.

9 Chicago is the great American city. New York is one of the capitals of the world and Los Angeles is a constellation of plastic, San Francisco is a lady, Boston has become Urban Renewal, Philadelphia and Baltimore and Washington wink like dull diamonds in the smog of Eastern Megalopolis, and New Orleans is unremarkable past the French Quarter. Detroit is a one-trade town, Pittsburgh has lost its golden triangle, St. Louis has become the golden arch of the corporation, and nights in Kansas City close early. The oil depletion allowance makes Houston and Dallas naught but checkerboards for this sort of game. But Chicago is a great American city. Perhaps it is the last of the great American cities.

—Norman Mailer, *Miami and the Siege of Chicago*, 1968

The bureaucratized, simplified cities, so dear to present-day city planners and urban designers . . . run counter to the processes of city growth and economic development. 1

—**Jane Jacobs,** *The Economy of Cities*, 1969

If you've seen one slum you've seen them all. 2

—**Spiro Agnew,** television interview, Detroit, Mich., Oct. 6, 1969

★ Vice President Agnew's attack style of political comment was new in its day. He resigned in disgrace in 1973—for past corruption—an exit hurried along so that he would not be in a position to succeed Pres. Richard Nixon, who was already tottering from the Watergate scandal. For a similar comment on trees, see Ronald Reagan under ENVIRONMENT.

The gardens of my heart are not found in the country, nor even small towns and villages. It is in great cities that the oases of the spirit lie, in cities, bridged and tunneled, and with pavement planted. 3

—**Richard Selzer**, *Letters to a Young Doctor*, 1982

Albany, New York

This large city lay in the landscape like an anthill in a meadow. 4

—**Harriett Martineau,** *Retrospect of Western Travel*, 1838

Joe: Now, you take Albany, New York. 5
Moe: No, *you* take Albany, New York.

—**Anonymous,** vaudeville routine

Those who are in Albany escaped Sing Sing, and those who are in Sing Sing were on their way to Albany. 6

—**Elbert Hubbard,** *The Roycroft Dictionary and Book of Epigrams*, 1923

★ The comment is directed more toward Albany as a seat of government than Albany as a community.

Amarillo, Texas

See also CITIES: AMARILLO & EL PASO

De vedder out here I do not like. De rain vas all vind, and de vind vas all sand. 7

—**Anonymous,** German settler in Amarillo, quoted in John Gunther, *Inside U.S.A.*, 1947

Amarillo & El Paso, Texas

Why, El Paso and Amarillo ain't no different from Sodom and Gomorrah. On a smaller scale, of course. 8

—**David O. Selznick,** *Duel in the Sun*, screenplay, 1946

★ The line is Walter Huston's. Selznick, the movie's producer, worked from an Oliver H. P. Garrett adaptation of Niven Busch's novel.

Amherst, Massachusetts

1 The Amherst heart is plain and whole and permanent and warm.
—**Emily Dickinson,** letter to J. K. Chickering, 1885

Arkansas City, Arkansas

2 We asked a passenger who belonged there what sort of a place it was. "Well," said he, after considering, and with the air of one who wishes to take time and be accurate, "It's a hell of a place." A description which was photographic for exactness.
—**Mark Twain,** *Life on the Mississippi*, 1883

Atlanta, Georgia

3 I heard it said that the "architecture" of Atlanta is rococola.
—**John Gunther,** *Inside U.S.A.*, 1947

Atwood, Kansas

4 Where else can you enjoy a cup of coffee at the local cafe, and everyone there is your friend?
—**Anonymous**, slogan, in *The New York Times*, March 3, 2005

Augusta, Georgia

5 A queer little rustic city called Augusta—a great broad street two miles long—old quaint looking shops—houses with galleries—ware-houses—trees—cows and negroes strolling about the side walks—plank roads—a happy dirty tranquillity generally prevalent.
—**William Makepeace Thackeray,** letter to Kate Perry, Feb. 14–16, 1856

6 I never saw so many cows in my life,—at least in the streets of an inhabited town.
—**G. A. Sala,** *America Revisited*, 1882

Aurora, Nevada

7 All quiet in Aurora. Five men will be hung in an hour.
—**Bob Howland,** city marshal, message to James Nye, governor of the Nevada Territory, in Albert Bigelow Paine, *Mark Twain, A Biography* [1924]

★ A ghost town today, Aurora's heyday as a silver-mining camp in the 1860s was brief because the veins of ore were shallow and soon worked out. Twain wrote in a letter of Feb. 8, 1862, that Howland was "known as the most fearless man in the Territory."

Austin, Texas

8 It reminds one somewhat of Washington; Washington *en petit*, seen through a reversed glass.
—**Frederick Law Olmsted,** *A Journey Through Texas*, 1857

★ Olmsted designed Central Park in Manhattan and Prospect Park in Brooklyn, N.Y.

Avon, New York

This Avon flows sweetly with nothing but whiskey and tobacco juice. 1
—**Frances Trollope,** *Domestic Manners of the Americans*, 1832

★ Frances Trollope was mother to the famous Anthony as well as the less famous Thomas, also a novelist and essayist. She was a frank travel writer, but had nice things to say about this country, too; see, for example, NATURE: SEASONS, and Memphis below.

Baltimore, Maryland

This is the dirtiest place in the world. 2
—**John Adams,** diary, Feb. 8, 1777

Wonderful little Baltimore. 3
—**Henry James,** *The American Scene*, 1907

The old charm, in truth, still survives in the town, despite the frantic efforts of the 4
boosters and boomers.
—**H. L. Mencken,** *Prejudices: Fifth Series*, 1926

Birmingham, Alabama

Birmingham is a new city in an old land. 5
—**Carl Carmer,** *Stars Fell on Alabama*, 1934

Boston, Massachusetts

This place abounds with pritty women who . . . are, for the most part, free and affa- 6
ble as well as pritty. I saw not one prude while I was here.
—**Alexander Hamilton,** August 16, 1744, *Itinerarium*

★ Boston in its youth was easygoing. The writer, Hamilton, was not the Founding Father of the same name, but an Annapolis physician, who traveled more than 1,600 miles during a four-month tour of the northern colonies.

Boston State-house is the hub of the solar system. 7
—**Oliver Wendell Holmes, Sr.,** *The Autocrat of the Breakfast-Table*, 1858

★ The opinion that 19th-century Bostonians had of themselves also is reflected in the remark that William Ewart Gladstone attributed to an anonymous citizen of the Athens of America, aka, the Hub of the Universe: "There are not ten men in Boston equal to Shakespeare."

A Boston man is the East wind made flesh. 8
—**Thomas Appleton,** attributed

We say the cows laid out Boston. Well, there are worse surveyors. 9
—**Ralph Waldo Emerson,** *Wealth*, in *The Conduct of Life*, 1860

Boston looks like a town that has been paid for; Boston has a balance at its bankers. 10
—**G. A. Sala,** *My Diary in America in the Midst of War*, 1865

1 A solid man of Boston.
A comfortable man with dividends,
And the first salmon and the first green peas.
—**Henry Wadsworth Longfellow,** *John Endicott*, in *The New England Tragedies*, 1868

2 Tonight I appear for the first time before a Boston audience—4,000 critics.
—**Mark Twain,** letter, Nov. 9, 1869

3 Boston is a state of mind.
—**Anonymous**

★ Attributions have been made to Mark Twain, Thomas Appleton, and Ralph Waldo Emerson.

4 I have learned enough never to argue with a Bostonian.
—**Rudyard Kipling,** *From Sea to Sea*, 1885

5 And this is good old Boston,
The home of the bean and the cod,
Where the Lowells talk to the Cabots,
And the Cabots talk only to God.
—**John Collins Bossidy,** toast at the Holy Cross alumni dinner, 1910

★ The toast was updated in 1952 by Franklin Pierce Adams (known as F.P.A.). He wrote: "And here's to the City of Boston, / The town of the cries and groans, / Where the Cabots can't see the Kabotschniks, / And the Lowells won't speak to the Cohns," *On the Aristocracy of Harvard, Revised*, in *F.P.A.'s Book of Quotations*, 1952.

6 It will make you or break you,
But never forsake you.
Southie is my home town.
—**Anonymous,** *Southie Is My Home Town*, c. 1910

★ This vaudeville song was the anthem of South Boston, sung by several generations of Irish politicians and their constituents.

7 It is not age which killed Boston, for no cities die of age; it is the youth of other cities.
—**W. L. George,** *Hail Columbia*, 1921

8 the Cambridge ladies who live in furnished souls
are unbeautiful and have comfortable minds.
—**E. E. Cummings,** *Realities*, I, in *Tulips and Chimneys*, 1923

9 I guess God made Boston on a wet Sunday.
—**Raymond Chandler,** letter, March 21, 1949

10 If you hear an owl hoot: "To whom" instead of "To who" you can make up your mind he was born and educated in Boston.
—**Anonymous,** in *F.P.A.'s Book of Quotations*, 1952

11 I have just returned from Boston. It is the only sane thing to do if you find yourself up there.
—**Fred Allen,** letter to Groucho Marx, June 12, 1953

This is a town where there are three pastimes: politics, sports, and revenge. 1

—**Lawrence C. Moulter,** in *The New York Times*, Feb. 17, 1993

★ Moulter, president of the New Boston Garden Corporation, also called the community "dysfunctional."

Buffalo, New York

Buffalo gals, won't you come out tonight, 2
And dance by the light of the moon?

—**Anonymous**, *Buffalo Gals*, c. 1848

★ Though commonly associated with boatmen on the Erie Canal, this probably began as a minstrel song. Cool White, an early blackface performer, published *Lubly Fan, Woncha Come Out Tonight* in 1844, according to *Folksong U.S.A.*, by John A. and Alan Lomax. The words were changed to "New York gals," "Bowery gals," "Philadelphia gals," and so on, depending on where the troupes were playing, with the "Buffalo" variant eventually becoming the most popular, probably for poetic reasons.

The street cars swing at a curve, 3
The middle class passengers witness low life.
The car windows frame low life all day in pictures.

—**Carl Sandburg,** *Slants at Buffalo, New York*, in *Cornhuskers*, 1918

Within the town of Buffalo 4
Are prosy men with leaden eyes,
Like ants they worry to and fro
(Important men in Buffalo.)
But only twenty miles away
A deathless glory is at play;
Niagara, Niagara . . .

—**Vachel Lindsay,** *Niagara*, 1917

Butte, Montana

Butte, "a mile high, a mile deep," built on the "richest hill on earth," and generally described as the greatest mining camp ever known . . . has a certain inferno-like magnificence, with lights appropriately copper-colored—I heard it called "the only electric-lit cemetery in the United States." 5

—**John Gunther,** *Inside U.S.A.*, 1947

★ Gunther rated Butte as "the toughest, bawdiest town in America, with the possible exception of Amarillo, Texas."

Cairo, Illinois

This dismal Cairo. 6

—**Charles Dickens,** *American Notes*, 1842

★ He hated the place. The American fad for giving ancient names to their towns dates to January 5, 1789, when the citizens of Vanderheyden's Ferry, N.Y., voted to change the name of their burg to Troy.

Carson City, Nevada

1 My informants declared that in and about Carson a dead man for breakfast was the rule; besides accidents perpetually occurring to indifferent or to peacemaking parties, they reckoned per annum fifty murders.

—**Richard Burton,** *The City of the Saints*, 1861

2 They shoot folks here somewhat and the law is rather partial than otherwise to first-class murderers.

—**Artemus Ward,** *Artemus Ward, His Travels*, 1865

Charleston, South Carolina

3 There prevails here [Charleston] a finer manner of life, and on the whole, there are more evidences of courtesy than in the northern cities.

—**Johann David Schoepf,** *Travels in the Confederation, 1783–1784* [1911]

4 Streets unpaved and narrow, small wooden houses, from among which rise, in every quarter of the town, stately mansions, surrounded from top to bottom with broad verandahs, and standing within little gardens full of orange trees, palmettos, and magnolias, are features which give Charleston an expression belonging rather to the south of Europe than to the Teutonic cities of the north. . . . In other respects, it is a noble monument of what human avarice can effect.

—**Francis Hall,** *Travels in Canada and the United States in 1816 and 1817*, 1818

★ Lt. Hall, a British visitor, found the climate of Charleston unbearable in summer, but noted that the fortunes to be made in rice, and the availability of slaves to cultivate the crop, led to the creation of the city.

5 In . . . [Charleston] you actually have to pin a man to the mat before you can do business with him.

—**Henry Miller,** *The Air-Conditioned Nightmare*, 1945

6 An old Charlestonian may think of his city first and last, his heart bound to the palm-lined Battery, where echoes linger from the blasts of the guns his forebears trained on two meddling foreign powers—Great Britain and the United States.

—**William Francis Guess,** *American Panorama: East of the Mississippi*, 1960

Chicago, Illinois

7 This is a great uninteresting place of 600,000 inhabitants.

—**Matthew Arnold,** letter to Frances Arnold, his sister, Jan. 23, 1884

★ But about two years later, Robert Browning noted in a letter to New York politician Chauncey M. Depew that in the whole world the place that "sends me the most intelligent and thoughtful criticism upon my poetry is Chicago."

8 Perhaps the most typically American place in America.

—**James Bryce,** *The American Commonwealth*, 1888

I have struck a city—a real city—and they call it Chicago. . . . I urgently desire never to see it again. It is inhabited by savages. **1**

—Rudyard Kipling, *American Notes*, 1891

Satan (impatiently) to *new-comer*. The trouble with you Chicago people is that you think you are the best people down here, whereas you are merely the most numerous. **2**

—Mark Twain, *Pudd'nhead Wilson's New Calendar*, in *Following the Equator*, 1897

Late one night when we were all in bed, **3**
Mrs. O'Leary lit a lantern in the shed.
Her cow kicked it over,
Then winked her eye and said,
"There'll be a hot time in the old town tonight."

—Anonymous, c. 1900

★ Sung to the tune of an 1896 popular hit, "A Hot Time in the Old Town" (music by Joe Hayden, lyrics by Theodore A. Metz), the anonymous verse commemorates the great Chicago fire of 1871, which destroyed a third of the city, and which may—or may not—have been started by one of the five cows that Kate O'Leary kept in a barn off DeKoven Street. The guilty cow was named Daisy, or Madeline, or Gwendolyn, depending on which version of the tale one chooses to believe. Analysis of property records in 1997 by Richard F. Bales, of the Chicago Title Insurance Co., suggested, however, that the man who said he saw the fire break out, Peg Leg Sullivan, couldn't actually have seen the O'Leary barn from where he said he was standing because intervening structures would have blocked his view. This raises the possibility that Peg Leg, who rescued a calf, was in the barn but didn't want to admit it. He may have started the fire himself, perhaps by dropping a pipe or, like an awkward cow, knocking over a lantern.

First in violence, deepest in dirt, lawless, unlovely, ill-smelling, irreverent, new; an overgrown gawk of a—village, the "tough" among cities, a spectacle for the nation. **4**

—Lincoln Steffens, *The Shame of the Cities*, 1904

★ Either Steffens mellowed or Chicago improved; see Steffens below.

In the twilight, it was a vision of power. **5**

—Upton Sinclair, *The Jungle*, 1906

Chicago is the product of modern capitalism, and, like other great commercial centers, is unfit for human habitation. **6**

—Eugene Debs, 1908, quoted in Kevin Tierney, *Darrow* [1979]

Hog butcher for the world, **7**
Tool maker, stacker of wheat,
Player with railroads and the nation's freight handler;
Stormy, husky, brawling,
City of the big shoulders.

—Carl Sandburg, *Chicago*, 1916

1 It's one of the most progressive cities in the world. Shooting is only a sideline.
—**Will Rogers,** *Weekly Articles*, June 22, 1930

2 Chicago will give you a chance. The sporting spirit is the spirit of Chicago.
—**Lincoln Steffens,** *The Autobiography of Lincoln Steffens*, 1931

3 Goodbye, God. We're going to Chicago.
—**Anonymous,** Midwestern farm boy, saying often quoted by Irv Kupcinet, columnist for the Chicago Sun-Times, c. 1950s

4 Chicago is a great American city. Perhaps it is the last of the great American cities.
—**Norman Mailer,** *Miami and the Siege of Chicago*, 1968

★ More at CITIES above.

5 Chicago was a town where nobody could forget how the money was made. It was picked up from floors still slippery with blood.
—**Ibid.**

6 The city that works.
—**Anonymous**, saying, called "recently traditional" in *The Economist*, March 3-9, 1979

★ Incidentally, the name *Chicago* is from an Miami-Illinois Indian word, *sheegahgwuh*, meaning 'wild leek' and used as the name of the Des Plaines River. The word originally meant 'skunk.'

Cincinnati, Ohio

7 I am sure I should have liked Cincinnati much better if the people had not dealt so very largely in hogs.
—**Frances Trollope,** *Domestic Manners of the Americans*, 1832

★ On Main Street, said Mrs. Trollope, "the chances were five hundred to one against my reaching the shady side without brushing by a snout fresh dripping from the kennel." On a stroll outside the city, she found to her distress that she had to cross a brook reddened from a nearby slaughterhouse, while her feet "literally got entangled in pigs' tails and jawbones."

8 Cincinnati is a beautiful city; cheerful, thriving, and animated.
—**Charles Dickens,** *American Notes*, 1842

★ In a letter of April 15, 1842, Dickens wrote: "Cincinnati is only fifty years old, but is a very beautiful city; I think the prettiest place I have seen here, except Boston. It has risen out of the forests like an Arabian night city; it is well laid out; ornamented in the suburbs with pretty villas; and, above all, for this is a rare feature in America, has smooth turf-plots and well kept gardens."

9 The Queen of the West.
—**Henry Wadsworth Longfellow,** *Catawba Wine*, 1854

★ The nickname dates from the 1830s, but this poem validated it. The poem is a thank-you from Longfellow to Nicholas Longworth of Cincinnati, who had given Longfellow some Catawba wine from vineyards that Longworth had established on the Ohio River. The full stanza reads: "And this Song of the Vine, / This greeting of mine, / The winds and the birds shall deliver / To the Queen of the West, / In her garlands dressed, / On the banks of the Beautiful River," quoted in *American Heritage*, February 1975.

I saw it first bathed in the mellow light of a declining sun. . . . hill beyond hill, clothed with the rich verdure of an almost tropical clime, slopes of vineyards just ready for the wine-press, magnolias with their fragrant blossoms, and that queen of trees, the beautiful ilanthus, the "tree of heaven," as it is called; and everywhere foliage so luxuriant that it looked as if autumn and decay could never come. 1

—**Isabella Bird,** description of Cincinnati in 1855

★ She, too, was a visitor from England.

Lying along the right bank of the Ohio River, with its wooded banks on both sides and its graceful reaches as it winds its course below the city, it is one of the most beautiful sites for a town I have ever seen. 2

—**Richard Cobden,** diary entry, 1859

★ Cobden, an English reformer, also mentioned the famous pork market that so struck Frances Trollope, but he was not put off by it. The city had a host of other industries, but nevertheless did earn the nickname "Porkopolis." The Bird and Cobden comments here are from *American Heritage*, December 1956.

Cleveland, Ohio

I know of no other metropolis with quite so impressive a record in the practical application of good citizenship to government. 3

—**John Gunther,** *Inside U.S.A.*, 1947

Colorado Springs, Colorado

Colorado Springs is a city of faith. A shining city at the foot of a hill . . . [It] is a city of moral fabulousness. It is a city of fables. 4

—**Jeff Sharlet**, *Soldiers of Christ*, in *Harper's*, May 2005

Columbia, South Carolina

There is about it an air of neatness and elegance which betokens it to be the residence of a superior class of people. 5

—**Charles Mackay,** *Travels in the United States in 1846–47*, 1850

★ Mackay did complain that the town was in the middle of nowhere, and that the government buildings were uninteresting, "their dimensions being very limited, and their style of a simple and altogether unambitious description."

Columbus, Ohio

Columbus is a town in which almost anything is likely to happen and in which almost everything has. 6

—**James Thurber,** *More Alarms at Night*, in *My Life and Hard Times*, 1933

Concord, Massachusetts

See also TRAVEL (Thoreau).

1 The biggest little place in America.
—**Henry James,** *The American Scene*, 1907

Dallas & Forth Worth, Texas

2 Dallas is a baby Manhattan; Fort Worth is a cattle annex.
—**John Gunther,** *Inside U.S.A.*, 1947

Denver, Colorado

3 There have been, during my two weeks sojourn, more brawls, more fights, more pistol-shots with criminal intent in this log city of one hundred and fifty dwellings, not three-fourths completed nor two-thirds inhabited, nor one-third fit to be, than in any community of no greater numbers on earth.
—**Horace Greeley,** *An Overland Journey from New York to San Francisco . . . in 1859*, 1860

4 Cash! why they create it here.
—**Walt Whitman,** *Specimen Days*, 1879, 1882

5 The air is so refined that you can live without much lungs.
—**Shane Leslie,** *American Wonderland*, 1936

Des Moines, Iowa

6 Des Moines has the largest per capita ice cream consumption in America.

The second largest gold fish farm in the world is located within seventy miles of Des Moines.

The best pair of overalls made on the American Continent came from Iowa.

There is no group of two and a half million people in the world who worship God as Iowans do.
—**Anonymous** (a professor at Iowa State College), quoted by H. L. Mencken, in *Americana*, 1925

7 In Des Moines, a man's eyes will light up at the mere mention of the word "corn."
—**Philip Hamburger,** *An American Notebook*, 1965

Detroit, Michigan

8 The capital of the new planet—the one, I mean, which will kill itself off—is of course Detroit.
—**Henry Miller,** *The Air-Conditioned Nightmare*, 1945

9 You can slip up on Detroit in the dead of night, consider it from any standpoint, and it's still hell on wheels.
—**George Sessions Perry,** *Cities of America*, 1947

Say nice things about Detroit! 1

—**Anonymous**, sign outside downtown Detroit pizzeria, quoted in *The New York Times*, August 23, 1995

Duluth, Minnesota

Duluth! The word fell upon my ear with peculiar and indescribable charm, like the 2
gentle murmur of a low fountain stealing forth in the midst of roses, or the soft, sweet accents of an angel's whisper in the bright, joyous dream of sleeping innocence. Duluth! 'Twas the name for which my soul had panted for years, as the hart panteth for water-brooks. But where was Duluth? Never in all my limited reading had my vision been gladdened by seeing the celestial word in print.

—**J. Proctor Knott,** speech, U.S. House of Representatives, Jan. 27, 1871

Zenith City of the Unsalted Seas. 3

—**Ibid.**

★ This uproarious half-hour speech by Rep. Knott of Kentucky turned the nation's attention to Duluth, an obscure, muddy village with a population of about three thousand. Knott was attacking a bill proposing to donate federal lands to build a railroad that would link Duluth, with its port on Lake Superior, to the St. Croix River in Wisconsin. His oration, which left his colleagues weak with laughter, killed the railway bill, but made Duluth famous—for which Knott was properly thanked at a banquet in his honor when he eventually visited "that terrestrial paradise."

El Paso, Texas

See also AMARILLO & EL PASO.

The city of the four C's—Climate, Cotton, Cattle, Copper. 4

—**John Gunther,** *Inside U.S.A.*, 1947

Florence, Italy

Everything about Florence seems to be colored with a mild violet, like diluted wine. 5

—**Henry James,** letter, to Henry James, Sr., Oct. 26, 1869

This is the fairest picture on our planet, the most enchanting to look upon, the most 6
satisfying to the eye and the spirit. To see the sun sink down, drowned in his pink and purple and golden floods, and overwhelm Florence with tides of color that make all the sharp lines dim and faint and turn the solid city to a city of dreams, is a sight to stir the coldest nature, and make a sympathetic one drunk with ecstasy.

—**Mark Twain,** entry 1892, *Mark Twain's Autobiography* [1924]

Fort Worth, Texas

See DALLAS & FORT WORTH.

Frankfort, Kentucky

1 Frankfort is the capital of Kentucky, and is as quietly a dull town as I ever visited. . . . The legislature of the state was not sitting when I was there, and the grass was growing in the streets.

—**Anthony Trollope,** *North America,* 1862

Hartford, Connecticut

2 Of all the beautiful towns it has been my fortune to see, this is the chief . . . Everywhere the eye turns it is blessed with visions of refreshing green. You do not know what beauty is if you have not been here.

—**Mark Twain,** letter to the San Francisco *Alta California,* Sept. 6, 1868

★ This was Twain's initial impression of the city in which he was to spend twenty of his happiest years (1871–1894)

3 The most underappreciated city in America . . . the passthrough city in the passthrough state.

—**Lary Bloom,** *Hartford Courant Sunday Magazine,* May 7, 1995

Hoboken, New Jersey

4 *Reporter.* Might beauty then be in both the lily and Hoboken?
Oscar Wilde. Something of the kind.

—**Oscar Wilde,** Jan. 3, 1882, cited in Richard Ellman, *Oscar Wilde,* 1987

★ When Wilde arrived in New York to tour America, reporters began querying him about the fine points of aesthetics even before he disembarked. This also was the occasion of one of his most famous bon mots (not recorded until much later). Asked, when passing through customs, if he had anything to declare, the great Oscar replied, "I have nothing to declare except my genius."

5 It's Heaven, Hell, or Hoboken.

—**Anonymous,** 1917

★ More at World War I.

Hollywood

See Los Angeles.

Houston, Texas

6 In Houston the air was warm and rich and suggestive of fossil fuel.

—**Joan Didion** *The White Album,* 1979

Kansas City, Missouri

7 Ev'rythin's up to date in Kansas City.

—**Oscar Hammerstein II,** *Kansas City,* in *Oklahoma!,* 1943

Laredo, Texas

As I walked out in the streets of Laredo, 1
As I walked out in Laredo one day,
I spied a dear cowboy wrapped up in white linen,
Wrapped up in white linen as cold as the clay.

—**Anonymous,** *The Streets of Laredo*, or *The Cowboy's Lament*, c 1860

★ Alan Lomax reported in *Folksong U.S.A.* that his collection of ballads includes more than one hundred examples of this song, set in almost as many western towns. In what may be the original version, an English ballad, the young man dies, not of a gunshot wound but of syphilis. In an Irish version, sung in Cork around 1790, the dying man is a soldier. In still other versions, it is a young woman who has gone astray. From the last evolved the famous *St. James Infirmary Blues*, which begins: "I was down in St. James Hospital, / My baby there she lay / Out on cold marble table. / Well, I looked and I turned away."

Las Vegas, Nevada

If you aim to leave Las Vegas with a small fortune, go there with a large one. 2

—**Anonymous,** saying, c. 1950

★ Gambling was legalized in Nevada in 1931 but did not become a major factor in the state's economy until after World War II. The first plush casino was opened December 26, 1946, by gangster Benjamin "Bugsy" Siegel, who called it the Flamingo, after the nickname of his mistress, Virginia Hill. Six months later he was killed in a mob hit (three rifle bullets to the head) while talking to an associate in the living room of Hill's home in Beverly Hills.

Vegas is the most extreme and allegorical of American settlements, bizarre and 3
beautiful in its venality and in its devotion to immediate gratification.

—**Joan Didion,** *Marrying Absurd*, in *Slouching Towards Bethlehem*, 1968

What happens here, stays here. 4

—**Jeff Candido & Jason Hoff,** for R&R Partners, *advertisement*

★ The advertisement for Las Vegas became a pop cultural tag-line at the start of the 21st century. After the conservative credentials of William J. Bennett, education secretary under Pres. Reagan, were somewhat tarnished when he was caught gambling by a surveillance camera at a Las Vegas casino, Mr. Bennett complained, "Apparently, 'What happens here, stays here' applies to everyone but me" (*The New York Times*, June 4, 2004).

Lincoln, Kansas

The Size of a Dime With the Heart of a Dollar 5

—**Anonymous,** slogan, in *The New York Times*, March 3, 2005

London, England

London is the epitome of our times and the Rome of today.

—**Ralph Waldo Emerson,** *English Traits*, 1856 6

1 The muddy tide of the Thames, reflecting nothing, and hiding a million unclean secrets within its breast . . . is just the dismal stream to glide by such a city.
—**Nathaniel Hawthorne,** *Our Old Home*, 1863

2 When it's three o'clock in New York, it's still 1938 in London.
—**Bette Midler,** quoted in the London *Times*, Sept. 21, 1978

Los Angeles, California

See also ART: THEATER, DRAMA, MOVIES, & MAGIC (Kusturica).

3 Want authority to rent barn in place called Hollywood for $75 a month.
—**C. B. DeMille,** telegram, 1913, in Richard de Mille, *My Secret Mother: Lorna Moon* [1998]

★ Richard was at once C.B.'s adopted son and nephew—despite the difference in the spellings of their last names.

4 Nineteen suburbs in search of a metropolis.
—**Aldous Huxley,** *Americana*, 1925

★ The still more sprawling "seventy-two suburbs in search of a city" has been attributed to Dorothy Parker and Alexander Woollcott, among others.

5 Thought is barred in this City of Dreadful Joy, and conversation is unknown.
—**Aldous Huxley,** *Jesting Pilate*, 1926

6 There are millions to be grabbed out here, and your only competition is idiots. Don't let this get around.
—**Herman Mankiewicz,** cable to Ben Hecht, 1926, quoted in *The New York Times* [Jan. 8, 1993]

7 A trip through a sewer in a glass-bottomed boat.
—**Wilson Mizner,** characterization of Hollywood, pre–1933, in Alva Johnson, *The Incredible Mizners* [1953]

8 A Sargasso of the imagination!
—**Nathanael West,** *The Day of the Locust*, 1939

★ The passage goes, "Just as that imaginary body of water [the Sargasso Sea] was a history of civilization in the form of a marine junkyard, the studio lot was one in the form of a dream dump. A Sargasso of the imagination!" The name of one of the characters in this novel has floated into the 21st century—Homer Simpson, protagonist of a cartoon series about an American family.

9 A dreary industrial town controlled by hoodlums of enormous wealth.
—**S. J. Perelman,** quoted on radio following his death, Oct. 18, 1979

10 A circus without a tent.
—**Carey McWilliams,** *Southern California Country*, 1946

11 An Island on the Land.
—**Carey McWilliams,** subtitle of *Southern California Country*, 1946

If you tilt the whole country sideways, Los Angeles is the place where everything will fall. 1

—**Frank Lloyd Wright,** attributed

Hollywood is a place where there is no definition of your worth earlier than your last picture. 2

—**Murray Kempton,** *The Day of the Locust*, in *Part of Our Time*, 1955

Strip the phoney tinsel off Hollywood and you'll find the real tinsel underneath. 3

—**Oscar Levant,** *Inquisition in Eden*, 1965

★ Levant—pianist, composer, actor, media celebrity, and mordant wit—went to Hollywood in the 1920s. He became a close friend of George Gershwin and a major interpreter of his music. Levant began self-destructing in the 1950s, taking pills of various sorts, which was a common path to addiction in that period.

It's redundant to die in L.A. 4

—**Truman Capote,** 1975, quoted in Jay Presson Allen's play *Tru* [1989]

★ More at CALIFORNIA.

In Hollywood, if you don't have happiness, you send out for it. 5

—**Rex Reed,** quoted in J. R. Colombo, *Colombo's Hollywood*, 1979

Hollywood ceased to be Hollywood when television moved into the American home . . . Hollywood today is unimpressive, seems outmoded, a pale memory of itself. 6

—**Alfred Kazin,** Introduction, 1983, to Nathanael West's *The Day of the Locust*

If you say what you mean in this town you're an outlaw. 7

—**Kevin Costner**, quoted in *Time*, June 26, 1989

★ Meaning Hollywood.

In Hollywood . . . there are more gun owners in the closet than homosexuals. 8

—**Charlton Heston,** in *The New York Times*, June 9, 1998

★ Mr. Heston made the comment after being inducted the previous day as president of the National Rifle Association.

Los Angeles is a first-rate third-world country. 9

—**Connie Rice,** on *Now* PBS television Channel 13, Feb. 20, 2004

★ On an international measure of the disparity between incomes of rich and poor, Los Angeles took fourth place after Calcutta.

Lubbock, Texas

Nobody minds Dust storms in Lubbock; 10
They don't create havoc,
Just hubbubbock.

—**Ogden Nash,** *The Dust Storm, or I've Got Texas in My Lungs* in *The Private Dining Room,* 1952

Memphis, Tennessee

1 The great height of the trees, the quantity of pendant vine branches that hang amongst them; and the variety of gay plumaged birds, particularly the small green parrot, made us feel we were in a new world.

—**Frances Trollope,** *Domestic Manners of the Americans*, 1832

2 A dreary, dingy, muddy, melancholy town.

—**Charles Mackay,** *Down the Mississippi*, in *Life and Liberty in America, or, Sketches of a Tour in the United States and Canada in 1857–1858*, 1859

★ This is the same Mackay who wrote the classic sociological study *Popular Delusions and the Madness of Crowds*.

Miami, Florida

3 Miami is . . . of unimaginable awfulness—much like other American seaside resorts but on an unprecedented scale: acres of cheap white shops, mountain ranges of white hotels.

—**Edmund Wilson,** letter to Elena Wilson, Nov. 26, 1949

4 Miami Beach is where neon goes to die.

—**Lenny Bruce,** quoted by Barbara Gordon, *Saturday Review*, May 20, 1972

5 In Miami Beach the air conditioning is pushed to that icy point where women may wear fur coats over their diamonds in the tropics.

—**Norman Mailer,** *Miami and the Siege of Chicago*, 1968

6 Miami is more American than America.

—**Garry Wills,** *Nixon Agonistes*, 1970

Milwaukee, Wisconsin

7 Milwaukee and its environs provided a gray landscape, drawn with hard lines and great attention to detail.

—**Cecil Beaton,** *It Gives Me Great Pleasure*, 1955

Mobile, Alabama

8 Mobile stays in the heart, the loveliest of cities.

—**Carl Carmer,** *Stars Fell on Alabama*, 1934

9 I have never once thought of work in connection with Mobile. *Not anybody working.*

—**Henry Miller,** *The Air-Conditioned Nightmare*, 1945

Moscow, Russia

10 It did look like the other side of the moon should look—gray, flat, and spooky.

—**Harpo Marx,** *Harpo Speaks*, 1961

The Russians have a saying . . . "Moscow is downhill from all the Russias," meaning that the best of everything flows down into Moscow. 1

—**Hedrick Smith,** *The Russians*, 1977

Muncie, Indiana

This sober, hopeful, well-meaning city. 2

—**Robert S. Lynd & Helen Merrell Lynd,** *Middletown in Transition*, 1937

★ This was a follow-up by the Lynds to *Middletown* (1929), in which they applied the methods of cultural anthropology to a typical American community. Their findings at first shocked the natives, many of whom regarded the Lynds as muckrakers or Marxists. But their studies eventually were accepted as classics of American sociology.

Middletown is *against* the reverse of the things it is for. 3

—**Ibid.**

Middletown is a marrying city. 4

—**Ibid.**

Nashville, Tennessee

The Athens of Dixie. 5

—**Anonymous,** motto, quoted in John Gunther, *Inside U.S.A.*, 1947

Newark, New Jersey

A city of strivers pushing forward from immigrant enclaves. 6

—**Grace Mirabella,** with Judith Warner, *In and Out of Vogue*, 1995

New Orleans, Louisiana

Great Babylon is come up before me. Oh, the wickedness, the idolatry of the place! 7
unspeakable the riches and splendor.

—**Rachel Jackson,** letter, April 27, 1821

★ Rachel was the wife of Andrew Jackson, hero of the Battle of New Orleans. She called the city "Babylon-on-the Mississippi," a well-earned sobriquet. New Orleans has adopted the identity with some pride. (Try "New Orleans" and "Babylon" on Google.) Quotes here are from Robert V. Remini's *The Life of Andrew Jackson,* 1977, and *The Battle of New Orleans,* 2000.

A city of sin and gayety unique on the North American continent. 8

—**Herbert Asbury,** *The French Quarter: An Informal History of the New Orleans Underworld*, 1936

There is no architecture in New Orleans except in the cemeteries. 9

—**Mark Twain,** *Life on the Mississippi*, 1883

★ Old New Orleans was built upon a cypress swamp, and it is impossible to dig conventional six-foot-deep graves except in some of the newer, higher parts of town: the water table is too close to the surface. As a result, above-ground tombs of varying degrees of ornateness have proliferated.

1 New Orleans is the unique American place.
—**Charles Kuralt,** *Charles Kuralt's America*, 1995

Newport, Rhode Island

See also EPITAPHS & GRAVESTONES (Longfellow).

2 [Newport,] where idleness ranks among the virtues.
—**Oscar Wilde,** letter to Charles Eliot Norton, c. July 15, 1882

3 Newport, Rhode Island, that breeding place—that stud farm, so to speak—of aristocracy; aristocracy of the American type; that auction mart where English nobilities come to trade hereditary titles for American girls and cash.
—**Mark Twain,** Feb. 4, 1907, in *The Autobiography of Mark Twain*, ed. by Charles Neider [1959]

4 Newport was charming, but it asked for no education and gave none.
—**Henry Adams,** *The Education of Henry Adams*, 1907

5 One hundred years after the declaration that "all men are created equal," there began to gather in Newport a colony of the rich, determined to show that some Americans were conspicuously more equal than others.
—**Alistair Cooke,** *America*, 1973

New York City, New York

For a view of New York Harbor in 1609, see under NEW YORK.

6 They [New Yorkers] talk very loud, very fast, and all together.
—**John Adams,** July 23, 1774, *The Diary* [1850]

7 The renowned and ancient city of Gotham.
—**Washington Irving,** *Salmagundi*, 1807–1808

★ Irving's allusion was to the folktales about the village of Gotham in Nottinghamshire, England. The so-called wise men of Gotham actually were fools. Thus, twelve Gothamites on a fishing expedition worried that one of their party had drowned because each man forgot to count himself. The sense of "gothamite" gradually improved over the years, however, from "fool" to "wise fool" to "wiseacre" or "know-it-all," which is how Irving used it when referring to New Yorkers.

8 Situated on an island, which I think it will one day cover, it rises like Venice, from the sea, and like the fairest of cities in the days of her glory, receives into its lap tribute of all the riches of the earth.
—**Frances Trollope,** *Domestic Manners of the Americans*, 1832

★ For a comment on New York society, see Ward McAllister at ELITE, THE.

New York is notoriously the largest and least loved of any of our great cities. 1
—***Harper's Monthly***, 1856

New York is a sucked orange. 2
—**Ralph Waldo Emerson,** *Culture*, in *The Conduct of Life*, 1860

I have never walked down Fifth Avenue alone without thinking of money. I have never walked there with a companion without talking of it. 3
—**Anthony Trollope,** *North America,* 1862

My own Manhattan, with spires and the sparkling and hurrying tides, and the ships. 4
—**Walt Whitman,** *When Lilacs Last in the Dooryard Bloom'd*, 1865–66

★ For more of this poem, see SORROW & GRIEF.

City of hurried and sparkling waters! City of spires and masts! City nested in bays! My city! 5
—**Walt Whitman,** *Mannahatta*, 1881

The Bow'ry, The Bow'ry. They say such things, and they do strange things on the Bow'ry. 6
—**Harry Conor,** *A Trip to Chinatown,* musical, 1891

East Side, West Side, all around the town, 7
The tots sang "Ring-a-rosie," "London Bridge is falling down";
Boys and girls together, me and Mamie O'Rourke,
Tripped the light fantastic on the sidewalks of New York.
—**James W. Blake,** *The Sidewalks of New York*, 1894

★ The last line echoes Milton: "Come, and trip it, as you go,/ On the light fantastic toe" (*L'Allegro,* 1631).

The Great White Way. 8
—**Albert Bigelow Paine,** play title, 1901

★ Broadway, of course.

Give my regards to Broadway, 9
Remember me to Herald Square,
Tell all the gang at Forty-second Street
That I will soon be there.
—**George M. Cohan,** *Give My Regards to Broadway*, from *Little Johnny Jones*, 1904

When you are away from old Broadway, you are only camping out. 10
—**George M. Cohan,** quoted in Fred R. Ringel, ed., *America as Americans See It* [1932]

★ Or as Fred Allen put it, "Everywhere outside New York City is Bridgeport, Connecticut," quoted in Alistair Cooke, *America*, 1973. See also the saying on Paul Volcker's ashtray under Anonymous below.

1 *Mammon, n.* The god of the world's leading religion. His chief temple is in the holy city of New York.

—**Ambrose Bierce,** *The Devil's Dictionary*, 1906

★ *Mammon* means "riches," or "money," in Aramaic. At *Matthew* 6:24, we are warned, "Ye cannot serve God and mammon." New Yorkers, however, may cite in their defense *Luke* 16:9, "Make to yourself friends of the mammon of unrighteousness."

2 Little old Bagdad-on-the-Subway.

—**O. Henry,** *A Madison Square Arabian Night*, in *The Trimmed Lamp*, 1907

★ Henry used the "Bagdad-on-the-Subway" phrase again in *Roads of Destiny, A Night in New Arabia*, and *What You Want*. Turning to another "on-the-Subway" epithet for New York, Henry wrote, "Well, little old Noisy-ville-on-the-Subway is good enough for me," *The Duel*, in *Strictly Business*, 1910.

3 New York is the great stone desert.

—**Israel Zangwill,** *The Melting Pot*, 1908

4 To Europe she was America, to America she was the gateway of the earth. But to tell the story of New York would be to write a social history of the world.

—**H. G. Wells,** *The War in the Air*, 1908

★ Wells foresaw in this novel, written five years after the Wright brothers flew the first airplane, the development not only of air warfare but of the atomic bomb.

5 It couldn't have happened anywhere but in little old New York.

—**O. Henry,** *A Little Local Color*, in *Whirligigs*, 1910

6 New York is the most fatally fascinating thing in America.

—**James Weldon Johnson,** *O, Black and Unknown Bards*, 1917

7 Harlem is the precious fruit in the Garden of Eden, the big apple.

—**Alain Locke,** c. 1919

★ An early example of the "big apple" metaphor, cited in Deirdre Mullane, ed., *Words to Make My Children Live: A Book of African American Quotations*, 1995. Locke who earned a B.A. and Ph.D. from Harvard University, was the first black Rhodes Scholar, and taught philosophy at Howard University. He edited *The New Negro*, 1925, an anthology that introduced the writers of the Harlem Renaissance to a wide audience.

8 Heartless, Godless, Hell's delight, / Rude by day, and lewd by night.

—**Anonymous,** popular prohibitionist poem, c. 1920

9 O Babylon! O Carthage! O New York!

—**Siegfried Sassoon,** *Storm on Fifth Avenue*, in the *London Mercury* magazine, April 1921

10 The great big city's a wondrous toy
Just made for a girl and boy.
We'll turn Manhattan
Into an isle of joy.

—**Lorenz Hart,** *Manhattan*, 1925

The city seen from the Queensboro Bridge is always the city seen for the first time, in its first wild promise of all the mystery and all the beauty in the world. **1**

—**F. Scott Fitzgerald,** *The Great Gatsby*, 1925

More than any other city in the world, it is the fullest expression of our modern age. **2**

—**Leon Trotsky,** *My Life*, 1930

The Bronx? **3**
No thonx!

—**Ogden Nash,** *Geographical Reflection,* in *Hard-Lines*, 1931

★ Bronxites were understandably outraged by this catchy couplet. In 1964, for the Bronx's golden jubilee, Nash delivered an apology, which read in part: "I wrote those lines 'The Bronx? No thonx!' / I shudder to confess them. Now I'm an older, wiser man / I cry, 'The Bronx, God bless them!' "

Hardly a day goes by, you know, that some innocent bystander ain't shot to death in New York City. **4**

—**Will Rogers,** Nov. 20, 1931, *More Letters of a Self-Made Diplomat* [1982]

★ Rogers's point was that it took a pretty good marksman to hit an innocent person in New York. "One day they shot four," he noted. "That's the best shooting ever done in this town. Any time you can find four innocent people in New York in one day you are doing well even if you don't shoot them."

New York is so situated that anything you want, you can get in the very block you live in. If you want to be robbed, there is one living in your block; if you want to be murdered, you don't have to leave your apartment house; if you want pastrami or gefilte fish, there is a delicatessen every other door; if it's female excitement you crave, your neighbor's wife will accommodate you. **5**

—**Ibid.**

Only the Dead Know Brooklyn. **6**

—**Thomas Wolfe,** story title, in *From Death to Morning*, 1935

★ See also Emmanuel Celler below.

New York had all the iridescence of the beginning of the world. **7**

—**F. Scott Fitzgerald,** *The Crack-up*, 1936

O sweep of stars over Harlem streets, **8**
O little breath of oblivion that is night.
A city building to a mother's song,
A city dreaming to a lullaby.

—**Langston Hughes,** *Stars*, in *From My People*

★ In a 1963 essay, *In Love with Harlem,* Hughes wrote: "Melting pot Harlem—Harlem of honey and chocolate and caramel and rum and vinegar and lemon and lime and gall. Dusky dream Harlem rumbling into a nightmare tunnel where the subway from the Bronx keeps right on downtown."

1 When I think of New York, I think of all the girls . . . the young girls at the football games with the red cheeks and when the warm weather comes, the girls in their summer dresses.

—Irwin Shaw, *The Girls in Their Summer Dresses,* in *The New Yorker,* Feb. 4, 1939

2 Suddenly New York blazes like a magnificent jewel in its fit setting of sea, and earth, and stars.

—Thomas Wolfe, *The Web and the Rock*, 1939

3 It was a cruel city, but it was a lovely one.

—Thomas Wolfe, *The Web and the Rock*, 1939

4 I like New York in June,
How about you?

—Ralph Freed, *How About You?*, 1941 (music by Burton Lane)

5 At all events there is in Brooklyn
something that makes me feel at home.

—Marianne Moore, *A Carriage from Sweden,* 1944

★ The poet moved to Brooklyn in 1929 and lived there until 1965.

6 New York, New York—a helluva town,
The Bronx is up but the Battery's down.

—Betty Comden & Adolph Green, *New York, New York*, 1945

★ The authors reworked the lyric slightly for the 1949 film of *On the Town*, bowdlerizing "helluva town" as "wonderful town."

7 A hundred times have I thought New York is a catastrophe and fifty times: It is a beautiful catastrophe.

—Le Corbusier, *The Fairy Catastrophe*, in *When Cathedrals Were White*, 1947

8 New York City isn't a melting pot, it's a boiling pot.

—Thomas E. Dewey, remark to John Gunther, *Inside U.S.A.*, 1947

★ For the original melting pot metaphor, see under Israel Zangwill at AMERICA & AMERICANS. In 1986, *US News & World Report*, April 14 issue, reported that a sign in Times Square read, "If the United States is a melting pot, then New York makes it bubble."

9 There are eight million stories in the naked city. This has been one of them.

—Albert Maltz & Malvin Wald, screenplay, *The Naked City,* 1948

★ These are the final words of this standout crime drama. It was developed as a television series, with this tag line repeated weekly.

10 New York is to the nation what the white church spire is to the village—the visible symbol of aspiration and faith, the white plume saying the way is up!

—E. B. White, *Here Is New York*, in *Holiday* magazine, April 1949

On any person who desires such queer prizes, New York will bestow the gift of loneliness and the gift of privacy. 1

—Ibid.

It can destroy an individual, or it can fulfill him. No one should come to New York to live unless he is willing to be lucky. 2

—Ibid.

The city, for the first time in its long history, is destructible. A single flight of planes no bigger than a wedge of geese can quickly end this island fantasy, burn the towers, crumble the bridges, turn the underground passages into lethal chambers, cremate the millions. The intimation of mortality is part of New York now: in the sound of jets overhead, in the black headlines of the latest edition. 3

—Ibid.

★ White died six years before September 11, 2001.

You Never Leave Brooklyn. 4

—Emmanuel Celler, title of autobiography, 1953

★ Celler served in the U.S. Senate from 1923 to 1972, but remained a Brooklyn loyalist, and continued to practice law—and politics—there until his death in 1981.

The only credential the city asked was the boldness to dream. For those who did, it unlocked its gates and its treasures, not caring who they were or where they came from. 5

—Moss Hart, *Act One*, 1959

Terrible things happen to young girls in New York City. 6

—Mary Margaret McBride, *A Long Way from Missouri*, 1959

There is no greenery. It is enough to make a stone sad. 7

—Nikita Khrushchev, quoted by Bruce Weber, *The New York Times* [June 21, 1992]

★ Khrushchev, the premier of the USSR, toured the U.S. in 1959.

This is Harlem, where anything can happen. 8

—Chester Himes, *The Crazy Kill*, 1959

★ The speaker is police detective Grave Digger Jones.

As usual in New York, everything is torn down 9
Before you have had time to care for it.

James Merrill, *An Urban Convalescence,* 1962

If you should happen after dark 10
To find yourself in Central Park
Ignore the paths that beckon you
And hurry, hurry to the zoo
And creep into the tiger's lair.
Frankly you'll be safer there.

—Ogden Nash, in *Everyone but Thee and Me*, 1964

1 New York was heaven to me. And Harlem was Seventh Heaven.
—Malcolm X, *The Autobiography of Malcolm X*, 1965

2 New York, thy name is irreverence and hyperbole. And grandeur.
—Ada Louise Huxtable, in *The New York Times*, July 20, 1975

3 Ford to City: Drop Dead.
—(New York) Daily News, headline, Oct. 30, 1975

★ Columnist Jimmy Breslin has said reporters William Brink and Michael O'Neill should be credited with this headline. At the time, Pres. Gerald Ford has just promised to veto any bill to provide bailout funds to the nearly bankrupt city. The line that prompted the outrage was penned by David Gergen in what he thought was a draft version likely to be toned down (*The New York Times*, August 29, 2004). "The people of this country will not be stampeded. They will not panic when a few desperate New York officials and bankers try scare New York's mortgage payments out of them." Ford later narrowly lost New York in the campaign that brought the presidency to Democrat Jimmy Carter. For another great headline, see Abel Green at MEDIA.

4 When you've left New York, you ain't going nowhere.
—Anonymous, legend on ashtray, spotted in 1980, on desk of Federal Reserve Board chairman Paul Volcker, according to Martin Mayer, *The Money Bazaars*, 1985

5 A lot of places can beat it for livability; almost any place can beat it for civility; and as for affordability—don't ask.
—The New York Times, *Joyful Noises of New York*, editorial, Feb. 27, 1991

6 New York is the true City of Light in any season.
—Charles Kuralt, *Charles Kuralt's America*, 1995

Niagara Falls, New York

See BUFFALO above, *and* NEW YORK (Vachel Lindsay).

7 I felt as if approaching the very residence of the Deity.
—Thomas Moore, letter to his mother, July 24, 1804

8 It is the fall of an ocean.
—Frances Trollope, *Domestic Manners of the Americans, 1832*

9 I was disappointed with Niagara—most people must be disappointed with Niagara. Every American bride is taken there, and the sight of the stupendous waterfall must be one of the earliest, if not the keenest disappointments in American married life.
—Oscar Wilde, *Impressions of America,* 1883

10 A deathless glory is at play:
Niagara, Niagara . . .
—Vachel Lindsay, *Niagara*, 1917

★ More at CITIES: BUFFALO

Nome, Alaska

You'll find a magic city 1
On the shore of Bering Strait.
Which shall be for you a station
To unload your arctic freight.
—**Sam Dunham,** *The Goldsmith of Nome*, 1901

Oakland, California

What was the use of my having come from Oakland . . . there is no there there. 2
—**Gertrude Stein,** *Everybody's Autobiography*, 1937

Pampa, Texas

Pampa was a Texas boom town and wilder than a woodchuck. 3
—**Woody Guthrie,** *Bound for Glory*, 1943

Paris, France

If you ask me what is the business of life here? I answer, pleasure. 4
—**Abigail Adams,** letter, 1784

A loud modern New York of a place. 5
—**Ralph Waldo Emerson,** *Journal*, July 1833

Good Americans when they die go to Paris. 6
—**Thomas Gold Appleton,** saying, c. 1850

★ Appleton, a Bostonian, is credited with this bon mot in Oliver Wendell Holmes's *The Autocrat of the Breakfast-Table*, 1858. Oscar Wilde posed the question, "And when bad Americans die, where do they go to?" The answer: "Oh, they go to America," *A Woman of No Importance*, 1893.

We were obviously in beautiful if not moral company. 7
—**Theodore Dreiser,** diary, 1911.

★ Dreiser also observed that Paris was "a perfect maelstrom of sex."

How you gonna keep 'em down on the farm after they've seen Paree? 8
—**Sam M. Lewis & Joe Young,** refrain and song title, 1919

★ "They" are American soldiers coming home from France.

Dinners, soirées, poets, erratic millionaires, painters, translations, lobsters, absinthe, music, promenade, oysters, sherry, aspirin, pictures, Sapphic heiresses, editors, books, sailors. *And How!* 9
—**Hart Crane,** postcard from Paris, 1929

America is my country and Paris is my home town. 10
—**Gertrude Stein,** *An American and France*, 1936

1 The last time I saw Paris, her heart was warm and gay,
I heard the laughter of her heart in every street cafe.
—**Oscar Hammerstein II,** *The Last Time I Saw Paris*, 1940

★ Music by Jerome Kern. France, beloved of many Americans, fell to Germany in 1940. See also Elliot Paul below.

2 The last time I see Paris will be on the day that I die. The city is inexhaustible and so is its memory.
—**Elliot Paul**, *The Last Time I Saw Paris*, 1942

★ Paul fought in World War I and stayed on in Europe, forging a successful career as journalist and book writer.

3 Paris seems to be full of American girls who are hiding from their mothers.
—**James Thurber,** *Credits and Curios*, 1962

4 Paris is a moveable feast.
—**Ernest Hemingway,** epigraph, *A Moveable Feast*, 1964

★ The sentence reads in full: "If you are lucky enough to have lived in Paris as a young man, then wherever you go for the rest of your life, it stays with you, for Paris is a moveable feast." Peter Yapp in *The Travelers' Dictionary of Quotations* traces this to a 1950 letter from Hemingway to a friend.

Paterson, New Jersey

5 Paterson lies in the valley under the Passaic Falls
its spent waters forming the outline of his back. He
lies on his right side, head near the thunder
of the waters filling his dreams.
—**William Carlos Williams,** *Six Poems from Paterson*

Peoria, Illinois

6 Will it play in Peoria?
—**Anonymous**

★ The origin of this query is obscure. Gorton Carruth and Eugene Ehrlich in *American Quotations*, 1988, cite it as a traditional phrase in America politics, and it may derive from vaudeville. Political lexicographer William Safire gives considerable credit to Pres. Richard Nixon's aide John Ehrlichman, who used the phrase, "It'll play in Peoria" to mean that a policy or plan was politically viable. Mr. Ehrlichman told William Safire that he first used the expression while running a course for political campaign workers in New York City in 1968. "Onomatopoeia was the only reason for Peoria, I suppose. And it personified—exemplified—a place, removed from media centers on the coasts, where the national verdict is cast, according to the Nixon doctrine" (*Safire's New Political Dictionary*, 1993). Earlier, around the turn of the century, Ambrose Bierce similarly recognized the symbolic status of Peoria. In his *Devil's Dictionary* (1906), he wrote, "According to the most trustworthy statistics the number of adult dullards in the United States is but little short of thirty millions. The intellectual center of the race is somewhere about Peoria, Illinois." Charles Dudley Warner used "Peoria" in the same generic, somewhat disparaging sense in an 1875 essay, *The Whims of Travel*: "Foreign peoples, life, manners, religion, cities, are to be studied in the soft glow of ancientness, and not in the sudden flare of a pitch-pine knot that you have brought from Peoria."

Philadelphia, Pennsylvania

Three Philadelphia lawyers are a match for the very devil himself. 1
—Anonymous, c. 1800

★ More at Lawyers.

Spitting and swearing are nearly out of fashion in Philadelphia . . . at this moment we 2
cannot recall more than two or three gentlemen who would think of such a thing as spitting on the carpet of a lady's drawing room.
—Philip Houlbrooke Nicklin, *A Pleasant Peregrination in Pennsylvania*, 1836, cited in Samuel Eliot Morison, *The Oxford History of the American People* [1965]

Philadelphia: Corrupt and Contented. 3
—Lincoln Steffens, title of three-part series of articles on Philadelphia, in *The Shame of the Cities*, 1904

I liked poor dear queer flat comfortable Philadelphia almost ridiculously (for what it 4
is—extraordinarily *cossu* and materially civilized).
—Henry James, letter to Edmund Gosse, Feb. 16, 1905

★ Gentlemen are not supposed to discuss money, which explains James's lapse into the French *cossu*, meaning "rich." The city's comfortable charms were of some years standing. As Benjamin Franklin said, when told that the British under Sir William Howe had taken Philadelphia in 1777, "I beg your pardon, Sir, Philadelphia has taken Howe."

I went to Philadelphia one Sunday. The place was closed. 5
—W. C. Fields, attributed

★ One of Fields's many jokes at the expense of his native city. See also Epitaphs & Gravestones.

Philadelphia, a metropolis sometimes known as the City of Brotherly Love, but 6
more accurately as the City of Bleak Afternoons.
—S. J. Perelman, *Westward Ha!*, 1948

Philadelphia, the home of respectability, and the city of respectable homes. 7
—Anonymous, saying, quoted in Nathaniel Burt, *The Perennial Philadelphians*, 1963

In Philadelphia, Philadelphians feel, the Right Thing is more natural and more 8
firmly bred into [them] than anywhere else.
—Stephen Birmingham, *The Golden Dream*, 1978

Pittsburgh, Pennsylvania

1 The land at the point is 20 or 25 feet above the common surface of of the water; and a considerable bottom of flat, well-timbered land all around it, very convenient for building.

—**George Washington,** *Journal*, 1754

★ This was Washington's view on a scouting mission of the future site of Fort Duquesne where the Allegheny and Monongahela rivers meet to form the Ohio. Washington lost his journal when he surrendered Fort Necessity, southeast of present-day Uniontown, Pa., to the French on July 4, 1754, and it was first published in Paris in 1756 by the French government as a propaganda document to justify their own activities in North America.

2 Pittsburgh is like Birmingham in England; at least its townspeople say so. . . . It certainly has a great quantity of black smoke hanging about it.

—**Charles Dickens,** *American Notes*, 1842

3 Hell with the lid taken off.

—**James Parton,** in *The Atlantic Monthly*, 1868

Plymouth, Massachusetts

4 Plymouth is a somewhat flourishing town even at this day, but its principal pride is its historical recollections.

—**Charles Francis Adams,** *Diary*, Sept. 14, 1835

Pocatello, Idaho

5 You can't go back to Pocatello.

—**Richard L. Neuberger,** remark c. 1943–1944, quoted in Jonathan Daniels, *Frontier on the Potomac* [1946]

★ Pocatello, Idaho, said to be a fine small city, here stands for any provincial community to which a Washington politician would not want to return. According to *Safire's New Political Dictionary*, the adage was coined during a lunch conversation between Daniels and Neuberger, later a senator from Oregon. They were discussing the tendency of politicians to settle in Washington after they have left office. Neuberger probably had in mind the Thomas Wolfe quote on going home; see HOME.

Portland, Maine

6 Often I think of the beautiful town
That is seated by the sea;
Often in thought go up and down
The pleasant streets of that dear old town,
And my youth comes back to me.

—**Henry Wadsworth Longfellow,** *My Lost Youth*, in *Putnam's Magazine*, 1855

★ Longfellow was born and raised in Portland.

Oh happy Portlanders, if they only knew their own good fortune! They get up early, and go to bed early. The women are comely and sturdy, able to take care of themselves without any fal-lal of chivalry; and the men are sedate, obliging, and industrious. 1

—**Anthony Trollope,** *North America,* 1862

Portland, Oregon

Portland produces lumber and jig-saw fittings for houses, and beer and buggies, and bricks and biscuit; and, in case you should miss the fact, there are glorified views of the town hung up in public places with the value of the products set down in dollars. All this is excellent and exactly suitable to the opening of a new country; but when a man tells you it is civilization, you object. 2

—**Rudyard Kipling,** *American Notes,* 1891

★ Kipling didn't like Portland much. There was a sewage problem when he was there.

Providence, Rhode Island

Where bay and tranquil river blend, 3
And leafy hillsides rise,
The spires of Providence ascend
Against the ancient skies.

—**H. P. Lovecraft,** *Providence,* 1924

Reno, Nevada

The biggest little city in the world. 4

—**Anonymous,** saying, pre–1960

★ Reno was Nevada's most populous city until surpassed by Las Vegas in the 1950s. It also was for many years the divorce capital of the United States, thanks to a 1931 law that allowed people to end their marriages there after just six weeks of legal residence—and to Reno's location on the western edge of Nevada, close to Californians desiring to shed their spouses.

Rochester, New York

The very streets seemed to be starting up of their own accord, ready-made, and looking as fresh and new, as if they had been turned out of the workmen's hands but an hour before—or that a great boxfull of new houses had been sent by steam from New York, and tumbled out onto the half-cleared land. 5

—**Basil Hall,** *Travels in North America,* 1829

★ Capt. Hall retired from the British navy in 1842 and took up traveling and book writing.

Rome, Italy

1 More imagination wanted at Rome than at home to appreciate the place.
—**Herman Melville,** *Journal of a Visit to Europe and the Levant*, 1857

2 I've seen Rome, and I shall go to bed a wiser man than I last rose—yesterday morning.
—**Henry James,** letter to William James, Oct. 30, 1869

3 Rome was a poem pressed into service as a city.
—**Anatole Broyard,** *The New York Times*, March 24, 1974

Salt Lake City, Utah

4 I packt up my duds & left Salt Lake, which is a 2nd Soddum & Gemorrer, inhabitid by as theavin & onprincipled a set of retchis as ever drew breth in eny spot on the globe.
—**Artemus Ward,** *A Visit to Brigham Young*, in *Artemus Ward, His Book*, 1862

5 One must thank the genius of Brigham Young for the creation of Salt Lake City,—an inestimable hospitality to the Overland Emigrants, and an efficient example to all men in the vast desert, teaching how to subdue and turn it to a habitable garden.
—**Ralph Waldo Emerson,** *Journals*, Oct. 1863

★ See also UTAH.

6 Salt Lake City was healthy—an extremely healthy city. They declared that there was only one physician in the place and he was arrested every week regularly and held to answer under the vagrant act for having "no visible means of support."
—**Mark Twain,** *Roughing It*, 1872

Samarkand, Uzbekistan

7 Look 'round thee now on Samarcand!
Is not she queen of the Earth? her pride
Above all cities? in her hand
Their destinies?
—**Edgar Allan Poe,** *Tamerlane*, 1827

San Francisco, California

8 The miners came in forty-nine,
The whores in fifty-one;
And when they got together
They produced the native son.
—**Anonymous,** song, 1852 (or later)

★ Virtuous women were in such short supply in San Francisco during the early years of the gold rush that some prominent pioneers married professional ones, especially favoring those who had accumulated substantial "doweries." Herbert Asbury reported in *The Barbary Coast* (1933) that this bawdy song was "still sung by San Franciscans who do not take their municipal glories too seriously."

I have seen purer liquors, better segars, truer guns and pistols, larger dirks and bowie knives, and prettier courtezans, here in San Francisco, than in any other place I have ever visited; and it is my unbiased opinion that California can and does furnish the best bad things that are obtainable in America. **1**

—**Hinton R. Helper,** *Land of Gold: Reality versus Fiction*, 1855

San Francisco is a mad city—inhabited for the most part by perfectly insane people whose women are of a remarkable beauty. **2**

—**Rudyard Kipling,** *American Notes*, 1891

San Francisco has only one drawback. 'Tis hard to leave. **3**

—**Ibid.**

If, as some say, God spanked the town **4**
For being over frisky,
Why did he burn the churches down
And save Hotaling's Whiskey?

—**Anonymous,** comment on the San Francisco fire, 1906

★ Eve Golden in a letter to *The New York Times*, July 25, 1993, quoted this ditty from memory. She was addressing the question of whether fires, floods, and other natural catastrophes are God's response to people's sinful ways.

Baghdad-by-the-Bay **5**

—**Herb Caen,** book title, 1949

★ Caen's nickname for San Francisco, popularized in his long-running (1938–1997) newspaper column, has stuck permanently. He himself was, according to a 1957 *Time* magazine profile, "the Caliph of Baghdad." See also O. Henry under NEW YORK CITY.

San Francisco is perhaps the most European of all American cities. **6**

—**Cecil Beaton,** *It Gives Me Great Pleasure*, 1955

When you get tired of walking around San Francisco, you can always lean against it. **7**

—**Transworld Getaway Guide,** *San Francisco*, 1975–76

Santa Fe, New Mexico

Santa Fe, New Mexico, is the strangest place for fashion in America. They dress in what goes well with a highly polished aura. I imagine people there dress for their past lives. **8**

—**Andrei Codrescu,** in *The New York Times*, Oct. 24, 1993

Savannah, Georgia

I pitched upon this place, not only for the pleasantness of the situation, but because . . . I thought it healthy; for it is sheltered from the western and southern winds by vast woods of pine-trees. **9**

—**James Edward Oglethorpe,** letter, Feb. 20, 1733

★ Gen. Oglethorpe, a British philanthropist as well as a military man, established the colony of Georgia as a refuge for debtors—and also to protect neighboring colonies from Spanish forays to the north. Savannah was Oglethorpe's first settlement, this letter having been written just eight days after his arrival on the spot.

1 Savannah is a living tomb about which there still clings a sensuous aura as in old Corinth.

—**Henry Miller,** *The Air-Conditioned Nightmare*, 1945

Seattle, Washington

2 Seattle is a comparatively new-looking city that covers an old frontier like frosting on a cake.

—**Winthrop Sargent,** in *The New Yorker*, June 26, 1978

Springfield, Illinois

See also PARTING (Lincoln).

3 In this, the City of my Discontent,
Sometimes there comes a whisper from the grass.
"Romance, Romance—is here. No Hindu town
Is quite so strange. No Citadel of Brass
By Sindbad found, held half such love and hate;
No picture-palace in a picture-book
Such webs of Friendship, Beauty, Greed, and Fate!"
In this, the City of my Discontent,
Down from the sky, up from the smoking deep
Wild legends new and old burn round my bed
While trees and grass and men are wrapped in sleep.
Angels come down, with Christmas in their hearts,
Gentle, whimsical, laughing, heaven-sent;
And, for a day, fair Peace have given me
In this the City of my Discontent.

—**Vachel Lindsay,** in *The Sangamon County Peace Advocate*, Dec. 1909

St. Louis, Missouri

4 The city of St. Louis is, in the solidity of its buildings, the extent of its commerce, and the reputed wealth of its capitalists, the third in importance in the States. I have seen no place in the interior which gives the same impression of solid wealth and extensive commerce.

—**Richard Cobden,** diary entry, 1859

5 It is the capital city of the great west, the frontier town between the prairie and the settled country.

—**Edward Dicey,** *Six Months in the Federal States*, 1863

★ Although he called St. Louis a "frontier town," Dicey noted, "There is no look left . . . of a newly settled city. The hotels are as handsome and as luxurious as in any of the elder States. The shop windows are filled with all the evidences of an old civilization." And he went on to praise the sophisticated reading habits of the residents.

Meet me in St. Louis, Louis, 1
Meet me at the fair.

—**Andrew B. Sterling,** *Meet Me in St. Louis*, 1904

★ The fair was the Louisiana Purchase Exposition, celebrating the centennial of the giant land acquisition in 1803.

St. Petersburg, Russia

A silent, lonely beauty. 2

—**Lillian Hellman,** referring to what was then Leningrad (1944), in *An Unfinished Woman*, 1969

Tulsa, Oklahoma

Tulsa, "oil capital of the world," as it calls itself, is a tough, get-rich-quick, heady 3
town about as sensitive as corduroy.

—**Edna Ferber,** *Cimarron*, 1930

Tulsa is a residential suburb of Claremore [Rogers's hometown], where we park our 4
millionaires to keep them from getting under our feet.

—**Will Rogers,** in Alex Ayres, ed., *The Wit and Wisdom of Will Rogers* [1993]

Van Horn, Texas

Come to Van Horn to live. The climate is so healthy we had to shoot a man to start 5
our graveyard.

—**Anonymous,** placard, Jackson House Hotel, pre-World War I, cited in Mody C. Boatright, *Folk Laughter on the American Frontier* [1949]

Venice, Italy

A city for beavers. 6

—**Ralph Waldo Emerson,** *Journal*, June 1833

White swan of cities slumbering in thy nest . . . 7
White phantom city, whose untrodden streets
Are rivers, and whose pavements are the shifting
Shadows of the palaces and strips of sky.

—**Henry Wadsworth Longfellow,** *Venice*, 1876

Venice is like eating an entire box of chocolate liqueurs at one go. 8

—**Truman Capote,** "Sayings of the Week," in the London *Observer*, Nov. 26, 1961

1 A wholly materialistic city is nothing but a dream incarnate. Venice is the world's unconscious.

—**Mary McCarthy,** *Venice Observed*, 1961

2 It is the city of mirrors, the city of mirages, at once solid and liquid, at once air and stone.

—**Erica Jong,** *A City of Love and Death: Venice*, in *The New York Times*, March 23, 1986

Washington, D.C.

See also CONGRESS; GOVERNMENT.

3 To Washington, central star of the constellation, may it enlighten the whole world.

—**[Marquis de] Lafayette,** toast, 1824

4 Look to the city of Washington, and let the virtuous patriots of the country weep at the spectacle. There corruption is springing into existence, and fast flourishing.

—**Anonymous,** *Letters of Wyoming . . . in Favour of Andrew Jackson*, 1824

★ Most of the letters, originally published in the Philadelphia *Columbian Observer* in June and July of 1823, were written by John H. Eaton, who became Jackson's secretary of war after he was elected president in 1828. Eaton is remembered in history mainly for marrying a beautiful but forward young woman, the daughter of a Washington innkeeper, who was rumored to have been his mistress—and, horrors, also mistress to others. This caused such an uproar, socially and politically, that Eaton had to resign his office in 1831.

5 It is sometimes called the City of Magnificent Distances, but it might with greater propriety be termed the City of Magnificent Intentions.

—**Charles Dickens,** *American Notes*, 1842

6 Washington is full of famous men and the women they married when they were young.

—**Fanny Dixwell Holmes,** to Pres. Theodore Roosevelt, at a gathering in honor of her husband, Supreme Court Justice Oliver Wendell Holmes, Jan. 8, 1903

7 Things get very lonely in Washington sometimes. The real voice of the great people of America sometimes sounds faint and distant in that strange city. You hear politics until you wish that both parties were smothered in their own gas.

—**Woodrow Wilson,** speech, St. Louis, Sept. 5, 1919

8 If I wanted to go crazy, I would do it in Washington because it would not be noticed.

—**Irwin S. Cobb,** attributed

9 The heart of America is felt less here [Washington] than at any place I have ever been.

—**Huey Long,** speech in the U.S. Senate, May 17, 1932

The fundamental fact about Washington is that it was created for a definite purpose and has been developed, with many modifications, according to a definite plan. Therein lies its unique distinction among American cities. 1

—**Federal Writers Project,** *Washington, D.C.: A Guide to the Nation's Capital,* 1942

If you want a friend in Washington, buy a dog. 2

—**Anonymous** saying, sometimes attributed to Pres. Harry S. Truman

There are a number of things wrong with Washington. One of them is that everyone has been too long away from home. 3

—**Dwight D. Eisenhower,** attributed, press conference, May 11, 1955

★ The remark somehow did not make it into the official transcript.

Washington isn't a city, it's an abstraction. 4

—**Dylan Thomas,** interview, in John Malcolm Brinnin, *Dylan Thomas in America*, 1956

The more I observed Washington, the more frequently I visited it, and the more people I interviewed there, the more I understood how prophetic L'Enfant was when he laid it out as a city that goes around in circles. 5

—**John Mason Brown,** *Through These Men*, 1956

Somebody once said that Washington is a city of Southern efficiency and Northern charm. 6

—**John F. Kennedy,** comment to trustees and advisory committee of the national cultural center, Nov. 14, 1961

Too small to be a state but too large to be an asylum for the mentally deranged. 7

—**Anne Gorsuch Burford,** speech, Vail, Colo., July 27, 1984

★ Burford, a Reagan administration appointee, headed the Environmental Protection Agency. Her tenure was distinguished by an apparent determination not to enforce environmental laws. She left after being cited for contempt of Congress. Her assistant administrator, Rita Lavelle, a protégé of Attorney General Edwin Meese, was convicted of perjury and served three months in prison. Burford, by the way, borrowed this comment from James Petigru; see SOUTH CAROLINA.

Washington is a company town, really. And the company is U.S. Inc. 8

—**Sir David Hannay,** in *The New York Times*, Dec. 16, 1996

★ Sir David was contrasting Washington with New York City, where he had lived while serving as head of Britain's delegation to the United Nations.

Washington is just Hollywood for ugly people. 9

—**Anonymous saying,** *The New York Times Week in Review* [July 11, 2004]

★ The observation is sometimes attributed to comedian-writer-producer Lizz Winstead. A variation, "Politics is show business for ugly people," also has been used (since at least 1996) by "Tonight Show" host Jay Leno. But politicians do not take this lying down. Thus, Sen. John McCain retaliated: "If Washington is Hollywood for ugly people, Hollywood is Washington for the simple-minded" (*Philadelphia Inquirer*, Feb. 20, 2003).

Weehawken, New Jersey

1 The domes of the Church of
the Paulist Fathers in Weehawken
against a smoky dawn—the heart stirred—
are beautiful as St. Peter's
approached after years of anticipation.

—**William Carlos Williams,** *January Morning*, "Suite," in *Al Que Quiere!*, 1917

★ This is a continuation of Williams's thoughts on travel; see TRAVEL.

Civil Disobedience

See LAW; PACIFISM & NONVIOLENCE; RESISTANCE.

Civilization

See also SCIENCE: GEOLOGY (Will Durant)

2 The civilized man has the habits of the house. His house is a prison.

—**Henry David Thoreau,** *Journal*, April 26, 1841

★ More at RACES & PEOPLES.

3 We think our civilization near its meridian, but we are yet only at the cock-crowing and the morning star.

—**Ralph Waldo Emerson,** *Politics*, in *Essays: Second Series*, 1844

4 Civilization degrades the many to exalt the few.

—**A. Bronson Alcott,** *Table Talk*, 1877

5 Our civilization is still in the middle stage: scarcely beast, in that it is no longer wholly guided by instinct; scarcely human, in that it is not yet wholly guided by reason.

—**Theodore Dreiser,** *Sister Carrie*, 1900

6 Civilization is the lamb's skin in which barbarism masquerades.

—**Thomas Bailey Aldrich,** "Leaves from a Notebook," *Ponkapog Papers*, 1903

7 Civilization advances by extending the number of important operations which we can perform without thinking about them.

—**Alfred North Whitehead,** *An Introduction to Mathematics*, 1911

★ See another Whitehead definition, from 1933, below.

8 Civilization and profits go hand in hand.

—**Calvin Coolidge,** speech, New York City, Nov. 27, 1920

You can't say civilization don't advance, however, for in every war they kill you in a new way. 1
—**Will Rogers,** *The New York Times*, Dec. 23, 1929

A general definition of civilization: a civilized society is one exhibiting the five qualities of truth, beauty, adventure, art, peace. 2
—**Alfred North Whitehead,** *Adventures of Ideas*, 1933

what man calls civilization 3
always results in deserts.
—**Don Marquis,** *what the ants are saying* in *archy does his part*, 1935

Civilization is the progress toward a society of privacy. 4
—**Ayn Rand,** *The Fountainhead*, 1943

The test of a civilization is in the way that it cares for its helpless members. 5
—**Pearl S. Buck,** *My Several Worlds*, 1954

In the end, our society will be defined not only by what we create but by what we refuse to destroy. 6
—**John Sawhill,** attributed

★ Sawhill was president of The Nature Conservancy, whose mission is the preservation and restoration of biodiversity. TNC staffers believed the quote is from a conservancy publication, but could not cite the exact source.

Civil War, 1861–1865

See also AMERICAN HISTORY: MEMORABLE MOMENTS; EPITAPHS & GRAVESTONES (U.S. Grant and Henry Timrod); MILITARY STRATEGY; SLAVERY; UNION, THE; WAR.

It is an irrepressible conflict between opposing and enduring forces. 7
—**William Henry Seward,** *The Irrepressible Conflict*, speech, Rochester, N.Y., Oct. 25, 1858

★ Seward, an influential senator from New York, and later Secretary of State, saw no way to avoid war over the slavery issue.

I, John Brown, am now certain that the crimes of this guilty land will never be purged away but with blood. 8
—**John Brown**, note handed to guard en route to the gallows, Dec. 2, 1859

★ For a statement at his trial, see AMERICAN HISTORY: MEMORABLE MOMENTS. For a spoken remark on his the way to to the gallows, see LAST WORDS. John Brown rejected any tactic to avoid execution, for example, by pleading insanity. He told his brother, "I am worth inconceivably more to hang than for any other purpose."

Say to the seceded states, "Wayward sisters, depart in peace." 9
—**Winfield Scott,** letter to William Henry Seward, March 3, 1861

★ Gen. Scott, who hoped to avoid civil war, thus counseled Seward, who was about to become Lincoln's Secretary of State. Scott, incidentally, had a long and distinguished career, despite his irreverent nickname: Old Fuss and Feathers. (He insisted that his troops display a sharp, military appearance, and was given to carrying a plumed hat on ceremonial occasions.) A day later, Pres. Abraham Lincoln urged in his inaugural address, "We must not be enemies." See PEACE for the entire passage.

1 I had no feeling of self-reproach, for I fully believed the contest was inevitable and was not of our seeking. The United States was called upon not only to defend its sovereignty, but its right to exist as a nation . . . To me it was simply a contest, politically speaking, as to whether virtue or vice should rule.

—**Abner Doubleday,** thoughts at Fort Sumter, April 12, 1861, in *Reminiscences of Forts Sumter and Moultrie*, 1860–61 [1876]

★ Capt. Doubleday (he ended up a general but did not invent baseball as is often claimed) was second-in-command at Sumter and fired the first cannon shot at the Confederates at about seven o'clock in the morning. By this time, the Confederates already had been pounding away for two-and-one-half hours. At 1:30 P.M., on April 13, after thirty-three hours of bombardment, the Union commander, Major Robert Anderson, ordered that the fort's flag be taken down. The fort was on fire and he had no more ammunition.

For Ralph Waldo Emerson's reaction to the attack on Sumter, see WAR.

2 See, there is Jackson, standing like a stone wall.

—**Barnard E. Bee,** first Battle of Bull Run, July 21, 1861

★ Bee, a Confederate general, who died in the battle, said this referring to the First Brigade of the Army of the Shenandoah under the command of Brigadier-General Thomas J. Jackson. One of Bee's officers interpreted the remark as a complaint that Jackson's Virginians (then lying flat on the ground, not standing) were not coming to his support. At the end of the day, though, the resolute stand of Jackson's brigade proved to be the key to reversing what appeared at first to be a certain defeat for the South. The nickname "Stonewall" rapidly replaced Jackson's given name and his men became known as "the Stonewall Brigade." For Jackson's military maxims, see MILITARY STRATEGY.

3 All quiet along the Potomac.

—**George B. McClellan,** dispatches to Washington, 1861

★ All was too quiet for Pres. Lincoln and public opinion in the North. Gen. McClellan, commander in chief of the Union armies, was supposed to be advancing on Richmond, capital of the Confederacy. His reluctance to go forward cost him his job. He regained the command after the second Battle of Bull Run and lasted through the Battle of Antietam. The regular appearance of the "all quiet" phrase in headlines, all too frequently accompanied by a subhead such as "A Picket Shot," inspired the mournful song below.

4 "All quiet along the Potomac," they say,
Except now and then a stray picket
Is shot as he walks on his beat to and fro,
By a rifleman hid in the thicket.
'Tis nothing—a private or two now and then
Will not count in the news of the battle;

Not an officer lost—only one of the men,
Moaning out, all alone, the death-rattle.

—Ethel Lynn Beers, *The Picket Guard*, in *Harper's Weekly*, Sept. 30, 1861

★ The music was by James Hewitt. The fifth and last verse follows below.

All quiet along the Potomac to-night; 1
No sound save the rush of the river;
While soft falls the dew on the face of the dead—
The picket's off duty forever.

—Ibid.

We must cut our way out as we cut our way in. 2

—Ulysses S. Grant, when told that he was surrounded, Belmont, Mo., Nov. 7, 1861, cited in Eugene Lawrence, *Grant on the Battle-Field*, in *Harper's New Monthly Magazine*, XXXIX, 1869

If McClellan is not using the army, I should like to borrow it for a while. 3

—Abraham Lincoln, comment, April 9, 1862

Mine eyes have seen the glory of the coming of the Lord. 4

—Julia Ward Howe, *Battle Hymm of the Republic*, 1862

★ This is the first line of the song that became the anthem of the Union cause. More at God.

No terms except an unconditional and immediate surrender can be accepted. I propose to move immediately upon your works. 5

—Ulysses S. Grant, message to Confederate Major General Simon Bolivar Buckner at Fort Donelson, Tenn., Feb. 16, 1862

★ Grant's message popularized the phrase "unconditional surrender," thanks partly to the coincidence of the initial letters with the first two initials of his own name. Buckner, commander of this Confederate fort on the Cumberland River, had asked to negotiate terms of surrender. Upon receiving this reply from Grant, he gave over the fort. This victory, along with the capture of Fort Henry across the river ten days earlier, marked a turning point in the war. "Unconditional Surrender" Grant had shown his mettle.

I can't spare this man. He fights. 6

—Abraham Lincoln, speaking of Gen. Ulysses S. Grant, April 1862

★ After the bloody Battle of Shiloh, a costly and scant victory for the Union, Lincoln was repeatedly urged to remove Grant as commander. This was the president's reply to A. K. McClure.

We are coming Father Abraham, three hundred thousand more.

—James Sloan Gibbons, first line of song, *New York Evening Post*, July 16, 1862 7

★ Gibbons, a Philadelphia Quaker who had moved to New York, wrote this popular marching song after Lincoln, hoping to make up Union losses in the Peninsular campaign, appealed to the states on July 2, 1862, to raise "three hundred thousand more" soldiers. The music for the song was composed by Stephen Foster.

1 No, Captain, the men are right. Kill the brave ones; they lead on the others.
—Thomas J."Stonewall" Jackson, remark, second battle of Manassas (called Bull Run by the Federals), August 29, 1862

★ This was Jackson's rebuke to an officer who told his men that they should have captured a Union major instead of killing him; the officer had gallantly led a cavalry charge.

2 All persons held as slaves . . . are, and henceforward shall be, free.
—Abraham Lincoln, *Emancipation Proclamation*, Jan. 1, 1863

★ See also SLAVERY.

3 Yes, we'll rally 'round the flag, boys, we'll rally once again,
Shouting the battle cry of freedom.
—George Frederick Root, *The Battle Cry of Freedom*, 1863

★ The phrase "rally 'round the flag" has been ascribed to Gen. Andrew Jackson at the Battle of New Orleans, and was used in political campaigns before Root picked it up for this popular war song.

4 A rich man's war and a poor man's fight.
—Anonymous, slogan of draft rioters in New York City, July 1863

★ A person who had $300 to pay for a substitute could avoid the draft.

5 The Father of Waters again goes unvexed to the sea.
—Abraham Lincoln, comment on the fall of Vicksburg, Miss., letter to James C. Conkling, August 26, 1863

★ With the conquest of Vicksburg on July 4, the North had gained control of the full length of the Mississippi. On the same day, Gen. Robert E. Lee began the Confederate retreat from Gettysburg, Penn., following three days of battle. So the tide of war turned on two fronts on the Fourth of July, 1863. Thanking Grant in a letter on July 13 for the victory at Vicksburg, Lincoln, who had harbored doubts about the general's tactics, did something that few people—and fewer presidents—ever do, saying, "I now wish to make personal acknowledgment that you were right, and I was wrong."

6 Fourscore and seven years ago, our fathers brought forth on this continent a new nation, conceived in liberty, and dedicated to the proposition that all men are created equal.
—Abraham Lincoln, Gettysburg Address, Nov. 19, 1863

★ More at GETTYSBURG ADDRESS.

7 I propose to fight it out on this line if it takes all summer.
—Ulysses S. Grant, dispatch to Washington, May 11, 1864

★ Grant had been beaten back by Gen. Robert E. Lee's forces at the Spottsylvania Court House. In this dispatch to Gen. Henry Wager Halleck, Grant announced his intention to persevere. Lincoln echoed Grant's words in a speech on June 16, saying, "We are going through on this line if it takes three more years."

Wherever the enemy goes, let our troops go also. 1

—**Ulysses S. Grant,** dispatch from City Point, Va., to Gen. Henry W. Halleck, August 1, 1864

Damn the torpedoes! Go ahead!

—**David Glasgow Farragut,** battle of Mobile Bay, August 5, 1864 2

★ In this bloody battle, Admiral Farragut headed a fleet of fourteen wooden ships and four monitors, iron-clad vessels first used in 1862. In order to be able to continue to command even if wounded, Farragut lashed himself to the rigging of his flagship, the *Hartford*. Torpedoes—actually mines—sank the Union's lead ship, the monitor *Tecumseh*, halting the advance of the fleet until Farragut issued the order to go on. The badly needed victory that followed bolstered Northern spirits and, together with Sherman's march through Georgia, revived Pres. Lincoln's chances of reelection.

Breckinridge, what do you think of the Dred Scott decision and the rights of the 3
South in the Territories now?

—**Jubal Early,** Shenandoah Valley, August 1864

★ Gen. Early of Virginia, who had not favored secession, to John Breckinridge of Kentucky, who ran in 1860 as a Southern Democrat against Northern Democrat Stephen Douglas, Republican Abraham Lincoln, and Whig John Bell. On this occasion, it was the middle of the night; the Confederate army had been devastated by Maj. Gen. Philip Sheridan, and was in retreat. Breckinridge was dozing on his horse when Early woke him with this question. Humor spiced Early's command style. In May, at the Battle of the Wilderness, Early had accosted a healthy soldier leaving the scene and ordered him back to the front. When the man protested that he was a chaplain, Early retorted, "Chaplain, chaplain, eh? You have been praying these many years to go to heaven, and now when you have a chance to get there in fifteen minutes, you are running away!" These accounts are from the memoirs of Major David French Boyd, *Reminiscences of the War in Virginia*, 1994. For the Dred Scott decision, see AMERICAN HISTORY: MEMORABLE MOMENTS.

Hold out. Relief is coming. 4

—**William Tecumseh Sherman,** signal to Gen. John Murray Corse, battle of Allatoona Pass, Oct. 5, 1864

★ Although wounded and with two-thirds of his small force fallen, Corse did hold out all day and night until Sherman's troops got to him. The popular version of the signal, "Hold the fort! for I am coming," is the wording used in an 1874 gospel song by Philip Paul Bliss.

The terrible grumble, and rumble, and roar, 5
Telling the battle was on once more,
And Sheridan twenty miles away.

—**Thomas B. Read,** *Sheridan's Ride*, Oct. 1864

★ Generations of schoolchildren (in the North) declaimed this poem, composed a few days after the battle of Cedar Creek on October 19. The poem tells how Gen. Philip H. Sheridan, returning from a conference in Washington, encountered panic-stricken troops and galloped on his great black Morgan, Rienzi, twenty miles to the battlefield, where he rallied his army and converted an apparent defeat into victory. Painter-poet Thomas B. Read was then a major on the staff of another author of some note, Gen. Lew *(Ben Hur)* Wallace.

1 "Hurrah! Hurrah! we bring the jubilee!
Hurrah! Hurrah! the flag that makes you free!"
So we sang the chorus from Atlanta to the sea,
While we were marching through Georgia.

—**Henry Clay Work,** *Marching Through Georgia*, Dec. 1864

★ This song by the author of *Father, Dear Father, Come Home with Me Now* (see ALCOHOL & DRINKING) was composed shortly after Sherman occupied Savannah on December 21. In a message to Grant on September 9, Sherman had predicted, "I can make this march and make Georgia howl." He cut a swathe of destruction up to sixty miles wide in a campaign that was a military triumph but a political disaster. The march, which Sherman continued from Savannah northward through the Carolinas, crippled the Confederacy and shortened the conflict, almost certainly saving lives, but it left Southerners permanently embittered. On December 22, Sherman telegraphed Lincoln: "I beg to present you as a Christmas gift the city of Savannah, with 150 heavy guns and plenty of ammunition, also about 25,000 bales of cotton." The song, as well as the bitterness, lived on. Adopted by other armies, including the British and Japanese, it was still played and sung in World War II.

2 With malice toward none, with charity for all, with firmness in the right, as God gives us to see the right, let us strive on to finish the work we are in; to bind up the nation's wounds, to care for him who shall have borne the battle, and for his widow, and for his orphan—to do all which may achieve and cherish a just and lasting peace among ourselves, and with all nations.

—**Abraham Lincoln,** Second Inaugural Address, March 4, 1865

★ With victory at hand, Lincoln called for charity and equal justice in the Southern states. Thousands stood in deep mud on Pennsylvania Avenue to hear his words. A little over a month later, he was dead. See also Lincoln at GOD.

3 The war is over—the rebels are our countrymen again.

—**Ulysses S. Grant,** April 9, 1865

★ Grant silencing his cheering troops after Robert E. Lee surrendered at Appomattox. See also Grant's call for peace in 1868 at AMERICAN HISTORY: MEMORABLE MOMENTS.

4 The real war will never get in the books. And so goodbye to the war.

—**Walt Whitman,** *The Real War Will Never Get in the Books*, 1882

★ Whitman served as a nurse to wounded soldiers in the Civil War. Robert E. Lee made a similar comment in 1868; see HISTORY.

5 In the South, the war is what A.D. is elsewhere; they date from it.

—**Mark Twain,** *Life on the Mississippi*, 1883

6 There will never be anything in America more interesting than the Civil War, never.

—**Gertrude Stein,** *Everybody's Autobiography*, 1937

Clothes

See FASHION & CLOTHES.

Colorado

See also CITIES (DENVER).

Pike's Peak or bust. 1
—**Anonymous,** 1858

★ The rallying cry of immigrants to Denver, after gold was found in Pike's Peak in 1858. Some wagons displayed the sign, "Busted, by gosh."

Colorado men are we, 2
From the peaks gigantic, from the great sierras and the high plateaus,
From the mine and from the gully, from the hunting trail we come,
Pioneers! O pioneers!
—**Walt Whitman,** *Pioneers! O Pioneers!*, 1865, in *Leaves of Grass* [1881]

Passing through your wonderful mountains and cañons I realize that this state is 3
going to be more and more the playground for the entire Republic. . . .You will see this is the real Switzerland of America.
—**Theodore Roosevelt,** remark during visit to Colorado, 1905

We found God lavish there in Colorado. 4
—**Hart Crane,** "Indiana," in *To the Brooklyn Bridge*, 1930

★ The poet adds, "But passing sly"; the passage concerns disappointment in the promise of fortunes to be made in Colorado following the discovery of gold there in 1858.

Colorado is a grand seat to see the world from. 5
—**Will Rogers,** Jan. 1, 1933, in *Weekly Articles, Vol. V* [1982]

Colorado, the most spectacular of the mountain states. 6
—**John Gunther,** *Inside U.S.A.*, 1947

This state has more sunshine and more bastards that any place on earth! 7
—**Anonymous,** utilities company executive, on being sentenced to prison by Denver Judge Benjamin Barr Lindsey, in John Gunther, *Ibid.*

★ Judge Lindsey (1869–1943) is best remembered for having established the first juvenile court system in the United States. Gunther called him "the greatest man the state ever produced," adding that he "was of course reviled by the city he worked so hard to improve."

Nil sine numine. 8
Nothing without Providence.
—Motto, state of Colorado

Comedy

See HUMOR.

Committees & Conferences

1 No grand idea was ever born in a conference, but a lot of foolish ideas have died there.

—**F. Scott Fitzgerald,** *The Crack-up,* 1945

2 Committee—a group of men who individually can do nothing but as a group decide that nothing can be done.

—**Fred Allen,** attributed, in Laurence J. Peter, *Quotations for Our Time* [1978]

3 Could *Hamlet* have been written by a committee, or the *Mona Lisa* been painted by a club? Could the New Testament have been composed as a conference report? Creative ideas do not spring from groups. They spring from individuals. The divine spark leaps from God to the finger of Adam.

—**A. Whitney Griswold,** speech, 1957

4 What is a committee? A group of the unwilling, picked from the unfit, to do the unnecessary.

—**Richard Harkness,** in *New York Herald Tribune,* June 15, 1960

5 Committees are consumers and sometimes sterilizers of ideas, rarely creators of them.

—**Henry A. Kissinger,** *The Necessity for Choice: Prospects of American Foreign Policy*, 1961

Commitment

See also Determination, Effort, Persistence, & Perseverance; Loyalty.

6 Hew to the line, let the chips fall where they may.

—**Roscoe Conkling,** nomination speech, Republican National Convention, June 5, 1880

★ Sen. Conkling of New York nominated Gen. Ulysses S. Grant for an unprecedented third term. The convention, however, went for James A. Garfield of Ohio.

7 Don't tell me how talented you are. Tell me how hard you work.

—**Artur Rubinstein,** in David Dubal, *Evenings with Horowitz* [1991]

8 The question should be, is it worth trying to do, not can it be done.

—**Allard K. Lowenstein,** 1966, cited in *The New York Times* [Nov. 7, 1993]

Common Sense

See also Knowledge & Information (Gertrude Stein); Wisdom.

9 Where sense is wanting, everything is wanting.

—**Benjamin Franklin,** *Poor Richard's Almanack*, 1754

10 Nothing astonished men so much as common sense and plain dealing.

—**Ralph Waldo Emerson,** *Art*, in *Essays: First Series*, 1841

Common sense always takes a hasty and superficial view. 1
—**Henry David Thoreau,** *A Week on the Concord and Merrimack Rivers*, 1849

Common sense is compelled to make its way without the enthusiasm of anyone; all 2
admit it grudgingly.
—**Edgar Watson Howe,** *The Indignations of E. W. Howe*, 1933

Common sense is the collection of prejudices acquired by age eighteen. 3
—**Albert Einstein,** attributed in *Scientific American* magazine [Feb. 1976]

I just want to take common sense to high places. 4
—**Jesse Jackson,** speech, Democratic National Convention, July 20, 1988

Communication

See also MANAGEMENT TECHNIQUES; MEDIA; SCIENCE: TECHNOLOGY.

We are in great haste to construct a magnetic telegraph from Maine to Texas, but 5
Maine and Texas, it may be, have nothing important to communicate.
—**Henry David Thoreau,** *Economy*, in *Walden*, 1854

★ Cited by Bill Henderson in an op-ed piece in *The New York Times*, March 16, 1994. Henderson, director of the Lead Pencil Club, a subsidiary of the Pushcart Press, observed that Thoreau wrote this with a lead pencil that he made himself. Thoreau's father, John Thoreau, was a leading pencil manufacturer. Thoreau was not impressed by most inventions and improvements. He continued: "We are eager to tunnel under the Atlantic and bring the Old World some weeks nearer to the New; but perchance the first news that will leak through into the broad, flapping American ear will be that the Princess Adelaide has the whooping cough." See also SCIENCE: TECHNOLOGY.

Well, if I called thc wrong number, why did you answer the phone? 6
—**James Thurber**, cartoon caption, *The New Yorker*, June 5, 1937

What we've got here is failure to communicate. 7
—**Frank R. Pierson,** *Cool Hand Luke*, screenplay, 1967

★ An ironic comment directed at prisoner Paul Newman by a nasty chain-gang boss, played by Strother Martin. This quickly became a byword in an era full of communication failures—between generations, races, sexes, computers, and so on.

Communism

See also SOCIALISM.

Communism is twentieth-century Americanism. 8
—**Earl Browder,** slogan of the U.S. Communist Party, 1930–1945

★ Browder was ousted as head of the party in 1945 for advocating international harmony. He explained in an interview in *American Heritage*, December 1971, that this statement "meant that America's revolutionary heritage had been inherited by the Communists, and America's role in the world was a revolutionary one."

1 The economy of communism is an economy which grows in an atmosphere of misery and want.

—Eleanor Roosevelt, *My Day*, Feb. 12, 1947

★ For the Cold War; see under Bernard Baruch at AMERICAN HISTORY: MEMORABLE MOMENTS.

2 From what I hear, I don't like it [Communism] because it isn't on the level.

—Gary Cooper, testifying as a friendly witness, House Committee on Un-American Activities, 1947

★ The committee, usually known as HUAC, was conducting a probe of alleged Communism in the movie business. Chaired by Rep. J. Parnell Thomas, a New Jersey Republican, the committee broke the ground for McCarthyism and made infamous the question: "Are you now or have you ever been a member of the Communist Party?" (To which John Larder replied: "I could answer . . . but if I did, I would hate myself in the morning.") Committee member Richard M. Nixon gained a nationwide reputation for anti-Communist zeal in his questioning of former State Department official Alger Hiss. For the first major strike by Sen. McCarthy, see AMERICAN HISTORY: MEMORABLE MOMENTS, his Wheeling, W. Va., speech.

3 Communism is a corruption of a dream of justice.

—Adlai Stevenson, speech, Urbana, Ill., 1951

4 Capitalism, it is said, is a system wherein man exploits man. And communism is—vice versa.

—Daniel Bell, *The End of Ideology*, 1960

5 Better Red than dead.

—Anonymous, slogan of the nuclear disarmament movement, c. 1960

★ Opponents of nuclear weapons in the U.S. picked up this slogan from the British. It was based on a passage from the philosopher Bertrand Russell. Also popular was the rejoinder, "Better dead than Red," used as a book title in 1964 by British author Stanley Reynolds.

6 [Communism] has never come to power in a country that was not disrupted by war or internal corruption or both.

—John F. Kennedy, speech, July 3, 1963

7 [Communism is] Facism with a human face.

—Susan Sontag, speech, rally for Polish Solidarity, New York City, 1982

Complaints

8 I hate to be a kicker, I always long for peace,
But the wheel that does the squeaking is the one that gets the grease.

—Josh Billings, *The Kicker* [Complainer], c. 1870

9 Never complain, never explain.

—Henry Ford II, saying

★ More at EXCUSES & EXPLANATIONS.

Conflict

See also ARGUMENTS; DIFFERENCES; RACES & PEOPLES (Tocqueville).

1 So strong is the propensity of mankind to fall into mutual animosities, that where no substantial occasion presents itself, the most frivolous and fanciful distinctions have been sufficient to kindle their unfriendly passions and excite their most violent conflicts. But the most common and durable source of factions has been the various and unequal distribution of property.
—**James Madison,** *The Federalist, No. 10*, 1787

2 A house divided against itself cannot stand.
—**Abraham Lincoln,** speech, Republican State Convention, Springfield, Ill., June 16, 1858

★ More at UNION, THE.

3 There is nothing I love so much as a good fight.
—**Franklin D. Roosevelt,** quoted in *The New York Times*, Jan. 22, 1911

★ This was at the outset of F.D.R.'s political career. Elected to the New York State senate the previous fall, he had aligned himself with insurgent Democrats in Albany in an effort to defeat a Tammany-backed candidate for the U.S. Senate. In the end, a compromise of sorts was reached, and both sides claimed victory.

4 The choice we face is not between progress with conflict and progress without conflict. The choice is between conflict and stagnation. . . . The totalitarians regard the toleration of conflict as our central weakness. So it may appear in an age of anxiety. But we know it to be basically our central strength.
—**Arthur M. Schlesinger, Jr.**, *The Vital Center: The Politics of Freedom*, 1949

Congress

See also CITIES (POCATELLO; WASHINGTON, D.C.); POLITICS & POLITICIANS.

5 We pour legislation into the senatorial saucer to cool it.
—**George Washington,** quoted in Moncure D. Conway, *Omitted Chapters of History Disclosed in the Life and Papers of Edmund Randolph* [1888]

★ Probably an apocryphal remark, but the "senatorial saucer" is in the news periodically. Thus, Democratic senators emphasized the virtues of cool and extended deliberation in 2005 when Republicans, then in the majority, began talking about changing the filibuster rule so that votes on judicial nominations could not be blocked by the minority. Ten years earlier, in 1995, when Georgia Republican Newt Gingrich pushed through a record-breaking volume of legislation in the first one hundred days of his tenure as Speaker of the House, Democrats also sought to slow the conservative counter-revolution in the senatorial saucer. As recounted by Conway, the image appeared initially in a conversation between Washington and Thomas Jefferson. The passage runs: "There is a tradition that, on his return from France, Jefferson called Washington to account at the breakfast-table for having agreed to a second chamber [in Congress]. 'Why,' asked Washington, 'did you pour that coffee into your saucer?' 'To cool it,' quoth Jefferson. 'Even so,' said Washington, 'We pour legislation into the senatorial saucer to cool it.' "

1 That 150 lawyers should do business together ought not to be expected.
—Thomas Jefferson, *Autobiography*, Jan. 6, 1821

2 I have been told I was on the road to Hell, but I had no idea it was just a mile down the road with a dome on it.
—Abraham Lincoln, quoted in Rep. Morris K. Udall, *Too Funny to Be President* [1988]

3 Whiskey is taken into the committee rooms in demijohns and carried out in demagogues.
—Mark Twain, *Notebooks*, 1868, quoted in Albert Bigelow Paine, *Mark Twain, A Biography* [1912]

4 To my mind, Judas Iscariot was nothing but a low, mean, premature Congressman.
—Mark Twain, letter to the editor, *New York Daily Tribune*, printed March 10, 1873

5 The finest Congress money can buy.
—Mark Twain, attributed

★ The closest citation in Twain's writings, according to the Library of Congress's *Respectfully Quoted*, is: "I think I can say, and say with pride, that we have some legislatures that bring higher prices than any in the world." This is from a speech written for a Fourth of July celebration in London in 1875, but the American ambassador, General Schenck, canceled all speakers after himself. See also note to Will Rogers, below.

6 It could probably be shown by facts and figures that there is no distinctly native American criminal class except Congress.
—Mark Twain, *Pudd'nhead Wilson's New Calendar*, in *Following the Equator*, 1897

7 The new Congressman always spends the first week wondering how he got there and the rest of the time wondering how the other members got there.
—Anonymous, *The Saturday Evening Post*, Nov. 4, 1899

8 [Question to the chaplain of the U.S. Senate:] Dr. Hale, do you pray for the senate? [Answer:] No, I look at the senators and pray for the people.
—Edward Everett Hale, quoted in Van Wyck Brooks, *New England: Indian Summer, 1865–1915* [1940]

★ Hale, best known as the author of *The Man Without a Country*, was a Unitarian minister and served as Senate chaplain from 1903 to his death in 1909. He probably did not mean the remark to be quite as sharp as it reads.

9 No man, however strong, can serve ten years as a schoolmaster, priest, or senator, and remain fit for anything else.
—Henry Adams, *The Education of Henry Adams*, 1907

You can't use tact with a Congressman! A Congressman is a hog! You must take a 1
stick and hit him on the snout!

—**Anonymous,** remark by cabinet member, quoted in Henry Adams, *The Education of Henry Adams*, 1907

★ *Bartlett's* names Jacob Dolson Cox, Secretary of the Interior, as the suspected perpetrator of this unkind comment.

A little group of willful men. 2

—**Woodrow Wilson,** March 1917

★ The president was referring to a dozen senators, led by Wisconsin's Robert M. La Follette, who by filibustering blocked passage of a bill to permit arming of U.S. merchant ships, which were under attack by German submarines. The full charge was, "A little group of willful men representing no opinion but their own have rendered the great government of the United States helpless and contemptible." The Senate subsequently adopted a rule allowing a two-thirds majority vote to cut off a filibuster (changed to a three-fifths majority in 1975).

Now and then an innocent man is sent to the legislature. 3

—**Frank McKinney "Kin" Hubbard,** *Abe Martin's Broadcast*, 1930

★ Folksy, savvy Abe Martin was Hubbard's alter ego.

The thing about my jokes is they don't hurt anybody. . . . But with Congress—every 4
time they make a joke it's a law. And every time they make a law it's a joke.

—**Will Rogers,** in P. J. O'Brien, *Will Rogers, Ambassador of Good Will, Prince of Wit and Wisdom* [1935]

★ Rogers had a lot of fun at the expense of Congress. "There are only a few original jokes," he said, "and most of them are in Congress," also called by Rogers "the national joke factory." Despite this, he believed the American Congress to be the best in the world—in fact, "the best Congress money can buy." See also Mark Twain, above.

People ask me where I get my jokes. Why, I just watch Congress and report the facts. 5

—**Will Rogers,** in Alex Ayres, ed., *The Wit and Wisdom of Will Rogers* [1962]

A congressman's first obligation is to get elected; his second is to get reelected. 6

—**Russell Long,** saying

★ Sen. Long of Louisiana was the son of demagogue-dictator Huey Long, who served as governor and senator.

Don't try to go too fast. Learn your job. Don't ever talk until you know what you're 7
talking about. . . . If you want to get along, go along.

—**Sam Rayburn,** traditional advice, quoted in Neil MacNeil, *Forge of Democracy, the House of Representatives* [1963]

★ U.S. Rep. Sam Rayburn of Texas came to Congress in 1913, and served as Speaker of the House under presidents Roosevelt, Truman, Eisenhower, and Kennedy. He was "Mr. Democrat."

Congress is so strange. A man gets up to speak and says nothing. Nobody listens— 8
and then everybody disagrees.

—**Boris Marshalov,** quoted by Sen. Alexander Wiley, *Laughing with Congress*, 1947

1 If you give Congress a chance to vote on both sides of an issue, it will always do it.
—Les Aspin, interview, *The New York Times*, Dec. 9, 1982

★ Rep. Aspin, a Democrat from Wisconsin, was an influential member of the House Armed Services Committee, and later briefly served as Secretary of Defense.

2 [Today's House of Representatives] where members choose their voters instead of voters choosing their members.
—Cokie Roberts, on *This Week* television news show, Feb. 27, 2005

★ Journalist Roberts said of this change in the character of the House, "It breaks my heart." Her father, Hale Boggs, served as House Majority Leader. After he died in a plane crash in Alaska, her mother, Lindy Boggs, was elected to the House. The change, by the way, has been wrought by gerrymandering.

Connecticut

3 The land of steady habits.
—Anonymous

★ Traditional epithet for Connecticut since the 18th century, perhaps because Connecticut voters so often supported political incumbents. And see Thomas Jefferson's interpretation below.

4 No one that can and will be diligent in this place need fear poverty nor the want of food and raiment.
—Sarah Kemble Knight, *Journal*, Dec. 24, 1704

★ *The Journal of Madam Knight* is one of the best-known colonial American travel diaries. It details the author's trip by horseback from Boston to New York and back during five months in 1704–1705.

5 "Farewell Connecticut," said I, as I passed along the bridge. "I have had a surfeit of your ragged money, rough roads, and enthusiastic people."
—Alexander Hamilton, *Itinerarium*, August 30, 1744

★ This is not the famous Hamilton who was shot by Burr, but an Annapolis physician; see Boston under CITIES for more on him.

6 Connecticut in her blue-laws, laying it down as a principle, that the laws of God should be the laws of man.
—Thomas Jefferson, letter to John Adams, Jan. 24, 1814

7 The last [state] expected to yield its steady habits (which were essentially bigoted in politics as well as religion).
—Thomas Jefferson, letter to Marquis de Lafayette, May 14, 1817

8 'Tis a rough land of earth and stone and tree,
Where breathes no castled lord or cabined slave;
Where thought, and tongues, and hands are bold and free,
And friends will find a welcome, foes a grave;
And where none kneel, save when to Heaven they pray,
Nor even then, unless in their own way.
—Fitz-Greene Halleck, *Connecticut*, c. 1820

I was born and reared in Hartford, in the State of Connecticut—anyway, just over the river in the country. So I am a Yankee of the Yankees—and practical; yes, and nearly barren of sentiment, I suppose—or poetry in other words. 1

—**Mark Twain,** *A Connecticut Yankee in King Arthur's Court*, 1889

The warm, the very warm heart of "New England at its best," such a vast abounding Arcadia of mountains and broad vales and great rivers and large lakes and white villages embowered in prodigious elms and maples. It is extraordinarily beautiful and graceful and idyllic—for America. 2

—**Henry James,** letter to Sir T. H. Warren, May 29, 1911

Little Connecticut, with but 4,800 square miles of area, lies just outside New York City, and is made up, in almost equal parts, of golf links and squalid factory towns. 3

—**H. L. Mencken,** *Americana*, 1925

Aggressive, pervasive, with a foot in every American door, they [Connecticut peddlers] gave the country at large its first clear notions of the New England character. . . . The word *Yankee* came to mean *Connecticut Yankee*, and throughout the Old South, long before Abolition Days, it came to be pronounced "Damyank." 4

—**Odell Shepard,** *Connecticut Past and Present*, 1939

★ Southerners may have picked up the expression from Dutch inhabitants of New York, who referred to Connecticut people as "damn Yankees" as early as 1798. They also used *Yankee* as a verb meaning "to cheat." The word apparently is of Dutch extraction, coming either from the *Jan Kees*, i.e., John Cheese, or *Janke*, Little John. The Yankees themselves did not adopt the term for themselves until 1776; see the song *Yankee Doodle* at AMERICAN & AMERICANS.

Qui transtulit sustinet. 5
He who transplanted still sustains.

—Motto, state of Connecticut

Conscience

See also RELIGION.

Keep Conscience clear, 6
Then never fear.

—**Benjamin Franklin**, *Poor Richard's Almanack*, Nov., 1749

Conscience is the inner voice which warns us somebody may be looking. 7

—**H. L. Mencken,** *A Mencken Chrestomathy*, 1949

I cannot and will not cut my conscience to suit this year's fashions. 8

—**Lillian Hellman,** letter to the chairman of the House Committee on Un-American Activities, May 19, 1952

★ Singer Paul Robeson, also in trouble for leftist views, put it: "I saw no reason my convictions should change with the weather," *Here I Stand*, 1958.

The one thing that doesn't abide by majority rule is a person's conscience. 9

—**Harper Lee,** *To Kill a Mockingbird*, 1960

1 The idea of making the century's great crime look dull is not banal. . . . Banality is the adopted disguise of a very powerful will to abolish conscience.
—**Saul Bellow**, *Mr. Sammler's Planet*, 1970

★ The reference is to the Holocaust; see Arendt at EVIL.

Conservatives

See POLITICS & POLITICIANS.

Consistency

2 A foolish consistency is the hobgoblin of little minds, adored by little statesmen and philosophers and divines. With consistency a great soul simply has nothing to do.
—**Ralph Waldo Emerson,** *Self-Reliance*, in *Essays: First Series*, 1841

★ See also Emerson at MEDIOCRITY and F. Scott Fitzgerald at MIND, THOUGHT, & UNDERSTANDING.

3 Do I contradict myself?
Very well then I contradict myself,
(I am large, I contain multitudes.)
—**Walt Whitman,** *Song of Myself*, in *Leaves of Grass*, 1855

4 Consistency requires you to be as ignorant today as you were a year ago.
—**Bernard Berenson,** *Notebook*, 1892

5 Let it be said that I am right rather than consistent.
—**John Marshall Harlan,** quoted in Tinsley E. Yarbrough, *Judicial Enigma: The First Justice Harlan* [1995]

★ Harlan, a Kentuckian, was referring to his conversion from a supporter of slavery to an advocate of civil rights. See Harlan at THE CONSTITUTION.

6 I don't intend to let anybody make my mind become so set on anything that I can't change it according to to the circumstances and conditions that I happen to find myself in.
—**Malcolm X**, interview, Dec., 1964, in *National Leader* [June 2, 1983]

7 Consistency is only a kind of chastity of the head.
—**Donald Barr**, *Who Pushed Humpty Dumpty?*, 1971

8 I happen to feel that the degree of a person's intelligence is directly reflected by the number of conflicting attitudes she can bring to bear on the same topic.
—**Lisa Alther**, *Kinflicks*, 1976

Constitution, the

See also BILL OF RIGHTS; FREEDOM; FREE SPEECH; PRESS, THE; RIGHTS; SUPREME COURT.

9 I have the happiness to know that it is a rising, and not a setting sun.
—**Benjamin Franklin,** Sept. 17, 1787, as the Constitution was being signed.

★ Franklin referred to a sun that was painted on the back of the chair occupied by George Washington, president of the constitutional convention. Noting to delegates sitting nearby that painters often had trouble distinguishing a rising sun from a setting one, Franklin said that he had "often and often, in the course of the session, looked at that behind the president, without being able to tell whether it was rising or setting." Only now, as the last members signed the document, did he have the happy answer. The observation was recorded by James Madison, whose notes provide the principal record of the convention's debates. Franklin's support of the Constitution had surprised some delegates, because he was known to favor a unicameral legislature. But he urged support for the document, noting that at his age, 81, he had grown to have more respect for the judgment of others. The speech was read for him by James Wilson, because Franklin's voice was too weak to be heard; but his message was eloquent. He explained that he consented to the Constitution, "because I expect no better, and because I am not sure that it is not the best." Franklin expressed the wish that other delegates "who may still have objections to it, would with me, doubt a little of their own infallibility."

We, the people of the United States, in order to form a more perfect union, establish justice, insure domestic tranquillity, provide for the common defense, promote the general welfare, and secure the blessings of liberty to ourselves and our posterity, do ordain and establish this Constitution for the United States of America. **1**

—**Constitution of the United States,** Preamble, Sept. 17, 1787

★ Delegates to the Federal Constitutional Convention signed the great document on this date; it became effective on June 21, 1788, when ratified by the required number of states, nine. The all-important Bill of Rights usually is said to include the first ten amendments, although strictly it is the first nine amendments; all ten amendments were adopted December 15, 1791. James Madison, more than any other delegate, was responsible for the shape of the Constitution as well as the Bill of Rights.

A bill of rights is what the people are entitled to against every government on earth. **2**

—**Thomas Jefferson,** letter to James Madison, Dec. 20, 1787

Our new Constitution is now established, and has an appearance that promises permanency; but in this world nothing can be said to be certain, except death and taxes. **3**

—**Benjamin Franklin,** letter to Jean-Baptiste Leroy, Nov. 13, 1789

In Europe, charters of liberty have been granted by power. America has set the example . . . of power granted by liberty. **4**

—**James Madison,** *Constitution* in *National Gazette,* Jan. 19, 1792

★ This distinction was cited by Supreme Court justice Stephen Breyer in a televised discussion with fellow justice Antonin Scalia on "Foreign Courts and United States Constitutional Law" (American University, C-Span television, Jan. 13, 2005). Breyer said that this passage by the Father of the Constitution served as reminder of a reason for Americans' deep aversion to being subject to a foreign court. Nevertheless, he observed that there are other considerations.

The basis of our political system is the right of the people to make and to alter their constitutions of government. But the constitution which at any time exists, till changed by an explicit and authentic act of the whole people, is sacredly obligatory upon all. **5**

—**George Washington,** Farewell Address, Sept. 17, 1796

1 The independence of judges once destroyed, the Consitution is gone; it is a dead letter.

—**Alexander Hamilton,** speech, New York City Bar Association, Feb. 1802

2 A constitution is framed for ages to come, and is designed to approach immortality as nearly as human institutions can approach it.

—**John Marshall,** *Cohens v. Virginia*, 1821

★ But Chief Justice Marshall also noted that "in a constitution intended to endure for ages to come" there is provision for it "to be adapted to the various CRISES of human affairs," *McCulloch v. Maryland*, 1819.

3 The people made the Constitution, and the people can unmake it.

—**John Marshall,** *Cohens v. Virginia*, 1821

4 It is, Sir, the people's Constitution.

—**Daniel Webster,** speech, U.S. Senate, Jan. 26, 1830

★ More at GOVERNMENT.

5 Let us then stand by the Constitution as it is, and by our country as it is, one, united, and entire. . . . We have one country, one Constitution, and one destiny.

—**Daniel Webster,** speech at Whig party meeting, Niblo's Saloon, New York City, March 15, 1837

6 A convenant with death and an agreement with hell.

—**William Lloyd Garrison,** resolutions of the Massachusetts Anti-Slavery Society, Jan. 27, 1843

★ Garrison, a fierce abolitionist, thus condemned the Constitution, which did not outlaw slavery. He publicly burned a copy of the Constitution on July 4, 1854. See also William Henry Seward below.

7 The Constitution of the United States was made not merely for the generation that then existed, but for posterity—unlimited, undefined, endless, perpetual posterity.

—**Henry Clay,** speech, U.S. Senate, Feb. 6, 1850

8 There is a higher law than the Constitution.

—**William Henry Seward,** speech, U.S. Senate, March 11, 1850

★ Seward, an influential New York abolitionist, and later Secretary of State, in this speech was protesting the Compromise of 1850, a set of bills that included tolerance of slavery in some parts of the U.S.

9 Your Constitution is all sail and no anchor.

—**Thomas Babington, Lord Macaulay,** letter to Thomas Jefferson biographer H. S. Randall, May 23, 1857

10 The [U.S. Constitution] is the most wonderful work ever struck off at a given time by the brain and purpose of man.

—**William Gladstone,** *Kin Beyond the Sea*, in *North American Review*, Sept.–Oct. 1878

★ Gladstone was prime minister of Great Britain four times between 1868 and 1894.

What's the Constitution between friends? **1**

—Timothy J. Campbell, attributed c. 1885

★ The anecdote underlying this story was recounted by Grover Cleveland in *Presidential Problems*, 1904. The story involves a legislator trying to persuade a friend and colleague to vote for a particular measure. When the friend remarked that the bill was unconstitutional, the legislator exclaimed, according to Pres. Cleveland, "What does the Constitution amount to between friends?" The remark is usually attributed to Campbell in the form given above.

Our Constitution is color-blind, and neither knows nor tolerates classes among citizens. In respect of civil rights, all citizens are equal before the law. The humblest is the peer of the most powerful. **2**

—John Marshall Harlan, dissent in *Plessy v. Ferguson*, 1896

★ *Plessy* established, over Harlan's sole dissent, the principle that segregation, or "separate but equal" facilities for blacks and whites, was acceptable under the U.S. Constitution. This was reversed in 1954 in *Brown v. the Board of Education*; see below, and AMERICAN HISTORY: MEMORABLE MOMENTS and RACES & PEOPLES. Harlan's dissent in *Plessy* popularized the phrase "separate but equal." The Louisiana statute that was challenged in this case used the wording "equal but separate," but the terms were commonly reversed. Harlan summarized the statute: "By the Louisiana statute, the validity of which is here involved, all railway companies . . . carrying passengers in that state are required to have separate but equal accommodations for white and colored persons," *ibid.*

The Constitution follows the flag. **3**

—Anonymous, dictum of the Democratic party, c. 1900

★ The Democrats took an anti-imperialist stand in the Spanish-American War, and opposed the acquisition of the Philippines. At the least, they argued, Constitutional rights should be extended to the newly subject people. The Democrats, however, were out of power, and as Mr. Dooley remarked, the Supreme Court could read the election results; see SUPREME COURT.

A constitution . . . is made for people of fundamentally differing views. **4**

—Oliver Wendell Holmes, Jr., *Lochner v. New York*, 1905

It is a fortunate thing for society that the courts do not get the same chance at the Ten Commandments that they do at the Constitution of the United States. **5**

—Philander C. Johnson, *Senator Sorghum's Primer of Politics*, 1906

The Constitution is what the judges say it is. **6**

—Charles Evans Hughes, speech, Elmira, N.Y., May 3, 1907

★ Hughes later had to protest the use of the quotable comment to suggest that constitutional law is a matter of caprice. In the 1907 speech he was speaking of the dignity of the courts: "The judiciary is the safeguard of our liberty and of our property under the Constitution," he said.

The American Constitution, one of the few modern political documents drawn up by men who were forced by the sternest circumstances to think out what they really had to face instead of chopping logic in a university classroom. **7**

—George Bernard Shaw, Preface, *Getting Married*, 1908

1 The best test of truth is the power of the thought to get itself accepted in the competition of the market. . . . That at any rate is the theory of our Constitution. It is an experiment, as all life is an experiment.

—**Oliver Wendell Holmes, Jr.,** *Abrams v. U.S.*, 1919

★ More at FREE SPEECH.

2 The makers of our Constitution . . . conferred, as against the Government, the right to be let alone—the most comprehensive of rights and the right most valued by civilized men.

—**Louis Brandeis,** *Olmstead v. U.S.*, dissenting opinion, 1928

3 If there is any principle of the Constitution that more imperatively calls for attachment than any other it is the principle of free thought—not free thought for those who agree with us but freedom for the thought that we hate.

—**Oliver Wendell Holmes, Jr.,** dissent, *U.S. v. Schwimmer*, 1929

★ The Supreme Court decided 6-3 in this case that Hungarian-born Rosika Schwimmer could not become a U.S. citizen because of her outspoken pacificism. This was Holmes's last great dissent. In 1946, the court reversed itself, deciding in *Girouard v. U.S.* that an applicant for U.S. citizenship did not have to swear to bear arms in the country's defense.

4 Our Constitution is so simple and practical that it is possible always to meet extraordinary needs by changes in emphasis and arrangement without loss of essential form.

—**Franklin D. Roosevelt,** First Inaugural Address, March 4, 1933

5 Under our constitutional system, courts stand against any winds that blow as havens of refuge for those who might otherwise suffer because they are helpless.

—**Hugo L. Black,** *Chambers v. Florida*, 1938

★ More at SUPREME COURT.

6 The United States Constitution has proved itself the most marvelously elastic compilation of rules of government ever written.

—**Franklin D. Roosevelt,** radio address, March 2, 1930

7 If the Constitution is to be construed to mean what the majority at any given period in history wish the Constitution to mean, why a written Constitution and deliberate processes of amendment?

—**Frank J. Hogan,** "Presidential Address," American Bar Association convention, San Francisco, July 10, 1939

★ Hogan, a legendary Washington attorney and insider, was a first cousin to another insider, Sen. James F. Byrnes, who went on to become Secretary of State,

8 If there is any fixed star in our constitutional constellation, it is that no official, high or petty, can prescribe what shall be orthodox politics, nationalism, religion, or other matters of opinion, or force citizens to confess by word or act that faith therein.

—**Robert H. Jackson,** Supreme Court ruling in *West Virginia Department of Education v. Barnette*, 1943

★ The court misspelled the name of the plaintiff, Walter Barnet.

The Constitution does not provide for first and second class citizens. **1**
—**Wendell L. Willkie,** *An American Program*, 1944

The choice is not between order and liberty. It is between liberty with order and anarchy without either. There is danger that, if the Court does not temper its doctrinaire logic with a little practical wisdom, it will convert the constitutional Bill of Rights into a suicide pact. **2**
—**Robert H. Jackson,** *Terminiello v. Chicago,* 1949

Separate educational facilities are inherently unequal. **3**
—**Earl Warren,** *Brown v. Board of Education of Topeka*, May 17, 1954

★ More at AMERICAN HISTORY: MEMORABLE MOMENTS.

The Fifth Amendment is an old friend and a good friend. It is one of the great landmarks in man's struggle to be free of tyranny, to be decent and civilized. **4**
—**William O. Douglas,** *An Almanac of Liberty*, 1954

★ The Fifth Amendment gives people the right not to incriminate themselves and thus reduces the usefulness of statements extracted by violence and threats. Justice Douglas's reminder was timely. In the 1950s, Americans were watching televised Congressional hearings into domestic Communism and gangsterism, and taking the Fifth Amendment had become, in the minds of many, tantamount to pleading guilty. See AMERICAN HISTORY: MEMORABLE MOMENTS for some of the high points of the McCarthy era. See under GOVERNMENT for Douglas on getting government off the backs of people.

Take such proceedings . . . as are necessary and proper to admit to public schools on a rational nondiscriminatory basis with all deliberate speed the parties to these cases. **5**
—**Earl Warren,** *Brown v. Board of Education*, follow-up ruling, 1955

★ The phrase "with all deliberate speed" was apparently suggested by Justice Felix Frankfurter, who had used this wording in a dissenting opinion in 1942 in *Chrysler Corp. v. United States*. Frankfurter was drawing on Justice Oliver Wendell Holmes, Jr., whose decision in *Virginia v. West Virginia*, 1911, included the sentence: "A state cannot be expected to move with the celerity of a private business man; it is enough if it proceeds with all deliberate speed." In a letter written in 1909, Holmes ascribed what he called this "delightful phrase" to the English Chancery. Fred Shapiro, however, editor of *The Oxford Dictionary of American Legal Quotations*, reports that scholars have been unable to verify this attribution. The phrase does appear in Sir Walter Scott's *Rob Roy* (1817) in a legal context and in a 1819 letter from Lord Byron to John Murray. In *The Hound of Heaven*, 1893, Francis Thompson wrote, "And with unperturbèd pace, / Deliberate speed, majestic instancy, / They beat . . . "

If the First Amendment means anything, it means that a state has no business telling a man, sitting alone in his own house, what books he may read or what films he may watch. Our whole constitutional heritage rebels at the thought of giving government the power to control men's minds. **6**
—**Thurgood Marshall,** *Stanley v. Georgia*, 1969

Most of the other provisions in the Bill of Rights protect specific liberties or specific rights of individuals. . . . In contrast, the free-press clause extends protection to an **7**

institution. The publishing business is, in short, the only organized private business that is given explicit constitutional protection.
—**Potter Stewart,** speech, Yale Law School, 1974

Conversation

See also ARGUMENTS; TALK.

1 The music that can deepest reach, / And cure all ill, is cordial speech.
—**Ralph Waldo Emerson,** *Merlin's Song*, in *May-Day and Other Pieces*, 1867

★ A character in A. R. Gurney's play *The Cocktail Hour* (1988) recalls this couplet, and must be deterred from interrupting the conversation to go look it up in *Bartlett's*. The quote, alas, fell from grace and was deleted from the 1992 edition of *Bartlett's*. The moral: never throw out a reference book.

2 Many can argue, not many converse.
—**A. Bronson Alcott,** *Concord Days*, 1872

3 In America, people talk either to say or to listen to *memorable* things—but there is no atmosphere.
—**John Butler Yeats,** letter to Ruth Hart, July 3, 1912

4 In the room the women come and go
Talking of Michelangelo.
—**T. S. Eliot,** *The Love Song of J. Alfred Prufrock*, 1917

5 Most conversations are simply monologues delivered in the presence of a witness.
—**Margaret Millar,** *The Weak-Eyed Bat*, 1942

6 If you can't say anything good about someone—sit right here by me.
—**Alice Roosevelt Longworth,** saying, *The New York Times*, obituary [1979]

★ According to *Bartlett's*, she had this embroidered on a pillow in her sitting room.

7 We do not talk—we bludgeon one another with facts and theories gleaned from cursory readings of newspapers, magazines, and digests.
—**Henry Miller,** *The Shadows*, in *The Air-Conditioned Nightmare*, 1945

8 He believed that the art of conversation was dead. His own small talk, at any rate, was bigger than most people's large.
—**Peter De Vries**, *Comfort Me with Apples*, 1956

9 The opposite of talking isn't listening. The opposite of talking is waiting.
—**Fran Lebowitz**, *Social Studies*, 1981

10 I think men talk to women so they can sleep with them and women sleep with men so they can talk to them.
—**Jay McInerney**, *Brightness Falls*, 1992

Cosmology

See SCIENCE: PHYSICS & COSMOLOGY.

Country Life & People

See also FARMS & FARMERS.

We do not believe any more in the superior innocence and virtue of a rural population. **1**

—**James Fenimore Cooper,** *New York*

They [tree stumps] warmed me twice—once while I was splitting them, and again when they were on the fire. **2**

—**Henry David Thoreau,** "Housewarming," *Walden*, 1854

★ From the proverbial, "Who splits his own wood warms himself twice."

Beneath her torn hat glowed the wealth **3**
Of simple beauty and rustic health.

—**John Greeleaf Whittier,** *Maud Muller*, 1854

I saw the spiders marching through air, **4**
Swimming from tree to tree that mildewed day
In latter August when the hay
Came creaking into the barn.

—**Robert Lowell,** *Mr. Edwards and the Spider*, 1946

★ Mr. Edwards is the 18th-century Calvinist theologian Jonathan Edwards. At about age 12, he wrote his observations of spiders; see NATURE: ANIMALS. For Edwards on moral behavior, see under VIRTUE.

Courage

See also FEAR; HEROES; MILITARY, THE.

The battle, sir, is not to be to the strong alone; it is to the vigilant, the active, the brave. **5**

—**Patrick Henry,** speech, Virginia Convention, March 23, 1775

One man with courage makes a majority. **6**

—**Andrew Jackson,** saying

★ See also Henry David Thoreau and Wendell Phillips at MAJORITIES & MINORITIES, and Calvin Coolidge at LAW.

Courage is resistance to fear, mastery of fear—not absence of fear. **7**

—**Mark Twain,** *Pudd'nhead Wilson's Calendar* in *Pudd'nhead Wilson*, 1894

★ See Twain at ETHICS & MORALITY for moral versus physical courage.

Courage is the price that life exacts for granting peace. **8**
The soul that knows it not, knows no release

From little things;
Knows not the livid loneliness of fear,
Nor mountain heights where bitter joy can hear
The sound of wings.
    —**Amelia Earhart,** *Courage*

★ Her plane went down in 1937. See also Charles Lindbergh at ADVENTURE.

1 Courage doesn't always roar. Sometimes courage is the quiet voice at the end of the day saying, "I will try again tomorrow."
    —**Mary Anne Radmacher,** poster, c. 2000

Craftiness

See also WISDOM, WORDS OF.

2 Many foxes grow gray, but few grow good.
    —**Benjamin Franklin,** *Poor Richard's Almanack*, 1749

3 The best place to hide anything is in plain view.
    —**Edgar Allan Poe,** *The Purloined Letter*, 1844

4 A good memory is often a great help; but knowing just when to forget things sometimes counts for more.
    —**Philander C. Johnson;** *Senator Sorghum's Primer of Politics*, 1906

5 Never write if you can speak; never speak if you can nod; never nod if you can wink.
    —**Martin M. Lomasney,** saying, in *The Boston Mahatma*, Stephen James Lomasney, Internet posting [1998]

★ Lomasney was a legendary Boston political boss, serving variously as an alderman, state representative, and state senator for nearly forty years, starting in 1892. This advice to fellow pols also has been attributed to him in slightly condensed form: "Don't write when you can talk; don't talk when you can nod your head." See also Earl Long below.

6 Never fight fair with a stranger, boy. You'll never get out of the jungle that way.
    —**Arthur Miller,** *Death of a Salesman*, 1949

7 Never put anything in writing that you can convey by a wink or a nod.
    —**Earl Long,** saying

★ Gov. Earl Long of Louisiana was Huey Long's younger brother. A. J. Liebling's marvelous account of the zany 1959 gubernatorial race in *The Earl of Louisiana* (1962) reveals Earl as in part a shrewd liberal, even on racial issues, in the guise of a semidemented good old boy. See also Martin Lomasney above.

8 Guile, vanity, dissembling . . . might be unattractive habits, but to the leader, they can be essential. He needs guile in order to hold together the shifting coalitions of often bitterly opposed interest groups that governing requires. He needs a certain measure of vanity in order to create the right public impression. He sometimes has to dissemble in order to prevail on crucial issues.
    —**Richard M. Nixon**, *Leaders*, 1982

Crime, Criminals, & Detectives

See also DANGER & DANGEROUS PEOPLE; EVIDENCE; LAW.

Character is always known. Thefts never enrich; alms never impoverish; murder will **1**
speak out of stone walls.

—Ralph Waldo Emerson; commencement address, Harvard Divinity School, 1838

★ The belief that murder will out, and even stones will bear witness is found in the Bible: "The stone shall cry out of the wall," *Habakkuk* 2:11 and *Luke* 19:14. Chaucer observed, "Mordre wol out, certeyn, it wol nat not faille," in "The Prioress's Tale," from the *Canterbury Tales*. Shakespeare wrote in *Macbeth*, "The very stones prate of my whereabout," II, i; and "Blood will have blood. / Stones have been known to move and trees to speak," III, iv. The thought that murder will out is expressed also in *Hamlet*, II, ii; *The Merchant of Venice*, II, ii; and in *Richard III*, I, iv. Prior to Shakespeare, John Webster, in *The Duchess of Malfi*, focused on the horror of murder: "Other sins only speak; murder shrieks out."

Commit a crime and the world is made of glass. **2**

—Ralph Waldo Emerson, *Compensation*, in *Essays: First Series*, 1841

The rich rob the poor, and the poor rob one another. **3**

—Sojourner Truth, saying, c. 1850

Frankie and Johnny were lovers, lordee, and how they could love, **4**
Swore to be true to each other, true as the stars above;
He was her man, but he done her wrong.

—Anonymous, ballad, c. 1840–90

★ Frankie discovers Johnny's infidelity. She shoots him with a forty-five revolver, and is hanged for the crime; see below. Many versions exist of this folk ballad, which Carl Sandburg called America's "classical gutter song." Frankie is a prostitute, and Johnny (or Albert or Allen) is her fancy man, who two-times her with Alice Fly (or Bly). The ballad has provided the plots for plays (notably by Mae West and John Huston), several films, and a ballet.

The sheriff took Frankie to the gallows, **5**
Hung her until she died;
They hung her for killing Johnny,
And the undertaker waited outside;
She killed her man, 'cause he done her wrong.

—Ibid.

We never sleep. **6**

—Allan Pinkerton; motto of the Pinkerton Agency, c. 1855

★ Known from its earliest days as "the Eye," the agency is apparently the origin of the phrase "private eye," meaning detective. Pinkerton also played a public role. Learning of a conspiracy to assassinate Lincoln en route to Washington for his inaugural, Pinkerton escorted the president-elect to the capital under cover of night. During the Civil War, he organized the U.S. Secret Service and ran espionage operations behind Confederate lines.

1 Let no guilty man escape.

—**Ulysses S. Grant,** July 29, 1875

★ Pres. Grant issued this order after learning the evidence concerning the malfeasance of the Whiskey Ring, a conspiracy of federal officials and distillers that cost the government millions of dollars in revenues.

2 Oh, the dirty little coward
That shot Mr. Howard,
Has laid poor Jesse in his grave.

—**Anonymous,** *The Ballad of Jesse James*, 1882

★ Robert Ford, in conspiracy with his brother Charles, shot Jesse James in the back of the head, on April 3, 1882. The Fords were members of the James gang, but had made a deal with the governor of Missouri to betray Jesse in return for amnesty and a $10,000 reward. Jesse was living in St. Joseph, Mo., under the alias of Thomas Howard. He was unarmed, standing on a chair, straightening a picture at the time of his death. Ford came to be despised for an act that was seemingly a favor to the body politic. Jesse's brother Frank surrendered, stood two trials, managed to get off both times, and died in 1915. The words of the ballad are echoed in the line that Jesse's mother had inscribed on her son's tombstone: "Murdered by a Traitor and Coward Whose Name Is Not Worthy to Appear Here."

3 Where justice is denied, where poverty is enforced, where ignorance prevails, and where any one class is made to feel that society is in an organized conspiracy to oppress, rob, and degrade them, neither persons nor property will be safe.

—**Frederick Douglass,** speech, 24th anniversary of Emancipation, Washington, D.C., April 1886

4 Early one June morning in 1872, I murdered my father—an act which made a deep impression on me at the time.

—**Ambrose Bierce,** *An Imperfect Conflagration*, 1886

5 Lizzie Borden took an ax
And gave her mother forty whacks.
When she saw what she had done,
She gave her father forty-one!

—**Anonymous,** 1893

★ Lizzie Borden was acquitted of the murder of her parents in a jury trial in June 1893 in her hometown of Falls River, Mass. People have been second-guessing the jury ever since, but at the time it wasn't even a close call. The jury came to their verdict in a little over an hour, and there was applause in the courtroom when it was announced. The jury may have been biased; or, if the verdict was correct, the murderer may have been the family maid.

6 Given a child falling into a river, an old person in a burning building, and a woman fainting in the street, a band of convicts would risk their lives to give aid as quickly at least as a band of millionaires.

—**Clarence Darrow,** *Resist Not Evil*, 1903

[Definition of "honest graft"]: I seen my opportunities and I took 'em. 1

—**George Washington Plunkitt,** quoted in William L. Riordan, *Plunkitt of Tammany Hall* [1905]

★ Dishonest graft, by Plunkitt's standards, consisted of "blackmailin' gamblers, saloonkeepers, disorderly people, etc." Plunkitt's "honest graft" was merely getting inside information. or "tips,"that abled him to make profits in real estate, contracting, and other businesses. See also Plunkitt at EPITAPHS & GRAVESTONES.

It was beautiful and simple, as all truly great swindles are. 2

—**O. Henry,** *The Octopus Marooned*, in *The Gentle Grifter,* 1908

Lack of respect for law is characteristic of the American people as a whole. Until we 3
acquire a vastly increased sense of civic duty we should not complain that crime is increasing or the law ineffective.

—**Arthur Train,** *Courts and Criminals*, 1912

While there is a lower class, I am in it. While there is a criminal class, I am of it. 4
While there is a soul in prison, I am not free.

—**Eugene Debs,** statement during trial on charges of violating the 1917 Espionage Act, June 16, 1918

★ The great Socialist leader was in jail twice, once following the Pullman strike of 1894 and again when convicted at this trial. He was the sort of man who made friends with wardens and inmates alike. His fellow-Hoosier and friend, poet James Whitcomb Riley, wrote of him, "And there's 'Gene Debs—a man 'at stands / And jes' holds out in his two hands / As warm a heart as ever beat / Betwixt here and the Jedgement Seat." And similarly, "God was feeling mighty good when He created 'Gene Debs, and He didn't have anything else to do all day."

It's awful hard to get people interested in corruption unless they can get some of it. 5

—**Will Rogers,** *Weekly Articles*, April 22, 1928

Any man might do a girl in 6
Any man has to, needs to want to
Once in a lifetime, do a girl in.

—**T. S. Eliot,** *Sweeney Agonistes*, 1932

Well, as through this world I ramble, 7
I've seen lots of funny men;
Some will rob you with a six-gun,
And some with a fountain pen.

—**Woody Guthrie,** *Pretty Boy Floyd,* c.1932

★ Actually, Charles Arthur "Pretty Boy" Floyd favored a machine gun. He held up so many banks in the Southwest that he became something of a folk hero to the many Okies whose mortgages had been foreclosed. He also killed at least a half dozen people before he himself was gunned down by the FBI in 1934.

They shoot horses, don't they? 8

—**Horace McCoy,** *They Shoot Horses, Don't They?*, 1935

★ Response to a police query: "Why did you kill her?"

1 Knights had no meaning in this game. It wasn't a game for knights.

—Raymond Chandler, *The Big Sleep*, 1939

★ See also Chandler at Heroes.

2 Round up the usual suspects.

—Julius Epstein, Philip Epstein, & Howard Koch, *Casablanca*, screenplay, 1942

3 Crime does not pay—enough.

—Clayton Rawson, motto of the Mystery Writers of America, 1945

4 [Q.] Why do you rob banks?

[A.] Because that's where the money is.

—Willie Sutton, attributed

★ Sutton, a notorious bank robber, is said to have given this response to a reporter's query. He drew on the quote for the title of his autobiography, *Where the Money Was* (1976), but denied that the words were actually his. "The credit belongs to some enterprising reporter who apparently felt a need to fill out his copy," he said.

5 Down these mean streets must go a man who is not himself mean; who is neither tarnished nor afraid.

—Raymond Chandler, *The Simple Art of Murder*, 1950

★ More at HEROES.

6 Crime is only a left-handed form of human endeavor.

—Ben Maddow & John Huston, *The Asphalt Jungle*, 1950

★ Classic film noir, from the novel by W. R. Burnett. Huston also directed.

7 I never cheated an honest man, only rascals. They may have been respectable but they were never any good. They wanted something for nothing. I gave them nothing for something.

—Joseph "Yellow Kid" Weil, in Jay Robert Nash, *Bloodletters and Bad Men* [1973]

★ Arguably the greatest con man in American history, Weil got his moniker because of his well known fondness for the comic strip, "Hogan's Alley," featuring a character named The Yellow Kid. The dandyish Weil, always well-dressed, with pince nez and well-combed beard, swindled his way across the country from about 1900 to 1934, when he retired, so he said, because he had become so famous that he could no longer enter a town without attracting the attention of local police. He spent some time in jail over the course of his career but not as much as he might have since, as he noted here, the people he cheated were also trying to beat the system, leaving them in poor position to complain after realizing that they had been fleeced.

8 Most people never have to face the fact that at the right time and right place, they're capable of anything.

—Robert Towne, *Chinatown* screenplay, 1974

If you can't do the time, don't do the crime. 1
—**Anonymous,** saying among criminals, cops, judges, etc.

★ Cited in Ed McBain, *Heat*, 1981, among many sources.

I don't know what it says about human nature, but there are few activities more stimulating than planning a crime. 2
—**Robert Plunket,** book review, *The New York Times*, Oct. 6, 1991

I love murder—always one less witness to worry about. 3
—**Murray Richman,** quoted in *The New Yorker*, Feb. 19 & 26, 2002

★ New York City defense attorney Richman was profiled in *The New Yorker*. He elaborated that murder is "assault without a witness"—at least the most important witness—and therefore, "It's defendable."

Crises

See BAD TIMES; PROBLEMS; TROUBLE.

Criticism

See also ART: CRITICISM.

He that criticizes out of Passion raises Revenge sooner than Repentance. 4
—**William Penn,** *Some Fruits of Solitude*, 1693

Don't throw stones at your neighbours, if your own windows are glass. 5
—**Benjamin Franklin,** *Poor Richard's Almanack*, August 1736

★ Proverbial.

I find the pain of a little censure, even when it is unfounded, is more acute than the pleasure of much praise. 6
—**Thomas Jefferson,** letter to Francis Hopkinson, March 13, 1789

If both factions, or neither, shall abuse you, you will probably be about right. Beware of being assailed by one and praised by the other. 7
—**Abraham Lincoln,** letter to Gen. John M. Schofield, May 27, 1863

It is not the critic who counts. 8
—**Theodore Roosevelt,** speech, the Sorbonne, Paris, France, April 23, 1910

★ More at ACTION & DOING.

A remark generally hurts in proportion to its truth. 9
—**Will Rogers,** in Alex Ayres, ed., *The Wit and Wisdom of Will Rogers* [1933]

★ Proverbial. For example in Thomas Fuller's 1632 compilation of proverbs, it is given as: "The Sting of Reproach is the Truth of it."

If any has a stone to throw 10
It is not I, ever or now.
—**Elinor Hoyt Wylie,** *The Pebble*, in *Collected Poems* [1932]

1 There is so much good in the worst of us,
And so much bad in the best of us,
That it ill behooves any of us
To find fault with the rest of us.
—Anonymous

2 Most people believe that, if any shot goes unanswered, it must be true.
—Chris Matthews, *Hardball: How Politics Is Played—Told by One Who Knows the Game*, 1988

Custom

See HABIT & CUSTOM.

Dakota Territory

See also NORTH DAKOTA; SOUTH DAKOTA.

3 O Dakota land, sweet Dakota land
As on thy burning soil I stand
And look away across the plains,
I wonder why it never rains,
Till Gabriel blows his trumpet sound
And says the rain has gone around.
We don't live here; we only stay
Cause we're too poor to get away.
—Anonymous, *O Dakota Land,* song

★ Dakota Territory, which included parts of present-day Montana and Wyoming, was acquired in the Louisiana Purchase. It was organized as an official Territory in 1861; in 1863 its boundaries were adjusted, and the resulting tract was incorporated into the Union in 1889 as two states, North and South Dakota. This song exists in many versions, sometimes complaining of drought, sometimes floods and always poverty. But humor prevails. One verse common to all versions runs on the lines, "Our chickens are too poor to eat,/ They've scratched the toes right off their feet." The conclusion is "Dakota . . . we think you're a honey." The lyrics sung to "Oh, Tannenbaum [Christmas Tree]." For the drought and farm failures in the Dakotas in the 1890s, see at BAD TIMES the quote from *On the Way Home*, 1962, by Rose Wilder Lane and Laura Ingalls Wilder.

Danger & Dangerous People

See also ADVENTURE; CRIME, CRIMINALS, & DETECTIVES; EVIL; RUTHLESSNESS; SECURITY & SAFETY; VIOLENCE.

4 Men who are familiarized to danger, meet it without shrinking, whereas those who have never seen service often apprehend danger where no danger lies.
—George Washington, letter to the president of the Continental Congress, Feb. 9, 1776

I will cut your throat whilst you are sleeping. . . . You know me! Look out! 1
—**Junius Brutus Booth,** letter to Pres. Andrew Jackson, July 4, 1835

★ Booth, a talented but unstable actor—his fencing in the roles of Hamlet and Richard III sometimes forced other actors to fight for their lives—was the son of an actor and the father of three actors: Junius Brutus, Edwin, and John Wilkes Booth, the assassin of Abraham Lincoln. Jackson was the first American president to face an assassination attempt. On January 30, 1835, during a funeral at the Capitol building, Richard Lawrence, an insane, unemployed house painter, shot twice at the president with two different pistols from close range. It was a damp day and the gunpowder failed to ignite.

I never quarrel, sir. But sometimes I fight, sir, and whenever I fight, sir, a funeral 2
follows.
—**Thomas Hart Benton,** remark in the U.S. Senate, 1850

★ Benton represented Missouri in the Senate 1821–51, and in the House 1853–55. He was eventually defeated for supporting the Union against the South. The painter of the same name was his grandnephew.

As soon as there is life, there is danger. 3
—**Ralph Waldo Emerson,** *Public and Private Education*, speech, Parker Fraternity, Boston, Mass., Nov. 27, 1864

When you call me that, *smile*. 4
—**Owen Wister,** *The Virginian*, 1902

★ A line in the all-American tradition that recently brought us Dirty Harry's "Make my day"; see Joseph Stinson below. The Virginian, too, was a gunslinger: "Trampas spoke: 'Your bet, you son-of-a——.' The Virginian's pistol came out, and his hand lay on the table, holding it unaimed. And with a voice as gentle as ever . . . he issued his orders to the man Trampas:—'When you call me that, *smile*.' " The line was immortalized for later generations by Gary Cooper in the film that was made from the book in 1929.

I acknowledge the Furies, I believe in them. I have heard the disastrous beating of 5
their wings.
—**Theodore Dreiser,** *To Grant Richards*, 1911

A good many things go around in the dark besides Santa Claus. 6
—**Herbert Hoover,** speech at the John Marshall Republican Club, St. Louis, Mo., Dec. 16, 1935

Considering how dangerous everything is, nothing is really very frightening. 7
—**Gertrude Stein,** *Everybody's Autobiography*, 1937

I'll get you, my pretty, and your little dog, too.
—**Noel Langley, Florence Ryerson, & Edgar Allan Wolfe,** *The Wizard of Oz*, 8
screenplay, 1939

★ The Wicked Witch of the West, played by Margaret Hamilton, in a memorable threat to Dorothy.

1 Even a man who's pure in heart
And says his prayers at night
May become a wolf when the wolfbane blooms
And the autumn moon is bright.

—Curt Siodmak, filmscript, *The Wolf Man*, 1941

★ The verse has been attributed to Gypsy folklore, but Siodmak actually made it up, along with the bits about the full moon and silver bullets that have since become part of the popular notion of the wolf-man.

2 On nights like that . . . meek little wives feel the edge of the carving knife and study their husbands' necks. Anything can happen.

—Raymond Chandler, *Red Wind*, 1946

3 God Forgives, Outlaws Don't.

—Anonymous, gravestone for motorcyclist killed in 1977 in Vietnam

4 There is no more exhilarating feeling than being shot at without result.

—Ronald Reagan, 1981

★ Pres. Reagan tended to borrow lines as needed. In this case, after he was wounded by a would-be assassin, he drew on Winston Churchill's "Nothing is more exhilarating as to be shot at without result," *The Story of the Malakan Field Force*, 1898. In a less literary allusion, he told his wife Nancy, when she rushed to his side in the hospital, that he should have ducked—see Jack Dempsey at SPORTS. See also under WAR for George Washington's reaction to bullets whistling.

5 Go ahead, make my day.

—Joseph C. Stinson, *Sudden Impact*, 1983

★ Clint Eastwood as tough cop Dirty Harry challenges a bad guy to make a move. Pres. Ronald Reagan used the line to threaten legislators who favored tax increases; see TAXES. The expression "make my day" is of some antiquity. For example, in 1936, P.G. Wodehouse wrote, "That will just make my day," *The Luck of the Bodkins*; and in 1908, Florence Louisa Barclay wrote in *The Rosary*, "I knew her presence made my day, and her absence meant the chill of night." Hollywood writer Dean Riesner claimed that he originated the Eastwood line for the 1976 movie *The Enforcer*, although the line was not used there.

6 When you're dancing with a bear, you have to make sure you don't get tired and sit down. You've got to wait till the bear is tired before you get a rest.

—Joycelyn Elders, quoted in *The New York Times*, Sept. 14, 1993

★ Dr. Elders was appointed Surgeon General by Pres. Bill Clinton. An outspoken African-American, she was controversial from the beginning, and was fired for comments on sex education in which she appeared to support teaching masturbation.

7 First rule of the witch hunt, don't limit yourself to witches.

—Dan Dworkin & Jay Beattie, *Cold Case* television show, Nov. 21, 2004

★ The story concerned the murder of a communist sympathizer in 1953, when investigation of "Reds" was beginning to be seen as a witch hunt.

Death

See also Epitaphs & Gravestones; Last Words.

Xerxes the Great did die, 1
And so must you and I.
—New England Primer, c. 1688

Death is but crossing the world, as friends do the seas; they live in one another still. 2
—William Penn, *Some Fruits of Solitude*, 1693

Death observes no ceremony. 3
—John Wise, *A Vindication of the Government of New England Churches*, 1717

★ Rev. Wise knew death and danger well. He served as chaplain on two military expeditions. He was later imprisoned for a tax protest, and took up the cause of the victims in the Salem witch trial.

A man is not completely born until he is dead. Why then should we grieve that a new 4
child is born among the immortals, a new member added to their happy society?
—Benjamin Franklin; letter to Miss E. Hubbard, Feb. 23, 1756

★ Hubbard was the stepdaughter of Franklin's late brother John. The letter reveals an aspect of Franklin that he did not often show in public. He went on to console her with another metaphor: "Our friend and we are invited abroad on a party of pleasure, which is to last for ever. His chair was ready first, and he is gone before us. We could not all conveniently start together; and why should you and I be grieved at this, since we are soon to follow, and know where to find him?"

I die hard but I am not afraid to go. 5
—George Washington, on his deathbed, Dec. 14, 1799

★ Washington said these words to Dr. James Craik, his old and friend and neighbor, and also his physician. He died the same day, a little before midnight; see Last Words.

Our machines have now been running seventy or eighty years, and we must expect 6
that, worn as they are, here a pivot, there a wheel, now a pinion, next a spring, will be giving way; and however we may tinker them up for a while, all will at length surcease motion.
—Thomas Jefferson, letter to John Adams, July 15, 1814

★ See also Jefferson at Seasons & Times.

This fever called "living" is conquered at last. 7
—Edgar Allan Poe, *For Annie*, 1849

There is no death, only a change of worlds. 8
—Seattle, speech, c. 1854, in W. C. Vanderwerth, ed., *Famous Speeches by Noted Indian Chieftans* [1971]

The long mysterious Exodus of death. 9
—Henry Wadsworth Longfellow, *The Jewish Cemetery at Newport*, 1858

1 Because I could not stop for Death—
He kindly stopped for me—
The Carriage held but just Ourselves—
And Immortality.
—**Emily Dickinson,** poem no. 712, c. 1863

2 The report of my death was an exaggeration.
—**Mark Twain,** June 1892

★ For more see THE PRESS.

3 The nearest friends can go
With anyone to death, comes so far short
They might as well not try to go at all.
—**Robert Frost,** *Home Burial*, 1914

4 I have a rendezvous with death
At some disputed barricade.
—**Alan Seeger,** *I Have a Rendezvous with Death*, 1916

★ More at WORLD WAR I.

5 So here it is at last, the distinguished thing.
—**Henry James,** on his approaching death, 1916, in Edith Wharton, *A Backward Glance* [1934]

6 It costs me never a stab nor squirm
To tread by chance upon a worm.
"Aha, my little dear," I say,
"Your clan will pay me back some day."
—**Dorothy Parker,** *Thoughts for a Sunshiny Morning*, in *Sunset Gun*, 1928

7 Of all escape mechanisms, death is the most efficient.
—**H. L. Mencken,** *A Book of Burlesques*, 1928

8 Down, down, down into the darkness of the grave
Gently they go, the beautiful, the tender, the kind,
Quietly they go, the intelligent, the witty, the brave
I know. But I do not approve. And I am not resigned.
—**Edna St. Vincent Millay,** *Dirge Without Music*, 1928

9 Why can't the dead die!
—**Eugene O'Neill,** *Mourning Becomes Electra*, 1931

10 Look, Daddy, Teacher says every time a bell rings an angel gets his wings.
—**Frances Goodrich, Albert Hackett, & Jo Swerling,** *It's a Wonderful Life*, 1946

★ The concluding line of the great Frank Capra film. The script was based on a short story, *The Greatest Gift*, by Philip Van Doren Stern, originally written by Stern as a Christmas card.

Life is a great surprise. I do not see why death should not be an even greater one. **1**

—Vladimir Nabokov, *Pale Fire,* 1962

Dying **2**
Is an art, like everything else

—Sylvia Plath, *Lady Lazarus*, 1962–63

★ More at SUICIDE.

It's not that I'm afraid to die. I just don't want to be there when it happens. **3**

—Woody Allen, *Death (A Play)*, in *Without Feathers*, 1975

★ In *The Early Essays* in the same collection, Allen pointed out, "On the plus side, death is one of the few things that can be done as easily lying down."

I often wonder how I'm going to die. You don't want to embarrass friends. **4**

—Cary Grant, quoted in *Variety*, Dec. 6, 1983

★ He didn't. A trouper to the end, the debonair Grant died of a massive stroke, aged 82, hours after a rehearsal for an appearance at the Adler Theater in, of all places, Davenport, Ia.

And again the dead have found **5**
a way into the hearts we swore were stone.

—Philip Levine, *Breath*, 2004

Decision

See also BOLDNESS & INITIATIVE; INDECISION; REGRET (Robert Frost).

If someone tells you that he is going to make a 'realistic decision,' you immediately understand that he has resolved to do something bad. **6**

—Mary McCarthy, *American Realistic Playwrights*, in *On the Contrary*, 1961

The rarest gift that God bestows on man is the capacity for decision. **7**

—Dean Acheson, speech, Freedom House, New York City, April 13, 1965

No decision has been made unless carrying it out in specific steps has become someone's work assignment and responsibility. **8**

—Peter F. Drucker, *The Effective Executive*, 1967

The understanding that underlies the right decision grows out of the clash and conflict of opinions and out of the serious consderation of competing alternatives. **9**

—Peter F. Drucker, *Management: Tasks, Responsibiliies, Practices*, 1974

Most important decisions in corporate life are made by individuals, not by committees. My policy always has been to be democratic all the way to the point of decision. Then I become the ruthless commander. "Okay, I've heard everybody," I say. "Now here's what we're going to do." **10**

—Lee Iacocca, with William Novak, *Iacocca: An Autobiography*, 1984

★ Iacocca had the distinction of seving both as president of Ford Motor Co. (1970–78) and then as president (1978–79) and chairman of rival Chrysler Corp.

1 The key is not to make quick decisions but to make timely decisions.
—Colin L. Powell, *My American Journey*, 1995

★ While chairman of the joint chiefs of staff (1989–93), Powell devised a formula, P = 40 to 70, where P stands for probability of success and the numbers represent the percentage of information needed for making a decision. "I don't act if I only have enough information to give me a less than 40 percent chance of being right," he said. "And I don't wait until I have enough facts to be 100 percent sure of being right, because by then it is almost always too late."

2 Most decisions are seat-of-the-pants judgments. You can create a rationale for anything. In the end, most decisions are based on intuition and faith.
—Nathan Myhrvold, observation, in Ken Auletta, *The Microsoft Provocateur*, in *The New Yorker*, May 12, 1997

★ Mr. Myhrvold was chief technology officer of Microsoft Corp. at the time.

Declaration of Independence

See also American Revolution; Independence Day.

3 Resolved: That these united colonies are, and of right ought to be, free and independent states.
—Richard Henry Lee, resolution presented at the Continental Congress, June 7, 1776

★ This resolution, introduced by Lee of Virginia and seconded by John Adams of Massachusetts, led to the Declaration of Independence.

The Declaration of Independence

4 When in the course of human events, it becomes necessary for one people to dissolve the political bands which have connected them with another, and to assume among the powers of the earth, the separate and equal station to which the Laws of Nature and Nature's God entitle them, a decent respect to the opinions of mankind requires that they should declare the causes which impel them to the separation.

We hold these truths to be self-evident, that all men are created equal, that they are endowed by their Creator with certain unalienable rights, that among these are life, liberty and the pursuit of happiness.—That to secure these rights, governments are instituted among men, deriving their just powers from the consent of the governed,—That whenever any form of government becomes destructive of these ends, it is the right of the people to alter or to abolish it, and to institute new government, laying its foundation on such principles and organizing its powers in such form, as to them shall seem most likely to effect their safety and happiness. Prudence, indeed, will dictate that governments long established should not be changed for light and transient causes; and accordingly all experience hath shown, that mankind are more disposed to suffer, while evils are sufferable, than to right themselves by abolishing the forms to which they are accustomed. But when a long train of abuses and usurpations, pursuing invariably the same object evinces a design to reduce them under absolute despotism, it is their right, it is their duty, to throw off such government, and to provide new guards for their future security.—Such has been the patient sufferance of these Colonies; and such is now the necessity which constrains them to alter their former Systems of Government. The history of the present King of Great Britain is a history of repeated injuries and usurpations, all having in direct object the establishment of an absolute tyranny over these States. To prove this, let facts be submitted to a candid world.

He has refused his assent to laws, the most wholesome and necessary for the public good.

He has forbidden his Governors to pass laws of immediate and pressing importance, unless suspended in their operation till his assent shall be obtained; and when so suspended, he has utterly neglected to attend to them.

He has refused to pass other laws for the accommodation of large districts of people, unless those people would relinquish the right of representation in the Legislature, a right inestimable to them and formidable to tyrants only.

He has called together legislative bodies at places unusual, uncomfortable, and distant from the depository of their public records, for the sole purpose of fatiguing them into compliance with his measures.

He has dissolved representative houses repeatedly, for opposing with manly firmness his invasions on the rights of the people.

He has refused for a long time, after such dissolutions, to cause others to be elected; whereby the legislative powers, incapable of annihilation, have returned to the people at large for their exercise; the State remaining in the mean time exposed to all the dangers of invasion from without, and convulsions within.

He has endeavored to prevent the population of these States; for that purpose obstructing the laws for naturalization of foreigners; refusing to pass others to encourage their migration hither, and raising the conditions of new appropriations of lands.

He has obstructed the administration of justice, by refusing his assent to laws for establishing judiciary powers.

He has made judges dependent on his will alone, for the tenure of their offices, and the amount and payment of their salaries.

He has erected a multitude of new offices, and sent hither swarms of officers to harass our people, and eat out their substance.

He kept among us, in times of peace, standing armies, without the consent of our legislatures.

He has affected to render the military independent of and superior to civil power.

He has combined with others to subject us to a jurisdiction foreign to our constitution, and unacknowledged by our laws; giving his assent to their acts of pretended legislation:

For quartering large bodies of armed troops among us:

For protecting them, by a mock trial, from punishment for any murders which they should commit on the inhabitants of these States.

For cutting off our trade with all parts of the world:

For imposing taxes on us without our consent:

For depriving us in many cases, of benefits of trial by jury:

For transporting us beyond seas to be tried for pretended offences:

For abolishing the free system of English laws in a neighbouring Province, establishing therein an arbitrary government, and enlarging its boundaries so as to render it at once an example and fit instrument for introducing the same absolute rule into these Colonies:

For taking away our Charters, abolishing our most valuable laws, and altering fundamentally the forms of our governments:

For suspending our own Legislatures, and declaring themselves invested with power to legislate for us in all cases whatsoever.

He has abdicated government here, by declaring us out of his protection and waging war against us.

He has plundered our seas, ravaged our coasts, burnt our towns, and destroyed the lives of our people.

He is at this time transporting large armies of foreign mercenaries to complete the works of death, desolation and tyranny, already begun with circumstances of cruelty & perfidy scarcely paralleled in the most barbarous ages, and totally unworthy the head of a civilized nation.

He has constrained our fellow citizens taken captive on the high seas to bear arms against their country, to become the executioners of their friends and brethren, or to fall themselves to their hands.

He has excited domestic insurrections amongst us, and has endeavoured to bring on the inhabitants of our frontiers, the merciless Indian savages, whose known rule of warfare, is an undistinguished destruction of all ages, sexes and conditions.

In every stage of these oppressions we have petitioned for redress in the most humble terms: Our repeated petitions have been answered only by repeated injury. A prince, whose character is thus marked by every act which may define a tyrant, is unfit to be the ruler of a free people.

Nor have we been wanting in attention to our British brethren. We have warned them from time to time of attempts by their legislature to extend an unwarrantable jurisdiction over us. We have reminded them of the circumstances of our emigration and settlement here. We have appealed to their native justice and magnanimity, and we have conjured them by the ties of our common kindred to disavow these usurpations, which, would inevitably interrupt our connections and correspondence. They too have been deaf to the voice of justice and of consanguinity. We must, therefore, acquiesce in the necessity, which denounces our separation, and hold them, as we hold the rest of mankind, enemies in war, in Peace Friends.—

We, Therefore, the *Representatives* of the *United States of America*, in General Congress, assembled, appealing to the Supreme Judge of the world for the rectitude of our intentions, do, in the name, and by authority of the good people of these Colonies, solemnly publish and declare, That these United Colonies are, and of right ought to be *Free and Independent States*; that they are absolved from all allegiance to the British Crown, and that all political connection between them and the State of Great Britain, is and ought to be totally dissolved; and that as Free and Independent States, they have full power to levy war, conclude peace, contract alliances, establish commerce, and to do all other acts and things which Independent States may of right do.—And for the support of this Declaration, with a firm reliance on the protection of Divine Providence, we mutually pledge to each other our lives, our fortunes and our sacred honor.

—**Thomas Jefferson,** July 4, 1776

★ In the opening section, Jefferson had written, "We hold these truths to be sacred and undeniable." Benjamin Franklin, a good editor, substituted "self-evident." Nearly a century earlier, John Locke, whose writings had been studied by most delegates to the Continental Congress, had declared that all men had rights to life, liberty, and property. The idea that a good government should promote happiness of the governed was not original to Jefferson, but his substitution of "pursuit of happiness" for "property" in the traditional Lockean formulation put a distinctively American imprint on the Declaration—and on the newborn nation itself.

We must indeed all hang together, or most assuredly we shall all hang separately. 1

—**Benjamin Franklin,** 1776

★ Dark humor from Franklin during the signing of the Declaration of Independence. According to tradition, Franklin said this in response to John Hancock's comment, "We must all be unanimous; there must be no pulling different ways; we must all hang together." The attribution, however, is rather late, dating from c. 1840.

Delaware

Delaware is like a diamond, diminutive, but having within it inherent value. 2

—**John Lofland,** 1847, quoted in Federal Writers' Project, *Delaware: A Guide to the First State*, 1938

A state that has three counties when the tide is out, and two when it is in. 3

—**John J. Ingalls,** speech, U.S. Senate, c. 1885

This is a small and measly state, owned by a single family, the Du Ponts. 4

—**H. L. Mencken,** *Americana*, 1925

Delaware has fought and bucked, hated, reviled, admired and fawned upon, ignored 5
and courted the Du Ponts, but in the end, it has invariably bowed to Du Pont's benevolent paternalism.

—**James Warner Bellah,** *Delaware*, in *American Panorama East of the Mississippi*, 1960

1 There are two political parties in Delaware: the Du Ponts and the anti-Du Ponts, with the proviso that many Du Ponts are members of the anti-Du Pont family.
—**James L. Phelan & Robert C. Pozen,** *The Company State*, 1973

2 Liberty and independence.
—Motto, state of Delaware

Delay

See also INDECISION.

3 Delay is preferable to error.
—**Thomas Jefferson,** letter to George Washington, May 16, 1792

4 Never do today what you can do as well tomorrow.
—**Aaron Burr,** quoted in James Parton, *The Life and Times of Aaron Burr* [1857]

5 Do not delay;
Do not delay; the golden moments fly!
—**Henry Wadsworth Longfellow,** *The Masque of Pandora*, 1875

6 Procrastination is the
art of keeping
up with yesterday
—**Don Marquis,** *certain maxims of archy*, in *archy and mehitabel*, 1927

7 Delay is itself a decision.
—**Theodore C. Sorensen**, *Decision-Making in the White House: The Olive Branch or the Arrows*, 1963

Democracy

See also GOVERNMENT; MAJORITIES & MINORITIES; PEOPLE, THE; POLITICS & POLITICIANS.

8 If the people be the governors, who shall be the governed?
—**John Cotton,** *The Bloody Tenent Washed and Made Clean in the Blood of the Lamb*, 1647

★ Cotton, a Boston minister, preferred monarchy or aristocracy to democracy. "They are both clearly approved and directed in the scriptures," he claimed. Cotton and Gov. John Winthrop were opposed by Roger Williams, who was eventually exiled and went on to found the Providence Plantation, the core of the Rhode Island colony.

9 Our real *disease* . . . is *democracy*.
—**Alexander Hamilton,** letter to Theodore Sedgwick, July 10, 1804

★ This letter was written the night before Hamilton's duel with Aaron Burr. Hamilton was mortally wounded and died July 12.

10 The sober second thought of the people shall be law.
—**Fisher Ames,** speech, Massachusetts Convention, Jan. 1788

★ He was speaking in support of biennial elections.

Though the will of the majority is in all cases to prevail, that will, to be rightful, must be reasonable. **1**

—**Thomas Jefferson,** First Inaugural Address, March 4, 1801

★ More at MAJORITIES & MINORITIES.

Democracy never lasts long. It soon wastes, exhausts, and murders itself. There never was a democracy yet that did not commit suicide. **2**

—**John Adams,** letter to John Taylor, April 15, 1814

★ For another perspective on democracy and survival see under AMERICA & AMERICANS for Abraham Lincoln's 1838 speech at the Young Men's Lyceum in Springfield, Ill.

The tendency of democracy is, in all things, to mediocrity. **3**

—**James Fenimore Cooper,** *The American Democrat*, 1838

Democracy as I understand it, requires me to sacrifice myself *for* the masses, not *to* them. Who knows not that, if you would save the people, you must often oppose them. **4**

—**Orestes A. Brownson,** *An Oration on the Scholar's Mission*

The ballot is stronger than the bullet. **5**

—**Abraham Lincoln,** speech, May 19, 1856

Government of the people, by the people, for the people. **6**

—**Abraham Lincoln,** Gettysburg Address, Nov. 19, 1863

★ More at GETTYSBURG ADDRESS.

I will not gloss over the appalling dangers of universal suffrage. **7**

—**Walt Whitman,** *Democratic Vistas*, 1871

The rise of democracy as an effective force in the nation came in with western preponderance under Jackson and William Henry Harrison, and it meant the triumph of the frontier—with all of its good and all of its evil elements. **8**

—**Frederick J. Turner,** *The Significance of the Frontier in American History*, 1893

The democracy born of free land, strong in selfishness and individualism, intolerant of administrative experience and education, and pressing individual liberty beyond its proper bounds, has dangers as well as its benefits. **9**

—**Ibid.**

Democracy is the theory that the common people know what they want, and deserve to get it good and hard. **10**

—**H. L. Mencken,** *Little Book in C Major*, 1916

★ See also FRONTIER, THE.; INDIVIDUALITY & INDIVIDUALISM.

The world must be made safe for democracy. **11**

—**Woodrow Wilson,** speech to the U.S. Congress, April 2, 1917

★ More at WORLD WAR I. For Franklin D. Roosevelt's call for the U.S. to be the arsenal of democracy, see under AMERICAN HISTORY: MEMORABLE MOMENTS.

1 The cure for the evils of democracy is more democracy!
—**H. L. Mencken,** *Notes on Democracy*, 1926

2 It is one of the happy incidents of the federal system that a single courageous state may, if its citizens choose, serve as a laboratory and try novel social and economic experiments without risk to the rest of the country.
—**Louis D. Brandeis,** dissent, *New State Ice Company v. Liebmann*, 1932

★ The quote is often given as: "[states can be] laboratories of democracy."

3 I swear to the Lord
I still can't see
Why Democracy means
Everybody but me.
—**Langston Hughes,** *The Black Man Speaks*, in *Jim Crow's Last Stand*, 1943

★ See also Hughes at AMERICA & AMERICANS.

4 The blind lead the blind. It's the democratic way.
—**Henry Miller,** *With Edgard Varèse in the Gobi Desert*, in *The Air-Conditioned Nightmare*, 1945

5 Democracy is the recurrent suspicion that more than half of the people are right more than half of the time.
—**E. B. White,** *The Wild Flag*, 1946

6 If our democracy is to flourish, it must have criticism; if our government is to function, it must have dissent.
—**Henry Steele Commager,** *Freedom, Loyalty, Dissent*, 1954

7 Under democracy, one party always devotes its chief efforts to trying to prove that the other is unfit to rule—and both commonly succeed and are right.
—**H. L. Mencken,** *Minority Report: H. L. Mencken's Notebooks* [1956]

8 The people's government has come to be less and less the people's business.
—**Joseph Alsop,** *The Reporter's Trade*, 1958

9 It is a mistake to expect all to practice democracy as we do. There are as many democratic ways of getting things done as there are uses of the imagination and vision. Free government is not so much a question of the form of the institution as it is a way of life of the people.
—**Earl Warren,** interview, *The Saturday Evening Post*, 1965

10 A democracy cannot flourish half rich and half poor, any more than it can flourish half free and half slave.
—**Felix G. Rohatyn,** *Ethics in America's Money Culture*, in *The New York Times*, June 3, 1987

11 The central tenet of every democracy in the end is trust.
—**Bill Clinton,** quoted in *The New York Times*, Sept. 9, 1993

I never vote—it only encourages them. 1

—Anonymous

★ According to a column by William Safire in *The New York Times*, January 22, 1995, comedian Steve Allen credited this insight to an anonymous feisty old woman.

Democrats

See Politics & Politicians.

Depression, the

See also American History: Memorable Moments; Bad Times (Wilder/Lane); Economics (Brandeis); Sports (Babe Ruth)

Wall St. Lays an Egg. 2

—Sime Silverman, headline, *Variety*, Oct. 30, 1929

★ The economic boom that began in 1922 was running on fumes by 1929. The overheated, highly speculative Wall St. securities market collapsed in "the Panic" of October and November. Two devastating crashes occurred in October—on the 24th, with 13 million shares traded, and on the 29th, with 16 million shares traded. By mid-November, $30 billion had been erased from the value of stocks. Losses more than doubled by 1932.

Prosperity is just around the corner. 3

—Herbert Hoover, attributed

★ This was the popular distillation of various statements of assurance made by Hoover and others following the 1929 stock market crash. According to Paul F. Boller, Jr., and John George in *They Never Said It*, the closest Hoover came to the popular version was in a 1931 speech to the U.S. Chamber of Commerce, when he declared, "We have now passed the worst and with continued unity of effort we shall rapidly recover. There is one certainty of the future of a people with the resources, intelligence, and character of the people of the United States—that is, prosperity." Eventually, the phrase became an ironic joke, used mockingly as as a political attack phrase by the Democrats.

The grass will grow in the streets of a hundred cities. 4

—Herbert Hoover, speech, Oct. 31, 1932

★ The warning became associated with the Depression, although Hoover was speaking in a different context; see under Economics.

Depressions are farm led and farm fed. 5

—Anonymous, saying, 1930s, quoted in Studs Terkel, *Hard Times: An Oral History of the Great Depression* [1970]

★ The speaker is farmer Emil Lorik, who joined the Minnesota state senate in 1927. In his first session, five hundred farmers marched up Capitol Hill. "It thrilled me," he said. "I didn't know farmers were smart enough to organize. They stayed there two days. It was a strength I didn't realize we had." As farmers' purchasing power shrank, farm-equipment manufacturers went out of business starting a spiral of economic decline.

1 Once I built a railroad, now it's done.
Brother can you spare a dime?
—E. Y. "Yip" Harburg, *Brother Can You Spare a Dime?*, song, 1932

★ The music was by Jay Gorney. The title repeats a common request by street beggars, and the song, Harburg's first major hit, was a sort of anthem of the Depression. Its blunt recognition of the national crisis probably helped Franklin D. Roosevelt in his campaign for the presidency.

2 With the slow menace of a glacier, depression came on. No one had any measure of its progress; no one had any plan for stopping it. Everyone tried to get out of its way.
—Frances Perkins, *People at Work*, 1934

★ Perkins, the first woman in the U.S. cabinet, was Secretary of Labor 1933–44. In the winter of 1931–32—when there was no unemployment insurance or other safety net—twenty percent of the labor force was unemployed, some ten million people. Vaudevillians, reacting to reports that business was improving, quipped, "Is Hoover dead?" See also the joke about Hoover's engineering expertise at INSULTS. The following winter, incredibly, the numbers grew worse: one third of the workforce, sixteen million people, unemployed. Industrial workers were making less than eight cents per hour, with some women getting a penny or two per hour. The first light of hope glimmered in Franklin D. Roosevelt's inaugural speech in March 1933; see AMERICAN HISTORY: MEMORABLE MOMENTS.

3 I see one-third of a nation ill-housed, ill-clad, ill-nourished.
—Franklin D. Roosevelt, Second Inaugural Address, Jan. 20, 1937

Desires

See also HAPPINESS.

4 If you desire many things, many things will seem but a few.
—Benjamin Franklin, *Poor Richard's Almanack*, 1732–1757

5 The fundamental principle of human action—the law that is to political economy what the law of gravitation is to physics—is that men seek to gratify their desires with the least exertion.
—Henry George, *Progress and Poverty*, 1879

★ George, one of the most popular and influential of American economists, regarded land as the key economic commodity from which all values derive. Consequently, he proposed a single tax on land.

6 Men have a thousand desires to a bushel of choices.
—Henry Ward Beecher, *Proverbs from Plymouth Pulpit*, 1887

7 Protect me from what I want.
—Jenny Holzer, saying

★ Holzer, a post-Conceptualist artist, incorporates aphorisms and condensed narratives in her multimedia exhibits.

Despair

See also Failure.

We should never despair. 1

—George Washington, letter to Maj. Gen. Philip Schuyler, July 15, 1777

★ More at Determination, Effort, Persistence, & Perseverance.

And that White Sustenance— 2
Despair—

—Emily Dickinson, poem no. 640, c. 1862

Safe Despair it is that raves— 3
Agony is frugal.
Puts itself severe away
For its own perusal.

—Emily Dickinson, poem no. 1243, c. 1873

Lord save us all from old age and broken health and a hope tree that has lost the faculty of putting out blossoms. 4

—Mark Twain, letter to Joe. T. Goodman, April 1891

And nothing to look backward to with pride, 5
And nothing to look forward to with hope.

—Robert Frost, *The Death of the Hired Man*, 1914

There is not one among us in whom a devil does not dwell; at some time, on some point, the devil masters each of us. . . . It is not having been in the Dark House, but having left it that counts. 6

—Theodore Roosevelt, letter to Edwin Arlington Robinson, March, 27, 1916

The damned don't cry. 7

—Eugene O'Neill, "The Haunted," *Mourning Becomes Electra*, 1931

In the real dark night of the soul, it is always three o'clock in the morning. 8

—F. Scott Fitzgerald, *The Hours*, in *The Crack-Up*, 1945

★ Fitzgerald was referring to the writings of the 16th-century mystic St. John of the Cross, who entitled a treatise *The Dark Night of the Soul*. In *The Ascent of Mount Carmel*, St. John spoke of the "the dark night of the soul through which the soul passes on its way to the Divine Light." A time of despair commonly precedes an intense mystical experience.

The despairing soul is a rebel. 9

—Joyce Carol Oates, *The One Unforgiveable Sin* in *The New York Times Book Review*, July 25, 1993

★ She observes that the despairing soul is dangerous to a controlling government. Despair "is a state of intense inwardness, thus independence."

Desperation

See DESPAIR; UNHAPPINESS.

Destiny

See FATE & DESTINY.

Details

See SMALLNESS, DETAILS, & LITTLE THINGS.

Detectives

See CRIME, CRIMINALS, & DETECTIVES.

Determination, Effort, Persistence, & Perseverance

See also ACTION & DOING; COMMITMENT; ENTHUSIASM & ZEAL; ENDURANCE; PATIENCE; RESISTANCE; WILL; WORK.

1 There are no gains without pains.
—Benjamin Franklin, *Poor Richard's Almanack*, 1745

★ This proverbial wisdom was used also by Adlai Stevenson in accepting the Democratic party's presidential nomination on July 26, 1952.

2 Little strokes
Fell great oaks.
—Benjamin Franklin, *Poor Richard's Almanack*, August 1750

★ Proverbial. For example, in the 16th century, John Lyly included in his *Euphues: The Anatomy of Wit*: "Many strokes overthrow the tallest oaks." And in *Henry VI, Part III*, Shakespeare wrote: "Many strokes, though with a little axe, / Hew down and fell the hardest timber'd oak."

3 We should never despair; our situation before has been unpromising and has changed for the better, so I trust, it will again. If new difficulties arise, we must only put forth new exertions and proportion our efforts to the exigency of the times.
—George Washington, letter to Maj. Gen. Philip Schuyler on the fall of Fort Ticonderoga, July 15, 1777

★ Washington's perseverance was rewarded. Ticonderoga was taken by the British under Gen. Burgoyne. Three months later, Burgoyne surrendered at Saratoga, turning point of the Revolution.

4 I am in earnest—I will not equivocate—I will not excuse—I will not retreat a single inch—AND I WILL BE HEARD!
—William Lloyd Garrison, *The Liberator*, first issue, Boston, Jan. 1, 1831

★ More at SLAVERY.

I know of no more encouraging fact than the unquestionable ability of man to elevate his life by a conscious effort. 1

—**Henry David Thoreau,** *Where I Lived and What I Lived For, in Walden*, 1854

Nothing in the world can take the place of persistence. Talent will not; nothing is more common than unsuccessful men with talent. Genius will not; unrewarded genius is almost a proverb. Education will not; the world is full of educated derelicts. Persistence and determination are omnipotent. The slogan "press on" has solved and always will solve the problems of the human race. 2

—**Calvin Coolidge,** attributed on the cover of the program for his memorial service, 1933

★ A famous but never verified quotation.

Quitters never win. Winners never quit. 3

—**Anonymous**, traditional adage for football locker rooms

What God requires of us is that we not stop trying. 4

—**Bayard Rustin,** c. 1970, quoted in *The New York Times Book Review* [Nov. 9, 2003]

Keep on truckin'. 5

—**Robert Crumb,** cartoon slogan, poster

Perseverance is the hard work you do after you get tired of doing the hard work you already did. 6

—**Newt Gingrich,** *Quotations from Speaker Newt*, 1995

Talent is cheaper than table salt. What separates the talented individual from the successful one is a lot of hard work. 7

—**Stephen King,** quoted in the London *Independent on Sunday*, March 10, 1996

If there's no struggle, there's no progress. 8

—**Rachel Robinson,** commencement ceremony, New York University, May 16, 1996

★ Ms. Robinson, widow of Jackie Robinson, who integrated major league baseball, and founder of a foundation named for him, spoke after receiving an honorary doctorate of humane letters.

Devil, the

See also EVIL.

That there is a Devil is a thing doubted by none but such as are under the influences of the Devil. For any to deny the being of a Devil must be from an ignorance or profaneness worse than diabolical. 9

—**Cotton Mather,** *The Wonders of the Invisible World*, 1693

★ Rev. Mather's concept of the devil and hell was quite scientific—as he understood science: "[The Devil] impregnates the air with such malignant salts, as meeting with the salt of our microcosm, shall immediately cast us into the fermentation and putrefaction which will utterly dissolve all the vital ties within us." The text is contemporaneous with the Salem witch trials, which Mather did not support but for which his writings nevertheless were an inspiration.

1 One of the principal objects of American reverence is the devil. There are multitudes who are shocked to hear his name mentioned lightly, and who esteem such mention profanity.
—**J. G. Holland,** *Everyday Topics*, 1876

2 As a rule, the devils have been better friends to man than the gods.
—**Robert G. Ingersoll,** speech, Boston, April 23, 1880

3 Demonology is the shadow of theology.
—**Ralph Waldo Emerson,** *Demonology*, in *Lectures and Biographical Sketches*, 1883

4 The Devil and me, we don't agree;
I hate him, and he hates me.
—**Anonymous,** Salvation Army Hymn, c. 1890

5 We may not pay Satan reverence, for that would be indiscreet, but we can at least respect his talents.
—**Mark Twain,** *Concerning the Jews*, in *Harper's Magazine*, Sept. 1899

6 A person [Satan] who has during all time maintained the imposing position of spiritual head of four-fifths of the human race, and political head of the whole of it, must be granted the possession of executive abilities of the loftiest order.
—**Ibid.**

7 The snake stood up for evil in the Garden.
—**Robert Frost,** *The Ax-Helve*, 1923

8 The death of Satan was a tragedy
For the imagination.
—**Wallace Stevens,** *Esthétique du Mal*, 1947

9 The devil made me do it.
—**Flip Wilson,** saying

★ Wilson, a stand-up comic, was a television star in the 1960s and early 1970s. This line was the favorite excuse of one his stock characters, Geraldine.

10 The devil usually gets the best lines.
—**Alex Ross,** in *The New Yorker*, May 9, 2005

Differences

See also CONFLICT; INDIVIDUALITY & INDIVIDUALISM; MADNESS & SANITY; MAJORITIES & MINORITIES; PEACE (Bill Clinton).

As long as the reason of man continues fallible, and he is at liberty to exercise it, different opinions will be formed. **1**

—**James Madison,** *The Federalist, No. 10*, 1787

Every difference of opinion is not a difference of principle. **2**

—**Thomas Jefferson,** First Inaugural Address, March 4, 1801

★ More at UNION, THE.

But the great Master said, "I see **3**
No best in kind, but in degree;
I gave a various gift to each,
To charm, to strengthen, and to teach."

—**Henry Wadsworth Longfellow,** *The Singers*, 1849

It were not the best that we should all think alike; it is difference of opinion that makes horse races. **4**

—**Mark Twain,** *Pudd'nhead Wilson's Calendar*, in *Pudd'nhead Wilson*, 1894

I never saw a purple cow, **5**
I never hope to see one;
But I can tell you, anyhow,
I'd rather see than be one.

—**Gelett Burgess,** *The Purple Cow*, in *The Lark* magazine, 1895

★ This wildly popular bit of silliness eventually embarrassed its author. In 1914, Burgess protested, "Ah, yes, I wrote "The Purple Cow"—I'm sorry, now, I wrote it! / But I can tell you anyhow, / I'll kill you if you quote it," *Confessional*, 1914. Burgess is remembered also for apparently coining one of the essential terms in the language of book publishing, *blurb*, and for originating the use of *bromide* for a trite and soothing thought; see Burgess at ART: CRITICISM.

There is very little difference between one man and another; but what little there is, is very important. **6**

—**William James,** quoting an unidentified carpenter, in *The Will to Believe*, 1897

Conformists die, but heretics live forever. **7**

—**Elbert Hubbard,** saying

★ Quoted in *The New York Times*, Jan. 25, 1996, in an article on the revival of the American Arts and Crafts Movement led by Hubbard and Gustav Stickley, approximately a century after its founding. Hubbard's arts-and-crafts center at the Roycroft Inn, near Buffalo, was also enjoying a renaissance.

To think is to differ. **8**

—**Clarence Darrow,** remark during the Scopes "monkey" trial, Dayton, Tenn., July 13, 1925

1 Human diversity makes tolerance more than a virtue; it makes it a requirement for survival.

—**René Dubos,** *Celebrations of Life*, 1981

2 Without deviation from the norm, progress is not possible.

—**Frank Zappa,** quoted in *New York* magazine, June 20, 1994

3 If you aren't doing something different, you aren't doing anything at all.

—**Neil Cargile,** motto, quoted in John Berendt, *High-heel Neil*, in *The New Yorker*, Jan. 16, 1995

★ Cargile, a prominent figure in Nashville society, is a pilot, independent businessman (heavy dredging operations), polo player, and cross-dresser. An even more prominent cross-dresser in American history was Lord Cornbury, who served as first governor of New York, from 1702 to 1708. He wore gowns on occasion, ostensibly to show his resemblance to his cousin Queen Anne.

4 There is only one truth, and many opinions. Therefore, most people are wrong most of the time.

—**Mordecai Kurz,** in *Fortune* magazine, April 3, 1995

★ Mr. Kurz, a professor of economics at Stanford University, was referring specifically to differences of opinion about the values of stocks.

Diplomacy

See also FOREIGN POLICY.

5 In statesmanship get the formalities right, never mind about the moralities.

—**Mark Twain,** *Pudd'nhead Wilson's New Calendar*, in *Following the Equator*, 1897

6 *Diplomacy, n.* The patriotic art of lying for one's country.

—**Ambrose Bierce,** *The Devil's Dictionary*, 1906

7 Diplomacy is utterly useless where there is no force behind it.

—**Theodore Roosevelt,** speech, Naval War College, Newport, R.I., June 2, 1897

★ See also Brezezinski below. TR's statement prefigured his "big stick" adage; see FOREIGN POLICY.

8 Diplomacy shall proceed always frankly and in the public view.

—**Woodrow Wilson,** "Fourteen Points" address to Congress, Jan. 8, 1918

★ More at FOREIGN POLICY.

9 Diplomacy is to do and say
The nastiest thing in the nicest way.

—**Isaac Goldberg,** *The Reflex*, Oct. 1927

10 [An ambassador:] A politician who is given a job abroad in order to get him out of the country.

—**Anonymous,** cited in H. L. Mencken, *A New Dictionary of Quotations* [1942]

Diplomats don't mind starting a war because it's a custom that they are to be brought safely home before the trouble starts. 1

—**Will Rogers,** in Alex Ayres, ed., *The Wit and Wisdom of Will Rogers* [1993]

Diplomacy . . . is not the art of asserting ever more emphatically that attitudes should not be what they clearly are. It is not the repudiation of actuality, but the recognition of actuality, and the use of actuality to advance our national interests. 2

—**Adlai Stevenson,** 1954, quoted in *American Heritage* [Oct. 1973]

Diplomacy has rarely been able to gain at the conference table what cannot be gained or held on the battlefield. 3

—**Walter Bedell Smith,** 1954

★ Gen. Smith made this remark on returning from the Geneva Conference on Indo-China.

The first requirement of a statesman is that he be dull. This is not always easy to achieve. 4

—**Dean Acheson,** in *The Observer*, June 21, 1970

Diplomacy not backed by power is an exercise in good will. 5

—**Zbigniew Brzezinski,** in *The New York Times*, Jan. 18, 1981

★ A modern, slightly softer version of Theodore Roosevelt's pronouncement above. This was Brzezinski's farewell interview with the press as national security adviser in the Carter administration.

Politics drives diplomacy, not vice versa. 6

—**James A. Baker, III**, *War and Peace, 1989–1992*, 1995

Dishonesty & Lies

See also HONESTY; TRUTH.

I can't tell a lie, Pa; you know I can't tell a lie. I did cut it with my hatchet. 7

—**George Washington,** attributed in Parson Weems, *Life of George Washington* [1800]

★ This famous confession, in which Washington as a boy admits to having cut down a prized cherry tree, is most likely entirely fictional.

He who permits himself to tell a lie once, finds it much easier to do a second and third time, till at length it becomes habitual; he tells lies without attending to it, and truths without the world's believing him. This falsehood of the tongue leads to that of the heart, and in time depraves all its good dispositions. 8

—**Thomas Jefferson,** *Notes on the State of Virginia*, 1781–1785

Sin has many tools, but a lie is the handle which fits them all. 9

—**Oliver Wendell Holmes, Sr.,** *The Autocrat of the Breakfast-Table*, 1858

I never seen anybody but lied, one time or another. 10

—**Mark Twain,** *Huckleberry Finn*, 1885

★ Huck is speaking. This is from the opening paragraph of the book.

1 A lie can get halfway around the world before the truth gets its boots on.
—Mark Twain, attributed

★ The line is commonly credited to Twain, but has never been found in his writings or records of his conversations. The internet site twainquotes.com, suggests that it may have originated with Charles Haddon Spurgeon, an English Baptist preacher, who said in a sermon on April 1, 1855, that "A lie will go round the world while truth is pulling its boots on." Spurgeon himself introduced it as a proverbial saying, however.

2 A lie is an abomination unto the Lord and an ever present help in time of need.
—John A. Tyler Morgan, comment in the U.S. Senate, c. 1890

★ The remark is attributed to Sen. Morgan in David McCullough's book on the building of the Panama Canal, *The Path Between the Seas*, 1977. Morgan, who represented Alabama in the Senate for many years, ardently favored a Nicaraguan canal. More recently, Democratic presidential candidate Adlai Stevenson made essentially the same observation on the useful lie in a speech in Springfield, Illinois, January 1951.

3 One of the most striking differences between a cat and a lie is that a cat has only nine lives.
—Mark Twain, *Pudd'nhead Wilson's Calendar*, in *Pudd'nhead Wilson*, 1894

4 Mendacity is a system that we live in.
—Tennessee Williams, *Cat on a Hot Tin Roof*, 1955

5 Don't lie if you don't have to.
—Leo Szilard, *Science*, No. 176, 1972

6 [Politician's motto:] Only lie about the future.
—Anonymous, desk sign, cited in *The Macmillan Dictionary of Political Quotations* [1993]

7 No one ever lies. People often do what they have to do to make their story sound right.
—William Ginsburg, cited in *The New York Times,* Feb. 2, 1998

★ Mr. Ginsburg, a California medical malpractice lawyer, then acting as attorney for the former White House intern, Monica Lewinsky, amazed many fellow members of the bar with this statement, which seemed to undercut his client, who had denied having an affair with President Clinton in a sworn affidavit. Four months later Ms. Lewinsky replaced Mr. Ginsburg with two Washington lawyers with extensive experience in criminal and civil law.

Divisions & Barriers

8 Something there is that doesn't love a wall.
—Robert Frost, *Mending Wall*, 1914

★ Apart from the symbolic resonance, Frost was referring literally to the tendency of stone walls to fall apart. He disliked the outdated state requirement that he help his neighbor to rebuild a stone wall. See NEIGHBORS.

Before I built a wall I'd ask to know
What I was walling in or walling out. 1
—Ibid.

★ John F. Kennedy jotted down a variant of this, "Don't ever take a fence down until you know the reason why it was put up," in a notebook that he kept in 1945–46. He attributed it to G. K. Chesterton, but the line has not been found in any of Chesterton's many works. Kennedy may have just been misremembering Frost.

A door is what a dog is perpetually on the wrong side of. 2
—Ogden Nash, *A Dog's Best Friend Is His Illiteracy*, in *The Private Dining Room*, 1953

Doctors & Medicine

See also Health; Illness & Remedies; Science: biology & physiology; Science: Psychology.

God heals and the doctor takes the fee. 3
—Benjamin Franklin, *Poor Richard's Almanack*, 1736

The inexperienced and presumptuous band of medical tyros let loose upon the world destroys more of human life in one year than all the Robin Hoods, Cartouches, and Macheaths do in a century. 4
—Thomas Jefferson, letter to Dr. Caspar Wistar, June 21, 1807

★ Cartouche was an 18th-century French highwayman. Macheath was the London cutthroat whom we know from John Gay's *Beggar's Opera* and Bertolt Brecht's *The Threepenny Opera*. The famous Robin Hood, obviously, was not regarded as such a hero in Jefferson's day as he is now.

Consider the deference which is everywhere paid to a doctor's opinion. Nothing more strikingly betrays the credulity of mankind than medicine. 5
—Henry David Thoreau, *A Week on the Concord and Merrimack Rivers*, 1849

Surgeons must be very careful 6
When they take the knife!
Underneath their fine incisions
Stirs the culprit—*life*!
—Emily Dickinson, poem no. 108, c. 1859

What I call a good patient is one, who having found a good physician, sticks to him till he dies. 7
—Oliver Wendell Holmes, Sr., lecture, New York City, March 2, 1871

When a doctor looks me square in the face and kant see no money in me, then I am happy. 8
—Josh Billings, *Josh Billings' Encyclopedia of Wit and Wisdom*, 1874

Your doctor bill should be paid like your income tax, according to what you have. There is nothing that keeps poor people poor as much as paying doctor bills. 9
—Will Rogers, *Weekly Articles*, July 13, 1930

1 [Re specialists:] Take the throat business. A doctor that doctors on the upper half of your throat doesn't even know where the lower part goes to.

—Will Rogers, in Alex Ayres, ed., *The Wit and Wisdom of Will Rogers* [1993]

2 I hate doctors! They'll do anything—anything to keep you coming to them. They'll sell their souls! What's worse, they'll sell yours, and you'll never know it until one day you find yourself in hell.

—Eugene O'Neill, *A Long Day's Journey into Night*, 1956

3 Healing . . . is not a science, but the intuitive art of wooing nature.

—W. H. Auden, *The Art of Healing*, in *Collected Poems*, 1967

★ Auden wrote this poem in memory of his physician, Dr. Richard Protech. The line itself is a quote from Auden's father, also a physician.

4 The kind of doctor I want is one who when he's not examining me is home studying medicine.

—George S. Kaufman, attributed in Howard Teichmann, *George S. Kaufman: An Intimate Portrait* [1972]

★ Kaufman, the funniest playwright of his generation, rarely joked about his health. He was a notorious hypochondriac.

5 Half of what you learn in medical school is wrong. The problem is figuring out which half.

—Anonymous

★ Dr. Dan A. Oren of the National Institute of Health reported in a letter to *The New York Times* (June 29, 1995) that at Yale University in the 1980s, medical students were taught this aphorism Dr. Oren's records trace the saying to England, possibly originated by Sidney Burwell. See also John Wanamaker at ADVERTISING & ADVERTISING SLOGANS.

6 To cure sometimes, to relieve often, to comfort always—this is our work. This is the first and great commandment. And the second is like unto it—Thou shalt treat thy patient as thou wouldest thyself be treated.

—Anonymous

★ The first part of the saying, frequently cited in medical literature, is apparently proverbial.

7 In its effects I believe that the pill ranks in importance with the discovery of fire.

—Ashley Montagu, quoted in David Allyn, *Make Love, Not War: The Sexual Revolution: An Unfettered History* [2000]

★ Anthropologist Ashley Montagu was referring to the first contraceptive pill approved by the Federal Food and Drug Administration in 1960.

Doing

See ACTION & DOING.

Doubt

See Indecision; Skepticism.

Dreams & Dreamers

See also Dreams & Sleep; Reality, Illusions, & Images; Ideas & Ideals; Vision & Perception.

If one advances confidently in the direction of his dreams, and endeavors to live the life which he has imagined, he will meet with a success unexpected in common hours. **1**

—**Henry David Thoreau,** "Conclusion," *Walden*, 1854

To make a prairie it takes a clover and one bee, **2**
One clover, and a bee,
And revery.
The revery alone will do,
If bees are few.

—**Emily Dickinson,** in *Poems, Third Series* [1896]

★ The date of the poem's composition is not known

Don't part with your illusions. When they are gone you may still exist but you have ceased to live. **3**

—**Mark Twain,** *Pudd'nhead Wilson's New Calendar*, in *Following the Equator*, 1897

Make strong old dreams lest this our world lose heart. **4**

—**Ezra Pound,** postscript to his first book of poems, *A Lume Spento*, 1908

There's a long, long trail a-winding **5**
Into the land of my dreams,
Where the nightingales are singing
And a white moon beams;
There's a long, long night of waiting
Until my dreams all come true,
Till the day when I'll be going down that
Long, long trail with you.

—**Stoddard King,** *There's a Long, Long Trail A-Winding*, 1913

★ Music by Alonzo "Zo" Elliott. King and Elliott wrote the song while undergraduates at Yale, but couldn't find a publisher for it. Elliott went on to Oxford University, where he taught it to other graduate students, who popularized the song by singing it as soldiers in World War I.

The republic is a dream. **6**
Nothing happens unless first a dream.

—**Carl Sandburg,** *Washington Monument by Night*, 1922

1 In Dreams Begin Responsibilities
—**Delmore Schwartz,** title of short story, *Partisan Review,* 1937.

2 There is always one dream left, one final dream, no matter how low you've fallen.
—**Eugene O'Neill,** press conference, 1946, cited in *The New Yorker* [June 1, 1998]

★ The press conference was occasioned by the Broadway opening of *The Iceman Cometh.* About the dream, O'Neill added: "I know because I saw it."

3 What happens to a dream deferred?
Does it dry up
Like a raisin in the sun? . . .
Or does it explode?
—**Langston Hughes,** *Harlem,* 1951

4 Only the imagination is real.
—**William Carlos Williams,** poem in *Pictures from Brueghel* [1963]

5 I have a dream today.
—**Martin Luther King, Jr.,** speech at the Lincoln Memorial, Washington, D.C., to the great civil rights march, August 28, 1963

★ More at AMERICAN HISTORY: MEMORABLE MOMENTS.

6 It isn't a calamity to die with dreams unfulfilled, but it is a calamity not to dream.
—**Benjamin E. Mays,**"What a Man Lives By," in *Best Black Sermons*, William M. Philpot, ed. [1972]

7 We all have the same dreams.
—**Joan Didion,** *The Book of Common Prayer*, 1977

8 If you can dream it, you can do it.
—**Walt Disney Company,** slogan, 1982

★ This is often attributed to Disney himself, but the company's archives source it to the Imagineering division, which designs and builds theme parks. In 1982, the company was building the Epcot Center.

9 To be an American is to aspire to a room of one's own.
—***The New York Times*,** editorial, April 19, 1987

Dreams & Sleep

10 A traveler five hours doth crave
To sleep, a student seven will have,
And nine sleeps every idle knave.
—**John Josselyn,** *An Account of Two Voyages to New England*, 1675

★ Josselyn included this ditty in his report on the settlements in Maine, annexed to Massachusetts in 1650. He liked Maine men in the north but didn't think much of those in the south, who had recently emigrated from Massachusetts. See also MAINE.

Up, sluggard, and waste not life; in the grave will be sleeping enough. 1
—**Benjamin Franklin,** *Poor Richard's Almanack*, 1741

Judge of your natural character by what you do in your dreams. 2
—**Ralph Waldo Emerson,** *Journal*, 1833

★ Lewis Mumford, in *American Heritage*, February 1969, also cited a passage from Emerson written in 1832: "Dreams and beasts are the two keys by which we are to find out the secrets of our own nature. All mystics use them." Mumford commented, "The theory of Beasts is Darwin and evolution; the theory of Dreams is Freud and the unconscious."

Wynken, Blynken, and Nod one night 3
Sailed off in a wooden shoe
Sailed on a river of crystal light
Into a sea of dew.
—**Eugene Field,** *Wynken, Blynken, and Nod*, c. 1880–95

Dreaming men are haunted men. 4
—**Stephen Vincent Benét,** *John Brown's Body*, 1928

In sleep we lie all naked and alone, in sleep we are united at the heart of night and darkness, and we are strange and beautiful asleep; for we are dying in the darkness, and we know no death. 5
—**Thomas Wolfe,** *Death the Proud Brother*, in *From Death to Morning*, 1935

A dream is a wish your heart makes. 6
—**Walt Disney,** *Sleeping Beauty*, 1959

Dreaming permits each and every one of us to be quietly and safely insane every night of our lives. 7
—**William Dement,** in *Newsweek*, Nov. 30, 1959

In a dream you are never eighty. 8
—**Anne Sexton,** *Old*

★ Sexton, subject to recurring periods of deep depression, was only forty-six when she committed suicide in 1974. See also Sadie Delaney below.

In our dreams, we are always young. 9
—**Sadie Delany,** *Having Our Say: The Delany Sisters' First 100 Years*, 1993

★ The Delany sisters were both over one hundred years old when their memoirs appeared in 1993.

Duty

See Action & Doing; Responsibility; Virtue.

Eating

See Food, Wine, & Eating.

Economics

See also Business; Capitalism & Capital v. Labor; Communism; Depression, the; Farms & Farming; Money & the Rich; Poverty & Hunger; Rich & Poor, Wealth & Poverty; Socialism.

1 A national debt, if it is not excessive, will be to us a national blessing.
—**Alexander Hamilton,** letter to Robert Morris, April 30, 1781

★ But see Hamilton below on debt and taxes, and Andrew Jackson for a different view.

2 All the perplexities, confusions, and distresses in America arise . . . from downright ignorance of the nature of coin, credit, and circulation.
—**John Adams,** letter to Thomas Jefferson, August 25, 1787

3 To extinguish a debt which exists and to avoid contracting more are ideas almost always favored by public feeling and opinion; but to pay taxes for the one or the other purpose, which are the only means of avoiding the evil, is always more or less unpopular.
—**Alexander Hamilton,** c. 1790–94

★ Thomas McGraw of the Harvard Graduate School of Business Administration in *The New York Times*, May 2, 1993, cited this quote and added that Hamilton had observed that one commonly sees the very people who declaim against public debt "vehement against every plan of taxation which is proposed to discharge old debts, or to avoid new." The debt that worried Hamilton and Pres. George Washington as well was the huge Revolutionary War bill of $75.4 million, fifteen times annual revenues. U.S. debt in 1993 was four times annual revenues. See also Andrew Jackson below.

4 Not worth a continental.
—**Anonymous,** c. 1790

★ A popular expression for worthlessness. The "continental currency" was paper money issued by Congress after the Revolution. The nation was deep in debt and could not back up the currency. The continental quickly inflated to the point that one silver dollar was equal to $40 in continentals.

5 As a very important source of strength and security, cherish public credit. One method of preserving it is to use it as sparingly as possible.
—**George Washington,** Farewell Address, Sept. 17, 1796

6 We might hope to see the nation's finances as clear and intelligible as a merchant's books, so that every member of [the] Union should be able to comprehend then to investigate abuses, and consequently to control them.
—**Thomas Jefferson,** letter to his Secretary of the Treasury, Albert Gallatin, April 1, 1802

7 We must not let our rulers load us with perpetual debt.
—**Thomas Jefferson,** letter to Samuel Kercheval, July 12, 1816

8 If a national debt is considered a national blessing, then we can get on by borrowing. But as I believe it is a national curse, my vow shall be to pay the national debt.
—**Andrew Jackson,** veto statement, Bank Renewal Bill, July 10, 1832

The Forgotten Man. 1

—William Graham Sumner, speech title, 1885

★ Professor Sumner, speaking at Yale University, said, "The forgotten man works and votes—generally he prays—but his chief business in life is to pay. . . . Who and where is the forgotten man in this case, who will have to pay for it all?" Roosevelt used the symbol of the forgotten man in 1932; see under POVERTY & HUNGER. See also Richard M. Nixon's "silent majority" under MAJORITIES & MINORITIES.

The problem of our age is the proper administration of wealth, so that the ties of 2
brotherhood may still bind together the rich and poor in harmonious relationship.

—Andrew Carnegie, *Wealth*, 1889

You shall not press down upon the brow of labor this crown of thorns. You shall not 3
crucify mankind upon a cross of gold.

—William Jennings Bryan, "Cross of Gold" speech, Democratic National Convention, Chicago, July 8, 1896

★ This stirring climax to a powerful speech won Bryan the presidential nomination on the fifth ballot. The convention was dominated by Midwestern and Western populists who opposed the exclusive gold standard for currency and favored the free coinage of silver. In debate in Congress in 1892, Bryan had called the post-Civil War law that had eliminated the silver dollar "the crime of 1873." New laws in 1878 and 1890 had reinstated the government purchase of silver to the point that the country was flooded with it. In 1893, the government, headed by Democrat Grover Cleveland, backed off support of silver, a retreat that the free-silver forces believed exacerbated the financial panic of 1893. The crisis split the Democratic party. The 1896 platform called for free silver coinage in a fixed ratio to gold of sixteen to one. Many Democrats, especially Easterners, had difficulty supporting the platform and the candidate; see, for example, David Bennett Hill at POLITICS & POLITICIANS.

There are those who believe that if you will only legislate to make the well-to-do 4
prosperous, their prosperity will leak through on those below. The Democratic idea, however, has been that if you make the masses prosperous, their prosperity will find its way up through every class which rests above them.

—Ibid.

★ Prosperity that will "leak through" to the masses is the same as prosperity that is supposed to "trickle down." See Franklin D. Roosevelt below.

If Americans are going to start worrying about whether they can afford a thing or 5
not, you are going to ruin the whole characteristic of our people.

—Will Rogers, in Alex Ayres, ed., *The Wit and Wisdom of Will Rogers* [1993]

★ "If we want anything, all we have to do is go and buy it on credit," Rogers observed. "So that leaves us without any economic problems whatsoever, except some day to have to pay for them." This was in *Daily Telegrams*, Sept. 6, 1928, about one year before the market crash.

When a great many people are unable to find work, unemployment results. 6

—Calvin Coolidge, attributed, in Stanley Walker, *City Editor* [1934]

★ Walker, legendary city editor of the *New York Herald Tribune,* did not cite his source, and the quotation is otherwise unverified.

1 There's no such thing as a free lunch.

—Anonymous

★ Often phrased, "There ain't no such thing as a free lunch." Slang authority Stuart Berg Flexner has dated "free lunches" to the 1840s in the West, where bars offered food to customers who bought drinks. Later, free lunches were served in schools. In 1934, New York City mayor Fiorello La Guardia on his inauguration day announced, "*È finita la cuccagna!*"—meaning, the free meal (graft) is over. The concept that lunch is never free emerged in the late 1930s. A *San Francisco News* editorial of June 1, 1949, apparently a reprint of a 1938 editorial, included the pronouncement, "There ain't no such thing as free lunch." The axiom became associated with conservative economist Milton Friedman, a Nobel Prize winner, who used the no-free-lunch phrase in a book title in 1975. The adage in the form of an acronym—TANSTAAFL—also was popularized by best-selling science-fiction writer Robert Heinlein in *The Moon Is a Harsh Mistress* (1966).

2 The first theory is that if we make the rich richer, somehow they will let a part of their prosperity trickle down to the rest of us. The second theory [is] that if we make the average of mankind comfortable and secure, their prosperity will rise upward . . . through the ranks.

—Franklin D. Roosevelt, campaign speech, Detroit, Oct. 2, 1932

★ This trickle-down theory is the same as the leak-through theory described by William Jennings Bryan. The trickle-down approach to wealth distribution more recently was advocated by Republican presidents Ronald Reagan and George H. W. Bush. Republicans commonly used the term "supply side" in place of "trickle down," however. As budget director David Stockman explained in an indiscreet interview in *The Atlantic* (Dec. 1981): "It's kind of hard to sell 'trickle down,' so the supply-side formula was the only way to get a tax policy that was really 'trickle-down.' " A supply-side policy is one that uses tax cuts and other means to favor suppliers, usually corporations. The theory is that as producers have more money, jobs will increase, and, in the general prosperity, tax revenue will rise. George H. W. Bush once called it "voodoo economics"; see below.

3 Credit is the lifeblood of business, the lifeblood of prices and jobs.

—Herbert Hoover, speech at Des Moines, Iowa, Oct. 4, 1932

★ Pres. Hoover spoke of perils facing the country, including the "strangulation of credit through the removal of $3 billions of gold and currency by foreign drains and by the hoarding of our own citizens from the channels of our commerce and business." See also Daniel Webster at BUSINESS.

4 The grass will grow in the streets of a hundred cities.

—Herbert Hoover, speech, Madison Square Garden, New York City, Oct. 31, 1932

★ A traditional image of economic catastrophe. Here, Pres. Hoover was speaking in favor of the Smoot-Hawley protective tariff that he promised to retain. Hoover predicted that if Franklin D. Roosevelt were to be elected and eliminate the tariff, disaster would strike nationwide. "Whole towns, communities, and forms of agriculture . . . have been built up under this system of protection," he said. "The grass will grow in the streets of a hundred cities, a thousand towns; the weeds will overrun millions of farms, if that protection is taken away."—Henry F. Woods in *American Sayings* (1945) pointed out that earlier politicians had used similar language. At the outbreak of the Civil War,

Southerners prophesied that when the North was deprived of Southern raw materials, grass would grow in Northern cities. The *Louisville Courier*, in July 1861, reported that the grass was already sprouting in New York City. William Jennings Bryan in his "Cross of Gold" speech (see above) also warned of grass in the streets; see FARMS & FARMERS. And, when campaigning for reelection in 1936, Roosevelt enjoyed remarking that he was still looking for the grass that was supposed to grow on city streets.

[Depression:] An emergency more serious than war. 1

—**Louis Brandeis,** U.S. Supreme Court dissenting opinion, *Ice Company v. Liebmann,* 1932

A lot of fellows nowadays have a B.A., M.D., or Ph.D. 2
Unfortunately, they don't have a J.O.B.

—**"Fats" Domino,** attributed

A recession is when your neighbor loses his job; a depression is when you lose yours. 3

—**Anonymous**

★ Pres. Harry S. Truman used this line, according to Ralph Keyes's *Nice Guys Finish Seventh*; so did Ronald Reagan in his 1980 presidential campaign.

I'm always looking for a one-armed economist [one who can't say "On the other hand"] 4

—**Harry S. Truman,** attributed by Howell Raines, editorial page editor of *The New York Times*

★ Peter J. Boyer, writing in *The New Yorker*, August 22 & 29, 1994, quoted Raines as saying that just as Truman looked for one-armed economists, he himself wanted one-armed editorial writers.

There is nothing sacred about the pay-as-you-go idea so far as I am concerned, except that it represents the soundest principle of financing that I know. 5

—**Harry S. Truman,** quoted in *The New York Times*, article on the proposed balanced-budget amendment to the Constitution [Jan. 26, 1995]

If a free society cannot help the many who are poor, it cannot save the few who are rich. 6

—**John F. Kennedy,** Inaugural Address, 1961

★ See also Andrew Carnegie at RICH & POOR.

I stressed to the President the importance of realizing that in economics, the majority is always wrong. 7

—**John Kenneth Galbraith,** c. 1962

★ Quoted in *Plain Tales from the Embassy*, excerpts from letters and quotes dating from Mr. Galbraith's tenure as ambassador to India, *American Heritage*, October 1969.

We are all Keynesians now. 8

—**Richard M. Nixon**, attributed

★ The quote is usually sourced to Nixon's announcement of a new economic policy on May 15, 1971, but he evidently made the remark somewhat later. The policy freed the dollar to float against foreign currencies, created temporary wage-price controls, established incentives for creating jobs, and so forth. This maneuver assumed principles developed by British economist John Maynard Keynes, that the cure for a recession is government spending and the cure for an overheated economy is government cooling, for example, by raising interest rates. Sometimes the quote is given to conservative economist Milton Friedman, but in context Friedman's similar comment is less sweeping.

1 Voodoo economics.

—George H. W. Bush, speech, April 1980

★ In the Republican presidential primary race in Pennsylvania, Bush thus characterized the "supply side" economic theory espoused by his opponent, Ronald Reagan. According to this theory, a tax cut would actually increase government revenues by stimulating the economy. After Bush became Reagan's running mate, the phrase came back to haunt him. "God I wish I hadn't said that," he remarked. He had it right, though. Pres. Reagan's budget chief David Stockman confided to a reporter for the *The Atlantic* magazine, that supply-side economics was "a Trojan horse," adding, "None of us really understands what is going on with all these numbers," November 1981. At a meeting on June 5, 1981, presidential chief of staff James Baker asked jokingly (sort of), "You mean it really is voodoo economics after all?" By 1988, Pres. Reagan—assisted by a Democratic Congress—had run up the national debt to a record $2 trillion. In 1991, the economy was the central theme in Bill Clinton's presidential campaign. See James Carville at POLITICAL SLOGANS.

2 Starve the beast.

—David Stockman, saying from c. 1981

★ The beast is big government. You starve it by cutting taxes and reducing revenues, so that programs must be cut back. Stockman was budget director in Ronald Reagan's first administration. In his book *The Triumph of Politics: Why the Reagan Administration Failed* (1986) he introduced this metaphor to the world. It has since been associated with conservative theorist Grover Norquist; see GOVERNMENT.

3 Economic forecasters exist to make astrologers look good.

—Robert B. Reich, speech, World Affairs Council, San Francisco, Cal., April 3, 1992

4 NAFTA will cause a giant sucking sound as jobs go south.

—H. Ross Perot, *Save Your Job, Save Our County,* Jan, 1, 1993

★ Debating the North American Free Trade Agreement with Vice President Al Gore on Nov. 9, 1993, Mr. Perot varied the wording slightly, predicting that "You're going to hear a giant sucking sound of jobs being pulled out of this country."

5 Irrational exuberance.

—Alan Greenspan, referring to the stock market bubble of the latter 1990s, *The Challenge of Central Banking in a Democratic Society,* speech, American Enterprise Institute for Public Policy Research, Dec. 5, 1996

★ The phrase was immediately identified as a sign that the Federal Reserve chairman thought stock prices were too high, even though the reference was in the form of a question: "But how do we know when irrational exuberance has unduly escalated asset values, which then become subject to unexpected and prolonged contractions as they have in Japan over the past decade?" Of course, even with this warning, lots of investors were caught in the downturn, especially of technology stocks, bringing to mind the observation of an earlier American economist, Benjamin Anderson: "The more intense the craze, the higher the type of intellect that succumbs to it," *Economics and the Public Welfare*, 1949. For a sharper warning from Greenspan, see BUSINESS.

We must shape this global economy, not shrink from it. 1
—**Bill Clinton,** State of the Unuion message, Jan. 27, 1998

You are what you measure. 2
—**Anonymous,** saying among economists, as in *Metrics: You Are What You Measure,* by John R. Hauser and Gerald M. Katz, *European Management Journal*, April 1998

★ See also SCIENCE: TECHNOLOGY for a similar insight.

In the history of the world, no one has ever washed the windows of a rented car. 3
—**Lawrence H. Summers**, dictum, cited in *The New York Times* [Feb. 6, 2003]

Economics . . . is the cosmology and theodicy of our contemporary culture. . . . [It] 4
offers the dominant creation narrative of our society, depicting the relation of each of us to the universe we inhabit, the relation of human beings to God.
—**Gordon Bigelow**, *Let There Be Markets*, in *Harper's*, May 2005

Education

See also BOOKS & READING; KNOWLEDGE & INFORMATION.

I regret the trifling, narrow, contracted education of the females of my own country. 5
—**Abigail Adams,** letter to John Adams, June 30, 1778

★ Earlier in the year, writing to John Thaxter on "the difference of education between the male and female sex," Abigail asked, "Why should your sex wish for such a disparity in those whom they one day intend for companions and associates?" And she answered the question in part herself, "I cannot help sometimes suspecting that this neglect arises in some measure from an ungenerous jealousy of rivals near the throne" (Feb. 15, 1778). See also Abigail Adams at WOMEN & MEN.

Where the press is free and every man able to read, all is safe. 6
—**Thomas Jefferson,** letter to Charles Yancey, 1816

★ See also Jefferson under THE PRESS.

It is, Sir, as I have said, a small college. And yet *there are those who love it.* 7
—**Daniel Webster,** argument in the U.S. Supreme Court case *Trustees of Dartmouth College v. Woodward*, March 10, 1818

1 Our object is not to teach that which is peculiar to any one of the professions, but to lay the foundation which is common to them all.

—**Jeremiah Day,** *The Report on the Course of Instruction,* 1828

★ Yale's liberal arts curriculum, as described by President Day in this report to the faculty, became a model for many other American institutions of higher education.

2 It is an axiom in political science that unless a people are educated and enlightened it is idle to expect the continuance of civil liberty or the capacity for self-government.

—**Texas Declaration of Independence,** March 2, 1836

3 It's a damn poor mind, indeed, which can't think of at least two ways to spell a word.

—**Andrew Jackson,** attributed

★ In fact, as noted by Jackson's biographer Robert Remini, the great man was quite capable of writing "a single word or name four different ways on the same page" (*The Life of Andrew Jackson,* 1988).

4 Let the children of the rich and poor take their seats together and know of no distinction save that of industry, good conduct, and intellect.

—**Townsend Harris,** attributed

★ Harris, a merchant, served on and headed New York City's board of education, and was the chief advocate for founding the present College of the City of New York in 1847. In the 1850s, he served successfully as a diplomat in Japan.

5 Education . . . is a great equalizer of the conditions of men—the balance wheel of the social machinery.

—**Horace Mann,** report as Secretary of the Massachusetts Board of Education, 1848

6 What does education often do? It makes a straight-cut ditch of a free meandering brook.

—**Henry David Thoreau,** *Journal,* 1850

7 The public school system of the several states is the bulwark of the American republic.

—**Republican Party,** national platform, 1876

★ This platform called for a constitutional amendment to forbid using public funds for any sectarian school.

8 The free school is the preserver of that intelligence which is to preserve us as a free nation.

—**Republican Party,** national platform, 1888

9 Soap and education are not as sudden as a massacre, but they are more deadly in the long run.

—**Mark Twain,** *The Facts Concerning the Recent Registration,* in *Sketches New and Old,* 1867

10 Training is everything. The peach was once a bitter almond; cauliflower is nothing but cabbage with a college education.

—**Mark Twain,** *Pudd'nhead Wilson's Calendar,* in *Pudd'nhead Wilson,* 1894

★ But see also the note under Skinner below.

Enter to grow in wisdom. **1**
Depart to serve better thy country and thy kind.

—**Charles William Eliot,** inscription on the 1890 gate to Harvard Yard

In the first place God made idiots. This was for practice. Then he made school boards. **2**

—**Mark Twain,** *Pudd'nhead Wilson's New Calendar,* in *Following the Equator,* 1897

Education, n. That which discloses to the wise and disguises from the foolish their lack of understanding. **3**

—**Ambrose Bierce,** *The Devil's Dictionary,* 1906

They know enough who know how to learn. **4**

—**Henry Brooks Adams,** *The Education of Henry Adams,* 1907

A teacher affects eternity. He can never tell where his influence stops. **5**

—**Ibid.**

Who dares to teach must never cease to learn. **6**

—**John Cotton Dana,** motto of Kean College of New Jersey, 1912

★ Dana, a librarian in Newark, was asked to find a suitable inscription for a new building at Newark State College, Union, N.J., which later became Kean College. Apparently lacking a good dictionary of quotations, he wrote this maxim, which eventually the college adopted as its motto.

You can lead a horticulture, but you can't make her think. **7**

—**Dorothy Parker,** attributed in *The Ten-Year Lunch,* documentary on the Algonquin Round Table [1987]

★ Parker is said to have made this pun during a round of a word game played by wits who gathered at the Algonquin Hotel in Manhattan. She was challenged to use the word *horticulture* in a sentence.

When eras die, their legacies **8**
Are left to strange police.
Professors in New England guard
The glory that was Greece.

—**Clarence Day,** *Thoughts on Deaths,* in *Thoughts Without Words,* 1928

School days, I believe, are the unhappiest in the whole span of human existence. They are full of dull, unintelligible tasks, new and unpleasant ordinances, brutal violations of common sense and common decency. **9**

—**H. L. Mencken,** *Travail,* in *Baltimore Evening Sun,* Oct. 8, 1928

[Princeton University:] A quaint and ceremonious village of puny demigods on stilts. **10**

—**Albert Einstein,** letter to the Queen of Belgium, Nov. 20, 1933

My boyhood saw Greek islands floating over Harvard Square. **11**

—**Horace Gregory,** *Chorus for Survival,* 1935

★ The speaker is Ralph Waldo Emerson.

1 He who enters a university walks on hallowed ground.

—James Bryant Conant, *Notes on the Harvard Tercentenary*, 1936

2 The whole educational system has become one massive quiz program, with the prizes going to the most enterprising, most repulsively well-informed person—the man with his hand up first.

—Harold Taylor, conference 1947

★ Dr. Taylor, chosen at age thirty to head Sarah Lawrence College, was the youngest college president in the United States. In later years, he pursued a distinguished career in education, the arts, and in support of world peace. He also observed, "What is wrong with a great deal of higher education in America is that it is simply boring." Both quotes here are from his *New York Times* obituary, February 2, 1993.

3 Separate educational facilities are inherently unequal.

—Earl Warren, *Brown v. Board of Education*, May 17, 1954

★ More at AMERICAN HISTORY: MEMORABLE MOMENTS and THE CONSTITUTION.

4 Like so many aging college people, Pnin had long since ceased to notice the existence of students on campus.

—Vladimir Nabokov, *Pnin*, 1957

★ Nabokov taught at Cornell.

5 I find that the three major administrative problems on campus are sex for the students, athletics for the alumni, and parking for the faculty.

—Clark Kerr, speech at the University of Washington, *Time* magazine, Nov. 17, 1958

★ Kerr headed the University of California.

6 One by one the solid scholars
Get the degrees, the jobs, the dollars.

—W. D. Snodgrass, *April Inventory*, 1959

7 The founding fathers in their wisdom decided that children were an unnatural strain on parents. So they provided jails called schools, equipped with torture called education.

—John Updike, *The Centaur*, 1963

8 We go to college to be given one more chance to learn to read in case we haven't learned in high school.

—Robert Frost, cited in Jay Parini, *Robert Frost: A Life* [1999]

9 Education is what survives when what has been learnt has been forgotten.

—B. F. Skinner, *Education in 1984* in *Scientist,* May 21, 1964

★ Similarly, Mark Twain wrote in his *Notebook*, published posthumously in 1935, "Education consists mainly in what we have unlearned."

10 Without education, you are not going anywhere in this world.

—Malcolm X, speech, Militant Labor Forum, New York, May 29, 1964

High school is closer to the core of the American experience than anything else I can think of. 1

—**Kurt Vonnegut,** Introduction, *Our Times Is Now: Notes from the High School Underground*, John Birmingham, ed., 1970

A teacher is someone who talks in our sleep. 2

—**Anonymous,** *Mad* magazine, saying of Mad's hero Alfred E. Neuman

★ Attributed to *Mad* illustrator Frank Kelly Freas in his obituary in *The New York Times* (Jan. 5, 2005). A similar joke has been attributed to W. H. Auden and others: "A professor is someone who talks in someone else's sleep."

An education enables you to earn more than an educator. 3

—**Anonymous,** in Hans Gaffon, *Resistance to Knowledge*, 1970

Only he who *can* should teach. 4

—**Uta Hagen,** *A Challenge for the Actor,* 1973

★ A response to George Bernard Shaw's assertion, "He who *can* does. He who *cannot* teaches," *Man and Superman: Maxims for Revolutionists,* 1903.

If you think education is expensive, try ignorance. 5

—**Derek Bok,** attributed

★ The saying was popular in the 1980s and appeared on bumper stickers. It is not known if it is original with Bok, who was then president of Harvard University.

Some people say that I proved that if you get a C average, you can end up being successful in life. 6

—**George W. Bush,** campaigning at a grade school, Bedford, N.H., Sept. 1, 1999

★ He was governor of Texas at the time. Amplifying the thought in a commencement address at Yale University on May 21, 2001, he said: "To those of you who received honors, awards, and distinctions, I say, well done. And to the C students—I say, you, too, can be President of the United States."

No Child Left Behind 7

—**official title of education act,** signed into law by Pres. George W. Bush, Jan. 8, 1902

★ The name for the national education program was lifted from the motto of the Children's Defense Fund, "Leave No Child Behind." Marion Wright Edelman, president of the Fund, was not pleased. In her words: "The Bush Administration's words say 'Leave no child behind.' The Bush Administration's deeds say 'Leave no millionaire behind' " (*The New York Times,* July 11, 2002).

It wasn't for children, seventh grade. 8

—**Jonathan Lethem,** *View From a Headlock,* in *The New Yorker,* July 28, 2003

★ The passage continues, "You could read the stress of even entering the building in the postures of the teachers, the security guards. Nobody could relax in such a racial and hormonal disaster area."

College presidents, provosts, and deans act as if they have discovered a constitutional right for students not to be offended. 9

—**Nat Hentoff**, Oct. 16, 2003

Effort

See DETERMINATION, EFFORT, PERSISTENCE, & PERSEVERANCE.

Elections

See DEMOCRACY; MAJORITIES & MINORITIES; PEOPLE, THE; POLITICAL SLOGANS; POLITICS & POLITICIANS.

Elite, the

See also MANNERS; MONEY & THE RICH.

1 Adam was never called *Master* Adam; we never read of Noah *Esquire*, Lot *Knight* and *Baronet*, nor the *Right Honorable* Abraham, Viscount Mesopotamia, Baron of Carian; no, no, they were plain men.

—**Benjamin Franklin,** *Dogood Papers*, 1722

★ On the subject of old families, see Andrew Lytle at FAMILY.

2 I am an aristocrat. I love liberty, I hate equality.

—**John Randolph,** quoted in W. C. Bruce, *John Randolph of Roanoke*, 1923

3 I agree with you that there is a natural aristocracy among men. The grounds of this are virtue and talents.

—**Thomas Jefferson,** letter to John Adams, Oct. 28, 1813

4 The social duties of a gentleman are of a high order. The class to which he belongs is the natural repository of the manners, tastes, tone, and, to a certain extent, the principles of a country.

—**James Fenimore Cooper,** *The American Democrat*, 1838

5 He comes of the Brahmin caste of New England. This is the harmless, inoffensive, untitled aristocracy.

—**Oliver Wendell Holmes, Sr.,** *The Brahmin Caste of New England*, 1860

6 There is fast forming in this country an aristocracy of wealth, the worst form of aristocracy that can curse the prosperity of any country.

—**Peter Cooper,** c. 1875, quoted in Peter Lyon, *The Honest Man*, in *American Heritage* [Feb. 1959]

★ Cooper, a self-made, successful manufacturer, gave away much of his fortune.

7 The Pedigree of Honey
Does not concern the Bee—
A Clover, any time, to him
Is Aristocracy.

—**Emily Dickinson,** poem no. 1627, c. 1884

8 There are only about four hundred people in New York society.

—**Ward McAllister,** quoted in the *New York Tribune*, 1888

The talented tenth. 1

—W. E. B. Du Bois, *The Souls of Black Folk*, 1903

★ More at RACES & PEOPLE.

You can always tell a Harvard man, but you can't tell him much. 2

—James Barnes, Princeton, 1891, attributed

Society is any band of folks that kinder throw in with each other, and mess around together for each other's discomfort. The ones with the more money have more to eat and drink at their affairs, and their clothes cost more, and so that's called high society. 3

—Will Rogers, *Weekly Articles*, August 10, 1930

The spenders and drinkers and socially secure. 4

—John O'Hara, *Appointment in Samarra*, 1934

★ This was the social set of the protagonist, Julian English

The D.A.R.lings 5
Chatter like starlings
Telling their ancestors' names,
While grimly aloof
With looks of reproof,
Sit the Colonial Dames.
And The Cincinnati
All merry and chatty
Dangle their badges and pendants,
But haughty and proud
Disdaining the crowd
Brood the Mayflower Descendants.

—Arthur Guiterman, in *The New Yorker*, 1936

★ The Society of the Cincinnati was found by veterans of the Revolutionary War. The organization was named for the fifth-century B.C. Roman general Lucius Quinctius Cincinnatus, who, after a great victory, declined civil office and returned to his farm. In the 1780s, the Cincinnati were suspected of undemocratic and even tyrannical tendencies, but criticism faded by the turn of the century.

The upper classes fight the hardest. They have the most to lose. 6

—Henry Breck, quoted in Evan Thomas, *The Very Best Men* [1995]

★ Mr. Breck was a CIA officer by way of Groton and Harvard. The book is about the early years of the agency, when it was populated largely by well-born Ivy Leaguers. The same was true of its WWII predecessor, the Office of Strategic Services, whose acronym, OSS, also was said to stand for Oh So Social.

What men value in this world is not rights but privileges. 7

—H. L. Mencken, *Minority Report: H. L. Mencken's Notebooks* [1956]

Eggheads, unite! You have nothing to lose but your yolks! 8

—Adlai Stevenson, remark, presidential campaign, 1952

★ Stevenson, a Democrat, was the last frankly intellectual presidential candidate to represent a major party. "Eggheads" had already become objects of contempt. According to

Stanley and Eleanor Hochman in *The Penguin Dictionary of Contemporary American History*, Stevenson was responding to a column by the influential Stewart Alsop. Quoting his brother, John Alsop, a prominent Republican, Stewart Alsop wrote, "Sure, all the eggheads are voting for Stevenson, but how many eggheads are there?" Stevenson not only dared to be an egghead, but in a seriously anti-Communist era, his quip was based on a passage in the Communist Manifesto, popularly rendered as "Workers of the world unite. You have nothing to lose but your chains." In the presidential campaign of 1972, Gov. George Wallace of Alabama, introduced a replacement for eggheads, the infamous "pointy-headed intellectuals."

1 I don't want to belong to any club that will accept me as a member.
—Groucho Marx, attributed

★ Groucho took credit for the line in his autobiography, *Groucho and Me*, 1959, saying he used it in a telegram when withdrawing from a group called the Delaney Club. His son Arthur and brother Zeppo said that the resignation was from the Friars Club. The original piece of paper, if ever found, will be quite a collector's item.

2 To the man-in-the street, who, I'm sorry to say
Is a keen observer of life,
The word *intellectual* suggests right away
A man who's untrue to his wife.
—W. H. Auden, *Note on Intellectuals*, in *Collected Shorter Poems, 1927–1957* [1966]

3 Privileged classes do not give up their privileges voluntarily.
—Martin Luther King, Jr., *The Open Mind: The New Negro* television discussion, Feb. 10, 1957

★ Rev. King had been asked whether blacks should act gradually in seeking rights. "I think it's better to be aggressive," he replied, giving the reason quoted above. He defined the "new Negro" as "a person with a new sense of dignity and destiny, with a new self-respect."

4 The Best and the Brightest.
—David Halberstam, book title, 1969

★ Halberstam's title refers ironically to the well-educated and intelligent political advisers who justified involvement in the disastrous Vietnam War. The phrase comes from an 1811 hymn by Reginald Heber: "Brightest and best of the sons of the morning,/ Dawn on our darkness, and lend us thine aid!" The phrase must have been in the air, for in 1822, the poet Percy Bysshe Shelley penned the line, "Best and brightest, come away!" *To Jane: An Invitation*. Thomas Carlyle used a similar phrase: "What is aristocracy? A corporation of the best, of the bravest," *Chartism*, 1840.

5 A spirit of national masochism prevails, encouraged by an effete corps of impudent snobs who characterize themselves as Americans.
—Spiro Agnew, speech, Republican fundraiser, New Orleans, Oct. 19, 1969

★ The vice president was eventually eased out of office after being accused of taking bribes when he was governor of Maryland. But in his prime, he was blessed with a couple of talented speech writers, presidential aides William Safire and Pat Buchanan. His attacks on the press and antiwar protesters included the memorable passage: "In the United States today, we have more than our share of nattering nabobs of negativism. They have joined their own 4-H club, the hopeless, hysterical hypochondriacs of history." Safire has denied having crafted the "effete corps" attack, or Agnew's notorious comment on slums; see CITIES.

In a world of more than six billion people, there are only 587 billionaires. It's an exclusive club. Would you like to join us? 1

—**Donald J. Trump,** with **Meredith McIver**, *Trump: Think Like a Billionaire: Everything You Need to Know About Success, Real Estate, and Life*, 2004

Emotions

See ANGER; ANXIETY & WORRY; DESPAIR; ENVY; HAPPINESS; HATE; HEART; LAUGHTER & MIRTH; LOVE; SORROW & GRIEF; PASSION; UNHAPPINESS.

There are moments in life, when the heart is so full of emotion 2
That if by chance it be shaken, or into its depths like a pebble
Drops some careless word, it overflows and its secret,
Spilt on the ground like water, can never be gathered together.

—**Henry Wadsworth Longfellow**, *The Courtship of Miles Standish*, 1858

Every person's feelings have a front-door and a side-door by which they may be entered. 3

—**Oliver Wendell Holmes, Sr.**, *The Autocrat of the Breakfast Table*, 1858

I wish thar was winders to my Sole, sed I, so that you could see some of my feelins. 4

—**Artemus Ward**, *The Showman's Courtship* in *Artemus Ward, His Book*, 1862

No emotion, any more than a wave, can long retain its own individual form. 5

—**Henry Ward Beecher**, *Proverbs from Plymouth Pulpit*, 1887

We sometimes underestimate the influence of little things; there is no more powerful factor than sentiment in the conduct of human affairs. 6

—**Charles W. Chesnutt**, *Obliterating the Color Line* in *The New York World*, Oct. 23, 1901

★ This was an unsigned editorial, evidently by African-American scholar Chesnutt. He was addressing the uproar in the South when Pres. Theodore Roosevelt invited Booker T. Washington to dinner at the White House.

Emotion is primarily about nothing, and much of it remains nothing to the end. 7

—**George Santayana**, *The Life of Reason: Reason in Art*, 1905–06

Only emotion endures. 8

—**Ezra Pound**, *A Retrospect*, in *Pavannes and Divagations*, 1918

Ninety percent of our lives is governed by emotion. Our brains merely register and act upon what is telegraphed to them by our bodily experience. 9

—**Alfred North Whitehead**, June 10, 1943, *Dialogues of Alfred North Whitehead* [1955], recorded by Lucien Price

1 Sentimentality is the emotional promiscuity of those who have not sentiment.
—**Norman Mailer**, *Cannibals and Christians*, 1966

2 Emotions are neuropeptides attached to receptors and stimulating an electrical charge on neurons.
—**Candace Pert**, in *National Geographic*, June, 1995

Ends & Means

See EXPEDIENCY; MODERN TIMES (Einstein).

Endurance

See also DETERMINATION, EFFORT, PERSISTENCE, & PERSEVERANCE; RESIGNATION.

3 Endurance is the crowning quality,
And patience all the passion of great hearts.
—**James Russell Lowell,** *Columbus*, 1844

4 Sorrow and silence are strong, and patient endurance is godlike.
—**Henry Wadsworth Longfellow,** *Evangeline*, 1847

5 By trying we can easily learn to endure adversity.
Another man's, I mean.
—**Mark Twain**, *Following the Equator*, 1879

Enemies

6 There is no little enemy.
—**Benjamin Franklin,** *Poor Richard's Almanack*, Sept. 1733

7 If we could read the secret history of our enemies, we should find in each man's life sorrow and suffering enough to disarm all hostility.
—**Henry Wadsworth Longfellow,** *Driftwood*, 1857

8 They love him for the enemies he has made.
—**Edward S. Bragg,** presidential nomination speech, Cleveland, Ohio, July 9, 1884

★ Bragg, a war hero, headed the Wisconsin delegation, which backed Grover Cleveland. Cleveland's enemies were machine politicians allied with Tammany Hall. Cleveland won the nomination and the election.

9 Your friends sometimes go to sleep; your enemies never do.
—**Thomas Brackett Reed,** speech, March 6, 1891

10 If you attend to your work, and let your enemy alone, someone else will come along some day, and do him up for you.
—**E. W. Howe,** *Country Town Sayings*, 1911

★ Similar to a proverb from India: "If you sit on the bank of a river and wait, your enemy's corpse will soon float by."

Judge me by the enemies I have made. 1
—**Franklin D. Roosevelt,** presidential campaign, 1932, cited by Richard Norton Smith, in "Ten Rules to Judge a President" [Nov. 23, 2003]

Keep your friends close, but your enemies closer. 2
—**Mario Puzo,** *The Godfather,* 1969

We have met the enemy and he is us. 3
—**Walt Kelly,** comment by Pogo the possum in the "Pogo" cartoon strip, used as Earth Day poster in 1971

★ See also Kelly at HUMANS & HUMAN NATURE. For the Oliver Hazard Perry original, see WAR OF 1812.

Never tell a man to go to hell unless you can send him there. 4
—**Lyndon B. Johnson,** quoted in Joseph A. Califano Jr., *Inside* [2004]

Know Your Enemy. 5
—**Anonymous,** military posters

★ *New York Times* columnist Bob Herbert wrote (April 19, 2004) that these posters were ubiquitous when he was in the service in the 1960s.

If you don't have enemies, you don't have character. 6
—**Paul Newman,** attributed

★ Actor-philanthropist Newman was included in President Richard Nixon's famous enemies list. The original list of 20 names (later greatly expanded) was compiled by White House aide Charles Colson in 1971. Mr. Newman was number 19. The notation was "California. Radic-lib causes. Heavy [presidential candidate Eugene] McCarthy involvement. Used effectively in nationwide T.V. commercials. [Presidential campaign of] '72 involvement uncertain." Mr. Newman has described inclusion in this list as one of his greatest accomplishments.

Friends come and go, but enemies accumulate. 7
—**Anonymous,** saying in government circles

★ Former Republican presidential speech writer Peggy Noonan cited this aphorism, which dates at least to the 1970's, on the Charlie Rose television show on Jan. 6, 1994. A variant is "Friends come and go, but enemies linger on."

Know your enemies: avoid them if you can; intimidate them, if you can't; subdue 8
them, if you must.
—**Thomas Szasz**, *Ethics*, in *The Untamed Tongue: A Dissenting Dictionary*, 1990

Never hate your enemy. It affects your judgment. 9
—**Mario Puzo**, *Godfather III*, screenplay, 1990

England & the English

See NATIONS.

Enthusiasm & Zeal

See also Determination, Effort, Persistence, & Perseverance; Excess; Passion.

1 Enthusiasm is the glory and hope of the world.
—**Bronson Alcott**, *Orphic Sayings* in *The Dial*, July 1840

2 Nothing great was ever achieved without enthusiasm.
—**Ralph Waldo Emerson,** *Circles*, in *Essays: First Series*, 1841

★ Also, "Every great and commanding moment in the annals of the world is the triumph of some enthusiasm," *The Reformer* lecture, Boston, January 25, 1841.

3 A fanatic is a man that does what he thinks th' Lord wud do if He knew th' facts iv th' case.
—**Finley Peter Dunne,** *Casual Observations*, in *Mr. Dooley's Opinions*, 1900

4 *Enthusiasm, n.* A distemper of youth, curable by small doses of repentance in connection with outward applications of experience.
—**Ambrose Bierce,** *The Devil's Dictionary*, 1906

5 Fanaticism consists in redoubling your efforts when you have forgotten your aim.
—**George Santayana,** *The Life of Reason: Reason in Common Sense*, 1905–1906

6 The greatest dangers to liberty lurk in insidious encroachment by men of zeal, well-meaning but without understanding.
—**Louis D. Brandeis,** *Olmstead v. the United States*, 1928

7 When fanatics are on top, there is no limit to oppression.
—**H. L. Mencken,** *Minority Report: H. L. Mencken's Notebooks* [1956]

★ More at Government.

8 Instead of clearing his own heart, the zealot tries to clear the world.
—**Joseph Campbell**, *The Hero with a Thousand Faces*, 1949

9 [To fanatics] all thought is divinely classified into two kinds—that which is their own and that which is false and dangerous.
—**Robert H. Jackson,** *Amercian Communications Association v. Douds*, 1950

10 Passionate intensity may serve as a substitute for confidence.
—**Eric Hoffer**, *The Ordeal of Change*, 1964

Environment

See also Midwest, the; Nature; West, the; Wilderness.

11 The earth is given as a common stock for man to labor and live on.
—**Thomas Jefferson,** letter to Rev. James Madison, Oct. 28, 1785

12 Methinks my own soul must be a bright invisible green.
—**Henry David Thoreau,** *A Week on the Concord and Merrimack Rivers*, 1849

Perhaps the hunter is the greatest friend of the animals hunted, not excepting the Humane Society. 1

—**Henry David Thoreau,** *Higher Laws*, in *Walden*, 1854

The whole civilized country is to some extent turned into a city. 2

—**Henry David Thoreau,** *Travel in Concord*, in *Excursions* [1863]

I'll scrape the mountains clean, my boys, 3
I'll drain the rivers dry,
A pocket full of rocks bring home,
So brothers, don't you cry!

—**Anonymous,** c. 1850

★ This verse, sung to the tune of *Oh! Susanna*, was popular among prospectors attracted by the discovery of gold in California in 1848.

A people who would begin by burning the fences and let the forest stand! 4

—**Henry David Thoreau,** *Walking*, 1862

Men as a general rule have very little reverence for trees. 5

—**Elizabeth Cady Stanton,** diary entry, 1900

The conservation of natural resources is the fundamental problem. Unless we solve that problem, it will avail us little to solve others. 6

—**Theodore Roosevelt,** speech to to the Deep Waterway Convention, Memphis, Tenn., Oct. 4, 1907

The nation behaves well if it treats its natural resources as assets which it must turn over to the next generation increased, and not impaired, in value. 7

—**Theodore Roosevelt,** speech, Colorado Livestock Association, Denver, Colo., August 29, 1910

Conservation means development as much as it does protection. 8

—**Theodore Roosevelt,** *The New Nationalism,* speech, Osawatomie, Kansas, August 31, 1910

★ Conservation was very much part of the progressive New Nationalism program that Roosevelt was developing in 1910, especially in this speech. Continuing his thoughts, Roosevelt made points very familar in the politics of conservation today: "I recognize the right and duty of this generation to develop and use the natural resources of our land; but I do not recognize the right to waste them, or to rob, by wasteful use, the generation that comes after us."

Here in the United States, we turn our rivers and streams into sewers and dumping grounds, we pollute the air, we destroy forests, and exterminate fishes, birds, and mammals—not to speak of vulgarizing charming landscapes with hideous advertisements. But at last it looks as if our people were awakening. 9

—**Theodore Roosevelt,** *Our Vanishing Wildlife*, in *The Outlook*, Jan. 25, 1913

1 Not one cent for scenery.

—**Joseph Cannon,** rejecting a request for a conservation appropriation, U.S. House of Representatives

★ "Uncle Joe" Cannon served in the House for forty-six years, and was Speaker 1903–11. The Library of Congress's *Respectfully Quoted*, notes that Pres. Lyndon B. Johnson had commented that conservation had been in eclipse since Theodore Roosevelt's day, and described Cannon's comment as ultimatum. "Well, today we are repealing Cannon's Law," Johnson said. "We are declaring a new doctrine of conservation" (speech, September 21, 1965, at signing ceremony making Assateague Island a national seashore area).

2 But when the birds are gone, and their warm fields
Return no more, where, then, is paradise?

—**Wallace Stevens,** *Sunday Morning*, 1923

3 A river is more than an amenity; it is a treasure.

—**Oliver Wendell Holmes, Jr.,** *New Jersey v. New York et al.*, 1931

★ This Supreme Court case concerned New York's diversion of the Delaware River. In an important argument for equitable sharing of natural resources, Justice Holmes continued, "It [a river] offers a necessity of life that must be rationed among those that have the power over it." He concluded that while New York had the power to cut off the downriver flow, "Such a power . . . could not be tolerated." See also Laura Gilpin at NATURE.

4 [Mankind is] a skin disease of the earth.

—**William C. Bullitt**, c. 1933, quoted in George F. Kennan, *Around the Cragged Hill* [1993]

★ Bullitt was ambassador to Russia (America's first) at the time, Kennan a young attaché.

5 it wont be long now it wont be long
man is making deserts of the earth
it wont be long now
before man will have it used up
so that nothing but ants
and centipedes and scorpions
can find a living on it.

—**Don Marquis,** *archy does his part*, 1935

6 Pity the Meek, for they shall inherit the earth.

—**Don Marquis,** quoted in Frederick B. Wilcox, *A Little Book of Aphorisms* [1947]

7 The nation that destroys its soil destroys itself.

—**Franklin D. Roosevelt,** letter to state governors, Feb. 26, 1937

8 One of the penalties of an ecological education is that one lives alone in a world of wounds.

—**Aldo Leopold,** *The Round River*, in *Round River: From the Journals of Also Leopold* [1953]

I must teach my children to know and to love the earth itself. If they can keep in contact with the land and the water and the sky, they can obtain all worthwhile that life holds. 1

—Charles A. Lindbergh, journal entry, April 1, 1938, *The Wartime Journals of Charles A. Lindbergh* [1970]

You can't tear up everything just to get a dollar out of it without suffering as a result. 2

—George Washington Carver, quoted by James H. Cobb, Jr. in *Atlanta Journal,* March 17, 1940

We abuse the land because we regard it as a commodity belonging to us. When we see land as a community to which we belong, we may begin to use it with love and respect. 3

—Aldo Leopold, *A Sand County Almanac*, 1949

★ See also Robert Frost at AMERICA & AMERICANS.

Conservation is a state of harmony between men and the land. 4

—Ibid.

A thing is right when it tends to preserve the integrity, stability, and beauty of the biotic community. It is wrong when it tends otherwise. 5

—Ibid.

★ This is the summation of Leopold's argument in the book's concluding essay, *The Land Ethic*, for considering questions of land use in ethical and esthetic as well as economic terms. He held that "A system of conservation based solely on economic self-interest is hopelessly lopsided. It tends to ignore, and thus eventually to eliminate many elements in the land community that lack commercial value, but that are (as far as we know) essential to its healthy functioning."

A culture is no better than its woods. 6

—W. H. Auden, *Bucolics*, in *Shield of Achilles*, 1955

★ The full passage runs: "This society is going smash; / They cannot fool us with how fast they go, / How much they cost each other and the gods! / A culture is no better than its woods."

The history of life on earth is the history of living things and their environment. 7

—Rachel Carson, *Silent Spring*, 1962

Over increasingly large areas of the United States, spring now comes unheralded by the return of the birds, and the early mornings are strangely silent where once they were filled with the beauty of bird song. 8

—Ibid.

As crude a weapon as a cave man's club, the chemical barrage has been hurled against the fabric of life. 9

—Ibid.

The supreme reality of our time is the vulnerability of our planet. 10

—John F. Kennedy, speech, June 28, 1963

1 The Quiet Crisis.

—**Stewart L. Udall,** book title, 1963

★ Then Secretary of the Interior, Udall wrote this book urging Americans to develop a "land ethic."

2 We have met the enemy and he is us.

—**Walt Kelly,** comment by Pogo the possum in the "Pogo" cartoon strip, used as Earth Day poster in 1971, *The Best of Pogo*, ed., Mrs. Walt Kelly & Bill Crouch, Jr.

★ See also Kelly at HUMANS & HUMAN NATURE.

3 A tree is a tree—how many do you need to look at?

—**Ronald Reagan,** speech to the Western Wood Products Association, Sept. 12, 1965

★ Former Reagan press representative Lyn Nofziger wrote in his autobiography (*Nofziger*, 1992) that in 1966, when Reagan was running for governor of California, he successfully denied making this remark. But Nofziger's secretary had it on tape. See also Reagan at NATURE: TREES.

4 I am a passenger on the spaceship, Earth.

—**R. Buckminster Fuller,** *Operating Manual for Spaceship Earth*, 1969

5 Now there is one outstandingly important fact regarding Spaceship Earth, and that is that no instruction book came out with it.

—**Ibid.**

6 They paved paradise
And put up a parking lot.

—**Joni Mitchell,** *Big Yellow Taxi,*1970

★ The lines came to Ms. Mitchell as she stood on the balcony of a hotel in Hawaii. The scenery in the distance was lovely. Then she looked down and saw an ugly concrete parking lot. That's how the song was born.

7 I speak for the trees, for the trees have no tongues.

—**Dr. Seuss (Theodore Seuss Geisel),** *The Lorax,* 1971

8 We have forgotten how to be good guests, how to walk lightly on the earth as its other creatures do.

—**Barbara Ward Jackson & René Dubos,** *Only One Earth* (report of the United Nations Stockholm Conference on the Human Environment), 1972

9 The wildness of the soil that we call fertility begins to diminish, and the soil itself flees from us in water and wind.

—**Wendell Berry,** *Getting Along with Nature* in *Home Economics,* 1982

10 Rape, ruin, and run.

—**Ansel Adams** on the policies of Interior Secretary James Watt allowing strip mining and timbering in national parks, in *Playboy,* May 1983

After one look at this planet any visitor from outer space would say "I WANT TO SEE THE MANAGER." 1

—**William S. Burroughs**, *"Woman: A Biological Mistake?"* in *The Adding Machine*, 1985

★ The writer was named for his grandfather, who established the family's fortune by inventing a calculator and forming the Burroughs Adding Machine Co. to make and market it.

Stewardship of the land should be based on the principle that resources are not given to us by our parents but are loaned to us by our children. 2

—**Larry D. Harris,** in *Los Angeles Times*, June 22, 1987

In the end, our society will be defined not only by what we create but by what we refuse to destroy. 3

—**John Sawhill,** in John A. Murray, ed., *The Quotable Nature Lover* [1999]

★ Dr. Sawhill was president of The Nature Conservancy. The observation, commonly quoted by others, appears in the 1999 collection, which was produced in conjunction with the Conservancy, but TNC staffers were unable to pinpoint the original source. It may be from a speech or an editorial in a Conservancy publication.

A lawn is nature under totalitarian rule. 4

—**Michael Pollan,** *Second Nature,* 1991

Why should deserts be asked to blossom? 5

—**Wallace Stegner,** Introduction, *Where the Bluebird Sings to the Lemonade Springs*, 1992

★ The introduction was based on Stegner's lecture *A Geography of Hope*, delivered at the University of Colorado, and published by the university's press in *A Society to Match Our Scenery*, 1991. Stegner reminds us that aridity is the natural condition of the West, and cannot be overcome except at an excessively high price. "You have to get over the color green," he wrote; "you have to quit associating beauty with gardens and lawn; you have to get used to an unhuman scale," *Thoughts in a Dry Land*, 1972. See also Stegner at WILDERNESS.

Envy

Envy is ignorance. 6

—**Ralph Waldo Emerson,** *Self-Reliance*, in *Essays: First Series*, 1841

Pain, n. An uncomfortable frame of mind that may have a physical basis in something that is being done to the body, or may be purely mental, caused by the good fortune of another. 7

—**Ambrose Bierce,** *The Devil's Dictionary*, 1906

Epitaphs & Gravestones

See also CRIME (G. W. Plunkitt); LAST WORDS; LINCOLN, ABRAHAM; SPORTS (Grantland Rice)

Behold and see as you pass by 8
As you are now, so once was I;

As I am now, so you will be—
Prepare for death and follow me.
—**Anonymous,** commonly used on gravestones in Colonial times

★ The verse dates back at least to 1376, when it was carved on the tomb of Edward, the Black Prince, according to Avon Neal in *American Heritage*, August 1970.

1 The body of B. Franklin, Printer (like the cover of an old book, its contents torn out and stripped of its lettering and gilding), lies here, food for worms; but the work shall not be lost, for it will (as he believed) appear once more in a new and more elegant edition, revised and corrected by the Author.
—**Benjamin Franklin,** *Epitaph on Himself*, 1728

★ Franklin died in 1790.

2 Here lyes John Purcell;
And whether he be in heaven or in hell
Never a one of us can tell.
—**Anonymous,** in Alexander Hamilton, *Itinerarium*, July 6, 1744

★ A proposed epitaph for a recently deceased New Yorker. See Boston under CITIES for details on this Hamilton, who is not Hamilton the Founding Father.

3 Here Skugg
Lies snug
As a bug
In a rug.
—**Benjamin Franklin,** letter to Georgiana Shipley, Sept. 26, 1772

★ Skugg was Miss Shipley's pet squirrel.

4 And the fellow died as well as he lived, but it is part of a sailor's life to die well. He had no talk, but he inspired all about him with ardor; he always saw the best thing to be done; he knew the best way to do it; and he had no more dodge in him than the mainmast.
—**Stephen Decatur,** on Captain James Lawrence, after his death in action between the U.S.S. *Chesapeake* and H.M.S. *Shannon* off Boston Harbor on June 1, 1813

5 Here was buried Thomas Jefferson, author of the Declaration of American Independence, of the statute of Virginia for religious freedom, and father of the University of Virginia.
—**Thomas Jefferson,** epitaph written by himself, inscribed on his tombstone at Monticello

★ This was found in the top drawer of Jefferson's desk after his death on July 4, 1826. Note that he made no mention of the high offices he had attained: governor of Virginia, minister to France, U.S. Secretary of State, Vice President and President. As for the Virginia law guaranteeing religious freedom, he and James Madison fought nine years to get it passed, and it is one of the sources of the religion clause in the First Amendment, which was written by Madison. See also Jefferson at TYRANNY.

He served his country faithfully forty-eight years and was much beloved and respected by all who knew him. **1**

—Anonymous, gravestone of Ichabod Crane on Staten Island

★ Crane, a hero of the War of 1812, did not resemble the easily afeared character that bore his name in Washington Irving's *Legend of Sleepy Hollow*, 1819.

Quoth the Raven, "Nevermore." **2**

—Edgar Allan Poe, *The Raven*, 1845, used on his gravestone in Baltimore

★ More at THE OCCULT.

On fame's eternal camping ground **3**
Their silent tents are spread
And glory guards with solemn round
The bivouac of the dead.

—Theodore O'Hara, *The Bivouac of the Dead*, 1847

★ The poem, written during the Mexican War, commemorates the American dead at the battle of Buena Vista, on February 22, 1847. By an act of Congress, the verse is displayed at every national cemetery.

He died as he must have wished to die, breathing his last in the Capitol, stricken down by the angel of death on the field of his civil glory. **4**

—Philip Hone, *Diary*, on the death of John Quincy Adams, Feb. 24, 1848

★ After leaving the presidency in 1829, Adams served seventeen years in the House, its oldest member at the time of his death, and still an able debater. See also Adams at LAST WORDS.

Gone are the living, but the dead remain, **5**
And not neglected; for a hand unseen,
Scattering its bounty like summer rain,
Still keeps their graves and their remembrance green.

—Henry Wadsworth Longfellow, *The Jewish Cemetery at Newport*, 1852

★ The 18th-century Sephardic cemetery at Newport, Rhode Island, had been abandoned by Longfellow's time. The associated synagogue itself still stands.

Unawed by opinion **6**
Unseduced by flattery
Undismayed by disaster
He confronted life with antique courage
And death with Christian hope.

—Anonymous, epitaph of James Petigru, Charleston, S.C., 1863

★ He confronted life with intelligence, too; see Petigru at SOUTH CAROLINA.

He was a gallant soldier, and a Christian gentleman. **7**

—Ulysses S. Grant, speaking of Thomas J. "Stonewall" Jackson, 1864

★ During the Wilderness Campaign, Grant chanced to stay overnight in the house where Jackson had died. Told of this, Grant uttered this impromptu epitaph, which would have pleased Jackson greatly. See also Jackson at LAST WORDS.

1 Sleep sweetly in your humble graves,
Sleep, martyrs of a fallen cause . . .
Stoop, angels hither from the skies!
There is no holier spot of ground
Than where defeated valor lies,
By mourning beauty crowned!

—**Henry Timrod,** *Ode on the Confederate Dead*, 1867

★ The poem was written to be sung as a hymn. Its full title tells the story: *Ode. Sung on the occasion of decorating the graves of the Confederate dead, at Magnolia Cemetery, Charleston, S.C.*, 1867.

2 When fades at length our lingering day,
Who cares what pompous tombstones say?
Read on the hearts that love us still,
Hic jacet Joe. *Hic jacet* Bill.

—**Oliver Wendell Holmes, Sr.,** *Bill and Joe*, 1868

★ *Hic jacet* means "here lies."

3 Here lies a man who never owned a dollar he could not take up to the Great White Throne.

—**Robert Collyer,** funeral address for Peter Cooper, April 7, 1883

★ Cooper's rare honesty and generosity, highlighted here by the Reverend Dr. Collyer, prompted a spontaneous popular expression of grief at his death. Flags in New York City were lowered to half-staff, and mourners followed the coffin for miles through the city while church bells tolled. See also Cooper at GOD and MONEY & THE RICH.

4 Called back.

—**Emily Dickinson,** on her gravestone in West Amherst, Mass., from her last letter, May 1886

5 Here lies Champ Clark, who, in the year of our Lord and Master one thousand eight hundred and ninety-four, stood in the American Congress and did battle for the principle that the great body of the American people should have cheaper clothing, cheaper food, cheaper medicine, cheaper necessaries of life, more luxuries, and be better able to educate their children.

—**Champ Clark,** speech, House of Representatives, Dec. 10, 1894

★ Clark, then a lame duck, offered this political epitaph for himself when taunted by a Republican for having lost in the November election. Reports of the Missouri Democrat's political demise were premature, however. Reelected in 1897, he served another twelve terms in the House and was Speaker from 1911 to 1919.

6 Here lies Frank Pixley—as usual.

—**Ambrose Bierce,** attributed

★ Pixley, a former California attorney general, founded *The Argonaut* in 1877, and

Bierce was one of the magazine's first editors. According to one of Pixley's descendants, English professor Sandra Dutton, Pixley fired Bierce, and after that, the two men found amusement in writing each other's epitaphs.

Warm summer sun, shine kindly here; **1**
Warm southern wind, blow softly here;
Green sod above, lie light, lie light—Good night, dear heart, good night, good night.

—**Mark Twain,** attributed, 1896

★ The verse is on the gravestone in Elmira, New York, of Twain's daughter Susy—"she that had been our wonder and our worship"—who died August 18, 1896. The poem actually was by an Australian, Robert Richardson, written c. 1885, and used with a slight change by Twain. In the original, "southern" read "northern," because the warm wind in Australia is from the north. Twain's friend and biographer, Albert Bigelow Paine, reports that when Twain heard that the lines were being attributed to him, he had Richardson's name cut beneath them on the monument. Still, Twain is often given credit for them.

He Seen His Opportunities and He Took 'Em. **2**

—**George W. Plunkitt,** suggested epitaph for himself, in William L. Riordan, *Plunkitt of Tammany Hall* [1905]

★ Plunkitt lived until 1924. The epitaph is basically his own definition of "honest graft." See CRIME, CRIMINALS, & DETECTIVES.

Epitaph, n. An inscription on a tomb showing that virtues acquired by death have a retroactive effect. **3**

—**Ambrose Bierce,** *The Devil's Dictionary*, 1906

★ The dictionary, originally called the *The Cynic's Word Book*—at the publisher's insistence—included definitions used in newspaper columns from as early as 1877. In the entry for *loss*, Bierce countered the retroactive effect of death as best he could in a proposed epitaph for railroad magnate C. P. Huntington: "Here Huntington's ashes long have lain / Whose loss is our own eternal gain, / For while he exercised all his powers, / Whatever he gained, the loss was ours."

Faithful to the cause of Prohibition— **4**
She hath done what she could.

—**Anonymous,** gravestone of Carry Nation, Belton, Mo., 1911

If, after I depart this vale, you ever remember me and have thought to please my ghost, forgive some sinner and wink your eye at some homely girl. **5**

—**H. L. Mencken,** in *Smart Set* magazine, Dec. 1921

God gave him a great vision. **6**
The devil gave him an imperious heart.
The proud heart is still.
The vision lives.

—**William Allen White,** editorial on the death of Pres. Woodrow Wilson, *Emporia Gazette*, Feb. 4, 1924

★ Wilson suffered a stroke while campaigning to win support for the League of Nations.

1 I never met a man I didn't like.

—Will Rogers, remark, Tremont Temple Baptist Church, Boston, June 15, 1930

★ This was not the first time Rogers expressed this thought. Speculating that he would have enjoyed meeting Trotsky if given the chance, he wrote in *There's Not a Bathing Suit in Russia* (1927), "I have never yet met a man that I dident [*sic*] like." Rogers continued: "When you meet people, no matter what opinion you might have formed of them beforehand, why, after you meet them and see their angle and their personality, why, you can see a lot of good in all of them." The later, more famous statement was made when he was asked by the church minister to address his congregation. Then he said that "When I die, my epitaph or whatever you call those signs on gravestones is going to read: 'I joked about every prominent man of my time, but I never met a man I didn't like.' I am so proud of that I can hardly wait to die so it can be carved. And when you come to my grave you will find me sitting there, proudly reading it." Five years later, Rogers died in a plane crash in Alaska. The abbreviated form of the sentiment is inscribed on his burial stone at the Will Rogers Memorial in Claremore, Oklahoma.

2 [Epitaph for a waiter:] By and by
God caught his eye.

—David McCord, "Remainders," *Bay Window Ballads*, 1935

★ Attributed in short form—"God caught his eye"—to playwright George Kaufman, a slightly younger contemporary of McCord's, by critic Howard Teichman in his 1972 biography of Kaufman. Most authoritative sources cite McCord, however.

3 Earth, receive an honored guest;
William Yeats is laid to rest.
Let the Irish vessel lie
Emptied of its poetry.

—W. H. Auden, *In Memory of W. B. Yeats*, 1940

4 And were an epitaph to be my story,
I'd have a short one ready for my own.
I would have written of me on my stone:
I had a lover's quarrel with the world.

—Robert Frost, *The Lesson for Today*, read at Harvard University, June 20, 1941

5 On the whole, I'd rather be in Philadelphia.

—W. C. Fields, attributed, epitaph for himself, 1946

★ See also Fields on Philadelphia under Cities.

6 My Jesus mercy.

—Anonymous, gravestone of Al Capone, Chicago, 1947

7 Well, it only proves what they always say—give the public something they want to see, and they'll come out for it.

—"Red" Skelton, on the huge crowd, filling two sound stages, that turned out for the funeral of movie mogul Harry Cohn, Mar. 2, 1958, in Bob Thomas, *King Cohn* [1967]

Now I've laid me down to die, 1
I pray my neighbors not to pry
Too deeply into sins that I,
Not only cannot here deny,
But much enjoyed as life flew by.

—**Preston Sturges,** epitaph from opening of unfinished autobiography

★ This great director of comedies with bleak undertones died in 1959.

Excuse my dust. 2

—**Dorothy Parker,** proposed epitaph

Over my dead body! 3

—**George S. Kaufman,** proposed epitaph, quoted in Robert E. Drennan, *The Algonquin Wits* [1968]

Say that I was a drum major for justice; say that I was a drum major for peace; I was a drum major for righteousness. 4

—**Martin Luther King, Jr.,** suggestions for his own funeral, sermon, Feb. 4, 1968

★ The epitaph on his gravestone is from the spiritual with which he ended his "I have a dream" speech at the Lincoln Memorial in the march on Washington in 1963; see AMERICAN HISTORY: MEMORABLE MOMENTS. The words are "Free at last! Free at last! Thank God Almighty, we are free at last!"

She did it the hard way. 5

—**Bette Davis,** headstone inscription, Forest Lawn, Hollywood, 1989

Equality

See also DEMOCRACY; MANNERS (De Vries); PEOPLE, THE; RACES & PEOPLES; WOMEN; WOMEN & MEN.

All men are created equal. 6

—**Thomas Jefferson,** *Declaration of Independence*, July 4, 1776

★ More at DECLARATION OF INDEPENDENCE.

An equality of property . . . is the very soul of a republic. 7

—**Noah Webster**, *An Examination into the Leading Principles of the Federal Constitution*, Oct. 10, 1787

★ The full sentence reads: "An equality of property, with a necessity of alienation, constantly operating to destroy combinations of powerful families, is the very soul of a republic."

Equal laws protecting equal rights . . . the best guarantee of loyalty and love of country. 8

—**James Madison,** letter to Jacob De La Motta, August 1820

★ Inscribed in the Madison Memorial Hall, Library of Congress.

1 The earth is the mother of all people, and all people should have equal rights upon it. You might as well expect the rivers to run backward as that any man who was born a free man should be contented when penned up and denied liberty.
—**Joseph the Younger,** *An Indian's View of Indian Affairs,* in *The North American Review*, no. 269, vol. 128, 1879

★ Though outranked by several older Nez Percé chiefs, Joseph the Younger, who succeeded his father as chief of the Wallowa band in 1871, was regarded by whites as the principal leader of the entire tribe. More at TALK.

2 There is no king who has not had a slave among his ancestors, and no slave who has not had a king among his.
—**Helen Keller,** *The Story of My Life*, 1902

3 All of us do not have equal talent, but all of us should have an equal opportunity to develop our talents.
—**John F. Kennedy,** speech, San Diego State College, June 6, 1963

4 A society that puts equality—in the sense of equality of outcome—ahead of freedom will end up with neither equality nor freedom. The use of force to achieve equality will destroy freedom, and the force, introduced for good purposes, will end up in the hands of people who use it to promote their own interests.
—**Milton Friedman & Rose Friedman,** *Free to Choose: A Personal Statement*, 1979

5 Every attempt at social leveling ends with leveling to the bottom, never to the top.
—**George F. Kennan,** *Around the Cragged Hill: A Personal and Political Philosophy*, 1993

Eras

See BAD TIMES; DEPRESSION, THE; GENERATIONS; GOOD TIMES; MODERN TIMES; PAST, THE; POLITICS & POLITICIANS; PRESENT, THE.

Error

See FAULTS & FAILINGS; MISTAKES.

Escape

6 The efforts which we make to escape from our destiny only serve to lead us into it.
—**Ralph Waldo Emerson,** *Fate,* in *The Conduct of Life*, 1860

7 The best way out is always through.
—**Robert Frost,** *A Servant to Servants*, in *North of Boston*, 1914

8 listen: there's a hell of a good universe next door: let's go.
—**E. E. Cummings,** *pity this busy monster, manunkind,* in *One Times One* (or *1* × *1*), 1944

Ethics, Morality & Values

See also CONSCIENCE; EXPEDIENCY; RIGHT; VIRTUE.

I have no confidence in any man who is not exact in his morals. **1**
—**John Adams,** letter to Abigail Adams, Nov. 5, 1775

My country is the world, and my religion is to do good. **2**
—**Thomas Paine,** *The Rights of Man*, 1791

★ In *The Age of Reason*, 1794, Paine elaborated: "The world is my country, all mankind are my brethren, and to do good is my religion."

The money and morality ov [sic] this world are a good deal alike, the principle never **3**
loses sight ov the interest.
—**Josh Billings,** *Jews Harps*, in *Everybody's Friend, or Josh Billing's Encyclopedia . . . of Wit and Humor*, 1874

Expedients are for the hour, but principles are for the ages. **4**
—**Henry Ward Beecher,** *Proverbs from Plymouth Pulpit*, 1887

It is best not to use our morals weekdays, it gets them out of repair for Sunday. **5**
—**Mark Twain,** *Notebook*, 1898

★ See also Twain at SIN, VICE, & NAUGHTINESS on our Moral Sense and Immoral Sense.

We can act *as if* there were a God; feel *as if* we were free; consider nature *as if* she **6**
were full of special designs; lay plans *as if* we were to be immortal; and we find then that these words do make a genuine difference in our moral life.
—**William James,** *The Varieties of Religious Experience*, 1902

It is curious that physical courage should be so common in the world and moral **7**
courage so rare.
—**Mark Twain,** *Mark Twain in Eruption*, unpublished memoirs edited by Bernard DeVoto [1940]

It has always been a peculiarity of the human race that it keeps two sets of morals in **8**
stock—the private and the real, and the public and the artificial.
—**Ibid.**

There has never been a large political or social question before the American people **9**
which did not quickly resolve itself into a moral question.
—**H. L. Mencken,** in *Smart Set*, 1914, from S. T. Joshi, ed., *Mencken's America* [2004]

I know only that what is moral is what you feel good after and what is immoral is **10**
what you feel bad after.
—**Ernest Hemingway,** *Death in the Afternoon*, 1932

The number of people with any criteria for distinguishing between good and evil is **11**
very small.
—**T. S. Eliot,** Virginia lectures, 1933

1 The world has achieved brilliance without conscience. Ours is a world of nuclear giants and ethical infants.

—Omar Bradley, speech, Armistice Day, 1948

★ Gen. Bradley commanded U.S. Forces in Normandy in 1944, and became chief of staff in 1949. He supported Pres. Harry S. Truman in his confrontation with Gen. Douglas MacArthur, who at one point advocated use of nuclear weapons in the Korean conflict. See under MacArthur at AMERICAN HISTORY: MEMORABLE MOMENTS.

2 Puritanism—the haunting fear that someone, somewhere, may be happy.

—H. L. Mencken, *A Mencken Chrestomathy*, 1949

3 A man does what he must . . . and that is the basis of all human morality.

—John F. Kennedy, *Profiles in Courage*, 1956

4 The hottest places in hell are reserved for those who in a period of moral crisis maintain their neutrality.

—John F. Kennedy, remarks in Bonn, June 24, 1963

★ Pres. Kennedy attributed this observation to Dante in the talk that he gave on the occasion of the signing of a charter establishing the German Peace Corps. Arthur M. Schlesinger, Jr., reported in *A Thousand Days* (1965) that he found this quotation, along with others from other famous men, in a loose-leaf notebook that JFK kept in 1945–46. The young Kennedy seems to have misremembered, however. The line does not appear in Dante's works, so Kennedy gets credit for it by default.

5 A true revolution of values will soon look uneasily on the glaring contrast of poverty and wealth.

—Martin Luther King, Jr., *Where Do We Go from Here? Chaos or Community*, 1967

6 We no longer know how to justify any value except in terms of expediency. Man . . . feels, acts, and thinks as if the sole purpose of the universe were to satisfy his needs.

—Abraham Joshua Heschel, *The Insecurity of Freedom: Essays on Human Existence*, 1967

7 The needs of society determine its ethics.

—Maya Angelou, *I Know Why the Caged Bird Sings*, 1969

8 Moral victories don't count.

—Anonymous, sign on a door in the Pentagon, 1988, cited in *The Macmillan Dictionary of Political Quotations* [1993]

9 The art of acting morally is behaving *as if everything we do matters.*

—Gloria Steinem, *The Birth of Ms.*, in *New York*, April 19, 1993

10 Our values are defined by what we will tolerate when it is done to others.

—William Greider, *One World, Ready or Not: The Manic Logic of Global Capitalism*, 1997

Evidence

See also JUSTICE; LAW.

The suppressing of evidence ought always to be taken for the strongest evidence. **1**
—Andrew Hamilton, argument in the trial of John Peter Zenger, Aug. 4, 1735

★ Note this is not Alexander Hamilton, but Andrew Hamilton of Phildelphia, possibly the original "Philadelphia lawyer, " that is, a very clever lawyer indeed. Zenger, a New York printer, had been imprisoned and brought to trial because an edition of his newspaper had published material suggesting that some colonials found the government to be arbitrary and oppressive. Under British law, truth could not be a defense in a libel case. The rule was, "The greater the truth, the greater the libel," meaning that one does maximum damage to a person's reputation by publicizing bad acts that the person actually performed. Hamilton insisted that the truthfulness of Zenger's paper should be a complete defense. That the court would not allow testimony as to the truthfulness of the text in question was, Hamilton argued, the strongest evidence in favor of Zenger. He told the jury it was their duty, not the court's to decide what was libelous and their verdict would "affect every Freeman that lives under a British government on the main of America." The unanimous verdict was "not guilty." Hamilton, by the way, paid his own expenses and did not charge a fee.

Some circumstantial evidence is very strong, as when you find a trout in the milk. **2**
—Henry David Thoreau, *Journal*, Nov. 11, 1850

★ The reference is to a common consumer fraud of the time—watering of milk. The line has proven to be a popular one with mystery writers, at least three of whom have used *A Trout in the Milk* as a book title, according to Jane Horning's *The Mystery Lover's Book of Quotations*.

Goddamn an eyewitness anyway. He always spoils a good story. **3**
—Col. Crisp, c. 1880s

★ In David McCullough's *Truman*, this "colonel by agreement" is described as a perennial Democratic congressional candidate and local orator.

It is a less evil that some criminals should escape than that the government should **4**
play an ignoble part [in gathering evidence].
—Oliver Wendell Holmes, Jr., dissent, *Olmstead v. U.S.*, 1928

★ One of Holmes's famous dissents. He led up to his conclusion this way: "It is desirable that criminals should be detected, and to that end all available evidence should be used. It is also desirable that the government should not itself foster crimes, when they are the means by which evidence is to be obtained. . . . We have to choose, and for my part I think it is a less evil . . . [etc.]" The case, which involved wiretapping of a bootlegger, was finally completely overturned in 1967 when the Supreme Court held in *Katz v. U.S.* that government agents had to obtain court orders to place taps. Justice Louis D. Brandeis also wrote a dissent in *Olmstead*; see PRIVACY.

If it walks like a duck, and quacks like a duck, then it just may be a duck. **5**
—Walter Reuther, attributed

★ William Safire, in his *New Political Dictionary*, writes that Mr. Reuther, head of the United Auto Workers, applied this logic to the question of how to identify a Communist.

1 Extraordinary claims require extraordinary evidence.
—Carl Sagan, *Cosmos* (TV series), 1980

★ Sagan became identified with this standard of proof by citing it frequently in later works but he was not the first to suggest it. The same rule was enunciated by Marcello Truzzi in his opening editorial in the first issue of *The Zetetic* (now *The Skeptical Inquirer*; Fall/Winter 1976), published by the Committee for the Scientific Investigation of Claims of the Paranormal. This high standard for accepting extraordinary claims is essentially a distilled restatement of the Scottish philosopher David Hume's conclusion that "no testimony is sufficient to establish a miracle, unless the testimony be of such a kind, that its falsehood would be more miraculous than the fact which it endeavors to establish" ("On Miracles," in *Enquiry concerning Human Understanding*, 1748). See also MIRACLES.

2 Although they speak softly, they never lie and they never forget.
—Clyde Collins Snow, *Witnessing from the Grave*, 1991

★ Snow, a forensic anthropologist, writes here of the value of skeletons as evidence.

3 The absence of evidence is not evidence of absence.
—Michael Papagiannis, quoted in C. D. B. Bryan, *Close Encounters of the Fourth Kind: Alien Abductions, UFOs, and the Conference at M.I.T.*, 1995

★ Papagiannis is an astronomer at Boston University.

4 If it doesn't fit, you must acquit.
—Johnnie Cochran, summation at O. J. Simpson trial, Sept. 27, 1995

★ The "it" was a glove, found at the scene of the murder of Mr. Simpson's wife and a young man who had the bad luck of being at the wrong place at the wrong time. Asked earlier in the trial to put the glove on, the defendant apparently had difficulty slipping it on to his hand. Mr. Cochran made much of this in the closing argument, and the jury did acquit. The rhyme, often misquoted as "If the glove doesn't fit, you must acquit," was suggested to Mr. Cochran by a member of his legal team, Gerald Uelmen, but was so strongly identified with him that, as he wrote in his 1996 memoir, *Journey to Justice*, he believed it was "the line by which I'll be remembered."And judging from his obituary in *The New York Times* (March 30, 2005), he was right.

Evil

See also CRIME, CRIMINALS, & DETECTIVES; DANGER & DANGEROUS PEOPLE; DEVIL, THE; SIN, VICE, & NAUGHTINESS.

5 There is a capacity of virtue in us, and there is a capacity of vice to make your blood creep.
—Ralph Waldo Emerson, *Journal*, 1831

6 I's wicked, I is.
—Harriet Beecher Stowe, *Uncle Tom's Cabin*, 1852

7 There are a thousand hacking at the branches of evil to one who is striking at the root.
—Henry David Thoreau, *Economy*, in *Walden*, 1854

No man is justified in doing evil on the grounds of expediency. **1**

—Theodore Roosevelt, *The Strenuous Life*, title essay, 1900

Who knows what evil lurks in the hearts of men? The Shadow knows! **2**

—Walter B. Gibson (writing as Maxwell Grant), 1930

★ Gibson's character, The Shadow, first appeared, so to speak, on the *Street & Smith Detective Hour* radio show. The great popularity of the show made this line famous; it opened each episode.

Between two evils, I always pick the one I never tried before. **3**

—Mae West, *Klondike Annie*, 1936

Fashions in sin change. **4**

—Lillian Hellman, *Watch on the Rhine*, 1941

Evil is unspectacular and always human **5**
And shares our bed and eats at our own table.

—W. H. Auden, *Herman Melville*, in *The Collected Poetry of W. H. Auden*, 1945

It is a sin to believe evil of others, but it is seldom a mistake. **6**

—H. L. Mencken, *A Mencken Chrestomathy*, 1949

We all have flaws, and mine is being wicked. **7**

—James Thurber, *The Thirteen Clocks,* 1950

★ The evil duke speaking.

He who accepts evil without protesting against it is really cooperating with it. **8**

—Martin Luther King, Jr., *Stride Toward Freedom*, 1958

★ King's thought parallels an observation that John F. Kennedy used in speeches: "The only thing necessary for the triumph of evil is for good men to do nothing." Kennedy attributed the remark to the British statesman and political philosopher Edmund Burke, but no one has been able to find it in Burke's writings. Perhaps, as Emily Morison Beck suggested in the preface to the 1980 edition of *Bartlett's Familiar Quotations*, the quote is a paraphrase of another statement by Burke: "When bad men combine, the good must associate; else they will fall, one by one," *Thoughts on the Cause of the Present Discontents*, April 23, 1770. Ultimately, one might trace the thought to the Bible: "He who is not with me is against me," *Matthew* 12:30.

The fearsome . . . *banality of evil.* **9**

—Hannah Arendt, *Eichmann in Jerusalem*, 1963

★ The book was based on professor Arendt's articles in the *The New Yorker* on the trial of Adolf Eichmann for war crimes. Eichmann, more of a bureaucrat than a demon, personified to Arendt the institutionalization of evil in a totalitarian society. Just before his trial, he remarked, "To sum it all up, I must say I regret nothing." Arendt wrote, "It was as though, in those last minutes, he was summing up the lessons that this long course in human wickedness had taught us—the lesson of the fearsome, word-and-thought-defying *banality of evil*." A similar thought was expressed by American poet Stephen Vincent Benét in *John Brown's Body*, 1928. Benét wrote that while "some men wish evil and accomplish it," most "just let it happen." He concluded, "The fault is no decisive villainous knife / But the dull saw that is the routine mind." See also Bellow at CONSCIENCE.

1 No man is a villain in his own heart.
—James Baldwin, *Blues for Mr. Charley*, introduction to the play, 1964

2 An axis of evil.
—George W. Bush, State of the Union address, Jan. 29, 2002

★ For more see AMERICAN HISTORY: MEMORABLE MOMENTS

Excellence

See also GRACE; METHOD; VIRTUE.

3 Strive to be the *greatest* man in your country, and you may be disappointed. Strive to be the *best* and you may succeed: he may well win the race that runs by himself.
—Benjamin Franklin, *Poor Richard's Almanack*, 1747

4 If a man can write a better book, preach a better sermon, or make a better mousetrap than his neighbor, though he builds his house in the woods, the world will make a beaten path to his door.
—Ralph Waldo Emerson, lecture, attributed in Sarah B. Yule and Mary S. Keene, *Borrowings* [1889]

★ This is how Yule remembered Emerson's insight, offered during a lecture in 1871 in California, either in San Francisco or Oakland. Emerson's writings contain only the wordier: "I trust a good deal to common fame, as we all must. If a man has good corn, or wood, or boards, or pigs, to sell, or can make better chairs or knives, crucibles or church organs, than anybody else, you will find a broad hard-beaten road to his house," *Journal*, February 1855. Of course, now that we have advertising instead of common fame, the proposition falters. See also Emerson at ACTION & DOING.

5 It is the privilege of any human work which is well done to invest the doer with a certain haughtiness.
—Ralph Waldo Emerson, *Wealth*, in *The Conduct of Life*, 1860

6 What is our praise or pride
But to imagine excellence, and try to make it?
What does it say over the door of Heaven
But *homo fecit*?
—Richard Wilbur, *For the New Railway Station in Rome*, in *Things of This World*, 1956

★ *Homo fecit* means 'man built it.'

7 The sad truth is that excellence makes people nervous.
—Shana Alexander, *Neglected Kids—The Bright Ones*, 1966, in *The Feminist Eye* [1970]

Strive for excellence, not perfection. 1

—H. Jackson Brown, Jr., *Life's Little Instruction Book*, 1991

Excess

See also ENTHUSIASM & ZEAL; LUXURY; PASSION; THINGS & POSSESSIONS.

I don't regret a single "excess" of my responsive youth—I only regret, in my chilled 2
age, certain occasions and opportunities I didn't embrace.

—Henry James, letter to Hugh Walpole, August 21, 1913

Never murder a man who is committing suicide. 3

—Woodrow Wilson, letter to Bernard Baruch, 1916

★ This was Pres. Wilson's hands-off strategy for dealing with Charles Evans Hughes, his Republican opponent in the 1916 election. He attributed the precept to "a friend, who says that he has always followed the rule never to murder a man who is committing suicide." Nevertheless, the election was quite close, with Wilson winning by less than 600,000 votes out of almost 18 million cast. The victor wasn't known until three days after the polls closed.

My candle burns at both ends; 4
It will not last the night;
But ah, my foes, and oh my friends—
It gives a lovely light.

—Edna St. Vincent Millay, *First Fig*, in *A Few Figs from Thistles*, 1920

★ Legendary Broadway director George Abbott countered, "I do not think burning the candle at both ends casts a lovely light; on the contrary, I am of the opinion that it is a dandy way to get a nervous breakdown." This was in his autobiography, written in 1963, when he was seventy-six; he continued to work until his death at age 107. Millay, in her later years, settled down to country living, but nevertheless died at age fifty-eight. On the other hand, she had won a Pulitzer Prize at age twenty-seven. See also Neil Young below.

Too much of a good thing can be wonderful. 5

—Mae West, quoted in Joseph Weintraub, ed., *The Wit and Wisdom of Mae West* [1967]

It's better to burn out 6
Than to fade away

—Neil Young, *My My, Hey Hey (Out of the Blue)*, in *Rust Never Sleeps*, album, 1979

★ See also Edna St. Vincent Millay above.

Excuses & Explanations

You needn't try to reason, 7
Your excuse is out of season,
Just kiss yourself goodbye.

—William Jerome, *Just Kiss Yourself Goodbye*, 1902

1 Never explain—your friends do not need it, and your enemies will not believe you anyway.

—Elbert Hubbard, *Notebook*, 1927

★ See also Henry Ford below.

2 Wisdom too often never comes, and so one ought not to reject it merely because it comes late.

—Felix Frankfurter, *Henslee v. Union Planters Bank*, 1949

3 [On being observed by his wife kissing a chorus girl:] I wasn't kissing her, I was whispering into her mouth.

—Chico Marx, attributed, in Groucho Marx and Richard J. Anobile, *Marx Brothers Scrapbook* [1973]

4 Never complain, never explain.

—Henry Ford II, saying

★ According to *The New York Times* obituary for Ford, he turned to this traditional saying after being arrested for drunk driving; the advice is also the title of Victor Lasky's biography of Ford. The thought, however, is essentially proverbial. Dean Acheson observed, "How vulnerable are those who explain," *Time* magazine, June 26, 1964. Abroad, Admiral of the Fleet John Arbuthnot Baron Fisher noted in a letter to the London *Times*, Sept. 5, 1919: "(It's only d——d fools who argue!) Never contradict. Never explain. Never apologize. (Those are the secrets of a happy life!)" The earliest attribution is to the English Prime Minister Benjamin Disraeli in John Morley's *The Life of William Gladstone*, 1903.

5 I'm a wiser man this morning than I was last night.

—Sam Rayburn, comment, July 14, 1960, in Arthur M. Schlesinger, Jr., *A Thousand Days* [1965]

★ Thus Rayburn explained to Lyndon B. Johnson why he was recommending that Johnson accept the 1960 Democratic vice presidential nomination, when, just hours before, he had given the opposite advice.

6 I am not pulling the cat's tail, I'm just holding it. The cat's doing the pulling.

—"Red" Skelton, Mean Widdle Kid routine

7 I know nothing.

—Bernard Fein & Albert S. Ruddy, creators of *Hogan's Heroes* 1965–1971

★ This was the signature line of the bumbling but crafty Nazi prison guard, Sgt. Schultz, one of the regulars in this sit com. Often the full excuse was used: "I see nothing, I hear nothing, I know nothing." Claims of ignorance of wrongdoing have been called the Schultz defense. For example, in 2002, Rep. Edward J. Markey (D., Mass.) observed that Enron chief Jeffrey K. Skilling was using the Sergeant Schultz defense. In 2001, Fox News commentator Brit Hume claimed that Hillary Rodham Clinton was acting like Schultz when denying knowledge of the details of a questionable presidential pardon in which her brother had a role.

The devil made me do it. 1

—**Flip Wilson,** saying

★ A note on Wilson is given at THE DEVIL.

Two wrongs don't make a right, but they make a good excuse. 2

—**Thomas Szasz,** *Social Relations*, in *The Second Sin*, 1973

It's not how you win or lose, it's how you place the blame. 3

—**Anonymous**

★ Baseball slugger Ralph Kiner used this quip while broadcasting a Mets game, but acknowledged it wasn't original with him. It's a play on the commonplace, "It's not how you win or lose, it's how you play the game." See Grantland Rice at SPORTS.

I . . . didn't inhale. 4

—**Bill Clinton,** television interview, March 29, 1992

★ Presidential candidate Clinton offering a classic excuse for a popular form of law-breaking. In full, "I experimented with marijuana a time or two. And I didn't like it, and didn't inhale, and never tried it again."

My counsel advises me that there is no controlling legal authority or case that says 5
there was any violation of the law whatsoever.

—**Al Gore,** press conference, March 3, 1997

★ The Vice President was explaining that soliciting campaign contributions in 1996 from his office was not illegal, thanks to a distinction between "hard money" and "soft money." He was raising the latter, he thought.

Exercise

See PHYSICAL FITNESS; SPORTS.

Expediency

See also DISHONESTY & LIES; PRESIDENCY, THE (John W. Dean III); RUTHLESSNESS.

In times like these in which we live, it will not do to be overscrupulous. 6

—**Alexander Hamilton,** letter to John Jay, May 7, 1800

We do what we must, and call it by the best names. 7

—**Ralph Waldo Emerson,** *Considerations by the Way*, in *The Conduct of Life*, 1860

Most of the great results of history are brought about by discreditable means. 8

—**Ibid.**

Expedients are for the hour, but principles are for the ages. 9

—**Henry Ward Beecher,** *Proverbs from Plymouth Pulpit*, 1887

No man is justified in doing evil on the grounds of expediency. 10

—**Theodore Roosevelt,** *The Strenuous Life*, title essay, 1900

1 In practice, such trifles as contradictions in principle are easily set aside; the faculty of ignoring them makes the practical man.
—**Henry Brooks Adams,** *The Education of Henry Adams*, 1907

2 "The true," to put it very briefly, is only the expedient in the way of our thinking, just as "the right" is only the expedient in our way of behaving.
—**William James,** *Pragmatism*, 1907

★ For a fuller explanation, see James at TRUTH.

3 With me it's simple. Whatever is good for Sammy Glick is right, and whatever is bad for Sammy Glick is immoral, unethical, unconstitutional. In other words, it stinks.
—**Bud Schulberg,** *What Makes Sammy Run?*, 1941

4 Expediency and justice frequently are not even on speaking terms.
—**Arthur H. Vandenberg,** speech, U.S. Senate, March 8, 1945

★ Sen. Vandenberg was referring to the Yalta agreement, in particular to abandoning Poland to Russia.

5 If the ends don't justify the means, what does?
—**Robert Moses,** maxim [d. 1981]

Experience

See also LIFE; SUFFERING & PAIN.

6 Experience keeps a dear school, but fools will learn in no other.
—**Benjamin Franklin,** *Poor Richard's Almanack*, Dec. 1743

★ *Dear* in the sense of *expensive*.

7 One thorn of experience is worth a whole wilderness of warning.
—**James Russell Lowell,** *Shakespeare Once More*, in *Among My Books*, 1870

8 We should be careful to get out of an experience only the wisdom that is in it—and stop there; lest we be like the cat that sits down on a hot stove-lid. She will never sit down on a hot stove-lid again—and that is well; but also she will never sit down on a cold one anymore.
—**Mark Twain,** *Pudd'nhead Wilson's New Calendar*, in *Following the Equator*, 1897

9 All experience is an arch, to build upon.
—**Henry Brooks Adams,** *The Education of Henry Adams*, 1907

10 I've been things and seen places.
—**Mae West,** *I'm No Angel*, 1933

11 We are creatures shaped by our experiences, we like what we know more often than we know what we like.
—**Wallace Stegner,** *Thoughts in a Dry Land*, 1972

Experience gives us the tests first and the lessons later. 1

—Naomi Judd, public radio interview, *Weekend Edition*, Jan. 29, 1994

Experts

See also DOCTORS & MEDICINE; LAWYERS.

An expert is one who knows more and more about less and less. 2

—Nicholas Murray Butler, attributed, commencement speech, Columbia University, New York City

An expert is somone who borrows your watch to tell you what time it is, and then 3
keeps the watch.

—John Rauch, saying

★ Rauch was an original partner (from 1964) in the architectural firm of Venturi, Scott-Brown and Associates.

Too bad all the people who know how to run the country are busy driving taxi cabs 4
and cutting hair.

—George Burns, quoted in *Life*, Dec., 1979

Facts

See also KNOWLEDGE & INFORMATION; LIFE (T. S. Eliot).

Facts are stubborn things; and whatever may be our wishes, our inclinations, or the 5
dictates of our passions, they cannot alter the state of facts and evidence.

—John Adams, speaking as defense attorney for British soldiers accused in the Boston Massacre trial, Dec. 3, 1770

★ For more from this speech, and the outcome of the trial, see Adams at LAW. Ronald Reagan made a charming slip of the tongue in a farewell speech to the Republican National Convention in 1988: "Facts are stupid things, uh, stubborn things, I should say," *The New York Times*, August 21, 1988.

If a man will kick a fact out of the window, when he comes back he finds it again in 6
the chimney corner.

—Ralph Waldo Emerson, *Journal*, 1842

★ But see also Emerson at TIME.

A little fact is worth a whole limbo of dreams. 7

—Ralph Waldo Emerson, *The Superlative*, 1847

The frontiers are not east or west, north or south, but wherever a man *fronts* a fact. 8

—Henry David Thoreau, *A Week on the Concord and Merrimack Rivers*, 1849

★ See also Thoreau under LIFE for going into the woods to front the essential facts of life.

Facts are contrary 'z mules. 9

—James Russell Lowell, *The Biglow Papers*, II, 1862

1 Let us not underrate the value of a fact; it will one day flower into a truth.
—Henry David Thoreau, *Excursions*, 1863

2 Get your facts straight first, and then you can distort them as much as you please.
—Mark Twain, 1889, quoted in Rudyard Kipling, *From Sea to Sea* [1899]

★ Kipling paid a visit to Twain at his brother-in-law's home in Elmira, N.Y., in the summer of 1889. Kipling was just twenty-four years old and as yet unknown—he was writing travel letters for Indian journals at the time—but he made quite an impression. In a section of his *Autobiography*, written August 11, 1906, Twain recalled telling his mother-in-law, "He [Kipling] is a stranger to me, but he is a most remarkable man—and I am the other one. Between us, we cover all knowledge; he knows all that can be known and I know the rest." For his part, Kipling, in a letter to India, called the meeting a "golden morning," and wrote: "All my preconceived notions [of Twain's personality] were wrong and beneath the reality. Blessed is the man who finds no disillusion when he is brought face to face with a revered writer." In 1902, Kipling told his American publisher: "I love to think of the great and godlike Clemens. He is the biggest man you have on your side of the water by a damn sight. . . . Cervantes was a relation of his."

3 The fatal futility of fact.
—Henry James, *Prefaces, 1907–1909*, preface to his *The Spoils of Poynton*

4 Let's look at the record.
—Al Smith, saying, presidential campaign speeches, 1928

5 Fact-finding is more effective than fault-finding.
—Carl Becker, *Progress and Power*, 1935

6 Facts are piffle.
—John Dickson Carr, *The Crooked Hinge*, 1938

★ From a great detective with a great name, Dr. Gideon Fell.

7 You Could Look It Up.
—James Thurber, story title, *The Saturday Evening Post*, 1941

★ A favorite saying of baseball manager Charles Dillon "Casey" Stengel, probably borrowed from Thurber's story about a manager who sends a midget up to bat in a critical situation. In 1951, flamboyant Bill Veeck—it rhymes with *wreck*—then owner of the St. Louis Browns, actually tried this tactic.

8 Just the facts, ma'am.
—Jack Webb, *Dragnet*, 1952-59

★ Jack Webb's signature line as Sgt. Joe Friday in the popular television series, which ran from Dec. 16, 1951, to Sept. 6, 1959.

9 Facts are all accidents. They all might have been different. They all may become different. They all may collapse together.
—George Santayana, *Persons and Places: My Host the World*, 1953

★ Published the year after Santayana's death.

You can't make the duchess of Windsor into Rebecca of Sunnybrook Farm. The facts of life are very stubborn things. 1

—Cleveland Amory, news report, Oct. 6, 1955

The reliability of the person giving you the facts is as important as the facts themselves. Keep in mind that facts are seldom facts, but what people think are facts, heavily tinged with assumptions. 2

—**Harold Geneen,** with **Alvin Moscow,** *Managing*, 1984

You're entitled to your own opinions but not your own facts. 3

—Anonymous

★ Attributed in various forms to Barnard Baruch and others. Used in exactly these words by Sen. Chris Dodd on *Meet the Press*, May 1, 2005

Failings

See FAULTS & FAILINGS.

Failure

See also DESPAIR; SUCCESS & FAME; WINNING & LOSING, VICTORY & DEFEAT.

When a man starts down hill everything is greased for the occasion. 4

—Josh Billings, saying, quoted in Albert Bigelow Paine, *Mark Twain, A Biography* [1912]

There is no failure except in no longer trying. 5

—Elbert Hubbard, *The Note Book*, 1927

The line between failure and success is so fine that we scarcely know when we pass it: so fine that we are often on the line and do not know it. 6

—Elbert Hubbard, *The Note Book*, 1927

No one here [at the End of the Line Cafe] has to worry about where they're going next, because there's no farther they can go. It's great comfort to them. 7

—Eugene O'Neill, *The Iceman Cometh*, 1946

★ O'Neill, whose plays are crowded with people at the bottom or heading there, himself experienced both misery and blazing success. He much preferred the latter. *New Yorker* magazine theater critic John Lahr wrote in a review of a 1993 revival of *Anna Christie* that in 1922, after collecting his second Pulitzer Prize in three years, the playwright happily pronounced himself "the Hot Dog of Drama." See also DESPAIR.

There is no loneliness greater than the loneliness of a failure. The failure is a stranger in his own house. 8

—Eric Hoffer, *The Passionate State of Mind*, 1954

Flops are part of life's menu. 9

—Rosalind Russell, *New York Herald Tribune*, April 11, 1957

1 You're dead, son. Now get yourself buried.
—**Clifford Odets & Ernest Lehman,** *Sweet Smell of Success*, screenplay, 1957

2 There can be no real freedom without the freedom to fail.
—**Eric Hoffer,** *The Ordeal of Change*, 1964

3 She knows there's no success like failure
And that failure's no success at all.
—**Bob Dylan,** *Love Minus Zero/No Limit*, 1965

4 Nothing succeeds like failure.
—**Sidney Zion,** *New York* magazine, Jan. 24, 1977

★ This was Mr. Zion's explanation of why a Hollywood "genius" was not fired after losing millions of dollars on a picture. "Only after nine straight flops was he eligible to become head of a studio," Zion concluded. This insight is a riff on the proverbial "Nothing succeeds like success." See also Laurence J. Peter's principle in WORK & WORKERS.

5 Failure is not an option.
—**William Broyles, Jr. & Al Reinart,** *Apollo 13*, 1995, screenplay

Faith

See also IMMORTALITY; RELIGION.

6 The way to see by faith is to shut the eye of reason.
—**Benjamin Franklin,** *Poor Richard's Almanack*, 1758

7 What is it that men cannot be made to believe!
—**Thomas Jefferson,** letter to Richard Henry Lee, April 22, 1786

8 Faith is sight and knowledge.
—**Henry David Thoreau,** *Journal*, April 10, 1841

★ More at VISION & PERCEPTION.

9 Faith, like a jackal, feeds among the tombs, and even from these dead doubts she gathers her most vital hope.
—**Herman Melville,** *Moby-Dick*, 1851

10 While men believe in the infinite, some ponds will be thought to be bottomless.
—**Henry David Thoreau,** *The Pond in Winter,* in *Walden*, 1854

11 Doctrine is nothing but the skin of truth set up and stuffed.
—**Henry Ward Beecher,** *Life Thoughts*, 1858

12 Faith always implies the disbelief of a lesser fact in favor of a greater.
—**Oliver Wendell Holmes, Sr.,** *The Professor at the Breakfast-Table*, 1860

13 Faith—is the Pierless Bridge
Supporting what We see
Unto the Scene that We do not—
—**Emily Dickinson,** poem no. 915, c. 1864

I never spoke with God 1
Nor visited in Heaven—
Yet certain am I of the spot
As if the checks were given—
—Emily Dickinson, poem no. 1052, c. 1865

The terrors of truth and dart of death 2
To faith alike are vain.
—Herman Melville, *The Conflict of Convictions*, in *Battle-Pieces*, 1866

The essence of belief is the establishment of a habit. 3
—C. S. Peirce, *Illustrations of the Logic of Science, II*, in *Popular Science Monthly*, Jan. 1878

Faith, n. Belief without evidence in what is told by one who speaks without knowledge of things without parallel. 4
—Ambrose Bierce, *The Devil's Dictionary*, 1906

Faith is believing what you know ain't so. 5
—Mark Twain, *Pudd'nhead Wilson's New Calendar*, in *Following the Equator*, 1897

★ Twain picked this up from an unnamed schoolboy (Feb. 2, 1894, in *Mark Twain's Notebook*, Albert Bigelow Paine, ed., 1935)

Not Truth, but Faith, it is 6
That keeps the world alive.
—Edna St. Vincent Millay, *Interim*, in *Renascence*, 1917

Faith may be defined briefly as an illogical belief in the occurrence of the improbable. 7
—H. L. Mencken, *Prejudices: Third Series*, 1922

Faith in a holy cause is to a considerable extent a substitute for the lost faith in ourselves. 8
—Eric Hoffer, *The True Believer*, 1951

Somebody Up There Likes Me. 9
—Rocky Graziano, with **Rowland Barber,** book title, 1955

★ The complete title is *Somebody Up There Likes Me: The Story of My Life So Far.*

Hundreds may believe, but each has to believe by himself. 10
—W. H. Auden, *Genius and Apostle*, in *The Dyer's Hand*, 1962

Absolute faith corrupts as absolutely as absolute power. 11
—Eric Hoffer, *Reflections on the Human Condition*, 1972

★ This is a play on Lord Acton's observation that "Power tends to corrupt, and absolute power corrupts absolutely"; for source details, see Hitz at SECRETS.

1 You gotta believe!

—Frank Edwin "Tug" McGraw, Jr., rallying cry, NY Mets baseball team, 1973

★ Left-handed relief pitcher Tug McGraw sparked the Mets' 1973 ascent from last place to the World Series.

2 We should live our lives as though Christ were coming this afternoon.

—Jimmy Carter, talk to Bible class, Marantha Baptist Church, Plains, Ga., March, 1976

★ Mr. Carter regularly conducted a Bible class at his hometown church before and after his presidency.

3 If you build it, he will come.

—W. P. Kinsella, *Shoeless Joe*, 1982

★ Adapted by Phil Alden Robinson for the 1989 movie *Field of Dreams*, the story is of an Iowa farmer who believes a voice that tells him that if he builds a baseball diamond in a cornfield, he can bring back the great but tarnished "Shoeless Joe" Jackson. The Canadian Kinsella often writes about baseball and once scouted for the Atlanta Braves. This line is sometimes misquoted as "If you build it, they will come," referring to a promise that tourists will come to the ballfield, and thereby save the family farm. In the movie, the relevant line is "People will come." For "Say it ain't so, Joe," see under SPORTS.

Fall

See NATURE: SEASONS.

Fame

See SUCCESS & FAME.

Familiarity

See INTIMACY & FAMILIARITY.

Family

See also CHILDREN; GENERATIONS; HOME; MARRIAGE; PARENTS.

4 Over the river and through the wood,
To Grandfather's house we go.

—Lydia Maria Child, *Thanksgiving Day*, in *Flowers for Children*, 1844–1846

★ The author did not, in fact, enjoy family life as a child. For more, see THANKSGIVING.

5 Who shall say I am not
the happy genius of my household?

—William Carlos Williams, *Danse Russe*, in *Al Que Quiere!*, 1917

6 One would be in less danger
From the wiles of the stranger
If one's own kin and kith
Were more fun to be with.

—Ogden Nash, *Family Court*, in *Hard Lines*, 1931

Big sisters are the crab grass in the lawn of life. **1**
—Charles M. Schulz, *Peanuts*, 1953

There's no vocabulary **2**
For love within a family, love that's lived in
But not looked at, love within the light of which
All else is seen, the love within which
All other love finds speech.
This love is silent.
—T. S. Eliot, *The Elder Statesman*, 1958

Families break up when people take hints you don't intend and miss hints you do intend. **3**
—Robert Frost, interview, *Writers at Work: Second Series*, 1963

No family is older than any other **4**
—Andrew Lytle, interview by Robert Wilson, c. 1978

★ Lytle, whose novels are based in the South, wrote in 1975 a history of his own Tennessee family, spanning two centuries.

Happiness is having a large, loving, caring, close-knit family in another city. **5**
—George Burns, *Newsweek*, special issue, Winter/Spring 1990

We must trust our parents, our children to hear us even in silence, in an age that fears silence. **6**
—John Updike, book review, *The New Yorker*, March 14, 2005

★ Updike wrote with reference to the T. S. Eliot passage above.

Fanaticism

See ENTHUSIASM & ZEAL.

Farewells

See PARTING.

Farms & Farmers

See also COUNTRY LIFE & PEOPLE; NATURE.

Those who labor in the earth are the chosen people of God, if He ever had a chosen people. **7**
—Thomas Jefferson, *Notes on the State of Virginia*, 1781–1785

Cultivators of the earth are the most valuable citizens. They are the most vigorous, the most independent, the most virtuous, and they are tied to their country and wedded to its liberty and interest by the most lasting bands. **8**
—Thomas Jefferson, letter to John Jay, August 23, 1785

1 When tillage begins, other arts follow. The farmers, therefore, are the founders of human civilization.

—**Daniel Webster,** *Remarks on the Agriculture of England*, speech, Boston State House, Jan. 13, 1840

2 Blessed be agriculture! If one does not have too much of it.

—**Charles Dudley Warner,** *My Summer in a Garden*, 1870

3 We have three crops—corn, freight rates, and interest. The farmers farm the land, and the businessmen farm the farmers.

—**Anonymous,** saying attributed to a Nebraska farm editor, c. 1880

★ Hard times in the nation's agricultural heartland extended from the end of the Civil War almost to the end of the century. In the 1890s, the Populist party, representing the interests of farmers and laborers, surged to a position of national power. Populist farmers vowed to "raise less corn and more hell," as advised by Mary Lease; see under KANSAS. William Jennings Bryan advocated Populist principles in his "Cross of Gold" speech; see below.

4 Burn down your cities and leave our farms, and your cities will spring up again as if by magic; but destroy our farms and the grass will grow in the streets of every city in the country.

—**William Jennings Bryan,** "Cross of Gold" speech, Democratic National Convention, Chicago, July 8, 1896

★ For the meaning of the "cross of gold," see ECONOMICS.

5 Depressions are farm led and farm fed.

—**Anonymous,** saying, 1930s

★ More at THE DEPRESSION.

6 No one hates his job so heartily as a farmer.

—**H. L. Mencken,** *What Is Going On in the World Now?*, in *American Mercury* magazine, Nov. 1933

7 Agriculture is the keystone of our economic structure. The wealth, welfare, prosperity, and even the future freedom of this nation are based upon the soil.

—**Louis Bromfield,** *Pleasant Valley*, 1945

8 Farming looks mighty easy when your plow is a pencil, and you're a thousand miles from the corn field.

—**Dwight D. Eisenhower,** speech, Peoria, Ill., Sept. 25, 1956

9 The barn is America at its fragrant and warmest best. It stands for the genius of a nation built of rich soil and fat cattle.

—**Robert P. Tristram Coffin,** *On the Green Carpet*, 1951

★ Coffin's family owned a farm on Casco Bay in Maine. He won a Pulitzer Prize in 1936 for his book of poetry *Strange Holiness*.

10 The farmer . . . is the *fundamental* citizen of any community, state, or nation.

—**Louis Bromfield,** quoted in Arnold Jaeger, *The Fate of Family Farming* [2004]

It was the best place to be, thought Wilbur, this warm delicious cellar, with the garrulous geese, the changing seasons, the heat of the sun, the passage of swallows, the nearness of rats, the sameness of sheep, the love of spiders, the smell of manure, and the glory of everything. 1

—**E. B. White,** *Charlotte's Web*, 1952

The farmer is the only man in our economy who buys everything he needs at retail, sells everything he sells at wholesale, and pays the freight both ways. 2

—**John F. Kennedy,** campaign speech, national plowing contest, Sioux Falls, S.D., Sept. 22, 1960

The farm is an infinite form. 3

—**Wendell Berry,** *From the Crest*, in *Clearing*, 1977

Farmers are totally dependent on oil companies, machinery companies, fertilizer and pesticide companies. Farmers are, in one sense, helpless subjects of the corporate kingdoms of agriculture. 4

—**Wes Jackson,** *Falsehoods of Farming,* in *Altars of Unhewn Stone,* 1987

Most people didn't dream, then, that before long a lot of little farmers would buy and borrow their way out of farming, and bigger and bigger farmers would be competing with their neighbors (or with doctors from the city) for the available land. The time was going to come—it is clear enough now—when there would not be enough farmers left. 5

—**Wendell Berry,** *Jayber Crow,* 2000

The hardy, independent farmers, whom Jefferson considered the bedrock of democracy, are a truly vanishing breed. The United States now has more prison inmates than farmers. 6

—**Eric Schlosser,** *Fast Food Nation,* 2002

Fashion & Clothes

If thou art clean and warm, it is sufficient, for more doth but rob the poor and please the wanton. 7

—**William Penn,** *Some Fruits of Solitude*, 1693

A little of what you call frippery is very necessary towards looking like the rest of the world. 8

—**Abigail Adams,** letter to John Adams, May 1, 1780

The fondness for dress among the women [of California] is excessive and is often the ruin of many of them. 9

—**Richard Henry Dana, Jr.,** *Two Years Before the Mast*, 1840

★ For more comments on these women of the West, see CALIFORNIA.

It is an interesting question, how far men would retain their relative rank if they were divested of their clothes. 10

—**Henry David Thoreau,** *Economy*, in *Walden*, 1854

1 Beware of all enterprises that require new clothes.
—**Ibid.**

2 The costume of woman . . . should conduce at once to her health, comfort, and usefulness . . . While it should not fail also to conduce to her personal adornment, it should make that end of secondary importance.
—**Amelia Jenks Bloomer**, *letter*, June, 1857

★ Ms. Bloomer did not invent the outfit—a knee-length skirt over baggy, Turkish-style pantaloons—that gave women more freedom of movement and which is named after her. That honor goes to another reform-minded woman, Elizabeth Smith Miller, a cousin of Elizabeth Cady Stanton. Ms. Bloomer popularized the style, however, by wearing the outfit in public and advertising it, starting in 1851, in *The Lily*, a paper that she edited for the Ladies' Temperance Society. Subsequently, "bloomers" came to refer the pantaloons alone; these were usually gathered at the knee.

3 One wants to be *very* something, *very* great, *very* heroic; or if not that, then at least very stylish and very fashionable.
—**Harriet Beecher Stowe,** *Dress, or Who Makes the Fashions, The Atlantic Monthly* magazine, 1864

4 The sense of being well-dressed gives a feeling of inward tranquility which religion is powerless to bestow.
—**Ralph Waldo Emerson**, *Social Aims*, in *Letters and Social Aims*, 1876, reporting a comment by a Miss C. F. Forbes.

5 All dressed up with nowhere to go.
—**William Allen White,** 1916

★ White, the influential editor of the *Emporia Gazette* in Kansas, thus described the Progressive Party after Theodore Roosevelt, its candidate in 1912, endorsed Republican presidential candidate Charles Evans Hughes in 1916. According to Henry F. Woods in *American Sayings* (1945), White's actual words were, "all dressed up in their fighting clothes, with nowhere to go."

6 Where's the man could ease a heart
Like a satin gown.
—**Dorothy Parker,** *The Satin Dress*, in *Enough Rope*, 1927

7 Brevity is the soul of lingerie.
—**Dorothy Parker,** attributed, in Alexander Woollcott, *While Rome Burns* [1934]

8 I tell you men are watching their styles. That's why they all look so funny.
—**Will Rogers,** *Weekly Articles*, May 20, 1928

9 Would you be shocked if I put on something more comfortable?
—**James Whale,** *Hell's Angels*, 1930

★ The line, purred by Jean Harlow, gave the phrase "put on something more comfortable" an internationally recognized new meaning.

10 ["Dogwhistle" fashion:] clothes with a pitch so high and special that only that only the thinnest and most sophisticated of women would hear their call.
—**Geraldine Stutz**, cited in her obituary, *The New York Times* [April 9, 2005]

★ As president of Henri Bendel in New York City from 1957 to 1986, Ms. Stutz was famous for stocking small clothes—rarely larger than size 10—for women who were young, sophisticated, and, some suspected, anorexic.

Fashion is in ceaseless pursuit of things that are about to look familiar and in uneasy flight from things that have just become a bore. **1**

—**Kennedy Fraser,** *The Fashionable Mind: Reflections on Fashion 1979–1981*, 1981

The bikini is the most important thing since the atom bomb. **2**

—**Diana Vreeland,** quoted in Grace Mirabella, with Judith Warner, *In and Out of Vogue*, 1995

Clothes never shut up. **3**

—**Susan Brownmiller,** *Femininity*, 1984

The neon sign of one's inner thought is the clothes that one puts on one's body. Fashion in many ways defines the self-concept and character of the individual, and it gives a message to the audience. One has to gear one's message to how seriously one wants to be taken. **4**

—**Al Sharpton,** in *The New York Times*, Oct. 24, 1993

★ Rev. Sharpton's personal style is theatrical. See also JUSTICE.

Wardrobe malfunction. **5**

—**Justin Timberlake,** Feb. 2, 2004

★ A catch phrase for any embarrassing clothing incident. Singer Justin Timberlake issued an apology for the "malfunction" viewed around the world when, during the Super Bowl halftime show, he flicked away the right cup of a bustier worn by co-star, Janet Jackson, revealing her breast, decorated with a silver star. His apology was, "I am sorry if anyone was offended by the wardrobe malfunction during the halftime performance at the Super Bowl. It was not intentional and it is regrettable." It was also expensive. The Federal Communications Commission fined broadcaster CBS $500,000.

In my dictionary, fashion means moment. **6**

—**Christina Kim,** in *The New York Times*, Oct. 31, 2004

Fate & Destiny

See also LIFE; LUCK.

Fate is a name for facts not yet passed under the fire of thought, for causes which are unpenetrated. **7**

—**Ralph Waldo Emerson,** *Fate*, in *The Conduct of Life*, 1860

Whatever limits us we call fate. **8**

—**Ibid.**

I claim not to have controlled events, but confess plainly that events have controlled me. **9**

—**Abraham Lincoln,** letter to A. G. Hodges, April 4, 1864

1 Superiority to fate
Is difficult to gain
'Tis not conferred of any
But possible to earn.
—**Emily Dickinson,** poem no. 1081, c. 1866

★ More at IMMORTALITY.

2 The current of destiny carries us along. None but a madman would swim against the stream, and none but a fool would exert himself to swim with it. The best way is to float quietly with the tide.
—**William Cullen Bryant,** letter to his mother, June 1821

★ Bryant, best remembered as the author of *Thanatopsis*, used this passage in announcing to his mother that he was getting married. He described himself as "trapped before I was aware" by the goodness of heart, intelligence, and other fine qualities of his bride.

3 We are spinning our own fates, good or evil, and never to be undone.
—**William James,** *The Principles of Psychology*, 1890

4 Destiny is not a matter of chance, it is a matter of choice; it is not a thing to be waited for, it is a thing to be achieved.
—**William Jennings Bryan,** speech, Washington, D.C., Feb. 22, 1899

5 If fate means you to lose, give him a good fight anyhow.
—**William McFee,** *Casuals of the Sea*, 1916

6 Any spoke will lead an ant to the hub.
—**Rex Stout,** *Fer de Lance*, 1934

★ A favorite saying of Stout's detective hero, Nero Wolfe.

7 In my beginning is my end.
—**T. S. Eliot,** *Four Quartets: East Coker*, 1940

★ See also Eliot at BEGINNINGS & ENDINGS.

8 The great appeal of fatalism . . . is as a refuge from the terror of responsibility.
—**Arthur M. Schlesinger, Jr.,** *The Decline of Greatness*, in *Saturday Evening Post*, Nov. 1, 1958

9 The wisest of realists are those who recognize that fate can indeed be shaped by human faith and courage.
—**Henry A. Kissinger,** *Golda Meir: An Appreciation*, Nov. 13, 1977, in *For the Record: Selected Statements, 1977–1980*, 1981

Fathers

See PARENTS.

Faults & Failings

See also INSULTS; MISTAKES; TEMPTATION.

None but the well-bred man knows how to confess a fault or acknowledge himself in error. 1

—**Benjamin Franklin,** *Poor Richard's Almanack*, Nov. 1738

There is no odor so bad as that which arises from goodness tainted. 2

—**Henry David Thoreau,** *Economy*, in *Walden*, 1854

It's not that he "bites off more than he can chaw," . . . but he chaws more than he bites off. 3

—**Clover Adams,** letter to her father, Dec. 1881

★ Occasionally true of the writer's husband, Henry Adams, but she was aiming here at the novelist Henry James. The quote is sometimes attributed to Henry James's brother, psychologist William James. The omitted material in the quote reads, "as T. G. Appleton said of Nathan." Appleton, a minor writer and artist, was a famous conversationalist and is remembered for his epigram on Americans and Paris; see under CITIES. Nathan, his father, was a successful businessman and politician. Clover Adams committed suicide in 1885 by ingesting potassium cyanide.

He's liked, but he's not well liked. 4

—**Arthur Miller,** *Death of a Salesman*, 1949

Falling short of perfection is a process that just never stops. 5

—**William Shawn,** quoted in *The New York Times*, obituary [Jan. 9, 1992]

★ Shawn, a notorious perfectionist, was the second editor of *The New Yorker*, succeeding the founding editor Harold Ross upon his death in 1951, and remaining until 1987, when he was dismissed by the magazine's new owner, S. I. Newhouse. When asked how he could afford to spend so much time on details, he answered, "It takes as long as it takes," *The New Yorker*, Dec. 28, 1992/Jan. 4, 1993.

Fear

See also COURAGE.

Fear is an instructor of great sagacity and the herald of all revolutions. . . . He indicates great wrongs which must be revised. 6

—**Ralph Waldo Emerson,** *Compensation*, in *Essays: First Series*, 1841

Nothing is to be so much feared as fear. 7

—**Henry David Thoreau,** *Journal*, Sept. 7, 1851

★ See also Pres. Franklin D. Roosevelt's first inaugural address at AMERICAN HISTORY: MEMORABLE MOMENTS.

It occurred to me at once that Harris had been as much afraid of me as I had been of him. This was a new view of the question I had never taken before; but it was one I never forgot afterwards. 8

—**Ulysses S. Grant,** *Memoirs*, 1885

★ Grant's epiphany took place at the end of July 1861, near Florida, Mo., when he was still a colonel. Leading his unit up a hill toward an encampment of rebels under

General Thomas Harris, he admitted to being so afraid that he "lacked the moral courage" to call a halt and reconsider plans. Gaining the crest, however, he saw that the enemy camp was deserted. One of the Missourians who fled at Grant's approach was his future publisher and also an author of some note, Mark Twain. In *The Private History of a Campaign That Failed* (1885), Twain wrote, "In time I came to know that Union colonel whose coming frightened me out of the war and crippled the Southern cause to that extent—General Grant. I came within a few hours of seeing him when he was as unknown as I was myself; at a time when anybody could have said, 'Grant?—Ulysses S. Grant? I do not remember hearing the name before.' It seems difficult to realize that there was once a time when such a remark could be rationally made but there *was*, and I was within a few miles of the place and the occasion, too, though proceeding in the other direction."

1 A fool without fear is sometimes wiser than an angel with fear.
—**Nancy Astor,** *My Two Countries*, 1920

2 I will show you fear in a handful of dust.
—**T. S. Eliot,** *The Waste Land,* 1922

★ The English novelist Evelyn Waugh used *A Handful of Dust* as the title of a grim comic novel fifteen years later.

3 The only thing we have to fear is fear itself.
—**Franklin D. Roosevelt,** First Inaugural Address, March 4, 1933

★ More at AMERICAN HISTORY: MEMORABLE MOMENTS.

4 Cowardice, as distinguished from panic, is almost always simply a lack of ability to suspend the functioning of the imagination.
—**Ernest Hemingway,** *Men at War*, 1942

5 Fatigue makes cowards of us all.
—**George S. Patton, Jr.,** *War As I Knew It*, 1947

6 Our tragedy today is a general and universal physical fear.
—**William Faulkner,** speech accepting the Nobel Prize for Literature, 1949

★ Faulkner was referring to fear of nuclear war.

7 We are not descended from fearful men.
—**Edward R. Murrow,** *Report on Sen. Joseph R. McCarthy*, in Murrow's *See It Now* documentary television series, March 7, 1954

★ More at AMERICAN HISTORY: MEMORABLE MOMENTS, (Murrow note).

8 Fear tastes like a rusty knife and do not let her into your house.
—**John Cheever,** *The Wapshot Chronicle*, 1957

9 Our problem is not to be rid of fear but rather to harness and master it.
—**Martin Luther King, Jr.**, *Strength to Love*, 1963

Flag, the

See PATRIOTISM & THE FLAG.

Flattery

Let those flatter who fear: it is not an American art. **1**

—Thomas Jefferson, *The Rights of British America*, 1774

We love flattery, even though we are not deceived by it, because it shows that we are **2**
of importance enough to be courted.

—Ralph Waldo Emerson, *Gifts*, in *Essays: Second Series*, 1844

Mountains of gold would not seduce some men, yet flattery would break them down. **3**

—Henry Ward Beecher, *Proverbs from Plymouth Pulpit*, 1887

For God's sake, don't say yes until I've finished talking. **4**

—Darryl Zanuck, quoted in Philip French, *The Movie Moguls* [1969]

★ The great movie producer—*The Grapes of Wrath, All About Eve*—reining in a yes-man.

Flattery is all right—if you don't inhale. **5**

—Adlai Stevenson, speech, Feb. 1, 1961

Florida

See also CITIES (MIAMI).

Florida . . . does beguile and gratify me—giving me my first and last (evidently) **6**
sense of the tropics, or à peu près, the subtropics, and revealing to me blandness in
nature of which I had no idea.

—Henry James, letter to Edmund Gosse, Feb. 16, 1905

The state with the prettiest name, **7**
the state that floats in brackish water,
held together by mangrove roots.

—Elizabeth Bishop, *Florida*, 1939

In summer the crackers live off the yams; in winter they live off Yanks. **8**

—Anonymous, Florida saying, in H. L. Mencken, *A New Dictionary of Quotations on Historical Principles*, 1942

Florida is the world's greatest amusement park. **9**

—Budd Schulberg, *Florida*, in *American Panorama: East of the Mississippi*, 1960

Florida is a golden word . . . The very name Florida carried the message of warmth **10**
and ease and comfort. It was irresistible.

—John Steinbeck, *Travels with Charley*, 1962

1 It is a speck of rock in pastel sea. Palms whisper. Songbirds sing. The place has never known a frost.

—Charles Kuralt, on Key West, in *Charles Kuralt's America*, 1995

2 In God we trust.

—Motto, state of Florida

Flowers

See NATURE: PLANTS & GARDENS.

Food, Wine, & Eating

See also ALCOHOL & DRINKING; HEALTH.

3 Eat to live, and not live to eat.

—Benjamin Franklin, *Poor Richard's Almanack*, May 1733

★ The idea dates to classical times, at least, and is ascribed to Socrates. See also Franklin at HEALTH.

4 Eat not to dullness; drink not to elevation.

—Benjamin Franklin, *Autobiography*, begun 1771

5 We never repent having eaten too little.

—Thomas Jefferson, "A Decalogue of Canons for observation in practical life," letter to Thomas Jefferson Smith, Feb. 21, 1825

6 What moistens the lip and what brightens the eye?
What calls back the past, like the rich pumpkin pie?

—John Greenleaf Whittier, *The Pumpkin*, 1844

★ More at THANKSGIVING.

7 The American does not drink at meals as a sensible man should. Indeed, he has no meals. He stuffs for ten minutes thrice a day.

—Rudyard Kipling, *American Notes*, 1891

8 Perhaps no bread in the world is quite so good as Southern corn bread, and perhaps no bread in the world is quite so bad as the Northern imitation of it.

—Mark Twain, *Autobiography* [1924]

9 Most vigitaryans I ever see look enough like their food to be classed as cannybals.

—Finley Peter Dunne, *Casual Observations,* in *Mr. Dooley's Philosophy,* 1900

10 I know the taste of watermelon which has been honestly come by, and I know the taste of watermelon which has been acquired by art. Both taste good, but the experienced know which tastes best.

—Mark Twain, *Autobiography* [1924]

★ This concludes Twain's paean to the watermelon: "I know how a prize watermelon looks when it is sunning its fat rotundity among pumpkin vines. . . . I know how inviting it looks when it is cooling itself in a tub of water under the bed, waiting; I know how it looks when it lies on the table in the sheltered great floor space between house and kitchen, and the children gathered for the sacrifice and their mouths watering; I know the crackling sound it makes when the knife enters its end. . . . I can see its halves fall apart and display the rich red meat and the black seeds, and the heart standing up, a luxury fit for the elect; I know how a boy looks behind a yard-long slice of that melon, and I know how he feels; for I have been there."

I doubt whether the world holds for anyone a more soul-stirring surprise than the **1**
first adventure with ice-cream.

—**Heywood Broun,** *Holding a Baby*, in *Seeing Things at Night*, 1921

I have eaten **2**
the plums
that were in the icebox

and which
you were probably
saving
for breakfast

Forgive me
they were delicious
so sweet
and so cold.

—**William Carlos Williams,** *This Is Just to Say*, 1922

★ Williams loved plums. In *To a Poor Old Woman* (1935), he described a woman on the street, carrying a paper bag of plums and eating one: "Comforted / a solace of ripe plums / seeming to fill the air / They taste good to her." See Wallace Stevens below for another poetic plum.

The plum survives its poems. **3**

—**Wallace Stevens,** *The Comedian as the Letter C*, 1923

★ And ice cream rules. See Stevens at HIGH POSITION: RULERS & LEADERS.

"It's broccoli, dear." **4**
"I say it's spinach, and I say the hell with it."

—**E. B. White,** caption for a Carl Rose cartoon, *The New Yorker*, Dec. 8, 1928

Beulah, peel me a grape. **5**

—**Mae West,** *I'm No Angel*, 1933

No matter how thin you slice it, it's still baloney. **6**

—**Al Smith,** saying, 1936 campaign speeches for Alf Landon

★ Smith definitely wasn't looking for votes from the processed-meat industry. Earlier, commenting on Roosevelt's monetary devaluation, he wrote, "I am for gold dollars as against baloney dollars," *The New Outlook*, December 1933. And even earlier, when he was governor of New York, he declined to pose with a trowel at the cornerstone ceremony of the New York State Office Building in Manhattan. "That's baloney," he said.

1 It's a naive domestic Burgundy without any breeding, but I think you'll be amused by its presumption.
—James Thurber, caption for a cartoon in *The New Yorker*, March 27, 1937

2 You can travel fifty thousand miles in America without once tasting a piece of good bread.
—Henry Miller, *The Staff of Life*, in *Remember to Remember*, 1947

3 The very discovery of the New World was the by-product of a dietary quest.
—Arthur M. Schlesinger, Jr., *Paths to the Present*, 1949

★ The quest was for Eastern spices and seasonings.

4 Avoid fried meats which angry up the blood.
—Leroy "Satchel" Paige, *How to Stay Young*, 1953

★ More at WISDOM, WORDS OF.

5 Gluttony is an emotional escape—a sign something is eating us.
—Peter De Vries, *Comfort Me with Apples*, 1956

6 More die in the United States of too much food than of too little.
—John Kenneth Galbraith, *The Affluent Society*, 1958

7 We prefer our coffee as strong as love, as black as sin, and as hot as Hades.
—T. Hale Boggs, tariff bill debate, 1960

★ Rep. Boggs, Democrat of Louisiana, supported of the addition of chicory, a key ingredient of New Orleans coffee, to the list of items that could be imported without duty.

8 A bottle of wine begs to be shared. I have never met a miserly wine lover.
—Clifton Fadiman, quoted in *The New York Times*, March 8, 1967

9 Food is our common ground, a universal experience.
—James Beard, *Beard on Food*, 1974

10 Never eat more than you can lift.
—Miss Piggy (Jim Henson), saying

11 There are bold mushroom hunters and there are old mushroom hunters. There are no old, bold mushroom hunters.
—Anonymous, saying cited by John Trott, Warrenton, Va., *Fauquier Times-Democrat*, April 24, 1996

12 People who eat white bread have no dreams.
—Diana Vreeland, quoted in *The New Yorker* [Sept. 22, 1996]

13 Remember, you are alone in the kitchen, and no one can see you.
—Julia Child, comment on The French Chef television show [*The New York Times,* obit, August 14, 2004]

★ The legend is that this remark was occasioned by dropping a roast or the like on the studio floor. Actually, it was a potato pancake that she inadvertently flipped out of the pan on to the work table, and then returned to the pan.

Fools & Stupidity

Who knows a fool must know his brother; 1
For one will recommend another.
—Benjamin Franklin, *Poor Richard's Almanack*, 1740

It is ill-manners to silence a fool, and cruelty to let him go on. 2
—Benjamin Franklin, *Poor Richard's Almanack*, 1757

There's nothing we read of in torture's inventions 3
Like a well-meaning dunce with the best of intentions.
—James Russell Lowell, *A Fable for Critics*, 1848

There's a sucker born every minute. 4
—Joseph Bessimer, c. 1850

★ Con man Joseph "Paper Collar" Bessimer was a friend of P. T. Barnum, to whom the quote is usually attributed. Robert Pelton, curator of the Barnum Museum in Bridgeport, Conn., cites Bessimer as the true source.

Minds so earnest and helpless that it takes them a half-an-hour to get from one idea to its immediately adjacent next neighbor, and then they lie down on it . . . like a cow on a doormat, so that you can get neither in nor out with them. 5
—William James, description of audience at a Chautauqua lecture, letter to his wife, July 1896

Let us be thankful for the fools. But for them, the rest of us could not succeed. 6
—Mark Twain, *Pudd'nhead Wilson's New Calendar*, in *Following the Equator*, 1897

★ For Twain on the preponderance of fools, see MAJORITIES & MINORITIES. For fools on school boards, see EDUCATION.

Never give a sucker an even break. 7
—Anonymous

★ H. L. Mencken credited speakeasy and nightclub owner Texas Guinan with popularizing this around 1925—she used to welcome patrons with the greeting, "Hello, sucker." The originator, however, may have been Edward F. Albee, co-owner of the Keith-Albee vaudeville theaters. W. C. Fields ad-libbed the line in the 1923 Broadway musical *Poppy*, and used it as a movie title in 1941.

Fool me once, shame on you. Fool me twice, shame on me. 8
—Anonymous

★ Listed as proverbial in *A Dictionary of American Proverbs* (1992), the saying was popularized by Lieutenant Commander Montgomery Scott on Episode 32 of *Star Trek* (aired Dec. 1, 1967). Pres. George W. Bush mangled it memorably in a speech in Nashville on Sept. 17, 2002, telling his audience that "There's an old saying in Tennessee—I know it's in Texas, probably Tennessee—that says, fool me once, shame on—shame on you. Fool me—you can't get fooled again."

1 We are the hollow men
We are the stuffed men
Leaning together
Headpiece filled with straw. Alas!
—T. S. Eliot, *The Hollow Men*, 1925

2 Ninety-nine percent of the people in the world are fools, and the rest of us are in great danger of contagion.
—Thornton Wilder, *The Matchmaker*, 1954

3 There are some people that if they don't know, you can't tell 'em.
—Louis Armstrong, c. 1956, Deirdre Mullane, ed., *Words to Make My Children Live: A Book of African American Quotations* [1995]

4 This life's hard, but it's harder if you're stupid.
—George V. Higgins, *The Friends of Eddie Coyle*, 1972

5 They have a saying in the provinces, "Ignorance is salvageable, but stupid is forever."
—Henry J. Hyde, speech in the U.S. House of Representatives, April 1995

★ Rep. Hyde of Illinois, a conservative in his tenth term in Congress, pulled out this folk saying in the heat of the debate on Congressional term limits favored by zealous younger conservatives. "New is always better?" Mr Hyde asked. "What in the world is conservative about that? Have we nothing to learn from the past? Tradition, history, institutional memory—don't they count anymore?"

Force

See POWER; STRENGTH & TOUGHNESS; VIOLENCE.

Foreigners

See also FOREIGN POLICY; NATIONS; RACES & PEOPLES; TRAVEL.

6 Against the insidious wiles of foreign influence . . . the jealousy of a free people ought to be constantly awake; since history and experience prove that foreign influence is one of the most baneful foes of republican government.
—George Washington, Farewell Address, Sept. 17, 1796

★ Thomas Jefferson, too, held a baneful view of foreigners, at least those in cities; see under CITIES.

7 They spell it Vinci and pronounce it Vinchy; foreigners always spell better than they pronounce.
—Mark Twain, *The Innocents Abroad*, 1869

8 Give me your tired, your poor,
Your huddled masses yearning to breathe free.
—Emma Lazarus, *The New Colossus: Inscription for the Statue of Liberty*, 1883

★ More at AMERICAN HISTORY: MEMORABLE MOMENTS.

Some Americans need hyphens in their names because only half of them has come over. 1

—**Woodrow Wilson,** speech, Washington, D.C., May 16, 1914

There is no room in this country for hyphenated Americanism. 2

—**Theodore Roosevelt,** speech, New York City, Oct. 12 (Columbus Day), 1915

★ With the war in Europe boiling, suspicion of the allegiance of immigrants was at a high, and often took the form of simple prejudice. See also the Roosevelt entry at PATRIOTISM & THE FLAG.

A closed country is a dying country. 3

—**Edna Ferber,** radio broadcast, 1947

We were afraid of foreigners; we distrusted them; we didn't like them. 4

—**Emmanuel Celler,** *You Never Leave Brooklyn,* 1953

★ Congressman Celler was explaining the motivation for the Immigration Act of 1924, which he had vigorously opposed. See Calvin Coolidge at AMERICA & AMERICANS.

A Nation of Immigrants 5

—**John F. Kennedy,** book title, 1958

America is not a melting pot. It is a sizzling cauldron. 6

—**Barbara A. Mikulski,** speech, Washington, D.C., June, 1970, in Esther Stineman, *American Political Women* [1980]

★ The Maryland Representative (and future Senator) was amending a well-established metaphor; see Zangwill (1908) at AMERICA & AMERICANS.

We are . . . a nation of immigrants, but some of us too often forget that fact. Sometimes we forget that the question isn't when we came here, but why we came here. 7

—**Jimmy Carter,** speech, New York City, Oct. 1976

WE WANT ORDER ON OUR BORDER 8

—**Anonymous,** bumper sticker protesting illegal immigration, southern California, 1990

Foreign Policy

See also AMERICA & AMERICANS (John Quincy Adams); AMERICAN HISTORY: MEMORABLE MOMENTS; DIPLOMACY; NATIONS.

It is our true policy to steer clear of permanent alliances, with any portion of the foreign world. 9

—**George Washington,** Farewell Address, Sept. 17, 1796

★ Washington was deeply suspicious of foreign ways. See also FOREIGNERS.

There can be no greater error than to expect or calculate upon real favors from nation to nation. 10

—**Ibid.**

1 Observe good faith and justice toward all nations. Cultivate peace and harmony with all.

—Ibid.

2 Peace, commerce, and honest friendship with all nations, entangling alliances with none.

—Thomas Jefferson, First Inaugural Address, March 4, 1801

★ A year later, however, when Jefferson learned that Spain had ceded the Louisiana territory to the French, he wrote to the U.S. minister in France, Robert Livingston, "The moment Napoleon takes possession of New Orleans, we must marry ourselves to the British fleet and nation."

3 America does not go abroad in search of monsters to destroy.

—John Quincy Adams, *speech,* July 4, 1821.

★ More at AMERICA & AMERICANS.

4 We owe it, therefore, to candor and to the amicable relations existing between the United States and those [European] powers to declare that we should consider any attempt on their part to extend their system to any portion of this hemisphere as dangerous to our peace and safety.

—James Monroe, message to Congress, Dec. 2, 1823

★ The principle that the entire Western Hemisphere is bound up with the national interests of the United States became known as the Monroe Doctrine, and has been widely accepted as a nonnegotiable element in U.S. foreign policy. In 1895, for example, Pres. Grover Cleveland, in ordering England to settle a boundary dispute with Venezuela, pronounced: "Today the United States is practically sovereign on this continent, and its fiat is law upon the subjects to which it confines its interposition." In the 20th century, in the midst of the Cold War, Cuba's disregard for the Monroe Doctrine counterpoised to U.S. dedication to that principle led to the embarrassing Bay of Pigs invasion, and subsequently brought the U.S. and Cuba's ally, Russia, to the brink of nuclear conflict. A passage in John F. Kennedy's presidential inauguration speech in 1961 signaled the trouble ahead: "And let every other power know that this hemisphere intends to remain master of its own house." See also Theodore Roosevelt below.

5 The open door.

—John Hay, description of the trade policy the government had negotiated with China, Jan. 2, 1900

★ Hay was Secretary of State.

6 Speak softly and carry a big stick.

—Theodore Roosevelt, speech, Minnesota State Fair, Sept. 2, 1901

★ The adage was not original with Roosevelt. He described it as a West African proverb. Carl Sandberg thought it was a Spanish proverb. Both may be right as many proverbs appear in widely separated cultures. An example of the big stick in practice is Roosevelt's famous admission in his memoirs, "I took Panama without consulting the cabinet." At the time of the takeover, in 1903, he had denied having any role in the revolution that separated the Panama territory from Columbia. Roosevelt was vice president when he made this speech at the State Fair, but within two weeks, he succeeded the assassinated William McKinley. In full, his statement was: "There is a homely adage which runs, 'Speak softly and carry a big stick.' If the American nation will speak softly and yet build and keep at a pitch of the highest training a thoroughly efficient navy, the Monroe Doctrine will go far." See also DIPLOMACY.

The steady aim of this nation, as of all enlightened nations, should be to strive to bring ever nearer the day when there shall prevail throughout the world the peace of justice. 1

—**Theodore Roosevelt,** State of the Union Address, Dec. 6, 1904

★ The speech is called the "First Corollary to the Monroe Doctrine." It extended the justification under which the U.S. might intervene in other nations. T.R. contrasted the peace of justice with the peace imposed by oppression: "Tyrants and oppressors have many times made a wilderness and called it peace." This derives from Tacitus, *Agricola,* "They make a desert and call it peace."

Dollar diplomacy. 2

—**Anonymous,** characterization of policies of Secretary of State Philander C. Knox, 1909–10

★ The phrase was not intended as a compliment, but today there seems nothing exceptional in Knox's efforts to promote American investment abroad and to protect American interests via financial negotiations. Knox served under Pres. William Howard Taft.

Our policy of watchful waiting. 3

—**Woodrow Wilson,** State of the Union Address, Dec. 2, 1913

★ This was the stance of the U.S. toward Mexico during the turbulent years 1913–20.

The freedom of the seas is the *sine qua non* of peace, equality, and cooperation. 4

—**Woodrow Wilson,** speech, U.S. Senate, Jan. 22, 1917

★ Freedom of navigation was one of the "Fourteen Points" in Pres. Wilson's famous speech of Jan. 8, 1918. The Fourteen Points were objectives that were later included in the November 1918 armistice. The points, or objectives, were: covenants of peace (see PEACE); freedom of the seas; abolition of trade barriers; general disarmament; adjustment of colonial claims; evacuation of conquered Russian territories; evacuation and restoration of Belgium; return of Alsace-Lorrain to France; adjustment of Italian frontiers; autonomy for subject peoples of Austria and Hungary; guarantees of the integrity of Serbia, Montenegro, and Romania; autonomy for the subject people of the Ottoman Empire (Turkey); an independent Poland; and "a general association of nations," which was eventually realized in the League of Nations; see AMERICAN HISTORY: MEMORABLE MOMENTS.

There shall be no private understandings of any kind, but diplomacy shall proceed always frankly and in the public view. 5

—**Woodrow Wilson,** "Fourteen Points" address to Congress, Jan. 8, 1918

Wilson and his Fourteen Points! Bah! Even God Almighty only had ten! 6

—**Anonymous,** French joke, c. 1919

★ This is sometimes attributed to Georges Clemenceau, the French premier. There were jokes in America, too, as Wilson stumbled in the complex peace negotiations and lost political ground at home. See William Allen White's memorial editorial at EPITAPHS & GRAVESTONES.

1 I don't know how a lot of these other nations have existed as long as they have till we could get some of our people around and show 'em how to be pure and good like us.
—Will Rogers, *More Letters*, Feb. 27, 1932

2 In the field of world policy, I would dedicate this nation to the policy of the good neighbor—the neighbor who resolutely respects himself and, because he does so, respects the rights of others—the neighbor who respects his obligations and who respects the sanctity of his agreements in and with a world of neighbors.
—Franklin D. Roosevelt, First Inaugural Address, March 4, 1933

3 He may be a son of a bitch, but he's our son of a bitch.
—Franklin D. Roosevelt, meaning Nicaraguan dictator Anastasio Somoza, in William Pfaff in *The New Yorker* [May 27, 1985] and other sources

★ Some forty years later, CIA chief William Casey, discussing the Panamanian dictator Manuel Noriega, said, "He's a bastard, but he's our bastard." This comment, made to U.S. Rep. Lee Hamilton, chair of the House Intelligence Committee, was reported in Haynes Johnson's *Sleepwalking Through History: America in the Reagan Years*, 1991.

4 Soviet pressure against the free institutions of the Western world is something that can be contained by the adroit and vigorous application of counterforce.
—George F. Kennan, *The Sources of Soviet Conduct*in *Foreign Affairs*, July 1947

★ The first articulation of a containment policy, a term still used today, more than 50 years later. Kennan, who signed the article "X" (he was with the U.S. Embassy at Moscow), saw containment as consisting of diplomacy and covert action.

5 [Atoms for Peace:] If the fearful trend of atomic military build-up can be reversed, this greatest of destructive forces can be developed into a great boon, for the benefit of all mankind.
—Dwight D. Eisenhower, speech, U. N. General Assembly, Dec. 8, 1953

★ This address offering a "hopeful alternative" to the Cold War build-up of atomic weapons was immediately referred to as proposing "atoms for peace," and is still so known. The idea was that Russia and the United States should lead the way in sharing nuclear capability for peaceful uses while controlling proliferation of weapons. The program was implemented eventually through the creation of the International Atomic Energy Agency, EURATOM, and related agencies. The risk that the program itself would lead to wider development of nuclear weapons was recognized but considered worth taking given the acute dangers of the time.

6 The United States pledges . . . to find the way by which the miraculous inventiveness of man shall not be dedicated to his death, but consecrated to his life.
—Ibid.

★ This pledge at the end of the Atoms for Peace speech led to a standing ovation from the 3,500 United Nations delegates.

7 Local defense must be reinforced by the further deterrent of massive retaliatory power.
—John Foster Dulles, speech to the Council on Foreign Relations, Jan. 12, 1954

★ Dulles was secretary of state under Eisenhower from 1953 to 1959, during the Cold War with Russia. His call for "massive retaliatory power"—almost immediately condensed by the media into "massive retaliation"—implied that the United States would respond with overwhelming nuclear strikes to any military threats by Communist nations, even if made only with conventional forces. An attraction of "massive retaliation" was that it was cheaper—in the short run, at least—than maintaining large conventional forces. In the words of then Defense Secretary Charles E. Wilson, it offered "a bigger bang for the buck." It was also a lot scarier because it was coupled with Dulles's predilection for "brinksmanship"; see below. Ernest Gross, who was in the audience for the "massive retaliation" speech, said later, "We all shook our heads and were really worried," *American Heritage*, June 1971.

You have to take chances for peace, just as you must take chances in war. . . . The ability to get to the verge without getting into the war is the necessary art. If you cannot master it, you inevitably get into war. If you try to run away from it, if you are scared to go to the brink, you are lost. . . . We walked to the brink and we looked it in the face. 1

—**John Foster Dulles,** interview with James Shepley, *Life* magazine, Jan. 16, 1956

★ Dulles's willingness to face down Russian and Chinese communists, even if it meant going to the brink of nuclear war, was derided by Adlai Stevenson and other Democrats as "brinksmanship," a term that probably was inspired by the popularity of Stephen Potter's humorous book *Gamesmanship* (1947). In 1953 and 1954, Dulles faced a series of crises in the Far East, centering on the Korean peace talks, the French defeat in Indo-China, and China's desire to recover Taiwan. He reacted with dramatic vigor. As John Kenneth Galbraith observed in a letter to Pres. John F. Kennedy, "The greatest difficulty with Dulles was his yearning for new and exciting variants in policy," October 9, 1961.

Today we are competing for men's hearts, and minds, and trust all over the world. In such a competition, what we are at home and what we do at home is even more important than what we say abroad. 2

—**Dwight D. Eisenhower,** renomination acceptance speech, San Francisco, August 23, 1956

Great nations like great men, should keep their word. 3

—**Hugo Black,** dissent, *Federal Power Commission and New York Power Authority v. Tuscarora Indian Nation*, 1960

★ Justice Black sided with the Indians in their losing suit to prevent the Niagara Power Authority from taking part of their reservation. He continued most eloquently: "The record does not leave the impression that the lands of their reservation are the most fertile, the landscape the most beautiful or their homes the most splendid specimens of architecture. But this is their home—their ancestral home. There they, their children, and their forebears were born. They, too, have their memories and their loves. Some things are worth more than money and the costs of a new enterprise. I regret that this court is the government agency that breaks faith with this dependent people." Chief Justice Earl Warren and Justice William O. Douglas joined in this opinion.

Let us never negotiate out of fear. But let us never fear to negotiate. 4

—**John F. Kennedy,** Inaugural Address, Jan. 20, 1961

1 A policy that can be accurately, though perhaps not prudently, defined as one of "peaceful coexistence."

—**James W. Fulbright,** speech in the U.S. Senate, March 27, 1964

★ "Peaceful co-existence" gradually became the desired conclusion to the Cold War. According to political lexicographer William Safire, the phrase may be of Russian origin. It surfaced at the Ninth All-Russian Congress of the Soviets in the form "peaceful and friendly co-existence." An early U.S. citation comes from a press conference with Pres. Dwight D. Eisenhower on June 30, 1954; both a reporter and the president used the phrase. The phrase became frontpage news when it was used by the Russian leader Nikita Khrushchev in a speech on January 6, 1961, just prior to the inauguration of John F. Kennedy.

2 The canal is ours. We stole it fair and square.

—**S. I. Hayakawa,** campaign remark, 1976

★ The noted semanticist, who went on to win election as senator for California, was objecting to a treaty, approved the following year, to return the Panama Canal Zone to Panama. The phrase lives on. For example, House Speaker Newt Gingrich's press secretary contended that Democrats "can't take it [the anti-crime issue] from us because we stole it fair and square" (*The New York Times,* Feb. 21, 1995). And following the 2000 presidential election, tee shirts and bumper stickers blossomed with the assertion that the Republicans "stole it fair and square."

3 The struggle between right and wrong, good and evil.

—**Ronald Reagan,** speech to the National Association of Evangelicals, March 9, 1983

★ Pres. Reagan here was characterizing the conflict between the U.S. and Russia in the last years of the Cold War. In the same speech, he called Russia "an evil empire," borrowing the name of the galactic enemy in the 1977 film *Star Wars* by George W. Lucas, Jr. Naturally, two weeks later, when Reagan proposed constructing a space-based missile-defense system—the Strategic Defense Initiative—the system was immediately dubbed "star wars."

4 Trust but verify.

—**Ronald Reagan,** negotiating slogan, 1980s

★ Pres. Reagan borrowed this Russian saying during nuclear-arms reduction negotiations with the Soviet Union. His counterpart was Mikhail Gorbachev, who won the 1990 Nobel Prize for Peace. For another expression of the same sentiment, see Mr. Dooley at TRUST

5 What is at stake here is more than one small country [Kuwait]. It is a big idea—a new world order, where diverse nations are drawn together in a common cause to achieve the universal aspirations of mankind: peace and security, freedom, and the rule of law.

—**George H. W. Bush,** State of the Union address, Jan. 29, 1991

6 If we're an arrogant nation, they'll resent us. If we're a humble nation but strong, they'll welcome us.

—**George W. Bush,** 2nd presidential debate, Oct. 11, 2000

★ Bush was debating the Democratic candidate, Vice President Al Gore. He was referring to foreign nations in general.

America has, and intends to keep, military strengths beyond challenge, thereby making the destabilizing arms races of other eras pointless, and limiting rivalries to trade and other pursuits of peace. 1

—**George W. Bush,** speech at West Point, June 1, 2002

We're an empire now, and when we act, we create our own reality. 2

—**Anonymous,** White House senior advisor, summer 2002, quoted by Ron Suskind, *The New York Times Magazine* [Oct. 17, 2004]

★ The advisor was quoted as referring to the "reality-based community" of people who "believe that solutions emerge from your judicious study of discernible reality." After the explanation of the reality of empire, given above, the advisor continued, "And while you're studying that reality—judiciously as you will—we'll act again, creating new realities, which you can study too, and that's how things will sort out. We're history's actors . . . and you, all of you, will be left to just study what we do."

Americans are from Mars and Europeans are from Venus. 3

—**Robert Kagan,** *Power and Weakness* in *Policy Review,* June/July 2002

★ The statement derives from a best-selling advice book by John Gray, *Men Are from Mars, Women Are from Venus* (1992). That book provoked women who didn't like the planet assignment. Kagan's famous essay was even more provocative in asserting that Americans and Europeans are fundamentally different and growing farther apart. "They agree on little and understand each other less," Kagan wrote. The planetary sentence reads in full: "On major strategic and international questions today, Americans are from Mars and Europeans are from Venus."

The United States has long maintained the option of preemptive actions to counter a sufficient threat to our national security. The greater the threat, the greater is the risk of inaction—and the more compelling the case for taking anticipatory action to defend ourselves, even if uncertainty remains as to the time and place of the enemy's attack. To forestall or prevent such hostile acts by our adversaries, the United States will, if necessary, act preemptively. 4

—**National Security Council,** *National Security Strategy,* Sept. 2002

★ This NSS (national security strategy) was described by critics as a dramatic change in policy, authorizing preemptive war. Supporters defended it as a practical extension of long-standing policy (see, for example, MEXICAN WAR, the objection by Abraham Lincoln.) The preemptive attack on Iraq was launched a half-year later. See IRAQ WAR.

We don't do empire. 5

—**Donald Rumsfeld,** press conference, response to a question from an *al-Jazeera* reporter, April 29, 2003

★ The Secretary of Defense elaborated, "We don't seek empires. We're not imperialistic. We never have been. I can't imagine why you'd even ask the question." See also Colin Powell at IRAQ WAR and Niall Ferguson at AMERICA AND AMERICANS.

America will never seek a permission slip to defend the security of our people. 6

—**George W. Bush,** State of the Union Address, Jan. 20, 2004

★ The president was seeking to refute criticisms that the U.S. had attacked Iraq without sufficient international backing. Insisting that "we have gained much support," Mr.

Bush continued: " There is a difference, however, between leading a coalition of many nations, and submitting to the objections of a few. American will never seek a permission slip, etc."

Forests

See ENVIRONMENT; WILDERNESS.

Forgiveness

1 Did man e'er live
Saw priest or woman yet forgive?
—James Russell Lowell, *Villa France, 1859*, in *Under the Willows and Other Poems*, 1868

2 Love scarce is love that never knows
The sweetness of forgiving.
—John Greenleaf Whittier, *Among the Hills*, 1869

3 Forgotten is forgiven.
—F. Scott Fitzgerald, "Notebooks," in *The Crack-Up*, 1945

4 What power has love but forgiveness?
—William Carlos Williams, *Asphodel, That Greeny Flower*, in *Journey to Love*, 1955

5 Forgive but never forget.
—John F. Kennedy, saying, attributed in Theodore Sorensen, *Kennedy* [1965]

★ Thomas Szasz amplified the thought this way in *The Second Sin* (1973): "The stupid neither forgive nor forget; the naive forgive and forget; the wise forgive but do not forget."

6 Forgiving presupposes remembering.
—Paul Tillich, *The Eternal Now*, 1963

Fourth of July

See INDEPENDENCE DAY.

France

See NATIONS.

Franklin, Benjamin

7 He Took Lightning from the Sky and the Scepter from the Tyrant's Hand.
—A. R. J. Turgot, inscription for the Houdon bust of Franklin, 1778

Turgot, the leading French economist and statesman of his day, referred here to his friend's experiments with lightning and revolution. The actual inscription is in Latin:

Eripuit fulmen sceptrumque tyrannis. When Thomas Jefferson presented his credentials as minister to France in 1785, the French foreign minister asked, "It is you who replace Monsieur Franklin?" To which Jefferson replied, "No one can replace him, Sir. I am only his successor."

Freedom

See also CONSTITUTION, THE; DEMOCRACY; FREE SPEECH; INDEPENDENCE DAY; RIGHTS.

Without freedom of thought there can be no such thing as wisdom; and no such thing as liberty without freedom of speech. **1**

—**Benjamin Franklin,** *Dogood Papers*, 1722

★ An early expression of the revolutionary spirit in the colonies. Franklin was sixteen when he wrote these essays for *The New England Courant* under the pen name Silence Dogood.

Proclaim liberty throughout the land unto all the inhabitants thereof. **2**

—**Bible,** *Leviticus* 25:10, inscribed on the Liberty Bell, 1752

Those who would give up essential liberties to purchase temporary safety deserve neither liberty nor safety. **3**

—**Benjamin Franklin,** speech, Pennsylvania Assembly, Nov. 11, 1755

★ A variant of this appears on a plaque in the stairwell of the Statue of Liberty on Bedloe's Island in New York Harbor.

One of the most essential branches of English liberty is the freedom of one's house. A man's house is his castle. **4**

—**James Otis,** argument on the Writs of Assistance, Boston, 1761

★ More at PRIVACY.

The God who gave us life, gave us liberty at the same time. **5**

—**Thomas Jefferson,** *Summary View of the Rights of British America*, 1775

Do thou, great liberty, inspire our souls, **6**
And make our lives in thy possession happy
Or our deaths glorious in thy just defense.

—**Joseph Addison,** *Cato*, 1713, used as the motto of the *Massachusetts Spy*, Nov. 22, 1771, to April 6, 1775

★ *Cato* may have been the first play published in America, and it was very popular. Nathan Hale borrowed from it in his final statement before execution; see AMERICAN REVOLUTION. The *Massachusetts Spy*, a weekly newspaper, was published by Isaiah Thomas, who went on to become the foremost book publisher in the United States.

Is life so dear, or peace so sweet, as to be purchased at the price of chains and slavery? Forbid it, Almighty God! I know not what course others may take, but as for me, give me liberty or give me death! **7**

—**Patrick Henry,** speech, Virginia Convention, March 23, 1775

★ A ringing declaration, but probably apocryphal. Neither Washington nor Jefferson, who were there, ever mentioned Henry's speech. As in the case of Henry's "if this be treason" challenge, cited in AMERICAN HISTORY: MEMORABLE MOMENTS, this speech was reconstructed many years after the fact by Henry's biographer William Wirt.

1 Where liberty dwells, there is my country.

—**Benjamin Franklin,** attributed

★ Also sometimes attributed to James Otis in the form of the Latin motto: *Ubi libertas, ibi patria.* For Franklin, the root of the attribution may be in a letter to David Hartley, December 4, 1789, in which Franklin wrote: "God grant that not only the love of liberty but a thorough knowledge of the rights of man may pervade all the nations of the earth, so that a philosopher may set his foot anywhere on its surface and say: 'This is my country.' "

2 Can the liberties of a nation be thought secure when we have removed their only firm basis, a conviction in the minds of the people that these liberties are the gifts of God? That they are not to be violated but with his wrath? Indeed I tremble for my country when I reflect that God is just.

—**Thomas Jefferson,** *Notes on the State of Virginia*, 1781–1785

★ Jefferson was warning in particular that slavery violated God's gift of liberty for us all.

3 The tree of liberty must be refreshed from time to time with the blood of patriots and tyrants. It is its natural manure.

—**Thomas Jefferson,** letter to Col. William S. Smith, Nov. 13, 1787

4 Wherever the standard of freedom and independence has been unfurled, there will [America's] heart, her benedictions, and her prayers be.

—**John Quincy Adams,** July 4, 1821

★ More at AMERICA & AMERICANS.

5 Independence now and forever!

—**Daniel Webster,** eulogy, August 2, 1826

★ Webster spoke in memory of Thomas Jefferson and John Adams, who both died on July 4, 1826. Four days earlier, when asked to suggest a toast to be made in his name, Adams had said, "It is my living sentiment, and by the blessing of God, it shall be my dying sentiment, Independence now and Independence forever." See also INDEPENDENCE DAY.

6 Liberty and independence, forever!

—**David Crockett,** Alamo journal, March 5, 1836, in *Colonel Crockett's Exploits and Adventures in Texas* [1837]

★ These are the final words of the journal once attributed to Crockett, killed later that day, along with all the other defenders of the San Antonio fortress, by Mexicans under General Santa Anna. The entire last paragraph reads: "Pop, pop, pop! Bom, bom, bom! throughout the day. No time for memorandums now. Go ahead! Liberty and independence forever!" For more on the Alamo and Crockett, see William Barrett Travis at AMERICAN HISTORY: MEMORABLE MOMENTS.

7 We should be men first, and subjects afterward.

—**Henry David Thoreau,** *Civil Disobedience*, 1849

Eternal vigilance is the price of liberty. 1

—Wendell Phillips, *Public Opinion*, speech, Massachusetts Anti-Slavery Society, Jan. 28, 1852

★ Sometimes attributed to Thomas Jefferson or Patrick Henry. The true source seems to be the Irish magistrate and orator John Philpot Curran, who in a speech delivered on July 10, 1790, stated: "The condition upon which God hath given liberty to man is eternal vigilance."

Those who deny freedom to others deserve it not for themselves. 2

—Abraham Lincoln, letter to H. L. Pierce et al., April 6, 1859

When I found I had crossed that line, I looked at my hands to see if I was the same 3
person. There was such a glory over everything.

—Harriet Tubman, description of her first escape to the North, quoted in Sarah H. Bradford, *Harriet, the Moses of Her People*, 1869

★ She got away for good in 1849, and dedicated herself to freeing others, leading more than 300 slaves out of bondage via the Underground Railroad. In the Civil War, she worked for the Union forces in coastal South Carolina, acting as a nurse, laundress, and spy. She was as eloquent as she was courageous.

I had reasoned this out in my mind: There was two things I had a right to, liberty and 4
death. If I could not have one, I would have the other, for no man should take me alive.

—Ibid.

Free at last! Free at last! 5
Thank God Almighty, we are free at last!

—Anonymous, spiritual

★ Quoted by Martin Luther King, Jr., to conclude his speech at the Lincoln Memorial in the march on Washington in 1963; see American History: Memorable Moments. This is his epitaph at South View Cemetery in Atlanta.

That buoyancy and exuberance which comes with freedom. 6

—Frederick J. Turner, *The Significance of the Frontier in American History*, 1893

★ More from this passage at America & Americans.

The cost of liberty is less than the price of repression. 7

—W. E. B. Du Bois, *The Legacy of John Brown*, 1909

You can only protect your liberties in this world by protecting the other man's free- 8
dom. You can only be free if I am free.

—Clarence Darrow, *People v. Lloyd*, 1920

I always say . . . if my fellow citizens want to go to hell, I will help them. It's my job. 9

—Oliver Wendell Holmes, Jr., letter to Harold J. Laski, March 4, 1920

The right to be let alone—the most comprehensive of rights. 10

—Louis D. Brandeis, *Olmstead v. the United States*, 1928

★ More at Privacy.

1 Freedom is never given; it is won.

—**A. Philip Randolph,** keynote speech, Second National Negro Congress, 1937

★ Randolph was the founder of the railway porters' union. He unionized the Pullman company, and was influential in persuading Pres. Harry S. Truman that the U.S. armed services should be integrated. Rev. Martin Luther King, Jr., made the same point some twenty-five years later; see below.

2 In the future days, which we seek to make secure, we look forward to a world founded upon four essential human freedoms.

—**Franklin D. Roosevelt,** State of the Union message, Jan. 6, 1941

★ The four freedoms cited by the president were: freedom of speech, freedom of worship, freedom from want, and freedom from fear. The "Four Freedoms" speech is quoted on a plaque in the stairwell of the Statue of Liberty. In 1839, John L. O'Sullivan, who coined the phrase, "manifest destiny," also spoke of the American mission to spread four freedoms; his four were "freedom of conscience, freedom of person, freedom of trade and business pursuits, universality of freedom and equality."

3 Freedom means the supremacy of human rights everywhere.

—**Franklin D. Roosevelt,** State of the Union message, Jan. 6, 1941

4 Liberty lies in the hearts of men and women; when it dies there, no constitution, no law, no court can save it; no constitution, no law, no court can even do much to help it.

—**Learned Hand,** "The Spirit of Liberty," speech at "I Am an American Day," New York City, May 21, 1944

5 Liberty is so much latitude as the powerful choose to accord to the weak.

—**Ibid.**

6 The spirit of liberty is the spirit which is not too sure that it is right.

—**Ibid.**

7 Freedom of speech and freedom of action are meaningless without freedom to think. And there is no freedom of thought without doubt.

—**Bergen Evans,** *The Natural History of Nonsense*, 1946

8 Caged birds accept each other but flight is what they long for.

—**Tennessee Williams,** *Camino Real*, 1953

9 Freedom is not a luxury that we can indulge in when at last we have security and prosperity and enlightenment; it is, rather an antecedent to all of these, for without it, we can have neither security nor prosperity nor enlightenment.

—**Henry Steele Commager,** *Freedom, Loyalty, Dissent*, 1954

10 And this nation, for all its hopes and boasts, will not be fully free until all its citizens are free.

—**John F. Kennedy,** civil rights speech to the nation, June 11, 1963

11 Freedom is never voluntarily given by the oppressor; it must be demanded by the oppressed.

—**Martin Luther King, Jr.,** letter from Birmingham city jail, 1963

★ See A. Philip Randolph, above.

Freedom's just another word for nothing left to lose. 1

—**Kris Kristofferson & Fred Foster,** *Me and Bobby McGee,* 1969

★ Sung most famously by Janis Joplin

Freedom is untidy. Free people are free to make mistakes and commit crimes and 2
do bad things.

—**Donald H. Rumsfeld,** press conference, April 11, 2003

★ The Defense Secretary was responding to questions about looting in Iraq. He added, "They're also free to live their lives and do wonderful things. And that's what's going to happen here." See also IRAQ WAR.

The best hope for peace in our world is the expansion of freedom in all the world. 3

—**George W. Bush,** Second Inaugural Address, Jan. 20, 2005

Free Speech

See also CONSTITUTION, THE; CENSORSHIP; FREEDOM; PRESS, THE; REVOLUTION (William Epton)

The most stringent protection of free speech would not protect a man falsely shout- 4
ing fire in a theater and causing a panic.

—**Oliver Wendell Holmes, Jr.,** *Schenck v. U.S.*, 1919

★ In the case at hand, the Supreme Court unanimously upheld the conviction of Charles T. Schenck, secretary of the Socialist party, for distributing a circular intended to encourage men to peacefully resist military recruitment. The decision set the precedent that the First Amendment freedoms of press and speech may be abridged when they constitute "a clear and present danger" to the community. Holmes emphasized the imperatives of war—see WAR. But the doctrine was used in the 1930s and 1940s to sustain convictions of people considered to be politically subversive.

When men have realized that time has upset many fighting faiths, they may come to 5
believe . . . that the ultimate good desired is better reached by the free trade in ideas—that the best test of truth is the power of the thought to get itself accepted in the competition of the market . . . That at any rate is the theory of our Constitution.

—**Oliver Wendell Holmes, Jr.,** dissent, *Abrams v. U.S.*, 1919

★ Holmes is called "the great dissenter," and indeed this often-cited statement was produced on the losing side of the argument. George F. Kennan, onetime U.S. ambassador to Russia, dissented in part from Holmes, pointing out: "The truth is sometimes a poor competitor in the market place of ideas—complicated, unsatisfying, full of dilemmas, always vulnerable to misinterpretation and abuse," *American Diplomacy: 1900–1950* (1951). Legal historian Alexander M. Bickel dissented in total, writing in *The Morality of Consent,* 1975, "The theory of the truth of the marketplace, determined ultimately by a count of noses—this total relativism—cannot be the theory of our Constitution." See also TRUTH.

One of the prerogatives of American citizenship is the right to criticize public men 6
and measures—and that means not only informed and responsible criticism but the freedom to speak foolishly and without moderation.

—**Felix Frankfurter,** *Baumgartner v. United States*, 1944

1 A function of free speech under our system of government is to invite dispute. It may indeed best serve its high purpose when it induces a condition of unrest, creates dissatisfaction with conditions as they are, or even stirs people to anger.
—**William O. Douglas,** *Terminiello v. Chicago*, 1949

2 All ideas having even the slightest redeeming social importance . . . have the full protection of the [First Amendment] guaranties. . . . But implicit in the history of the First Amendment is the rejection of obscenity as utterly without redeeming social importance.
—**William J. Brennan, Jr.,** *Roth v. United States*, 1957

★ The key phrase is often misquoted as "redeeming social value." For more on defining obscenity, see Brennan at SEX and Potter Stewart at CENSORSHIP.

3 Speech concerning public affairs is more than self-expression; it is the essence of self-government.
—**William J. Brennan, Jr.,** *Garrison v. Louisiana*, 1964

4 Constitutional protection should be accorded only to speech that is explicitly political.
—**Robert H. Bork,** *Neutral Principles and Some First Amendment Problems*, in *Indiana Law Journal*, 1, 1971

★ This controversial article provided ammunition that helped Bork's critics torpedo his nomination to the United States Supreme Court in 1987. Nearly a decade later it remained the seventh most frequently cited law review article of all time, according to a 1996 study by Yale Law School librarian Fred R. Shapiro.

5 One man's vulgarity is another man's lyric.
—**John M. Harlan,** *Cohen v. California,* 1971

★ The "vulgarity" in this Vietnam Era case was a "single four-letter expletive" on a man's jacket that expressed his opinion of what should be done to the draft. Noting that "we cannot indulge the facile assumption that one can forbid particular words without running a substantial risk of suppressing ideas," the court concluded (with three dissenters) that the state may not make the word's simple public display a criminal offense.

6 You can cage the singer but not the song.
—**Harry Belafonte,** with reference to South Africa, *International Herald Tribune*, Oct. 3, 1988

Free Will

See WILL.

Friends & Friendship

7 A brother may not be a friend, but a friend will always be a brother.
—**Benjamin Franklin,** *Poor Richard's Almanack*, May 1752

8 True friendship is a plant of slow growth.
—**George Washington,** letter to his nephew Bushrod Washington, Jan. 15, 1783

And the song from beginning to end, **1**
I found again in the heart of a friend.
—Henry Wadsworth Longfellow, *The Arrow and the Song*, 1845

★ The last two lines of one of Longfellow's most famous if least successful poems, which begins, "I shot an arrow in the air, / It fell to earth, I know not where." And continues, " . . . I breathed a song into the air, / It fell to earth I know not where. . . . / Long, long afterward in an oak, / I found the arrow, still unbroke; / And the song, from beginning to end," etc.

A friend may well be reckoned the masterpiece of nature. **2**
—Ralph Waldo Emerson, *Friendship*, in *Essays: First Series*, 1841

A friend is person with whom I may be sincere. Before him, I may think aloud. **3**
—Ibid.

Our friends have no place in the graveyard. **4**
—Henry David Thoreau, *A Week on the Concord and Merrimack Rivers*, 1849

★ In our memories they live and inspire us even after death.

The ornament of a house is the friends who frequent it. **5**
—Ralph Waldo Emerson, *Domestic Life*, in *Society and Solitude*, 1870

The holy passion of friendship is of so sweet and steady and loyal and enduring a **6**
nature that it will last through a whole lifetime, if not asked to lend money.
—Mark Twain, *Pudd'nhead Wilson's Calendar*, in *Pudd'nhead Wilson*, 1894

Friends are born, not made. **7**
—Henry Adams, *The Education of Henry Adams*, 1907

One friend in a life is much, two are many, three are hardly possible. **8**
—Ibid.

★ See Power for Adams on a friend in power.

There is nothing final between friends. **9**
—William Jennings Bryan, May 1914

★ Secretary of State Bryan was referring to a strain in relations between Japan and the U.S. occasioned by a California law forbidding Japanese to own real estate. The Japanese ambassador had not been happy with Bryan's explanation that there was little that he could do about the situation, and had asked, "I suppose, Mr. Secretary, this decision is final?" In fact, matters were patched up subsequently.

Only solitary men know the full joys of friendship. Others have their families; but to **10**
a solitary and an exile his friends are everything.
—Willa Cather, *Shadows on the Rock*, 1931

Louis, I think this is the beginning of a beautiful friendship. **11**
—Julius Epstein, Philip Epstein, & Howard Koch, *Casablanca*, 1942

★ Humphrey Bogart to Claude Rains. According to Aljean Harmetz in her 1992 book on the movie, producer Hal Wallis wrote this great closing line.

1 It is not often that someone comes along who is a true friend and a good writer.
—E. B. White, *Charlotte's Web*, 1952

2 The friend who holds your hand and says the wrong thing is made of dearer stuff than the one who stays away.
—Barbara Kingsolver, *Stone Soup*, 1995, in *High Tide in Tucson: Essays from Now or Never*, 1996

Frontier, the

See also MIDWEST, THE; WEST, THE.

3 [In America there is] room enough for our descendants to the thousandth and thousandth generation.
—Thomas Jefferson, First Inaugural Address, March 4, 1801

4 It is sometimes said that the abundance of vacant land operates as the safety valve of our system.
—George Bancroft, *Reform*, in *New England Magazine*, Jan. 1832

★ See also the "manifest destiny" quotes from John L. O'Sullivan under AMERICA & AMERICANS.

5 So long as cheap land continues to be abundant, so long you cannot drive the wages of labor to the starvation point.
—Robert Rantoul, Jr., 1848, quoted in Luther Hamilton, *Memoirs, Speeches, and Writings of Robert Rantoul, Jr.*

★ Rantoul was a Democratic congressman from Gloucester, Massachusetts.

6 Go west, young man.
—Horace Greeley, saying

★ Greeley, editor of the *New York Tribune*. offered essentially this advice, beginning in the early 1850s, but never in his newspaper in these precise words. More at THE WEST.

7 Come my tan-faced children
Follow well in order, get your weapons ready,
Have you your pistols? have you your sharp-edged axes?
Pioneers! O pioneers!
. . . O you youths, Western youths,
So impatient, full of action, full of manly pride and friendship,
Plain I see you Western youths, see you tramping with the foremost,
Pioneers! O pioneers!
. . . All the past we leave behind,
We debouch upon a newer, mightier world, varied world,
Fresh and strong the world we seize, world of labor and the march,
Pioneers! O pioneers!
—Walt Whitman, *Pioneers! O Pioneers*, 1865, in *Leaves of Grass* [1881]

Do not be afraid of any man, 1
no matter what his size.
Just call on me,
and I will equalize.

—Anonymous, on the virtues of the Colt revolver, c. 1875

★ The Colt .45 caliber Peacemaker, also called "The Equalizer,"was introduced in 1873 and swiftly became the sidearm of choice in the American west.

The existence of an area of free land, its continuous recession, and the advance of American settlement westward, explain American development. 2

—Frederick J. Turner, *The Significance of the Frontier in American History*, 1893

★ For a similar observation by Turner, see WEST, THE. Gertrude Stein, too, thought that empty space shaped the American character; see AMERICA & AMERICANS. For the political and cultural impact of the frontier, see Turner at DEMOCRACY. Turner's fine essay was first read to the American Historical Association. In the scope of a few pages, Turner defined the role of the frontier in American history and announced the frontier's disappearance. See below.

The frontier is productive of individualism. 3

—Ibid.

The frontier has gone, and with its going has closed the first period of American history. 4

—Ibid.

★ Turner, a young scholar—just thirty-two years old—at the University of Wisconsin, recognized the significance of a little noticed passage in a bulletin from the Superintendent of Census for 1890: "Up to and including 1880, the country had a frontier of settlement, but at present the unsettled area has been so broken into by isolated bodies of settlement that there can hardly be said to be a frontier line. . . . It cannot, therefore, any longer have a place in the census reports." But Turner foresaw that the expansionist spirit of Americans would continue: "He would be a rash prophet who should assert that the expansive character of American life has now entirely ceased. Movement has been its dominant fact, and, unless this training has no effect upon people, the American energy will continually demand a wider field for its exercise."

If there was a road, I could not make it out in the faint starlight. There was nothing but land: not a country at all, but the material out of which countries are made. 5

—Willa Cather, *My Antonia*, 1918

★ This is Nebraska—Black Hawk in the novel, Red Cloud in reality.

It is a forest full of innocent beasts. It is America but not yet. 6

—W. H. Auden, *Paul Bunyan*, libretto for opera with Benjamin Britten, 1941

We stand today at the edge of a new frontier. 7

—John F. Kennedy, presidential nomination acceptance speech, Democratic National Convention, Los Angeles, July 15, 1960

★ More at POLITICAL SLOGANS.

1 Space—the final frontier.
—Gene Roddenberry, *Star Trek* lead-in, 1966–69

★ More at ADVENTURE, EXPLORATION & DISCOVERY.

Future, the

See also ENVIRONMENT, THE; TIME;

2 I know no way of judging the future but by the past.
—Patrick Henry, speech, Virginia Convention, March 23, 1775

3 I like the dreams of the future better than the history of the past.
—Thomas Jefferson, letter to John Adams, August 1, 1816

4 We shall be obliged to gnaw the very crust of the earth for nutriment.
—Henry David Thoreau, *Travel in Concord*, in *Excursions* [1863]

★ Thoreau was reacting to the wholesale cutting of timber and the view that this kind of timbering is a basic right, "as if individual speculators were to be allowed to export the clouds out of the sky, or the stars out of the firmament, one by one."

5 The day will come when no badge or uniform or star will be worn.
—Ralph Waldo Emerson, quoted in Lewis Mumford, *Have Courage!*, in *American Heritage* magazine, Feb. 1969

6 The future is no more uncertain than the present.
—Walt Whitman, *Song of the Broad-Axe*, 1856

7 I have seen the future and it works.
—Lincoln Steffens, letter to Marie Howe, after visiting Russia, April 3, 1919

★ In his *Autobiography*, published in 1931, Steffens states that he made almost the same remark to Bernard Baruch at about the same time: "I have been over into the future and it works." Steffens used the observation repeatedly.

8 You ain't heard nothin' yet, folks.
—Al Jolson, *The Jazz Singer*, 1927

★ This was the first talking motion picture. The line was ad-libbed.

9 I'll think of it all tomorrow at Tara. . . . After all, tomorrow is another day.
—Margaret Mitchell, *Gone with the Wind*, 1936

10 Today we hold tomorrow in our hands.
—Grover Whalen, at groundbreaking for Theme Center of New York's World's Fair of 1939–40, August, 16, 1937

11 I never worry about the future. It comes soon enough.
—Albert Einstein, aphorism, 1945–46, in Alice Calaprice, *The Expanded Quotable Einstein* [2000]

In a foreseeable future we shall be smothered by our own numbers. . . . Preoccupation with survival has set the stage for extinction. 1
—John Steinbeck, *Sweet Thursday*, 1954

Time and space—time to be alone, space to move about—these may well be the greatest scarcities of tomorrow. 2
—Edwin Way Teale, *Autumn Across America*, 1956

Due to a lack of interest, tomorrow has been canceled. 3
—Anonymous, graffito, 1980s, cited in Leonard Roy Frank, *Quotationary* [2001]

The coming century is probably going to be one in which the amount of suffering reaches its maximum. 4
—Linus Pauling, quoted in *The New York Times*, obituary, August 21, 1994

★ For a place striving to prevent the future, see VERMONT, the quote from Charles Kuralt.

We don't have option of turning away from the future. 5
—Bill Gates, *The Road Ahead,* 1995

★ More at SCIENCE: TECHNOLOGY.

Games

See also LAW (Charles Bruce Darrow); SPORTS.

Wrapped in the speculations of this wretched game [chess] you destroy your constitution. 6
—Benjamin Franklin, *Dialogue between Franklin and the Gout*, 1780

★ Franklin, a talented chess buff, regretted the addictive aspects of the game, which drew him away from "the finest gardens and walks, a pure air, beautiful women, and the most agreeable and instructive conversation." Occasionally, though, he managed to combine pleasures—for instance, by playing chess with a friend—Madame Brillon—while she bathed. (Her tub had a wooden cover.) One evening they became so absorbed that Franklin did not get home to Passy until eleven o'clock. Madame Brillon who was less than half Franklin's age, was blessed with an understanding husband, and she must have been extremely clean.

[Gambling:] The child of avarice, the brother of iniquity, and the father of mischief. 7
—George Washington, letter, Jan. 15, 1783

★ Washington was no prude. Neither was Thomas Jefferson, who wrote: "Gaming corrupts our dispositions, and teaches us a habit of hostility against all mankind," letter to Martha Jefferson, 1787.

A stereotyped but unconscious despair is concealed even under what are called the games and amusements of mankind. 8
—Henry David Thoreau, "Economy," *Walden*, 1854

★ This is part of the passage that begins with the observation that most of us lead desperate lives; see LIFE.

1 The serene confidence which a Christian feels in four aces.
—Mark Twain, letter to *The Golden Era*, San Francisco, May 22, 1864

2 A man's idee in a card game is war—crool, devastatin', an' pitiless. A lady's idee iv it is a combynation iv larceny, embezzlement, an' burglary.
—Finley Peter Dunne, *On the Game of Cards*, in *Mr. Dooley on Making a Will*, 1919

3 I've seen a game iv cards start among frinds, but I never see frinds in a game iv cards.
—Ibid.

4 I like the moment when I break a man's ego.
—Bobby Fischer, in *Newsweek*, July 31, 1972

★ On the following September 1, Mr. Fischer became the first American to win the world chess championship.

Gardens

See NATURE: PLANTS & GARDENS.

Generations

See also AGES; FAMILY.

5 Every man is a quotation from all his ancestors.
—Ralph Waldo Emerson, *Plato, or The Philosopher*, in *Representative Men*, 1850

6 You are all a lost generation.
—Gertrude Stein, letter to Ernest Hemingway, 1926

★ The observation is the epigraph of Hemingway's *The Sun Also Rises*, 1926. A *Bartlett's* footnote states that Stein first heard this from a garage owner in the Midi, who called his young mechanics "*une génération perdue*."

7 Each generation wastes a little more of the future with greed and lust for riches.
—Don Marquis, *archy and mehitabel*, 1927

8 This generation is sowing the seeds of ultimate dissolution.
—Hiram Johnson, letter, 1930

★ Johnson was a reformist governor of California, a Republican, and Theodore Roosevelt's running mate on the Progressive Party ticket in 1912. He served in the U.S. Senate from 1917 to his death in 1945.

9 We are always telling 'em [young people] what we used to not do. We didn't do it because we didn't think of it. We did everything we could think of.
—Will Rogers, in Alex Ayres, ed., *The Wit and Wisdom of Will Rogers* [1993]

10 Every generation revolts against its fathers and makes friends with its grandfathers.
—Lewis Mumford, *The Brown Decades*, 1931

I have moments of real terror when I think we may be losing this generation. **1**
—Eleanor Roosevelt, May 1934, quoted in Joseph P. Lash, *Eleanor and Franklin* [1971]

There is a mysterious cycle in human events. To some generations much is given. Of others much is expected. This generation of Americans has a rendezvous with destiny. **2**
—Franklin D. Roosevelt, presidential nomination acceptance speech, Democratic National Convention, June 27, 1936

★ *Safire's New Political Dictionary* notes that the president may have had in mind Alan Seeger's "I have a rendezvous with death"; see under WORLD WAR I.

What has posterity ever done for me? **3**
—Groucho Marx, attributed

I saw the best minds of my generation destroyed by madness. **4**
—Allen Ginsberg, *Howl*, 1956

★ More at MADNESS.

Let the word go forth from this time and place, to friend and foe alike, that the torch has been passed to a new generation of Americans. **5**
—John F. Kennedy, Inaugural Address, Jan. 20, 1961

Don't trust anyone over thirty. **6**
—Anonymous, c. 1965

★ More at YOUTH.

Any given generation gives the next generation advice that the given generation should have been given by the previous one but now it's too late. **7**
—Roy Blount, Jr., *Don't Anybody Steal These,* in Daniel Halpern, ed., *Antaeus: Journals, Notebooks and Diaries*, 1988

Genius

See also CITIES: HOBOKEN (WILDE), MIND, THOUGHT, & UNDERSTANDING.

Towering genius disdains a beaten path. It seeks regions hitherto unexplored. **8**
—Abraham Lincoln, speech, Jan. 27, 1838

Great geniuses have the shortest biographies. **9**
—Ralph Waldo Emerson, *Representative Men*, 1850

In every work of genius, we recognize our own rejected thoughts; they come back to us with a certain alienated majesty. **10**
—Ralph Waldo Emerson, cited in Robert D. Richardson, Jr., *Emerson: The Mind on Fire* [1995]

Genius . . . means little more than the faculty of perceiving in an unhabitual way. **11**
—William James, *The Principles of Psychology*, 1890

1 Genius is one percent inspiration and ninety-nine percent perspiration.
—Thomas Alva Edison, c. 1903, quoted by M. A. Rosanoff, *Harper's Monthly Magazine* [Sept. 1932]

2 It takes a lot of time to be a genius, you have to sit around so much doing nothing, really doing nothing.
—Gertrude Stein, *Everybody's Autobiography*, 1937

3 Genius is an African who dreams up snow.
—Vladimir Nabokov, *The Gift*, 1937–38

★ *The Gift* was Nabokov's last novel written in Russian. The dates are of the censored serialized versions; it was not published in full until 1952. The author, who came to the U.S. in 1940, collaborated with Michael Scammell on an English translation in which verse and prose merge, and are printed without lineation. Leona Toker, writing in *The Reader's Encyclopedia of American Literature*, calls this "one of the greatest feats of translation."

4 Geniuses are the luckiest of mortals because what they must do is the same as what they most wanted to do.
—W. H. Auden, foreword for Dag Hammarskjöld, *Markings*, 1964

Georgia

See also CITIES: (Atlanta, Savannah).

5 My native State! My cherished home!
—"R.M.C.," *Georgia*, in *Augusta Mirror*, 1839

6 In the small towns of the country, however, we found the hospitality of the residents all that we could desire, and more than we could enjoy.
—J. S. Buckingham, *The Slave States of America, 1839*, 1842

7 A resistless feeling of depression falls slowly upon us, despite the gaudy sunshine and the green cotton-fields. This, then, is the Cotton Kingdom, the shadow of a marvelous dream.
—W. E. B. Du Bois, *The Souls of Black Folk*, 1903

★ From a passage on southern Georgia in summer, when the heat is "dull, determined." "The whole land seems forlorn and forsaken," Du Bois observed.

8 I am determined that at the end of this administration we shall be able to stand up anywhere in the world—in New York, California, or Florida—and say "I'm a Georgian," and be proud of it.
—Jimmy Carter, Inaugural Gubernatorial Address, Atlanta, Jan. 12, 1971

9 Wisdom, justice, and moderation.
—Motto, state of Georgia

Germany

See NATIONS.

Gettysburg Address

See also CIVIL WAR.

Fourscore and seven years ago, our fathers brought forth on this continent a new nation, conceived in liberty, and dedicated to the proposition that all men are created equal. 1

Now we are engaged in a great civil war, testing whether that nation or any nation so conceived and so dedicated can long endure. We are met on a great battlefield of that war. We have come to dedicate a portion of that field, as a final resting place for those who here gave their lives that a nation might live. It is altogether fitting and proper that we should do this.

But, in a larger sense, we cannot dedicate—we cannot consecrate—we cannot hallow—this ground. The brave men, living and dead, who struggled here have consecrated it far above our power to add or detract. The world will little note nor long remember what we say here, but it can never forget what they did here. It is for us, the living, rather to be dedicated here to the unfinished work which they who fought here have thus far so nobly advanced. It is rather for us to be here dedicated to the great task remaining before us—that from these honored dead we take increased devotion to that cause for which they gave the last full measure of devotion; that we here highly resolve that these dead shall not have died in vain; that this nation, under God, shall have a new birth of freedom; and that government of the people, by the people, for the people, shall not perish from earth.

—Abraham Lincoln, Gettysburg Address, Nov. 19, 1863

★ Lincoln spoke at the dedication of a permanent cemetery on the Gettysburg battlefield. Edward Everett of Massachusetts was the principal speaker, but the superintendent of the enterprise, David Wills, asked Lincoln to make "a few appropriate remarks." The battle at Gettysburg, Pennsylvania, was the greatest battle of the war, marking the limit of the Confederacy's advance north. The fighting lasted from July 1 to July 3; on July 4, Gen. Robert E. Lee began to retreat across the Potomac. Lee blundered at Gettysburg by attacking an entrenched army. "All this has been my fault, it is I that have lost this fight," Lee said to Gen. C. M. Wilcox as the remnants of Pickett's division returned from their futile charge. Meanwhile, the Union commander, Gen. George Meade, failed to exploit the victory by pursuing Lee's forces. The Union took 23,000 casualties and the Confederates about 25,000. The greatness of Lincoln's address was not appreciated right away, not even by himself. The president told his friend Ward Lamon as he returned to his seat that the speech was "a flat failure." *The New York Times* called it "dull and commonplace," but Edward Everett wrote Lincoln: "I should be glad if I could flatter myself that I came as near the central idea of the occasion in two hours as you did in two minutes." The phrase "government of the people, by the people, for the people," in the last sentence of the speech, may have derived from an 1830 speech by Daniel Webster in the U.S. Senate, which referred to "government, made for the people, made by the people, and answerable to the people"; see under GOVERNMENT. In 1850, in a speech in Boston, Theodore Parker declaimed, "This is what I call the American idea—a government of all the people, by all the people, for all the people."

Giving

See CHARITY & PHILANTHROPHY.

God

See also POLITICS (Sen. George Mitchell); RELIGION.

1 The Lord has more truth and light yet to break forth out of his Holy Word.
—**John Robinson,** speech as the Pilgrims left for America, 1620

★ Robinson, an English nonconformist, was pastor of the Pilgrim community in Holland. He supported emigration to the New World, and would have made the journey himself if the majority of his congregation had decided to go.

2 The longer I live, the more convincing proofs I see of this truth, that God governs in the affairs of men. And if a sparrow cannot fall to the ground without his notice, is it probable than an empire can rise without his aid?
—**Benjamin Franklin,** at the Constitutional Convention, 1787

★ A Deist in his youth, Franklin became more religious with age, and at the convention asked that each session begin with a prayer. All but a handful of delegates voted against this motion, but, according to Henry Steele Commager, their main reason was a lack of money to hire a chaplain (*American Heritage*, Dec. 1958). In 2004, the nation's attention was drawn again to this passage when the second sentence was used by Vice President Dick Cheney in his Christmas card.

3 In God we trust.
—**U.S. Motto**

★ Francis Scott Key originated the motto in 1814 in the form "In God is our trust" in the fourth verse of *The Star-Spangled Banner*. The more familiar version began appearing on U.S. coins in 1864. This arose from a suggestion made to Secretary of the Treasury Salmon P. Chase by Rev. M. R. Watkinson of Ridleyville, Penn. Rev. Watkinson had been dismayed by Union losses early in the Civil War, and felt that the defeats were linked to "our national shame in disowning God." Therefore, he proposed that God be recognized in some form on coins. The motto was adopted officially by Congress in 1956 and is used now on all coins and paper money.

4 God is our name for the last generalization to which we can arrive.
—**Ralph Waldo Emerson,** *Journals*, 1836

5 Dare to love God without mediator or veil.
—**Ralph Waldo Emerson,** *Divinity School Address*, 1838

6 God enters by a private door into every individual.
—**Ralph Waldo Emerson,** *Intellect*, in *Essays: First Series*, 1841

7 One, on God's side, is a majority.
—**Wendell Phillips,** speech on John Brown, Brooklyn, N.Y., Nov. 1, 1859

8 The only money of God is God. He never pays with any thing less, or any thing else.
—**Ralph Waldo Emerson,** *Worship*, in *The Conduct of Life*, 1860

God Himself does not speak prose, but communicates with us by hints, omens, inference, and dark resemblances in objects lying all around us. 1

—Ralph Waldo Emerson, *Poetry and Imagination*, in *Letters and Social Aims* [1876]

Mine eyes have seen the glory of the coming of the Lord; 2
He is trampling out the vintage where the grapes of wrath are stored;
He hath loosed the fateful lightning of His terrible, swift sword;
His truth is marching on.

—Julia Ward Howe, *Battle Hymn of the Republic*, 1862

★ Howe based the *Battle Hymn* on an army marching song that concluded "John Brown's body lies a-moldering in the ground; His soul is marching on." Her song became the anthem of the Union forces. After the war, Howe took up the cause of world peace; see PACIFISM & NONVIOLENCE.

In the beauty of the lilies Christ was born across the sea, 3
With a glory in His bosom that transfigures you and me;
As he died to make men holy, let us die to make men free.

—Ibid.

The Almighty has His own purposes. 4

—Abraham Lincoln, Second Inaugural Address, March 4, 1865

★ The conclusion of a passage in which Lincoln comments that in the Civil War both sides prayed to the same God. "The prayers of both could not be answered," Lincoln wrote. "That of neither has been answered fully."

God is and all is well. 5

—John Greenleaf Whittier, *My Birthday*, 1871

God is love, love in action—love universal. 6

—Peter Cooper, c. 1875, quoted in Peter Lyon, *The Honest Man*, in *American Heritage* [Feb. 1959]

★ In the circles of the wealthy, Cooper was an unusually ardent advocate of social responsibility; see under BUSINESS and MONEY & THE RICH.

Our Father-Mother-God, all-harmonies. 7

—Mary Baker Eddy, *Science and Health with Key to the Scriptures*, 1875

Though the mills of God grind slowly, yet they grind exceedingly small; 8
Though with patience He stands waiting, with exactness grinds He all.

—Henry Wadsworth Longfellow, translation of Friedrich von Logau's *Retribution*, 1654

An honest God is the noblest work of man. 9

—Robert G. Ingersoll, *The Gods, and Other Lectures*, 1876

★ Also in the *Notebooks* of the 19th-century English writer Samuel Butler.

As man now is, God once was; as God now is, man may be. 10

—Lorenzo Snow, address, Sunday, Sept. 18, 1898

★ Snow was the fifth president of the Church of Latter-day Saints. This saying, now a Mormon adage, first came to him in June 1840, according to his sister Eliza Snow. She was a poet, the second wife of Joseph Smith, and later married Brigham Young. The same thought was expressed, in April, 1844, by Smith in his Discourse at the funeral of his friend King Follett. "God himself was once as we are now, and is an exalted man, and sits enthroned in yonder heavens!"

1 I believe that our Heavenly Father invented man because he was disappointed in the monkey.

—**Mark Twain,** dictation for his autobiography, Nov. 24, 1906

2 I myself believe that the evidence for God lies primarily in inner personal experiences.

—**William James,** *Pragmatism*, 1907

3 God, I can push the grass apart,
And lay my finger on thy heart.

—**Edna St. Vincent Millay,** *Renascence*, in *Renascence and Other Poems*, 1917

4 God: The John Doe of philosophy and religion.

—**Elbert Hubbard,** *Roycroft Dictionary and Book of Epigrams*, 1923

5 No reason can be given for the nature of God, because that nature is the ground of rationality.

—**Alfred North Whitehead,** *Science and the Modern World*, 1925

6 God is in me or else is not at all (does not exist).

—**Wallace Stevens,** *Adagia*, in *Opus Posthumous* [1957]

7 God is a mother.

—**Eugene O'Neill,** *Strange Interlude*, 1928

8 It takes a long while for a naturally trusting person to reconcile himself to the idea that after all God will not help him.

—**H. L. Mencken,** *Minority Report: H. L. Mencken's Notebooks* [1956]

9 Sometimes there's a God so quickly.

—**Tennessee Williams,** *A Streetcar Named Desire*, 1947

10 *Raffiniert ist der Herr Gott, aber boshaft ist er nicht.* God is subtle, but malicious he is not.

—**Albert Einstein,** inscription in Fine Hall, Princeton University

★ Einstein's own translation, according to Alan L. Mackay in *The Harvest of a Quiet Eye*, was "God is slick, but he ain't mean." For Einstein on God and dice, see SCIENCE: PHYSICS & COSMOLOGY.

11 What really interests me is whether God could have created the world any differently; in other words, whether the demand for logical simplicity leaves any freedom at all.

—**Albert Einstein**, comment, in Alice Calaprice, ed., *The Expanded Quotable Einstein* [2000]

★ The remark was made in answer to a question about whether God had any choice in the design of the world.

God and the imagination are one. 1

—Wallace Stevens, *Final Soliloquy of the Interior Paramour,* 1950

It is the final proof of God's omnipotence that he need not exist in order to save us. 2

—Peter De Vries, *Mackeral Plaza*, 1958

Gods do not answer letters. 3

—John Updike, *Hub Fans Bid Kid Adieu*, in *The New Yorker*, Oct. 22, 1960

★ The God in this instance was Theodore [Ted] Samuel Williams, aka the Kid or the Splendid Splinter, who concluded a Hall of Fame baseball career on Sept. 26, 1962, by hitting a home run, his 521st, on his final turn at bat in Boston's Fenway Park. Refusing to budge from past practice, Williams declined to acknowledge the cheers of Updike and other fans by coming out of the dugout and tipping his cap. It says something about New England weather—the day was cold—but about Boston, too, that only 10,454 people showed up for the occasion. But when Williams came to Fenway for the 1999 All-Star game, his last appearance there, all hard feelings were forgotten, with fans cheering and players gathering around Williams, so eager to talk to him that the game was delayed.

God is the Celebrity-Author of the World's Best Seller. We have made God into the 4
biggest celebrity of all, to contain our own emptiness.

—Daniel J. Boorstin, *The Image*, 1962

God is a verb. 5

—R. Buckminster Fuller, *No More Secondhand God*, 1963

★ Possibly derived from Ulysses S. Grant; see ACTION & DOING.

Like anybody, I would like to live a long life. Longevity has its place. But I'm not 6
concerned about that now. I just want to do God's will. And he's allowed me to go up to the mountain. And I've looked over, and I've seen the promised land. I may not get there with you, but I want you to know tonight that we as a people will get to the promised land. . . . So I'm happy tonight. I'm not worried about anything. I'm not fearing any man. Mine eyes have seen the glory of the coming of the Lord.

—Martin Luther King, Jr., speech to sanitation workers, Memphis, Tenn., April 3, 1968

★ Dr. King was shot the next day.

The Buddha, the Godhead, resides as comfortably in the circuits of a digital com- 7
puter or the gears of a cycle transmission as he does at the top of a mountain or in the petals of a flower.

—Robert Pirsig, *Zen and the Art of Motorcycle Maintenance*, 1974

★ See Pirsig also at SCIENCE: TECHNOLOGY.

There is no more powerful ally one can claim in a debate than Jesus Christ, or God, 8
or Allah or whatever one calls his Supreme Being. But, like any other powerful weapons, the use of God's name on one's behalf should be used sparingly.

—Barry Goldwater, *Conservatism, Religion, and Politics*, speech, 1981

★ The Republican senator from Arizona, speaking as one who had spent quite "a number of years carrying the flag of the 'old conservatism,' " here lamented the intrusion of the Moral Majority and other religious groups into politics. For a similar conclusion by a senator from the other end of the political spectrum, see George Mitchell at POLITICS & POLITICIANS.

1 A philosophy is needed that is built on time and space. Time and space are both attributes of God.

—Isaac Bashevis Singer, *The Certificate* [1992]

★ The speaker is the novel's protagnonist, David Bendinger. Originally serialized in 1967 in the Yiddish weekly, *The Forward*, the novel probably was written many years earlier.

2 People see God every day; they just don't recognize him.

—Pearl Bailey, in Eric V. Copage, *Black Pearls*, 1993

3 Coincidence is God's way of remaining anonymous.

—Bill Moyers, in *The New York Times,* Mar. 20, 1998

Goodness

See ETHICS & MORALITY; KINDNESS; VIRTUE.

Good Times

4 The Era of Good Feelings.

—Anonymous

★ A name for the peaceful terms of Republican presidents James Monroe and John Quincy Adams, 1816 to 1828. Jacksonian Democrats had a different name for the period: "The Era of Corruption."

5 The era of wonderful nonsense.

—Westbrook Pegler, saying

★ Pegler was referring to the 1920s. Henry F. Woods, in *American Sayings* (1945), writes that Pegler originated the phrase in an article later titled *Mr. Gump Himself* and included in his book *'Tain't Right*. Pegler liked the phrase and used it often.

6 Happy days are here again,
The skies above are clear again:
Let us sing a song of cheer again,
Happy days are here again!

—Jack Yellen, *Happy Days Are Here Again*, 1929

★ The song, with music by Milton Ager, enlivened the 1932 Democratic National Convention, and many thereafter. The incumbent president, Franklin D. Roosevelt used it as a campaign song.

7 A golden age of poetry and power
Of which this noonday's the beginning hour.

—Robert Frost, inauguration of John F. Kennedy, Jan. 20, 1961

This is the dawning of the age of Aquarius. **1**
—James Rado & Gerome Ragni, *Aquarius*, in the musical, *Hair*, 1967

Government

See also BUSINESS; CITIES (POCATELLO; WASHINGTON, D.C.); CONGRESS; DEMOCRACY; ECONOMICS; INSTITUTIONS; MAJORITIES & MINORITIES; MANAGEMENT TECHNIQUES; POLITICS & POLITICIANS; PRESIDENCY, THE; SUPREME COURT.

Society in every state is a blessing, but government, even in its best state, is but a **2**
necessary evil; in its worst state, an intolerable one.
—Thomas Paine, *Common Sense*, 1776

Government, like dress, is the badge of lost innocence; the palaces of kings are built **3**
upon the ruins of the bowers of paradise.
—Thomas Paine, *Common Sense*, 1776

The happiness of society is the end of government. **4**
—John Adams, *Thoughts on Government*, 1776

The legitimate powers of government extend to such acts only as are injurious to **5**
others.
—Thomas Jefferson, *Note on the State of Virginia*, 1784

★ In coming years, Jefferson came to see a broader role for government; see below. See also Jefferson at THE PEOPLE.

Why has government been instituted at all? Because the passions of men will not **6**
conform to the dictates of reason and justice, without constraint.
—Alexander Hamilton, *Federalist*, No. 15, 1787–88

What is government itself, but the greatest of all reflections on human nature? If **7**
men were angels, no government would be necessary. If angels were to govern men, neither external nor internal controls on government would be necessary. In framing a government which is to be administered by men over men, the great difficulty lies in this; you must first enable the government to control the governed; and in the next place oblige it to control itself.
—James Madison, *Federalist* No. 51, 1788

The natural progress of things is for liberty to yield and government to gain ground. **8**
—Thomas Jefferson, letter to Col. Edward Carrington, May 27, 1788

★ This may be the genesis of another quotation commonly but apparently incorrectly attributed to Jefferson: "Eternal vigilance is the price of liberty." See Wendell Phillips at FREEDOM.

The whole art of government consists in being honest. **9**
—Thomas Jefferson, *Works*, VI

The very idea of the power and the right of the people to establish government pre- **10**
supposes the duty of every individual to obey established government.
—George Washington, Farewell Address, Sept. 17, 1796

1 What more is necessary to make us wise and happy people? Still one thing more, fellow citizens—a wise and frugal government, which shall restrain men from injuring one another, which shall leave them otherwise free to regulate their own pursuits of industry and improvement, and shall not take from the mouth of labor the bread it has earned. This is the sum of good government, and this is necessary to close the circle of our felicities.

—**Thomas Jefferson,** First Inaugural Address, March 4, 1801

2 Sometimes it is said that man cannot be trusted with the government of himself. Can he then be trusted with the government of others?

—**Ibid.**

★ Jefferson was optimistic. He answered the question affirmatively, characterizing the new American form of government as "the world's best hope." But at the same time, he accepted resistance to government as natural and sometimes desirable; see RESISTANCE and REVOLUTION.

3 The care of human life and happiness, and not their destruction, is the first and only legitimate object of good government.

—**Thomas Jefferson,** message to the citizens of Washington County, Maryland, March 31, 1809

★ A few years later, Jefferson restated this view a little more broadly: "The only orthodox object of the institution of government is to secure the greatest degree of happiness possible to the general mass of those associated under it," letter to F. A. van der Kemp, March 22, 1812.

4 The world is too much governed.

—**Francis P. Blair,** motto of the *Washington Globe*, Dec. 1830

★ Blair, editor of the *Argus of Western America* in Kentucky, was summoned to Washington in 1830 to found a newspaper that would express the views of Pres. Andrew Jackson and his supporters. See also O'Sullivan below.

5 It is, Sir, the people's Constitution, the people's government, made for the people, made by the people, and answerable to the people.

—**Daniel Webster,** speech, U.S. Senate, Jan. 26, 1830

★ Webster was replying to Sen. Robert Y. Hayne of South Carolina, and indirectly to Vice President John C. Calhoun. They had proposed that states had the right within their boundaries to nullify any federal law. Webster countered that the Constitution belonged not to individual states but to the people. See GETTSYBURG ADDRESS and the note on Lincoln's reference to "government of the people, by the people, for the people."

6 All government is evil. . . . The best government is that which governs least.

—**John L. O'Sullivan,** *The United States Magazine and Democratic Review*, 1837

★ This view was prevalent in the era—see Emerson below, for example—and prevalent especially among Democrats. See above for the motto Francis Blair chose for the *Washington Globe*. The motto of the *Democratic Review* was: "That government is best which governs least." Among Democrats, mistrust of central government was allied with support for states' rights, and this alliance with Southern views eventually cost the party dearly. For a response to the least-is-best concept, see Walter Lippman below. For a modern Republican view, see Ronald Reagan under AMERICA & AMERICANS.

The less government we have, the better. 1

—**Ralph Waldo Emerson,** *Politics*, in *Essays: Second Series*, 1844

★ In the same year, Thoreau, in the opening of his essay *Civil Disobedience,* used the quote, "That government is best which governs least"; see John L. O'Sullivan above.

In every society some men are born to rule, and some to advise. 2

—**Ralph Waldo Emerson,** *The Young American*, in *Addresses and Lectures*, 1849

No man is good enough to govern another man without that other's consent. 3

—**Abraham Lincoln,** speech, Peoria, Ill., Oct. 16, 1854

Government of the people, by the people, for the people, shall not perish from the 4
earth.

—**Abraham Lincoln,** Gettsyburg Address, Nov. 19, 1863

★ More at GETTSYBURG ADDRESS.

A public office is a public trust. 5

—**Anonymous,** motto of Pres. Grover Cleveland's administrations

★ The thought was phrased many ways over the years. Henry Clay, in a speech in Ashland, Kentucky, in 1829, said: "Government is a trust, and the officers of the government are trustees; and both the trust and the trustees are created for the benefit of the people." John C. Calhoun, speaking on February 13, 1835, said: "The very essence of a free government consists in considering offices as public trusts, bestowed for the good of the country, and not for the benefit of an individual or party." In 1872, Charles Sumner noted, "The phrase 'public office is a public trust' has of late become common property." Grover Cleveland, among many references to this concept, wrote in accepting the Democratic presidential nomination in 1892: "Public officers are the trustees of the people." See also Thomas Jefferson on assuming a public trust at POLITICS & POLITICIANS.

Government is force. 6

—**John Adams Ingalls,** article, New York *World*, 1890

★ For more see under Ingalls at POLITICS & POLITICIANS.

It is perfectly true that the government is best which governs least. It is equally true 7
that the government is best which provides most.

—**Walter Lippmann,** *A Preface to Politics*, 1913

★ A response to John L. O'Sullivan; see above.

Neither snow, nor rain, nor heat, nor gloom of night stays these couriers from the 8
swift completion of their appointed rounds.

—**General Post Office,** New York City, inscription, 1913

★ Adapted from a passage in Herodotus, *The Histories*, 5th cent. B.C. More at NATURE: WEATHER.

1 Our government is the potent, the omnipresent teacher. For good or ill, it teaches the whole people by its example. Crime is contagious. If the government becomes the lawbreaker, it breeds contempt for law, it invites every man to become a law unto himself, it invites anarchy.

—**Louis Brandeis,** *Olmstead v. U.S.*, dissenting opinion, 1928

2 It is one of the happy incidents of the federal system that a single courageous state may, if its citizens choose, serve as a laboratory; and try novel social and economic experiments without risk to the rest of the country.

—**Louis Brandeis,** *New State Ice Company v. Liebmann,* dissenting opinion, 1932

3 Governments can err, Presidents do make mistakes, but the immortal Dante tells us that divine justice weighs the sins of the cold-blooded and the sins of the warm-hearted in different scales. Better the occasional faults of a Government that lives in a spirit of charity than the consistent omissions of a Government frozen in the ice of its own indifference.

—**Franklin D. Roosevelt,** speech accepting the Democratic Party's presidential nomination, June 27, 1936

★ Thus F.D.R. justified spending on governmental programs to aid people hurt by the Depression even though this meant breaking his promise to balance the budget.

4 I am against government by crony.

—**Harold L. Ickes,** resigning as Secretary of the Interior, Feb. 1946

5 We must remember that the people do not belong to the government but that government belongs to the people.

—**Bernard Baruch**, speech, U.N. Atomic Energy Commission, June 14, 1946

6 No man should be in public office who can't make more money in private life.

—**Thomas E. Dewey,** maxim, cited in Richard Norton Smith, *Thomas E. Dewey* [1982]

7 The worst government is the most moral. One composed of cynics is often very tolerant and humane. But when fanatics are on top, there is no limit to oppression.

—**H. L. Mencken,** *Minority Report: H. L. Mencken's Notebooks* [1956]

8 Where there is a lack of honor in the government, the morals of the whole people are poisoned.

—**Herbert Hoover**, quoted in *The New York Times* [August 9, 1964]

9 A government that is big enough to give you all you want is big enough to take it all away.

—**Barry Goldwater,** speech, Oct. 21, 1964

★ A popular theme in the resurgence of conservative Republicanism. See also Ronald Reagan below.

10 Today, government is involved in almost every aspect of our lives.

—**Bernard Baruch,** presenting his papers to Princeton University, May 11, 1964

Government is like a big baby—an alimentary canal with a big appetite at one end and no responsibility at the other. 1

—**Ronald Reagan,** saying, used in the gubernatorial campaign, 1965

★ Reagan continued to use this simile, for example, in a speech on March 11, 1981, in a joint session of Parliament in Ottawa, Canada.

Yet as I read the Constitution, one of its essential purposes was to take government off the backs of people and keep it off. 2

—**William O. Douglas,** dissenting opinion, in *W. E. B. Du Bois Clubs v. Clark*, 1967

If it ain't broke, don't fix it. 3

—**Bert Lance,** *Nation's Business*, May 27, 1977

★ A bit of proverbial wisdom popularized by Pres. Jimmy Carter's first budget director. As elucidated in *Nation's Business*: "Bert Lance believes he can save Uncle Sam billions if he can get the government to adopt a single motto: 'If it ain't broke, don't fix it.' He explains: 'That's the trouble with government: Fixing things that aren't broken and not fixing things that are broken.' "

In this present crisis, government is not the solution to our problem; government is the problem. 4

—**Ronald Reagan,** First Inaugural Address, Jan. 20, 1981

★ The crisis was economic distress, high inflation in particular. The reference to the crisis is usually dropped from the quote. Earlier, Reagan observed, "Government does not solve problems, it subsidizes them," speech, Dec. 11, 1972.

We do not get all the government we pay for—thank God. 5

—**Milton Friedman,** quoted by George Will, *David Brinkley Show*, American Broadcasting Corp., Oct. 4, 1992

The era of big government is over. 6

—**Bill Clinton,** radio address, Jan. 27, 1996

★ Less than ten years later, with the federal deficit projected at a record $427 billion, political scholar Marshall Wittman noted, "The era of big government being over is over," *The New York Times*, Feb. 13, 2005

I don't want to abolish government. I simply want to reduce it to the size where I can drag it into the bathroom and drown it in the bathtub. 7

—**Grover Norquist,** interview, National Public Radio, Morning Edition, May 25, 2001

★ This drastic reduction is sometimes called "starving the beast"; see David Stockman at ECONOMICS.

We govern our democracy either through leadership or crisis. 8

—**Leon Panetta,** former chief of staff for Pres. Bill Clinton, on C-Span 2, Jan. 18, 2005

Grace

See also SIMPLICITY.

1 'Tis the gift to be simple,
'Tis the gift to be free,
'Tis the gift to come down
Where we ought to be.
—**Anonymous,** *Simple Gifts*, Shaker song, c. 1848

2 Grace under pressure.
—**Ernest Hemingway,** c. 1926

★ This was Hemingway's definition of *guts* according to Dorothy Parker, *The Artist's Reward*, in *The New Yorker*, Nov. 20, 1929. He evidently also used the phrase in 1926 to describe Gerald Murphy's first efforts at downhill skiing, as recounted in Honoria Murphy Donnelly and Richard N. Billings, *Sara & Gerald*, 1982. The phrase was echoed in Hemingway's articles on bullfighting; see under SPORTS. And it was quoted memorably by John F. Kennedy in *Profiles in Courage*.

3 To learn to dance by practicing dancing or to live by practicing living, the principles are the same. . . . One becomes, in some area, an athlete of God.
—**Martha Graham,** May 15, 1945

4 The sign of grace is luck.
—**Garry Wills,** *The Kennedy Imprisonment: A Meditation on Power*, 1981

Greatness

5 It is not in the still calm of life, or in the repose of pacific station that great characters are formed. . . . Great necessities call out great virtues.
—**Abigail Adams,** letter to John Quincy Adams, Jan. 19, 1780

6 Lives of great men all remind us.
We can make our lives sublime.
And, departing, leave behind us
Footprints on the sands of time.
—**Henry Wadsworth Longfellow,** *A Psalm of Life*, 1839

7 To be great is to be misunderstood.
—**Ralph Waldo Emerson,** *Self-Reliance*, in *Essays; First Series*, 1841

8 A great man is always willing to be little.
—**Ralph Waldo Emerson,** *Compensation*, in *Essays: First Series*, 1841

★ See Emerson at VIRTUE for "the essence of greatness."

9 Great men, great nations, have not been boasters and buffoons, but perceivers of the terror of life, and have manned themselves to face it.
—**Ralph Waldo Emerson,** *Fate*, in *The Conduct of Life*, 1860

There is no indispensable man. 1

—**Franklin D. Roosevelt,** campaign speech, New York, Nov. 3, 1932

★ He was borrowing from Woodrow Wilson; see under HUMANS & HUMAN NATURE.

Great men can't be ruled. 2

—**Ayn Rand,** *The Fountainhead*, 1943

★ See also Richard M. Nixon at HIGH POSITION: RULERS & LEADERS.

An article of the democratic faith is that greatness lies in each person. 3

—**Bill Bradley**, commencement address, Middlebury [Conn.] College, May, 1989

Greece

See NATIONS.

Grief

See DEATH; SORROW & GRIEF.

Guests

See also HOSPITALITY.

My evening visitors, if they cannot see the clock, should be able to find the time in my face. 4

—**Ralph Waldo Emerson,** *Journal*, 1842

A dinner invitation, once accepted is a sacred obligation. If you die before the dinner takes place, your executor must attend the dinner. 5

—**Ward McAllister,** 1890

★ Quoted in *American Heritage*, April 1975. McAllister was the chap who said that there were only four hundred people in New York society; see ELITE, THE.

Some people can stay longer in an hour than others can in a week. 6

—**William Dean Howells,** attributed

To be an ideal guest, stay at home. 7

—**Edgar Watson Howe,** *Country Town Sayings*, 1911

My father used to say "Superior people never make long visits." 8

—**Marianne Moore,** *Silence*, in *Collected Poems*, 1935

Gulf War, 1991

See also FOREIGN POLICY (GEORGE H. W. BUSH).

Just two hours ago, allied air forces began an attack on military targets in Iraq and Kuwait. These attacks continue as I speak. 9

—**George H. W. Bush,** Jan. 16, 1991

★ The president addressed the nation on television, which was already broadcasting air attacks on Baghdad. The war was precipitated by Iraq's invasion of Kuwait in 1990.

1 Our strategy for going after this army is very, very simple. First, we are going to cut it off, and then, we are going to kill it.

—**Colin Powell,** press conference, Jan. 23, 1991

★ Gen. Powell was referring to the Iraqi army, considered at that time to be the fourth-greatest army in the world. See also IRAQ WAR (note to "shock and awe").

2 Seven months ago, America and the world drew a line in the sand. We declared that aggression against Kuwait would not stand, and tonight America and the world have kept their word.

—**George H. W. Bush,** Feb. 27, 1991

★ Allied forces, led by the U.S., drove Iraqi troops out of Kuwait and back toward Baghdad. When the war ended, however, Iraqi leader Saddam Hussein was still in power, supported by a considerable military presence.

3 Saddam Hussein still has his job. Do you?

—**Anonymous,** bumper sticker, 1991–92

★ The nation was in a recession, with high unemployment. In the presidential election, Democratic challenger Bill Clinton ousted Pres. George H. W. Bush.

4 Seldom have so many gathered for a war eventually fought by so few.

—**Edward N. Luttwak,** in Robert Cowley and Geoffrey Parker, eds., *The Reader's Companion to Military History* [1996]

★ The American-led coalition began this war with well over 600,000 ground troops in place (more than three times the number involved in launching the IRAQ WAR.) Luttwak was playing on the famous Winston Churchill tribute to the Royal Air Force in World War II—"Never in the field of human conflict was so much owed by so many to so few," speech in the House of Commons, Aug. 20, 1940.

Habit & Custom

5 Customs represent the experiences of mankind.

—**Henry Ward Beecher,** *Proverbs from Plymouth Pulpit*, 1887

6 Habit is . . . the enormous flywheel of society, its most precious conservative agent. It alone is what keeps us all within the bounds of ordinance.

—**William James,** *The Principles of Psychology*, 1890

7 Nothing so needs reforming as other people's habits.

—**Mark Twain,** *Pudd'nhead Wilson's Calendar*, in *Pudd'nhead Wilson*, 1894

8 Most of the things we do, we do for no better reason than that our fathers have done them or our neighbors do them, and the same is true of a larger part than what we suspect of what we think.

—**Oliver Wendell Holmes, Jr.,** speech, Boston, Jan. 8, 1897

9 No written law has ever been more binding than unwritten custom supported by popular opinion.

—**Carrie Chapman Catt,** *Why We Ask for the Submission of an Amendment*, speech at Senate hearing on woman's suffrage, Feb. 13, 1900

Habit is stronger than reason. 1

—**George Santayana,** *Interpretations of Poetry and Religion*, 1900

For the ordinary business of life, an ounce of habit is worth a pound of intellect. 2

—**Thomas B. Reed,** speech at Bowdoin College, Maine, July 25, 1902

Laws are sand, customs are rock. Law can be evaded and punishment escaped, but 3
an openly transgressed custom brings sure punishment.

—**Mark Twain,** *The Gorky Incident*, 1906

★ See also Adlai Stevenson below.

Habit is far stronger than the lessons of experience. 4

—**Helen McCloy,** *Cue for Murder*, 1942

★ The speaker is Dr. Basil Willing, a psychiatrist-detective.

Laws are never as effective as habits. 5

—**Adlai Stevenson,** speech, New York City, August 28, 1952

I don't have any bad habits. They might be bad habits for other people, but they're 6
all right for me.

—**Eubie Blake,** *Eubie*, 1979

Happiness

See also Desires; Pleasure & Hedonism; Utopia.

My heart is like a feather and my spirits are dancing. 7

—**Abigail Adams,** letter, April 1776

★ She was happy because she had just received a packet of letters—"a feast to me"—from her husband, John.

Human felicity is produced not so much by great pieces of good fortune that seldom 8
happen, as by little advantages that occur every day.

—**Benjamin Franklin,** *Autobiography* [1791]

It is neither wealth nor splendor, but tranquility and occupation, which give happi- 9
ness.

—**Thomas Jefferson,** letter to Mrs. A. S. Marks, 1788

A man needs only three things to be happy: a good gun, a good horse, and a good 10
wife.

—**Daniel Boone,** saying, cited in *Daniel Boone: The Life and Legend of an American Pioneer,* John Mack Faragher [1992]

★ The saying was remembered by Boone's son-in-law, Joseph Scholl. Other hoary maxims of the pioneer that were recalled by his granddaughter, Delinda Boone Craig, in an interview in 1866 with the Wisconsin historian, Lyman Copeland Draper, were "Better mend a fault than find a fault" and "If we can't say good, we should say no harm."

1 Little deeds of kindness,
Little words of love
Help to make earth happy
Like the heavens above.
—**Julia Carney,** *Little Things*, 1845

★ More at SMALLNESS, DETAILS & OTHER LITTLE THINGS.

2 Happiness remains the only sanction of life; where happiness fails, existence remains a mad and lamentable experiment.
—**George Santayana,** *The Life of Reason: Reason in Common Sense*, 1905–1906

3 That is happiness; to be dissolved into something complete and great.
—**Willa Cather,** *My Antonia*, 1918

★ This line is inscribed on the author's gravestone in Jaffrey, N.H.

4 We were very tired, we were very merry—
We had gone back and forth all night on the ferry.
—**Edna St. Vincent Millay,** *Recuerdo*, in *A Few Figs from Thistles*, 1920

5 There are two things to aim at in life: first to get what you want; and, after that, to enjoy it. Only the wisest of mankind achieve the second.
—**Logan Pearsall Smith,** *Afterthoughts*, 1931

6 Happiness lies not in the mere possession of money; it lies in the joy of achievement, in the thrill of creative effort.
—**Franklin D. Roosevelt,** First Inaugural Address, March 4, 1933

7 toujours gai, archy, toujours gai.
—**Don Marquis,** *the life of mehitablel* in *archy's life of mehitabel*, 1933

8 Somewhere over the rainbow
Bluebirds fly.
Birds fly over the rainbow—
Why then, oh why can't I?
—**E. Y. "Yip" Harburg,** *Over the Rainbow*, in the movie *The Wizard of Oz*, 1939

★ Metro-Goldwyn-Mayer studio executives and the movie's director, Victor Fleming, wanted to drop the rainbow number—the start of the movie was too slow, they thought. Harburg and composer Harold Arlen protested and Louis B. Mayer finally ruled, "Let the boys have the damn song . . . it can't hurt."

9 Don't let's ask for the moon! We have the stars!
—**Olive Higgins Prouty,** *Now, Voyager*, 1941

★ A Bette Davis line in the 1942 movie version.

10 Happiness Makes Up in Height for What It Lacks in Length.
—**Robert Frost,** poem title, 1942

11 Happiness is a warm puppy.
—**Charles Schulz,** *Peanuts*, April 25, 1960

★ The words were spoken by Lucy Van Pelt, aka "Fussbudget," to Snoopy.

Happiness isn't a moral force. It's a duty. 1

—**W. H. Auden,** quoted in *Wystan and Chester: A Personal Memoir of W. H. Auden and Chester Kallman,* Thekla Clark [1996]

Happiness is an imaginary condition, formerly often attributed by the living to the 2
dead, now usually attributed by adults to children, and by children to adults.

—**Thomas Szasz,** *Emotions*, in *The Second Sin*, 1973

Happiness is a decision. 3

—**Lionel R. Ketchian**, *Food for Thought*, quoted in *The New York Times* [April 17, 2005]

Follow your bliss. 4

—**Joseph Campbell,** motto, *The Power of Myth* [1988]

★ Published the year after Campbell's death. His best known book was *The Hero with a Thousand Faces*, 1949. Some of his ideas are reflected in the megamovie *Star Wars*, 1977.

Still, it's embarrassing this happiness 5
Who's satisfied simply with what's good for us,
When has the ordinary ever been news?

—**Rita Dove,** *Cozy Apologia,* in *American Smooth,* 2005

We must risk delight. We can do without pleasure, but not delight. Not enjoyment. 6
We must have
the stubborness to accept our gladness in the ruthless
furnace of this world.

—**Jack Gilbert,** *A Brief for the Defense,* in *Refusing Heaven*, 2005

Harding, Warren G.

I suppose I ought to be thankful for one thing: that you're a boy. If you'd been born 7
a girl, by this time, every boy in town would have had his way with you.

—**George T. Harding,** attributed

★ Harding's father is reported to have said this to his son about 1880, when Warren was fifteen; quoted in Mark Sullivan, *Our Times*, 1935.

A tin-horn politician with the manner of a rural corn doctor and the mien of a ham 8
doctor.

—**H. L. Mencken,** on Warren Harding, *Lodge, Baltimore Evening Sun*, June 15, 1920

A fitting representative of the common aspirations of his fellow citizens. 9

—**Calvin Coolidge,** accepting the vice-presidential nomination, Republican National Convention, July 27, 1920

★ This was as far as Coolidge was willing to go in praise of his party's candidate for president. Harding's own campaign manager, Harry M. Daugherty, predicted that his selection would take place in "a smoke-filled room" and be based more on exhaustion than preference; see POLITICS & POLITICIANS. Daugherty was right, and Harding became known as "everybody's second choice." Harding's performance as candidate and president inspired a wealth of creative insults, and he still represents the nadir of presidential competence. In 1981, when consumer advocate Ralph Nader told a reporter, "Ronald Reagan is the most ignorant president since Warren Harding," he meant just about as ignorant as a man can be and still find his way to the Oval Office. Nevertheless, Harding was likeable, and Americans responded to his call for a return to "normalcy," despite the infelicity of the term; see AMERICAN HISTORY: MEMORABLE MOMENTS. Contrary to some accounts, he probably did *not* say in 1921, "When a lot of people are out of work, unemployment results." On the other hand, he evidently invented the ever-useful phrase "Founding Fathers." According to Richard Hanser, in *American Heritage* magazine (June 1970), Harding used the phrase in speeches in 1918, 1920, and most prominently in his inaugural address on March 4, 1921: "I must utter my belief in the divine inspiration of the founding fathers." Harding died suddenly in 1923, and thus missed the unraveling of the Teapot Dome scandal, in which the pervasive corruption of his administration became painfully clear.

1 He writes the worst English I have ever encountered. It reminds me of a string of wet sponges; it reminds me of tattered washing on the line; it reminds me of stale bean soup, of college yells, of dogs barking idiotically through endless nights. It is so bad that a sort of grandeur creeps into it. It drags itself out of the dark abysm (I was about to write abscess!) of pish, and crawls insanely up to the topmost pinnacle of posh. It is rumble and bumble. It is flap and doodle. It is balder and dash.

—**H. L. Mencken,** *Baltimore Evening Sun*, March 7, 1921

2 His speeches left the impression of an army of pompous phrases moving over the landscape in search of an idea. Sometimes these meandering words would actually capture a straggling thought and bear it triumphantly a prisoner in their midst, until it died of servitude and overwork.

—**William G. McAdoo,** quoted in Leon A. Harris, *The Fine Art of Political Wit* [1964]

★ Sen. McAdoo was a leader of the Democratic opposition.

3 He has a bungalow mind.

—**Woodrow Wilson,** quoted in Thomas A. Bailey, *Woodrow Wilson and the Great Betrayal* [1945]

4 If ever there was a he-harlot, it was this same Warren G. Harding.

—**William Allen White,** attributed, c. 1926

5 the only man, woman, or child who wrote a simple declarative sentence with seven grammatical errors is dead.

—**E. E. Cummings,** *the first president to be loved by his*, in *Viva*, 1931

6 Harding was not a bad man. He was just a slob.

—**Alice Roosevelt Longworth,** *Crowded Hours*, 1933

Haste v. Going Slow

See also SPEED.

Nothing is more vulgar than haste. 1
—**Ralph Waldo Emerson,** *The Conduct of Life*, 1860

★ More at MANNERS.

No man who is in a hurry is quite civilized. 2
—**Will Durant,** *What Is Civilization?*

If a thing is worth doing, it is worth doing slowly . . . very slowly. 3
—**Gypsy Rose Lee,** in *Leo Rosten's Carnival of Wit* [1994]

★ Ms. Lee, née Rose Louise Hovick, was a graceful and intelligent ecdysiast—a thinking man's stripper—though she also is said to have said, "Men aren't attracted to me by my mind, but what I don't mind."

Never hurry and never worry! 4
—**E. B. White,** *Charlotte's Web*, 1952

★ Charlotte's advice to Wilbur—what a friend!

Hate

See also POLITICS & POLITICIANS (Henry Adams).

To be loved is to be fortunate, but to be hated is to achieve distinction. 5
—**Minna Antrim,** *Naked Truth and Veiled Allusions*, 1902

I tell you, there is such a thing as creative hate! 6
—**Willa Cather,** *The Song of the Lark*, 1915

I think I know enough of hate 7
To say that for destruction ice
Is also great
And would suffice.
—**Robert Frost,** *Fire and Ice*, 1923

★ More at THE WORLD.

I've played the traitor over and over; 8
I'm a good hater but a bad lover.
—**Elinor Hoyt Wylie,** *Peregrine*, in *Collected Poems* [1932]

Fear of something is at the root of hate for others, and hate within will eventually 9
destroy the hater.
—**George Washington Carver,** *George Washington Carver: Man of God*, 1954

Hatred paralyzes life; love releases it. 10
—**Martin Luther King, Jr.,** *Strength to Love*, 1963

★ More at LOVE.

1 Hate cannot drive out hate. Only love can do that.

—**Martin Luther King, Jr.,** *Where Do We Go from Here: Chaos or Community?*, 1967

2 The price of hating other human beings is loving oneself less.

—**Eldridge Cleaver,** *On Becoming*, in *Soul on Ice*, 1968

3 Those who hate you don't win unless you hate them—and then you destroy yourself.

—**Richard M. Nixon,** good bye remarks to his White House staff the day after resigning as president, August 9, 1974

4 Hate is too great a burden to bear. It injures the hater more than it injures the hated.

—**Coretta Scott King**, speech, First National Conference on the Black Family and Crack Cocaine, San Francisco, April 14, 1989

5 Anger, yes, but not hatred. A man remains in ignorance as long as he hates. I hate what someone does, but I don't hate him.

—**John "Buck" O'Neil**, remark, *Nightline*, ABC-TV, Sept, 26, 1994

★ A famous first baseman for the Kansas City Monarchs in the Negro Leagues, Mr. O'Neil was barred from Major Leagues Baseball on account of his race. Not until after his playing days were over did he reach the majors, initially with the Chicago Cubs as a scout and then a coach.

Haves & Have-nots

See CAPITALISM & CAPITAL V. LABOR; RICH & POOR, WEALTH & POVERTY.

Hawaii

See also ENVIRONMENT (Mitchell).

6 That peaceful land, that beautiful land, that far-off home of solitude and soft idleness, and repose, and dreams, where life is one long slumberous Sabbath, the climate one long summer day, and the good that die experience no change, for they but fall asleep in one heaven and wake up in another.

—**Mark Twain,** speech, April 1889

★ The occasion was a dinner in honor of a baseball team captained by Albert Spalding that had returned from a worldwide tour via what were then the Sandwich Islands—"these enchanted islands," as Twain called them at the time of his visit there in 1866. Similarly, in a letter to H. P. Wood, secretary of the Hawaii Promotion Committee, Twain identified Hawaii as "the loveliest fleet of islands that lies anchored in any ocean." See also Twain on baseball at SPORTS.

7 Mr. President, we want those islands. We want them because they are the stepping stone across the sea. Necessary to our safety, they are necessary to our commerce.

—**Henry M. Teller,** addressing Pres. William McKinley, 1898

★ Sen. Teller was a Republican from Colorado.

We need Hawaii just as much and a good deal more than we did California. It is manifest destiny. 1

—**William McKinley,** remark to his aide George Cortelyou, 1898

★ In this year, Hawaii was annexed, a move favored by Pres. McKinley.

The Hawaiian people have been from time immemorial lovers of poetry and music, and have been apt in improvising historic poems, songs of love, and chants of worship. 2

—**Lydia Kamekeha Liliuokalani,** *Hawaii's Story*, 1898

★ For an example of Hawaiian law in poetry, see Kamehameha I at PRAYERS.

In what other land save this one is the commonest form of greeting not "Good day," nor "How d'ye do," but "Love"? That greeting is *Aloha*—love, I love you, my love to you. . . . It is a positive affirmation of the warmth of one's own heart-giving. 3

—**Jack London,** *My Hawaiian Aloha*, 1916

Hawaii is a paradise—and I can never cease proclaiming it; but I must append one word of qualification: *Hawaii is a paradise for the well-to-do*. 4

—**Ibid.**

Hawaii is the only place I know where they lay flowers on you while you are alive. 5

—**Will Rogers,** in Alex Ayres, ed., *The Wit and Wisdom of Will Rogers* [1993]

The spiritual destiny of Hawaii has been shared by a Calvinist theory of paternalism enacted by the descendants of missionaries who carried it there: a will to do good for unfortunates regardless of what the unfortunates thought about it. 6

—**Francine Du Plessix Gray,** *Hawaii: The Sugar-Coated Fortress*, 1972

Ua mau ke ea o ka aina i ka pono. The life of the land is perpetuated by righteousness. 7

—Motto, state of Hawaii

Health

See also ALCOHOL & DRINKING; DOCTORS & MEDICINE; FOOD, WINE, & EATING; ILLNESS & REMEDIES; PHYSICAL FITNESS; TOBACCO.

To lengthen thy life lessen thy meals. 8

—**Benjamin Franklin,** *Poor Richard's Almanack*, Oct. 1733

Early to bed and early to rise, makes a man healthy, wealthy, and wise. 9

—**Benjamin Franklin,** *Poor Richard's Almanack*, Oct. 1735

★ James Thurber suggested, "Early to rise and early to bed makes a man healthy, wealthy, and dead," *The Shrike and the Chipmunks*, in *Fables for Our Times*, 1940. Rarely is Thurber bested on his own ground, but George Ade has a lighter touch with, "Early to bed and early to rise, and you never meet any prominent people," quoted in Carl Sandburg, *The Proverbs of a People*, in *Good Morning, America*, 1928.

Nine men in ten are suicides. 10

—**Benjamin Franklin,** *Poor Richard's Almanack*, 1749

1 Measure your health by your sympathy with morning and spring.
—**Henry David Thoreau,** *Journal*, Feb. 25, 1859

2 The first wealth is health.
—**Ralph Waldo Emerson,** *Power*, in *The Conduct of Life*, 1860

★ For another quote on wealth and health, see John Greenleaf Whittier at COUNTRY LIFE & PEOPLE.

3 If you mean to keep as well as possible, the less you think about your health the better.
—**Oliver Wendell Holmes, Sr.,** *Over the Teacups*, 1891

4 He had much experience of physicians, and said, "The only way to keep your health is to eat what you don't want, drink what you don't like, and do what you'd druther not."
—**Mark Twain,** *Pudd'nhead Wilson's New Calendar*, in *Following the Equator*, 1897

5 It's not the men in my life that counts, it's the life in my men.
—**Mae West,** *I'm No Angel*, 1933

6 Live clean, think clean, and don't go to burlesque shows.
—**Charles Atlas,** saying

★ Atlas was the most famous bodybuilder in the world from about 1925 into the 1950s. For more, see under Charles Roman at ADVERTISING, ADVERTISING SLOGANS, & PUBLICITY.

7 Avoid fried meats which angry up the blood. If your stomach disputes you, lie down and pacify it with cool thoughts.
—**Leroy "Satchel" Paige,** *How to Stay Young*, 1953

★ More at WISDOM, WORDS OF.

8 [The key to longevity:] Keep breathing.
—**Sophie Tucker,** newspaper reports, Jan. 13, 1964

9 If I'd known I was going to live this long, I'd have taken better care of myself.
—**Eubie Blake,** attributed

★ A popular saying, widely attributed. Blake, a legendary ragtime pianist and composer, performed into his nineties. Born in 1883, the son of former slaves, he lived to be 100—old enough to see the Broadway musical based on his life, *Eubie!*, produced in 1979. The saying was also used by the great Yankee slugger Mickey Mantle, who came from a family affected by Hodgkin's disease. Many of the males in the Mantle family died young, including his father, at age thirty-nine; a son, at age thirty-six; his grandfather and two uncles. Mantle was a famous carouser, and decades of heavy drinking and cancer killed him in 1995 at age sixty-three.

10 Health is infinite and expansive in mode, and reaches out to be filled with the fullness of the world; whereas disease is finite and reductive in mode, and endeavors to reduce the world to itself.
—**Oliver Sacks,** *Perspectives*, in *Awakenings*, 1974

Slender people bury the dead. 1
—**Eileen Ford,** on *The Dick Cavett Show*, quoted in Michael Gross, *Model* [1995]

★ See also Barbara Paley at MONEY.

Heart

See also LOVE; EMOTIONS

The heart is like a viper, hissing and spitting poison at God. 2
—**Jonathan Edwards,** *The Freedom of the Will*, 1754

The heart has its sabbaths and jubilees in which the world appears as a hymeneal 3
feast, and all natural sounds and the circle of the seasons are erotic odes and dances.
—**Ralph Waldo Emerson,** *Love*, in *Essays: First Series*, 1841

★ For Emerson on God's temple in the heart, see RELIGION.

Never mind the ridicule, never mind the defeat: up again, old heart! 4
—**Ralph Waldo Emerson,** *Experience* in *Essays: Second Series*, 1844

The heart is forever inexperienced. 5
—**Henry David Thoreau,** *A Week on the Concord and Merrimack Rivers*, 1849

It is the heart, and not the brain, 6
That to the highest doth attain.
—**Henry Wadsworth Longfellow,** *The Building of the Ship*, 1849

What other dungeon is so dark as one's own heart! 7
—**Nathaniel Hawthorne,** *The House of the Seven Gables*, 1851

★ More at SELF.

The holiest of holidays are those 8
Kept by ourselves in silence and apart;
The secret anniversaries of the heart.
—**Henry Wadsworth Longfellow,** *Holidays*, in *The Mask of Pandora and Other Writings*, 1875

The heart hath its own memory, like the mind. 9
—**Henry Wadsworth Longfellow,** *From My Arm-chair*, 1879

★ More at CHARITY & PHILANTHROPY.

The Heart Is a Lonely Hunter 10
—**Carson McCullers,** title of a novel, 1940

★ The title came from a line in a poem, *The Lonely Hunter* (1896), by "Fiona Macleod" (pseudonym of William Sharp): "My heart is a lonely hunter that hunts on a lonely hill."

The desires of the heart are as crooked as corkscrews. 11
—**W. H. Auden,** *Death's Echo*, 1937

1 Pity me that the heart is slow to learn
What the swift mind beholds at every turn.
—Edna St. Vincent Millay, *Sonnets*, 1941

2 One should have a heart for every fate.
—Emanuel Celler, remark to the press, 1972

★ Mr. Celler, after fifty years in the U.S. House of Representatives, was defeated in an upset by political newcomer Elizabeth Holtzman.

3 The heart is a resilient muscle.
—Woody Allen, *The New York Times*, May 23, 1986

Heavens, the

See NATURE: THE HEAVENS, THE SKY.

Hedonism

See PLEASURE & HEDONISM.

Hell

4 Easy it is for God, when he pleases, to cast his enemies down to Hell.
—Jonathan Edwards, *Sinners in the Hands of an Angry God*, sermon, July 8, 1741

5 If there is no Hell, a good many preachers are obtaining money under false pretenses.
—William A. "Billy" Sunday

★ Billy Sunday, who died in 1936, was a mesmerizing revivalist preacher. Wherever he pitched his tent, the crowds would come. H. L. Mencken included this adage in his dictionary of quotations. He also cites the American proverb just below.

6 Cheer up, there ain't no hell.
—Anonymous, American proverb

7 To work hard, to live hard, to die hard, and then to go to hell after all would be too damned hard.
—Carl Sandburg, *The People, Yes*, 1936

8 Hell is oneself.
—T. S. Eliot, *The Cocktail Party*, 1949

★ Robert Lowell said almost the same thing; see below. By contrast, Jean-Paul Sartre claimed "Hell is others," *No Exit*, 1944.

9 I myself am hell.
—Robert Lowell, *Skunk Hour*, 1959

★ More at MADNESS.

People in hell—where do they tell people to go? 1

—**"Red" Skelton,** comedy routine, cited in his obituary, *The New York Times*, Sept. 18, 1997

Heroes

See also VIRTUE.

Self-trust is the essence of heroism. 2

—**Ralph Waldo Emerson,** *Heroism*, in *Essays: First Series*, 1841

Every hero becomes a bore at last. 3

—**Ralph Waldo Emerson,** *Representative Men*, 1850

A hero cannot be a hero unless in an heroic world. 4

—**Nathaniel Hawthorne,** *Journals*, May 7, 1850

Like an armed warrior, like a plumed knight, James G. Blaine marched down the 5
halls of the American Congress and threw his shining lance full and fair against the brazen foreheads of the defamers of his country and the maligners of his honor.

—**Robert Ingersoll,** nomination speech for Sen. James G. Blaine, Republican National Convention, Cincinnati, 1876

★ The Chicago *Times* wrote that in response to this emotional acclaim "the overwrought thousands fell back in an exhaustion of unspeakable wonder and delight." Sen. Blaine of Maine was a skilled political leader, but possibly corrupt. He failed to get the nomination in 1876, despite Ingersoll's efforts. When Blaine was successfully nominated in 1884, mugwump Republicans supported the Democratic candidate, Grover Cleveland; for more on *mugwump*, see LANGUAGE & WORDS. For another hero politician, see "the happy warrior" below.

The chief business of the nation, as a nation, is the setting up of heroes, mainly 6
bogus.

—**H. L. Mencken,** *Prejudices: Third Series*, 1923

He is the happy warrior of the political battlefield. 7

—**Franklin D. Roosevelt,** nominating Al Smith for president, Democratic National Convention, June 26, 1924

★ Roosevelt was alluding to Wordsworth's *Character of the Happy Warrior*, 1807: "Who is this happy Warrior? Who is he/ That every man in arms should wish to be?" The speech, including the poetic phrase, was drafted by Judge Joseph Proskauer, manager of Smith's New York gubernatorial campaigns in 1920 and 1922. Roosevelt resisted using the literary reference, but Proskauer overcame his objections. Smith held on for a record 103 ballots at the convention before losing to John W. Davis, who was wiped out by Calvin Coolidge in November. For more on the *happy warrior*, see Roosevelt at AMERICAN HISTORY: MEMORABLE MOMENTS.

This thing about being a hero, about the main thing to do is to know when to die. 8
Prolonged life has ruined more men than it ever made.

—**Will Rogers,** *The Autobiography of Will Rogers* [1949]

1 In the spring of '27, something bright and alien flashed across the sky, a young Minnesotan who seemed to have nothing to do with his generation did a heroic thing, and for a moment, people set down their glasses in country clubs and speakeasies and thought of their old best dreams.

—**F. Scott Fitzgerald,** on Charles Lindbergh, quoted in *Bartlett's*, 16th edition

2 Show me a hero and I will write you a tragedy.

—**F. Scott Fitzgerald,** *Notebooks* [1978]

3 A fiery horse with the speed of light, a cloud of dust, and a hearty, "Hi-yo, Silver!"

—**Fran Stryker,** announcer's introduction, *The Lone Ranger* radio show, March 11, 1933

★ The show first aired on February 2, but it took the writer several weeks to come up with the signature shout. "Hi-yo, Silver!" The introduction continued, "With his faithful Indian companion Tonto, the daring and resourceful masked rider of the plains led the fight for law and order in the early West. Return with us now to those thrilling days of yesteryear. The Lone Ranger rides again!"

4 Faster than a speeding bullet! More powerful than a locomotive! Able to leap tall buildings in a single bound! Look! Up in the sky! It's a bird! It's a plane! It's Superman!

—**Jerry Siegel & Joe Shuster,** *Superman* comic strip, June 1938

★ This thrilling passage became famous as the lead-in to the Superman radio show, first broadcast, Feb. 12, 1940. Bud Collyer as Superman recited the first three sentences. A chorus of voices followed, and then Jackson Beck, announced, "It's Superman! Yes, it's Superman—strange visitor from the plant Krypton who came to earth with amazing physical powers far beyond those of mortal men, and who, disguised as Clark Kent, mild-manner reporter for a great metropolitan newspaper, wages a never-ending battle for truth and justice." The Superman character was created in 1934 by Jerry Siegel, a graduate of Glenville High School in Cleveland who had little luck with girls. Siegel's partner in a would-be career in comics was Joe Shuster, who improved the character with tights, a cape, and a handsome face. After moving to New York, and meeting hard times, they sold the character in March 1938 to DC Comics for $130. In June, the first Superman comic book appeared, and it was immediately obvious that the young men had made a disastrous mistake. They were never able to gain a share of Superman's earnings. Siegel worked most of his life as a clerk-typist, Shuster as a messenger.

5 The hero is a feeling, a man seen
As if the eye was an emotion,
As if in seeing we saw our feeling
In the object seen.

—**Wallace Stevens,** *Examination of the Hero in Time of War, 1942*

6 The hero must not take unfair advantage of anyone, including the bad guys. He must not hit anyone smaller than himself. He must always keep his word. He must not smoke or drink in public, and he must not kiss the girl.

—**Gene Autry,** the singing cowboy's code, cited in his obituary, *The New York Times* [Oct. 3, 1998]

You're a good man, Charlie Brown. **1**

—Charles Schulz, *Peanuts*

★ Charlie made his first appearance in the comic strip on Oct. 2, 1950. He was named after an aquaintance of the cartoonist, who recalled the original as "a very bright young man with a lot of enthusiasm for life. I began to tease him about his love for parties and I used to say, 'Here comes good ol' Charlie Brown, now we can have a good time' "(*The New York Times,* Feb. 14, 2000).

No hero is mortal till he dies. **2**

—W. H. Auden, *A Short Ode to a Philologist*, 1962

Down these mean streets must go a man who is not himself mean; who is neither **3**
tarnished nor afraid.

—Raymond Chandler, *The Simple Art of Murder*, 1950

★ Chandler also said of his hero-detective: "He must be, to use a rather weathered phrase, a man of honor, by instinct and inevitability, and certainly without saying it. He must be the best man in his world, and a good enough man for any world."

The dead hero becomes immortal. He becomes more vital with the passage of time. **4**

—Daniel J. Boorstin, *The Image*, 1962

★ Distinguishing between the hero and the celebrity, Boorstin wrote, "The hero created himself; the celebrity is created by the media."

Every hero mirrors the time and place in which he lives. He must reflect men's **5**
innermost hopes and beliefs in a public way.

—Marshall Fishwick, *The Hero, American Style*, 1969

One must think like a hero to behave like a merely decent human being. **6**

—May Sarton, *Journal of a Solitude*, 1973, used as the epigraph to John Le Carré's *Russia House*

A Hero Ain't Nothin' but a Sandwich. **7**

—Alice Childress, book title, 1973

★ For our far-flung readers, a "hero" is a sandwich on a hero roll, which is a long roll.

A hero is a man who would argue with the gods, and so awakens devils to contest his **8**
vision.

—Norman Mailer, Special Preface, First Berkely Edition, *The Presidential Papers*, 1976

No man is a hero to his septic tank cleaner. **9**

—David Owen, *The Walls Around Us*, 1991

★ The theme on which this varies is "No man is a hero to his valet," Anne Bigot de Cornuel, *Lettres de Mme. Aissé*, August 13, 1728.

Heroes are pretty well all washed up in America these days. **10**

—Russell Baker, column on Washington, D.C., Mayor Marion S. Barry, Jr., quoted by Marilyn Stasio, *The New York Times Book Review*, Oct. 14, 1990.

1 True heroism is remarkably sober, very undramatic. It is not the urge to surpass all others at whatever cost, but the urge to serve others at whatever cost.
—**Arthur Ashe**, in *Points to Ponder*, in *Reader's Digest*, August, 1994

High Position: Rulers & Leaders

See also GOVERNMENT; CONGRESS; POLITICS & POLITICIANS; POWER; PRESIDENCY, THE; VICE PRESIDENCY, THE.

2 There are men, who by their sympathetic attractions, carry nations with them, and lead the activity of the human race.
—**Ralph Waldo Emerson,** *Power*, in *The Conduct of Life*, 1860

3 All kings is mostly rapscallions.
—**Mark Twain,** *The Adventures of Huckleberry Finn*, 1885

4 Every man who has attained to high position is a sincere believer of the survival of the fittest.
—**Philander C. Johnson,** *Senator Sorghum's Primer of Politics*, 1906

5 The only emperor is the emperor of ice-cream.
—**Wallace Stevens,** *The Emperor of Ice-Cream*, 1923

6 A king can stand people's fighting, but he can't last long if people start thinking.
—**Will Rogers,** *The Autobiography of Will Rogers*, 1949

7 My first qualification for this great office is my monumental personal ingratitude.
—**Fiorello La Guardia,** comment on importuning office seekers, 1934

★ La Guardia, of course, was mayor of New York. The quote is from Ernest Cuneo, *Life with Fiorello*, 1995

8 The real leader has no need to lead—he is content to point the way.
—**Henry Miller,** *The Wisdom of the Heart*, 1941

9 The final test of a leader is that he leaves behind him in other men the conviction and the will to carry on.
—**Walter Lippmann,** *Roosevelt Has Gone*, in the *New York Herald Tribune*, April 14, 1945

10 All very successful commanders are prima donnas and must be so treated.
—**George S. Patton, Jr.,** *War As I Knew It*, 1947

11 You cannot be a leader, and ask other people to follow you, unless you are willing to follow, too.
—**Sam Rayburn,** saying

★ This is from *The Leadership of Speaker Sam Rayburn, Collected Tributes of his Congressional Colleagues*, a compilation of tributes paid him on June 12, 1961, when he had served as Speaker of the House for sixteen years and 273 days—twice as long as any predecessor.

Great leaders make their own rules. 1

—**Richard M. Nixon,** *Leaders,* 1982

★ See also Ayn Rand at GREATNESS and Mr. Nixon's expansive view of the chief executive's powers at PRESIDENCY, THE.

History is filled with undistinguished leaders who succeeded because they had a flair 2
for selecting sound counselors.

—**George W. Ball,** *Kennedy Up Close,* in *New York Review of Books,* Feb. 3, 1994

History

See also PAST, THE; REVOLUTION.

I consider the true history of the American Revolution, and the establishment of our 3
present Constitution, as lost forever; and nothing but misrepresentations, or partial accounts of it, will ever be recovered.

—**John Adams,** quoted in Lt. Francis Hall, *Travels in Canada and the United States in 1816 and 1817,* 1818

★ In particular, Adams referred to the lack of records of speeches in meetings of the Continental Congresses from 1774 to 1776. A century later, Robert E. Lee (see below) and Walt Whitman (see CIVIL WAR) expressed similar skepticism, doubting that the truth about the Civil War would ever be told.

A morsel of genuine history is a thing so rare as to be always valuable. 4

—**Thomas Jefferson,** letter to John Adams, Sept. 8, 1817

History fades into fable; fact becomes clouded with doubt and controversy; the 5
inscription molders from the tablet; the statue falls from the pedestal. Columns, arches, pyramids, what are they but heaps of sand; and their epitaphs, but characters written in the dust?

—**Washington Irving,** *The Sketch Book,* 1820

I am ashamed to see what a shallow village tale our so-called history is. 6

—**Ralph Waldo Emerson,** *History,* in *Essays; First Series,* 1841

What we call History, considered as giving a record of notable events, or transac- 7
tions, under names and dates . . . I conceive to be commonly very much of a fiction.

—**Horace Bushnell,** "The Age of Homespun,"August 14, 1851, in *Work and Play,* 1864

★ This "secular sermon," as Bushnell, a Congregational minister, called it, was occasioned by the centennial of Litchfield, Conn.

Fellow citizens, we cannot escape history. We . . . will be remembered in spite of 8
ourselves.

—**Abraham Lincoln,** second annual message to Congress, Dec. 1, 1862

It is history that teaches us to hope. 9

—**Robert E. Lee,** letter to Charles Marshall, c. 1866

1 The time is not come for impartial history. If the truth were told just now, it would not be credited.

—**Robert E. Lee,** c. 1868, in David McCrae, *The Americans at Home,* 1870

★ Similar to Walt Whitman's, "The real war will never get in the books"; see CIVIL WAR. See also Philip Graham at THE PRESS.

2 History doesn't repeat itself, but it rhymes.

—**Mark Twain,** attributed

★ The quote is rendered in many forms, among them: "History [or sometimes "The past"] doesn't repeat itself, at best it rhymes," or "it sure does rhyme," or "it sometimes rhymes." See also Madeline K. Albright and Maya Angelou below.

3 Bismarck, when asked what was the most important fact in modern history, replied: "The fact that North America speaks English."

—**Gurney Benham,** *Benham's Book of Quotations* [1948]

4 *History, n.* An account mostly false, of events mostly unimportant, which are brought about by rulers, mostly knaves, and soldiers, mostly fools.

—**Ambrose Bierce,** *The Devil's Dictionary,* 1906

5 The history of every country begins in the heart of a man or a woman.

—**Willa Cather,** *O Pioneers!.* 1913

6 History is more or less bunk.

—**Henry Ford,** quoted in the *Chicago Tribune,* May 25, 1916

★ Ford made this comment in an interview with journalist Charles N. Wheeler. "Records of old wars mean nothing to me," he said. "History is more or less bunk. It's tradition."

7 History has many cunning passages, contrived corridors
and issues.

—**T. S. Eliot,** *Gerontion,* 1920

8 The history of the world is the record of a man in quest of his daily bread and butter.

—**Hendrik Willem Van Loon,** *The Story of Mankind,* 1921

★ See also Will Durant at SCIENCE: BIOLOGY & PHYSIOLOGY for a similar view of the influence of the body on our history.

9 Upon this point, a page of history is worth a volume of logic.

—**Oliver Wendell Holmes, Jr.,** *New York Trust Co. v. Eisner,* 1921

10 All history is modern history.

—**Wallace Stevens,** *Adagia,* in *Opus Posthumous* [1957]

11 Men make history and not the other way around.

—**Harry S. Truman,** quoted in *This Week* magazine, Feb. 22, 1959

★ See Abraham Lincoln under FATE for a different view.

The only thing new in the world is the history you don't know. **1**
—Harry S. Truman, quoted by Merle Miller in *Plain Speaking* [1982]

History consists of the inside of the outside. **2**
—Howard Nemerov, *The Homecoming Game,* 1957

★ Also stated, in the opening scene, as: "The historian examines the outsides of past events, with a view to discovering what their insides were."

History is, strictly speaking, the study of questions; the study of answers belongs to anthropolgy and sociology. **3**
—W. H. Auden, *The Dyer's Hand,* 1962

Man is a history-making creature. **4**
—Ibid.

★ More at PAST, THE.

History is . . . very chancy. **5**
—Samuel Eliot Morison, *The Oxford History of the American People,* 1965

History is a relay of revolutions. **6**
—Saul Alinsky, *Rules for Radicals,* 1971

The main thing history teaches us that history teaches us—nothing. **7**
—Truman Capote, 1975, quoted in Jay Presson Allen, *Tru* [1989]

The End of History **8**
—Francis Fukuyama, essay in *The National Interest,* summer 1989

★ Professor Fukuyama argued in this famous essay that liberal democracy had conquered all competing ideologies, such as monarchy, fascism, and communism. Thus liberal democracy may constitute the "end point of mankind's ideological evolution" and the final form of government. As such, it marks the end of history.

History is a strange teacher. It never repeats itself exactly, but you ignore its general lessons at your peril. **9**
—Madeline K. Albright, *The Role of the United States in Central Europe*, 1991

★ For the "Four Lessons of History," see Charles Beard at WISDOM, WORDS OF.

History is a guide to navigation in perilous times. **10**
—David McCullough, quoted in Harold L. Klawans, *Life, Death and In Between,* 1992

History, despite its wrenching pain, **11**
Cannot be unlived, but if faced
With courage, need not be lived again.
—Maya Angelou, *On the Pulse of Morning*, 1993

★ Ms. Angelou read the poem at the first inauguration of Pres. Bill Clinton (Jan. 20, 1993).

Holidays

See also CHRISTMAS; INDEPENDENCE DAY; NEW YEAR; THANKSGIVING.

1 The holiest of all holidays are those
Kept by ourselves in silence and apart.
—**Henry Wadsworth Longfellow,** *Holidays*

★ More at HEART, THE.

2 Every holiday ought to be named Labor Day.
—**Will Rogers,** in Alex Ayres, ed., *The Wit and Wisdom of Will Rogers* [1993]

Home

See also FAMILY; PARTING (Lincoln).

3 A man's house is his castle.
—**James Otis,** argument on the Writs of Assistance, Boston, 1761

★ More at PRIVACY.

4 Abstracted from home, I know no happiness in this world.
—**Thomas Jefferson,** letter to Lt. de Unger, 1780

5 'Mid pleasures and palaces though we may roam,
Be it ever so humble, there's no place like home.
—**John Howard Payne,** *Home, Sweet Home,* song for the opera *Clari, or The Maid of Milan*, 1823

★ The song, with music by Henry R. Bishop, was popular for decades and was used in concert by the most popular sopranos of the era—Adelina Patti, Jenny Lind, Dame Nellie Melba.

6 Home is the kingdom and love is the king.
—**William Rankin Duryea,** *A Song for Hearth and Home,* in the *New York Home Journal,* 1866

7 As the homes, so the state.
—**A. Bronson Alcott,** *Tablets*, 1868

★ Alcott, an educator and reformer, was the father of Louisa May Alcott.

8 The best thing about traveling is going home.
—**Charles Dudley Warner,** *The Whims of Travel,* Sept. 12, 1875

★ More at TRAVEL.

9 Eden is that old-fashioned House
We dwell in every day
Without suspecting our abode
Until we drive away.
—**Emily Dickinson,** poem no. 1657

[On decorating the home:] I believe in plenty of optimism and white paint. 1
—Elsie de Wolfe, *The House in Good Taste,* 1913.

★ De Wolfe essentially invented the profession of interior decorating. Abhorring the dark, ornate Victorian homes of her childhood, she emphasized "simplicity and suitability." Her book still seemed fresh when reprinted in 2004.

[Husband:] "Home is the place where, when you have to go there, 2
They have to take you in."
[Wife:] "I should have called it
Something you somehow haven't to deserve."
—Robert Frost, *The Death of the Hired Man,* 1914

Home is where the heart is. 3
—Anonymous, in Elbert Hubbard, *A Thousand and One Epigrams,* 1914

★ An old saying, sometimes attributed to the Roman writer Pliny.

It takes a heap o' livin' in a house t' make it home. 4
—Edgar A. Guest, *Home,* in *The Collected Works of Edgar A. Guest,* 1934

★ Ogden Nash pointed out that to make a house a home also "takes a heap o' payin'," *A Heap o' Livin'*.

You Can't Go Home Again. 5
—Thomas Wolfe, book title, 1940

★ For going home to Pocatello, see CITIES (POCATELLO).

Home is where one starts from. 6
—T. S. Eliot, *Four Quartets: East Coker,* 1940

★ Eliot started in St. Louis and eventually attended Harvard University. In 1913, while he was traveling abroad on a postgraduate fellowship, war erupted. He could not get back to the U.S., and he became in time thoroughly English.

How does it feel 7
To be on your own
With no direction home
Like a complete unknown
Like a rolling stone?
—Bob Dylan, *Like a Rolling Stone*, 1965

A man's home may seem to be his castle on the outside; inside it is more often his 8
nursury.
—Clare Boothe Luce, *Bulletin of the Baldwin* [Penn.] *School*, Sept. 1974

Honesty

See also DISHONESTY & LIES; EXPEDIENCY; HONOR; TRUTH; VIRTUE.

Of more worth is one honest man to society, and in the eyes of God, than all the 9
crowned ruffians that ever lived.
—Tom Paine, *Common Sense,* 1776

1 I hope I shall always possess firmness and virtue enough to maintain (what I consider the most enviable of all titles) the character of an "Honest Man."

—**George Washington,** letter to Alexander Hamilton, August 28, 1788

★ See also below.

2 I hold the maxim no less applicable to public than to private affairs, that honesty is always the best policy.

—**George Washington,** Farewell Address, Sept. 17, 1796

★ The maxim is an old one; Cervantes, for example, used it in *Don Quixote*. Washington stood by this principle, and his reputation for honesty inspired the fable promulgated by an early biographer, Mason Lock "Parson" Weems, that as a boy he cut down a cherry tree and confessed his guilt, saying, "I cannot tell a lie." Thanks to his invariable integrity, Washington was asked by friends and neighbors to serve as executor of their estates—so many that his own estate suffered as a result.

3 One great error is that we suppose mankind more honest than they are.

—**Alexander Hamilton,** speech, Constitutional Convention, Philadelphia, June 22, 1787

4 Men are disposed to live honestly, if the means of doing so are open to them.

—**Thomas Jefferson,** letter to M. Barré de Marbois, June 14, 1817

5 Nothing astonishes men so much as common sense and plain dealing.

—**Ralph Waldo Emerson,** *Art.* in *Essays: First Series,* 1841

6 There is no well-defined boundary line between honesty and dishonesty.

—**O. Henry,** *Bexar Scrip No. 2692,* in *Rolling Stones,* 1912

7 honesty is a good
thing but
it is not profitable to its possesser
unless it is
kept under control.

—**Don Marquis**, *archygrams*, in *archys life of mehitabel*, 1933

8 You can't cheat an honest man.

—**W. C. Fields,** saying and film title, 1939

9 Honesty may not be the best policy, but it is worth trying once in a while.

—**Richard M. Nixon,** quoted by Herbert Stein, in *The New York Times,* July 31, 1996

10 Sincerity: if you can fake it, you've got it made.

—**Daniel Schorr,** *International Herald Tribune*, May 18, 1992

★ The quotation by Schorr comes from *The Columbia World of Quotations* (1996), but the thought appears to be proverbial. It also is attributed in various forms to George Burns, among them: "The secret of acting is sincerity, etc.," "The most important thing to succeed in show business is sincerity, etc.," and, from a 1995 news summary, included in *Simpson's Contemporary Quotations* (1997), "Sincerity is the secret of success. If you can fake that, you've got it made." Schorr himself said in a talk at the Library of Congress in 2001 that the advice about faking sincerity had been given to him by a producer at the outset of his career in television broadcasting forty-eight years before.

Honor

See also HEROES; HONESTY; VIRTUE.

I would lay down my life for America, but I cannot trifle with my honor. 1
—John Paul Jones, letter to A. Livingston, Sept. 4, 1777

When faith is lost, when honor dies, 2
The man is dead!
—John Greenleaf Whittier, *Ichabod*, 1850

★ The poem is a denunciation of Daniel Webster for supporting the Compromise of 1850, which included a stringent fugitive slave law.

The louder he talked of his honor, the faster we counted our spoons. 3
—Ralph Waldo Emerson, *Worship*, in *The Conduct of Life*, 1860

Honor knows no statute of limitations. 4
—Samuel E. Moffett, in *Mark Twain's Autobiography* [1924]

★ Writing in 1909, Twain said that this "happy remark" by his late nephew had "traveled around the globe." Twain introduced the comment in connection with his account of the collapse of his publishing company. Friends urged Twain to declare personal bankruptcy, but he felt morally bound to assume the firm's debts. In sorting out his affairs, he was aided greatly by Henry H. Rogers, a Standard Oil lawyer who belied his cutthroat reputation on Wall Street by telling Twain: "Business has its laws and customs and they are justified; but a literary man's reputation is his life; he can afford to be money poor, but he cannot afford to be character poor; you must earn the cent per cent, and pay it." But Rogers managed to save Twain's copyrights.

The nation's honor is dearer than the nation's comfort; yes, than the nation's life 5
itself.
—Woodrow Wilson, speech, Jan. 26, 1919

A man of honor, by instinct and inevitability. 6
—Raymond Chandler, *The Simple Art of Murder*, 1950

★ More at HEROES.

Hope

See also OPTIMISM & PESSIMISM.

He that lives upon hope will die fasting. 7
—Benjamin Franklin, "Preface: Courteous Reader," *Poor Richard's Almanack*, 1758

★ Or, in the adult version: "He that lives upon hope, dies farting," *Poor Richard's Almanack*, 1736.

1 “Hope” is the thing with feathers—
That perches in the soul—
And sings the tune without the words—
And never stops—at all—
—Emily Dickinson, poem no. 254, c. 1861

2 Hope is a strange invention—
A Patent of the Heart—
In unremitting action
Yet never wearing out—
—Emily Dickinson, poem no. 1392, c. 1877

3 Hope is the only universal liar who never loses his reputation for veracity.
—Robert G. Ingersoll, speech, Manhattan Liberal Club, printed in *Truth-Seeker*, weekly periodical, Feb. 28, 1892

4 There is nothing so well known as that we should not expect something for nothing—but we all do and call it Hope.
—Edgar Watson Howe, *Country Town Sayings*, 1911

5 When hope is taken away from a people, moral degeneration follows swiftly after.
—Pearl S. Buck, letter to *The New York Times*, Nov. 15, 1941

6 What man is strong enough to reject the possibility of hope?
—Paul Auster, *The Locked Room*, 1986

Hospitality

See also GUESTS; MANNERS.

7 Hospitality consists in a little fire, a little food, and an immense quiet.
—Ralph Waldo Emerson, *Journal*, 1856

8 When an American says, “Come and see me,” he *means* it.
—Wilkie Collins

★ Collins, one of the originators of the modern mystery novel, was one of the few 19th-century travelers in the U.S. who had nice things to say about the young country. This quote is cited in Catherine Peters, *The King of Inventors: A Life of Wilkie Collins*, Princeton University Press, 1993.

9 Why don’t you come up sometime, ’n see me?
—Mae West, *She Done Him Wrong*, 1933

★ Essentially the same line is in her play *Diamond Lil*, 1928.

10 *Entertaining Is Fun!*
—Dorothy Draper, book title, 1946

★ In this classic guide, primarily for women, the author urges the hostess to avoid the “Will to Be Dreary,” that is “being resigned to life and terribly serious about it.”

I hate cocktail parties. They're for people who're not good enough to invite for dinner—then they *stay* to dinner. 1

—**Elsa Maxwell,** quoted in a letter to *The New York Times* from Harvard Hollenberg of New York City [Dec. 22, 1989]

You can never have less than the graces nor more than the muses. 2

—**Henry Steele Commager,** on the appropriate size of a dinner party, quoted at his memorial service [May 9, 1998]

★ Meaning that the company should number between three and nine.

Humans & Human Nature

See also DIFFERENCES; DREAMS & SLEEP (Emerson); INDIVIDUALITY & INDIVIDUALISM; PEOPLE, THE.

Men and melons are hard to know. 3

—**Benjamin Franklin,** *Poor Richard's Almanack*, 1733

★ See also Franklin below and at HYPOCRISY.

Man: A tool-making animal. 4

—**Benjamin Franklin,** quoted by James Boswell, entry for April 7, 1778, *Life of Johnson* [1791]

★ Boswell told Samuel Johnson that he thought Dr. Franklin's definition was a good one, but the great lexicographer disagreed. "But many a man never made a tool," he objected, "and suppose a man without arms, he could not make a tool." Nevertheless, Franklin deserves credit for expressing the basic idea long before the better-known statement by Thomas Carlyle: "Man is a tool-using animal. . . . Without tools he is nothing, with tools he is all," *Sartor Resartus*, 1833–34. In our own time, humorist Tim Allen has observed, "Man is the only animal to borrow tools," cited by Robert L. Welsch, *Natural History*, April 1994.

In this world, a man must be either anvil or hammer. 5

—**Henry Wadsworth Longfellow,** *The Story of Brother Bernardus*, in *Hyperion*, 1839

I am a parcel of vain strivings tied 6
By a chance bond together.

—**Henry David Thoreau,** *Sic Vita*, 1841

Mankind are earthen jugs with spirits in them. 7

—**Nathaniel Hawthorne,** notebook entry, 1842, in *Passages from the American Notebooks* [1868]

The savage in man is never quite eradicated. 8

—**Henry David Thoreau,** *Journal*, 1859

1 Man is everywhere a disturbing agent. Whenever he plants his foot, the harmonies of nature are turned to discords.

—**George Perkins Marsh,** *Man and Nature*, 1864

★ Marsh was a lawyer, scholar, politician, and diplomat—minister to Turkey and the first U.S. minister to Italy. He was also a pioneer in conservation, whose work took hold and flourished in his native state, Vermont.

2 Be ashamed to die until you have won some victory for humanity.

—**Horace Mann,** graduation address, Antioch College, Ohio, 1859

3 Nothing is so hard to understand as that there are human beings in this world besides one's self and one's set.

—**William Dean Howells,** *Their Wedding Journey*, 1872

4 If you pick up a starving dog and make him prosperous, he will not bite you. This is the principal difference between a dog and a man.

—**Mark Twain,** *Pudd'nhead Wilson's Calendar*, in *Pudd'nhead Wilson*, 1894

5 The deepest principle of human nature is the craving to be appreciated.

—**William James,** letter, April 6, 1896

★ This is from Professor James's thank-you note to Radcliffe students in Philosophy 2A, who had presented him with an azalea plant. The gift made him realize that he had omitted this "deepest principle" from his classic *Principles of Psychology* because, as he told the students, "I had never had it gratified till now."

6 Man is the only animal that blushes. Or needs to.

—**Mark Twain,** *Pudd'nhead Wilson's New Calendar*, in *Following the Equator*, 1897

7 You tell me whar a man gits his corn-pone, en I'll tell you what his 'pinions is.

—**Mark Twain,** *Corn-Pone Opinions*, 1901

★ In this reminiscence, Twain is quoting Jerry, a young slave, whose eloquence deeply impressed the even younger Twain, who was about fifteen. Jerry's point was that people adopt the views held by the majority of those around them. In retrospect, Twain decided that the process was profound and unconscious. "We are creatures of outside influences; as a rule we do not think, only imitate," Twain concluded. "Broadly speaking, corn-pone stands for self-approval. Self-approval is acquired mainly from the approval of other people. The result is conformity." Similarly in his autobiography, Twain wrote: "In the matter of slavish imitation, man is the monkey's superior all the time. The average man is destitute of independence of opinion."

8 Herein lies the tragedy of the age: . . . that men know so little of men.

—**W. E. B. Du Bois,** *The Souls of Black Folk*, 1903

9 *Man, n.* An animal so lost in rapturous contemplation of what he thinks he is as to overlook what he indubitably ought to be. His chief occupation is extermination of other animals and his own species, which, however, multiplies with such insistent rapidity as to infest the whole habitable earth and Canada.

—**Ambrose Bierce,** *The Devil's Dictionary*, 1906

There is no indispensable man. 1

—**Woodrow Wilson,** presidential nomination acceptance speech, Democratic National Convention, August 7, 1912

★ Wilson was advocating a campaign on issues. He said, "A presidential campaign may easily degenerate into a mere personal contest and so lose its real dignity. There is no indispensable man." His opponents were the incumbent William Howard Taft, a Republican, and former president Theodore Roosevelt, running as a Progressive. Franklin Roosevelt also used this aphorism while campaigning in 1932; see under GREATNESS. The French say, "Il n'y a point d'homme nécessaire."

Science may have found a cure for most evils; but it has found no remedy for the 2
worst of them all—the apathy of human beings.

—**Helen Keller,** *My Religion*, 1927

I never met a man I didn't like. 3

—**Will Rogers,** remark, June 15, 1930

★ More at EPITAPHS & GRAVESTONES.

Pity this busy monster, manunkind, not. 4

—**E. E. Cummings,** *Pity this busy monster, manunkind*, in *One Times One* (or *1 × 1*), 1944

★ More at PROGRESS.

You can't eat the orange and throw the peel away—a man is not a piece of fruit. 5

—**Arthur Miller,** *Death of a Salesman*, 1949

★ See also Miller at KINDNESS.

I decline to accept the end of man. . . . I believe that man will not merely endure: he 6
will prevail. He is immortal, not because he alone among creatures has an inexhaustible voice, but because he has a soul, a spirit capable of compassion and sacrifice and endurance.

—**William Faulkner,** speech accepting the Nobel Prize for Literature, Dec. 10, 1950

Humanity is just a work in progress. 7

—**Tennessee Williams,** *Camino Real*, 1953

★ The preceding line is, "We are all of us guinea pigs in the laboratory of God."

We has met the enemy and it is us. 8

—**Walt Kelly,** comment by Pogo the possum in the "Pogo" cartoon strip

★ A variation was used as a slogan on an Earth Day poster in 1971; see ENVIRONMENT. In *Respectfully Quoted*, published by the Library of Congress, editor Suzy Platt turned up this earlier version: "Resolve then, that on this very ground, with small flags waving and tinny blasts on tiny trumpets, we shall meet the enemy, and not only may he be ours, he may be us," *The Pogo Papers*, Foreword, 1953. For Oliver Hazard Perry's military dispatch, see WAR OF 1812.

1 The people who are always hankering the loudest for some golden yesteryear usually drive new cars.

—**Russell Baker,** *Poor Russell's Almanac*, 1972

2 We need words to keep us human. Being human is like playing an instrument. It takes practice.

—**Michael Ignatieff**, *The Needs of Strangers*, 1984

Humor

See also ART: THEATER, DRAMA & MAGIC (Gwenn); INSULTS & PUT-DOWNS; LAUGHTER & MIRTH.

3 Wit makes its own welcome and levels all distinctions.

—**Ralph Waldo Emerson,** *The Comic*, in *Letters and Social Aims*, 1876

4 The quality of wit inspires more admiration than confidence.

—**George Santayana,** *The Sense of Beauty*, 1896

5 The secret source of humor itself is not joy but sorrow. There is no humor in heaven.

—**Mark Twain,** *Pudd'nhead Wilson's New Calendar*, in *Following the Equator*, 1897

★ For distinctively Western humor, see Twain's biographer Albert Bigelow Paine at WEST, THE.

6 It's hard to be funny when you have to be clean.

—**Mae West,** from Joseph Weintraub, ed., *The Wit and Wisdom of Mae West* [1967]

7 Everything is funny as long as it is happening to somebody else.

—**Will Rogers,** *Warning to Jokers: Lay Off the Prince*, in *The Illiterate Digest*, 1924

8 coarse
jocosity
catches the crowd
shakespeare
and I
are often
low browed.

—**Don Marquis,** *archy and mehitabel*, 1927

9 Wit is the only wall
Between us and the dark.

—**Mark van Doren,** *Wit*, in *A Winter Diary and Other Poems*, 1935

10 Everybody likes a kidder, but nobody lends him money.

—**Arthur Miller,** *Death of a Salesman*, 1949

Comedy is the last refuge of the nonconformist mind. **1**
—Gilbert Seldes, *The New Republic*, Dec. 20, 1954

The wit makes fun of other persons; the satirist makes fun of the world; the humorist makes fun of himself. **2**
—James Thurber, in Edward R. Murrow television interview

★ For the difference between vivacity and wit, as defined by Josh Billings, see the note under Mark Twain on lightning and the lightning bug at LANGUAGE & WORDS.

Comedy deals with that portion of our suffering that is exempt from tragedy. **3**
—Peter De Vries, quoted in *The New Yorker* [May 24, 2004]

Humor . . . is emotional chaos remembered in tranquillity. **4**
—James Thurber, *New York Post*, Feb. 29, 1960

★ Thurber was referring to William Wordsworth, "Poetry . . . takes its origin from emotion remembered in tranquillity," Preface to the 2nd edition of *Lyrical Ballads*, 1800.

This is not an easy time for humorists because the government is far funnier than we are. **5**
—Art Buchwald, speech, international meeting of satirists and cartoonists, 1987

★ Mr. Buchwald was speaking during President Reagan's second term. It also helped those on the inside to have a sense of humor; see below.

Humor is the shock absorber of life; it helps us take the blows. **6**
—Peggy Noonan, *What I saw at the Revolution: A Political Life in the Reagan Era*, 1990

★ She wrote speeches for the president. See also Buchwald above.

Hunger

See POVERTY & HUNGER.

Hurrying

See HASTE V. GOING SLOW; SPEED.

Hypocrisy

Mankind are very odd creatures: one half censure what they practice, the other half practice what they censure; the rest always say and do as they ought. **7**
—Benjamin Franklin, *Poor Richard's Almanack*, 1752

As for conforming outwardly, and living your own life inwardly, I don't think much of that. **8**
—Henry David Thoreau, letter to Harrison Blake, August 9, 1850

We live in an atmosphere of hypocrisy throughout. The men believe not in the women, nor the women in the men. **9**
—Walt Whitman, *Democratic Vistas*, 1871

1 A hypocrite is a person who—but who isn't?
—Don Marquis, attributed in Frederick B. Wilcox, *A Little Book of Aphorisms* [1947]

2 I am shocked, shocked to discover that gambling is going on here.
—Julius Epstein, Philip Epstein, & Howard Koch, *Casablanca*, screenplay, 1942

★ Spoken by the French police chief (Claude Rains), who closes Rick's (Humphry Bogart's) nightclub while tucking his winnings into his pocket.

3 Hypocrisy is the vice of vices. . . . Integrity can indeed exist under the cover of all other vices except this one. . . . Only the hypocrite is really rotten to the core.
—Hannah Arendt, *On Revolution*, 1963

Idaho

See also CITIES (POCATELLO).

4 It is a melancholy strange-looking country, one of fractures and violence and fire.
—John C. Frémont, 1843

5 Idaho is torn, above all, between two other states, between the pull of Washington in the north, that of Utah in the south. Half of Idaho belongs to Spokane, I heard it said, and the other half to the Mormon church.
—John Gunther, *Inside U.S.A.*, 1947

6 I asked an Idaho patriot why potatoes were so big. Answer: "We fertiliz'em with cornmeal and irrigate them with milk."
—John Gunther, *Inside U.S.A.*, 1947

7 Dice 'em, hash 'em, boil 'em, mash 'em! Idaho, Idaho, Idaho!
—Anonymous, football cheer, quoted by Charles Kuralt, *Dateline America*, 1979

★ The reference is to Idaho's dominant crop, potatoes. By the 1990s, however, Idaho was attracting reverse immigration from California, and farming was receding somewhat in importance while electronic industries were gaining ground.

8 *Esto perpetua.* May she endure forever. (Also translated: "May she be perpetual.")
—Motto, state of Idaho

Ideas & Ideals

See also DREAMS & DREAMERS; VIRTUE.

9 There was never an idea started that woke up men out of their stupid indifference but its originator was spoken of as a crank.
—Oliver Wendell Holmes, Sr., *The Autocrat of the Breakfast-Table*, 1858

★ Mark Twain said the same thing. See NEW THINGS.

I died for Beauty—but was scarce 1
Adjusted in the Tomb
When One who died for Truth, was lain
In an adjoining Room—

—Emily Dickinson, poem no. 449, c. 1862

★ This is the first stanza. The third reads: "And so, as Kinsmen, met at Night, / We talked between the Rooms / Until the Moss had reached our lips— / And covered up—our names—"

All our scientific and philosophic ideals are altars to unknown gods. 2

—William James, *The Dilemma of Determinism*, 1884

Loyalty to petrified opinion never yet broke a chain or freed a human soul. 3

—Mark Twain, attributed, inscribed beneath his bust in the Hall of Fame

There is no force so democratic as the force of an ideal. 4

—Calvin Coolidge, speech, New York City, Nov. 27, 1920

An idea isn't responsible for the people who believe in it. 5

—Don Marquis, *The Sun Dial*

★ Marquis wrote columns for the New York *Sun* 1913–22, and then moved on to the *New York Tribune*.

To die for an idea: it is unquestionably noble. But how much nobler would it be if 6
men died for ideas that were true.

—H. L. Mencken, *Prejudices: Fifth Series*, 1926

Men are mortal; but ideas are immortal. 7

—Walter Lippmann, *A Preface to Morals*, 1929

There is nothing wrong with Americans except their ideals. 8

—G. K. Chesterton, in *The New York Times*, Feb. 1, 1931

★ More at AMERICA & AMERICANS.

You can't shoot an idea. 9

—Thomas E. Dewey, debate with Harold Stassen on whether to outlaw the Communist Party, 1948

If you believe in an ideal, you don't own it, it owns you. 10

—Raymond Chandler, quoted in Frank MacShane, *The Life of Raymond Chandler* [1978]

Every man with an idea has at least two or three followers. 11

—Brooks Atkinson, *Once Around the Sun*, 1951

A man may die, nations may rise and fall, but an idea lives on. Ideas have endurance 12
without death.

—John F. Kennedy, speech, Greenville, N.C., Feb. 8, 1963

1 If a man hasn't discovered something that he will die for, he isn't fit to live.
—**Martin Luther King, Jr.,** speech, Detroit, June 23, 1963

2 To maintain one's ideals in ignorance is easy.
—**Uta Hagan,** *Respect for Acting*, 1973

3 Ideas move fast when their time comes.
—**Carolyn Heilbrun,** *Toward a Recognition of Androgeny*, 1973

★ The allusion is to the saying, expressed by Victor Hugo in *Histoire d'un Crime*: "An invasion of armies can be resisted, but not an idea whose time has come" (written 1851–52, but not published until 1877).

4 Ideas that we do not know we have, have us.
—**William Appleman Williams,** *Empire as a Way of Life*, in the *Nation*, August 2, 1980

Illinois

See also CITIES (CAIRO, CHICAGO, PEORIA, SPRINGFIELD).

5 The official language of the State of Illinois shall be known henceforth as the American language, and not as the English language.
—**Acts of the Legislature of Illinois,** ch. 127, sec. 178, 1923, in H. L. Mencken, *New Dictionary of Quotations on Historical Principles*, 1942

6 Its women are lovely and stubborn, its men angry and ingenious. Is there a land anywhere like southern Illinois?
—**Baker Brownell,** *The Other Illinois*, 1958

7 Illinois is perhaps the most American of all the states. It's the U.S.A. in a capsule. Here our virtues and our faults are most exaggerated and magnified. Here somehow the heroes seem more heroic, the villains more villainous, the buffoons more comic. Here violence is more unrestrained, and the capacity for greatness is as limitless as the sweep of unending cornfields.
—**Clyde Brion Davis,** *Illinois*, in *American Panorama: East of the Mississippi*, 1960

8 State sovereignty—national union.
—Motto, state of Illinois

Illness & Remedies

See also DOCTORS & MEDICINE; SUFFERING & PAIN.

9 We forget ourselves and our destinies in health, and the chief use of temporary sickness is to remind us of these concerns.
—**Ralph Waldo Emerson,** *Journal*, 1821

There was a little bird, 1
Its name was Enza,
I opened the window
And in-flu-enza.

—**Anonymous,** 1918

★ The lethal swine flu epidemic of 1918, called at the time Spanish influenza, killed 21 million people, about the same number that died in World War I. More than a half million died in the United States.

Ivry sick man is a hero, if not to th' wurruld or aven to th' fam'ly, at laste to himsilf. 2

—**Finley Peter Dunne,** *Going to See the Doctor*, in *Mr. Dooley on Making a Will*, 1919

Illness is the night-side of life, a more onerous citizenship. Everyone who is born 3
holds dual citizenship, in the kingdom of the well and the kingdom of the sick.

—**Susan Sontag,** *Illness as Metaphor*, 1977

★ See also Ralph Waldo Emerson at SUFFERING & PAIN.

There is a healthy way to be ill. 4

—**George Sheehan,** *The New York Times*, obituary, Nov. 2, 1993

★ Cardiologist Sheehan became one of the great amateur runners of his day after taking up the sport at age forty-three. He continued to run after developing cancer seven years before his death.

Cancer is the subversive sea licking at the shores of everything supposed to be estab- 5
lished and safe.

—**Alfred Kazin**, journal, 1993–95, in *A Lifetime Burning in Every Moment* [1996]

Ask not what disease the person has, but rather what person the disease has. 6

—**Oliver Sacks,** Epigraph, *An Anthropologist on Mars: Seven Paradoxical Tales*, 1995

I look at everything as a temporary assignment. 7

—**Bob Schieffer,** news reports, April 2005

★ Schieffer, age 68 and a survivor of bladder cancer, commenting on the extension of his interim assignment, four months earlier, to replace Dan Rather as anchor of the CBS Evening News.

Illusions

See DREAMS & DREAMERS; REALITY, ILLUSIONS, & IMAGES.

Images

See REALITY, ILLUSIONS, & IMAGES.

Imagination

See DREAMS & DREAMERS; GOD (WALLACE STEVENS); MIND, THOUGHT & UNDERSTANDING; VISION & PERCEPTION.

Immortality

1 Superiority to Fate
Is difficult to gain
'Tis not conferred of Any
But possible to earn

A pittance at a time
Until to Her surprise
The soul with strict economy
Subsist till Paradise.
—**Emily Dickinson,** poem no. 1081, c. 1866

2 The only secret people keep
Is immortality.
—**Emily Dickinson,** poem no. 1748, undated

3 The fact of having been born is a bad augury for immortality.
—**George Santayana,** *The Life of Reason*, 1905–1906

4 Immortality is not a gift,
Immortality is an achievement;
And only those who strive mightily
Shall possess it.
—**Edgar Lee Masters,** *The Village Atheist*, in *The Spoon River Anthology*, 1915

5 The universe is a stairway leading nowhere unless man is immortal.
—**Edgar Young Mullins,** *The Father Almighty*, quoted in Joseph Fort Newton, *My Idea of God*, 1926

6 The truth is, no one really believes in immortality. Belief must mean something more than desire or hope.
—**Clarence Darrow,** *The Story of My Life*, 1932

7 Millions long for immortality who don't know what to do with themselves on a rainy Sunday afternoon.
—**Susan Ertz,** *Anger in the Sky: A Novel*, 1943

8 He had decided to live forever or die in the attempt.
—**Joseph Heller,** *Catch-22*, 1961

9 Our current obsession with creativity is the result of our continued striving for immortality in an era when most people no longer believe in an after-life.
—**Ariana Huffington**, *The Female Woman*, 1974

I don't want to achieve immortality through my work. . . . I want to achieve it through not dying. 1

—**Woody Allen,** quoted in E. Lax, *Woody Allen and His Comedy*, 1975

Indecision

See also DECISION; DELAY.

There is no more miserable human being than one in whom nothing is habitual but indecision. 2

—**William James,** *The Principles of Psychology*, 1890

He who hesitates is sometimes saved. 3

—**James Thurber,** *The Glass in the Field*, in *Fables for Our Time*, 1940

It is human nature to stand in the middle of a thing. 4

—**Marianne Moore,** *A Grave*, in *Collected Poems*, 1951

Some problems are so complex that you have to be highly intelligent and well informed just to be undecided about them. 5

—**Laurence J. Peter,** *Peter's Almanac*, 1982

★ In the same book, Peter also condensed a wordy statement by Harvey G. Cox in *On Not Leaving It to the Snake*, 1967, into the pithy: "Not to decide is to decide."

I've made up my mind both ways. 6

—**Charles Dillon "Casey" Stengel,** quoted in the Ken Burns television series *Baseball*, part IV [1994]

Independence Day

See also DECLARATION OF INDEPENDENCE; FREEDOM.

It will be celebrated by succeeding generations as the great anniversary festival. It ought to be commemorated as the day of deliverance, by solemn acts of devotion to God almighty. It ought to be solemnized with pomp and parade, with shows, games, sports, guns, bells, bonfires, and illuminations from one end of this continent to the other, from this time forward forevermore. 7

—**John Adams,** 2d letter to Abigail Adams, July 3, 1776

★ Adams had in mind celebrating July 2, when the independence resolution was adopted in committee. Traditionally, we celebrate on July 4, the date the Continental Congress approved the Declaration of Independence. Adams, and everyone else, soon came to regard July 4 as the memorable occasion.

Is it the Fourth? 8

—**Thomas Jefferson,** last words, July 3, 1826

★ His doctor assured him that it soon would be; the day would be the fiftieth anniversary of independence. Jefferson became delirious shortly afterward, but did live to the fourth. John Adams survived him by about two hours. See also Adams at LAST WORDS.

1 Independence forever!

—**John Adams,** July 4, 1826

★ Adams was responding to the sound of canon firing in celebration of the great anniversary. See also LAST WORDS and Daniel Webster at FREEDOM.

2 What to the Slave Is the Fourth of July?

—**Frederick Douglass,** title of speech, July 5, 1852

Indiana

See also CITIES (MUNCIE).

3 Blest Indiana! in whose soil
Men seek the sure rewards of toil,
And honest poverty and worth
Find here the best retreat on earth,
While hosts of preachers, doctors, lawyers,
All independent as wood-sawyers,
With men of every hue and fashion,
Flock to the rising "Hoosier" nation.

—**John Finley,** *The Hoosiers' Nest*, c. 1830

★ Finley gave the 1830 date for this poem, claiming to have published it originally in the *Richmond* (Indiana) *Palladium*; no one has been able to verify this. The poem was used as a New Year's greeting by newspaper carrier boys in 1832 (*Indiana Democrat*) and 1833 (*Indianapolis Journal*, which published the work on January 1). The origin of the term *Hoosier* is unknown, the most colorful guess—by James Whitcomb Riley, "the Hoosier poet"—is that as a result of people biting off each other's ears in drunken brawls, the question sometimes arose, "Whose ear is this?" Other guesses are that it comes from "husher," or "whoosher," or the greeting, "Who's yere?" The 4th edition of the *American Heritage Dictionary* gives as the most likely source the English dialect word *hoozer*, used in the 19th century of anything unusually large or, as we might say, "larger than life." In this case, the original reference may have been to the "big men" from the mountains of Kentucky who were among Indiana's first settlers.

4 Oh the moonlight's fair tonight along the Wabash.
From the fields there comes the breath of new-mown hay;
Thro' the sycamores the candle lights are gleaming,
On the banks of the Wabash far away.

—**Paul Dresser,** *On the Banks of the Wabash Far Away*, 1897

5 I come from Indiana, the home of more first-rate second-class men than any state in the Union.

—**Thomas Riley Marshall,** *Recollections*, 1925

★ Marshall was Woodrow Wilson's vice president, most remembered today for his insight into the country's need for a really good five-cent cigar; see TOBACCO.

6 The crossroads of America.

—Motto, state of Indiana

Indians

See RACES & PEOPLES.

Individuality & Individualism

See also DIFFERENCES; SELF.

He may well win the race that runs by himself. **1**
—Benjamin Franklin, *Poor Richard's Almanack*, 1747

★ More at EXCELLENCE.

Individuality is the aim of political liberty. **2**
—James Fenimore Cooper, *The American Democrat*, 1838

If a man does not keep pace with his companions, perhaps it is because he hears a **3**
different drummer. Let him step to the music which he hears, however measured or far away.
—Henry David Thoreau, *Conclusion*, in *Walden*, 1854

Individualism in America has allowed a laxity in regard to governmental affairs **4**
which has rendered possible the spoils system and all the manifest evils that follow from the lack of a highly developed civic spirit.
—Frederick J. Turner, *The Significance of the Frontier in American History*, 1893

★ See also Turner at AMERICA & AMERICANS and THE FRONTIER for more on American individualism. For the spoils system, see William Marcy at POLITICS & POLITICIANS.

Rugged individualism. **5**
—Herbert Hoover, speech, New York City, Oct. 22, 1928

★ More at AMERICA & AMERICANS.

One is hip or one is square, one is a rebel or one conforms, one is a frontiersman in **6**
the Wild West of American night life, or else a square cell, trapped in the totalitarian tissues of American society, doomed willy-nilly to conform if one is to succeed.
—Norman Mailer, *The White Negro*, 1957

There is always the danger that if you speak a language that recognizes only individ- **7**
ual rights, you will become a people that can think only about individuals.
—Mary Ann Glendon, quoted in Bill Moyers, *A World of Ideas*, 1989

In the United States we try to accomplish on an individual level what we've given up **8**
trying to do on a social one.
—Anonymous editor, call out for review of Judith Warner, *Perfect Madness: Motherhood in the Age of Anxiety*, in *The New York Times Book Review*, Feb. 20, 2005

Information

See KNOWLEDGE & INFORMATION.

Injustice

See also JUSTICE.

1 This is an age of the world where nations are trembling and convulsed. A mighty influence is abroad, surging and heaving the world, as with an earthquake. And is America safe? Every nation that carries in its bosom great and unredressed injustice has in it the elements of this last convulsion.

—Harriet Beecher Stowe, *Uncle Tom's Cabin*, 1852

★ This is from the last chapter. The book's immense popularity itself contributed to the coming convulsion.

2 There is but one blasphemy, and that is injustice.

—Robert Ingersoll, lecture, Chicago, Sept. 20, 1880

3 Injustice anywhere is a threat to justice everywhere.

—Martin Luther King, Jr., letter from Birmingham city jail, April 16, 1963

4 There comes a time when . . . men are no longer willing to be plunged into an abyss of injustice.

—Ibid.

★ More at RESISTANCE.

Institutions

See also GOVERNMENT.

5 The safety and happiness of society are the objects at which all political institutions aim and to which all such institutions must be sacrificed.

—James Madison, *Federalist* No. 45, 1788

6 An institution is the lengthened shadow of one man.

—Ralph Waldo Emerson, *Self-Reliance*, in *Essays: First Series*, 1841

★ In his *Journal*, in 1832, Emerson wrote, "We do not make a world of our own, but fall into institutions already made, and have to accommodate ourselves to them to be useful at all."

7 In a changing world, worthy institutions can be conserved only by adjusting them to the changing time.

—Franklin D. Roosevelt, speech, Syracuse, N.Y., Sept. 29, 1936

8 Man is as the Lord made him. But we can change our institutions.

—Louis D. Brandeis· letter to Arnold Lief, Dec. 7, 1940

9 What is any established institution but a Society for the Prevention of Change?

—Lewis Mumford, *The Conduct of Life*, 1951

10 The people in this country come first—not the institutions.

—Joseph Kennedy III, interview, May 7, 1989

Insults

See also ELITE, THE (Adlai Stevenson and Spiro Agnew); FAULTS & FAILINGS; FOOLS & STUPIDITY; HARDING, WARREN G.

You and I were long friends: you are now my enemy, and I am yours, B. Franklin 1

—**Benjamin Franklin,** letter to William Strahan, of London, England, July 5, 1775

★ Strahan was a fellow printer (of Samuel Johnson's *Dictionary of the English Language*, among other works) as well as—the occasion for this letter—a Member of Parliament. Franklin was thinking of patriot blood shed at Lexington and Bunker Hill when he wrote this letter, but he did what wise people generally do with letters that are written in anger: he never mailed it. Thus, the old friends remained friends despite the war between their nations.

[He] means well, very well. But he means it feebly. 2

—**Gouverneur Morris,** on the French foreign minister, the Comte de Montmorin, 1790

★ Morris was America's third minister to France, following Benjamin Franklin and Thomas Jefferson, and he had the most dangerous tour of duty, staying in Paris throughout the Reign of Terror. Morris was both shrewd and brave. Of Lafayette he wrote, "If the sea runs high, he will be unable to hold the helm." The quotes here were cited by Arnold Whitridge in *A Representative of America*, in *American Heritage*, June 1976.

He is a man of splendid abilities but utterly corrupt. He shines and stinks like rotten 3
mackerel by moonlight.

—**John Randolph,** speaking of Rep. Edward Livingston of New York, c. 1800, cited in William Cabell Bruce, *John Randolph of Roanoke* [1922]

★ Randolph, commonly called John Randolph of Roanoke, served almost continuously in Congress from 1799 to 1833. He was well educated, highly intelligent, and famed for his venomous wit. For his comment on the appointment in 1825 of Richard Rush as Secretary of the Treasury, see below. Of Martin Van Buren's political tactics, he said, "He rowed to his object with muffled oars." On at least one occasion, however, he was bested. Meeting Henry Clay on a narrow walkway in a muddy Washington street, he refused to let the other man pass, declaring, "Sir, I never give way for a scoundrel." To which Clay, gallantly stepping aside, replied, "I always do."

Never were abilities so much below mediocrity so well rewarded; no, not when 4
Caligula's horse was made Consul.

—**John Randolph,** speaking of Pres. John Quincy Adams's appointment of Richard Rush as Secretary of the Treasury, published as an appendix to a speech in the U.S. House of Representatives, Feb. 1, 1828

★ In 1828, Rush was Adams's vice-presidential running mate in a bid for reelection. Adams was beaten by Andrew Jackson, and took up a new, if more modest career as a U.S. Representative. Speaking of Caligula, Randolph was an odd bird, himself—distinctly feminine in appearance, which was the cause of much comment and no doubt pain to Randolph. John Quincy Adams said of him, according to Edward Boykin's *Wit and Wisdom of Congress* (1961), "His face is livid, gaunt his whole body, his breath is green with gall; his tongue drips poison." Congressman Tristram Burges was even more pointed, implying that Randolph was "impotent of everything but malevolence of purpose," and concluding, "I rejoice that the father of lies can never become the father of liars," quoted in William Cabell Bruce, *John Randolph of Roanoke*, 1922. Politically, Randolph was an ardent libertarian and protector of states' rights and the Constitution, as he saw it. He fought a duel with Henry Clay, and became increasingly eccentric in his later years.

1 One might as well try to spoil a rotten egg as to damage Dan's character.
—**George Templeton Strong,** in Allan Nevins, ed., *The Diary of George Templeton Strong*, entry c. 1859

★ On February 27, 1859, U.S. Congressman Daniel E. Sickles of New York City shot to death Washington, D.C., district attorney Philip Barton Key—son of Francis Scott Key, author of *The Star-Spangled Banner*. Sickles, a notorious ladies' man himself, killed Key for having an affair with Sickles's wife. The congressman pleaded temporary insanity—an unprecedented plea in American courts, and was acquitted by a sympathetic jury. Sickles went on to serve as a general in the Civil War, playing a near disastrous role at Gettysburg (and losing a leg in the process) when he advanced his corps without orders, moving so far in front of the rest of the Union line that he could be attacked on both flanks. After the war, Sickles continued to mix public service with private scandals until his death at age ninety-five. George Templeton Strong was a New York lawyer and a friend of Abraham Lincoln. He produced a colorful and historically valuable diary.

2 You take the lies out of him, and he'll shrink to the size of your hat; you take the malice out of him, and he'll disappear.
—**Mark Twain,** *Life on the Mississippi*, 1833

3 He is useless on top of the ground; he ought to be under it, inspiring the cabbages.
—**Mark Twain,** *Pudd'nhead Wilson's Calendar*, in *Pudd'nhead Wilson*, 1894

4 He saw nearly all things as through a glass eye, darkly.
—**Mark Twain,** *Fenimore Cooper's Literary Offenses*, 1895

5 No more backbone than a chocolate éclair.
—**Theodore Roosevelt,** characterization of Pres. William McKinley, c. 1897, cited in V. C. Jones *Last of the Rough Riders*, in *American Heritage* [July 1969]

★ Roosevelt, then Assistant Secretary of the Navy, may have picked up the image from Thomas B. Reed, Speaker of the House of Representatives. Variants from the same era include Ulysses S. Grant's opinion that James A. Garfield was "not possessed of the backbone of an angleworm" and another comment by T.R., reflecting his disappointment by a Supreme Court decision of Oliver Wendell Holmes, Jr.: "I could carve out of a banana a judge with more backbone than that."

6 A rather cheap character [similar to his father in displaying] levity, lack of sobriety, lack of permanent principle, and an inordinate thirst for that cheap form of admiration which is given to notoriety.
—**Theodore Roosevelt,** describing Winston Churchill and in passing Randolph Churchill, letter from 1908, first made public by Library of Congress, 2004

They never open their mouths without subtracting from the sum of human knowledge. 1

—Thomas Brackett Reed, remark about two colleagues in the House of Representatives, quoted in Samuel W. McCall, *The Life of Thomas Brackett Reed*, 1914

★ "Czar" Reed, a Maine Republican, served as Speaker of the House 1889–91 and 1895–99. Of another colleague in that august body—William M. Springer of Illinois—he said in 1881, "If I ever 'made light' of his remarks, it is more than he ever made of them himself."

A scab is a two-legged animal with a corkscrew soul, a waterlogged brain, a combination backbone of jelly and glue. Where others have hearts, he carries a tumor of rotten principles. 2

—Jack London, *A Scab*, in *C.I.O. News* [Sept. 13, 1946]

★ See also London at CAPITALISM & CAPITAL V. LABOR.

The covers of this book are too far apart. 3

—Ambrose Bierce, attributed, in C. H. Grattan, *Bitter Bierce*, 1929

There is less in this than meets the eye. 4

—Tallulah Bankhead, remark to Alexander Woollcott at Maurice Maeterlinck's play *Aglavaine and Selysette*, Jan. 3, 1922

★ Attribution by *Bartlett's*. For a quote about Tallulah, see Howard Dietz below.

And it is that word "hummy," my darlings, that marks the first place in *The House at Pooh Corner* at which Tonstant Weader fwowed up. 5

—Dorothy Parker, *Constant Reader* column, *The New Yorker*, Oct. 20, 1928

★ Parker is also said to have coined the terse review: "It is not a novel to be thrown aside lightly. It should be thrown aside with great force"; quoted in A. Johnston, *Legend of a Sport*, in *The New Yorker*. See her theater reviews below.

That woman speaks eighteen languages, and can't say No in any of them. 6

—Dorothy Parker, in Alexander Woollcott, *While Rome Burns* [1934]

★ Or as it also was said of Moe Berg, a light-hitting but scholarly baseball catcher (Princeton *magna cum laude*, Columbia Law), "He knew twelve languages but couldn't hit in any of them."

[On being told that former Pres. Calvin Coolidge had died:] How do they know? 7

—Wilson Mizner, 1933, attributed, in *The International Dictionary of 20th Century Biography*, Edward Vernoff and Rima Shore, eds., [1987]

★ Also attributed to Dorothy Parker and Alice Roosevelt Longworth.

[Pres. Herbert] Hoover is the world's greatest engineer: he's drained, ditched, and damned the United States. 8

—Anonymous, joke, c. 1931

★ Hoover, a distinguished engineer and a decent, generally competent man, was overwhelmed by the economic catastrophe that hit the country in 1929. His tendency to deny the depth of the problem ruined his credibility. People tended to ascribe to him dumb comments that he probably or certainly did not make; see "Prosperity is just around the corner," for example, at THE DEPRESSION, or this attribution: "Many people have left their jobs for the more profitable one of selling apples," quoted by Robert Dallek in his biography of Lyndon Johnson, *Lone Star Rising*.

1 She ran the whole gamut of emotions from A to B.

—**Dorothy Parker,** commenting on Katharine Hepburn in the play *The Lake*, 1933, attributed

2 *House Beautiful* is play lousy.

—**Dorothy Parker,** theater review, *The New Yorker*, 1933

★ Another production was dismissed with the advice, "If you don't knit, bring a book," quoted in *The New Yorker* in an essay on Parker by Joan Acocella, August 16, 1993.

3 My dear, I don't give a damn.

—**Margaret Mitchell,** *Gone with the Wind*, 1936

★ Rhett Butler's definitive dismissal of Scarlett O'Hara. In the screenplay by Sidney Howard, the line is, "Frankly, my dear, I don't give a damn." Producer David O. Selznik kept the "damn," and paid a $5,000 fine for breaking the Motion Picture Production Code. The code administrators had argued for "Frankly, my dear, I don't care."

4 A labor-baiting, poker-playing, whiskey-drinking, evil old man whose name is Garner.

—**John L. Lewis,** testimony, Labor Committee, U. S. House of Representatives, July 27, 1939

★ Lewis headed both the United Mine Workers of America and the Congress of Industrial Organizations (C.I.O.) at the time. John Nance Garner was vice president of the United States.

5 There goes the famous good time that was had by all.

—**Bette Davis,** speaking of a starlet, attributed in Leslie Halliwell, *The Filmgoer's Book of Quotes* [1990]

6 She looked as though butter wouldn't melt in her mouth or anywhere else.

—**Elsa Lanchester,** speaking of a starlet, attributed in Leslie Halliwell, *The Filmgoer's Book of Quotes* [1990]

7 There but for the grace of God goes God.

—**Herman J. Mankiewicz,** c. 1941, quoted by Pauline Kael in *The New Yorker*, 1971

★ Mankiewicz and Orson Welles wrote the 1941 movie *Citizen Kane*. Welles also directed and starred in the classic film, and is the butt of this gentle gibe.

8 [Dewey is like] the little man on the wedding cake.

—**Alice Roosevelt Longworth,** attributed 1944

★ The bon mot has been credited to a number of people, including Harold Ickes, Walter Winchell, and Ethel Barrymore. Mrs. Longworth told William Safire that she heard it from a friend, Grace Hodgson Flandrau. Dewey—short, mustachioed, and young (42) for a presidential candidate—proved to be a lightning rod for witticisms. The New York Republican was "The Boy Orator of the Platitude," according to one anonymous pundit. Former Interior Secretary Harold Ickes described him as the kind of person "who, when he had nothing to do, went home and cleaned his bureau drawers." In 1948, when he announced his candidacy for the presidency for a second time, Ickes said that "Dewey has thrown his diaper into the ring," while Mrs. Longworth dismissed his chances with the observation, "You can't make a soufflé rise twice." Upon his loss to Truman that year, wise heads nodded sagely and agreed that he had "snatched defeat from the jaws of victory."

To err is Truman. 1

—Anonymous, c. 1946

★ Truman, during the first years of his presidency, was often regarded as something of an embarrassment. Another joke compared him unfavorably with Franklin Delano Roosevelt: "For years, we had the champion of the common man in the presidency. Now we have the common man." Truman answered tit for tat. For example, he called Sen. J. William Fulbright of Arkansas "half-bright"—when Fulbright suggested, after Democrats were swamped in the 1946 congressional elections, that Truman appoint a Republican Secretary of State to succeed him and then resign. For Truman's attack on the music critic who didn't like his daughter's singing, see ART: CRITICISM.

Not even wrong. *Ganz falsch.* 2

—Wolfgang Pauli, comment, cited in *Scientific American* [June 1994]

★ Himself a child prodigy and Nobel Prize-winner, Pauli was famous for dismissing wrong-headed ideas of other physicists in this way. Literally, *ganz falsch* means "completely wrong," but Pauli gave the expression a more withering twist.

What a dump! 3

—Lenore Coffee, *Beyond the Forest*, 1949

★ In this movie, Bette Davis had the line and made it famous. But it was used also in *Night Court*, 1932, with a similar delivery by Anita Page.

A day away from Tallulah is like a month in the country. 4

—Howard Dietz, ascribed

★ In a brief profile on Bankhead, Brendan Gill, in *The New Yorker*, reported that Tallulah spoke at the rate of almost seventy thousand words per day, "the equivalent of a short novel." Dietz, by the way, was one of those multitalented, competent people that we seem to have fewer of lately. He was a successful lyricist—e.g., *Dancing in the Dark*—librettist—opera as well as musical comedy—and publicity executive with MGM, credited with creating the Leo the Lion trademark.

It is a pity that his wisdom, his judgment, his tact, and his sense of humor lag so far 5
behind his ambition.

—Dwight D. Eisenhower, note to a friend re Senate Majority Leader William Knowland of California, 1953, quoted in Stephen E. Ambrose, *Eisenhower: The President* [1983]

★ The very conservative and notoriously dim Knowland prompted the president to comment in his diary "There seems to be no final answer to the question, 'How stupid can you get?' " The Eisenhower administration itself drew a few barbs. His cabinet was described in *The New Republic's* anonymous TRB column—written by Richard Strout—as "eight millionaires and a plumber"; the labor secretary had formerly headed the plumbers' union, the rest were a corporate lawyer, John Foster Dulles, and businessmen, three from the auto industry. Defeated Democratic candidate Adlai Stevenson remarked, "The New Dealers have all left Washington to make way for the car dealers."

1 [Re William Jennings Bryan:] His mind was like a soup dish, wide and shallow.
—**Irving Stone,** *They Also Ran*, 1966

2 Television is a triumph of equipment over people, and the minds that control it are so small that you could put them in a gnat's navel with room left over for two caraway seeds and an agent's heart.
—**Fred Allen,** in *CoEvolution Quarterly,* Winter 1977

3 Every word she writes is a lie, including "and" and "the."
—**Mary McCarthy,** on fellow writer Lillian Hellman, television interview on *The Dick Cavett Show*, 1979

★ This remark prompted a two-and-a-quarter million dollar lawsuit by Hellman against McCarthy, Cavett, and the Public Broadcasting System. McCarthy and Hellman, formidable figures of the literary world, were both difficult. Poet Randall Jarrell wrote of McCarthy's famous smile, "Torn animals were removed at sunset from that smile," *Pictures from an Institution.* Fiction writer Jean Stafford dubbed Hellman "Old Scaly Bird." The lawsuit blighted the last years of both plaintiff and defendant. It was dismissed following Hellman's death in 1984.

4 You have Van Gogh's ear for music.
—**Billy Wilder,** to actor Cliff Ormand, reported Dec. 31, 1982

5 He is a man who was born on third base and thinks he hit a triple.
—**Jim Hightower,** Democratic National Convention, 1988

★ Hightower, a populist Texas Democrat, applied this to Republican presidential candidate George H. W. Bush. Also applied by Texas Governor, Democrat Ann Richards, and others to Bush's son and also a successful presidential candidate, George W. Bush.

6 You get the feeling that Dan Quayle's golf bag doesn't have a full set of irons.
—**Johnny Carson,** *The Johnny Carson Show,* c. 1988 quoted in his *New York Times* obituary [Jan. 24, 2005]

★ Vice-President Quayle, a handsome man, was the butt of endless jokes suggesting his intellect was weak. The form of the insult is an American tradition. People play cards with less than a full deck, or are missing some of their marbles. Carson also suggested that "Col. Qaddafi [leader of Libya] must have left a few of his dresser drawers open," [*Best of Johnny Carson,* April 11, 1984.] Incidentally, Quayle was such an enthusiastic golfer that once when it was suggested that a female lobbyist was being overly friendly during a golf game, Quayle's wife, Marilyn, dismissed the incident, remarking, "Anyone who knows Dan, knows he would rather play golf than have sex any day."

As I used to say about my old Yonkers Raceway boss Al Tananbaum—if I ever need a heart transplant I want his, because it hardly ever has been used. 1

—**Irving Rudd,** *The Sporting Life*, 1990

★ Rudd was a press agent—not a PR person, please. See under ADVERTISING, ADVERTISING SLOGANS, & PUBLICITY.

He inherited some good instincts from his Quaker forebears, but by diligent hard work, he overcame them. 2

—**James Reston,** comment on Pres. Richard Nixon, *Deadline: Our Times and The New York Times*, 1991

I call them girlie-men. 3

—**Arnold Schwarzenegger,** speech, July 17, 2004

★ The governor of California was referring to Democrats who were delaying passage of the state budget at the behest, he claimed, of special interests. The insult came from a recurring skit, 20 years earlier, on the Saturday Night Live television show. Two fake, comic Austrian body-builders would apply the epithet to men of normal build. Schwarznegger re-used the joke at the Republican National Convention in September 2004, urging people who were pessimistic about the economy, "Don't be economic girlie-men!" Writers for Saturday Night Live did not invent the insult, however. Thus, *American Speech* (Spring 2005) included this example from the *Newark* [Ohio] *Daily Advocate* of April 11, 1894: "The girl man is soon cast aside and has to flock by himself when a real man comes along."

The only time he opens his mouth is to change his foot. 4

—**Anonymous,** 2005

★ The joke, which circulated in academic circles and beyond, referred to Harvard president Lawrence H. Summers, who, in January 2005, suggested that "innate differences" might explain why males outnumber females on the faculties of math and science at his university. This was just the latest of a series of impolitic remarks from Mr. Summers.

Intimacy & Familiarity

Familiarity breeds contempt—and children. 5

—**Mark Twain,** *Mark Twain's Notebooks*, Albert B. Paine, ed. [1935]

★ The adage, minus the reference to children, dates to ancient times and is the moral of Aesop's fable *The Fox and the Lion*. For an up-to-date comment on the effects of a certain intimacy, see David Owen at HEROES.

Familiarity breeds contentment. 6

—**George Ade,** *The Uplift That Moved Sideways*, in *Hand-Made Fables*, 1920

Familiarity breeds attempt. 7

—**Jane Ace,** observation on *The Easy Aces* radio show, 1930–45, in Goodman Ace, *The Fine Art of Hypochondria* [1996]

Iowa

See also CITIES (DES MOINES).

1 Ioway, Ioway, that's where the tall corn grows!
—Anonymous, c. 1840

2 There is no group of two and a half million people in the world who worship God as Iowans do.
—Anonymous, professor at Iowa State College, quoted by H. L. Mencken, in *Americana*, 1925

★ More at CITIES (DES MOINES).

3 The gold mines and the diamond mines of the world are cheap and trivial compared to the produce that Iowa breeds out of its land every year.
—Phil Stong, *Hawkeyes*, 1940

★ *Hawkeyes* is a history of Iowa. Stong's novel *State Fair*, 1932, was made into a movie three times, the first version starring Will Rogers. Iowans are called Hawkeyes after the Indian warrior Chief Black Hawk, who survived the massacre of his band in 1832, and was later set free in Iowa, where he spent his last days.

4 The character of Iowa is essentially bucolic in the best senses of that word (and, to be quite honest, occasionally in some of the worst).
—Ibid.

5 Iowa spells agriculture, and agriculture in this part of the world spells corn. This is the heart of agrarian America.
—John Gunther, *Inside U.S.A.*, 1947

6 "Is this heaven?"
"It's Iowa."
"I could have sworn it was heaven."
—W. P. Kinsella, *Shoeless Joe*, 1982

★ Adapted by Phil Alden Robinson for the 1989 movie *Field of Dreams* Kinsella, a Canadian, studied at the Iowa Writer's Workshop at the U. of Iowa. See FAITH for the most famous line from the movie.

7 Iowa—where exciting things happen.
—Anonymous, information center highway sign, cited in *The New York Times*, Oct. 7, 2004.

8 Our liberties we prize and our rights we will maintain.
—Motto, state of Iowa

Iraq War, 2003– .

9 You break it, you own it.
—Colin L. Powell, in private remarks, 2003

★ Secretary of State Powell called this the Pottery Barn rule, and applied it to Administration plans to invade Iraq, according to Bob Woodward, in *Plan of Attack*

(2004). Woodward reported that in a meeting with President George W. Bush on January 13, 2003, Mr. Powell pledged his support but commented, "You know you're going to be owning this place?" Later, the Pottery Barn company protested that it did not charge customers for accidental breakage. *New York Times* columnist William Safire verified that Powell had picked up the "rule" from speeches by Tom Friedman of *The Times*, who had recollected a china-shop rule from years earlier. Friedman's column of of February 12, 2003, called it the "pottery store rule." Friedman told Safire, "I was a little surprised to see Powell being quoted as saying that to the President. I was also pleased. I only wish the president had paid attention."

Shock and Awe. 1

—**Harlan K. Ullman,** quoted on CBS News, January 24, 2003

★ The "Shock and Awe" battle plan was developed at the National Defense University, with Ullman evidently its main author. He and James Wade wrote a book with that title in 1996. The idea is to use overwhelming and demoralizing massive air strikes. One model is Hiroshima. Prior to the Iraq War, Ullman told CBS, "We want them to quit. We want them not to fight." The broadcast added, "If Shock and Awe works, there won't be a ground war" (CBSNEWS.com). The Iraq air attacks were not as crushing as expected, in part because the US changed its war plan to strike directly at Saddam Hussein. Nevertheless, in the ensuing weeks, Iraq military forces mounted almost no resistance. The basic "shock-and-awe" strategy was first described about 500 B.C. by military writer Sun Tzu. (There is an anecdote involving imperial courtesans who failed to march in proper order, until one was pulled aside and beheaded.) In modern times, the German military strategist Gen. Karl von Clausewitz expressed a similar approach, calling war "fog, friction and fear." The standard American formulation has been "overwhelming force." The precept that one should not attack with less is often called the "Powell doctrine," after its best-known advocate, Colin Powell. See also Powell at GULF WAR and MILITARY STRATEGY.

I really do believe that we will be greeted as liberators. 2

—**Dick Cheney,** *Meet the Press*, March 16, 2003

Mission Accomplished. 3

—**Anonymous,** sign on board USS *Abraham Lincoln*, May 1, 2003

★ The sign was very prominent as Pres. George W. Bush, wearing a flight suit, congratulated the assembled forces on their successful mission. Later, when casualities post-May 1 had exceeded those pre–May 1, the White House attempted to distance itself from the sign. Eventually sources agreed that the sign had been proposed by the Navy and created by the Administration.

We're the dog that caught the car. Now what do we do with it? 4

—**Dave Pere,** remark, 2003

★ Marine Lt. Col. Pere is quoted in the Prologue to *A Time of Our Choosing*, by Todd S. Purdum, 2003

Bring 'em on. 5

—**George W. Bush,** press conference, July 2, 2003

★ The president was referring to insurgents in Iraq attacking American troops. "There are some that feel like—that if they attack us—that we may leave prematurely . . . My answer is, bring 'em on."

1 We are not occupiers. . . We came here as liberators.
—**Colin Powell,** in Iraq, Sept. 14, 2003

★ It was the Secretary of State's first visit to Iraq following the fall of Saddam Hussein. See also Donald Rumsfeld at FOREIGN POLICY on empire.

2 I actually did vote for the $87 billion before I voted against it.
—**John Kerry,** presidential campaign speech, Marshall University, W. Va., March 16, 2004

★ The $87 billion was in the Emergency Supplemental Appropriations Act for Afghanistan and Iraq, which the Senate passed on Oct. 17, 2003, with Sen. Kerry voting nay. It is true that he had earlier supported a bill with the same funding that included an amendment revoking Bush administration tax cuts for those earning more than $400,000 per year. But considering that Kerry had earlier voted to give Pres. Bush the authority to go to war in Iraq if necessary, this comment instantly became emblematic of Kerry's often muddled message. Within two days, the Bush campaign had an ad out featuring this quote.

3 Tell me how this ends.
—**David H. Petraeus,** in Rick Atkinson, *In the Company of Soldiers*, 2004

★ Maj. Gen. Petraeus was commander of the 101st Airborne Division.

4 Catastrophic success.
—**George W. Bush,** interview in *Time* magazine, August 29, 2004

★ Characterization of the Iraq War: "Had we to do it over again," the president said, "we would look at the consequences of catastrophic success, being so successful, so fast, that an enemy that should have surrendered or been done in, escaped and lived to fight another day." The phrase was used earlier by Secretary of Defense Donald Rumsfeld on at least a couple of public occasions (interview with Jim Lehrer on the PBS NewsHour, Feb. 20, 2003, and during a Pentagon press conference, April 11, 2003). Others who employed it prior to the president included the former commander in Iraq, Gen. Tommy Franks, in his book *American Soldier*, and military historian Frederick Kagan.

5 As you know, you go to war with the army you have, not the army you might want or may wish to have at a later time.
—**Donald H. Rumsfeld,** Kuwait, Dec. 8, 2004

★ Secretary of Defense Rumsfeld was speaking to about 2,300 troops headed to Iraq. He was answering an unexpected question about why soldiers were having to scrounge through dumps to find scrap materials to armor vehicles. See also Rumsfeld at FREEDOM.

6 But when those guns start blazing and our friends get hit,
That's when our hearts start racing and our stomach gets whoozy,
Cuz for y'all this is just a show, but we live in this movie.
—**Richmond Shaw,** rap lyric, quoted in *The New York Times*, Feb. 20, 2005

Ireland & the Irish

See Nations & Regions

Italy & Italians

See Nations & Regions

Jackson, Andrew

If General Jackson wants to go to Heaven, who's to stop him? 1
—Anonymous

★ Perhaps apocryphal, but this is said to be the response of one of Jackson's slaves, who, after Jackson's death, was asked whether he thought the great man had gone to heaven. See also Jackson at Last Words.

Little advanced in civilization over the Indians with whom he made war. 2
—Elijah Hunt Mills, in Marquis James, *Andrew Jackson—Portrait of a President* [1933]

A natural king 3
With a raven wing,
Cold no more,
Weary no more,
Old, old,
Old, old,
Andrew Jackson.
—Vachel Lindsay, *Old, Old, Old, Old Andrew Jackson*, spoken by the author, Jefferson's Birthday Dinner, Spokane, Wash., April 15, 1925

Japan

See Nations & Regions

Jefferson, Thomas

See also Epitaphs & Gravestones; Independence Day; Last Words; Tyranny.

He lives and will live in memory and gratitude of the wise and good, as a luminary of science, as a votary of liberty, as a model of patriotism, and as a benefactor of human kind. 4
—James Madison, in memory of Thomas Jefferson, 1826

[Jefferson was] perhaps the most incapable executive that ever filled the presidential chair. . . . It would be difficult to imagine a man less fit to guide a state with honor and safety through the stormy times that marked the opening of the present century. 5
—Theodore Roosevelt, *The Naval War of 1812*, 1882

1 I think this is the most extraordinary collection of human talent, of human knowledge, that has ever been gathered at the White House—with the possible exception of when Thomas Jefferson dined alone.

—**John F. Kennedy,** speech, dinner honoring 49 Nobel Prize winners, in *The New York Times*, April 30, 1962

Judges

See also CONSTITUTION, THE (Alexander Hamilton); LAW.

2 The acme of judicial distinction means the ability to look a lawyer straight in the eye for two hours and not hear a damned word he says.

—**John Marshall,** quoted in Albert J. Beveridge, *The Life of John Marshall* [1916–1919]

3 The perfect judge fears nothing—he could go front to front before God, Before the perfect judge all shall stand back—life and death shall stand back—heaven and hell shall stand back.

—**Walt Whitman,** *Great Are the Myths*, in *Leaves of Grass*, 1860

4 Even judges sometimes progress.

—**Emma Goldman,** *The Social Aspects of Birth Control*, in *Mother Earth* magazine, April 1916

5 We are not final because we are infallible, but we are infallible only because we are final.

—**Robert H. Jackson,** *Brown v. Allen,* 1952

★ Justice Jackson was concurring in this case, which upheld the Supreme Court as the court of last resort.

6 There has been much undiscriminating eulogy of dissenting opinions. . . . Each dissenting opinion is a confession of failure to convince the writer's colleagues and the true test of a judge is his influence in leading, not in opposing, his court.

—**Robert H. Jackson,** *The Supreme Court in the American System of Government*, 1955

7 Always go for the jugular. Never agonize in an opinion.

—**Hugo Black,** c. 1970, quoted in Linda Greenhouse, *Becoming Justice Blackmun* [2005]

★ Justice Black was advising new Supreme Court Justice Harry Blackmun.

8 Judges are the weakest link in our system of justice, and they are also the most protected.

—**Alan Dershowitz,** *Newsweek*, Feb. 20, 1978

9 Judicial restraint is but another form of judicial activism.

—**Laurence H. Tribe,** *American Constitutional Law*, 1978

We must never forget that the only real source of power that we as judges can tap is the respect of the people. 1

—**Thurgood Marshall,** in the *Chicago Tribune*, August 15, 1981

I don't care what the law is, tell me who the judge is. 2

—**Roy M. Cohn,** saying, c. 1983, in Nicholas von Hoffman, *Citizen Cohn* [1988]

★ Cohn, a feared New York defense attorney, first gained notoriety as a young counsel to Red-hunting Sen. Joseph McCarthy.

Judicial independence is the judge's right to do the right thing or, believing it to be the right thing, to do the wrong thing. 3

—**Adolpho A. Birch, Jr.,** in *The New York Times*, Dec. 10, 1998

★ Mr. Birch, a Tennessee judge, spoke at a conference of state judges, lawyers, and legal scholars in Philadelphia.

If we are to be a nation of laws and not of men, judges must be impartial referees who defend Constitutional principles from attempts by particular interests (or even the people as a whole) to overwhelm them. 4

—**Clarence Thomas**, Francis Boyer Lecture, American Enterprise Institute, Feb. 13, 2001

★ Justice Thomas restated his "judge-as-referee" analogy on April 13, 2005, when he and Justice Anthony Kennedy appeared before a Congressional subcommittee to defend the Supreme Court's proposed budget and, incidentally, a number of criticisms. Justice Thomas added on this occasion that referees should not expect to be popular. When a football game is over, he said, "the referees get out of there fast. They don't stand around high-fiving people."

July Fourth

See INDEPENDENCE DAY.

Juries

In controversies respecting property, and in suits between man and man, the ancient trial by jury is preferable to any other, and ought to be held sacred. 5

—**Virginia Declaration of Rights,** 1776

Juries . . . have the effect . . . of placing the law in the hands of those who would be most apt to abuse it. 6

—**James Fenimore Cooper,** *The Redskins*, 1846

A jury too frequently have at least one member, more ready to hang the panel than hang the traitor. 7

—**Abraham Lincoln,** letter to Erastus Corning et al., June 12, 1863

We have a criminal justice system which is superior to any in the world; and its efficiency is only marred by the difficulty of finding twelve men every day who don't know anything and can't read. 8

—**Mark Twain,** *Americans and the English*, speech, July 4, 1872

1 The jury system puts a ban upon intelligence and honesty, and a premium upon ignorance, stupidity, and perjury.

—**Mark Twain,** *Roughing It*, 1872

2 *Jury, n.* A number of persons appointed by a judge to assist the attorneys in preventing law from degenerating into justice.

—**Ambrose Bierce,** *The Devil's Dictionary*, 1906

3 I never saw twelve men in my life that if you could get them to understand a human case, were not true and right.

—**Clarence Darrow,** summation in the Sweet case, Detroit, 1926

★ When not in the process of flattering jurors, Darrow recognized a number of exceptions; for example, he wrote in *Attorney for the Defense*: "Never take a wealthy man on a jury. He will convict, unless the defendant is accused of violating the anti-trust law, selling worthless stocks or bonds, or something of that kind. Next to the Board of Trade, for him, the penitentiary is the most important of all public buildings," *Esquire*, May 1936.

4 Trial by jury is a rough scales at best.

—**Learned Hand,** *United States v. Brown*, 1935

★ Hand was the most influential and respected U.S. judge not to make it to the highest court, and was often referred to as the tenth Supreme Court justice.

5 Every jury trial in the land is a small daily miracle of democracy in action.

—**Robert Traver,** *Anatomy of a Murder*, 1958

★ Traver (psudonym of John D. Voelker) was a prosecutor and judge as well as bestselling author.

6 A court is only as sound as its jury, and a jury is only as sound as the men who make it up.

—**Harper Lee,** *To Kill a Mockingbird*, 1960

7 I would rather have my fate in the hands of twenty-three representative citizens of the country [the grand jury] than in the hands of a politically appointed judge.

—**Robert M. Morgenthau,** quoted in *Time,* April 8, 1985

8 Why should anyone think that twelve persons brought in from the street, selected in various ways for their lack of general ability, should have any special capacity for deciding controversies between persons?

—**Erwin Griswold,** quoted in Stephen J. Adler, *The Jury*, 1994

★ Griswold was dean of Harvard Law School. In the *Harvard Law Review*, in 1899, Oliver Wendell Holmes acknowledged that jurors show no great insight or unusual judgment. "They will introduce into their verdict a certain amount—a very large amount, so far as I have observed—of popular prejudice," he said. But he also speculated that this is in fact an advantage, for "thus [they] keep the administration of the law in accord with the wishes and feelings of the community," *Law in Science and Science in Law.*

Justice

See also INJUSTICE; JUDGES; JURIES; LAW.

Without justice, courage is weak. **1**

—Benjamin Franklin, *Poor Richard's Almanack*, Jan. 1734

Until the infallibility of human judgment shall have been proved to me, I shall persist in demanding the abolition of the death penalty. **2**

—[Marquis de] Lafayette, letter, August 17, 1830

Justice is always in jeopardy. **3**

—Walt Whitman, *Democratic Vistas*, 1870

The laws of changeless justice bind **4**
Oppressor and oppressed;
And close as sin and suffering joined,
We march to fate abreast.

—John Greenleaf Whittier, *At Port Royal*, 1862

★ The occasion of the poem was the capture by Union forces of Port Royal, South Carolina, on November 7, 1861. This liberated some 10,000 slaves on islands between Charleston and Savannah, who then became part of an abolitionist venture in which the freed people were educated and set up as cotton farmers.

We are the whirlwinds that winnow the West— **5**
We scatter the wicked like straw!
We are the Nemeses, never at rest—
We are Justice, and Right, and the Law!

—Margaret Ashmun, *The Vigilantes*, in *The Pacific Monthly*, 1907

It is higher and nobler to be kind. . . . If we should deal out justice only, in this world, who would escape? **6**

—Mark Twain, *Autobiography* [1924]

Even the wicked get worse than they deserve. **7**

—Willa Cather, *One of Ours*, 1921

★ In this instance the wicked one is the chief steward of a troopship en route to France, who has been hoarding oranges and eggs needed by soldiers suffering from influenza and who, toward the end of the voyage, comes down with the lethal disease himself.

Injustice is relatively easy to bear; what stings is justice. **8**

—H. L. Mencken, *Prejudices, Third Series*, 1922

Justice is not to be taken by storm. She is to be wooed by slow advances. **9**

—Benjamin Cardozo, *The Growth of the Law*, 1924

There is no such thing as justice—in or out of court. **10**

—Clarence Darrow, interview, *The New York Times*, April 19, 1936

1 The most odious of all oppressions are those which mask as justice.
—**Robert H. Jackson,** concurring opinion, *Krulewitch v. United States*, 1949

2 Thou shalt not ration justice.
—**Learned Hand,** speech to the Legal Aid Society of New York, Feb. 16, 1951

3 Your justice would freeze beer!
—**Arthur Miller,** *The Crucible*, 1953

4 Swift justice demands more than just swiftness.
—**Potter Stewart,** dissenting opinion in *Henderson v. Bannan*, 6th Circuit, 1958

5 No, no, we are not satisfied, and we will not be satisfied until justice rolls down like waters and righteousness like a mighty stream.
—**Martin Luther King, Jr.,** speech at the Lincoln Memorial in Washington, D.C., to 200,000 civil rights marchers, August 28, 1963

★ More at AMERICAN HISTORY: MEMORABLE MOMENTS.

6 Rush to Judgment.
—**Mark Lane,** book title, 1966

★ The title has become a tag for any hurried and biased approach to deciding who or what is responsible for a wrong. Lane was writing about the Warren Commission report on the assassination of Pres. John F. Kennedy.

7 The court doesn't exist to give them justice . . . But to give them a chance for justice.
—**David Mamet,** screenplay, *The Verdict*, 1982, based on the Barry Reed novel

8 You go . . . lookin' for justice, and that's what you find, Just-Us.
—**Richard Pryor,** quoted in Mel Watkins, *On the Real Side* [1994]

9 No justice. No peace.
—**Al Sharpton,** saying, c. 1994

★ Rev. Al Sharpton is an African-American activist and politician, based in New York City. He ran for the Democratic nomination for president in 2004.

10 People who are well-represented at trial do not get the death penalty.
—**Ruth Bader Ginsburg,** speech, University of the District of Columbia, April 9, 2001

★ The Supreme Court Justice spoke in favor of a moratorium in Maryland on capital punishment.

11 Whether we bring our enemies to justice, or bring justice to our enemies, justice will be done.
—**George W. Bush,** address to joint session of Congress, Sept. 20, 2001

★ This was nine days after Sept. 11, 2001.

12 Compassion is no substitute for justice.
—**Rush Limbaugh,** quoted by newscaster Aaron Brown, CNN, Jan. 23, 2004

Kansas

Bleeding Kansas. 1

—Anonymous, popular epithet for the Kansas territory in the 1850s

★ After the Kansas-Nebraska Act of 1854, which opened the possibility that Kansas could become a slave state if its residents so chose, the territory became a battleground between free-soil (antislavery) and pro-Southern forces. Kansas became a state in 1861.

The Crime against Kansas. 2

—Charles Sumner, title of speech in the U.S. Senate, May 19–20, 1856

★ An impassioned antislavery speech, larded with rich personal invective: Sumner described supporters of slavery as "hirelings picked from the drunken spew and vomit of an uneasy civilization." Senators Andrew P. Butler and Stephen A. Douglas, the authors of the Kansas-Nebraska Act (see above), were portrayed as the Don Quixote and Sancho Panza of "the harlot, slavery." All this led to the lowest of low points in congressional history: to avenge family and Southern honor, Preston S. "Bully" Brooks, a representative from South Carolina and a distant cousin of Butler, invaded the Senate chamber on May 22, and, catching Sumner unawares at his desk, nearly beat him to death with a stout cane.

It takes three log houses to make a city in Kansas, but they begin *calling* it a city as 3
soon as they have staked out the lots.

—Horace Greeley, *An Overland Journey from New York to San Francisco . . . in 1859*, 1860

In God we trusted, in Kansas we busted. 4

—Anonymous, 1870s

★ Sign on wagons of would-be western pioneers who didn't make it. Quoted by Wallace Stegner in *Thoughts in a Dry Land*, 1972.

The roosters lay eggs in Kansas. 5
The roosters lay eggs as big as beer kegs.
And the hair grows on their legs in Kansas.

—Anonymous, song, c. 1880

Oh, they chew tobacco in Kansas, 6
Oh, they say that drink's a sin in Kansas.

—Anonymous, folk song, in John Gunther, *Inside U.S.A.* [1947]

What you Kansas farmers ought to do is raise less corn and more hell. 7

—Mary Lease, attributed, speech, 1890

★ Roger Butterfield in *The American Past* (1957) wrote that this advice may have originated with a newspaper reporter.

What's the Matter with Kansas? 8

—William Allen White, title of editorial, *Emporia Gazette*, August 15, 1896

★ The answer, according to this famous editorial, is that the state's top politicians were a bunch of loonies and failures. White loved Kansas, though. He concluded, "Kansas is all right. She has started to raise hell, as Mrs. Lease advised, and she seems to have an overproduction." In 2004, a bestseller by Thomas Frank asked in its title, *What's the Matter with Kansas: How Conservatives Won the Heart of America.*

1 When anything is going to happen in this country, it happens first in Kansas.
—**William Allen White,** editorial, *Emporia Gazette*, 1922

★ White went on to list the following "firsts:" "Abolition, Prohibition, Populism, the Bull Moose, the exit of the roller towel, the appearance of the bank guarantee, the blue sky law, the adjudication of industrial disputes as distinguished from the arbitration of industrial differences—these things come popping out of Kansas like bats out of hell."

2 The only way you could tell a citizen from a bootlegger in Kansas was the bootlegger was sober.
—**Will Rogers,** quoted in Alex Ayres, ed., *The Wit and Wisdom of Will Rogers* [1993]

3 Toto, I've a feeling we're not in Kansas any more.
—**Noel Langley, Florence Ryerson, & Edgar Allen Wolfe,** *The Wizard of Oz*, screenplay, 1939

4 Kansas is the child of Plymouth Rock.
—**William Allen White,** *Autobiography*, 1946

5 A kind of gravity point for American democracy.
—**John Gunther,** *Inside U.S.A.*, 1947

6 First in freedom, first in wheat.
—**Anonymous,** Kansas saying, quoted in Dwight D. Eisenhower, *Eisenhower Speaks*, 1948

7 Kansas, by reason of history and location at the heart of our continental power, is a kind of social, political, and cultural barometer for all America.
—**Adlai Stevenson,** *A Kind of Prophecy*, speech, Wichita, Kansas, Oct. 7, 1954

8 Well, if we blow up Kansas, the world may not hear of it for years.
—**Richard Maibaum,** *Diamonds Are Forever*, screenplay, 1971

★ The movie is based on Ian Fleming's novel, and the speaker is the villain, Blofeld. He has just been told that his satellite-based death ray is over Kansas.

9 Kansas, in sum, is one of our finest states and lives a sane, peaceful, and prosperous life.
—**Pearl S. Buck,** *America*, 1971

10 *Ad astra per aspera.* To the stars through difficulties.
—Motto, state of Kansas

Kentucky

See also CITIES (FRANKFORT); MEXICAN WAR (Zachary Taylor).

He's gone to hell or Kentucky. 1
—Anonymous, c. 1785

★ The saying, which was popular in Virginia, referred to a man who had disappeared, leaving behind debts or indictments.

Heaven is a Kentuck of a place. 2
—Timothy Flint, *Recollections of the Last Ten Years Passed in Occasional Residences and Journeyings in the Valley of the Mississippi*, 1826

★ The comparison of fertile Kentucky to Heaven was made so often by early visitors—as well as by local boosters—that "Kentuck" or "Kentucky" became synonymous for any ideal place, as in, "(New York) is a real Kentuck of a place," W. A. Caruthers, *A Kentuckian in New York*, 1834.

The dark and bloody ground. 3
—Theodore O'Hara, *The Bivouac of the Dead*, 1847

★ Though the name KENTUCKY is sometimes said to be an Indian term meaning "dark and bloody ground," it is really a Seneca Iroquois word meaning "at the meadowlands." Henry F. Woods noted in *American Sayings*, however, that the Cherokee chief Dragging Canoe did warn in 1775 that the land was a "bloody ground"—evidently from the hunting, battles, and burials there—and that it would be dark and hard to settle. Possibly he was trying to scare off representatives of the Transylvania Land Company that acquired the land by treaty that year. The phrase, "Sons of the dark and bloody ground" was used by poet and soldier Theodore O'Hara in *The Bivouac of the Dead*, quoted above.

Great, tall, raw-boned Kentuckians, attired in hunting shirts, and trailing their loose 4
joints over a vast extent of territory with the easy lounge peculiar to the race.
—Harriet Beecher Stowe, *Uncle Tom's Cabin*, 1852

Here's a health to old Kentucky, 5
Where the fathers through the years,
Hand down the courtly graces
To the sons of cavaliers;
Where the golden age is regnant,
And each succeeding morn
Finds "the corn is full of kernels,
And the Colonels full of corn."
—William J. Lampton, *To Old Kentucky*

★ The phrase in quotations in the last couplet is a bit of traditional folk wit, author unknown, with the final "corn" being short for "corn whisky." The pun dates to at least the opening decades of the 19th century. In 1825, Chief Justice John Marshall penned the ditty: "In the blue grass region, / A paradox was born: / The corn was full of kernels / and the *colonels* full of corn."

1 The sun shines bright in the old Kentucky home.
—**Stephen Foster,** *My Old Kentucky Home*, 1853

2 Weep no more, my lady;
Oh, weep no more today!
We will sing one song for the old Kentucky home,
For the old Kentucky home, far away.
—**Stephen Foster,** *My Old Kentucky Home*, 1853

3 The songbirds are the sweetest
In Kentucky;
The thoroughbreds are fleetest
In Kentucky;
Mountains tower proudest,
Thunder peals the loudest,
The landscape is the grandest—
And politics—the damnedest
In Kentucky.
—**James H. Mulligan,** *In Kentucky,* late 19th century

4 Wherever a Kentuckian may be, he is more than willing to boast of the beauties and virtues of the native state. He believes without reservation that Kentucky is the garden spot of the world, and is ready to dispute with anyone who questions the claim.
—**Federal Writers' Project,** *Kentucky: A Guide to the Bluegrass State*, 1939

5 United we stand, divided we fall.
—Motto, state of Kentucky

Kindness

See also VIRTUE.

6 I expect to pass through this world but once; any good thing, therefore, that I can do, or any kindness that I can show to any fellow creature, let me do it now; let me not defer or neglect it, for I shall not pass this way again.
—**Anonymous**

★ *Bartlett's* points out that this has been attributed to many people, and most often to Stephen Grellet, a French Quaker cleric, but no attribution has been verified.

7 By Chivalries as tiny,
A Blossom, or a Book,
The seeds of smiles are planted—
Which blossom in the dark.
—**Emily Dickinson,** poem no. 55, c. 1858

8 If I can stop one Heart from breaking,
I shall not live in vain
If I can ease one Life the Aching
Or cool one Pain

Or help one fainting Robin
Unto his Nest again
I shall not live in Vain.

—**Emily Dickinson,** poem no. 919, c. 1864

It is higher and nobler to be kind. 1

—**Mark Twain,** *Autobiography* [1924]

★ More at JUSTICE.

I have always depended on the kindness of strangers. 2

—**Tennessee Williams,** *A Streetcar Named Desire*, 1947

★ Blanche DuBois's exit line.

Attention must be paid. 3

—**Arthur Miller**, *Death of A Salesman*, 1949

★ The passage runs, "He [the salesman, Willy Loman] is a human being, and a terrible thing is happening to him, so attention must be paid. He's not to be allowed to fall into his grave like an old dog. Attention, attention must be finally paid to such a person."

Nothing has happened today except kindness. 4

—**Gertrude Stein,** *A Diary*, in *Alphabets and Birthdays*, 1957

A kinder, gentler, nation. 5

—**George H. W. Bush,** presidential nomination acceptance speech, Republican National Convention, New Orleans, August 18, 1988

★ More information at POLITICAL SLOGANS.

Knowledge & Information

See also EDUCATION; FACTS.

Forewarned, forearmed. 6

—**Benjamin Franklin,** *Poor Richard's Almanack*, 1736

★ Another proverb recycled by Franklin. Cervantes included it in *Don Quixote*, 1615.

Knowledge . . . is the great sun in the firmament. Life and power are scattered with 7
all its beams.

—**Daniel Webster,** speech at the laying of the cornerstone, Bunker Hill Monument, June 17, 1825

Knowledge is the knowing that we cannot know. 8

—**Ralph Waldo Emerson,** *Representative Men*, 1850

It is better to know nothing than to know what ain't so. 9

—**Josh Billings,** *Josh Billings' Encyclopedia of Wit and Wisdom*, 1874

★ This is essentially a proverb, used in various forms by Benjamin Franklin and others. Abroad, Friedrich Wilhelm Nietzsche wrote in *Thus Spake Zarathustra* (1883–91),

"Better know nothing than half know many things." John Maynard Keynes opined, "It is better to be approximately right than precisely wrong." See also Thomas Jefferson at THE PRESS—the note after his comment on there being nothing in newspapers that can be believed.

1 Many men are stored full of unused knowledge . . . they are stuffed with useless ammunition.

—**Henry Ward Beecher,** *Proverbs from Plymouth Pulpit*, 1887

2 Knowledge is the recognition of something absent; it is a salutation, not an embrace.

—**George Santayana,** *The Life of Reason: Reason in Common Sense*, 1905–1906

3 Knowledge is always accompanied with accessories of emotion and purpose.

—**Alfred North Whitehead,** *Adventures of Ideas*, 1933

4 Die knowing something. You are not here long.

—**Walker Evans,** unpublished text for his subway photographs, c. 1940, quoted in Belinda Rathbone, *Walker Evans* [1995]

★ The full passage runs: "Stare. It is the way to educate your eye, and more. Stare, pry, listen, eavesdrop. Die knowing something . . . (etc.)" Evans was one of America's great photographers, most remembered for his photos of Alabama tenant farmers in the Depression, published in *Let Us Now Praise Famous Men*, 1938, with a text by James Agee.

5 Everybody gets so much information all day long that they lose their common sense.

—**Gertrude Stein,** untitled essay from 1946, in *Reflection on the Atomic Bomb* [1973]

6 To live effectively is to live with adequate information.

—**Norbert Wiener,** *The Human Use of Human Beings*, 1954

7 So much has already been written about everything that you can't find out anything about it.

—**James Thurber,** *The New Vocabularianism*, in *Lanterns and Lances*, 1961

8 Information is power.

—**Arthur Sylvester,** remarks, Sigma Delta Chi dinner, New York City, Dec. 6, 1962

★ A common observation. Assistant Defense Secretary Sylvester made more waves when he asserted that the "government's right, if necessary, to lie." This was just after the Cuban missile crisis.

9 The greater our knowledge increases, the more our ignorance unfolds.

—**John F. Kennedy,** speech, Rice University, Sept. 12, 1962

10 Information wants to be free.

—**Stewart Brand,** *Whole Earth Review*, May 1985

★ The quotation comes from the transcript of the first Hackers' Conference in the fall of 1984. Mr. Brand elucidated the thought in a book, *The Media Lab* (1987), in a section that begins: "Information Wants To Be Free. Information also wants to be expensive. Information wants to be free because it has become so cheap to distribute, copy, and recombine—too cheap to meter. It wants to be expensive because it can be immeasurably valuable to the recipient. The tension will not go away. It leads to endless wrenching debate about price, copyright, 'intellectual property,' the moral rightness of casual distribution, because each round of new devices makes the tension worse, not better."

As knowledge expands globally, it is being lost locally. 1

—**Wendell Berry,** *Life Is a Miracle,* 2000

★ In particular, Berry was concerned by loss of knowledge of the history and character of rural lands and places.

Korean War, 1950–1953

The attack upon Korea makes it plain beyond all doubt that Communism has passed beyond the use of subversion to conquer independent nations, and will now use armed invasion and war. 2

—**Harry S. Truman,** comment to the press, June 27, 1950

★ The division of Korea along the 38th parallel, into North Korea, dominated by the Soviet and Chinese Communists, and the South, governed by the United Nations, persisted after the end of World War II. In 1948, elections in South Korea created a democratic state. On June 24, 1950, the Communist People's Army invaded South Korea. The U.N. Security Council called for all members to help repel the invaders. (The Council was being boycotted by the U.S.S.R., which otherwise could have vetoed the resolution.) Pres. Truman ordered the first U.S. military response on June 27.

Retreat, hell! We're only attacking in another direction. 3

—**Oliver P. Smith,** vicinity of Chosin Reservoir, Korea, Dec. 4, 1950

★ Maj. Gen. Smith conducted an epic retreat when his 1st Marine Division, surrounded by Chinese troops and outnumbered by more than ten to one, fought its way back to the coast, bringing their dead with them. The troops were evacuated by ship.

In the simplest of terms, what we are doing in Korea is this: We are trying to prevent a third world war. 4

—**Harry S. Truman,** address to the nation, April 16, 1951

★ The occasion of the president's address was his recall of Gen. Douglas MacArthur for insubordination.

In war there is no substitute for victory. 5

—**Douglas MacArthur,** speech, joint session of Congress, April 19, 1951

★ From his "old soldiers never die" speech; see AMERICAN HISTORY: MEMORABLE MOMENTS. A couple of weeks earlier, in a letter to House Speaker Joseph Martin, Jr., Gen. MacArthur had used the same phrase: "There is no substitute for victory." Martin, a Republican, read the letter aloud in the House on April 5, despite knowing that it might lead to the general's downfall, for MacArthur was challenging the authority of his commander in chief, Pres. Harry S. Truman. MacArthur in his letter advocated "meeting force with maximum counterforce." The target was China, which had intervened on the side of North Korea against South Korea and its American allies. MacArthur advised bombing China and calling in the Nationalist forces of Gen. Chiang Kai-shek. Truman relieved MacArthur of command on April 11.

1 This strategy would involve us in the wrong war, at the wrong place, at the wrong time, and with the wrong enemy.

—Omar Bradley, testimony, U. S. Senate, May 15, 1951

★ The subject was widening the war, as advocated by Gen. Douglas MacArthur. Gen. Bradley was testifying as chairman of the Joint Chiefs of Staff in combined hearings of the Foreign Relations and Armed Services committees investigating the dismissal of Gen. MacArthur by Pres. Harry S. Truman. See also THE MILITARY.

2 I shall go to Korea.

—Dwight D. Eisenhower, campaign speech, Detroit, Mich., Oct. 25, 1952

★ Eisenhower, who was running for president, promised to restart stalled peace talks. As president-elect, he did go to Korea at the end of November. The armistice was signed in July 1953.

3 This was a police action, a limited war, whatever you want to call it, to stop aggression and to prevent a big war.

—Harry S. Truman, in Merle Miller, *Plain Speaking* [1974]

★ This unpopular, costly, and indecisive conflict never involved a U.S. declaration of war. The euphemistic "police action" arose in a roundabout way. On June 29, 1950, at Truman's first press conference following North Korea's invasion of South Korea, the president said that the United States was "not at war" but just suppressing a raid by "a bunch of bandits." A reporter then asked if it would be fair "to call this a police action under the United Nations?" "Yes. That is exactly what it amounts to," Truman replied, thus justifying such headlines the next day as "Truman Calls Intervention 'Police Action.'" The anonymous reporter, in turn, may have picked up the phrase from a Senate speech by William F. Knowland. Speaking of the air force's mission, the California Republican declared: "The action this government is taking is a police action against a violator of the law of nations and the Charter of the United Nations."

Labor

See CAPITALISM & CAPITAL V. LABOR; WORK & WORKERS.

Language & Words

See also AMERICA & AMERICANS (Whitman on American names); ART: STYLE IN WRITING & EXPRESSION; ART: WRITING; NORTH CAROLINA (Walker on Buncombe); FREE SPEECH; NATURE: SEASONS (James on "summer afternoon"); TALK.

4 Morals and manners will rise or decline with our attention to grammar.

—Jason Chamberlain, inaugural speech, University of Vermont, 1811

5 I very seldom during my whole stay in the country heard a sentence elegantly turned and correctly pronounced from the lips of an American. There is always something either in the expression or the accent that jars the feelings and shocks the taste.

—Frances Trollope, *Domestic Manners of the Americans*, 1832

★ Like most British visitors of the period (see also Capt. Marryat below), Mrs. Trollope did not agree with the American view that they spoke a superior English. For example, James Fenimore Cooper asserted in *Notions of the Americans* (1828) that "The people of the United States, with the exception of a few of German or French descent, speak, as a body, incomparably better English than the people of the mother country." Cooper reached this conclusion, despite noting serious faults in American English; see below.

The common faults of American language are ambition of effect, a want of simplicity, and turgid abuse of terms. 1

—**James Fenimore Cooper,** *The American Democrat*, 1838

It is remarkable how very debased the language has become in a short period in America. 2

—**Frederick Marryat,** *A Diary in America*, 1839

★ Capt. Marryat—a former British navy officer and author of *Mr. Midshipman Easy* and other novels—was personally disconcerted by one such "debasement" while accompanying a young woman to view Niagara Falls. After she slipped from a rock, he asked if she had hurt her "leg." Consternation! She turned away from him, "evidently much shocked, or much offended." He begged to know why, and after some hesitation she explained that "the word *leg* was never mentioned before ladies." The proper term turned out to be *limb*. She herself was not nearly as particular as some people, she told the Captain, "for I know those who always say limb of a table, or limb of a piano-forte."

Every word was once a poem. Every new relation is a new word. 3

—**Ralph Waldo Emerson,** *The Poet*, in *Essays: Second Series*, 1844

Language is the archives of history. 4

—**Ibid.**

Each word was at first a stroke of genius. 5

—**Ibid.**

Language is fossil poetry. 6

—**Ibid.**

She dealt her pretty words like Blades— 7
As glittering they shone—
And every One unbared a Nerve
Or wantoned with a Bone.

—**Emily Dickinson,** poem no. 479, c. 1862, in *Further Poems* [1924]

A word is dead 8
When it is said,
Some say.

I say it just
Begins to live
That day.

—**Emily Dickinson,** poem no. 1212, c. 1872

A *mugwump* is a fellow with his mug on one side of the fence and his wump on the other. 9

—**Anonymous,** possibly c. 1884

★ The most famous early mugwumps, or political independents, were Republican liberals, led by Carl Schurz of Missouri, who in 1884 supported Democrat Grover

Cleveland rather than the Republican candidate, James G. Blaine. The anonymous definition, which has been tracked in print only to the 1930s, has been credited to Rep. Albert J. Engel, who used it in a 1936 speech, and to Harold Willis Dodds, president of Princeton from 1933 to 1937, but it is almost certainly older. *Mugwump* itself is a Massachusett Indian word for *chief* and was used by the Rev. John Eliot in 1663 in place of *duke* when translating the Old Testament for Native Americans. For more on Blaine, see Robert Ingersoll at HEROES. See Horace Porter at POLITICAL SLOGANS for additional information on mugwumps.

1 The difference between the *almost*-right word and the *right* word is really a large matter—it's the difference between the lightning bug and the lightning.

—Mark Twain, letter to George Bainton, Oct. 15, 1888, reprinted as *Reply to the Editor of "The Art of Authorship,"* 1890

★ Twain may have lifted this image from his good friend Josh Billings (Henry Wheeler Shaw), who had died five years before. Billings's immensely popular sayings included the observation that "the difference between vivacity and wit is the same as the difference between the lightning-bug and the lightning." The plagiarism almost certainly was unconscious. Twain, who was about the last writer in need of stealing from others, had done this sort of thing inadvertently before. The dedication of his first book, *Innocents Abroad* (1869), repeated the dedication of a collection of poems by Oliver Wendell Holmes, Sr. Twain had read the poems but forgotten the dedication. He was mortified when the unintentional theft was pointed out to him, wrote an abject apology to Holmes, and was immediately and completely forgiven. See also Twain at ART: STYLE IN WRITING & EXPRESSION.

2 The only people that should use the word "we" are editors, kings, and persons with tapeworms.

—Mark Twain, attributed in *The New Yorker*, Talk of the Town [May 1, 1989]

★ Attributed to Twain in several forms, but we editors have not been able to verify it.

3 Words are slippery.

—Henry Brooks Adams, *The Education of Henry Adams*, 1907

4 The short words are the best.

—William Jay Gaynor, saying

★ Judge Gaynor was Tammany Hall's candidate for New York City mayor in 1909. An erudite and testy man, he proved to be uncontrollably honest—and blunt. One of his unhappy opponents was William Randolph Hearst, who used his paper the New York *Morning Journal* as a base for attacks on Gaynor. The judge and reform prevailed in the election, but in August 1910, a disgruntled city worker, who was a *Journal* reader, shot and seriously wounded Gaynor; the mayor never fully recovered. A photographer from Joseph Pulitzer's *Evening World* by chance caught the shooting in a now-famous photograph. The city editor is said to have reacted with delight: "Blood all over him—and exclusive, too!" See the note at the Zelda Fitzgerald quote at ADVERTISING, ADVERTISING SLOGANS, & PUBLICITY for more on Gaynor.

5 A shorter and more ugly word.

—Theodore Roosevelt, 1907

★ Roosevelt apparently hesitated to accuse financier Edward H. Harriman explicitly of lying. But this was his implicit characterization of a published claim by Harriman that in 1904 Roosevelt had agreed in essence to exchange an ambassadorship for much needed campaign funds. Roosevelt did call the claim "a deliberate and willful untruth," adding, "by rights it should be characterized by an even shorter and more ugly word." The word "lie" is one of those terms that almost guarantee that a libel suit will be filed, and one had best be sure of winning it.

One of our defects as a nation is a tendency to use what have been called "weasel words." 1

—**Theodore Roosevelt,** speech, St. Louis, May 31, 1916

★ Roosevelt was attacking Woodrow Wilson's call for universal voluntary military training. "You can have universal training, or you can have voluntary training," Roosevelt said, "but when you use the word 'voluntary' to qualify the word 'universal,' you are making a 'weasel word'; it has sucked all the meaning out of 'universal.' " Roosevelt heard of weasel words as a young man while visiting Maine. He stayed with the Sewall family, whom he liked very much, excepting perhaps Sam Sewall, a deacon. Roosevelt wrote that Sam was "very adroit in using fair-sounding words which completely nullified the meaning of other fair-sounding words which preceded them." Deacon Sewall's brother, Dave, explained, "His words weasel the meaning of the words in front of them, just like a weasel when he sucks the meat out of an egg and leaves nothing but the shell." Roosevelt commented, "I always remembered 'weasel words' as applicable to certain forms of oratory, especially political oratory," *My Debt to Maine* in the anthology *Maine My State*, 1919.

Omit needless words. 2

—**William Strunk, Jr.,** *The Elements of Style*, 1918

★ More at ART: STYLE IN WRITING & EXPRESSION.

I have fallen in love with American names . . . 3
The plumed war-bonnet of Medicine Hat,
Tucson and Deadwood and Lost Mule Flat . . .
You may bury my body in Sussex grass,
You may bury my tongue at Champmedy,
I shall not be there. I shall rise and pass.
Bury my heart at Wounded Knee.

—**Stephen Vincent Benét,** *American Names*, 1927

Honeyed words like bees, 4
Gilded and sticky, with a little sting.

—**Elinor Hoyt Wylie,** *Pretty Words*, in *Collected Poems* [1932]

I love smooth words, like gold-enameled fish 5
Which circle slowly with a silken swish.

—**Ibid.**

Words are weapons, and it is dangerous . . . to borrow them from the arsenal of the enemy. 6

—**George Santayana,** *Obiter Scripta*, 1936

1 You can stroke people with words.

—F. Scott Fitzgerald, *The Crack-Up*, 1945

2 When I split an infinitive, God damn it, I split it so it will stay split.

—Raymond Chandler, letter to Edward A. Weeks, Jan. 18, 1947, in Frank MacShane, *Life of Raymond Chandler* [1976]

★ Weeks was editor of *The Atlantic Monthly*. Chandler was objecting to the unwelcome ministrations of a purist proofreader.

3 Words are chameleons, which reflect the color of their environment.

—Learned Hand, *Commissioner v. National Carbide Corp.*, 1948

4 Man does not live by words alone, despite the fact that sometimes he has to eat them.

—Adlai Stevenson, speech, Denver, Col., Sept. 5, 1952

★ By contrast, Robert Louis Stevenson claimed, "Man does not live by bread alone, but principally by catchwords," *Virginibus Puerisque*, title essay, 1881.

5 Slang is a language that rolls up its sleeves, spits on its hands, and goes to work.

—Carl Sandburg, *The New York Times*, Feb. 13, 1959

6 I can answer you in two words—im possible.

—Samuel Goldwyn, attributed

★ Fake quotes—malapropisms especially—collected around movie producer Samuel Goldwyn (born Goldfish) in much the same way as they did later around baseball star Yogi Berra. The "im possible" is an old vaudeville gag; Charlie Chaplin took credit for managing to attach it to Goldwyn, according to biographer A. Scott Berg (*Goldwyn*, 1989). Among other reputed Goldwynisms (possibly the work of Goldwyn's publicist, Pete Smith) are: "Gentlemen, include me out," "Quick as a flashlight," "You've got to take the bull by the teeth," and "If nobody wants to see your picture, there's nothing you can do to stop them." See also Goldwyn at ART: THEATER, DRAMA, MOVIES & MAGIC, LAW, and SCIENCE: PSYCHOLOGY.

7 Words are a great trap.

—Marianne Moore, answering a question from the audience, 92nd St. Y, New York City, 1968

8 Only where there is language is there world.

—Adrienne Rich, *The Demon Lover*, in *Leaflets*, 1969

9 The use of language is all we have to pit against death and silence.

—Joyce Carol Oates, speech, National Book Awards, 1969

10 One man's vulgarity is another man's lyric.

—John M. Harlan, *Cohen v. California*, 1971

★ The "vulgarity" in this Vietnam Era case was a "single four-letter expletive" on a man's jacket that expressed his opinion of the draft. Noting that "we cannot indulge the facile assumption that one can forbid particular words without running a substantial risk of suppressing ideas," the court concluded (with three dissenters) that the state may not make the simple public display of the word a criminal offense.

Language is a virus from outer space. 1

—**William S. Burroughs,** quoted in *Home of the Brave*, multimedia production by Laurie Anderson, 1985

Ugly things should be called by ugly names. 2

—**Francis H. Wade,** report to a convention of the Episcopal Diocese of Washington, Jan. 30, 1988

★ Rev. Dr. Wade was explaining why a commission on racism decided not to change its name.

The minute any word has that much power, everyone on the planet should scream it. 3

—**Quentin Tarantino**, quoted in *Empire*, Nov. 1994

★ The word was the taboo word "nigger," used frequently in Tarantino's film *Pulp Fiction*.

It depends on what the meaning of *is* is. 4

—**Bill Clinton**, grand jury testimony, Aug. 17, 1998

★ The issue was whether the president should have corrected his lawyer during a deposition eight months earlier when the lawyer said, regarding an affidavit by former White House intern Monica Lewinsky, "There is absolutely no sex of any kind in any manner, shape or form." Because the lawyer had used the present tense, and because he himself had not engaged in "improper contact" with Ms. Lewisky for some time previously, Mr. Clinton maintained that he was not obligated to make a correction.

Words alter, words add, words subtract. 5

—**Susan Sontag,** *The Photographs Are Us,* in *The New York Times Magazine,* May 23, 2004

★ This observation related to Secretary of Defense Donald Rumsfeld's comment in a May 4, 2004 press conference on the treatment of Iraqi prisoners in Abu Graib prison. "My impression is that what has been charged thus far is abuse, which I believe technically is different from torture. And therefore I'm not going to address the 'torture' word."

A sentence is an idea. An idea with urgency. 6

—**Linda Gregg**, *The Problem of Sentences*, in *The New Yorker*, Feb. 14 & 21, 2005

Last Words

See also ART: THEATER, DRAMA, MAGIC & MOVIES (Edmund Gwenn); DEATH; EPITAPHS & GRAVESTONES; FREEDOM (David Crockett); LIFE (Crowfoot); SUICIDE.

To be like Christ is to be a Christian. 7

—**William Penn,** last words, May 30, 1718

I only regret that I have but one life to lose for my country. 8

—**Nathan Hale,** at the gallows in the British Artillery Park, N.Y., c. Sept. 22, 1776

★ See AMERICAN REVOLUTION for more on Hale, and for his doomed counterpart in the British army, Maj. John André.

1 'Tis well.

—George Washington, Dec. 14, 1799

★ Washington had already told his doctor that he was dying hard but not afraid; see DEATH. He was, however, frightened of being buried alive—something that probably happens more often than we like to think. Just before death, he instructed his secretary, Tobias Lear, "I am just going. Have me decently buried, and do not let my body be put into the vault in less than three days after I am dead. Do you understand me?" When Lear nodded, Washington then spoke his last, and died a few hours later, close to midnight.

2 Sixty-four years ago, it pleased the Almighty to to call me into existence—here on this spot, in this very room; and now shall I complain that he is pleased to call me hence?

—Gouverneur Morris, on his deathbed, 1816

★ Morris was a wealthy, handsome, patrician libertine, who played a major role in the Revolution and at the Constitutional Convention in 1787. He helped to write and edit the document, and was one of the few to call for an end to slavery.

3 Is it the Fourth?

—Thomas Jefferson, last words, July 3, 1826

★ Jefferson did live one day more day, reaching the fiftieth anniversary of the Fourth of July, as he had hoped.

4 Thomas Jefferson survives.

—John Adams, July 4, 1826

★ Jefferson had died about two hours earlier; see also INDEPENDENCE DAY. At the time of John Adam's death, his son John Quincy Adams was president of the United States.

5 This is the last of earth! I am content.

—John Quincy Adams, Feb. 23, 1848

★ Adams, after serving as the sixth president of the U.S., went on to represent Massachusetts in the U.S. House of Representatives for seventeen years. He suffered a stroke there on February 21 and died two days later. See also Philip Hone on Adams at EPITAPHS & GRAVESTONES.

6 Oh, do not cry—be good children and we will all meet in heaven.

—Andrew Jackson, June 8, 1845

★ Jackson, on his deathbed, to his griefstricken household.

7 The South! The South! God knows what will become of her.

—John C. Calhoun, March 31, 1850

8 An American kneels only to his god, and faces his enemy.

—W. H. Crittenden, Havana, August 16, 1851

★ On being ordered by a Spanish officer to kneel down before being shot as a filibusterer—a soldier of fortune—in Cuba.

This *is* a beautiful country. **1**

—John Brown, on his way to the gallows, Dec. 2, 1859

★ To the hangman he said, "Do not keep me waiting. I am ready at any time." For his last written words, see CIVIL WAR. For his statement at his trial, see AMERICAN HISTORY: MEMORABLE MOMENTS.

One world at a time. **2**

—Henry David Thoreau, remark in the last week of his life, 1862

★ This is said to have been Thoreau's answer when a visitor, somewhat impertinently, asked how "the opposite shore" appeared to him. Other reports of last, or nearly last, words from Thoreau include: "I did not know we had ever quarreled, aunt," in response to his aunt Louisa's inquiry as to whether he had made his peace with God; and, to his sister Sophie, "Now comes good sailing."

Texas. Texas. **3**

—Samuel Houston, attributed last words, 1863

Let us cross over the river and rest under the shade of the trees. **4**

—Thomas J. "Stonewall" Jackson, May 10, 1863

★ Gen. Jackson, a victim of friendly fire, was shot inadvertently on May 2 by his own troops while returning from a nighttime reconaissance of Union lines during the battle of Chancellorsville. The deeply religious Jackson had written in an 1862 letter: "God has fixed the time for my death. I do not concern myself about that, but to be always ready, no matter when it may overtake me.—That is the way all men should live, and then all would be equally brave." See under CIVIL WAR for Jackson's nickname and under EPITAPHS & GRAVESTONES for U. S. Grant on Jackson's character.

Strike the tent. **5**

—Robert E. Lee, attributed last words, Oct. 12, 1870

★ Some accounts say Lee prefaced these words with "Tell Hill he *must* come up," but Emory Thomas concluded in *Robert E. Lee* (1995) that all these "last words" were part of the process of making Lee's life into a legend even as he lay dying. In truth, Lee suffered a massive stroke on September 28 that left him passive and apparently speechless for the last two weeks of his life.

Now comes the mystery. **6**

—Henry Ward Beecher, March 8, 1887

[Life] is the little shadow which runs across the grass and loses itself in the sunset. **7**

—Crowfoot, last words, 1890

★ More at LIFE.

Not our will, but His be done. **8**

—William McKinley, on his deathbed, Sept. 11, 1901

★ President McKinley was shot by an anarchist.

Put out the light. **9**

—Theodore Roosevelt, last words, Jan. 6, 1919

1 *Adieu, mes amis. Je vais à la gloire.* (Farewell, my friends. I am going to glory.)
—**Isadora Duncan,** attributed, as she got into a car in Nice on the evening of Sept. 14, 1927, in Mary Desti, *Isadora Duncan's End* [1929]

★ Neither La Duncan nor the driver of the open car noticed that one end of her long silk scarf had become entangled in the spokes of a rear wheel. As the car sped away, she was pulled over the car's side, thrown with great force onto the cobblestone street, and died instantly.

2 It is very beautiful over there.
—**Thomas Edison,** Oct. 18, 1931

3 I'm glad it was me instead of you, Frank. The country needs you.
—**Anton Cermak,** remark to Franklin D. Roosevelt, Miami, Feb. 15, 1933

★ Cermak, the mayor of Chicago, was standing next to president-elect Roosevelt's car when Giuseppe Zangara, an out-of-work bricklayer, fired shots in their direction. Cermak was wounded in the abdomen and died a few days later.

4 Rosebud.
—**Herman J. Mankiewicz & Orson Welles,** *Citizen Kane*, screenplay, 1941

★ Kane's last communication. *Rosebud* was the name of Kane's sled when he was a boy. See also REGRET.

5 I have a terrific pain in the back of my head.
—**Franklin D. Roosevelt,** suffering a cerebral hemorrhage, April 12, 1945

★ The ailing president was in the living room of the Little White House in Warm Springs, Ga., working and reading. With him were his cousins Margaret Lynch (Daisy) Suckley and Laura Delano, Lucy Mercer Rutherfurd, and a portrait painter, Elizabeth Shoumatoff. The last words have also been recorded as, "I have a terrific headache." He collapsed immediately and never recovered consciousness. The news flew round the world. In Germany, Propaganda Minister Goebbels telephoned Hitler, "My Führer! I congratulate you. Roosevelt is dead. . . . It is the turning point!"

6 What is the answer? [*I was silent.*] In that case, what is the question?
—**Gertrude Stein,** last words, 1946, reported in Alice B. Toklas, *What Is Remembered* [1963]

7 Seventeen whiskeys. A record, I think.
—**Dylan Thomas,** after a fatal bout of drinking at the White Horse Tavern in Manhattan in 1953

★ Thomas was Welsh, of course, but his spirit is very much alive in this American bar, where he was a regular for a time.

8 I had rather be a servant in the house of the Lord than sit in the seat of the mighty.
—**Alben Barkley,** April 30, 1956

★ He was vice president under Harry S. Truman, 1949–53.

9 Like anybody, I would like to live a long life. Longevity has its place. But I'm not concerned about that now. I just want to do God's will. And he's allowed me to go up to

the mountain. And I've looked over, and I've seen the promised land. I may not get there with you, but I want you to know tonight that we as a people will get to the promised land. . . . So I'm happy tonight. I'm not worried about anything. I'm not fearing any man. Mine eyes have seen the glory of the coming of the Lord.

—**Martin Luther King, Jr.,** speech to sanitation workers, Memphis, Tenn., April 3, 1968

★ King was shot the next morning. The speech is renowned for its sense of impending death. Seconds before he was hit, King said to his friend Ben Branch, "Ben, make sure you play *Precious Lord, Take My Hand*. Play it real pretty for me."

Vancouver, Vancouver, this is it. 1

—**David Johnston,** at the eruption of Mount St. Helens, May 18, 1980

★ U.S. Geological Survey scientist Johnston was on duty at the volcano when it erupted. He was one of 57 people killed in the explosion. The viewing site Johnston Ridge Observatory is named for him.

I now begin the journey that will lead me into the sunset of my life. I know that for 2
America there will always be a bright dawn ahead.

—**Ronald Reagan,** letter of farewell to the American people announcing his affliction with Alzheimer's disease, Nov. 5, 1994

Too bad you can only live so long. 3

—**Richard Versalle,** Jan. 5, 1996

★ The tenor was standing on a ladder as he sang this line from the opening scene of Leoš Janáček's *The Makropulos Case* at New York City's Metropolitan Opera House when his voice faltered and he fell to the stage and died.

Laughter & Mirth

See also HUMOR.

A human being should beware how he laughs, for then he shows all his faults. 4

—**Ralph Waldo Emerson,** *Journals*, 1836

A laugh's the wisest, easiest answer to all that's queer. 5

—**Herman Melville,** *Moby-Dick*, 1851

Mirth is the Mail of Anguish. 6

—**Emily Dickinson,** poem no. 165, c. 1860

★ *Mail* in the sense of armor.

Laughing has always been considered by theologians as a crime. 7

—**Robert G. Ingersoll,** speech, Chicago, Nov. 26, 1882

Against the assault of laughter, nothing can stand. 8

—**Mark Twain,** *The Mysterious Stranger* [1922]

We laugh and laugh. Then cry and cry—Then feebler laugh. Then die. 9

—**Mark Twain,** *Notebook* [1935]

1 Laugh, and the world laughs with you;
Weep, and you weep alone;
For the sad old earth must borrow its mirth,
But has trouble enough of its own.
—**Ella Wheeler Wilcox,** *Solitude*, in *Collected Poems*, 1917

2 One horse-laugh is worth ten thousand syllogisms.
—**H. L. Mencken,** *Prejudices: Fourth Series*, 1924

3 There's a lot to be said for making people laugh.
—**Preston Sturges,** *Sullivan's Travels,* screenplay, 1941

4 Frivolity is the species' refusal to suffer.
—**John Lahr,** *Vaudeville,* PBS television, Nov. 26, 1997

★ Critic John Lahr's father, Bert Lahr, was a vaudeville star, although now best remembered as the Cowardly Lion in the movie *The Wizard of Oz*.

Law

See also CONSTITUTION, THE; CRIME, CRIMINALS, & DETECTIVES; EVIDENCE; HABIT & CUSTOM (Santayana and Stevenson); JUDGES; JURIES; JUSTICE; LAWYERS; SUPREME COURT; WEST, THE (Anonymous).

5 Laws like to cobwebs catch small flies;
Great ones break through before your eyes.
—**Benjamin Franklin,** *Poor Richard's Almanack*, 1734

★ An update from Solon, 7th century B.C.: "Laws are like spiders' webs: If some poor weak creature come up against them, it is caught; but a big one can break through and get away," quoted in Diogenes Laërtius, *Lives of Eminent Philosophers*, third century A.D.

6 Laws too gentle are seldom obeyed; too severe, seldom executed.
—**Benjamin Franklin,** *Poor Richard's Almanack*, 1756

7 It is of more importance to the community that innocence should be protected than it is that guilt should be punished; for guilt and crimes are so frequent in the world that all of them cannot be punished; and many times they happen in such a manner that it is not of much consequence to the public whether they are punished or not.
—**John Adams,** closing statement for the defense, second Boston Massacre trial, Dec. 3, 1770

★ In one of the finest moments of his long public career, Adams took on the exceedingly unpopular task of defending the British captain and eight soldiers charged with murder for firing on a Boston mob the previous March, killing three people outright and wounding two fatally. The officer and men were tried separately. The captain was acquitted in October and six of the eight soldiers in December. The two remaining men were found guilty of manslaughter, punished by having their thumbs branded, and discharged from the army. See also Benjamin Franklin below and Adams at FACTS.

A government of laws, and not of men. **1**

—John Adams, "Novanglus" papers, No. 7, *Boston Gazette*, 1774

★ Adams credited the phrase to the English political writer James Harrington, who used the expression in his Utopian work, *The Commonwealth of Oceana*, 1656. Thanks to Adams, the phrase appears in Article 30 of the Declaration of Rights in the Massachusetts Constitution, 1780.

That it is better one hundred guilty persons should escape than that one innocent person should suffer is a maxim that has been long and generally approved. **2**

—Benjamin Franklin, letter to Benjamin Vaughan, March 14, 1785

★ The maxim, identified as such, was also cited by Voltaire: " 'Tis much more prudence to acquit two persons, though actually guilty, than to pass sentence of condemnation on one that is virtuous and innocent," *Zadig*, 1749. It is enshrined in Sir William Blackstone's *Commentaries on the Laws of England* (1765–69): "It is better that ten guilty persons escape than one innocent suffer." See also the first John Adams quote above. In more recent times, early in the McCarthy era of communist-hunting, judge Learned Hand said, "I would rather take the chance that some traitors will escape detection than spread abroad a spirit of general suspicion and distrust, which accepts rumor and gossip in place of undismayed and unintimidated inquiry," speech to the Board of Regents, University of the State of New York, Oct. 24, 1952.

Laws are a dead letter without courts to expound their true meaning and operation. **3**

—Alexander Hamilton, *The Federalist*, No. 22, 1788

The execution of the laws is more important than the making of them. **4**

—Thomas Jefferson, letter to the Abbé Arnoux, July 19, 1789

Law is whatever is boldly asserted and plausibly maintained. **5**

—Aaron Burr, attributed, quoted in James Parton, *The Life and Times of Aaron Burr* [1857]

In general, the great can protect themselves, but the poor and humble require the arm and shield of the law. **6**

—Andrew Jackson, letter to John Quincy Adams, August 26, 1821

Scarcely any political question arises in the United States that is not resolved, sooner or later, into a judicial question. **7**

—Alexis de Tocqueville, *Democracy in America*, 1835

Good men must not obey the laws too well. **8**

—Ralph Waldo Emerson, *Politics*, in *Essays: Second Series*, 1844

It is not desirable to cultivate a respect for the law, so much as for the right. **9**

—Henry David Thoreau, *Civil Disobedience*, 1849

★ In 1843, Thoreau refused to pay a state tax as a protest against the legality of slavery in the U.S. Constitution. He was arrested in 1846 by constable and tax collector Samuel Staples, who was trying to get his accounts in order preparatory to resigning. Thoreau spent only one night in jail; a woman—probably his Aunt Maria—paid the tax. Actually, according to Thoreau scholar Walter Harding, Thoreau probably should not have been in jail at all: the applicable law mandated seizure of property to cover any unpaid tax. But then we would not have this essay on civil disobedience, which is the seminal text advocating passive resistance as a political tool. See also Thoreau at MEXICAN WAR.

1 There is more law in the end of policeman's nightstick than in a decision of the Supreme Court.

—**Alexander S. Williams,** attributed c. 1870, in Herbert Asbury, *The Gangs of New York* [1937]

★ Inspector "Clubber" Williams earned his soubriquet while a patrolman in Hell's Kitchen, on the west side of Manhattan. Moving across town, he became a captain in the Gas House district, where he subdued the notorious Gas House Gang with a squad of club-swinging policemen. In 1876, he went on to serve in the 29th precinct, in the center of Manhattan, which acquired a new name when Williams told a friend, "I've had nothing but chuck steak for a long time, and now I'm going to get a little of the tenderloin."

2 The life of the law has not been logic: it has been experience.

—**Oliver Wendell Holmes, Jr.,** *The Common Law*, 1881

3 The law embodies the story of a nation's development through many centuries, and it cannot be dealt with as if it contained only the axioms and corollaries of a book of mathematics.

—**Ibid.**

4 Hear ye! Hear ye! This honorable court's now in session; and if any galoot wants to snort afore we start, let him step up the bar and name his pizen.

—**Roy Bean,** attributed

★ Numerous sources report—with minor variations in wording—that this is how Judge Bean opened court sessions following his appointment in 1882 as justice of the peace in Langtry, Texas. Bean's fame stretched so far that train passengers often stopped off at Langtry to get a look at the "Law West of the Pecos" (in the words of the sign that graced his saloon-cum-court). When he died in 1903, newspapers all over the nation ran his obituary. See also Bean at TEXAS in the note on the anonymous quote regarding the absence of law west of the Pecos.

5 The law is not the place for the artist or the poet. . . . The law is the calling of thinkers.

—**Oliver Wendell Holmes, Jr.,** *The Profession of the Law*, lecture to Harvard undergraduates, Feb. 17, 1886

6 Law is merely the expression of the will of the strongest for the time being, and therefore, laws have no fixity, but shift from generation to generation.

—**Brooks Adams,** *The Law of Civilization and Decay*, 1896

7 No man is above the law and no man is below it; nor do we ask any man's permission when we require him to obey it.

—**Theodore Roosevelt,** 3rd annual message, Dec. 7, 1903

8 Great cases like hard cases make bad law.

—**Oliver Wendell Holmes, Jr.,** *Northern Securities Co. v. U.S.*, 1904

★ Holmes is alluding to the legal byword: "Hard cases make bad law."

General propositions do not decide concrete cases. **1**
—**Oliver Wendell Holmes, Jr.,** dissent, *Lochner v. New York*, 1905

It is a fortunate thing for society that the courts do not get the same chance at the Ten Commandments as they do at the Constitution of the United States. **2**
—**Philander C. Johnson,** *Senator Sorghum's Primer of Politics*, 1906

Lawsuit, n. A machine which you go into as a pig and come out as a sausage. **3**
—**Ambrose Bierce,** *The Devil's Dictionary*, 1906

If facts are changing, law cannot be static. **4**
—**Felix Frankfurter,** speech, 1912

It cannot be helped, it is as it should be, that the law is behind the times. **5**
—**Oliver Wendell Holmes, Jr.,** speech, Harvard Law School Association of New York, Feb. 15, 1913

No great idea in its beginning can ever be within the law. How can it be within the law? The law is stationary. The law is fixed. The law is a chariot wheel which binds us all regardless of conditions or place or time. **6**
—**Emma Goldman,** *Address to the Jury*, in *Mother Earth*, July 17, 1917

One with the law is a majority. **7**
—**Calvin Coolidge,** speech, July 27, 1920

Law never is, but is always about to be. **8**
—**Benjamin Cardozo,** lecture, *The Nature of the Judicial Process*, Yale Law School, 1921

I must say that as a litigant I should dread a lawsuit beyond anything else short of sickness and death. **9**
—**Learned Hand,** *The Deficiencies of Trials to Reach the Heart of the Matter*, in *Lectures on Legal Topics*, 1921

★ Hand was a judge in federal courts from 1909 to 1951. On the theme of the fallibility of trials, see also Hand at JURIES.

The law must be stable but it must not stand still. **10**
—**Roscoe Pound,** *Introduction to the Philosophy of Law*, 1922

★ Pound, who became dean of the Harvard School of Law, was one of nation's foremost legal theorists.

A nuisance may be merely a right thing in the wrong place,—like a pig in the parlor instead of the barnyard. **11**
—**George Sutherland,** *Euclid v. Amber Realty Co.*, 1926

Go to jail. Go directly to jail. Do not pass Go. Do not collect $200. **12**
—**Charles Bruce Darrow,** Community Chest card in Monopoly, 1931

★ Darrow created the popular board game.

If we would guide by the light of reason, we must let our minds be bold. **13**
—**Louis D. Brandeis,** *N. Y. State Ice Co. v. Liebmann*, 1932

1 Legal concepts are supernatural entities which do not have a verifiable existence except to the eyes of faith.
—Felix S. Cohen, *Transcendental Nonsense and the Functional Approach*, 1935

2 The law [is] a horrible business.
—Clarence Darrow, interview, *The New York Times*, April 19, 1936

3 I am the law.
—Frank Hague, quoted in *The New York Times*, Nov. 11, 1937

★ Hague, the boss of Jersey City and Hudson County, was testifying in a legislative investigation when he made this comment. He had been asked by what right he had prohibited picketing and the distribution of prolabor literature.

4 Under our constitutional system, courts stand against any winds that blow as havens of refuge for those who might otherwise suffer because they are helpless, weak, outnumbered, or because they are non-conforming victims of prejudice and public excitement.
—Hugo L. Black, *Chambers v. Florida*, 1938

★ More from this decision is given at SUPREME COURT.

5 While it may not be true that laws and constitutions do not act to right wrong and overturn established folkways overnight, it is also true that the reaffirmation of these principles of democracy builds a body of public opinion in which rights and privileges of citizenship may be enjoyed.
—Thurgood Marshall, in the N.A.A.C.P. magazine, *The Crisis*, July, 1939

6 A verbal contract isn't worth the paper it's written on.
—Samuel Goldwyn, attributed

★ Unlike most other Goldwynisms—see LANGUAGE & WORDS—which were purely fictitious, this quote is a distortion of something the movie producer actually said. Referring to Joseph M. Schenck, a Hollywood executive whose word was considered his bond, Goldwyn declared, according to *They Never Said It* (1989) by Paul F. Boller, Jr., and John George: "His verbal contract is worth more than the paper it's written on." The mangled version made a better story, however, and this is the one that press agents and columnists popularized.

7 There is no surer way to misread any document than to read it literally.
—Learned Hand, dissent, *Guiseppe v. Walling*, 1944

8 The law is bigger than money, but only if the law works hard enough.
—Thomas E. Dewey, quoted in Richard Norton Smith, *Thomas E. Dewey* [1982]

9 The history of American freedom is, in no small measure, the history of procedure.
—Felix Frankfurter, *Malinski v. New York*, 1945

★ Justice Frankfurter made the same point in similar words in *McNabb v. United States*, 1943. For a later, metaphorical expression of the same idea, see Robert Cover, et al., below.

We don't give a damn about the law. Down here we make our own law. 1

—**Eugene "Bull" Connor,** quoted in *The Afro-American*, Nov. 22, 1958

★ Connor, the Public Safety Commissioner of Birmingham, Ala., was responding to a question about the legality of arresting for vagrancy three African-American ministers from Montgomery, who had come to Birmingham to confer with a colleague.

Morality cannot be legislated but behavior can be regulated. Judicial decrees may 2
not change the heart, but they can restrain the heartless.

—**Martin Luther King, Jr.,** *Strength to Love*, 1963

An individual who breaks a law that conscience tells him is unjust, and who willingly 3
accepts the penalty of imprisonment in order to arouse the conscience of the community over its injustice, is in reality expressing the highest respect for the law.

—**Martin Luther King, Jr.,** *Why We Can't Wait*, 1964

To live outside the law, you must be honest. 4

—**Bob Dylan,** *Absolutely Sweet Marie*, in the album, *Blonde on Blonde*, 1966

An impeachable offense is whatever a majority of the House of Representatives con- 5
siders [it] to be at a given moment in history.

—**Gerald R. Ford,** April 15, 1970

★ Rep. Ford was speaking in the House on the proposed impeachment of liberal Supreme Court Justice William O. Douglas. Four years later, Ford was Vice President, and as such succeeded the impeached president Richard Nixon, who resigned.

Procedure is the blindfold of justice. 6

—**Robert M. Cover, Owen M. Fiss, & Judith Resnik,** *Procedure*, 1988

★ See also Felix Frankfurter above in *McNabb v. United States.*

A state of war is not a blank check when it come to the rights of the nation's citizens. 7

—**Sandra Day O'Connor,** Supreme Court majority opinion, *Hamdi v. Rumsfeld*, June 28, 2004

★ American citizen Esam Hamdi had been designated an enemy combatant by Department of Defense Secretary Donald Rumsfeld. The Administration argued that this designation can be applied to citizens and non-citizens alike, and that it cancels all rights under U.S. law.

Lawyers

One thing I supplicate your majesty: that you will give orders, under a great penalty, 8
that no bachelors of law should be allowed to come here [the New World]; for not only are they bad themselves, but they also make and contrive a thousand iniquities.

—**Vasco Nuñez de Balboa,** to Ferdinand V of Spain, 1513

In no country, perhaps, in the world is the law so general a study. The profession 9
itself is numerous and powerful, and in most provinces [in America] it takes the lead.

—**Edmund Burke,** speech in Parliament moving his resolution on conciliation with the colonies, March 22, 1775

1 Accuracy and diligence are much more necessary to a lawyer than great comprehension of mind or brilliancy of talent.

—**Daniel Webster,** letter to Thomas Merrill, Nov. 11, 1803

2 The New England folks have a saying that three Philadelphia lawyers are a match for the very devil himself.

—**Anonymous,** *Salem Observer*, March 13, 1824

★ The reputation of Philadelphia lawyers was already several decades old. Fred R. Shapiro in *American Legal Quotations* (1993) cites a reference from 1788 in the *Columbian Magazine*: "They have a proverb here [in London] . . . in speaking of a difficult point, they say, *'it would puzzle a Philadelphia lawyer.'* " Shapiro speculates that the reputation of Philadelphia lawyers may stem from Andrew Hamilton's defense of publisher John Peter Zenger in New York in 1735. Zenger was charged with libel, and his acquittal helped to establish truth as a defense in such cases.

3 The lawyers of the United States form a party which is but little feared and scarcely perceived. . . . But this party extends over the whole community, and penetrates into all the classes which compose it; it acts upon the country imperceptibly, but finally fashions it to suit its own purposes.

—**Alexis de Tocqueville,** *Democracy in America*, 1835

4 Civil laws are familiarly known only to lawyers, whose direct interest it is to maintain them as they are, whether good or bad, simply because they themselves are conversant with them.

—**Ibid.**

5 Resolve to be honest at all events: and if in your judgment you cannot be an honest lawyer, resolve to be honest without being a lawyer. Choose some other occupation.

—**Abraham Lincoln,** notes for a lecture, 1850

6 Weary lawyers with endless tongues.

—**John Greenleaf Whittier,** *Maud Muller*, 1854

7 You cannot live without the lawyers, and certainly you cannot die without them.

—**Joseph H. Choate,** speech, *The Bench and the Bar,* May 3, 1879

8 Mr. Evarts, rising, hands in pockets: "Does it not seem unusual to this gathering that a professional humorist should appear to be funny?" Mr. Twain: "Does it not also appear strange to this assembly that a lawyer should have his hands in his own pockets?"

—**Mark Twain,** in *The Wit & Wisdom of Mark Twain*, Alex Ayres, ed. [1987]

★ William M. Evarts, one of the most distinguished lawyers of the second half of the nineteenth century, also served as U.S. Attorney General, Secretary of State, and Senator from New York. The exchange with Twain is said to have taken place at a banquet in New England.

9 To succeed in other trades, capacity must be shown; in the law, concealment will do.

—**Mark Twain,** *Pudd'nhead Wilson's New Calendar*, in *Following the Equator*, 1897

The government of the United States is, and always has been, a lawyer's government. **1**
—Chauncey M. Depew, speech, New York City, Nov. 5, 1898

Lawyer, n. One skilled in circumvention of the law. **2**
—Ambrose Bierce, *The Devil's Dictionary*, 1906

Dice, n. Small polka-dotted cubes of ivory, constructed like a lawyer to lie on any **3**
side, but commonly on the wrong one.
—Ibid.

A law, Hennessy, that might look like a wall to you or me would look like a triumphal **4**
arch to the experienced eye of a lawyer.
—Finley Peter Dunne, *Mr. Dooley on the Power of the Pres*, in *American Magazine*, no. 62, 1906

America is the paradise of lawyers. **5**
—David J. Brewer, attributed

★ Justice Brewer was credited with this by Champ Clark, who was Speaker of the House 1911–19, in his autobiography, *My Quarter Century of American Politics*, 1920.

Why is there always a secret singing **6**
When a lawyer cashes in?
Why does a hearse horse snicker
Hauling a lawyer away?
—Carl Sandburg, *The Lawyers Know Too Much*, in *Smoke and Steel*, 1920

★ Sandburg also used a popular joke about lawyers in *The People, Yes*; see below.

Lawyer: The only man in whom ignorance of the law is not punished. **7**
—Elbert Hubbard, *Roycroft Dictionary and Book of Epigrams*, 1923

People are getting smarter nowadays; they are letting lawyers instead of their con- **8**
science be their guide.
—Will Rogers, *How to Stop the Bootleggin'*, weekly column, April 8, 1923

★ The joke reappears in the screenplay of *Detective Story*, 1951, by Philip Yordan and Robert Wyler: "What do you got in place of a conscience? Don't answer. I know—a lawyer." Wyler was the brother of the director, William Wyler. The movie was an adaptation of Sidney Kingsley's Broadway play of the same title.

There are two things wrong with almost all legal writing. One is its style. The other **9**
is its content.
—Fred Rodell, *Goodbye to Law Reviews*, in *Virginia Law Review*, 38, 1936

★ Yale Law Professor Rodell's article raised quite a storm. David Margolick described it in 1980 in the *National Law Journal* as "perhaps the most widely read—and most controversial article in all of legal literature." But it did no good, at least not in the eyes of Professor Rodell, who dismissed law-review authors generally as "professional purveyors of pretentious poppycock" in a 1980 follow-up, *Goodbye to Law Reviews—Revisited*.

1 "Have you a criminal lawyer in this burg?"
"We think so, but we haven't been able to prove it on him yet."
—Carl Sandburg, *The People, Yes*, 1936

2 Daniel Webster: You seem to have an excellent acquaintance with the law, sir.
The Devil: Sir, that is no fault of mine. Where I come from, we have always gotten the pick of the Bar.
—Stephen Vincent Benét, *The Devil and Daniel Webster*, 1939

3 There's gotta be a law—even for lawyers.
—Harry Ruskin & Niven Busch, *The Postman Always Rings Twice*, screenplay, 1946

★ Lana Turner to her lawyer, Hume Cronyn.

4 Courage is the most important attribute of a lawyer. . . . It should pervade the heart, the halls of justice, and the chambers of the mind.
—Robert F. Kennedy, speech, University of San Francisco Law School, Sept. 29, 1962

5 A lawyer with his briefcase can steal more than a hundred men with guns.
—Mario Puzo, *The Godfather*, 1969

6 Ninety percent of our lawyers serve ten percent of our people. We are over-lawyered and under-represented.
—Jimmy Carter, speech, 100th anniversary of the Los Angeles County Bar Association, May 4, 1978

7 I'm not a potted plant. I'm here as a lawyer. That's my job.
—Brendan Sullivan, hearing in the U.S. Senate, July 9, 1987

★ Attorney Sullivan was justifying his aggressive tactics in defense of his client, Col. Oliver North.

8 Like an usher in a dark movie theater, holding the client by the hand, the lawyer guides him through the maze of law and regulation which now enmeshes all our lives.
—Simon H. Rifkind, speech, 1984, quoted in *The New York Times* [Nov. 11, 1995]

9 Lawyers are the high priests of America.
—Tony Kushner, *Angels in America*, 1992

Laziness

See also Dreams & Sleep (first two entries).

10 Laziness travels so slowly that poverty soon overtakes it.
—Benjamin Franklin, *The Way to Wealth*, July 7, 1757

The man who does not betake himself at once and desperately to sawing is called a loafer, though he may be knocking at the doors of heaven all the while. 1
—**Henry David Thoreau,** *The Pond in Winter*, in *Walden*, 1854

Lazy fokes' stummucks don't git tired. 2
—**Joel Chandler Harris,** *Nights with Uncle Remus*, 1883

Leaders

See HIGH POSITION: RULERS & LEADERS.

Leisure

It is a great art to saunter. 3
—**Henry David Thoreau,** *Journal*, April 26, 1841

★ In *Walking*, 1862, Thoreau suggests that *saunter* comes from the French la Sainte Terre, the Holy Land. In the Middle Ages, wandering beggars would claim to be going à la Sainte Terre, and thus came to be called *Saint-Terrers*. Professional etymologists reject this charming theory in favor of the view that *saunter* comes from the Middle English *santren*, to muse, or the 15th-century *saunteryng*, aimless talk. In any case, Thoreau thought that the saunter was the right gait for travel; see SPEED.

I loaf and invite my soul; 4
I lean and loaf at my ease, observing a spear of
Summer grass.
—**Walt Whitman,** *Song of Myself*, 1855

There can be no high civilization where there is not ample leisure. 5
—**Henry Ward Beecher,** *Proverbs from Plymouth Pulpit*, 1887

It takes application, a fine sense of value, and a powerful community spirit for a people to have serious leisure, and this has not been the genius of the Americans. 6
—**Paul Goodman,** *Growing Up Absurd*, 1960

Turn on, tune in, drop out. 7
—**Timothy Leary,** saying, 1960s

Leisure does not automatically develop the soul. And this is the real dilemma of Americans. 8
—**Margaret Mead,** in *Life* magazine, August 23, 1968

Liberals

See POLITICS & POLITICIANS.

Liberty

See FREEDOM.

Lies

See DISHONESTY & LIES.

Life

See also FATE & DESTINY; TIME; WORLD

1 Our days begin with trouble here,
Our life is but a span,
And cruel death is always near,
So frail a thing is man.
—**The New England Primer,** c. 1683

2 Dost thou love life, then do not squander time, for that's the stuff life is made of.
—**Benjamin Franklin,** *Poor Richard's Almanack*, June 1746

★ Franklin, however, had a weakness for that great time-waster, chess; see GAMES. See also Franklin at TIME.

3 Wish not so much to live long as to live well.
—**Benjamin Franklin,** *Poor Richard's Almanack*, June 1746

4 We are always getting ready to live but never living.
—**Ralph Waldo Emerson,** *Journal*, April 13, 1834

★ For another Emerson view of life, from 1847, see below.

5 Tell me not in mournful numbers,
Life is but an empty dream!
For the soul is dead that slumbers,
And things are not what they seem.

Life is real! Life is earnest!
And the grave is not its goal;
Dust thou art, to dust returnest,
Was not spoken of the soul.
—**Henry Wadsworth Longfellow,** *A Psalm of Life*, 1839

6 Life is a series of surprises.
—**Ralph Waldo Emerson,** *Circles*, in *Essays: First Series*, 1841

★ See also Emerson at PATTERNS.

7 These struggling tides of life that seem
In wayward, aimless course to tend,
Are eddies of the mighty stream
That rolls to its appointed end.
—**William Cullen Bryant,** *The Crowded Street*, 1843

8 Life consists in what a man is thinking of all day.
—**Ralph Waldo Emerson,** *Journal*, July–Aug. 1847

My life has been the poem I would have writ, 1
But I could not both live and utter it.
—Henry David Thoreau, *A Week on the Concord and Merrimack Rivers*, 1849

Life is made up of marble and mud. 2
—Nathaniel Hawthorne, *The House of Seven Gables*, 1851

The mass of men lead lives of quiet desperation. What is called resignation is confirmed desperation. 3
—Henry David Thoreau, *Economy,* in *Walden*, 1854

I went to the woods because I wished to live deliberately, to front only the essential facts of life, and see if I could not learn what it had to teach, and not, when I came to die, discover that I had not lived. 4
—Henry David Thoreau, *Where I Lived, and What I Lived For, Ibid.*

I love a broad margin to my life. 5
—Henry David Thoreau, *Solitude, Ibid.*

Ships that pass in the night, and speak each other in passing, 6
Only a signal shown and a distant voice in the darkness;
So on the ocean of life we pass and speak one another,
Only a look and a voice; then darkness again and a silence.
—Henry Wadsworth Longfellow, *The Theologian's Tale: Elizabeth*, in *Tales of a Wayside Inn*, 1863–74

The outward wayward life we see, 7
The hidden springs we may not know—
It is not ours to separate
The tangled skein of will and fate.
—John Greenleaf Whittier, *Snow-Bound*, 1866

That it will never come again 8
Is what makes life so sweet.
—Emily Dickinson, poem no. 1741

Life is a shadowy, strange, and winding road. 9
—Robert G. Ingersoll, speech, Chicago, Nov. 26, 1882

I think that, as life is action and passion, it is required of a man that he should share the action and passion of his time at peril of being judged not to have lived. 10
—Oliver Wendell Holmes, Jr., Memorial Day speech, Keene, N.H., 1884

★ See also Holmes at PASSION.

What is life? It is the flash of a firefly in the night. It is the breath of a buffalo in the wintertime. It is the little shadow which runs across the grass and loses itself in the sunset. 11
—Crowfoot, last words, 1890

1 Life is the game that must be played.
—Edwin Arlington Robinson, *Ballade by the Fire: Envoy,* in *The Children of the Night,* 1897

2 Believe that life *is* worth living, and your belief will help create the fact.
—William James, *The Will to Believe*, 1897

3 The events of life are mainly small events—they only seem large when we are close to them.
—Mark Twain, *Autobiography* [1924]

★ See also Twain at MIND, THOUGHT, & UNDERSTANDING.

4 Life is a dangerous business—few indeed get out of it alive.
—Elbert Hubbard, *Little Journies to the Homes of English Authors*, Vol. Six, (Robert Burns), 1900

5 That life is worth living is the most necessary of assumptions and, were it not assumed, the most impossible of conclusions.
—George Santayana, *Life of Reason: Reason in Common Sense,* 1905

6 Life is just one damn thing after another.
—Elbert Hubbard, *Philistine*, Dec., 1909

★ The quote also has been attributed to New York *Sun* reporter Ward O'Malley, according to *Nice Guys Finish Seventh* by Ralph Keyes. For a response, see Edna St. Vincent Millay, below.

7 Life is painting a picture, not doing a sum.
—Oliver Wendell Holmes, Jr., *The Class of '61*, speech, Cambridge, Mass., June 28, 1911

8 And life is too much like a pathless wood.
—Robert Frost, *Birches*, 1916

9 The proper function of man is to live, not to exist. I shall not waste my days in trying to prolong them. I shall use my time.
—Jack London, to friends, 1916, reported in San Francisco *Bulletin*, Dec. 2, 1916

★ Known as London's credo, this speech began: "I would rather be ashes than dust! I would rather that my spark burn out in a brilliant blaze than it be stifled by dry-rot. I would rather be a superb meteor, every atom of me in magnificent glow, than a sleepy and permanent planet." A life of adventure and extraordinary achievement broke his health and he died two months later, at forty.

10 I have measured out my life with coffee spoons.
—T. S. Eliot, *The Love Song of J. Alfred Prufrock*, 1917

11 I want to love first, and live incidentally.
—Zelda Fitzgerald, letter to F. Scott Fitzgerald, 1919

12 Pray for the dead and fight like hell for the living!
—Mother Jones, *Autobiography*, 1925

Life is for each man a solitary cell whose walls are mirrors. **1**
—Eugene O'Neill, *Lazarus Laughed*, 1927

Strange interlude! Yes, our lives are merely strange dark interludes in the electrical **2**
display of God the Father!
—Eugene O'Neill, *Strange Interlude*, 1928

★ See also O'Neill at THE PRESENT.

It's not true that life is one damn thing after another—it's one damn thing over and **3**
over.
—Edna St. Vincent Millay, letter to Arthur Davison Ficke, Oct. 24, 1930

Birth, copulation, and death. **4**
That's all the facts when you come to brass tacks.
—T. S. Eliot, *Sweeney Agonistes*, 1932

Life is an offensive, directed against the repetitious mechanism of the universe. **5**
—Alfred North Whitehead, *Adventures of Ideas*, 1933

Life is a succession of second bests. **6**
—George Santayana, letter to George Sturgis, July 9, 1934

Do any human beings ever realize life while they live it?—every, every minute? **7**
—Thornton Wilder, *Our Town*, 1938

Time that is intolerant **8**
Of the brave and the innocent,
And indifferent in a week
To a beautiful physique.
—W. H. Auden, *In Memory of W. B. Yeats*, 1940

★ Auden later deleted this and the next two verses.

Life, as it is called, is for most of us one long postponement. **9**
—Henry Miller, *The Enormous Womb*, in *The Wisdom of the Heart*, 1941

i thank You God for most this amazing **10**
day . . .
i who have died am alive again this day
—E. E. Cummings, *I thank You God for most this amazing*, in *Xaipe*, 1950

The song sparrow, who knows how brief and lovely life is, says, "Sweet, sweet, sweet **11**
interlude; sweet, sweet, sweet interlude."
—E. B. White, *Charlotte's Web*, 1952

Our existence is but a brief crack of light between two eternities of darkness. **12**
—Vladimir Nabokov, *Speak, Memory*, 1947

★ Or, hardly more cheery: "Human life is but a series of footnotes to a vast obscure unfinished manuscript," *Pale Fire*, 1962.

1 Let's face it, life is mainly wasted time.

—John Berryman, 1954

★ Poet Berryman made this remark to a promising student, Philip Levine, who included it in his *The Bread of Time: Toward an Autobiography*, 1994.

2 You're only here for a short visit. Don't hurry. Don't worry. And be sure to smell the flowers along the way.

—Walter C. Hagen, *The Walter Hagen Story,* 1956

3 Life is the process of finding out, too late, everything that should have been obvious at the time.

—John D. MacDonald, *The Only Girl in the Game*, 1960

4 We are involved in a life that passes understanding, and our highest business is our daily life.

—John Cage, *Where Are We Going? And What Are we Doing?*, in *Silence*, 1961

5 There is always inequity in life. Some men are killed in a war, and some men are wounded, and some men never leave the country. . . . Life is unfair.

—John F. Kennedy, press conference, March 23, 1962

6 Man's life is not a business.

—Saul Bellow, *Herzog*, 1964

★ Herzog makes this point in a letter to the president protesting that IRS regulations are turning Americans into a nation of bookkeepers.

7 Like sands through the hourglass, so are the days of our lives.

—Ted Corday & Irna Phillips, signature line, *Days of Our Lives* soap opera, 1965

★ The line, spoken by star Macdonald Carey and written by the show's creators, includes a loose reference to the last verse of the 23rd Psalm: "Surely goodness and mercy shall follow me all the days of my life: and I will dwell in the house of the Lord for ever."

8 There must be more to life than having everything.

—Maurice Sendak, *Higglety, Pigglety Pop!*, 1967

9 Dying is no big deal. The least of us can manage that. Living is the trick.

—Walter "Red" Smith, funeral eulogy for golf impresario Fred Corcoran, 1977

10 Life is something to do when you can't get to sleep.

—Fran Lebowitz, *Metropolitan Life*, 1978

11 Our lives carry us along in ways we cannot control, and almost nothing stays with us.

—Paul Auster, *The Locked Room*, 1986

12 Life is short, and it's up to you to make it sweet.

—Sadie Delany, *Having Our Say: The Delany Sisters' First 100 Years*, 1993, written with her sister, Bessie Delany

★ The Delany sisters were both over one hundred years old when this book was published.

A man is many men in his life. 1

—**William Manchester,** remark near end of his life, quoted in obituary, *The Hartford Courant,* June 14, 2004

★ Manchester was a war hero, foreign correspondent, family man, professor, historian, and a prodigious writer.

Like all good things 2
Life tend to go too long.

—**John Ashbery**, *Broken Tulips,* in *Where Shall I Wander*, 2005

Lincoln, Abraham

★ *Note to the reader:* Beware of Lincoln quotes that fit contemporary political debates. Fakes abound. In particular, since 1916, a number of maxims invented by Rev. William John Henry Boetcker have been misidentified as sayings of Lincoln and widely promulgated. For example, Ronald Reagan, addressing the Republican National Convention in 1992, quoted Lincoln thus: "You cannot strengthen the weak by weakening the strong. You cannot help the wage earner by pulling down the wage payer. You cannot help the poor by destroying the rich. You cannot help men permanently by doing for them what they could and should do for themselves." That is Boetcker speaking, not Lincoln, as *New York Times* writer Herbert Mitgang promptly pointed out. Other counterfeits include "You cannot keep out of trouble by spending more than your income" and "You cannot establish sound security on borrowed money."

In 1954, Postmaster General Summerfield used these same all-too-apt Boetcker-Lincoln quotes, and he, too, was corrected, by scholar Roy Basler and Democratic National Committee Chairman Stephen A. Mitchell in an Associated Press article. George Seldes, in *The Great Quotations*, claims that Summerfield's most immediate source was a 1942 leaflet from the Committee for Constitutional Government. A convicted German agent, Edward A. Rumely, was one of the leaders of that committee.

The infamous anti-Catholic "Lincoln warning," which alludes to a "dark cloud coming from Rome," is also spurious. And serving the other extreme of political spectrum, lines such as "All that serves labor serves the nation" are not authentic Lincoln.

Fox populi. 3

—**Anonymous**, *Vanity Fair*, 1863

★ A negative evaluation of the president, punning on *vox populi* and Lincoln's respect for ordinary citizens. As Carl Sandberg wrote in *Abraham Lincoln, the War Years*, "To him the great hero was The People. He could not say too often that he was merely their instrument." For more on *vox populi*, see under William Tecumseh Sherman at THE PEOPLE.

He is a barbarian, Scythian, Yahoo, a gorilla in respect of outward polish, but a most sensible, straight-forward old codger. 4

—**George Templeton Strong,** in Allan Nevins, ed., *The Diary of George Templeton Strong*

★ Strong, a wealthy New York lawyer, was a friend of Lincoln.

1 Now he belongs to the ages.
—Edwin Stanton, at Lincoln's deathbed, April 15, 1865

★ War Secretary Stanton's view of Lincoln had changed over time from contempt to admiration. He wept as he pronounced this eulogy. The moment was recorded in the diary of John Hay, a secretary to Lincoln. He and Stanton "rushed into the little room across from the theater where Lincoln lay . . . a look of unspeakable peace came upon his worn features. It was Stanton who broke the silence by saying, 'Now he belongs to the ages.' "

2 I mourned and yet shall mourn with ever-returning spring.
—Walt Whitman, *When Lilacs Last in the Dooryard Bloom'd*, 1865–66

★ From Whitman's lyric elegy for Lincoln; more at SORROW & GRIEF. See also below. In the war, Whitman served as a volunteer helping to care for wounded Union soldiers.

3 O Captain! my Captain! our fearful trip is done,
The ship has weathered every rack, the prize we sought is won.
—Walt Whitman, *O Captain! My Captain!*, 1865-66

★ The reference is to the Civil War and the death of Lincoln, and the poem ends "on the deck my Captain lies, / Fallen cold and dead."

4 His heart was as great as the world, but there was no room in it to hold a memory of a wrong.
—Ralph Waldo Emerson, *Greatness*, in *Letters and Social Aims*, 1876

5 And when he fell in whirlwind, he went down
As when a lordly cedar, green with boughs,
Goes down with a great shout against the hills,
And leaves a lonesome place against the sky.
—Edwin Markham, *Lincoln, the Man of the People*, in *Lincoln and Other Poems*, 1901

6 The prairie-lawyer, master of us all.
—Vachel Lindsay, *Abraham Lincoln Walks at Midnight*, 1914

7 In this temple, as in the hearts of the people for whom he saved the Union, the memory of Abraham Lincoln is inscribed forever.
—Royal Cortissoz, inscription, Lincoln Memorial, Washington, D.C., dedicated Memorial Day, 1922

★ The author was art critic at the *New York Herald Tribune*.

8 A lonesome train on a lonesome track,
Seven coaches painted black . . .
A slow train, a quiet train,
Carrying Lincoln home again.
—Millard Lampell, *The Lonesome Train*, 1943

Loneliness

See SOLITUDE & LONELINESS.

Losers

See FOOLS & STUPIDITY; SPORTS; WINNING & LOSING, VICTORY & DEFEAT.

Louisiana

See also AMERICAN HISTORY: MEMORABLE MOMENTS (Livingston on the Louisiana Purchase); CITIES (NEW ORLEANS).

The thousands of warblers and thrushes, the richly blossoming magnolias, the holly, **1**
beech, tall yellow poplar, red clay earth, and hilly ground delighted my eye.

—**John James Audubon,** *Journal*, 1820

★ Audubon was visiting at Oakley Farm, near Bayou Sara.

Smoothly the ploughshare runs through the soil, as a keel through the water. **2**
All the year round the orange-groves are in blossom; and grass grows
More in a single night than in a whole Canadian summer.
Here, too, numberless herds run wild and unclaimed in the prairies.

—**Henry Wadsworth Longfellow,** *Evangeline*, 1847

★ The narrative poem is based on an apparently true story of a young couple separated when England exiled some 6,000 French settlers from Acadia in Nova Scotia. The poem was an immediate success, and is required reading in Louisiana, where a large group of exiles formed what we now call Cajun communities. Huey Long turned the story to his political advantage in one of the great speeches of his era; see below.

In Louisiana, the live-oak is the king of the forest, and the magnolia is its queen. **3**

—**Joseph Jefferson,** *The Autobiography of Joseph Jefferson*, 1917

And it is here, under this oak where Evangeline waited for her lover, Gabriel. . . . But **4**
Evangeline is not the only one who has waited here in disappointment. Where are the schools that you have waited for your children to have, that have never come? Where are the roads and highways that you send your money to build, that are no nearer now than before? Where are the institutions to care for the sick and disabled? Evangeline wept bitter tears in her disappointment, but it lasted through only one lifetime. Your tears in this country, around this oak, have lasted for generations. Give me the chance to dry the tears of those who still weep here!

—**Huey P. Long,** speech, 1927

★ Long was running for governor, and was elected with massive popular support. He combined a yen for absolute power with a compelling vision of social justice. He was assassinated in 1935.

The poor people of Louisiana have only three friends: Jesus Christ, Sears and **5**
Roebuck, and Earl Long.

—**Ron Shelton,** *Blaze*, screenplay, 1989

★ Paul Newman, playing Earl Long, speaks this line in the film about Governor Long's infatuation with stripper Blaze Starr; the movie drew on her book, *Blaze Starr*, written with Huey Perry. According to Ralph Keyes's *Nice Guys Finish Seventh*, however, the line had an earlier incarnation in Georgia, where the reference was to that state's governor Eugene Talmadge.

1 Union, justice, and confidence.
—Motto, state of Louisiana

Love

See also HEART; MARRIAGE; SEX; WOMEN & MEN.

2 If you would be loved, love and be loveable.
—**Benjamin Franklin,** *Poor Richard's Almanack*, 1755

3 Love is little; Love is low;
Love will make our spirit grow;
Grow in peace,
Grow in light,
Love will do the thing that's right.
Shaker song, c.1800

4 Tell me whom you love, and I'll tell you who you are.
—**Anonymous,** Creole proverb, quoted in Richard Newman, *African American Quotations* [1998]

5 O, there is nothing holier in this life of ours than the first consciousness of love—the first fluttering of its silken wings; the first rising sound and breath of that wind, which is soon to sweep through the soul, to putrify or to destroy!
—**Henry Wordsworth Longfellow,** *Hyperion*, 1839

6 Love is omnipresent in nature as motive and reward. Love is our highest word and the synonym of God.
—**Ralph Waldo Emerson,** *Love*, in *Essays: First Series*, 1841

7 The passion of love is not felt with the same intensity by either sex in this country as even in France; still less so than in England, and with nothing approaching the ardour with which this passion burns in Portugal, in Spain, in Italy.
—**J. S. Buckingham,** *The Slave States of America, 1839*, 1842

8 Love keeps the cold out better than a cloak. It is food and raiment.
—**Henry Wadsworth Longfellow,** *The Spanish Student*, 1843

9 Give all to love;
Obey thy heart.
—**Ralph Waldo Emerson,** *Give All to Love*, in *Poems*, 1847

10 Better to be wounded, a captive and a slave, than always to walk in armor.
—**Margaret Fuller,** *Summer on the Lakes*, 1844

11 Love is the bright foreigner, the foreign self.
—**Ralph Waldo Emerson,** *Journal*, 1849

Oh, the earth was *made* for lovers. **1**
—Emily Dickinson, poem no. 1, *Valentine Week*, c. 1850

Love—is anterior to life— **2**
Posterior—to death—
Initial of Creation, and
The Exponent of Earth.
—Emily Dickinson, poem no. 917, 1864

Unable are the Loved to die, **3**
For Love is Immortality,
Nay, it is Deity—
—Emily Dickinson, poem no. 1809, c. 1864

Love iz like the meazles; we kant have it bad but onst, and the later in life we have it the tuffer it goes with us. **4**
—Josh Billings, *Josh Billings: His Sayings*, 1865

So blind is life, so long at last is sleep, **5**
And none but love to bid us laugh or weep.
—Willa Cather, *Evening Song*, in *April Twilights*, 1903

The love we give away is the only love we keep. **6**
—Elbert Hubbard, *The Note Book* [1927]

Earth's the right place for love: **7**
I don't know where it's likely to go better.
—Robert Frost, *Birches*, 1916

I want to love first, and live incidentally. **8**
—Zelda Fitzgerald, letter to F. Scott Fitzgerald, 1919

What thou lovest well is thy true heritage. **9**
—Ezra Pound, *Hugh Selwyn Mauberley: E.P. Ode pour l'élection de son sepulchre*, 1920

Love at the lips was touch **10**
As sweet as I could bear;
And once that seemed too much;
I lived on air.
—Robert Frost, *To Earthward*, 1923

Love is an emotion experienced by the many and enjoyed by the few. **11**
—George Jean Nathan, *Attitude Toward Love and Marriage*, in *The Autobiography of an Attitude*, 1925

★ Nathan, the most distinguished and feared theater critic of his day, also observed, "Love is the emotion that a woman feels always for a poodle dog and sometimes for a man," *General Conclusions About the Coarse Sex*, in *The Theater, the Drama, the Girls*, 1921.

1 and kisses are a better fate than wisdom.
—E. E. Cummings, *since feeling is first*, in *Is 5*, 1926

2 By the time you swear you're his,
Shivering and sighing,
And he vows his passion is
Infinite, Undying—
Lady, make a note of this:
One of you is lying.
—Dorothy Parker, *Unfortunate Coincidence*, in *Enough Rope*, 1927

3 Oh, life is a glorious cycle of song,
A medley of extemporanea;
And love is a thing that can never go wrong;
And I am Marie of Roumania.
—Dorothy Parker, *Comment*, in *Enough Rope*, 1927

4 What is love? . . . It is the morning and the evening star.
—Sinclair Lewis, *Elmer Gantry*, 1927

5 As the rain falls
so does
your love
bathe every
open
object of the world
—William Carlos Williams, *Rain*, in *Poems*, 1930

6 Love is
unworldly
and nothing
comes of it but love.
—Ibid.

7 Three great mysteries there are in the lives of mortal beings: the mystery of birth at the beginning; the mystery of death at the end; and greater than either, the mystery of love. Everything that is most precious in life is a form of love. Art is a form of love, if it be noble; labor is a form of love, if it be worthy; thought is a form of love, if it be inspired.
—Benjamin N. Cardozo, officiating at a wedding, 1931, in Andrew L. Kaufman, *Cardozo* [1998]

8 We must love one another or die.
—W. H. Auden, *September 1, 1939*, 1939

★ This dark poem became darker yet when Auden decided the famous line was "a damned lie." We are going to die anyway. He changed it to, "We must love one another and die."

★ See also Williams at FORGIVENESS.

love is the whole and more than all. **1**

—E. E. Cummings, *my father moved through dooms of love*, 1940

Love is more serious than philosophy. **2**

—W. H. Auden, *For the Time Being: A Christmas Oratorio*, In Memoriam Constance Rosalie Auden, 1870–1941

love is a deeper season **3**
than reason;
my sweet one
(and april's where we're).

—E. E. Cummings, *yes is a pleasant country*, in *One Times One* (or *1* × *1*), 1944

When I'm not near the girl I love, **4**
I love the girl I'm near.

—E. Y. "Yip" Harburg, *When I'm Not Near the Girl I Love*, in *Finian's Rainbow*, 1947

Love is the delusion that one woman differs from another. **5**

—H. L. Mencken, *A Mencken Chrestomathy*, 1949

I am the least difficult of men. All I want is boundless love. **6**

—Frank O'Hara, *Meditations in an Emergency*, 1957

Love is born of faith, lives on hope, and dies of charity. **7**

—Gian Carlo Menotti, notebook for opera *Maria Golovin*, 1958

Love is that condition in which the happiness of another person is essential to your own. **8**

—Robert A. Heinlein, *Stranger in a Strange Land*, 1961

Make love not war. **9**

—Gershon Legman, lecture, Ohio University, 1963

★ Legman claimed to be the author of this popular slogan protesting the Vietnam war, according to his obituary in the *International Herald Tribune*, Mar. 15, 1999. We see no reason to doubt him. He specialized in the scholarly study of such sexually laden subjects as dirty jokes, limericks, and erotic folklore.

Hatred paralyzes life; love releases it. Hatred confuses life; love harmonizes it. Hatred darkens life; love illumines it. **10**

—Martin Luther King, Jr., *Strength to Love*, 1963

Love means not ever having to say you're sorry. **11**

—Erich Segal, *Love Story*, 1970

★ In the movie, the line is, "Love means never having to say you're sorry."

1 Love is purely a creation of the human imagination . . . the most important example of how the imagination continually outruns the creature it inhabits.
—**Katherine Anne Porter,** in *Contemporary Novelists*, 1976

2 Sometimes love is stronger than man's convictions.
—**Isaac Bashevis Singer,** in *The New York Times Magazine,* Nov. 26, 1978

3 If all of us just loved and cared for one person each. That is all it takes. Love breeds love. Maybe then we will be able to prevent each other from going insane.
—**Yoko Ono,** letter to world, following murder of her husband, John Lennon, Dec. 8, 1980

4 If love is the answer, could you rephrase the question?
—**Lily Tomlin,** in David Housham and John Frank-Keyes, *Funny Business* [1992]

5 You don't love because, you love despite; not for the virtues, but despite the faults.
—**William Faulkner,** quoted in Willie Morris, *Faulkner's Mississippi* in *National Geographic* [March 1989]

6 Love is an irresistible desire to be irresistibly desired.
—**Robert Frost,** in *Life* magazine [April 1992]

7 Nobody loves me but my mother,
And she could be jiving, too.
—**B. B. King,** blues lyric, quoted by Roy Blount, Jr., *The New York Times Book Review* [Dec. 11, 1994]

Love, Expressions of

8 If ever two were one, then surely we.
If ever man were loved by wife, then thee.
If every wife was happy with a man,
Compare with me ye women if you can.
—**Anne Bradstreet,** *To My Dear and Loving Husband* [1678]

★ Anne Bradstreet grew up in Sempringham Castle in England, where her father, Thomas Dudley, was steward to the earl of Lincoln. She married Simon Bradstreet at about age sixteen—the date of her birth is uncertain. She and her husband and parents came to America two years later in the company of Gov. John Winthrop and other Puritans. She was the first important poet in the colonies. She raised eight children; seven survived her, a rare record in that harsh environment. She lived to age fifty-eight.

9 Thou wast that all to me, love,
For which my soul did pine—
A green isle in the sea, love,
A fountain and a shrine,
All wreathed with fairy fruits and flowers,
And all the flowers were mine.
—**Edgar Allan Poe,** *To One in Paradise*, 1834

Thou art to me a delicious torment. **1**

—Ralph Waldo Emerson, *Friendship*, in *Essays: First Series*, 1841

I was a child and she was a child **2**
In this kingdom by the sea,
But we loved with a love that was more than love—
I and my Annabel Lee.

—Edgar Allan Poe, *Annabel Lee*, 1849

Why don't you speak for yourself, John? **3**

—Henry Wadsworth Longfellow, *The Courtship of Miles Standish*, 1858

★ Priscilla Mullens posed this question to John Alden, who had been wooing her in behalf of his friend Miles Standish, the military leader of the Plymouth colony—but an older man. Moreover, the object of his affection is not pleased by this approach to courtship. "If I am not worth the wooing, I surely am not worth the winning," she remarks. Longfellow was a descendant of John and Priscilla, and the famous question had been handed down in family lore. Alden, incidentally, was one of the signers of the Mayflower Compact, agreed to aboard ship in 1620.

A woman waits for me, she contains all, nothing is lacking. **4**

—Walt Whitman, *A Woman Waits for Me*, in *Leaves of Grass*, 1871

Around her neck she wore a yellow ribbon, **5**
She wore it for her lover who was far, far away.

—Anonymous, folk song, in Oscar Brand, *Bawdy Songs and Back-Room Ballads* [1960]

★ Union soldiers during the Civil War wore yellow neckerchiefs and tradition has it that their wives and sweethearts remembered them by wearing yellow ribbons. This may be the source of the folk song, which provided the theme and title for the 1949 John Ford movie about cavalrymen on the plains, *She Wore a Yellow Ribbon*, as well as the 1971 incident, reported by Pete Hamill in the *New York Post*, in which a woman in Brunswick, Georgia, let her husband, returning from four years in prison in New York, know that she still loved him by tying twenty or thirty yellow handkerchiefs around a tree in the middle of the town. Hamill's story formed the basis for the 1973 hit song by Irwin Levine and L. Russell Brown, *Tie a Yellow Ribbon Around the Ole Oak Tree*, and this song, in turn, inspired Penne Laingen, of Bethesda, Maryland, wife of one of the Americans held hostage in Iran for 444 days in 1979–81, to start a campaign to remember the captives with yellow ribbons. A decade later, during the Gulf War of 1990–91, trees and lamposts around the nation again were festooned with yellow ribbons, signifying support for the war itself as well as for Americans sent to fight it. Yellow ribbons, mainly in the form of magnetic replicas affixed to automobiles, also were displayed following the 2003 attack on Iraq to show support for American troops.

Will you love me in December as you do in May? **6**

—James J. Walker, *Will You Love Me in December?*, song

★ Jimmy Walker borrowed from John Alexander Joyce, who wrote: "I shall love you in December / With the love I gave in May!" Walker's verse was set to music in 1905 by Ernest R. Ball. Walker went on to become mayor of New York City in the 1920s. As an earlier quote master, Bergen Evans, pointed out, Walker's whoopee lifestyle was scandalous, even for the roaring twenties. Evans commented, "The answer of the public to the query in his song was 'No.' "

1 Music I heard with you was more than music,
And bread I broke with you was more than bread.
Now that I am without you, all is desolate;
And all that once was so beautiful is dead.
—Conrad Aiken, *Bread and Music*, 1914

2 I wish they were emeralds.
—Charles MacArthur, offering peanuts to Helen Hayes, c. 1925

★ The line worked. And twenty years later, he gave her emeralds. "I wish they were peanuts," he said.

3 Why is it no one ever sent me yet
One perfect limousine, do you suppose?
Ah no, it's always just my luck to get
One perfect rose.
—Dorothy Parker, *One Perfect Rose*, in *Enough Rope*, 1927

4 If you want to buy my wares
Follow me and climb the stairs . . .
Love for sale.
—Cole Porter, *Love for Sale*, in *The New Yorkers*, 1930

★ The Federal Communications Commission banned the song's lyrics from the nation's airwaves for many years. Playing the music alone was permissible. It was okay for listeners to sing along in the privacy of their homes and automobiles.

5 Spices hung about him. He was a glance from God.
—Zora Neale Hurston, *Their Eyes Were Watching God*, 1937

6 Here's looking at you, kid.
—Julius Epstein, Philip Epstein, & Howard Koch, *Casablanca*, screenplay, 1942

★ Humphrey Bogart to Ingrid Bergman.

7 He was my North, my South, my East and West,
My working week and my Sunday rest,
My noon, my midnight, my talk, my song;
I thought that love would last forever: I was wrong.
—W. H. Auden, *Songs and Older Musical Pieces*, III, in *The Collected Poetry of W. H. Auden* [1945]

8 Lolita, light of my life, fire of my loins. My sin. My soul.
—Vladimir Nabokov, *Lolita*, 1955

★ The novel's opening line.

Him that I love, I wish to be 1
Free—
Even from me.
—**Anne Morrow Lindbergh,** *Even*, in *The Unicorn and Other Poems, 1935–1955*, 1956

Love me tender, love me sweet, 2
Never let me go.
—**Elvis Presley,** with Vera Matson, *Love Me Tender*, 1956

There is something I want to say to you. I've wanted to say it for years. World, I love 3
you. I have always loved you . . . or almost always.
—**Edna Ferber,** *A Kind of Magic*, 1963

★ See also WORLD, THE.

Loyalty

See also AMBITION & ASPIRATION (Jackson); CHANGE (Lincoln); UNITY.

True to friend and foe. 4
—**William F. "Buffalo Bill" Cody,** personal motto, in announcer's spiel prior to the star's entrance in his touring Wild West show, from 1883

An ounce of loyalty is worth a pound of discretion. 5
—**Elbert Hubbard,** *The Note Book*, 1927

I meant what I said 6
And I said what I meant—
An elephant's faithful
One hundred per cent!
—**Dr. Seuss** (Theodor Seuss Geisel), *Horton Hatches the Egg*, 1940

Keep the faith, baby! 7
—**Adam Clayton Powell, Jr.,** motto and book title, 1967

★ Based on the Bible, *II Timothy*, 4:7, "I have fought a good fight, I have finished my course, I have kept the faith." Powell succeeded his father as pastor of the Abyssinian Baptist Church in Harlem in 1937 and later became the nation's most famous African-American congressman.

Loyalty is a very attractive quality, but it doesn't get you anything. 8
—**Richard Norton Smith,** remark, *The New York Times Week in Review,* Dec. 14, 2003

★ More at POLITICS & POLITICIANS.

Luck

See also FATE & DESTINY.

Shallow men believe in luck. . . . Strong men believe in cause and effect. 9
—**Ralph Waldo Emerson,** *Worship*, in *The Conduct of Life*, 1860

1 The only sure thing about luck is that it will change.
—Bret Harte, *The Outcasts of Poker Flat*, 1869

2 Luck is not chance—
It's toil—
Fortune's expensive smile
Is earned—
—Emily Dickinson, poem no. 1350, c. 1876

3 Sometimes a crumb falls
From the tables of joy
Sometimes a bone
Is flung
To some people love is given
To others
Only heaven.
—Langston Hughes, *Luck*, in *Fields of Wonder*, 1947

4 now and then
there is a person born
who is so unlucky
that he runs into accidents
which started out to happen to somebody else.
—Don Marquis, *archy's life of mehitabel*, 1933

5 Luck is not something you can mention in the presence of self-made men.
—E. B. White, *Control*, in *One Man's Meat*, 1944

6 Luck Is the Residue of Design.
—Branch Rickey, lecture title, 1950

★ Rickey, then running the Brooklyn Dodgers, expanded the thought in this way: "Things worthwhile generally just don't happen. Luck is a fact, but should not be a factor. Good luck is whatever is left over after intelligence and effort have combined at their best" (from *Branch Rickey's Little Blue Book*, John J. Monteleone, ed., 1995).

7 If it wasn't for bad luck, I wouldn't have no luck at all.
—Albert King, *Born under a Bad Sign*, 1963

★ A folk saying that takes many forms, including this, from King's blues classic.

8 Luck is what happens when preparation meets opportunity.
—Darrell Royal, quoted in James A. Michener, *Sports in America*, 1976

★ Royal had considerable "luck," coaching U. of Texas football teams to 167 victories.

9 Luck is a dividend of sweat. The more you sweat, the luckier you get.
—Ray Kroc, quoted by Penny Moser, *The McDonald's Mystique*, in *Fortune* magazine, July 4, 1988

★ Mr. Kroc got into the fast-food business in 1955 by purchasing a franchise in Des Plaines, Ill., from Richard and Maurice McDonald, who had developed assembly-line techniques for hamburger restaurants in California. In 1961 Kroc bought out the brothers, and the rest, as they say, is history.

Hard work and a proper frame of mind prepare you for the lucky breaks that come along—or don't. **1**

—Harrison Ford, quoted by Glenn Plaskin, *The Real Harrison Ford*, in *San Francisco Chronicle*, August 13, 1990

Luxury

See also EXCESS; THINGS & POSSESSIONS.

It is for cake that we all run in debt. **2**

—Ralph Waldo Emerson, *Journals*, 1840

Most of the luxuries, and many of the so-called comforts, of life are not only not indispensable, but positive hindrances to the elevation of mankind. **3**

—Henry David Thoreau, *Economy*, in *Walden*, 1854

In the affluent society no useful distinction can be made between luxuries and necessaries. **4**

—John Kenneth Galbraith, *The Affluent Society*, 1958

Give me the luxuries in life and I will willingly do without the necessities. **5**

—Frank Lloyd Wright, *The New York Times*, obituary, April 9, 1959

A luxury once sampled becomes a necessity. Pace yourself. **6**

—Andrew Tobias, *My Vast Fortune*, 1997

Madness & Sanity

See also ALIENATION; DIFFERENCES; SCIENCE: PSYCHOLOGY.

Sanity is very rare. **7**

—Ralph Waldo Emerson, *Journal*, 1836

Here's an object more of dread **8**
Than aught the grave contains—
A human form with reason fled,
While wretched life remains.—

—Abraham Lincoln, letter to William Johnston, Sept. 6, 1846

★ Lincoln himself suffered from severe depressions, and perhaps for this reason was impressed by the misfortune of a childhood acquaintance who became insane at age nineteen and never recovered. Probably the young man suffered from schizophrenia.

Men have called me mad; but the question is not yet settled, whether madness is or is not the loftiest intelligence—whether much that is glorious—whether all that is profound—does not spring from the disease of thought—from moods of mind exalted at the expense of the general intellect. **9**

—Edgar Allan Poe, *Eleonora*, 1850

1 Much Madness is divinest sense—
To a discerning Eye—
Much Sense—the starkest Madness—
'Tis the Majority
In this, as All, prevail—
Assent—and you are sane—
Demur—you're straightway dangerous—
And handled with a Chain.
—**Emily Dickinson,** poem no. 435, c. 1862

2 Our occasional madness is less wonderful than our occasional sanity.
—**George Santayana,** *The Life of Reason: Reason in Common Sense*, 1905–1906

3 When we remember that we are all mad, the mysteries disappear and life stands explained.
—**Mark Twain,** *Mark Twain's Notebook,* Albert Bigelow Paine, ed. [1935]

4 Sanity is madness put to good uses.
—**George Santayana,** *Little Essays*, 1921

5 Insanity runs in my family. It practically *gallops*!
—**Joseph Kesserling,** *Arsenic and Old Lace*, 1941

★ Mortimer Brewster's explanation of why he can't get married.

6 Even paranoids have enemies.
—**Delmore Schwartz,** saying

7 I saw the best minds of my generation destroyed by madness, starving hysterical naked,
dragging themselves through the negro streets at dawn looking for an angry fix
angelhead hipsters burning for the ancient heavenly connection to the starry
dynamo in the machinery of the night.
—**Allen Ginsberg,** *Howl*, 1956

8 The only people for me are the mad ones, the ones who are mad to live, mad to talk, mad to be saved, desirous of everything at the same time, the ones who never yawn or say a commonplace thing, but burn, burn like fabulous yellow roman candles exploding like spiders across the stars and in the middle you see the blue centerlight pop and everybody goes "Aww!"
—**Jack Kerouac,** *On the Road*, 1957

9 My mind's not right.
. . . I myself am hell;
nobody's here.
—**Robert Lowell,** *Skunk Hour*, 1959

★ For a similar quote, see T. S. Eliot at HELL. Both poets refer to Milton's *Paradise Lost*, in which Satan declares, "Myself am hell."

I think perhaps all of us go a little crazy at times. 1
—**Robert Bloch,** *Psycho*, 1959

★ An observation by Norman Bates.

What's madness, but a nobility of soul 2
At odds with circumstance?
—**Theodore Roethke,** *In a Dark Time*, in *The Far Field*, 1964

★ The collection was published a year after the death of the poet, who had suffered periodic mental breakdowns since the mid–1930s.

All that makes a lunatic are very ordinary ideas of mankind shut up very tight inside a man's head. 3
—**Diane Arbus,** *Notebook*, 1960, cited in Patricia Bosworth, *Diane Arbus* [1985]

If you talk to God, you are praying. If God talks to you, you have schizophrenia. 4
—**Thomas Szasz,** *Emotions*, in *The Second Sin*, 1973

Depression is a wimp of a word for a howling tempest in the brain. 5
—**William Styron,** *Darkness Visible*, 1990

You ask me if I have a God complex? Let me tell you something. I *AM* God. 6
—**Aaron Sorkin,** *Malice* screenplay, 1993

To be mad is not necessarily to be creative, or there'd be a Shelley on every corner. 7
—**The New York Times,** editorial, *Making Art of Madness*, Oct. 15, 1993

Sanity is like a clearing in the jungle where the humans agree to meet from time to time and behave in certain fixed ways that even a baboon could master. 8
—**Wilfrid Sheed,** *In Love with Daylight*, 1995

Maine

See also CITIES (PORTLAND).

Land of the Bad People (*Terra Onde di Mala Gente*). 9
—**Giovanni Da Verrazzano,** May 1524

★ This was the name Verrazzano gave the Maine coast near Casco Bay on account of the "crudity and evil manners" of the local Abnaki Indians. But the Abnaki were not nearly as "bad" as the Caribs who met Verrazzano as he waded ashore in 1528 on an island in the Lesser Antilles, probably Guadeloupe. They killed and ate him immediately.

The people of the province of Maine may be divided into magistrates, husbandmen or planters, and fishermen; of the magistrates some be royalists, the rest perverse 10 spirits, the like are the planters and fishers, of which some be planters and fishers both, others mere fishers.

—**John Josselyn,** *An Account of Two Voyages to New England*, 1675

★ An early view of the land of lobsters and potatoes. See also Josselyn at DREAMS & SLEEP.

1 This is what you might call a brand-new country.

—**Henry David Thoreau,** *The Maine Woods*, 1850

2 Maine, perhaps, will soon be where Massachusetts is. A good part of her territory is already as bare and commonplace as much of our neighborhood, and her villages generally are not so well shaded as ours.

—**Henry David Thoreau,** *Travel in Concord*, in *Excursions* [1863]

3 As Maine goes, so goes the nation.

—**Anonymous,** political observation, from c. 1840

★ The maxim generally held true for presidential elections in the second half of the 19th century and until Franklin D. Roosevelt's victory in 1932. Maine, a Republican stronghold, held its state elections before the national elections. In a Republican-dominated era, Maine voters seemed in tune with the nation. But in 1936 Maine was one of only two states to support Alf Landon (the "Kansas Coolidge"). "As Maine goes, so goes Vermont," quipped Roosevelt's campaign manager, James A. Farley, after the election. Farley had predicted a sweep except for these two states. The bottom line on Maine and presidential elections: It has supported more presidential losers than any other state. See also Political Slogans (the note on "Tippecanoe and Tyler, too").

4 In Maine they have not a summer but a thaw.

—**Ralph Waldo Emerson,** *Journal*, undated, c. 1844

5 Here's to the state of Maine, the land of the bluest skies, the greenest earth, the richest air, the strongest, and what is better, the sturdiest men, the fairest, and what is best of all, the truest women under the sun.

—**Thomas B. Reed,** speech, Portland, Maine, August 7, 1900

★ Reed, one of Maine's most famous politicians, served twenty-two years in the House of Representatives, six of them as Speaker. His nickname was "Czar Reed."

6 Maine has as much geology as some states that are twice her size, which is highly creditable to her, of course.

—**Irvin S. Cobb,** *Land of Balsam Pillows and Filling Stations*, in his *American Guyed Book* series

7 Maine was the first state to vote dry and, if I am one to say, will be among the last to become so.

—**Ibid.**

8 I am lingering in Maine this winter, to fight wolves and foxes. The sun here is less strong than Florida's, but so is the spirit of development.

—**E. B. White,** *A Report in January*, 1958

"Don't ever ask directions of a Maine native," I was told. 1
"Why ever not?"
"Somehow we think it is funny to misdirect people and we don't smile when we do it, but we laugh inwardly. It is our nature."
—**John Steinbeck,** *Travels with Charley*, 1962

★ Note the state's motto, below.

Dirigo. 2
I direct. [Or, "I guide."]
—Motto, state of Maine

Majorities & Minorities

See also DEMOCRACY; DIFFERENCES; RACES & PEOPLES.

All, too, will bear in mind this sacred principle, that though the will of the majority 3
is in all cases to prevail, that will to be rightful must be reasonable; that the minority possess their equal rights, which equal law must protect, and to violate which would be oppression.
—**Thomas Jefferson,** First Inaugural Address, March 4, 1801

Tyranny of the Majority. 4
—**Alexis de Tocqueville,** section title, *Democracy in America*, 1835

★ Tocqueville was worried by the "irresistible strength of democratic institutions" in the U.S., and by "the inadequate securities which one finds there against tyranny."

A man more right than his neighbors constitutes a majority of one. 5
—**Henry David Thoreau,** *Civil Disobedience*, 1849

★ See also Andrew Jackson at COURAGE, Calvin Coolidge at LAW, and Wendell Phillips below.

One, on God's side, is a majority. 6
—**Wendell Phillips,** speech on John Brown, Brooklyn, N.Y., Nov. 1, 1859

Shall we judge a country by the majority or by the minority? By the minority, surely. 7
—**Ralph Waldo Emerson,** *Considerations by the Way*, in *The Conduct of Life*, 1860

The history of most countries has been that of majorities—mounted majorities, clad 8
in iron, armed with death, treading down the ten-fold more numerous minorities.
—**Oliver Wendell Holmes, Sr.,** speech to the Massachusetts Medical Society, May 30, 1860

Neither current events nor history show that the majority rules, or ever did rule. 9
—**Jefferson Davis,** letter to James Frazier Jacquess & James R. Gilmore, July 17, 1864

★ Davis was president of the Confederacy, 1861–65.

1 Hain't we got all the fools in town on our side? and ain't that a big enough majority in any town?

—**Mark Twain,** *Huckleberry Finn*, 1884

★ The "king" addresses this question to the "duke."

2 The majority is always in the wrong.
Whenever you find that you are on the side of the majority, it's time to reform — (or pause and reflect).

—**Mark Twain,** Oct. 13, 1904, in Albert Bigelow Paine, ed., *Mark Twain's Notebook* [1935]

3 When great changes occur in history, when great principles are involved, as a rule the majority are wrong. The minority are right.

—**Eugene Debs,** speech in his own defense in federal court, Cleveland, Sept. 12, 1918, in *Speeches of Eugene V. Debs* [1928]

★ For denouncing the prosecution of opponents of World War I under the Espionage Act of 1917, Debs was himself, tried, convicted, and sentenced to ten years in prison. In 1920, running from a prison cell for president on the Socialist ticket, he garnered more than 900,000 votes. In 1921, the winning candidate, Warren Harding, pardoned him.

4 A majority can do anything.

—**Joseph G. Cannon,** saying, quoted in the Baltimore *Sun*, March 4, 1923

★ The *Sun*'s article marked the retirement of "Uncle Joe" Cannon, who served in the House for forty-six years, and as Speaker 1903–11.

5 All politics are based on the indifference of the majority.

—**James Reston,** in *The New York Times*, June 12, 1968

6 You, the great silent majority of my fellow Americans.

—**Richard M. Nixon,** speech to the nation on the Vietnam War, Nov. 3, 1969

★ Nixon appealed directly to Americans who were worried by the antiwar, counterculture protests of the 1960s. "And so tonight," he said, "to you, the great silent majority of my fellow Americans—I ask for your support." The phrase "silent majority" had been employed previously by Nixon, along with such variants as "silent center," "quiet majority," and when accepting the Republican presidential nomination in August of 1968, the "quiet voice in the tumult of the shouting . . . . the voice of the great majority of Americans," but this was the speech that popularized the expression in a political sense. (Back in the 19th century, "silent majority" referred to those who had died and outnumbered the living.) John F. Kennedy employed the same antithesis in 1956 in *Profiles in Courage*, referring to congressmen who "may have been representing the actual sentiments of the silent majority of their constituents in opposition to the screams of a vocal minority." See also William Graham Sumner's "forgotten man" under ECONOMICS.

7 Columbus did not seek a new route to the Indies in response to a majority directive.

—**Milton Friedman,** *Reader's Digest*, June 1, 1978

8 In any great organization, it is far, far safer to be wrong with the majority than to be right alone.

—**John Kenneth Galbraith,** Manchester *Guardian*, July 28, 1989

Management Techniques

See also BUSINESS; GOVERNMENT; METHOD; MILITARY STRATEGY.

Praise in public, penalize in private. **1**

—U. S. Navy adage

★ The principle is venerable: *A Dictionary of American Proverbs* (1992) traces "Praise publicly; blame privately" to Erasmus, c. 1526, and there is no reason to think that the Dutch scholar and theologian coined it.

A memorandum is written not to inform the reader but to protect the writer. **2**

—Dean Acheson, quoted in the *Wall Street Journal* [Sept. 8, 1977]

Guidelines for bureaucrats: (1) When in charge, ponder. (2) When in trouble, delegate. (3) When in doubt, mumble. **3**

—James H. Boren, *The New York Times*, Nov. 8, 1970

★ An experienced governmental bureaucrat who had metamorphosed into an independent consultant, Boren was founder and president of NATAPROBU, the National Association of Professional Bureaucrats. He explained that NATAPROBU had dedicated itself to "optimize the status quo by fostering adjustive adherence to procedural abstractions and rhetorical clearances," *Time* magazine, Nov. 23, 1970.

Efficiency is doing things right. Effectiveness is doing the right things. **4**

—Peter F. Drucker, quoted in Robert K. Cooper, *The Performance Edge*, 1990

★ See also Bennis below.

Have three people do five jobs but pay them like four. **5**

—Arnold W. Donald, in *Fortune People*, *Fortune* magazine, Sept. 1991

Leaders are people who do the right thing. Managers are people who do things right. . . . a profound difference. **6**

—Warren Bennis, *Fortune* magazine, Sept. 19, 1994

★ And see Drucker above.

Manners

See also CONVERSATION; ELITE, THE; GRACE; GUESTS; HOSPITALITY; STYLE.

In the Presence of Others Sing not to yourself with a humming Noise, nor Drum with your Fingers or Feet. **7**

—George Washington, copybook, *Rules of Civility & Decent Behavior In Company and Conversation*, c. 1747

★ Washington laboriously copied the 110 *Rules* as guidance for his personal conduct. Other maxims in the set, originally codified in the sixteenth-century by Jesuit priests for the benefit of French aristocrats: "When you Sit down, Keep your Feet firm and Even, without putting one on the other or Crossing them," "Kill no Vermin as Fleas, lice ticks &c in the Sight of Others," "Shew not yourself glad at the Misfortune of another though he were your enemy," and "Use no reproachfull Language against any one, neither Curse nor Revile."

1 A gentleman makes no noise; a lady is serene.
—**Ralph Waldo Emerson,** *Manners*, in *Essays: Second Series*, 1844

2 Manners are the happy way of doing things.
—**Ralph Waldo Emerson,** *Behavior*, in *The Conduct of Life*, 1860

3 Manners make the fortune of the ambitious youth.
—**Ibid.**

4 Manners require time, as nothing is more vulgar than haste.
—**Ibid.**

5 Never be haughty to the humble; never be humble to the haughty.
—**Jefferson Davis,** speech, Richmond, Va., July 22, 1861

★ Davis was unable to master this excellent advice himself. In the words of the editor of the *Southern Literary Messenger*, he was "cold, haughty, peevish, narrow-minded, pig-headed, *malignant*."

6 To attempt to describe any phase of American manners without frequent reference to the spittoon is impossible. It would be like the play of Hamlet with the part of Hamlet omitted.
—**G. A. Sala,** *My Diary in America in the Midst of War*, 1865

★ Oscar Wilde agreed. "America is one long expectoration," he announced in a newspaper interview during his 1882 tour of the U.S.

7 Good manners are made up of petty sacrifices.
—**Ralph Waldo Emerson,** *Letters and Social Aims*, 1876

8 The stately manners of the old school.
—**Henry Wadsworth Longfellow,** *Michael Angelo*, 1883

9 Good breeding consists in concealing how much we think of ourselves and how little we think of the other person.
—**Mark Twain,** in Albert Bigelow Paine, ed., *Mark Twain's Notebook* [1935]

10 To do *exactly as your neighbors* do is the only sensible rule.
—**Emily Post,** *Etiquette*, 1922

11 Etiquette can be at the same time a means of approaching people and of staying clear of them.
—**David Riesman**, *The Lonely Crowd*, 1950

12 Morals are three-quarters manners.
—**Felix Frankfurter,** saying

★ The Supreme Court Justice was quoted in Harlan Phillips, *Felix Frankfurter Reminiscences* [1960].

13 You never want to give a man a present when you know he's feeling good. You want to do it when he's down.
—**Lyndon B. Johnson,** quoted in Doris Kearns Goodwin, *Lyndon Johnson and the American Dream* [1976]

The trouble with treating people as equals is that the first thing you know they may be doing the same thing to you. 1

—**Peter De Vries,** *The Prick of Noon*, 1985

Ordinary politeness, including even a certain charitable reticence, can easily conceal feelings of a quite different nature. Outward deference, as everyone knows who has ever occupied a high executive position, easily slips over into unctuousness and flattery. 2

—**George F. Kennan,** *Around the Cragged Hill: A Personal and Political Philosophy*, 1993

Marines

See MILITARY, THE.

Marriage

See also FAMILY; HOME; LOVE; PARENTS; WOMEN & MEN.

Keep your eyes wide open before marriage, half shut afterwards. 3

—**Benjamin Franklin,** Poor Richard's *Almanack*, June 1738

★ For more on marriage, see Poor Richard at SIN, VICE, & NAUGHTINESS.

A single man . . . is an incomplete animal. He resembles the odd half of a pair of scissors. 4

—**Benjamin Franklin,** letter to a young man, June 25, 1745

★ A couple of hundred years later, much-married actress Zsa Zsa Gabor agreed—sort of: "A man is incomplete until he has married. Then he is finished," *Newsweek*, March 28, 1960.

In the new code of laws, which I suppose it will be necessary for you to make . . . Do not put such unlimited power into the hands of husbands. Remember all men would be tyrants if they could. 5

—**Abigail Adams,** letter to John Adams, March 31, 1776

★ More at WOMEN & MEN.

I'll be no submissive wife, 6
No, not I; no, not I.
I'll not be slave for life,
No, not I; no, not I.

—**Alexander Lee,** *I'll Be No Submissive Wife*, 1835

★ As this song indicates, women's liberation was in the air early in America.

I have now come to the conclusion never again to think of marrying, and for this reason: I can never be satisfied with anyone who would be blockhead enough to have me. 7

—**Abraham Lincoln,** April 1, 1838, after being rejected by Mary Owen

1 Is not marriage an open question, when it is alleged . . . that such as are in the institution wish to get out, and such as are out wish to get in?

—Ralph Waldo Emerson, *Representative Men*, 1850

★ The great French essayist Montaigne made just this allegation when he wrote in 1580 that marriage "happens as with cages: the birds without despair to get in, and those within despair of getting out."

2 Reader, my story ends with freedom; not in the usual way, with marriage.

—Harriet Jacobs, *Incidents in the Life of a Slave Girl: Written by Herself*, 1861

3 Brigham Young has two hundred wives. He loves not wisely but two hundred well.

—Artemus Ward, quoted in *The Windsor Magazine* [1895]

4 The husband and wife are one, and that one is the husband.

—Anonymous, Harvard Law School professor, c. 1855

★ From D. M. Marshman, Jr., *The Four Ages of Joseph Choate* in *American Heritage* magazine, April 1975. The unnamed professor is said to have promulgated this maxim as the basic principle in marital law. The more gracious side of 19th-century marital relationships was illustrated by the eminent lawyer Joseph Choate, who, when asked at a dinner party who he would most like to be if he were not Joseph H. Choate, replied, "Why, Mrs. Choate's second husband."

5 Marriage, to women as to men, must be a luxury, not a necessity; an incident of life, not all of it.

—Susan B. Anthony, speech, 1875

6 The men that women marry,
And why they marry them, will always be
A marvel and a mystery to the world.

—Henry Wadsworth Longfellow, *Michael Angelo*, 1883

7 Who was that lady I saw you with last night?
She ain't no lady; she's my wife.

—Joseph Weber & Lew Fields, vaudeville lines, 1887

8 It takes patience to appreciate domestic bliss; volatile spirits prefer unhappiness.

—George Santayana, *The Life of Reason*, 1905–1906

9 *Marriage, n.* a community consisting of a master, a mistress, and two slaves, making in all, two.

—Ambrose Bierce, *The Devil's Dictionary*, 1906

10 Love, the strongest and deepest element in all life, the harbinger of hope, of joy, of ecstasy; love, the defier of all laws, of all conventions; love, the freest, the most powerful molder of human destiny; how can such an all-compelling force be synonymous with that poor little State and Church-begotten weed, marriage?

—Emma Goldman, *Marriage and Love* in *Anarchism and Other Essays*, 1911

★ Goldman's free spirit is consistent with a quote often attributed to her: "If I can't dance, I don't want to be in your revolution." Alas, *Bartlett's* reports that this can only be dated to a 1973 T-shirt slogan, not Goldman's writings.

Who marries who is a small matter after all. **1**
—Willa Cather, *The Song of the Lark*, 1915

★ The speaker is the novel's heroine, opera singer Thea Kronborg. Joan Acocella, in *The New Yorker* (Nov. 27, 1995), wrote: "This scene is a kind of turning point in the history of literature. . . . In the bulk of literature about women, who marries whom—or, at least, who goes to bed with whom—is not simply not a small matter; it is the subject."

Two can live cheaper than one. **2**
—Ring Lardner, *Big Town*, 1921

★ Lardner may not have coined this proverb but his is the earliest example of the thought in Oxford University Press's *A Dictionary of American Proverbs*, 1992.

Love, the quest; marriage, the conquest; divorce, the inquest. **3**
—Helen Rowland, *A Guide to Men*, 1922

The sanctity of the institution of marriage shall be upheld. Pictures shall not infer [*sic*] that low forms of sex relationships are the accepted or common thing. **4**
—Motion Picture Producers and Distributors, Inc., *A Code for the Industry*, 1930

"That's bigamy." **5**
"Yes, and it's big of me, too. It's big of all of us. I'm sick of these conventional marriages. One woman and one man was good enough for your grandmother. But who wants to marry your grandmother?"
—Groucho Marx, in *Animal Crackers*, 1930

Married women are kept women, and they are beginning to find it out. **6**
—Logan Pearsall Smith, *Other People*, in *Afterthoughts*, 1931

Most everybody in the world climbs into their graves married. **7**
—Thornton Wilder, *Our Town*, 1938

Love-making is the red-tape of marriage. **8**
—Billy Wilder, 1938

★ A line for Gary Cooper to say to Claudette Colbert in *Bluebeard's Eighth Wife*, as recollected by film critic Vincent Canby, *The New York Times*, May 10, 1991.

A husband, a good marriage, is earth. **9**
—Anne Morrow Lindbergh, diary entry, 1944, *Diaries and Letters* [1972]

There's nothing so nice as a new marriage. **10**
—Ben Hecht, *Spellbound*, screenplay, 1945

★ The line, spoken by a Viennese psychiatrist, continues "No psychoses yet, no aggressions, no guilt complexes." The movie was adapted from a book, *The House of Dr. Edwardes* by Francis Beeding, and was directed, of course, by Alfred Hitchcock.

1 I married beneath me—all women do.
—Nancy Astor, speech, Oldham, England, 1951

★ The American-born Lady Astor was the first woman to sit in the House of Commons, from 1919 to 1945. Her husband, Waldorf Astor, was a politician and publisher.

2 The best part of married life is the fights. The rest is merely so-so.
—Thornton Wilder, *The Matchmaker*, 1954

3 Take my wife—please!
—Henny Youngman, saying

★ An old vaudeville line; see also CITIES (ALBANY). Another Youngman routine goes: Q: "How's your wife?" A: "Compared to what?"

4 Love and marriage, love and marriage,
Go together like a horse and carriage.
—Sammy Cahn, song, *Love and Marriage*, 1955

5 The married are those who have taken the terrible risk of intimacy and, having taken it, know life without intimacy to be impossible.
—Carolyn Heilbrun, *Marriage is the Message*, in *Ms*, August 1974

6 Some people claim that marriage interferes with romance. There is no doubt about it. Anytime you have a romance, your wife is bound to interfere.
—Groucho Marx, *The Groucho Phile*, 1976

7 If you think of him first, he will think of you first; that's a good marriage.
—Abigail Van Buren, interview with Phil Donohue, NBC-TV, March 1, 1988

8 Every marriage is a battle between two families struggling to reproduce themselves.
—Carl A. Whitaker, obituary, *The New York Times* [April 25, 1995]

★ Dr. Whitaker was a pioneer in psychotherapy with families.

9 The heart of marriage is memories.
—Bill Cosby, *Love and Marriage*, 1989

10 Marriage is a romance in which the hero dies in the first chapter.
—Anonymous, quoted in Barbara Gowdy, *Fallen Angels*, 1990

Maryland

See also CITIES (BALTIMORE).

11 Heaven and earth never agreed to frame a better place for man's habitation.
—John Smith, on Chesapeake Bay, 1606

★ More at VIRGINIA.

12 Our summer in Maryland was delightful. . . . In no part of North America are the natural productions of the soil more various, or more beautiful.
—Frances Trollope, *Domestic Manners of the Americans*, 1832

★ She wrote in particular of the abundance of delicious strawberries and other fruit.

Maryland! My Maryland! 1

—**James Ryder Randall,** song title, 1861

★ Traditionally played—to the tune of *O Tannenbaum*—at the Preakness Stakes, the second event of racing's triple crown, this is a fiercely anti-Northern song. Written by a native Baltimorean just after a mob of Southern sympathizers had attacked the 6th Massachusetts Regiment as it proceeded through the city en route to Washington, the song begins, "The despot's heel is on thy shore," and concludes, "Huzza! she spurns the Northern scum! / She breathes! she burns! she'll come! she'll come! / Maryland! My Maryland!"

In truth he had never seen a finished landscape; but Maryland was a raggedness of a new kind. 2

—**Henry Adams,** *The Education of Henry Adams*, 1907

Fatti maschii, parole femine. 3
Manly deeds; womanly words.

—Motto, state of Maryland

Massachusetts

See also CITIES (AMHERST, BOSTON, CONCORD, PLYMOUTH).

The first public love of my heart is the Commonwealth of Massachusetts. 4

—**Josiah Quincy,** speech, U.S. House of Representatives, Jan. 14, 1811

The State of Massachusetts is made up of the enterprise of its inhabitants. 5

—**Charles Francis Adams,** *Diary*, Sept. 21, 1835

No slave-hunt in our borders—no pirate on our strand! 6
No fetters in the Bay State—no slave upon our land!

—**John Greenleaf Whittier,** *Massachusetts to Virginia*, 1843

Nantucket! . . . a mere hillock, and elbow of sand; all beach without a background. Some gamesome wights will tell you that they have to plant weeds there; they don't grow naturally; that pieces of wood in Nantucket are carried about like bits of the true cross in Rome; that one blade of grass makes an oasis, three blades in a day's walk a prairie. 7

—**Herman Melville,** *Moby-Dick*, 1851

Down to the Plymouth Rock, that had been to their feet as a doorstep 8
Into a world unknown,—the cornerstone of a nation!

—**Henry Wadsworth Longfellow,** *The Courtship of Miles Standish*, 1858

Massachusetts has a good climate, but it needs a little anthracite coal. 9

—**Ralph Waldo Emerson,** *Journal*, 1857–58

A man may stand there [Cape Cod] and put all America behind him. 10

—**Henry David Thoreau,** *Cape Cod* [1865]

1 Have faith in Massachusetts!
—**Calvin Coolidge,** speech, state legislature, Jan. 7, 1914

2 Flowers through the window
lavender and yellow
changed by white curtains—
smell of cleanliness—
Sunshine of late afternoon—
On the glass tray
a glass pitcher, the tumbler
turned down, by which
a key is lying—And the
immaculate white bed
—**William Carlos Williams,** *Nantucket*, 1934

3 Settlers of Massachusetts
Were of two sets:
Those by grace of God elected;
Those rejected.
One way to tell the sainted
From the tainted
Was that those whose prayers were heeded
Had succeeded.
As a rule it therefore followed
That the hallowed
Were the favored upper classes
Not the masses.
—**Gilman M. Ostrander,** *The Social Structure of Early Massachusetts*, in *American Heritage*, Feb. 1958

4 We yearn for the long waves and beach grass; we see white wings on morning air, and in the afternoon, the shadows cast by the doorways of history.
—**Stewart L. Udall,** Secretary of the Interior, dedication of Cape Cod National Seashore, *The New York Times*, June 5, 1966

5 *Ense petit placidam sub libertate quietem.* By the sword he seeks peace, but peace only under liberty.
—Motto, state of Massachusetts

Mathematics

See SCIENCE: MATHEMATICS & STATISTICS.

Maturity

See EXPERIENCE; MIDDLE AGE & MIDLIFE CRISIS.

Media

See also ADVICE (Nathanael West); CITIES (LOS ANGELES); PRESS, THE; VIETNAM WAR (Michael Arlen).

Who will underrate the influence of loose popular literature in debauching the popular mind? 1

—**Walt Whitman,** article in the *Brooklyn Daily Times* 1857

Spoken speech is one thing, written speech is quite another. Print is the proper vehicle for the latter, but it isn't for the former. The moment "talk" is put into print you recognize that it is not what it was when you heard it. 2

—**Mark Twain,** letter to Edward Bok, c. Dec. 1888

★ Twain was commenting on the text of an interview that Bok, editor of *Ladies' Home Journal*, had conducted with him. Seeing his words in print, said Twain, made him realize that this interview, like most, was "pure twaddle and valueless."

Publishers are demons, no doubt about it. 3

—**William James,** attributed, in John Winokur, *Writers on Writing* [1986]

Publicity is justly commended as a remedy for social and industrial diseases. Sunlight is said to be the best of disinfectants; electric light the most efficient policeman. 4

—**Louis D. Brandeis,** *What Publicity Can Do*, in *Harper's Weekly*, Dec. 20, 1913

The New Yorker will be the magazine that is not edited for the old lady in Dubuque. 5

—**Harold Ross,** prospectus for the magazine, 1924

One picture is worth a thousand words. 6

—**Fred R. Barnard,** in *Printers' Ink*, March 10, 1927

★ Barnard called this a Chinese proverb, but actually it is a rewrite of an earlier Bernard aphorism, "One look is worth a thousand words," *Printers' Ink*, Dec. 8, 1921.

Good evening, Mr. and Mrs. America—and all the ships at sea! This is Walter Winchell in New York. Let's go to press! 7

—**Walter Winchell,** signature radio broadcast opening, from 1934

★ Winchell's 15-minute Sunday night show—a broadcast version of his newspaper gossip column, delivered staccato style and punctuated by the sound of a telegraph ticker—attracted some fifty million listeners weekly during its peak years, 1932–42. A subhead, so to speak, was "Dots and dashes and lots of flashes, from border to border and coast to coast."

Sticks Nix Hick Pix. 8

—**Abel Green,** headline, *Variety*, July 17, 1935

★ VARIETY was famous for its boffo headlines. This one means that movies with rural subjects don't do well in rural communities. For a famous headline on an urban theme, from the *Daily News*, see CITIES (NEW YORK).

I believe television is going to be the test of the modern world, and that in this new opportunity to see beyond the range of our vision, we shall discover either a new and 9 unbearable disturbance of the general peace or a saving radiance in the sky. We shall stand or fall by television.

—E. B. White, *Removal*, in *Harper's Magazine*, 1938

1 The problem with television is that people must sit and keep their eyes glued to the screen; the average American family hasn't time for it. Therefore the showmen are convinced that for this reason, if no other, television will never be a serious competitor of broadcasting.

—The New York Times, editorial, March 1939

★ Good analysis, wrong conclusion.

2 The hand that rules the press, the radio, the screen, and the far-spread magazine rules the country.

—Learned Hand, memorial speech for Justice Louis Brandeis, Dec. 21, 1942

3 Joe Gillis: You used to be in pictures. You used to be big.
Norma Desmond: I am big. It's the pictures that got small.

—Charles Brackett, Billy Wilder, & D. M. Marshman, Jr., *Sunset Blvd.*, screenplay, 1950

★ Desmond's last line: "All right, Mr. DeMille, I'm ready for my close-up now."

4 Some television programs are so much chewing gum for the eyes.

—John Mason Brown, interview, July 28, 1955

★ This quote also has been attributed to Frank Lloyd Wright and Fred Allen.

5 [Television:] a medium, so called because it is neither rare nor well done.

—Ernie Kovacs, quoted in Leslie Halliwell, *The Filmgoer's Book of Quotes* [1973]

★ The epitaph on Kovacs' gravestone, "Nothing in Moderation," was used by David G. Walley as the title of his 1975 biography of this highly inventive TV comedian, who died in a car crash.

6 In television we have the greatest instrument for mass persuasion in the history of the world.

—Budd Schulberg, *A Face in the Crowd*, screenplay, 1957

7 During the peak viewing periods, television in the main insulates us from the realities of the world in which we live. If this state of affairs continues, we may alter an advertising slogan to read: *look now, pay later*.

—Edward R. Murrow, speech to radio and television news directors, Chicago, 1958

8 [If you watch television from morning through night] I can assure you that you will observe a vast wasteland.

—Newton Minow, speech to the National Association of Broadcasters, May 9, 1961

★ The wasteland charge, which seems mild now, was startling at the time, the equivalent of announcing that the emperor is not wearing clothes. Moreover, the speaker was the head of the Federal Communications Commission, and he had the support of Pres. John F. Kennedy. Minow's specific charges are depressingly familiar: "You will see a procession of game shows, violence, audience participation shows, formula comedies about totally unbelievable families, blood and thunder, mayhem, violence, sadism, murder, western bad men, western good men, private eyes, gangsters, more violence, and cartoons. And endlessly, commercials—many screaming, cajoling, and offending." Minow, by the way, had been a law partner of Adlai Stevenson.

It is not enough to cater to the nation's whims, you must also meet the nation's needs. **1**

—**Newton Minow,** speech to the National Association of Broadcasters, May 9, 1961

★ And he threatened not to renew their licenses if they failed to meet the nation's needs.

It [television] is a medium of entertainment which permits millions of people to listen to the same joke at the same time, and yet remain lonesome. **2**

—**T. S. Eliot,** quoted in the *New York Post*, Sept. 22, 1963

Because television can make so much money doing its worst, it often cannot afford to do its best. **3**

—**Fred W. Friendly,** *Due to Circumstances Beyond Our Control*, 1967

Unlike the print media, television writes on the wind. **4**

—**Lyndon B. Johnson,** speech, 1968

★ This "Power of the Media" speech was given shortly after Pres. Johnson announced that he would not seek reelection. More follows.

Where there's great power, there must also be great responsibility. This is true for broadcasters just as it's true for presidents. **5**

—**Ibid.**

Television pollutes identity. **6**

—**Norman Mailer,** *St. George and the Godfather*, 1972

The publishing business is . . . the only organized private business that is given explicit constitutional protection. **7**

—**Potter Stewart,** speech, Yale Law School, 1974

Television is a triumph of equipment over people. **8**

—**Fred Allen,** in *CoEvolution Quarterly*, [Winter 1977]

★ More at INSULTS.

Nothing is real unless it happens on television. **9**

—**Daniel Boorstin,** in *The New York Times*, Feb. 19, 1978

★ Two decades later, writer-director-actor Buck Henry similarly observed, "You aren't anybody in America if you're not on TV. In short, you don't exist unless you're on TV," quoted by Bernard Weinraub, *The New York Times*, Oct. 10, 1995.

1 TV . . . is how we dream out loud about ourselves.

—John Leonard, *Smoke and Mirrors: Violence, Television, and Other American Cultures*, 1997

2 Imitation is the sincerest form of television.

—Charles Osgood on *The Charlie Rose Show*, April 7, 2004

★ Commentator Osgood referred to this as a "saying."

3 There is no writer's block in the newsroom. Only unemployment block.

—Carl Hiaasen, *The New York Times Magazine*, July 25, 2004

4 If it bleeds, it leads.

Anonymous, newsroom saying

★ Cited by John Tierney as an "old rule of television," in a column bemoaning the media focus on bombings and other violent and gruesome events, *The New York Times* [May 10, 2005]

Medicine

See DOCTORS & MEDICINE.

Mediocrity

5 I hope in these days we have heard the last of conformity and consistency. . . . Let us affront and reprimand the smooth mediocrity and squalid contentment of the times.

—Ralph Waldo Emerson, *Self-Reliance*, in *Essay: First Series*, 1841

★ See also CONSISTENCY.

6 Blessed are those who have no talent!

—Ralph Waldo Emerson, *Journal*, Feb. 1850

7 The mediocrity of everything in the great world of today is simply appalling. We live in intellectual slums.

—George Santayana, letter to Victor Wolfgang von Hagen, Nov. 5, 1934

8 Intolerance of mediocrity has been the main prop of my independence.

—Elsa Maxwell, *R.S.V.P.*, 1954

9 Women want mediocre men, and men are working hard to be as mediocre as possible.

—Margaret Mead, in *Quote Magazine*, May 15, 1958

10 Some men are born mediocre, some men achieve mediocrity, and some men have mediocrity thrust upon them. With Major Major it had been all three.

—Joseph Heller, *Catch-22*, 1961

★ The Shakespeare quote underlying Heller's joke is: "Some are born great, some achieve greatness, and some have greatness thrust upon 'em," *Twelfth Night*, II, v.

Even if he is mediocre, there are lots of mediocre judges, and people, and lawyers. They are entitled to a little representation, too, aren't they. **1**

—Roman L. Hruska, Senate hearings on the nomination of G. Harrold Carswell to the Supreme Court, 1970

★ Sen. Hruska of Nebraska, a Republican, was trying to defend a nomination made by Pres. Richard Nixon. It didn't help. The Senate rejected Judge Carswell.

The only sin is mediocrity. **2**

—Martha Graham, quoted in *The New York Times*, March 31, 1985

If you hire mediocre people, they will hire mediocre people. **3**

—Tom Murphy, CEO of Capital Cities/ABC, Inc. *Fortune*, May 6, 1991

Memory

See also CRAFTINESS (Philander C. Johnson); PAST, THE.

[Memory is] the thread on which the beads of man are strung, making the personal identity which is necessary to moral action. **4**

—Ralph Waldo Emerson, *Memory,* 1857

When I was younger I could remember anything, whether it happened or not, but I am getting old, and soon I shall remember only the latter. **5**

—Mark Twain, quoted in prefatory note to Albert Bigelow Paine, *Mark Twain, A Biography* [1912]

★ Twain played with this idea in various forms. On another occasion, according to Paine, he paraphrased a remark by Josh Billings, saying: "It isn't so astonishing the things that I can remember, as the number of things I can remember that aren't so."

Some memories are realities, and are better than anything that can ever happen to one again. **6**

—Willa Cather, *My Ántonia*, 1918

In memory, everything seems to happen to music. **7**

—Tennessee Williams, *The Glass Menagerie*, 1944

★ See also Williams at PRESENT, THE.

Americans are impatient with memory. **8**

—Jamaica Kincaid, *Alien Soil*, in *The New Yorker*, June 21, 1993

Nobody belongs to us except in memory. **9**

—John Updike, *Grandparenting*, 1994

The older I get, the better I used to be. **10**

—Connie Hawkins, quoted by John McEnroe, on *Charlie Rose*, WNET [Feb. 4, 1999]

★ Tennis star McEnroe was applying to himself, somewhat ruefully, the insight by basketball star Hawkins. Deemed by those who know to be the best playground basketball player ever in New York City history, Hawkins went on to a Hall-of-Fame professional career. Another basketball star, Charles Barkley, had a similar but more specific memory: "The older I get, the faster I was" (interview with Bob Costa, NBC-TV, Jan. 22, 1995).

Men

See also HUMANS & HUMAN NATURE; MEDIOCRITY (Heller); WOMEN & MEN.

1 All men would be tyrants if they could.
—**Abigail Adams,** letter to John Adams, March 31, 1776

★ More at WOMEN & MEN. Cf. Daniel Defoe: "Nature has left this tincture in the blood./That all men would be tyrants if they could," *The History of the Kentish Petition*, 1701.

2 A man is a god in ruins.
—**Ralph Waldo Emerson,** *Nature*, 1836

3 All daring and courage, all iron endurance of misfortune—make for a finer, nobler type of manhood.
—**Theodore Roosevelt,** *The Strenuous Life,* 1900

4 *Male n.* A member of the unconsidered, or negligible sex. The male of the human race is commonly known (to the female) as Mere Man. The genus has two varieties: good providers and bad providers.
—**Ambrose Bierce,** *The Devil's Dictionary*, 1906

5 Men build bridges and throw railroads across deserts, and yet they contend successfully that the job of sewing on a button is beyond them. Accordingly, they don't have to sew buttons.
—**Heywood Broun,** *Holding a Baby*, in *Seeing Things at Night*, 1921

6 A man in the house is worth two in the street.
—**Mae West,** *Belle of the Nineties*, 1934

★ For the life in her men, see HEALTH. Ms. West's self-proclaimed fondness for men inspired many bon mots, some of which she may actually have said at one time or another. Among them: "I like only two kinds of men, domestic and foreign," "So many men, so little time," "A hard man is good to find," and, in rare defensive mode, "Give a man a free hand, and he'll run it all over you."

7 What's the use of being a little boy if you are going to grow up to be a man?
—**Gertrude Stein,** *Everybody's Autobiography*, 1937

8 A man's role is uncertain, undefined, and perhaps unnecessary.
—**Margaret Mead,** *Male and Female*, 1948

9 A man can be destroyed but not defeated.
—**Ernest Hemingway,** *The Old Man and the Sea*, 1952

Why can't a woman be more like a man?
Men are so honest, so thoroughly square;
Eternally noble, historically fair. 1

—**Alan Jay Lerner,** *My Fair Lady*, 1956

★ Music by Frederick Loewe. The show was adapted from George Bernard Shaw's play *Pygmalion* (1913).

Most men never mature; they simply grow taller. 2

—**Leo Rosten,** quoted in *Saturday Review*, April 4, 1970

Most men act so strong and tough on the outside because on the inside, we are scared, weak, and fragile. Men, not women, are the weaker sex. 3

—**Jerry Rubin,** quoted in *Chicago Tribune*, March 16, 1978

Now me, when I want ready-made trouble, I dig up a handsome man. 4

—**Gloria Naylor,** *The Women of Brewster Place*, 1982

Most men become men at the cost of a certain innate sense of decency. 5

—**Norman Mailer,** quoted in *Norman Mailer: Stormin' No More, San Francisco Sunday Examiner & Chronicle*, No. 24, 1991

Men & Women

See WOMEN & MEN.

Mental Illness

See MADNESS & SANITY.

Method

See also EXCELLENCE; MANAGEMENT TECHNIQUES; MILITARY STRATEGY.

Method goes far to prevent trouble in business. 6

—**William Penn,** *Some Fruits of Solitude*, 1693

★ More at BUSINESS.

There are some enterprises in which a careful disorderliness is the true method. 7

—**Herman Melville,** *Moby-Dick*, 1851

There is a best way of doing everything, if it be to boil an egg. 8

—**Ralph Waldo Emerson,** *Behavior*, in *The Conduct of Life*, 1860

Chaos often breeds life, when order breeds habit. 9

—**Henry Adams,** *The Education of Henry Adams*, 1907

There's a way to do it better—Find it. 10

—**Thomas Alva Edison,** directive to a research assistant, c. 1919, cited in Robert Debs Heinl, *Dictionary of Military and Naval Quotations*, 1966

1 Take a method and try it. If it fails, admit it frankly and try another.
—**Franklin D. Roosevelt,** speech, Oglethorpe University, Atlanta, Ga., May 22, 1932

★ More at ACTION & DOING.

2 A good plan violently executed *Now* is better than a perfect plan next week.
—**George S. Patton, Jr.,** *War As I Knew It*, 1947

3 Chaos is a friend of mine.
—**Bob Dylan,** explaining his music, quoted in *Newsweek*, Dec. 9, 1985

Mexican War, 1846–1848

See also EPITAPHS & GRAVESTONES (O'Hara).

4 It is for the interest of mankind that its [the United States'] power and territory should be extended—the farther the better.
—**Walt Whitman,** editorial, *Brooklyn Eagle*, Dec. 2, 1847

★ Whitman was writing in defense of this war, which was precipitated by the annexation of Texas late in 1845. Whitman essentially accepted John L. O'Sullivan's manifest-destiny concept; see AMERICA & AMERICANS. Thoreau, however, viewed the war very differently; see below. For the loss of the Alamo in 1836, one of the events leading to the Mexican War, see AMERICAN HISTORY: MEMORABLE MOMENTS.

5 Tell him to go to hell.
—**Zachary Taylor,** reply to Gen. Santa Anna's demand for surrender, Buena Vista, Feb. 22, 1847

★ Gen. Taylor's forces were reduced at this time, and the battle was Mexico's best chance at a major victory. But the U.S. troops prevailed, and the Mexicans withdrew.

6 Hurrah for Old Kentucky! That's the way to do it. Give 'em hell, damn'em.
—**Zachary Taylor,** rallying cry, to the 2d Kentucky Brigade, Battle of Buena Vista, Mexico, Feb. 23, 1847

7 Allow the president to invade a neighboring nation whenever he shall deem it necessary to repel an invasion, . . . and you allow him to make war at pleasure.
—**Abraham Lincoln,** letter to William H. Herndon, Feb. 15, 1848

★ Rep. Lincoln's opposition to President James Polk's rationale for the Mexican War—that Mexico might invade the U.S.—was not politically popular. After his Congressional term ended, Lincoln resumed the private practice of law.

8 How does it become a man to behave toward this American government today? I answer that he cannot without disgrace be associated with it.
—**Henry David Thoreau,** *Civil Disobedience*, 1849

★ Thoreau saw the war as an illegitimate design to extend slavery. As an abolitionist, he had stopped paying the Massachusetts poll tax (a head tax) in 1843, and as a result was arrested in 1846 and spent one night in prison. His subsequent essay on civil disobedience is a key text in pacifist resistance movements. See also Thoreau under LAW. In 1914, the U.S. intervened in Mexico again, during the revolution, and Lincoln Steffens commented later in his autobiography, "We Americans can't seem to get it that you can't commit rape a little." Will Rogers added a few years later, "We could never understand why Mexico wasn't crazy about us. We always had their goodwill, oil, coffee, and minerals at heart," in Alex Ayres, ed., *The Wit and Wisdom of Will Rogers* (1993). It was in the Mexican War, incidentally, that American marines reached the "halls of Montezuma"; see THE MILITARY.

Poor Mexico! So far from God and so close to the United States.
—Porfirio Díaz, attributed, in John S. D. Eisenhower, *The U.S. War with Mexico, 1846–1848* [1989] 1

★ Gen. Díaz was president of Mexico from 1877 to 1911.

Mexico

See NATIONS.

Michigan

See also CITIES (DETROIT).

Milton must have travelled in Michigan before he wrote the garden parts of *Paradise Lost.* 2
—Harriet Martineau, *Society in America*, 1837

The Michiganders were a people without identity, without community of purpose or past, without tradition. Then Ford. 3
—Leonard Lanson Cline, in Ernest H. Gruening, ed., *These United States*, 1924

Michigan . . . is the skyscraper, the mass-production line, and the frantic rush into what the machine will some day make of us, and at the same time, it is golden sand, 4
blue water, green pine trees on empty hills, and a wind that comes down from the cold spaces, scented with the forests that were butchered by hard-handed men in checked flannel shirts and floppy pants. It is the North Country wedded to the force that destroyed it.
—Bruce Catton, *Michigan*, in *American Panorama, East of the Mississippi*, 1960

The earth was generous and outgoing here in the heartland.
—John Steinbeck, *Travels with Charley*, 1962 5

Si quaeris peninsulam amoenam, circumspice.
If you seek a pleasant peninsula, look around you. 6
—Motto, state of Michigan

★ A play on architect Sir Christopher Wren's epitaph in St. Paul's Cathedral, London: *Si monumentum requiris circumspice,* If you would see his monument, look around you.

Middle Age & Mid Life

See also AGES.

After thirty, a man wakes up sad every morning, excepting perhaps five or six, until 7
the day of his death.
—Ralph Waldo Emerson, *Journal*, 1834

1 Men, like peaches and pears, grow sweet a little while before they begin to decay.
—Oliver Wendell Holmes, Sr., *The Autocrat of the Breakfast-Table*, 1858

2 A man reaches the zenith at forty, the top of the hill. From that time forward he begins to descend. If you have any great undertaking ahead, begin it now. You will never be so capable again.
—John Hay, remark to Mark Twain, quoted in Alfred Bigelow Paine, *Mark Twain, A Biography* [1912]

3 Forty is ten years older than thirty-nine.
—Frank Irving Cobb, c. 1912

★ Cobb, chief editor on Joseph Pulitzer's New York *World*, wrote this in a note to Pulitzer. To Pulitzer himself he ascribed the view that "Everybody is a damn fool until he is forty, and not necessarily very intelligent after that." Quoted in Louis M. Starr, *Joseph Pulitzer and His Most 'Indegoddampendent' Editor*, in *American Heritage*, June 1968.

4 By the time a person has achieved years adequate for choosing a direction, the die is cast and the moment has long since passed which determined the future.
—Zelda Fitzgerald, *Save Me the Waltz*, 1932

5 Life Begins at Forty.
—Walter Pitkin, book title, 1932

6 One of the pleasures of middle age is to *find out* that one WAS right, and that one was much righter than one knew at say 17 or 23.
—Ezra Pound, *ABC of Reading*, 1934

7 [Middle age] is the time when a man is always thinking that in a week or two he'll feel just as good as ever.
—Don Marquis, attributed in B. Wilcox, *A Little Book of Aphorisms,* [1947]

8 The only time you really live fully is from thirty to sixty . . . The young are slaves to dreams; the old servants of regrets. Only the middle-aged have all their five senses in the keeping of their wits.
—Hervey Allen, *Anthony Adverse*, 1936

9 Years ago we discovered the exact point, the dead center of middle age. It occurs when you are too young to take up golf and too old to rush the net.
—Franklin Pierce Adams, *Valentine* in *Nods and Becks,* 1944

10 Middle age is when you've met so many people that every new person you meet reminds you of someone else.
—Ogden Nash, *Versus*, 1949

11 Then there is a time in life when you just take a walk: And you walk in your own landscape.
—Willem de Kooning, quoted in *The New York Times,* [March 23, 1997]

They call that [44 years] middle age, but I don't know too many 88-year-olds. **1**

—Burt Reynolds, quoted in *The New York Times*, July 24, 1980

★ The screen star was commenting ruefully on his own advancing years.

[On turning fifty:] When you're planning to live to one hundred, it's only halftime. **2**

—Joe Namath, quoted in *The New York Times*, Jan. 29, 1994

Middle Class

The whole country seems to have melded into one middle class. **3**

—Alexis de Tocqueville, *Democracy in America*, 1835

The middle class is always a firm champion of equality when it concerns a class **4**
above it; but it is the inveterate foe when it concerns elevating a class below it.

—Orestes A. Brownson, *The Laboring Classes*, 1840

The booboisie. **5**

—H. L. Mencken, neologism for the bourgeoisie, c. 1922

His name was George F. Babbitt [and] he was nimble in the calling of selling houses **6**
for more than people could afford to pay.

—Sinclair Lewis, *Babbitt*, 1922

★ See also Babbitt at SCIENCE: TECHNOLOGY and UNHAPPINESS.

Us middle class never have to worry about having old furniture to point out to our **7**
friends. We buy it on payments, and before it's paid for, it's plenty antique.

—Will Rogers, in Alex Ayres, ed., *The Wit and Wisdom of Will Rogers,* [1993]

For a number of years I've wondered if people like us are the forgotten. We're not **8**
the poor, and we're not the rich. We're not the very young or the aged. We're the average American family.

—Donna Alexander, letter to Texas state treasurer Ann Richards, 1988

★ Ms. Richards quoted from this letter from a constituent in Lorena, Tex., in her keynote address to the Democratic National Convention in Atlanta, Ga., July 18, 1988

Midwest, the

See also FRONTIER, THE; WEST, THE.

[The Great Prairies] A vast country, incapable of sustaining a dense population. **9**

—James Fenimore Cooper, *The Prairie*, 1827

There, in the Mississippi Valley, beyond a question, and in a very brief time, will be **10**
cities and towns to rival any in the world in population, in commercial enterprise, and in the production of art, in the refinements of cultivated life and manners, and I fear, in *luxury*.

—Calvin Colton, *Manual for Emigrants to America*, 1832

1 In the Western settlements we may behold democracy arrived at its utmost limits.
—**Alexis de Tocqueville,** *Democracy in America*, 1835

2 The new states of the West are already inhabited, but society has no existence among them.
—**Ibid.**

3 In this country you can look farther and see less than any other place in the world.
—**Anonymous,** 19th century

★ The saying dates from the time when grassland plains extended from Indiana to the foot of the Rockies.

4 These are the gardens of the desert, these
The unshorn fields, boundless and beautiful,
For which the speech of England has no name—
The prairies.
—**William Cullen Bryant,** *The Prairies*, 1833

5 A world of grass and flowers stretched around me, rising and falling in gentle undulations, as if an enchanter had struck the ocean swell, and it was at rest forever.
—**Eliza Steele,** *Summer Journey in the West*, 1841

★ She traveled from Chicago to Peoria in 1840. Quoted in *The New York Times*, Feb. 15, 1995.

6 The clean, bright, gardened townships spoke of country fare and pleasant summer evenings on the stoop. It was a sort of paradise.
—**Robert Louis Stevenson,** *Across the Plains*, 1892

★ Stevenson's account is of his trip across the United States in 1879.

7 The grass was the country, as the water is the sea.
—**Willa Cather,** *My Ántonia*, 1918

★ The scene is Nebraska. See also Cather at THE FRONTIER.

8 July came on with that breathless, brilliant heat which makes the plains of Kansas and Nebraska the best corn country in the world. It seemed as if we could hear the corn growing in the night; under the stars one caught a faint cracking in the dewy, heavy odoured cornfields where the feathered stalks stood so juicy and green.
—**Willa Cather,** *My Ántonia*, 1918

9 The Corn Belt is a gift of the gods—the rain god, the sun god, the ice god, and the gods of geology.
—**J. Russell Smith,** *North America*, 1925

10 Nobody can possibly understand the Middle West who has not, for fun or profit, once looked through the catalogue of a great mail order company.
—**John Gunther,** *Inside U.S.A.*, 1947

11 The Midwest is exactly what one would expect from a marriage between New England puritanism and rich soil.
—**Ibid.**

The withered towns are empty, but not uninhabited. 1

—**Wright Morris,** *The Works of Love*, 1951

Bland, boring and beige. 2

—**Dan S. Kaercher,** quoted in *The New York Times*, April 27, 1987

★ Thus, Mr. Kaecher, editor of *Midwest Living*, summarized the typical outsider's view of the American heartland.

Military Strategy

See also GULF WAR (Colin Powell); IRAQ WAR (Harlan K. Ullman).

Get there first with the most men. 3

—**Nathan Bedford Forrest,** saying during the Civil War

★ The advice of Gen. Forrest, a highly effective Confederate calvary commander, sometimes is phrased, "Git thar fustest with the mostest." But there is no evidence that Forrest (later the first grand wizard of the Ku Klux Klan) spoke nonstandard or silly English. American humorists of the period leaned heavily on such misspellings, as in this passage from Artemus Ward's *Shakespeare Up-to-Date*: "Twice is he armed that hath his quarrel just, / And three times he who gets his fist in fust."

The art of war is simple enough. Find out where your enemy is. Get at him as soon 4
as you can. Strike at him as hard as you can and as often as you can, and keep moving on.

—**Ulysses S. Grant,** attributed

Always mystify, mislead, and surprise the enemy, if possible. 5

—**Thomas J. "Stonewall" Jackson,** strategical motto, during Civil War

★ This is the distilled version of Jackson's strategic vision. In the *Battles and Leaders* series published in *Century* magazine and then in book form (1888), one of Stonewall's officers, John D. Imboden, said that long before Jackson became famous he often cited the two following maxims: "Always mystify, mislead, and surprise the enemy, if possible; and when you strike and overcome him, never let up in the pursuit so long as your men have strength to follow; for an army routed, if hotly pursued, becomes panic-stricken, and can then be destroyed by half their number. The other rule is, never fight against heavy odds, if by any possible manoeuvering you can hurl your own force on only a part, and that the weakest part, of your enemy and crush it. Such tactics will win every time, and a small army may thus destroy a large one in detail, and repeated victory will make it invincible."

There is no better way of defending a long line than by moving into the enemy's ter- 6
ritory.

—**Robert E. Lee,** letter to Gen. John R. Jones, CSA, March 21, 1863

★ The letter presaged Lee's advance into Pennsylvania that summer, which culminated in the Battle of Gettysburg.

Call no council of war. It is proverbial that councils of war never fight. 7

—**Henry W. Halleck,** telegram to Gen. George Gordon Meade, July 13, 1863

★ Halleck, General-in-Chief of the Union Armies, wanted Gen. Meade, who had won at Gettysburg ten days before, to engage Lee's army again. But Meade, whose forces also had suffered terribly at Gettysburg, already had been talked out of an attack by his corps commanders at a council of war on the 12th. After hearing that the Confederates had been allowed to retreat to safety across the Potomac on the night of the 13th, Lincoln cried "Great God! . . . Our Army held the war in the hollow of their hand and they would not close it."

1 The "fog of war" works both ways. The enemy is as much in the dark as you are. BE BOLD!!!!!

—George S. Patton, *Notebook*, 1921–1922

2 A pint of sweat will save a gallon of blood.

—George S. Patton, message to troops, Oct. 1942

3 All experience goes to show that wars cannot be won by bombing alone.

—Walter Lippmann, *Washington Post*, June 22, 1965

★ The implication, of course, is that the infantry is always needed. As Lippmann also observed in the *Post* earlier that year, on February 18: "Nobody has yet found a way of bombing that can prevent foot soldiers from walking." At the time the U.S. was emphasizing bombing in the Vietnam War.

4 When you get into a war, you should win as quick as you can, because your losses become a function of the duration of the war. . . . Get everything you need and win it.

—Dwight D. Eisenhower, press conference, March 15, 1968

5 Budget drives strategy.

—Maxwell D. Taylor, quoted on *MacNeil-Lehrer News Hour*, PBS [Feb. 13, 1989]

★ Gen. Taylor's posts included a tour as chairman of the joint chiefs of staff (1962-64).

6 The conventional army loses if it does not win. The guerrilla wins if he does not lose.

—Henry A. Kissinger, *The Vietnam Negotiations, Foreign Affairs*, Jan. 1969

Military, the

See also EPITAPHS & GRAVESTONES; HIGH POSITION: RULERS & LEADERS (Patton); MILITARY STRATEGY; WAR.

7 Discipline is the soul of an army. It makes small numbers formidable; procures success to the weak and esteem to all.

—George Washington, letter to the captains of the Virginia Regiments, July 1759

★ In general orders on July 6, 1777, Washington wrote, "Discipline more than numbers gives one army superiority over another."

8 Without a respectable navy—alas America!

—John Paul Jones, letter to Robert Morris, Oct. 17, 1776

To place any dependence upon militia, is assuredly, resting upon a broken staff. **1**

—George Washington, letter to the president of Congress, Sept. 24, 1776

★ Washington found local militia units to be useful in harrying the British in guerrilla-type actions, but in the spring of 1780, after nearly four years of war, he still cautioned against reliance on them, telling Virginians when Nathanael Greene assumed command in the South: "We must have a permanent force, not a force that is constantly fluctuating and sliding from under us as a pedestal of ice would do from a statue in a summer's day."

I intend to go *in harm's way*. **2**

—John Paul Jones, letter, Nov. 16, 1778

★ More at AMERICAN REVOLUTION.

[United under one government, we] will avoid the necessity of those overgrown military establishments, which, under any form of government, are inauspicious to liberty, and which are to be regarded as particularly hostile to republican liberty. **3**

—George Washington, Farewell Address, Sept. 17, 1796

★ Another great general who became president, Dwight D. Eisenhower, made a similar point; see below.

Bravery is a quality not to be dispensed with in officers—like charity, it covers a great many defects. **4**

—Benjamin Stoddert, letter to James Simons, Dec. 13, 1798

★ Stoddert was the first Secretary of the Navy.

The spirit of this country is totally adverse to a large military force. **5**

—Thomas Jefferson, letter to Chandler Price, Feb. 28, 1807

For a people who are free, and who mean to remain so, a well-organized and armed militia is their best security. **6**

—Thomas Jefferson, message to Congress, Nov. 8, 1808

★ Jefferson was more approving of militias than was Washington—see above—but he had not the field experience in leading them.

Every citizen [should] be a soldier. This was the case with the Greeks and the Romans, and must be that of every free state. **7**

—Thomas Jefferson, letter to James Monroe, 1813

Long may she ride, our Navy's pride, **8**
And spur to resolution:
And seaman boast, and landsmen toast,
The Frigate Constitution.

—Anonymous, U.S. Navy song, *The Frigate Constitution*, c. 1813

★ Also called "Old Ironsides," this forty-four-gun frigate is probably the most famous American naval vessel. She was launched in 1797, and took part in the undeclared war with France, the battles against Barbary pirates based in Tripoli, and the War of 1812. (Her most celebrated victory was over the British frigate, the Guerrière, on August 19, 1812. Before the war, the *Constitution*'s captain, Isaac Hull, and the British captain, James Dacres, had made a friendly wager of a hat on the outcome should their ships ever meet in combat. After Dacres offered his sword in surrender following the furious engagement off Nova Scotia, Hull replied: "I will not take a sword from one who knows so well how to use it but, I tell you, Dacres. I will trouble you for that hat.") When the *Constitution* was scheduled to be scrapped in 1830, a patriotic poem by Oliver Wendell Holmes, Sr., aroused a popular protest that saved the vessel. She is now at the Boston naval yard. See also Holmes at PATRIOTISM & THE FLAG.

1 It is part of a sailor's life to die well.

—**Stephen Decatur,** on Captain James Lawrence, after his death in action on June 1, 1813

★ More at EPITAPHS & GRAVESTONES.

2 From the halls of Montezuma,
To the shores of Tripoli,
We fight our country's battles,
On the land as on the sea.

—**Anonymous,** *The Marines' Hymn*, 1847

★ Tripoli was the capital of one of the Barbary States, Tripolitania, now part of Libya. Government-sponsored piracy along the Barbary Coast plagued U.S. shipping in the early 19th century, especially 1800–15, the period of the so-called Tripolitan War. The great hero of these hostilities was Stephen Decatur; see PATRIOTISM & THE FLAG. *Halls of Montezuma* refers to the National Palace in Mexico City, seized by American troops in September 1847, in the battle of Chapultepec in the Mexican War. For a marine's prayer, see under WORLD WAR II, the anonymous epitaph for a marine killed at Guadalcanal.

3 A soldier has a hard life, and but little consideration.

—**Robert E. Lee,** letter to his wife, Nov. 5, 1855

4 If it moves, salute it. If it doesn't move, pick it up. If you can't pick it up, paint it.

—**Anonymous,** U.S. Navy saying

5 A man who is good enough to give his blood for his country is good enough to be given a square deal afterwards.

—**Theodore Roosevelt,** speech, Springfield, Ill., July 4, 1903

★ More at POLITICAL SLOGANS.

6 Militarism is the great preserver of our ideals of hardihood, and human life with no use for hardihood would be contemptible.

—**William James,** *The Moral Equivalent of War*, 1910

★ For more of James's thinking on the value of rigorous training, see PACIFISM & NONVIOLENCE.

7 *Semper paratus.* Always Ready.

—**U.S. Coast Guard,** motto, 1915

8 I have a rendezvous with death
At some disputed barricade.

—**Alan Seeger,** *I Have a Rendezvous with Death*, 1916

★ More at WORLD WAR I.

First in the fight. Always faithful. **1**

—U.S. Marines, recruiting poster, World War I

All a soldier needs to know is how to shoot and salute. **2**

—John J. Pershing, attributed

★ After commanding the American Expeditionary Force in Europe in World War I, Pershing served as army chief of staff from 1921 until his retirement in 1924.

Military intelligence—a contradiction in terms. **3**

—Oswald Garrison Villard, lecture c. 1920, personal report from a member of the audience, Lt. Donald Armstrong

★ Armstrong later became a brigadier general. Villard published *The Nation* magazine.

You can't pick up a paper without seeing where the Marines were landed to keep **4**
some nation from shooting each other, and if necessary we shoot them to keep them from shooting each other.

—Will Rogers, *Weekly Articles*, July 5, 1925

Men do not take good iron to make nails nor good men to make soldiers. **5**

—Pearl S. Buck, *The Young Revolutionist*, 1932

★ Prescient of the fatal flaws in the Nationalist Chinese army.

Gung ho! **6**

—Evans Fordyce Carlson, motto, Second Raider Battalion, U.S. Marines, from Feb. 1942

★ The expression, which attained wide popularity as a byword for zealous, enthusiastic performance of one's duty, does not come, as battalion commander Col. Carlson himself thought—and as reported in some dictionaries—from the Chinese words for "work together," but from the abbreviated name for the Chinese Industrial Cooperative Societies first formed in 1939. For more details, see Hugh Rawson's *Devious Derivations*, 1994.

Spartan simplicity must be observed. Nothing will be done merely because it con- **7**
tributes to beauty, convenience, comfort, or prestige.

—U. S. Army, message from the Office of the Chief Signal Officer, May 29, 1945

Look at an infantryman's eyes, and you can tell how much war he has seen. **8**

—Bill Mauldin, *Up Front*, 1945

With pride we hide, three knots to nowhere. **9**

—Anonymous, submariner saying

No sane man is unafraid in battle, but discipline produces in him a form of vicarious **10**
courage.

—George S. Patton, Jr., *War As I Knew It*, 1947

Any commander who fails to obtain his objective, and who is not dead or severely **11**
wounded, has not done his full duty.

—Ibid.

1 It is sad to remember that when anyone has fairly mastered the art of command, the necessity for that art usually expires—either through the termination of the war or through the advanced age of the commander.
—Ibid.

2 When I joined the Army, even before the turn of the century, it was the fulfillment of all my hopes and dreams. The hopes and dreams have long since vanished. But I still remember the refrain of one of the most popular barracks ballads of that day, which proclaimed most proudly that, "Old soldiers never die. They just fade away."
—Douglas MacArthur, speech, joint session of Congress, April 19, 1951

★ More at AMERICAN HISTORY: MEMORABLE MOMENTS. The song is an old one. The Library of Congress's volume of quotations suggests that the song is a parody of a 19th-century gospel hymn, *Kind Words Can Never Die*, which was known to cadets at West Point, where MacArthur was in the class of 1903. The earliest printed version dates from 1917 in England in *Tommy's Tunes*, compiled by Frederick T. Nettleton. There are small differences in the wording in different versions of the song.

3 Every gun that is made, every warship launched, every rocket fired signifies, in the final sense, a theft from those who hunger and are not fed, those who are cold and are not clothed.
—Dwight D. Eisenhower, speech, April 16, 1953, Washington, D.C.

4 There are all sorts of things to be done in this country. . . . I see no reason why the sums which are now going into these sterile, negative mechanisms that we call war munitions shouldn't go into something positive.
—Dwight D. Eisenhower, quoted in Stephen E. Ambrose, *Eisenhower: The President* [1983]

5 If there is one basic element in our Constitution, it is civilian control of the military.
—Harry S. Truman, *Memoirs*, 1955

6 The deterrence of war is the primary objective of the armed forces.
—Maxwell D. Taylor, *The Uncertain Trumpet*, 1960

★ Gen. Taylor was army chief of staff from 1955 to 1959, resigning in protest of the Eisenhower administration's reliance on massive retaliation; see John Foster Dulles at FOREIGN POLICY. Taylor was appointed chairman of the Joint Chiefs of Staff by Pres. John F. Kennedy in 1962. His statement here is one of many versions of "Washington's maxim," which derives from the Roman writer Vegetius; see George Washington and Theodore Roosevelt at WAR.

7 In the councils of government, we must guard against the acquisition of unwarranted influence, whether sought or unsought, by the military-industrial complex. The potential for the disastrous rise of misplaced power exists and will persist.
—Dwight D. Eisenhower, Farewell Address, Jan. 17, 1961

★ Pres. Eisenhower's original warning, according to physicist Robert L. Park, was against a "military-industrial-scientific complex." Professor Park, writing in *The New York Times* on June 27, 1994, said that science adviser James Killian persuaded the president to drop the reference to science. See also Eisenhower at PEACE.

There was only one catch and that was Catch-22, which specified that a concern for one's own safety in the face of dangers that were real and immediate was the process of a rational mind. Orr was crazy and could be grounded. All he had to do was ask; and as soon as he did he would no longer be crazy and would have to fly more missions. Orr would be crazy to fly more missions and sane if he didn't, but if he was sane he had to fly them. If he flew them he was crazy and didn't have to; but if he didn't want to he was sane and had to. Yossarian was moved deeply by the absolute simplicity of this clause of Catch-22 and let out a respectful whistle. 1

—**Joseph Heller,** *Catch-22*, 1961

★ The now-famous paradoxical Catch-22 was originally dubbed Catch–18. But Leon Uris that same year had a great success with *Mila 18*, which led Heller to change the number in his title from 18 to 22 shortly before publication. *Catch-22* garnered mixed, mostly poor reviews, and never made it to *The New York Times* best-seller list. But it went on to become one of the great publishing successes of the century.

Catch-22 says they [superior officers] have a right to do anything we can't stop them from doing. 2

—**Ibid.**

You seldom hear of the fleets except when there's trouble and then you hear a lot. 3

—**John S. McCain, Jr.,** *Norfolk Star Ledger*, August 4, 1964

★ McCain oversaw the Vietnam War at its height as Commander-in-Chief of the Pacific Command. During the whole of his tour in charge, 1968–72, his eldest son, John S. McCain III, a naval pilot who later became a Republican senator from Arizona, was a prisoner of war in Hanoi.

A nation that continues year after year to spend more money on military defense than on programs of social uplift is approaching spiritual death. 4

—**Martin Luther King, Jr.,** *Where Do We Go from Here? Chaos or Community?*, 1967

When I was in the military, they gave me a medal for killing two men, and a discharge for loving one. 5

—**Leonard Matlovich,** the inscription on Sgt. Matlovich's tombstone, cited by Anna Quindlen, *The New York Times* [June 27, 1993]

★ Sgt. Matlovich, who served three tours of duty in Vietnam, made headlines—including the cover of *Time* magazine—when he declared his homosexuality in 1975, then fought the Air Force's attempt to give him a general, or less than honorable, discharge. A U.S. Court of Appeals ruled in Matlovich's favor in 1978, but rather than pursue the case when the government appealed to the Supreme Court, he settled for an honorable discharge and a tax-free payment of $160,000. Ten years later he died of AIDS.

I don't care if a soldier is straight as long as he can shoot straight. 6

—**Barry Goldwater,** attributed, c. 1993

★ Goldwater, a Republican senator from Arizona who ran for president in 1964, was an old-fashioned libertarian Republican. In the 1990s, he became something of a hero among homosexual Americans for his outspoken conviction that government should not be concerned with people's private lives.

1 You go to war with the army you have, not the army you might want.
—Donald H. Rumsfeld, speaking in Kuwait, Dec. 8, 2004.

★ More at IRAQ WAR.

2 Marines never die. They just go to hell and regroup.
—Anonymous, U.S. Marines, saying, most recently cited, National Public Radio Morning Edition, Jan. 31, 2005 memorial service in Hawaii for 30 Marines and one U.S. Navy sailor killed in helicopter crash in Iraq.

Mind, Thought, & Understanding

See also GENIUS; IDEAS & IDEALS; VISION & PERCEPTION; WILL, WISDOM.

3 What is the hardest task in the world? To think.
—Ralph Waldo Emerson, *Intellect*, in *Essays: First Series*, 1841

4 There is no such thing as being too profound.
—Edgar Allan Poe, *The Murders in the Rue Morgue*, 1841

★ The speaker is C. Auguste Dupin, the most famous forefather of the modern fictional detective.

5 What are the earth and all its interests beside the deep surmise which pierces and scatters them?
—Henry David Thoreau, *A Week on the Concord and Merrimack Rivers*, 1849

6 A moment's insight is sometimes worth a life's experience.
—Oliver Wendell Holmes, Sr., *The Professor at the Breakfast-Table*, 1860

7 The Brain—is wider than the Sky—
For—put them side by side—
The one the other will contain
With ease—and You—beside.
—Emily Dickinson, poem no. 632, 1862

8 The Brain is just the weight of God—
For—Heft them—Pound for Pound—
And they will differ—if they do—
As Syllable from Sound.
—Ibid.

9 You are good for nothing unless you are clever.
—Henry James, *Washington Square*, 1880

★ This Dr. Sloper's response to his sister Lavinia's question, "Do you think it is better to be clever than good?" The subject of the conversation is the doctor's daughter, Catherine, the heiress.

Imagination is the secret and marrow of civilization. It is the very eye of faith. **1**

—Henry Ward Beecher, *Proverbs from Plymouth Pulpit*, 1887

As the brain changes are continuous, so do all these consciousnesses melt into each **2**
other like dissolving views. Properly they are but one protracted consciousness, one unbroken stream.

—William James, *The Principles of Psychology*, 1890

★ This is from the highly influential chapter "The Stream of Thought," in which the term "stream of consciousness" first appears. This flow of consciousness, or what French writer Édouard Dujardin earlier called "the interior monologue," is at the center of many of the great novels of the 20th century, including, most famously, *Ulysses*, by James Joyce.

Our dignity is not in what we do but what we understand. The whole world is doing **3**
things.

—George Santayana, *Winds of Doctrine*, 1913

Life does not consist mainly—or even largely—of facts and happenings. It consists **4**
mainly of the storm of thoughts that is forever blowing through one's head.

—Mark Twain, *Autobiography* [1924]

★ Note the similarity between the observations of Twain and William James, above. Awareness of the constant activity of the mind in shaping perceived reality was very much in the air in this era. Referring to the "storm of thoughts," Twain continued: "Could you set them down stenographically? No. . . . Fifteen stenographers hard at work couldn't keep up. Therefore, a full autobiography has never been written, and it never will be." Twain's own autobiography was never finished. He wrote passages for it over many years, and it was published posthumously.

If you make people think they're thinking, they'll love you: but if you really make **5**
them think, they'll hate you

—Don Marquis, *archy and mehitabel*, 1927

Imagination is more important than knowledge. **6**

—Albert Einstein, in *What Life Means to Einstein*, in *The Saturday Evening Post*, Oct. 26, 1929

The test of a first-rate intelligence is the ability to hold two opposed ideas in the **7**
mind at the same time, and still retain the ability to function. One should, for example, be able to see that things are hopeless and yet be determined to make them otherwise.

—F. Scott Fitzgerald, *The Crack-Up*, originally published in *Esquire* magazine, 1936

★ See also Ralph Waldo Emerson at CONSISTENCY.

Understanding is a very dull occupation. **8**

—Gertrude Stein, *Everybody's Autobiography*, 1937

Men are not prisoners of fate, but only prisoners of their own minds. **9**

—Franklin D. Roosevelt, speech, Pan American Day, April 15, 1939

1 Intelligence is quickness to apprehend as distinct from ability, which is capacity to act wisely on the thing apprehended.
—**Alfred North Whitehead,** *Dialogues,* Dec. 15, 1939

2 The mind is an enchanting thing, is an enchanted thing.
—**Marianne Moore,** *The Mind Is an Enchanting Thing*, 1944

3 The Power of Positive Thinking.
—**Norman Vincent Peale,** book title, 1952

★ The very successful Rev. Peale was an all-American cleric. "Pray big! Believe Big! Act Big!" he urged. His politics were conservative, his theology vaguely liberal. He campaigned for Dwight D. Eisenhower, prompting Adlai Stevenson to joke that he found "Paul appealing, and Peale appalling" (*Skeptical Inquirer*, winter 94, Martin Gardner review of *God's Salesman* by Carol V. R. George, 1933).

4 The mind is the expression of the soul, which belongs to God and must be let alone by government.
—**Adlai Stevenson,** speech, Salt Lake City, Utah, Oct. 14, 1952

5 Imagination continually outruns the creature it inhabits.
—**Katherine Anne Porter,** in *Contemporary Novelists*, 1976

★ More at Love.

6 I believe in an open mind, but not so open that your brains fall out.
—**Arthur Hays Sulzberger,** quoted by Lawrence Krauss, OpEd column, *The New York Times* [July 29, 1996]

★ Identified by Dan Glickman, head of the Motion Picture Association of America, as a Yiddish saying in the form, "It's good to be open-minded, but if you are too open-minded, your brains fall out," *The New York Times*, Feb. 6, 2005. Or as science and science fiction writer L. Sprague de Camp, put it, referring to credulous believers in the paranormal: "Many people have developed minds that are not only open, but gaping"(founding conference of the Committee for the Scientific Investigation of Claims of the Paranormal, April 30-May 1, 1976, Buffalo, N.Y., in *Skeptical Inquirer*, March-April 2005).

7 A mind is a terrible thing to waste.
—**United Negro College Fund,** advertising slogan, adopted 1983

★ Reportedly garbled by Vice President Dan Quayle into "What a waste it is to lose one's mind," quoted in Douglas Brinkley, *The Majic Bus: An American Odyssey*, 1993.

8 The mind is what the brain does.
—**Stephen M. Kosslyn,** quoted in *The New York Times*, science section, April 22, 1986

9 An open mind is a prequisite to an open heart.
—**Robert M. Sapolsky,** *Open Season*, in *The New Yorker*, May 30, 1998

10 Your brain is not in charge.
—**Candace Pert,** *Your Body Is Your Subconscious Mind*, audio tape, 2000

Minnesota

See also Cities (Duluth); Heroes (F. Scott Fitzgerald).

What a glorious new Scandinavia might not Minnesota become! . . . None of [the American states] appear to me to have a greater or more beautiful future before them than Minnesota. 1

—**Fredrika Bremer,** *Homes of the New World*, 1853

Lake Wobegon, where all the women are strong, all the men are good looking, and all the children are above average. 2

—**Garrison Keillor,** *A Prairie Home Companion*, signature line, radio show, started 1974

Minnesotans are just different, that's all. 3

—**Charles Kuralt,** *Dateline America*, 1979

★ In particular, Kuralt noted that "with the wind-chill factor hovering at fifty-seven below . . . there were all these Minnesotans running around outdoors, happy as lambs in the spring." And he took up the "different" theme in his next book, too; see below.

Minnesotans are different from the rest of us . . . Minnesotans don't smoke . . . Minnesotans recycle . . . Minnesotans return the grocery cart to the store. Minnesotans do not consume butterfat . . . Minnesotans bike with their helmets on. Minnesotans fasten their seat belts. Minnesotans hold the door for you. Minnesota men don't leave the toilet seat up. Minnesotans do not blow their horn behind you when the light turns green; they wait for you to notice. Minnesotans are nicer than other people. 4

—**Charles Kuralt,** *Charles Kuralt's America*, 1995

Minnesota . . . has a stubbornness, it has a persistence. It treasures its own landscape. 5

—**Garrison Keillor,** interview, *The New York Times,* Dec. 21, 2004

L'Étoile du Nord. The Star of the North. 6

—Motto, state of Minnesota

Minorities

See Majorities & Minorities; Races & Peoples.

Miracles

See also America & Americans (Thomas Wolfe); Evidence (Carl Sagan).

Men talk about Bible miracles because there is no miracle in their lives. Cease to gnaw that crust. There is ripe fruit over your head. 7

—**Ralph Waldo Emerson,** *Journal*, June 1850

To me every hour of the light and dark is a miracle, Every cubic inch of space is a miracle. 8

—**Walt Whitman,** *Miracles*, 1881

1 Miracles are laughed at be a nation that r-reads thirty millyon newspapers a day an' supports Wall sthreet.

—**Finley Peter Dunne,** *Casual Observations*, in *Mr. Dooley's Opinions*, 1900

2 Miracles are propitious accidents, the natural causes of which are too complicated to be readily understood.

—**George Santayana,** *The Ethics of Spinoza*, 1901

3 One miracle is just as easy to believe as another.

—**William Jennings Bryan,** at the Scopes "monkey" trial, Dayton, Tenn., July 21, 1925

4 Miracles are to come. With you I leave a remembrance of miracles.

—**E. E. Cummings,** Introduction, *New Poems*, in *Collected Poems*, 1938

5 Expect a miracle!

—**Oral Roberts,** signature line for faith-healing TV broadcasts, from c. 1947

6 It's a very mixed blessing to be brought back from the dead.

—**Kurt Vonnegut,** Palm Sunday sermon, St. Clement's Episcopal Church, New York City, quoted by John Leonard, *The New York Times*, April 30, 1980

7 Do you believe in miracles? Yes!

—**Al Michaels,** Winter Olympics, 1980

★ In a Cold War battle at Lake Placid, New York, the U.S. hockey team of rag-tag college players ousted the formidable Russians. Sportscaster Michaels' emotional broadcast inspired the title, "Miracle," for the 2004 film on the team and the game, sometimes called the greatest upset in sports history.

8 Coincidence is God's way of performing miracles anonymously.

—**Sophy Burnham,** *Angel Letters*, 1991

Misanthropy

See also ALIENATION.

9 Any man who hates dogs and babies can't be all bad.

—**Leo C. Rosten,** speaking of W. C. Fields, Masquer's Club, 1939

★ Often attributed to Fields in the form: "Anyone who hates children and dogs can't be all bad." One of columnist William Safire's correspondents unearthed a 1937 version by Cedric Worth in *Harper's* magazine: "No man who hates dogs and children can be all bad." Worth, in turn, was recalling a comment by a *New York Times* reporter, Byron Darton, following a party in 1930 at which the conversation was dominated by a man who detested dogs.

10 I am free of all prejudice. I hate everyone equally.

—**W. C. Fields,** in Jerome Beatty, Jr., *Trade Winds*, column, *Saturday Review* [Jan. 28, 1967]

There are no innocent bystanders. What were they doing there in the first place? 1
—**William S. Burroughs,** *My Education: A Book of Dreams*, 1995

Mississippi

Mississippi will drink wet and vote dry—so long as any citizen can stagger to the polls. 2
—**Will Rogers,** attributed, pre–1919 and the start of Prohibition

Mississippi begins in the lobby of a Memphis, Tennessee, hotel and extends south to the Gulf of Mexico. It is dotted with little towns concentric about the ghosts of the horses and mules once tethered to the hitch-rail enclosing the county courthouse and it might almost be said to have only two directions, north and south, since until a few years ago it was impossible to travel east or west in it unless you walked or rode on the horses or mules. 3
—**William Faulkner,** *Mississippi*, in *American Panorama: East of the Mississippi*, 1960

When you're in Mississippi, the rest of America doesn't seem real. And when you're in the rest of America, Mississippi doesn't seem real. 4
—**Bob Parris Moses,** c. 1961, quoted by Jack Newfield, *Amite County*, in *Bread and Roses Too* [1971]

Virtute et armis. By valor and arms. 5
—Motto, state of Mississippi

Missouri

See also CITIES (KANSAS CITY, ST. LOUIS).

As an agricultural region, Missouri is not surpassed by any state in the Union. It is indeed the farmers' kingdom. 6
—**Anonymous,** *The History of Jackson County*, 1881

I am from Missouri. You've got to show me. 7
—**Willard D. Vandiver,** speech, U.S. Navy Yard, Philadelphia, 1899

★ The passage reads in full: "I come from a state that raises corn and cotton and cockleburs and Democrats, and frothy eloquence neither convinces or satisfies me. I am from Missouri. You've got to show me." Henry F. Woods in *American Sayings* (1945) notes that the key comment was not original with Vandiver, but he was one of the first to take pride in a characteristic previously linked to an alleged inability among Missourians to grasp instructions quickly. Pride prevailed, and Missouri became popularly known as the "show-me state," in honor of Missourians' commonsensical skepticism. Vandiver was a member of the U. S. House of Representatives. Woods differs from other sources in giving a date of 1902 for the speech. It first became widely known in the 1912 presidential race, when Champ Clark of Missouri was a candidate. For more on Clark, see the note with Richard Nixon's "Checkers" speech at AMERICAN HISTORY: MEMORABLE MOMENTS. Being "from Missouri" eventually dropped its geographical anchor and became a metaphor for being sceptical. In 1923, Elbert Hubbard wrote, "Be from Missouri, of course; but for God's sake forget it occasionally," *The Roycroft Dictionary and Book of epigrams*, 1923.

1 *Salus populi suprema lex esto.*
The welfare of the people shall be the supreme law.
—Motto, state of Missouri

Mistakes

See also FAULTS & FAILINGS.

2 Mistakes have been made.
—Ulysses S. Grant, report to Congress, Dec. 5, 1876

★ With these words, in an unprecedented apology that Grant appended to his final annual report to Congress the president acknowledged the scandals that had plagued his two administrations. At the same time, he distanced himself from them. Later political leaders in this country and abroad have found the passive-evasive construction to be equally useful. For example, Pres. Bill Clinton side-stepped responsibility for improper Democratic Party fundraising activities by saying, "Mistakes were made" (press conference, Jan. 20, 1998); Israeli Prime Minister Benjamin Netanyahu reacted to news that he had escaped indictment in a scandal with the same "Mistakes were made" (*The New York Times*, Apr. 21, 1998); and Pol Pot, onetime leader of Cambodia, glossed over the killing by the Kymer Rouge of some two million of his fellow citizens, with the similarly bland, "Our movement made mistakes" (*The New York Times*, Oct. 23, 1998). Back in the United States, on Dec. 23, 2004, a far more likeable criminal, impeached ex-governor John Rowland of Connecticut, speaking to the press after pleading guilty to a federal corruption charge, explained, "Obviously mistakes have been made throughout the last few years, and I accept responsibility for those." The many mistakes in the Rowland years elevated Connecticut to a credible contender with New Jersey for corruption capital of the U.S.

3 The only one who makes no mistakes is one who never does anything.
—Theodore Roosevelt, saying, inscribed on the house in which he was born, the Theodore Roosevelt National Historical Site in New York City

4 When I make a mistake, it's a beaut!
—Fiorello H. La Guardia, remark to Judge Justine Wise Polier, in William Manners, *Patience and Fortitude: Fiorello La Guardia, A Biography* [1976]

★ LaGuardia ("the Little Flower") didn't make many political mistakes; he was mayor of New York from 1934 to 1945. The mistake here was the appointment of Herbert O'Brien to be a children's court judge. O'Brien turned out to be sympathetic to fascist ideas. His colleague, judge Justine Wise Polier (daughter of Rabbi Stephen Wise), claimed that when O'Brien asked for a low license plate number, he was given IQ 16—and didn't get the joke.

5 Admitting Error clears the Score
And proves you Wiser than before.
—Arthur Guiterman, *Of Apology*, in *A Poet's Proverbs*, 1924

6 A reign of error.
—Robert K. Merton, *The Self-Fulfilling Prophecy*, 1948

★ The sentence in full reads: "The specious validity of the self-fulfilling prophecy perpetuates a reign of error." More at SCIENCE.

We're all proud of making little mistakes. It gives us the feeling that we don't make any big ones. 1

—**Andy Rooney,** *Not That You Asked*, 1990

Modern Times

See also BAD TIMES; SCIENCE: TECHNOLOGY.

All the modern inconveniences. 2

—**Mark Twain,** *Life on the Mississippi*, 1883

The age demanded an image 3
Of its accelerated grimace,
Something for the modern stage,
Not, at any rate, an Attic grace.

—**Ezra Pound,** *Hugh Selwyn Mauberley: E. P. Ode pour l'élection de son sépulchre*, 1920

One of the crying needs of the time is for a suitable burial service for the admittedly damned. 4

—**H. L. Mencken,** *Prejudices*, 1919–1927

In the nightmare of the dark 5
All the dogs of Europe bark,
And the living nations wait,
Each sequestered in its hate.

—**W. H. Auden,** *In Memory of W. B. Yeats*, 1940

The century on which we are entering can be and must be the century of the common man. 6

—**Henry A. Wallace,** speech, May 8, 1942

★ Wallace was Pres. Franklin Roosevelt's vice president in 1942. Subsequently, he ran for president on the Progressive Party ticket in 1948.

We have grasped the mystery of the atom and rejected the Sermon on the Mount. 7

—**Omar Bradley, speech,** Armistice Day, 1948

★ Gen. Bradley led the U.S. forces in the invasion of Normandy, and as commander of the 12th Army group was a key commander in the victory in Europe. See also Martin Luther King, Jr., at SCIENCE: TECHNOLOGY.

At this very moment, we have the necessary techniques, both material and psychological, to create a full and satisfying life for everyone. 8

—**B. F. Skinner,** *Walden Two*, 1948

Perfection of means and confusion of goals seem, in my opinion, to characterize our age. 9

—**Albert Einstein,** *Out of My Later Years*, 1950

1 There are evidently limits to the achievements of science; and there are irresolvable contradictions both between prosperity and virtue, and between happiness and "the good life," which had not been anticipated in our philosophy. The discovery of these contradictions threatens our culture with despair.
—**Reinhold Niebuhr,** *The Irony of American History*, 1952

2 I saw the best minds of my generation destroyed by madness.
—**Allen Ginsberg,** *Howl*, 1956

★ More at MADNESS.

3 Like it or not, we live in interesting times.
—**Robert F. Kennedy**, TV biography [Jan. 28, 1992]

★ The observation recalls the ancient Greek curse: "May you live in interesting times."

4 They paved paradise
And put up a parking lot.
—**Joni Mitchell,** *Big Yellow Taxi,* 1969

Money & the Rich

See also BUSINESS; CAPITAL & CAPITALISM V. LABOR; ECONOMICS; ELITE, THE; LUXURY; RICH & POOR, WEALTH & POVERTY; *success*

5 Nothing but money
Is sweeter than honey.
—**Benjamin Franklin,** *Poor Richard's Almanack*, 1735

6 There are three faithful friends—an old wife, an old dog, and ready money.
—**Benjamin Franklin,** *Poor Richard's Almanack*, Jan. 1738

7 I would rather have it said, *he lived usefully*, than, *He died rich.*
—**Benjamin Franklin,** letter to his mother, 1751

8 If you would know the value of money, go and try to borrow some.
—**Benjamin Franklin,** *Poor Richard's Almanack*, 1758

9 A penny saved is a penny earned.
—**Anonymous,** proverb often attributed to Benjamin Franklin

★ For all his advice about money, records of the Bank of North America in Philadelphia show that Franklin was overdrawn at least three times a week.

10 Hardly anything but money remains to create strongly marked differences between them [Americans] and to raise some of them above the common level.
—**Alexis de Tocqueville,** *Democracy in America*, 1835

★ Tocqueville introduced this observation with the general comment, "When the reverence that belonged to what is old has vanished, birth, condition, and profession no longer distinguish men." See also Tocqueville at AMERICA & AMERICANS.

The almighty dollar, that great object of universal veneration throughout our land. **1**

—Washington Irving, *The Creole Village*, in *The New Yorker*, Nov. 12, 1836

★ The passage recalls Ben Jonson's "That for which all virtue now is sold, / And almost every vice—almighty gold," *Epistle to Elizabeth, Countess of Rutland*, in *Epigrams*, 1616.

Of all the sources of human pride, mere wealth is the basest and most vulgar-minded. Real gentlemen are almost invariably above this low feeling. **2**

—James Fenimore Cooper, *The American Democrat*, 1838

Money, which represents the prose in life, and which is hardly mentioned in parlors without an apology, is, in its effects and laws, as beautiful as roses. **3**

—Ralph Waldo Emerson, *Nominalist and Realist*, in *Essays: Second Series*, 1844

A man is rich in proportion to the number of things which he can afford to let alone. **4**

—Henry David Thoreau, *Where I lived and What I Lived For*, in *Walden*, 1854

That man is the richest whose pleasures are the cheapest. **5**

—Henry David Thoreau, *Journal*, March 3, 1856

Moral principle is a looser bond than pecuniary interest. **6**

—Abraham Lincoln, speech, Oct. 1856

The production of wealth is not the work of any one man, and the acquisition of great fortunes is not possible without the cooperation of multitudes of men; . . . therefore the individuals to whose lot these fortunes fall . . . should never lose sight of the fact that as they hold them by the will of society expressed in statute law, so they should administer them as trustees for the benefit of society as inculcated by moral law. **7**

—Peter Cooper, c. 1875, quoted in Peter Lyon, *The Honest Man*, in *American Heritage* [Feb. 1959]

★ Cooper practiced what he preached, spending the fortune that he made on philanthropic ventures. See also Cooper at BUSINESS; THE ELITE; and REVOLUTION; as well as Robert Collyer's eulogy at EPITAPHS & GRAVESTONES.

Conspicuous consumption of valuable goods is a means of reputability to the gentleman of leisure. **8**

—Thorstein Veblen, *The Theory of the Leisure Class*, 1899

In order to stand well in the eyes of the community, it is necessary to come up to a certain, somewhat indefinite, conventional standard of wealth. **9**

—Ibid.

I risked much, but I made much. **10**

—P. T. Barnum

★ A *New York Times* article from August 29, 1993, on the Barnum Museum in Bridgeport, Conn., stated that while Barnum did not say anything about suckers being born every minute—see FOOLS & STUPIDITY—he did say this.

1 Money is always fashionable.

—Henry Goldman, attributed, in Lisa Endlich, *Goldman Sachs: The Culture of Success* [1999]

★ Henry was the son of Marcus Goldman, co-founder of the firm in 1869 with his son-in-law Sam Sachs.

2 I believe the power to make money is a gift of God. . . . I believe it is my duty to make money and still more money and to use the money I make for the good of my fellow man according to the dictates of my conscience.

—John D. Rockefeller, interview, 1905

★ Mr. Dooley explained Rockefeller's divine mandate thus: "He's kind iv a society f'r the previntion of croolty to money. If he finds a man misusing his money, he takes it away fr'm him an' adopts it," Finley Peter Dunne, *Mr. Dooley Says*, 1910.

3 It is difficult to get a man to understand something when his salary depends on his not understanding.

—Upton Sinclair, *The Jungle,* 1906

★ Sinclair got America to understand what was wrong with the meat business with a visceral approach, as he explained in *Cosmopolitan,* Oct. 1906: "I aimed at the public's heart, and by accident I hit it in the stomach."

4 *Impunity, n*. Wealth.

—Ambrose Bierce, *The Devil's Dictionary*, 1906

5 *Money, n*. A blessing that is of no advantage to us excepting when we part with it.

—Ibid.

6 Malefactors of great wealth.

—Theodore Roosevelt, speech, Provincetown, Mass., August 20, 1907

★ Pres. Roosevelt, who had created legislation to regulate the railroads, was blamed by financiers for the stock market panic of 1907. In this speech, he suggested that "certain malefactors of great wealth" might have conspired to bring on the crisis and discredit regulation. Meanwhile, the financiers, many of whom had contributed to Roosevelt's election campaign in 1904, felt that they had been double-crossed. Henry Clay Frick, who had supported T.R. to the tune of $100,000, is credited with the complaint that "We bought the son of a bitch, and then he didn't stay bought."

7 Let me tell you about the very rich. They are different from you and me.

—F. Scott Fitzgerald, *The Rich Boy*, 1926

★ Peter De Vries noted in the *Washington Post*, July 30, 1989: "The rich aren't like us—they pay less taxes." See also Ernest Hemingway below and Leona Helmsley at TAXES.

8 When a man tells you that he got rich through hard work, ask him: "Whose?"

—Don Marquis, quoted in Edward Anthony, *O Rare Don Marquis* [1962]

9 What's a thousand dollars? Mere chicken feed. A poultry matter.

—Groucho Marx, *The Cocoanuts*, 1929

No one can live on one salary any more. **1**
—Will Rogers, *Daily Telegrams*, Oct. 19, 1929

There are few sorrows, however poignant, in which a good income is of no avail. **2**
—Logan Pearsall Smith, *Afterthoughts*, 1931

Money is like an arm or a leg—use it or lose it. **3**
—Henry Ford, interview in *The New York Times*, Nov. 8, 1931

Man was lost if he went to a usurer, for the interest ran faster than a tiger upon him. **4**
—Pearl S. Buck, *The First Wife*, in *The First Wife and Other Stories*, 1933

The rich were dull and they drank too much. **5**
—Ernest Hemingway, *The Snows of Kilimanjaro*, 1936

★ In the next paragraph of the story, Hemingway refers to the Fitzgerald quote above about the rich being different from you and me, and includes a retort, "Yes, they have more money." Hemingway accepted credit for this quip, but evidently the remark was made by critic Mary Colum at a lunch in 1936 with Hemingway and famed editor Maxwell Perkins. It was directed not at Fitzgerald but at Hemingway, who had boasted, "I am getting to know the rich." Colum replied, "The only difference between the rich and other people is that the rich have more money," Matthew J. Bruccoli, *Scott and Ernest*, 1978.

Money is power, freedom, a cushion, the root of all evil, the sum of blessings. **6**
—Carl Sandburg, *The People, Yes*, 1936

★ The biblical allusion is to *1 Timothy* 6:10: "The love of money is the root of all evil."

I do want to get rich but I never want to do what there is to do to get rich. **7**
—Gertrude Stein, *Everybody's Autobiography*, 1937

★ She also noted, "There are so many ways of earning a living and most of them are failures."

When money talks, few are deaf. **8**
—Charles Belden, with **Chandler Sprague,** *Charlie Chan in Honolulu*, screenplay, 1938

They say money doesn't stink. I sometimes wonder. **9**
—Raymond Chandler, *Farewell My Lovely*, 1940

A full pocketbook often groans more loudly than an empty stomach. **10**
—Franklin D. Roosevelt, speech, Nov. 1, 1940

Not even a collapsing world looks dark to a man who is about to make his fortune. **11**
—E. B. White, *Intimations*, in *One Man's Meat*, 1944

Money should circulate like rainwater . . . setting up a little business here and furnishing a good time there. **12**
—Thornton Wilder, *The Matchmaker*, 1956

Money will not make you happy, and happy will not make you money. **13**
—Groucho Marx, saying, attributed in *The New York Times* [Jan. 29, 1955]

1 Never invest in anything that eats or needs repainting.
—Billy Rose, in the *New York Post*, Oct. 25, 1957

2 If you can actually count your money, then you are not really a rich man.
—J. Paul Getty, quoted in the London *Observer*, Nov. 3, 1957

★ Billionaire Getty was one of the world's richest men at the time, possibly the richest.

3 Money, it turned out, was exactly like sex. You thought of nothing else if you didn't have it and thought of other things if you did.
—James Baldwin, *The Black Boy Looks at the White Boy*, in *Nobody Knows My Name*, 1961

4 A billion here and a billion there and pretty soon you're talking real money.
—Everett M. Dirksen, attributed

★ Dirksen of Illinois, a Republican, was Senate minority leader from 1959 to his death in 1969. This comment is widely attributed to him, but the curator at the Dirksen Congressional Center was unable to track down the quote for the *Wall Street Journal*. That paper reported, however, on January 1, 1985, that the curator added, "That doesn't mean he didn't say it."

5 You can never be too skinny or too rich.
—Barbara "Babe" Paley, saying, attributed

★ She was the wife of CBS founder and head, Bill Paley. The quote has also been attributed to Gloria Vanderbilt, Rose Kennedy, Truman Capote, and the Duchess of Windsor (who had it embroidered on a pillow). See also Eileen Ford at HEALTH.

6 Follow the money.
—William Goldman, screenplay, *All the President's Men*, 1976

★ The injunction from "Deep Throat," the mysterious source (now known to have been FBI associate director W. Mark Felt) who helped reporters Bob Woodward and Carl Bernstein penetrate the Watergate conspiracy, is so memorable that people tend to forget that the line first appeared in the movie based on their book, not the book itself.

7 It is better to lose opportunity than capital.
—Susan M. Byrne, on *Wall Street Week in Review*, Feb. 15, 1985

8 Greed is healthy.
—Ivan Boesky, speech, University of California Business School in Berkeley, 1986

★ Boesky, a high-flying financier, was later charged with fraud and jailed. He was the model for the villain, Gordon Gekko, in the 1987 movie *Wall Street*, co-authored and directed by Oliver Stone. Gekko tells stockholders, "Greed, for lack of a better word, is good. Greed is right. Greed works."

9 Show me the money!
—Cameron Crowe, screenplay, *Jerry Maguire*, 1996

10 What we do is determined by who pays us.
—Lawrence Joseph, *Lawyerland*, 1997

Money follows power. 1

—**Larry Makinson,** Deputy Director, Center for Responsive Politics, quoted in *The New York Times,* Nov. 12, 1997

★ This is Makinson's Maxim.

This is an impressive crowd—the haves and the have-mores. 2

—**George W. Bush,** Alfred E. Smith Memorial Dinner, Oct. 20, 2000

★ Presidential candidate Bush added, "Some people call you the elites; I call you my base." This annual dinner is an occasion for politicians to show off a sense of humor.

Money, like water, will always find an outlet. 3

—**Sandra Day O'Connor & John Paul Stevens,** U.S. Supreme Court majority opinion upholding major portions of the McCain-Feingold campaign finance law, Dec. 10, 2003

Marrying for money: It is not done. Rather one mingles with the rich and marries for 4
love.

—**Anonymous,** aphorism, cited in *The New York Times,* Fashion Diary, Guy Trebay, Feb. 22, 2005

Montana

See also CITIES (BUTTE).

Montana's real trouble . . . is that her graveyards aren't big enough. 5

—**Arthur Fisher,** quoted in Ernest Gruening, ed., *These United States, A Symposium,* 1923

Montana: High, Wide, and Handsome. 6

—**Joseph Kinsey Howard,** book title, 1943

I am in love with Montana. . . . Montana seems to me to be what a small boy would 7
think Texas is like from hearing Texans.

—**John Steinbeck,** *Travels with Charley,* 1962

Montana is a great splash of grandeur. 8

—**Ibid.**

[Montana:] The last best place on earth. 9

—**Anonymous,** motto, cited in exhibit of art and crafts from Montana at The Silo in New Milford, Conn., [1999]

Oro y plata. 10
Gold and silver.

—Motto, state of Montana

Moon

See NATURE: THE HEAVENS, THE SKY.

Morality

See ETHICS & MORALITY; VIRTUE.

Morning

See NATURE: TIMES OF DAY.

Mothers

See PARENTS.

Movies

See ART: THEATER, DRAMA, MOVIES & MAGIC.

Mysticism & Mystery

1 Mystery is the antagonist of truth. It is a fog of human invention that obscures truth and represents it in distortion.

—**Tom Paine,** *The Age of Reason*, 1794

2 It is true that the unknown is the largest need of the intellect, although for this no one thinks to thank God.

—**Emily Dickinson,** letter to her cousins, Louise and Frances Norcross, 1876, in Alfred Kazin, *God & the American Writer* [1997]

3 In the deepest heart of all of us there is a corner in which the ultimate mystery of things works sadly.

—**William James,** *The Will to Believe*, 1897

4 The mystic is, in short, *invulnerable*, and must be left, whether we relish it or not, in undisturbed enjoyment of his creed.

—**William James,** *The Varieties of Religious Experience*, 1902

5 The mystic can live happily in the droning consciousness of his own heart-beats and those of the universe.

—**George Santayana,** *Winds of Doctrine*, 1913

6 Mystics always hope that science will some day overtake them.

—**Booth Tarkington,** *Looking forward to the Great Adventure*, 1926

7 The most beautiful thing we can experience is the mysterious. It is the source of all true art and science.

—**Albert Einstein,** *What I Believe*, 1930

8 I said to my soul, be still, and let the dark come upon you which shall be the darkness of God.

—**T. S. Eliot,** *Four Quartets: East Coker*, 1940

★ The allusion is *Psalms* 46:10: "Be still, and know that I am God."

Penetrating so many secrets, we cease to believe in the unknowable. But there it sits nevertheless, calmly licking its chops. 1

—**H. L. Mencken,** *Minority Report: H. L. Mencken's Notebooks* [1956]

In mysticism . . . the attempt is given up to know God by thought, and it is replaced by the experience of union with God in which there is no more room—and no need—for knowledge about God. 2

—**Erich Fromm,** *The Art of Loving*, 1956

The greatest mystery is why there is something instead of nothing, and the greatest something is this thing called life. 3

—**Allan Sandage,** quoted in Alan Lightman and Roberta Brawer, *Through a Window*, 1990

★ As an astronomer, Mr. Sandage has sought to determine how and when the universe was formed by peering through telescopic windows at the furthest, oldest objects in it.

Nations & Regions

See also CITIES; FOREIGNERS; FOREIGN POLICY; MEXICAN WAR; RACES & PEOPLES; SPANISH-AMERICAN WAR.

Africa

It is still yesterday in Africa. It will take millions of tomorrows to rectify what has been done here. 4

—**Lorraine Hansberry,** *Les Blancs*, 1972

Ancient World

See also GREECE.

The Naiad airs have brought me home 5
To the glory that was Greece,
And the grandeur that was Rome.

—**Edgar Allan Poe,** *To Helen*, 1831

Argentina

A shadow state gripped by psychoses because the world has passed it by. 6

—**John Gunther,** *Inside South America*, 1967

Australia

Australia, n. A country lying in the South Sea, whose industrial and commercial development has been unspeakably retarded by an unfortunate dispute among geographers as to whether it is a continent or an island. 7

—**Ambrose Bierce,** *The Devil's Dictionary*, 1906

Brazil

1 It's such a useless thing for a man to want to be: the p-p-president of Brazil.
—Truman Capote, *Breakfast at Tiffany's*, 1957

Canada

2 Canada is a mighty good neighbor and a mighty good customer. That's a combination that is hard to beat.
—Will Rogers, in Alex Ayres, ed., *The Wit and Wisdom of Will Rogers* [1993]

3 I don't even know what street Canada is on.
—Al Capone, remark, 1931, quoted in Roy Greenaway, *The News Game* [1966]

4 Nobody wants to talk about Canada.
—Brian Moore, *The Luck of Ginger Coffee*, 1960

★ Canadians can be hard upon themselves; see also Bruce McCall below. Moore, who always described himself as a Canadian author, took up residence in the United States in 1959, the year before his novel won the Governor General's Award.

5 Geography has made us neighbors. History has made us friends. Economics has made us partners, and necessity has made us allies. Those whom God has so joined together, let no man put asunder.
—John F. Kennedy, address, Canadian Parliament, May 17, 1961

6 We tended to imagine Canada as a kind of vast hunting preserve convenient to the United States.
—Edmund Wilson, *O Canada*, 1965

7 Heaven was the word for Canada, and the Negro sang of the hope that his escape on the Underground Railroad would carry him there.
—Martin Luther King, Jr., quoted in *The New York Times,* [Nov. 23, 2003]

8 Canada is a bore.
—Bruce McCall, *Thin Ice: Coming of Age in Canada*, 1997

★ Born and bred in Canada, McCall moved to the United States in the early 1960s. See also Brian Moore above.

9 Blame Canada
—Trey Parker and Marc Shaiman, song title, *South Park: Bigger, Longer & Uncut*, 1999

10 Newfoundland is, or was, full of interesting people. . . .
In short there was a higherer capita percentage of interesting people
there than almost anywhere on earth, but the population was small,
which meant not too many interesting people
—John Ashbery, *Newfoundland,* in *Where Shall I Wander*, 2005

China

[Re the maxim that the word of a Chinese man is as good as his bond:] That might have been in the old days, but not since the missionaries and businessmen come in. Chinese are just as human as anybody now. 1
—**Will Rogers,** in Alex Ayres, ed., *The Wit and Wisdom of Will Rogers* [1993]

England

See also CITIES, CITIES ABROAD: LONDON.

The extremes of opulence and of want are more remarkable, and more constantly obvious, in this country than in any other I ever saw. 2
—**John Quincy Adams,** diary, Nov. 8, 1816

An Englishman who has lost his fortune is said to have died of a broken heart. 3
—**Ralph Waldo Emerson,** *English Traits*, 1856

An Englishman is never so natural as when he's holding his tongue. 4
—**Henry James,** *The Portrait of a Lady*, 1881

England and the United States are natural allies, and should be the best of friends. 5
—**U. S. Grant,** *Memoirs*, 1885

We have really everything in common with America nowadays except, of course, language. 6
—**Oscar Wilde,** *The Canterville Ghost*, 1887

★ George Bernard Shaw often is credited with much the same thought—"England and America are two countries divided by a common language"—but the line has not been found in his writings, according to the *Oxford Dictionary of Quotations* (2004).

England is the paradise of individuality, eccentricity, heresy, anomalies, hobbies, and humors. 7
—**George Santayana,** *Soliloquies in England*, 1922

To be an Englishman is to belong to the most exclusive club there is. 8
—**Ogden Nash,** *England Expects*, in *I'm a Stranger Here Myself*, 1938

In England's case, uniquely, God and Mammon *are* one. 9
—**John Gunther,** *Inside Europe*, 1938

The English never abolish anything. They put it in cold storage. 10
—**Alfred North Whitehead,** *Dialogues of Alfred North Whitehead*, Jan. 19, 1945, recorded by Lucien Price [1955]

Great Britain has lost an empire and has not yet found a role. 11
—**Dean Acheson,** speech, U.S. Military Academy, West Point, Dec. 5, 1962

Europe

1 Can we never extract the tapeworm of Europe from the brain of our countrymen?
—Ralph Waldo Emerson, *Culture*, in *The Conduct of Life*, 1860

2 Europe's old dynastic slaughterhouse (Area of murder-plots of thrones, with scent yet left of wars and scaffolds everywhere).
—Walt Whitman, *Song of the Redwood Tree*, 1873

3 America has never quite forgiven Europe for having been discovered somewhat earlier in history than itself.
—Oscar Wilde, *The American Man*, in *Court and Society Review*, April 1887

4 Every time Europe looks across the Atlantic to see the American Eagle, it observes only the rear end of an ostrich.
—H. G. Wells, *America*, 1907

5 You're thinking of Europe as Germany and France. I don't. I think that's old Europe.
—Donald Rumsfeld, Jan. 22, 2003

★ The Defense Secretary caused an uproar in Europe with this and similar comments at a foreign corps press conference on the intensifying US-Iraq hostility. "Germany has been a problem and France has been a problem," he said. But, he added, "the center of gravity is shifting to the East."

France

See also CITIES, CITIES ABROAD: PARIS.

6 When our king goes out they [French people] fall down and kiss the earth. . . Then they go to kissing one another. This is the truest wisdom. They have as much happiness in one year as one Englishman in ten.
—**Thomas Jefferson,** quoted in Gore Vidal, *Inventing a Nation*, 2003

7 All is orderly and beautiful—everything is charming to the eye.
—Mark Twain, *The Innocents Abroad,* 1869

8 France has neither winter, summer, nor morals—apart from these drawbacks it is a fine country.
—Mark Twain, in *Notebook* [1935], written before 1910

9 [France is] a country where the money falls apart but you can't tear the toilet paper.
—Billy Wilder, quoted in Maurice Zolotow, *Billy Wilder in Hollywood* [1977]

10 Fifty million Frenchmen can't be wrong.
—Anonymous, saying of American troops in World War I, 1917–18

11 In France, every argument becomes a matter of principle; the practical results are relegated to second place.
—Edward C. Banfield, 1961, quoted by Michael Lind, *The New York Times Book Review*, July 23, 1995

Germany

Whenever the literary German dives into a sentence, that is the last you are going to see of him till he emerges on the other side of the Atlantic with his verb in his mouth. **1**
—Mark Twain, *A Connecticut Yankee in King Arthur's Court*, 1889

Greece

See also ANCIENT WORLD.

They [the Greeks] were the first Westerners; the spirit of the West, the modern spirtit, is a Greek discovery. **2**
—Edith Hamilton, *The Greek Way*, 1930

Greece is the home of the Gods. **3**
—Henry Miller, *The Colossus of Maroussi*, 1941

Ireland

The Irish with their glowing hearts and reverent credulity, are needed in this cold age of intellect and skepticism. **4**
—Lydia Maria Child, *Letters from New York*, No. 33, Dec. 8, 1842

I'm troubled, I'm dissatisfied, I'm Irish. **5**
—Marianne Moore, *Spenser's Ireland*, 1941

★ The 16th-century English poet Edmund Spenser wrote one prose work, *A View of the Present State of Ireland.* Moore's poem begins: "Spenser's Ireland / has not altered:— / a place as kind as it is green, / the greenest place I've never seen. / Every name is a tune."

To be Irish is to know that in the end the world will break your heart. **6**
—Daniel Patrick Moynihan, attributed, in Thomas Cahill, *How the Irish Saved Civilization*, 1995

★ The observation was occasioned by the assassination of Pres. John F. Kennedy.

Italy

See also CITIES: FLORENCE, ROME, VENICE.

Italy is well deserving the character it has acquired of being the Garden of Europe— and of being likewise the abode of poverty, villainy—filth and extortion. **7**
—Washington Irving, *Journal*, April 22, 1805

Italy gives us antiquity with good roads, cheap living, and above all, a sense of freedom from responsibility. **8**
—James Russell Lowell, *Leaves from My Journal in Italy and Elsewhere*, 1854

Say that the Creator made Italy from designs by Michael Angelo! **9**
—Mark Twain, *The Innocents Abroad*, 1869

1 I am inclined to notice the ruin in things, perhaps because I was born in Italy.
—**Arthur Miller,** *A View from the Bridge*, 1955

Italy v. Switzerland

2 In Italy for thirty years under the Borgias, they had warfare, terror, murder, bloodshed. They produced Michaelangelo, Leonardo da Vinci, and the Renaissance. In Switzerland, they had brotherly love, five hundred years of democracy, and peace, and what did they produce? The cuckoo clock.
—**Orson Welles,** *The Third Man*, 1949

★ The screenplay was by Graham Greene, but Welles is said to have added this passage himself.

Japan

3 I think we have thrown Japan morally backward a thousand years; she is going to adopt our vices (which are much too large for her).
—**Lafcadio Hearn,** letter to Basil Hall Chamberlain, Jan. 14, 1893

★ Japan was changing quickly. The last rebellion of the feudal samurai had been crushed in 1877; the army adopted the German general-staff system in 1878; political parties formed in 1881; a constitution was promulgated in 1889. A slogan of the period was *fukoku-kyohei*, rich country—strong army. And see below.

4 The development of the mathematical faculty in the race—unchecked by our class of aesthetics and idealisms—ought to prove a serious danger to western civilization at last.
—**Lafcadio Hearn,** letter to Basil Hall Chamberlain, Feb. 1895

★ Hearn's reasoning is questionable—Western aesthetics and idealisms proved to be weak moral reeds in the 20th century—but he knew which way the wind was blowing. The Sino-Japanese War, a quick victory on land and sea for Japan, was winding down as he wrote. The subsequent war with Russia (1904–1905) was another quick victory for Japan, this time over a Western power.

5 Under all the amazing self-control and patience, there exists an adamantine something very dangerous to reach.
—**Lafcadio Hearn,** *Out of the East*, 1895

★ Hearn, incidentally, felt at home in Japan; married a Japanese, became a citizen of the country, and taught there.

6 I saw the native home in Japan as a supreme study in elimination—not only of dirt, but the elimination of the insignificant . . . . I found this ancient Japanese dwelling to be a perfect example of the modern standardizing I had myself been working out.
—**Frank Lloyd Wright,** c. 1914 in *An Autobiography* [1979]

7 [On the Japanese:] They got everything we got, and if they haven't, you show it to 'em and they will make it.
—**Will Rogers,** *Weekly Articles*, Jan. 17, 1932

While we spend energy and imagination on new ways of cleaning the floors of our houses, the Japanese solve the problem by not dirtying them in the first place. 1
—**Bernard Rudofsky,** *The Kimono Mind: An Informed Guide to Japan*, 1965

The Japanese have perfected good manners and made them indistinguishable from rudeness. 2
—**Paul Theroux,** *The Great Railway Bazaar*, 1975

Liberia

A little America, destined to shine gem-like in the heart of darkest Africa. 3
—**James Monroe,** on the founding of Liberia, 1821

★ Liberia was colonized by former American slaves under the program of the American Colonization Society. It declared independence in 1847. President Monroe's optimistic vision seems anachronistic today for several reasons, one of which is that Liberia's vast rain forest is probably its most precious asset. Monroe's "christening" of Liberia was quoted by William Power, *The New York Times Op Ed,* Jan. 10, 2005

Mexico

See also MEXICAN WAR.

Napoleon has no right to Mexico. Mexico may deserve a licking. That is possible enough. Most people do. But nobody has any right to lick Mexico except the United States. We have a right, I flatter myself, to lick the entire continent, including ourselves, any time we want to. 4
—**Artemus Ward,** *Artemus Ward (His Travels) Among the Mormons* [1863], 1865

Poor Mexico! So far from God and so close to the United States. 5
—**Porfirio Díaz,** attributed, in John S. D. Eisenhower, *The U.S. War with Mexico, 1846–1848* [1989]

★ Gen. Díaz was president and dictator of Mexico 1876–80 and 1884–1911.

Russia

See also CITIES: MOSCOW, ST. PETERSBURG; FUTURE, THE (Steffens).

Russia seems at present the great bug-bear of the European politicians on the land, as the British Leviathan is on the water. 6
—**James Madison,** letter to Richard Rush, Nov. 20, 1821

You can take the whole of the United States of America, from Maine to California and from Lake Superior to the Gulf of Mexico, and set it down in the middle of Siberia, without touching anywhere the boundaries of the latter's territory. 7
—**George Kennan,** *Siberia and the Exile System*, 1891

Russia is omnipotence. . . . who can ever penetrate that polar mystery? 8
—**Henry Adams,** letter to Brooks Adams, June 5, 1895

1 The Russians are devout believers in an eye for an eye, or if possible two.
—**John Gunther,** *Inside Russia Today*, 1962

2 In a Russian tragedy, everybody dies. In a Russian comedy, everybody dies, too. But they die happy.
—**Barry Farber,** in his radio talk show, WMCA, New York City, cited in Suzy Platt, ed., *Respectfully Quoted*, Library of Congress [1989]

3 The brain is ill-equipped to comprehend the meaning of a nation that encompasses eleven time zones.
—**Hedrick Smith,** *The Russians*, 1977

4 The Russians are connoisseurs of the cold.
—**Ibid.**

5 At the Cabinet meeting this morning Zbig [national security adviser Zbigniew Brzezinski] made an interesting comment that under Lenin the Soviet Union was like a religious revival, under Stalin like a prison, under Khrushchev like a circus, and under Brezhnev like the U.S. Post Office.
—**Jimmy Carter,** diary, Nov. 7, 1977

6 When they go to take a bite out of the world, the Soviets are not fussy eaters.
—**Richard M. Nixon,** *The Real War*, 1980

7 An evil empire.
—**Ronald Reagan,** speech, National Association of Evangelicals, March 8, 1983

★ Russia was the evil empire, according to Pres. Reagan. The label was borrowed from the 1977 film *Star Wars* by George W. Lucas, Jr. See also FOREIGN POLICY.

Scandinavia

8 The folk who live in Scandinavia
Are famous for their odd behavia.
They have the frigidest of climates
And avoid their bellicose fellow-primates.
Though salesmen cluster at their door,
They don't want anybody's war.
It isn't that they put on airs;
They merely mind their own affairs.
—**Ogden Nash,** *Fellow Creatures III: The Northerners*, in *I'm a Stranger Here Myself*, 1938

South America

9 Few South Americans have ulcers.
—**John Gunther,** *Inside South America*, 1967

"You must not judge people by their country," a lady advised me. "In South America, it is always wise to judge people by their altitude." 1
—**Paul Theroux,** *The Old Patagonian Express*, 1979

Spain

If the people of Spain have one common trait it is pride, and, if they have another, it is common sense, and if they have a third, it is impracticality. 2
—**Ernest Hemingway,** *Death in the Afternoon*, 1932

Sweden

If ever there was a Yankeer than Yankee, he's a Swede. 3
—**Henry Adams,** letter to Elizabeth Cameron, Sept. 10, 1901

Switzerland

See also ITALY V. SWITZERLAND.

Continually since I have been in Switzerland have I been struck with the similarity in sentiment and manners between the Swiss and the Americans—It is impossible this nation can always be kept under, the love of liberty burns too strongly in their bosoms. 4
—**Washington Irving,** *Journal*, May 8, 1805

Switzerland is a small, steep country, much more up and down than sideways, and is all stuck over with brown hotels built on the cuckoo clock style of architecture. 5
—**Ernest Hemingway,** in the *Toronto Star Weekly*, March 4, 1922

The Swiss who are not a people so much as a neat clean small quite solvent business. 6
—**William Faulkner,** *Intruder in the Dust*, 1948

The Pacific

The power that rules the Pacific . . . is the power that rules the world. 7
—**Albert J. Beveridge,** speech, U.S. Senate, 1900

★ A farsighted global view from the American heartland: Sen. Beveridge, a Republican, represented Indiana from 1899 to 1911.

Turkey

A humorless soldierly people whose arts are courage, honor, and bloodletting. 8
—**Nelson Algren,** *Who Lost an American?*, 1963

Before World War I, Turkey was known as the "Sick Man of Europe"; now it is almost a terminal case. 9
—**Richard M. Nixon,** *The Real War*, 1980

Venezuela

1 This pioneer democracy, built on foundations, not of rock, but blood hard as rock.
—**Robert Lowell,** *Caracas I*, in *Notebook*, 1970

Native Americans

See RACES & PEOPLES.

Nature

See also COUNTRY LIFE & PEOPLE; ENVIRONMENT; FARMS & FARMERS; MIDWEST, THE; SCIENCE; UNIVERSE, THE; WEST, THE; WILDERNESS.

2 It were happy if we studied nature more in natural things, and acted according to nature, whose rules are few, plain, and most reasonable.
—**William Penn,** *Some Fruits of Solitude*, 1693

3 With beauty before me, I walk
With beauty behind me, I walk
With beauty above and about me, I walk,
It is finished in beauty,
It is finished in beauty.
—**Anonymous,** Navaho night chant, in Frank Bergon & Zeese Papaniklas, *Looking Far West* [1978]

4 Everything in nature contains all the powers of nature. Everything is made of one hidden stuff.
—**Ralph Waldo Emerson,** *Compensation*, in *Essays: First Series*, 1841

★ For Emerson on nature's secrets, see SCIENCE.

5 Nature, as we know her, is no saint.
—**Ralph Waldo Emerson,** *History*, in *Essays: First Series*, 1841

6 Nature provides exceptions to every rule.
—**Margaret Fuller,** *The Great Lawsuit: Man versus Men, Woman versus Women*, in *The Dial*, July 1843

7 Nature is one and continuous everywhere.
—**Henry David Thoreau,** *A Week on the Concord and Merrimack Rivers*, 1849

8 Heaven is under our feet as well as over our heads.
—**Henry David Thoreau,** *The Pond in Winter*, in *Walden*, 1854

9 Nature is full of genius, full of the divinity; so that not a snowflake escapes its fashioning hand.
—**Henry David Thoreau,** *Journal*, Jan. 5, 1856

10 I believe in the forest, and in the meadow, and in the night in which the corn grows.
—**Henry David Thoreau,** *Walking*, 1862

Mountains are earth's undecaying monuments. 1
—**Nathaniel Hawthorne,** *The Notch of the White Mountains* [1868]

There are no short cuts in evolution. 2
—**Louis D. Brandeis,** speech, Boston, April 22, 1904

★ For William Jennings Bryan on evolution, see SCIENCE: BIOLOGY.

There are no sermons in stones. It is easier to get a spark out of a stone than a moral. 3
—**John Burroughs,** *Time and Change*, 1912

Nature, n. The Unseen Intelligence which loved us into being, and is disposing of us 4
by the same token.
—**Elbert Hubbard,** *The Roycroft Dictionary and Book of Epigrams*, 1923

The earth is all I know of wonder. 5
—**Marsden Hartley,** *To The Nameless One*

Nothing is so cruel, so wanton, so unfeeling as nature; she moves with the weight of 6
a glacier carrying everything before her.
—**Clarence Darrow,** *The Story of My Life*, 1932

Only to the white man was nature a wilderness, and only to him was the land 7
"infested" with "wild" animals and "savage" people. To us it was tame. Earth was bountiful, and we were surrounded with the blessings of the Great Mystery.
—**Luther Standing Bear,** *Land of the Spotted Eagle*, 1933

★ He was chief of the Oglala Sioux.

Perhaps nature is our best assurance of immortality. 8
—**Eleanor Roosevelt,** *My Day*, newspaper column, April 24, 1945

Nature always deceives. . . . There is in Nature a marvelous system of spells and wiles. 9
—**Vladimir Nabokov,** *Good Readers and Good Writers*, 1948

★ Nabokov continues, "The art of fiction only follows Nature's lead." See Nabokov also at STORIES.

A river seems a magic thing. A magic, moving, living part of the very earth itself. 10
—**Laura Gilpin,** *The Rio Grande*, 1949

In nature, there is less death and destruction than death and transmutation. 11
—**Edwin Way Teale,** *Circle of the Seasons*, 1953

Whatever Nature has in store for mankind, unpleasant as it may be, men must 12
accept, for ignorance is never better than knowledge.
—**Enrico Fermi,** quoted in Laura Fermi, *Atoms in the Family*, 1955

★ Fermi pioneered the way in unleashing the power of the atom—for better or for worse. See Arthur Holly Compton in SCIENCE: TECHNOLOGY.

The "control of nature" is a phrase conceived in arrogance. 13
—**Rachel Carson,** *Silent Spring*, 1962

★ More at SCIENCE: TECHNOLOGY.

1 Nature writes with a spray can, not a ballpoint pen.
—**Lotfi Asker Zadeh,** saying, *Skeptical Inquirer* [Sept./Oct., 1995]

★ Zadeh invented so-called "fuzzy logic," which differs from classical black-and-white Aristotelian logic in having more tolerance for the impreciseness so often encountered in the real world.

2 Nature uses only the longest threads to weave her patterns, so each small piece of her fabric reveals the organization of the entire tapestry.
—**Richard Feynman,** personal papers, quoted in James Gleick, *Genius: The Life and Science of Richard Feynman*, 1992

3 We are already engaged in World War III. It is a war against nature.
—**Norman Myers,** quoted by G. Tyler Miller, *Living in the Environment,* 1996

4 We didn't invent nature. Nature invented us. Nature bats last, the saying goes, but, even more importantly, it's her playing field. We would be wise to learn the ground rules and play by them.
—**Kenny Ausubel,** speech, Bioneers Conference, Oct. 7, 2003

Nature: Animals

See also HAPPINESS (Schulz)

5 Everything belonging to the spider is admirable.
—**Jonathan Edwards,** *The Spider*, c. 1714

★ Edwards was about age twelve when he wrote about spiders. See Robert Lowell at COUNTRY LIFE & PEOPLE for a poem about Edwards and his observation of spiders.

6 I wish the bald eagle had not been chosen as the representative of our country; he is a bird of bad moral character . . . like those among men who live by sharping and robbing, he is generally poor, and often very lousy . . . The turkey . . . is a much more respectable bird, and withal a true original native of America.
—**Benjamin Franklin,** letter to Sarah Bache, Jan. 26, 1784

7 The air was literally filled with Pigeons, and the noon-day light was obscured as by an eclipse.
—**John James Audubon,** *Passenger Pigeon*, in *Ornithological Biography*, 1831–39

★ Audubon was describing the flight of Passenger Pigeons over the Kentucky barrens in 1813. He also wrote that the sound of approaching pigeons—sometimes in flocks of more than a billion—was like that of a hard gale at sea. The mass of pigeons was so thick that they could be knocked down with poles. When they alit, the weight of their numbers caused branches to break. The uproar continued all night. These birds were easy to kill with clubs, and Audubon described the men in his company taking large numbers that night, and setting hogs on the pigeons remaining. The species became extinct when the last passenger pigeon, named Martha Washington, died in the Cincinnati Zoo, at age twenty-nine, on September 1, 1914.

There is something in the unselfish and self-sacrificing love of a brute, which goes directly to the heart of him who has had frequent occasion to test the paltry friendship and gossamer fidelity of mere man. **1**

—Edgar Allan Poe, *The Black Cat*, 1843

The country before us thronged with buffalo. They were crowded so densely together that in the distance their rounded backs presented a surface of uniform blackness. **2**

—Francis Parkman, *The Oregon Trail*, 1847

★ At that time some sixty million bison roamed the plains along the Oregon Trail. White settlers and hunters then killed almost all of them within a few years.

The bluebird carries the sky on its back. **3**

—Henry David Thoreau, *Journal*, April 3, 1852

I think I could turn and live with animals, they are so placid and self-contained **4**

I stand and look at them long and long.

—Walt Whitman, *Song of Myself*, 1855

Split the Lark—and you'll find the Music— **5**
Bulb after Bulb, in Silver rolled—
Scantily dealt to the Summer Morning
Saved for your Ear when Lutes be old.

—Emily Dickinson, poem no. 861, c. 1864

Bees are Black, with Gilt Surcingles— **6**
Buccaneers of Buzz.

—Emily Dickinson, poem no. 1405, c. 1877

★ A surcingle is a belt or girth.

MAJOR **7**
Born a Dog
Died a Gentleman.

—Anonymous

★ Identified in *American Heritage*, Feb. 1973, as a line on an old Maryland gravestone for a dog.

Cats and monkeys, monkeys and cats—all human life is there. **8**

—Henry James, *The Madonna of the Future*, 1879

A jay hasn't got any more principle than a Congressman. A jay will lie, a jay will steal, a jay will deceive, a jay will betray; and four times out of five, a jay will go back on his solemnest promise. **9**

—Mark Twain, *Jim Baker's Blue Jay Yarn*, in *A Tramp Abroad*, 1880

A noiseless patient spider. **10**

—Walt Whitman, *A Noiseless Patient Spider*, 1881

The dog was created especially for children. He is the god of frolic. **11**

—Henry Ward Beecher, *Proverbs from Plymouth Pulpit*, 1887

1 Of all God's creatures there is only one that cannot be made the slave of the lash. That one is the cat. If man could be crossed with the cat, it would improve man, but it would deteriorate the cat.

—**Mark Twain,** *Notebook* [1935]

2 Oh, a wondrous bird is the pelican!
His beak holds more than his belican.
He takes in his beak
Enough food for a week.
But I'll be darned if I know how the helican.

—**Dixon Lanier Merritt,** in the *Nashville Banner*, April 22, 1913

3 The bull is godlike.

—**William Carlos Williams,** *The Bull*, 1922

4 At evening, casual flocks of pigeons make
Ambiguous undulations as they sink.
Downward to darkness, on extended wings.

—**Wallace Stevens,** *Sunday Morning*, 1923

5 Pigeons on the grass alas.

—**Gertrude Stein,** *Four Saints in Three Acts*, 1927

6 The turtle lives 'twixt plated decks
Which practically conceal its sex.
I think its clever of the turtle.
In such a fix to be so fertile.

—**Ogden Nash,** *Autres Bêtes, Autres Moeurs*, in *Hard Lines* 1931

7 As the cat
climbed over
the top of

the jamcloset
first the right
forefoot

carefully then the hind
stepped down

into the pit of
the empty
flowerpot.

—**William Carlos Williams,** *Poem*, c. 1930–31

8 An elephant's faithful
One hundred per cent!

—**Dr. Seuss** (Theodor Seuss Geisel), *Horton Hatches the Egg*, 1940

★ More at LOYALTY.

The trouble with a kitten is 1
THAT
Eventually it becomes a
CAT.

—Ogden Nash, *The Kitten*, in *The Face Is Familiar*, 1941

The song of canaries 2
Never varies,
And when they're moulting
They're pretty revolting.

—Ogden Nash, *The Canary*, in *The Face Is Familiar*, 1941

★ Canaries were popular pets in this era, and people put a lot of effort into their care and encouraging them to sing. Dorothy Parker called her canary Onan, because he spilled his seed upon the ground.

Dogs display reluctance and wrath 3
If you try to give them a bath.
They bury bones in hideaways,
And half the time they run sideaways.

—Ogden Nash, *An Introduction to Dogs*, in *The Face Is Familiar*, 1941

If a dog jumps in your lap, it is because he is fond of you. If a cat does the same thing, it is because your lap is warmer. 4

—Alfred North Whitehead, *Dialogues of Alfred North Whitehead*, recorded by Lucien Price [1955]

The best thing about animals is that they don't talk much. 5

—Thornton Wilder, *The Skin of Our Teeth*, 1942

I saw the spiders marching through air. 6

—Robert Lowell, *Mr. Edwards and the Spider*, 1946

★ More at Country Life & People.

Booming and booming of the new-come bee. 7

—Wallace Stevens, *Notes Toward a Supreme Fiction*, 1947

Our ability to perceive quality in nature begins, as in art, with the pretty. It expands through successive stages of the beautiful to values as yet uncaptured by language. The quality of cranes lies, I think, in this higher gamut, as yet beyond the reach of words. 8

—Aldo Leopold, *A Sand County Almanac*, 1949

★ Within the reach of words, Leopold described cranes in flight as "a great echelon of birds."

People on horses look better than they are. 9

—Marya Mannes, *More in Anger*, 1958

★ The next line is "People in cars look worse than they are."

1 It's not that easy being green.
—Joe Raposo, lyric for Kermit the Frog on Jim Henson's *Sesame Street*, television show, from 1969

2 If we had better hearing, and could discern the descants of sea birds, the rhythmic tympani of schools of mollusks, or even the distant harmonics of midges hanging over meadows in the sun, the combined sound might lift us off our feet.
—Lewis Thomas, *The Lives of a Cell*, 1974

3 Nothing to be done really about animals. Anything you do looks foolish. . . . It's almost as if we were put here on earth to show how silly they aren't.
—Russell Hoban, *Turtle Diary*, 1975

4 The basis of all animal rights should be the Golden Rule; we should treat *them* as we would wish them to treat us.
—Christine Stevens, in Michael Fox, *Returning to Eden*, 1980

Nature: Plants & Gardens

See also ENVIRONMENT; NATURE: TREES; WILDERNESS (for forests).

5 But though I am an old man, I am but a young gardener.
—Thomas Jefferson, letter to Charles Wilson Peale, August 20, 1811

6 The rose that lives its little hour
Is prized beyond the sculptured flower.
—William Cullen Bryant, *A Scene on the Banks of the Hudson*, 1828

7 Earth laughs in flowers.
—Ralph Waldo Emerson, *Hamatreya*, in *Poems*, 1847

8 A weed is no more than a flower in disguise.
—James Russell Lowell, *A Fable for Critics*, 1848
★ See also Emerson below.

9 One of the attractive things about the flowers is their beautiful reserve.
—Henry David Thoreau, *Journal*, June 17, 1853

10 I have great faith in a seed. Convince me that you have a seed there, and I am prepared to expect wonders.
—Henry David Thoreau, *The Dispersion of Seeds,* from his journal, published in Bradley P. Dear, ed., *Faith in a Seed* [1993]

11 I was determined to know beans.
—Henry David Thoreau, *The Beanfield, Walden*, 1854

12 Flowers are the sweetest things God ever made and forgot to put a soul into.
—Henry Ward Beecher, *Life Thoughts*, 1858

The Amen! of nature is always a flower. 1
—Oliver Wendell Holmes, Sr., *The Autocrat of the Breakfast-Table*, 1858

When lilacs last in the dooryard bloom'd. 2
—Walt Whitman, *When Lilacs Last in the Dooryard Bloom'd*, 1865–66

★ More at SORROW & GRIEF.

To own a bit of ground, to scratch it with a hoe, to plant seeds and watch their renewal of life—this is the commonest delight of the race, the most satisfactory thing a man can do. 3
—Charles Dudley Warner, *My Summer in a Garden*, 1870

★ But see also Warner at FARMS & FARMERS.

What is a weed? A plant whose virtues have not yet been discovered. 4
—Ralph Waldo Emerson, *Fortune of the Republic*, 1878

★ See also James Russell Lowell above.

The Dandelion's pallid tube 5
Astonishes the Grass,
And Winter instantly becomes
An infinite Alas—
—Emily Dickinson, poem no. 1519, c. 1881

Rose is a rose is a rose. 6
—Gertrude Stein, *Sacred Emily*, 1913

[On picking blueberries:] It's a nice way to live, 7
Just taking what Nature is willing to give,
Not forcing her hand with harrow and plow.
—Robert Frost, *Blueberries*, in *North of Boston*, 1914

As long as one has a garden, one has a future, and as long as one has a future, one is alive. 8
—Frances Hodgson Burnett, *In the Garden*, written 1924

★ This essay borrows its title from a chapter in the author's famous novel *The Secret Garden* (1911). In the last year of her life, when sick with cancer, Burnett tended her garden in Plandome, Long Island, and wrote this piece, which was published posthumously.

Nature abhors a garden. 9
—Michael Pollan, *The Botany of Desire*, 2001.

★ A play on Spinoza's "Nature abhors a vacuum."

Nature: Seas & Oceans

See also SHIPS & SAILING.

The sea is feline. It licks your feet. 10
—Oliver Wendell Holmes, Sr., *The Professor at the Breakfast-Table*, 1860

1 Implacable I, the implacable sea;
Implacable most when most I smile serene—
Pleased not appeased by myriad wrecks in me.
—**Herman Melville,** *Pebbles*, in *John Marr and Other Sailors*, 1888

2 The sea is woman, the sea is wonder—
Her other name is fate.
—**Edwin Markham,** *Virgilia*, 1905

3 The seas are the heart's blood of the earth.
—**Henry Beston,** *The Headlong Wave*, in *The Outermost House*, 1928

4 The sea hates a coward.
—**Eugene O'Neill,** *Mourning Becomes Electra*, 1931

5 The sea has many voices,
Many gods and many voices.
—**T. S. Eliot,** *Four Quartets: The Dry Salvages*, 1941

6 For all at last returns to the sea—to Oceanus, the ocean river, like the everflowing stream of time, the beginning and the end.
—**Rachel Carson,** last sentence, *The Sea Around Us*, 1951

7 it's always ourselves we find in the sea.
—**E. E. Cummings,** *maggie and millie and molly and may*, in *95 Poems*, 1958

8 It is an interesting biological fact that all of us have, in our veins the exact same percentage of salt in our blood that exists in the ocean, and, therefore, we have salt in our blood, in our sweat, in our tears. We are tied to the ocean. And when we go back to the sea, whether it is to sail or to watch it, we are going back from whence we came.
—**John F. Kennedy,** remarks, dinner for America's Cup crews, Newport, R.I., Sept. 14, 1962

9 The sea is mother-death . . . the one who wins.
—**Anne Sexton,** entry, Nov. 19, 1971, *A Small Journal*, in Howard Moss, ed., *The Poet's Story* [1974]

Nature: Seasons

See also Seasons & Times.

10 The melancholy days are come, the saddest of the year,
Of wailing winds, and naked woods, and meadows brown and sere.
—**William Cullen Bryant,** *The Death of the Flowers*, 1825

11 In . . . the fall, the whole country goes to glory.
—**Frances Trollope,** *Domestic Manners of the Americans*, 1832

Spring in the world! **1**
And all things are made new!
—**Henry Wadsworth Longfellow,** *Hyperion*, 1839

And what is so rare as a day in June? **2**
Then, if ever, come perfect days.
—**James Russell Lowell,** *The Vision of Sir Launfal*, 1846

★ In the prelude, Lowell wrote, "No price is set on the lavish summer; / June may be had by the poorest comer."

These are the days when Birds come back— **3**
A very few—a Bird or two—
To take a backward look.

These are the days when the skies resume
The old—old sophistries of June—
A blue and gold mistake.
—**Emily Dickinson,** poem no. 130, c. 1859

There's a certain Slant of light, **4**
Winter Afternoons—
That oppresses, like the Heft
Of Cathedral Tunes—
—**Emily Dickinson,** poem no. 258, c. 1861

The word May is a perfumed word. It is an illuminated initial. It means youth, love, **5**
song, and all that is beautiful in life.
—**Henry Wadsworth Longfellow,** journal entry, May 1, 1861

[On the beginning of summer:] The season of hope and promise is passed, and **6**
already the season of small fruits has arrived. We are a little saddened because we
begin to see the interval between our hopes and their fulfillment.
—**Henry David Thoreau,** *The Dispersion of Seeds,* in *Faith in a Seed* [1993]

★ This essay is one of several on botanical subjects that Thoreau had in the works at the time of his death in 1862. *Faith in a Seed* marked its first publication.

Then came the lovely spring with a rush of blossoms and music, **7**
Flooding the earth with flowers, and the air with melodies vernal.
—**Henry Wadsworth Longfellow,** *The Theologian's Tale,* in *Tales of a Wayside Inn*, 1863–74

Spring is the Period **8**
Express from God.
—**Emily Dickinson,** poem no. 844, c. 1864

1 November always seemed to be the Norway of the year.
—**Emily Dickinson,** letter to Dr. and Mrs. J. G. Holland, 1864

2 Our Summer made her light escape
Into the Beautiful.
—**Emily Dickinson,** poem no. 1540, c. 1865

3 The sun that brief December day
Rose cheerless over hills of gray,
And, darkly circled, gave at noon
A sadder light than waning moon.
—**John Greenleaf Whittier,** *Snow-Bound; A Winter Idyl*, 1866

4 November is the most disagreeable month in the whole year.
—**Louisa May Alcott,** *Little Women*, 1868

5 A little Madness in the Spring
Is wholesome even for the King.
—**Emily Dickinson,** poem no. 1333, c. 1875

★ The correct dates for Dickinson's poems do not always match the traditional numerical order.

6 O, it sets my heart a-clickin' like the tickin' of a clock,
When the frost is on the punkin and the fodder's in the shock.
—**James Whitcomb Riley,** *When the Frost Is on the Punkin*, 1883

7 The scarlet of the maples can shake me like a cry
Of bugles going by.
And my lonely spirit thrills
To see the frosty asters like a smoke upon the hills.
—**Bliss Carman,** *A Vagabond Song*, in *Songs in Vagabondia*, 1894

8 In the Good Old Summer Time.
—**Ren Shields,** song title, 1902

★ Music by George Evans.

9 Summer afternoon—summer afternoon; to me those have always been the two most beautiful words in the English language.
—**Henry James,** quoted in Edith Wharton, *A Backward Glance* [1934]

★ See also Tim Russert at SPORTS.

10 Spring came on forever,
Spring came on forever,
Said the Chinese nightingale.
—**Vachel Lindsay,** *The Chinese Nightingale*, 1917

11 Winter is icumen in,
Lhude sing Goddamm,
Raineth drop and staineth slop,

And how the wind doth ramm!
Sing: Goddamm.
—Ezra Pound, *Ancient Music*, 1917

★ A play on the anonymous *Cuckoo Song* from about 1250: "Sumer is icumen in, / Lhude sing cuccu! / Groweth sed, and bloweth med, / And springth the wude nu— / Sing cuccu!"

The leaves fall early this autumn, in wind. 1
The paired butterflies are already yellow with August
Over the grass in the West garden;
They hurt me. I grow older.
—Ezra Pound, *The River Merchant's Wife: A Letter (After Rihaku)*

Blaze the mountains in the windless autumn, 2
Frost-clear, blue-nooned, apple-ripening days.
—Sarah N. Cleghorn, *Vermont*, in *Portraits and Protests*, 1917

Winter lies too long in country towns; hangs on until it is stale and shabby, old and 3
sullen.
—Willa Cather, *My Antonia*, 1918

★ The town in the novel is Black Hawk, Nebraska. The author grew up in Red Cloud, Nebraska.

April 4
Comes like an idiot, babbling and strewing flowers.
—Edna St. Vincent Millay, *Spring*, in *Second April*, 1921

April is the cruellest month, breeding 5
Lilacs out of the dead land, mixing
Memory and desire, stirring
Dull roots with spring rain.
—T. S. Eliot, *The Waste Land*, 1922

The way a crow 6
Shook down on me
The dust of snow
From a hemlock tree
Has given my heart a change of mood
And saved some part
Of a day I had rued.
—Robert Frost, *Dust of Snow*, 1923

When the world is puddle-wonderful. 7
—E. E. Cummings, *Chansons Innocentes*, 1923

★ The season is "Just- / spring when the world is mud- / luscious."

1 A wind has blown the rain away and blown
the sky away and all the leaves away,
and the trees stand. I think I too have known
autumn too long.
—**E. E. Cummings,** *Realities*, V, in *Tulips and Chimneys*, 1923

2 O sweet spontaneous
earth how often
has the naughty thumb of science prodded
thy
beauty
thou answereth them only with
spring.
—**E. E. Cummings,** *Tulips and Chimneys*, 1924

3 Spring, the cruelest and fairest of the seasons, will come again. And the strange and buried men will come again, in flower and leaf the strange and buried men will come again, and death and the dust will never come again, for death and the dust will die.
—**Thomas Wolfe,** *Look Homeward Angel*, 1929

4 In summer the song
sings itself
—**William Carlos Williams,** *The Botticellian Trees*, 1930

5 All things on earth point home in old October: sailors to sea, travelers to walls and fences, hunters to field and hollow and the long voice of the hounds, the lover to the love he has forsaken.
—**Thomas Wolfe,** *Of Time and the River*, 1935

6 Summertime
And the livin' is easy,
Fish are jumpin', and the cotton is high.
—**Ira Gershwin,** *Porgy and Bess*, 1935

★ Music by George Gershwin.

7 These are the desolate, dark weeks.
—**William Carlos Williams,** *These*, 1938

8 The year plunges into night
and the heart plunges
lower than night.
—**William Carlos Williams,** *These*, 1938

9 When the short day is brightest, with forest and fire,
The brief sun flames the ice, on pond and ditches,
In windless cold that is the heart's beat,
Reflecting in a watery mirror
A glare that is blindness in the early afternoon.
—**T. S. Eliot,** *Four Quartets: Little Gidding*, 1942

The house was quiet and the world was calm. 1
The reader became the book; and the summer night
Was like the conscious being of the book.
The house was quiet and the world was calm.

—**Wallace Stevens,** *The House Was Quiet and the World Was Calm*, in *Transport to Summer*, 1947

August creates as she slumbers, replete and satisfied. 2

—**Joseph Wood Krutch,** *August*, in *Twelve Seasons*, 1949

One swallow does not make a summer, but one skein of geese, cleaving the murk of a March thaw, is the spring. 3

—**Aldo Leopold,** *A Sand County Almanac*, 1949

★ And, Leopold added, "A March morning is only as drab as he who walks in it without a glance skyward, ear cocked for geese."

All things seem possible in May. 4

—**Edwin Way Teale,** *North with the Spring*, 1951

For man, autumn is a time of harvest, of gathering together. For nature, it is a time of sowing, of scattering abroad. 5

—**Edwin Way Teale,** *Autumn Across America*, 1956

Over increasingly large areas of the United States, spring now comes unheralded by the return of birds. 6

—**Rachel Carson,** *The Silent Spring*, 1962

★ More at ENVIRONMENT.

One snow in a winter is happiness. Two snows are too many. Three snows are a penance visited on cities that are unjust. 7

—**Russell Baker,** *Poor Russell's Almanac*, 1972

The seasons . . . are authentic; there is no mistake about them, they are what a symphony ought to be: four perfect movements in intimate harmony with one another. 8

—**Arthur Rubinstein**, *My Young Years*, 1973

Nature: The Heavens, the Sky

The man who has seen the rising moon break out of the clouds at midnight has been present like an archangel at the creation of light and of the world. 9

—**Ralph Waldo Emerson,** *History*, in *Essays: First Series*, 1841

The sky is the daily bread of the eyes. 10

—**Ralph Waldo Emerson,** *Journal*, May 25, 1843

Silently, one by one, in the infinite meadows of heaven, 11
Blossomed the lovely stars, the forget-me-nots of the angels.

—**Henry Wadsworth Longfellow,** *Evangeline*, 1847

1 Give me the splendid silent sun with all his beams full-dazzling.
—**Walt Whitman,** *Give Me the Splendid Silent Sun*, 1865

2 Lo, the moon ascending,
Up from the east, the silvery round moon,
Beautiful over the house-tops, ghastly, phantom moon,
Immense and silent moon.
—**Walt Whitman,** *Song of the Universal*, 1881

3 The moon? It is a griffin's egg
Hatching tomorrow night . . .
Yet gentle will the griffin be,
Most decorous and fat,
And walk up to the Milky Way
And lap it like a cat.
—**Vachel Lindsay,** *Yet Gentle Will the Griffin Be (What Grandpa Told the Children)*, 1912

4 The book of moonlight is not written yet.
—**Wallace Stevens,** *The Comedian as the Letter C*, in *Harmonium*, 1923

★ See below for another Stevens line on the moon.

5 Blessed moon
noon
of night
that through the dark
bids Love
stay.
—**William Carlos Williams,** *Full Moon*, first version, 1924

6 who knows if the moon's
a balloon, coming out of a keen city
in the sky—filled with pretty people?
—**E. E. Cummings,** *who knows if the moon's a balloon*, in & [*And*], 1925

7 Blue skies
Smiling at me
Nothing but blue skies
Do I see.
—**Irving Berlin,** *Blue Skies*, song, 1926

8 The moon is the mother of pathos and pity.
—**Wallace Stevens,** *Lunar Paraphrase*, in *Harmonium*, 1931

9 The moon is a friend for the lonesome to talk to.
—**Carl Sandburg,** *Moonlight and Maggots*, in *Complete Poems*, 1950

10 Comets are the nearest thing to nothing that anything can be and still be something.
—**National Geographic,** press release, March 31, 1955

The moon is a different thing to each one of us. 1

—**Frank Borman,** from Apollo 8, Dec. 24, 1968

★ For the moon landing, see SCIENCE: TECHNOLOGY.

Our passionate preoccupation with the sky, the stars, and a God somewhere in outer space is a homing impulse. We are drawn back to where we came from. 2

—**Eric Hoffer,** in *The New York Times*, July 21, 1969

★ Mr. Hoffer was interviewed on the previous day in connnection with the first manned landing on the moon.

Space changes nobody. You bring back from space what you bring into space. 3

—**Stuart A. Roosa,** comment to Andrew Chaiken, quoted in Chaiken's *Man on the Moon*, 1994

★ Roosa flew on the Apollo 14 moon mission in 1971, remaining in orbit and doing scientific experiments while Alan Shepard and Edgar Mitchell were on the moon.

Although the earth is vast, its most vulnerable point is the atmosphere, which is surprisingly thin. As the late Carl Sagan used to say, it's like a coat of varnish on a globe. 4

—**Al Gore,** *Our World Is Facing a Climate Crisis*, speech excerpted in MoveOn.org ad, *The New York Times*, Jan. 15, 2004

Nature: Times of Day

Blue evening falls, 5
Blue evening falls;
Nearby in every direction,
It sets the corn tassels trembling.

—**Anonymous,** song of the Papago Indians of southern Arizona and northern Sonora, Mexico

The lark is up to meet the sun, 6
The bee is on the wing,
The ant his labor has begun,
The woods with music ring.
Shall bird and bee and ant be wise
While I my moments waste?
Oh, let me with the morning rise
And to my duties haste.

—**William McGuffey,** *Third Reader*, 1837

★ McGuffey's *Readers* educated millions of American schoolchildren, from the 1830s into the 1920s, teaching them not so incidentally the author's socially correct and politically conservative views.

The day is done, and the darkness 7
Falls from the wings of night,
As a feather is wafted downward
From an eagle in his flight.

—**Henry Wadsworth Longfellow,** *The Day Is Done*, 1845

1 And the night shall be filled with music,
And the cares, that infest the day,
Shall fold their tents, like the Arabs,
And as silently steal away.
—**Ibid.**

2 You've gut to git up airly
Ef you want to take in God.
—**James Russell Lowell,** *The Biglow Papers*, 1848

3 I'll tell you how the Sun rose—
A Ribbon at a time—
—**Emily Dickinson,** poem no. 318, 1862

4 In the long, sleepless watches of the night.
—**Henry Wadsworth Longfellow,** *The Cross of Snow*, 1879

5 Oh! How I Hate to Get Up in the Morning.
—**Irving Berlin**, in *Yip! Yip! Yaphank, 1918*

★ Sgt. Berlin wrote the revue while stationed at Camp Upton in Yaphank, N.Y.

6 I have been one acquainted with the night.
I have walked out in the rain—and back in the rain.
I have outwalked the furthest city light.
—**Robert Frost,** *Acquainted with the Night*, 1928

7 Night falls fast.
Today is in the past.
—**Edna St. Vincent Millay,** *Not So Far as the Forest*, in *Huntsman, What Quarry?*, 1939

8 Oh, what a beautiful mornin'
Oh, what a beautiful day.
—**Oscar Hammerstein,** *Oh, What a Beautiful Mornin'*, in *Oklahoma!*, 1943

9 Outside the open window
The morning air is all awash with angels.
—**Richard Wilbur,** *Love Calls Us to the Things of This World*, 1956

10 Beware thoughts that come in the night.
—**William Least Heat-Moon,** *Blue Highways*, 1983

★ The book's opening sentence.

11 It's completely usual for me to get up in the morning, take a look around, and laugh out loud.
—**Barbara Kingsolver**, title essay, in *High Tide in Tucson: Essays from Now or Never*, 1996

Nature: Trees

See also ENVIRONMENT (Reagan); NATURE: SEASONS (Bliss Carman); WILDERNESS (for forests)

The groves were God's first temples. 1
—William Cullen Bryant, *A Forest Hymn*, 1825

Woodman, spare that tree! 2
Touch not a single bough!
In youth it sheltered me,
And I'll protect it now.
—George Pope Morris, *Woodman, Spare That Tree!*, 1830

The birch, most shy and ladylike of trees. 3
—James Russell Lowell, *An Indian Summer Reverie*, 1846

The pine is the mother of legends. 4
—James Russell Lowell, *The Growth of a Legend*, 1847

I like trees because they seem more resigned to the way they have to live than other 5
things do.
—Willa Cather, *O Pioneers!*, 1913

I think that I shall never see 6
A poem lovely as a tree.
—Joyce Kilmer, *Trees*, 1913

★ See also Ogden Nash at ADVERTISING.

Poems are made by fools like me, 7
But only God can make a tree.
—Ibid.

One could do worse than be a swinger of birches. 8
—Robert Frost, *Birches*, 1916

There's a tree that grows in Brooklyn. Some people call it the Tree of Heaven. No 9
matter where its seed falls, it makes a tree which struggles to reach the sky.
—Betty Smith, *A Tree Grows in Brooklyn*, 1943

★ The ailanthus tree has many negative features: seeds that scatter in profusion, weak limbs, and unpleasantly odiferous flowers. But it is an inner city survivor.

The redwoods, once seen, leave a mark or create a vision that stays with you al- 10
ways. . . . they are ambassadors from another time.
—John Steinbeck, *Travels with Charley*, 1962

Once you've seen one redwood, you've seen them all. 11
—Ronald Reagan, quoted by Ted Morgan, *The Good Life*, in *The New York Times Magazine*, July 4, 1976

★ The former California governor and future president had a limited appreciation for trees; see also his 1965 remark at ENVIRONMENT.

1 The forests are sanctuaries not only of wildlife, but also of the human spirit. And every tree is a compact between generations.
—**George H. W. Bush,** speech, Sioux Falls, S.D., Sept. 18, 1989

Nature: Weather

2 Thunder is the voice of God, and, therefore, to be dreaded.
—**Increase Mather,** *Remarkable Providences*, 1684

3 I expand and live in the warm day like corn and melons.
—**Ralph Waldo Emerson,** *Nature*, 1836

4 Through woods and mountain passes
The winds, like anthems, roll.
—**Henry Wadsworth Longfellow,** *Midnight Mass for the Dying Year*, 1839

5 How beautiful is the rain!
After the dust and heat,
In the broad and fiery street,
In the narrow lane,
How beautiful is the rain!
—**Henry Wadsworth Longfellow,** *Rain in Summer*, 1846

6 Everybody talks about the weather, but nobody does anything about it.
—**Mark Twain,** editorial, Hartford *Courant*, August 24, 1897

★ Twain is the probable author of this observation. He was living in Hartford at the time, and *Bartlett's* points out that Robert Underwood Johnson, in his memoirs, quotes Twain as saying, "We all grumble about the weather, but nothing is *done* about it." On the other hand, Charles Dudley Warner, associate editor of the *Courant*, was a witty man in his own right and may have coined the joke himself. Or the line could just have been going around the town. Twain, though, was very weather conscious. For example, in a speech to the New England Society in New York City, on December 22, 1876, he advised, "If you don't like the weather in New England, just wait a few minutes." See also Twain at NEW ENGLAND.

7 Neither snow, nor rain, nor heat, nor gloom of night stays these couriers from the swift completion of their appointed rounds.
—**General Post Office,** New York City, inscription, 1913

★ Adapted from a passage in Herodotus, *The Histories*, 5th cent. B.C. Herodotus was describing the couriers used by the Persian king Xerxes to carry news across his empire: "Nothing mortal travels so fast as these Persian messengers," the historian wrote, describing a relay method similar to the American pony express. "These men will not be hindered from accomplishing . . . the distance which they have to go, either by snow, or rain, or heat, or by the darkness of night."

The fog comes 1
on little cat feet.
It sits looking
over the harbor and city
on silent haunches
and then moves on.
—**Carl Sandburg,** *Fog*, 1916

Thank heavens, the sun has gone in, and I don't have to go out and enjoy it. 2
—**Logan Pearsall Smith,** *Afterthoughts*, 1931

It ain't a fit night out for man or beast. 3
—**W. C. Fields,** *The Fatal Glass of Beer*, 1933

★ Fields originally used the line in a sketch in Earl Carroll's Broadway show *Vanities*, and then as a title for a Mack Sennett movie. In a letter of February 8, 1944, he spoke of making the phrase a byword, and added that he was not the originator. He suspected that it came from an old melodrama.

what if a much of which of a wind 4
gives the truth to summer's lie;
bloodies with dizzying leaves the sun
and yanks immortal stars awry.
—**E. E. Cummings,** *what if a much of a which of a wind*, in *One Times One* (or *1 × 1*), 1944

[To his cat, who disliked rain:] I know what's wrong, my dear, but I really do not 5
know how to turn it off.
—**Albert Einstein,** quoted in Banesch Hoffmann, *Albert Einstein: Creator and Rebel* [1972]

It could be rain 6
It could be snow
Weathermen never know.
—**Willard Scott,** *The Today Show*, NBC-TV, Nov. 27, 1995

Navy

See Military, the.

Nebraska

In regard to this extensive section of the country, I do not hesitate in giving the opin- 7
ion that it is almost wholly unfit for cultivation, and, of course, uninhabitable by a
people depending on agriculture for their subsistence.
—**Stephen H. Long,** c. 1820

★ Major Long, an explorer, is quoted in James C. Olson, *History of Nebraska*, 1966. Long was wrong. Nebraska is the Corn Husker State.

1 Hurrah for Greer county! The land of the free,
The land of the bedbug, grasshopper, and flea;
I'll sing of its praises, I'll tell of its fame,
While starving to death on my government claim.
—Anonymous, song, c. 1870

★ Fleas were a serious problem in pioneer sod homes; they lived in the walls. Another verse, apparently from the same song, warns of even more critters: "How happy am I when I crawl into bed; / A rattlesnake hisses a tune at my head! / A gay little centipede, all without fear, / Crawls over my pillow and into my ear," quoted in *American Heritage*, August 1973.

2 We were at sea—there is no other adequate expression—on the plains of Nebraska.
—Robert Louis Stevenson, *Across the Plains with Other Memories and Essays*, 1892

3 The green plain ran till it touched the skirts of heaven.
—Ibid.

4 What livelihood can repay a human creature for a life spent in this huge sameness? . . . A sky full of stars is the most varied spectacle that he can hope for.
—Ibid.

5 It is almost unheard of to find a town in Nebraska that has a past; it is sometimes rather difficult to find one that has a present, though all of them have, or think they have, a future.
—Willa Cather, article on the fortieth anniversary of the founding of Brownville, Nebr., 1894, reprinted in *American Heritage* [Oct. 1970]

★ In 2005, the population of Brownville was 439. It was about 5,000 in 1880.

6 I don't care how well she [Willa Cather] writes, I don't give a damn what happens in Nebraska.
—H. L. Mencken, attributed, in *The New York Times* [April 29, 1998]

★ Mencken was not always so dyspeptic. Reviewing Cather's *My Antonia*, which is set in Nebraska, he wrote in 1919, a year after the book's publication: "I know of no novel that makes the remote folk of the western prairies more real . . . and I know of none that makes them seem better worth knowing."

7 Here the Middle West merges with the West.
—Federal Writers' Project, *Nebraska: A Guide to the Cornhusker State*, 1939

8 A mile wide, an inch deep, stand it on end and it will reach to heaven, so muddy that the catfish have to come up to sneeze.
—Anonymous, characterization of the South Platte River, *Life*, August 30, 1943

9 Equality before the law.
—Motto, state of Nebraska

Necessity

Necessity never made a good bargain. 1
—Benjamin Franklin, *Poor Richard's Almanack*, April 1735

Great necessities call out great virtues. 2
—Abigail Adams, letter to John Quincy Adams, Jan. 19, 1780

★ For an example of great necessity from the era, see George Washington at AMERICAN REVOLUTION, entry for Dec. 25, 1776.

I know this—a man got to do what he got to do. 3
—John Steinbeck, *The Grapes of Wrath*, 1939

Negotiation

See DIPLOMACY; FOREIGN POLICY (John F. Kennedy).

Neighbors

See also MANNERS (Emily Post).

I am as desirous of being a good neighbor as I am of being a bad subject. 4
—Henry David Thoreau, *Civil Disobedience*, 1849

Good fences make good neighbors. 5
—Robert Frost, *Mending Wall*, 1914

★ This proverbial saying is spoken in the poem by a farmer, a neighbor of Frost's, who urges the reluctant poet to help in rebuilding a fence, some of which, at least, was on the farmer's property. Such mutual fence maintenance was a duty mandated by a 1790 Vermont law. The idea behind the law was that fences, which control wandering livestock, are in the common good and therefore the responsibility of repairing them should be shared. Frost, in this poem, takes a different view: "My apple trees will never get across [the fence line] / And eat the cones under his pines, I tell him." This cuts no ice with the farmer. In 1989, the Vermont Supreme Court, citing changing land-use patterns, found the law unconstitutional. See also DIVISIONS & BARRIERS.

I do not love my neighbor as myself, and apologize to no one. 6
—Edgar Watson Howe, *Success Easier Than Failure*, 1917

This is the grave of Mike O'Day, 7
Who died defending his right of way.
His right was clear, his will was strong,
But he's just as dead as if he'd been wrong.
—Anonymous, 20th century

It's easier to love humanity as a whole than to love one's neighbor. 8
—Eric Hoffer, in *The New York Times Magazine*, Feb. 15, 1959

Nevada

See also CITIES (AURORA, CARSON CITY, LAS VEGAS, RENO).

1 The country looks something like a singed cat, owing to the scarcity of shrubbery, and also resembles that animal in the respect that it has more merits than its personal appearance would seem to indicate.

—**Mark Twain,** *Washoe.—'Information Wanted,'* c. May 1, 1864, in Tom Quirk, ed., *Tales, Speeches, Essays, and Sketches/Mark Twain* [1994]

2 Nevada—it's freedom's last stand in America.

—**Will Rogers,** in Alex Ayres, ed., *The Wit and Wisdom of Will Rogers* [1993]

3 Anyone who is under the impression that the world is becoming too crowded should move to Nevada.

—**J. B. Priestley,** *Midnight on the Desert*, 1937

4 The desolation of Nevada is awesome.

—**Neil Morgan,** *Westward Tilt—The American West Today*, 1963

5 Neon looks good in Nevada.

—**John McPhee,** *Basin and Range*, 1980

6 All for our country.

—Motto, state of Nevada

New England

See also CITIES (BOSTON)]

7 I have lived in a country seven years, and all that time I never heard one profane oath, and all that time I never did see a man drunk in that land. Where was that country? It was New England.

—**Giles Firmin,** sermon to the Lords and Commons, c. 1675

★ On this subject, H. L. Mencken, in his quotations dictionary, cites J. G. Holland, who wrote that in the early colonial records of New England "rigidity of doctrine . . . and definitive laws against every form of social vice, go hand in hand with every form of vice. There was adultery in high places and adultery in low," *Everyday Topics*, 1876.

8 The New Englanders are a people of God, settled in those which were once the Devil's territories.

—**Cotton Mather,** *Wonders of the Invisible World*, 1693

9 The sway of the clergy in New England is indeed formidable. No mind beyond mediocrity dares there to develop itself.

—**Thomas Jefferson,** letter to Horatio Gates Spafford, 1816

10 The great vice of this New England people is their adoration of Mammon.

—**Charles Francis Adams,** *Diary*, Oct. 6, 1833

★ Adams was himself a New Englander to the bone, the son of one president and the grandson of another. For another comment on New Englanders and Mammon, see John Updike, below.

The Brahmin Caste of New England. **1**

—Oliver Wendell Holmes, Sr., book title, 1860

★ See also THE ELITE.

I saw but one drunken man through all New England, and he was very respectable. **2**

—Anthony Trollope, *North America*, 1862

★ Trollope continued: "He was, however, so uncommonly drunk that he might be allowed to count for two or three."

You can always tell the Irish, **3**
You can always tell the Dutch,
You can always tell a Yankee,
But you cannot tell him much.

—Anonymous, folk saying, probably 19th century

★ "Dutch" here may refer to German immigrants, the *Deutsch* as they called themselves, but which native Americans misheard as the more familiar term.

There is a sumptuous variety about the New England weather that compels the stranger's admiration—and regret . . . . In the spring, I have counted one hundred and thirty-six different kinds of weather inside of twenty-four hours. **4**

—Mark Twain, speech to the New England Society, New York City, Dec. 22, 1876

★ This was the society's seventy-first dinner. See also Twain at NATURE: WEATHER.

The one great poem of New England is her Sunday. **5**

—Henry Ward Beecher, *Proverbs from Plymouth Pulpit*, 1887

Use it up, wear it out; **6**
Make it do, or do without.

—Anonymous, New England maxim

Here where the wind is always north-northeast, **7**
And children learn to walk on frozen toes.

—Edwin Arlington Robinson, *New England,* in *Collected Poems,* 1921

The most serious charge which can be brought against New England is not Puritanism but February. **8**

—Joseph Wood Krutch, *The Twelve Seasons*, 1949

[In New England:] The ghosts of Hawthorne and Melville still sit on those green hills. The worship of Mammon is also somewhat lessened there by the spirit of irony. **9**

—John Updike, quoted in the London *Observer*, Mar. 25, 1979

The New England conscience . . . does not stop you from doing what you shouldn't—it just stops you from enjoying it. **10**

—Cleveland Amory, in *The New Yorker*, May 5, 1980

New Hampshire

1 Men hang out their signs indicative of their respective trades: shoemakers hang out a gigantic shoe; jewlers, a monster watch; and the dentist hangs out a gold tooth; but up in the mountains of New Hampshire, God Almighty has hung out a sign to show that there He makes men.

—Daniel Webster, *On the Old Man of the Mountain*, attributed

★ The reference is to the rock outcrop in the Cannon Mountains that resembled a craggy face in profile. Familiarly called "The Old Man of the Mountain," it was iconic of New Hampshire, appearing on the state emblem and featured in Nathaniel Hawthorne's story *The Great Stone Face*. The outcrop, estimated to be some 30,000 years old, collapsed to the ground on May 3, 2003.

2 The god who made New Hampshire
Taunted the lofty land with little men.

—Ralph Waldo Emerson, *Ode Inscribed to W. H. Channing*, 1846

★ This is Emerson's response to Webster's claim.

3 She's one of the two best states in the Union.
Vermont's the other.

—Robert Frost, *New Hampshire*, 1923

★ Frost came from Vermont. See also Maxfield Parrish at VERMONT.

4 Politically, New Hampshire is as unproductive as an abandoned farm.

—Ralph D. Paine, in Ernest Gruening, ed., *These United States*, 1924

★ Perhaps unproductive, but hardly uninfluential—its presidential primary is now a major early indicator of candidates' relative strength.

5 If two New Hampshire men aren't a match for the devil, we might as well give the country back to the Indians.

—Stephen Vincent Benét, *The Devil and Daniel Webster*, 1936

6 I like your nickname, "The Granite State." It shows the strength of character, firmness of principle, and restraint that have long characterized New Hampshire.

—Gerald Ford, speech, Concord, N.H., April 17, 1975

7 Live free or die.

—Motto, state of New Hampshire

New Jersey

See also CITIES (HOBOKEN, NEWARK, PATERSON, WEEHAWKEN).

8 The new proprietors [of New Jersey] inveigled many over by this tempting account of the country: that it was a place free from those three great scourges of mankind—priests, lawyers, and physicians. Nor did they tell a word of a lie, for the people were as yet too poor to maintain these learned gentlemen.

—William Byrd, 1728, cited in *American Heritage*, June 1976

[New Jersey is like] a beer barrel, tapped at both ends, with all the live beer running into Philadelphia and New York. 1

—Benjamin Franklin, attributed by Abram Browning, speech, Centennial Exposition in Philadelphia [1876]

On our left, the bold features of nature [the Palisades] rise as in the days of yore, unimpaired, unchangeable; grey cliffs, like aged battlements, tower perpendicularly from the water to their height of several hundred feet. 2

—Francis Hall, *Travels in Canada and the United States in 1816 and 1817*, 1818

★ Lt. Hall, an English visitor, traveled up the Hudson.

Like China, New Jersey absorbs the invader. 3

—Federal Writers' Project, *New Jersey: A Guide to Its Present and Past*, 1939

I'm empty and aching and I don't know why. 4
Counting the cars on the New Jersey Turnpike.
They've all come to look for America.

—Paul Simon, *America*, 1967

Liberty and prosperity. 5

—Motto, New Jersey

★ A more down-to-earth motto, "New Jersey: you got a problem with that?", was suggested by a character in Eric Dezenhall's novel, *Shakedown Beach* (2004).

New Mexico

See also CITIES (SANTA FE).

In New Mexico he always awoke a young man. . . . His first consciousness was a sense of the light dry wind blowing in through the windows, with the fragrance of hot sun and sagebrush and sweet clover; a wind that made one's body feel light and one's heart cry, "Today, today," like a child's. 6

—Willa Cather, *Death Comes for the Archbishop*, 1927

The mesa plain had an appearance of great antiquity, and of incompleteness; . . . The country was still waiting to be made into a landscape. 7

—Ibid.

Space is the keynote of the land—vast, limitless stretches of plain, desert, and lofty mountains, with buttes and mesas and purple distances to rest the eye. 8

—Federal Writers' Project, *New Mexico: A Guide to the Colorful State*, 1940

Stone, stone 9
layered and beaten
under the confessed brilliance
of this desert noon.

—William Carlos Williams, *New Mexico*, 1949

1 New Mexico is old, stupendously old and dry and brown, and wind-worn by the ages.
—**Charles Kuralt,** *Charles Kuralt's America*, 1995

2 It grows as it goes.
—Motto, state of New Mexico

Newspapers

See MEDIA; PRESS, THE.

New Things

See also EXCELLENCE (Emerson's mousetrap); SCIENCE: TECHNOLOGY.

3 The man with a new idea is a crank until the idea succeeds.
—**Mark Twain,** *Pudd'nhead Wilson's New Calendar*, in *Following the Equator*, 1897

★ See also Oliver Wendell Holmes, Sr., at IDEAS & IDEALS for a similar quote.

4 Even in slight things, the experience of the new is rarely without some stirring of foreboding.
—**Eric Hoffer,** *The Ordeal of Change*, 1964

New Year

5 Every New Year is the direct descendant, isn't it, of a
long line of proven criminals?
—**Ogden Nash,** *Good-by, Old Year or Why Don't They Pay the Bonus?*, in *The Primrose Path*, 1935

6 Across East River in the night
Manhattan is ablaze with light.
No shadow dares to criticize
The popular festivities.
Hard liquor causes everywhere
A general *détente*, and Care
For this state function of Good Will
Is diplomatically ill;
The Old Year dies a noisy death.
—**W. H. Auden,** *New Year Letter*, Jan. 1, 1940

New York

See also CITIES (ALBANY, AVON, BUFFALO, NEW YORK CITY, NIAGARA FALLS, ROCHESTER).

7 The lands were pleasant, with grass and flowers and goodly trees . . . and very sweet smells came from them.
—**Robert Juet,** *Juet's Journal of Hudson's Voyage*, [1841]

★ Juet was an officer on the *Half Moon*. He is describing here New York Harbor in late summer, 1609.

A bleak, blackguard, beggarly climate, of which I can say no good, except that it suits me and some others of the same or similar persuasion whom (by all rights) it ought to kill. 1

—**Robert Louis Stevenson,** letter to Miss Ferrier, April 1888

★ Stevenson wrote this from Trudeau sanitarium at Saranac, to which he had come in a vain attempt to cure his "persuasion," i.e., tuberculosis. Sufferers rarely named their disease, much as a later generation avoided "cancer."

Fresh green breast of the New World. 2

—**F. Scott Fitzgerald,** *The Great Gatsby*, 1925

★ Long Island as described in the closing passage of the novel.

Excelsior. 3
Ever upward.

—Motto, state of New York

Night

See NATURE: TIMES OF DAY.

Nonviolence

See PACIFISM & NONVIOLENCE.

North Carolina

Surely there is no place in the world where the inhabitants live with less labor than in North Carolina. 4

—**William Byrd,** *A Journey to the Land of Eden in 1733* [1866]

★ Byrd's observation was not intended as a compliment. A cultivated Virginia squire (his plantation at Westover featured a billiard table, upon which, according to his diary, he once gave his wife a "flourish"), Byrd looked down on uncouth backwoodsmen, who worked only as hard as they had to—not a great strain by Byrd's lights, given the felicity of the climate and the ease of raising crops. He dismissed North Carolina as "Lubberland." See also Timothy Dwight at VERMONT.

I'm talking to Buncombe. 5

—**Felix Walker,** debate, U.S. House of Representatives, 1820

★ This is the source of our word *bunk*. The story is that Rep. Walker, whose district included Buncombe County, N.C., interrupted debate on the Missouri Compromise with a long, tedious, and irrelevant speech. When told that it was no use to go on because other members were leaving the House, Walker replied, "Never mind; I'm talking to Buncombe." Afterward, whenever any congressman made a speech only for the sake of getting his name in the newspapers back home, he was said to be "talking to (or for) Buncombe." The term subsequently acquired the broader sense of nonsense or humbug and was converted first to *bunkum* and then, by 1900, to the modern *bunk*.

1 First at Bethel, furthest at Gettysburg, and last at Appomattox.
—**Anonymous,** characterization of the state's military prowess

★ The slogan was popularized by the 1st North Carolina Volunteers, who became known as the Bethel Regiment, after participating in the first clash between Federal and Confederate troops at Bethel Church, Virginia, on June 10, 1861.

2 The Land of the Sky.
—**Christian Reid,** novel title, 1876

3 North Carolina is a valley of humility between two mountains of conceit.
—**Anonymous**

★ The Library of Congress, in *Respectfully Quoted*, selected this version rather than Mencken's, "valley of humiliation." The mountains of conceit are Virginia and South Carolina. A similar comment, which Mencken attributes to a journalist named Stewart from Charleston, South Carolina, is: "A strip of land lying between two states," c. 1861.

4 I'm a Tar Heel born,
I'm a Tar Heel bred,
And when I die,
I'll be a Tar Heel dead.
—**Anonymous,** University of North Carolina fight song

★ *Tar Heel* was originally an insult, referring to a Civil War Battle in which a North Carolinian brigade failed to hold its position. Mississippians said that they had forgotten to tar their heels that morning. Tar (and turpentine) made from North Carolina's pines were important materials, especially in the building and rigging of ships, and the state was known for these valuable exports.

5 In my honest and unbiased judgment, the good Lord will place the Garden of Eden in North Carolina when he restores it to earth. He will do this because he will have so few changes to make in order to achieve perfection.
—**Sam J. Ervin, Jr.,** *Humor of a Country Lawyer*, 1983

★ Senator Ervin of North Carolina won international acclaim as chairman of the Senate committee that investigated the Watergate scandal; see WATERGATE. His skillful performance belied his repeated assertions that he was just a country lawyer. Actually, he graduated from Harvard Law School.

6 *Esse quam videri.*
To be rather than to seem.
—Motto, state of North Carolina

North Dakota

See also DAKOTA TERRITORY.

7 North Dakota is a doomed state. In twenty years, it will revert to the Indian and the buffalo. We must be moving on.
—**Anonymous,** early settler, quoted in Frank P. Stockbridge, *The North Dakota Man Crop, World's Work* magazine, Nov. 1912

I would never have been president if it had not been for my experiences in North Dakota. **1**

—Theodore Roosevelt, quoted in Elwyn B. Robinson, *History of North Dakota* [1966]

A state of unbounded plains and hills and badlands. **2**

—Federal Writers' Project, *North Dakota: A Guide to the Northern Prairie State*, 1938

Freely admitted is the rural character of the state, and there is seldom an attempt to cover native crudities with a veneer of Eastern culture. **3**

—Ibid.

We have four distinct seasons—three are absolutely beautiful, one is *very* distinct. **4**

—Anonymous, slogan, northwestern North Dakota, in *The New York Times*, March 3, 2005

Liberty and union, now and forever, one and inseparable. **5**

—Motto, state of North Dakota

★ This is drawn from a toast by Daniel Webster; see UNION, THE.

Occult, the

Once upon a midnight dreary, while I pondered, weak and weary, **6**
Over many a quaint and curious volume of forgotten lore—
While I nodded, nearly napping, suddenly there came a tapping,
As of someone gently rapping, rapping at my chamber door.

—Edgar Allan Poe, *The Raven*, 1845

★ What the cryptic Raven utters was used on Poe's gravestone; see EPITAPHS & GRAVESTONES.

Us ignorant people laugh at spiritualists, but when they die, they go mighty peaceful and happy. **7**

—Will Rogers, *Daily Telegrams*, July 7, 1930

Belief in magic is older than writing. **8**

—Zora Neale Hurston, *Mules and Men*, 1935

I have gone out, a possessed witch, **9**
haunting the black air, braver at night;
dreaming evil, I have done my hitch
over the plain houses, light by light.

—Anne Sexton, *Her Kind*, in *To Bedlam and Partway Back*, 1960

May the Force be with you. **10**

—George Lucas, *Star Wars*, 1977

Oceans

See NATURE: SEAS & OCEANS.

Ohio

See also CITIES (CINCINNATI, CLEVELAND, COLUMBUS).

1 Ohio is the farthest west of the east and the farthest north of the south.
—**Louis Bromfield,** attributed, in Peter Yapp, *The Traveller's Dictionary of Quotations* [1983]

2 [Ohio:] A giant carpet of agriculture studded by great cities.
—**John Gunther,** *Inside U.S.A.*, 1947

3 Why, O why, O why-o
Why did I ever leave Ohio,
Why did I wander
To see what lies yonder
When life was so happy at home?
—**Betty Comden & Adolph Green,** *Wonderful Town*, 1953

★ This terrific musical, composed by Leonard Bernstein, was based on the 1941 play *My Sister Eileen* by Joseph Fields and Jerome Chodorov, which was derived from Ruth McKenney's 1938 best-seller, *My Sister Eileen*. Eileen and her husband, novelist Nathanael West, died in an automobile crash three days before the Broadway opening of *My Sister Eileen*. The Wests were on their way to the funeral of F. Scott Fitzgerald.

4 With God, all things are possible.
—Motto, state of Ohio

Oklahoma

See also CITIES (TULSA).

5 You just throw anything out in Oklahoma, and all you have to do is come back and harvest it.
—**Will Rogers,** *How to Be Funny*, May 29, 1926

★ Rogers was a native of Oklahoma, "the Garden of Eden of the West."

6 They swarmed on Oklahoma from every state in the Union.
—**Edna Ferber,** *Cimarron*, 1930

★ They swarmed twice. In 1889, Indian territory was opened for settlement at noon on April 22. Speculators and would-be settlers lined up at the boundary; those who crossed early were called "sooners," which is how Oklahoma came to be known as the Sooner state. Ferber wrote in this popular novel that the inflow was much more dramatic a few years later, when people came from all corners of the nation hoping to get rich from Oklahoma oil.

7 Okie use' ta mean you was from Oklahoma. Now it means you're a dirty son-of-a-bitch. Okie means you're scum. Don't mean nothing itself, it's the way they say it.
—**John Steinbeck,** *The Grapes of Wrath*, 1939

★ You don't hear "Okie" much anymore, but it was still a term of derision almost twenty years after the migrations out of Oklahoma and other midwestern prairie states in the 1930s. Drought and erosion turned twenty-five thousand square miles to dust.

Oklahoma, 1
Where the wind comes sweepin' down the plain,
And the wavin' wheat
Can sure smell sweet
When the wind comes right behind the rain.
—**Oscar Hammerstein II,** *Oklahoma!*, title song of the musical *Oklahoma!*, 1943

We know we belong to the land, and the land we belong to is grand! 2
—**Ibid.**

★ This great show, with music by Richard Rodgers, was dismissed at its New Haven tryout by producer Mike Todd, who specialized in extravaganzas, and who in middle age became Elizabeth Taylor's third husband. "No legs, no jokes, no chance," he pronounced—as recalled in a *New York Times* editorial, Feb. 7, 1993.

Labor omnia vincit. 3
Works conquers all things.
—Motto, state of Oklahoma

Old Age

See also AGES; MIDDLE AGE & MIDLIFE CRISIS.

The older I grow, the more apt I am to doubt my own judgment, and to pay more respect to the judgment of others. 4
—**Benjamin Franklin,** speech, Constitutional Convention, Sept. 17, 1787

★ Franklin, with this gentle, self-deprecating remark, made on the last day of the convention, urged delegates to put aside whatever objections they might have and adopt the Constitution. More at THE CONSTITUTION.

By my rambling digressions I perceive myself to be growing older. 5
—**Benjamin Franklin,** *Autobiography* [1798]

★ Franklin, the old man among our young founding fathers, wrote his autobiography off and on from 1771 to shortly before his death in 1790; the book covers the first part of his life. Despite the disclaimer in this quotation, Franklin remained sharp to the end. William Pierce, a fellow delegate to the Constitutional Convention said of him in 1787: "He is 82 years old, and possesses an activity of mind equal to a youth of 25 years of age."

Tranquility is the old man's milk. I go to enjoy it in a few days, and to exchange the roar and tumult of bulls and bears for the prattle of my grandchildren and senile rest. 6
—**Thomas Jefferson,** letter to Edward Rutledge, June 24, 1797

★ Jefferson was vice president at the time and evidently bored. His desire for senile rest did not last, and he served as president 1801–1809. In 1820, approaching his seventy-seventh birthday, he returned to this theme: "Tranquility is the *summum bonum* ('greatest good') of old age," he wrote to Mark L. Hill, on April 5. Jefferson and John Adams both died on July 4, 1826; see INDEPENDENCE DAY.

1 My one fear is that I may live too long. This would be a subject of dread to me.
—Thomas Jefferson, letter to Philip Mazzai, March 1801

2 Whenever a man's friends begin to compliment him about looking young, he may be sure that they think he is growing old.
—Washington Irving, *Bachelors*, in *Bracebridge Hall*, 1822

3 It is time to be old,
To take in sail.
—Ralph Waldo Emerson, *Terminus*, in *Poems*, 1847

4 A person is always startled when he hears himself seriously called an old man for the first time.
—Oliver Wendell Holmes, Sr., *The Autocrat of the Breakfast-Table*, 1858

★ Or as Leon Trotsky observed in his *Diary in Exile, 1935*: "Old age is the most unexpected of all the things that can happen to a man."

5 For age is opportunity no less
Than youth itself, though in another dress,
And as the evening twilight fades away,
The sky is filled with stars invisible by day.
—Henry Wadsworth Longfellow, *Morituri Salutamus*, 1875

6 To be seventy years young is sometimes far more cheerful and hopeful than to be forty years old.
—Oliver Wendell Holmes, Sr., letter to Julia Ward Howe on her 70th birthday, May 27, 1889

7 Old age is like an opium-dream. Nothing seems real except what is unreal.
—Oliver Wendell Holmes, Sr., *Over the Teacups*, 1891

8 I grow old . . . I grow old . . .
I shall wear the bottoms of my trousers rolled.
—T. S. Eliot, *The Love Song of J. Alfred Prufrock*, 1917

★ He will roll his trousers as his stature shrinks with age.

9 Here I am, an old man in a dry month,
Being read to by a boy, waiting for rain.
—T. S. Eliot, *Gerontion*, 1920

10 The older I grow the more I distrust the familiar doctrine that age brings wisdom.
—H. L. Mencken, *Prejudices, Third Series*, 1922

11 One aged man—one man—can't fill a house.
—Robert Frost, *An Old Man's Winter Night*, in *Mountain Interval*, 1923

dance mehitabel dance 1
caper and shake a leg
what little blood is left
will fizz like wine in a keg.

—**Don Marquis,** *mehitabel dances with boreas*, in *archy and mehitabel*, 1927

Between the years of ninety-two and a hundred and two, however, we shall be the ribald, useless, drunken, outcast person we have always wished to be. . . . We look forward to a disreputable, vigorous, unhonored, and disorderly old age. 2

—**Don Marquis,** *The Almost Perfect State*, 1927

★ Some of the outrageous details of this state: "We shall not walk at all, but recline in a wheel chair and bellow for alcoholic beverages . . . write ribald songs against organized society" . . . shoot out the lights at night with a .45 caliber revolver, and address public meetings (to which we have been invited because of our wisdom) in a vein of jocund malice."

The riders in a race do not stop short when they reach the goal. There is a little finishing canter before coming to a standstill. There is time to hear the kind voice of friends and to say to one's self, "The work is done." 3

—**Oliver Wendell Holmes, Jr.,** radio broadcast honoring his ninetieth birthday, March 8, 1931

Oh, to be seventy again! [At age ninety-two, upon seeing a pretty, young woman.] 4

—**Oliver Wendell Holmes, Jr.,** attributed, 1933

★ The remark is also attributed to French Premier Georges Clemenceau, who lived to be eighty-eight, and, possibly the progenitor, French writer Bernard le Bouvier de Fontenelle, who died in 1757 at age 100. Holmes, who was born in 1841, served on the Supreme Court 1902–32, that is, into his nineties. He died in 1935. See also Mark Twain on still appreciating young women at age seventy, at WOMEN.

The last years of life are the best, if you are a philosopher. 5

—**George Santayana,** quoted by F. Champion Ward, former chancellor of the New School for Social Research, Op-Ed page, *The New York Times*, Sept. 24, 1993

There is no such thing as old age, there is only sorrow. 6

—**Edith Wharton,** *A Backward Glance*, 1934

No memory of having starred 7
Atones for later disregard,
Or keeps the end from being hard.

—**Robert Frost,** *Provide, Provide*, 1936

★ For Frost's unsentimental solution to this problem, see CHARITY & PHILANTHROPY, where the Frost quote is the next verse from this poem.

As de old folks always say, Ah'm born but Ah ain't dead. No tellin' what Ah'm liable tuh do yet. 8

—**Zora Neale Hurston,** *Their Eyes Were Watching God*, 1937

1 Oh, it's a long, long while
From May to December,
But the days grow short,
When you reach September.

—Maxwell Anderson, *September Song*, music by Kurt Weill, *Knickerbocker Holiday*, 1938

2 Oh, the days dwindle down
To a precious few . . .
And these few precious days
I'll spend with you.

—Ibid.

3 Don't grow old without money, honey.

—Lena Horne, quoted in *People* magazine, April 7, 1980

★ Ms. Horne was interviewed on the occasion of her retirement from show business at 62. But like many entertainers, she had second thoughts and returned to Broadway the following year with a one-woman show. See also Sophie Tucker at AGES.

4 A beautiful young lady is an act of nature. A beautiful old lady is a work of art.

—Louis Nizer, remark, cited in *The New York Times* [Nov. 11, 1994]

★ Presenting Sara Delano Roosevelt, mother of Pres. Franklin D. Roosevelt, at a banquet, Nizer concluded: "I introduce you to a work of art."

5 [Old age:] It's the only disease you don't look forward to being cured of.

—Herman J. Mankiewicz & Orson Welles, *Citizen Kane*, screenplay, 1941

6 A man is not old until regrets take the place of dreams.

—John Barrymore, quoted in Gene Fowler, *Good Night, Sweet Prince*, [1943]

7 It is a terrible thing for an old woman to outlive her dogs.

—Tennessee Williams, Prologue, *Camino Real*, 1953

8 To me, old age is always fifteen years older than I am.

—Bernard Baruch, quoted in the press on his eighty-fifth birthday, August 20, 1955

9 Nobody knows what's going to happen to anybody besides the forlorn rags of growing old.

—Jack Kerouac, *On the Road*, 1957

10 I'll never make the mistake of being seventy again.

—Charles Dillon "Casey" Stengel, remark to the press, on being fired as manager of the New York Yankees, 1960

★ Stengel, whose teams had won ten American League pennants and seven World Series in a dozen years, was dismissed five days after the Yankees lost the 1960 Series to the Pittsburgh Pirates. The quote is from Robert W. Creamer's *Stengel: His Life and Times*, 1984. See also Stengel below.

When everything else physical and mental seems to diminish, the appreciation of beauty is on the increase. 1

—**Bernard Berenson,** *Sunset and Twilight*, 1963

Most people my age are dead at the present time. 2

—**Charles Dillon "Casey" Stengel,** quoted in the Ken Burns television series *Baseball* [part IV, 1994]

Being seventy is not a sin. 3

—**Golda Meir,** quoted by David Reed, *Reader's Digest*, July 1971

Getting old ain't for sissies. 4

—**Bette Davis,** quoted by Paul Newman, on *60 Minutes* television show [Sept. 3, 1995]

★ The line is given in various forms, among them: "Old age is no place for sissies," "Old age ain't for sissies," and "Old age is not for sissies," the last of which was used as the title for a book by Art Linkletter in 1988.

One advantage of getting "old." So many people do not share my past that I am free to invent it. 5

—**Alfred Kazin,** *journal*, 1978–93, in *A Lifetime Burning in Every Moment* [1996]

How old would you be if you didn't know how old you was? 6

—**Leroy "Satchel" Paige,** attributed

What's wrong with me? I'm old. I'm getting old and coming apart. 7

—**Thurgood Marshall,** response to a reporter's question, press conference on his retirement from the Supreme Court, 1992

The elderly have a duty to die and get out of the way. 8

—**Richard D. Lamm**, quoted in *The New York Times*, Oct. 1, 1993

★ Lamm, then governor of Colorado, was so upset about the rising costs of health care that he made his case in a more quotable manner than he probably intended.

[I attribute my longevity to] Red meat and gin. 9

—**Julia Child**, in the *Minneapolis Star Tribune*, quoted in *Reader's Digest*, Jan., 1997

★ Ms. Child was 84 at the time.

Opportunity

Only that day dawns to which we are awake. 10

—**Henry David Thoreau,** *Conclusion,* in *Walden*, 1854

America has been another name for opportunity. 11

—**Frederick J. Turner,** *The Significance of the Frontier in American History*, 1893

1 Unlimited opportunities can be as potent a cause of frustration as a paucity or lack of opportunities.
—**Eric Hoffer,** *The True Believer: Thoughts on the Nature of Mass Movements*, 1951

2 There is no security on this earth; there is only opportunity.
—**Douglas MacArthur,** quoted in, Courtney Whitney, *MacArthur: His Rendezvous with History* [1955]

3 It ain't enough to get the breaks. You gotta know how to use 'em.
—**Huey P. Long,** saying

4 Know Your Opportunity—Seize It.
—**Tennessee Williams,** family motto

5 You got to get it while you can.
—**Janis Joplin,** *Get It While You Can*, in *Pearl*, album, 1971

★ Lyrics by Jerry Ragovoy and Mort Shuman.

6 It is better to lose opportunity than capital.
—**Susan M. Byrne,** *Wall Street Week in Review* television show, Feb. 15, 1985

Oppression

See Races & Peoples; Tyranny.

Optimism & Pessimism

See also Despair; Hope.

7 'Tis always morning somewhere.
—**Henry Wadsworth Longfellow,** *The Birds of Killingsworth*, in *Tales of a Wayside Inn*, 1863–74

8 The nearer the dawn, the darker the night.
—**Ibid.**

★ The thought is proverbial: "It is always darkest just before the day dawneth" (Thomas Fuller, *Pisgah Sight of Palestine*, 1650).

9 The man who is a pessimist before forty-eight knows too much; the man who is an optimist after he is forty-eight knows too little.
—**Mark Twain,** *Mark Twain's Notebook*, Albert Bigelow Paine, ed. [1935]

★ Twain composed the aphorism upon the occasion of his own forty-eighth birthday in 1883.

10 A pessimist is a man who thinks all women are bad. An optimist is a man who hopes that they are.
—**Chauncey Depew,** attributed, c. 1898

★ Attorney Depew was much in demand as an after-dinner speaker. For a more serious comment, see Lawyers.

Cheer up, the worst is yet to come. 1

—**Philander Chase Johnson,** *Shooting Stars*, in *Everybody's Magazine*, May 1920

The optimist proclaims that we live in the best of all possible worlds; and the pessimist fears this is true. 2

—**James Branch Cabell,** *The Silver Stallion*, 1926

★ The same thought was expressed later and more forcefully by J. Robert Oppenheimer: "The optimist thinks this is the best of all possible worlds, and the pessimist knows it," *The Bulletin of Atomic Scientists*, Feb. 1951.

an optimist is a guy 3
that has never had
much experience.

—**Don Marquis,** *archy and mehitabel*, 1927

A pessimist is a man who has been compelled to live with an optimist. 4

—**Elbert Hubbard,** *The Note Book*, 1927

★ Or, from the same era, Don Marquis: "A pessimist is a person who has had to listen to too many optimists," quoted in Frederick B. Wilcox, *A Little Book of Aphorisms*, 1947.

Optimism is the content of small men in high places. 5

—**F. Scott Fitzgerald,** "Note-Books," in *The Crack-Up* [1945]

O, merry is the optimist, 6
With the troops of courage leaguing.
But a dour trend
In any friend
Is somehow less fatiguing.

—**Phyllis McGinley,** *A Pocketful of Rye*, 1940

An optimist . . . is a person who thinks the future is uncertain. 7

—**Russel Crouse & Howard Lindsay,** *State of the Union*, 1948

Every day, in every way, things are getting worse and worse. 8

—**William F. Buckley, Jr.,** in *The National Review*, July 2, 1963

I have a very low regard for cynics. I think it's the beginning of dying. 9

—**Robert Redford,** in *Time*, March 29, 1976

Perpetual optimism is a force multiplier. 10

—**Colin Powell,** *My American Journey*, 1995

★ Gen. Powell, who was chairman of the Joint Chiefs of Staff in the Gulf War, included a set of maxims in his autobiography. This was number thirteen. For another, see ACTION & DOING.

Oregon

See also CITIES (PORTLAND).

1 Or lose thyself in the continuous woods
Where rolls the Oregon, and hears no sound
Saving his own dashings.
—**William Cullen Bryant,** *Thanatopsis*, 1817

2 I must walk toward Oregon and not toward Europe.
—**Henry David Thoreau,** *Walking*, 1862

★ More at THE WEST.

3 Oregon is seldom heard of. Its people believe in the Bible, and hold that all radicals should be lynched. It has no poets and no statesmen.
—**H. L. Mencken,** in *The American Mercury*, 1925

4 She flies with her own wings.
—Motto, state of Oregon

★ Formerly, "The Union."

Pacific, the

See NATIONS; WORLD WAR.

Pacifism & Nonviolence

See also LAW (Martin Luther King, Jr., 2nd quote); PEACE; VIOLENCE.

5 Disarm, disarm. The sword of murder is not the balance of justice. Blood does not wipe out dishonor, nor violence indicate possession.
—**Julia Ward Howe,** peace proclamation, London, 1870

★ Howe, author of *The Battle Hymn of the Republic*—see under GOD—was repelled by the bloodshed of the Civil War and the Franco-Prussian War. In 1872, she established June 2 as Mothers' Peace Day, dedicated to world peace. She organized the annual holiday in Boston, and in 1915, Pres. Woodrow Wilson authorized a national Mother's Day holiday.

6 So long as antimilitarists propose no substitute for war's disciplinary function, no *moral equivalent of war*, . . . so long they fail to realize the full inwardness of the situation.
—**William James,** *The Moral Equivalent of War*, in *Memories and Studies*, 1911

★ James proposed a national martial training program to prepare young men for responsible citizenship. See also James at THE MILITARY.

7 There is such a thing as a man being too proud to fight.
—**Woodrow Wilson,** speech to foreign-born citizens, Philadelphia, May 10, 1915

★ See also Wilson at PEACE. Oswald Garrison Villard claimed in *Fighting Years*, 1939, that he originated this saying.

I am not only a pacifist, but a militant pacifist. I am willing to fight for peace. . . . Is it not better for a man to die for a cause in which he believes, such as peace, than to suffer for a cause in which he does not believe, such as war? **1**

—**Albert Einstein,** interview, 1931, in Alfred Lief, ed., *The Fight Against War,* [1933]

Nonviolence is a powerful and just weapon. . . . It is a sword that heals. **2**

—**Martin Luther King, Jr.,** *Why We Can't Wait*, 1963

We must rise to the majestic heights of meeting physical force with soul force. **3**

—**Martin Luther King, Jr.,** speech at the Lincoln Memorial in Washington, D.C., to 200,000 civil rights marchers, August 28, 1963

★ More at AMERICAN HISTORY: MEMORABLE MOMENTS.

That's all nonviolence is—organized love. **4**

—**Joan Baez,** *Daybreak*, 1966

Nonviolence, pacifism, that's the greatest thing that I think the human species has to aspire to, because otherwise it's not going to be around. **5**

—**Martin Scorsese,** TV interview with Charlie Rose, PBS, Jan. 16, 1998

Pain

See SUFFERING & PAIN.

Painting

See ART: VISUAL.

Parents

See also CHILDREN; FAMILY.

Men are what their mothers made them. **6**

—**Ralph Waldo Emerson,** *Fate*, in *The Conduct of Life*, 1860

What is home without a mother? **7**

—**Thomas Alva Edison,** diary, July 12, 1885

★ Edison was musing on the home life of chickens in the technological future. William Holzer, the brother of his deceased wife, was developing an electric incubator. "Just think," Edison wrote, "electricity employed to cheat a poor hen out of the pleasures of maternity. Machine-born chickens. What is home without a mother?"

There is no slave out of heaven like a loving woman; and, of all loving women, there is no such slave as a mother. **8**

—**Henry Ward Beecher,** *Proverbs from Plymouth Pulpit*, 1887

What the mother sings to the cradle goes all the way down to the coffin. **9**

—**Ibid.**

★ For the importance of "the hand that rocks the cradle," see W. R. Wallace at WOMEN.

1 A mother's advice is safest for a boy to follow.
—Henry Thomas Burn, speech, Tennessee House of Representatives, August 1920

★ At the urging of his mother, Burn cast a tie-breaking vote in favor of the 19th Amendment, granting suffrage to American women; see AMERICAN HISTORY: MEMORABLE MOMENTS.

2 wot in hell
have I done to deserve
all these kittens.
—Don Marquis, *archy and mehitabel*, 1927

3 Mother Knows Best.
—Edna Ferber, story title, 1927

4 There are no illegitimate children—only illegitimate parents.
—Judge Léon R. Yankwich, decision in *Zipkin v. Mozon*, June 1928

★ M. J. Cohen says in *The Penguin Thesaurus of Quotations* that Yankwich was quoting the columnist O. O. McIntyre.

5 Mothers are the only race of people that speak the same tongue. A mother in Manchuria could converse with a mother in Nebraska and never miss a word.
—Will Rogers, radio broadcast, May 11, 1930

6 I doubt if a charging elephant, or a rhino, is as determined or as hard to check as a socially ambitious mother.
—Will Rogers, *Daily Telegrams* column, May 10, 1932

7 my father moved through dooms of love.
—E. E. Cummings, poem title, 1940

8 Trust yourself. You know more than you think you do.
—Benjamin Spock, *Baby and Child Care*, 1946

★ Dr. Spock's advice to new parents, the opening line of his classic text.

9 I have found the best way to give advice to your children is to find out what they want and then advise them to do it.
—Harry S. Truman, television interview, May 27, 1955

10 The thing that impresses me most about America is the way parents obey their children.
—Duke of Windsor (Edward VIII), in *Look* magazine, March 5, 1957

11 A boy's best friend is his mother.
—Joseph Stefano, screenplay of *Psycho*, 1960

★ The speaker is Norman Bates, played by Tony Perkins. The movie was based on Robert Bloch's novel of the same name.

A Jewish man with parents alive is a fifteen-year-old boy, and will remain a fifteen-year-old boy till they die. 1
—**Philip Roth,** *Portnoy's Complaint*, 1969

Most American children suffer too much mother and too little father. 2
—**Gloria Steinem,** in *The New York Times*, August 26, 1971

Everything our parents said was good is bad. Sun, milk, red meat, college. 3
—**Woody Allen,** *Annie Hall* screenplay, 1977

Loving someone as a parent can produce a cloud that conceals from vision what correct behavior is. 4
—**John Irving,** *The Cider-House Rules*, 1985

No one who has not experienced it can realize the determination of an American mother defending one of her children. 5
—**Harold Macmillan,** in Alistair Horne, *Harold Macmillan. Vol. I* [1988]

★ Like Winston Churchill, former Prime Minister Macmillan had a formidable American mother. Here he was recalling for his official biographer how his mother pevented him as a young man from converting to Roman Catholicism, a step that she feared would interfere with her ambitions for her son.

I may be dead, but I'm still your mother. 6
—**Nicky Silver,** *Raised in Captivity*, 1995

Parting

With a heart full of love and gratitude, I now take my leave of you. 7
—**George Washington,** farewell to his officers, Fraunces Tavern, New York City, Dec. 4, 1783

★ More at AMERICAN HISTORY: MEMORABLE MOMENTS.

No one, not in my situation, can appreciate my feeling of sadness at this parting. To this place, and the kindness of these people, I owe everything. Here I have lived a quarter of a century, and have passed from a young to an old man. Here my children have been born, and one is buried. I now leave not knowing when or whether ever I may return, with a task before me greater than that which rested upon Washington. 8
—**Abraham Lincoln,** farewell remarks on leaving Springfield, Ill., for Washington, D.C., Feb. 11, 1861

Parting is all we know of heaven, 9
And all we need of hell.
—**Emily Dickinson,** poem no. 1732, in *Poems*, V [1891]

A man never knows how to say goodbye; a woman never knows when to say it. 10
—**Helen Rowland,** *Reflections of a Bachelor Girl*, 1909

1 If that plane leaves the ground and you're not with him, you'll regret it. Maybe not today, maybe not tomorrow, but soon and for the rest of your life.
—**Julius Epstein, Philip Epstein, & Howard Koch,** *Casablanca*, screenplay, 1942

★ See also LOVE, EXPRESSIONS OF.

2 There is a time for departure, even when there is no certain place to go.
—**Tennessee Williams,** *Camino Real*, 1953

Passion

See also ENTHUSIASM & ZEAL; EXCESS; LOVE.

3 Passion is a sort of fever in the mind, which ever leaves us weaker than it found us.
—**William Penn,** *Some Fruits of Solitude*, 1693

4 A man in a passion rides a wild horse.
—**Benjamin Franklin,** *Poor Richard's Almanack*, 1749

5 The end of passion is the beginning of repentance.
—**Ibid.**

6 Men are often false to their country and their honor, false to duty and even to their interest, but multitudes of men are never long false or deaf to their passions.
—**Fisher Ames,** speech, Boston, Feb. 8, 1800

7 Passion, though a bad regulator, is a powerful spring.
—**Ralph Waldo Emerson,** *Considerations by the Way*, in *The Conduct of Life*, 1860

8 Through our great good fortune, in our youth our hearts were touched with fire. It was given to us to learn at the outset that life is a profound and passionate thing.
—**Oliver Wendell Holmes, Jr.,** Memorial Day speech, Keene, N.H., 1884

★ See also Holmes at LIFE.

9 The way to avoid evil is not by maiming our passions, but by compelling them to yield their vigor to our moral nature.
—**Henry Ward Beecher,** *Proverbs from Plymouth Pulpit*, 1887

10 Life is action and passion.
—**Oliver Wendell Holmes, Jr.,** speech, to Harvard Law School alumni, New York City, Feb. 1916

★ More at LIFE.

11 Violent physical passions do not in themselves differentiate men from each other, but rather tend to reduce them to the same state.
—**T. S. Eliot,** *After Strange Gods*, 1934

Birth is the starting point of passion, **1**
Passion is the beginning of death,
How can you turn your back from birth?
How can you say no to passion?
How can you bid death hold off?
—**Carl Sandburg,** *Fog Numbers*, in *Honey and Salt*, 1963

Passion makes the world go round. Love just makes it a safer place. **2**
—**Ice-T,** *The Ice Opinion* (with Heidi Sigmund), 1994

Past, the

See also HISTORY; MEMORY; PRESENT, THE; TIME.

We are not free to use today, or to promise tomorrow, because we are already mortgaged to yesterday. **3**
—**Ralph Waldo Emerson,** *Journal*, 1858

The dogmas of the quiet past are inadequate to the stormy present. **4**
—**Abraham Lincoln,** annual message to Congress, Dec. 1, 1862

We have to do with the past only as we can make it useful to the present and the future. **5**
—**Frederick Douglass,** *The Life and Writings of Frederick Douglass*, Philip S. Foner, ed., Vol. II [1950]

There is no time like the old time, when you and I were young. **6**
—**Oliver Wendell Holmes, Sr.,** *No Times Like the Old Time*, 1865

Those who cannot remember the past are condemned to repeat it. **7**
—**George Santayana,** *The Life of Reason*, 1905–1906

I tell you the past is a bucket of ashes. **8**
—**Carl Sandburg,** *The Prairie*, 1918

★ H. L. Mencken, in his dictionary of quotations, includes this Sandburg statement but as an anonymous saying.

The precious, incommunicable past. **9**
—**Willa Cather,** *My Ántonia*, 1918

★ From the last line of the book: "Whatever we had missed, we possessed together the precious, incommunicable past."

Ignorance of the past does not guarantee freedom from its imperfections. **10**
—**Reinhold Niebuhr,** entry, 1928, in *Leaves from the Notebook of a Tamed Cynic* [1930]

Yesterday, **11**
A night-gone thing
A sun-down name.
—**Langston Hughes,** *Youth*, in *From My People*

1 If she [America] forgets where she came from, if the people lose sight of what brought them along, if she listens to the deniers and mockers, then will begin the rot and dissolution.

—**Carl Sandburg,** *Remembrance Rock*, 1948

2 Don't look back. Something may be gaining on you.

—**Leroy "Satchel" Paige,** from his autobiography, *How to Stay Young*, 1953

★ Not original with Paige, but identified with him. More at WISDOM, WORDS OF.

3 The past is the present, isn't it? It's the future, too.

—**Eugene O'Neill,** *Long Day's Journey into Night*, 1956

4 Only the past when you were happy is real.

—**Ibid.**

5 The past is never dead. It is not even past.

—**William Faulkner,** *Requiem for a Nun*, 1959

6 Which of us has overcome his past?

—**James Baldwin,** *Alas, Poor Richard*, 1961

★ But the past can point the way to a better future, Baldwin advised: "Know whence you came. If you know whence you came, there is really no limit to where you can go," *The Fire Next Time*, 1962.

7 Man is a history-making creature who can neither repeat his past nor leave it behind.

—**W. H. Auden,** *D. H. Lawrence*, in *The Dyer's Hand*, 1962

8 Every journey into the past is complicated by delusions, false memories, false namings of real events.

—**Adrienne Rich,** *Of Woman Born*, 1976

9 Hindsight is always twenty-twenty.

—**Billy Wilder,** attributed, in J. R. Colombo, *Colombo's Hollywood: Wit and Wisdom of the Moviemakers*, 1979

10 The past is always dozing in the ice, waiting to alter the present.

—**Roger Rosenblatt,** in *US News & World Report*, Oct. 24, 1988

11 The Past Is What Catches Up With Us

—**Thomas Fleming,** article title, in *The New York Times Book Review*, Jan. 12, 1992

Patience

See also DETERMINATION, EFFORT, PERSISTENCE, & PERSEVERANCE.

12 Patience and Diligence, like Faith, move Mountains.

—**William Penn,** *Some Fruits of Solitude*, 1693

Learn to labor and to wait. 1
—Henry Wadsworth Longfellow, *A Psalm of Life*, 1839

★ More at ACTION & DOING.

Patience all the passion of great hearts. 2
—James Russell Lowell, *Columbus*, 1844

★ More at ENDURANCE.

Sorrow and silence are strong, and patient endurance is godlike. 3
—Henry Wadsworth Longfellow, *Evangeline*, 1847

Patience, n. A minor form of despair disguised as a virtue. 4
—Ambrose Bierce, *The Devil's Dictionary*, 1906

The marvel of all history is the patience with which men and women submit to bur- 5
dens unnecessarily laid upon them by their governments.
—William E. Borah, in Otto L. Bettmann, *A Word from the Wise* [1977]

★ Among the burdens that the longtime (1907–40) Republican senator from Idaho opposed were the National Recovery Administration and other New Deal measures for coping with the great depression of the 1930s.

However often the thread may be torn out of your hands, you must develop enough 6
patience to wind it up again and again.
—Walter Gropius, on fortitude for completing tasks, in *The New York Times*, July 8, 1969

Patriotism & the Flag

See also AMERICA & AMERICANS; AMERICAN HISTORY: MEMORABLE MOMENTS; SERVING ONE'S COUNTRY.

I am not a Virginian, but an American. 7
—Patrick Henry, speech in the First Continental Congress, Philadelphia, Oct. 14, 1774

The summer soldier and the sunshine patriot. 8
—Tom Paine, *The American Crisis*, Dec., 1776

★ More at AMERICAN REVOLUTION.

I would go to hell for my country. 9
—Thomas Jefferson, upon being appointed commissioner to France, 1785

Guard against the postures of pretended patriotism. 10
—George Washington, Farewell Address, Sept. 17, 1796

Oh, say, can you see by the dawn's early light, 11
What so proudly we hailed at the twilight's last gleaming?
Whose broad stripes and bright stars, through the perilous fight,

O'er the ramparts we watched were so gallantly streaming?
And the rockets' red glare, the bombs bursting in air,
Gave proof through the night that our flag was still there.
Oh, say, does that star-spangled banner yet wave
O'er land of the free and the home of the brave.

—**Francis Scott Key,** *The Star-Spangled Banner*, Sept. 14, 1814

★ Key watched the nighttime attack on Fort McHenry, one of the harbor defenses of Baltimore, and wrote *The Star-Spangled Banner* the next day. He had been detained by the British Commander Admiral Cockburn after successfully negotiating the release of a Washington physician taken along as a hostage by the British when they evacuated that city. The poem quickly became famous and was set to the music of *To Anacreon in Heaven*, an English drinking song that had been adapted to American sentiments under the title *Adams and Liberty*. The *Star-Spangled Banner* became the official U.S. anthem in 1931. Lines from its fourth verse gave us our national motto; see under GOD.

1 Our country! In her intercourse with foreign nations, may she always be in the right; but our country, right or wrong.

—**Stephen Decatur,** toast at dinner in his honor, Norfolk, Va., April 1816

★ Commodore Decatur was feted nationwide for his 1815 campaign against the pirates of the Barbary Coast of North Africa; see *The Marine Hymn* under MILITARY, THE. This version of his patriotic toast is from the 1848 biography by Alexander Slidell Mackenzie. According to *Bartlett's*, an account in the *Niles' Weekly Register* of Baltimore, April 20, 1816, quoted Decatur as saying, "Our Country—In her intercourse with foreign nations, may she always be in the right, and always successful, right or wrong." On August 1, 1816, John Quincy Adams wrote to his father John Adams, "My toast would be, may our country be always successful, but whether successful or otherwise, always right." Near the end of the century, Carl Schurz offered, "Our country, right or wrong. When right, to be kept right. When wrong, to be put right," in a speech at the Anti-Imperialistic Conference, in Chicago, Ill., October 17, 1899; see also Adams below. The English writer G. K. Chesterton, in an essay on patriotism, likened Decatur's toast to "My mother, drunk or sober."

2 When a whole nation is roaring Patriotism at the top of its voice, I am fain to explore the cleanliness of its hands and the purity of its heart.

—**Ralph Waldo Emerson,** *Journal*, 1824

3 Let our object be, Our Country, our whole Country, and nothing but our Country.

—**Daniel Webster,** speech at the setting of the cornerstone, Bunker Hill monument, June 17, 1825

4 Ay, tear her tattered ensign down!
Long has it waved on high.
And many an eye has danced to see
That banner in the sky.

—**Oliver Wendell Holmes, Sr.,** *Old Ironsides*, 1830

★ The poem was written to protest the proposed scrapping of the frigate USS *Constitution*. See MILITARY, THE for more on this famous ship.

I name thee Old Glory! 1
—William Driver, 1831

★ Capt. Driver, the originator of "Old Glory" as a name for the U.S. flag, first used the phrase in saluting a new flag flown on his brig, the *Charles Dogget*, which was setting sail from Salem, Mass., to the South Pacific. Three decades later, in 1862, Driver's "Old Glory" was flown from the dome of the state capitol in Nashville, Tenn., after Union forces had recaptured the city. Driver, a bold supporter of the Union, had hidden the flag in the coverlet of his bed to save it from Confederate partisans.

My country, 'tis of thee, 2
Sweet land of liberty,
Of thee I sing;
Land where my fathers died,
Land of the pilgrims' pride,
From every mountain side
Let freedom ring.
—Samuel Francis Smith, *America*, Fourth of July program, Boston Sabbath School Union, 1831

Nothing is more embarrassing in the ordinary intercourse of life than this irritable 3
patriotism of Americans.
—Alexis de Tocqueville, *Democracy in America*, 1835

Say not thou, "My country right or wrong," 4
Nor shed thy blood for an unhallowed cause.
—John Quincy Adams, *Congress, Slavery, and an Unjust War*, c. 1847

Rally 'round the flag, boys. 5
—George Frederick Root, *The Battle Cry of Freedom*, 1863

★ More at CIVIL WAR.

"Shoot, if you must, this old gray head, 6
But spare your country's flag," she said.
—John Greenleaf Whittier, *Barbara Frietchie*, in *The Atlantic*, Oct. 1863

★ The poem refers to an alleged incident in the Civil War, when troops under Stonewall Jackson had occupied Frederick, Maryland, in September 1862. Barbara Frietchie, then over ninety-five years old, is said to have waved the American flag in front of the Confederate troops. Gen. Jackson cut short the confrontation. " 'Who touches a hair of yon gray head/ Dies like a dog! March on!' he said."

Gold is good in its place, but living, brave, patriotic men are better than gold. 7
—Abraham Lincoln, remarks, at the White House, Nov. 10, 1864

There is the national flag. He must be cold, indeed, who can look upon its folds rip- 8
pling in the breeze without pride of country.
—Charles Sumner, *Are We a Nation?*, Nov. 19, 1867

★ Sen. Sumner was an ardent abolitionist and a harsh enemy of the South during Reconstruction. See also SLAVERY.

1 [The American flag:] Beautiful as a flower to those who love it, terrible as a meteor to those who hate it, it is the symbol of the power and glory, and the honor, of . . . Americans.

—**George Frisbie Hoar,** 1878

★ Sen. Hoar, a Massachusetts Republican, opposed the expansionist program of Pres. William McKinley, his party's leader.

2 I think patriotism is like charity—it begins at home.

—**Henry James,** *The Portrait of a Lady*, 1881

3 The virtue of patriotism is subordinate in most souls to individual and family aggrandizement.

—**Elizabeth Cady Stanton & Susan B. Anthony,** *History of Woman Suffrage*, written with Mathilda Joslyn Gage, 1881

4 I pledge allegiance to my flag and the republic for which it stands: one nation, indivisible, with liberty and justice for all.

—**Francis Bellamy,** in *Youth's Companion*, Sept. 8, 1892

★ Allegiance to the flag was first pledged at the dedication of the World's Fair Grounds in Chicago, on October 21, 1892; this was also the first celebration of Columbus Day; Bellamy was chairman of the executive committee listed in the program for the celebration. Various changes have been made in wording over the years, including most significantly, and controversially, the phrase "under God," added by law in 1945. The pledge today reads: "I pledge allegiance to the flag of the United States of America, and to the republic for which it stands, one nation under God, indivisible, with liberty and justice for all."

5 Don't haul down the flag.

—**Anonymous,** slogan c. 1898

★ While some Americans deplored the era's imperialism—see SPANISH-AMERICAN WAR—others welcomed the sight of Old Glory flying on foreign shores.

6 It is the duty of the good citizen not to be silent.

—**Charles Eliot Norton,** *True Patriotism*, 1898

★ More at WAR.

7 In the beginning of a change, the patriot is a scarce man, and brave, and hated and scorned. When his cause succeeds, the timid join him, for then it costs nothing to be a patriot.

—**Mark Twain,** *Notebook* [1935]

8 I'm a Yankee Doodle Dandy.
A Yankee Doodle do or die;
A real live nephew of my Uncle Sam's,
Born on the Fourth of July.

—**George M. Cohan,** *Yankee Doodle Dandy*, from *Little Johnny Jones*, 1904

★ For the original *Yankee Doodle*, dating to 1755, see Anonymous at this date under AMERICA & AMERICANS.

Patriot, n. One to whom the interests of a part seem superior to those of the whole. The dupe of statesmen and the tool of conquerers. **1**

—Ambrose Bierce, *The Devil's Dictionary*, 1906

Oh, it's home again and home again, America for me! **2**
I want a ship that's westward bound to plough the rolling sea
To the blessed land of Room Enough beyond the ocean bars,
Where the air is full of sunlight and the flag is full of stars.

—Henry van Dyke, *America for Me*, June 1909

The flag is the embodiment, not of sentiment, but of history. **3**

—Woodrow Wilson, speech, June 14, 1915

★ This was a Flag Day speech, the anniversary of the official adoption of the flag on June 14, 1777.

The hyphenated American always hoists the American flag undermost. **4**

—Theodore Roosevelt, *Fear God and Take Your Own Part*, 1916

★ A slur on immigrants. Similarly, Pres. Woodrow Wilson complained in a speech on May 16, 1914, "Some Americans need hyphens in their names, because only part of them has come over." He stated that he was not putting all immigrants into this category. But he maintained that, with World War I in progress, there was too much partisanship based on national origins. See also Roosevelt's 1918 pronouncement against fifty-fifty Americans under AMERICA & AMERICANS, and against hyphenated Americanism at FOREIGNERS.

Patriotism which is bought and paid for is not patriotism. **5**

—Calvin Coolidge, 1924

★ The president was explaining his veto of the World War Veterans Act. The Act passed despite the veto, granting each veteran a bonus of $1 per day for service at home, $1.25 per day for service abroad. But anyone owed more than $50 would not be paid until 1945. This delayed award was understandably called the Tombstone Bonus. After the Depression hit Congressman Wright Patman of Texas tried in 1929 and 1932 to pass legislation paying out the money. In 1932, a ragged "Bonus Army" of veterans gathered in Washington D.C. seeking relief. Nine thousand of them were routed by the real Army, including Douglas A. MacArthur, George S. Patton, and Dwight D. Eisenhower (who called it "a pitiful scene"). In 1936, the Patman legislation finally passed.

Whenever you hear a man speak of his love for his country it is a sign that he expects to be paid for it. **6**

—H. L. Mencken, *A Mencken Chrestomathy*, 1949

Patriotism is not a short and frenzied outburst of emotion, but the tranquil and steady dedication of a lifetime. **7**

—Adlai Stevenson, speech, New York City, Aug. 27, 1952

1 You're not supposed to be so blind with patriotism that you can't face reality. Wrong is wrong, no matter who does it or who says it.
—Malcolm X, *Malcolm X Speaks*, 1965

2 U.S.A.—Love It or Leave It.
—Anonymous, bumper sticker, c. 1970

3 There are those things that at one time we all accepted as more important than our comfort or discomfort—if not our very lives: duty, honor, country! There was a time when all was to be set aside for these.
—Clarence Thomas, Francis Boyer Lecture, American Enterprise Institute, Feb. 13, 2001

Patterns

4 The life of man is a self-evolving circle.
—Ralph Waldo Emerson, *Circles*, in *Essays: First Series*, 1841

5 Christ! What are patterns for?
—Amy Lowell, *Patterns*, in *Men, Women, and Ghosts*, 1916

★ More at WAR.

6 The desires of the heart are as crooked as corkscrews
Not to be born is best for man
The second best is a formal order
The dance's pattern, dance while you can.
—W. H. Auden & Louis MacNeice, *Letter from Iceland*, 1937

7 Life has taught me that it knows better plans than we can imagine, so that I try . . . to accept what comes, and to make the most of it . . . there is a Pattern, larger and more beautiful than our short vision can weave.
—Julia M. Seton, epilogue, *By a Thousand Fires: Nature Notes and Extracts from the Life and Unpublished Journals of Ernest Thompson Seton*, 1967

Peace

See also PACIFISM & NONVIOLENCE; RESISTANCE.

8 There never was a good war or a bad peace.
—Benjamin Franklin, letter to Josiah Quincy, Sept. 11, 1783

★ Franklin was one of the negotiators who in Paris, on September 3, 1783, signed the peace treaty with Great Britain ending the Revolutionary War.

9 Peace hath higher tests of manhood
Than battle ever knew.
—John Greenleaf Whittier, *The Hero*, 1853

10 We must not be enemies. Though passion may have strained, it must not break our bonds of affection. The mystic chords of memory, stretching from every battlefield

and patriot grave, to every heart and hearthstone, all over this broad land, will yet swell the chorus of the Union, when again touched, as surely they will be, by the better angels of our nature.

—Abraham Lincoln, First Inaugural Address, March 4, 1861

★ Arthur M. Schlesinger, Jr., pointed out in a letter to *American Heritage* magazine (Oct. 1999) that a draft for this speech, done by William H. Seward, the Secretary of State-designate, concluded: "The mystic chords which proceeding from so many battlefields and so many patriot graves pass through all our hearts and all the heaths in this broad continent will yet again harmonize in the ancient music when breathed upon by the guardian angel of the nation." Lincoln's reworking of the orotund draft shows that he was, in Schlesinger's words, "not only a great writer. He was a great editor."

A just and lasting peace. **1**

—Abraham Lincoln, Second Inaugural Address, March 4, 1865

★ More at CIVIL WAR.

Let us have peace. **2**

—Ulysses S. Grant, presidential nomination acceptance speech, May 29, 1868

Better to live in peace than begin a war and lie dead. **3**

—Joseph the Younger, cited in Time-Life Books, *The Indians* [1973]

★ The Nez Percé leader's Indian name was Hinmatowyalahtkit, probably meaning "(thunder) travels up from low places." He surrendered in Montana after the battle of Bear Paw Mountains in 1877. See also RESIGNATION.

There is a price which is too great to pay for peace, and that price can be put in one word. One cannot pay the price of self-respect. **4**

—Woodrow Wilson, speech, Des Moines, Iowa, Feb. 1, 1916

★ See also Wilson at RIGHT; and for a different Wilson view, see him at PACIFISM & NONVIOLENCE. For his call for peace near the end of World War I, see AMERICAN HISTORY: MEMORABLE MOMENTS.

Only a peace between equals can last. **5**

—Woodrow Wilson, speech to the U.S. Senate, Jan. 22, 1917

Open covenants of peace, openly arrived at. **6**

—Woodrow Wilson, "Fourteen Points" address to Congress, Jan. 8, 1918

★ This speech, which prefigured the proposal to create a League of Nations, featured a program of peace as its first point: "The program of the world's peace, therefore, is our program; and that program, the only possible program, as we see it, is this: Open covenants of peace, openly arrived at, after which there shall be no private understandings of any kind but diplomacy shall proceed always frankly and in the public view." For more on the speech, see FOREIGN POLICY and AMERICAN HISTORY: MEMORABLE MOMENTS.

You and me, we've made a separate peace. **7**

—Ernest Hemingway, *In Our Time*, 1924

1 Peace cannot be kept by force. It can only be achieved by understanding.

—**Albert Einstein,** *Militant Pacificism,* in *Cosmic Religion*, 1931

2 Peace, like charity, begins at home.

—**Franklin D. Roosevelt,** speech, August 14, 1936

3 Let us not deceive ourselves: we must elect world peace or world destruction.

—**Bernard Baruch,** speech, United Nations Atomic Energy Commission, June 14, 1946

★ See also Baruch at SCIENCE: TECHNOLOGY.

4 God and the politicians willing, the United States can declare peace upon the world and win it.

—**Ely Culbertson,** *Must We Fight Russia?*, 1946

★ Culbertson, a bridge expert, was the inventor of the first successful bidding system. Born in Rumania, he was captain of the U.S. team in 1933, 1934, and 1937, and founded and edited *Bridge World.* From 1940, he devoted much time and effort to promoting world peace.

5 It isn't enough to talk about peace. One must believe in it. And it isn't enough to believe in it. One must work at it.

—**Eleanor Roosevelt,** *Voice of America* radio broadcast, Nov. 11, 1951

6 America's leadership and prestige depend, not merely upon on our unmatched material progress, riches and military strength, but on how we use our power in the interests of world peace and human betterment.

—**Dwight D. Eisenhower,** Farewell Address, Jan. 17, 1961

★ This is the same speech in which Eisenhower warned about the dangers of "the military-industrial complex." See Eisenhower at MILITARY, THE.

7 Arms alone are not enough to keep the peace. It must be kept by men.

—**John F. Kennedy,** State of the Union message, 1963

8 Peace is a process—a way of solving problems.

—**John F. Kennedy,** speech, American University, 1963

9 There is no way to peace—peace is the way.

—**A. J. Muste,** *Debasing Dissent*, in *The New York Times* [Nov. 16, 1967]

★ This was Muste's credo. A minister and radical pacifist, he saw "peace" not as a noun but as a verb.

10 The real differences around the world today are not between Jews and Arabs, Protestants and Catholics; Muslims, Croats and Serbs. The real differences are between those who embrace peace and those who would destroy it; between those who look to the future and those who cling to the past; between those who open their arms and those who are determined to clench their fists.

—**Bill Clinton,** message to the people of Sarajevo, Dec. 22, 1997

Pennsylvania

See also CITIES (PHILADELPHIA; PITTSBURGH).

Pennsylvania is heaven for farmers, paradise for artisans, and hell for officials and preachers. **1**

—Gottlieb Mittelberger, *Journey to Pennsylvania,* 1754

★ Mittelberger visited Pennsylvania in the years 1750–1754, working as a school teacher and organist. He recorded the miseries of his fellow voyagers destined to be indentured servants. He had kinds words, too, for the state; see AMERICA & AMERICANS.

Pennsylvania is the Keystone of the Democratic arch. **2**

—Pennsylvania Democratic Committee, address, 1803, in H. M. Jenkins, *Pennsylvania* [1903]

★ This is the earliest example in *The Oxford English Dictionary* of "keystone" in the sense of "Keystone State," Pennsylvania's most common nickname today.

The cradle of toleration and freedom of religion. **3**

—Thomas Jefferson, letter to Thomas Cooper, Nov. 2, 1822

The Pennsylvania mind, as minds go, was not complex; it reasoned little and never talked; but in practical matters it was the steadiest of all American types; perhaps the most efficient; certainly the safest. **4**

—Henry Adams, *The Education of Henry Adams*, 1907

Still the pine-woods scent the noon; still the catbird sings his tune; **5**
Still the autumn sets the maple-forest blazing;
Still the grape-vine through the dusk flings her soul-compelling musk;
Still the fire-flies in the corn make night amazing!
The things that truly last when men and times have passed,
They are all in Pennsylvania this morning!

—Rudyard Kipling, *Philadelphia*, in *Rewards and Fairies*, 1910

Virtue, liberty, and independence. **6**

—Motto, state of Pennsylvania

People, the

See also DEMOCRACY; HUMANS & HUMAN NATURE; PUBLIC OPINION & THE PUBLIC.

The people are the only sure reliance for the preservation of our liberty. **7**

—Thomas Jefferson, letter to James Madison, 1787

The will of the people is the only legitimate foundation of government, and to protect its free expression should be our first object. **8**

—Thomas Jefferson, letter to Benjamin Waring, March 1801

There is but little virtue in the action of masses of men. **9**

—Henry David Thoreau, *Civil Disobedience*, 1849

1 The measure of the progress of civilization is the progress of the people.
—George Bancroft, speech, New-York Historical Society, 1854

2 Why should there not be a patient confidence in the ultimate justice of the people? Is there any better or equal hope in the world?
—Abraham Lincoln, First Inaugural Address, 1861

3 You may fool all the people some of the time; you can even fool some of the people all of the time; but you can't fool all of the people all the time.
—Abraham Lincoln, attributed

★ Possibly apocryphal. *Barlett's* cites Alexander K. McClure, who in *Lincoln's Yarns and Stories*, 1904, recounts that the president made this remark to a caller at the White House. There are numerous updates to the thought. The newspaper columnist F.P.A. (Franklin Pierce Adams) declared in *Nods and Becks*, 1944, that "The trouble with this country is that there are too many politicians who believe, with a conviction based on experience, that you can fool all of the people all of the time." James Thurber noted, "You can fool too many of the people too much of the time," *The Owl Who Was God*, in *The New Yorker*, April 25, 1949. Movie producer Joseph Levine quipped, "You can fool all the people if the advertising is right and the budget is big enough," *The New York Times*, obituary, August 1, 1987.

4 *Vox populi, vox humbug.*
—William Tecumseh Sherman, letter to his wife, June 2, 1863

★ Sherman was referring to the historic "*Vox populi, vox Dei*—The voice of the people is the voice of God," attributed to Alcuin, c. A.D. 800. He may also have known Alexander Pope's "The people's voice is odd; It is, and it is not, the voice of God," *Imitations of Horace* (1733–38). Alexander Hamilton, too, found the voice of the people suspect: "The voice of the people has been said to be the voice of God; . . . it is not true in fact. The people are turbulent and changing; they seldom judge or determine right." Also attributed to him in an argument with Thomas Jefferson is the rejoinder, "Your people, sir, your people is a great beast!" See also Hamilton at RICH & POOR, WEALTH & POVERTY and, for a punning variation, the anonymous *Vanity Fair* quote under ABRAHAM LINCOLN.

5 Government of the people, by the people, for the people.
—Abraham Lincoln, Gettysburg Address, Nov. 19, 1863

★ More at GETTYSBURG ADDRESS.

6 The pitifulest thing out is a mob.
—Mark Twain, *Huckleberry Finn*, 1885

7 I am the people—the mob—the crowd—the mass.
Do you know that all the great work of the world is done through me?
—Carl Sandburg, *I Am the People, the Mob*, 1916

8 The apparition of these faces in the crowd;
Petals on a wet, black bough.
—Ezra Pound, *In a Station of a Metro*, 1916

★ Pound studied Oriental poetry, as is evident in this famous couplet. For other faces in the crowd, see W. H. Auden below.

No one . . . has ever lost money by underestimating the intelligence of the great masses of the plain people. **1**

—H. L. Mencken, *Notes on Journalism, Chicago Tribune*, Sept. 19, 1926

★ Popularized as: "No one ever went broke underestimating the intelligence of the American people." Roland Marchand, historian of advertising, reports that in the same era Hearst editor Arthur Brisbane posted a sign in the Hearst city rooms: "You *cannot* underestimate the intelligence of the American public."

Private faces in public places **2**
Are wiser and nicer
Than public faces in private places.

—W. H. Auden, *Orators*, 1932

★ From the dedication, which is to Stephen Spender.

The people will live on. **3**
The learning and blundering people will live on.
They will be tricked and sold and again sold
And go back to the nourishing earth for rootholds.

—Carl Sandburg, *The People, Yes*, 1936

The total collapse of the public opinion polls shows that this country is in good health. A country that developed an airtight system of finding out in advance what was in people's minds would be uninhabitable. **4**

—E. B. White, *Polling, The New Yorker*, Nov. 13, 1948

★ This essay was written just after Harry S. Truman's totally unexpected (by pollsters) victory in the presidential election over Thomas E. Dewey.

About one-fifth of the people are against everything all the time. **5**

—Robert F. Kennedy, speech, University of Pennsylvania, May 6, 1964

The silent majority. **6**

—Richard M. Nixon, speech, Nov. 3, 1969

★ More at MAJORITIES & MINORITIES. The "silent majority" recalls William Graham Sumner's "forgotten man"; see under ECONOMICS.

The people have spoken—the bastards! **7**

—Morris K. Udall, informal remark, Feb. 24, 1976

★ Rep. Udall had just come in second to former Georgia governor Jimmy Carter in New Hampshire's Democratic presidential primary.

The American people have the Constitutional right to be wrong. **8**

—Warren Rudman, comment in the Senate Select Committee hearing on the Iran-Contra affair, July 1987

Legitimacy [of governments] is not bought by force; it is earned by consensus of the people. **9**

—George H. W. Bush, press conference, Jan. 13, 1991

Perception

See VISION & PERCEPTION.

Perseverance & Persistence

See COMMITMENT; DETERMINATION, EFFORT, PERSISTENCE, & PERSEVERANCE; ENDURANCE; PATIENCE; WINNING & LOSING, VICTORY & DEFEAT.

Pessimism

See OPTIMISM & PESSIMISM.

Philanthropy

See CHARITY & PHILANTHROPY.

Philosophy

See also REALITY, ILLUSIONS, & IMAGES.

1 The test of a religion or philosophy is the number of things it can explain.
—Ralph Waldo Emerson, *Journal*, 1836

2 To be a philosopher is . . . so to love wisdom as to live according to its dictates, a life of simplicity, independence, magnaminity, and trust.
—Henry David Thoreau, *Economy, Walden*, 1854

3 Let us not pretend to doubt in philosophy what we do not doubt in our hearts.
—C. S. Peirce, *Collected Papers*, Vol. V, para. 265

★ See also Peirce at SKEPTICISM and in the note on the William James quote at TRUTH.

4 The philosophy which is so important in each of us is not a technical matter; it is our more or less dumb sense of what life honestly and deeply means.
—William James, *Pragmatism*, 1907

★ See also James at EXPEDIENCY and TRUTH.

5 In the end, every philosopher has to walk alone.
—George Santayana, letter to Susan Sturgis de Sastre, Oct. 1, 1913

6 Every philosophy is tinged with the coloring of some secret imaginative, which never emerges explicitly into its trains of reasoning.
—Alfred North Whitehead, *Science and the Modern World*, 1925

7 Most philosophical treatises show the human cerebrum loaded far beyond its Plimsoll mark.
—H. L. Mencken, *Prejudices*, 1919–27

The safest general characterization of the European philosophical tradition is that it consists of a series of footnotes to Plato. 1

—**Alfred North Whitehead,** *Process and Reality*, 1929

Philosophy begins in wonder. And at the end, when philosophic thought has done its best, the wonder remains. 2

—**Alfred North Whitehead,** *Modes of Thought*, 1938

Metaphysics is almost always an attempt to prove the incredible by an appeal to the unintelligible. 3

—**H. L. Mencken,** *Minority Report: H. L. Mencken's Notebooks* [1956]

Philosophy is concerned with two matters: soluble questions that are trivial and critical questions that are insoluble. 4

—**Stefan Kanfer,** in *Time* magazine, April 19, 1982

In the information age, you don't teach philosophy as they did after feudalism. You perform it. If Aristotle were alive today, he'd have a talk show. 5

—**Timothy Leary,** in London *Evening Standard*, Feb. 8, 1989

Photography

See ART: VISUAL.

Physical Fitness

See also HEALTH; SPORTS.

The sovereign invigorator of the body is exercise, and of all the exercises, walking is best. 6

—**Thomas Jefferson,** letter to Thomas Mann Randolph, Jr., August 27, 1786

★ Randolph later married Jefferson's daughter Martha.

Keep the faculty of effort alive in you by a little gratuitous exercise every day . . . so that when the hour of need draws nigh, it may find you not unnerved and untrained to stand the test. 7

—**William James,** *The Principles of Psychology*, 1890

I wish to preach, not the doctrine of ignoble ease, but the doctrine of the strenuous life. 8

—**Theodore Roosevelt,** speech at the Hamilton Club, Chicago, April 10, 1899

★ See William James at POVERTY & HUNGER for the strenuous life lived by the poor.

I have never taken any exercise, except sleeping and resting, and I never intend to take any. Exercise is loathsome. 9

—**Mark Twain,** speech, on his 70th birthday, Delmonico's, New York City, Dec. 5, 1905

1 Whenever the urge to exercise comes upon me, I lie down for a while and it passes.
—**Robert Maynard Hutchins,** quoted in Harry S. Ashmore, *Unseasonable Truths: The Life of Robert Maynard Hutchins* [1989]

★ Hutchins headed the University of Chicago from 1929 to 1951. He enjoyed good health and died at age seventy-eight.

2 Avoid running at all times.
—**Leroy "Satchel" Paige,** *How to Stay Young*, 1953

★ More at WISDOM, WORDS OF.

3 We are underexercised as a nation. We look instead of play. We ride instead of walk. Our existence deprives us of the minimum physical activity essential for healthy living.
—**John F. Kennedy,** speech, National Football Foundation, Dec. 5, 1961

4 Exercise is the yuppie version of bulimia.
—**Barbara Ehrenreich,** *Food Worship*, in *The Worst Years of Our Lives*, 1991

Physics

See SCIENCE: PHYSICS & COSMOLOGY.

Physiology

See SCIENCE: BIOLOGY & PHYSIOLOGY.

Plants

See NATURE: PLANTS & GARDENS.

Pleasure & Hedonism

See also SIN, VICE & NAUGHTINESS

5 Pain wastes the body, pleasure the understanding.
—**Benjamin Franklin,** *Poor Richard's Almanack*, 1735

6 I do not agree that an age of pleasure is no compensation for a moment of pain.
—**Thomas Jefferson,** letter to John Adams, August 1, 1816

7 That man is richest whose pleasures are the cheapest.
—**Henry David Thoreau,** *Journal*, March 11, 1856

8 *Debauchee, n.* One who has so earnestly pursued pleasure that he has had the misfortune to overtake it.
—**Ambrose Bierce,** *The Devil's Dictionary*, 1906

9 Drink and dance and laugh and lie,
Love, the reeling midnight through,

For tomorrow we shall die!
(But, alas, we never do.)
—**Dorothy Parker,** *The Flaw in Paganism*, in *Death and Taxes*, 1931

Liquor and love 1
rescue the cloudy sense
banish its despair
give it a home.
—**William Carlos Williams,** *The World Narrowed to a Point*, in *Poetry* magazine, Nov. 1940

People seem to enjoy things more when they know a lot of other people have been left out of the pleasure. 2
—**Russell Baker,** *The Sport of Counting Each Other Out*, in *The New York Times*, Nov. 2, 1967

Ninety percent [of my salary] I'll spend on good times, women, and Irish whiskey. The other ten percent I'll probably waste. 3
—**"Tug" McGraw,** *Sports Illustrated,* April 21, 1975

★ McGraw, then in the employ of the Philadelphia Phillies, was very pleased with his new contract for $75,000, which seemed to him like a lot of money for throwing baseballs. Times change.

Poetry

See ART: POETRY.

Political Parties

See POLITICS & POLITICIANS.

Political Slogans

Stand with Washington. 4
—**Anonymous,** slogan of the Federalist party, 1790s

★ The Federalists, the party of Alexander Hamilton, favored a strong central authority and republican, rather than purely democratic, government. By contrast, Thomas Jefferson's Republican Democrats (later simply Democrats) favored states' rights and power vested directly with the people. Pres. Washington, who belonged to no party, eventually appeared to favor the Federalists, and thus this slogan arose.

A corrupt bargain. 5
—**Anonymous,** rallying cry of Jacksonian Democrats, 1827–28

★ The phrase refers to the appointment of Henry Clay as secretary of state by Pres. John Quincy Adams. Clay, the Speaker of the House, was a loser in the presidential campaign of 1824, in which four candidates split the vote. Jackson received a plurality of the popular vote but fell well short of the required majority in the electoral college. The decision, therefore, went to the House of Representatives, where Clay, having no chance for the presidency himself, and heartily detesting Jackson, assembled the necessary majority of thirteen states for Adams. He persuaded his own state, Kentucky, to vote for Adams, contrary to the instructions of the state legislature to support Jackson. Naturally, Clay's subsequent appointment was seen as a quid pro quo. Jackson went on to win in 1828.

1 Root, hog, or die.

—Anonymous, political saying, c. 1830s

★ A pithy summation of the political spoils system, popularized in the Jacksonian period. An 1836 publican, in *Calumet and War Club*, put it this way: "Root, hog, or die—work for your office, or leave it—support the party, right or wrong—are the terms of our agreement." The expression probably arose among farmers, who turned hogs loose in the woods and prairies to fend for themselves. Davy Crockett used the admonition in his 1834 attributed autobiography, referring to it there as an "old saying." He used it to mean: work hard or suffer undesirable consequences. See also William Marcy at POLITICS & POLITICIANS.

2 Two dollars a day and roast beef.

—Anonymous, slogan of the Whig party, 1840

★ See also the quotes directly below, as well as "the full dinner pail" and "a chicken in every pot" slogans also below. In the presidential campaign of 1840, Democratic incumbent Martin Van Buren was handicapped by a national financial crisis. The full slogan of the Whigs, who were running William Henry Harrison, was: "Van's policy, fifty cents a day and French soup. Our policy, two dollars a day and roast beef." The "French soup" was a reference to Van Buren's allegedly elegant lifestyle.

3 Tippecanoe and Tyler too.

—Anonymous, Whig campaign slogan, 1840

★ The Whig candidates in 1840 were William Henry Harrison, "the Hero of Tippecanoe," and, for the vice-presidency, John Tyler. They bested Democratic incumbent Martin Van Buren. Harrison was famous for defeating (more or less) the Shawnee Indians in battle at the Tippecanoe River in Indiana in 1811. The slogan was incorporated in a popular campaign song: "And have you heard the news from Maine, / And what old Maine can do? / She went hell-bent for Governor Kent, / And Tippecanoe and Tyler too, / And Tippecanoe and Tyler too." Gov. Kent was Edward Kent, whose victory in that summer's Maine election—until 1958 Maine voted in advance of the national election in November—was the first sign of a Whig sweep nationally. This also seems to be the source of the saying, "As Maine goes, so goes the nation"; see MAINE.

4 Farewell, dear Van,
You're not our man;
To guide the ship,
We'll try old Tip.

—Anonymous, Whig campaign song, 1840

★ Van is Martin Van Buren; Tip is William Henry Harrison; see note above. Sharp-witted Martin Van Buren, a loyal Jacksonian Democrat, gained a reputation as an overly elegant elitist, while the rather dim Harrison, who came from a wealthy family, was portrayed as a simple man of the people, raised in a log cabin. This election also popularized the expression "O.K." A humorous abbreviation of "Oll [or "Orl"] Korrect," it became associated with Van Buren because of the coincidence of the initials with those of his nickname, "Old Kinderhook," referring to his hometown in New York. Van Buren's supporters in New York, for example, formed a Democratic O.K. Club. After the election, victorious Whigs claimed that O.K. actually stood for an Arabic phrase which, when read backward, translated as "Kicked Out."

Fifty-four forty or fight. **1**

—William Allen, attributed, Democratic presidential campaign slogan, 1844

★ Sen. William Allen ("Earthquake Allen") of Ohio, a supporter of James K. Polk for president, is said to have invented this catchy slogan. The reference is to a latitude in the Oregon territory; the territory was controlled by Great Britain, but jointly occupied by Americans and British. Sen. Allen spoke in favor of a U.S. acquisition as far north as Alaska. Polk won, but in 1846, the U.S. and Britain settled their differences amicably. The U.S. took over Oregon territory up to the forty-ninth parallel, dividing the Oregon tract approximately in half. Included in the U.S. portion was land that is now divided into the states of Washington, Oregon, and Idaho.

Vote early and vote often. **2**

—Anonymous

★ In *The Age of Jackson*, Arthur M. Schlesinger, Jr., associates this with New York City political strongman, journalist, and iconoclast Mike Walsh. A bold friend of the underprivileged, Walsh headed the Spartan Band, a group of rowdies who participated actively in local elections. On March 31, 1858, in a speech in the U.S. Congress, Rep. William Porcher Miles referred to the "vote early and often" adage as "advice openly displayed on the election banners in one of our northern cities."

I think I hear his cheerful voice, **3**
"On column! Steady! Steady!"
So handy and so prompt was he,
We called him Rough and Ready.

—Anonymous, Whig presidential campaign song, 1848

★ Old Rough and Ready, Zachary Taylor, gained his appealing nickname in a marginally successful assault on outnumbered Seminole Indians in Florida in 1837. He was popularly regarded as a hero for his exploits in the Mexican War, and became the presidential candidate of the Whig party in 1848. He died after a year in office and was succeeded by Millard Fillmore.

We Polked you in '44, we shall Pierce you in '52. **4**

—Anonymous, Democratic campaign slogan, 1852

★ Franklin Pierce became the nation's fourteenth president, defeating his commander in the Mexican War, Whig candidate Gen. Winfield Scott. His failure to implement his party's expansionist foreign policy and his pro-Southern domestic policy ruined his standing in his own party, and he was not renominated.

Free soil, free men, Frémont. **5**

—Anonymous, Republican campaign slogan, 1856

★ Abolitionist William C. Frémont was the first presidential nominee of the Republican party. "Free-soil" meant no slavery, and the free-soil battleground was

Kansas. The Republican slogan was inspired by the Free Soil Party's 1848 rallying cry: "Free Soil, Free Speech, Free Labor, and Free Men." Despite a stirring campaign, Frémont lost to Democrat James Buchanan.

1 I know nothing but my Country, my whole Country, and nothing but Country.
—Anonymous, American (Know-Nothing) Party slogan, 1856

★ The Know-Nothing movement, dating to the 1840s, was so-called because its leading members belonged to secret organizations and would profess to know nothing when questioned as to their aims and their leaders. The movement was anti-immigrant and nationalistic. The Know-Nothings emerged from the semisecret Order of the Star-Spangled Banner, formed in New York in 1849. As the numbers of Catholic immigrants swelled, and their political influence increased, the Know-Nothings became more respectable, re-forming as the American party in 1854. Despite considerable success in congressional elections, the party was politically inept, and almost immediately divided on the slavery issue. The Know-Nothing candidate in 1856 was former president Millard Fillmore; he hoped to unite North and South, but of course failed. In 1855, Abraham Lincoln made the following observation: "As a nation we began by declaring that '*all men are created equal.*' We now practically read it, 'all men are created equal, *except negroes*.' When the Know-Nothings get control, it will read 'all men are created equal, except negroes, *and foreigners, and Catholics*,'" in a letter to Joshua Speed.

2 Don't swap horses.
—Anonymous, Republican presidential campaign slogan, 1864

★ This derived from a comment by Pres. Lincoln on the inadvisiblity of changing horses in midstream; see CHANGE. Democrats recycled this bit of folk wisdom in F.D.R.'s reelection campaigns of 1940 and 1944. They also used an ironic twist in 1932 when, with the nation's economy in shambles and Herbert Hoover running for reelection, the Dems maintained that the Republican motto must be "Don't swap barrels while going over Niagara."

3 Turn the rascals out.
—Charles A. Dana, slogan, presidential election of 1872

★ Dana, the editor of the New York *Sun*, made this phrase famous while urging the defeat of Pres. Ulysses S. Grant. Horace Greeley, editor of the *New York Tribune*, was running against Grant as a candidate of both the Democratic party and the Liberal Republican party—not a label likely to be revived these days. Grant won.

4 Rum, Romanism, and rebellion.
—Samuel Dickinson Burchard, remark, New York City, Oct. 9, 1884

★ Rev. Dr. Burchard, at a reception for Republican presidential candidate James G. Blaine, commented, "We are Republicans, and don't propose to identify ourselves with the party whose antecedents have been rum, Romanism, and rebellion." Blaine lost to Grover Cleveland, in part because he failed to distance himself, as we now say, from this inflammatory insult. The remark became a rallying cry for the Democrats.

5 A mugwump is a person educated beyond his intellect.
—Horace Porter, slogan, presidential election of 1884

★ In 1884, Republican mugwumps, or, more politely, political independents, deserted presidential candidate James G. Blaine in favor of Democrat Grover Cleveland.

Another reason that Blaine lost was a supporter's indiscreet reference to Democrats as belonging to the party of "rum, Romanism, and rebellion"; see Samuel Dickinson Burchard above. Maine's Thomas Reed described mugwumps as "longtailed birds of paradise." See also LANGUAGE & WORDS. Horace Porter served under Ulysses S. Grant both in the Army and the White House. In 1897, he became ambassador to France, and at the end of his tour, in 1905, he brought back the body of John Paul Jones.

Blaine, Blaine, James G. Blaine, 1
The Continental liar from the state of Maine.

—Anonymous, heckling slogan, 1884

★ A piece of simpleminded doggerel aimed at the Republican presidential candidate. For the Republican rejoinder, see below.

Ma, Ma, where's my Pa? 2

—Anonymous, heckling slogan, 1884

★ The question was popularly directed at Democratic presidential candidate Grover Cleveland, who admitted having fathered, or possibly fathered, an illegitimate child; at any rate he supported the child. The popular Democratic rejoinder was, "Gone to the White House, ha, ha, ha," and Cleveland did indeed go there.

Sixteen to one. 3

—Anonymous, Democratic party slogan, 1896

★ The Democratic platform called for the free coinage of silver in a ratio of sixteen to one to gold. See also William Jennings Bryan's "Cross of Gold" speech at ECONOMICS.

Four more years of the full dinner pail. 4

—Anonymous, Republican party slogan, 1900

★ The Republicans promised continuing prosperity with the reelection of William McKinley over William Jennings Bryan.

No crown of thorns, no cross of gold. 5

—Anonymous, Democratic party slogan, 1900

★ The reference is to candidate Bryan's "Cross of Gold" speech; see ECONOMICS.

McKinley drinks soda water; Bryan drinks rum; McKinley is a gentleman, Bryan is a 6
bum.

—Anonymous, heckling verse, presidential campaign, 1900

We'll stand pat. 7

—Mark Hanna, remark to reporter on campaign strategy, 1900

★ Sen. Hanna of Ohio—"the kingmaker"—was referring to his strategy for reelecting William McKinley. The stand-pat notion was included four years later in an unmemorable Republican slogan in support of Theodore Roosevelt, who had succeeded the assassinated McKinley, "Same old flag and victory—stand pat." Sixty years later, candidate Richard M. Nixon, running against John F. Kennedy, asserted repeatedly, "America cannot stand pat." He dropped the slogan after it was pointed out that his wife's name was Pat. Instead he used, "America cannot stand still."

1 We demand that big business give people a square deal.
—Theodore Roosevelt, 1901

★ Roosevelt was referring to setting limits on U.S. Steel. The term "square deal" was his favorite metaphor for fairness. In his autobiography, Roosevelt added to his original thought, "In turn, we must insist that when anyone engaged in big business honestly endeavors to do right, he shall himself be given a square deal." In a famous speech at Springfield, Ill., on July 4, 1903, Roosevelt said, "A man who is good enough to give his blood for his country is good enough to be given a square deal afterwards. More than that no man is entitled to, less than that no man shall have." On the campaign trail, his pledge to the American people was "I stand for the square deal." In 1910, in *The New Nationalism*, he explained, "When I say I am for the square deal, I mean not merely that I stand for fair play under the present rules of the game, but that I stand for having those rules changed so as to work for a more substantial equality of opportunity and of reward for equally good service." A square deal in card games is a fair, equitable deal, as in, for example, "Thought I had better give him a square deal," Mark Twain, *Life on the Mississippi*, 1883. According to William Safire in his *New Political Dictionary*, Lincoln Steffens claimed to have suggested the square-deal metaphor to Roosevelt. Use of card-playing metaphors in politics is traditional, witness the "New Deal" and the "Fair Deal"; see below. The redoubtable Colonel David (Davy) Crockett noted in his *Life of Martin Van Buren*, 1835, that "Statesmen are gamesters, and the people are the cards they play with . . . the way they cut and shuffle is a surprise to all beginners."

2 Get on the raft with Taft.
—Anonymous, Republican campaign slogan, 1908

★ Taft had been Pres. Theodore Roosevelt's Secretary of War—now called Secretary of Defense. He defeated William Jennings Bryan.

3 A New Nationalism.
—Theodore Roosevelt, campaign motto, 1912

4 A New Freedom.
—Woodrow Wilson, campaign motto, 1912

★ The voters preferred the New Freedom.

5 He kept us out of war.
—Martin H. Glynn, keynote address, Democratic National Convention, 1916

★ The convention selected incumbent Woodrow Wilson for president. Glyn's statement became a campaign slogan.

6 Harding, you're the man for us.
We think the country's ready
For another man like Teddy.
We need another Lincoln
To do the country's thinkin.
Mister Harding,
You're the man for us.
—Al Jolson, campaign song, 1920

Return to normalcy. 1

—**Warren G. Harding,** campaign slogan, 1920

★ See Harding at AMERICAN HISTORY: MEMORABLE MOMENTS, and also WARREN G. HARDING.

Law and Order. 2

—**Anonymous,** motto on banners waved by supporters of Calvin Coolidge for the vice-presidential nomination at the 1920 Republican National Convention

★ Coolidge became the "law and order" candidate because as governor of Massachusetts he reacted with force to a strike by police; see CAPITALISM & CAPITAL V. LABOR. The call for "law and order" has arisen frequently in American politics, usually in a conservative context. Thus, in 1842, the Law and Order Party in Rhode Island opposed extending the right to vote to males who didn't own property, and in 1857 the proslavery party in Kansas changed its name to the Law and Order Party. In the 1960s, "law and order" was a rallying cry for Republicans who hoped to turn back the liberal tide of that era.

Cox and cocktails. 3

—**Anonymous,** Democratic presidential campaign slogan, 1920

★ Presidential candidate James Middleton Cox of Ohio favored the League of Nations and the repeal of Prohibition. He lost badly in a three-way race against Warren Harding and Eugene Debs. Cox's running mate was Franklin D. Roosevelt.

Convict No. 9653 for President. 4

—**Anonymous,** Socialist presidential campaign slogan for Eugene Debs, 1920

★ Debs, the great socialist leader, who was regarded with affection even by many of his political enemies, was serving a ten-year prison term in 1920. His crime was publicly denouncing the federal prosecution of persons charged with sedition under the 1917 Espionage Act. Nevertheless, he got nearly 920,000 votes. Pres. Harding ordered his release in 1920. But Debs, age sixty-five, was finished as a major political figure.

Keep cool with Coolidge. 5

—**Anonymous,** campaign slogan for Republican presidential candidate Calvin Coolidge, 1924

Coolidge or chaos. 6

—**Anonymous,** campaign slogan for Republican presidential candidate Calvin Coolidge, 1924

★ In 1924, Coolidge, who had inherited the presidency from Warren Harding, ran against two major candidates, Democrat John W. Davis and the Progressive Party's Robert M. La Follette. There were also six minor parties in the race, including the Prohibition Party, the Socialist Labor Party, and the Communist Party.

A chicken in every pot, a car in every garage. 7

—**Anonymous,** Republican presidential campaign slogan, 1928

★ The slogan often is attributed mistakenly to Pres. Herbert Hoover. As the Republican incumbent, he prophesied an end to poverty in the U.S. in his nomination acceptance speech (see AMERICAN HISTORY: MEMORABLE MOMENTS), but not in these terms. The closest that he came was in a speech on Oct. 22 when he said that "The slogan of progress is changing from the full dinner pail to the full garage." The slogan was used in campaign flyers as well as in the headline, "A chicken in every pot and a car in every garage, to boot," of an ad that was placed in the New York *World* by "Republican Businessmen, Inc." The ultimate source of the phrase is Henry IV of France, who reputedly said, "I want there to be no peasant in my realm so poor that he will not have a chicken in his pot every Sunday."

1 Every man a king!

—Huey Long, slogan in the 1928 Louisiana gubernatorial campaign and title of Long's autobiography, 1933

★ Populist to some, demagogue to others, Long won in this campaign, and, in 1932, was elected to the U.S. Senate. He declared for the presidency in 1934. Will Rogers commented, "He found me and pinned a button on me, called *every man a king*, and it said everybody was to divide up their wealth. I am working with him on a percentage." Will Rogers died in a plane crash in 1935. A month later Long was assassinated.

2 Share our wealth.

—Huey Long, political slogan, carved on his tomb in the Capitol in Baton Rouge, La.

★ In February 1934, Long announced the creation of the Share Our Wealth Society, calling for a more equal distribution of wealth among rich and poor. Share Our Wealth clubs sprang up nationally, but especially in the impoverished South.

3 A new deal for the American people.

—Franklin D. Roosevelt, presidential nomination acceptance speech, Democratic National Convention, Chicago, July 2, 1932

★ See also AMERICAN HISTORY: MEMORABLE MOMENTS.

4 Happy days are here again.

—Jack Yellen, *Happy Days Are Here Again*, 1929

★ More at GOOD TIMES.

5 Life, liberty, and Landon.

—Anonymous, Republican presidential campaign slogan for Alf Landon, 1936

★ Landon won only Maine and Vermont.

6 Roosevelt for ex-President.

—Anonymous, Republican presidential campaign slogan, 1940

★ The Republican candidate Wendell Willkie, an industrialist, had been a Democrat until 1940. He did better than any other contender against Roosevelt, tallying more than 22 million votes.

7 Let's re- re- re-elect Roosevelt.

—Anonymous, Democratic presidential campaign slogan, 1944

8 Had enough?

—Anonymous, Republican presidential campaign slogan, 1944

★ The Republican candidate was Thomas Dewey, and the voters answered no.

Give 'em hell, Harry! 1

—Anonymous, Democratic rallying cry, 1948

★ Pres. Harry S. Truman, apparently running behind the Republican challenger Thomas Dewey, was cheered on by this popular slogan. He first heard the cry in Seattle, and it followed him to victory. Going into the home stretch, he told Vice President Alben Barkley "I'm going to fight hard. I'm going to give them hell," Sept. 27, 1948. See also Truman at TRUTH.

I like Ike. 2

—Anonymous, Republican campaign slogan for Dwight D. "Ike" Eisenhower, 1952

★ A great slogan—almost everybody did like Ike—derived from the song, "They Like Ike," in Irving Berlin's 1950 Broadway hit, *Call Me Madam*, and recycled in 1956 as "I still like Ike."

You never had it so good. 3

—Anonymous, Democratic campaign slogan for candidate Adlai Stevenson, 1952

★ A good effort, much better than the weak 1956 slogans "We need Adlai badly" and "We're madly for Adlai." Stevenson also pledged that his administration would be in tune with "a new America," anticipating John F. Kennedy's "New Frontier."

A New Frontier. 4

—John F. Kennedy, presidential campaign slogan, 1960

★ The tag line came from his nomination acceptance speech at the Democratic convention in Los Angeles on July 15, 1960: "We stand today at the edge of a new frontier—the frontier of the 1960s, a frontier of unknown opportunities and paths, a frontier of unfulfilled hopes and threats." He explained, "The new frontier of which I speak is not a set of promises, it is a set of challenges. It sums up not what I intend to *offer* the American people but what I intend to *ask* of them." In his inaugural speech, he returned to the concept of citizen service; see SERVING ONE'S COUNTRY. The "new frontier" idea was not new. In 1934, Henry Wallace published a book entitled *New Frontiers*, and in 1936, Alf Landon, the Republican candidate for president also spoke of "a new frontier . . . a frontier of invention and new wants." Kennedy, though, made the phrase his own, his equivalent of F.D.R.'s New Deal and Truman's Fair Deal. The programs that typified Kennedy's New Frontier were in space exploration, civil rights, education, medical care for the aged, and farm policy. In 1979, Pres. Jimmy Carter and speechwriter Rick Herzberg introduced A New Foundation, but it did not catch on.

All the way with LBJ. 5

—Anonymous, Democratic presidential campaign slogan for Lyndon Baines Johnson, 1964

The Great Society. 6

—Lyndon B. Johnson, political slogan, 1964

★ In *The Penguin Dictionary of Contemporary American History*, Stanley and Eleanor Hochman point out that President Johnson first tried the tag line "a better deal" to describe the type of government he hoped to bring to the American people. When that flopped, he recalled the phrase "a great society" in a speech written for him by Richard Goodwin, March 4, 1964. He successfully launched the slogan on April 23 at a Democratic fundraiser in Chicago: "We have been called upon—are you listening?—to build a great society of the highest order, a society not just for today or tomorrow, but for three or four generations to come." The best publicized occasion of its use was in May at the University of Michigan; see AMERICAN HISTORY: MEMORABLE MOMENTS. Great Society programs were introduced in a flood of legislation designed to end poverty and promote civil rights. Republicans noted that a 1914 book by Graham Wallace titled *The Great Society* was a socialist text. The Vietnam War, however, ended Johnson's social initiatives.

1 In your heart you know he's right.

—**Anonymous,** Republican campaign slogan for presidential candidate Barry Goldwater, 1964

★ Republicans also advertised that Goldwater offered "a choice, not an echo," picking up on Goldwater's announcement on Jan. 3, 1964, of his candidacy: "I will not change my beliefs to win votes. I will offer a choice not an echo." Ironically, thirty years later, Goldwater, the old warrior of the right, came to be considered too libertarian, too free-thinking, and too liberal for contemporary Republicans.

2 Nixon's the one.

—**Anonymous,** Republican campaign slogan aimed at winning the presidential nomination for Richard Nixon, 1968

★ Nixon's supporters prevailed and the phrase entered the language, but was easily turned against Nixon. For example, after the 1972 campaign, when the official party slogan was "Nixon now more than ever," skeptics resurrected "Nixon's the one" with reference to the national Watergate whodunit.

3 Unbought and Unbossed.

—**Shirley Chisholm,** Congressional campaign, 1968

★ Chisolm won an upset victory in Brooklyn, N.Y., becoming the first black woman to serve in Congress. In 1970, she used the slogan as a book title. In 1972, she ran for president. Advocates for women's rights often referred to her comment to an Associated Press reporter in 1982, "When I ran for Congress, when I ran for president, I met more discrimination as a woman than for being black."

4 Are you better off today than you were four years ago?

—**Paul Simmons,** slogan for Illinois Gov. Jim Thompson, late 1970s

★ It was picked up and used to great effect by Republican presidential candidate Ronald Reagan in 1980. His target was Pres. Jimmy Carter.

5 It's morning in America.

—**Anonymous,** theme of campaign commercial for re-election of President Reagan, 1984

★ He won handily.

6 A kinder, gentler nation.

—**George H. W. Bush,** presidential nomination speech, Republican National Convention, New Orleans, August 18, 1988

★ This instantly famous phrase was selected by speechwriter Peggy Noonan to distinguish Vice President Bush from Pres. Ronald Reagan, who was often accused of a bland heartlessness. Nancy Reagan caught on fast. When Bush announced, "I want a kinder, gentler nation," she is said to have asked immediately, "Kinder and gentler than who?" This speech also included the reference to "a thousand points of light"; see AMERICA & AMERICANS.

It's the economy, stupid. **1**

—James Carville, saying, 1992

★ Carville, campaign manager for Bill Clinton, put up a sign with this message in his headquarters in Little Rock, Ark. The sign also bore the statements—"Change vs. more of the same"and "Don't forget health care"—but it was the first one, meaning that attention to the faltering economy was the key to victory, that got the most attention. Woodrow Wilson made the same point more politely; see POLITICS & POLITICIANS.

Compassionate conservatism. **2**

—George W. Bush, slogan, from 1999

★ When accepting the Republican presidential nomination at the party's national convention in Philadelphia, Mr. Bush explained the meaning of the slogan this way: "Big government is not the answer, but the alternative to bureaucracy is not indifference. It is to put conservative values and conservative ideas into the thick of the fight for justice and opportunity. This is what I mean by compassionate conservatism" (August 8, 2000).

Freedom is on the march. **3**

—George W. Bush, presidential campaign slogan, 2004

★ The reference was to the Iraq War and other efforts aimed at increasing democracy in the Middle East. It echoed his father's "because we have been resolute, liberty is on the march" (fundraising speech, Tyson's Corner, Virginia, March 8, 1990).

Politics & Politicians

See also COMMUNISM; CONGRESS; DEMOCRACY; GOVERNMENT; MAJORITIES & MINORITIES; POLITICAL SLOGANS; PRESIDENCY, THE; SOCIALISM.

I agree with you that in politics the middle way is none at all. **4**

—John Adams, letter to Horatio Gates, March 23, 1776

An attachment to different leaders ambitiously contending for preeminence and **5**
power . . . [has] divided mankind into parties, inflamed them with mutual animosity, and rendered them much more disposed to vex and oppress each other than to co-operate for their common good.

—James Madison, *Federalist*, No. 10, 1787–88

The meekness of Quakerism will do in religion, but not in politics. **6**

—De Witt Clinton, c. 1803

★ Clinton dominated New York politics in the first quarter of the 19th century as assemblyman, state senator, U.S. senator, mayor of New York City, and three-term governor of the state. Among other good works, he promoted public schools, public sanitation, relief for the poor, the abolition of slavery, and—his crowning achievement—the construction of the Erie Canal.

1 When a man assumes a public trust, he should consider himself as public property.
—**Thomas Jefferson,** remark to Baron von Humboldt, attributed in Rayner, *Life of Jefferson* [1834]

★ See also Grover Cleveland's motto—"A public office is a public trust"—at GOVERNMENT, author anonymous.

2 [The Democrats] see nothing wrong in the rule that to the victors belong the spoils of the enemy.
—**William Marcy,** speech, U.S. Senate, Jan. 25, 1832

★ Sen. Marcy of New York was defending Pres. Andrew Jackson's policy of appointing his own supporters to government positions. In particular, he was defending the appointment of Martin Van Buren as ambassador to Great Britain. This "spoils system," which Jackson called "rotation in office," is taken for granted today. Jackson himself replaced less than ten percent of office holders in his first eighteen months. See also Richard Croker, Huey Long, and Fiorello LaGuardia below.

3 We are reformers in spring and summer; in autumn and winter, we stand by the old; reformers in the morning, conservers at night. Reform is affirmative, conservatism negative; conservatism goes for comfort, reform for truth.
—**Ralph Waldo Emerson,** *The Conservative*, lecture, Boston, May 9, 1841

4 Conservatism makes no poetry, breathes no prayer, has no invention; it is all memory. Reform has no gratitude, no prudence, no husbandry.
—**Ibid.**

5 A party is perpetually corrupted by personality.
—**Ralph Waldo Emerson,** *Politics*, in *Essays: Second Series*, 1844

6 It is the fashion of a certain set to assume to despise "politics." . . . But to our view, the spectacle is always a grand one—full of the most august and sublime attributes.
—**Walt Whitman,** *American Democracy*, in the *Brooklyn Eagle*, April 20, 1847

7 An honest politician is one who when he's bought stays bought.
—**Simon Cameron,** attributed, c. 1850

★ Cameron was the Republican boss of Pennsylvania, widely accused of doing a lot of political buying and selling. George Seldes, in *The Great Quotations*, wrote that fellow politician Thomas B. Reed attributed this line to Cameron. See also Cameron below and Charles Brayton, below, on honest voters.

8 I never said all Democrats were saloon-keepers. What I said was that all saloon-keepers are Democrats.
—**Horace Greeley,** attributed, c. 1860

9 What is conservatism? Is it not adherence to the old and tried against the new and untried?
—**Abraham Lincoln,** speech, Feb. 27, 1860

10 You scratch my back, I'll scratch yours.
—**Simon Cameron,** attributed

★ Cameron did so much scratching as Lincoln's Secretary of War that it became a national scandal, and he had to be eased from office. Lincoln named him ambassador to Russia.

The Democratic party is like a mule. It has neither pride of ancestry nor hope of posterity. 1

—**Ignatius Donnelly,** speech, Minnesota legislature, 1860

★ Donnelly, who enjoyed a long political career, including three terms as a Republican representative in Congress, was a genuine American crackpot, holding forth in best-selling books that Bacon wrote Shakespeare, that a close call with a comet had caused the ice ages, and that the biblical Eden was in the lost continent of Atlantis.

My pollertics, like my religion, bein of a exceedin accommodatin character. 2

—**Artemus Ward,** *The Crisis* in *Artemus Ward: His Book,* 1862

There are always two parties, the party of the past and the party of the future: the establishment and the movement. 3

—**Ralph Waldo Emerson,** *Historic Notes of Life and Letters in New England,* 1867

Politics makes strange bedfellows. 4

—**Charles Dudley Warner,** *My Summer in a Garden,* 1870

★ Warner, editor of the *Hartford Courant* and *Harper's Magazine*, probably had in mind Shakespeare's "Misery acquaints a man with strange bedfellows," *The Tempest*, Act 2, Scene 2.

Waving the bloody shirt. 5

—**Oliver Perry Morton,** saying, c. 1876

★ Sen. Morton of Indiana made this phrase popular as a description of the tendency of post-Civil War Republicans to appeal to sectionalism and anti-Confederate sentiment to get votes. The "bloody shirt," sometimes euphemized by Victorians as "the ensanguined garment," has a pre-Civil War history. The idea is to inflame emotions by displaying bloodstained clothes of someone who's been killed. The oldest example of "bloody shirt" in this sense in *The Oxford English Dictionary* is from Sir Philip Sidney's *Arcadia* (pre–1586).

An honest voter is one who stays bought. 6

—**Charles R. "Boss" Brayton,** attributed saying

★ Brayton was a notorious GOP operative in Rhode Island. The politics of his era was captured by Lincoln Steffens in 1905. See RHODE ISLAND.

He serves his party best who serves the country best. 7

—**Rutherford B. Hayes,** Inaugural Address, March 5, 1877

Politics are impossible without spoils. . . . You have to deal with men as they are . . . 8
You must bribe the masses with spoils.

—**Richard Croker,** quoted in Richard Norton Smith, *Thomas E. Dewey* [1982]

★ "Boss" Croker of New York City flourished in the late 1880s. He was the political descendant of William Marcy, see above.

1 The purification of politics is an iridescent dream.
—**John James Ingalls,** article, *New York World*, 1890

★ Sen. Ingalls of Kansas was a nationally popular orator. In this cynical assessment of the political arena, he continued, "Government is force. . . . The Decalogue and the Golden Rule have no place in a political campaign. The commander who lost the battle through the activity of his moral nature would be the derision and jest of history."

2 There are two things that are important in politics. The first is money, and I can't remember what the second one is.
—**Mark Hanna,** attributed, 1895

3 I am a Democrat still—very still.
—**David Bennett Hill,** comment to reporter following the nomination of William Jennings Bryan in 1900

★ Hill, a former governor of New York and presidential candidate, had difficulty supporting the convention's free-silver policies and its candidate, William Jennings Bryan. See also ECONOMICS. Four years earlier, when Bryan won the first of his three nominations for the presidency, Hill had commented, "I am a Democrat, but not a revolutionist."

4 I am as strong as a bull moose and you can use me to the limit.
—**Theodore Roosevelt,** letter to Sen. Mark Hanna, June 27, 1900

★ Roosevelt's references to himself as a bull moose gave the Progressive Party, founded in 1912, its nickname.

5 Reformers Only Morning Glories.
—**George Washington Plunkitt,** title of speech, c. 1900

★ Plunkitt, a Tammany Hall state senator, observed: "The fact is that a reformer can't last in politics. He can make a show of it for a while, but he always comes down like a rocket." See also Plunkitt at CRIME, CRIMINALS & DETECTIVES for a definition of "honest graft."

6 Th' dimmycratic party ain't on speakin' terms with itsilf.
—**Finley Peter Dunne,** *Mr. Dooley Discusses Party Politics*, in *Mr. Dooley's Opinions*, 1900

7 A statesman is a successful politician who is dead.
—**Thomas Brackett Reed,** attributed

★ "Czar" Reed represented Maine from 1877 to 1899, and was Speaker in 1889–91 and 1895–99. He made this observation to Rep. Henry Cabot Lodge, according to Edward Boykin's *The Wit and Wisdom of Congress*, 1961. Harry S. Truman, another politician who waited long to be called a statesman, used the same thought: "A statesman is a politician who's been dead ten or fifteen years," *New York World-Telegram & Sun*, April 12, 1958.

8 If we would vote in mass on the more promising ticket, or, if the two are equally bad, would throw out the party that is in, and wait till the next election, and then throw out the other party that is in—then, I say, the commerical politician would feel a demand for good government and he would supply it.
—**Lincoln Steffens,** *Shame of the Cities*, 1904

Politics is the art of turning influence into affluence. **1**

—Philander C. Johnson, *Senator Sorghum's Primer of Politics*, 1906

★ And vice versa.

Somehow a party platform always reminds me a lot of New Year's resolutions. **2**

—Ibid.

The man who goes into politics because he needs the money isn't likely to do as **3**
much harm as the man who goes into it merely because he has money to burn.

—Ibid.

A true politician never forgets a favor; that is to say, if by chance he does someone **4**
else a favor, he never forgets it.

—Ibid.

Practical politics consists in ignoring facts. **5**

—Henry Adams, *The Education of Henry Adams*, 1907

Politics, as a practice, whatever its professions, has always been the systematic **6**
organization of hatreds.

—Ibid.

Knowledge of human nature is the beginning and end of political education. **7**

—Ibid.

Modern politics is, at bottom, a struggle not of men but of forces. **8**

—Ibid.

Prosperity is necessarily the first theme of a political campaign. **9**

—Woodrow Wilson, speech, Sept. 4, 1912

★ See also James Carville at POLITICAL SLOGANS.

Men who form the lunatic fringe in all reform movements. **10**

—Theodore Roosevelt, *Autobiography*, 1913

★ The passage runs: "Among the wise and high-minded people who in self-respecting and genuine fashion strive earnestly for peace, there are the foolish fanatics always to be found in such a movement and always discrediting it— the men who form the lunatic fringe in all reform movements."

In a smoke-filled room in some hotel. **11**

—Harry M. Daugherty, quoted in *The New York Times*, Feb. 21, 1920

★ Daugherty was Warren G. Harding's campaign manager, and the TIMES quoted his prediction that at the Republican Convention in June, his candidate would be selected for the presidential nomination. "The convention will be deadlocked," he predicted, "and after the other candidates have gone their limit, some twelve or fifteen men, worn out and bleary-eyed for lack of sleep, will sit down around a table in a smoke-filled room in some hotel and decide the nomination. When that time comes, Harding will be selected." Daugherty later denied using the phrase "smoke-filled room," but he had the scenario right, and the smoke-filled room came to symbolize professional party politics.

1 Nationalism is an infantile disease. It is the measles of mankind.
—**Albert Einstein,** statement to G. S. Vereck, 1921, in Helen Dukas and Banesh Hoffmann, *Albert Einstein, the Human Side* [1979]

2 I never took a quarter from anyone who couldn't afford it.
—**James Curley,** quoted in Jack Beatty, *The Rascal King* [1993]

★ Mayor Curley of Boston was the model for Edwin O'Connor's Irish city boss, Frank Skeffington, in *The Last Hurrah*, 1956.

3 I tell you folks, all politics is applesauce.
—**Will Rogers,** *The Illiterate Digest*, 1924

4 Any party which takes credit for the rain must not be surprised if its opponents blame it for the drought.
—**Dwight W. Morrow,** remark, quoted in William Safire, *Safire's New Political Dictionary* [1993]

★ A lawyer, banker, and diplomat, Morrow also was father of Anne Morrow Lindbergh.

5 Politics has got so expensive that it takes a lot of money to even get beat with nowadays.
—**Will Rogers,** *Daily Telegrams*, June 28, 1931

6 Politicians, after all, are not over a year behind public opinion.
—**Will Rogers,** *The Autobiography of Will Rogers* [1949]

★ And in another bit of faint praise: "Politicians are doing the best they can according to the dictates of no conscience"; quoted in Alex Ayres, ed., *The Wit and Wisdom of Will Rogers*, 1993.

7 Politics is the best show in America.
—**Will Rogers,** *Weekly Articles*, Dec. 18, 1932

8 You can't adopt politics as a profession and remain honest.
—**Louis McHenry Howe,** speech, Jan. 17, 1933

★ Howe was a trusted, invaluable aide to Franklin D. Roosevelt.

9 The man who pulls the plow gets the plunder in politics.
—**Huey P. Long,** speech, U.S. Senate, Jan. 30, 1934

10 A conservative is a man who has plenty of money and doesn't see any reason why he shouldn't always have plenty of money. . . . A Democrat is a fellow who never had any money but doesn't see why he shouldn't have some money.
—**Will Rogers,** quoted in Alex Ayres, ed., *The Wit and Wisdom of Will Rogers* [1993]

11 I am not a member of any organized political party—I am a Democrat.
—**Will Rogers,** quoted in P. J. O'Brien, *Will Rogers, Ambassador of Good Will, Prince of Wit and Wisdom*, 1935

★ Rogers also remarked, "You've got to be [an] optimist to be a Democrat, and you've got be a humorist to stay one," *Gold Gulf* radio show, June 24, 1934.

All politics is local. 1

—Thomas P. "Tip" O'Neill, saying

★ Speaker of the House from 1977 to 1987, Tip O'Neill was the last of Boston's larger-than-life Irish politicians. In his autobiography, *Man of the House*, O'Neill credited his father with this line. Possibly his father picked it up from Finley Peter Dunne, who was the first to make this observation, according to *The Macmillan Dictionary of Political Quotations* [1993].

A liberal is a man who is willing to spend someone else's money. 2

—Carter Glass, quoted in an Associated Press interview, Sept. 24, 1938

★ This may not have been original with Sen. Glass, but as a newspaper publisher he knew how to exploit a good line. Glass, a conservative Virginia Democrat, staunchly opposed Pres. Franklin D. Roosevelt's New Deal, and fought for states' rights and segregation.

To the victor belongs the responsibility of good government. 3

—Fiorello La Guardia, epigraph, *New York Advancing: World's Fair Edition*, Rebecca B. Rankin, ed., 1939

★ The New York City mayor's emendation of Sen. Marcy's observation above.

A radical is a man with both feet firmly planted in the air. 4

—Franklin D. Roosevelt, radio speech, Oct. 26, 1939

A conservative is a man with two perfectly good legs who, however, has never 5
learned how to walk forward.

—Ibid.

A reactionary is a somnambulist walking backward. 6

—Ibid.

Honesty is no substitute for experience. 7

—Anonymous

★ The saying sometimes is attributed to Erastus Corning, 2nd, longtime (1941–83) mayor of Albany, N.Y. Others say that it is the time-honored motto of the Brooklyn, N.Y., Democrat machine.

a politician is an arse upon 8
which everyone has sat except a man.

—E. E. Cummings, *a politician*, in *One Times One* (or *1* × *1*), 1944

The object of liberalism has never been to destroy capitalism . . . only to keep the 9
capitalists from destroying it.

—Arthur M. Schlesinger, Jr., *The Age of Jackson*, 1945

We mean by "politics" the people's business—the most important business there is. 10

—Adlai Stevenson, speech, Chicago, Nov. 19, 1955

An independent is a guy who wants to take the politics out of politics. 11

—Adlai Stevenson, *The Art of Politics*, 1955

1 Money is the mother's milk of politics.

—**Jesse Unruh,** saying, quoted in *The New York Times*, obituary [Aug. 6, 1987]

★ Unruh, speaker of the California assembly, was a dominant Democrat.

2 Political action is the highest responsibility of a citizen.

—**John F. Kennedy,** speech, Oct. 20, 1960

3 Little old ladies in tennis shoes.

—**Stanley Mosk,** report on right-wing political activity in California, 1961

★ This became a catch-phrase in the 1960s to describe ultra-conservative women supporters of Barry Goldwater and Ronald Reagan. In full, Mr. Mosk, a Democrat then attorney general of California, wrote that "The cadre of the John Birch Society seems to be formed primarily of wealthy businessmen, retired military officers, and little old ladies in tennis shoes." His office received mailbags full of worn and mismatched tennis shoes as a result.

4 Sometimes I think this country would be better off if we could just saw off the Eastern Seaboard and let it float out to sea.

—**Barry Goldwater,** press conference report, Chicago *Tribune*, Sept. 30, 1961

★ The conservative Arizona Republican may have made the remark half in jest, but it revealed a basic fault-line in American politics. By winning the Republican nomination for president in 1964, Goldwater began the process of marginalizing the moderate Republican establishment of the northeast, then led by New York's Gov. Nelson Rockefeller. He thus paved the way for the Reagan "revolution" and for the red-state/blue-state divide at the start of the twenty-first century.

5 Politics is not the art of the possible. It consists in choosing between the disastrous and the unpalatable.

—**John Kenneth Galbraith,** letter to Pres. John F. Kennedy, March 2, 1962, in *Ambassador's Journal* [1969]

★ Galbraith is referring to Otto von Bismarck's "Politics is the art of the possible, the attainable . . . the next best," conversation with Meyer von Waldeck, August 11, 1867.

6 Sometimes party loyalty asks too much.

—**John F. Kennedy,** quoted in Arthur M. Schlesinger, Jr., *A Thousand Days: John F. Kennedy in the White House* [1965]

7 The difference between expediency and morality in politics is the difference between selling out a principle and making small concessions to win larger ones. The leader who shrinks from this task reveals not his purity but his lack of political sense.

—**Bayard Rustin,** c. 1963, *The Collected Writings of Bayard Rustin* [2003]

8 All politics are based on the indifference of the majority.

—**James Reston,** *The New York Times*, June 12, 1968

9 The liberals can understand everything but people who don't understand them.

—**Lenny Bruce,** in John Cohen, *Essential Lenny Bruce*, 1970

Politics is supposed to be the second oldest profession. I have come to realize that it bears a very close resemblance to the first. 1

—**Ronald Reagan,** conference remarks, Los Angeles, March 2, 1977

The difference between a campaign contribution and a bribe is almost a hairline's difference. 2

—**Russell B. Long,** quoted in *The New York Times,* obituary [May 11, 2003]

★ Sen. Long was from that larger-than-life family of Louisiana politicians that included Huey Long and Earl Long.

A conservative is a liberal who was mugged the night before. 3

—**Frank Rizzo,** saying

★ Rizzo was mayor of Philadelphia from 1972 to 1980. The converse is: "A liberal is a conservative who's been arrested," quoted in Tom Wolfe, *The Bonfire of the Vanities*, 1987.

We campaign in poetry, but when we're elected, we're forced to govern in prose. 4

—**Mario Cuomo,** speech, Yale University, 1985

We're the party that wants to see an America in which people can still get rich. 5

—**Ronald Reagan,** dinner for Republicans in Congress, May 4, 1982

Although he is regularly asked to do so, God does not take sides in American politics. 6

—**George Mitchell,** comment in Senate Select Committee hearing on the Iran-Contra affair, July 1987

★ Sen. Mitchell of Maine was reprimanding Col. Oliver North for implying that he and God were of the same mind on covert political activities. See also Lincoln at PRAYER and Barry Goldwater at GOD.

Politics is knowing when to pull the trigger. 7

—**Mario Puzo,** *Godfather III*, screenplay, 1990

You want to win this election, you better change the subject. You wanna change the subject, you better have a war. It's show business. 8

—**Hilary Henkin & David Mamet,** from book by Larry Beinhart, *Wag the Dog*, screenplay, 1997

★ Comment delivered by Robert DeNiro as a political operative who distracts the nation from a presidential sex scandal with a fake global conflict cooked up by a Hollywood producer (Dustin Hoffman). The title comes from the old joke: Why does a dog wag its tail? Because a dog is smarter than its tail. If the tail was smarter, the tail would wag the dog."

This vast right wing conspiracy . . . has been conspiring against my husband since the day he announced for president. 9

—**Hillary Clinton,** on the NBC *Today Show,* Jan. 27, 1998

★ The First Lady was reacting to stories that her husband had been having an affair with White House intern Monical Lewinsky, a scandal that led to his impeachment. The reference to a vast right-wing conspiracy was not entirely new. *American Speech* (Winter 2000) found examples back to 1991.

1 The American people are conservative. What they want to conserve is the New Deal.
—**George Will,** quoted in Alan Brinkley, *Liberalism and Its Discontents,* 1998

2 Creative betrayal is the essence of successful statesmanship. The other side of the coin is that loyalty is a very attractive quality, but it doesn't get you anything.
—**Richard Norton Smith,** comment, *The New York Times Week in Review,* Dec. 14, 2003

★ Historian Smith is the director of the Abraham Lincoln Presidential Library.

3 We [Republicans] want you to get rich and the Democrats don't. They want to tax you as if you were rich already.
—**Grover Norquist,** quoted in *The New York Times Week in Review,* Feb. 1, 2004

4 Spin pays.
—**Jack Rosenthal,** The Sunday Group, roundtable discussion of spinning the news, Washington, Conn., April 18, 2004

★ Rosenthal is president of The New York Times Foundation.

Possessions

See Luxury; Things & Possessions.

Poverty & Hunger

See also Economics; Money & the Rich; Rich & Poor, Wealth & Poverty.

5 Light purse, heavy heart.
—**Benjamin Franklin,** *Poor Richard's Almanack*, 1749

6 They are slaves who fear to speak
For the fallen and the weak.
—**James Russell Lowell,** *Stanzas on Freedom*, 1843

7 Poverty demoralizes.
—**Ralph Waldo Emerson,** *Wealth*, in *The Conduct of Life*, 1860

8 Over the hill to the poor-house, I'm trudging my weary way.
—**Will Carleton,** *Over the Hill to the Poor-house*, in *Farm Ballads*, 1873

9 The awful phantom of the hungry poor.
—**Harriet Prescott Spofford,** *A Winter's Night*, c. 1875

10 Poverty indeed *is* the strenuous life—without brass bands, or uniforms, or hysteric popular applause, or lies, or circumlocutions.
—**William James,** *The Varieties of Religious Experience*, 1902

★ James was referring to Theodore Roosevelt's call to all to take up the strenuous life; see Physical Fitness.

11 It's no disgrace t'be poor, but it might as well be.
—**Frank McKinney "Kin" Hubbard,** *Short Furrows*, 1911

No man can worship God or love his neighbor on an empty stomach. **1**
—Woodrow Wilson, speech, New York City, May 23, 1912

I was once so poor I didn't know where my next husband was coming from. **2**
—Mae West, in the movie *She Done Him Wrong*, from her play *Diamond Lil*, 1928

The forgotten man at the bottom of the economic pyramid. **3**
—Franklin D. Roosevelt, radio speech, April 7, 1932

★ Roosevelt, then governor of New York, compared the economic crisis of the Depression to the war crises of 1917, saying that the nation must regain faith in the forgotten man, and "build from the bottom up not the top down." Roosevelt took the phrase from a famous 1885 speech by William Graham Sumner; see under ECONOMICS. See also Roosevelt's Second Inaugural Address, AMERICAN HISTORY: MEMORABLE MOMENTS.

It's the anarchy of poverty **4**
delights me.
—William Carlos Williams, *The Poor,* 1938

There is something about poverty that smells like death. Dead dreams dropping off **5**
the heart like leaves in a dry season and rotting around the feet.
—Zora Neale Hurston, *Dust Tracks on a Road*, 1942

A hungry man is not a free man. **6**
—Adlai Stevenson, speech, Sept. 6, 1952

If a free society cannot help the many who are poor, it cannot save the few who are **7**
rich.
—John F. Kennedy, Inaugural Address, 1961

People who are much too sensitive to demand of cripples that they run races ask of **8**
the poor that they get up and act just like everyone else in society.
—Michael Harrington, *The Other America*, 1962

There is a monotony about the injustices suffered by the poor that perhaps accounts **9**
for the lack of interest the rest of society shows in them. Everything seems to go wrong with them. They never win. It's just boring.
—Dwight Macdonald, review of Michael Harrington's *The Other America*, in *The New Yorker*, 1963

★ Macdonald's review helped to catalyze Lyndon B. Johnson's War on Poverty.

This administration . . . declares unconditional war on poverty in America. **10**
—Lyndon B. Johnson, State of the Union speech, Jan. 8, 1964

★ More at AMERICAN HISTORY: MEMORABLE MOMENTS.

We been down so long we got no way to go but up. **11**
—Fannie Lou Hamer, saying c. 1964, quoted in *In This Affluent Society*, television documentary, WNET [Jan. 16, 1995]

★ Hamer was an influential African-American leader, one of the founders of the Mississippi Freedom Democratic Party, which, in 1972, unseated the regular delegation at the Democratic National Convention. Another Hamer saying, which is on her tombstone, is,"I'm sick and tired of being sick and tired."

1 We could use less foreign aid and more home aid.
—Pearl Bailey, *Pearl's Kitchen*, 1973

2 The working poor are the major philanthropists of our society.
—Barbara Ehrenreich, *Nickel and Dimed: On (Not) Getting By in America*, 2001

★ Because they give so much more than they get.

Power

See also STRENGTH & TOUGHNESS; VIOLENCE; TYRANNY.

3 All men would be tyrants if they could.
—Abigail Adams, letter to John Adams, Nov. 27, 1775

★ More at WOMEN & MEN.

4 I am more and more convinced that man is a dangerous creature and that power, whether vested in many or a few, is ever grasping, and like the grave, cries, "Give, Give."
—Abigail Adams, letter to John Adams, March 31, 1776

5 Power always follows property.
—John Adams, letter to James Sullivan, May 26, 1776

★ Adams and Sullivan (a member of the Provincial congress of Massachusetts) wrote back and forth on who should be allowed to vote. Adams was a member of the Second Continental Congress at the time. In this letter, Adams opposed the more liberal Sullivan, arguing that only property owners should have the right to vote. The key sentences read, "Harrington has shown that power always follows property. This I believe to be as infallible a maxim in politics, as that action and reaction are equal in mechanics." James Harrington was a contemporaneous (d. 1776) English political writer. See also PROPERTY.

6 In the general course of human nature, a power over a man's subsistence amounts to a power over his will.
—Alexander Hamilton, *The Federalist*, No. 79, 1788

★ Hamilton was worried about the implications of the legislature having power over judges' salaries. The solution was lifetime appointments for federal judges.

7 An honest man can feel no pleasure in the exercise of power over his fellow citizens.
—Thomas Jefferson, letter to John Melish, Jan. 13, 1813

8 Power always thinks it has a great soul and vast views beyond the comprehension of the weak, and that it is doing God's service, when it is violating all His laws.
—John Adams, letter to Thomas Jefferson, Feb. 2, 1816

Where the people possess no authority, their rights obtain no respect. **1**

—George Bancroft, *To the Workingmen of Northampton*, in the *Boston Courier*, Oct. 22, 1834

Power ceases in the instant of repose. **2**

—Ralph Waldo Emerson, *Self-Reliance*, in *Essays: First Series*, 1841

You shall have joy, or you shall have power, said God; you shall not have both. **3**

—Ralph Waldo Emerson, *Journal*, Oct. 1842

Life is a search after power. **4**

—Ralph Waldo Emerson, *Power*, in *The Conduct of Life*, 1860

Power is the first good. **5**

—Ralph Waldo Emerson, *Inspiration*, in *Letters and Social Aims*, 1876

A friend in power is a friend lost. **6**

—Henry Brooks Adams, *The Education of Henry Adams*, 1907

Power intoxicates men. It is never voluntarily surrendered. It must be taken from them. **7**

—James F. Byrnes, quoted in *The New York Times*, May 15, 1956

★ See also Charles Beard at WISDOM, WORDS OF for a quote on the destructive effects of power.

Power never takes a back step—only in the face of more power. **8**

—Malcolm X, *Malcolm X Speaks Out*, 1965

We have, I fear, confused power with greatness. **9**

—Stewart Udall, commencement speech, Dartmouth College, 1965

The Arrogance of Power **10**

—J. William Fulbright, book title, 1967

★ After initially favoring U.S. intervention in Vietnam, Fulbright, chairman of the Senate foreign relations committee, was having serious second thoughts. He originally used the title for a lecture, part of a series on foreign policy that he gave the previous year at Johns Hopkins University in Baltimore. He may have taken the phrase from John F. Kennedy's speech at the dedication of the Robert Frost Library at Amherst College on Oct. 26, 1963: "When power leads man toward arrogance, poetry reminds him of his limitations." For more, see Kennedy at ART: POETRY.

It's good to be the king. **11**

—Mel Brooks, *The Producers*, screenplay, 1968

★ Spoken by Zero Mostel as Max Bialystock.

Power is the great aphrodisiac. **12**

—Henry Kissinger, in *The New York Times*, Jan. 19, 1971

The most dangerous thing about power is to employ it where it is not applicable. **13**

—David Halberstam, *The Best and the Brightest*, 1972

1 A man in power must have men around him whom his awesome power does not intimidate.

—**William Safire,** *Before the Fall: An Inside View of the Pre-Watergate White House*, 1975

2 Power is wonderful, and absolute power is absolutely wonderful.

—**Ross Perot,** interview with Charlie Rose, PBS, Oct. 18, 1994

★ This is another variation on Lord Acton's classic axiom; see also Hitz at SECRETS.

Prairies

See MIDWEST, THE.

Prayer

See also GOD; PRAYERS; RELIGION.

3 In his prayers he says, thy will be done: but means his own, at least acts so.

—**William Penn,** *Some Fruits of Solitude*, 1693

4 Prayer is the contemplation of the facts of life from the highest point of view.

—**Ralph Waldo Emerson,** *Self-Reliance*, in *Essays: First Series*, 1841

5 Prayer as a means to effect a private end is theft and meanness.

—**Ibid.**

6 Of course—I prayed—
And did God Care?
He cared as much as on the Air
A Bird—had stamped her foot
And cried "Give Me."

—**Emily Dickinson,** poem no. 376, c. 1862

7 Prayer is the little implement
Through which Men reach
Where Presence—is denied them.

—**Emily Dickinson,** poem no. 437, c. 1862

8 Both [North and South] read the same Bible, and pray to the same God; and each invokes His aid against the other. It may seem strange that any men should dare to ask a just God's assistance in wringing their bread from the sweat of other men's faces; but let us judge not, that we be not judged.

—**Abraham Lincoln,** Second Inaugural Address, 1865

9 "Why Should We Not Pray to Our Mother Who Art in Heaven, As Well As to Our Father?"

—**Susan B. Anthony,** *Feminist* newspaper headline, March 18, 1869

Prayer is not to be used as a confessional, to cancel sin. **1**
—Mary Baker Eddy, *Science and Health, with Key to the Scriptures,* 1875

You can't pray a lie. **2**
—Mark Twain, *Huckleberry Finn,* 1885

Pray, v. To ask that the rules of the universe be annulled in behalf of a single petitioner, confessedly unworthy. **3**
—Ambrose Bierce, *The Devil's Dictionary,* 1906

Prayer, among sane people, has never superseded practical efforts to secure the desired end. **4**
—George Santayana, *The Life of Reason: Reason in Religion,* 1905–1906

The prayers of all good people are good. **5**
—Willa Cather, *My Ántonia,* 1918

The trouble with our praying is, we just do it as a means of last resort. **6**
—Will Rogers, *Weekly Articles,* May 11, 1930

The family that prays together stays together. **7**
—Al Scalpone, slogan, 1947

★ First used on the Family Theater weekly radio series, developed by a Roman Catholic priest, Father Patrick Peyton, and aired over the Mutual Broadcasting System from 1947 to 1969, the slogan was adopted—and further publicized on billboards throughout the country—as the motto of Father Peyton's Family Rosary Crusade. Mr. Scalpone, a young advertising copywriter who donated his services to Family Theater, also devised "A world at prayer is a world at peace" for the radio series.

One of the greatest of all efficiency methods is prayer power. **8**
—Norman Vincent Peale, *The Power of Positive Thinking,* 1952

★ See also Rev. Peale at MIND, THOUGHT, & UNDERSTANDING.

I cannot see how an "official religion" is established by letting those who want to say a prayer say it. . . . to deny the wish of these school children to join in reciting this prayer is to deny them the opportunity of sharing in the spiritual heritage of our Nation. **9**
—Potter Stewart, *Engel v. Vitale,* dissenting, 1962

★ For another view of the value of school prayer, see Anna Quindlen below.

The only decent activity in the world [is] to pray for everyone, in solitude. **10**
—Jack Kerouac, quoted in *The New York Times Book Review* [April 9, 1995]

Do not pray for easy lives. Pray to be stronger men. **11**
—John F. Kennedy, at a prayer breakfast, Washington, D.C., Feb. 7, 1963

I think the dying pray at the last not please but thank you as a guest thanks his host at the door. **12**
—Annie Dillard, *Pilgrim at Tinker Creek,* 1974

1 School prayer . . . bears about as much resemblance to real spiritual experience as that freeze-dried astronaut food does to a nice standing rib roast.
—**Anna Quindlen,** OpEd column, *The New York Times*, Dec. 7, 1994

★ A dissent, in effect, from Potter Stewart's dissent above.

Prayers & Blessings

2 O my people,
Honor thy god;
Respect alike men great and humble;
See to it that our aged, our women, and our children
Lie down to sleep by the roadside
Without fear of harm.
Disobey, and die.
—**Kamehameha I,** *Law of the Splintered Paddle*

★ Kamehameha, king of Hawaii, also called Kamehameha the Great, conquered the chiefs of the other islands in the archipelago by 1810, establishing a dynasty that lasted until the death of Kamehameha V in 1872.

3 Lord, grant that I may always be right, for Thou knowest I am hard to turn.
—**Anonymous**

★ An anonymous Scotch-Irish prayer, quoted in *Truman* by David McCullough [1992]

4 May you be in heaven for twenty minutes before the Devil discovers that you're dead.
—**Anonymous,** Saint Patrick's Day greeting

5 God, give us grace to accept with serenity the things that cannot be changed, courage to change the things which should be changed, and the wisdom to distinguish the one from the other.
—**Reinhold Niebuhr,** *The Serenity Prayer*, 1943

6 Give strength to their arms, stoutness to their hearts, steadfastness in their faith.
—**Franklin D. Roosevelt,** D-day prayer, June 6, 1944

★ More at WORLD WAR II.

7 I thank You God for most this amazing
day: for the leaping greenly spirits of trees
and a blue true dream of sky; and for everything
which is natural which is infinite which is yes.
—**E. E. Cummings,** *I Thank You God for Most This Amazing*, in *Xiape*, 1950

8 God bless mother and daddy, my brother and sister, and save the King. And, oh God, do take care of yourself, because if anything happens to you, we're all sunk.
—**Adlai Stevenson,** speech, quoting a child's prayer, Harvard Business School, June 6, 1959

9 Forgive, O Lord, my little jokes on Thee
And I'll forgive Thy great big one on me.
—**Robert Frost,** *Cluster of Faith*, in *In the Clearing*, 1962

Prejudice

See also RACES & PEOPLES.

No man is prejudiced in favor of a thing knowing it to be wrong. He is attached to it on the belief of it being right. **1**
—**Tom Paine,** *The Rights of Man*, 1791

It is never too late to give up our prejudices. **2**
—**Henry David Thoreau,** *Economy*, in *Walden*, 1854

We are chameleons, and our partialities and prejudices change places with an easy and blessed facility. **3**
—**Mark Twain,** *When in Doubt, Tell the Truth*, in Albert Bigelow Paine, ed., *Speeches* [1923]

Prejudice, n. A vagrant opinion without visible means of support. **4**
—**Ambrose Bierce,** *The Devil's Dictionary*, 1906

I ran across a Prejudice. **5**
That quite cut off the view.
—**Charlotte Perkins Gilman,** *The Obstacle*, undated

There is a tendency to judge a race, a nation, or a distinct group by its least qualified members. **6**
—**Eric Hoffer,** *The True Believer*, 1951

Everyone is a prisoner of his own prejudices. No one can eliminate prejudices—just recognize them. **7**
—**Edward R. Murrow,** Dec. 31, 1955

There are no "white" or "colored" signs on the foxholes or graveyards of battle. **8**
—**John F. Kennedy,** civil rights message to Congress, June 19, 1963

★ The president proposed a sweeping piece of legislation to outlaw racial discrimination in many aspects of American life, to guarantee voting rights, and to put more teeth into existing prohibitions. Southern congressmen bitterly resisted the bill and it was not signed into law until July 2, 1964, some seven months after Kennedy's assassination and more than a year after he had proposed it. Only one southern senator, Ralph Yarborough, of Texas, voted for the act.

Ignorance is stubborn, and prejudice dies hard. **9**
—**Adlai Stevenson,** speech, Oct. 1, 1963

Present, the

See also MODERN TIMES; PAST, THE; TIME.

The vanishing volatile froth of the present, which any shadow will alter, any thought blow away, any event annihilate, is every moment converted into the adamantine record of the past. **10**
—**Ralph Waldo Emerson,** *Journal*, 1832

1 With the past, as past, I have nothing to do; nor with the future as future. I live now, and will verify all past history in my own moments.
—Ibid.

2 We can see well into the past; we can guess shrewdly into the future; but that which is rolled up and muffled in impenetrable folds is today.
—Ibid.

3 The dogmas of the quiet past are inadequate to the stormy present.
—Abraham Lincoln, annual message to Congress, Dec. 1, 1862

4 Each day the world is born anew
For him who takes it rightly
—James Russell Lowell, *Gold Egg: A Dream Fantasy*, in *Under the Willows and Other Poems*, 1868

5 Let anyone try . . . to notice or attend to the *present* moment of time. One of the most baffling experiences occurs. Where is it, this present? It has melted in our grasp, fled ere we could touch it, gone in the instant of becoming.
—William James, *The Principles of Psychology*, 1890

6 We want to live in the present, and the only history that is worth a tinker's damn is the history we make today.
—Henry Ford, in the *Chicago Tribune*, May 25, 1916

7 The only living life is in the past and future—the present is an interlude—strange interlude in which we call on past and future to bear witness we are living.
—Eugene O'Neill, *Strange Interlude*, 1928

★ See also the O'Neill quote from this play at LIFE.

8 Exhaust the little moment. Soon it dies.
And be it gash or gold it will not come
Again in this identical guise.
—Gwendolyn Brooks, *Exhaust the Little Moment*, in *Annie Allen*, 1949

9 Life is all memory, except for the one present moment that goes by you so quick you hardly catch it going.
—Tennessee Williams, *The Milk Train Doesn't Stop Here Any More*, 1963

10 The word "now" is like a bomb through the window, and it ticks.
—Arthur Miller, *After the Fall*, 1964

11 Today is the first day of the rest of your life.
—Anonymous, saying, c. 1970s

★ This upbeat adage is sometime attributed to Charles Dederich, who founded Synanon in 1958. The reputation of this self-help community for substance abusers faded in the 1970s as Dederich and other members of the organization were charged with civil and criminal wrongdoing.

Every day you wake up is a beautiful day. 1

—John Wayne, quoted in Lauren Bacall, *Now* [1994]

★ The actor, dying of cancer, spoke in response to a movie crew member who said to him, "Boy, it's a beautiful day!"

Presidency, the

Every vital question of state will be merged in the question, "Who will be the next 2
president?"

—Alexander, Hamilton, *The Federalist*, 1787–88

My movements to the chair of government will be accompanied by feelings not 3
unlike those of a culprit who is going to the place of his execution.

—George Washington, letter to Henry Knox, April 1, 1789

[The presidency] is but a splendid misery. 4

—Thomas Jefferson, letter to Elbridge Gerry, May 13, 1797

★ More at VICE PRESIDENCY, THE.

May none but honest and wise men ever rule under this roof. 5

—John Adams, letter to Abigail Adams, Nov. 2, 1800

★ Written from "The President's House," later called The White House, after spending his first night there. By order of Pres. Franklin D. Roosevelt this was inscribed on the mantelpiece in the State Dining Room.

I have learned to expect that it will rarely fall to the lot of imperfect man to retire 6
from this station with the reputation and the favor which bring him into it.

—Thomas Jefferson, First Inaugural Address, March 4, 1801

No man who ever held the office of president would congratulate a friend on obtain- 7
ing it. He will make one man ungrateful, and a hundred men his enemies, for every office he can bestow.

—John Adams, to his son John Quincy Adams, elected president in 1824

★ Presidents were required to make hundreds of government appointments personally, a burden that was somewhat lightened with the establishment of the Civil Service system in the 1880s. See James A. Garfield below.

I can with truth say mine is a situation of dignified slavery. 8

—Andrew Jackson, letter to Robert J. Chester, Nov. 30, 1829

The president is the direct representative of the American people . . . responsible to 9
them.

—Andrew Jackson, message protesting his censure by the Senate, April 15, 1834

★ This concept, a commonplace today, was daring in its time. Robert Remini, in his biography of Jackson, describes the outrage among those who held that the president was directly responsible to Congress. Daniel Webster immediately counterattacked, referring to presidential accountability to the people as an "airy and unreal responsibility." As for the president being the representative of the people, Webster boomed, "This is not the language of the Constitution. The Constitution no where calls him the representative of the American people; still less their direct representative. . . . I hold this, Sir, to be a mere assumption, and dangerous assumption." The protest message was co-authored by Secretary of the Treasury Roger Taney and Attorney General Benjamin Butler. The issue that led to censure was the government's withdrawal of funds from the Bank of the United States.

1 The farmer imagines power and place are fine things. But the president has paid dear for his White House. It has commonly cost him all his peace and the best of his manly attributes. To preserve for a short time so conspicuous an appearance before the world, he is content to eat dust before the real masters who stand behind the throne.

—**Ralph Waldo Emerson,** *Compensation*, in *Essays: First Series*, 1841

2 No president who performs his duties faithfully and conscientiously can have any leisure.

—**James K. Polk,** diary, Sept. 1, 1847

★ Polk also complained, "Though I occupy a very high position, I am the hardest working man in the country." Hard work took its toll, and he died three months after leaving office. Polk, a Tennessee Democrat, had not sought the office. He emerged as a compromise candidate when ex-president Martin Van Buren of New York and Lewis Cass of Michigan deadlocked at the 1844 convention.

3 I had rather be right than be president.

—**Henry Clay,** speech, U. S. Senate, 1850

★ Clay made this remark when taunted in the Senate for once again setting on a course away from the White House. Clay had five times sought the presidency without success. On this occasion, he was speaking in defense of the series of resolutions originated by him in 1848 to avoid civil war over issues of slavery and states' rights. The package of compromises collectively is now called the Compromise of 1850. In 1890, Rep. William McK. Springer, speaking in the House, resurrected Clay's "I would rather be right than be president," and the Speaker, Thomas Brackett Reed, known as "Czar Reed," retorted, "Well, the gentleman need not be disturbed. He will never be either." And referring to William Jennings Bryan, the Speaker said that he had "rather be wrong than president."

4 If forced to choose between the penitentiary and the White House for four years, I would say the penitentiary, thank you.

—**William Tecumseh Sherman,** letter to Gen. Henry W. Halleck, Sept. 1864

★ Sherman's attitude stiffened further after observing the unhappy experience of his fellow warrior Ulysses S. Grant as president; see Sherman below.

5 After the White House what is there to do but drink?

—**Franklin Pierce,** remark, in Philip Kunhardt, Jr., et al., *The American President* [1999]

★ Pierce, who had given up alcohol in 1840, began drinking heavily following the death of his wife in 1863.

We elect a king for four years and give him absolute power within certain limits, which after all he can interpret for himself. **1**

—**William Seward,** remark to a British journalist, 1868

★ This observation by Lincoln's secretary of state is quoted in theologian Michael Novak's *Choosing Our King*, 1974. Novak himself wrote, "We may wish it otherwise, but he is king—king in the sense of decisive, symbolic focal point of our power and destiny."

My God, what is there in this place that a man should ever want to get in it? **2**

—**James A. Garfield,** 1881

★ Pres. Garfield suffered particularly from the importuning of job seekers. He wrote, "Once or twice I felt like crying out in the agony of my soul against the greed for office and its consumption of my time," quoted in *American Heritage* magazine, April 1974. A few weeks later, he was shot by a disgruntled office seeker; when he rallied, more office seekers rushed to his bedside; he died two months later.

I will not accept if nominated, and will not serve if elected. **3**

—**William Tecumseh Sherman,** telegram to the Republican National Convention, June 5, 1884

★ Commonly rendered as, "If nominated, I will not accept. If elected, I will not serve." But the simpler wording is as quoted by Sherman's son, Thomas. The convention nominated James G. Blaine, who lost to Grover Cleveland; see POLITICAL SLOGANS.

Great men are not chosen president, firstly, because great men are rare in politics; secondly, because the method of choice does not bring them to the top; thirdly, because they are not, in quiet times, absolutely needed. **4**

—**James Bryce,** *The American Commonwealth*, 1888

Presidency, n. The greased pig in the field game of American politics. **5**

—**Ambrose Bierce,** *The Devil's Dictionary*, 1906

I'll be damned if I am not getting tired of this. It seems to be the profession of a president simply to hear other people talk. **6**

—**William Howard Taft,** comment to an aide, 1910

★ Quoted in *American Heritage* magazine, April 1974.

My hat is in the ring. **7**

—**Theodore Roosevelt,** remark, Feb. 21, 1912

★ Roosevelt, speaking during a railroad stop in Ohio, added, "The fight is on and I am stripped to the buff." On February 24, he wrote seven state governors: "I will accept the nomination for the presidency if it is tendered to me." Roosevelt ran as a third-party candidate against his former friend and fellow Republican, the incumbent president, William Howard Taft. His Progressive party was popularly called the Bull Moose party. It split the Republican vote, leading to the election of Woodrow Wilson.

I am glad to be going. The White House is the lonesomest place in the world. **8**

—**William Howard Taft,** remark to his successor, Woodrow Wilson, 1913

1 The Office of the President requires the constitution of an athlete, the patience of a mother, and the endurance of an early Christian. . . . The President is a superior kind of slave.

—**Woodrow Wilson,** quoted in *The New York Times* [Oct. 8, 1995]

2 The White House is a bully pulpit.

—**Theodore Roosevelt,** remark to George Haven Putnam

★ Putnam quoted this remark at his eulogy for Roosevelt at the Century Club in New York City, 1919; also cited in Hamilton Basso, *Mainstream*. In Putnam's introductory essay to *The Works of Theodore Roosevelt*, vol. 9, he explains that he had accused the president of a tendency to preach, and Roosevelt had replied, "Yes, Haven, most of us enjoy preaching, and I've got such a bully pulpit."

3 The president cannot be disturbed.

—**Charles E. Hughes, Jr.,** Nov. 1916

★ Charles Evans Hughes, the Republican candidate for president, retired on election night in the belief that he had won. A New York reporter called after midnight to tell him that, unexpectedly, the California vote looked close. Someone, evidently Hughes's son, put off the reporter as quoted above. "Well, when he wakes up," the reporter advised, "just tell him he isn't president." That was a guess, but a good one. Hughes did indeed lose to incumbent Woodrow Wilson.

4 To announce that there must be no criticism of the president, or that we are to stand by the president, right or wrong, is not only unpatriotic and servile, but is morally treasonable to the American public.

—**Theodore Roosevelt,** *Kansas City Star,* May 7, 1918

5 "Afther lookin' the candydates over," said Mr. Dooley, "an' studyin' their qualifications carefully, I can't truthfully say that I see a prisidintial possibility in sight."

—**Finley Peter Dunne,** *Mr. Dooley on Baseball*, in *Mr. Dooley on Making a Will and Other Necessary Evils*, 1919

6 As democracy is perfected, the office of president represents, more and more closely, the inner soul of the people. On some great and glorious day, the plain folks of the land will reach their heart's desire at last, and the White House will be adorned by a downright moron.

—**H. L. Mencken,** *Bayard vs. Lionheart* in *Baltimore Evening Sun,* July 26, 1920

7 I do not choose to run for president in 1928.

—**Calvin Coolidge,** statement to reporters, at the White House, August 2, 1928

8 Every man has a few mental hair shirts and . . . presidents differ only by their larger wardrobe.

—**Herbert Hoover,** letter to President Thompson of Ohio State University, 1930

9 [The presidency:] It is preeminently a place of moral leadership.

—**Franklin D. Roosevelt,** quoted in *The New York Times*, Sept. 11, 1932

The first twelve years are the hardest. **1**

—**Franklin D. Roosevelt,** remark on the presidency, press conference, Jan. 19, 1945

You must not ask the president of the United States to get down in the gutter with a guttersnipe. **2**

—**Harry S. Truman,** 1951

★ This was Truman's response to a suggestion that he could destroy Sen. Joseph McCarthy by leaking a dossier on McCarthy's sex life. The remark was recorded by writer John Hersey, who was there, gathering material for a *New Yorker* profile of the president, and who included it in his *Aspects of the Presidency*, 1980. Truman continued in this vein: "Nobody, not even the president of the United States, can approach too close to a skunk, in skunk territory, and expect to get anything out of it except a bad smell. If you think somebody is telling a big lie about you, the only way to answer is with the whole truth."

In America any boy may become president. I suppose it's one of the risks he takes. **3**

—**Adlai Stevenson,** speech, Indianapolis, Ind., Sept. 26, 1952

★ As he had noted a month earlier, "They pick a president and then for four years they pick on him" (speech August 28, 1952).

He'll sit right here and he'll say do this, do that! And nothing will happen. Poor Ike—it won't be a bit like the Army. **4**

—**Harry S. Truman,** Nov. 1952

★ Truman made this remark after meeting with Gen. Dwight D. Eisenhower, the president-elect. The quote is from Margaret Truman's biography of her father.

The president is the representative of the whole nation, and he's the only lobbyist that all the 160 million people in this country have. **5**

—**Harry S. Truman,** speech, Columbia University, April 27, 1959

★ For Truman's reaction when he first inherited the presidency, see AMERICAN HISTORY: MEMORABLE MOMENTS. And for some negative reactions to his performance in office, see INSULTS.

No *easy* problems ever come to the president of the United States. If they are easy to solve, someone else has solved them. **6**

—**Dwight D. Eisenhower,** quoted by John F. Kennedy in *Parade* magazine, April 8, 1962

The function and responsibility of the president is to set before the American people the unfinished business, the things we must do if we are going to succeed as a nation. **7**

—**John F. Kennedy,** comment, Crestwood, Mo., Oct. 22, 1960

In the White House, the future rapidly becomes the past; and delay is itself a decision. **8**

—**Theodore Sorensen,** *Nation's Business*, June 1963

1 Don't let it be forgot
That once there was a spot
That for one brief shining moment was known
As Camelot.

—**Alan Jay Lerner,** *Camelot* [1960]

★ Jacqueline Kennedy told the journalist Theodore H. White in an interview on November 29, 1963, just a week after President Kennedy's assassination, that her husband had so loved this song from the Broadway musical that she would get out of bed in the cold of night to play it for him on an old Victrola. After reading White's notes on the interview, she added in pencil, "And all she could think of was, tell people there will never be that Camelot again." White did so, and Camelot became indelibly associated with the Kennedy presidency after the interview was published in the December 6, 1963, issue of *Life* magazine.

2 The office of the presidency is the only office in this land of all the people.

—**Lyndon B. Johnson,** speech, 1964

3 A president's hardest task is not to do what is right but to know what is right.

—**Lyndon B. Johnson,** State of the Union speech, Jan. 4, 1965

4 The White House is another world. Expediency is everything.

—**John W. Dean III,** quoted by Mary McGrory, *New York Post*, June 18, 1973

★ See also WATERGATE.

5 He must summon his people to be with him—yet stand above, not squat beside them. He must question his own wisdom and judgment but not too severely. He must hear the opinion and heed the powers of others—but not too abjectly. He must be aggressive without being contentious, decisive without being arrogant, and compassionate without being confused.

—**Emmet John Hughes,** *The Living Presidency*, 1973

6 Presidents must take care lest their tentative suggestions close off discussion or be disseminated after the meetings as clear presidential preferences.

—**I. M. Destler,** *National Security Advice to Presidents: Some Lessons from Thirty Years*, in *World Politics*, Jan. 1977

7 When the president does it, that means that it is not illegal.

—**Richard M. Nixon,** television interview with David Frost, May 4, 1977

★ Pres. Nixon was speaking of his approval of a domestic surveillance plan that involved burglaries and opening mail.

8 Remembering him [Truman] reminds people what a man in that office ought to be like. It's character, just character. He stands like a rock in memory now.

—**Eric Sevareid,** interview with David McCullough for his biography, *Truman* [1992]

9 The best way to get the news is from objective sources, and the most objective sources I have are the people on my staff who tell me what's happening in the world.

—**George W. Bush,** interview with Britt Hume, Fox News, Sept. 22, 2003.

Press, the

See also ADVERTISING, ADVERTISING SLOGANS, & PUBLICITY; CENSORSHIP; CONSTITUTION, THE (Potter Stewart); FREE SPEECH; MEDIA.

The freedom of the press is one of the great bulwarks of liberty, and can never be restrained but by despotic governments. **1**

—**George Mason,** *Virginia Bill of Rights*, June 12, 1776

The liberty of the press is essential to the security of the state. **2**

—**John Adams,** Free-Press Clause, Massachusetts Constitution, 1780

Our liberty depends on the freedom of the press, and that cannot be limited without being lost. **3**

—**Thomas Jefferson,** letter to Dr. James Currie, Jan. 28, 1786

★ Jefferson was keenly aware of the faults of the press. Just before the statement above, he wrote, "I deplore . . . the putrid state into which the newspapers have passed," but added, "It is, however, an evil for which there is no remedy."

Were it left to me to decide whether we should have a government without newspapers, or newspapers without a government, I should not hesitate a moment to prefer the latter. **4**

—**Thomas Jefferson,** letter to Col. Edward Carrington, Jan. 16, 1787

No government ought to be without censors; and where the press is free, no one ever will. **5**

—**Thomas Jefferson,** letter to George Washington, Sept 9, 1792

It is better to leave a few of its [the press's] noxious branches to their luxuriant growth, than by pruning them away, to injure the vigor of those yielding the proper fruits. **6**

—**James Madison,** *Report on the Virginia Resolutions*, 1799–1800, in Jonathan Elliot, *Debates on the Adoption of the Federal Constitution* [1876]

Nothing can now be believed which is seen in a newspaper. **7**

—**Thomas Jefferson,** letter to J. Norville, June 14, 1807

★ Newspapers, incidentally, were more vicious in Jefferson's day than now, with less regard for the truth. Later in this letter, Pres. Jefferson suggested: "Perhaps an editor might begin a reformation in some way such as this. Divide his paper into four chapters, heading the 1st, Truths. 2nd, Probabilities. 3d, Possibilities. 4th, Lies. the first chapter would be very short." He also claimed, "The man who never looks into a newspaper is better informed than he who reads them, inasmuch as he who knows nothing is nearer to the truth than he whose mind is filled with falsehoods and errors."

The only security of all is in a free press. **8**

—**Thomas Jefferson,** letter to Marquis de Lafayette, 1823

We live under a government of men and morning newspapers. **9**

—**Wendell Phillips,** speech, Jan. 28, 1852

★ See also Jefferson's letter to Charles Yancey under EDUCATION.

1 I will never again command an army in America if we must carry along paid spies. I will banish myself to some foreign country first.

—William Tecumseh Sherman, letter to his wife, Feb. 1863

★ Sherman hated the press not only because of news reports critical of him, but also because he thought that reporters provided intelligence to the Confederates either privately or in the course of reporting news. He is said to have complained, "Napoleon himself would have been defeated with a free press." He came close to executing one journalist as a spy; Pres. Lincoln intervened.

2 It is a newspaper's duty to print the news and raise hell.

—*The Chicago Times*, 1861

3 The average consumption of newspapers by an American must amount to about three a day.

—Anthony Trollope, *North America*, 1862

4 When a dog bites a man that is not news. But when a man bites a dog, that is news.

—Charles A. Dana, "What Is News?" New York *Sun*, 1882

★ Dana was the owner and publisher of the *Sun*, the top newspaper of its era. Its motto was "If you see it in the *Sun* it's so." The quote is sometimes attributed to *Sun* editor John B. Bogart, as in Frank M. O'Brien's *The Story of the Sun*, where the statement runs: "When a dog bites a man that is not news, because it happens so often. But if a man bites a dog, that is news."

5 Newspapers are read at the breakfast and dinner tables. God's great gift to man is appetite. Put nothing in the paper that will destroy it.

—W. R. Nelson, quoted by H. L. Mencken, *A New Dictionary of Quotations* [1942]

★ Nelson was the publisher of the *Kansas City Star*.

6 All the news that's fit to print.

—Adolph Simon Ochs, motto of *The New York Times*, 1896

★ Ochs made the point in full in a speech upon assuming ownership of the paper on August 18, 1896: "It will be my earnest aim that the New-York Times give the news, all the news, in concise and attractive form, in language that is permissible in good society." He also pledged that the paper would give the news early, and "impartially, without fear or favor, regardless of party, sect, or interest involved," and that the paper would provide a forum for "intelligent discussion from all shades of opinion." Similar idealistic statements from the same period include: "We shall tell no lies about persons or policies for love, malice, or money," E. W. Scripps, founder of the Scripps-Howard chain; C. L. Knight, founder of the present Knight-Ridder chain, told his son, John, "Better you should set fire to your plant, and leave town by the light of it, than to remain a human cash-register editor." According to Joan Konner, who cited these comments in a paper, *Is Journalism Losing Its Standards?*, excerpted in the *Columbia Journalism Review*, Nov./Dec. 1995, owners today no longer lead the way on standards.

7 The report of my death has been grossly exaggerated.

—Mark Twain, quoted in a cable from London, Associated Press, 1897

★ The *New York Journal* ran the story on June 2, with the quote as, "The report of my death was an exaggeration." The press had confused Twain with his cousin Dr. James

Ross Clemens, who had been ill in London when Twain, too, was there. Reports circulated that Twain himself was near death or indeed dead. A young Associated Press reporter, sent to check on the writer's health, showed Twain his cabled instructions: "If Mark Twain very ill, five hundred words. If dead, send one thousand." Twain handed back the cable, saying, "You don't need as much as that. Just say the report of my death has been grossly exaggerated." The young man took this seriously and was almost back at his office before he saw the joke, which he then relayed to the world.

Most people don't think for themselves. They lean on newspapers. **1**

—**Thomas J. Pendergast,** saying quoted in David McCullough, *Truman* [1992]

★ Pendergast, the "Big Boss" of Kansas City, sponsored the young Harry S. Truman. See also Pendergast at WISDOM, WORDS OF.

Th' newspaper does ivrything f'r us. It . . . comforts th' afflicted, afflicts th' comfort- **2**
able, buries th' dead an' roasts thim aftherward.

—**Finley Peter Dunne,** *Observations by Mr. Dooley*, 1902

★ In the omitted section of the quote, Mr. Dooley observes that newspapers also run the police, and banks, and the military, and the legislature, as well as baptizing the young and marrying the foolish. The reference to affliction is based on the adage, "The duty of a newspaper is to comfort the afflicted and afflict the comfortable."

The first duty of an editor is to gauge the sentiment of his readers, and then tell them **3**
what they like to believe. . . . His second duty is to see that nothing is said in the news items or editorials which may discountenance any claims made by his advertisers, discredit their standing or good faith, or expose any weakness or deception in any business venture that is or may become a valuable advertiser.

—**Thorstein Veblen,** *The Theory of Business Enterprise*, 1904

I don't care what the papers say about me as long as they spell my name right. **4**

—**"Big Tim" Sullivan,** saying

★ The thought also has been attributed to P. T. Barnum, George M. Cohan, Samuel Goldwyn, and others. Sullivan, by the way, was a Tammany Hall luminary around the turn of the century—the 19th to 20th century. One of his political colleagues was "Little Tim" Sullivan. Big Tim is remembered as one of the first large-scale political bosses. Later in life, he experienced a decline, possibly due to Alzheimer's. He was found dead on train tracks in Eastchester, N.Y., and was not immediately identified. He is responsible for making Columbus Day a legal holiday in New York and for making it a felony to carry a concealed weapon.

The men with the muckrakes are often indispensable to the well-being of society, **5**
but only if they know when to stop raking the muck, and to look upward to the celestial crown above them. . . . If they gradually grow to feel that the whole world is nothing but muck, their power of usefulness is gone.

—**Theodore Roosevelt,** speech for the laying of the cornerstone of the House Office Building, April 14, 1906

★ Roosevelt popularized the term "muckraker" for those who expose society's ills. His patience with muckrackers wore thin with the publication of David Graham Phillips's series of articles titled *The Treason of the Senate*. The term *muckraker* comes from John Bunyan's *The Pilgrim's Progress* (1678): "A man that could look no way but downwards with a muckrake in his hand."

1 Sunlight is said to be the best of disinfectants.
—**Louis D. Brandeis,** *What Publicity Can Do*, in *Harper's Weekly*, Dec. 20, 1913

★ More at MEDIA.

2 [Editor:] A person employed on a newspaper, whose business it is to separate the wheat from the chaff and see to it that the chaff is printed.
—**Elbert Hubbard,** *Roycroft Dictionary and Book of Epigrams*, 1923

3 All I know is just what I read in the newspapers.
—**Will Rogers,** saying, used as a lead-in for his comedy and commentary routines

4 The funnies occupy four pages of the paper and editorials two columns. That proves that merit will tell.
—**Will Rogers,** *Weekly Articles*, August 2, 1925

5 [Strategy for dealing with the press during World War II:] Don't tell them a thing. After it's over, tell them who won.
—**Ernest J. King,** cited by Christopher Buckley, *The New York Times Book Review* [March 12, 1995]

★ Admiral King was Chief of Naval Operations.

6 The difference between burlesque and the newspapers is that the former never pretended to be performing a public service by exposure.
—**I. F. Stone,** *I. F. Stone's Weekly*, Sept. 7, 1952

7 People everywhere confuse
What they read in the newspapers with news.
—**A. J. Liebling,** *A Talkative Something or Other*, in *The New Yorker*, April 7, 1956

8 Freedom of the press is guaranteed only to those who own one.
—**A. J. Liebling,** *Do You Belong in Journalism?* in *The New Yorker*, May 14, 1960

9 Once a newspaper touches a story, the facts are lost forever, even to the protagonists.
—**Norman Mailer,** in *Esquire*, June 1960

10 A good newspaper . . . is a nation talking to itself.
—**Arthur Miller,** in *The Observer*, Nov. 26, 1961

11 If the myth gets bigger than the man, print the myth.
—**Dorothy Johnson,** *The Man Who Shot Liberty Valance*

★ John Ford directed the 1962 movie based on Johnson's 1949 short story, adapted by Warner Bellan and Willis Goldbeck.

12 [Journalism:] The first rough draft of history.
—**Philip Graham,** April 29, 1963

★ A popular shortening of remarks by the *Washington Post's* publisher to *Newsweek* correspondents in London. The full sentence is: "So let us today drudge on about our inescapably impossible task of providing every week a first rough draft of a history that will never be completed about a world we can never really understand."

The press is the enemy. 1

—Richard M. Nixon, remark to aides, 1969

★ The same year, he also observed, "If we treat the press with a little more contempt, we'll probably get better treatment."

The primary purpose [of the Constitutional protection of the press was] to create a fourth institution outside the government as an additional check on the three official branches. 2

—Potter Stewart, *Or of the Press* in *Hastings Law Journal,* 1975

The Third World never sold a newspaper. 3

—Rupert Murdoch, in *The Oberver*, Jan. 1, 1978

Only a fool expects the authorities to tell him what the news is. 4

—Russell Baker, *The Good Times*, 1989

Journalists, like teachers, are society's narrators. The good ones discern our fears, anxieties, and curiosities and tell stories that make life meaningful and manageable. 5

—Max Frankel, *The New York Times Magazine*, June 29, 1997

The press is tough on everybody. The nature of the news business is that conflict is news. 6

—Mark McKinnon, quoted by Ken Auletta, *Fortress Bush,* in *The New Yorker,* Jan. 19, 2004

★ McKinnon was advertising director for George W. Bush's campaign in 2000.

They [reporters] don't represent the public any more than other people do. In our democracy, the people who represent the public stood for election. 7

—Andrew Card, White House chief of staff, quoted in *The New Yorker,* Jan 19, 2004.

Pride & Vanity

Pride is said to be the last vice the good man gets clear of. 8

—Benjamin Franklin, *Poor Richard's Almanack*, 1732–57

Pride breakfasted with Plenty, dined with Poverty, and supped with Infamy. 9

—Ibid.

Pride costs us more than hunger, thirst, and cold. 10

—Thomas Jefferson, "A Decalogue of Canons for observation in practical life," letter to Thomas Jefferson Smith, Feb. 21, 1825

Pride ruined the angels. 11

—Ralph Waldo Emerson, *The Sphinx*, in *The Dial*, Jan. 1841

There was one who thought he was above me, and he was above me until he had that thought. 12

—Elbert Hubbard, *Roycroft Dictionary and Book of Epigrams*, 1923

1 I never wanted to be a crumb. If I had to be a crumb, I'd rather be dead.

—Charles "Lucky" Luciano, quoted in Richard Norton Smith, *Thomas E. Dewey* [1982]

★ Luciano is given much of the credit for organizing the mafia into a national crime syndicate in the 1930s. Imprisoned in 1936, he used his connections on the New York City docks and in Sicily to help U.S. military intelligence during World War II and was rewarded with early release and deportation in 1946.

2 Half of the harm that is done in this world
Is due to people who want to feel important.

—T. S. Eliot, *The Cocktail Party*, 1950

3 When you've got it, flaunt it.

—Mel Brooks, *The Producers*, screenplay, 1968

4 I'm the straw that stirs the drink.

—Reggie Jackson, remark in spring training with the Yankees, May 1977

★ In the 1977 World Series, on October 18, Jackson hit three consecutive home runs, on the first pitches from three different pitchers.

5 I'm in awe of myself.

—Mark McGwire, quoted in *The New York Times*, Sept. 28, 1996

★ Mr. McGwire, of the St. Louis Cardinals, finished the season with a flourish, hitting two homeruns the previous day, bringing his total for the year to a then-record 70. But the awesome achievement was tarnished considerably when he repeatedly declined to answer questions about use of muscle-enhancing steroids in an appearance before a committee of the U.S. House of Representatives on March 17, 2005.

Privacy

See also Secrets; Security & Safety; Solitude & Loneliness.

6 One of the most essential branches of English liberty is the freedom of one's house. A man's house is his castle; and whilst he is quiet, he is as well guarded as a prince in his castle.

—James Otis, argument on the Writs of Assistance, Boston, Feb. 24, 1761

★ The Writs of Assistance allowed customs officers to break into ships, shops, houses, or any place in search of smuggled goods. In opposition, Otis referred to an axiom of common law, also stated by the great English jurist Sir Edward Coke: "For a man's house is his castle, *et domus sua cuique tutissimum refugium,*" *Third Institute*, 1644. The Latin translates, "One's home is the safest refuge to everyone." This comes from the ancient world, *The Pandects*, or *Digest of Justinian*.

7 The saint and poet seek privacy.

—Ralph Waldo Emerson, *Culture*, in *The Conduct of Life*, 1860

★ The full sentence is: "The saint and poet seek privacy to ends the most public and universal."

The right to be let alone—the most comprehensive of rights and the right most valued by civilized men. 1

—**Louis D. Brandeis,** *Olmstead v. the U.S.*, 1928

★ Justice Brandeis wrote that the framers of the Constitution conferred this right upon individuals as against the government. See also Justice Holmes's dissent at EVIDENCE.

Civilization is the progress toward a society of privacy. 2

—**Ayn Rand,** *The Fountainhead*, 1943

Gentlemen do not read each other's mail. 3

—**Henry L. Stimson,** *On Active Service in Peace and War*, with McGeorge Bundy, 1948

★ The former Secretary of State gave this as his reason for closing down American codebreaking operations in 1929 by withdrawing department support from the Military Information Department's Cipher Bureau, informally known as the American Black Chamber. Such high-minded considerations now seem quaint. As longtime CIA Director Alan Dulles said in *The Craft of Intelligence* (1963): "When the fate of a nation and the lives of its soldiers are at stake, gentlemen do read each other's mail—if they can get their hands on it." In any case, after 1929, the Army and Navy continued to work on codes and code breaking, with the result that the U.S. learned to read Japanese and German coded messages during World War II.

We are rapidly entering the age of no privacy, where everyone is open to surveillance at all times; where there are no secrets from government. 4

—**William O. Douglas,** dissenting opinion, *Osborn v. the United States*, 1966

If the right of privacy means anything, it is the right of the *individual*, married or single, to be free from unwarranted governmental intrusion into matters so fundamentally affecting a person as the decision whether to bear or beget a child. 5

—**William J. Brennan, Jr.,** *Eisenstadt v. Baird*, 1972

★ This ruling, which applied to contraception, carried forward the Supreme Court's precedent in another contraception case, *Griswold v. Connecticut*, 1965, in which Justice William O. Douglas wrote, "Would we allow the police to search the sacred precincts of marital bedrooms for telltale signs of contraceptives?" Justice Brennan's decision prefigured the court's landmark decision in *Roe v. Wade* the following year; see AMERICAN HISTORY: MEMORABLE MOMENTS. The court's support of a person's right to choice in reproduction ran counter to a 1927 decision, in *Buck v. Bell*, which upheld compulsory sterilization of a reputedly retarded woman whose family allegedly had a history of retardation. "Three generations of imbeciles are enough," concluded Justice Oliver Wendell Holmes, Jr. Recent research has suggested that the woman targeted here, Carrie Buck, and her daughter, who died young, actually may have been of normal intelligence, and certainly were not imbeciles. The *Buck* decision is an embarrassment; Holmes's belief in eugenics evidently clouded his judgment.

The right of privacy . . . is broad enough to encompass a woman's decision whether or not to terminate her pregnancy. 6

—**Harry A. Blackmun,** *Roe v. Wade*, 1973

★ The Court's conclusion is given at AMERICAN HISTORY: MEMORABLE MOMENTS.

1 Our house is made of glass . . .and our lives are made of glass; and there is nothing we can do to protect ourselves.
—**Joyce Carol Oates,** *American Appetites*, 1988

2 In their vigorous advocacy of the public's right to know, the media frequently violate a right that has a higher standing—the individual's right to privacy.
—**Richard M. Nixon,** *In the Arena: A Memoir of Victory, Defeat and Renewal*, 1990

★ As President, Mr. Nixon fought vigorously to keep many things private; see WATERGATE.

Problems

See also TROUBLE.

3 There is always a well-known solution to every human problem—neat, plausible, and wrong.
—**H. L. Mencken,** *Prejudices: Second Series*, 1920

4 Problems are only opportunities in work clothes.
—**Henry J. Kaiser,** saying

5 Our problems are man-made. Therefore, they can be solved by man.
—**John F. Kennedy,** speech, The American University, June 10, 1963

6 All progress is precarious, and the solution of one problem brings us face to face with another problem.
—**Martin Luther King, Jr.,** *Strength to Love*, 1963

★ See also Stephen Jay Gould at SCIENCE.

7 You're either part of the solution or part of the problem.
—**Eldridge Cleaver,** speech, San Francisco Barristers' Club, Sept. 1968

★ Making a point somewhat similar to Cleaver's, Buell Gallagher, president of the City College of New York, told the graduating class of 1964, "Be part of the answer, not part of the problem, as the American revolution proceeds."

8 There is no such thing as a single problem . . . all problems are interrelated.
—**Saul Alinsky,** *Reveille for Radicals*, 1969

9 Those who are most moral are furthest from the problem.
—**Saul Alinsky,** *Rules for Radicals*, 1971

10 The solution to a problem changes the nature of the problem.
—**John Peers,** introduction, *1,001 Logical Laws, Accurate Axioms, Profound Principles, etc.*, 1979

Procrastination

See DELAY; INDECISION.

Professions

See Doctors & Medicine; Lawyers; New Jersey (William Byrd).

Progress

See also Civilization.

And step by step, since time began, **1**
I see the steady gain of man.
—**John Greenleaf Whittier,** *The Chapel of the Hermits*, 1851

Every step of progress the world has made has been from scaffold to scaffold, and from stake to stake. **2**
—**Wendell Phillips,** speech, Oct. 15, 1851

The history of progress is written in the blood of men and women who have dared to espouse an unpopular cause, as, for instance, the black man's right to his body, or the woman's right to her soul. **3**
—**Emma Goldman**, *What I Believe*, in *New York World*, July 19, 1908

Human progress is furthered, not by conformity, but by aberration. **4**
—**H. L. Mencken,** *Prejudices: Third Series*, 1922

Change is not always progress. . . . A fever of newness has everywhere been confused with the spirit of progress. **5**
—**Henry Ford**, in Daniel J. Boorstin, *Democracy and Its Discontents: Reflections on Everyday America* [1975]

Life means progress, and progress means suffering. **6**
—**Hendrik Willem van Loon,** *Tolerance*, 1925

Today, the notion of progress in a single line without goal or limit seems perhaps the most parochial notion of a very parochial century. **7**
—**Lewis Mumford**, *Technics and Civilization*, 1934

Progress might have been all right once, but it has gone on too long. **8**
—**Ogden Nash,** attributed

Pity this busy monster, manunkind, **9**
not. Progress is a comfortable disease.
—**E. E. Cummings,** *Pity this busy monster, manunkind*, in *One Times One* (or *1* × *1*), 1944

Progress is our most important product. **10**
—**General Electric Corp.**, slogan, from 1950

All progress has resulted from people who took unpopular positions. **11**
—**Adlai E. Stevenson,** speech at Princeton University, March 22, 1954

★ Robert Ingersoll put it: "The history of progress is written in the lives of infidels," in a speech in New York City, May 1, 1881.

1 Progress imposes not only new possibilities for the future but new restrictions.
—**Norbert Wiener,** *The Human Use of Human Beings*, 1954

★ Wiener, a leading mathematician and pioneer in the mathematics of information theory, originated the term *cybernetics*, from the Greek word for "helmsman."

2 All progress is precarious.
—**Martin Luther King, Jr.,** *Strength to Love*, 1963

★ More at PROBLEMS.

3 There can be no progress if people have no faith in tomorrow.
—**John F. Kennedy,** *Berlin East and West*, in *The Pursuit of Justice*, 1964

4 Progress is what people who are planning to do something terrible almost always justify themselves on the grounds of.
—**Russell Baker,** *Poor Russell's Almanac*, 1972

5 Progress robs us of past delights.
—**Sam Ervin, Jr.,** *Humor of a Country Lawyer*, 1983

★ Sen. Ervin, a Democrat from North Carolina, chaired the Senate committee that investigated the Watergate scandal in 1973. He was given to prefacing needle-sharp observations with the comment, "I'm just a country lawyer." See also WATERGATE.

6 We have made progress in everything, yet nothing has changed.
—**Derrick Bell,** *And We Are Not Saved*, 1987

★ Professor Bell left Harvard University Law School after the law school refused to meet his demand that a minority woman be appointed to the faculty.

Property

See also CAPITALISM & CAPITAL V. LABOR; LUXURY; THINGS & POSSESSIONS.

7 Mine is better than ours.
—**Benjamin Franklin,** *Poor Richard's Almanac,* 1756

8 Such is the frailty of the human heart that very few men who have no property have any judgment of their own. They talk and vote as they are directed by some man of property who has attached their minds to his interest.
—**John Adams,** letter to James Sullivan, May 26, 1776

★ This is from the "property follows power letter"; see POWER.

9 Whenever there is in any country, uncultivated lands and unemployed poor, it is clear that the laws of property have been so far extended as to violate natural right. The earth is given as a common stock for man to labor and live on.
—**Thomas Jefferson,** letter to James Madison, Oct. 28, 1785

10 Property is surely a right of mankind as really as liberty.
—**John Adams,** *A Defense of the Constitutions of Government of the United States of America,* 1787

★ For more on this topic, see James Madison and Woodrow Wilson at RIGHTS.

Private property therefore is a creature of society, and is subject to the calls of that society, whenever its necessities shall require it, even to its last farthing. 1
—Benjamin Franklin, *On the Legislative Branch,* 1789

In no country in the world is the love of property more active and more anxious than in the United States. 2
—Alexis de Tocqueville, *Democracy in America,* 1835

We did not inherit the land from our fathers.We are borrowing it from our children. 3
—Anonymous, Amish Proverb

I am amused to see from my window here how busily a man has divided and staked off his domain. God must smile at his puny fences running hither and thither everywhere over the land. 4
—Henry David Thoreau, *Journal,* Feb. 20, 1842

What we call real estate—the solid ground to build a house on—is the broad foundation on which nearly all the guilt to the world rests. 5
—Nathaniel Hawthorne, *The House of Seven Gables,* 1851

By right or wrong, Lands and goods go to the strong. 6
Property will brutely draw
Still to the proprietor;
Silver to silver creep and wind.
And kind to kind.
—Ralph Waldo Emerson, *Initial Demonic and Celestial Love,* 1867

Property is the most fundamental and complex of social facts, and the most important of human interests; it is, therefore, the hardest to understand, the most delicate to meddle with, and the easiest to dogmatize about. 7
—William Graham Sumner, *The Family and Property,* 1888

Few rich men own their own property. Their property owns them. 8
—Robert G. Ingersoll, speech, New York City, Oct. 29, 1896

The instinct of ownership is fundamental in man's nature. 9
—William James, *The Varieties of Religious Experience,* 1902

Proverbs

See Quotations & Proverbs.

Prudence & Practical Wisdom

See Wisdom, Words of.

Psychology

See Science: Psychology.

Publicity

See ADVERTISING, ADVERTISING SLOGANS, & PUBLICITY; MEDIA; PRESS, THE.

Public Opinion & the Public

See also PEOPLE, THE.

1 The public must and will be served.
—William Penn, *Some Fruits of Solitude*, 1693

2 I have learned to hold popular opinion of no value.
—Alexander Hamilton, letter to George Washington, 1794

3 In a democracy, as a matter of course, every effort is made to seize upon and create public opinion, which is, substantially, securing power.
—James Fenimore Cooper, *The American Democrat*, 1838

4 Public opinion in this country is everything.
—Abraham Lincoln, speech, Columbus, Ohio, Sept. 16, 1859

★ Lincoln gave public opinion considerable weight in his deliberations. Prior to this statement, he observed, "A universal feeling, whether well or ill founded, cannot be safely disregarded," speech, Peoria, Ill., October 16, 1854. Similarly, "With public sentiment, nothing can fail; without it, nothing can succeed," speech, Ottawa, Ill., July 31, 1858.

5 In the modern world, the intelligence of public opinion is the one indispensable condition of social progress.
—Charles William Eliot, address upon inauguration as president of Harvard, 1869

6 The public be damned.
—William H. Vanderbilt, comment to a news reporter, Oct. 2, 1882

★ More at BUSINESS.

7 There is nothing that makes more cowardly and feeble men than public opinion.
—Henry Ward Beecher, *Proverbs from Plymouth Pulpit*, 1887

8 The most dangerous thing for a bad cause is to expose it to the opinion of the world. The most certain way that you can prove that a man is mistaken is by letting all his neighbors know what he thinks, by letting all his neighbors discuss what he thinks, and if he is in the wrong you will notice that he will stay at home, he will not walk on the street. He will be afraid of their judgment of his character.
—Woodrow Wilson, speech, Pueblo, Colo., 1919

★ For another favorable comment on public opinion, see Mark Twain at ART: CRITICISM.

9 We are ruled by public opinion, not by statute law.
—Elbert Hubbard, *The Note Book*, 1927

There is no group in America that can withstand the force of an aroused public opinion. 1

—Franklin D. Roosevelt, remark on signing the National Industrial Recovery Act, June 16, 1933

The problem with polls lies not in turning the heads of voters but in destroying what little spine remains in politicians. . . . We've created a nation of office seekers and office holders who operate like windsocks. 2

—Chuck Bowden, quoted in *USA Today*, Oct. 13, 1988

★ Mr. Bowden was editor of the Tucson, Ariz., *City Magazine* at the time.

In the world of public opinion, the person with the bullhorn is king. 3

—Helen Alvaré, quoted in the *Washington Post*, June 2, 1991

★ Ms. Alvaré spoke as director of communications for the National Conference of Catholic Bishops.

Questions & Answers

Who are we? *Where* are we? 4

—Henry David Thoreau, *Ktaadn*, written 1848, in *The Maine Woods* [1864]

★ The whole passage reads: Talk of mysteries! Think of our life in nature—daily to be shown matter, to come in contact with it—rocks, trees, wind on our cheeks! the *solid* earth! the *actual* world! the *common sense! Contact! Contact! Who* are we? *Where* are we?"

And so I leave it to all of you: 5
Which came out of the opened door,—the lady, or the tiger?

—Frank R. Stockton, *The Lady or the Tiger*, in *Century Magazine*, Nov. 1882

★ Originally called *The King's Arena*, this enormously popular tale has become an American classic. The story involves a young hero who dares to fall in love with a king's daughter, and she responds in kind. The cruel king, after discovering the romance, condemns the youth to enter a great arena and open one of two doors. Behind one is a beautiful maiden whom he may marry; behind the other is a tiger. The princess learns which door conceals what. She directs her beloved to open the door on the right. And then the fable ends with the famous query.

The outcome of any serious research can only be to make two questions grow where only one grew before. 6

—Thorstein Veblen, *The Place of Science in Modern Civilization and Other Essays*, 1919

Who he? 7

—Harold Ross, editorial query

★ Ross, the first editor of *The New Yorker*, was famous for irreverent questions, this being one of his favorites. In a birthday tribute to Ross, Roger Angell asked, "Who we?," *The New Yorker*, Nov. 9, 1992.

To ask the hard question is simple. 8

—W. H. Auden, poem no. 27, *Poems*, 1933

1 It is better to ask some of the questions than to know all of the answers.
—James Thurber, *The Scottie Who Knew Too Much*, in *The Thurber Carnival*, 1945

2 What is the answer? [*I was silent.*] In that case, what is the question?
—Gertrude Stein, last words, 1946, reported in Alice B. Toklas, *What Is Remembered* [1963]

3 The questions which one asks oneself begin, at last, to illuminate the world, and become one's key to the experience of others.
—James Baldwin, *Nobody Knows My Name*, 1961

4 The answer, my friend, is blowin' in the wind.
—Bob Dylan, *Blowin' in the Wind*, 1962

5 There aren't any embarrassing questions—just embarrassing answers.
—Carl Rowan, *The New Yorker*, Dec. 7, 1963

★ Journalists find this a useful defense when criticized for asking impertinent questions. Sydney Harris, in the *Chicago Daily News*, March 27, 1958, wrote "More trouble is caused in the world by indiscreet answers than by indiscreet questions."

6 Where's the Rest of Me?
—Ronald Reagan, with **Richard Hubler,** book title, 1965

★ Reagan wrote that he selected this line from one of his films, *King's Row* (1942), as the title for his autobiography because he had always felt that a part of him was missing. In the film, which Reagan felt was the best he ever made, the reference was tragically literal. As Drake McHugh, he utters the question upon waking up in a hospital bed and discovering that his legs are gone. After an accident a railroad yard, both legs have been unnecessarily amputated at the hip by a doctor in revenge for McHugh's having romanced his daughter.

7 Some questions don't have answers, which is a terribly difficult lesson to learn.
—Katharine Graham, quoted by Jane Howard, *Ms. Magazine*, Oct. 1974

8 God may be in the details, but the goddess is in the questions. Once we begin to ask them, there's no turning back.
—Gloria Steinem, *Doing Sixty*, reprinted in *Moving Byond Words*, 1994

Quotations & Proverbs

See also Wisdom, Words of.

9 Nothing gives an author so much pleasure as to find his works respectfully quoted by other learned authors.
—Benjamin Franklin, *Poor Richard's Almanack*, 1758

10 I hate quotation. Tell me what you know.
—Ralph Waldo Emerson, *Journal*, May 1849

Proverbs are the sanctuary of the intuitions. 1
—**Ralph Waldo Emerson,** *Compensation*, in *Essays: First Series*, 1841

Though old the thought and oft expressed, 2
'Tis his at last who says it best.
—**James Russell Lowell,** *For an Autograph*, 1868

The use of proverbs is characteristic of an unlettered people. They are invaluable 3
treasures to dunces with good memories.
—**John Hay,** *Castilian Days*, 1871

★ Hay was a private secretary to Lincoln, and later was posted to Spain. He served as Secretary of State under presidents William McKinley and Theodore Roosevelt and framed the Open Door policy; see under FOREIGN POLICY.

Next to the originator of a good sentence is the first quoter of it. 4
—**Ralph Waldo Emerson,** *Quotation and Originality*, in *Letters and Social Aims*, 1876

★ For a different type of quotation, see Emerson at GENERATIONS.

By necessity, by proclivity, and by delight, we all quote. 5
—**Ibid.**

[Proverbs:] the ready money of human experience. 6
—**James Russell Lowell,** *My Study Windows*, 1871

Quotation, n. The act of repeating erroneously the words of another. 7
—**Ambrose Bierce**, *The Devil's Dictionary*, 1906

The surest way to make a monkey of a man is to quote him. 8
—**Robert Benchley**, *My Ten Years in a Quandary*, 1936

Famous remarks are very seldom quoted correctly. 9
—**Simeon Strunsky,** *No Mean City*, 1944

Few things are more tempting to a writer than to repeat, admiringly, what he has 10
said before.
—**John Kenneth Galbraith**, *Economics and the Public Purpose*, 1973

A quotation, like a pun, should come unsought and then be welcomed only for some 11
propriety or felicity justifying the intrusion.
—**Robert W. Chapman**, *The Art of Quotation*, in *Writer's Digest*, May 1977

Proverbs contain the value system of the time of their origin. 12
—**Wolfgang Mieder**, *Proverbs Are Never Out of Season: Popular Wisdom in the Modern Age*, 1993

Races & Peoples

See also CITIES (NEW YORK CITY, quotes on Harlem); FOREIGNERS; INJUSTICE; LANGUAGE & WORDS (Francis H. Wade); MAJORITIES & MINORITIES; NATIONS; POVERTY & HUNGER; RESISTANCE; SLAVERY; SOUTH, THE.

1 I believe the Indian to be in body and mind equal to the white man.
—**Thomas Jefferson,** letter to François Jean de Beauvoir, Chevalier de Chastellux, June 7, 1785

2 These lands are ours. No one has a right to remove us, because we were the first owners. The Great Spirit above has appointed this place for us, on which to light our fires, and here we will remain.
—**Tecumseh,** 1810

★ The Shawnee chief sent this message to Pres. James Madison via Joseph Barron. See also Tecumseh at RESISTANCE.

3 When the white man had warmed himself before the Indian's fire and filled himself with their hominy, he became very large. With a step he bestrode the mountains, and his feet covered the plains and the vallies [sic]. His hand grasped the Eastern and Western sea, and his head rested on the moon.
—**Speckled Snake,** speech, *Savannah Mercury*, July 8, 1829

★ The Creek warrior was reacting to Pres. Andrew Jackson's plan to move the Cherokees, Chickasaws, Chocktaws, Creeks, and Seminoles west of the Mississippi River; see Jackson at SUPREME COURT.

4 Brothers! I have listened to a great many talks from our great father. But they always began and ended in this— "get a little further; you are too near me."
—**Ibid.**

5 What a happy country this will be, if the whites will listen.
—**David Walker,** *Walker's Appeal*, Sept. 28, 1829

6 We first crush people to the earth, and then claim the right of trampling on them forever, because they are prostrate.
—**Lydia Maria Child,** *An Appeal on Behalf of That Class of Americans Called Africans*, 1833

7 We told them [the white men] to let us alone, and keep away from us; but they followed on, and beset our paths, and they coiled themselves among us like the snake.
—**Black Hawk,** speech, Prairie du Chien, Wisc., August 1835

8 The danger of a conflict between the white and the black inhabitants perpetually haunts the imagination of the Americans like a bad dream.
—**Alexis de Tocqueville,** *Democracy in America*, 1835

9 The Indian . . . stands free and unconstrained in nature, is her inhabitant and not her guest, and wears her easily and gracefully. But the civilized man has the habits of the house. His house is a prison.
—**Henry David Thoreau,** *Journal*, April 26, 1841

Their name is on your water— 1
Ye may not wash it out.
—**Lydia Huntley Sigourney,** *Indian Names*, 1841

If the Negro be a soul, if the woman be a soul, apparelled in flesh, to one master only are they accountable. 2
—**Margaret Fuller,** *The Great Lawsuit: Man versus Men, Woman versus Women*, in *The Dial*, July 1843

They [the Irish] are looked upon with contempt for their want of aptitude in learning new things; their ready and ingenious lying; their eye-service. These are the faults of an oppressed race, which must require the aid of better circumstances through two or three generations to eradicate. 3
—**Margaret Fuller,** untitled essay, in Alice Rossi, ed., *The Feminist Papers* [1973]

The doom of extinction is over this wretched nation [the Indians in the Oregon Territory]. The hand of Providence is removing them to give place to a people more worthy of so beautiful and fertile a country. 4
—**Gustavus Hines,** 1850

★ Hines was a Methodist minister. With the influx of white people along the Oregon Trail, the Indians in their path died in huge numbers of smallpox, cholera, measles, and other diseases to which they had no immunity. This quote was cited in *The New York Times*, June 1, 1993.

When the last red man shall have vanished from this earth, and his memory is only a story among the whites, these shores will still swarm with the invisible dead of my people. And when your children's children think they are alone in the fields, the forests, the shops, the highways, or the quiet of the woods, they will not be alone. . . . Your lands will throng with the returning hosts that once filled them and still love this beautiful land. The white man will never be alone. 5
—**Seattle,** speech, c. 1854

★ The speech was probably given in the Lushootseed language to the governor of the Washington Territory. A translation by Dr. Henry Smith was published in 1887. Since then, Seattle's words have been richly embellished. In the 1971 film *Home*, the speech was transformed into an ecological manifesto.

By the shores of Gitche Gumee, 6
By the shining Big-Sea-Water,
Stood the wigwam of Nokomis,
Daughter of the Moon, Nokomis
—**Henry Wadsworth Longfellow,** *The Song of Hiawatha*, 1855

★ For generations of school children, Hiawatha was one of a mere handful of admirable Indians to appear in their lessons. Longfellow, of course, was flexible in his history, but his hero, a man of peace, was evidently modeled on the Ojibway leader of that name who founded the Iroquois Confederacy (and his meter on that of the Finnish national epic, the *Kalevala*). The poem has inspired a number of parodies, including *The Song of Milkanwatha* by George A. Strong, included in Franklin P. Adams, *Innocent Merriment*, 1942: "When he killed the Mudjokivis, / Of the skin he made him mittens, / Made them with the fur side inside, / Made them with the skin side outside; / He, to get the warm side inside, / Put the inside skin side outside; / He, to get the cold side outside, / Put the warm side fur side inside. / That's why he put the fur side inside, / Why he put the skin side outside, / Why he turned them inside outside."

1 All I ask for the Negro is that if you do not like him, let him alone. If God gave him but little, that little let him enjoy.

—**Abraham Lincoln,** speech, July 17, 1858

2 These people [native Americans in the Great Plains] must die out—there is no help for them. God has given this earth to those who will subdue and cultivate it, and it is vain to struggle against his righteous decree.

—**Horace Greeley,** *An Overland Journey,* 1859

3 The destiny of the colored American . . . is the destiny of America.

—**Frederick Douglass,** speech, Emancipation League, Boston, Mass., Feb. 12, 1862

4 The relation subsisting between the white and colored people of this country is the great, paramount, imperative and all-commanding question for this age and nation to solve.

—**Frederick Douglass,** speech, Church of the Puritans, New York City, May 1863

★ See also W. E. B. Du Bois, below.

5 The only good Indians I ever saw were dead.

—**Philip H. Sheridan,** remark to the Comanche chief Toch-a-way, Jan. 1869

★ According to various accounts of the time, Gen. Sheridan uttered this retort to the chief at Fort Cobb in Indian Territory after Toch-a-way identified himself as a "good Indian." The remark was widely reported and popularly condensed to: "The only good Indian is a dead Indian." Sheridan denied that he had ever made the comment, and it is possible that the quote became attached to him because of his reputation as an Indian fighter. Or, some believe, the culprit may have been a subordinate, possibly Capt. Charles Nordstrum. Certainly, the sentiment was not original to Sheridan. Ralph Keyes reports in *Nice Guys Finish Seventh* that J. M. Cavanaugh, delegate from the Montana Territory, told the House on May 28 of the previous year, "I have never in my life seen a good Indian (and I have seen thousands) except when I have seen a dead Indian."

6 When you first came, we were very many, and you were few; now, you are many, and we are getting very few, and we are poor.

—**Red Cloud,** speech, Cooper Union, New York City, July 16, 1870

★ For Justice Hugo Black's comments on the relations between the U.S. and the Indian nations, see FOREIGN POLICY.

7 I will fight no more forever.

—**Joseph the Younger,** speech at the end of the Nez Percé War, 1877

★ More at RESIGNATION. See also Chief Joseph at PEACE.

The earth is the mother of all people, and all people should have equal rights upon it. **1**

—Joseph the Younger, *An Indian's View of Indian Affairs*, in *The North American Review*, no. 269, vol. 128, 1879

★ More at EQUALITY and TALK.

There are surely bad races and good races . . . and the Irish belong to the category of the impossible. **2**

—Henry James, letter to Mrs. Henry James, Sr., Feb. 7, 1881

★ More quotes on the Irish are at NATIONS.

A Century of Dishonor. **3**

—Helen Hunt Jackson, title of her history of the government's treatment of Indians, c. 1881

Do you know who I am? **4**

—Sitting Bull, question directed to a delegation of U.S. senators, Standing Rock Sioux reservation, 1883

The life of white men is slavery. They are prisoners in towns or farms. **5**

—Sitting Bull, quoted in Robert M. Utely, *The Lance and the Shield: The Life and Times of Sitting Bull* [1993]

In all the relations of life and death, we are met by the color line. **6**

—Frederick Douglass, speech, Convention of Colored Men, Louisville, Ky., Sept. 24, 1883

Once I moved about like the wind. Now I surrender to you, and that is all. **7**

—Geronimo, March 27, 1886

★ The great Apache warrior escaped from military custody the next day, but on September 3 gave himself up for good—the last Native American to surrender formally to the U.S. To catch him and his band of about fifty men, the U.S. and Mexico had combined forces, the Americans deploying forty-two companies of infantry and cavalry, while Mexico contributed another four thousand troops. Exiled to Florida for a time, Geronimo spent his last years in Oklahoma, dying at Fort Sill in 1909.

The sure guarantee of the peace and security of each race is the clear, distinct, unconditional recognition by our governments, national and state, of every right that inheres in civil freedom, and of the equality before the law of all citizens of the United States, without regard to race. **8**

—John Marshall Harlan, dissent in *Plessy v. Ferguson*, 1896

★ For more from this great dissent, see CONSTITUTION, THE. It was in *Plessy* that the Supreme Court accepted the argument that so-called separate but equal accommodations for black and white were Constitutional. Harlan saw clearly that the claim that segregated accommodations would be equal was a "thin disguise." *Plessy v. Ferguson* was reversed in 1954 in *Brown v. the Board of Education*; see below and under AMERICAN HISTORY: MEMORABLE MOMENTS.

We have ground the manhood out of them, and the shame is ours and not theirs, and we should pay for it. **9**

—Mark Twain, letter to Francis Wayland, Dean of the Yale Law School

★ In this letter, Twain offered to pay the tuition of a black student at law school. In addition to supporting this student, he also paid the costs at a Southern school of a black student who went on to become a minister.

1 The difference between the brain of the average Christian and that of the average Jew—certainly in Europe—is about the difference between a tadpole's and an archbishop's. It's a marvelous race, by long odds the most marvelous race the world has produced, I suppose.

—Mark Twain, letter to Rev. Joseph Twitchell, Oct. 23, 1897

2 The little brown brother.

—William Howard Taft, 1900

★ More at SPANISH-AMERICAN WAR.

3 The problem of the twentieth century is the problem of the color line.

—W. E. B. Du Bois, *To The Nations of the World*, speech, Pan-African conference, London, 1900

4 One ever feels his twoness—an American, a Negro; two souls, two thoughts, two unreconciled strivings; two warring ideals in one dark body, whose dogged strength alone keeps it from being torn asunder. The history of the American Negro is the history of this strife—this longing to attain self-conscious manhood, to merge his double self into a better and truer self.

—W. E. B. Du Bois, *The Souls of Black Folk*, 1903

★ In 1993, referring to this passage, Charles Johnson wrote in *The New York Times Book Review*, "Four generations of black artists, scholars, and community leaders have accepted these powerful words as their point of departure when deliberating on the complex phenomenon of race."

5 The talented tenth.

—Ibid.

★ Du Bois introduced the concept of a talented elite in this book and in his essay *The Talented Tenth*, 1903. The tenth, according to Du Bois, were those black leaders who by talent, education, and fortune could immediately begin to lead the way out of "contamination and death." He wrote, "The Negro race, like all races, is going to be saved by its exceptional men." He referred mainly to Northern, urban, college-educated men and women.

6 America is God's crucible, the great melting pot.

—Israel Zangwill, *The Melting Pot*, 1908

★ More at AMERICA & AMERICANS.

7 The Pilgrim Fathers landed on the shores of America and fell upon their knees. Then they fell upon the aborigines.

—Anonymous

★ The date of this witticism is not known, but early 20th century may be about right. It has been attributed to William Maxwell Evarts, who printed a version of it in the *Louisville Courier-Journal* on July 4, 1913, and also to Oliver Wendell Holmes, Sr., Bill Nye, and George Frisbie Hoar. Incidentally, the original families, who arrived in 1620, lived for a time at peace with the native people of New England. But that era ended catastrophically fifty-four years later with the outbreak of King Philip's War. For a description of the Pilgrims falling to their knees, see William Bradford at AMERICAN HISTORY: MEMORABLE MOMENTS.

All blood runs red. *Tout le Sang qui coule est rouge.* **1**

—Eugene J. Bullard, motto on his Spad fighter plane, 1916, cited by John H. Lienhard, "Engines of Our Ingenuity," No. 997

★ A dashing expatriate African-American—a prizefighter and Parisan nightclub owner—Bullard fought for France in World War I as an infantryman in the French Foreign Legion and as a flyer, shooting down two German planes. The motto accompanied a rendering of a heart with a knife through it. When Germany invaded France in 1940, Bullard rejoined his old infantry unit. After the fall of France, he made his way via Spain to the United States, where he wound up as an elevator operator in New York City's RCA Building.

If George [King George V] comes to Chicago, I'll crack him in the snoot. **2**

—William Hale Thompson, 1927

★ An alleged Anglo menace figured prominently in the 1927 Chicago mayoralty campaign. Thompson, running for a third term, promised to weed out nefarious British tendencies in the public schools. According to Henry F. Woods in *American Sayings* (1945), Thompson's prime targets were the king of England and the superintendent of schools.

My forefathers didn't come over on the *Mayflower*, but they met the boat. **3**

—Will Rogers, saying

★ Rogers was referring to his Cherokee ancestors.

Bury my heart at Wounded Knee. **4**

—Stephen Vincent Benét, *American Names*, 1927

★ On December 29, 1890, U.S. troops massacred two hundred Sioux warriors, women, and children at Wounded Knee Creek in South Dakota. This was the last important "battle" in the Indian Wars. For preceding lines, see Benét at LANGUAGE & WORDS.

One of the things that makes a Negro unpleasant to white folk is the fact that he suffers from their injustice. He is thus a standing rebuke to them. **5**

—H. L. Mencken, *Notebooks*, 1930, in *Minority Report: H. L. Mencken's Notebooks* [1956]

The white imagination sure is something when it comes to blacks. **6**

—Josephine Baker, remark, 1931, in Ken Burns, *Jazz* [2001]

★ The observation was inspired by her immense appeal to French audiences. At the same time, some of her stage-show costumes—a few feathers in La Revue Nègre in 1925 and a "skirt"of bananas at the Folies-Bergères the next year—didn't leave a lot to anyone's imagination.

To be a Jew is destiny. **7**

—Vicki Baum, *And Life Goes On*, 1932

1 Only to the white man was nature a wilderness, and only to him was the land "infested" with "wild" animals and "savage" people.

—**Luther Standing Bear,** *Land of the Spotted Eagle*, 1933

★ More at NATURE.

2 Among the thousand white persons, I am a dark rock surged upon, and overswept.

—**Zora Neale Hurston,** *Mules and Men*, 1935

3 No democracy can long survive which does not accept as fundamental to its very existence the recognition of the rights of minorities.

—**Franklin D. Roosevelt,** letter to the National Association for the Advancement of Colored People, June 25, 1938

4 We live here and they live here. We black and they white. They got things and we ain't. They do things and we can't. It's just like living in jail.

—**Richard Wright,** *Native Son*, 1940

5 It is not healthy when a nation lives within a nation, as colored Americans are living inside America. A nation cannot live confident of its tomorrow if its refugees are among its own citizens.

—**Pearl S. Buck,** *What America Means to Me*, 1942

6 Let a new earth rise. Let another world be born. Let a bloody peace be written in the sky. Let a second generation full of courage issue forth; let a people loving freedom come to growth.

—**Margaret Walker,** *For My People*, 1942

★ Publication of the poem, the first by a black writer to win the Yale Series of Younger Poets competition, was an important event in African-American literary history. A generation later the poem resonated more powerfully than ever with civil rights activists.

7 I swear to the Lord
I still can't see
Why Democracy means
Everybody but me.

—**Langston Hughes,** *The Black Man Speaks*, in *Jim Crow's Last Stand*, 1943

8 The Eskimos are a gentle people. I like gentle people, because there are so many in the world who are not gentle. Sometimes in a big city, I just sit all day in my room, with my head down, afraid to go out and talk to tough people. I expect Eskimos have spells like that too.

—**Ernie Pyle,** *Home Country* [1947]

★ The most beloved correspondent of World War II because he wrote about people rather than battles, Pyle was killed by Japanese machine gun fire on an island near Okinawa in 1945.

9 As long as the Negroes are held down by deprivation and lack of opportunity, the other poor people will be held down alongside them.

—**James "Big Jim" Folsom,** Christmas speech, 1949

I am an invisible man. 1

—**Ralph Ellison,** *Invisible Man*, 1952

★ The opening line of Ellison's instantly successful and still influential novel. A few lines later, the speaker explains, "I am invisible, understand, simply because people refuse to see me." The book, at the end, suggests that we may all be to a degree invisible. The last line reads: "Who knows but that, on the lower frequencies, I speak for you?"

We conclude that in the field of public education "separate but equal" has no place. 2

—**Earl Warren,** *Brown v. Board of Education*, May 17, 1954

★ More at AMERICAN HISTORY: MEMORABLE MOMENTS. See also THE CONSTITUTION, and John Marshall Harlan, above, whose dissenting view in 1896 became the law of the land in 1954 when the Supreme Court, headed by Earl Warren, handed down its unanimous decision in *Brown*.

The history of an oppressed people is hidden in the lies and the agreed-upon myths 3
of its conquerors.

—**Meridel Le Sueur,** *Crusaders*, 1955

We shall overcome, we shall overcome, 4
We shall overcome some day,
Oh, deep in my heart, I do believe
We shall overcome some day.

—**Anonymous,** civil rights song of the 1960s

★ According to *Bartlett's*, the song dates from the mid–19th century and was made into a Baptist hymn, titled *I'll Overcome Some Day*, by C. Albert Tindley about 1900. It became well known as a labor protest song when used by black workers on strike in Charleston, S.C., in 1946.

The American economy, the American society, the American unconscious are all 5
racist.

—**Michael Harrington,** *The Other America*, 1962

If we do not now dare everything, the fulfillment of that prophecy, recreated from 6
the Bible in a song by a slave, is upon us:
"God gave Noah the rainbow sign,
No more water, the fire next time!"

—**James Baldwin,** *The Fire Next Time*, 1963

★ This work was first published in *The New Yorker* in 1962, and caused an uproar. Liberal white readers were unaccustomed to being criticized in one of their own magazines, a point underlined by critic Clifton Fadiman, who wrote, "The crime of the whites, he [Baldwin] thinks, lies less in their cruelty than in their bland assumption of innocence," *Book- of-the-Month Club News*, 1963. See also below. For an earlier invocation of fire, see Frederick Douglass at ACTION & DOING.

The American Negro has the great advantage of having never believed that collec- 7
tion of myths to which white Americans cling: that their ancestors were all freedom-
loving heroes, that they were born in the greatest country the world has ever seen,

or that Americans are invincible in battle and wise in peace, that Americans have always dealt honorably with Mexicans and Indians and all other neighbors or inferiors, that American men are the world's most direct and virile, that American women are pure.

—**James Baldwin,** *The Fire Next Time*, 1963

1 If you're born in America with a black skin, you're born in prison.

—**Malcolm X,** interview, June 1963

2 Segregation now. Segregation tomorrow. Segregation forever.

—**George Wallace,** inauguration speech as governor of Alabama, 1963

★ These notorious lines reportedly were written by Asa Earl Carter, a right-wing extremist with a somewhat flexible persona. Under the pseudonym Forrest Carter, he wrote the well-received, politically correct memoirs of an Indian named Little Tree.

3 I have a dream that one day on the red hills of Georgia, the sons of former slaves and the sons of former slaveowners will be able to sit down together at the table of brotherhood.

—**Martin Luther King, Jr.,** speech at the Lincoln Memorial in Washington, D.C., August 28, 1963

★ More at AMERICAN HISTORY: MEMORABLE MOMENTS. See also King and Richard Pryor at JUSTICE.

4 I have a dream that my four little children will one day live in a nation where they will not be judged by the color of their skin but by the content of their character.

—**Ibid.**

5 We didn't land on Plymouth Rock, my brothers and sisters—Plymouth Rock landed on *us*.

—**Malcolm X,** *The Autobiography of Malcolm X*, 1965

6 I firmly believe that Negroes have the right to fight against these racists by any means that are necessary.

—**Ibid.**

★ "By any means necessary" emerged as a rallying call for militant action. It is now associated mostly with African-American radical action, but in the 1960s it had a general appeal. Thus, Abbie Hoffman, one of the founders of the Youth International Party, whose members were called Yippies, pledged in 1968, "We'll build our society in the vacant lots of the old, and we'll do it by any means necessary."

7 You do not wipe away the scars of centuries by saying, "Now, you are free to go where you want, do what you desire, and choose the leaders you please." You do not take a man who, for years, has been hobbled by chains, liberate him, bring him to the starting line of the race, saying, "You are free to compete with the others."

—**Lyndon B. Johnson,** speech, Howard University, 1965

8 Being a star has made it possible for me to get insulted in places where the average Negro could never hope to get insulted.

—**Sammy Davis, Jr.,** *Yes I Can*, 1965

To be a Negro in this country and to be relatively conscious is to be in a rage almost **1**
all the time.

—James Baldwin, *Time*, August 1965

Black is beautiful. **2**

—Anonymous, slogan, c. 1966

★ The phrase was linked with the Black Power movement (see below), but the idea was expressed decades earlier by Langston Hughes, who wrote in *The Negro Artist and the Racial Mountain*, "Why should I want to be white? I am a Negro—and beautiful!" (*The Nation*, June 23, 1926). Similarly, in his poem *Negro*, from the same year, Hughes wrote, "I am a Negro: / Black as the night is black, / Black like the depths of my Africa." Finally, of course, going back to the Bible, the Douay version of *The Song of Solomon*, 1:5, has the sentence, "I am black but beautiful."

Black power . . . is a call for black people in this country to unite, to recognize their **3**
heritage, to build a sense of community. . . . It is a call to reject the racist institutions and values of this society.

—Stokely Carmichael & Charles Vernon Hamilton, *Black Power!*, 1967

★ Carmichael is usually credited with inventing the phrase "black power"; he certainly popularized it in the summer of 1966 while leading the continuation of a civil rights walk by James Meredith, who was shot and wounded on June 6, 1966. But the phrase and the concept were in the air that year. For example, the more moderate Adam Clayton Powell, Jr., in a speech at Howard University on May 29, 1966, said, "Our life must be purposed to implement human rights. . . . To demand these God-given rights is to seek black power—the power to build black institutions of splendid achievement."

Say It Loud: I'm Black and I'm Proud.

—James Brown, song title, 1968 **4**

Death is a slave's freedom.

—Nikki Giovanni, speech at the funeral of Martin Luther King, Jr., 1968 **5**

Our nation is moving toward two societies, one black, one white—separate and
unequal. **6**

—Otto Kerner, Jr., *Report of the National Advisory Commission on Civil Disorders*, 1968

stupid america, hear that chicano
shouting curses on the street **7**
he is a poet without paper and pencil
and since he cannot write
he will explode.

—Lalo Delgado, *Stupid America*, 1969

The time may have come when the issue of race could benefit from a period of **8**
"benign neglect."

—Daniel Patrick Moynihan, White House memo, March 2, 1970

★ Moynihan was then urban affairs adviser to President Richard M. Nixon. The quoted phrase came from the earl of Durham's 1839 recommendation to Queen Victoria that Canada be allowed to govern herself, since she had done so well on her own "through a period of benign neglect."

1 White men, whether they are the majority or the minority, must find a way to purge themselves completely of racism, or face an ultimate fateful confrontation which will shake the very foundations of civilization.

—Ralph J. Bunche, speech, 1971, quoted in *The New York Times* [May 7, 1986]

★ This was the last public speech of Dr. Bunche, who won a Nobel Prize—the first African-American to do so—for negotiating a settlement to the 1948 Israeli-Arab war.

2 A racially integrated community is a chronological term timed from the entrance of the first black family to the exit of the last white family.

—Saul Alinsky, *Rules for Radicals,* 1971

3 My only concern was to get home after a hard day's work.

—Rosa Parks, *Time* magazine, Dec. 15, 1975

★ Parks, an African-American seamstress from Montgomery, Ala., was speaking of December 1, 1955, when she refused to give up her seat at the front of a bus to a white man. For this defiance of the rule that blacks had to sit in the back of a bus, she was arrested; and this led to a black boycott of buses in the city. The successful protest was led by a young minister, Martin Luther King, Jr. Elsewhere, Parks acknowledged that she had felt for some time that she would never again give up her seat on demand; she was not simply too tired to move. "The only tired I was, was tired of giving in," she said in *Rosa Parks: My Story*, written with Jim Haskins, 1992.

4 In order to get beyond racism, we must first take account of race. There is no other way.

—Harry A. Blackmun, *University of California Regents v. Bakke*, 1978

★ Allan Bakke, a white man, was twice turned down at the medical school of the University of California at Davis, where some places were set aside for minority applicants. His suit against the California Board of Regents required the Supreme Court to take a position on affirmative action programs, designed to make opportunities for people of color more nearly equal with those of whites. Justice Blackmun's famous pronouncement was borrowed, without attribution, from Harvard dean McGeorge Bundy, "To get past racism, we must here take account of race. There is no other present way," *The Atlantic Monthly*, November, 1977. A four-four tie on the Court gave the final word on *Bakke* to Justice Lewis Powell, who concluded that affirmative action was constitutionally permissable but quotas were not.

5 In light of the sorry history of discrimination and its devastating impact on the lives of Negroes, bringing the Negro into the mainstream of American life should be a state interest of the highest order. To fail to do so is to ensure that America will remain forever a divided society.

—Thurgood Marshall, *University of California Regents v. Bakke*, 1978

6 Our nation is a rainbow—red, yellow, brown, black, and white—and we're all precious in God's sight.

—Jesse Jackson, Democratic National Convention, San Francisco, July 17, 1984

★ More at AMERICA & AMERICANS.

7 We don't have to be what you want us to be.

—Bill Russell, quoted by George Vecsey, *The New York Times*, 1985

★ Bill Russell played center for the Boston Celtics when they ran up one of the finest records of any team in sports, winning eleven championships in thirteen years, 1956-69. As player-coach for the last two years of that stretch, he was the first black leader of a major U.S. professional sports team.

I am somebody. 1
—**Jesse Jackson,** motto

The history of the white man's use of the earth in America is a scandal. 2
—**Wendell Berry,** *The Hidden Wound,* 1989

My Daddy told me it doesn't matter if it's a white snake or a black snake, it can still 3
bite you.
—**Thurgood Marshall,** saying

★ Carl Rowan, author of a biography of Justice Marshall, said that he applied this specifically to Clarence Thomas, a conservative Republican, nominated to the Supreme Court by Pres. George H. W. Bush after Marshall's retirement in 1991.

A white man with a million dollars is a millionaire, and a black man with a million 4
dollars is a nigger with a million dollars.
—**Anonymous,** saying used by New York City mayor David Dinkins, 1980s

★ This bitter comment had been around for several decades at least. Mayor Dinkins was quoted by Ellis Cose in *The Rage of the Privileged Class* [1993]

Racism is not an excuse to not do the best you can. 5
—**Arthur Ashe,** *Sports Illustrated*, July 1991

The most basic fact of American life is that sometime within the next 50 or so years, 6
non-Hispanic white people will become demographically just another minority group.
—**William A. Henry III,** *In Defense of Elitism,* 1994

Reality, Illusions, & Images

See also Appearances; Art: Aesthetics; Dreams & Dreamers.

Things are not what they seem. 7
—**Henry Wadsworth Longfellow,** *A Psalm of Life*, 1839

★ More at Life.

All that we see or seem 8
Is but a dream within a dream.
—**Edgar Allan Poe,** *A Dream Within a Dream,* 1848–49

A true account of the actual is the rarest poetry, for common sense always takes a 9
hasty and superficial view.
—**Henry David Thoreau,** *A Week on the Concord and Merrimack Rivers*, 1849

Be it life or death, we crave only reality. 10
—**Henry David Thoreau,** *Where I Lived and What I Lived For,* in *Walden*, 1854

1 We wake from one dream into another dream.
—Ralph Waldo Emerson, *Illusions*, in *The Conduct of Life*, 1860

2 Certainty generally is an illusion, and repose is not the destiny of man.
—Oliver Wendell Holmes, Jr., *The Path of the Law*, 1897

3 Between the idea and the reality
Between the motion
And the act
Falls the Shadow.
—T. S. Eliot, *The Hollow Men*, 1925

4 Humankind
Cannot bear very much reality.
—T. S. Eliot, *Murder in the Cathedral*, 1935

★ The same sentence is in Eliot's *Burnt Norton* in *Four Quartets*, 1943. See also Eliot at SCIENCE: PHYSICS & COSMOLOGY.

5 In the American metaphysic, reality is always material reality, hard, resistant, unformed, impenetrable, and unpleasant.
—Lionel Trilling, *Reality in America*, in *The Liberal Imagination*, 1950

6 It helps to see the actual world to visualize a fantastic world.
—Wallace Stevens, Milton J. Bates, ed., expanded *Opus Posthumous,* [1989]

7 Life is washed in the speechless real.
—Jacques Barzun, *The House of Intellect*, 1959

8 We suffer primarily not from our vices or our weaknesses, but from our illusions. We are haunted, not by reality, but by those images we have put in place of reality.
—Daniel J. Boorstin, Introduction, *The Image*, 1962

9 Obsessed by a fairy tale, we spend our lives searching for a magic door and a lost kingdom of peace.
—Eugene O'Neill, *More Stately Mansions*, 1964

10 First baseball umpire: "Balls and strikes, I call them as I sees them."
Second umpire: "Balls and strikes, I call them as they are."
Third umpire: "Balls and strikes, they ain't nothing until I call them."
—Anonymous, in Alan L. Mackay, ed., *The Harvest of a Quiet Eye*, 1977

11 Each person paints their picture of reality with a brush dipped in the pigments of the past.
—Jerry Andrus, conference, Center for the Scientific Investigation of Claims of the Paranormal, Seattle, Wash., June 1994

★ Andrus, a magician, delighted the audience with demonstrations of how expectations based on past experience mislead us in perceiving present events. See also magician Dai Vernon at ART: THEATER, DRAMA, & MAGIC.

Reality is our ally. 1
—**Russ Rymer,** Editor's Note, *Mother Jones*, May/June 2005

Reasons & Reasonable People

So convenient a thing it is to be a *reasonable creature*, since it enables one to find or make a reason for everything one has a mind to do. 2
—**Benjamin Franklin,** *Autobiography*, started 1771 [published in full, 1868]

Every man's own reason must be his oracle. 3
—**Thomas Jefferson,** letter to Dr. Benjamin Rush, March 6, 1813

Nature hates calculators. 4
—**Ralph Waldo Emerson,** *Nature*, in *Essays: Second Series*, 1844

There are few things more exciting to me . . . than a psychological reason. 5
—**Henry James,** *The Art of Fiction*, 1888

A man always has two reasons for what he does—a good one and the real one. 6
—**John Pierpont Morgan,** quoted in Owen Wister, *Roosevelt: The Story of a Friendship* [1930]

Come now, let us reason together. 7
—**Lyndon B. Johnson,** saying

★ From *Isaiah* 1:18: "Come now, and let us reason together."

A study of the art of motorcycle maintenance is really a miniature study of the art of rationality itself. 8
—**Robert Pirsig,** *Zen and the Art of Motorcycle Maintenance*, 1974

★ More at SCIENCE: TECHNOLOGY.

You don't convince people to support you for your reasons. You convince them to support you for their reasons. 9
—**Gary Jacobson,** *The New York Times*, Sept. 17, 1995

Regret

See also OLD AGE (John Barrymore)

To regret deeply is to live afresh. 10
—**Henry David Thoreau,** *Journal*, Nov. 13, 1839

Why should I mourn at the untimely fate of my people? Tribe follows tribe, and nation follows nation, and regret is useless. 11
—**Seattle,** speech, c. 1854

★ For more from and about this speech, see Seattle under RACES & PEOPLES.

For of all sad words of tongue or pen, 12
The saddest are these: "It might have been!"
—**John Greenleaf Whittier,** *Maud Muller*, 1856

1 I shall be telling this with a sigh
Somewhere ages and ages hence:
Two roads diverged in a wood, and I—
I took the one less traveled by,
And that has made all the difference.
—**Robert Frost,** *The Road Not Taken*, 1916

2 The follies which a man regrets most, in his life, are those which he didn't commit when he had the opportunity.
—**Helen Rowland,** *A Guide to Men*, 1922

3 Footfalls echo in the memory
Down the passage which we did not take
Towards the door we never opened
Into the rosegarden.
—**T. S. Eliot,** *Four Quartets: Burnt Norton*, 1935

4 I could have had class. I could've been a contender. I could've been somebody. Instead of a bum, which is what I am.
—**Budd Schulberg,** *Waterfront*, 1955

★ The novel appeared a year after the film, *On the Waterfront*, written by Schulberg and starring Marlon Brando as Terry Malloy, who "could've been a contender."

5 Maybe Rosebud was something he couldn't get or something he lost. Anyway, it wouldn't explain a man's life. No, I guess Rosebud is just a piece in a jigsaw puzzle, a missing piece.
—**Herman J. Mankiewicz & Orson Welles,** *Citizen Kane*, screenplay, 1941

★ Kane's deathbed whisper was "Rosebud," and the movie turns on the search for why he said this. See also LAST WORDS.

6 It's not what you are; it's what you don't become that hurts.
—**Oscar Levant**, ad-lib line, *Humoresque*, 1946

7 Never, never waste a moment on regret. It's a waste of time.
—**Harry S. Truman,** in Janet Landman, *Regret: The Persistance of the Possible* [1993]

8 My one regret in life is that I am not someone else.
—**Woody Allen,** epigraph, in Eric Lax, *Woody Allen and His Comedy* [1975]

9 Maybe all one can do is hope to end up with the right regrets.
—**Arthur Miller,** *The Ride Down Mount Morgan*, 1991

Religion

See also ATHEISM; FAITH; GOD; MIRACLES; PRAYER; PRAYERS.

10 Job feels the rod,
Yet blesses God.
—**The New England Primer,** c. 1688

To be like Christ is to be a Christian. 1
—**William Penn,** last words, 1718

It does me no injury for my neighbor to say there are twenty gods, or no God. 2
—**Thomas Jefferson,** *Notes on the State of Virginia*, 1782

★ The observation is part of an argument for freedom of religion. In full, Jefferson wrote, "The legitimate powers of government extend to such acts only as are injurious to others. But it does me no injury for my neighbor to say there are twenty gods, or no God. It neither picks my pocket nor breaks my leg." See also Jefferson below and at TYRANNY (letter to Benjamin Rush).

Every man, conducting himself as a good citizen, and being accountable to God alone for his religious opinions, ought to be protected in worshipping the Deity according to the dictates of his own conscience. 3
—**George Washington,** letter to the United Baptist Churches in Virginia, May 1789

I believe in one God and no more, and I hope for happiness beyond this life. I believe in the equality of man; and I believe that religious duties consist in doing justice, loving mercy, and endeavoring to make our fellow creatures happy. 4
—**Tom Paine,** *The Age of Reason*, 1794

★ See also Paine at ETHICS & MORALITY.

Priests and conjurors are of the same trade. 5
—**Ibid.**

Any system of religion that has anything in it that shocks the mind of a child cannot be a true system. 6
—**Ibid.**

Believing with you that religion is a matter which lies solely between man and his God, that he owes account to none other for his faith or his worship, that the legislative powers of government reach actions only, and not opinions, I contemplate with sovereign reverence that act of the whole American people which declared that their legislature should "make no law respecting an establishment of religion, or prohibiting the free exercise thereof," thus building a wall of separation between Church and State. 7
—**Thomas Jefferson,** letter to Nehemiah Dodge, Ephraim Robbins, and Stephen S. Nelson, of the Danbury [Conn.] Baptist Association, Jan. 1, 1802

★ This is the source of the famous wall between Church and State, based on but not in the First Amendment; see BILL OF RIGHTS. The phrase was used in the mid-20th century by Justice Hugo Black in a major Supreme Court decision; see below. The Baptists in New England were in the forefront of the struggle for religious freedom. The recipients of this letter, a committeee of the Danbury association, had written to President Jefferson approving his religious views. Jefferson was proud of having previously constructed such a wall of separation, though without using those words, in his bill for establishing religious freedom in Virginia. The key paragraph of this bill, drafted by

Jefferson in 1777, much debated, and at length adopted in 1786, stated that "no man shall be compelled to frequent or support any religious worship, place, or ministry whatsoever" and concluded with the declaration that "all men shall be free to profess, and by argument to maintain, their opinions in matters of religion, and that the same shall in no wise diminish, enlarge, or affect their civil capacities." See also Jefferson above and at EPITAPHS & GRAVESTONES.

1 Democracy has given to conscience absolute liberty.

—**George Bancroft,** address to the Democratic Elector of Massachusetts, *Boston Post*, Oct. 16, 1835

★ For a comment on the variety of churches associated with that liberty, see Frances Trollope at AMERICA & AMERICANS.

2 If a man entertains heretical sentiments, who shall be his judge? Our creator has not delegated this power to man. He is himself the only competent judge; and it concerns him much more than it does us to define the crime and inflict the penalty.

—**Richard M. Johnson,** address to Barnabas Bates et al., *New York Evening Post*, April 1, 1840

★ Col. Johnson of Kentucky, hero of the Battle of the Thames in the War of 1812, was a popular congressman, a great defender of the common people, and served as vice president for one term under Andrew Jackson. A tendency to venality in the management of his financial affairs, and an interracial liaison, undermined his political career.

3 I like the silent church before the service begins, better than any preaching.

—**Ralph Waldo Emerson,** *Self-Reliance*, in *Essays: First Series*, 1841

4 For every Stoic was a Stoic; but in Christendom where is the Christian?

—**Ibid.**

5 God builds his temple in the heart on the ruins of churches and religions.

—**Ralph Waldo Emerson,** *Worship*, in *The Conduct of Life*, 1860

6 Some keep the Sabbath going to Church—
I keep it, staying at Home—
With a Bobolink for a Chorister—
And an Orchard for a Dome.

—**Emily Dickinson,** poem no. 324, 1862

7 I am approached with the most opposite opinions and advice, and that by religious men, who are equally certain that they represent the divine will. I hope it will not be irreverent for me to say that if it is probable that God would reveal his will to others, on a point so connected with my duty, it might be supposed that he would reveal it directly to me.

—**Abraham Lincoln,** remark to a group of ministers, Sept. 1862

8 Once we had wooden chalices and golden priests, now we have golden chalices and wooden priests.

—**Ralph Waldo Emerson,** *The Preacher*, 1867

Leave the matter of religion to the family altar, the church and the private school, supported entirely by private contributions. Keep the church and state forever separate. 1

—**Ulysses S. Grant,** speech, Des Moines, Iowa, 1875

The country that has got the least religion is the most prosperous, and the country that has got the most religion is the least prosperous. 2

—**Robert G. Ingersoll,** speech, Boston, April 23, 1880

Religion . . . is a man's total reaction upon life. 3

—**William James,** *The Varieties of Religious Experience*, 1902

Religion is a monumental chapter in the history of human egotism. 4

—**Ibid.**

Heathen, n. A benighted creature who has the folly to worship something that he can see and feel. 5

—**Ambrose Bierce,** *The Devil's Dictionary*, 1906

The Bible is literature, not dogma. 6

—**George Santayana,** *The Ethics of Spinoza*, 1910

★ See also Mark Twain at ATHEISM.

Religion is the love of life in the consciousness of impotence. 7

—**George Santayana,** *Winds of Doctrine*, 1913

Give me that old-time religion, 8
It's good enough for me.

—**Anonymous,** hymn

The cosmic religious experience is the strongest and noblest driving force behind scientific research. 9

—**Albert Einstein,** *Cosmic Religion*, 1931

As society is now constituted, a literal adherence to the moral precepts scattered throughout the gospels would mean sudden death. 10

—**Alfred North Whitehead,** *Adventures of Ideas*, 1933

It ain't necessarily so— 11
The things that you're liable
To read in the Bible—
It ain't necessarily so.

—**Ira Gershwin,** *Porgy and Bess*, 1935

★ Music by George Gershwin.

Science without religion is lame, religion without science is blind. 12

—**Albert Einstein**, *Science, Philosophy, and Religion*, symposium contribution, New York City, 1940

1 Caesar and Christ had met in the arena, and Christ had won.
—**William Durant,** *The Story of Civilization*, Vol. 3, 1944

2 We must respect the other fellow's religion, but only in the sense and to the extent that we accept his theory that his wife is beautiful and his children smart.
—**H. L. Mencken,** *Minority Report: H. L. Mencken's Notebooks* [1956]

3 Fear of death and fear of life both become piety.
—**Ibid.**

4 If you really want to make a million, the quickest way is to start your own religion.
—**L. Ron Hubbard,** lecture, Eastern Science Fiction Association, Newark, N.J., 1947

★ Hubbard was the founding spirit of Scientology, which was incorporated as a church in 1965. The quote comes courtesy of Sam Moscowitz, attributed in B. Corydon and L. Ron Hubbard, Jr., *L. Ron Hubbard*, 1987. Moscowitz said that Hubbard observed that writing science fiction for about a penny a word was no way to make a living, especially as compared to founding a religion.

5 The First Amendment has erected a wall between church and state. That wall must be kept high and impregnable. We could not approve the slightest breach.
—**Hugo L. Black,** *Everson v. Board of Education,* 1947

★ The metaphor of the wall derives from Thomas Jefferson; see his letter above to the Danbury Baptist Association.

6 We are a religious people whose institutions presuppose a Supreme Being.
—**William O. Douglas,** *Zorach v. Clauson*, 1952

★ Justice Douglas was trying to carve out some ground on which church and State could co-exist. Otherwise, among other mundane examples that he cited, "Municipalities would not be permitted to render police or fire protection to religious groups. Policemen who helped parishioners into their places of worship would violate the Constitution. Prayers in our legislative halls; the appeals to the Almighty in the messages of the Chief Executive; the proclamations making Thanksgiving Day a holiday . . . these and all other references to the Almighty that run through our laws, our public rituals, our ceremonies would be flouting the First Amendment."

7 The day that this country ceases to be free for irreligion it will cease to be free for religion—except for the sect that can win political power.
—**Robert H. Jackson,** *Zorach v. Clausen*, dissenting, 1952

8 I am a deeply religious nonbeliever. . . . This is a somewhat new kind of religion.
—**Albert Einstein,** letter to Hans Muehsam, March 30, 1954

9 I was the accuser, God the accused. My eyes were open and I was alone—terribly alone in a world without God and without man.
—**Elie Wiesel,** *Night*, 1958

10 Every day, people are straying away from the church and going back to God.
—**Lenny Bruce,** quoted in *The Essential Lenny Bruce*, compiled and edited by John Cohen [1970]

The church must be reminded that it is not the master or the servant of the state, but rather the conscience of the state. 1

—**Martin Luther King, Jr.,** *Strength to Love*, 1963

I read about an Eskimo hunter who asked the local missionary priest, "If I did not know about God and sin, would I go to hell?" "No," said the priest, "not if you did not know." "Then why," asked the Eskimo earnestly, "did you tell me?" 2

—**Annie Dillard,** *Pilgrim at Tinker Creek*, 1974

People don't come to church for preachments, of course, but to daydream about God. 3

—**Kurt Vonnegut,** Palm Sunday sermon, St. Clement's Episcopal Church, New York City, quoted by John Leonard in *The New York Times*, April 30, 1980

The yearning for an afterlife is the opposite of selfish; it is love and praise for the world that we are privileged, in this complex interval of light, to witness and experience. 4

—**John Updike,** *Self-Consciousness: Memoirs*, 1989

Religion enables us to ignore nothingness and get on with the joke of life. 5

—**Ibid.**

Catholics believe in forgiveness. Jews believe in guilt. 6

—**Tony Kushner,** *Angels in America*, 1993

It ain't often that a man's reputation outlasts his munny. 7

—**Josh Billings,** *Josh Billings: Hiz Sayings*, 1866

Republicans

See POLITICS & POLITICIANS.

Reputation

See also HONOR; VIRTUE (Lincoln).

What people say behind your back is your standing in the community. 8

—**E. W. Howe,** *Country Town Sayings*, 1911

Reputation, like a face, is the symbol of its possessor and creator, and another can use it only as a mask. 9

—**Learned Hand,** *Yale Electric Company v. Robertson*, 1928

★ This was a trademark case.

If we disregard what the world says of someone, we live to repent it. 10

—**Logan Pearsall Smith,** *All Trivia*, 1935

1 Until you've lost your reputation, you never realize what a burden it was, or what freedom really is.
—**Margaret Mitchell,** *Gone With the Wind*, 1936
★ Scarlett O'Hara speaking.

2 Some say she do and some say she don't.
—**Anonymous,** African-American folksaying

3 All a man has got to show for his time here on earth is what kind of name he had.
—**Muhammad Ali,** on refusing induction into the U.S. Army, 1967
★ See also Ali at VIETNAM WAR.

4 A bad reputation is like a hangover. It takes a while to get rid of, and it makes everything else hurt.
—**James Preston**, in *Fortune* magazine, Feb. 10, 1992
★ Mr. Preston was CEO of Avon Products at the time.

Resignation

See also ENDURANCE; PATIENCE.

5 What is called resignation is confirmed desperation.
—**Henry David Thoreau,** "Economy," *Walden*, 1854
★ More at LIFE.

6 Hear me, my chiefs, I am tired; my heart is sick and sad. From where the sun now stands, I will fight no more forever.
—**Joseph the Younger,** speech at the end of the Nez Percé War, October 1877
★ Chief Joseph was known as a skilled orator.

7 There is no good arguing with the inevitable. The only argument available with an east wind is to put on your overcoat.
—**James Russell Lowell,** *Democracy*, Oct. 6, 1884

8 Teach us to care and not to care.
Teach us to sit still.
—**T. S. Eliot,** *Ash Wednesday*, 1930

Resistance

See also AMERICAN HISTORY: MEMORABLE MOMENTS (quotes on the Alamo); DETERMINATION, EFFORT, PERSISTENCE, & PERSEVERANCE; LAW (Henry David Thoreau, Martin Luther King, Jr.); REVOLUTION; WAR (Charles Eliot Norton); TYRANNY.

9 The spirit of resistance to government is so valuable on certain occasions that I wish it to be always kept alive. It will often be exercised when wrong, but better so than not to be exercised at all.
—**Thomas Jefferson,** to Abigail Adams, Feb. 22, 1787
★ See also Jefferson on resistance to tyrants at TYRANNY.

Our lives are in the hands of the Great Spirit. He gave to our ancestors the lands which we possess. We are determined to defend our lands, and if it is His will, our bones shall whiten upon them, but we will never give them up. 1

—**Tecumseh,** speech to Maj. Gen. Henry Procter of the British army, Sept. 1813

★ The Shawnee chief had allied his people with the British, and he covered Procter's retreat into Canada. Tecumseh was killed on October 5 in the battle of the Thames River.

He is whipped oftenest, who is whipped easiest, and that slave who has the courage to stand up for himself against the overseer, although he may have many hard stripes at the first, becomes, in the end, a freeman even though he sustain the formal relation of a slave. 2

—**Frederick Douglass,** *My Bondage and My Freedom*, 1855

★ Douglass escaped from slavery on his second try, in 1838, and found work in New Bedford, Mass., where he became a spokesman and leader of the abolitionist cause, with a national following. See also Douglass at SLAVERY.

We beg no longer; we entreat no more; we petition no more. We defy them. 3

—**William Jennings Bryan,** "Cross of Gold" speech, Democratic National Convention, Chicago, July 7, 1896

★ See ECONOMICS for more on this speech. "Them" in this passage refers to Eastern financiers.

There comes a time when the cup of endurance runs over, and men are no longer willing to be plunged into an abyss of injustice where they experience the blackness of corroding despair. 4

—**Martin Luther King, Jr.,** letter from Birmingham city jail, April 16, 1963

★ King was addressing fellow ministers in the South, white men who recognized the injustice of segregation but had deplored the confrontations and civil disobedience used in opposing it.

You may trod me in the very dirt 5
But still, like dust, I'll rise.

—**Maya Angelou,** *Still I Rise*, in *And Still I Rise*, 1978

The office of the independent counsel can indict my dog, they can indict my cat, but I am not going to lie about the President. 6

—**Webster L. Hubbell,** press interview, in *The New York Times*, May 1, 1998

★ A longtime friend of President and Mrs. Clinton, as well as a former law partner of hers, Hubbell was indicted, along with his wife, his accountant, and his lawyer, on ten counts of tax evasion and fraud in what was widely viewed as an attempt by Independent Counsel Kenneth Starr to pressure him into testifying against the Clintons in connection with the so-called Whitewater investigation into a failed real estate venture in Arkansas in the 1970s. Hubbell, who insisted that he knew of no wrongdoing by the Clintons, pleaded guilty in 1999 to a felony charge of lying and was sentenced to a year's probation. Charges against the others were dropped, and so was the charge against Hubbell following a Supreme Court ruling in his favor in 2000.

Responsibility

1 Only aim to do your duty, and mankind will give you credit where you fail.
—**Thomas Jefferson,** *The Rights of British America*, 1774

2 They are slaves who fear to speak
For the fallen and the weak.
—**James Russell Lowell,** *Stanzas on Freedom*, 1843

3 Duty, oh duty,
Why are thou not a
Sweetie or a cutie?
—**Ogden Nash,** 1935

★ This version of Nash's ditty is cited, without a title, in Robert Debs Heinl, *Dictionary of Military and Naval Quotations*, 1966. A longer version is included in Nash's *The Face Is Familiar*, 1941. It is titled *Kind of an Ode to Duty*, and reads: "Oh duty, / Why hast thou not the visage of a sweetie or a cutie?"

4 I believe that every right implies a responsibility; every opportunity, an obligation; every possession, a duty.
—**John D. Rockefeller,** speech, July 8, 1941

5 A burden in the bush is worth two on your hands.
—**James Thurber,** *The Hunter and the Elephant*, in *Fables for Our Times*, 1943

6 The buck stops here.
—**Harry S. Truman,** motto

★ In *Truman* (1992), David McCullough relates that Truman's faithful friend Fred Canfil saw a sign with this motto on the warden's desk at the federal reformatory in El Reno, Oklahoma, and had a copy made for Truman, who briefly kept it on his desk in the White House. Word maven William Safire has explained that the buck was a marker, often a silver dollar, used in poker games to indicate the upcoming dealer. The buck could be passed on if a player did not want the responsibility of dealing. Sen. Daniel Patrick Moynihan, however, told Mr. Safire that, in the Navy, the buck is a small dining-table marker that shows which officer is to be served first. It is moved from place to place daily. If the buck stops at one place, that officer always is served first—not the image we associate with the Truman saying.

7 But this nation was not founded solely on citizens' rights. Equally important, though too often not discussed, is the citizens' responsibility. Our privileges can be no greater than our obligations. The protection of our rights can endure no longer than the performance of our responsibilities.
—**John F. Kennedy,** convocation address, Vanderbilt University, May 18, 1963

8 "Once the rockets go up, who cares where they come down?
That's not my department," says Wernher von Braun.
—**Tom Lehrer**, *Wernher von Braun*, song, 1965

★ Von Braun headed Germany's program to develop the V-2 rocket used against Britain in World War II. Working for the U.S. after the war, he led the team that developed the Saturn booster rocket used in the Apollo missions to the moon.

In a free society, all are involved in what some are doing. Some are guilty, all are responsible. 1

—**Abraham Joshua Heschel,** speech, Town Hall, New York City, 1966

★ Rabbi Heschel was speaking against the Vietnam war. He made the statement in slightly different ways on different occasions. A common variation, often quoted, is "In a free society, where terrible wrongs exist, some are guilty, all are responsbile."

Responsible persons are mature people who have taken charge of themselves and their conduct, who *own* their actions and *own up* to them—who answer for them. 2

—**William J. Bennett,** *The Book of Virtues: A Treasury of Great Moral Stories*, 1993

Revenge

Gentlemen: You have undertaken to ruin me. I will not sue you for the law takes too long. I will ruin you. 3

—**Cornelius Vanderbilt,** letter to Charles Morgan and Cornelius Garrison, 1854

★ Morgan and Garrison were plotting to ruin a Vanderbilt transit company in order to replace it with a venture of their own. Vanderbilt was called the Commodore because he established himself in shipping before turning to railroads.

Living well is the best revenge. 4

—**Gerald Murphy & Sara Murphy,** personal motto

★ The quote usually is associated with the Murphys, expatriate friends of Scott and Zelda Fitgerald, and the models for Dick and Nicole Diver in *Tender Is the Night* (1934). The thought is proverbial, however. George Herbert recorded it in this exact form in his 1640 collection of *Outlandish Proverbs*.

When a man's partner is killed he is supposed to do something about it. It doesn't make any difference what you thought of him. He was your partner and you're supposed to do something about it. 5

—**Dashiell Hammett,** *The Maltese Falcon*, 1930

★ Spoken by the private detective Sam Spade, and uttered most memorably by Humphrey Bogart in the 1941 movie of the same title—the third to be made from the book.

Don't get mad, get even. 6

—**Joseph Patrick Kennedy,** attributed

Revenge is a dish that tastes best when it is eaten cold. 7

—**Mario Puzo,** *The Godfather*, 1969

★ Proverbial insight. H. L. Mencken identified it as English, not recorded earlier than the 19th century. His version is, "Vengeance is a dish best eaten cold." We do not have an Italian citation. Presumably the godfather and friends would not agree with the wise Italian proverb, "Revenge is a morsel reserved for God."

Revenge is a form of nostalgia. 8

—**Sheldon B. Kopp,** *What Took You So Long?*, 1979

Revolution

See also American Revolution; Future, the (Lincoln Steffens); History (Saul Alinsky); Resistance; Ruthlessness; Tyranny; Violence.

1 A little rebellion now and then is a good thing, and as necessary in the political world as storms in the physical.
—**Thomas Jefferson,** letter to James Madison, Jan. 30, 1787

★ Jefferson was referring to Shays' Rebellion, an antitax revolt in Massachusetts.

2 The tree of liberty must be refreshed from time to time with the blood of patriots and tyrants. It is its natural manure.
—**Thomas Jefferson,** letter to Col. William S. Smith, Nov. 13, 1787

3 A share in two revolutions is living to some purpose.
—**Tom Paine,** quoted in Eric Foner, *Tom Paine and Revolutionary America,* [1976]

4 An oppressed people are authorized, whenever they can, to rise and break their fetters.
—**Henry Clay,** speech in the Congress, March 24, 1818

5 The great wheel of political revolution began to move in America.
—**Daniel Webster,** speech for the the laying of the cornerstone for the Bunker Hill Monument, June 17, 1825

6 Every revolution was at first a thought in one man's mind.
—**Ralph Waldo Emerson,** *History*, in *Essays: First Series*, 1841

★ Similarly, Wendell Phillips said of John Brown: "Insurrection of thought always precedes insurrection of arms," speech, Harpers Ferry, November 1, 1859.

7 God gave Noah the rainbow sign, No more water, the fire next time!
—**Anonymous,** slave song, cited by James Baldwin in *The Fire Next Time* [1963]

★ See Baldwin at Races & Peoples.

8 All men recognize the right of revolution.
—**Henry David Thoreau,** *Civil Disobedience*, 1849

9 A mighty influence is abroad, surging and heaving the world, as with an earthquake.
—**Harriet Beecher Stowe,** *Uncle Tom's Cabin*, 1852

★ More at Injustice.

10 Be not deceived. Revolutions do not go backward.
—**Abraham Lincoln,** speech, May 19, 1856

★ The same thought was expressed by the abolitionist William Henry Seward in his speech *The Irrepressible Conflict:* "Revolutions never go backward," Rochester, N.Y., October 25, 1858. And abolitionist Wendell Phillips made the same remark in a speech on February 17, 1861. We do not immediately think of the Civil War as a revolution, but to abolitionists it was indeed.

Revolutions are not made by men in spectacles. 1

—**Oliver Wendell Holmes, Sr.,** *The Young Practitioner*, speech, New York City, March 2, 1871

There may at some future day be a whirlwind precipitated upon the moneyed men of this country. 2

—**Peter Cooper,** c. 1875, quoted in Peter Lyon, *The Honest Man*, in *American Heritage* [Feb. 1959]

★ Cooper was a wealthy, self-made manufacturer and philanthropist.

Revolutions are born of hope. 3

—**Crane Brinton,** *The Anatomy of Revolution*, 1938

The Revolution of Rising Expectations 4

—**Harlan Cleveland,** title of speech at Colgate University, Hamilton, N.Y., 1949

★ The full title of the speech from which the famous phrase came was "Reflections on the Revolution of Rising Expectations."

What happens to a dream deferred? 5
Does it dry up
Like a raisin in the sun? . . .
Or does it explode?

—**Langston Hughes,** *Harlem*, 1951

Every revolution has its counterrevolution—that is a sign the revolution is for real. 6

—**C. Wright Mills**, *Listen, Yankee: The Revolution in Cuba*, 1960

Those who make peaceful revolution impossible will make violent revolution inevitable. 7

—**John F. Kennedy,** remarks to Latin American diplomats at the White House, March 13, 1962

Revolution is bloody, revolution is hostile, revolution knows no compromise, revolution overturns and destroys everything that gets in its way. 8

—**Malcolm X,** *Message to the Grass Roots*, Nov. 1963

A revolution is like a forest fire. It burns everything in its path. 9

—**Malcolm X,** interview with A. B. Spellman, *Monthly Review*, May 1964

Burn, baby, burn. 10

—**William Epton,** street-corner speech, New York City, July 18, 1964

★ Mr. Epton spoke as Harlem erupted in riot as a result of the shooting death of a teenager by a police officer two days before. His words, recorded by an undercover officer, became a test of the limits on free speech in a time of stress. After being convicted of criminal anarchy, and sentenced to a year in jail, Mr. Epton appealed to New York's highest court, the Court of Appeals. While agreeing that there was no evidence he had caused the riot, this court held that his speech was not protected under the First Amendment of the Constitution. Some speculated that his real offense in the eyes of the court was not so much the "Burn, baby, burn" as his statement that "We're going to have to kill a lot of cops, a lot of judges." See also FREE SPEECH.

1 Our own revolution has ended the need for revolution forever.
—**William C. Westmoreland,** speech to Daughters of the American Revolution, quoted in Daniel Berrigan, *America Is Hard to Find* [1972]

★ Gen. Westmoreland commanded the U.S. forces in Vietnam from 1964 to 1968.

2 Life in this society being, at best, an utter bore and no aspect of society being at all relevant to women, there remains to civic-minded, responsible, thrill-seeking females only to overthrow the government, eliminate the money system, institute complete automation and destroy the male sex.
—**Valerie Solanas,** *The SCUM Manifesto*, 1968

★ Ms. Solanas' fifteen minutes of fame came the same year that her book was published when she shot and wounded Andy Warhol. *SCUM* is an acronym for *S*ociety for *C*utting *U*p *M*en.

3 It is well known that the most radical revolutionary will become a conservative on the day after the revolution.
—**Hannah Arendt,** in *The New Yorker, Sept. 12, 1970*

4 All successful revolutions are the kicking in of a rotten door. The violence of revolutions is the violence of men charging into a vacuum.
—**John Kenneth Galbraith,** *The Age of Uncertainty*, 1977

Revolutionary War

See AMERICAN REVOLUTION.

Rhode Island

See also CITIES (NEWPORT, PROVIDENCE).

5 Aquethneck shall henceforth be called the Ile of Rhods or Rhod-Island.
—**Rhode Island Colonial Assembly,** March 13, 1694

★ Roger Williams, founder of the colony, apparently had read a translation of Giovanni da Verrazzano's account of his voyage along the New England coast in 1524 in which he reported discovering "an island in the form of a triangle, distant from the mainland 10 leagues, about the bigness of the Island of Rhodes." Williams erred in supposing that Verrazzano meant Aquidneck, or Aquethneck, future site of Newport, according to Samuel Eliot Morison's *The European Discovery of America: The Northern Voyages*. Nevertheless, the name stuck and was transferred to the colony as a whole. Variations in the spelling of the name, by the way, are of no significance.

6 The country people in the island, in general, are very unpolished and rude.
—**Alexander Hamilton,** *Itinerarium*, August 18, 1744

★ For background on Dr. Hamilton, see Boston under CITIES.

7 The political condition of Rhode Island is notorious, acknowledged, and it is shameful. Rhode Island is a state for sale, and cheap.
—**Lincoln Steffens,** *Rhode Island: A State for Sale,* 1905

★ Little Rhode Island's troubles with corruption continued into the 21st century, when, in 2002, Vincent "Buddy" Cianci, widely credited with rejuvenating Providence, was convicted of racketeering. See also the anonymous bumper sticker below and Charles "Boss" Brayton at POLITICS & POLITICIANS.

Rhode Island was settled and is made up of people who found it unbearable to live anywhere else in New England. 1
—**Woodrow Wilson,** speech, New York City, Jan. 29, 1911

Texas could wear Rhode Island as a watch fob. 2
—**Pat Neff,** quoted in John Gunther, *Inside U.S.A.* [1947]

★ Neff was governor of Texas, 1921–25.

This state has the best politicians money can buy. 3
—**Anonymous,** bumper sticker, *The New Yorker,* Sept. 2, 2002

★ While the bumper sticker was reported to be popular in Rhode Island at this time, the same message was in national circulation.

Hope. 4
—Motto, state of Rhode Island

Rich & Poor, Wealth & Poverty

See also CAPITALISM & CAPITAL V. LABOR; ECONOMICS; ELITE, THE; MONEY & THE RICH; POVERTY & HUNGER; WORK & WORKERS.

It is a reproach to religion and government to suffer so much poverty and excess. 5
—**William Penn,** *Some Fruits of Solitude*, 1693

The most common and durable source of factions has been the various and unequal distribution of property. 6
—**James Madison,** *The Federalist, No. 10*, 1787

★ More at CONFLICT.

All communities divide themselves into the few and the many. The first are the rich and well-born, the other the mass of the people. 7
—**Alexander Hamilton,** speech, Constitutional Convention, 1787

★ Hamilton described the second group, the people, as "turbulent and changing." He advocated giving the first group a permanent share in government, and predicted that it would be in their own interest to maintain good government. See also Hamilton at THE PEOPLE, in the note under William T. Sherman.

Each belongs here or anywhere as much as the well off . . . just as much as you or I. Each has his or her place in the procession. 8
—**Walt Whitman,** *Leaves of Grass*, 1855

The problem of our age is the proper administration of wealth, so that the ties of brotherhood may still bind together the rich and poor in harmonious relationship. 9
—**Andrew Carnegie,** *Wealth*, in *North American Review*, June, 1889

★ This is the opening sentence of Carnegie's essay. The great philanthropist-to-be went on to declare that "The man who dies . . . rich dies disgraced." See also John F. Kennedy at ECONOMICS.

1 How the Other Half Lives.

—**Jacob A. Riis,** book title, 1890

★ Riis's book described the horrific conditions of life in New York City tenements. The photographs are still shocking.

2 To be a poor man is hard, but to be a poor race in a land of dollars is the very bottom of hardships.

—**W. E. B. Du Bois,** *The Souls of Black Folk*, 1903

★ See also Du Bois at RACES & PEOPLES and Frederick Douglass at CRIME, CRIMINALS, & DETECTIVES.

3 The golf links lie so near the mill
That almost every day
The laboring children can look out
And see the men at play.

—**Sarah N. Cleghorn,** *The Golf Links Lie So Near the Mill*, Franklin P. Adams's column, *The Conning Tower*, in the *New York Tribune*, 1919

4 The transmission from generation to generation of vast fortunes by will, inheritance, or gift is not consistent with the ideals and sentiments of the American people.

—**Franklin D. Roosevelt,** message to Congress, June 19, 1935

★ The message accompanied a bill that represented FDR's first attempt to use taxes as an instrument of social as well as fiscal policy. Arthur M. Schlesinger, Jr., reports in *The Politics of Upheaval* (1960) that House Democrats cheered the message, while Senators sat in silence—and the Senate finance committee went on to eliminate the president's proposal for an inheritance tax from the 1935 revenue act.

5 The test of our progress is not whether we add more to the abundance of those who have much; it is whether we provide enough for those who have too little.

—**Franklin D. Roosevelt,** Second Inaugural Address, Jan. 20, 1937

6 I've been rich and I've been poor. Rich is better.

—**Sophie Tucker,** attributed

★ Some think Joe E. Lewis said it first but, as Ralph Keyes points out in *Nice Guys Finish Seventh* (1992), Lewis and Tucker often performed together and either might have borrowed it from the other.

7 The Two Americas.

—**James P. Cannon,** speech, 13th National Convention of the Socialist Workers Party, July 1, 1948

★ Remiscent of British Prime Minster Benjamin Disraeli's observation some 100 years earlier: "The Privileged and the People Form Two Nations," *Sybil*, 1845. See also Jacob Riis, above, and Michael Harrington's *The Other America* at POVERTY. Cannon wrote of his divided Americas, "One is the America of the imperialists, of the little clique of capitalists, landlords, and militarists who are threatening and terrifying the world. . . . There is the other America—the America of the workers and farmers and the "little people."

The only incurable troubles of the rich are troubles that money can't cure, 1
Which is a kind of trouble that is even more troublesome if you are poor.
—**Ogden Nash,** *The Terrible People*, in *Verses from 1929 On*, 1959

The meek shall inherit the earth but not the mineral rights. 2
—**J. Paul Getty,** attributed

Being poor is like being a child. Being rich is like being an adult: you get to do what- 3
ever you want. Everyone is nice when they have to be; rich people are nice when they feel like it.
—**Fran Lebowitz,** quoted in James Atlas, *What They Look Like to the Rest of Us*, in *The New York Times Magazine*, Nov. 19, 1995

Right

See also ETHICS & MORALITY; VIRTUE.

Be always sure you're right—then go ahead. 4
—**David Crockett,** his motto from the War of 1812, cited in *Narrative of the Life of David Crockett*, 1834

They are slaves who dare not be 5
In the right with two or three.
—**James Russell Lowell,** *Stanza on Freedom*, 1843

It is not desirable to cultivate a respect for the law, so much as for the right. 6
—**Henry David Thoreau,** *Civil Disobedience*, 1849

★ More at LAW. See also Thoreau at MAJORITIES & MINORITIES for "a man more right than his neighbors."

Let us have faith that right makes might. 7
—**Abraham Lincoln,** speech at Cooper Union, New York City, Feb. 27, 1860

★ More at VIRTUE.

The humblest citizen of all the land, when clad in the armor of a righteous cause, is 8
stronger than all the hosts of error.
—**William Jennings Bryan,** speech, Democratic National Convention, Chicago, July 8, 1896

Always do right. This will gratify some people and astonish the rest. 9
—**Mark Twain,** speech, Greenpoint Presbyterian Church, Brooklyn, N.Y., 1901

★ See also Twain at VIRTUE.

1 "The right" is only the expedient in our way of behaving.
—William James, *Pragmatism*, 1907

★ More at EXPEDIENCY.

2 The world is divided into people who think they are right.
—Anonymous

3 If I must choose between righteousness and peace, I choose righteousness.
—Theodore Roosevelt, *America and the World War*, 1915

4 The right is more precious than peace.
—Woodrow Wilson, speech to Congress, April 2, 1917

★ This is from the speech in which he asked Congress to enter the war to make the world safe for democracy; see WORLD WAR I.

5 The time is always ripe to do right.
—Martin Luther King, Jr., letter from Birmingham city jail, April 16, 1963

6 You cannot make yourself feel something you do not feel, but you can make yourself do right in spite of your feelings.
—Pearl S. Buck, *My Neighbor's Son*, in *To My Daughters With Love*, 1967

7 May God prevent us from becoming "right-thinking men"—that is to say, men who agree perfectly with their own police.
—Thomas Merton, *The New York Times*, obituary, Dec. 11, 1968

★ Merton, a Trappist monk and priest, and an excellent writer, was one of the most effective advocates of his day for Catholicism, mysticism, and the life of the spirit.

8 Rise above principle and do what's right.
—Walter Heller, testimony to Congress, May 7, 1985

Rights

See also CONSTITUTION, THE; DEMOCRACY; EQUALITY (Madison); FREEDOM; FREE SPEECH; PRESS, THE; PRIVACY; SUPREME COURT.

9 [All men] are endowed by their Creator with certain inalienable rights.
—Thomas Jefferson, *The Declaration of Independence*, July 4, 1776

★ More at DECLARATION OF INDEPENDENCE.

10 A bill of rights is what the people are entitled to against every government on earth.
—Thomas Jefferson, letter to James Madison, Dec. 1787

★ Two years later, Jefferson wrote urgently to Madison, "If we cannot secure all our rights, let us secure what we can" (March 15, 1789).

11 As a man is said to have a right to his property, he may be equally said to have a property in his rights.
—James Madison, *Property*, 1792

★ See also CONSTITUTION, THE; PROPERTY.

They have rights who dare maintain them. **1**
—**James Russell Lowell,** *The Present Crisis*, 1884

I am the inferior of any man whose rights I trample under foot. **2**
—**Robert G. Ingersoll,** *Prose Poems and Selections*, 1884

What I am interested in is having the government of the United States more concerned about human rights than about property rights. **3**
—**Woodrow Wilson,** speech in Minneapolis, Sept. 19, 1912

There is no such thing as rights anyhow. It is a question of whether you can put it over. In any legal sense or practical sense, whatever is, is "a right." **4**
—**Clarence Darrow,** debate on Prohibition, quoted in Kevin Tierney, *Darrow* [1979]

It is fair to judge peoples by the rights they will sacrifice the most for. **5**
—**Clarence Day,** *This Simian World*, 1920

I hold it the inalienable right of anybody to go to hell in his own way. **6**
—**Robert Frost,** speech, Berkeley, Calif., 1935

The rights of every man are diminished when the rights of one man are threatened. **7**
—**John F. Kennedy,** address to the nation, June 11, 1963

★ The president explained in this speech why he had federalized the Alabama National Guard in order to ensure that the University of Alabama would admit two black students. Gov. George C. Wallace, who had fulfilled a public vow to personally block the entrance to university's registration building, beat a retreat when Guardsmen arrived on the campus, and the students were registered that same evening

A right is not what someone gives you; it's what no one can take from you. **8**
—**Ramsey Clark,** in *The New York Times*, Oct. 2, 1977

The American idea is that government exists to protect, not to give, the most fundamental rights which, as Jefferson wrote . . . are "inalienable" because they exist independent of, and prior to, government. **9**
—**George F. Will**, *Speaking of Free Speech . . .*, in *Newsweek*, July 8, 1996

Roosevelt, Eleanor

See VIRTUE (Adlai Stevenson).

Roosevelt, Franklin Delano

Two-thirds mush and one-third Eleanor. **10**
—**Alice Roosevelt Longworth,** on her cousin F.D.R., quoted in George Wolfskill and John A. Hudson, *All but the People: Franklin D. Roosevelt and his Critics, 1933–39* [1969]

Meeting Roosevelt was like uncorking your first bottle of champagne. **11**
—**Winston Churchill,** quoted on *The American Experience* television show, Public Broadcasting System [March 17, 1995]

Roosevelt, Theodore

1 I don't think my name will mean much to the bear business, but you're welcome to use it.

—Theodore Roosevelt, letter to Morris Michtom of Brooklyn, New York, who asked permission to use the president's nickname for a line of toy stuffed bears, c. 1903

★ In November 1902, Roosevelt had refused to shoot a bear that had been run down by dogs and lassoed. A cartoon by Clifford Berryman made the incident instantly famous, and Roosevelt was dubbed Teddy Bear.

2 I am as strong as a bull moose.

—Theodore Roosevelt, letter to Sen. Mark Hanna, June 27, 1900

★ More at POLITICS & POLITICIANS.

3 Now look, that damned cowboy is president of the United States.

—Mark Hanna, remark to Hermann H. Kohlsaat, Sept. 16, 1901, quoted in Kohlsaat, *From McKinley to Harding* [1923]

★ This conversation took place in a Pullman railroad car shortly after the train pulled out of Buffalo, N.Y., where President McKinley, shot on September 6, had died two days before. Hanna—Marcus Alonzo Hanna, in full—an Ohio industrialist, Republican Party power broker, U.S. Senator, and manager of McKinley's successful 1896 presidential campaign, had agreed only grudgingly to T.R.'s nomination for the vice presidency in 1900—mainly, it was said, to get rid of "that wild man." With Kohlsaat's discreet intercession, Hanna and the president reached a working accommodation that lasted until Hanna's death in 1904.

4 An interesting combination of St. Vitus and St. Paul.

—John Morley, description of Roosevelt

★ Morley, British statesman and author, also remarked when Roosevelt was president, "The two outstanding natural phenomena of America are Niagara Falls and Theodore Roosevelt," quoted in Mark Sullivan, *Our Times*, Vol. II, 1927.

5 He was pure act.

—Henry Adams, *The Education of Henry Adams*, 1907

★ Adams wrote in full, "Roosevelt, more than any other man living within the range of notoriety, showed the singular primitive quality . . . that medieval theology assigned to God—he was pure act."

6 A charlatan of the very highest skill.

—H. L. Mencken, *Prejudices: Second Series*, 1920

7 He was a walking day of judgment.

—John Burroughs, in *Forest and Stream*, Jan. 1928

★ The comment was made with affection.

8 He wanted to be the bride at every wedding and the corpse at every funeral.

—Nicholas Roosevelt, *A Front Row Seat*, 1953

Rulers

See HIGH POSITION: RULERS & LEADERS.

Rumor

Rumor travels faster, but it don't stay put as long as truth. **1**
—Will Rogers, *Politics Getting Ready to Jell*, in *The Illiterate Digest*, 1924

So the rumors are true? **2**
Rumors are always true. You know that.
—Michael Tolkin, *The Player*, screenplay, 1992

★ Especially in Hollywood. Tolkin also wrote the novel on which the movie was based. Robert Altman directed.

All truths begin as hearsay. **3**
—Matt Drudge, speech, National Press Club., Washington, D.C., June 2, 1998

Russia

See NATIONS.

Ruthlessness

See also DANGER & DANGEROUS PEOPLE; EXPEDIENCY; REVOLUTION; STRENGTH & TOUGHNESS; VIOLENCE;

The cat in gloves catches no mice. **4**
—Benjamin Franklin, *Poor Richard's Almanack*, Feb. 1754

When you strike at a king you must kill him. **5**
—Ralph Waldo Emerson, attributed

★ According to *Bartlett's*, this was recalled by Oliver Wendell Holmes, Jr., and quoted in Max Lerner, *The Mind and Faith of Justice Holmes*, 1943. Emerson penned a slightly longer version of the same thought as a *Journal* entry in September 1843: "Never strike a king unless you are sure you shall kill him."

When you see a rattlesnake poised to strike, you do not wait until he has struck **6**
before you crush him.
—Franklin D. Roosevelt, fireside radio talk, Sept. 11, 1941

★ A justification for so-called preventive war. The strategy was, in fact, not used by the U.S., and three months later, Japan attacked Pearl Harbor. See WORLD WAR II.

Safety

See SECURITY & SAFETY.

Sailing & Sailors

See MILITARY, THE; SHIPS & SAILING.

Scandinavia

See NATIONS.

Scepticism

See SKEPTICISM.

Science

1 Every science has for its basis a system of principles as fixed and unalterable as those by which the universe is regulated and governed. Man cannot make principles; he can only discover them.

—**Tom Paine,** *The Age of Reason*, 1794

2 Nature tells every secret once.

—**Ralph Waldo Emerson,** *Behavior*, in *The Conduct of Life*, 1860

3 "Faith" is a fine invention
When Gentlemen can see—
But *Microscopes* are prudent
In an Emergency.

—**Emily Dickinson,** poem no. 185, c. 1860

4 Men love to wonder, and that is the seed of our science.

—**Ralph Waldo Emerson,** *Works and Days*, in *Society and Solitude*, 1870

5 Science is a first-rate piece of furniture for a man's upper chamber, if he has common sense on the ground-floor.

—**Oliver Wendell Holmes, Sr.,** *The Poet at the Breakfast-Table*, 1872

6 To be a Naturalist is better than to be a King.

—**William Beebe,** journal entry, 1893

★ Beebe was 16 when he made this entry. He went on to become the most celebrated popularizer of science in his day, as well as an important naturalist and explorer. He advised Theodore Roosevelt on the preservation of species and habitats and was a mentor to Rachel Carson.

7 There's always wan encouragin' thing about th' sad scientific facts that come out ivry week in th' pa-apers. They're usually not thrue.

—**Finley Peter Dunne,** *On the Descent of Man*, in *Mr. Dooley on Making a Will*, 1919

8 The outcome of any serious research can only be to make two questions grow where only one grew before.

—**Thorstein Veblen,** *The Place of Science in Modern Civilization*, 1919

9 No one but a theorist believes his theory; everyone puts faith in a laboratory result but the experimenter himself.

—**Albert Einstein,** remark, 1922, from an interview with Dr. Herman A. Mark in the *Jerusalem Post*, March 22, 1979, and cited in Peter L. Galison, *Einstein's Compass*, in *Scientific American* [Sept. 2004]

Familiar things happen, and mankind does not bother about them. It requires a very unusual mind to undertake the analysis of the obvious. 1

—**Alfred North Whitehead,** *Science and the Modern World*, 1925

Every science begins as philosophy and ends as art. 2

—**Will Durant,** *The Story of Philosophy*, 1926

★ Contemporaneously, new fields of science were struggling to come of age—quantum physics, psychology, and anthropology. The last was dismissed by the influential American lawyer and racist Madison Grant as "the gossip of natives." His chief opponent was struggling anthropologist Franz Boas. In the short run, Grant triumphed with the passage of the strict exclusionary immigration bill of 1924. See Calvin Coolidge at AMERICA & AMERICANS.

Every great advance in science has issued from a new audacity of imagination. 3

—**John Dewey,** *The Quest for Certainty*, 1929

Theory like mist on eyeglasses. Obscure facts. 4

—**Earl Derr Biggers,** *Charlie Chan in Egypt*, 1935

★ Biggers published six mystery stories between 1925 and 1932 featuring Charlie Chan. Having a Chinese-American as a detective hero was something of a departure at a time when Asian males typically were portrayed as villians or houseboys. The novels were well received but it was the series of Charlie Chan movies—more than forty in all beginning in 1926—that made the character famous. Those from the 1930s and early 1940s, including this 1935 film, starring Warner Oland, are the best of the lot.

Most of the fundamental ideas of science are essentially simple, and may, as a rule, be expressed in a language comprehensible to anyone. 5

—**Albert Einstein,** with Leopold Infeld, *The Evolution of Physics*, 1938

Science must enter into the consciousness of the people. 6

—**Albert Einstein,** remarks, opening day of New York World's Fair, April 39, 1939

★ See also Einstein below.

Every chaos is a wrong appearance. 7

—**Kurt Gödel,** saying, quoted in Jim Holt, *Time Bandits* in *The New Yorker* [Feb. 28, 2005]

★ Everything has a hidden order or motive. Gödel was a great mathematician and inclined toward paranoia.

I am become Death, the shatterer of worlds. 8

—**J. Robert Oppenheimer,** quoting from the *Bhagavad Gita* at the test of the first atom bomb, July 16, 1945, in N. P. Davis, *Lawrence and Oppenheimer,* [1986]

★ See also Martin Luther King, Jr., at SCIENCE: TECHNOLOGY.

In some sort of crude sense which no vulgarity, no humor, no overstatement can quite extinguish, the physicists have known sin; and this is a knowledge that they cannot lose. 9

—**J. Robert Oppenheimer**, *Physics in the Contemporary World*, lecture, Massachussetts Institute of Technology, Nov. 25, 1947

1 The self-fulfilling prophecy is, in the beginning, a *false* definition of the situation evoking a new behavior which makes the originally false conception come *true*. The specious validity of the self-fulfilling prophecy perpetuates a reign of error.

—**Robert K. Merton,** *The Self-Fulfilling Prophecy*, 1948

★ Merton was one of the founders of the sociology of science, and had the unusual distinction in his field of being admired both by academics and a much wider audience. An example of a self-fulfilling prophecy would be a case in which a teacher is told *falsely* that a group of students is exceptionally talented (or dull); experiments show that the teacher is likely then to treat the students in such a way that they actually display exceptional talent (or lack of it).

2 The degradation of the position of the scientist as independent worker and thinker to that of a morally irresponsible stooge in a science-factory has proceeded even more rapidly and devastatingly than I had expected.

—**Norbert Wiener,** in *Bulletin of the Atomic Scientists*, Nov. 4, 1948

3 You imagine that I look back on my life's work with calm satisfaction, but from nearby it looks quite different. There is not a single concept of which I am convinced it will stand firm, and I feel uncertain whether I am in general on the right track.

—**Albert Einstein,** letter to Maurice Solovine, March 28, 1949

4 The whole of science is nothing more than a refinement of everyday thinking.

—**Ibid.**

5 Science is the attempt to make the chaotic diversity of our sense-experience correspond to a logically uniform system of thought.

—**Albert Einstein,** *Out of My Later Years*, 1950

6 Science is the search for truth.

—**Linus Pauling,** *No More War!*, 1958

7 I am sorry to say that there is too much point to the wisecrack that life is extinct on other planets because their scientists were more advanced than ours.

—**John F. Kennedy,** speech, Dec. 11, 1959

8 In science, the excellent is not just better than the ordinary; it is almost all that matters.

—**U.S. President's Science Advisory Committee,** *Scientific Progress, the Universities and the Federal Government*, 1960

9 To solve any problem that has not been solved before, you have to leave the door to the unknown ajar. You have to permit the possibility that you do not have it exactly right.

—**Richard P. Feynman,** lecture, April, 1963, in Feynman, *The Meaning of It All* [1998]

★ See also Feynman at SKEPTICISM.

10 If all else fails, immortality can be assured by spectacular error.

—**John Kenneth Galbraith,** *Money: Whence It Came, Where It Went,* 1975

The pleasure of discovery in science derives not only from the satisfaction of new explanations but also, if not more so, from fresh (and often more difficult) puzzles that the novel solutions generate. 1

—**Stephen Jay Gould**, in *Natural History* magazine, Jan. 1991

★ See also Martin Luther King, Jr. at PROBLEMS.

Science [is] a candle in the dark. 2

—**Carl Sagan,** from subtitle of his book *The Demon-Haunted World: Science as a Candle in the Dark*, 1996

While natural selection drives Darwinian evolution, the growth of human culture is largely Lamarckian: new generations of humans inherit the acquired discoveries of generations past, enabling cosmic insight to grow slowly, but without limit. 3

—**Neil de Grasse Tyson**, *The Beginning of Science*, in *Natural History* magazine, Feb. 2001

Science: Biology & Physiology

See also DOCTORS & MEDICINE; HEALTH; NATURE (Brandeis).

Of physiology from top to toe I sing. 4

—**Walt Whitman,** *I Sing the Body Electric*, c. 1870

There is no more reason to believe that man descended from some inferior animal than there is to believe that a stately mansion has descended from a small cottage. 5

—**William Jennings Bryan,** in the Scopes "monkey" trial, Dayton, Tenn., July 28, 1925

★ High school teacher John Scopes was tried for teaching Darwin's theory of evolution. Bryan aided the prosecution and Clarence Darrow participated in the defense. The law under which Scopes was tried—and convicted—remained on the books in Tennessee until 1967.

Science is taking on a new aspect that is neither purely physical nor purely biological. It is becoming the study of organisms. Biology is the study of the larger organisms; whereas physics is the study of the smaller organisms. 6

—**Alfred North Whitehead,** *Science and the Modern World*, 1926

Amoebas at the start 7
Were not complex;
They tore themselves apart and started Sex.

—**Arthur Guiterman,** *Sex*

We wish to suggest a structure for the salt of deoxyribose nucleic acid (D.N.A). This structure has novel features which are of considerable biological interest. . . . It has not escaped our attention that the specific paring we have postulated immediately suggests a possible copying mechanism for the genetic material. 8

—**J. D. Watson & F. H. C. Crick,** *A Structure for Deoxyribose Nucleic Acid*, in *Nature*, April 25, 1953

★ The opening and closing lines of the anouncement of the twentieth century's most important biological discovery: the DNA double helix that carries hereditary information.

1 Human history is a fragment of biology. Man is one of countless millions of species and, like all the rest, is subject to the struggle for existence and the competition of the fittest to survive.

—**Will Durant,** *Heroes of History,* published posthumously [2001]

2 We live in evolutionary competition with microbes—bacteria and viruses. There is no guarantee that we will be the survivors.

—**Joshua Lederberg,** *Emerging Viruses, Emerging Threat,* in *Science*, Jan. 19, 1990

Science: Geology

3 Civilization exists by geological consent, subject to change without notice.

—**Will Durant,** attributed

★ This observation, quoted widely in course syllabi and other documents relating to geology, came to general attention following the devastating tsunami of 2005. The source has not, however, been found in Durant's writings. It may have been a remark or an anonymous compaction of ideas in his texts. Also George Will made a very similar remark. See below.

4 To the geologic eye, all the surface of the earth is a fluid form, and man moves upon it as insecurely as Peter walking on the waves to Christ.

—**Will & Ariel Durant,** *Lessons of History,* 1968

★ The chapter ("History and the Earth") concludes: "Man, not the earth, makes civilization."

5 Geology has joined biology in lowering mankind's self-esteem. Geology suggests how mankind's existence is contingent upon the geological consent of the planet.

—**George Will,** review of Simon Winchester's *Krakatoa,* 2003

Science: Mathematics & Statistics

6 The union of the mathematician with the poet, fervor with measure, passion with correctness, this surely is the ideal.

—**William James,** *Clifford's Lectures and Essays*, 1879

7 Figures won't lie, but liars will figure.

—**Charles H. Grosvenor,** saying

★ Rep. Grosvenor, Republican from Ohio, was referring to the process of predicting election outcomes. He may have had in mind Thomas Carlyle's comment, "A witty statesman said, you might prove anything by figures." At any rate, Grosvenor himself was a famous forecaster of presidential elections, which earned him the nickname "Old Figgers." Another whiz with figures was New York governor and Democratic presidential candidate Al Smith. "He could make statistics sit up, beg, roll over, and bark," said Robert Moses.

There are three kinds of lies: lies, damned lies, and statistics. 1
—**Mark Twain,** *Autobiography*, 1924

★ Twain said that he was quoting British statesman Benjamin Disraeli. The actual author is not known for certain.

The science of pure mathematics . . . may claim to be the most original creation of 2
the human spirit.
—**Alfred North Whitehead,** *Science and the Modern World*, 1925

Prayers for the condemned man will be offered on an adding machine. Numbers 3
constitute the only universal language.
—**Nathanael West,** *Miss Lonelyhearts*, 1933

I don't believe in mathematics. 4
—**Albert Einstein**, café conversation with Gustave Ferrière, in Denis Brian, *Einstein—A Life* [1996]

In mathematics, you don't understand things, you just get used to them. 5
—**John von Neumann,** observation, cited in Gary Zukav, *The Dancing Wu Li Masters* [1979]

★ This was von Neumann's reply to a young physicist who said he didn't understand the method that von Neumann suggested for solving a particularly knotty problem at the government's Los Alamos, New Mexico, laboratory, where von Neumann served as a consultant following World War II.

There's a lot we don't know about nothing. 6
—**John Baez,** in *How Is the Universe Built?* in *The New York Times,* Dec. 7, 1999

Science: Physics & Cosmology

See also Universe, the.

The world we live in is but thickened light. 7
—**Ralph Waldo Emerson,** *The Scholar*, 1883

The more important fundamental laws and facts of physical science have all been 8
discovered, and these are now so firmly established that the possibility of their ever being supplanted in consequence of new discoveries is exceedingly remote.
—**Albert Abraham Michelson,** dedication ceremony, Ryerson Physical Laboratory, University of Chicago, 1894

★ The work of Michelson, the first American to win a Nobel Prize in physics, paved the way for the Einsteinian revolution, beginning barely ten years after he spoke.

What is actual is actual only for one time 9
And only for one place.
—**T. S. Eliot,** *Ash Wednesday*, 1930

Physical concepts are free creations of the human mind, and are not, however it may 10
seem, uniquely determined by the external world.
—**Albert Einstein,** with Leopold Infeld, *The Evolution of Physics*, 1938

1 God does not play dice with the universe.

—Albert Einstein, saying, attributed

★ In Philipp Frank, *Einstein, His Life and Times*, 1947, the wording is given as, "I shall never believe that God plays dice with the world." Einstein here was objecting to the randomness at the heart of the theory of quantum mechanics, in which probabilities replace precise measurements and predictions. Werner Heisenberg's uncertainty principle states that one cannot determine both the momentum and position of a particle at any given time—which allows for all sorts of bizarre events, at least in theory. John Wheeler of Princeton University likes to tell students, "If you aren't confused by quantum physics, then you haven't really understood it." He ascribes this insight to Niels Bohr, the father of quantum physics. Bohr, however, was not moved by complaints about his theory. He responded to Einstein, "Nor is it our business to prescribe to God how he should run the world." See also Einstein at God, and Wheeler and Daniel Greenberger below.

2 There is nothing in the world except empty curved space. Matter, charge, electromagnetism, and other fields are only manifestations of the curvature of space.

—John A. Wheeler, 1957, quoted in *New Scientist* [Sept. 26, 1974]

3 There once was a twin brother named Bright
Who could travel faster than light.
He departed one day, in a relative way,
And came home on the previous night.

—Anonymous, *Newsweek*, Feb. 3, 1958

4 Neutrinos, they are very small.
They have no charge and have no mass
And do not interact at all.
The earth is just a silly ball
To them, through which they simply pass,
Like dustmaids down a drafty hall
Or photons through a sheet of glass.

—John Updike, *Cosmic Gall*, in *Telephone Poles and Other Poems*, 1963

★ Physicists have since rethought the no-mass proposition.Thus, when the theoretical physicist Murray Gell-Mann cited this poem in a lecture, he changed the second line to "scarcely interact at all."

5 There is no democracy in physics. We can't say that some second-rate guy has as much right to an opinion as Fermi.

—Luis Alvarez, in D. S. Greenberg, *The Politics of Pure Science*, 1967

6 More Is Different.

—Philip W. Anderson, article title, *Science*, 177, 1972

★ With great increases in complexity, new laws emerge.

7 A black hole has no hair.

—John A. Wheeler, *Gravitation*, with Charles W. Misner & Kip S. Thorne, 1973

★ The idea was that a black hole, with its immense gravitational force, sucks in everything within its event horizon and allows nothing to escape. No hair, no radiation, nothing exists in the vicinity of a black hole. But in 1974, British astrophysicist Stephen Hawking deduced that black holes emit a few whisps of hair, random particles. This only raised a new question because the randomness contradicted an important principle in quantum physics, namely that information cannot be obliterated (which randomness would do). Hawking and Kip Thorne of the California Institute of Technology made a famous bet with John Peskill of Cal Tech that "information swallowed by a black hole is forever hidden and can never be revealed." In the summer of 2004, some 30 years later, Hawking announced that his view had changed and he had lost the bet. He postulated that, "a black hole only appears to form but later opens up and releases information about what fell inside. So we can be sure of the past and predict the future." But the mathematics of this view and other efforts to solve the paradox have not yet proved satisfactory. See also Wheeler below.

There is in space a small black hole **1**
Through which, say our astronomers,
The whole damn thing, the universe,
Must one day fall. That will be all.

—**Howard Nemerov,** *Cosmic Comics*, 1975

Laws of thermodynamics: 1) You cannot win. 2) You cannot break even. 3) You cannot get out of the game. **2**

—**Anonymous,** in Alan L. Mackay, ed., *The Harvest of a Quiet Eye*, 1977

Einstein said that if quantum mechanics is right, then the world is crazy. Well, Einstein was right. The world is crazy. **3**

—**Daniel Greenberger,** quoted in John Horgan, *Quantum Philosophy*, in *Scientific American* magazine, July 1992

All material wants to return to its most stable form, chaos. **4**

—**William D. Wixom,** *The New York Times*, Apr. 21, 1998

★ Mr. Wixom's observation was inspired by the need to renovate the Cloisters in upper Manhattan, a project that he oversaw in his capacity as chairman of the department of medieval art at the Metropolitan Museum of Art.

We will first recognize how simple the universe is when we recognize how strange it is. **5**

—**John A. Wheeler,** saying, cited in *The New York Times*, Dec. 12, 2000

★ See also Wheeler above and below.

Gravity—it's not just a good idea. It's the Law. **6**

—**Anonymous,** popular bumper sticker, c. 2000, cited in *The New York Times* [Nov. 11, 2003]

It from bit. **7**

—**John A. Wheeler,** saying, quoted in Seth Lloyd and Y. Jack Ng, *Black Hole Computers* in *Scientific American*, [Nov. 2004]

★ In three words, Wheeler sums up the concept that the existence of an object and its information content (bits of information) are inextricably linked.

Science: Psychology

See also DREAMS & SLEEP (Emerson); MADNESS & SANITY; MIND, THOUGHT, & UNDERSTANDING.

1 I wished by treating psychology *like* a natural science, to help her become one.
—**William James,** *A Plea for Psychology as a Natural Science*, 1892

2 Psychology which explains everything
explains nothing,
and we are still in doubt.
—**Marianne Moore,** *Marriage*, in *Collected Poems*, 1951

3 Cured, I am frizzled, stale, and small.
—**Robert Lowell,** *Home After Three Months Away*, 1959

4 All neurotics are petty bourgeois. Madmen are the aristocrats of mental illness.
—**Mary McCarthy,** *The Group*, 1963

5 Any man who goes to a psychiatrist should have his head examined.
—**Samuel Goldwyn,** quoted in Norman Zierold, *Moguls*, 1969

★ But the provenance of many Goldwyn quotes is somewhat dubious; see the note on him at LANGUAGE & WORDS.

6 Of course, behaviorism "works." So does torture.
—**W. H. Auden,** *A Certain World*, 1970

7 I'm O.K.—You're O.K.
—**Thomas Harris**, book title, 1969

8 If you talk to God, you are praying. If God talks to you, you have schizophrenia.
—**Thomas Szasz,** *Emotions*, in *The Second Sin*, 1973

9 Depression is the common cold of mental illness.
—**The New York Times**, May 14, 1986

10 I've spent fifteen years in therapy. One more year, and I'm going to Lourdes.
—**Woody Allen,** quoted by Charles Krauthammer, *Weekly Standard*, May 6, 1996

Science: Technology

See also MEDIA; MODERN TIMES; PROGRESS.

11 Railroad iron is a magician's rod, in its power to evoke the sleeping energies of land and water.
—**Ralph Waldo Emerson,** *The American Scholar*, first delivered at the Phi Beta Kappa Society, Harvard University, August 31, 1837, in *Essays: First Series*, 1841

The advancement of the arts, from year to year, taxes our credulity and seems to presage the arrival of that period when human improvement must end. 1

—**Henry L. Ellsworth,** report to Congress from the Patent Office, 1843

★ This seems to be the source of the story that a commissioner of the patent office once resigned because there was nothing left to invent. In context, Commissioner Ellsworth's comment seems to have been ironical. He did not resign.

What hath God wrought! 2

—**Samuel F. B. Morse,** electric telegraph message, May 24, 1844

★ This biblical quotation, from *Numbers* 23:23, was suggested to Morse by Annie Ellsworth, daughter of the U.S. Commissioner of Patents. The occasion was the formal opening of the first telegraph line, between Washington and Baltimore. Other messages had been sent earlier. On May 1, when the line from Washington extended only to Annapolis Junction, a colleague of Morse telegraphed to Washington the surprising news that the Whig national convention in Baltimore had picked an unknown, Theodore Frelinghuysen, to run for vice president with Henry Clay in the national election that fall. When Morse read the message in the Capitol, "The ticket is Clay and Frelinghuysen," many people refused to believe it. Even after the news was confirmed by convention delegates returning to Washington by train, some who doubted that the new invention really worked suggested that Morse had just made a lucky guess.

Is it fact, or have I dreamt it—that, by means of electricity, the world of matter has become a great nerve, vibrating thousands of miles in a breathless point of time. 3

—**Nathaniel Hawthorne,** *The House of the Seven Gables*, 1851

Our inventions are wont to be pretty toys, which distract our attention from serious things. They are but improved means to an unimproved end. 4

—**Henry David Thoreau,** *Walden*, 1854

★ Thoreau also wrote in *Walden*, "We do not ride on the railroad; it rides upon us." And see Thoreau at COMMUNICATION and in the next quote below.

Men have become the tools of their tools. 5

—**Henry David Thoreau,** *Economy*, in *Walden*, 1854

Have you heard of the wonderful one-hoss shay, 6
That was built in such a logical way
It ran a hundred years to the day?

—**Oliver Wendell Holmes, Sr.,** *The Deacon's Masterpiece*, in *The Autocrat of the Breakfast-Table*, 1858

As for the Yankees, they have no other ambition than to take possession of this new continent [the moon], and to plant upon the summit of its highest elevation the star-spangled banner of the United States. 7

—**Jules Verne,** *From the Earth to the Moon*, 1865

Mr. Watson, come here, I want to see you. 8

—**Alexander Graham Bell,** to his assistant, Thomas A. Watson, March 10, 1876

★ These were the first words communicated by telephone. The message was sent in Bell's laboratory-lodgings in Boston. Bell was in the bedroom and Watson, his assistant, in the laboratory down the hall, with two closed doors between them. See also Edison below.

1 Hello!

—**Thomas Alva Edison,** letter to T.B.A. David, August 15, 1877

★ The first telephone lines were constantly open, necessitating a signal or greeting of some sort to get the attention of the other party. Alexander Graham Bell (see above) favored the nautical "Ahoy," but Edison's suggestion quickly won out. The 1877 letter in which Edison proposed "hello," which "can be heard ten to twenty feet away," to Mr. David, president of the Central District and Printing Co. in Pittsburgh, was discovered in AT&T archives in 1993 by Allen Koenigsburg, a professor at Brooklyn College in New York.

2 Success. Four flights Thursday morning all against twenty-one mile wind. Started from level with engine power alone. Average speed through air thirty-one miles. Longest fifty-seven seconds. Inform press. Home Christmas. Oreville [*sic*] Wright.

—**Wilbur Wright & Orville Wright,** telegram to their father, Bishop Milton Wright of Dayton, Ohio, from Kitty Hawk, N.C., Dec. 17, 1903

3 [The automobile] is a picture of the arrogance of wealth. . . . Nothing has spread socialist feeling more than the use of the automobile.

—**Woodrow Wilson,** 1906

★ Wilson was president of Princeton at this time. This remark was cited in *Goggles & Side Curtains* by Gerald Carson, *American Heritage*, April 1967.

4 To George F. Babbitt . . . his motor-car was poetry and tragedy, love and heroism.

—**Sinclair Lewis,** *Babbitt*, 1922

5 People can have the model T in any color—so long as it's black.

—**Henry Ford,** quoted in Allan Nevins, with Frank Ernest Hill, *Ford*, v. 2, 1957

6 In the past human life was lived in a bullock cart; in the future it will be lived in an aeroplane; and the change of speed amounts to a difference in quality.

—**Alfred North Whitehead,** *Science and the Modern World*, 1925

7 Bridges are America's cathedrals.

—**Anonymous,** in *Respectfully Quoted: A Dictionary of Quotations Requested from the Congressional Research Service*, Suzy Platt, ed., Library of Congress [1989]

★ American bridges have inspired awe and affection. In *American Heritage* (Dec. 1973) an unnamed staff writer described bridges as "those gaunt and wistful structures on whose weathered surfaces can be read so much of our history." See also Hart Crane and Langston Hughes below.

8 O sleepless as the river under thee,
Vaulting the sea, the prairies' dreaming sod,
Unto us lowliest sometime sweep, descend
And of the curveship lend a myth to God.

—**Hart Crane,** *To Brooklyn Bridge*, in *The Bridge*, 1930

De railroad bridge's 1
A sad song in the air.
—**Langston Hughes,** *Homesick Blues*

The clock, not the steam engine, is the key-machine of the modern industrial age. 2
—**Lewis Mumford,** *Technics and Civilization*, 1934

The machine yes the machine 3
never wastes anybody's time
never watches the foreman
never talks back.
—**Carl Sandburg,** *The People, Yes*, 1936

The Italian Navigator has reached the New World. 4
—**Arthur Holly Compton,** telephone message to James B. Conant, Dec. 2, 1942

★ With this coded message on an unsecure phone, Dr. Compton announced the dawning of the Atomic Age. The "navigator" was Enrico Fermi, leader of a team of physicists that had just produced the first self-sustaining nuclear chain reaction. The test was conducted in a reactor assembled in a squash court beneath the football stadium of the University of Chicago. Continuing the coded conversation, Dr. Conant, head of the National Defense Research Committee, asked, "And how did he find the Natives?" "Very friendly," Compton replied. The conversation was reported by Laura Fermi in a memoir, *Atoms in the Family* (1955). See also Fermi at NATURE.

Three fundamental Rules of Robotics. . . . one, a robot may not injure a human 5
being, or, through inaction, allow a human being to come by harm. Two, a robot must obey the orders given it by human beings, except where such orders would conflict with the first law. And three, a robot must protect its own existence, as long as such protection does not conflict with the First or Second Laws.
—**Isaac Asimov,** *Run Around* in *Astounding Science*, March 1942, reprinted in *I, Robot* [1950]

★ Evidently this was the first use of the term "robotics."

Everything in life is somewhere else, and you get there in a car. 6
—**E. B. White,** *Fro-Joy*, in *One Man's Meat*, 1944

We are here to make a choice between the quick and the dead. 7
—**Bernard Baruch,** introducing plan for international control of atomic energy, United Nations Atomic Energy Commission, June 14, 1946

★ See also PEACE.

Do not fold, spindle, or mutilate. 8
—**Anonymous,** instructions on punched cards used with early computers, from the 1950s

★ The punched cards—flexible and hence called software—were devised by a statistician, Dr. Herman Hollerith, for tabulating the 1890 census, which otherwise would not have been finished before the next one was conducted in 1900. Sensing that his automated accounting system might have commercial applications, he set up the

Computing-Tabulating-Recording Co. Through mergers, this firm evolved into International Business Machines, while the cards, using "Hollerith Coding," became known generically as "IBM cards." Without Hollerith's cards, it would not have been possible for Frederick Jackson Turner to discern in 1893 the end of a significant epoch in American history; see Turner at THE FRONTIER.

1 Garbage in, garbage out.

—**Anonymous,** 1950s

★ A succinct explanation of why computer findings may be errant, sometimes summarized in the acronymn *gigo*. A related aphorism from the same period is: "To err is human, but to really foul things up requires a computer."

2 The automobile changed our dress, manners, social customs, vacation habits, the shape of our cities, consumer purchasing patterns, common tastes, and positions in intercourse.

—**John Keats,** *The Insolent Chariots*, 1958

3 The "control of nature" is a phrase conceived in arrogance, born of the Neanderthal age of biology and the convenience of man.

—**Rachel Carson,** *Silent Spring*, 1962

4 Our scientific power has outrun our spiritual power. We have guided missiles and misguided men.

—**Martin Luther King, Jr.,** *Strength to Love*, 1963

★ See also Gen. Omar Bradley and Albert Einstein at MODERN TIMES, and J. Robert Openheimer at SCIENCE above.

5 That's one small step for [a] man, one giant leap for mankind.

—**Neil A. Armstrong,** disembarking from the Eagle moon lander, July 20, 1969

★ "A man" is the wording in the official version of the Apollo 11 mission. But according to recordings of this moment—the first step on the moon—the "a" was lost in transmission. This first moon landing, which incidentally fulfilled Jules Verne's prediction of 1865 (see above), bordered on the miraculous. But some observers, for various reasons, stood apart from the general enthusiasm. W. H. Auden wrote, "The moon is a desert. I have seen deserts." Later, conspiracy theorists abroad and at home developed the idea that the entire venture was faked.

6 Here men from the planet Earth first set foot on the moon, July 1969 A.D. We came in peace for all mankind.

—**NASA (National Aeronautic and Space Administration),** plaque on the moon

★ For a moon flight that went wrong, see James A. Lovell, Jr., at AMERICAN HISTORY: MEMORABLE MOMENTS.

7 The real problem is not whether machines think but whether men do.

—**B. F. Skinner,** *Contingencies of Reinforcement*, 1969

8 Old elephants limp off to the hills to die; old Americans go out to the highway and drive themselves to death with huge cars.

—**Hunter S. Thompson,** *Fear and Loathing in Las Vegas*, 1972

A motorcycle functions entirely in accordance with the laws of reason, and a study of the art of motorcycle maintenance is really a miniature study of the art of rationality itself. 1

—**Robert Pirsig,** *Zen and the Art of Motorcycle Maintenance*, 1974

★ Pirsig objected to the "barriers of dualistic thought that prevent a real understanding of what technology is—not an exploitation of nature, but a fusion of nature and the human spirit into a new kind of creation that transcends both," *ibid*. See also GOD.

If true computer music were ever written, it would be listened to only by other computers. 2

—**Michael Crichton,** *Electronic Life: How to Think About Computers*, 1983

For a successful technology, reality must take precedence over public relations, for Nature cannot be fooled. 3

—**Richard P. Feynman,** appendix to presidential commission report on the explosion of the space shuttle *Challenger* following a cold-weather liftoff, Jan. 28, 1986

★ Feynman, a Nobel Prize winner and one of the most imaginative and charming of modern physicists, served on the presidential panel that investigated the *Challenger* disaster, in which all seven crew members were killed. Cutting through the ponderous, defensive, televised proceedings, Feynman dropped into a glass of ice water a sample of the rubber used for the O-ring seals that connected segments of the booster rockets. This demonstrated on the spot that cold destroyed the material's resiliency. Not for another month, however, did NASA concede that joint failure was the most likely cause of the explosion.

Thanks to modern technology . . . history now comes equipped with a fast-forward button. 4

—**Gore Vidal,** *Screening History*, 1992

Beware the technological juggernaut, reckon the terrible costs, understand the worlds being lost in the world being gained, reflect on the price of the machine and its systems in your life, pay attention to the natural world and its increasing destruction, resist the seductive catastrophe of industrialism. 5

—**Kirkpatrick Sale,** *Rebels Against the Future: Lessons for the Computer Age*, 1995

We don't have the option of turning away from the future. No one gets to vote on whether technology is going to change our lives. 6

—**Bill Gates,** *The Road Ahead,* 1995

Never send a human to do a machine's job. 7

—**Andy & Larry Wachowski ("The Wachowski Brothers"),** line for Agent Smith, *The Matrix* 1999,

You Get What You Measure. 8

—**"Sharky,"** title of Shark Tank column, *Computer World,* June 30, 2003

★ A saying indicating that results in a computer analysis will be skewed according to what you measure. See a similar, anonymous quote at ECONOMICS.

Seas

See NATURE: SEAS & OCEANS.

Seasons & Times

See also MODERN TIMES; NATURE: SEASONS; TIME

1 There is a fullness of time when men should go, and not occupy too long the ground to which others have a right to advance.
—**Thomas Jefferson,** letter to Dr. Benjamin Rush, 1811

2 You must remember this, a kiss is just a kiss,
A sigh is just a sigh;
The fundamental things apply,
As time goes by.
—**Herman Hupfield,** *As Times Goes By*, 1931

★ The song was featured in the 1942 film, *Casablanca*; see ART: MUSIC.

3 Death and taxes and childbirth! There's never any convenient time for any of them!
—**Margaret Mitchell,** *Gone with the Wind*, 1936

4 There's a time in every man's life, and I've had plenty of them.
—**Charles Dillon "Casey" Stengel,** quoted in the Ken Burns television series *Baseball*, part IV, 1994

5 The time to repair the roof is when the sun is shining.
—**John F. Kennedy,** State of the Union address, 1962

★ The thought is proverbial. "Thatch your roof before rainy weather" is a variant, dated to the nineteenth century but probably a lot older, included in *A Dictionary of American Proverbs* (1992).

Secrets

See also SECURITY & SAFETY.

6 Three may keep a secret, if two of them are dead.
—**Benjamin Franklin,** *Poor Richard's Almanack*, July 1735

7 Everyone is a moon, and has a dark side which he never shows to anybody.
—**Mark Twain,** *Pudd'nhead Wilson's New Calendar*, in *Following the Equator*, 1897

8 Secrecy necessarily breeds suspicion.
—**Louis D. Brandeis,** letter to Cyrus Adler, August 10, 1915

9 We dance round in a ring and suppose,
But the Secret sits in the middle and knows.
—**Robert Frost,** *The Secret Sits*, in *The Witness Tree*, 1942

While all deception requires secrecy, all secrecy is not meant to deceive. **1**
—**Sissela Bok,** *Secrets*, 1983

Men with secrets tend to be drawn to each other . . . because they need the company **2**
of the like-minded, the fellow afflicted.
—**Don DeLillo,** *Libra*, 1988

Absolute secrecy corrupts absolutely. **3**
—**Fred Hitz,** interview, *The New York Times*, July 30, 1995

★ Hitz, the Inspector General of the CIA, adapted Lord Acton's classic, "Power tends to corrupt, and absolute power corrupts absolutely," letter to Bishop Mandell Creighton, April 5, 1887. For other variations on this theme, see Hoffer at FAITH and Perot at POWER.

Security & Safety

See also PRIVACY; SECRETS; TALK (Anonymous).

He that's secure is not safe. **4**
—**Benjamin Franklin,** *Poor Richard's Almanack*, August 1748

There is no safety in numbers, or in anything else. **5**
—**James Thurber,** *The Fairly Intelligent Fly*, in *The New Yorker*, Feb. 4, 1939

There is no home here. There is no security in your mansions or your fortresses, your **6**
family vaults or your banks or your double beds. Understand this fact, and you will
be free. Accept it, and you will be happy.
—**Christopher Isherwood,** *Los Angeles*, 1947, in *Exhumations* [1966]

★ Isherwood is speaking of California, "this untamed, undomesticated, aloof, prehistoric landscape which relentlessly reminds the traveler of his human condition and the circumstances of his tenure upon the earth."

My only solution for the problem of habitual accidents . . . is to stay in bed all day. **7**
Even then, there is always the chance you may fall out.
—**Robert Benchley,** *Safety Second,* in *Chips off the Old Benchley*, 1949

Security is like liberty in that many are the crimes that are committed in its name. **8**
—**Robert H. Jackson,** dissenting opinion in *U.S. v. Shaughnessy*, 1950

Carelessness about our security is dangerous; carelessness about our freedom is also **9**
dangerous.
—**Adlai Stevenson,** speech, Oct. 7, 1952

Most people want security in this world, not liberty. **10**
—**H. L. Mencken,** *Minority Report: H. L. Mencken's Notebooks* [1956]

Unsafe at any speed. **11**
—**Ralph Nader,** *Unsafe at Any Speed*, book title, 1965

★ Mr. Nader's exposé of the flaws in automobile manufacturing led to passage by congress of the traffic and motor vehicle safety act of 1966. It also provided the seed money, after General Motors settled a suit for siccing prvate detectives on him, for Mr. Nader's activities on behalf of consumers over the next forty years or so.

1 Safety has really killed all our business.
—Lee Iacocca, complaint to Pres. Richard Nixon, 1971

★ Iacocca and Henry Ford II were lobbying privately against safety rules. They were caught on the White House tape recorder. Nixon responded by delaying all new federal safety regulations.

2 The guarding of military and diplomatic secrets at the expense of informed representative government provides no real security for our Republic.
—Hugo Black, *New York Times v. United States*, 1971

★ This was the Pentagon Papers case in which the court ruled 6-3 (with each judge writing an opinon) that the government could not halt publication of the massive history of U.S. involvement in southeast Asia that had been leaked to the press by Daniel Ellsberg.

3 If the national security is involved, anything goes. There are no rules.
—Helen Gahagan Douglas, quoted in *Ms.*, Oct. 1973

4 When America is stronger, the world is safer.
—George H. W. Bush, address to congress, Feb. 9, 1989

5 The best homeland security is the kind where we get the enemy before he gets us.
—Tom Ridge, remark to Jay Leno, *The Tonight Show*, Nov. 22, 2002

★ Mr. Ridge was the first director of the Department of Homeland Security.

Self

See also SELF-RELIANCE

6 Trust thyself: every heart vibrates to that iron string.
—Ralph Waldo Emerson, *Self-Reliance*, in *Essays: First Series*, 1841

7 Nothing can bring you peace but yourself. Nothing can bring you peace but the triumph of principles.
—Ibid.

★ The last sentences of this classic essay.

8 The Imp of the Perverse
—Edgar Allan Poe, story title, in *Graham's Lady's and Gentleman's Magazine (The Casket and Gentleman's United)*, July 1850

★ The Imp is the perverse human impulse to act in ways that are contrary to one's best interests—to procrastinate when delay means ruin, for example, or the temptation to jump from a height that is sure to result in one's death. The unwieldy publication title was the result of an 1841 merger of two previously independent magazines.

9 What other dungeon is so dark as one's own heart! What jailer so inexorable as one's self.
—Nathaniel Hawthorne, *The House of the Seven Gables*, 1851

I should not talk so much about myself if there were anybody else whom I knew as well. 1

—**Henry David Thoreau,** *Economy*, in *Walden*, 1854

I celebrate myself, and sing myself. 2

—**Walt Whitman,** *Song of Myself*, in *Leaves of Grass*, 1855

★ In celebrating himself, Whitman, did not exclude others. Thus the opening lines of this poem read: "I celebrate myself, / And what I assume you shall assume, / For every atom belonging to me as good belongs to you." For Whitman on contradicting himself, see CONSISTENCY.

I dote on myself, there is that lot of me and all so luscious. 3

—**Ibid.**

Not in the clamor of the crowded street, 4
Not in the shouts and plaudits of the throng,
But in ourselves, are triumph and defeat.

—**Henry Wadsworth Longfellow,** *The Poets*, 1876

To understand oneself is the classic form of consolation; to elude oneself is the romantic. 5

—**George Santayana,** *The Genteel Tradition in American Philosophy*, in *Winds of Doctrine*, 1913

I Yam What I Yam 6

—**Elzie Segar,** title, Popeye animated cartoon, released Sept. 29, 1933

★ The muscular sailor man first appeared in Segar's "Thimble Theater" comic strip on Jan. 17, 1929. He quickly edged other characters aside and went on to greater fame on the screen, following his debut on July 14, 1933, in "Popeye the Sailor." So great was Popeye's popularity during the depresssion of the 1930s that growers of spinach, the sailor's favorite food, credited him with saving their industry by increasing spinach consumption some 33%. Another famous Popeye quote: "That's all I can stands, I can't stands no more."

Men can starve from a lack of self-realization as much as they can from a lack of bread. 7

—**Richard Wright,** *Native Son*, 1940

I myself am hell. 8

—**Robert Lowell**, *Skunk Hour*, 1959

★ More at MADNESS.

If you want inner peace, find it in solitude, not speed, and if you would find yourself, look to the land from which you came and to which you go. 9

—**Stewart L. Udall,** *The Quiet Crisis*, 1963

People often say that this or that person has not yet found himself. But the self is not something one finds; it is something one creates. 10

—**Thomas Szasz,** *The Second Sin*, 1973

1 *I, I, I!*—a burden to be surrendered.
—**Tennessee Williams,** *Mes Cahiers Noirs*, diary, c. 1979

2 Part of me suspects that I'm a loser, and the other part of me thinks I'm God Almighty.
—**John Lennon,** to David Steff, interview with Lennon and Yoko Ono, *Playboy*, Jan. 1981

★ The interview was published a month after Lennon was shot to death in New York City.

3 In our society that is so self-absorbed, begin to look less at yourself and more at each other. Learn more about the face of your neighbor, and less about your own.
—**Sargent Shriver,** commencement address, Yale University, 1994

4 Self-knowledge is always bad news.
—**John Barth,** quoted by David Bouchier, *Morning Edition* radio show, National Public Radio, Dec. 12, 1994

5 You have to trust to your inner knowledge. If you have a clear mind and an open heart, you won't have to search for direction. Direction will come to you.
—**Phil Jackson,** with Hugh Delehanty, *Sacred Hoops: Spiritual Lessons of a Hardwood Warrior*, 1995

Self-Reliance

See also SELF.

6 God helps them that help themselves.
—**Benjamin Franklin,** *Poor Richard's Almanack*, June 1736

★ An old saying. Aesop, in *Hercules and the Waggoner*, expressed the same idea: "The gods help them that help themselves."

7 We will walk on our own feet; we will work with our own hands; we will speak our own minds.
—**Ralph Waldo Emerson,** *The American Scholar*, oration before the Phi Beta Kappa Society, Harvard University, August 31, 1837, reprinted in *Essays: First Series*, 1841

★ The above sentence immediately precedes the conclusion of Emerson's oration: "The study of letters shall no longer be a name for pity, for doubt, and for sensual indulgence. The dread of man and the love of man shall be a wall of defence and a wreath of joy around all. A nation of men will for the first time exist, because each believes himself inspired by the Divine Soul which also inspires all men."

8 Discontent is the want of self-reliance.
—**Ralph Waldo Emerson,** *Self-Reliance*, in *Essays: First Series*, 1841

★ More at UNHAPPINESS.

9 Voyager upon life's sea, to yourself be true,
And whate'er your lot may be, paddle your own canoe.
—**Anonymous,** *Harper's Monthly*, May 1854

★ This is the earliest known American example of "paddle your own canoe." The basic idea is ancient. Steering one's own boat was used as a metaphor for independence and self-reliance by Euripides in *Cyclops*, c. 440 B.C.

He was a self-made man who owed his lack of success to nobody. 1

—Joseph Heller, *Catch-22*, 1961

To me, the whole process of being a brushstroke in someone else's painting is a little difficult. 2

—Madonna, interview, *Vanity Fair*, April 1991

Serving One's Country

See also PATRIOTISM & THE FLAG.

The Moral Equivalent of War. 3

—William James, book title, 1910

★ James, a pacifist, believed in drafting young men into national service as the moral equivalent of war. See also James at PACIFISM & NONVIOLENCE and THE MILITARY.

And so my fellow Americans: ask not what your country can do for you—ask what you can do for your country. 4

—John F. Kennedy, Inaugural Address, Jan. 20, 1961

★ In his presidential nomination acceptance, Kennedy had said that he would be calling upon Americans to take action to help their country. See POLITICAL SLOGANS, note under Kennedy's New Frontier. The call to serve the nation in the great inaugural address was not entirely original with Pres. Kennedy. *Bartlett's* cites a number of predecessors, including a Memorial Day address by Oliver Wendell Holmes, Jr., in 1884: "We pause . . . to recall what our country has done for each of us, and to ask ourselves what we can do for our country in return." *The Oxford Dictionary of Quotations* found a similar exhortation in the funeral oration for John Greenleaf Whittier in 1892. Warren G. Harding, surprisingly, urged, "We must have a citizenship less concerned about what the government can do for it, and more anxious about what it can do for the nation," Republican National Convention, June 7, 1916. Kennedy advisor and biographer Arthur Schelsinger wrote in *A Thousand Days* (1965) that Kennedy, in 1945, had copied into a notebook an observation from Jean Jacques Rousseau: "As soon as any man says of the affairs of the state, 'What does it matter to me?' the state may be given up as lost." Historian Thurston Clarke reported in his book on the inaugural address (*Ask Not,* 2004) that Kennedy's prep school headmaster used to say, "[It's] not what Choate can do for you, but what you can do for Choate." The basic idea probably is proverbial. Thus, one of Robert Greene's guides to the Elizabethan underworld, *The Defence of Cony-Catching* (1592), includes the line, "*Nascimur pro patria*: We are born for the country."

I challenge a new generation of young Americans to a season of service. 5

—Bill Clinton, Inaugural Address, Jan. 20, 1993

Sex

See also LOVE; SCIENCE: PHYSIOLOGY & BIOLOGY (Guiterman); SIN, VICE, & NAUGHTINESS.

1 Eighth and lastly. They are so grateful!!
—**Benjamin Franklin,** letter to a young friend (sometimes identified as *Reasons for Preferring an Elderly Mistress*), June 25, 1745

2 Sex contains all, bodies, souls,
Meanings, proofs, purities, delicacies, results, promulgations,
Songs, commands, health, pride, the maternal mystery, the seminal milk,
All hopes, benefactions, bestowals, all the passions, loves,
beauties, delights of the earth.
—**Walt Whitman,** *A Woman Waits for Me*, 1856

3 I have an inalienable constitutional and natural right to love whom I may, to love as long or as short a period as I can, to change that love every day if I please!
—**Victoria Claflin Woodhull,** in *Woodhull and Claflin's Weekly*, Nov. 20, 1871

4 Higgamus hoggamus, woman's monogamous;
Hoggamus higgamus, men are polygamous.
—**Anonymous**

★ Apparently from the last part of the 19th century. On the issue of polygamy, in about 1925, Pres. Calvin Coolidge and his wife are said to have visited a poultry farm, separately and with different guides. Mrs. Coolidge asked how often the rooster performed his duty, and was told "several times a day." She replied, "Tell that to Mr. Coolidge." Upon receiving the news, the president asked whether the rooster always performed with the same hen, and was told, "No, each time with a different hen." The president responded, "Tell that to Mrs. Coolidge." This version of the story is courtesy of Kenneth Maxwell, *The Sex Imperative*.

5 Men seldom make passes
At girls who wear glasses.
—**Dorothy Parker,** *News Item*, in *Enough Rope*, 1927

6 He had that nameless charm, with a strong magnetism, which can only be called "It."
—**Elinor Glyn,** *It*, 1927

★ "It" is so thoroughly associated with women—Clara Bow, who starred in the movie made from Glyn's bestselling novel became famous as the "It Girl"—that people tend to forget the author herself did not limit the term by gender. "It" itself has been around for awhile, as evidenced by it's appearance in Kipling's *Traffics and Discoveries* (1904): "Tisn't beauty, so to speak, nor good talk, necessarily. It's just It. Some women stay in a man's memory if they once walk down a street."

7 Is Sex Necessary?
—**James Thurber & E. B. White,** book title, 1929

8 If you want to buy my wares / Follow me and climb the stairs . . . / Love for sale.
—**Cole Porter,** *Love for Sale*, in *The New Yorkers*, 1930

★ The Federal Communications Commission banned the song's lyrics from the nation's airwaves for many years. Playing the music alone was permissible. It was okay for listeners to sing along in the privacy of their homes and automobiles.

It's better to be looked over than overlooked. **1**

—Mae West, *Belle of the Nineties*, 1934

A laugh at sex is a laugh at destiny. **2**

—Thornton Wilder, *The Journals of Thornton Wilder*, 1939–1961

But did thee feel the earth move? **3**

—Ernest Hemingway, *For Whom the Bells Toll*, 1940

My big trouble is that I always think whoever I'm necking with is a pretty intelligent person. **4**

—J. D. Salinger, *The Catcher in the Rye*, 1951

★ The great novelist and poet Thomas Hardy suffered from a similar flaw according to biographer Martin Seymour-Smith: "The least sign of passion or sexual interest from a woman was enough to set him off into the belief that she must be capable of good writing," *Hardy*, 1994.

Years from now—when you talk about this—and you will!—be kind. **5**

—Robert Anderson, *Tea and Sympathy*, 1953

★ This, the last line of the play was spoken, originally, by Deborah Kerr, who is married, not happily, to a gung-ho football coach at an all-male prep school. She befriends a troubled student accused of being a homosexual (Tony Perkins followed John Kerr—no relation to Deborah Kerr—in the role).

Sex and obscenity are not synonymous. **6**

—William J. Brennan, Jr., *Roth v. United States*, 1957

★ For more from this decision, see Brennan at FREE SPEECH.

You mustn't force sex to do the work of love or love to do the work of sex. **7**

—Mary McCarthy, *The Group*, 1963

You show me a happy homosexual, and I'll show you a gay corpse. **8**

—Mart Crowley, *The Boys in the Band*, 1968

Is sex dirty? Only if it's done right. **9**

—Woody Allen, screenplay, *Everything You Always Wanted to Know About Sex*, 1972

I've looked on a lot of women with lust. I've committed adultery in my heart many times. This is something that God recognizes that I will do—and I have done it—and God forgives me for it. **10**

—Jimmy Carter, interview in *Playboy*, Oct. 1976

I hear America swinging, **11**
The carpenter with his wife or the mason's wife, or even the mason,

The mason's daughter in love with the boy next door, who is in love with the boy next door to him,
Everyone free, comrades in arms together, freely swinging.
—**Peter De Vries,** *I Hear America Swinging*, 1976

★ A takeoff, of course, on the Whitman poem; see AMERICA & AMERICANS.

1 Sex Is Never an Emergency.
—**Elaine Pierson,** title of guide for college students, 1971

★ The title in full is *Sex Is Never an Emergency: A Guide for the Young.*

2 Females have their own agenda.
—**Pascal Gagneux,** in *The New York Times,* May 27, 1997

★ Professor Gagneux of the University of California at San Diego was one of a team who reported in the science journal *Nature* the 54 percent of baby chimpanzees in a group being studied in the Tai forest in Ivory Coast were not fathered by any of the group's males. Despite the instant fame attached to this finding, subsequent studies have indicated that female chimps do not stray from home regularly. In 2001, a team led by Dr. Anne E. Pusey of the University of Minnesota corrected the earlier work. Nevertheless, the agenda of chimp females does seem to differ from that of the alpha males who attempt to dominate their sex lives. About half of all offspring are sired by lower-status but friendlier males.

3 Everybody lies about sex. People lie during sex. If it weren't for lies, there'd be no sex.
—**Jerry Seinfeld,** in *The New York Times,* Dec. 18, 1998

★ Comment on the then burning national question: Whether Pres. Bill Clinton should be impeached for lying about sex.

4 Success in the boardroom guarantees success in the bedroom.
—**Anonymous,** proverbial saying, *The New York Times, Week in Review* [July 11, 2004]

Ships & Sailing

See also BUSINESS (quote from John Woolman); MILITARY, THE (for the U.S.S. *Constitution*); NATURE: SEAS & OCEANS.

5 I wish to have no connection with any ship that does not sail *fast.*
—**John Paul Jones,** letter, Nov. 16, 1778

★ More at AMERICAN REVOLUTION.

6 There is not so helpless and pitiable an object in the world as a landsman beginning a sailor's life.
—**Richard Henry Dana, Jr.,** *Two Years Before the Mast*, 1840

7 He was a true sailor, every finger a fishhook.
—**Ibid.**

Christ save us all from a death like this. **1**
On the reef of Norman's Woe!
—Henry Wadsworth Longfellow, *The Wreck of the Hesperus*, 1841

★ This extremely popular poem was based on the 1839 shipwreck of the schooner *Hesperus* off Norman's Reef near Gloucester, Massachusetts. More than twenty bodies washed ashore.

You are freedom's swift-winged angels, that fly around the world. **2**
—Frederick Douglass, *Narrative of the Life of Frederick Douglass, An American Slave, Written by Himself*, 1845

Build me straight, O worthy Master! **3**
Staunch and strong, a goodly vessel.
—Henry Wadsworth Longfellow, *The Building of the Ship*, 1849

★ The reference is to the "ship of state." See AMERICA & AMERICANS.

A whale ship was my Yale College and my Harvard. **4**
—Herman Melville, *Moby-Dick*, 1851

I love to sail forbidden seas. **5**
—Ibid.

★ More at TRAVEL.

I remember the black wharves and the slips, **6**
And the sea-tides tossing free;
And the Spanish sailors with bearded lips,
And the beauty and majesty of the ships,
And the magic of the sea.
—Henry Wadsworth Longfellow, *My Lost Youth*, in *Putnam's Magazine*, August 1855

The wonder is always new that any sane man can be a sailor. **7**
—Ralph Waldo Emerson, *English Traits*, 1856

O Captain! my Captain! our fearful trip is done. **8**
—Walt Whitman, *O Captain! My Captain!*, 1865-66

★ More at ABRAHAM LINCOLN.

We said there warn't no home like a raft, after all. Other places do seem so cramped up and smothery, but a raft don't. You feel mighty free and easy and comfortable on a raft. **9**
—Mark Twain, *Huckleberry Finn*, 1885

Any man who has to ask about the annual upkeep of a yacht can't afford one. **10**
—John Pierpont Morgan, attributed

Ships at a distance have every man's wish on board. **11**
—Zora Neale Hurston, *Their Eyes Were Watching God*, 1937

Sickness

See ILLNESS & REMEDIES.

Silence

See also TALK.

1 Three silences there are: the first of speech,
The second of desire, the third of thought.
—Henry Wadsworth Longfellow, *The Three Silences of Molinos*, for John Greenleaf Whittier's 70th birthday, Dec. 18, 1877

2 We shall walk in velvet shoes:
Wherever we go
Silence will fall like dews
On white silence below.
—Elinor Hoyt Wylie, *Velvet Shoes*, 1921

3 It is a good practice to leave a few things unsaid.
—Elbert Hubbard, *The Roycroft Dictionary and Book of Epigrams*, 1923

4 Drawing on my fine command of language, I said nothing.
—Robert Benchley, *Chips off the Old Benchley*, 1949

5 Try as we may to make a silence, we cannot.
—John Cage, *Silence*, 1961

6 Nobody ever got in trouble keeping his mouth shut.
—Elmore Leonard, *52 Pick-up*, 1974

7 Only Talk When It Improves the Silence
—Chris Matthews, chapter title in *Hardball: How Politics Is Played—Told by One Who Knows the Game*, 1998

Simplicity

See also ART: AESTHETICS; ART: STYLE IN WRITING & EXPRESSION; COUNTRY LIFE & PEOPLE; GRACE.

8 A refined simplicity is the characteristic of all high bred deportment, in every country.
—James Fenimore Cooper, *The American Democrat*, 1838

9 Our life is frittered away by detail. . . . Simplify, simplify.
—Henry David Thoreau, *Where I Lived, and What I Lived For*, in *Walden*, 1854

★ Making the point at greater length in the same passage, Thoreau wrote: "Simplicity, simplicity, simplicity! I say, let your affairs be as two or three, and not a hundred or a thousand; instead of a million, count half a dozen, and keep your accounts on your thumb-nail."

I had three chairs in my house: one for solitude, two for friendship, three for society. **1**
—Henry David Thoreau, *Visitors,* in *Walden*, 1854

The art of art, the glory of expression, and the sunshine of the light of letters, is simplicity. **2**
—Walt Whitman, Preface, *Leaves of Grass*, 1855

Seek simplicity and distrust it. **3**
—Alfred North Whitehead, *The Concept of Nature*, 1920

★ Whitehead said that this should be "the guiding motto in the life of every natural philosopher."

Less is more. **4**
—Ludwig Mies van der Rohe, motto

★ For more information, see the note on Mies under ART: AESTHETICS.

The ability to simplify means to eliminate the unnecessary so that the necessary may speak. **5**
—Hans Hofmann, *Search for the Real*, 1930

Everything should be made as simple as possible, but not simpler. **6**
—Albert Einstein, quoted in *The Reader's Digest* [Oct. 1977]

★ The original source of this oft-quoted remark has not been found despite much searching. Alice Calaprice, editor of *The Expanded Quotable Einstein* (2000), speculated that it might be a paraphrase of one of Einstein's other statements about simplicity. Another possibility, she suggested, is that the quote is a version of the philosophical rule known as Ockham's Razor—in essence, one should always pick the simplest of competing theories or explanations—that has been mistakenly attributed over the years to Einstein.

The bare necessities, the simple bare necessities **7**
Forget about your worries and your strife.
—Terry Gilkyson, *The Bare Necessities*, in *The Jungle Book*, animated film, 1967

Kelly's Law: Nothing is ever as simple as it first seems. **8**
—Anonymous, *Farmer's Almanac*, 1978

★ If this particular Kelly ever existed, nothing is known about him.

No endeavor that is worthwhile is simple in prospect; if it is right, it will prove simple in retrospect. **9**
—Edward Teller, *The Pursuit of Simplicity*, 1980

It's just that simple. **10**
—H. Ross Perot, presidental campaign signature line, 1992

Sin, Vice, & Naughtiness

See also ALCOHOL & DRINKING; EPITAPHS & GRAVESTONES (Preston Sturges); EVIL; PLEASURE & HEDONISM; SEX; TEMPTATION.

1 Where there's marriage without love, there will be love without marriage.
—**Benjamin Franklin,** *Poor Richard's Almanack*, May 1734

2 What maintains one vice would bring up two children.
—**Benjamin Franklin,** *Poor Richard's Almanack*, Sept. 1747

3 Folks who have not vices have generally very few virtues.
—**Anonymous,** saying quoted by Abraham Lincoln as reported in F. B. Carpenter, *Six Months at the White House with Abraham Lincoln*, 1866

4 Sin travels faster than they that ride in chariots.
—**Charles Dudley Warner,** *My Summer in a Garden*, 1871

5 [In colonial New England] there was adultery in high places and adultery in low.
—**J. G. Holland,** *Everyday Topics*, 1876

★ More at NEW ENGLAND, in the note under the Giles Firmin quote.

6 We're poor little lambs who've lost our way.
Baa! Baa! Baa!
We're little black sheep who've gone astray,
Baa—aa—aa!
Gentleman rankers out on the spree,
Damned from here to eternity,
God ha' mercy on such as we,
Baa! Yah! Baa!
—**Rudyard Kipling,** *Gentlemen Rankers*, c. 1890

★ The Ballad is probably better known in America than in England. It is called here "The Whiffenpoof Song," after the Yale University singing group.

7 There is a Moral Sense, and there is an Immoral Sense. History shows us that the Moral Sense enables us to perceive morality and how to avoid it, and that the Immoral Sense enables us to perceive Immorality and how to enjoy it.
—**Mark Twain,** Epigraph, *Following the Equator: A Journey Around the World*, 1897

8 There is a charm about the forbidden that makes it unspeakably desirable.
—**Mark Twain,** *Mark Twain's Notebook*, Albert Bigelow Paine, ed. [1935]

9 The probable fact is that we are descended not only from monkeys but from monks.
—**Elbert Hubbard,** *The Roycroft Dictionary and Book of Epigrams*, 1923

10 We are punished by our sins, not for them.
—**Elbert Hubbard,** *The Note Book* [1927]

"Goodness, what beautiful diamonds!" **1**
"Goodness had nothing to do with it, dearie."
—**Mae West,** *Diamond Lil*, 1928

★ The same joke is in West's 1932 debut movie *Night After Night*. The line was one of her favorites, and she titled her autobiography, *Goodness Had Nothing to Do with It*, 1959.

When I'm good, I'm very, very good, but when I'm bad, I'm better. **2**
—**Mae West,** *I'm No Angel*, 1933

I used to be Snow White—but I drifted. **3**
—**Mae West,** quoted in Joseph Weintraub, *The Wit and Wisdom of Mae West* [1967]

★ An improvement on "She was pure as the driven snow, but she drifted,"characterized as a cliché as far back as 1940 by folklorist Harold W. Thompson in *Body, Boots, and Britches*.

Enjoyed it! One more drink and I'd have been under the host. **4**
—**Dorothy Parker,** on being asked if she'd enjoyed a cocktail party, quoted in Howard Teichmann, *George S. Kaufman* [1972]

★ See also Parker at PLEASURE & HEDONISM.

If all the girls attending it [the Yale prom] were laid end to end—I wouldn't be at all **5**
surprised.
—**Dorothy Parker,** quoted in Alexander Woollcott, *While Rome Burns*, 1934

All the things I really like to do are either immoral, illegal, or fattening. **6**
—**Alexander Woollcott,** quoted in Howard Teichmann, *George S. Kaufman* [1972]

★ "Woolly," as he was called, grew larger than life, so large that someone quipped that "he was all Woollcott and a yard wide." He was the model for the outrageously egocentric Sheridan Whiteside in *The Man Who Came to Dinner* by Moss Hart and George Kaufman, and he took over the role on the road.

Home is heaven and orgies are vile, **7**
But you need an orgy once in a while.
—**Ogden Nash,** *Home 99 44/100% Sweet Home*, in *The Primrose Path*, 1935

The only people who should really sin **8**
Are the people who can sin with a grin.
—**Ogden Nash,** *Inter-Office Memorandum*, in *I'm a Stranger to Myself*, 1938

I'm shocked, shocked to discover that gambling is going on here! **9**
—**Julius J. Epstein, Philip G. Epstein & Howard Koch,** *Casablanca*, 1943

Maybe just whistle. You know how to whistle, don't you, Steve? You just put your lips **10**
together and blow.
—**Jules Furthman & William Faulkner,** *To Have and Have Not*, screenplay, 1944

★ In this scene, a young Lauren Bacall tells Humphrey Bogart that if he needs her, he should whistle. In real life, the two later married, and she gave him a silver whistle to call her. An earlier Hollywood film, *The Son of the Sheik* (1926), presented whistling rather less romantically: "I don't know her name. When I want her, I whistle" (script by Frances Marion and Fred de Gresac, from a novel by Edith Maude Hall). Whistling for one's beloved has a long literary history. A Beaumont and Fletcher play, *Wit Without Money*, written in 1639, includes the line, "Whistle and she'll come to you." And in the 18th century, a charming if headstrong young lady in a Robert Burns poem promises, "O whistle, and I'll come to you, my lad: / Tho' father and mother and a' should gae mad." In this connection, note that the proverb, "A whistling girl and a crowing hen always come to the same bad end," also has been traced back to 18th-century Scotland.

1 I'm pure as the driven slush.

—Tallulah Bankhead, quoted in *Saturday Evening Post*, April 12, 1947

★ Tallulah, in her 1952 autobiography said that she had three phobias: "I hate to go to bed, I hate to get up, and I hate to be alone." Tallulah was terrific but tiring. See Howard Dietz at INSULTS.

2 Never practice two vices at once.

—Tallulah Bankhead, *Tallulah*, 1952

3 Go very light on the vices, such as carrying on in society.

—Leroy "Satchel" Paige, *How to Stay Young*, 1953

★ More at WISDOM, WORDS OF.

4 A house is not a home.

—Polly Adler, *A House Is Not a Home*, memoir, 1954

★ Ms. Adler ran one of New York City's fanciest brothels during the 1920s and '30s.

5 The worst thing about having a mistress are those two dinners you have to eat.

—Oscar Levant, *The Unimportance of Being Oscar,* 1968

6 For travelers going sidereal
The danger they say is bacterial.
I don't know the pattern
On Mars or Saturn
But on Venus it must be venereal.

—Robert Frost, *For Travelers Going Sidereal*, c. 1962

★ The final adjective is technically correct, but American newspapers have always steered away from it when reporting interplanetary probes, preferring "Venerean," "Venerial," or, most often, "Venusian," instead of "Venereal," for obvious reasons.

7 All sin tends to be addictive, and the terminal point of addiction is what is called damnation.

—W. H. Auden, *Hell*, in *A Certain World*, 1970

8 I am all for bringing back the birch but only between consenting adults.

—Gore Vidal, television interview with David Frost, quoted in *Sunday Times Magazine*, Sept. 16, 1973

[Re baseball players who break curfew:] It ain't getting it that hurts them, it's staying up all night looking for it. They got to learn that if you don't get it by midnight, you ain't gonna get it, and if you do, it ain't worth it. 1
—**Charles Dillon "Casey" Stengel,** quoted in Robert Creamer, *Stengel* [1984]

Is that a gun in your pocket or are you just glad to see me? 2
—**Mae West,** *Sextette*, 1978

★ One of her most famous lines, but not recorded by her in a film until she was doddering 85; screenplay by Herbert Baker, based on a play by Herself.

Adultery is hard on a small town because it can cause sudden population loss, and usually it's the wrong people who get run out. 3
—**Garrison Keillor,** *The New York Times*, Op-Ed article, 1994

Skepticism

Ignorance is preferable to error; and he is less remote from the truth who believes nothing, than he who believes what is wrong. 4
—**Thomas Jefferson,** *Notes on the State of Virginia*, 1781–85

The pragmatist knows that doubt is an art which has to be acquired with difficulty. 5
—**C. S. Peirce,** *Collected Papers* [1931-58]

★ See also Peirce at PHILOSOPHY.

Skepticism is the chastity of the intellect. 6
—**George Santayana,** *Skepticism and Animals Faith*, 1923

One never know, do one? 7
—**Thomas "Fats" Waller,** saying, used in the movie *Stormy Weather*, 1943

There is no freedom of thought without doubt. 8
—**Bergen Evans,** *The Natural History of Nonsense*, 1946

★ More at FREEDOM.

To be constanty skeptical is to believe in doubt, which is after all a form of faith. 9
—**Crane Brinton,** *The Anatomy of Revolution*, 1952

Doubt is not to be feared . . . If you know that you are not sure, you have a chance to improve the situation. 10
—**Richard P. Feynman,** lecture, April, 1963, in Feynman, *The Meaning of It All* [1998]

★ See also Feynman at SCIENCE.

We must scale the walls of the people's skepticism, not with our words but with our deeds. 11
—**Bill Clinton,** Inaugural Address, Jan. 20, 1993

Sky, the

See NATURE: THE HEAVENS, THE SKY.

Slavery

See also AMERICAN HISTORY: MEMORABLE MOMENTS (John Brown); CIVIL WAR, THE; INJUSTICE; RACES & PEOPLES; RESISTANCE; SOUTH, THE.

1 I tremble for my country when I reflect that God is just.

—**Thomas Jefferson,** *Notes on the State of Virginia*, 1781–85

★ Jefferson was warning that liberties come from God and that enslaving fellow human beings would call down His wrath. More at FREEDOM.

2 We raise de wheat,
Dey gib us de corn,
We bake de bread,
Dey gib us de cruss,
We sif de meal
Dey gib us de huss [husks].

—**Anonymous,** slave verse, date not certain, cited in Mel Watkins, *On the Real Side* [1994]

3 On this subject, I do not wish to think, or speak, or write with moderation. . . . I am in earnest—I will not equivocate—I will not excuse—I will not retreat a single inch—AND I WILL BE HEARD!

—**William Lloyd Garrison,** in *The Liberator*, Boston, Jan. 1, 1831

★ Garrison, who had already been jailed in Baltimore for his ardent abolitionist writings, promised here, in the first issue of *The Liberator*, not to give quarter to his enemies, although he was in danger in Boston, too. The final sentence above is inscribed on his monument in Boston. See also Garrison and William Henry Seward at THE CONSTITUTION.

4 When Israel was in Egypt's land,
Let my people go;
Oppressed so hard they could not stand,
Let my people go.

—**Anonymous,** *Go Down, Moses*, early 19th century

5 We need not always weep and moan,
Let my people go;
And wear these slavery chains forlorn,
Let my people go.
What a beautiful morning that will be,
Let my people go;
When time breaks up in eternity,
Let my people go.

—**Ibid.**

Wide through the landscape of his dreams 1
The lordly Niger followed;
Beneath the palm trees on the plain,
Once more a king he strode.

—Henry Wadsworth Longfellow, *The Slave's Dream*, in *Poems on Slavery*, 1842

Every nation that carries in its bosom great and unredressed injustice has in it the elements of this last convulsion. 2

—Harriet Beecher Stowe, *Uncle Tom's Cabin*, 1852

★ More at INJUSTICE. *Uncle Tom's Cabin* sold 300,000 copies its first year in print, and was an extraordinarily effective political document. It did as much to arouse Americans against slavery as the Communist Manifesto did to arouse workers against capitalism. When Pres. Abraham Lincoln first met Mrs. Stowe, in 1862, during the Civil War, he is reported to have said, "So you're the little woman who wrote the book that started this great war!" Harriet Beecher Stowe, incidentally, stood less than five feet.

Slavery is founded in the selfishness of man's nature—opposition to it, in his love of justice. 3

—Abraham Lincoln, speech, Peoria, Ill., Oct. 16, 1854

★ Lincoln had served a term in Congress, 1847–49, but was not widely known until he made this speech. Foreseeing the terrible struggle to come, he continued, "These principles are in eternal antagonism; and when brought into collision so fiercely, as slavery extension brings them, shocks, and throes, and convulsions must ceaselessly follow."

A peculiar institution. 4

—New York Tribune, article, Oct. 19, 1854

★ The phrase had been around for a while, in the sense that slavery was regarded as an institution peculiar to the South. The earliest example of it in writing comes in the plural form in James S. Buckingham's *The Slave States of America*, 1842: "Slavery is usually called here 'our peculiar institutions.' "

You have seen how a man was made a slave; you shall see how a slave was made a man. 5

—Frederick Douglass, *The Narrative of the Life of Frederick Douglass*, 1845

★ Thus Douglass begins his account of how he fought back when his master of the moment, Edward Covey, a so-called "nigger-breaker," tried to punish him. His resistance so intimidated Covey that he never attempted to lay a finger on Douglass again. This was "the turning-point" for Douglass: "My long-crushed spirit rose, cowardice departed, bold defiance took its place; and I now resolved that, however long I might remain a slave in form, the day had passed forever when I could be a slave in fact. I did not hesitate to let it be known of me that the white man who succeeded in whipping me must also succeed in killing me." The *Narrative* was a best-seller for its period, selling some thirty thousand copies in its first five years and influencing many people, Harriet Beecher Stowe among them. See also Douglass at RESISTANCE.

This government cannot endure permanently half slave and half free. 6

—Abraham Lincoln, speech, Republican State Convention, Springfield, Ill., June 16, 1858

★ More at THE UNION; see also Dred Scott at AMERICAN HISTORY: MEMORABLE MOMENTS.

1 As I would not be a *slave*, so I would not be a *master*.

—**Abraham Lincoln,** handwritten note, c. August 1, 1858

2 My paramount object in this struggle *is* to save the Union, and is *not* either to save or destroy slavery. If I could save the Union without freeing *any* slave, I would do it; if I could save it by freeing *all* the slaves, I would do it; and if I could do it by freeing some and leaving others alone, I would also do that.

—**Abraham Lincoln,** reply to Horace Greeley, August 19, 1862

★ Greeley had asked Lincoln to make emancipation a government goal. Lincoln resented Abolitionist pressure, but was at the point of espousing their goal. See below.

3 Thenceforward, and forever free.

—**Abraham Lincoln,** Preliminary Emancipation Proclamation, Nov. 22, 1862

★ Lincoln issued the so-called Preliminary Emancipation Proclamation following the narrow victory at Antietam. The document ordered: "On the first day of January in the year of our Lord, one thousand eight hundred and sixty-three, all persons held as slaves within any state, or designated part of a state, the people whereof shall then be in rebellion against the United States shall be then, thenceforward, and forever free." The formal Proclamation was issued Jan. 1, 1863. The Thirteenth Amendment to the Constitution, which abolished slavery, was passed in 1865. See also Civil War.

4 In giving freedom to the slave, we assure freedom to the free—honorable alike in what we give and what we preserve. We shall nobly save or meanly lose the last, best hope of earth.

—**Abraham Lincoln,** second annual message to Congress, Dec. 1, 1862

★ Here Lincoln ties emancipation to his most beloved cause, saving the Union, "The last, best hope of earth." Lincoln may have had in mind Thomas Jefferson's first inaugural address, March 4, 1801, in which the president referred to the government of the United States as "the world's best hope."

5 Where slavery is, there liberty cannot be; and where liberty is, there slavery cannot be.

—**Charles Sumner,** *Slavery and the Rebellion*, speech, Cooper Institute, New York, Nov. 5, 1864

★ The senator from Massachusetts was a staunch abolitionist and one of the early organizers of the Republican party. He is perhaps best remembered for suffering a near fatal beating on the Senate floor from Preston S. Brooks, nephew of Sen. Andrew Pickens Butler of South Carolina.

6 Now the war begun.

—**Sojourner Truth,** on being sold to a harsh master, *Narrative of Sojourner Truth*, 1878

★ She took her name, she reported, after she left "the house of bondage." "I wa'n't goin' to keep nothin' of Egypt on me," she explains. "And the Lord gave me Sojourner because I was to travel up an' down the land showin' the people their sins, an' being a sign unto them." After a time, she asked for a second name, "and the Lord gave me Truth, because I was to declare the truth to the people."

I know why the caged bird sings, ah me, 1
When his wing is bruised and his bosom sore,
When he beats his bars and he would be free;
It is not a carol of joy or glee,
But a prayer that he sends from his heart's deep core.

—**Paul Laurence Dunbar,** *Sympathy,* 1899

★ Born the son of former slaves, Dunbar became a nationally known poet. The first line here was used by Maya Angelou in her celebrated autobiography, *I Know Why the Caged Bird Sings*, 1969.

The slave system on our place, in large measure, took the spirit of self-reliance and 2
self-help out of the white people.

—**Booker T. Washington,** *Up from Slavery,* 1901

Sleep

See Dreams & Sleep.

Slowness

See Haste v. Going Slow.

Smallness, Details, & Little Things

See also Bigness.

A little neglect may breed great mischief . . . for want of a nail the shoe was lost; for 3
want of a shoe the horse was lost; for want of a horse the rider was lost.

—**Benjamin Franklin,** *Poor Richard's Almanack,* June 1758

★ The thought is sometimes extended with, "For the want of a rider the battle was lost." Franklin, himself, after stating the proverb, added that the rider was "overtaken and slain by the enemy, all for want of care about a horse-shoe nail." It is proverbial, included, for example, in George Herbert's *Jacula Prudentum*, 1651. See also Poor Richard at Determination, Effort, Persistence, & Perseverance.

Large streams from little fountains flow, 4
Tall oaks from little acorns grow.

—**David Everett,** *Lines written for a school declamation,* New Ipswich, N.H., 1791

★ Based on a proverbial saying about acorns and oaks—and appropriate in context, the student orator being all of eleven years old.

Little drops of water, 5
Little grains of sand,
Make the mighty ocean
And the pleasant land.
So the little minutes,

Humble though they be,
Make the mighty ages
Of eternity.

—Julia Carney, *Little Things*, 1845

1 Little deeds of kindness,
Little words of love
Help to make earth happy
Like the heaven above.

—Ibid.

2 Our life is frittered away by detail.

—Henry David Thoreau, *Where I Lived and What I Lived For,* in *Walden*, 1854

★ More at SIMPLICITY.

3 We sometimes underestimate the influence of little things.

—Charles W. Chesnutt, *Obliterating the Color Line* in *The World*, Oct. 23, 1901

★ More at EMOTIONS.

4 We think in generalities but we live in detail.

—Alfred North Whitehead, in W. H. Auden and Louis Kronenberger, *The Viking Book of Aphorisms* [1966]

5 Make no little plans; they have no magic to stir men's blood and probably themselves will not be realized.

—Daniel H. Burnham, attributed, 1910

★ Burnham, a great Chicago architect, expressed this idea in a paper to the Town Planning Conference in London. His exact words are not known, but his San Francisco partner, Willis Polk, reconstructed his remarks and used them on Christmas cards in 1912, following Polk's death.

6 Nothing little counts.

—A. Philip Randolph, speech, policy conference, March on Washington Movement, Detroit, Sept. 26, 1942

★ More at BIGNESS.

7 It takes five hundred small details to add up to one favorable impression.

—Cary Grant, quoted in Graham McCann, *Cary Grant: A Life Apart* [1997]

8 Think Little.

—Wendell Berry, chapter title, *A Continuous Harmony*, 1972

★ The thought was in the air. A year later British economist Ernst Friedrich Schumacher published *Small Is Beautiful,* a major popular work on the virtues of small ventures. The subtitle was "Economics As If People Mattered."

9 God is in the details.

—Anonymous

★ Probably of European origin, popularized here by architect Ludwig Mies van der Rohe and others. Sometimes attributed to Gustave Flaubert: "*Le bon Dieu est dans le détail*." See also Vladimir Nabokov on details in writing and reading at BOOKS & READING. A variant is "The devil is in the details."

I always trust the microcosm over the macrocosm. 1
—**Gloria Steinem,** Postscript, *Revaluing Economics*, reprinted in *Moving Beyond Words*, 1994

Socialism

See also COMMUNISM.

I am for socialism because I am for humanity. 2
—**Eugene Debs,** speech, Jan. 1, 1897

Any man who is not something of a socialist before he is forty has no heart. Any man who is still a socialist after he is forty has no head. 3
—**Wendell L. Willkie,** quoted in Richard Norton Smith, *Thomas E. Dewey* [1982]

Soldiers

See EPITAPHS & GRAVESTONES; MILITARY, THE.

Solitude & Loneliness

See also ALIENATION; PRIVACY.

No man should live where he can hear his neighbor's dog bark. 4
—**Nathaniel Macon,** saying

In the solitude to which every man is always returning, he has a sanity and revelations, which in his passage into new worlds he will carry with him. 5
—**Ralph Waldo Emerson,** *Experience* in *Essays: Second Series*, 1844

I went to the woods because I wished to live deliberately. 6
—**Henry David Thoreau,** *Where I Lived and What I Lived For*, in *Walden*, 1854

★ More at LIFE.

I never found the companion that was so companionable as solitude. 7
—**Henry David Thoreau,** *Solitude*, in *Walden*, 1854

The holiest of holidays are those 8
Kept by ourselves in silence and apart.
—**Henry Wadsworth Longfellow,** *Holidays*, in *The Mask of Pandora and Other Writings*, 1873

★ More at THE HEART.

I am lonely, lonely 9
I was born to be lonely,
I am best so!
—**William Carlos Williams,** *Danse Russe*, in *Al Que Quiere!*, 1917

1 Avoid the reeking herd,
Shun the polluted flock,
Live like that stoic bird
The eagle of the rock.

—**Elinor Hoyt Wylie,** *The Eagle and the Mole*, 1921

2 I want to be alone.

—**Greta Garbo,** saying and also one of her lines in the movie *Grand Hotel*, 1932

★ Garbo's *New York Times* obituary in 1990 stated that she actually said, "I want to be let alone." The screenplay for *Grand Hotel* was written by William A. Drake, from the novel by Vicki Baum.

3 We're all of us sentenced to solitary confinement inside our own skins for life!

—**Tennessee Williams,** *Orpheus Descending*, 1957

4 The cure for loneliness is solitude.

—**Anne Morrow Lindbergh,** saying, reported by her daughter, Reeve; quoted by Dr. John Lienhard, *Engines of Our Ingenuity, No.1857* [Dec. 4, 2003]

5 Solitude is the playfield of Satan.

—**Vladimir Nabokov,** *Pale Fire*, 1962

6 If you would find inner peace, look to solitude not speed.

—**Stewart L. Udall,** *The Quiet Crisis,* 1963

★ More at SELF.

7 Solitude is un-American.

—**Erica Jong,** *Fear of Flying*, 1973

8 Solitude is the salt of personhood. It brings out the authentic flavor of every experience.

—**May Sarton,** *Rewards of a Solitary Life*, in *The New York Times*, 1990

Sorrow & Grief

See also REGRET; SUFFERING & PAIN; UNHAPPINESS.

9 Grief drives men into habits of serious reflection, sharpens the understanding, and softens the heart.

—**John Adams,** letter to Thomas Jefferson, May 6, 1816

10 Every man has his secret sorrows which the world knows not; and oftentimes we call a man cold, when he is only sad.

—**Henry Wadsworth Longfellow,** *Hyperion*, 1839

11 Sorrow makes us all children again.

—**Ralph Waldo Emerson,** *Journal*, 1842

★ His five-year-old son Waldo died Jan. 27, 1842.

When lilacs last in the dooryard bloom'd,
And the great star early droop'd in the western sky in the night,
I mourn'd, and yet shall mourn with ever-returning spring. 1

—Walt Whitman, *When Lilacs Last in the Dooryard Bloom'd*, 1865–66

★ An elegy for Lincoln; see also *O Captain! My Captain!* at ABRAHAM LINCOLN.

Sorrow is my own yard
where the new grass
flames as it has flamed
often before but not
with the cold fire
that closes round me this year. 2

—William Carlos Williams, *The Widow's Lament in Springtime*, in *Sour Grapes*, 1921

Between grief and nothing, I will take grief. 3

—William Faulkner, *The Wild Palms*, 1939

Grief is the price we pay for love. 4

—Queen Elizabeth II, message of condolence to the United States, Sept. 20, 2001

★ The Queen's message, occasioned by the attack on the World Trade Center, was read by the British ambassador, Sir Christopher Meyer, at a prayer service in St. Thomas' Church on Fifth Avenue in New York City. The line may not have been original to the Queen, or her speechwriter. The *Oxford Dictionary of Quotations* (2004) describes it as a "late 20th century saying."

Soul, the

See also IMMORTALITY; MYSTICISM (Eliot).

Dust thou art, to dust returnest,
Was not spoken of the soul. 5

—Henry Wadsworth Longfellow, *A Psalm of Life*, 1839

★ More at LIFE.

With all your science, can you tell me how it is, and whence it is that light comes into the soul? 6

—Henry David Thoreau, *Travel in Concord*, in *Excursions* [1863]

My soul an't yours Mas'r! You haven't bought it,—ye can't buy it! It's been bought and paid for, by one that is able to keep it. 7

—Harriet Beecher Stowe, *Uncle Tom's Cabin*, 1852

The windows of my soul I throw
Wide open to the sun. 8

—John Greenleaf Whittier, *My Psalm*, 1859

1 The soul can split the sky in two,
And let the face of God shine through.
—**Edna St. Vincent Millay,** *Renascence,* in *Renascence and Other Poems*, 1917

2 My soul has grown deep like the rivers.
—**Langston Hughes,** *The Negro Speaks of Rivers*, 1926

3 He [man] is immortal, not because he alone among creatures has an inexhaustible voice, but because he has a soul, a spirit capable of compassion and sacrifice and endurance.
—**William Faulkner,** speech accepting the Nobel Prize for Literature, 1949

★ More at HUMANS & HUMAN NATURE.

4 Teach me, like you, to drink creation whole
And casting out my self, become a soul.
—**Richard Wilbur,** *The Aspen and the Stream,* in *Advice to a Prophet and Other Poems*, 1961

5 My soul is a witness for my Lord.
—**James Baldwin,** *Malcolm and Martin,* in *Esquire*, April 1972 (meaning Malcolm X and Martin Luther King, Jr.)

South America

See NATIONS & REGIONS.

South Carolina

See also CITIES (CHARLESTON, COLUMBIA).

6 One of the greatest and fayrest havens in the world.
—**Jean Ribaut,** *The Whole and True Discouerye of Terra Florida*, 1563

★ Ribaut established a short-lived colony on Parris Island as an asylum for French Huguenots. Archaeologists discovered the site of the colony's fort in 1996 on the edge of what is now a golf course on the Parris Island Marine training base.

7 In South Carolina, the spirit and the links of social life are aristocratic to a degree which I cannot approve of, however much I may like certain people there. And aristocracy there has this in common with aristocracies of the present time; that, while the aristocratic virtues and greatness have vanished, merely the pretension remains.
—**Frederika Bremer,** *The Homes of the New World: Impressions of America*, 1853

8 South Carolina is too small for a republic and too large for an insane asylum.
—**James L. Petigru,** remark to Robert Barnwell Rhett, Christmas week, 1860

★ The remark was a response to a question from Rhett, a leader of the secessionist movement. Rhett wanted to know if Petigru supported the secessionist cause. He did not, and unfortunately for the South, his realistic assessment was largely ignored. South

Carolina, in particular, paid a heavy price in 1865 when Sherman's men assaulted the state that had started the war. "The whole army is burning with insatiable desire to wreak vengeance on South Carolina," Sherman wrote Gen. Henry Halleck. "I almost tremble at her fate but feel that she deserves all that seems to be in store for her." The destruction was much greater than in Sherman's more famous march through Georgia. One of Sherman's generals, John A. Logan, is credited with the ditty, sung by his corps as they marched: "Hail Columbia, happy land; / If I don't burn you, I'll be damned!" Another officer wrote home, "In Georgia, few houses were burned; here few escaped." For more on Petigru, see EPITAPHS & GRAVESTONES. For a recycled version of the quote here, see Anne Gorsuch Burford at CITIES (WASHINGTON, D.C.).

South Carolinians are among the rare folk in the South who have no secret envy of the Virginians. **1**

—**Federal Writers' Project,** *South Carolina: A Guide to the Palmetto State*, 1941

The South Carolinian has fire in his head, comfort in his middle, and a little lead in his feet. Proud of his past, often scornful of innovations, he is not willing to adapt unless thoroughly convinced that it is a good thing. **2**

—**Ibid.**

Animis opibusque parati. **3**
Prepared in mind and resources.

—Motto, state of South Carolina

Dum spiro spero. **4**
While I breathe, I hope.

—Motto, state of South Carolina

South Dakota

See also DAKOTA TERRITORY

A part of hell with the fires burnt out. **5**

—**George Armstrong Custer,** speaking of the Bad Lands in southwestern South Dakota, c. 1874, attributed, in John Gunther, *Inside U.S.A.* [1947]

I was not prepared for the Bad Lands. They deserve this name. They are like the work of an evil child. **6**

—**John Steinbeck,** *Travels with Charley*, 1962

I guess it is the physical and cultural remoteness of South Dakota that compels everyone to memorialize almost every South Dakotan who has ever left the state and achieved some recognition. As a child I would pore over newspapers and magazines, looking for some sign that the rest of the world knew we existed. **7**

—**Tom Brokaw,** in John Milton, *South Dakota: A Bicentennial History*, 1977

Under God, the people rule. **8**

—Motto, state of South Dakota

South, the

See also SLAVERY.

1 The South! The South! God knows what will become of her!
—John C. Calhoun, deathbed words, March 31, 1850

2 Way down upon the Swanee ribber,
Far, far away,
Dere's where my heart is turning ebber,
Dere's where de old folks stay.
—Stephen Foster, *Old Folks at Home*, 1851

★ The Suwannee River runs from Georgia through north Florida to the Gulf of Mexico.

3 Cotton Is King; or, the Economical Relations of Slavery.
—David Christy, book title, 1855

★ Christy opposed slavery, but was not a typical abolitionist—he favored colonization of American slaves. Cotton, the dominant crop in the South in the 19th century, declined in importance slowly but steadily after the Civil War, almost disappearing by the 1970s. Twenty years later, however, it showed signs of resurgence. In 1995, the price of cotton topped $1 per pound for the first time since the Civil War, and Southern farmers rushed to plant cotton again. See also W. E. B. Du Bois at GEORGIA for a quote on the kingdom of cotton.

4 I wish I was in de land ob cotton,
Old times dar am not forgotten.
Look away, look away,
Look away, Dixie Land.
—Daniel Decatur Emmet, *I Wish I Was in Dixie's Land*, 1859

★ Written by a famous minstrel, an Ohioan as it happens, this song was first sung by Bryant's Minstrels at Mechanics' Hall on Broadway in New York City on April 4, 1859. It quickly became popular in the North as well as the South, but the Confederates made it their own, playing it at Jefferson Davis's inauguration as provisional president in Montgomery, Ala., on February 18, 1861, and treating it as their national anthem. Lincoln reclaimed *Dixie* for the reformed Union after Lee's surrender on April 9, 1865, requesting a military band to play the tune, which, he said, "is federal property" now. The next day, when a crowd gathered at the White House to celebrate the war's end, Lincoln elaborated. "I have always thought 'Dixie' one of the best tunes I ever heard," he stated. "I have heard that our adversaries over the way have attempted to appropriate it as a national air. I insisted yesterday that we had fairly captured it. I presented the question to the Attorney General, and he gave his opinion that it is our lawful prize. I ask the band to give us a good turn on it. "The song is now usually sung minus the original dialect and "Dixie's," as in "In Dixie's land, I'll take my stan'! / To lib an' die in Dixie," is almost always rendered "Dixie." The origin of the term *Dixie* has been much debated. It probably derives from the French *dix* 'ten,' printed on ten-dollar notes issued prior to the Civil War by the Citizens Bank of Louisiana, the term being applied first to New Orleans where the bills circulated and then to the entire South. Despite Lincoln's efforts, the song still belongs to the South.

Forty acres and a mule. 1

—Anonymous, catch phrase describing the Freedman's Bureau Act of 1865

★ This 1865 law required that abandoned and confiscated land in the South be divided into forty-acre lots for rental and sale to former slaves and white refugees loyal to the Union. Abolitionists had called for giving liberated slaves "ten acres and a mule" in 1862, according to lexicographer Stuart Berg Flexner. The increase to forty acres in the law stemmed from Gen. William Tecumseh Sherman's special field order No. 15, of Jan. 16, 1865. This order allocated tens of thousands of acres for former slaves, with the head of each family to receive "a plot of not more than forty acres of tillable ground," and authorized the lending of Army mules to the settlers. The law was signed by Pres. Abraham Lincoln, but under Pres. Andrew Johnson it was abrogated; the land was returned to former owners; the black settlers were required to sign labor contracts, and if they refused, they were evicted.

Oh, I'm a good old rebel, that's what I am 2
. . . I won't be reconstructed, and I don't give a damn.

—Innes Randolph, *A Good Old Rebel*, c. 1870

★ An early appearance of the good old boy, historically not necessarily good, not a boy, and not usually old either.

The wrecks of slavery are fast growing a fungus crop of sentiment. 3

—William Dean Howells, *Their Wedding Journey*, 1872

The solid South. 4

—John S. Mosby, letter, 1876

★ Mosby, who had been an exceptionally bold Confederate general, used this phrase in a letter announcing that he would abandon sectional loyalty and support the Republican candidate for president, Rutherford B. Hayes. The South was solidly, ardently Democratic for some eighty years, from the end of the Civil War to the rise of the Dixiecrat movement in 1948. At that time, states' rights Democrats opposed to their party's strong civil rights platform, named Gov. Strom Thurmond of South Carolina and Gov. Fielding L. Wright of Mississippi to head a presidential ticket. Gradually, white Southerners simply joined the Republicans, leading to a dramatic reversal of fortune for the Democratic party in the South. See also Hubert Humphrey at AMERICAN HISTORY, MEMORABLE MOMENTS and Fannie Lou Hamer at POVERTY & HUNGER.

A southerner talks music. 5

—Mark Twain, *Life on the Mississippi*, 1883

The South has been very tenderly dealt with in recent years. 6

—Charles W. Chesnutt, *Obliterating the Color Line*, unsigned editorial in *The World*, Oct. 23, 1901

★ Chesnutt, who claimed authorship of this editorial, was reacting to the uproar when Pres. Theodore Roosevelt invited Booker T. Washington to dine at the White House. For example, the Atlanta *Constitution* announced "President Roosevelt Proposes to Coddle Descendants of Ham." For the break in the Democratic Party's tender treatment of the South, see Hubert Humphrey at AMERICAN HISTORY: MEMORABLE MOMENTS.

1 Tortured with history.

—Hart Crane, *The River (Mississippi)*, in *The Bridge*, 1930

2 *I don't. I don't! I don't hate it! I don't hate it!*

—William Faulkner, *Absalom, Absalom!* 1936

★ The last line of the novel, spoken by Quentin Compson.

3 Southern trees bear strange fruit,
Blood on the leaves and blood at the root.
Black bodies swinging
In the southern breeze
Strange fruit hanging
From the poplar trees.

—Lewis Allan, *Strange Fruit*, 1939

★ Popularized by Billie Holiday, melody by Edward B. Marks. Lewis Allan was the pen name of Abel Meeropol, who formed it by combining the names of his sons, Lewis and Allan, who had died in infancy. Meeropol and his wife later adopted the sons of Julius and Ethel Rosenberg, Michael and Robert, after their parents were executed in 1953 for passing atomic-bomb secrets to Russia.

4 The old South was plowed under. But the ashes are still warm.

—Henry Miller, *The Air-Conditioned Nightmare*, 1945

5 There's nothing I treasure more as a writer than being a Southerner.

—Alex Haley, remark, c. 1990, quoted in *The New York Times* [July 31, 1994]

6 You can't be Southern without being black, and you can't be a black Southerner without being white.

—Ralph Ellison, comment, 1994, quoted in *The New York Times* [July 31, 1994]

★ At Harvard University in 1973, Ellison said, "All of us are part white, and all of y'all are part colored."

7 Southern behavior was devious, depending on indirection, a fuzzy flirtation that relied on strategic hinting.

—Bobbie Ann Mason, *Clear Springs: A Memoir*, 1999

Spain

See Nations & Regions.

Spanish-American War, 1898

See War (Charles Eliot Norton).

8 I should welcome any war. The country needs one.

—Theodore Roosevelt, 1897

★ Roosevelt was Assistant Secretary of the Navy. He got his wish a year later. The quote is from V. C. Jones, *Last of the Rough Riders*, in *American Heritage*, July 1969.

Remember the Maine. 1

—Anonymous, war slogan, 1898

★ The slogan was popularized in Hearst and Pulitzer newspapers after the U.S. battleship *Maine*, anchored in Havana harbor, was destroyed by an explosion of unknown origin on Feb. 15, 1898. Two hundred and sixty Americans died; ninety survived. A U.S. government report in March suggested that Spain was either directly or indirectly responsible. A popular children's rhyme sprang up: "Remember the Maine! / To hell with Spain!" The U.S. declared war against Spain in April; the war ended in December. Cuba was liberated from Spain but put under the tutelage of the U.S. See also Elbert Hubbard's "message to Garcia" at ACTION & DOING.

You furnish the pictures and I'll furnish the war. 2

—William Randolph Hearst, telegram allegedly sent to artist Frederic Remington in Havana, Cuba, March 1898

★ Reporter James Creelman related the story of this perhaps apocryphal cable. Hearst denied sending such a message but did not object to the content: his *New York Journal* called the brief war "the *Journal*'s war." U.S. business interests and popular opinion supported insurgents against the Spanish government in Cuba and the Philippines. Historian Brooks Adams, bicycling with Oliver Wendell Holmes, remarked, "This war is the first gun in the battle for the ownership of the world."

You may fire when you are ready, Gridley. 3

—George Dewey, order at Manila Bay, May 1, 1898

★ With these words, Commodore Dewey began the Battle of Manila Bay, destroying the Spanish fleet of ten vessels, with no American casualties. Dewey's friend Capt. Charles Vernon Gridley was captain of the flagship *Olympia*. He was ill and died a few months later. Under the December peace treaty, the U.S. acquired the Philippines for $20 million. It was a troubled acquisition; see William Howard Taft below.

Rough-tough, we're the stuff! We want to fight and we can't get enough! 4

—Rough Riders (1st U.S. Volunteer Cavalry), attributed, rallying cry while en route to Cuba, June 1898

Don't cheer, men; the poor devils are dying. 5

—John Woodward Philip, the battle of Santiago, July 3, 1898

★ The dying men were from the Spanish flagship *Viscaya*, a cruiser that exploded under American fire. Capt. Jack Philip commanded the USS *Texas*, part of the North Atlantic squadron blockading Santiago harbor. Admiral Cervera's fleet of four cruisers and three destroyers attempted to escape the blockade and were all sunk in the U.S. attack. There was later a dispute as to who should be honored for the victory: Commodore Winfield S. Schley, who directed the actual battle, or his superior, Commodore William T. Sampson, who was a little distance away. "There's glory enough for all," said Schley.

It has been a splendid little war, begun with the highest motives, carried on with 6
magnificent intelligence and spirit, favored by that fortune which loves the brave.

—John Hay, letter to Theodore Roosevelt, July 27, 1898

★ Hay, once and future Secretary of State, was ambassaador to Great Britain at the time. The mugwumps, who opposed imperialist power politics, saw it differently. They quipped, “Dewey took Manila with the loss of one man—and all our institutions.” At the end of this four-month war, America had suddenly acquired a colonial empire.

1 Take up the White Man’s burden—
Send forth the best ye breed—
Go bind your sons to exile
To serve your captives’ need.
—Rudyard Kipling, *The White Man’s Burden*, 1899

★ A few lines from Kipling’s sardonic warning to Americans that imperialism is a hard undertaking.

2 The little brown brother.
—William Howard Taft, 1900

★ Taft, Commissioner of the Philippines, was enlightened for his time and intended the unfortunate “little brown brother” designation to inspire decent treatment of the Philippine people. Meanwhile, the conquered Filipinos resisted American domination with stinging guerrilla attacks. The Americans were not happy. “He may be a brother of big Bill Taft, / But he ain’t no brother of mine,” wrote Robert F. Morrison in the *Manila Sunday Times*. As for the pejorative *little*, it may be somewhat forgivable in the case of Taft, who weighed more than 300 pounds—they had to make special chairs for him when he taught at his alma mater, Yale. Even rather large persons looked little to him.

Speed

See also BOLDNESS & INITIATIVE; HASTE V. GOING SLOW; SCIENCE: TECHNOLOGY.

3 In skating over thin ice, our safety is in our speed.
—Ralph Waldo Emerson, *Prudence*, in *Essays: First Series*, 1841

4 The swiftest traveler is he that goes afoot.
—Henry David Thoreau, *Economy*, in *Walden*, 1854

★ See also Thoreau at LEISURE.

5 Black care rarely sits behind the rider whose pace is fast enough.
—Theodore Roosevelt, quoted in David McCullough, *Truman* [1992]

6 Speed and curves—what more do you want?
—Anonymous, quoted in Carl Sandburg, *The Proverbs of a People*, in *Good Morning, America*, 1928

7 With all deliberate speed.
—Earl Warren, *Brown v. Board of Education*, follow-up ruling, 1955

★ More at THE CONSTITUTION.

Sports

See also ART: WRITING ("Red" Smith); MIRACLES (Al Michaels); WINNING & LOSING, VICTORY & DEFEAT.

Offense is the best defense. 1

—Anonymous

★ Traced to the 1700s in Bartlett Jere Whiting, ed., *Early American Proverbs and Proverbial Phrases*, 1977.

Base ball [*sic*] has been known in the Northern States as far back as the memory of 2
the oldest inhabitant reacheth, and must be regarded as the national pastime, the same as cricket is by the British.

—Anonymous, *Porter's Spirit of the Times*, Jan. 31, 1857

★ Fans began referring proudly to baseball as the "national pastime" or "national game" as early as 1856, but it became truly national during the Civil War, when what had been a city game was introduced to soldiers from all areas.

Oh, somewhere in this favored land the sun is shining bright; 3
The band is playing somewhere, and somewhere hearts are light,
And somewhere men are laughing, and somewhere children shout;
But there is no joy in Mudville—mighty Casey has struck out.

—Ernest Lawrence Thayer, *Casey at the Bat: A Ballad of the Republic, Sung in the Year 1888*, June 3, 1888

★ At Harvard, Thayer was *Lampoon* editor and William Randolph Hearst was business manager. Thayer graduated magna cum laude and wrote *Casey*. Hearst, who had been expelled, printed it in the San Francisco *Examiner*.

Baseball is the very symbol of the outward and visible expression of the drive and 4
push and rush and struggle of the raging, tearing, booming nineteenth century.

—Mark Twain, speech, April 1889

★ Twain spoke at a dinner honoring a team captained by Albert Spalding. Twain also used the occasion to praise a place that they had visited; see HAWAII.

Slide, Kelly, Slide. 5

—J. W. Kelly, song title, 1889

★ The song came from the chant that arose whenever Michael "King" Kelly, catcher for the old Boston Nationals, got on base. A fine all-around player, and later Hall of Famer, Kelly turned base-stealing into an art; he once stole six bases in a single game.

[Golf:] A good walk spoiled. 6

—Mark Twain, attributed

★ The attribution is commonly accepted, but Britt Gustafson at the Mark Twain House in Hartford cannot find the source in Twain's writings.

Hit 'em where they ain't. 7

—William "Wee Willie" Keeler, personal motto, from 1897

★ In 1897, Keeler, the diminutive (five-foot-four, 140-pound) right fielder for the

Baltimore Orioles, was on a tear—he wound up the year hitting .432. When Abe Yager of the Brooklyn *Eagle* asked how he did it, Keeler answered, "Simple. I keep my eyes clear and hit 'em where they ain't."

1 The bigger they come, the harder they fall.

—**John L. Sullivan,** saying, c. 1900

★ An old adage, but often associated with this fearless boxer and with the slightly younger Robert "Ruby Bob" Fitzsimmons, an Australian-English fighter, who is said to have used the line before his 1899 bout with the much heavier Jim Jeffries. "Gentleman Jim" Corbett may have directed the remark to Sullivan himself before beating him in a heavyweight championship bout in New Orleans in 1897. Another provocative Sullivan saying was, "I can lick any man in the house!"

2 He too serves a purpose who only stands and cheers.

—**Henry Brooks Adams,** *The Education of Henry Adams*, 1907

3 Take me out to the ballgame,
Take me out with the crowd,
Buy me some peanuts and Cracker Jack,
I don't care if I never get back;
Let me root, root, root for the home team.
If they don't win, it's a shame;
For it's one, two, three strikes,
You're out, at the old ballgame.

—**Jack Norworth,** *Take Me Out to the Ballgame*, 1908

★ The music is by Albert Von Tilzer. This is the chorus, by the way. The verse is about a female fan who went to every home game, knew all the players by their first names, corrected the umpires loudly, and cheered for the home team. "Katie Casey was baseball mad, / Had the fever and had it bad." When her young beau called on a Saturday and asked if she'd like to go to a show, "Miss Kate said, 'No, / I'll tell you what you can do.' " Chorus.

4 These are the saddest of possible words,
"Tinker-to-Evers-to-Chance."

—**Franklin Pierce Adams,** *Baseball's Sad Lexicon* in the *New York Mail*, July 1910

★ The Chicago Cubs trio of shortstop Joe Tinker, second baseman Johnny Evers, and first baseman Frank Chance made it into baseball's Hall of Fame as a unit in 1946 partly on the strength of this poem. Despite FPA's lament (he was a New York Giant fan), they did not make very many double plays by modern standards. As Chicago sportswriter Warren Brown reported in *Don't Believe Everything You Read* (*The Second Fireside Book of Baseball*, 1958), during their glory years, 1906–1909, the Tinker-to-Evers-to-Chance combination accounted for a grand total of—hold your breath—just 29 double plays!

5 Under the wide and starry sky
Dig the grave and let me lie;
Gladly I've lived and gladly die

Away from the world of strife;
These be the lines you grave for me;
Here he lies where he wants to be;
Lies at rest by the nineteenth tee,
Where he lied all through his life."

—**Grantland Rice,** *The Duffer's Requiem (with Apologies to R.L.S.)*, in *The Winning Shot*, with Jerome D. Traverse, 1915

Say it ain't so, Joe. 1

—**Anonymous,** Sept. 1920

★ Plea allegedly made by a tearful boy to Chicago White Sox great "Shoeless" Joe Jackson, one of eight members of the team who had been charged with taking bribes to throw the 1919 World Series to the Cincinnati Reds. All were banned from baseball for life, going down in baseball history as "The Black Sox." Another boy who was there, the future novelist James T. Farrell, remembered a less euphonious plea. He told sportswriter Ira Berkow that the tearful boy actually said "Say it ain't true, Joe" (*The New York Times*, Nov. 1, 1998).

Win this one for the Gipper. 2

—**Knute Rockne,** exhortation to the Notre Dame football team, from 1921

★ Legend has it that as George Gipp, Notre Dame's first All-American, lay dying of a strep infection on December 14, 1920, he asked coach Rockne to use his name to inspire the team someday when it was down. Such sentiment doesn't sound true for Gipp, a wild-living, hard-drinking, big-gambling man, but it was in character for Rockne to employ it, and he apparently did so more than once, most famously to motivate the Irish to upset Army in 1928. Rockne also has been credited with "When the going gets tough, the tough get going"; see under STRENGTH & TOUGHNESS. In the movie, *Knute Rockne, All American*, 1940, writer Robert Buckner cleaned up Gipp's character. Ronald Reagan as Gipp brought tears to millions of eyes with a plaintive but manly deathbed request: "Someday when things are tough, maybe you can ask the boys to go in there and win just one for the Gipper."

Quitters never win. Winners never quit. 3

—**Anonymous,** traditional adage for football locker rooms

Gentlemen, you are now going out to play football against Harvard. Never again in your whole life will you do anything so important. 4

—**T. A. D. Jones,** Yale University locker room, Nov. 24, 1923

★ Inspired by coach Jones, the Bulldogs beat Harvard 13-0, breaking a string of four Crimson victories.

Outlined against a blue-gray October sky, the Four Horsemen rode again. In dramatic lore they are known as Famine, Pestilence, Destruction, and Death. These are only aliases. Their real names are Stuhldreher, Miller, Crowley, and Layden. 5

—**Grantland Rice,** article on a Notre Dame-Army football game, *New York Tribune*, Oct. 19, 1924

★ The game was played at the Polo Grounds in New York. Notre Dame won 13-7, thanks in large part to the Four Horsemen in the backfield: Harry Stuhldreher, quarterback; and Don Miller, Jim Crowley, and Elmer Layden, running backs. Led by these four fearsome players, Notre Dame went on to enjoy an undefeated season including victory in the Rose Bowl over Stanford.

1 A streak of fire, a breath of flame,
Eluding all who reach the clutch;
A gray ghost thrown into the game
That rival hands may never touch.

—Grantland Rice, description of Harold "Red" Grange

★ Grange became a professional in 1925 and for two years thrilled crowds as an open-field runner for the Chicago Bears. A knee injury in 1927 forced him to develop other skills. Defense became the strongest part of his game and he was team captain as well. As an undergraduate he led Illinois to an extraordinary victory over the University of Michigan, which had been undefeated for three years. He returned the opening kick for a touchdown; scored three more td's in ten minutes, and in the second half, ran for a fifth touchdown, and passed for a sixth. It was a home game, October 18, 1924, the day that the Illini dedicated Memorial Stadium at Champaign. Illinois won 39–14 before a crowd of 65,000. Grange became known as "the galloping ghost." Robert Gallagher quoted this verse by Rice in an *American Heritage* interview with Grange, December 1974. Gallagher did not date the verse, but presumably Rice was not at the Illinois–Michigan game, since he was in New York City one day later writing up the Notre Dame–Army game with the Four Horsemen; see above. So the "gray ghost" verse probably came some time later.

2 Tennis anyone?

—Anonymous

★ The line is a proverbial theatrical device for getting characters off the stage in a scene change. Humphrey Bogart was said to have actually spoken such a line in a play in the 1920s, but he denied it, and no one has found a citation.

3 Honey, I just forgot to duck.

—Jack Dempsey, telephone call to his wife, Sept. 23, 1926

★ Dempsey had lost the heavyweight title to Gene Tunney, and called his wife from the dressing room. In 1981, Pres. Ronald Reagan re-used the rueful remark in conversation with his wife, Nancy, after being shot and wounded by a would-be assassin, John Hinckley.

4 What the hell has Hoover got to do with it? I had a better year than he did.

—Babe Ruth, attributed, on being asked if he deserved to be paid $5,000 more than the president, cited in *The New York Times* [Oct. 14, 1992]

★ The Babe's salary for 1930 was $80,000. And he had had a pretty good year in 1929, batting .345, with 46 homers and 154 RBIs.

5 For when the One Great Scorer comes to write against your name,
He marks—not that you won or lost—but how you played the game.

—Grantland Rice, *Alumnus Football*, last two lines, 1930

★ Pres. Richard M. Nixon, in his memoirs, wrote with affection of his football coach at Whittier College, Wallace Newman: "He had no tolerance for the view that how you play the game counts more than whether you win or lose. He used to say, 'Show me a good loser and I'll show you a loser.' " Newman was following the footsteps of Knute Rockne; see WINNING & LOSING, VICTORY & DEFEAT. See also football coach Alonzo

Gaither below. Baseball coach Billy Martin also had no respect for good losers. "If there is such a thing as a good loser, then the game is crooked," he said, according to sportswriter Douglas Martin, *The New York Times*, June 27, 1993.

We wuz robbed! **1**

—Joe Jacobs, remark after the Max Schmeling–Jack Sharkey heavyweight title fight, June 21, 1932

★ Jacobs was Schmeling's manager, and the fight ended in a controversial split decision for Sharkey. In a fight two years earlier, Sharkey had kayoed Schmeling, but because the winning punch was a low blow, Schmeling was awarded the title. Sharkey failed in his single defense of his title, in 1933. The giant Prima Carnera, whom he had beaten in 1931, got revenge with a right-hand uppercut knockout. Sharkey's last fight was against the young Joe Louis in 1936.

I should've stood in bed. **2**

—Joe Jacobs, remark after the opening game of the 1935 World Series, in Detroit

★ This was the first major league ball game that Jacobs, who was more familiar with boxing (see above), had attended. It was a frigid day, Jacobs was ill, and he had bet on the Cubs, who lost.

Always Alert / Be Better / Concentrate Constantly / Don't Dally / Ever Earnest / Fair Feeling / Get Going / Hit Hard / Imitate Instructor / Just Jump / Keep Keen / Less Loafing / Move Meaningly / Never New / Only Over / Praise Partner / Quash Qualms / Relax Rightly / Stand Straight / Take Time / Umpire Usually / Vary Volleys / Work Wiles / Xceed Xpectations / Yell Yours / Zip Zip. **3**

—Hazel Hotchkiss Wightman, "Letters of Advice: Mrs. Wightman's Tennis Alphabet" in her book *Better Tennis*, 1937

★ Mrs. Wightman was America's first great woman tennis champion, winning national titles in singles and doubles from 1909 to 1943.

The race is not always to the swift nor the battle to the strong—but that's the way to bet it. **4**

—Damon Runyon, *More Than Somewhat,* 1937

★ The allusion is to *Ecclesiastes* 9:11: "The race is not to the swift, nor the battle to the strong, neither yet bread to the wise, nor yet riches to men of understanding, nor yet favor to men of skill; but time and chance happeneth to them all."

I zigged when I should have zagged. **5**

—Jack Roper, attributed, explanation of how heavyweight champion Joe Louis knocked him out, April 17, 1939

I'll moider der bum. **6**

—Tony Galento, threat prior to heavyweight championship bout, June 28, 1939

★ "Two-ton" Tony was fighting Joe Louis, and he didn't murder him—he lost.

He can run but he can't hide. **7**

—Joe Louis, remark to the press, 1946

★ Louis was speaking of Billy Conn prior to their rematch fight in June 1946. Conn was the quicker man but not as strong. In their first match, in 1941, Conn was ahead until round thirteen, when Louis knocked him out. Conn lasted eight rounds in 1946. He lost to Louis once more, on a decision in a six-round exhibition match in 1948. The phrase has since become a bellicose political cliché. In 1985, after U.S. fighters intercepted a plane carrying the four men who had hijacked the *Achille Lauro* from Egypt to Italy, Pres. Ronald Reagan declared, "These young Americans sent a message to terrorists everywhere . . . You can run but you can't hide." In 1991, at the outset of the Gulf War, Pres. George H. W. Bush said of Iraq's dictator Saddam Hussein, "He can run but he can't hide." Saddam was eventually tracked down more than a decade later, during the the Iraq War. Meanwhile, Pres. George W. Bush had said of Al Qaeda terrorist leader, Osama bin Laden, "He can run [etc.]" On the domestic front, Charles Jarvis, president of USA Next, a conservative lobbying group, atacked AARP for opposing Pres. Bush 43's plan to revamp Social Security by accusing the retirees' origanization of supporting same-sex marriage, and saying "They can run, but they can't hide" (*The New York Times*, Feb. 24, 2005).

1 Our tools for the pursuit of wildlife improve faster than we do, and sportsmanship is a voluntary limitation in the use of these armaments. It is aimed to augment the role of skill and shrink the role of gadgets in the pursuit of wild things.

—**Aldo Leopold,** *A Sand County Almanac*, 1949

2 I can teach a lot more character winning than I can losing.

—**Alonzo Gaither,** saying, *The New York Times*, obituary [Feb. 10, 1994]

★ This legendary football coach at historically black Florida A&M held a win-loss-tie record from 1945 to 1969 of 203-36-4.

3 The Sweet Science.

—**A. J. Liebling,** book title, 1956

★ This collection of articles on boxing, written for *The New Yorker*, popularized this name for the sport. Liebling based it on the English writer Pierce Egan's *Boxiana* (1829) in which boxing is described as "The Sweet Science of Bruising." Liebling explained his interest in the sport, writing, "A boxer, like a writer, must stand alone."

4 He had the three great requisites of a matador: courage, skill in his profession, and grace in the presence of the danger of death.

—**Ernest Hemingway,** *The Dangerous Summer*, 1958

★ Hemingway was referring to Antonio Ordoñez. *The Dangerous Summer* is based on Hemingway's articles on bullfighting in LIFE magazine. See also Hemingway at GRACE.

5 Whoever wants to know the heart and mind of America had better learn baseball, the rules and realities of the game—and do it by watching first some high school or small-town teams.

—**Jacques Barzun,** *God's Country and Mine*, 1954

6 Zest, they've zest.
"Hope springs eternal in the Brooklyn breast."

—**Marianne Moore,** *Hometown Piece for Messrs. Alston and Reese*, 1956

★ A lifelong Brooklyn resident, Moore wrote this paean at World Series time. The

Dodgers had beaten the Yankees 4-3 in the 1955 series, their first World Series victory. In 1956 they lost by the same margin.

It was hard to say, about football as about games in general, which was more impressive, the violence or the rationality. 1

—Howard Nemerov, *The Homecoming Game*, 1957

My business is hurting people. 2

—Sugar Ray Robinson, testimony, New York State Boxing Commission, May 23, 1962

Can't *anybody* play this here game? 3

—Charles Dillon "Casey" Stengel, remark, 1962

★ Casey was talking about the New York Mets, who lost 120 games in this, their first season—the most defeats by a major league team since 1899. With the words slightly transposed to "Can't anybody here play this game," Casey's saying was publicized widely as the Met's badge of ineptitude, according to Robert W. Creamer's *Stengel: His Life and Times*, 1984.

Run to Daylight 4

—Vince Lombardi, with **W. C. Heinz,** book title, 1963

★ The reference is to coach Lombardi's favorite play for his Green Bay Packers, the power sweep. The ominous "run to darkness" describes the tendency of players to charge futilely into a wall of opponents, television commentary, New York Giants v. Baltimore Ravens, Nov. 21, 2004

Pitching is a large subject. 5

—Marianne Moore, *Baseball and Writing*, in *Tell Me, Tell Me*, 1966

In America, it is sport that is the opiate of the masses. 6

—Russell Baker, *The New York Times*, Oct. 3, 1967

The game isn't over till it's over. 7

—Yogi Berra, saying, attributed

★ A variation on the traditional remark, "The game isn't over until the last man is out." See also ENDINGS. Berra made this observation in 1973 while the New York Mets, then managed by him, were embroiled in a tight pennant race, which they eventually won. This is one of many quotations popularly attributed to Berra, but usually without much evidence. Many of them are malapropisms, perhaps reflecting the complex thought patterns of Casey Stengel, who managed the New York Yankees when Berra played catcher. Among the better-known Berra-isms:

You can observe a lot by watching. (An actual remark, made Oct. 24, 1963, at the press conference at which he was introduced as the new manager of the New York Yankees.)

It's like *déjà vu* all over again (but it's unlike Berra to lapse into French).

The future ain't what it used to be. (A kind of corollary to the above.)

Nobody ever goes there anymore. It's too crowded. (Said by his wife and friends to be a real quote but, as Ralph Keyes pointed out in *Nice Guys Finish Seventh*, the same line also appears in a 1943 *New Yorker* short story by John McNulty.)

When you arrive at a fork in the road, take it.

Anybody who is popular is bound to be disliked.

You have got to be very careful if you don't know where you are going, because you might not get there.

Ninety percent of this game is half mental.

You can't win all the time. There are guys out there who are better than you. (But in Berra's case, not many, and he has ten World Series rings to prove it.)

1 Float like a butterfly,
Sting like a bee!
Rumble young man! Rumble!
Waa!

—Muhammad Ali & Drew "Bundini" Brown, their "war cry," *The Greatest: My Own Story*, 1975

★ For another fighter's line that has passed into general usage, see Joe Louis on Billy Conn—"He can run, but he can't hide"—above.

2 Football isn't a contact sport, it's a collision sport. Dancing is a contact sport.

—Vince Lombardi, quoted in James A. Michener, *Sports in America* [1976]

★ See also Lombardi at WINNING & LOSING, VICTORY & DEFEAT.

3 In our family there was no clear line between religion and fly fishing.

—Norman MacLean, *A River Runs Through It*, 1976

★ The opening line of this great Montana novel.

4 The point of the game is not how well the individual does but whether the team wins. That is the beautiful heart of the game, the blending of personalities, the mutual sacrifices for group success.

—Bill Bradley, *Life on the Run*, 1976

5 [Baseball:] It breaks your heart. It is designed to break your heart.

—A. Bartlett Giamatti, *The Green Fields of the Mind*, in *Yale Alumni Magazine*, 1977

6 Thank you, God, for giving me strength and making me a ballplayer.

—Jim "Catfish" Hunter, on Catfish Hunter Day at Yankee Stadium, Sept. 16, 1979

7 It's [boxing's] most immediate appeal is that of the spectacle, in itself wordless, lacking a language, that requires others to define it, celebrate it, complete it.

—Joyce Carol Oates, *On Boxing*, 1987

8 Merit will win, it was promised by baseball.

—A. Bartlett Giamatti, *Take Time for Paradise*, 1989

Baseball . . . expresses our longing for the rule of law while licensing our resentment of law givers. **1**

—A. Bartlett Giamatti, quoted in *The New York Times* [Oct. 1, 1997]

★ Meaning umpires.

There's no crying in baseball. **2**

—Lowell Ganz & Babaloo Mandel, screenplay, *A League of Their Own*, 1992

Football combines the two worst features of modern American life: it's violence punctuated by committee meetings. **3**

—George Will, in *Baseball*, produced by Ken Burns, Public Broadcasting System, 1994

There is a fine line between boxing and chaos. **4**

—Gordon Fink, AP, July 9, 1997

★ Fink, a Nevada Deputy Attorney General, was asking the state's boxing commission to revoke the license of heavyweight Mike Tyson, who had bit above the belt, chomping an opponent's ear.

Rowing is such a beautiful small, obscure sport. **5**

—Craig Lambert, *Mind Over Water: Lessons of Life From the Art of Rowing*, 1998

Baseball. If there's a more beautiful word in the English language, I have yet to hear it. **6**

—Tim Russert, *Big Russ and Me*, 2004

★ This is a riff on Henry James, who would have disagreed with Mr. Russert or, perhaps, his ghostwriter, William Novak. See James at NATURE: SEASONS.

[Boxing:] a sport of the poor, set up to the entertain the middle class. **7**

—Pete Hamill, *Ring of Fire*, television documentary, 2005

Spring

See NATURE: SEASONS.

Statistics

See SCIENCE: MATHEMATICS & STATISTICS.

Stories

See also BOOKS & READING.

There are only two or three human stories, and they go on repeating themselves as fiercely as if they had never happened before. **8**

—Willa Cather, *O Pioneers!*, 1913

All stories, if continued long enough, end in death. **9**

—Ernest Hemingway, *Death in the Afternoon*, 1932

1 Listen, little Elia: draw your chair up close to the edge of the precipice and I'll tell you a story.

—**F. Scott Fitzgerald,** in Edmund Wilson, ed., *The Crack-Up, Notebook E* [1945]

2 To call a story a true story is an insult to both art and nature. Every writer is a great deceiver, but so is that arch-cheat Nature.

—**Vladimir Nabokov,** *Good Readers and Good Writers*, 1948

★ More at NATURE.

3 We tell ourselves stories in order to live.

—**Joan Didion,** *The White Album: A Chronicle of Survival in the Sixties*, in *New West*, June 4, 1979

4 What stories can do . . . is make things present.

—**Tim O'Brien,** *The Things They Carried*, 1990

5 We think that we are reading nature by applying rules of logic and laws of matter to our observations. But we are often telling stories—in the good sense, but stories nevertheless.

—**Stephen Jay Gould,** *Bully for Brontosaurus*, 1991

6 For what is story if not relief from the pain
of the inconclusive, from dread of the meaningless.

—**Mon Van Duyn,** *Endings* in *Firefall*, 1992

Strength & Toughness

See also ALASKA (Robert W. Service); BIGNESS; RUTHLESSNESS; VIOLENCE.

7 Concentration is the secret of strength in politics, in war, in trade, in short in all management of human affairs.

—**Ralph Waldo Emerson,** *The Conduct of Life*, 1860

8 There is a homely adage which runs: "Speak softly and carry a big stick; you will go far."

—**Theodore Roosevelt,** speech, Sept. 2, 1901

★ For background on this adage, see T.R. at FOREIGN POLICY.

9 The world breaks everyone, and afterwards many are strong at the broken places.

—**Ernest Hemingway,** *A Farewell to Arms*, 1929

10 A nation does not have to be cruel to be tough.

—**Franklin D. Roosevelt,** radio speech, Oct. 13, 1940

11 Physical strength can never permanently withstand the impact of spiritual force.

—**Franklin D. Roosevelt,** speech, May 4, 1941

12 If you can't stand the heat, get out of the kitchen.

—**Harry S. Truman,** saying

★ David McCullough in *Truman*, 1992, said this is an old Missouri saying that Truman first heard in the 1930s.

When the going gets tough, the tough get going. 1
—**Anonymous**

★ This maxim was popularized by John N. Mitchell, attorney general (1969–72) in the first Nixon administration, but used earlier by John F. Kennedy's father, Joseph P. Kennedy, according to J. H. Cutler's *Honey Fitz* (1962). It also has been attributed to football coach Knute Rockne.

The more rapidly the styles succeed and displace one another, the more offensive 2
they are to sound taste.
—**Thorstein Veblen,** *The Theory of the Leisure Class*, 1899

Stupidity

See FOOLS & STUPIDITY.

Style

See also ART: STYLE IN WRITING & EXPRESSION; FASHION & CLOTHES; GRACE.

Style is the ultimate morality of the mind. 3
—**Alfred North Whitehead,** *The Aims of Education*, in *The Organization of Thought*, 1917

Elegance is refusal. 4
—**Diana Vreeland,** quoted by Holly Brubach, *The New York Times Magazine* [Jan. 12, 1997]

★ Vreeland was editor-in-chief of *Vogue* from 1963 to 1971.

Style is character. 5
—**Joan Didion,** *Georgia O'Keeffe*, 1976, in *The White Album* [1979]

★ Reminiscent of the most famous dictum on style: "*Le style est l'homme même*"—"The style is the man himself"—by Georges Louis Leclerc de Buffon, *Discours sur le style*, 1753.

People are much too concerned about having good taste. . . . It's not a character flaw 6
if you don't have good taste.
—**Paige Rense,** editor of *Architectural Digest*, quoted in *The New York Times*, Oct. 25, 1993

Style is about surviving, about having been through a lot and making it look easy. 7
—**C. Z. Guest,** quoted in Annette Tapert and Diana Edkins, *The Power of Style* [1994]

Success & Fame

See also WINNING & LOSING, VICTORY & DEFEAT.

Success has ruined many a man. 8
—**Benjamin Franklin,** *Poor Richard's Almanack*, 1752

1 The sublime and the ridiculous are often so nearly related that it is difficult to class them separately. One step above the sublime makes the ridiculous, and one step above the ridiculous makes the sublime again.

—**Tom Paine,** *The Age of Reason,* 1794

★ Paine appears to be the first with this wording. Napoleon is credited with remarking to the Abbé de Pradt in 1812, *Du sublime au ridicule il n'ya qu'un pas*—"From the sublime to the ridiculous is only a step." He was referring to his retreat from Russia. The comment has also been attributed to the French foreign minister Talleyrand. Heinrich Heine made the same observation in *Reisebilder,* 1826.

2 There is always room at the top.

—**Daniel Webster,** attributed

3 How dreary—to be Somebody!
How public—like a Frog—
To tell your name—the livelong June—
To an admiring Bog.

—**Emily Dickinson,** poem no. 288, 1861

4 Fame is a bee,
It has a song—
It has a sting—
Ah, too, it has a wing.

—**Emily Dickinson,** poem no. 67, c. 1859

5 Success is counted sweetest
By those who ne'er succeed.

—**Emily Dickinson,** *Success*, in *Poems*, V [1890]

6 All you need in this life is ignorance and confidence, and then success is sure.

—**Mark Twain,** letter to Mrs. Foote, Dec. 2, 1887

7 Fame is a vapor, popularity an accident; the only earthly certainty is oblivion.

—**Mark Twain,** *Notebook*, c. 1868–1869

8 Success is to be measured not so much by the position that one has reached in life as by the obstacles which he has overcome while trying to succeed.

—**Booker T. Washington,** *Up from Slavery*, 1901

9 He has achieved success who has lived well, laughed often and loved much.

—**Bessie Anderson Stanley,** "Success," 1904

★ *Bartlett's* notes that this opening to a definition of "success" was the prize-winner in a contest conducted by *Brown Book Magazine*.

10 The highest form of vanity is love of fame.

—**George Santayana,** *The Life of Reason: Reason in Society*, 1905–1906

11 The moral flabbiness born of the exclusive worship of the bitch-goddess SUCCESS. That—with the squalid cash interpretation put on the word success—is our national disease.

—**William James,** letter to H. G. Wells, Sept. 11, 1906

Success, like charity, covers a multitude of sins. **1**
—Alfred Thayer Mahan, *Naval Strategy*, 1911

★ More at WINNING & LOSING, VICTORY & DEFEAT.

Success consists in the climb. **2**
—Elbert Hubbard, *The Roycroft Dictionary and Book of Epigrams*, 1923

Pray that success will not come any faster than you are able to endure it. **3**
—Ibid.

Some men succeed by what they know; some by what they do; and a few by what **4**
they are.
—Ibid.

Success has killed more men than bullets. **5**
—Texas Guinan, saying used in nightclub act, c. 1920s

Fame always brings loneliness. Success is as ice cold and lonely as the North Pole. **6**
—Vicki Baum, *Grand Hotel*, 1931

Be nice to people on your way up because you'll need them on your way down. **7**
—Wilson Mizner, quoted in Alva Johnson, *The Incredible Mizners*, from *New Yorker* profiles [1942, 1950]

★ Also attributed to Jimmy Durante.

Success is relative. **8**
—T. S. Eliot, *The Family Reunion*, 1939

Sweet smell of success. **9**
—Ernest Lehman, *Tell Me About It Tomorrow*, 1950

★ The title of the novella was changed to *Sweet Smell of Success* in its reincarnations as a screenplay (1957) and musical (2002). The phrase originally appeared in this context: "I allowed the soothing music and the muted sounds of the city and the rich sweet smell of success that permeated the room to lull my senses."

Success is always dangerous, and early success is deadly. **10**
—Calder Willingham, *The New York Times* obituary [Feb. 21, 1995], quoting interview, 1953

★ In 1947, Willingham, age twenty-four, became an overnight success with his novel *End as a Man*, about bad times at a military school similar to the Citadel in South Carolina. He never equaled this achievement as a novelist but had a good career in the movies, most famously as the writer, with Buck Henry, of the screenplay for *The Graduate* (1967). See BUSINESS for advice to the graduate re "plastics."

Once we find the fruits of success, the taste is nothing like what we had anticipated. **11**
—William Inge, introduction to collection of his major plays [1990]

★ Inge in the 1950s was one of America's most successful playwrights; his hits included *Come Back, Little Sheba* and *Picnic*. In the 1960s his reputation declined, and in 1973 he committed suicide.

1 The celebrity is a person who is known for his well-knownness.
—**Daniel J. Boorstin,** *The Image*, 1962

2 A sign of a celebrity is often that his name is worth more than his services.
—**Ibid.**

3 In the future, everyone will be world-famous for fifteen minutes.
—**Andy Warhol,** *Andy Warhol's Exposures*, catalogue of his photographs, exhibition in Stockholm, Sweden, 1968

4 Whenever a friend succeeds, a little something in me dies.
—**Gore Vidal,** *The New York Times Sunday Magazine*, Sept. 16, 1973

5 Eighty percent of success is showing up.
—**Woody Allen,** saying

★ Politicians of different persuasions popularized variations of this remark. Pres. George H. W. Bush several times remarked that "Ninety percent of life is showing up," while New York governor Mario Cuomo fudged with, "Most of life is just a matter of showing up." Word columnist William Safire queried Allen on the matter, and Allen confirmed that he had used the eighty-percent figure in an interview and that he had been talking about success, not life generally (*The New York Times Magazine*, August 13, 1989). See also Theodore Roosevelt at WISDOM.

6 You like me, right now, you like me!
Sally Field, upon winning her second Oscar, 1985

★ Her first was in 1980, for *Norma Rae.* The second was for *Places in the Heart.*

7 Success breeds arrogance and complacency.
—**Ross Perot,** *Frontline* television documentary on General Motors, Oct. 12, 1993

8 Success is a lousy teacher. It seduces smart people into thinking they can't lose.
—**Bill Gates,** *The Road Ahead,* 1995

9 Those whom the gods wish to destroy, they first make famous.
—**Joyce Carol Oates,** *Down the Road* in *The New Yorker*, March 27, 1995

★ A variation on the ancient saying, "Those whom God wishes to destroy, he first makes mad." This earliest version is from a fragment by Euripides

Suffering & Pain

See also ILLNESS & REMEDIES; SORROW; TROUBLE; UNHAPPINESS.

10 No pain, no palm; no thorns, no throne; no gall, no glory; no cross, no crown.
—**William Penn,** *No Cross, No Crown*, 1669

11 There are people who have an appetite for grief. Pleasure is not strong enough and they crave pain.
—**Ralph Waldo Emerson,** *The Tragic,* in *Uncollected Prose, Dial Essay,* 1844

He has seen but half the universe who has not been shown the house of pain. 1
—**Ralph Waldo Emerson,** letter to his aunt Mary Moody Emerson

★ Also, the opening sentence of his 1844 essay, *The Tragic Dial.*

Know how sublime a thing it is 2
To suffer and be strong.
—**Henry Wadsworth Longfellow,** *The Light of the Stars*, in *Voices of the Night*, 1839

A *Wounded* Deer—leaps highest. 3
—**Emily Dickinson,** poem no. 165, c. 1860

After great pain, a formal feeling comes. 4
—**Emily Dickinson,** poem no. 341 c. 1862

Pain—Has an element of Blank— 5
It cannot recollect
When it begun—or if there were
A time when it was not—
—**Emily Dickinson,** poem no. 650, c. 1862

If pain could have cured us, we should long ago have been saved. 6
—**George Santayana,** *The Life of Reason: Reason in Common Sense*, 1905–1906

God will not look you over for medals, degrees, or diplomas, but for scars! 7
—**Elbert Hubbard,** *The Note Book*, 1927

About suffering they were never wrong, 8
The Old Masters: how well they understood
Its human position; how it takes place
While someone else is eating or opening a window or just walking dully along.
—**W. H. Auden,** *Musée des Beaux Arts*, in *Another Time*, 1940

Don't look forward to the day you stop suffering, because when it comes you'll *know* you're dead. 9
—**Tennessee Williams,** quoted in London *Observer*, Jan. 26, 1958

Perhaps the worst thing about suffering is that it finally hardens the hearts of those around it. 10
—**Gloria Steinem,** *Ruth's Song* in *Outrageous Acts and Everyday Rebellions*, 1983

I feel your pain. 11
—**Bill Clinton,** during the primary campaign, March 26, 1992

Suicide

The question is whether [suicide] is the way *out*, or the way *in*. 12
—**Ralph Waldo Emerson,** *Journal*, 1839

1 Razors pain you;
Rivers are damp;
Acid stains you;
And drugs cause cramp;
Guns aren't lawful;
Nooses give;
Gas smells awful;
You might as well live.
—Dorothy Parker, *Résumé*, in *Enough Rope*, 1927

2 To my friends: My work is done. Why wait?
—George Eastman, suicide note, March 14, 1932

★ Eastman, the great inventor, manufacturer, and philanthropist, was plagued by illness in his final years.

3 Dying
Is an art, like everything else.
I do it exceptionally well.
—Sylvia Plath, *Lady Lazarus*, 1962–63

★ *Lady Lazarus* is one of the *Ariel* poems, which Plath wrote during the half year before her suicide in 1963.

4 A suicide kills two people . . . that's what it's for.
—Arthur Miller, *After the Fall*, 1964

★ Miller was married for five years to film star Marilyn Monroe, who committed suicide in 1962.

Summer

See NATURE: SEASONS.

Supreme Court

See also CONSTITUTION, THE; PRIVACY (Brennan).

5 John Marshall has made his decision, now let him enforce it.
—Andrew Jackson, 1832

★ Pres. Jackson was making the point that the Supreme Court must depend on the executive branch of government to enforce its decisions. The decision that riled Jackson came in a case involving Indian rights. Chief Justice Marshall and the court had ruled on March 3, 1832, against the state of Georgia, which sought to annex territories belonging to the Creeks and Cherokees. (Gold had been discovered in Cherokee country in 1828.) The remark, reported by Horace Greeley, has a decidedly Jacksonian ring and many historians accept it. Jackson's sympathies were all with the state. Robert Remini demurs, however, concluding in his 1988 *Life of Andrew Jackson* that Old Hickory never said it, there being no reason for him to do so: The court had not issued any orders that required enforcement by the executive branch. Whatever the case, Jackson did ignore the court's ruling. The Creeks and then the Cherokees were pressured into relinquishing their lands by treaty and in 1838 were exiled west of the Mississippi. For the Cherokees, this forcible removal along what came to be called

"The Trail of Tears" cost them nearly a quarter of their population of 18,000. See also Speckled Snake at RACES & PEOPLES.

Th' supreme coort follows th' iliction returns. 1

—**Finley Peter Dunne,** *The Supreme Court's Decision*, in *Mr. Dooley's Opinions*, 1900

★ This was the era of the Spanish-American War and American empire building, which was largely a Republican venture. The Democrats, taking a liberal view of the rights of people conquered by Americans, contended that "the Constitution follows the flag." In particular, they argued that the Constitution should apply to the people of the newly acquired Philippine Islands. The Democrats, however, failed to wrest the presidency from William McKinley, and the Supreme Court failed to find that the Constitution applied in the Philippines. As Mr. Dooley noted, in full: "No matther whether th' constitution follows th' flag or not, th' supreme coort follows th' iliction returns."

The Nine Old Men. 2

—**Drew Pearson & Robert S. Allen,** book title, 1936

★ This was not meant as a compliment.

Under our constitutional system, courts stand against any winds that blow as havens of refuge for those who might otherwise suffer because they are helpless, weak, outnumbered, or because they are non-conforming victims of prejudice and public excitement. . . . No higher duty, or more solemn responsibility, rests upon this Court than that of translating into living law and maintaining this Constitutional shield deliberately planned and inscribed for the benefit of every human being subject to our Constitution—of whatever race, creed, or persuasion. 3

—**Hugo L. Black,** *Chambers v. Florida*, 1938

★ Black, a former senator from Alabama, had once been a member of the Ku Klux Klan; the membership was confirmed after Black joined the Supreme Court in 1937. H. L. Mencken joked, "Hugo won't have to buy any new robes. All he'll have to do is dye his old ones black" (quoted by Johnny Greene, in *The Dixie Smile*, in *Harper's*, Sept. 2, 1946). Black, however, was not a racist at heart, and when Chief Justice Charles Evan Hughes gave him a chance to redeem his reputation in the *Chambers* case, he rose to the occasion with a magnificent decision. In this case, four black murder suspects had confessed following an all-night police "interrogation." Their confessions led to convictions, and they had been sentenced to die.

The people have seemed to feel that the Supreme Court, whatever its defects, is still the most detached, dispassionate, and trustworthy custodian that one system affords for the translation of abstract into concrete constitutional comands. 4

—**Robert H. Jackson,** *The Supreme Court in the American System of Government*, 1955

If this country wanted its Supreme Court to reflect the immediate social or political wishes of the people, it would provide for the election of the Court. And if the Founding Fathers had wanted it that way, they could have said so—or at least hinted at it. They did just the opposite: they designed a system that tried to immunize the Court from the changing moods and passions of the people. 5

—**Mario Cuomo,** speech to American Bar Association, New York City, in *The New York Times*, August 12, 1986

Sweden

See NATIONS & REGIONS.

Switzerland

See NATIONS & REGIONS.

Talk

See also CONVERSATION; LANGUAGE & WORDS; SILENCE.

1 Great talkers, little doers.
—Benjamin Franklin, "Preface: Courteous Reader," *Poor Richard's Almanack*, 1733

★ *Poor Richard* was based on skillful honing of proverbs and aphorisms. For example an earlier, wordier version of this saying goes, "The greatest talkers are the least doers," James Howell, *Lexicon Tetraglotten*, London, 1660.

2 Here comes the orator! with his flood of words, and his drop of reason.
—Benjamin Franklin, *Poor Richard's Almanack*, Oct. 1735

3 A word to the wise is enough, and many words won't fill a bushel.
—Benjamin Franklin, "Preface: Courteous Reader," *Poor Richard's Almanack*, 1758

4 A sharp tongue is the only edged tool that grows keener with constant use.
—Washington Irving, *Rip Van Winkle*, in *The Sketch Book*, 1820

5 No, never say nothin' without you're compelled tu,
An' then don't say nothin' thet you can be held tu.
—James Russell Lowell, *The Courtin'* in *The Biglow Papers* Series II, 1866

6 The chief effect of talk on any subject is to strengthen one's own opinion.
—Charles Dudley Warner, *Sixth Study*, in *Backlog Studies*, 1873

7 I have heard talk and talk, but nothing is done. Good words do not last long unless they amount to something.
—Joseph the Younger, in *An Indian's View of Indian Affairs*, in *The North American Review*, no. 269, vol. 128, 1879

★ Chief Joseph of the Nez Percé, was referring to the broken promises of white men. He continued: "Words do not pay for my dead people. They do not pay for my country, now overrun by white men. They do not protect my father's grave. They do not pay for all my horses and cattle. Good words will not give me back my children." More at EQUALITY.

8 The only bird that can talk is the parrot, and he doesn't fly very well.
—Wilbur Wright, saying

★ This was attributed to aviation pioneer Wright by astronaut Neil Armstrong in a speech at the White House on July 20, 1994, the twenty-fifth anniversary of the first moon landing. From the same era as the Wright brothers, John D. Rockefeller, in his later years, liked to recite another bit of wisdom based on a bird: "A wise old owl lived in an oak / The more he saw, the less he spoke / The less he spoke, the more he heard / Why aren't we all like that old bird?" A close variant of this verse appeared in the English humor magazine *Punch* in 1875.

If you don't say anything, you won't be called on to repeat it. **1**
—Calvin Coolidge, attributed

★ Historian Sheldon Stern has pointed out that so-called "Silent Cal" actually made more speeches than any of his predecessors, while holding more press conferences per month than F.D.R. (*The New York Times*, Dec. 28, 1997). Perhaps his reputation for silence was influenced by his flinty Yankee appearance. Alice Roosevelt Longworth, in *Crowded Hours*, 1933, passed along a Coolidge joke, a comment that her doctor attributed to one of his patients: "Though I yield to no one in my admiration for Mr. Coolidge, I do wish he did not look as if he had been weaned on a pickle." Coolidge had a light side, however. See his comment on the virility of the rooster, in the note on the anonymous "Higgamus, hoggamus" verse at SEX.

Talking's something you can't do judiciously unless you keep in practice. **2**
—Dashiell Hammett, *The Maltese Falcon*, 1930

Loose lips sink ships. **3**
—Anonymous, World War II slogan

When you're leading, don't talk. **4**
—Thomas E. Dewey, remark during the 1948 presidential campaign, Richard Norton Smith, *Thomas E. Dewey* [1982]

Talk is an old man's last vice. **5**
—Louise Erdrich, *Tracks*, 1988

Taxes

Taxation without representation is tyranny. **6**
—James Otis, attributed by John Adams and others, 1763

★ The aphorism circulated in many forms in reaction to the taxes imposed on the colonies in the 1760s by Great Britain. Otis's exact words are not known. In 1764, he wrote in *Rights of the Colonies*, "No parts of His Majesty's dominions can be taxed without their consent." See also AMERICAN HISTORY: MEMORABLE MOMENTS, the anonymous slogan from 1765.

The united voice of all His Majesty's free and loyal subjects in America—liberty and **7**
property and no stamps.
—Anonymous, newspaper motto, 1765–1766

★ The Stamp Act of 1765 was the first direct tax applied by the British in the American colonies. Newspapers, legal bills, and other documents were required to bear a stamp, which had to be purchased from official stamp distributors. *Bartlett's* states that this quote was the motto of various colonial newspapers.

In this world nothing can be said to be certain, except death and taxes. **8**
—Benjamin Franklin, letter to Jean-Baptiste Leroy, Nov. 13, 1789

★ More at THE CONSTITUTION.

1 The power to tax involves the power to destroy.
—John Marshall, *McCulloch v. Maryland*, March 6, 1819

★ Chief Justice Marshall here rejected the claim of the state of Maryland that it had a right to tax the Bank of the United States. In so doing, he expanded and bolstered the power of the federal government. Daniel Webster, one of the attorneys for the bank, had argued: "An *unlimited* right to tax implies a right to destroy." See also the second quote from Oliver Wendell Holmes, Jr., below for more on the power to destroy.

2 The wisdom of man never yet contrived a system of taxation that would operate with perfect equality.
—Andrew Jackson, *Proclamation to the People of South Carolina*, Dec. 10, 1832

3 Of all debts, men are least willing to pay taxes. What a satire is this on government!
—Ralph Waldo Emerson, *Politics*, in *Essays: First Series*, 1844

4 The beggar is taxed for a corner to die in.
—James Russell Lowell, *The Vision of Sir Launfal*, 1848

5 The thing generally raised on city land is taxes.
—Charles Dudley Warner, *My Summer in a Garden*, 1870

6 The tax-gatherer is viewed as a representative of oppression.
—Frederick J. Turner, *The Significance of the Frontier in American History*, 1893

★ Life on the frontier promotes individualism, Turner wrote, adding: "The tendency is anti-social. It produces antipathy to control"—including imposition of taxes. See also Turner at AMERICA & AMERICANS.

7 I am in favor of an income tax. When I find a man who is not willing to bear his share of the burdens of the government which protects him, I find a man who is unworthy to enjoy the blessings of a government like ours.
—William Jennings Bryan, speech, Democratic National Convention, July 8, 1896

8 What is the difference between a taxidermist and a tax collector? The taxidermist takes only your skin.
—Mark Twain, notebook entry, Dec. 30, 1902, in Albert Bigelow Paine, ed., *Mark Twain's Notebook* [1935]

9 Taxes are what we pay for civilized society.
—Oliver Wendell Holmes, Jr., *Compañía General de Tabacos de Filipinas v. Collector of Internal Revenue*, 1904

10 The income tax has made more liars out of the American people than golf has.
—Will Rogers, *The Illiterate Digest*, 1924

★ This first appeared as one of his weekly articles, April 8, 1923, entitled "Helping the Girls with their Income Taxes." See also Barry Goldwater below.

11 The power to tax is not the power to destroy while this court sits.
—Oliver Wendell Holmes, Jr., *Panhandle Oil Co., v. Mississippi ex rel. Knox*, 1930

Taxes are paid in the sweat of every man who labors. **1**

—**Franklin D. Roosevelt,** speech, Pittsburgh, Oct. 19, 1932

Anyone may arrange his affairs so that his taxes may be as low as possible; he is not bound to choose the pattern which will best pay the Treasury; there is not even a patriotic duty to increase one's taxes. **2**

—**Learned Hand,** *Helvering v. Gregory*, 1934

★ One keeps taxes low through the use of legal tax umbrellas. As explained in an anonymous verse, probably from this era, "The rain, it raineth all around, / Upon the just and unjust fellas, / But more upon the just because / The unjust have the just's umbrellas," *American Heritage*, Dec. 1973.

Taxes, after all, are the dues that we pay for the privileges of membership in an organized society. **3**

—**Franklin D. Roosevelt,** campaign speech, Worcester, Mass., Oct. 21, 1936

Why shouldn't the American people take half my money from me? I took all of it from them. **4**

—**Edward Filene,** quoted in Arthur M. Schlesinger, Jr., *The Coming of the New Deal*, 1959

★ Filene founded the famous Filene's department store in Boston.

Don't tax you, **5**
Don't tax me,
Tax that man behind the tree.

—**Anonymous,** political saying

★ Sen. Russell B. Long described this as the basic principle of tax reform, *Forbes* magazine, Dec. 15, 1976.

[We should] have a tax structure which looks like someone designed it on purpose. **6**

—**William E. Simon,** quoted in *Blueprints for Tax Reform*, 1977

I have only one thing to say to the tax increasers: Go ahead, make my day. **7**

—**Ronald Reagan,** speech, American Business Conference, Washington, D.C., March 13, 1985

★ The president was threatening to veto legislation increasing taxes. He borrowed a line from the Dirty Harry movie *Sudden Impact*; see under Stinson at DANGER & DANGEROUS PEOPLE.

We don't pay taxes. Only the little people pay taxes. **8**

—**Leona Helmsley,** quoted in *The New York Times*, July 12, 1989

★ A witness in the trial of Helmsley on charges of tax evasion alleged that the "hotel queen" made this imprudent remark. As provocative as "Let them eat cake"—words that Marie-Antoinette probably never uttered, —the quote helped to convict the elderly Helmsley and send her to jail. See also Peter De Vries at MONEY & THE RICH.

The Congress will push me to raise taxes, and I'll say, no, and they'll push, and I'll say no, and they'll push again. And all I can say to them is, read my lips: No new taxes. **9**

—**George H. W. Bush,** presidential nomination acceptance speech, Republican National Convention, August 18, 1988

★ This rousing and wildly applauded pledge was the emotional high point of the convention. But it was perhaps too memorable, for Congress did push, and in 1990, Pres. Bush did raise taxes, which ignited a political firestorm from which he never recovered. Bush was trying to adopt the Hollywood-style menace popularized by his predecessor Ronald Reagan, who posed as "Dirty Harry" when threatening to veto tax increases; see above. Bush's "read my lips" was borrowed from the 1973 screenplay for *Magnum Force*, by John Milius and Michael Cimino. The phrase has roots in rock music and is the title of a 1957 song by Joe Greene and a 1978 album by Tim Curry. Mr. Curry told William Safire of *The New York Times* that he picked up the phrase from an Italian-American recording engineer. More from this speech at AMERICA & AMERICANS and AMERICAN HISTORY: MEMORABLE MOMENTS.

1 The income tax created more criminals than any other single act of government.
—**Barry Goldwater,** interview, *Firing Line*, PBS, Nov. 18, 1989

★ See also Will Rogers above.

Technology

See SCIENCE: TECHNOLOGY.

Television

See MEDIA.

Temptation

See also SIN, VICE, & NAUGHTINESS.

2 It is not the great temptations that ruin us; it is the little ones.
—**John W. De Forest,** *Seacliff, or The Mystery of the Westervelts*, 1859

3 There are several good protections against temptation, but the surest is cowardice.
—**Mark Twain,** *Pudd'nhead Wilson's New Calendar*, in *Following the Equator*, 1897

4 We should be judged, not by our acts, but by our temptations.
—**Elbert Hubbard,** *The Roycroft Dictionary and Book of Epigrams*, 1923

5 The last temptation is the greatest treason:
To do the right deed for the wrong reason.
—**T. S. Eliot,** *Murder in the Cathedral*, 1935

6 I generally avoid temptation unless I can't resist it.
—**Mae West,** *My Little Chickadee*, 1940

★ Similar to Oscar Wilde's "I can resist everything except temptation," *Lady Windemere's Fan*, 1892.

Tennessee

See also CITIES (MEMPHIS, NASHVILLE).

The Bostonian looks down upon the Virginian—the Virginian on the Tennessean. 1
—***Southern Literary Messenger***, XIX, 1853

The Perfect Thirty-six. 2
—**Anonymous,** designation for Tennessee, the 36th state to ratify the 19th Amendment, giving women the right to vote, August 18, 1920

★ The amendment required ratification by two-thirds of the states, or thirty-six states. Tennessee put the amendment over the top. The deciding vote was cast by Henry Thomas Burn (see AMERICAN HISTORY: MEMORABLE MOMENTS) acting on the advice of his mother (see WOMEN). The phrase "perfect thirty-six" was used in newspapers to refer not only to the number of states but also to supposedly perfect female dimensions: 36-24-36.

Tennessean's lives are unhurried. Though they may complain about weather, poor crops, bad business and politics, beneath all is a certain feeling of security. The farmer will leave his plowing, the attorney his lawsuit, the business man his accounts, for a moment's or an hour's conversation with stranger or friend. 3
—**Federal Writers' Project,** *Tennessee: A Guide to the State*, 1939

What you need for breakfast, they say in East Tennessee, is a jug of good corn liquor, a thick beefsteak, and a hound dog. Then you feed the beefsteak to the hound dog. 4
—**Charles Kuralt,** *Dateline America*, 1979

Tennessee—America at its best. Agriculture and Commerce. 5
—Motto, state of Tennessee

Texas

See also CITIES (AMARILLO, AUSTIN, DALLAS, EL PASO, HOUSTON, LAREDO, LUBBOCK, PAMPA, VAN HORN).

The province of Techas will be the richest state of our Union without any exception. 6
—**Thomas Jefferson,** letter to James Monroe, May 15, 1820

No person will be admitted as a settler, who does not produce satisfactory evidence of having supported the character of a moral, sober, and industrious citizen. 7
—**Stephen F. Austin,** *Permit and Conditions for Colonization,* Nov. 23, 1821

★ This was the first of the "General Regulations Relative to the Colony," issued by Austin, who came to be called "The Father of Texas."

The people are universally kind and hospitable. . . . Everybody's house is open, and table spread, to accommodate the traveler. There are no poor people here, and none are rich. 8
—**Mary Austin Holley,** letter from Bolivar, Texas, Dec., 1831

★ She was a first cousin to Stephen Austin. The letter goes on to explain that "poor and rich . . . get the same quantity of land on arrival, and if they do not continue equal, it is for want of good management on the one part, or superior industry and sagacity on the other."

1 I must say, as to what I have seen of Texas, it is the garden spot of the universe. The best land and the best prospects for health I ever saw, and I do believe it is a fortune to any man to come here. There is a world of country here to settle.

—**David Crockett,** letter to his daughter, Margaret, and her husband, Wiley Flowers, Jan. 19, 1836

2 Remember the Alamo!

—**Sidney Sherman,** battle cry, April 21, 1836

★ More at AMERICAN HISTORY: MEMORABLE MOMENTS.

3 If I owned Texas and Hell, I would rent out Texas and live in Hell.

—**Philip H. Sheridan,** remark, Officers' Mess, Fort Clark, Texas, 1855

★ Sheridan was two years out of West Point. He went on to become commanding general of the U.S. Army.

4 Texas has an arcadian preeminence of position among our States, and an opulent future before her, that only wanton mismanagement can forfeit.

—**Frederick Law Olmsted,** *A Journey Through Texas,* 1857

★ Olmsted, the greatest American landscape architect, was also a social reformer and what we would call an ecologist. He designed Central Park in Manhattan and Prospect Park in Brooklyn, both with Calvert Vaux.

5 Texas. Texas.

—**Samuel Houston,** last words, 1863

6 There is no law west of the Pecos.

—**Anonymous,** saying 1880s

★ Justice of the Peace Roy Bean was an exception, of sorts, to this general observation. In his saloon-courtroom, The Jersey Lily, in Langtry, Texas, Bean advertised himself as "Judge Roy Bean, Notary Public" and "The Law West of the Pecos." Both the saloon and town were named by Bean in honor of the actress Lillie Langtry. Among Bean's many colorful legal pronouncements was a cause-of-death ruling: "The gent met his death at the hands of an unknown party who was a damned good pistol shot," attributed, c. 1895. It is said that Bean once fined a dead man forty dollars for carrying a concealed weapon, but when a friend of Bean's was charged with the same offense, he ruled that the man was not guilty because he was standing still when arrested and so could not be said to be "carrying" a weapon. On another occasion, he supposedly freed the murderer of a Chinese railroad worker because he could find no law on the books that made it a crime "to kill a Chinaman."

7 The rattlesnake bites and the scorpion stings,
The mosquito delights with its buzzing wings;
The sand burs prevail and so do the ants,
And those who sit down need soles on their pants.
The summer heat is a hundred and ten—
Too hot for the Devil, too hot for men;

The wild boar roams thru the black chaparral— 1
'Tis a Hell of a place is this Texas Hell.

—**E. U. Cook,** last two verses, *Hell in Texas*, 1886

★ Cook, manager of Keystone Land and Cattle Co., wrote this poem following the drought of 1885–86. It was very popular among all those Texans not dead of heat stroke. In the poem, the Lord gives a decidedly poor piece of property along the Rio Grande to the Devil, who furnishes it with thorns, fleas, tarantulas, and similar amenities.

The place where there are the most cows and the least milk, and the most rivers and the least water in them, and where you can look the furthest and see the least. 2

—**Anonymous,** c. 1880s, in H. L. Mencken, *A New Dictionary of Quotations on Historical Principles from Ancient and Modern Sources* [1942]

I'm going to leave old Texas now, 3
For they've got no use for the longhorn cow;
They've plowed and fenced my cattle range,
And the people there are all so strange.

—**Anonymous,** *The Texas Song,* c. 1890, in Clark C. Spence, ed., *The American West* [1966]

The sun shines bright 4
Deep in the heart of Texas.

—**June Hershey,** *Deep in the Heart of Texas,* music by Don Swander, 1941

In Texas the cattle come first, then the men, then the horses and last the women. 5

—**Edna Ferber,** *Giant,* 1952

★ Identified as "an old Texas saying."

A local umbry—gets hold of oil and money, why, he's liable to want to be Governor of Texas. Or worse. 6

—**Edna Ferber,** *Giant*, 1952

★ "Umbry" is a local pronunciation of "hombre," the umbry in question being the novel's anti-hero, Rink Jett.

Here was a society dominated entirely by the masculine principle. 7

—**J. B. Priestley,** *Journey Down a Rainbow*, 1955

Texas, in the eyes of its inhabitants and in maps supplied to visitors, occupies all of the North American continent but a fraction set aside for the United States, Canada, and Mexico. 8

—**Lord Kinross,** *The Innocents at Home*, 1959

Texas is a state of mind. Texas is an obsession. Above all, Texas is a nation in every sense of the word. 9

—**John Steinbeck,** *Travels with Charley*, 1962

★ Or in the words of the state's tourism slogan: "Texas: It's Like a Whole Other Country."

1 Once you are in Texas it seems to take forever to get out, and some people never make it.

—Ibid.

2 The Texas legislature consists of 181 people who meet for 140 days every two years. This catastrophe has now occurred 63 times.

—Molly Ivins, *The Atlantic,* May 1975

★ On the positive side, Ms. Ivans recommended the legislature as "the finest free entertainment in Texas."

3 In Texas, we regard politics as a contact sport.

—Lloyd Bentsen, attributed

★ A common observation, most often attributed to Lloyd Bentsen, with Ann Richards a close second. Both, as Texas Democrats, took their share of hard hits. Often the phrase is "full-contact sport," as in Karl Rove, longtime advisor to George W. Bush. "In both states [Texas and Louisiana], we look upon politics as sort of like Friday night high school football; it's a full-contact sport" (television interview, Oct. 12, 2003).

4 If God had meant Texans to ski, he would have made bullshit white.

—Anonymous, *The Texas Observer,* Sept. 19, 1980

5 When I die, bury me in Texas because I want to remain politically active.

—Jack Valenti, quoted by William Safire, *The New York Times,* Jan. 3, 2000

6 In Texas, we don't do nuance.

—George W. Bush, remark to CNN reporter Candy Crowley, quoted in William Safire's column, *The New York Times Magazine* [March 28, 2004]

7 Friendship.

—Motto, state of Texas

Thanksgiving

8 Ah! on Thanksgiving day, when from east and from west,
From North and from South come the pilgrim and guest.

—John Greenleaf Whittier, *The Pumpkin*, 1844

9 What moistens the lip and what brightens the eye?
What calls back the past, like the rich pumpkin pie?

—Ibid.

10 Over the river and through the wood,
To grandfather's house we go.
The horse knows the way
To carry the sleigh
Through the white and drifted snow.
Trot fast my dapple gray!
Spring over the ground
Like a hunting-hound!

For this is Thanksgiving Day!
Over the river and through the wood—
Now grandmother's cap I spy!
Hurrah for the fun!
Is the pudding done?
Hurrah for the pumpkin pie!

—**Lydia Maria Child,** *Thanksgiving Day*, in *Flowers for Children*, 1844–46

★ Note, it is "grandfather's" house in the original, not "grandmother's." The author's paternal grandfather, Benjamin Francis, had a house in Medford, Massachusetts. He was a veteran of the Revolutionary War, and both of his wives had died before the author was born. Lydia Maria Child, a prominent reformer and author, did not in fact have happy memories of family life. "Cold, shaded, and uncongenial was my childhood and youth," she reported in an interview in 1877. "Whenever reminiscences rise before me, I turn my back on them as quickly as possible."

The year which is drawing toward its close has been filled with the blessings of fruitful fields and healthful skies. . . . I do, therefore, invite my fellow citizens . . . to set apart and observe the last Thursday of November next as a day of thanksgiving and praise to our beneficent Father who dwelleth in the heavens. 1

—**Abraham Lincoln,** Oct. 3, 1863

★ This proclamation was the fruit of a thirty-year campaign by Sarah Hale, the editor of *Godey's Lady's Book*, to establish Thanksgiving as a national holiday.

And therefore I, William Bradford 2
(By the grace of God today,
And the franchise of this good people),
Governor of Plymouth, say—
Through virtue of vested power—ye
Shall gather with one accord,
And hold it the month of November,
Thanksgiving unto the Lord.

—**Margaret Junkin Preston,** *The First Thanksgiving*, c. 1875

Dear the people coming home, 3
Dear glad faces long away,
Dear the merry cries, and dear
All the glad and happy play.
Dear the thanks, too, that we give
For all of this Thanksgiving Day.

—**Harriet Prescott Spofford,** *Every Day Thanksgiving Day*, in *Poems*, 1881

Heap high the board with plenteous cheer and gather to the feast, 4
And toast that sturdy Pilgrim band whose courage never ceased.

—**Alice Williams Brotherton,** *The First Thanksgiving Day*

'Twas founded be th' Puritans to give thanks f'r bein' presarved fr'm th' Indians, an' . . . we keep it to give thanks we are presarved fr'm th' Puritans. 5

—**Finley Peter Dunne,** *Thanksgiving*, in *Mr. Dooley's Opinions*, 1900

Theater

See ART: THEATER, DRAMA, & MAGIC.

Things & Possessions

See also LUXURY; PROPERTY.

1 Things have their laws as well as men; things refuse to be trifled with.
—Ralph Waldo Emerson, *Politics*, in *Essays: Second Series*, 1844

2 Things are of the snake.
—Ralph Waldo Emerson, *Ode Inscribed to W. H. Channing*, in *Poems*, 1847

★ The Satanic snake.

3 Things are in the saddle,
And ride mankind.
—Ralph Waldo Emerson, *Ode Inscribed to W. H. Channing*, in *Poems*, 1847

4 A coin, sleeve button, or collar button dropped in a bedroom will hide itself and be hard to find. A handkerchief in bed *can't* be found.
—Mark Twain, *Mark Twain's Notebook*, Albert Bigelow Paine, ed. [1935]

5 The mortality of all inanimate things is terrible to me, but that of books most of all.
—William Dean Howells, letter to Charles Eliot Norton, April 6, 1903

6 No ideas but in things.
—William Carlos Williams, *A Sort of a Song*

★ More at ART: WRITING.

7 The goal of all inanimate objects is to resist man and ultimately to defeat him.
—Russell Baker, in *The New York Times*, June 18, 1968

8 Inanimate objects are classified scientifically into three major categories—those that don't work, those that break down, and those that get lost.
—Ibid.

9 The difference between men and boys
is the price of their toys.
—Malcolm S. Forbes, *The Sayings of Chairman Malcolm: The Capitalist's Handbook*, 1978

★ Mr. Forbes's toys included lead soldiers, hot air balloons, motorcycles, Fabergé; Easter eggs, and a yacht. A 1990 biography of him was aptly entitled *The Man Who Had Everything*.

10 To delight in possession is to allow the conceivability of dispossession.
—Richard Ellman, lecture, Bennington, Vt., Sept. 28, 1983, reprinted in *a long the riverrun*, 1988

Thought

See MIND, THOUGHT, & UNDERSTANDING.

Time

See also Future, the; Life; Past, the; Present, the; Seasons & Times.

Lost time is never found again. **1**
—Benjamin Franklin, *Poor Richard's Almanack*, Jan. 1748

★ See also Poor Richard on time and life, at Life.

Remember that time is money. **2**
—Benjamin Franklin, *Advice to a Young Tradesman*, 1748.

★ See also Franklin at Money.

Time makes more converts than reason. **3**
—Tom Paine, Introduction, *Common Sense*, 1776

Look not mournfully into the past. It comes not back again. Wisely improve the present. It is thine. Go forth to meet the shadowy future, without fear, and with a manly heart. **4**
—Henry Wadsworth Longfellow, *Hyperion*, 1839

Time dissipates to shining ether the solid angularity of facts. **5**
—Ralph Waldo Emerson, *History*, in *Essays: First Series*, 1841

★ See also Emerson at Facts.

So the little minutes, **6**
Humble though they be,
Make the mighty ages
Of eternity.
—Julia Carney, *Little Things*, 1845

★ More at Details & Other Small Things.

As if you could kill time without injuring eternity. **7**
—Henry David Thoreau, *Economy*, in *Walden*, 1854

Time is but the stream I go a-fishing in. **8**
—Henry David Thoreau, *Where I Lived and What I Lived For*, in *Walden*, 1854

★ Thoreau continued the metaphor of the stream this way: "I drink at it; but while I drink I see the sandy bottom and detect how shallow it is. Its thin current slides away, but eternity remains."

Backward, turn backward, O Time, in your flight, **9**
Make me a child again just for tonight!
—Elizabeth Akers Allen, *Rock Me to Sleep*, 1860

★ Along with *Casey at the Bat* (see Sports) and *The Night Before Christmas* (see Christmas), *Rock Me to Sleep* was one of the great 19th-century recitation pieces.

Time flies over us, but leaves its shadow behind. **10**
—Nathaniel Hawthorne, *The Marble Faun*, 1860

1 The surest poison is time.
—Ralph Waldo Emerson, *Old Age*, in *Society and Solitude*, 1870

2 Time has laid his hand
Upon my heart, gently, not smiting it,
But as a harper lays his open palm
Upon his harp to deaden its vibrations.
—Henry Wadsworth Longfellow, *The Cloisters*, in *The Golden Legend*, 1872

3 Ah, the clock is always slow.
It is later than you think.
—Robert W. Service, *Songs of a Sourdough*, 1907, retitled *The Spell of the Yukon*, 1915

4 The small intolerable drums
Of time are like slow drops descending.
—Edwin Arlington Robinson, *The Poor Relation*, in *Man Against the Sky*, 1916

5 Time is a great legalizer, even in the field of morals.
—H. L. Mencken, *Prejudices: First Series*, 1919

6 Our life is spent trying to find something to do with the time we have rushed through life trying to save.
—Will Rogers, *The Autobiography of Will Rogers* [1949]

7 Time present and time past
Are both perhaps present in time future,
And time future contained in time past.
—T. S. Eliot, *Four Quartets: Burnt Norton*, 1935

8 Time is the school in which we learn,
Time is the fire in which we burn.
—Delmore Schwartz, *For Rhoda*, 1938

9 Time wounds all heels.
—Jane Sherwood Ace, c. 1930s

★ This play on the proverbial "Time heals all wounds" was attributed by Goodman Ace to his wife in *The Fine Art of Hypochondria; or, How Are You?* (1966). Ace might be suspected of bias in crediting her for the *bon mot*, but it fits with her reputation for producing malapropisms (e.g., "Congress is still in season" and "I'm really in a quarry") on their long-running (1930–45) radio show, *The Easy Aces.* The line also has been attributed to Groucho Marx, who used it in *The Marx Brothers Go West* (1940).

10 Time the destroyer is time the preserver.
—T. S. Eliot, *Four Quartets: The Dry Salvages*, 1941

11 Time is the longest distance between two places.
—Tennessee Williams, *The Glass Menagerie*, 1945

For us believing physicists, the distinction between past, present, and future is only an illusion, even if a stubborn one. 1

—**Albert Einstein,** letter to Michele Angelo Besso's son after his father's death, March 21, 1955

I must govern the clock, not be governed by it. 2

—**Golda Meir,** quoted by Oriana Fallaci, in *L'Europeo*, 1976

People spend so much time fretting about what they did yesterday and dreading what might happen tomorrow, they miss out on all their todays. 3

—**John D. MacDonald,** *One Fearful Yellow Eye*, 1960

Father Time and Mother Earth, A marriage on the rocks. 4

—**James Merrill,** *The Broken Home,* 1966

Time is what prevents everything from happening at once. 5

—**John A. Wheeler,** in *The American Journal of Physics*, 1978

One reason God created time was so that there would be a place to bury the failures of the past. 6

—**James Long,** in *Leadership Magazine,* Winter 1997

Times

See Good Times; Bad Times; Seasons & Times.

Times of Day

See Nature: Times of Day.

Tobacco

I remember with shame how formerly, when I had taken two or three pipes, I was presently ready for another, such a bewitching thing it is; but I thank God he has now given me power over it; sure there are many who may be better employed than sucking a stinking tobacco-pipe. 7

—**Mary Rowlandson,** *A True History of the Captivity and Restoration of Mrs. Mary Rowlandson*, 1682

★ Mary Rowlandson was among those abducted by Indians who attacked Lancaster, Massachusetts, on February 10, 1676. The captives became pawns in a larger game—King Philip's War—but she was ransomed after eleven weeks and five days. During her captivity, she overcame many hardships—and also gave up smoking. Her account became a 17th-century best-seller.

Tobacco is a filthy weed, 8
That from the devil does proceed;
It drains your purse, it burns your clothes,
And makes a chimney of your nose.

—**Benjamin Waterhouse,** 1754–1846

★ This verse was recalled by Oliver Wendell Holmes Sr., who had been vaccinated by Dr. Waterhouse. One of the three founding professors of Harvard Medical School,

Waterhouse was the first American physician to vaccinate patients as a matter of routine. He began in 1800 with his five-year-old son, using thread impregnated with vaccine against smallpox that he had obtained from Edward Jenner in England.

1 The believing we do something when we do nothing is the first illusion of tobacco.
—**Ralph Waldo Emerson,** *Journal*, 1859

2 Some things are better eschewed than chewed; tobacco is one of them.
—**George Dennison Prentice,** *Prenticeana*, 1860

3 A man of no conversation should smoke.
—**Ralph Waldo Emerson,** *Journal*, 1866

4 The roots of tobacco plants must go clear through to hell.
—**Thomas Alva Edison,** diary, July 12, 1885

★ Edison had a tobacco habit; he chewed tobacco, smoked heavy cigars and knew they were making him sick. Still, he lived to be eighty-four. This day's diary entry was cited in *American Heritage*, Dec. 1970.

5 I have made it a rule never to smoke more than one cigar at a time. I have no other restrictions as regards smoking.
—**Mark Twain,** speech, on his seventieth birthday, Delmonico's, New York City, Dec. 5, 1905

★ Twain confided that (like Edison) he didn't exercise either; see PHYSICAL FITNESS.

6 Tobacco is as indispensable as the daily ration. We must have thousands of tons of it without delay.
—**John Joseph Pershing,** cable to Washington, 1917

★ Gen. Pershing was commander in chief of the American Expeditionary Force in World War I.

7 What this country needs is a really good five-cent cigar.
—**Thomas Riley Marshall,** remark in the U.S. Senate, reported in the *New York Tribune*, Jan. 4, 1920

★ Vice President Marshall, a former governor of Indiana, reportedly made this remark to John Crockett, chief clerk of the Senate, during a tedious Senate debate on the needs of the nation. See also Franklin P. Adams at VALUE and, for another astute Marshall observation, VICE PRESIDENCY.

8 [This cigarette] is a revolutionary nicotine delivery device.
—**Barbara Reuter,** confidential memo for R.J. Reynolds Co., cited by the U.S. Food and Drug Administration, *Washington Post*, Dec. 9, 1995

★ The cigarette delivered less tar but ample nicotine. The statement was helpful to the FDA, which was seeking regulatory authority over tobacco products.

Tolerance

See also Government (Mencken).

Error of opinion may be tolerated where reason is left free to combat it. 1
—Thomas Jefferson, First Inaugural Address, March 4, 1801

If you want to be free, there is but one way; it is to guarantee an equally full meas- 2
ure of liberty to all your neighbors.
—Carl Schurz, in George Seldes, *The Great Quotations* [1960]

The highest result of education is tolerance. 3
—Helen Keller, *Optimism*, 1903

If there is but one truth, and you have that truth completely, toleration of differences 4
means an encouragement to error, crime, evil, sin.
—Crane Brinton, *The Anatomy of Revolution*, 1952

Shallow understanding from people of goodwill is more frustrating than absolute 5
misunderstanding. Lukewarm acceptance is much more bewildering than outright rejection.
—Martin Luther King, Jr., letter from Birmingham city jail, 1963

Travel

[Traveling] makes men wiser but less happy. 6
—Thomas Jefferson, letter to Peter Carr, August 10, 1787

No man should travel until he has learned the language of the country he visits. 7
Otherwise he voluntarily makes himself a great baby—so helpless and so ridiculous.
—Ralph Waldo Emerson, *Journal*, 1833

Traveling is a fool's paradise. 8
—Ralph Waldo Emerson, *Self-Reliance*, in *Essays: First Series*, 1841

★ Emerson wrote that it is "for want of self culture" that educated Americans had created "the idol of traveling." After calling travel "a fool's paradise," he noted, "We owe to our first journeys the discovery that place is nothing."

Generally speaking, a howling wilderness does not howl; it is the imagination of the 9
traveler that does.
—Henry David Thoreau, *Maine Woods,* 1846

★ Thoreau attributes this to his guide, Joe Polis, a sophisticated and well-to-do Penobscot Indian.

I love to sail forbidden seas, and land on barbarous coasts. 10
—Herman Melville, *Moby-Dick*, 1851

I have traveled a good deal in Concord. 11
—Henry David Thoreau, *Economy,* in *Walden*, 1854

★ Thoreau preferred to travel by foot; see Leisure and Speed.

1 We go to Europe to be Americanized.
—Ralph Waldo Emerson, *Culture,* in *The Conduct of Life*, 1860

2 I can wish the traveller no better fortune than to stroll forth in the early evening with as large a reserve of ignorance as my own.
—Henry James, *Collected Travel Writings* [1993]

3 In order to travel one must have a home, and one that is loved and pulling a little at the heart-strings all the while; for the best thing about traveling is going home.
—Charles Dudley Warner, *The Whims of Travel*, Sept. 12, 1875

4 To forget pain is to be painless; to forget care is to be rid of it; to go abroad is to accomplish both.
—Mark Twain, letter to Dr. John Brown, June 22, 1876

5 Afoot and light-hearted I take to the open road,
Healthy, free, the world before me
The long brown path before me leading wherever I choose.
—Walt Whitman, *Song of the Open Road*, 1881

★ In our time, poet Louis Simpson asked, "Where are you, Walt? / The Open Road goes to the used-car lot" (*Walt Whitman at Bear Mountain Bridge,* 1963)

6 "The road to the City of Emeralds is paved with yellow brick," said the Witch, "so you cannot miss it."
—L. Frank Baum, *The Wonderful Wizard of Oz*, 1900

7 Why do people so love to wander? I think the civilized parts of the world will suffice for me in the future.
—Mary Cassatt, letter to Louisine Havemeyer, Feb. 11, 1911

8 I have discovered that most of
the beauties of travel are due to
the strange hours we keep to see them.
—William Carlos Williams, *January Morning*, "Suite," in *Al Que Quiere!*, 1917

★ See also CITIES (WEEHAWKEN).

9 My heart is warm with the friends I make,
And better friends I'll not be knowing;
Yet there isn't a train I wouldn't take,
No matter where it's going.
—Edna St. Vincent Millay, *Travel*, in *Second April*, 1921

10 The woods are lovely, dark and deep.
But I have promises to keep,
And miles to go before I sleep,
And miles to go before I sleep.
—Robert Frost, *Stopping by Woods on a Snowy Evening*, 1923

Men travel faster now, but I do not know if they go to better things. **1**
—**Willa Cather,** *Death Comes for the Archbishop*, 1927

Winter is coming and tourists will soon be looking for a place to mate. **2**
—**Will Rogers,** *Daily Telegram*, Oct. 27, 1932

★ Tourists bothered Rogers. He wrote to Pres. Calvin Coolidge from Europe in 1926, "We, unfortunately, don't make a good impression collectively. . . . There ought to be a law prohibiting over three Americans going anywhere abroad together."

Come with me to the Casbah. **3**
—**Anonymous,** from c. 1938

★ The quote often is attributed to Charles Boyer, who is supposed to have said it, with a heavy dose of Gallic innuendo, in the 1938 movie *Algiers*. But as Tom Burnham pointed out in *More Misinformation*, Boyer never uttered the line in any film or stage appearance. He said that his press agent of the time invented the invitation.

We shall not cease from exploration **4**
And the end of all our exploring
Will be to arrive where we started
And know the place for the first time.
—**T. S. Eliot,** *Four Quartets: Little Gidding*, 1940

I rather expect that from now on I shall be travelling north until the end of my days. **5**
—**E. B. White,** *Stuart Little*, 1945

What a long, strange trip it's been. **6**
—**The Grateful Dead band,** *Truckin*, words by Robert Hunter, first performed Aug. 18, 1970

Thanks to the interstate highway system, it is now possible to travel from coast to coast without seeing anything. **7**
—**Charles Kuralt,** *On the Road*, 1980

First you fall in love with Antarctica, and then it breaks your heart. **8**
—**Kim Stanley Robinson,** *Antarctica*, 1998

Trees

See NATURE: TREES.

Trouble

See also ANXIETY & WORRY; BAD TIMES; DANGER & DANGEROUS PEOPLE; DEPRESSION, THE; ILLNESS & REMEDIES; PROBLEMS; SORROW; SUFFERING & PAIN; UNHAPPINESS.

Into each life some rain must fall, **9**
Some days must be dark and dreary.
—**Henry Wadsworth Longfellow,** *The Rainy Day*, 1842

1 And the cares that infest the day,
Shall fold their tents like the Arabs,
And as silently steal away.
—Henry Wadsworth Longfellow, *The Day Is Done*, 1845

★ More at ART: MUSIC.

2 Every calamity is a spur and valuable hint.
—Ralph Waldo Emerson, *Fate* in *The Conduct of Life*, 1860

3 If you see ten troubles coming down the road, you can be sure that nine will run into the ditch before they reach you, and you will have to battle with only one of them.
—Calvin Coolidge, saying

★ Herbert Hoover, who inherited the results of Pres. Coolidge's laissez-faire approach to national affairs, had a comment on this Yankee saying: "The trouble with this philosophy was that when the tenth trouble reached him, he was wholly unprepared. . . . The outstanding instance was the rising boom and orgy of mad speculation which began in 1927," quoted by John Kenneth Galbraith, *The Days of Boom or Bust*, in *American Heritage*, August 1958.

4 The kiss of death.
—Al Smith, remark, 1926

★ Smith, the Democratic governor of New York, was referring to his old enemy William Randolph Hearst, who had come out in support of Republican Ogden Mills in the 1926 gubernatorial election. When Smith got the news, he commented happily, "It's the kiss of death!" He was right and went on to a fourth term.

5 "Difficulties" is the name given to things which it is our business to overcome.
—Ernest J. King, graduation address, U.S. Naval Academy, Annapolis, Md., June 19, 1942

★ Admiral King had been named Chief of Naval Operations the preceding March.

6 If anything can go wrong, it will.
—Edward A. Murphy, Jr., c. 1949

★ The search for Murphy, the originator of "Murphy's law," rivaled the hunt for Kilroy, but seems to have been more successful. Various authorities (e.g., Robert L. Forward in *Science 83*, Jan.-Feb 1983, and George E. Nichols in the *Listener*, Feb. 16, 1984) have assigned credit for the law to Capt. Edward A. Murphy, a development engineer from the Wright Field Aircraft Laboratory, in Ohio, then working on crash research tests at Edwards Air Force Base in California. After tracing a malfunction in a strain gauge he had designed to the botched wiring of a particular technician, he is said to have observed, "If there's a way to do it wrong, he will." The law has inspired many variations. Thus, Murphy's First Law of Biology is "Under any given set of environmental conditions an experimental animal behaves as it damn well pleases." Murphy's Law of Thermodynamics reads: "Things get worse under pressure." The law's corollaries include "Nothing is as easy as it looks" and "Everything takes longer than you think."

7 Everybody fasten your seat belts. It's going to be a bumpy night.
—Joseph L. Mankiewicz, *All About Eve*, 1950

★ Bette Davis speaking.

Great crises produce great men and great deeds of courage. **1**

—John F. Kennedy, *Profiles in Courage*, 1956

It's not the tragedies that kill us; it's the messes. **2**

—Dorothy Parker, interview, *Paris Review,* Summer 1956

If you can keep your head when all about you are losing theirs, it's just possible you haven't grasped the situation. **3**

—Jean Kerr, *Please Don't Eat the Daisies*, 1957

★ The reference, of course, is to Rudyard Kipling's poem *If*, from 1910, which contains the lines "If you can keep your head when all about you / Are losing theirs, and blaming it on you,"—and if you can do a lot of other mature and heroic things—then "Yours is the earth and everything that's in it, / And—which is more—you'll be a man, my son!"

When written in Chinese, the word *crisis* is composed of two characters. One represents danger and the other represents opportunity. **4**

—John F. Kennedy, speech, United Negro College Fund, Indianapolis, Ind., April 12, 1959

★ See also Charles Beard at WISDOM, WORDS OF for a quote on the dark and bright aspects of adversity

The Perfect Storm. **5**

—Sebastian Junger, book title, 1991

★ The title is now used to describe confluences of bad events of all sorts. The subject of the book was a vicious storm off the Northeast Coast of America in October 1991, in which the fishing boat *Andrea Gail* was lost.

Adversity introduces a man to himself. **6**

—Alonzo Mourning, quoted in *The New York Times,* May 16, 1999

★ Mourning played center for the Miami Heat basketball team, which had been upset in a playoff series by their arch-rivals, the New York Knicks.

Trust

See also FOREIGN POLICY (Reagan)

Trust men and they will be true to you. **7**

—Ralph Waldo Emerson, *Prudence*, in *Essays: First Series*, 1841

Our distrust is very expensive. **8**

—Ralph Waldo Emerson, *Man the Reformer*, lecture, Boston, Jan. 25, 1841

I think we may safely trust a good deal more than we do. **9**

—Henry David Thoreau, *Economy*, in *Walden,* 1854

Thrust [trust] ivrybody—but cut th' ca-ards. **10**

—Finley Peter Dunne, *Casual Observations*, in *Mr. Dooley's Opinions*, 1900

I never trust a man I can't buy. **11**

—Benjamin Franklin Keith, attibuted, in *Vaudeville*, WNET, [Nov. 26, 1997]

★ Keith teamed up Edward Franklin Albee in 1885 and formed the national Keith-

Albee circuit of theaters. The quote also has been attributed to Abraham Lincoln Erlanger, partner with Marc Klaw in the rival Theatrical Syndicate.

1 In God we trust. All others, we virus scan.
—**Anonymous,** *Quote Garden,* internet, 2004

Truth

See also CENSORSHIP; DISHONESTY & LIES; SKEPTICISM.

2 Truth often suffers more by the heat of its defenders than from the arguments of its opposers.
—**William Penn,** *Some Fruits of Solitude*, 1693

3 Such is the irresistible nature of truth that all it asks, and all it wants, is the liberty of appearing.
—**Tom Paine,** *The Rights of Man*, 1791–92

4 There is not a truth existing which I fear, or would wish unknown to the world.
—**Thomas Jefferson,** letter to Henry Lee, 1826

5 There is nothing so powerful as truth—and often nothing so strange.
—**Daniel Webster,** argument in the case of the murder of Captain White, April 26, 1830

6 The ability to discriminate between that which is true and that which is false is one of the last attainments of the human mind.
—**James Fenimore Cooper,** *The American Democrat*, 1838

7 Truth crushed to earth shall rise again.
—**William Cullen Bryant,** *The Battlefield*, 1839

★ See also Bryant at THE WORLD.

8 God offers to every mind its choice between truth and repose. Take which you please—you can never have both.
—**Ralph Waldo Emerson,** *Intellect*, in *Essays: First Series*, 1841

★ See Emerson on a similar choice between power and joy at POWER.

9 Truth forever on the scaffold.
—**James Russell Lowell,** *The Present Crisis*, 1844

★ More at TYRANNY.

10 It takes two to speak the truth—one to speak, and another to hear.
—**Henry David Thoreau,** *A Week on the Concord and Merrimack Rivers*, 1849

11 Truth is the silliest thing under the sun. Try to get a living by the truth—and go to the soup societies. Heavens! Let any clergyman try to preach the truth from its very stronghold, the pulpit, and they would ride him out of his church on his own pulpit banister.
—**Herman Melville,** letter to Nathaniel Hawthorne, June 1851

Rather than love, than money, than fame, give me truth. **1**
—Henry David Thoreau, "Conclusion," *Walden*, 1854

Truth is tough. **2**
—Oliver Wendell Holmes, Sr., *The Autocrat at the Breakfast-Table*, 1858

As scarce as truth is, the supply has always been in excess of the demand. **3**
—Josh Billings, *Josh Billings: Hiz Sayings*, 1866

Who dares **4**
To say that he alone has found the truth?
—Henry Wadsworth Longfellow, *The New England Tragedies*, 1868

Tell all the Truth, but tell it slant— . . . **5**
The Truth must dazzle gradually
Or every man be blind—
—Emily Dickinson, poem no. 1129, c. 1868

Truth is such a rare thing, it is delightful to tell it. **6**
—Emily Dickinson, letter to Col. Thomas Wentworth Higginson, August, 1870

★ He was one of the few men in her life. They corresponded for twenty-four years, from the time she was thirty-two until her death in 1886.

Truth is the only safe ground to stand upon. **7**
—Elizabeth Cady Stanton, *The Woman's Bible*, 1895

The man who finds a truth lights a torch. **8**
—Robert G. Ingersoll, *The Truth*, 1897

When in doubt, tell the truth. **9**
—Mark Twain, *Pudd'nhead Wilson's New Calendar*, in *Following the Equator*, 1897

Truth is stranger than Fiction, but it is because Fiction is obliged to stick to possibilities; Truth isn't. **10**
—Ibid.

Truth is the most valuable thing we have. Let us economize it. **11**
—Ibid.

Truth is mighty and will prevail. There is nothing the matter with this, except that it ain't so. **12**
—Mark Twain, *Mark Twain's Notebook*, Albert Bigelow Paine, ed., [1935]

Truth *happens* to an idea. It *becomes* true, is *made* true by events. Its verity *is* in fact an event, a process. **13**
—William James, *Pragmatism*, 1907

★ James, a pragmatist philosopher, took up the central question of what it means to say that a statement or theory is true. He argued that it means that we can specify "what definite difference" the statement will make at "definite instants" of our life. The meaning and truth of ideas depend upon their "practical consequences," "usefulness," and "workability." This contrasted with traditional notions that one can deduce absolute truths, as well as with the equally traditional suspicion that there may not be any such thing as truth. On the latter question, C. S. Peirce, who coined *pragmatism* in its philosophical sense, wrote: "Every man is fully satisfied that there is such a thing as truth or he would not ask any questions," *Collected Papers*, vol. V, para. 211. See also Albert Einstein below.

1 "The true," to put it very briefly, is only the expedient in the way of our thinking.
—**William James,** *Pragmatism*, 1907

2 There are no whole truths; all truths are half-truths.
—**Alfred North Whitehead,** prologue, *Dialogues of Alfred North Whithead* [1955], recorded by Lucien Price

3 Most of the change we think we see in life
Is due to truths being in and out of favor.
—**Robert Frost,** *The Black Cottage*, 1914

4 The best test of truth is the power of the thought to get itself accepted in the competition of the market.
—**Oliver Wendell Holmes, Jr.,** *Abrams v. U.S.*, 1919

★ More at FREE SPEECH.

5 The truth is always modern, and there never comes a time when it is safe to give it voice.
—**Clarence Darrow,** writing on Voltaire, cited in George Seldes, ed., *The Great Quotations* [1960]

★ One of Mr. Seldes's own books was titled *Tell the Truth and Run*.

6 For truth there is no deadline.
—**Heywood Broun,** *The Nation* magazine, Dec. 30, 1939

7 Too much truth
Is uncouth.
—**Franklin Pierce Adams,** *From the New England Primer* in *Nods and Becks,* 1944

8 I never give them hell. I just tell the truth and they think it's hell.
—**Harry S. Truman,** saying

★ Truman started giving the Republicans hell in 1948 during his railroad trip across the U.S.; see also AMERICAN HISTORY: MEMORABLE MOMENTS; POLITICAL SLOGANS.

9 Truth is what stands the test of experience.
—**Albert Einstein,** *Out of My Later Years*, 1950

10 The most casual student of history knows that, as a matter of fact, truth does *not* necessarily vanquish. . . . The cause of truth must be championed, and it must be championed dynamically.
—**William F. Buckley, Jr.,** *God and Man at Yale*, 1951

11 "Truth" has been displaced by "believability" as the test of the statements that dominate our lives.
—**Daniel J. Boorstin,** *The Image: A Guide to Pseudo-Events in America*, 1961

The great enemy of the truth is very often not the lie . . . but the myth. **1**
—John F. Kennedy, commencement address, Yale University, June 11, 1962

I don't care what anybody says about me as long as it isn't true. **2**
—Truman Capote, in David Frost, *The Americans*, 1970

★ Also attributed to Dorothy Parker.

There's a saying: Only children and old folks tell the truth. **3**
—Bessie Delany, *Having Our Say: The Delany Sisters' First 100 Years*, written with her sister, Sadie, 1993

The truth never arrives neatly wrapped. **4**
—Thomas Powers, *The Sins of a President*, in *The New York Times Book Review*, Nov. 30, 1997

Turkey

See NATIONS & REGIONS.

Tyranny

See also JUSTICE (Whittier); REVOLUTION.

Rebellion to tyrants is obedience to God. **5**
—Thomas Jefferson, personal motto, written on his seal

★ Jefferson was insired to adopt this motto after hearing Patrick Henry's "If this be treason" speech, according to Saul Padover's biography of the third president; for details on Henry, see AMERICAN HISTORY: MEMORABLE MOMENTS. Decades later, on February 24, 1823, Jefferson wrote Edward Everett that he believed that the maxim originated with one of the regicides of Charles I of England. *Bartlett's* notes that he probably was referring to John Bradshaw (1602–1659). See also Jefferson at REVOLUTION for his observation that the tree of liberty must be refreshed with the blood of patriots and tyrants.

All men would be tyrants if they could. **6**
—Abigail Adams, letter to John Adams, March 31, 1776

★ More at WOMEN & MEN.

Tyranny, like hell, is not easily conquered. **7**
—Tom Paine, *The American Crisis*, Dec. 23, 1776

I have sworn upon the altar of God, eternal hostility against every form of tyranny over the mind of men. **8**
—Thomas Jefferson, letter to Benjamin Rush, Sept. 23, 1800

★ The tyranny to which Jefferson referred included assaults on his character and presidential candidacy by the Christian clergy, particularly in Philadelphia. Rush, a Philadelphia physician, had written his friend Jefferson to report an apparently coordinated series of anti-Jefferson sermons. Jefferson responded to his accusers in this letter, with sentiments that are now inscribed on the rotunda of the Jefferson Memorial in Washington—without identification of Jefferson's target, of course. See also Jefferson at EPITAPHS & GRAVESTONES; RELIGION; RESISTANCE; as well as at UNION, THE, below.

1 Truth forever on the scaffold,
Wrong forever on the throne.
—**James Russell Lowell,** *The Present Crisis*, 1844

2 Repression is the seed of revolution.
—**Daniel Webster,** speech, 1845

3 Mounted majorities, clad in iron, armed with death.
—**Oliver Wendell Holmes, Sr.,** speech, Massachusetts Medical Society, May 30, 1860

★ More at MAJORITIES & MINORITIES.

4 The more complete the despotism, the more smoothly all things move on the surface.
—**Elizabeth Cady Stanton,** *History of Woman Suffrage*, written with Susan B. Anthony and Mathilda Gage, 1881

5 How hard the tyrants die!
—**Elbert Hubbard,** *The Roycroft Dictionary and Book of Epigrams*, 1923

6 Fascism is capitalism plus murder.
—**Upton Sinclair,** *Singing Jailbirds*, 1924

7 It Can't Happen Here.
—**Sinclair Lewis,** book title, 1935

★ The novel posits a fascist take-over of the United States in 1936; the ironic title is a perennial warning that unexpectedly bad things can happen.

8 Under conditions of tyranny it is far easier to act than to think.
—**Hannah Arendt,** quoted in W. H. Auden, *A Certain World*, 1971

9 As nightfall does not come at once, neither does oppression. In both instances, there is a twilight when everything remains seemingly unchanged. And it is in such twilight that we all must be most aware of change in the air—however slight—lest we become unwitting victims of the darkness.
—**William O. Douglas,** quoted by Professor Gary T. Marx, Massachusetts Institute of Technology, letter to *The New York Times* [August 15, 1989]

Unhappiness

See also ALIENATION; SORROW; SUFFERING & PAIN; TROUBLE.

10 Discontent is the want of self-reliance: it is infirmity of will.
—**Ralph Waldo Emerson,** *Self-Reliance*, in *Essays: First Series*, 1841

11 If misery loves company, misery has company enough.
—**Henry David Thoreau,** *Journal*, Sept. 1, 1851

The mass of men lead lives of quiet desperation. 1
—**Henry David Thoreau,** *Economy*, in *Walden*, 1854

★ More at LIFE.

I've never done a single thing I've wanted to in my whole life! I don't know's I've accomplished anything except just get along. 2
—**Sinclair Lewis,** *Babbitt*, 1922

Nobody loves me, 3
Everybody hates me,
Going into the garden
To eat worms.
—**Anonymous,** nursery verse, probably of English derivation, included in Iona and Peter Opie, *I Saw Esau*, rev. ed. [1992]

Unless one has learned to work in spite of extreme unhappiness, one will never accomplish much. One's lifetime will not be long enough. 4
—**Glenway Wescott,** journal, April 11, 1952, in Robert Phelps with Jerry Rosco, *Continual Lessons* [1990]

★ Wescott made this entry on his fifty-first birthday.

Years ago a person, he was unhappy, didn't know what to do with himself—he'd go to church, start a revolution—*something*. Today you're unhappy? Can't figure it out? What is the salvation? Go shopping. 5
—**Arthur Miller,** *The Price*, 1968

It's not what isn't, it's what you wish *was* that makes unhappiness. 6
—**Janis Joplin,** quoted in Gary Herman, *Rock 'N' Roll Babylon* [1982]

Union, the

See also UNITY.

Every difference of opinion is not a difference of principle. We have been called by different names brethren of the same principle. We are all Republicans—we are all Federalists. If there be any among us who would wish to dissolve this Union or to change its republican form, let them stand undisturbed as monuments to the safety with which error of opinion may be tolerated where reason is left free to combat it. 7
—**Thomas Jefferson,** First Inaugural Address, 1801

Liberty and Union, now and forever, one and inseparable! 8
—**Daniel Webster,** speech in Congress, Jan. 1830

★ This line marks the high point of the Hayne-Webster debate, in which Webster opposed the claim of Robert Hayne of South Carolina that a state had the right to nullify a federal law as unconstitutional. The Southern position, Webster phrased as "Liberty first and Union afterwards."

Our Federal Union! It must and shall be preserved. 9
—**Andrew Jackson,** April 30, 1830

★ At a formal birthday dinner, Pres. Jackson offered this toast to John Calhoun of South Carolina. Calhoun's counter toast was: "The Union, next to our liberty most dear. May we all remember that it can be preserved only by respecting the rights of states." Robert Remini, in his biography *The Life of Andrew Jackson*, observes that Jackson's personal slogan was "Our Federal Union, It Must Be Preserved."

1 Sail on, O Union, strong and great!

—Henry Wadsworth Longfellow, *The Building of the Ship*, 1849

★ More at AMERICA & AMERICANS.

2 All your strength is in your union.
All your danger is in discord.

—Henry Wadsworth Longfellow, *The Song of Hiawatha*, 1855

★ More at UNITY.

3 A house divided against itself cannot stand. I believe this government cannot endure permanently half slave and half free. I do not expect the Union to be dissolved. I do not expect the house to fall, but I do expect it will cease to be divided.

—Abraham Lincoln, speech, Republican State Convention, Springfield, Ill., June 16, 1858

★ In accepting the Republican nomination for the U.S. Senate, before he confronted the incumbent Democrat, Stephen A. Douglas, in a series of instantly famous debates, Lincoln succinctly described the crisis facing the nation. The reference to "a house divided" has two biblical sources. *Mark* 3:25 reads: "If a house be divided against itself, that house cannot stand." *Matthew* 12:25 is more colorful and prophetic in terms of American history: "Every kingdom divided against itself is brought to desolation; and every city or house divided against itself, shall not stand." Lincoln had been warned that a speech this blunt might cost him the election. He responded, "The time has come when those sentiments should be uttered, and if it is decreed that I should go down because of this speech, then let me go down linked with the truth—let me die in the advocacy of what is just and right."

4 A Union that can only be maintained by swords and bayonets, and in which strife and civil war are to take the place of brotherly love and kindness, has no charm for me.

—Robert E. Lee, letter to his son, Jan. 1861

★ Lee was still a colonel. The Union was coming apart as he wrote. South Carolina had seceded the previous month. Mississippi, Alabama, Georgia, and Louisiana did so in January. On April 18, the day after Virginia, Lee's own state, seceded, Gen. Winfield Scott offered to make him field commander of the Union army, but Lee declined, saying, "Save in defense of my native state, I never desire again to draw my sword." Scott, Lee's friend and also a Virginian, replied, "You have made the greatest mistake of your life, but I feared it would be so."

5 My paramount object in this struggle *is* to save the Union, and is *not* either to save or destroy slavery.

—Abraham Lincoln, reply to Horace Greeley, August 19, 1862

★ More at SLAVERY.

We shall nobly save or meanly lose the last, best hope of earth.
—**Abraham Lincoln,** second annual message to Congress, Dec. 1, 1862 1

★ More at SLAVERY.

"Neighbor, how stands the Union?" 2
—**Daniel Webster,** attributed, in Stephen Vincent Benét, *The Devil and Daniel Webster*, 1937

★ Webster's timeless question, according to Benét, came from a story that was told in the border country, where Massachusetts joins Vermont and New Hampshire. "Every time there's a thunderstorm around Marshfield [Mass.], they say you can hear his rolling voice in the hollows of the sky. And they say that if you go to his grave and speak loud and clear, 'Dan'l Webster—Dan'l Webster!' the ground will begin to shiver and the trees begin to shake. And after a while you'll hear a deep voice saying, 'Neighbor, how stands the Union?' Then you better answer that the Union stands as she stood, rock-bottomed and copper-sheathed, one and indivisible, or he's liable to rear right out of the ground."

United States Motto

See under GOD.

Unity

See also AMERICA & AMERICANS (*E pluribus unum*); DECLARATION OF INDEPENDENCE (Benjamin Franklin); LOYALTY; UNION, THE.

Then join hand in hand, brave Americans all! 3
By uniting we stand, by dividing we fall.
—**John Dickinson,** *The Liberty Song*, 1768

All your strength is in your union. 4
All your danger is in discord;
Therefore be at peace henceforward,
And as brothers live together.
—**Henry Wadsworth Longfellow,** *The Song of Hiawatha*, 1855

A house divided against itself cannot stand. 5
—**Abraham Lincoln,** Republican State Convention, Springfield, Ill., June 16, 1858

★ More at UNION, THE.

Universe, the

See also NATURE; SCIENCE: PHYSICS & COSMOLOGY; WORLD, THE.

The universe is all chemistry, with a certain hint of a magnificent *Whence* or *Whereto*. 6
—**Ralph Waldo Emerson,** letter to Caroline Sturgis Tappan, in Stephen E. Whicher, ed., *Selections from Ralph Waldo Emerson*, [1960]

1 I accept the universe.
—Margaret Fuller, attributed

★ We have been unable to find good authority for this common attribution. Some reliable reference works, such as *Bartlett's*, list no source; others do not list the quote. Nevertheless, the alleged remark comes complete with an alleged reaction: "By gad, she'd better," by Thomas Carlyle—and he did meet Fuller in London in 1846. William James, in *The Varieties of Religious Experience* (1902), not only passed along the Fuller remark, he added that it "is reported to have been a favorite utterance."

2 Law rules throughout existence, a law which is not intelligent, but Intelligence.
—Ralph Waldo Emerson, *Fate*, in *The Conduct of Life*, 1860

3 O amazement of things—even the least particle!
—Walt Whitman, *Song at Sunset*, 1860

4 A man said to the universe:
"Sir, I exist."
"However," replied the universe,
"The fact has not created in me
A sense of obligation."
—Stephen Crane, *War Is Kind and Other Lines*, 1899

5 Whenever we try to pick out anything by itself, we find it hitched to everything else in the universe.
—John Muir, quoted by John T. Nichols, *Natural History* magazine, [Nov. 1992]

6 The universe is not hostile, nor yet is it friendly. It is simply indifferent.
—John Haynes Holmes, *The Sensible Man's View of Religion*, 1933

7 The more the universe seems comprehensible, the more it also seems pointless.
—Steven Weinberg, *The First Three Minutes*, 1977

8 The universe is a spiraling Big Band in a polka-dotted speakeasy, effusively generating new light every one-night stand.
—Ishmael Reed, quoted in Jim (James A.) Haskins, *The Cotton Club*, 1977

★ For a similar thought, see Philip Roth at ART: THEATER, DRAMA, & MAGIC.

Usefulness

9 What good is a newborn baby?
—Benjamin Franklin, remark at first balloon ascension, Champs de Mars, France, August 27, 1783

★ Franklin, fascinated by the invention, was responding to someone in the huge crowd who asked, "What good is it?" This balloon was an unmanned hydrogen balloon that traveled fifteen miles. As it came down, it was attacked and destroyed by terrified peasants. Franklin also had a good view of the first free flight of a manned balloon, which was launched near his Paris house about three months later. This was a hot-air balloon invented by the Montgolfier brothers.

Democratic nations . . . will habitually prefer the useful to the beautiful, and they will require that the beautiful be useful. 1

—Alexis de Tocqueville, *Democracy in America*, 1835

Aim above morality. Be not simply good; be good for something. 2

—Henry David Thoreau, letter to Harrison G. O. Blake, Mar. 27, 1848

Nothing useless is, or low. 3

—Henry Wadsworth Longfellow, *The Builders*, 1849

Utah

See also CITIES (SALT LAKE CITY).

This is the place! 4

—Brigham Young, at first sight of the Great Salt Lake valley, July 24, 1847

★ Young recognized it as the place he had seen in a vision—possibly, though he didn't say this, inspired by a long conversation the preceding month with Jim Bridger, the famous mountain man and guide, who knew the territory like the back of his hand.

Let the Mormons have the territory to themselves—it is worth very little to others. 5

—Horace Greeley, *An Overland Journey from New York to San Francisco . . . in 1859*, 1860

Utah has always had a way of doing things different. 6

—Federal Writers' Project, *Utah: A Guide to the State*, 1941

Water in Utah is precious, savored as champagne might be in another land. Life does not come easy. . . . Utah's loveliness is a desert loveliness, unyielding and frequently sterile. 7

—Federal Writers' Project, *Utah: A Guide to the State*, 1941

Utah is the only place in the world where Jews are Gentiles. 8

—Anonymous, quoted in John Gunther, *Inside U.S.A.*, 1947

★ Non-Mormons are classified as Gentiles.

Industry. 9

—Motto, state of Utah

Utopia

In my Kosmis there will be no feeva of discord . . . all my immotions will function in hominy and kind feelings. 10

—George Joseph Herriman, *Krazy Kat*

★ The cartoon strip was first published in 1913. Many connoisseurs of this art form regard it as the best strip ever.

In the Big Rock Candy Mountains 11
There's a land that's fair and bright
Where the hand-outs grow on bushes

And you sleep out every night;
Where the box cars all are empty,
And the sun shines every day
On the birds and the bees
And the cigarette trees,
And the lemonade springs
Where the blue bird sings—
In the Big Rock Candy Mountains.
—Anonymous, c. 1920

★ Folk song experts John and Alan Lomax called this a favorite hobo chantey. Wallace Stegner used the verse as a symbol of the popular perception that the riches of the American West are inexhaustible. He noted that the ballad was supposedly written by Harry "Haywire Mac" McClintock in 1928. But Stegner heard his own father sing it long before then. In *Thoughts in a Dry Land* (1972), Stegner wrote that some people call Utah's Sigurd, or Pahvant, Mountain the Big Rock Candy Mountain. It is as colorful as a peppermint stick, he said.

1 [In Willoughby] a man can slow down to a walk and live his life full measure.
—Rod Serling, *A Stop At Willoughby*, 1960

★ In this classic from the first season of *Twilight Zone*, an unhappy commuter dreams of an idyllic, 19th-century New England town, and tries to get there.

Value & Values

See also Ethics, Morality, & Values.

2 When the well's dry, we know the worth of water.
—Benjamin Franklin, *Poor Richard's Almanack*, Jan. 1746

★ The rule is proverbial. See, for example, Thomas Fuller: "We never know the worth of water till the well is dry" (*Gnomologia*, 1732). Or both may have drawn on a proverbial saying.

3 What we obtain too cheap, we esteem too lightly; it is dearness [high cost] only that gives everything its value.
—Tom Paine, *The American Crisis*, 1776–1783

4 In short, I conceive that a great part of the miseries of mankind are brought upon them by the false estimates they have made of the value of things, and by their giving too much for their whistles.
—Benjamin Franklin, letter to Madame Brillon, Nov. 10, 1779

5 Labor is the true standard of value.
—Abraham Lincoln, speech, Pittsburgh, Pa., Feb. 15, 1861

6 There is no such thing as absolute value in this world. You can only estimate what a thing is worth to you.
—Charles Dudley Warner, *My Summer in a Garden*, 1871

7 What is false in the science of facts may be true in the science of values.
—George Santayana, *Interpretations of Poetry and Religion*, 1900

What this country needs is a good five-cent nickel. **1**

—**Franklin P. Adams,** in Robert E. Drennan, ed., *The Algonquin Wits* [1968]

★ A quip that played on an observation by Vice President Thomas Marshall; see TOBACCO.

Diamonds Are a Girl's Best Friend **2**

—**Leo Robin,** song title, *Gentlemen Prefer Blondes*, 1949

★ The successful musical, starring Carol Channing, was adapted from Anita Loos's 1925 novel of the same title.

Nothing is intrinsically valuable; the value of everything is attributed to it, assigned **3**
to it from outside the thing itself, by people.

—**John Barth,** *The Floating Opera*, 1956

Price is what you pay. Value is what you get. **4**

—**Warren Buffett,** in Janet Lowe, comp., *Warren Buffett Speaks: Wit and Wisdom from the World's Greatest Investor* [1997]

A true revolution of values will soon look uneasily on the glaring contrast of poverty **5**
and wealth.

—**Martin Luther King, Jr.,** *Where Do We Go from Here? Chaos or Community*, 1967

We no longer know how to justify any value except in terms of expediency. Man . . . **6**
feels, acts, and thinks as if the sole purpose of the universe were to satisfy his needs.

—**Abraham Joshua Heschel,** *The Insecurity of Freedom: Essays on Human Existence*, 1967

Variety

See DIFFERENCES.

Venezuela

See NATIONS & REGIONS.

Vermont

I lift up my eyes to the hills. **7**
From whence does my help come?
My help comes from the Lord, who made heaven and earth.

—**Bible,** *Psalms* 121:1-2

★ In Vermont, Psalm 121 is known as "the Vermont Psalm."

A Sunday-school teacher asked a child . . . "In what state were mankind left after the **8**
fall?"—"In the state of Vermont."

—**Harriet Martineau,** *Society in America*, 1837

1 Vermont, O maiden of the hills,
My heart is there with thee!

—**Wendell Phillips Stafford,** *Song of Vermont,* in *The Land We Love*, 1916

★ For the hills in autumn, see Sarah Cleghorn at NATURE: SEASONS.

2 These men cannot live in regular society. They are too idle, too talktative, too passionate, too prodigal, too shiftless, to acquire either property or character. They are impatient of the restraints of law, religion, morality; grumble about taxes by which rulers, ministers, and schoolmasters, are supported; and complain incessantly, as well as bitterly, of the extortions of mechanics, farmers, merchants, and physicians, to whom they are always indebted.

—**Timothy Dwight,** *Travels in New England and New York*, 1821

★ A not uncommon view of frontiersmen by those who lived along the more civilized seaboard. Compare the assessment of Dwight, a president of Yale, with William Byrd's earlier opinion of backwoodsmen in NORTH CAROLINA.

3 Statistics prove that no Vermonter ever left the state unless transportation was furnished in advance. She is what you call a "hard-boiled state." The principal ingredients are granite, rock salt, and Republicans. The last being the hardest of the three.

—**Will Rogers,** March 29, 1925, quoted in Donald Day, *The Autobiography of Will Rogers* [1949]

★ But Vermonters have elected Democratic governors in recent years.

4 I love Vermont because of her hills and valleys, her scenery and invigorating climate, but most of all, because of her indomitable people. They are a race of pioneers who have almost beggared themselves to serve others. If the spirit of liberty should vanish in other parts of the union, and support of our institutions should languish, it could all be replenished from the generous store held by the people of this brave little state of Vermont.

—**Calvin Coolidge,** speech, Bennington, Vt., Sept. 21, 1928

5 This state bows to nothing: the first legislative measure it ever passed was "to adopt the laws of God . . . until there is time to frame better."

—**John Gunther,** *Inside U.S.A.*, 1947

6 I live in New Hampshire so I can get a better view of Vermont.

—**Maxfield Parrish,** *Vermont Life*, 1952

★ Parrish was an extremely successful book illustrator and muralist. See also Robert Frost at NEW HAMPSHIRE.

7 Vermont's a place where barns come painted
Red as a strong man's heart,
Where stout carts and stout boys in freckles
Are highest forms of art.

—**Robert Tristram Coffin,** *Vermont Looks Like a Man*, 1955

★ According to *Simpson's Contemporary Quotations*, by James B. Simpson, this is the last poem that Coffin contributed to the *New York Herald Tribune*'s editorial page prior to his death on January 20, 1955.

All in all, Vermont is a jewel state, small but precious. 1
—Pearl S. Buck, *Pearl Buck's America*, 1971

They deliberately chose Vermont, and a hard-working, old-fashioned life. I hear this 2
attitude of Vermonters described as "preventing the future."
—Charles Kuralt, *Charles Kuralt's America*, 1995

Freedom and unity. 3
—Motto, state of Vermont

Vice Presidency, the

My country has in its wisdom contrived for me the most insignificant office that ever 4
the invention of man contrived or his imagination conceived.
—John Adams, letter to Abigail Adams, Dec. 19, 1793

★ Adams was the first vice president, and most politicians since have agreed with his assessment of the job. In 1993, Vice President Al Gore, while visiting the former Soviet republic of Kyrgyzstan, was asked at a town meeting whether he dreamed of being president. Embarrassed, he replied, "Would you believe me if I told you that since I was a young child I dreamed of becoming *Vice* President of the United States?" Even in Kyrgyzstan that got a big laugh. Thomas Jefferson, though, professed to think that the vice presidency was a pretty good post; see below.

The second office of the land is honorable and easy, the first is but a splendid misery. 5
—Thomas Jefferson, letter to Elbridge Gerry, May 13, 1797

★ Jefferson was vice president when he wrote this; Adams was president. Jefferson himself became president in 1801.

I do not propose to be buried until I am really dead. 6
—Daniel Webster, attributed response when offered the vice-presidential position on the Whig ticket, 1848

The vice president of the United States is like a man in a cateleptic state: he cannot 7
speak; he cannot move; he suffers no pain; and yet he is perfectly conscious of everything that is going on around him.
—Thomas Riley Marshall, statement to the press, c. 1920

★ From H. L. Mencken's dictionary of quotations. The citation is vague, but the attribution is probably okay. Marshall was vice president under Woodrow Wilson, 1913–21.

The vice presidency isn't worth a pitcher of warm spit. 8
—John Nance Garner, attributed, c. 1934

★ "Spit," it generally is agreed, is a euphemism for "piss," a word that was rarely put in print at that time. A former Texas congressman and Speaker of the House, "Cactus Jack" served as vice president during Franklin D. Roosevelt's first two terms (1933–41). See also Garner below.

A spare tire on the automobile of government. 9
—John Nance Garner, speaking of the vice presidency, to the press, June 19, 1934

1 [Re the vice presidency:] Here is one instance in which it is the man who makes the office, not the office the man.

—Harry S. Truman, *Years of Decision*, 1955

2 I think the vice president should do anything the president wants him to do.

—Richard M. Nixon, quoted in Earl Mazo, *Richard Nixon: A Political and Personal Portrait*, 1959

3 [On vice presidential duties:] Inside work with no heavy lifting.

—Robert J. Dole, quoted on *This Week*, ABC-TV, July 24, 1988

Vietnam War, 1961–1975

See also ELITE, THE (Halberstam).

4 You have the broader considerations that might follow what you would call the "falling domino" principle. You have a row of dominos set up, you knock over the first one, and what will happen to the last one is the certainty that it will go over very quickly

—Dwight D. Eisenhower, press conference, April 7, 1954

★ The states of Southeast Asia were the stack of dominos. In Vietnam, the Communist Viet Minh were fighting to break French control, and the U.S. was backing the French. After defeating the French in 1954, the Viet Minh took control of the north, and Western-oriented South Vietnam became the key "domino" the U.S. had to prop up.

5 We are not going to send American boys nine or ten thousand miles away from home to do what Asian boys ought to be doing for themselves.

—Lyndon B. Johnson, speech, Akron University, Akron, Ohio, Oct. 21, 1964

★ At this time, Johnson was trying to draw a clear political line between himself and Republican presidential candidate Barry Goldwater, who was calling for an American air strike against North Vietnam. For example, in a speech on September 25, Johnson said, "There are those who say, you ought to go north and drop bombs. . . . We don't want our American boys to do the fighting for Asian boys. We don't want to get involved in a nation with 700 million people and get tied down in a land war in Asia." But as revealed in the Pentagon Papers, the administration had already determined that air attacks against North Vietnam would be used—once the election was over. As for the efficacy of bombing, see Walter Lippman at MILITARY STRATEGY.

6 Hey, hey, LBJ, how many kids did you kill today?

—Anonymous, heckling slogan of the 1960s anti–Vietnam War movement

7 You don't need a weatherman to know which way the wind blows.

—Bob Dylan, *Subterranean Homesick Blues*, 1965

★ This line from Dylan's song became an antiwar slogan with overtones of menace in 1969, when a group from Students for a Democratic Society adopted the line as a title of a program calling on white liberals to support liberation movements worldwide. The most militant and violent of this group formed a splinter organization, Revolutionary Youth Movement I, which called itself the Weathermen and went in for bombings and robberies.

Keep asking me, no matter how long 1
On the war in Viet Nam, I sing this song
I ain't got no quarrel with the Viet Cong.
—**Muhammad Ali,** press conference, Miami, Fla., Feb. 1966

★ Ali, then world heavyweight boxing champion, read the poem after his local draft board had promoted him from I-Y, deferred status, to I-A, making him eligible for the draft. A year later, when he received his army induction notice, he declined on religious grounds to serve. Neither the courts nor boxing authorities accepted this reason. He was sentenced to five years in prison and stripped of his title. On appeal, however, his conviction was reversed and his boxing license restored. He returned to the ring in 1970 and regained the heavyweight crown in 1974. See REPUTATION for his explanation of his reason for sticking by his beliefs.

I believe there is a light at the end of what has been a long and lonely tunnel. 2
—**Lyndon B. Johnson,** speech, Sept. 21, 1966

★ "Light at the end of the tunnel" had been used earlier in this context—by John F. Kennedy in a press conference in 1962 and by Joseph Alsop in a 1965 column, among others, and it was to be repeated so many times that it became an ironic catchphrase summing up the futility of the Vietnam War. In *Day by Day* (1977), Robert Lowell wrote that "If we see light at the end of the tunnel, / It's the light of the oncoming train."

Declare the United States the winner and begin de-escalation. 3
—**George Aiken,** speech, U.S. Senate, Oct. 19, 1966

★ Wise advice from Vermont's canny senior senator.

It is our will and not our strength that is being tried. 4
—**Lyndon B. Johnson,** State of the Union Address, Jan. 17, 1968

It became necessary to destroy the town to save it. 5
—**Anonymous,** U.S. Army Major on the bombing of the town of Ben Tre, quoted by the Associated Press, Feb. 8, 1968

The Living-Room War 6
—**Michael J. Arlen,** book title, 1968

★ Pictures of what was happening on the six o'clock TV news did more than reporters' descriptions in print to increase public opposition to the war.

If when the chips are down, the world's most powerful nation, the United States of America, acts like a pitiful, helpless giant, the forces of totalitarianism and anarchy will threaten free nations and institutions throughout the world. 7
—**Richard M. Nixon,** speech, April 30, 1970

★ The frightening image of a helpless United States was used by the president in this televised address to the nation to explain the necessity for a major offensive into Cambodia. Nixon went all out, stating "I would rather be a one-term president and do what I believe is right than to be a two-term president at the cost of seeing America becoming a second-rate power and to see this nation accept its first defeat in its proud 190-year history." Despite the powerful rhetoric, the reaction of the war-weary public was largely negative. The U.S. had not won the "hearts and minds" of the Vietnamese—a basic goal of the struggle—nor even of its own people. For an early use of "hearts and minds," see John Adams at AMERICAN REVOLUTION, letter to Hezekiah Niles, 1818.

1 How do you ask a man to be the last man to die in Vietnam? How do ask a man to be the last man to die for a mistake?

John J. Kerry, statement, Senate Foreign Relations Committee, April 23, 1971

★ At this time, Kerry a decorated, former Navy lieutenant, was a spokesman for Vietnam Veterans Against the War.

2 The war the soldiers tried to stop.

—**John F. Kerry,** speech at antiwar rally, Washington D.C., April 26, 1971

★ This was how Kerry hoped the war would be remembered.

3 I love the smell of napalm in the morning. It smells like victory.

—**Francis Ford Coppola,** *Apocalypse Now*, screenplay, 1979

★ For another reaction to the smell of war, see Ralph Waldo Emerson at WAR.

4 Vietnam was the first war ever fought without censorship. Without censorship, things can get terribly confused in the public mind.

—**William C. Westmoreland,** 1982, quoted in Stanley Hochman & Eleanor Hochman, eds., *The Penguin Dictionary of Contemporary American History* [1997]

★ Gen. Westmoreland commanded American forces in Vietnam 1964–68. He urged a major commitment of troops, which did not lead to victory but did fire up war protests back home.

5 In the end, we simply cut and ran. The American national will had collapsed.

—**Graham A. Martin,** on the tenth anniversary of the fall of Saigon, *The New York Times*, April 30, 1985

★ Martin was the last American ambassador to South Vietnam.

Violence

See also CRIME, CRIMINALS, & DETECTIVES; DANGER & DANGEROUS PEOPLE; PACIFISM & NONVIOLENCE; REVOLUTION; RUTHLESSNESS; STRENGTH & TOUGHNESS.

6 Force cannot give right.

—**Thomas Jefferson,** *Summary View of the Rights of British America*, 1774

7 The sword of murder is not the balance of justice. Blood does not wipe out dishonor, nor violence indicate possession.

—**Julia Ward Howe,** peace proclamation, London, 1870

★ More at PACIFISM & NONVIOLENCE.

8 A gun is a tool . . . no better or no worse than any other tool, an axe, a shovel or anything. A gun is as good or bad as the man using it.

—**A. B. Guthrie, Jr.,** screenplay, *Shane,* 1953

★ The line is spoken by the gunfighter, Alan Ladd, to the young boy who idolizes him, Marion, played by Brandon de Wilde. Guthrie distilled the wording in the 1949 novel by Jack Schaefer on which the movie was based. A lesson in screenwriting 101: "A gun is just a tool. No better or worse than any other tool, a shovel—or an axe or a saddle or a stove or anything. Think of it always that way. A gun is as good—and as bad—as the man who carries it."

In violence, we forget who we are. **1**
—Mary McCarthy, *On the Contrary*, 1961

Be peaceful, be courteous, obey the law, respect everyone; but if someone puts his **2**
hand on you, send him to the cemetery.
—Malcolm X, *Malcom X Speaks* [1965]

I say violence is necessary. It is as American as apple pie. **3**
—H. "Rap" Brown, press conference at the Student Nonviolent Co-ordinating Committee headquarters, Washington, D.C., July 27, 1967

⋆ Brown was defending the use of violence in the pursuit of civil rights. This kind of talk challenged the leadership of Martin Luther King, Jr., and signaled a sea change in the civil rights movement. It obviously represented a radical transformation of the Student Nonviolent Co-ordinating Committee.

Returning violence for violence multiples violence, adding deeper darkness to a **4**
night already devoid of stars.
—Martin Luther King, Jr., *Where Do We Go from Here: Chaos or Community?*, 1967

This world is ruled by violence / But I guess that's better left unsaid. **5**
—Bob Dylan, *Union Sundown*, song on *Infidels*, 1960

Violence is an admission that one's ideas and goals cannot prevail on their own mer- **6**
its.
—Edward M. Kennedy, speech, June 10, 1970, in Thomas P. Collins and Louis M. Savary, eds., *A People of Compassion: The Concerns of Edward Kennedy* [1972]

A little violence never hurt anybody. **7**
—Benjamin Ruggiero, c. 1978, in Joseph D. Pistone, with Richard Woodley, *Donnie Brasco*, 1987

⋆ "Donnie Brasco" was the name that FBI agent Pistone used when he infiltrated the Mafia. In the 1997 movie that was made from the book, the part of "Lefty" (short for "Lefty Guns") Ruggiero was played by Al Pacino.

Violence is one of the most fun things to watch. **8**
—Quentin Tarantino, comment, Cannes Fillm Festival, screening of *Pulp Fiction*, March 1994

Violence is not the problem; it is a consequence of the problem. **9**
—Jim Wallis, *The Soul of Politics: A Practical and Prophetic Vision for Change*, 1994

Virginia

See also South Carolina (Federal Writers' Project).

1 We found shoal water, where we smelt so sweet and so strong a smell, as if we had been in the midst of some delicate garden abounding with all kinds of odoriferous flowers, by which we were assured that the land could not be far distant.

—**Arthur Barlowe,** quoted in *The First Voyage Made to North America*, July 2, 1584, in Richard Hakluyt, *Principall Navigations . . . of the English Nation* [1598–1600]

★ Barlow was a ship captain.

2 If Virginia had but horses and kine in some reasonable proportion, I dare assure myself, being inhabited with English, no realm in Christendom were comparable to it.

—**Ralph Lane,** 1585, in Richard Hakluyt, *Principall Navigations . . . of the English Nation* [1598–1600]

3 Virginia,
Earth's onely paradise.
Where nature hath in store
Fowle, venison and fish
And the fruitfull'st soyle
Without your toyle
Three harvests more,
All greater than you wish.

—**Michael Drayton,** *To the Virginian Voyage*, 1606

★ Drayton composed the ballad for the departure from London on December 20, 1606, of the 120 colonists who founded Jamestown. The early colonists spent more time looking for gold than farming, however, with the result that most died of starvation and disease. The survivors were preparing to abandon the colony in 1610 when reinforcements arrived with ample supplies.

4 Heaven & earth never agreed to frame a better place for mans habitation.

—**John Smith,** on Chesapeake Bay, 1607, in *A Map of Virginia with a Description of the Country*, 1612

★ Capt. Smith added the proviso, "were it fully manured and inhabited by industrious people." He continued, "Here are mountaines, hils, plaines, valleyes, rivers, and brookes, all running most pleasantly into a faire Bay, compassed but for the mouth, with fruitfull and delightsome land."

5 The country is not mountanous nor yet low but such pleasant plaine hils & fertle valleyes, one prettily crossing an other, and watered so conveniently with their sweete brookes and christall springs, as if art it selfe had devised them.

—**Ibid.**

★ Nevertheless, the first wave of settlers probably would have perished had it not been for the effective leadership of Capt. Smith. He established some semblance of order in Jamestown and made friends with the local chieftan, Powhatan—thanks apparently to the intercession of Powhatan's daughter Pocahontas.

The Virginians have little money and great pride, contempt of Northern men, and great fondness for a dissipated life. They do not understand grammar. **1**

—Noah Webster, *Letter from Williamsburg, Va.*, c. 1785

On the whole, I find nothing anywhere else, in point of climate, which Virginia need envy to any part of the world. **2**

—Thomas Jefferson, letter to Martha Jefferson Randolph, May 31, 1791

The higher Virginians seem to venerate themselves as men. **3**

—John Davis, *Travels of Four Years and a Half in the United States of America*, 1803

Our society is neither scientific nor splendid, but independent, hospitable, correct, and neighborly. **4**

—Thomas Jefferson, letter to Nathaniel Bowditch, Oct. 26, 1818

The good Old Dominion, the blessed mother of us all. **5**

—Thomas Jefferson, *Thoughts on Lotteries*, Feb. 1826

★ Jefferson's thoughts were occasioned by terrible debts. Fearful of being thrown out of Monticello, he proposed to pay off his most pressing obligations by selling properties around it through a lottery. News of his plight led citizens in New York, Boston, Philadelphia, Richmond, and other cities to hold public meetings at which funds quickly were raised for the old and ailing patriot. Thus, when he died five months later, it was peacefully in his own home.

You can work for Virginia, to build her up again, to make her great again. You can teach your children to love and cherish her. **6**

—Robert E. Lee, to the daughter of Dr. Prosser Tabb, at White Marsh, Gloucester County, Va., May 1870

Carry me back to old Virginny, **7**
That's where the cotton and the corn and taters grow.

—James A. Bland, *Carry Me Back to Old Virginny*, 1875

Red river, red river, **8**
Slow flow heat is silence
No will is as still as a river
Still.

—T. S. Eliot, *Virginia*, 1934

Never ask people where they are from. If they are from Virginia, they will tell you so; **9**
if not, it will embarrass them to have to confess that they aren't.

—Anonymous, quoted in H. L. Mencken, *A New Dictionary of Quotations* [1942]

That, without any fear of succeeding, the intrepid native Virginian will dauntlessly **10**
attempt to conceal his superiority to everybody else, remains a tribal virtue which has not escaped the comment of anthropologists.

—James Branch Cabell, *Let Me Live*, 1947

1 His [the Virginian's] dream was to found an aristocratic republic, in which superior individuals would emerge to rule the many.
—**Clifford Dowdey,** *Virginia*, in *American Panorama: East of the Mississippi*, 1960

2 *Sic semper tyrannis.*
Thus ever to tyrants.
—Motto, state of Virginia

★ John Wilkes Booth uttered this after shooting Pres. Lincoln; see AMERICAN HISTORY: MEMORABLE MOMENTS.

Virtue

See also CHARACTER; ETHICS & MORALITY; HEROES; HONESTY; HONOR; IDEAS & IDEALS; KINDNESS; REPUTATION; RESPONSIBILITY; RIGHT

3 Resolved, never to do anything which I should be afraid to do if it were the last hour of my life.
—**Jonathan Edwards,** *Seventy Resolutions,* 1722

4 The happiness of man as well as his dignity consists in virtue.
—**John Adams,** *Thoughts on Government*, 1776

★ See below for a second thought three years later.

5 Virtue is not always amiable.
—**John Adams,** diary entry, Feb. 9, 1779

6 Hands to work; hearts to God.
—**Shaker** motto

★ The first Shaker community was founded in 1774 in Mount Lebanon, New York, by Mother Ann Lee. She and eight others had come to America from England to escape religious persecution. Membership in Shaker communities reached six thousand by 1860, but had died out some one hundred years later. The Shakers believed in communal ownership of property, equality of the sexes, and celibacy (four of Mother Lee's children had died young).

7 Virtue is the governor, the creator, the reality.
—**Ralph Waldo Emerson,** *Self-Reliance*, in *Essays: First Series*, 1841

8 The essence of greatness is the perception that virtue is enough.
—**Ralph Waldo Emerson,** *Heroism*, in *ibid.*

★ See also Emerson at COMMON SENSE.

9 The only reward of virtue is virtue.
—**Ralph Waldo Emerson,** *Friendship*, in *Essays: First Series*, 1841

10 Are the honorable, the just, the high-minded and compassionate, the majority anywhere in the world?
—**Harriet Beecher Stowe,** final chapter, or afterword, to *Uncle Tom's Cabin*, 1852

★ See also Thoreau, who writing in defense of John Brown's raid on Harpers Ferry said, "I hear many condemn these men because they were so few"—the rest follows two quotes below.

As for doing good, that is one of the professions which are full. 1
—Henry David Thoreau, *Economy,* in *Walden,* 1854

When were the good and the brave ever in a majority? 2
—Henry David Thoreau, *A Plea for Captain John Brown,* 1859

Let us have faith that right makes might, and in that faith, let us, to the end, dare to 3
do our duty as we understand it.
—Abraham Lincoln, speech at Cooper Union, New York City, Feb. 27, 1860

Character is like a tree and reputation like its shadow. The shadow is what we think 4
of it; the tree is the real thing.
—Abraham Lincoln, in Anthony Gross, *Lincoln's Own Stories,* [1912]

Dearest says that is the best kind of goodness: not to think about yourself, but to 5
think about other people.
—Frances Hodgson Burnett, *Little Lord Fauntleroy,* 1885

★ "Dearest" is what little Fauntleroy calls his mother. He was modeled on the author's son Vivian, who grew up to be a successful editor and enthusiastic sportsman. He died of a heart attack in 1937 on Long Island Sound, a few minutes after rescuing four people whose boat had capsized. While many passages in his mother's famous book are now cloying, the story is pretty good, and she herself was no prude.

Be noble! and the nobleness that lies 6
In other men, sleeping, but never dead,
Will rise in majesty to meet thine own.
—James Russell Lowell, *Sonnet IV,* in *The Complete Poetical Works of James Russell Lowell* [1900]

★ Inscribed at Union Station, Washington, D.C. A similar thought from Lowell was selected by Harvard University president Charles W. Eliot for inscription in the main reading room of the Library of Congress: "As one lamp lights another, nor grows less, / So nobleness enkindleth nobleness," *Yussouf,* in *ibid.*

★ See also Twain at RIGHT.

Character, not circumstances, makes the man. 7
—Booker T. Washington, Jan. 31, 1896

★ Cited in Deirdre Mullane, ed., *Words to Make My Children Live: A Book of African American Quotations,* [1995]

Few things are harder to put up with than the annoyance of a good example. 8
—Mark Twain, *Pudd'nhead Wilson's Calendar,* in *Pudd'nhead Wilson,* 1894

Be good and you will be lonesome. 9
—Mark Twain, *Pudd'nhead Wilson's New Calendar,* in *Following the Equator,* 1897, motto for frontispiece

1 Always do right. This will gratify some people and astonish the rest.
—Mark Twain, speech, Greenpoint Presbyterian Church, Brooklyn, N.Y., 1901

2 *Saint, n.* a dead sinner revised and edited.
—Ambrose Bierce, *The Devil's Dictionary*, 1906

3 No one can build his security upon the nobleness of another person.
—Willa Cather, *Alexander's Bridge*, 1912

4 Some persons are likeable in spite of their unswerving integrity.
—Don Marquis, quoted in Edward Anthony, *O Rare Don Marquis* [1962]

5 Let us honor if we can
The vertical man
Though we value none
But the horizonal one.
—W. H. Auden, *To Christopher Isherwood*, in *Poems*, 1930

6 No good deed goes unpunished.
—Clare Boothe Luce, attributed, William Safire, *The New York Times Magazine* [Jan. 9, 1994]

★ One of numerous attributions for this cynical observation, which exists in several variations, as Safire pointed out in this article. For example, the Rev. William Sloane Coffin produced the wordier, "In my experience, good deeds usually do not go unpunished," in an October, 1984, speech in support of the Sanctuary Program for protecting refugees.

7 It is often easier to fight for principles than to live up to them.
—Adlai Stevenson, speech, New York City, August 27, 1952

8 She would rather light candles than curse the darkness, and her glow has warmed the world.
—Adlai Stevenson, eulogy for Eleanor Roosevelt, United Nations, Nov. 9, 1962

★ See also the Christopher Society motto under ACTION & DOING.

9 Service Above Self.
—Benjamin Franklin Collins, motto for Rotary International, adopted 1989

★ Introduced in 1910 in the form of "Service, Not Self," Collins' motto was used for many years by Rotary along with "He profits most who serves best," a slogan proposed by A. F. Sheldon in 1922. The organization approved both mottos at its 1950 convention, but officially adopted the present wording as its primary slogan in 1989.

10 Just say no.
—Nancy Reagan, motto, campaign against drug abuse

★ The First Lady gave this advice initially to schoolchildren in Oakland, Cal., in 1984. It became the motto of the Nancy Reagan Drug Abuse Fund, founded in 1985. In *The Penguin Dictionary of Contemporary American History* (1997), Stanley and Eleanor Hochman remind readers that this venture had a limited impact. At the 1988 Democratic National Convention, Rev. Jesse Jackson stated, "We need a real war on drugs. We can't just say no. It's deeper than that."

Vision & Perception

See also DREAMS & DREAMERS; MIND, THOUGHT, & UNDERSTANDING.

We are as much as we see. Faith is sight and knowledge. The hands only serve the eyes. **1**
—Henry David Thoreau, *Journal*, April 10, 1841

People see only what they are prepared to see. **2**
—Ralph Waldo Emerson, *Journal*, 1863

Try to be one of the people on whom nothing is lost. **3**
—Henry James, *The Art of Fiction*, 1888

Cynic, n. a blackguard whose faulty vision sees things as they are, not as they ought to be. **4**
—Ambrose Bierce, *The Devil's Dictionary*, 1906

The fellow that can only see a week ahead is always the popular fellow, for he is looking with the crowd. But the one that can see years ahead, he has a telescope, but he can't make anybody believe he has it. **5**
—Will Rogers, *The Autobiography of Will Rogers* [1949]

The floo floo bird . . . the peculiar and especial bird who always flew backward . . . because it didn't give a darn where it was going, but just had to see where it had been. **6**
—Frank Lloyd Wright, speech, 1938

★ Wright was referring to cultural vision in particular—see ART. But the backward-looking bird has been cited in a variety of contexts. William Safire, for example, likened people who continue to argue about whether the U.S. should have gone to war in Iraq with the floo floo bird (*The New York Times*, April 5, 2004).

Stare. It is the way to educate your eye, and more. **7**
—Walker Evans, unpublished text for his subway photographs, c. 1940

★ More at KNOWLEDGE.

I don't believe anything I see unless I see it with my own eyes. **8**
—Anonymous, *The New York Times* [Nov. 12, 1998]

★ One of the fractured phrases from boxing managers and trainers collected over the years by Harry Markson, boxing director at New York City's Madison Square Garden for twenty-five years, starting in 1948, and included in his obituary. Another, truly punch-drunk example: "I'm in a terrible squandry. I just gave my daughter $400 for intuition at college. The tax people want me to atomize my expenses, and my home was ramshackled by burglars."

We should not be surprised that the Founding Fathers didn't foresee everything, when we see that the current Fathers hardly ever foresee anything. **9**
—Henry Steele Commager, interview in *American Heritage*, Feb. 1970

If I didn't believe it with my own mind, I never would have seen it. **10**
—Anonymous, graffito, Bard College, Annandale-on-Hudson, N.Y., c. 1971, book review, *The New York Times*, Feb. 12, 1996

1 We are not victims of the world we see. We are victims of the way we see the world.
—**Shirley MacLaine**, *Dancing in the Light*, 1985

2 The vision thing.
—**George H. W. Bush,** phrase, 1987

★ Unfortunately for Vice President Bush, his use of this phrase was picked up by the popular press as emblematic of a decline in political rhetoric and, of course, vision. Thus Marci McDonald, writing in *MacLean's* (Dec. 9, 1991), commented that Bush's supposed "inability to come to grips with what he used to repeatedly refer to as 'the vision thing' . . . haunted him, however undeservedly, through early 1988." Nevertheless, he was elected president, and served one term.

3 Nobody sees a flower—really—it is so small—we haven't time—and to see takes time.
—**Georgia O'Keeffe,** in *The New York Times*, Nov. 1, 1987

4 The important thing is not the camera but the eye.
—**Alfred Eisenstaedt,** interview, *The New York Times*, Sept. 26, 1994

★ Eisenstaedt was on the staff of the first *Life* magazine in 1936. In 1994, at age ninety-five, he was still coming in to the office every day. He died the following year.

War

See also AMERICAN REVOLUTION; CIVIL WAR, THE; GULF WAR; IRAQ WAR; KOREAN WAR; MEXICAN WAR; MILITARY, THE; MILITARY STRATEGY; PEACE; SPANISH-AMERICAN WAR; VIETNAM WAR; WAR OF 1812; WORLD WAR I; WORLD WAR II.

5 I heard the bullets whistle; and believe me, there is something charming in the sound.
—**George Washington,** letter to his mother, May 3, 1754

★ This was after the battle of Great Meadows in the French and Indian War. Others have reacted similarly; for example, see Ralph Waldo Emerson below and Ronald Reagan at DANGER & DANGEROUS PEOPLE.

6 He who is the author of a war lets loose the whole contagion of hell and opens a vein that bleeds a nation to death.
—**Tom Paine,** *The American Crisis*, no. V, March 21, 1778

7 It is the object only of war that makes it honorable.
—**Ibid.**

8 There never was a good war or a bad peace.
—**Benjamin Franklin,** letter to Josiah Quincy, Sept. 11, 1783

9 To be prepared for war is one of the most effectual means of preserving peace.
—**George Washington,** first annual address to Congress, Jan. 8, 1790

★ The president spoke to both houses of Congress—what has since come to be known as the annual State of the Union speech. Here Washington paraphrased part of a passage he admired from *De rei militari*, written in the fourth century by Vegetius: "He, therefore, who desires peace should prepare for war. He who aspires to victory should spare no pains to form his soldiers. And he who hopes for success should fight on principle, not chance." In 1990, Pres. George H. W. Bush, as he prepared the nation for the Gulf War, also drew on the maxims of Vegetius and Washington. See also Theodore Roosevelt below,.

Sometimes gunpowder smells good. **1**

—**Ralph Waldo Emerson,** April 1861, cited in Samuel Eliot Morison, *The Oxford History of the American People* [1965]

★ Emerson was referring to the attack on Fort Sumter. Like many other Northerners, he was glad that the issue of slavery would at last be settled, "Now we have a country again," he wrote. For the smell of napalm, see Francis Ford Coppola at VIETNAM WAR.

War is an organized bore. **2**

—**Oliver Wendell Holmes, Jr.,** remark to a visitor after being wounded at Antietam, 1862

★ Holmes enlisted in the Union army before completing his senior year at Harvard and was wounded three times in three years, twice severely.

It is well that war is so terrible, or we should grow too fond of it. **3**

—**Robert E. Lee,** remark to Gen. James Longstreet, Battle of Fredericksburg, Dec. 13, 1862

★ Lee had just seen an attack by Union forces repulsed. Not everyone is so susceptible to war's attractions. Lee, himself, was much amused by a black cook who explained that he had managed to avoid being wounded because, "I stays back wid de ginerals."

War is cruelty, and you cannot refine it. **4**

—**William Tecumseh Sherman,** letter to James M. Calhoun, mayor of Atlanta, Sept. 12, 1864

The legitimate object of war is a more perfect peace. **5**

—**William Tecumseh Sherman,** speech, St. Louis, July 20, 1865

★ The epigram is inscribed upon his statue in Washington, D.C.

All wars are boyish and are fought by boys. **6**

—**Herman Melville,** *The March into Virginia*, in *Battle-Pieces*, 1866

War is hell. **7**

—**William Tecumseh Sherman,** attributed, graduation speech, Michigan Military Academy, June 19, 1879

★ The passage, for which there is no contemporary verification, reportedly ran thus: "I am sick and tired of war. Its glory is all moonshine. It is only those who have never fired a shot nor heard the shrieks and groans of the wounded who cry aloud for blood, more vengeance, more desolations. War is hell." Similarly, in a speech in Columbus, Ohio, on August 11, 1880, Sherman was reported in a local paper to have said, "There is many a boy here today who looks on war as all glory, but, boys, it is all hell."

War educates the senses, calls into action the will, perfects the physical constitution, brings men into such swift and close collision in critical moments that man measures man. **8**

—**Ralph Waldo Emerson,** *War*, in *Miscellanies* [1884]

1 War loses a great deal of its romance after a soldier has seen his first battle.
—John Singleton Mosby, *War Reminiscences*, 1887

2 It is not merely cruelty that leads men to love war, it is excitement.
—Henry Ward Beecher, *Proverbs from Plymouth Pulpit*, 1887

3 They were going to look at war, the red animal—war, the blood-swollen god.
—Stephen Crane, *The Red Badge of Courage*, 1895

4 Preparation for war is the surest guaranty for peace.
—Theodore Roosevelt, *Washington's Forgotten Maxim*, speech, Naval War College, 1897

★ Here Assistant Secretary of the Navy Roosevelt referred to Washington's advice that military preparedness helps to prevent wars; see above. Roosevelt's speech called for "a great navy . . . an armament fit for the nation's needs, not primarily to fight, but to avert fighting." Roosevelt, however, was less than sincere here. He was an enthusiastic warrior, some would say warmonger. Washington, on the other hand, while advocating preparedness, was suspicious of military establishments; see THE MILITARY.

5 The voice of protest, of warning, of appeal is never more needed than when the clamor of fife and drum, echoed by the press and too often by the pulpit, is bidding all men fall in and keep step and obey in silence the tyrannous word of command. Then, more than ever, it is the duty of the good citizen not to be silent.
—Charles Eliot Norton, *True Patriotism*, 1898

★ The SPANISH-AMERICAN WAR was whipped up by the press as well as the politicians.

6 It has been a splendid little war.
—John Hay, letter to Theodore Roosevelt, July 27, 1898

★ More at SPANISH-AMERICAN WAR.

7 A pattern called a war.
Christ! What are patterns for?
—Amy Lowell, *Patterns*, in *Men, Women, and Ghosts*, 1916

8 War is the only place where a man really lives.
—George S. Patton, letter to Gen. John J. "Black Jack" Pershing, quoted in Carlo D'Este, *A Genius for War* [1995]

★ Patton's first battle experience was in Mexico in Gen. Pershing's 1916–17 expedition against the rebel leader Pancho Villa.

9 Every nation has its war party. It is not the party of democracy. It is the party of autocracy. It seeks to dominate absolutely. It is commercial, imperialistic, ruthless. . . . If there is no sufficient reason for war, the war party will make war on one pretext, then invent another.
—Robert La Follette, in *The Progressive* magazine, June 1917

10 The first casualty when war comes is truth.
—Hiram Johnson, remark in the U. S. Senate, 1918

★ This has long been attributed to Sen. Johnson. Suzy Platt, editor of *Respectfully Quoted*, published by the Library of Congress, could not verify the attribution, but does give an earlier and similar source for the same idea: Samuel Johnson, "Among the calamities of war, may be justly numbered the diminution of the love of truth, by the falsehoods which interest dictates, and credulity encourages," *The Idler*, Nov. 11, 1758.

When a nation is at war many things that might be said in a time of peace are such a hindrance to its effort that their utterance will not be endured. **1**

—**Oliver Wendell Holmes, Jr.,** dissent in *Schenck v. U.S.*, 1919

★ For more from *Schenck*, see FREE SPEECH.

What Price Glory? **2**

—**Maxwell Anderson & Laurence Stallings,** title of antiwar play about World War I, 1924

You can't say civilization don't advance, however, for in every war they kill you in a new way. **3**

—**Will Rogers,** *The New York Times*, Dec. 23, 1929

All wars are planned by old men **4**
In council rooms apart.

—**Grantland Rice,** *Two Sides of War*, 1930

★ See also Herbert Hoover below.

Wars may be fought with weapons, but they are won by men. **5**

—**George S. Patton,** in the *Cavalry Journal*, Sept. 1933

Take the profits out of war, and you won't have any war. **6**

—**Will Rogers,** *Daily Telegrams*, Dec. 14, 1934

Sometime they'll give a war and nobody will come. **7**

—**Carl Sandburg,** *The People, Yes*, 1936

I have seen war. . . . I hate war! **8**

—**Franklin D. Roosevelt,** speech at Chautauqua, N.Y., August 14, 1936

There is money in war. There is money in fear of war. **9**

—**John Gunther,** *Inside Europe*, rev. ed., 1937

War is a contagion. **10**

—**Franklin D. Roosevelt,** "Quarantine the Aggressors" speech, Chicago, Oct. 5, 1937

Although war is evil, it is occasionally the lesser of two evils. **11**

—**McGeorge Bundy,** essay, Yale College, 1940

★ Bundy graduated first in his class at Yale and, as special assistant for national security affairs for Presidents Kennedy and Johnson from 1961 to 1966, was one of "the best and the brightest" who presided over the war in Vietnam.

As a woman I can't go to war, and I refuse to send anyone else. **12**

—**Jeanette Rankin,** c. 1941, quoted in Hannah Josephson, *Jeanette Rankin: First Lady in Congress* [1974]

1 You can no more win a war than you can win an earthquake.
—Ibid.

★ Rep. Rankin of Montana, the first woman elected to Congress, cast the only vote against declaring war on Japan in 1941. This was consistent with her position on April 6, 1917, when she was in her first term. "I want to stand by my country, but I cannot vote for war," she said then, concluding, "I vote no."

2 Help me to remember somewhere out there a man died for me today. As long as there be war, I must ask and answer, "Am I worth dying for?"
—Anonymous, prayer kept by Eleanor Roosevelt at her bedside during World War II

3 I want you to remember that no bastard ever won a war by dying for his country. He won it by making the other poor dumb bastard die for his country.
—George S. Patton, addressing troops prior to an invasion, attributed

★ The quote opens the six-minute monologue by the general, played by George C. Scott, at the beginning of the 1970 film, *Patton.* The monologue is a pastiche, composed by screenwriters Francis Ford Coppola and Edmund H. North, from pieces of speeches made by Patton at different times and places. Most people who knew the man agree that the film portrayal was on the mark, except that the general's richly profane language had to be toned down for public consumption.

4 God help me, I love it.
—George S. Patton, after a tank battle, attributed

5 When Statesmen gravely say, "We must be realistic,"
The chances are they're weak and, therefore, pacifistic,
But when they speak of Principles, look out: perhaps
Their generals are already poring over maps.
—W. H. Auden, from *Shorts*, in *Collected Shorter Poems 1927–1957*

6 Older men declare war. But it is youth that must fight and die. And it is youth who must inherit the tribulation, the sorrow, and the triumphs that are the aftermath of war.
—Herbert Hoover, speech, Republican National Convention, June 27, 1944

7 War may make a fool of man, but it by no means degrades him; on the contrary it tends to exalt him.
—H. L. Mencken, *Minority Report: H. L. Mencken's Notebooks* [1956]

8 No one won the last war, and no one will win the next.
—Eleanor Roosevelt, letter to Harry S. Truman, Nov. 5, 1948

9 A wonderful time—the War:
when money rolled in
and blood rolled out.
But blood
was far away

from here—
Money was near.
—Langston Hughes, *Green Memory*, 1949

In war there is no second prize for the runner-up. 1
—Omar Bradley, *USA: In Military Review*, Feb. 1950

In war there is no substitute for victory. 2
—Douglas MacArthur, speech, joint session of Congress, April 19, 1951

★ From his "old soldiers never die" speech; see AMERICAN HISTORY: MEMORABLE MOMENTS, and KOREAN WAR.

The wrong war, at the wrong place, at the wrong time, and with the wrong enemy. 3
—Omar Bradley, testimony to committees on Armed Services and Foreign Affairs, U.S. Senate, May 15, 1951

★ More at KOREAN WAR.

It is fatal to enter any war without the will to win it. 4
—Douglas MacArthur, speech, Republican National Convention, 1952

War will never cease until babies begin to come into the world with larger cerebrums 5
and smaller adrenal glands.
—H. L. Mencken, *Minority Report: H. L. Mencken's Notebooks* [1956]

War is the unfolding of miscalculations. 6
—Barbara Tuchman, *The Guns of August*, 1962

Make love not war. 7
—Gershon Legman, lecture, Ohio University, 1963

★ A ubiquitous slogan on buttons and placards at student rallies against the Vietnam war. See Legman at LOVE for background on him.

That's the way it is in war. You win or lose, live or die—and the difference is just an 8
eyelash.
—Douglas MacArthur, *Reminiscences*, 1964

All the gods are dead except the god of war. 9
—Eldridge Cleaver, *Soul on Ice*, 1968

War is a bore interrupted only by moments of sheer terror when men die. 10
—NBC News, voice of correspondent, Vietnam, May 1969

Either man is obsolete or war is. 11
—Buckminster Fuller, *I Seem to Be a Verb*, 1970

There will be no veterans of World War III. 12
—Walter Mondale, speech, Sept. 5, 1984

★ Sen. Mondale, a Democrat, ran for president against Republican Ronald Reagan. Mondale's lack of martial spirit and, worse, his commitment to raise taxes, doomed his candidacy.

1 War is a central expression of a nation, revealing the values for which it is willing to sacrifice its treasure and its young.

—R. Michael Schiffer & Michael P. Rinzler, "No News Is No News," OpEd page, *The New York Times*, Jan. 25, 1991

2 History is replete with examples of empires mounting impressive military campaigns on the cusp of their impending economic collapse.

—Eric Alterman, *Sound and Fury: The Washington Punditocracy and the Collapse of American Politics*, 1992

3 War is a ghost that haunts the living.

—John Cory, *The Ghosts of War*, August 12, 2004

War of 1812, 1812–1814 (Treaty of Ghent) or *1812–1815* (Battle of New Orleans)

4 If you wish to avoid foreign collision, you had better abandon the ocean—surrender your commerce, give up all your prosperity.

—Henry Clay, speech, U.S. House of Representatives, Jan. 22, 1812

★ The U.S. and Great Britain had been battling at sea for years. War was declared on June 18.

5 For the hotter the war, boys, the quicker the peace.

—Anonymous, Republican broadside, Boston, just after declaration of the War of 1812

6 Don't give up the ship.

—James Lawrence, June 1, 1813

★ Reports vary on the exact words of Lawrence, who was mortally wounded this day, but he gave this order in essence as his frigate, the USS *Chesapeake*, was being boarded by British sailors from HMS *Shannon*. Lawrence, by some accounts, said, "Tell the men to fire faster and not to give up the ship. Fight her till she sinks." He lingered in a delirium until June 4, repeating many times, "Don't give up the ship." The captain of the *Shannon*, too, died from wounds suffered in the battle. Some prefer to credit the famous order to Oliver Hazard Perry, who conveyed this signal by a flag during the Battle of Lake Erie, see below. For more on Lawrence see Stephen Decatur at EPITAPHS & GRAVESTONES.

7 We have met the enemy and they are ours—two ships, two brigs, one schooner, and one sloop.

—Oliver Hazard Perry, message to Gen. William Henry Harrison, Battle of Lake Erie, Sept. 10, 1813

★ For Pogo's version, see Walt Kelly under HUMANS & HUMAN NATURE.

8 Oh, say, can you see by the dawn's early light,
What so proudly we hailed at the twilight's last gleaming?

—Francis Scott Key, *The Star-Spangled Banner*, Sept. 14, 1814

★ More at PATRIOTISM & THE FLAG.

By the Eternal, they shall not sleep on our soil! 1

—**Andrew Jackson,** Dec. 23, 1814

★ The reaction of Gen. Jackson upon learning that twelve thousand British troops were disembarking in New Orleans. He orchestrated their defeat at the battle of New Orleans on January 8, without knowing that the Treaty of Ghent, formally ending the war, had been signed two weeks earlier.

The last American war was to us only something to talk or read about; but to the Americans, it was the cause of misery in their own homes. 2

—**Samuel Taylor Coleridge,** *Table-Talk*, May 3, 1830

War with Mexico

See MEXICAN WAR.

Washington

See also CITIES (SEATTLE).

Rainier, from Puget Sound, is a sight for the gods, and when one looks upon him he feels that he is in the presence of the gods. 3

—**Paul Fountain,** *The Eleven Eaglets of the West*, 1905

Washington is a puzzling state. We think of it as cool, pristine and evergreen. Yet the civilization around Puget Sound is industrial, cosmopolitan, intense, wracked by economic boom and bust. 4

—**Neal R. Pierce,** *The Pacific States of America*, 1972

Alki. 5

By and by.

—Motto, state of Washington

★ *Alki* is a Chinook Jargon word.

Washington, D.C.

See CITIES.

Washington, George

See also DEATH (Washington); LAST WORDS (Washington); PRESIDENCY, THE.

George Washington, Commander of the American armies, who, like Joshua of old, commanded the sun and the moon to stand still, and they obeyed him. 6

—**Benjamin Franklin,** attributed, toast at a state dinner in France, c. 1784

★ Franklin's biographer James Parton relates that Franklin is said to have made this toast after the British ambassador had announced, "England—the sun—whose bright beams enlighten and fructify the remotest corners of the earth," and the French ambassador had proposed, "France—the moon—whose mild, steady and cheering rays are the delight of all nations, consoling them in darkness." Parton did not, however, find the story particularly credible: "If such toasts were given, it must have been late in the third bottle or at the opening of the fourth," *The Life and Times of Benjamin Franklin*, 1864. Franklin served as ambassador to France during and after the Revolution. On March 5, 1780, he wrote back to Washington, "Here [in France] you would know and enjoy what posterity will say of Washington. For a thousand leagues have nearly the same effect with a thousand years." (*Note:* We would say "as a thousand years.") Franklin genuinely admired Washington, which is reflected in a codicil that he added to his will on June 23, 1789: "My fine crab-tree walking-stick, with a gold head curiously wrought in the form of the cap of liberty, I give to my friend and the friend of mankind, General Washington. If it were a scepter, he has merited it and would become it."

1 O, Washington! thou hero, patriot sage,
Friend of all climes, and pride of every age!
—Tom Paine, attributed

2 He has not the imposing pomp of a *Maréchal de France* who gives *the order*. A hero in a republic, he excites another sort of respect which seems to spring from the sole idea that the safety of each individual is attached to his person. . . . The goodness and benevolence which characterize him are evident in all that surrounds him, but the confidence that he calls forth never occasions improper familiarity.
—François Jean de Chastellux, *Travels in North America*, 1786

★ The Marquis de Chastellux met Washington after coming to America as a major general in Rochambeau's army in 1780. They became friends, and in 1787, Washington wrote de Chastellux a bantering letter of congratulations upon his marriage at age fifty-four to a pretty Irish woman of about twenty-eight. The following year de Chastellux died.

3 The character and services of this gentlemen are sufficient to put all those men called kings to shame. . . . He accepted no pay as commander-in-chief; he accepts none as President of the United States.
—Tom Paine, *The Rights of Man*, 1791–92

★ But in a letter to Washington, written July 30, 1796, Paine called him "treacherous in private friendship . . . and a hypocrite in public life, the world will be puzzled to decide whether you are an apostate or an imposter; whether you have abandoned good principles, or whether you ever had any." Paine had been imprisoned in France in 1793–94 and felt that Washington could have intervened to save him.

4 [Washington] errs as other men do, but errs with integrity.
—Thomas Jefferson, letter to William B. Giles, Dec. 31, 1795

5 *Der Landes Vater* [The father of his country]
—Francis Bailey, caption for portrait of Washington, *Nordamericanische Kalendar*, 1799

6 First in war, first in peace, first in the hearts of his countrymen.
—Henry Lee, eulogy, passed as a resolution in the U.S. Congress, Dec. 26, 1799

★ Lee, nicknamed "Light Horse Harry," was a devoted friend to Washington. In the early 20th century, baseball writer Charles Dryden parodied the eulogy to characterize the old Washington Senators baseball team: "Washington—first in war, first in peace, and last in the American League."

I can't tell a lie, Pa; you know I can't tell a lie. I did cut it with my hatchet. 1

—**Mason Locke "Parson" Weems,** *The Life and Memorable Actions of George Washington*, 5th edition

★ Washington was honored for his honesty, but there is no basis for the story that as a boy he confessed to chopping down a cherry tree.

He was, indeed, in every sense of the words, a wise, a good, and a great man. 2

—**Thomas Jefferson,** letter to Walter Jones, Jan. 2, 1814

The character of Washington . . . is a fixed star in the firmament of great names, 3
shining without twinkling or obscuration, with a clear, steady, beneficent light.

—**Daniel Webster,** letter to the New York Committee for the Celebration of the Birthday of Washington, Feb. 20, 1851

G. Washington was about the best man this country ever sot eyes on. He was a clear- 4
heded, warm-hearted, and stiddy goin man. He never slopt over! The prevailin' weakness of most public men is to *slop over*! . . . Washington never slopt over. That wasn't George's stile. He luved his country dearly. He wasn't after the spiles [spoils]. He was a human angil in a 3 kornered hat and knee britches.

—**Artemus Ward,** "Fourth of July Oration," 1859

Watergate

A third-rate burglary attempt. 5

—**Ronald L. Ziegler,** press conference, Key Biscayne, Florida, June 19, 1972

★ Presidential press secretary Ziegler was characterizing the break-in on June 17 at the offices of the Democratic National Committee in Washington's Watergate complex. Presciently, one of the Watergate burglars, E. Howard Hunt, an ex-CIA man who wrote mystery stories on the side, had noted in *Angel Eyes*, 1961: "Don't think I can't smell a cover-up."

Katie Graham's gonna get her tit caught in a big fat wringer if that's published. 6

—**John N. Mitchell,** telephone interview, Sept. 29, 1972, quoted in Carl Bernstein and Bob Woodward, *All the President's Men* [1974]

★ Attorney General Mitchell, chairman of the Committee to Re-elect the President (CREEP), was referring here to *Washington Post* publisher, Katharine Graham. Bernstein was checking a lead accusing Mitchell of controlling a secret fund that financed the Watergate break-in and other political espionage operations. The next day, after the story appeared, minus the anatomical reference, deleted at the order of editor Ben Bradlee, publisher Graham, who had been told of it, disconcerted Bernstein by asking if he had any more messages for her. Incidentally, Mitchell's quaint "wringer" metaphor was already archaic thanks to the development of automatic clothes dryers.

1 Well, I think we ought to let him hang there. Let him twist slowly, slowly in the wind.
—**John D. Ehrlichman,** telephone conversation with presidential counsel John W. Dean III, March 6, 1973

★ Presidential adviser Ehrlichman's proposed victim was L. Patrick Gray III, whose nomination as director of the FBI was stalled in the Senate because Gray did not have answers for senators' questions about Watergate.

2 We have a cancer within, close to the presidency, that is growing. It is growing daily.
—**John W. Dean III,** to Pres. Richard M. Nixon, White House tape, March 21, 1973

3 It's a limited hang-out. It's not an absolute hang-out.
—**John W. Dean III,** to Pres. Richard M. Nixon, White House tape, March 22, 1973

★ Presidential counsel Dean was recommending that the White House cooperate minimally with the Senate Watergate Committee in order to get the president himself "up above and away from" the breaking Watergate scandal. Presidential adviser John Ehrlichman called it a "modified limited hang-out." That term has endured. More than 20 years later, Maureen Dowd wrote on another problematic issue, "The White House's Iraq policy has gone from a total charade to a limited modified hangout," *The New York Times,* Dec. 23, 2004. The transposition of adjectives evidently is not significant.

4 I don't give a shit what happens. I want you all to stonewall it.
—**Richard M. Nixon,** White House tape, March 22, 1973

★ Pres. Nixon's use of "stonewall" probably derives from the resolute defense by Confederate General Thomas J. "Stonewall" Jackson at the first Battle of Bull Run in 1861. The term also has been used in Australia and New Zealand to describe parliamentary tactics that involve long-winded speeches and other delaying actions, but there the allusion is to a batter in cricket who is said "to stonewall" when playing purely defensively.

5 This is the operative statement. The others are inoperative.
—**Ronald L. Ziegler,** press conference, April 17, 1973

★ Ziegler was retracting almost a year's worth of denials that the White House had been involved in covering up the Watergate break-in.

6 I asked him what he meant by "deep six." He leaned back in his chair and said: "You cross the [Potomac] river at night, don't you? Well, when you cross over the river on your way home, just toss the briefcase into the river."
—**John W. Dean III,** Senate Watergate Committee hearings, June 25, 1973

★ Dean was reporting John Ehrlichman's advice about disposing of a briefcase found in the White House office safe of Watergate burglar E. Howard Hunt, Jr. "Deep six" is old naval slang for jettisoning cargo or gear, presumably six fathoms (thirty-six feet) deep.

7 There was also maintained what was called an "enemies list," which was rather extensive and continually being updated.
—**John W. Dean III,** Senate Watergate Committee hearings, June 25, 1973

The central question is simply put: What did the president know and when did he know it? 1

—**Howard H. Baker, Jr.,** Senate Watergate Committee hearings, June 25, 1973

★ Sen. Baker, a Republican and the minority leader of the Senate Watergate Committee, learned the answer to this oft-repeated question on August 5, 1974, when Pres. Nixon acceded to a unanimous Supreme Court decision and released transcripts of conversations with his chief of staff, H. R. Haldeman, that were, as Mr. Nixon described it, "at variance with" his previous denials that he had known about the Watergate coverup prior to John Dean's "cancer on the presidency" speech; see above. The incriminating conversations, dating from June 23, 1972, just six days after the Watergate break-in, represented undeniable direct evidence ("a smoking gun," as Rep. Barber Conable put it) that Mr. Nixon had been part of the Watergate cover-up conspiracy. Facing impeachment, Mr. Nixon resigned on August 9, 1974. See below.

I'm not a crook. 2

—**Richard M. Nixon,** press conference, Disney World, Nov. 11, 1973

★ The president's remarks in full were: "I made my mistakes, but in all my years of public life, I have never, *never* profited from public service. . . . I welcome this kind of examination because people have got to know whether or not their president is a crook. Well, I'm not a crook."

I have never been a quitter. To leave office before my term is completed is abhorrent to every instinct in my body. 3

—**Richard M. Nixon,** announcing his resignation as president, national radio address, August 8, 1974

★ See also, under HATE, his comments to his staff the next morning.

Our long national nightmare is over. Our Constitution works. 4

—**Gerald Ford,** inaugural statement upon succeeding Richard M. Nixon as president, August 9, 1974

I screwed up terribly in what was a little thing and it became a big thing. 5

—**Richard M. Nixon,** television interview with David Frost, May 4, 1977

I brought myself down. I gave them a sword. And they stuck it in, and they twisted it with relish. And I guess if I had been in their position, I'd have done the same thing. 6

—**Ibid.**

Wealth

See MONEY & THE RICH; POVERTY & HUNGER; RICH & POOR, WEALTH & POVERTY.

Weather

See NATURE: WEATHER.

West, the

See also CITIES and entries for states; DAKOTA TERRITORY; FRONTIER, THE; MIDWEST, THE; WISDOM, WORDS OF (Anonymous cowboy sayings).

1 Few people even know the true definition of the term "West"; and where is its location?—phantom-like it flies before us as we travel.

—**George Catlin,** *Letters and Notes on the Manners, Customs, and Conditions of the North American Indians*, 1841

2 Eastward I go only by force; but westward I go free. . . . I must walk toward Oregon and not toward Europe.

—**Henry David Thoreau,** *Walking*, 1862

★ Speaking of his inclination to leave behind cities and walk west into the wilderness, Thoreau wrote, "Something like this is the prevailing tendency of my countrymen."

3 Ain't no law west of St. Louis, ain't no God west of Fort Smith.

—**Anonymous,** saying, 19th century

★ Fort Smith is in Arkansas. See a similar anonymous comment at TEXAS.

4 Go west, young man, and grow up with the country.

—**Horace Greeley,** editorial, *New York Tribune*

★ Traditionally credited to John B. L. Soule, editor of the *Terre Haute* (Ind.) *Express*, "go west, young man" was long assumed to have been popularized by Greeley, editor of the *New York Tribune,* when he reprinted an 1851 article of Soule's as an editorial in the *Tribune*. But Thomas Fuller reports in the *Indiana Magazine of History* (Sept. 2004) that researchers can't find either the supposed article or editorial in back issues of the two papers. Thus, Greeley alone should be credited for the expression, since he often gave this advice, verbally and in print, though perhaps never in exactly these words.

5 Home, home on the range,
Where the deer and the antelope play;
Where seldom is heard a discouraging word,
And the skies are not cloudy all day.

—**Anonymous,** cowboy song, 1860s or earlier

★ Folk music expert John A. Lomax first recorded this song in San Antonio, Texas, in 1908, from a "Negro singer who ran a beer saloon out beyond the Southern Pacific depot, in a scrubby mesquite grove" (*Folk Song U.S.A.*). Not sung so often nowadays is the third verse: "The red man was pressed from this part of the West, / He's likely no more to return / To the banks of the Red River where seldom if ever / Their flickering campfires burn."

6 Oh, bury me not on the lone prairie,
Where the wild coyote will howl over me,
In a narrow grave just six by three,
Oh, bury me not on the lone prairie!

—**Anonymous,** cowboy song

★ In *Folk Song U.S.A.*, John A. and Alan Lomax say that this song derives from an English sailors' song.

Come along, boys, and listen to my tale 1
I'll tell you of my troubles on the old Chisholm trail.

—**Anonymous,** *The Old Chisholm Trail*

★ The Chisholm Trail was the major route for cattle drives from Texas to Kansas just after the Civil War, and this song, according to John A. and Alan Lomax in *Folk Song U.S.A.*, was sung by most cowboys. New verses were made up constantly, furnishing in aggregate a vivid record of cowboy life.

In this country you can look farther and see less than any other place in the world. 2

—**Anonymous,** 19th century

★ The saying dates from the time when grassland plains extended from Indiana to the foot of the Rockies. See also NEBRASKA.

To the West, to the West, to the land of the free, 3
Where the mighty Missouri rolls down to the sea,
Where a man is a man, even though he must toil
And the poorest may gather the fruits of the soil.

—**Anonymous,** ballad recalled by Andrew Carnegie (d. 1919) toward the end of his life, in Samuel Gompers, *Seventy Years of Life and Labor* [1925]

O you youths, Western youths, 4
So impatient, full of action, full of manly pride and friendship,
Plain I see you Western youths, see you tramping with the foremost,
Pioneers! O pioneers!

—**Walt Whitman,** *Pioneers! O Pioneers*, 1865, in *Leaves of Grass* [1881]

★ More at THE FRONTIER.

[Out West] change has grown to metamorphosis. The sons of civilization, drawn by the fascinations of a fresher and bolder life, thronged to the western wilds in multitudes which blighted the charm that had lured them. 5

—**Francis Parkman,** preface, 1892 edition of *The Oregon Trail*

★ See under NATURE: ANIMALS for his description of buffalo along the Oregon Trail.

American history has been in a large degree the history of the colonization of the Great West. 6

—**Frederick J. Turner,** *The Significance of the Frontier in American History*, 1893

★ See also Turner at THE FRONTIER.

Out where the handclasp's a little stronger, 7
Out where the smile dwells a little longer,
That's where the West begins.

—**Arthur Chapman,** *Out Where the West Begins*, 1917

Western humor . . . grew out of a distinct condition—the battle with the frontier. . . . It is the freshest, wildest humor in the world, but there is tragedy behind it. 8

—**Albert Bigelow Paine,** *Mark Twain, A Biography*, 1924

1 Everything in the West is on a grander scale, more intense, vital, dramatic.
—Edward Weston, diary entry, c. 1937, quoted in Nancy Newhall, ed., *From the Daybooks of Edward Weston: California* [1966]

2 Don't Fence Me In
—Cole Porter, song title, introduced by Roy Rogers in the film, *Hollywood Canteen*, 1944

★ The song, which became an instant international hit, was written originally for a film that was canceled in 1935, *Adios, Argentina!* Porter took the song's title and some of the phraseology from a poem by Robert W. Fletcher, an engineer in the Montana State Highway Department, paying him $250 for the rights to use the material, according to William McBrien's biography, *Cole Porter* (1998).

3 Nobody watches TV westerns more avidly than cowboys.
—Larry McMurtry, *Cowboys, Movies, Myths and Cadillacs: Realism in the Western*, in W. R. Robinson, ed., with George Garrett, *Man and the Movies*, 1967

4 I've always acted alone. Americans admire that enormously. Americans admire the cowboy leading the caravan alone astride his horse, the cowboy entering a village or city alone on his horse.
—Henry A. Kissinger, interview with Oriana Fallaci, *The New Republic*, Dec. 16, 1972

★ This was the then national security adviser's response to Ms. Fallaci's question about how he had attained "incredible superstar status," becoming "almost more famous and popular than the president," i.e., Richard M. Nixon.

5 The true West differs from the East in one great, pervasive, awesome way: space.
—William Least Heat-Moon, *Blue Highways*, 1982

6 The West at large is hope's native home.
—Wallace Stegner, *Where the Bluebird Sings to the Lemonade Springs*, Introduction, 1992

★ This introduction was based on Stegner's *A Geography of Hope*, a lecture delivered at the University of Colorado, and published by the university's press in *A Society to Match Our Scenery*, 1991.

7 Ghost towns and dust bowls, like motels, are western inventions.
—Ibid.

8 There is no more West. We are the West. So we've got to take care of what we have.
—Wendy Glen, an Arizona rancher, quoted in *The Ecology of Hope*, 1997

West Virginia

9 The state is one of the most mountainous in the country; sometimes it is called the "little Switzerland" of America, and I once heard an irreverent local citizen call it the "Afghanistan of the United States."
—John Gunther, *Inside U.S.A.*, 1947

We West Virginians are very tired of being considered inhabitants of just a dominion of the Old Dominion; we would like to make it clear that our state has been independent for ninety years. Some residents take a very strong line about this and always refer to it in conversation as "*West*—By God—Virginia!" 1

—**John Knowles,** *West Virginia*, in *American Panorama: East of the Mississippi*, 1960

Here is hard-core unemployment, widespread and chronic; here is a region of shacks and hovels for housing; here are cliffs and ravines without standing room for a cow or chickens. In this region of steep mountains, a person is exceptionally fortunate if he is able to hack out two or three ten-foot rows of land for potatoes or beans. 2

—**Erskine Caldwell,** *Around America*, 1964

Country roads, take me home 3
To the place I belong,
West Virginia, mountain momma
Take me home, country roads.

—**John Denver,** with Bill Danoff & Taffy Nivert, *Take Me Home, Country Roads*, 1971

Almost Heaven. 4

—**Anonymous,** bumper stickers, c. 1976, reported in Gorton Carruth & Eugene Ehrlich, *American Quotations*, 1988

Montani semper liberi. 5
Mountaineers are always free.

—Motto, state of West Virginia

Whites

See RACES & PEOPLES.

Wilderness

See also ENVIRONMENT; FRONTIER, THE; NATURE; WEST, THE.

There is something in the proximity of the woods which is very singular. It is with men as it is with plants and animals that grow and live in the forests; they are entirely different from those that live in the plains. 6

—**Michel Guillaume Jean de Crèvecoeur,** *Letters from an American Farmer*, 1782

This is the forest primeval. The murmuring pines and the hemlocks, 7
Bearded with moss, and in garments green, indistinct in the twilight,
Stand like Druids of old, with voices sad and prophetic.

—**Henry Wadsworth Longfellow,** *Evangeline, A Tale of Acadie*, 1847

1 I went to the woods because I wished to live deliberately, to front only the essential facts of life.

—**Henry David Thoreau,** *Where I Lived, and What I Lived For,* in *Walden,* 1854

★ More at LIFE.

2 In wildness is the preservation of the world.

—**Henry David Thoreau,** *Walking*, 1862

★ The motto of the Wilderness Society. See also Thoreau at TRAVEL.

3 The most alive is the wildest.

—**Ibid.**

4 It is a wild rank place, and there is no flattery in it.

—**Henry David Thoreau,** *Cape Cod*, 1865

★ See also Thoreau under MASSACHUSETTS re Cape Cod.

5 In God's wildness lies the hope of the world—the great fresh, unblighted, unredeemed wilderness.

—**John Muir,** note from Alaska, 1890

6 There are no words that can tell the hidden spirit of the wilderness, that can reveal its mystery, its melancholy, and its charm.

—**Theodore Roosevelt,** *African Game Trails*, 1910

★ Written on safari in East Africa.

7 The clearest way into the universe is through a forest wilderness.

—**John Muir,** *John of the Mountains*, 1938

8 Wilderness is the raw material out of which man has hammered the artifact called civilization.

—**Aldo Leopold,** *A Sand County Almanac*, 1949

9 Something will have gone out of us as a people if we ever let the remaining wilderness be destroyed.

—**Wallace Stegner,** "the wilderness letter," to David Pesonen, University of California Wildlands Research Center, 1960

★ Stegner, whose novels were set in the American West, was a lifelong advocate of conservation of natural resources.

10 God made the wilderness for man and all other creatures to use, to adore, but not to destroy.

—**William O. Douglas,** *My Wilderness: The Pacific West*, 1962

11 A Wilderness Bill of Rights.

—**William O. Douglas,** book title, 1965

★ Douglas, a leader of liberal causes on the Supreme Court, was also a prominent environmentalist.

12 You must have certain noble areas of the world left in as close-to-primal condition as possible. You must have quietness and a certain amount of solitude. You must be

able to touch the living rock, drink the pure waters, scan the great vistas, sleep under the stars and awaken to the cool dawn wind. Such experiences are the heritage of all people.

—**Ansel Adams,** *Give Nature Time,* commencement address, Occidental College, June 11, 1967

The remaining western wilderness is the geography of hope. **1**

—**Wallace Stegner,** Introduction, *Where the Bluebird Sings to the Lemonade Springs*, 1992

★ This was a saying of Stegner's, also used in *A Geography of Hope*, a lecture delivered at the University of Colorado, and published by the university's press in *A Society to Match Our Scenery*, 1991. See also THE WEST.

Will

See also DETERMINATION, EFFORT, PERSISTENCE, & PERSEVERANCE.

A fat kitchen, a lean will. **2**

—**Benjamin Franklin,** *Poor Richard's Almanack*, 1732-57

Will springs from the two elements of moral sense and self-interest. **3**

—**Abraham Lincoln,** speech, Springfield, Ill., June 26, 1857

"There's no free will," says the philosopher; **4**
"To hang is most unjust."
"There is no free will," assents the officer;
"We hang because we must."

—**Ambrose Bierce,** *Collected Works*, VIII, 1911

Will and wisdom are both mighty leaders. Our times worship will. **5**

—**Clarence Day,** *Humpty-Dumpty and Adam*, in *The Crow's Nest*, 1921

"Where there is a will, there is a way," says the proverb. Not entirely true; but it is **6**
true that where there is no will, there is no way.

—**Thomas Szasz,** *The Second Sin*, 1973

We have to believe in free will. We've got no other choice. **7**

—**Isaac Bashevis Singer,** London, *Times*, June 21, 1982

Wine

See FOOD, WINE, & EATING.

Winning & Losing, Victory & Defeat

See also FAILURE; SPORTS; SUCCESS & FAME.

To the victors belong the spoils. **8**

—**William Marcy,** speech, U.S. Senate, Jan. 25, 1832

★ More at POLITICS & POLITICIANS.

1 [I feel] somewhat like the boy in Kentucky who stubbed his toe while running to see his sweetheart. The boy said he was too big to cry, and far too badly hurt to laugh.

—**Abraham Lincoln,** reply when asked to comment on the Democrats winning state elections in New York, quoted in *Leslie's Illustrated Weekly*, Nov. 22, 1862

★ Adlai Stevenson, after losing in the 1952 presidential election, used this same anecdote, crediting Lincoln. "I'm too old to cry, but it hurts too much to laugh," he said.

2 Too much success is not wholly desirable; an occasional beating is good for men—and nations.

—**Alfred Thayer Mahan,** *Life of Nelson*, 1897

3 Errors and defeats are more obviously illustrative of principles than successes are. . . . Defeat cries aloud for explanation; whereas success, like charity, covers a multitude of sins.

—**Alfred Thayer Mahan,** *Naval Strategy*, 1911

4 Defeat may serve as well as victory
To shake the soul and let the glory out.

—**Edwin Markham,** *Victory in Defeat*, in *The Shoes of Happiness*, 1913

★ Al Gore quoted these lines when finally (after the Supreme Court had weighed in) conceding the 2000 presidential election to George W. Bush, but credited them mistakenly to his father, Sen. Albert Gore, Sr.

5 Winners never give up.

—**Anonymous,** "work-incentive" poster, 1920s

★ This slogan accompanied a picture of George Washington, and was preceded by "When others lost heart and quit, Washington fought on—and won." See also the perennial locker room advice at SPORTS. And for another uplifting workplace slogan, AMBITION & ASPIRATION.

6 Show me a good and gracious loser, and I'll show you a failure.

—**Knute Rockne,** comment to Wisconsin basketball coach Walter Meanwell, 1920s

★ See also SPORTS, the note to the Grantland Rice quote, and the Vince Lombardi quote, below.

7 Winning isn't worthwhile unless one has something finer and nobler behind it.

—**Amos Alonzo Stagg,** *Touchdown!*, 1927

★ Stagg's football teams won 315 games during his 71-year career, spent mainly at the University of Chicago. He is credited with introducing the huddle, the snap from center, the man in motion, the line shift, and cross blocking.

8 Lose as if you like it; win as if you were used to it.

—**Tommy Hitchcock,** saying c. 1935

★ Hitchcock was a famous and dashing polo player.

9 There can only be one winner, folks, but isn't that the American way?

—**Horace McCoy,** *They Shoot Horses, Don't They?*, 1935

Nice guys finish last. 1

—Leo Durocher, July 5, 1946

★ Popular version of comment by Brooklyn Dodgers' manager Durocher on the New York Giants baseball team. The aphorism was spotlighted by sportswriter Jimmy Cannon and used as a book title by Durocher in 1975. The comment in full ran: "I called off his [Giant manager Mel Ott's] players' names as they came marching up the steps behind him, 'Walker Cooper [who had a brother named Morton Cooper], Mize, Marshall, Kerr, Gordon, Thomson. Take a look at them. All nice guys. They'll finish last. Nice guys. Finish last.' " By the way, the Giants did finish last—thirty-six games out—but on the last day of the season, they beat the Dodgers, forcing them into a playoff with St. Louis, which the Dodgers lost 2-0.

You know what makes a good loser? Practice. 2

—Ernest Hemingway, speaking to his son Gregory "Gig" H. Hemingway, quoted in *Papa, a Personal Memoir* [1976]

Never have so few lost so much so stupidly and so fast. 3

—Dean Acheson, 1951, quoted in Daniel Yergin, *The Prize*, 1991

★ Secretary of State Acheson was referring to the huge British losses when Iran nationalized the oil industry. The comment plays on Winston Churchill's, "Never in the field of conflict was so much owed by so many to so few," August 1940. Churchill was expressing gratitude to the Royal Air Force for battling German bombers and fighters.

You can't win them all. 4

—Raymond Chandler, *The Long Goodbye*, 1954

★ Eric Partridge dated this expression to c. 1940 in *A Dictionary of Catch Phrases*, but Chandler's use is the earliest given in *The Concise Oxford Dictionary of Proverbs*. It did not become common until the 1960s.

Sometimes it's worse to win a fight than to lose. 5

—Billie Holiday, *Lady Sings the Blues*, 1956

Winning isn't everything, it's the only thing. 6

—Vincent Lombardi, attributed

★ Lombardi coached the formidable Green Bay Packers 1959-69, and this quote was widely associated with him. It may have originated, however, with coach Henry "Red" Sanders of Vanderbilt University. *Respectfully Quoted*, published by The Library of Congress, credits Sanders with this c. 1948. Melville Shavelson, producer-screenwriter of a 1953 movie, *Trouble Along the Way*, also credited Sanders for the line, which is uttered in the film by the twelve-year-old daughter of a football coach (one of John Wayne's less memorable performances). Sanders was later quoted in *Sports Illustrated* as quipping, "Sure winning isn't everything. It's the only thing," December 26, 1955. Lombardi tried to persuade people that what he himself said was something gentlemanly on the lines of "Winning isn't everything, but wanting (or making the effort) to win is." Others recollect him taking the harder position. Later he told writer James A. Michener that he wished he had never said "the damn thing," that he had meant that it was important to make an effort and to have a goal: "I sure as hell didn't mean for people to crush human values and morality," *Sports in America*, 1976.

1 Close only counts in horseshoes and hand grenades.

—**George C. Wallace,** saying, attributed, *The New York Times* [May 26, 2003]

★ The first part of the statement is proverbial; the second is a recent amplification; the whole is still used often in sports commentary. In 1962, Governor Wallace of Alabama was a fierce segregationist; see RACES & PEOPLES. As a third-party, right-wing presidential candidate in 1968, he didn't come close to winning, but did get 9.9 million votes. In 1972, he was shot while campaigning in the Democratic presidential primary and was paralyzed from the waist down. Meanwhile, he expressed regret for his earlier racial positions, and finished his career with a fourth election to be governor of Alabama. In the end, he had significant support from African-American voters.

2 Winning is a habit. Unfortunately so is losing.

—**Vincent Lombardi**, attributed, *The New York Times* [June 3, 1999]

3 There's an old saying that victory has a hundred fathers and defeat is an orphan.

—**John F. Kennedy,** press conference, State Department, Washington, D.C., April 21, 1961

★ Kennedy made the "old saying" famous on this occasion by taking on his own shoulders as "the responsible officer of the government" full blame for the aborted invasion of Cuba at the Bay of Pigs four days before. The saying—Kennedy himself couldn't remember at the time where he had picked it up—apparently comes from *The Ciano Diaries: 1939–43*, in which Mussolini's foreign minister, Count Galeazzo Ciano, noted on September 9, 1942: "As always, victory finds a hundred fathers, but defeat is an orphan."

4 When you're playing for the national championship, it's not a matter of life and death. It's more important than that.

—**Duffy Daugherty,** attributed

★ Daugherty's Michigan State University football team shared a national championship with the University of Alabama in 1965. He also is credited with the insight that "A tie is like kissing your sister." During his nineteen years at MSU, Mr. Daugherty had 109 wins, 69 losses, and 5 brotherly kisses.

5 A man's not finished when he's defeated; he's finished when he quits.

—**Richard M. Nixon,** letter to Sen. Edward Kennedy after the accident at Chappaquiddick, July 18, 1969

★ Quoted by William Safire after former Pres. Nixon's death in 1994. See also Nixon at HATE.

6 It's easy to do anything in victory. It's in defeat that a man reveals himself.

—**Floyd Patterson,** in Henry Mullan, *The Book of Boxing Quotations* [1988]

★ Patterson, a soft-spoken boxer, won the heavyweight championship in 1956 at age twenty-one. He lost to Swedish fighter Ingemar Johansson in 1959, but regained the crown by beating Johansson in 1960—becoming the first heavyweight champ to win back that title. In 1962, he fell to a glowering Sonny Liston in a first-round K.O., lost to Liston again the next year, and despite a long effort never again reached the first rank.

Losing is the only American sin. 1

—**John R. Tunis,** quoted by Mark Shields, *The MacNeil/Lehrer NewsHour* [March 19, 1992]

★ Shields called Tunis "the greatest American sports writer." For the value of moral victory, see the anonymous Pentagon sign at ETHICS, MORALITY & VALUES.

If you lose, you're out of the family. 2

—**Jeff Martin,** *The Simpsons* television show, Nov. 15, 1990

★ Homer to his son, Bart, who is about to play in a miniature golf game. Homer has bet on Bart.

If you want to have a lot of friends, lose. 3

—**John Thompson,** *The Wall Street Journal*, May 5, 1997

★ The *Journal's* source was Nike sportswear chairman Philip Knight, who quoted Thompson, longtime Georgetown University basketball coach, while making the point that when one is successful, one develops enemies.

Confidence is a fragile thing. Momentum is a fragile thing. 4

—**Bill Cowher,** coach of the Steelers football team, in *Pittsburgh Tribune Review*, Sept. 27, 2003

★ Also, attributed to quarterback Joe Montana, "Confidence is a very fragile thing."

You like to think that the incentive for winning games is winning games. 5

—**Joe Torre,** summer 2004

★ Torre, manager of the New York Yankees, murmured this remark following an 11–10 loss to their arch-rivals Boston Red Sox, reported by Roger Angell, *The New Yorker*, Nov. 22, 2004.

Winter

See NATURE: SEASONS.

Wisconsin

See also CITIES (MILWAUKEE).

Wisconsin is the soul of a great people. She manifests the spirit of the conqueror, 6
whose strength has subdued the forest, quickened the soil, harvested the forces of nature and multiplied production. From her abundance she serves food to the world.

—**Fred L. Holmes,** *Old World Wisconsin*, 1944

Wisconsin's politics have traditionally been uproar politics—full of the yammer, the 7
squawk, the accusing finger, the injured howl. Every voter is an amateur detective, full of zeal to get out and nip a little political inequity in the bud.

—**George Sessions Perry,** *Cities of America*, 1947

Forward. 8

—Motto, state of Wisconsin

Wisdom

See also ADVICE; COMMON SENSE; EXCUSES & EXPLANATIONS (Frankfurter); MIND, THOUGHT & UNDERSTANDING.

1 It is a characteristic of wisdom not to do desperate things.

—**Henry David Thoreau,** *Economy,* in *Walden*, 1854

2 Wisdom is of the soul.

—**Walt Whitman,** *Song of the Open Road*, in *Leaves of Grass*, 3d ed., 1860

3 It is the province of knowledge to speak, and it is the privilege of wisdom to listen.

—**Oliver Wendell Holmes, Sr.,** *The Poet at the Breakfast-Table*, 1872

4 Wisdom is wealth.

—**Joseph Wheeler,** speech, U.S. House of Representatives, Feb. 1883

★ More at BOOKS & READING.

5 The art of being wise is the art of knowing what to overlook.

—**William James,** *The Principles of Psychology*, 1890

6 Wisdom comes by disillusionment.

—**George Santayana,** *The Life of Reason: Reason in Common Sense*, 1905–1906

7 Nine-tenths of wisdom consists in being wise in time.

—**Theodore Roosevelt,** speech, June 14, 1917

8 Wise Man: One who sees the storm coming before the clouds appear.

—**Elbert Hubbard,** *The Roycroft Dictionary and Book of Epigrams*, 1923

9 To know when to be generous and when firm—this is wisdom.

—**Ibid.**

10 The hallmark of the conventional wisdom is acceptability. It has the approval of those to whom it is addressed.

—**John Kenneth Galbraith,** *The Affluent Society*, 1958

★ In *A Journey Through Economic Time* (1994), Galbraith remarked that he created the disparaging phrase "conventional wisdom" to refer to the attempt "to justify the disparity in well-being."

11 Good people are good because they've come to wisdom through failure. We get very little wisdom through success, you know.

—**William Saroyan,** quoted in New York *Journal-American*, August 23, 1961

12 Wisdom is the tears of experience, the bridge of experience and imagination over time.

—**Daniel Bell,** commencement address, Brandeis University, May 26, 1991

Wisdom, Words of

See also ADVICE; CRAFTINESS; HEALTH; QUOTATIONS & PROVERBS; SEASONS & TIMES (Kennedy).

You have the world before you. Stoop as you go through it, and you will miss many hard bumps. **1**

—**Cotton Mather,** advice to Benjamin Franklin, 1724

★ Franklin, in a letter to his son, May 12, 1784, revealed that Mather had given him this advice some sixty years earlier.

Work as if you were to live a hundred years, **2**
Pray as if you were to die tomorrow.

—**Benjamin Franklin,** *Poor Richard's Almanack,* May 1757

Be moderate in prosperity and patient in adversity. **3**

—**Lucinda Howe Storrs,** motto

★ The motto appears in a diary that Mrs. Storrs (1758–1839) kept about her religious life. The wife of Col. Constant Storrs, she lived in Lebanon, N.H.

The bigger the mouth, the better it looks when shut. **4**
Only a fool argues with a skunk, a mule, or a cook.
Kickin' never gets you nowhere, 'les'n you're a mule.
There ain't no hoss that can't be rode.
It's sometimes safer to pull your freight than pull your gun.
Faint heart never filled a flush.
Never call a man a liar because he knows mor'n you do.

—**Anonymous,** cowboy sayings, in Ramon F. Adams, *Western Words: A Dictionary of the American West* [1968]

Put all your eggs in one basket—and watch that basket! **5**

—**Mark Twain,** *Pudd'nhead Wilson's Calendar,* in *Pudd'nhead Wilson,* 1894

★ By rights this should be credited to Andrew Carnegie, but so many authorities, including *Bartlett's,* cite Twain that we stay with the attribution to avoid confusion. As early as 1912, however, Twain's biographer Albert Bigelow Paine revealed that the canny comment was delivered by Andrew Carnegie at a dinner with Twain and others on April 6, 1893. Trying to persuade Carnegie to join him in investing in an automatic typesetting machine, Twain quoted the old adage (it appears in *Don Quixote,* but Cervantes is unlikely to have invented it) that the wise man should not put all his eggs in one basket. "Carnegie regarded him through half-closed eyes as was his custom," wrote Paine, "and answered, 'That's a mistake. Put all your eggs in one basket . . . etc.' " The investment, incidentally, was a major factor in Twain's subsequent bankruptcy; see also Moffett at HONOR above.

Live all you can; it's a mistake not to. It doesn't so much matter what you do in particular, so long as you have your life. **6**

—**Henry James,** *The Ambassadors,* 1903

★ Louis Lambert Strether's advice to Little Bilham distills the essence of the novel.

1 Be prepared.
—Boy Scouts, motto

★ The founder of the Scouts, Sir Robert Baden-Powell, explained, "The scouts' motto is founded on my initials, it is: *be prepared*, which means you are always to be in a state of readiness in mind and body to do your DUTY," *Scouting for Boys*, 1908.

2 Work hard, keep your mouth shut, and answer your mail.
—Thomas J. Pendergast, advice to Harry S. Truman, 1934

★ Pendergast, the political boss of Kansas City, gave this advice to Truman upon his departure for his first term in the U.S. Senate.

3 To get along, go along.
—Sam Rayburn, saying

★ More at CONGRESS.

4 When it is dark enough you can see the stars.
Whom the Gods would destroy they first make mad with power.
The bee fertilizes the flower it robs.
Though the mills of God grind slowly, they grind exceedingly small.
—Charles Beard, *The Four Lessons of History* in *Reader's Digest*, Feb. 1941

★ The first is a variant on the proverbial, "It is darkest before dawn"; see Longfellow at OPTIMISM & PESSIMISM. The second (minus the words "with power") is from Euripides via the Romans via the English and others. The third also sounds proverbial but we have not found it; in this context, it relates to cultural influences. The fourth is from the German via Longfellow; see GOD.

5 Never trust a man who combs his hair straight from the left armpit.
—Alice Roosevelt Longworth, quoted in Michael Teague, *Mrs. L.: Conversations with Alice Roosevelt* [1991]

★ Mrs. L., daughter of Teddy Roosevelt, was speaking specifically of Gen. Douglas MacArthur, who wore his hair in strands over the top of his head.

6 Avoid fried meats which angry up the blood. If your stomach disputes you, lie down and pacify it with cool thoughts. Keep the juices flowing by jangling around gently as you move. Go very light on the vices, such as carrying on in society. The social ramble ain't restful. Avoid running at all times. Don't look back. Something may be gaining on you.
—Leroy "Satchel" Paige, from his autobiography, *How to Stay Young*, 1953

★ Some of the credit for this appealing advice—maybe most of it—should go to *Collier's* magazine writer Richard Donovan, who wrote a profile of Paige, a legendary star of the Negro leagues, and one of the greatest and most enduring of baseball pitchers. (He was 42 when finally admitted into organized baseball in 1948 and made his last appearance in a major league game in 1965.) According to *Good Advice* (1982) by brothers William Safire and Leonard Safir, when Donovan's editor asked for some "typical Paige quotes" to use in a box, Donovan "cooked up" these words of wisdom. Paige later appropriated them. What isn't clear is how close Donovan came to comments actually made by Paige.

Keep your eyes open and your mouth shut. 1

—John Steinbeck, *Sweet Thursday*, 1954

Never eat at a place called Mom's. Never play cards with a man named Doc. And never lie down with a woman who's got more troubles than you. 2

—Nelson Algren, *What Every Young Man Should Know*, in *A Walk on the Wild Side*, 1956

★ Advice from Cross-Country Kline. Algren said that he learned this from "a nice old Negro lady." He and others sometimes used slightly different formulations. For example, mystery writer Ross Macdonald advises in *Black Money* (1966), "Never sleep with anyone whose troubles are worse than your own."

If it ain't broke, don't fix it. 3

—Anonymous, folk adage

★ Given widespread currency in 1977 by Bert Lance, director of the Office of Management and Budget under Pres. Jimmy Carter. Lance could not fix his own problems with investigations into personal banking irregularities, and he resigned the same year.

The first rule of wing walking—never let go of what you are holding onto until you grab hold of something else. 4

—Anonymous, *Wall Street Journal*, Nov. 20, 1991

★ Reporter Stanley W. Angrist cited this rule with reference to resigning from one job before getting another. But the admonition originally was meant literally. Donald Herzberg, dean of Georgetown University's graduate school, told Allan L. Otten, of the *Journal*, that the rule dates to days of airshows by barnstorming pilots (Paul Dickson, *The Official Rules*, 1978).

Have fun. And go home when you're tired. 5

—George Abbott, saying, *The New York Times*, obituary, Feb. 2, 1995

Women

See also WOMEN & MEN.

Men of sense of all ages abhor those customs which treat us only as the vassals of your sex. 6

—Abigail Adams, letter to John Adams, March 31, 1776

★ Abigail was urging her husband to write laws fair to women. More at WOMEN & MEN.

A woman's whole life is a history of the affections. 7

—Washington Irving, *The Broken Heart*, in *The Sketch Book of Geoffrey Crayon, Gent.*, 1819–20

There is in every true woman's heart a spark of heavenly fire which lies dormant in the broad daylight of prosperity; but which kindles up, and beams and blazes in the dark hour of adversity. 8

—Washington Irving, *The Wife*, in *The Sketch Book of Geoffrey Crayon, Gent.*, 1819–20

1 If I were asked . . . to what the singular prosperity and growing strength of that people [Americans] ought mainly to be attributed, I should reply: to the superiority of their women.

—Alexis de Tocqueville, *Democracy in America*, 1835

2 A woman should always challenge our respect, and never move our compassion.

—Ralph Waldo Emerson, *Journal*, 1836

3 As men become aware that few have had a fair chance, they are inclined to say that no woman has had a fair chance.

—Margaret Fuller, *Woman in the Nineteenth Century*, 1845

4 If the first woman God ever made was strong enough to turn the world upside down all alone, these women together ought to be able to turn it back, and get it right side up again!

—Sojourner Truth, Women's Rights Convention, Akron, Ohio, May 29, 1851

5 [That little man in black says] woman can't have as much rights as man because Christ wasn't a woman. Where did your Christ come from? . . . From God and a woman. Man has nothing to do with him.

—Ibid.

★ The man in black was a clergyman in the audience.

6 America is now wholly given over to a damned mob of scribbling women.

—Nathaniel Hawthorne, letter, 1855, quoted in Caroline Ticknor, *Hawthorne and His Publisher* [1913]

7 A Lady with a Lamp shall stand
In the great history of the land,
A noble type of good,
Heroic womanhood.

—Henry Wadsworth Longfellow, *Santa Filomena*, 1858

8 A beautiful woman is a practical poet.

—Ralph Waldo Emerson, *Beauty*, in *The Conduct of Life*, 1860

9 All native American women are intelligent. It seems to be their birthright.

—Anthony Trollope, *North America*, 1862

★ Trollope especially admired women in the eastern cities, whom he thought were graceful, beautiful, charming companions, lacking "nothing that a lover can desire in his love." About western women he had reservations: "They are as sharp as nails, but then they are also as hard. They know, doubtless, all that they ought to know, but then they know so much more than they ought to know. They are tyrants to their parents, and never practice the virtue of obedience till they have half-grown-up daughters of their own."

10 The hand that rocks the cradle
Is the hand that rules the world.

—W. R. Wallace, *The Hand That Rules the World*, c. 1865

Join the union, girls, and together say, "Equal Pay for Equal Work!" 1

—**Susan B. Anthony,** in *The Revolution*, March 18, 1869

A sufficient measure of civilization is the influence of good women. 2

—**Ralph Waldo Emerson,** *Civilization*, in *Society and Solitude*, 1870

Woman must not depend upon the protection of man, but must be taught to protect 3
herself.

—**Susan B. Anthony,** speech, July 1871

I promulgate new races of teachers, and of perfect women, indispensable to endow 4
the birth-stock of a new world.

—**Walt Whitman,** *Democratic Vistas*, 1871

The queens in history compare favorably with the kings. 5

—**Elizabeth Cady Stanton & Susan B. Anthony,** *History of Woman Suffrage*, written with Mathilda Joslyn Gage, 1881

The prolonged slavery of women is the darkest page in human history. 6

—**Ibid.**

Our young women are haunted by the idea that they ought . . . to "improve" their 7
minds. They are utterly unconscious of the pathetic impossibility of improving those poor little hard, thin, wiry, one-stringed instruments which they call their minds, and which haven't range enough to master one big emotion much less to express it in words or figures.

—**Henry Adams,** letter to the American Historical Association, 1885

★ This letter was written in the same year that his wife, Marian, usually called Clover, committed suicide. They had been married for thirteen years.

The Bible teaches that woman brought sin and death into the world, that she pre- 8
cipitated the fall of the race, that she was arraigned before the judgement seat of Heaven, tried, condemned and sentenced. Marriage for her was to be a condition of bondage, maternity a period of suffering and anguish, and in silence and subjection, she was to play the role of a dependent on man's bounty for all her material wants.

—**Elizabeth Cady Stanton,** *The Woman's Bible,* Vol. I, 1895

Girls are charming creatures. I shall have to be twice seventy years before I change 9
my mind as to that.

—**Mark Twain,** in *Autobiography* [1924]

★ The thought was occasioned by fond memories of a visit to Vassar twenty-one years before—and by anticipation of a talk that he planned to give at Barnard College that afternoon.

A thoroughly beautiful woman and a thoroughly homely woman are creations which 10
I love to gaze upon, and which I cannot tire of gazing upon, for each is perfect in her own line.

—**Ibid.**

1 What a woman wants is what you're out of. She wants more of a thing when it's scarce.

—**O. Henry,** *Cupid à la Carte*, in *Heart of the West*, 1907

2 At first a woman doesn't want anything but a husband, but as soon as she gets one, she wants everything else in the world.

—**Edgar Watson Howe,** *Country Town Sayings*, 1911

3 A free race cannot be born of slave mothers.

—**Margaret Sanger,** *Women and the New Race*, 1920

4 Hurray and vote for suffrage.

—**Febb Ensminger Burn,** letter to her son, August 1920

★ "Be a good boy," she urged. And Henry Thomas Burn, age twenty-three, was. He broke a tie in the Tennessee legislature, tipping the balance to ratification of the Nineteenth Amendment, giving women the right to vote; see AMERICAN HISTORY: MEMORABLE MOMENTS.

5 I was, being human, born alone;
I am, being woman, hard beset;
I live by squeezing from a stone
The little nourishment I get.

—**Elinor Hoyt Wylie,** *Let No Charitable Hope*, in *Collected Poems* [1932]

6 No lady is ever a gentleman.

—**James Branch Cabell,** *Something About Eve*, 1927

7 It won't be no time till some woman will become so desperate politically and just lose all prospectus of right and wrong and maybe go from bad to worse and finally wind up in the Senate.

—**Will Rogers,** *Weekly Articles*, March 31, 1929

8 Can we today measure devotion to husband and children by our indifference to everything else?

—**Golda Meir,** *The Plough Woman*, 1930

9 The true worth of a race must be measured by the character of its womanhood.

—**Mary McLeod Bethune,** speech, A *Century of Progress of Negro Women*, Chicago Women's Federation, June 3, 1933

10 A Woman Is a Sometime Thing.

—**Ira Gershwin,** song title, *Porgy and Bess*, 1935

★ Music by George Gershwin.

11 Never Underestimate the Power of a Woman

—**Leo Lionni & Betty Kidd,** N. W. Ayer ad campaign for *Ladies' Home Journal*, from 1939

12 All elegant women have acquired a technique of weeping which has no . . . fatal effect on the makeup.

—**Anaïs Nin,** *Winter of Artifice*, 1939

It was a blonde. A blonde to make a bishop kick a hole in a stained glass window. 1
—**Raymond Chandler,** *Farewell, My Lovely*, 1940

A woman's work is seldom done. 2
—**Thornton Wilder,** *The Skin of Our Teeth*, 1942

★ A play on the old saying, "Man may work from sun to sun, / But woman's work is never done."

Women have simple tastes. They can get pleasure out of the conversation of children 3
in arms and men in love.
—**H. L. Mencken,** *Sententiae*, in *A Mencken Crestomathy*, 1949

When women kiss it always reminds one of prize-fighters shaking hands. 4
—**Ibid.**

There Is Nothing Like a Dame. 5
—**Oscar Hammerstein II,** song title, in *South Pacific*, 1949

★ Music by Richard Rodgers

A woman's best protection is a little money of her own. 6
—**Clare Boothe Luce,** attributed

A liberated woman is one who has sex before marriage and a job after. 7
—**Gloria Steinem,** quoted in *Newsweek* magazine, March 28, 1960

Women's virtue is man's greatest invention. 8
—**Cornelia Otis Skinner**, quoted in *Paris '90*, perhaps c. 1960

Women would rather be right than reasonable. 9
—**Ogden Nash,** *Frailty, Thy Name Is a Misnomer*, in *Marriage Lines*, 1964

Many women do not recognize themselves as discriminated against; no better proof 10
could be found of the totality of their conditioning.
—**Kate Millett,** *Sexual Politics*, 1969

Raging hormonal tides. 11
—**Edgar Berman,** characterization of a causative factor in women's behavior, 1970

★ Dr. Berman, an adviser to Vice President Hubert Humphrey, was forced to resign from the Democratic National Committee's planning council after announcing that hormonal tides interfered with women's competence.

If I have to, I can do anything. 12
I am strong, I am invincible, I am woman.
—**Helen Reddy,** *I Am Woman*, 1972

So few grown women like their lives. 13
—**Katharine Graham,** quoted by Jane Howard, *Ms. Magazine*, Oct. 1974

A strong woman is determined 14
To do something that others are determined not to be done.
—**Marge Piercy,** *For a Strong Woman*, in *Chrysalis*, No. 4, 1977

1 Some of us are becoming the men we wanted to marry.
—**Gloria Steinem,** speech, Yale University, Sept. 1981

2 The meaning of what it is to be a woman has never been more open-ended and therefore more filled with anxiety.
—**Nancy Friday,** *Woman on Top*, 1991

Women & Men

See also CONVERSATION (McInerney); MEN; WOMEN.

3 In the new code of laws, which I suppose it will be necessary for you to make, I desire you remember the ladies, and be more generous and favorable to them than your ancestors. Do not put such unlimited power into the hands of husbands. Remember all men would be tyrants if they could. . . . [We women] will not hold ourselves bound by any laws in which we have no voice or representation. . . Men of sense of all ages abhor those customs which treat us only as the vassals of your sex.
—**Abigail Adams,** letter to John Adams, March 31, 1776

★ See also Abigail Adams at EDUCATION.

4 I cannot say that I think you are very generous to the ladies; for, whilst you are proclaiming peace and good will to men, emancipating all nations, you insist upon retaining an absolute power over wives.
—**Abigail Adams,** letter to John Adams, May 7, 1776

5 I will never consent to have our sex considered an inferior point of light. Let each planet shine in their own orbit. God and nature designed it so—if man is Lord, woman is *Lordess*—that is what I contend for.
—**Abigail Adams,** letter to Eliza Peabody, her sister, July 19, 1779

6 There exists, in the world of men, a tone of feeling towards women as towards slaves, such as is expressed in the common phrase, "Tell that to women and children."
—**Margaret Fuller,** *The Great Lawsuit: Man versus Men, Woman versus Women*, in *The Dial*, July 1843

7 We hold these truths to be self-evident; that all men and women are created equal.
—**Elizabeth Cady Stanton,** *Declaration of Sentiment*, First Woman's Rights Convention, Seneca Falls, N.Y., July 19, 1848

8 As unto the bow, the cord is,
So unto the man is woman,
Though she bends him, she obeys him,
Though she draws him, yet she follows,
Useless each without the other.
—**Henry Wadsworth Longfellow,** *The Song of Hiawatha*, 1855

9 Man has his will—but woman has her way.
—**Oliver Wendell Holmes, Sr.,** *The Autocrat of the Breakfast-Table*, 1858

Men, their rights and nothing more; women, their rights and nothing less. 1
—**Susan B. Anthony,** 1868

★ The motto of *The Revolution*, a newspaper founded by Anthony in 1868, was "The True Republic—men, their rights and nothing more," etc.

The men believe not in the women, nor the women in the men. 2
—**Walt Whitman,** *Democratic Vistas*, 1871

★ More at HYPOCRISY.

A woman never forgets her sex. She would rather talk with a man than an angel, any day. 3
—**Oliver Wendell Holmes, Sr.,** *The Poet at the Breakfast-Table*, 1872

The masculine tone is passing out of the world. It's a feminine, a nervous, hysterical, chattering, canting age. 4
—**Henry James,** *The Bostonians*, 1886

No matter how much women prefer to lean, to be protected and supported, nor no matter how much men desire to have them do so, they must make the voyage of life alone. 5
—**Elzabeth Cady Stanton,** speech, *The Solitude of Self*, in *The Woman's Journal*, Jan. 23, 1893

★ Ms. Stanton gave this speech twice on January 18—to the Judiciary Committee of the U.S. House of Represenatives and when resigning as president of the National American Woman Suffrage Association. Two days later she delivered it again to the U.S. Senate Committee on Woman Suffrage. She regarded the speech as "the best thing I have ever written." And it was very well received. The House committee ordered that 10,000 copies be reprinted from the Congressional Record for distribution around the country.

Hogamus higamus, 6
Men are polygamous,
Higamous hogamous
Women monogamous.
—**Anonymous,** c. 1895

★ The verse has several variations.

You are not permitted to kill a woman who has wronged you, but nothing forbids you to reflect that she is growing older every minute. You are avenged 1,440 times a day. 7
—**Ambrose Bierce,** *Epigrams*

Scratch a lover, and find a foe. 8
—**Dorothy Parker,** *Ballads of a Great Weariness*, in *Enough Rope*, 1927

Where women cease from troubling and the wicked are at rest. 9
—**Anonymous,** slogan on the barroom floor of the Princeton Club in New York

★ The floor was demolished and the slogan not carried forward into the nineties—1990s.

1 Me Tarzan, you Jane.

—**Johnny Weissmuller,** to Maureen O'Sullivan, *Tarzan the Ape Man*, 1932

★ The oft-quoted line appeared in *Photoplay Magazine* (1932) but is not actually in the soundtrack. Rather, Ms. O'Sullivan says "Jane" and points to herself, then says "Tarzan" and points to him. Slowly the ape man catches on and says, while pointing back and forth, "Tarzan . . . Jane . . . Tarzan . . . Jane." Ms. O'Sullivan recalled, according to her obituary in *The New York Times* (June 24, 1998), that the interchange arose as a result of a bit of horseplay. The two actors were sitting on a branch of an MGM tree between takes when Mr. Weismuller pretended to push Ms. O'Sullivan off, and she pretended to push back. "He said 'Jane.' She said 'Tarzan.' He said 'Jane.' Then he said 'Me Tarzan, you Jane.'"

2 A woman will always have to be better than a man in any job she undertakes.

—**Eleanor Roosevelt,** *My Day*, Nov. 29, 1945

3 There is no spectacle on earth more appealing than a beautiful woman in the act of cooking dinner for someone she loves.

—**Thomas Wolfe,** quoted in *The American Heritage Cookbook* [1964]

4 Maleness in America is not absolutely defined; it has to be kept and re-earned every day, and one essential element in the definition is beating women in every game that both sexes play.

—**Margaret Mead,** *Male and Female*, 1948

★ See also Mead at MEDIOCRITY.

5 Men have a much better time of it than women. For one thing, they marry later. For another thing, they die earlier.

—**H. L. Mencken,** *A Mencken Chrestomathy*, 1949

6 If men could get pregnant, abortion would be a sacrament.

—**Florynce Kennedy,** quoted in *Ms.* magazine, March 1973

★ Kennedy, a lawyer and civil rights activist, was speaking in the year of *Roe v. Wade*; see AMERICAN HISTORY: MEMORABLE MOMENTS.

7 Sometimes I wonder if men and women really suit each other. Perhaps they should live next door and just visit now and then.

—**Katharine Hepburn,** attributed, in Deborah Brodie, *Untying the Knot* [1999]

8 Men and women belong to different species, and communication between them is a science still in its infancy.

—**Bill Cosby,** *Love and Marriage*, 1989

9 Their relationship consisted
In discussing if it existed.

—**Thom Gunn,** *Jamesian*, in *The Men With Night Sweats*, 1992

★ The one-couplet poem was displayed on New York City subway cars and buses as part of the transit system's "Poetry in Motion" series. It could apply to a relationship of any sort; the poet himself was gay.

It takes a smart woman to fall in love with a good man. 1

—**Sadie & Bessie Delany,** *Having Our Say: The Delany Sisters' First 100 Years*, 1993

Men Are from Mars, Women Are from Venus 2

—**John Gray,** book title, 1992

★ See also Donald Kagan at FOREIGN POLICY.

A woman without a man is like a fish without a bicycle. 3

—**Gloria Steinem,** *US News & World Report*, Sept. 27, 1993

★ Though generally credited to Ms. Steinem, the graffito, "A woman needs a man like a fish needs a bicycle," was common in the 1970s, according to *The New Penguin Dictionary of Modern Quotations* (2001). A male chauvinist variation, pre-dating Ms. Steinem by nearly thirty years, "A woman without a man is like a trailer without a car; it ain't going nowhere," crops up in the 1964 film, *Kiss Me Stupid*, written by Billy Wilder and I. A. L. Diamond.

Woods

See WILDERNESS.

Words

See LANGUAGE & WORDS.

Work & Workers

See also CAPITALISM & CAPITAL V. LABOR; ACTION & DOING; EXCELLENCE; FARMS & FARMERS.

Love labor: . . . It is wholesome for thy body and good for thy mind. 4

—**William Penn,** *Some Fruits of Solitude*, 1693

The used key is always bright. 5

—**Benjamin Franklin,** *Poor Richard's Almanack*, July 1744

I shall never ask, never refuse, nor ever resign an office. 6

—**Benjamin Franklin,** *Autobiography*, begun 1771 [published in full, 1868]

When men are employed they are best contented. 7

—**Ibid.**

Wherever and whenever one person is found adequate to the discharge of a duty by close application thereto, it is worse executed by two persons, and scarcely done at all if three or more persons are employed therein. 8

—**George Washington,** letter to Secretary of War Henry Knox, Sept. 24, 1792

★ Washington was ahead of his time in realizing that more hands do not necessarily result in better work; see also Whitehead below.

1 O sing me a song of the Factory Girl
So merry and glad and free—
The bloom on her cheeks, of health it speaks!—
O a happy creature is she.
—**John H. Warland,** *Song of the Manchester Factory Girl*

★ Arthur M. Schlesinger, Jr., in *The Age of Jackson*, notes that Warland, a defender of the privileged classes, wrote many Whig campaign songs.

2 We put our love where we have put our labor.
—**Ralph Waldo Emerson,** *Journal*, 1836

★ See also Emerson at EXCELLENCE.

3 The life of labor does not make men, but drudges.
—**Ibid.**

4 Under the spreading chestnut tree
The village smithy stands;
The smith a mighty man is he
With large and sinewy hands.
And the muscles of his brawny arms
Are strong as iron bands.
His brow is wet with honest sweat,
He earns whate'er he can,
And looks the whole world in the face,
For he owes not any man.
—**Henry Wadsworth Longfellow,** *The Village Blacksmith*, 1842

5 And blessed are the horny hands of toil!
—**James Russell Lowell,** *A Glance Behind the Curtain*, in *The Democratic Review*, Sept. 1843

★ One of those lines that school children tend to remember for the wrong reasons.

6 Men for the sake of getting a living forget to live.
—**Margaret Fuller,** *Summer on the Lakes*, 1844

7 It is not necessary that a man should earn his living from the sweat of his brow unless he sweats easier than I do.
—**Henry David Thoreau,** *Economy*, in *Walden*, 1854

8 Every man's task is his life-preserver.
—**Ralph Waldo Emerson,** *Worship*, in *The Conduct of Life*, 1860

9 Labor is the superior of capital, and deserves much the higher consideration.
—**Abraham Lincoln,** first annual message to Congress, Dec. 3, 1861

★ More at CAPITALISM & CAPITAL V. LABOR.

10 Join the union, girls.
—**Susan B. Anthony,** in *The Revolution* newspaper, March 18, 1869

★ More at CAPITALISM & CAPITAL V. LABOR.

John Henry told his captain, 1
"A man ain't nothin' but a man,
And before I'd let that steam-drill beat me down,
I'd die with this hammer in my hand."

—Anonymous, folk song, 1870s

★ John Henry, an African-American steel driver for the C.&O. railroad company, is thought by many to have died during construction of the Big Bend Tunnel in West Virginia in 1870–72. He evidently bested a newly developed steam drill in a steel-driving contest, and in legend, that contest killed him. But other possibilities exist. According to John and Alan Lomax in *Folksong U.S.A.*, John Henry died in a rock fall, one of many, perhaps hundreds of men killed while building that tunnel. Still other folklore researchers believe that a contest took place, but about fifteen years later during construction of tunnels near Birminham, Ala., for the old Columbus & Western Railway.

Labor disgraces no man. 2

—Ulysses S. Grant, speech, Midland International Arbitration Union, Birmingham, England, 1877

★ More at CAPITALISM & CAPITAL V. LABOR.

Work is not the curse, but drudgery is. 3

—Henry Ward Beecher, *Proverbs from Plymouth Pulpit*, 1887

Raise less corn and more hell. 4

—Mary Lease, attributed, speech to Kansas farmers, 1890

★ More at KANSAS.

No race can prosper till it learns there is as much dignity in tilling a field as in writ- 5
ing a poem.

—Booker T. Washington, speech, Atlanta Exposition, Sept. 18, 1895

Every child should be taught that useful work is worship and that intelligent labor is 6
the highest form of prayer.

—Robert G. Ingersoll, *How to Reform Mankind*, 1896

Far and away the best prize that life offers is the chance to work hard at work worth 7
doing.

—Theodore Roosevelt, Labor Day speech, Syracuse, N.Y., Sept. 7, 1903

Come all you rounders for I want you to hear 8
The story of a brave engineer.
Casey Jones was the rounder's name,
On a big eight-wheeler of a mighty fame.

—Anonymous, c. 1907

★ There are many versions of this popular ballad. Most readers know Carl Sandburg's verses in *The American Songbook*, 1927. He drew on the rendition of the vaudevellian Tallifero Laurence Sibert (or Siebert) dating from 1909. And Sibert's work was based on an earlier song by Wallace Saunders, who apparently deserves credit for the original ballad. In *Folksong U.S.A.*, John and Alan Lomax say that Saunders, "a Negro engine wiper," cleaned the blood of his friend Casey Jones from the cab of engine No. 638.

Another railroad worker, Cornelius Steen, heard a railroad ballad in Kansas City that Saunders adapted in memory of Jones. See also below.

1 Casey Jones! Orders in his hand.
Casey Jones! Mounted to his cabin,
Took his farewell trip to the promised land.
—**Anonymous,** c. 1907

★ Engineer John Luther Jones, from Cayce, Kentucky, was famous for his skill in getting the most out of his engine on the Illinois Central's famed "Cannonball"express between Chicago and New Orleans. Jones also made the most of a train's whistle, producing a memorable, mournful sound. After another engineer reported in sick on the evening of April 29, 1906, Casey took over on the night run on the section of the Cannonball's route from Memphis, Tennessee, to Canton, Mississippi. The inscription on Jones's monument in Calvary Cemetery in Jackson, Tennessee, are the lines from the ballad describing his mission: "For I'm going to run till she leaves the rail / Or make it on time with the southbound mail." Shortly before 4:00 A.M., as he came around a curve Jones sighted boxcars ahead, and told his fireman to jump. Jones died at his post, braking and sounding the whistle. Jones had a pretty good safety record up to then, other than a few derailments, and derailments were common, as witness this perhaps apocryphal engineer's communication from the same period: "Off again, on again, gone again. Finnegan."

2 You may tempt the upper classes
With your villainous demitasses,
But Heaven will protect the working girl.
—**Edgar Smith,** *Heaven Will Protect the Working Girl*

★ Sung by Marie Dressler in *Tillie's Nightmare*, 1910

3 No work with interest is ever hard. I am always certain of results. They always come if you work hard enough.
—**Henry, Ford,** *My Life and Work*, 1922

4 The average male gets his living by such depressing devices that boredom becomes a sort of natural state to him.
—**H. L. Mencken,** *In Defense of Women*, 1922

5 Working people have a lot of bad habits, but the worst of them is work.
—**Clarence Darrow,** quoted in Lincoln Steffens, *Autobiography*, 1931

6 There is no substitute for hard work.
—**Thomas Alva Edison,** *Life*, 1932

7 Figure it out. Work a lifetime to pay off a house. You finally own it, and there's no one to live in it.
—**Arthur Miller,** *Death of a Salesman*, 1949

8 The bitter and sweet come from the outside, the hard from within, from one's own efforts.
—**Albert Einstein,** *Out of My Later Years*, 1950

When you cease to make a contribution, you begin to die. 1

—**Eleanor Roosevelt,** letter to Mr. Horne, Feb. 19, 1960

Here on earth God's work must truly be our own. 2

—**John F. Kennedy,** Inaugural Address, Jan. 20, 1961

If work was a good thing the rich would have it all and not let you do it. 3

—**Elmore Leonard,** *Split Images*, 1961

Work is a four-letter word. 4

—**Anonymous,** bumper sticker, from a comment by Yippie founder Abbie Hoffman, 1960s

★ Cf. Tennessee Williams below.

I am the cry of the poor 5
Who work in the fields
Who water the earth
With our sweat . . .
Long have we suffered
Being sold like slaves
Now we can all see
Our triumph is coming.

—**Epifanio Camacho,** *Strike of the Roses*, 1965, in Stan Steiner, *La Raza: The Mexican Americans* [1969]

★ Camacho, a rose grafter, led a strike that began on May 3, 1965, at Mount Arbor Nurseries, in McFarland, California. This was the first strike of Cesar Chavez's National Farm Workers Association, organized in September of 1962.

The working class is loyal to friends, not ideas. 6

—**Norman Mailer,** *The Armies of the Night*, 1968

In a hierarchy, every employee tends to rise to his level of incompetence. 7

—**Laurence J. Peter,** *The Peter Principle*, 1969

★ Nor do corporate disasters necessarily impede the employee's rise; see Zion at FAILURE.

There is no prestige whatsoever attached to actually working. Workers are invisible. 8

—**Marge Piercy,** *The Grand Coolie Damn*, in Robin Morgan ed., *Sisterhood Is Powerful*, 1970

The loveliest of all four-letter words—Work! 9

—**Tennessee Williams,** *Memoirs*, 1975

Eight people will do ten people's work better than twelve people. 10

—**Jack W. Whiteman,** *Whiteman's Finding: The First Corollary to Parkinson's Law*, in Paul Dickson, *The Official Explanations*, 1980

★ C. Northcote Parkinson, Raffles Professor of History at the University of Malaya, initially proclaimed his great law in the *Economist* (1955): "Work expands so as to fill the time available for its completion." See also George Washington above.

1 I never retired. I just did something else.
—Doris Day, quoted in *Time*, July 29, 1985

2 When you've been living in the sunshine all your life, you don't want to move into the shade.
—Don Hewitt, quoted in *The New York Times*, April 17, 2005

★ Mr. Hewitt, the longtime executive director of the television news show *60 Minutes*, resisted retirement until 2004, when he was 81.

World, the

See also LIFE; LOVE, EXPRESSIONS OF (Edna Ferber); NATURE; RELIGION (John Updike); UNIVERSE, THE.

3 Abstract yourself with a holy violence from the dung heap of this world.
—Roger Williams, to John Winthrop, governor of the Massachusetts Bay Colony, c. 1635

★ Williams, who challenged the authority of the colony's government, was banished in 1635, and abstracted himself to the Rhode Island region, where he founded Providence.

4 The world is a severe schoolmaster, for its frowns are less dangerous than its smiles and flatteries, and it is a difficult task to keep in the path of wisdom.
—Phillis Wheatley, letter to John Thornton, Oct. 30, 1774

★ Wheatley was kidnapped from Africa at about age eight, and arrived in Boston in 1761. She began to write poetry at age fourteen, and finding no publisher in America, traveled to England. Her *Poems on Various Subjects, Religious and Moral*, published in 1773 in England, is the first book by an African-American. She was freed in the mid–1770s, and died in poverty some ten years later.

5 Look on this beautiful world, and read the truth
In her fair pages.
—William Cullen Bryant, *The Ages*, 1821

6 To different minds, the same world is a hell, and a heaven.
—Ralph Waldo Emerson, *Journal*, Dec. 20, 1822

7 This curious world which we inhabit is more wonderful than it is convenient; more beautiful than it is useful; it is more to be admired and enjoyed, then, than it is to be used.
—Henry David Thoreau, *The Commercial Spirit of Modern Times,* commencement address at Harvard, 1837

8 Good-bye proud world! I'm going home.
Thou art not my friend and I'm not thine.
—Ralph Waldo Emerson, *Good-bye*, in *Poems*, 1847

9 I came into this world, not chiefly to make this a good place to live in, but to live in it, be it good or bad.
—Henry David Thoreau, *Civil Disobedience*, 1849

The world is so big, and I am so small, **1**
I do not like it at all at all.
—Woodrow Wilson, quoted by Adlai Stevenson, in Leon Harris, *The Fine Art of Political Wit* [1965]

O world, I cannot hold thee close enough! **2**
—Edna St. Vincent Millay, *God's World*, 1917

Some say the world will end in fire, **3**
Some say in ice.
From what I've tasted of desire
I hold with those who favor fire.
But if it had to perish twice,
I think I know enough of hate
To say that for destruction ice
Is also great
And would suffice.
—Robert Frost, *Fire and Ice*, 1923

This is the way the world ends **4**
Not with a bang but a whimper.
—T. S. Eliot, *The Hollow Men*, 1925

No. I do not weep at the world—I am too busy sharpening my oyster knife. **5**
—Zore Neale Hurston, *Colored Me*, in *World Tomorrow*, 1928

The world is a fine place and worth fighting for. **6**
—Ernest Hemingway, *For Whom the Bell Tolls*, 1940

I had a lover's quarrel with the world. **7**
—Robert Frost, *The Lesson for Today*, read at Harvard University, June 20, 1941

★ More at EPITAPHS & GRAVESTONES.

The world only exists in your eyes—your conception of it. You can make it as big or as small as you want to. **8**
—F. Scott Fitzgerald, *The Crack-Up*, 1945

The material of this world may be real enough (as far as reality goes) but does not exist at all as an accepted entirety; it is chaos. **9**
—Vladimir Nabokov, *Good Readers and Good Writers*, 1948

★ Nabokov explained that it is the artist who makes sense of the chaos: ". . . the author says 'go!' allowing the world to flicker and to fuse. It is now recombined in its very atoms, not merely in its visible and superificial parts."

The most incomprehensible thing about the world is that it is comprehensible. **10**
—Albert Einstein, obituary, *The New York Times*, April 19, 1955

The world is a force, not a presence. **11**
—Wallace Stevens, *Adagia*, in *Opus Posthumous* [1957]

1 The world's perverse,but it could be worse.

—**Mona Van Duyn,** *Sonnet for Minimalists* in *Letters from a Father and Other Poems,* 1982

2 There is no one way the world is because the world is still in creation, still being hammered out.

—**Christopher A. Fuchs,** letter to Howard Barnum & Tony Sudbury, August 18, 2003, quoted in *Scientific American,* Sept. 2004

3 The ruthless furnace of this world.

—**Jack Gilbert**, *A Brief for the Defense,*in *Refusing Heaven*, 2005

★ More at HAPPINESS.

World War I, 1914–1918 (U.S. entered in 1917)

4 We're going to try to get the boys out of the trenches by Christmas.

—**Henry Ford**, statement to the press, Nov. 1915

★ Ford's promise has been reported in several versions. This is from Allan Nevins and Frank Ernest Hill, *Ford: Expansion and Challenge, 1915–1933* (1957). (In 1915, two years before America entered the European war, Ford, who was a pacifist, had chartered a ship and sailed for the Continent with a peace delegation. The venture was ridiculed by the press, but Ford never regretted the effort: "I wanted to see peace," he commented later. "I at least tried to bring it about. Most men did not even try.") Christmas is a traditional target date for ending conflicts, and some question whether the Christmas reference here was an embellishment of Ford's actual words. Gen. John J. Pershing was also credited, later, with aiming to get troops home by Christmas; see the note to the anonymous quote below on Hoboken. In 1951, people hoped that the Korean conflict would be decided by Christmas, after Gen. Douglas MacArthur launched a major U.S.-U.N. offensive in Korea on November 24, the day after Thanksgiving. He hoped to reach the Yalu River before December 25, but ran into several hundred thousand Chinese troops who had come to the aid of North Korea, and he barely escaped total disaster.

5 Wake up America.

—**Augustus P. Gardner**, speech, Oct. 16, 1916

6 I have a rendezvous with death
At some disputed barricade,
When spring comes round with rustling shade
And apple blossoms fill the air.
. . .
But I've a rendezvous with death
At midnight in some flaming town,
When spring trips north again this year,
And I to my pledged word am true.
I shall not fail that rendezvous.

—**Alan Seeger,** *I Have a Rendezvous with Death*, 1916

★ Seeger was killed in 1916, while fighting with the French Foreign Legion. The poem may have been the inspiration for Franklin D. Roosevelt's "This generation of

Americans has a rendezvous with destiny." The poem was a favorite of John F. Kennedy.

It must be a peace without victory. **1**

—Woodrow Wilson, speech, U.S. Senate, Jan. 22, 1917

★ The president was describing the kind of peace that he believed was needed to end war in Europe. More at AMERICAN HISTORY: MEMORABLE MOMENTS.

The world must be made safe for democracy. **2**

—Woodrow Wilson, speech to the U.S. Congress asking for a declaration of war, April 2, 1917

★ In this speech, the president recommended declaring war on Germany. "The right is more precious than peace," he said, "and we shall fight for the things which we have always carried nearest our hearts." Those things were democracy, the rights and liberties of small nations, and the freedom of all peoples. Wilson is sometimes associated with the argument that the war would be "the war that will end war." H. G. Wells, however, is the apparent author of the phrase, and used it as a book title in 1914. The British statesman Lloyd George is said to have remarked, "This war, like the next war, is a war to end war."

It is a war against all nations. **3**

—Ibid.

If it be not treason, it grazes the edge of treason. **4**

—John Sharp Williams, debate, U.S. Senate, April 4, 1917

★ Sen. Williams, Democrat of Mississippi, thus characterized comments by George W. Norris, an isolationist Republican from Nebraska, who opposed the decision to declare war.

Food will win the war. **5**

—Anonymous, slogan, 1917

★ The slogan was associated with the voluntary—later mandated—food programs run by Herbert Hoover. A witticism of the times was, "But how do we get the Krauts here to eat it?"

It's heaven, hell, or Hoboken. **6**

—Anonymous, 1917

★ U.S. troops left for and returned from the war at the port of Hoboken, New Jersey. Thus soldiers on their way overseas realized that they would end up at one of these three places. The phrase was published in verses by Albert Jay Cook in *Stars and Stripes*. In 1918, Gen. John J. Pershing is said to have pledged, "Hell, heaven, or Hoboken by Christmas."

You're in the Army now, **7**
You're not behind a plow.
You'll never get rich,
You son of a bitch.
You're in the Army now.

—Anonymous, soldier's song, c. 1917

1 And we won't come back till it's over over there.
—George M. Cohan, *Over There*, 1917

2 Lafayette, we are here.
—Charles E. Stanton, at the tomb of the Marquis de Lafayette, Paris, July 4, 1917

★ Probably the best-remembered statement by an American in World War I. The comment has been attributed to both Gen. John Pershing and Col. Stanton, a nephew of Lincoln's Secretary of War, Edwin M. Stanton. People who were there remember different speakers, but Pershing himself credited Stanton. Henry F. Woods in *American Sayings* (1945) writes that the famous line was the closing sentence in a short speech by Stanton: "America has joined forces with the Allied Powers, and what we have of blood and treasure are yours. Therefore it is that with loving pride we drape the colors in tribute of respect to this citizen of your great republic. And here and now, in the presence of the illustrious dead, we pledge our hearts and our honor in carrying this war to a successful issue. Lafayette, we are here."

3 There lie many fighting men,
Dead in their youthful prime.
Never to laugh nor love again
Nor taste the summertime.
—Joyce Kilmer, *Rouge Bouquet*, March 7, 1918

★ *Rouge Bouquet* was a woods and battleground.

4 The first hundred years are the hardest.
—Anonymous, saying among members of the American Expeditionary Force, c. 1918

5 Come on you sons of bitches! Do you want to live forever?
—Daniel Daly, battle cry, June 4, 1918

★ Marine Sergeant Daly used this rallying call in the Battle of Belleau Wood. The late word expert Stuart Flexner reported that in World War I, U.S. soldiers used the phrase "son of a bitch" so often that the French called them *les sommobiches.* As with "don't fire until you see the whites of their eyes"—see AMERICAN REVOLUTION—this battle cry has a precedent. On June 18, 1757, at Kolin, Frederick the Great is said to have shouted at his Guards, "Rascals, would you live forever?"

6 This war was a commercial and industrial war. It was not a political war.
—Woodrow Wilson, speech, St. Louis, Sept. 5, 1919

7 There died a myriad,
And of the best, among them,
For an old bitch gone in the teeth,
For a botched civilization.
—Ezra Pound, *Hugh Selwyn Mauberley: E.P. Ode pour l'élection de son sépulchre*, 1920

World War II, 1939–1945 (U.S. entered in 1941)

This is—London. 1

—Edward R. Murrow, opening line for his radio broadcasts from London, 1939–45

★ Murrow's reports brought the war into American living rooms, eroding isolationist sentiment and inspiring affection for the beleaguered British.

On this tenth day of June 1940, the hand that held the dagger has struck it into the back of its neighbor. 2

—Franklin D. Roosevelt, speech, University of Virginia, June 10, 1940

★ The "stab in the back," as it was popularly known, was struck by Italy, when it declared war on France, already conquered and occupied by German troops.

I shall say it again and again and again. Your boys are not going to be sent into any foreign wars. 3

—Franklin D. Roosevelt, campaign speech, Boston, Oct. 30, 1940

★ But the president did believe that the country should help the nations that were fighting fascism and tyranny. Two months later, he made his "arsenal of democracy" speech; see AMERICAN HISTORY: MEMORABLE MOMENTS. After the attack on Pearl Harbor and the German declaration of war on the U.S., American boys were in the war.

It is significant that despite the claims of air enthusiasts no battleship has yet been sunk by bombs. 4

—Anonymous, caption for photograph of the U.S.S. *Arizona*, Army-Navy Game program, Nov. 29, 1941, cited in Walter Lord, *Day of Infamy* [1957]

★ The *Arizona* was bombed and sunk in Pearl Harbor, December 7, 1941.

Praise the Lord and pass the ammunition. 5

—Howell M. Forgy, Pearl Harbor, Dec. 7, 1941

★ With these words, Forgy, a navy chaplain on the cruiser *New Orleans*, encouraged sailors hoisting shells to the guns firing on Japanese warplanes. They were widely repeated and later used in a popular song by Frank Loesser. The rallying cry has also been attributed to another Pearl Harbor navy chaplain, William A. Maguire (1890–1953); according to *They Never Said It*, by Paul F. Boller, Jr., and John George, it was used as far back as the Civil War.

Yesterday, December 7, 1941—a date which will live in infamy—the United States of America was suddenly and deliberately attacked by naval and air forces of the empire of Japan. 6

—Franklin D. Roosevelt, message to Congress requesting that it declare a state of war existing between the U.S. and Japan, Dec. 8, 1941

We are now in this war. We are all in it, all the way. 7

—Franklin D. Roosevelt, message to the nation, Dec. 9, 1941

We are going to win the war, and we are going to win the peace that follows. 8

—Ibid.

1 Sighted sub. Sank same.

—Donald F. Mason, radio dispatch, Jan. 28, 1942

★ Mason, an aviation machinist's mate, 1st class, in the U.S. Navy, was flying a patrol plane over the Atlantic, when he spotted an enemy submarine, dropped depth charges, and radioed this message to his base. He received a Distinguished Flying Cross and promotion to chief aviation machinist's mate but, as was learned at the end of the war, he did not sink the sub.

2 This war is a new kind of war. It is warfare in terms of every continent, every island, every sea, every air lane in the world.

—Franklin D. Roosevelt, fireside radio talk, Feb. 23, 1942

3 We're the battling bastards of Bataan;
No momma, no papa, no Uncle Sam;
No aunts, no uncles, no nephews, no nieces,
No rifles, no planes or artillery pieces,
And nobody gives a damn.

—Anonymous, military song, Bataan peninsula, Philippines, winter 1941–42

★ Following the attack on Pearl Harbor, the eighty thousand American and Filipino troops on Bataan were doomed to defeat. Despite pleas from their commander, Gen. Douglas MacArthur, no reinforcements were sent, and MacArthur was reassigned in March. In April, the overwhelmed defenders, under Gen. Jonathan Wainwright, surrendered. Ten thousand had died in battle; fourteen thousand died in the Death March that followed. See also William Thomas Cummings at ATHEISM and MacArthur below.

4 I shall return.

—Douglas MacArthur, remark, March 11, 1942

★ Gen. MacArthur first made this pledge to his fellow officers and friends as he left the Philippines, according to Henry F. Woods in *American Sayings* (1945). Upon landing in Melbourne, Australia, on March 20, he again announced, "I came through and I shall return." See also MacArthur below.

5 No army has ever done so much with so little.

—Douglas MacArthur, comment on the fall of Bataan, quoted in *The New York Times*, April 11, 1942

6 And when he goes to heaven
To Saint Peter he will tell:
Another Marine reporting, sir;
I've served my time in hell.

—Anonymous, epitaph, grave of Marine Pfc. Cameron, Guadalcanal, 1942

★ The battle for the island of Guadalcanal in the Solomon Sea lasted from August 7, 1942, to February 9, 1943. The costly American victory led to the first Japanese retreat in the Pacific islands. Nine marines were awarded the Medal of Honor for their part in the struggle.

7 Oversexed, overfed, over here.

—Anonymous, British saying

★ From 1942 to 1944, American troops were stationed in Britain in great numbers.

They were both admired and resented, as reflected in this quip, which is sometimes attributed to entertainer Tommy Trinder.

Berlin was an orchestrated hell—a terrible symphony of death and flames. 1

—**Edward R. Murrow,** CBS radio broadcast from London, Dec. 3, 1943

★ Murrow had flown on an RAF bombing raid the previous night. Two other reporters on other planes did not get back. CBS would not allow Murrow to go again.

I seen my duty and I done it. 2

—**James H. Howard,** Jan. 1944

★ Flying a P-51 Mustang fighter, Howard became separated from his squadron but spotted a group of B–17 bombers returning from a raid in Germany. The Flying Fortresses were under attack by German fighters. For more than a half hour, he fought off some thirty German planes, downing at least four. He was awarded the Medal of Honor, and retired from the U.S. Air Force with the rank of brigadier general. Earlier in the war, he had been a member of Col. Claire L. Chennault's volunteer Flying Tigers, who fought the Japanese in Burma and China.

The eyes of the world are upon you. The hopes and prayers of liberty-loving people 3
everywhere march with you.

—**Dwight D. Eisenhower,** order to troops preparing to invade Normandy, June 6, 1944

Gentlemen, we are being killed on the beaches. Let's go inland and be killed. 4

—**Norman D. Cota,** Omaha Beach, France, June 6, 1944

★ Brig. Gen. "Dutch" Cota's comment may have been improved in recollection. Stephen Ambrose in his 1994 book on D-day gives the quote as: "Don't die on the beaches. Die up on the bluff, if you have to die. But get off the beaches or you're sure to die." The same day, Cota also gave the U.S. Army Rangers their motto, "Rangers lead the way," when he told the Ranger commander, "I'm expecting the Rangers to lead the way."

Almighty God: Our sons, pride of our nation, this day have set upon a mighty 5
endeavor, a struggle to preserve our republic, our religion, and our civilization, and to set free a suffering humanity. Lead them straight and true: Give strength to their arms, stoutness to their hearts, steadfastness in their faith.

—**Franklin D. Roosevelt,** D-day prayer, June 6, 1944

★ This is from a long prayer read by Pres. Roosevelt over the radio at 10:00 P.M. on D-day.

We sure liberated the hell out of this place. 6

—**Anonymous,** U.S. soldier in a French village, 1944, quoted in Max Miller, *The Far Shore* [1945]

The Third Fleet's sunken and damaged ships have been salvaged and are retiring at 7
high speed toward the enemy.

—**William F. Halsey,** radio dispatch, Oct. 15, 1944

★ Admiral Halsey's response to Japanese reports that the American fleet had been destroyed. The message was addressed to Admiral Chester Nimitz.

1 Follow me!

—Aubrey S. Newman, battle cry, Oct. 20, 1944

★ In the return of American troops to the Philippines, Col. Newman's infantry regiment was pinned down by Japanese fire on the beach at Leyte. He shouted this order, leading a charge that was credited with saving his men. Col. Newman won a Distinguished Service Cross, and the 24th Infantry Division adopted his cry as a motto. Later, Army recruiting posters urged, "Get up and get moving! Follow me!"

2 I have returned. By the grace of almighty God, our forces stand again on Philippine soil.

—Douglas MacArthur, landing at Leyte, Oct. 20, 1944

3 I'll run away again if I have to go out there.

—Eddie D. Slovik, confession, introduced at his court-martial, Nov. 11, 1944

★ Pvt. Slovik, never soldier material, landed at Omaha Beach in 1944, but quickly lost heart and hid in his foxhole. He reported for duty six weeks later, but acknowledged he could not face the fighting. He was killed by a firing squad in January 1945, the last U.S. soldier to be executed for desertion. See also Joseph Heller at THE MILITARY.

4 Nuts!

—Anthony McAuliffe, reply to German query as to whether he was ready to surrender Bastogne, Battle of the Bulge, Dec. 22, 1944

★ Brig. Gen. McAuliffe, known affectionately as "Old Crock," most probably used a stronger term. Kurt Vonnegut, Jr., an infantry scout, remarked later, "Can you imagine the commanding general of the 101st Airborne saying anything but 'shit'?" McAuliffe's defiant rejoinder recalled Maj. Charles W. Whittlesey's "They can go to hell," in World War I when Germans asked him to surrender his "Lost Battalion," isolated in a ravine in the Meuse-Argonne battle in Oct. 1918. He won the Medal of Honor for his valor.

5 Uncommon valor was a common virtue.

—Chester Nimitz, 1945

★ Adm. Nimitz was referring to the Marines' conquest of Iwo Jima. More than 5,000 were killed; 17,400 were wounded. Of 23,000 Japanese defenders, only 216 were taken alive.

6 From my mother's sleep I fell into the State,
And hunched in its belly till my wet fur froze.
Six miles from earth, loosed from its dream of life,
I woke to black flak and the nightmare fighters.
When I died they washed me out of the turret with a hose.

—Randall Jarrell, *The Death of the Ball Turret Gunner*, 1945

★ Jarrell served in the Air Force. This is probably the most famous World War II combat poem by an American.

7 Kilroy was here.

—Anonymous, U.S. military graffito slogan, World War II

★ No one knows for sure the origin of this slogan, which was emblazoned all over the world on walls, ships, tanks, and anything else that could be written upon. Wherever one went, Kilroy seemed to have been there first. Troops hitting beaches in the second wave of an invasion often were greeted with signs announcing "Kilroy was here." Leading candidates as the source of the phrase include an inspector of military equipment, James J. Kilroy, who chalked his name on items that he checked, and Francis J. Kilroy, Jr., a sergeant in the Army Air Transport Command, who had a friend or friends who made a game of writing his name wherever they went.

The flags of freedom fly all over Europe. 1

—**Harry S. Truman,** VE [Victory in Europe]-Day, May 8, 1945

★ The president, speaking on radio at nine in the morning, told the nation that Germany had surrendered.

I am become Death, the shatterer of worlds. 2

—**J. Robert Oppenheimer,** quoting from the *Bhagavad-Gita* at the test of the first atom bomb, July 16, 1945, cited in N. P. Davis, *Lawrence and Oppenheimer* [1986]

★ See also Martin Luther King, Jr., at SCIENCE: TECHNOLOGY.

The war's over. One or two of those things, and Japan will be finished. 3

—**Leslie R. Groves,** remark to deputy after first atomic bomb test, July 16, 1945

★ Gen. Groves was in charge of the Manhattan Project that developed the bomb.

Sixteen hours ago an American plane dropped one bomb on Hiroshima. . . . It is an 4
atomic bomb. It is a harnessing of the basic power of the universe. The force from which the sun draws its power has been loosed against those who brought war to the Far East.

—**Harry S. Truman,** message to the nation, August 6, 1945

* * * Official Truman Announces Japanese Surrender * * * 5

—**The New York Times,** message on electric "zipper" sign, August 14, 1945

★ At 7:03 P.M., this message ran on the illuminated moving headlines sign that ran around the Times Tower on Times Square in New York. Thousands of people below were waiting for this official confirmation of Japan's surrender. The zipper sign, incidentally, ran and conveyed news continuously from 1928 to 1963, and was operated off and on after that.

To save your world you asked this man to die: 6
Would this man, could he see you now, ask why?

—**W. H. Auden,** *Epitaph for an Unknown Soldier*, 1945

Writers & Writing

See ART: STYLE IN WRITING & EXPRESSION; BOOKS & READING.

Wyoming

Whoopee ti yi yo, git along, little dogies, 7
It's your misfortune and none of my own;

Whoopee ti yi yo, git along, little dogies,
For you know Wyoming will be your new home.
—Anonymous, cowboy song, c. 1870

★ A series of relatively mild winters encouraged cattlemen to make greater use of open ranges in Wyoming in the 1870s and early 1880s.

1 I looked into a gulf seventeen hundred feet deep with eagles and fish hawks circling far below. And the sides of that gulf were one wild welter of color—crimson, emerald, cobalt, ochre, amber, honey splashed with port wine, snow white, vermilion, lemon, and silver gray, in wide washes. . . . So far below that no sound of its strife could reach us, the Yellowstone River ran—a finger-wide strip of jade green.
—Rudyard Kipling, *American Notes*, 1891

★ Kipling reported riding in a buggy through Yellowstone with "an adventurous old lady from Chicago and her husband, who disapproved of [the] scenery as being 'ongodly.' I fancy it scared them." Robert Louis Stevenson, who visited the state at about the same time, found the scenery depressing: "Sagebrush, eternal sagebrush; over all, the same weariful and gloomy coloring, grays warming into brown, grays darkening toward black; and for sole sign of life, here and there a few fleeing antelopes," *Across the Plains*, 1892.

2 Wyoming is a land of great open spaces with plenty of elbow room . . . There are sections of the state where it is said you can look farther and see less than any other place in the world.
—Federal Writers' Project, *Wyoming: A Guide to Its History, Highways, and People*, 1941

3 About the only thing that will make a Wyoming cattleman reach for his gun nowadays is to call him a "farmer." A "rancher," he wants it clearly understood, drinks only canned milk, never eats vegetables, and grows nothing but hay and whiskers.
—John Gunther, *Inside U.S.A.*, 1947

4 [Wyoming:] One of my favorite states—of existence.
—Vladimir Nabokov, introducing his poem *The Ballad of Longwood Glen*, at the 92nd St. Y, New York City, 1964

5 Equal rights.
—Motto, state of Wyoming

Youth

See also Ages; Children.

6 In our youth is our strength; in our inexperience, our wisdom.
—Herman Melville, *White-Jacket*, 1850

★ More at America & Americans.

7 A boy's will is the wind's will,
And the thoughts of youth are long, long thoughts.
—Henry Wadsworth Longfellow, *My Lost Youth*, 1858

8 So nigh is grandeur to our dust,
So near is God to man,

When Duty whispers low, *Thou must*,
The youth replies, *I can*.
—**Ralph Waldo Emerson,** *Voluntaries*, 1867

In America, the young are always ready to give to those who are older than themselves the full benefits of their inexperience. 1
—**Oscar Wilde,** *The American Invasion*, in *Court and Society Review*, March 1887

One may return to the place of his birth. 2
He cannot go back to his youth.
—**John Burroughs,** *The Return*, in *Bird and Bough*, 1906

One could do worse than be a swinger of birches. 3
—**Robert Frost,** *Birches*, 1916

All lovely things will have an ending, 4
All lovely things will fade and die,
And youth that's now so bravely spending,
Will beg a penny by and by.
—**Conrad Aiken,** *All Lovely Things*, in *Twins and Moves*, 1916

★ Aiken's own youth was blighted at age ten, when he heard gun shots and found the bodies of his father and mother—killed by his father in a murder-suicide.

No time to marry, no time to settle down; 5
I'm a young woman, and I ain't done runnin' around.
—**Bessie Smith,** *Young Woman's Blues*, 1927

Little brown boy, 6
Slim, dark, big-eyed,
Crooning love songs to your banjo
Down at the Lafayette—Gee, boy, I love the way you hold your head,
High sort of and a bit to one side,
Like a prince, a jazz prince.
—**Helene Johnson,** *Poem*, in Countee Cullen, ed., *Caroling Dusk: An Anthology of Verse by Negro Poets*, 1927

Youth is the pollen 7
That blows through the sky
And does not ask why.
—**Stephen Vincent Benét,** *John Brown's Body*, 1928

The American ideal is youth—handsome, empty youth. 8
—**Henry Miller,** *The Wisdom of the Heart*, 1941

The secret of eternal youth is arrested development. 9
—**Alice Roosevelt Longworth,** quoted in *American Heritage*, Feb. 1969

1 We have a saying in the movement that we don't trust anybody over thirty.
—Jack Weinberg, interview, *San Francisco Chronicle*, c. 1965, cited in the *Washington Post*, March 23, 1970

★ The saying was associated with the free speech movement at the University of California, which started in the early 1960s, and with the Youth International Party, which was founded in 1968 and whose members were called Yippies. The originator may indeed be Weinberg, then a twenty-four-year-old student at the Berkeley campus of the University of California. Years later, he told Ralph Keyes, author of *Nice Guys Finish Seventh*, that he had called it a saying in order to give the words more zing. Actually, he had made them up on the spot, he said, and believed that they were original to him.

2 No one thinks anything of *you* where you grow up.
—Diane Johnson, *Le Divorce*, 1997

Zeal

See ENTHUSIASM & ZEAL.

Author Index

Abbott, George (1887–1995), *theatrical director, producer, playwright;* burning the candle at both ends (note), 241:4; have fun, 727:5; motivation & your job, 71:5

Ace, Jane Sherwood (1905–1974), *radio show host;* familiarity breeds attempt, 343:7; time wounds, 670:9

Acheson, Dean (1893–1971), *secy. of state;* decision, 183:7; explain, those who (note), 242:4; Great Britain, 447:11; a memorandum, 403:2; never have so few lost so much, 721:3; a statesman, 199:4

Acocella, Joan, *cultural critic, biographer;* who marries who (note), 407:1

Acton, Lord (John Emerich Edward Dalberg-Acton, 1st Baron Acton) (1834–1902), *English historian, M.P.;* power (note), 611:3

Acts of the Legislature of Illinois, official language, 330:5

Adams, Abigail (1744–1818), *letter-writer;* customs which treat us only as vassals, 727:6; education of females (& note), 211:5; frippery, 253:8; give, give, 534:4; Lord & Lordess, 732:5; men would be tyrants, 732:3; my heart is like a feather, 301:7; necessities, great, 298:5; Paris, 137:4; power, 534:4; wives, absolute power over, 732:4

Adams, Ansel [Easton] (1902–1984), *photographer, conservationist;* art & life, 59:7; noble areas of the world, 718:12; a photograph, 73:6; rape, ruin & run, 226:10

Adams, Brooks (1848–1927), *lawyer, historian;* law, 372:5; this war is the first gun (note), 468:5

Adams, Charles Francis (1807–1886), *amb. to Great Britain;* action, 1:5; Massachusetts, 409:5; New England & worship of Mammon, 476:10; Plymouth, 140:4

Adams, [Marian Hooper] Clover (1843–1885), *Washington, D.C., hostess;* chaws more than he bites off, 257:3

Adams, Franklin Pierce (1881–1960) *newspaper columnist, versifier, translator, editor;* Boston (note), 116:5; middle age, 420:0; Tinker-to-Evers-to-Chance, 642:4; too much truth, 680:7; what this country needs, 689:1; you can fool all of the people (note), 508:3

Adams, Henry [Brooks] (1838–1918), *historian, novelist, biographer, autobiographer;* the America mind, 26:2; chaos v. order, 417:9; cheers, who stands and, 642:2; contradictions in principle, 244:1; experience, 244:9; friend, one, 279:8; friends are born, 279:7; learn, know how to, 213:4; Maryland, 409:2; Newport, 130:4; the Pennsylvania mind, 507:4; political education, 527:7; politics, 527:5,6,8; power, a friend in, 535:6; [Roosevelt, T.:] pure act, 594:5 & note; Russia, 451:8; schoolmaster, priest, or senator, 160:9; a teacher, 213:5; women, our young, 729:7; words, 362:3; Yankee & a Swede, 453:3

Adams, John (1735–1826), *lawyer; delegate from Mass. to 1st & 2nd Continental Congresses; commissioner to France; amb. to Great Britain; 1st vice pres., 2nd pres.;* [Baltimore:] dirtiest place, 115:2; coin, credit & circulation, 206:2; day of deliverance, 333:7; democracy, 189:2; facts, 245:5; government & happiness, 293:4; government of laws & not of men, 371:1; grief, 632:9; history of the American Revolution, 315:3; independence forever (note), 274:5; innocence should be protected, 370:7; Jefferson still survives, 366:4; morals, 235:1; [New Yorkers] talk loud, 130:6; office, most insignificant, 691:4; a poet in your pocket, 66:7; politics & the middle way, 523:4; power, 534:5,8; president, the office of, 541:5,7; press, liberty of, 547:2; property, have no, 556:8; property is surely a right, 556:10; revolution was in the hearts and minds of the people, 51:3; virtue, 698:4,5

Adams, John Quincy (1767–1848), *U.S. sen. from Mass., secy. of state, 6th pres., U.S. rep. from Mass.;* abroad in search of monsters, 21:6; dictatress of the world (note), 21:6; freedom, wherever standard of unfurled, 21:6; his face is livid (note), 337:4; I am content, 366:5; opulence & want, 447:2; our country always right (note), 500:1; say not "My country right or wrong", 501:4

Adams, Samuel (1722–1803), *revolutionary leader, gov. of Mass.;* country shall be independent, 33:4; glorious morning for America, 48:2

Addams, Jane (1860–1935), *social reformer, feminist, pacifist;* private beneficence, 107:2

Addison, Joseph (1672–1719), *English essayist, poet, playwright, govt. official;* liberty, 273:6; we can die but once (note), 49:2

Ade, George (1866–1944), *newspaperman, humorist, playwright;* the cocktail, 14:6; early to bed (note), 307:9 (note); familiarity breeds, 343:6

Adler, Polly (1900–1962), *Russian-born brothel-keeper, memoirist;* house is not a home, 624:4

Adler, Stella (1902–1992), *"method" acting teacher;* actors, 73:1

Agnew, Spiro T[heodore] (1918–1996), *gov. of Md., 39th vice pres.;* effete corps of impudent

prescribe to (note), 602:1; quantum physics (note), 602:1

Bok, Derek (b. 1930), *educator and author; pres. of Harvard;* if you think education is expensive, 215:5

Bok, Sissela (b. 1934), *Swedish-born philosopher, writer;* secrecy, 611:1

Boone, Daniel (1734–1820), *frontiersman, hunter, Va. state rep., American icon;* fault, better mend a (note), 301:10; gun, horse & wife, 301:10; say no harm (note), 301:10

Boorstin, Daniel J. (1914–2004), *historian;* advertising, 8:6; a celebrity, 654:2; the celebrity, 654:1; God, 291:4; the hero, 313:4; a pseudo-event, 8:7; reality & images, 574:8; television, 413:9; truth, 680:11

Booth, John Wilkes (1838–1965), *assassin of Lincoln, actor;* the South is avenged!, 36:5

Booth, Junius Brutus (1796–1852), *English-born actor;* I will cut your throat, 179:1

Borah, William E[dgar] (1865–1940), *U.S. sen. from Idaho;* patience, 499:5

Boren, James H. (b. 1925), *business consultant;* guidelines for bureaucrats, 403:3

Bork, Robert H[eron] (b. 1927), *U.S. solicitor gen.; federal judge;* speech, explicitly political, 278:4

Borman, Frank (b. 1928), *astronaut; commander, Apollo VIII;* the moon, 469:1

Bossidy, John Collins (1860–1928), *physician, poet;* Boston [toast to], 116:5

Boston Globe, Red Sox Complete Sweep, 47:3

Bowden, Charles ["Chuck"] (b. c. 1945), *journalist, author;* problem with polls, 559:2

Boykin, William G. ["Gerry"], *U.S. army lt. gen.;* my God v. his idol, 85:5

Brackett, Charles (1892–1969), Wilder, Billy (1906–2002), & D. M. Marshman, Jr., *screenwriters: Brackett and Wilder also directed and produced; Brackett also journalist, drama critic, novelist;* love-making, 407:8; the pictures got small, 412:3; I'm ready for my close-up (note), 303:9

Bradford, William (1590–1657), *English-born gov. of Plymouth Colony;* actions, great and honorable, 1:1; pilgrims, 18:6; they fell upon their knees, 32:6

Bradley, Bill [given forenames, William Warren] **(b. 1943),** *U.S. sen. from N.J.; forward, New York Knickerbockers;* greatness in each person, 299:3; the point of the game, 648:4

Bradley, Omar [Nelson] (1893–1981), *U.S. army gen.; 1st chm. Joint Chiefs of Staff;* the atom v. Sermon on the Mount, 437:7; ethical infants, 236:1; wrong war/wrong place, 360:1; war, 707:1

Bradstreet, Anne [Dudley] (c. 1612–1672), *English-born poet; author of 1st book of American poetry;* if ever two were one, 392:8; youth & middle age & old age, 10:7

Bragg, Edward S[tuyvesant] (1827–1912), *U.S. rep. from Wisc.;* enemies he has made, 220:8

Brand, Stewart (b. 1938), *designer, writer, founding editor-publisher of* The Whole Earth Catalog; information wants to be free, 358:10 & note

Brandeis, Louis D[embitz] (1856–1941), *public-interest lawyer; assoc. just., U.S. Supreme Court (1st Jew on Court);* if we would guide by the light of reason, 373:13; [Depression, the] more serious than war, 209:1; evolution, 455:2; federal system as laboratory, 190:2; government, 296:1; man is as the Lord made him, 336:8; the right to be let alone, 168:2, 553:1; secrecy, 610:8; sunlight, 411:4; zeal, men of, 222:6

Brando, Marlon [Jr.] (1924–2004), *actor;* an actor (note), 72:2

Brayton, Charles R. "Boss" (1840–1910), *Union Army general, politician;* honest vote, 525:6

Breck, Henry R., *C.I.A. officer, investment mgr.;* the upper classes, 217:6

Bremer, Frederika (1801–1865), *Swedish novelist, poet;* Minnesota, 443:1; South Carolina, 634:7

Brennan, William J[oseph], Jr. (1906–1997), *assoc. just., U.S. Supreme Court;* damn obscenity thing (note), 103:4; privacy, the right of, 553:5; sex & obscenity, 617:6; social importance, without redeeming, 278:2; speech concerning public affairs, 278:3

Brewer, David J. (1837–1910), *assoc. just., U.S. Supreme Court;* America is the paradise of lawyers, 377:5

Brinton, [Clarence] Crane (1898–1968), *historian;* revolutions, 587:3; skeptical, 626:9; toleration, 673:4

Brisbane, Albert (1809–1890), *popularizer of Charles Fourier's ideas in U.S.;* society as it is now, 78:2

Brisbane, Arthur (1864–1936), *newspaper editor;* intelligence of public (note), 509:1

Britt, Steuart Henderson (1907–1979), *advertising consultant;* doing business without advertising, 8:3

Brokaw, Tom [given forenames, Thomas John] **(b. 1940),** *TV journalist, news anchor;* South Dakota, 635:7

Bromfield, Louis (1896–1956), *novelist, essayist, farmer;* agriculture & our economic structure, 252:7; the farmer, 252:10; Ohio, 484:1

Brooks, Gwendolyn [Mrs. Henry Blakely] **(1917–2000),** *poet, novelist;* the little moment, 540:8

Brooks, Mel [born Melvin Kaminsky] **(b. 1926),** *director, producer, screenwriter;* flaunt it, 552:3; good to be king, 535:11

Brooks, Peter C. (fl. 1845), corporations, 91:8

Brooks, Phillips (1835–1893), *Episcopal bishop, writer;* O little town of Bethlehem, 110:7

Brotherton, Alice Williams (1848–1930), *poet, short-story writer, lecturer;* heap high the board, 667:4

Broun [Matthew] Heywood [Campbell] (1888–1939), *journalist, novelist;* ice cream, 261:1; men, 416:5; truth, 680:6

Browder, Earl Russell (1891–1973), *secy. gen. of American Communist Party; candidate for pres.;* communism, 157:8

Brown, Drew ["Bundini"] (1928–1987), *asst. boxing trainer, actor;* float like a butterfly, 648:1

Brown, H[ubert Geroid] "Rap" [adopted name,

Jamil Abdullah al-Amin] **(b. 1943),** *black-power activist, Muslim leader;* violence, 695:3

Brown, H. Jackson, Jr. (b. 1940), *adv. agency owner;* power to change, 105:7; strive for excellence, 241:1

Brown, James ("the godfather of soul") (b. 1934), *singer;* I'm black and proud, 571:4

Brown, John (1800–1859), *abolitionist, insurrectionist; tried and executed for attacking fed. arsenal, Harper's Ferry, Va. (now W. Va.);* crimes, purged with blood, 149:8; forfeit my life (note), 35:2; I am worth more to hang (note), 149:8; not wrong but right, 35:5; this is a beautiful country, 367:1

Brown, John Mason (1900–1969), *drama critic, essayist;* tv. programs & chewing gum, 412:4; Washington [D.C.], 147:5

Brownell, Baker (1887–1965), *teacher, writer, social philosopher;* southern Illinois, 330:6

Browning, Robert (1812–1889), *English poet;* Chicago (note), 118:7; less is more (note), 60:6

Brownmiller, Susan (b. 1935), *feminist writer, historian;* clothes, 255:3

Brownson, Orestes A[ugustus] (1803–1876), *editor, novelist;* classes of society, 99:4; democracy, 189:4

Broyard, Anatole (1920–1990), *critic;* Rome, 142:3

Bruce, Lenny [born Leonard Alfred Schneider] **(1925–1966),** *nightclub comedian;* church & God, 580:10; liberals, 530:9; Miami Beach, 128:4

Bryan, William Jennings (1860–1925), *3-time Dem. pres. candidate; secy. of state; prosecutor in Scopes "Monkey Trial";* burn down your cities & leave our farms, 252:4; cross of gold, 207:3; destiny, 256:4; friends, nothing final between, 279:9; income tax, 660:7; man & some inferior, 599:5; miracle, one, 434:3; prosperity [that] will leak through, 207:4; a righteous cause, 591:8; we defy them, 583:3

Bryant, William Cullen (1794–1878), *poet, editor, critic;* destiny, 256:2; the groves, 471:1; life, tides of, 380:7; the melancholy days, 462:10; the Oregon, 492:1; the prairies, 422:4; the rose, 460:6; truth, 678:7; world, this beautiful 740:5

Bryce, James [1st Viscount Bryce] (1838–1922), *British jurist, historian, politician; amb. to U.S.;* cities, the government of, 111:9; most typically American place, 118:8; president, great men not chosen, 543:4

Brzezinski, Zbigniew (b. 1928), *Polish-born writer, nat. security advisor to pres.;* diplomacy, 199:5

Buchwald, Art[hur] (b. 1925), *humorous writer, lecturer;* humorists, 327:5

Buck, Pearl S[ydenstricker] [Mrs. Richard Walsh] **(1892–1973),** *novelist, short-story writer, translator;* civilization & its helpless members, 149:5; colored Americans, 568:5; do right, 592:6; hope is taken away, 322:5; Kansas, 354:9; soldiers, 427:5; a usurer & interest, 441:4; Vermont, 691:1

Buckingham, J[ames] S[ilk] (1786–1855), *British journalist, author, traveler; M.P.;* Alabama, 11:6; hospitality [in Georgia], 286:6; love in this country, 388:7

Buckley, William F[rank], Jr. (b. 1925), *editor, writer, columnist, TV host, novelist;* truth, 680:10; worse and worse, 491:8

Buckner, Robert [Henry] (1906–1989), *screenwriter, producer;* win just one for the Gipper (note), 643:2

Buffett, Warren (b. 1930), *financier;* value, 689:4

Buffon, Georges Louis Leclerc [Comte de] (1707–1788), *French naturalist;* style (note) 651:5

Bullard, Eugene J. (1894–1971), *boxer, nightclub owner;* all blood runs red, 567:1

Bullitt, William C[hristian] (1891–1967), *amb. to Russia, France; secy. of navy;* mankind, 224:4

Bunche, Ralph J[ohnson] (1903–71), *U.N. diplomat;* racism, 572:1

Bundy, McGeorge (1919–1996), *dean, Harvard Coll.; spec. asst. for nat. sec;* no other present way (note), 572:4; war, 705:11

Bunyan, John (1628–1688), *English minister and religious writer;* a muckrake in his hand (note), 549:5

Burchard, Samuel Dickinson (1812–1891), *pastor;* Rum, Romanism and rebellion, 516:4

Burford, Anne M[cGill] Gorsuch (1942–2004), *1st woman to head Environmental Protection Administration;* Washington [D.C.], 147:7

Burges, Tristram (1770–1853), *U.S. rep. from R.I.;* the father of lies (note), 337:4

Burgess, [Frank] Gelett (1866–1951), *humorist; writer, epigrammatist, coiner of words;* I know what I like, 62:2; purple cow, 197:5

Burke, Edmund (1729–1797), *Irish-born British political theorist, writer, orator; M.P.;* America, 19:5; the profession [the law] is numerous and powerful, 375:9; when bad men combine (note), 239:8

Burn, Phoebe ["Febb"] Ensminger (1873–1945), *homemaker, suffragist;* vote for suffrage, 730:4

Burn, Henry ["Harry"] Thomas (1895–1977), *Tenn. state rep.,* a mother's advice, 494:1; to free 17 million from political slavery, 38:4

Burnham, Daniel (1864–1912), *architect;* make no plans, 630:5

Burnham, Sophy (b. 1936), *novelist, journalist, nonfiction writer, playwright;* coincidence & miracles, 434:8

Burnett, Frances [Eliza] Hodgson (1849–1924), *English-born writer of novels, children's stories, plays;* as long as one has a garden, 461:8; goodness, the best kind of, 699:5

Burns, George [born Nathan Birnbaum] **(1896–1996),** *comedian, actor;* happiness, 251:5; people who know how to run the country, 245:4; sincerity (note), 320:10

Burns, Robert (1759–1796), *Scottish poet;* O whistle, and I'll come to you (note), 623:10

Burr, Aaron (1756–1836), *lt. col. in Continental army, U.S. sen. from N.Y., 3rd vice. pres.; killed Alexander Hamilton in pistol duel;* law, 371:5; never do today what you can do tomorrow, 188:4

Burroughs, John (1837–1921), *naturalist, essayist, poet;* stones, no sermons in, 455:3; [T. Roosevelt] was a walking day of judgment, 594:7; youth, 751:2

Burroughs, William S[eward] (1914–1997), *novelist;* language, 365:1; this planet, 227:1

Burton, [Sir] Richard [Francis] (1821–1890), *British army capt., explorer, travel writer, translator;* a dead man for breakfast, 118:1

Burton, Robert (1577–1640), *English vicar, librarian, writer;* Columbus & America & God, 18:5

Busch, Niven (1903–1991) & Ruskin, Harry (1894–1969), *screenwriters: Busch also mag. ed., novelist, producer; Ruskin also lyricist, producer;* there's gotta be a law, 378:3

Bush, George [Herbert Walker] (b. 1924), *navy pilot in WWII, U.S. rep. from Texas, amb. to U.N., C.I.A. dir., 43rd vice pres., 41st pres., losing pres. candidate;* allied air forces began an attack, 299:9; a classic bully (note), 7:7; cold war, 46:3; forests, 472:1; legitimacy, 509:9; light, a thousand points of, 31:4; a line in the sand, 300:2; nation, a kinder, gentler, 522:6; new world order, 270:5; taxes, no new, 661:9; the vision thing, 702:2; voodoo economics, 210:1; world is safer, 612:4

Bush, George W[alker] [b. 1946], *businessman, gov. of Texas, 43rd pres.;* a C average (& note), 215:6; America & military strengths, 270:1; axis of evil, 47:1; bring 'em on, 345:5; catastrophic success, 346:4 & note; compassionate conservatism, 523:2; exploration not an option, 5:4; fool me once (note), 263:8; freedom is on the march, 523:3; in Texas, 666:6; justice, 352:11; nation, humble but strong, 270:6; peace & freedom in world, 277:3; permission slip, 271:6; what's happening in the world, 546:9

Bushnell, Horace (1802–1876), *Congregational minister, theologian;* history, 315:7

Butler, Nicholas Murray (1862–1947), *pres., Columbia U.; vice pres. candidate;* an expert, 245:2

Byrd, William, II (1674–1744), *lawyer, public official, writer;* North Carolina, 481:4; priests, lawyers, and physicians, 478:8

Byrne, Susan M. (b. 1946), *mutual fund mgr.;* capital v. opportunity, 95:5

Byrnes, James F[rancis] ["Jimmy"] (1882–1972), *U.S. rep. and sen. from S.C.; assoc. just., U.S. Supreme Court; secy. of state; gov. of S.C.;* power intoxicates, 535:7

Cabell, James Branch (1879–1958), *novelist, essayist, poet;* no lady is a gentleman, 730:6; the optimist & pessimist, 491:2; Virginian, the intrepid native, 697:10

Caen, Herb[ert Eugene] (1916–1997), *newspaper columnist;* Baghdad-by-the-Bay, 143:5

Cage, John [Milton] (1912–1992), *composer, author;* beauty, 80:12; life, 384:4; silence, 620:5

Cahn, Sammy [born Samuel Cohen] **(1913–1993),** *song lyricist;* love and marriage, 408:4

Caldwell, Erskine [Preston] (1903–1987), *novelist, screenwriter;* here is hard-core unemployment, 717:2

Calhoun, John C[aldwell] (1782–1850), *U.S. rep. from S.C., secy. of war, 7th vice pres., U.S. sen. from S.C., secy. of state;* the cohesive power of banks, 91:7; offices as public trusts (note), 295:5; the South! the South!, 366:7; the Union & the rights of states (note), 683:1

Calonne, Charles-Alexander de (1734–1802), *French lawyer, official;* difficult & impossible [note]. 4:2

Camacho, Epifanio, *Mexican-American farmworker, union organizer, poet;* I am the cry of the poor, 739:5

Cameron, Simon (1799–1889), *newspaper publisher, financier, secy. of war, amb. to Russia, U.S. sen. from Pa., Rep. state party boss;* honest politician stays bought, 524:7; back, scratch my, 524:10

Campbell, Joseph (1904–1987), *teacher, mythologist, writer;* bliss, follow your, 303:4; the zealot, 222:8

Campbell, Timothy J[ohn] (1840–1904), *U.S. rep. from N.Y.;* the Constitution between friends, 167:1

Candido, Jeff & Hoff, Jason (fl. 2004), *advertising copywriters* what happens here [Las Vegas], 125:4

Cannon, James P[atrick] (1890–1974), *Trotskyist leader; a founder of U.S. Communist Party and Socialist Workers Party;* The Two Americas, 590:7

Cannon, Joseph G[urney] ["Czar"] (1836–1926), *U.S. rep. from Ill., speaker;* a majority, 402:4; not one cent for scenery, 224:1

Caples, John R. (1900–90), *advertising copywriter;* all laughed when I sat down at the piano, 6:6

Capone, Al[fonso] (1899–1947), *Chicago crime syndicate boss;* Canada, 446:3

Capote, Truman [born Truman Streckfus Persons] **(1924–1984),** *novelist, short-story writer, journalist, dramatist, screenwriter, celebrity;* California, 97:12; Brazil, to want to be president of, 446:1; history, 307:7; Venice, 145:8; what anyone says about me, 681:2

Card, Andrew [Jr.] (b. 1947), *lobbyist, secy. of trans., White House chief of staff;* they [reporters], 551:7

Cardozo, Benjamin N[athan] (1870–1938), *judge, N.Y. appeals ct,; assoc. just., U.S. Supreme Court;* justice, 351:9; law never is, 373:8; three great mysteries, 390:7

Carey, Macdonald (1913–1994). See Corday, Ted

Cargile, Neil [Hastings Jr.] (1928–1995), *cross-dressing businessman;* doing something different, 198:3

Carleton, Will[iam McKendree] (1845–1912), *poet, journalist;* over the hill to the poor-house. 532:8

Carlson, Evans Fordyce (1896–1947), *U.S. marine gen.;* gung ho, 427:6

Carlyle, Thomas (1795–1881), *Scottish-born English essayist and historian;* best & bravest (note), 218:4; man is a tool-using animal (note), 323:4

Carman, [William] Bliss (1861–1929), *Canadian poet, essayist, journalist;* maples, the scarlet of, 464:7

Carmer, Carl [Lamson] (1893–1976), *writer, editor, radio broadcaster, folklorist;* Alabama, 12:1; Birmingham, 115:5; Mobile, 128:8

Carmichael, Stokeley [Standiford Churchill] [adopted name, Kwame Touré] **(1941–1998) & Hamilton, Charles, Vernon (b. 1929),** *Trinidad-born "black power" activist, Hamilton a political scientist, teacher, writer;* Black power, 571:3

Carnegie, Andrew (1838–1919), *Scottish-born industrialist, philanthropist, writer;* administration of wealth, 207:2; put all your eggs in one basket (note), 725:5

Carney, Julia (1823–1908), *poet, teacher;* little drops of water, 629:5; little deeds of kindness, 630:1

Carr, John Dickson (1906–1977), *"locked room" mystery writer;* facts, 246:6

Carson, Johnny [born John William Carson] **(1925–2005),** *TV personality, "Tonight Show" host;* Dan Quayle's golf bag, 341:6

Carson, Rachel [Louise] (1907–1964), *marine biologist, science writer and editor, environmentalist;* all returns to the sea 462:6; the chemical barrage, 225:9; life on earth, 225:7; nature, control of, 608:3; spring [is] strangely silent, 225:8

Carter, Elliott C[ook], [Jr.] (b. 1908), *composer, teacher;* music & architecture, 55:5

Carter, Jimmy [James Earl, Jr.] (b. 1922), *U.S. navy officer, Ga. state sen. and gov., 39th pres.;* adultery in my heart, 617:10; California, 98:1; I'm a Georgian, 286:8; immigrants, we are a nation of, 265:7; live as though Christ coming in afternoon, 250:2; over-lawyered, 378:6; the Soviet Union, 452:5

Carver, George Washington (1864–1943), *director of agricultural research at Tuskegee Institute;* can't tear up everything, 225:2; fear & hate, 305:9

Carville, James (b. 1944), *political consultant, pundit;* the economy, stupid, 523:1

Casey, William (1913–1987), *lawyer, politician, C.I.A. dir.;* our bastard (note), 268:3

Cassatt, Mary (1845–1926), *painter, printmaker; settled in France;* the civilized parts of the world, 674:7

Cather, Willa [Sibert] (1873–1947), *novelist, short-story writer, journalist, editor, poet;* corn country, 422:8; friendship & solitary men, 279:10; the grass was the country, 422:7; happiness, 302:3; hate, creative, 305:6; history begins in the heart, 316:5; human stories, 649:8; land, there was nothing but, 280:5; love, 389:5; memories, 415:6; the mesa plain, 479:7; Nebraska, 474:5; New Mexico, 479:6; nobleness, 700:3; past, the precious, 497:9 & note; prayers, 537:5; the thing not named, 60:2; travel faster now, 675:1; trees, 471:5; who marries who, 407:1; wicked ones get worse, 351:7; winter, 465:3

Catlin, George (1796–1872), *painter, writer, explorer of American west;* "West," the term, 714:1

Catt, Carrie Chapman (1859–1947), *suffragist, pacifist; a founder of the League of Women Voters;* custom & opinion, 300:9

Catton, Bruce (1899–1978), *historian, journalist, govt. official;* Michigan, 419:4

Cavanaugh, J[ames] M[ichael] (1823–1878), *U.S. rep. from Minn.;* good Indian, never seen (note), 564:5

Celler, Emmanuel (1888–1981), *U.S. rep. from N.Y.;* Brooklyn, 134:4; foreigners, afraid of, 265:4; a heart for every fate, 310:2

Cermak, Anton [Joseph] ["Pushcart Tony"] (1873–1933), *Bohemian-born Chicago mayor;* glad it was me instead of you, Frank, 368:3

Chaffee, John H[ubbard] (1922–1999), *R.I gov., U.S. sen.;* preservation not just about brick and mortar

Chamberlain, Jason (fl. 1811), *clergyman; pres., U. of Vt.;* morals & manners & grammar, 360:4

Chandler, Raymond [Thornton] (1888–1959), *hard-boiled detective-story writer, screenwriter;* art & redemption, 58:12; a blonde, 731:1; Boston, 116:9; carving knife & husband's necks, 180:2; an ideal, 329:10; knights, 176:1; down these mean streets a man must go, 312:3; a man of honor 313:3; money, 441:9; split an infinitive, 364:2; win them all, you can't, 721:4

Chaplin, Ralph (1887–1961), *labor activist, songwriter, poet;* solidarity forever, 100:4

Chapman, Arthur (1873–1935) *poet, journalist, novelist, historian;* where the West begins, 715:7

Chapman, Robert W., *writer;* a quotation, 561:11

Charles of Prussia [Prince] (fl. c. 1745), whites of their eyes [note], 48:3

Chase, Alexander (b. 1926), *journalist, editor;* the movie actor, 72:4

Chastellux, François Jean [Marquis de] (1734–1788), *French soldier, writer, philosopher;* goodness and benevolence [of George Washington], 710:2

Chaucer, Geoffrey (c. 1343–1400), *English poet, diplomat, govt. official, M.P.;* mordre wol out (note), 173:1; your own thing (note), 1:7

Chayevsky, Paddy (1923–1981), *playwright, producer;* I'm mad as hell, 53:3

Cheever, John (1923–1981), *novelist, short-story writer;* fear, 258.8

Chesnutt, Charles W[addell] (1858–1932), *teacher, lawyer* sentiment, 219:6; The South, 637:6

Chesterton, G[ilbert] K[eith] (1874–1936), *English novelist, essayist, poet;* Americans & their ideals, 28:2; my country right or wrong (note), 500:1

Cheney, Dick [given forenames, Richard Bruce] **(b. 1941),** *White House chief of staff, U.S. rep. from Wyo., secy. of def., 46th vice pres.;* greeted as liberators, 345:2

Chiat/Day, *advertising agency;* it keeps going and going, 9:10

Chicago Times, print news & raise hell, 548:2

Chicago Tribune, Dewey Defeats Truman, 41:1

Child, Julia [McWilliams] (1912–2004), *chef, popularizer of French cooking on TV, cookbook author;* alone in the kitchen, 262:13; red meat and gin, 489:9

Child, Lydia Maria (1802–1880), *editor, novelist, versifier, abolitionist, feminist;* grandfather's house, 666:10; the Irish, 449:4; the United States is a warning, 23:6; we first crush people to the earth, 562:6

Collyer, Robert (1823–1912), *English-born clergyman, writer;* a dollar to the Great White Throne, 230:3

Colombani, Jean-Marie (b. 1948), *Senegal-born French journalist;* we are all Americans, 46:7

Colson, Charles W[endell] ["Chuck"] (b. 1931), *spec. counsel to Pres. Nixon;* enemies list (note), 221:6

Colton, Calvin (1789–1857), *clergyman, journalist, teacher, writer;* in the Mississippi Valley, 421:10

Columbus, Christopher [birth name, Christoforo Colombo; in Spanish, Cristóbal Colón] **(1451–1506),** *Italian-born explorer for Spain;* I went into the ocean, 32:5

Comden, Betty (b. 1919) & Green, Adolph (1915–2002), *lyricists, librettists;* New York, 134:6; why did I ever leave Ohio?, 484:3

Commager, Henry Steele (1902–1998), *historian, teacher, writer, editor;* criticism & dissent, 190:6; Founding Fathers & current Fathers, 701:9; freedom, 276:9; less than the graces, 323:2

Compton, Arthur Holly (1892–1962), *physicist;* the Italian navigator, 607:4

Computer World, what you measure, 609:8

Conable, Barber B[enjamin], Jr. (1922–2003), *U.S. rep. from N.Y;* what did president know? (note), 713:1

Conant, James Bryant (1893–1978), *chemist, pres. of Harvard, amb. to West Germany;* a university [is] hallowed ground, 214:1

Conkling, Roscoe (1829–1888), *U.S. rep. and sen. from N.Y.;* hew to the line, 156:6

Connor, [Theophilus] Eugene ["Bull"] (1897–1973), *longtime commissioner of public safety, Birmingham, Ala.;* we make our own law, 375:1

Conor, Harry (c. 1856–1931), *actor, singer, comedian;* the Bow'ry, 131:6

Conrad, Joseph [born Teodor Jósef Konrad Korzeniowski] **(1857–1924),** *Polish-born English novelist;* the discovery of America, 27:6

Constitution of the United States, Preamble, 165:1

Cook, E. U. (fl. c. 1885), *cattleman, versifier;* this Texas Hell, 664:7

Cooke, [given name, Alfred] **Alistair (1908–2004),** *English-born journalist, TV host, writer;* Newport, 130:5

Coolidge, [John] Calvin (1872–1933), *gov. of Mass., 29th vice pres., 30th pres.;* business & the American people, 27:8; [Harding:] a fitting representative, 303:9; ideal, force of an, 329:4; if you don't say anything, 659:1; the law & a majority, 373:7; Massachusetts, 410:1; patriotism, 503:5; persistence, 195:2; president, not choose to run for, 544:7; strike, no right to, 101:1; tell that to Mrs. Coolidge (note), 616:4; troubles, 767:3; Vermont, 690:4; work & unemployment, 207:6

Cooper, Gary [born Frank James Cooper] **(1901–1961),** *actor;* [Communism:] I don't like it, 158:2

Cooper, James Fenimore [born James Cooper] **(1789–1851),** *novelist, naval historian;* democracy & mediocrity, 189:3; a gentleman, 216:4; individuality & freedom, 335:2; juries, 349:6; language, American, 361:1; Prairies, the Great, 421:9; public opinion, 558:3; a rural population 171:1; simplicity, 620:8; true, that which is, 678:6; wealth, mere, 439:2

Cooper, Peter (1791–1883), *industrialist, philanthropist; candidate for pres.;* an aristocracy of wealth, 216:6; dealers in money, 92:4; God, 289:6; moneyed men, 587:2; wealth, the production of, 439:7

Coppola, Francis Ford (b. 1939) and Edmund H. North (1911–1990), *screenwriters; Coppola also director, producer;* napalm in the morning, 694:3

Corbusier, Le. See Le Corbusier

Corday, Ted (1908–1966) & Phillips, Irna (c. 1901–1973), *soap opera scriptwriters, producers; Corday also directed;* days of our lives (spoken by Macdonald Carey), 384:7

Cornfeld, Bernard (1927–1995), *Turkish-born mutual fund hustler;* rich?, sincerely want to be, 8:5

Cornuel, Anne Bigot (1605–1694), *wit, letter-writer;* no man a hero (note), 313:9

Cortissoz, Royal (1869–1948), *journalist, critic and lecturer on art, writer;* Abraham Lincoln, 386:7

Corey, Irwin ["Professor"] (b. 1914), *stand-up comedian, actor;* change (note), 105:9

Cory, John, *journalist, author;* war is a ghost, 708:3

Cosby, Bill [William Henry Cosby, Jr.] **(b. 1937),** *actor, comedian;* marriage, 408:9; men and women, 734:8

Costner, Kevin [Michael] (b. 1955), *actor, director;* if you say what you mean in [Hollywood], 127:7

Cota, Norman D. ["Dutch"] (1893–1971), *U.S. army gen.; asst. commander during WWII Normandy invasion;* let's go inland and be killed, 747:4; Rangers lead the way (note), 747:4

Cotton, John (1584–1652), *English born cleric, writer;* if the people be governors, 188:8

Cover, Robert M; Fiss, Own, M. & Resnick, Judith, *law professors;* procedure & justice, 375:6

Cowher, ["Bill"] William (b. 1957), *pro football player and coach;* confidence, 723:4

Cowley, [David] Malcolm (1898–1990), *editor, poet, critic;* criticism & writing books, 62:5

Crane, Hart (1899–1937), *poet;* Colorado, 155:4; [Paris:] dinners, soirées, poets, etc., 137:9; tortured with history, 638:1; vaulting the sea, 606:8

Crane, Stephen (1871–1900), *novelist, short-story writer, poet;* the universe, 686:4; war, 704:3

Creelman, James [Ashmore] (c. 1901–1941) and Rose, Ruth (1896–1978), *screenwriters;* beauty killed the beast, 80:8

Crèvecoeur, Michel Guillaume Jean de [pen name, J. Hector St. John] **(1735–1813),** *French-born writer; French consul in N.Y.C.;* forests, 717:6; melted into a new race, 20:10; what then is the American?, 20:9

Crichton, Michael D. (b. 1942), *novelist, screenwriter, director;* computer music, 609:2

Crick, Francis H. C. See under Watson, James D.

Crisp, Col. (fl. late 19th cent.), *politician, orator;* an eyewitness, 237:3

Eakins, Thomas (1844–1916), *painter, teacher, photographer, sculptor;* in a big picture, 73:5
Earhart, Amelia [Putnam] (1898–1937), *aviator;* courage, 171:8
Early, Jubal [Anderson] (1816–1894), *Confederate general, lawyer;* Dred Scott, 153:3; praying to go to heaven (note), 153:3
Eastman, George (1854–1932), *inventor, industrialist;* why wait?, 656:2; you press the button, 6:3
Eddy, Mary [Morse] Baker [Glover Patterson] (1821–1910), *founder of Christian Science movement, writer;* Father-Mother-God, 289:7; prayer, 537:1
Edelman, Marion Wright (b. 1939), *lawyer;* Bush Administration's words v. deeds (note), 215:7
Edison, Thomas Alva (1847–1931), *inventor, industrialist;* beautiful over there, 368:2; genius, 286:1; hello!, 606:1; a mother, 493:7; tobacco, 672:4; way, a better, 417:10; work, hard, 738:6
Education Act, No Child Left Behind, 215:7
Edward VIII. See Windsor, Duke of.
Edwards, Jonathan (1703–1758), *theologian, philosopher, missionary; pres., Princeton U.;* the heart is like a viper, 309:2; hell, 310:4; last hour of my life, 698:3; the spider, 456:5
Ehrenreich, Barbara (b. 1941), *sociologist, writer;* exercise, 512:4; working poor, 534:2
Ehrlichman, John [Daniel] (1925–1999), *asst. to pres. for domestic affairs, novelist;* hang out, a limited (note), 712:3; Peoria (note), 138:6; twist slowly, slowly in the wind, 755:1
Eichmann, Adolf [Otto] (1906–1962), *German Nazi, SS lt. col. in charge of deporting Central European Jews to death camps in Eastern Europe;* I regret nothing (note), 239:9
Einstein, Albert (1879–1955), *German-born theoretical physicist;* common sense, 157:3; deeply religious nonbeliever, 580:8; efforts, one's own, 738:8; the future, 282:11;goals, confusion of, 437:9; God & logical simplicity, 290:11; God does not play dice, 602:1; God is not malicious, 290:10; I feel uncertain, 598:3; I know what's wrong, 473:5; imagination, 431:6; mathematics, 601:4; the mysterious, 444:7; nationalism, 528:1; pacifist, 493:1; past, present & future, 671:1; peace, 506:1; physical concepts, 601:10; [Princeton:] a village, 213:10 religious experience, the cosmic, 579:9; religion and science, 579:12; science, 598:4,5, 597:5,6; simple as possible, as, 621:6; theorist, 596:9; truth, 680:9; whether I am on the right track, 598:3; world, incomprehensible thing about the, 741:10
Eisenhower, Dwight D[avid] ("Ike") (1890–1969), *U.S. army gen.; commander allied forces in Europe; army chief of staff; pres., Columbia U.; NATO commander; 34th pres.;* [Atoms for Peace] for the benefit of all mankind, 268:5; bridge to Asia, 13:4; dominos, a row of, 692:4; the eyes of the world are upon you, 747:3; farming, 252:8; hearts & minds, we are competing for, 269:2; inventiveness of mankind concentrated to his life, 268:6; it is a pity, 341:5; Knowland, William, 341:5 & note; I shall go to Korea, 360:2; military-industrial establishment, 428:7; problems, no easy, 545:6; war munitions, 428:4; Washington [D.C.], 147:3; win as quick as you can, 424:4; world peace, 506:6
Eisenstaedt, Alfred (1898–1995), *German-born photojournalist, writer;* the eye, 702:4
Eisner, Michael (b. 1942), *business executive;* promise v. perform, 85:6
Elders, M[innie] Jocycelyn [Lee] (b. 1933), *physician, U.S. surgeon gen. (1st African-American in post);* dancing with a bear, 180:6
Eliot, Charles William (1834–1926), *pres., Harvard U.;* public opinion, 558:5; wisdom, to grow in, 213:1
Eliot, T[homas] S[tearns] (1888–1965), *U.S.-born English poet, critic, editor, playwright;* actual, what is, 601:9; April, 465:5; beginning, in my, 256:7; beginning is often the end, 81:2; birth, copulation, & death, 383:4; a cold coming we had of it, 111:2; do a girl in, 175:6; exploration, we shall not cease from, 675:4; fear, 258:2; God, the darkness of, 444:8; good & evil, 235:11; half of the harm, 552:2; hell is oneself, 310:8; history, 316:7; here I am an old man, 486:9; hollow men, 264:1; home, 319:6; I have measured out my life in coffee spoons, 382:10; love within a family, 251:2; a medium of entertainment, 413:2; music, 65:8; objective correlative, 60:1; old, I grow, 486:8; talking of Michelangelo, 170:4; the passage which we did not take, 576:3; people who want to feel important, 552:2; passions, violent physical, 496:11 poetry, genuine, 67:10; poets, 67:6; reality, 574:4; red river, 696:8; the sea, 462:5; Shadow, falls the, 574:3; success, 693:8; temptation, 662:5; time, 670:7,10; to care & not to care, 582:8; world ends, this is the way, 741:4; when the short day is brightest, 466:9
Elizabeth II [Queen] (b. 1926), *queen of Great Britain and Northern Ireland;* grief, 633:4
Ellington, Duke [given names, Edward Kennedy] **(1899–1974),** *jazz pianist, composer, conductor;* swing, that, 65:4
Ellison, Ralph [Waldo] (1914–1994), *novelist, essayist, teacher;* invisible man, 569:1 & note; I may speak for you (note), 569:1; Southern, be, 638:6; white, part (note), 638:6
Ellman, Richard (1918–1987), *biographer, literary critic;* delight in possession, 668:10
Ellsworth, Henry L[eavitt] (1791–1858), *1st comm. of U.S. patent office;* advancement of arts, 605:1
Elvas, Knight [or Gentleman] of (fl. 1540), *Spanish explorer, historian;* trees & woods [in Arkansas], 56:5
Emerson, Mary Moody (1774–1863), *proto-transcendentalist intellectual;* do what you are afraid to do, 1:4
Emerson, Ralph Waldo (1803–1882), *one-time Unitarian minister, poet, essayist, transcendentalist philosopher;* America is a country of young men, 24:1; America means opportunity, 23:8; Americanism, shallow, 24:2; ancestors, 284:5; art is a jealous mistress, 58:3; a beautiful woman, 80:3;

better book, sermon, mousetrap, 240:4; boil at different degrees, 52:5; book that is not a year old, 87:11; books, 87:5, 88:1; born to rule, 295:2; Boston, 115:9; cake & debt, 397:2; calamity, every, 676:2; calculators, 575:4; California days, 96:7; calmness, 98:3; chalices & priests, 578:8; a child, 107:9; children, 107:10, 108:5; Christian, where is the, 578:4; church, I like the silent, 578:3; cities degrade us, 111:7; [Venice:] a city for beavers, 145:6; civilization, our, 148:3; civilization & a good woman, 729:2; common sense and plain dealing, 320:5; conformity & consistency & mediocrity, 414:5; concentration, 650:7; conservatism & reform, 524:3,4; consistency, a foolish, 164:2; cool, keep, 98:4; crime, commit a, 173:2; the day will come when no badge or uniform, 282:5; demonology, 196:3; destiny, our, 234:6; discontent, 682:10; distrust, 677:8; do your thing, 1:7; dream, we wake from one, 574:1; Dreams & Beasts (note), 205:2; dreams & natural character, 205:2; duty whispers, when, 750:8; an Englishman who has lost his fortune, 447:3; embattled farmers, 51:4; enthusiasm, 221:2 & note; envy, 227:6; Europe, the tapeworm of, 448:1; Europe to be Americanized, 674:1; fact, 245:6, 7; fate, 255:7, 8; fear, 257:6; flattery, 259:2; flowers, 460:7; a friend, 279:2,3; friends, 279:5; genius, work of, 285:10; geniuses & biographies, 285:9; a gentleman & a lady, 404:1; a giver, 106:6; God, 288:4, 5, 6, 8; 289:1; God builds his temple in the heart, 578:5; God who made New Hampshire, 478:2; government, less, 295:1; great, to be, 298:7; a great man, 298:8; great men, 298:9; grief, appetite for, 654:11; gunpowder smells good, 703:1; hand that feed us, 106:6; haste, 305:1; health, 308:2; 330:9; heart, 309:3,4; heart great as the world, 386:4; hero, every, 311:3; heroism, 311:2; history, our so-called, 315:6; hitch your wagon to a star, 17:8; honor, the louder he talked of his, 321:3; hospitality, 322:7; an institution, 336:6 & note; I live now, 540:1; institutions (note), 336:6; identity, personal, 415:4; it will be all the same 100 years hence, 98:4; king, strike at, 595:5 & note; knowledge, 357:8; labor, 736:2,3; lands and goods go to the strong, 557:6; language, 361:4,6; laughs, beware how he, 369:4; law rules through out existence, 686:2; laws, obey, 371:8; life & danger, 179:4; life & thinking, 380:8; life is a series of surprises, 380:6; life—a self-evolving circle, 504:4; living, never, 380:4; London, 125:6; love, 388:6,9,11; lover, all mankind love a, 388:6; luck, 395:9; Maine, 400:4; the majority or the minority, 401:7; man is a god in ruins, 416:2; manners, 404:2,3,4,7; marriage, 406:1; Massachusetts, 409:9; means, discreditable, 243:8; men & mothers, 493:6; men who lead, 314:2; miracles, 433:7; money, 439:3; moon, the rising, 467:9; mousetrap, better, 240:4; murder will speak out, 173:1; music, 64:2; nature, 454:4,5; nature & calculators, 575:4; nature & every secret, 596:2; [New York:] a sucked orange, 131:2; now, I live, 540:1; old, time to be, 486:3; pain, the house of, 655:1; [Paris:] a loud modern place, 137:5; a party corrupted by personality, 524:5; the party of the past and the party of future: the establishment and the movement, 525:3; passion, 496:7; past, adamantine record of, 539:10; patriotism, 500:2; peace & yourself, 612:7; place is nothing (note), 673:8; poet, world waiting for its, 67:2; poetry, 67:3; poverty, 532:7; power, 535:2,3,4,5; prayer, 536:4,5; present, the, 539:10, 540:1,2; the president has paid dear for his White House, 542:1; pride, 551:11; proverbs, 561:1; quotation, I hate, 560:10; quote, we all, 561:5; quoter, the first, 561:4; railroad iron is a magician's rod, 604:11; reading, 87:6; revolution & a thought, 586:6; a sailor, 619:7; the saint & poet & privacy, 552:7; Salt Lake City, 142:5; sanity, 397:7; see only what they are prepared to see, 701:2; shot heard round the world, 51:4; size, no virtue goes with, 81:8; the sky, 467:10; smoke, man of no conversation should, 672:3; solitude, 631:5; sorrow, 632:11; speech, cordial, 170:1; speech, short and positive, 69:2; spoons, the faster we counted, 321:3; suicide, 655:12; talent, those who have no, 414:6; task, every man's, 736:8; taxes, willing to pay, 660:3; the test of a religion or philosophy, 510:1; thin ice & speed, 640:3; things, 668:1,2,3; a thing well done, 2:2; think, to, 430:3; thirty, after, 419:7; time, 669:5, 670:1; time & facts, 669:5; times hard/money scarce, 78:5; thyself, trust, 612:6; tobacco, 672:1; today, 540:2; torment, delicious, 393:1; toys, strewn (note), 107:9; travel & language, 673:7; traveling, 673:8 & note; trust men, 677:7; truth v. repose, 678:8; universe, the, 685:6; virtue, 698:7,8,9; virtue in us & vice, 238:5; visitors, 299:4; war, 703:8; the warm day, 472:3; way, a best, 417:8; we are the builders of our fortunes, 2:6; we do what we must, 243:7; we will walk, 614:7 & note; weed? what is a, 461:4; we have a country again (note), 703:1; well-dressed, being, 254:4; wit, 326:3; a woman, 728:2; woman, a beautiful, 80:3; wonder & science, 596:4; word, 361:3,5; word, expunged, 102:4; work done well, 240:5; world, the same, 740:6; world, proud, 740:8; the world & its poet, 67:2; world is but thickened light, 601:7; writing & God, 74:3; yesterday, mortgaged to, 497:3; yourself & principles, 612:7; the youth replies I can, 750:8

Emmet, Daniel Decatur (1815–1904), *minstrel, songwriter;* Dixie's Land, 636:4

Epstein, Julius J. (1909–2000) and Philip G. (1909–1952) & Koch, Howard (1902–1995), *screenwriters, also producers;* friendship, a beautiful, 279:11; here's looking at you 394:6; I am shocked, 328:2; play it, Sam, 65:9; the usual suspects, 176:2; regret it, you'll, 496:1

Epton, William (1932–2002), *local N.Y.C. radical labor leader;* burn baby burn, 587:10

Erdrich, Louise (b. 1954), *poet, novelist, short-story writer;* talk, 659:5

Erlanger, Abraham Lincoln (1860–1930), *theater owner, producer;* never trust a man (note), 677:11

Ertz, Susan (1894–1985), *English-born (of American parents) novelist;* immorality, 332:7

Ervin, Sam[uel James], Jr. (1896–1985), *U.S. sen. from N.C.; chm., Watergate comm.;* I'm just a coun-

try lawyer (note), 556:5; North Carolina, 482:5; progress, 556:5
Euripides (485 or 480–406 B.C.), *Greek tragic playwright;* those gods wish to destroy (note), 654:9
Evans, Bergen [Baldwin] (1904–1978), *teacher, radio show host, writer;* freedom to think & doubt, 276:7
Evans, Walker (1903–1975), *photographer, magazine editor;* die knowing something, 358:4 & note
Evarts, William M[axwell] (1818–1901), *lawyer, U.S. atty. gen., secy. of state, U.S. sen. from N.Y.;* professional humorist, 376:8
Everett, David (1770–1813), *lawyer, journalist;* oaks & acorns, 629:4
Everett, Edward (1794–1865), *Unitarian minister, orator; U.S. rep. from and gov. of Mass.; pres., Harvard U.; secy. of state; U.S. sen. from Mass.;* glad if I could flatter myself (note), 287:1

Fadiman, Clifton [Paul] ["Kip"] (1904–1999), *editor, writer, critic;* crime of the whites (note), 569:6; wine, 262:8
Farber, Barry (b. 1930) *radio talk-show host, lecturer, writer;* Russian tragedy/comedy, 452:2
Farley, James A[loysius] (1888–1976), *politician, businessman;* Maine & Vermont (note), 400:3
Farragut, David Glasgow (1801–1870), *naval officer;* damn the torpedoes, 153:2
Faulkner, William [Cuthbert] (1879–1962), *novelist, screenwriter;* fear, 258:6; grief, 633:3; I don't, 638:2; if a writer has to rob his mother, 75:7; man will prevail, 325:6; Mississippi, 435:3; the past is never dead, 498:5; a soul, a spirit, 634:3; the Swiss, 454:6; writer's only, responsibility, 75:6; you don't love because, 392:5; you know how to whistle, don't you?, 623:10
Federalist Party, stand with Washington, 513:4
Federal Writers' Project, [Arizona:] land of extremes, 56:1; a Kentuckian, 356:4; [Nebraska:] Middle West merges with the West, 474:7; New Jersey, 479:3; [New Mexico:] keynote of the land, 479:8; [North Dakota:] rural character, 483:3; [North Dakota:] unbounded plains and hills, 483:2, South Carolinians, 635:1,2; Tennessean's lives, 663:3; Utah, 687:6,7; Washington [D.C.], 147:1; Wyoming, 750:2
Fein, Bernard ["Bernie"] & Ruddy, Albert S. (b. 1930), *scriptwriters, producers; Fein also an actor, director;* I know nothing, 242:7
Ferber, Edna (1887–1968) *novelist, playwright, short-story writer;* country, closed & dying, 265:3; governor of Texas, 665:5; I love you, 395:3; in Texas, 665:4; mother knows best, 494:3; Oklahoma, 484:6; Tulsa, 145:3
Ferguson, Niall C. (b. 1964), *English-born Harvard teacher, historian, writer;* U.S. as empire, 32:3
Fermi, Enrico (1901–1954), *Italian-born physicist;* whatever nature has in store, 455:12
Feynman, Richard P[hillips] (1918–1988), *physicist, teacher, memoirist;* doubt is feared, 626:10; nature, 456:2; solve any problem, 598:9; technology, 609:3
Field, Eugene (1850–1895), *poet, journalist;* Wynken, Blynken & Nod, 205:3
Field, Sally (b. 1946), *actor, producer director;* you like me, 654:6
Fields, Lew[is Maurice] (1867–1941), *comedian; partner of Joe Weber in vaudeville;* wife, she's my, 406:7
Fields, W. C. [born William Claude Dukenfeld] **(1879–1946),** *comedian;* ain't a fit night out, 473:3; hates children and dogs (note), 434:9; honest man, 320:8; Philadelphia, 139:5, 232:5; sucker (note), 263:7
Filene, Edward [Albert] (1860–1937), *innovative retailer;* [tax] money, 661:4
Fink, Gordon, *lawyer, dpty. atty. gen. of Nevada;* boxing & chaos, 649:4
Fink, Mike (1770?-1823), *rowdy keelboat-man, hunter, trapper, folk hero;* I'm a Salt River roarer!, 84:1
Finley, John (1797–1866), *versifier; mayor, Richmond, Ind.;* Hoosier nation, 334:3
Firmin, Giles (c. 1614–1670), *English-born preacher, writer;* New England, 475:7
Fischer, Bobby [given names, Robert James] **(b. 1943),** *U.S. chess champion, world champion;* break a man's ego, 284:4
Fisher, John Arbuthnot [1st Baron Fisher] (1841–1920), *British admiral;* never explain (note), 242:4
Fisher, Arthur (b. 1931), *magazine editor, writer;* Montana's graveyards, 443:5
Fishwick, Marshall [William] (b. 1923), *teacher, editor, writer;* hero, every, 313:5
Fitzgerald, F[rancis] Scott (1896–1940), *novelist, short-story writer;* a conference & ideas, 156:1; adventure, premature, 5:1; American lives, no second acts in, 29:1; breast of the new world, 481:2; dark night of the soul, 193:8; forgotten is forgiven, 272:3; a hero, 312:2; a heroic thing, 312:1; intelligence, a first rate, 431:7; New York, 133:7; [New York:] seen from Queensboro Bridge, 133:1; optimism, 491:5; rich, the very, 440:7; words, you can stroke people with, 364:1; tell you a story, 650:1; the world, 741:8; young Minnesotan did a heroic thing, 312:1; young person (note), 5:1
Fitzgerald, Zelda [Sayre] (1900–1948), *writer;* advertising, 7:4; I still believe [in advertisements] (note), 6:6; love first, and live incidentally, 382:11; the moment which determined the future, 420:4
Fitzsimmons, Robert (1862–1918), *English boxer;* the bigger they come (note), 641:1
Flaubert, Gustav (1812–1880) *French novelist, short-story writer; le détail* [note], 630:9
Fleischer, [Lawrence] Ari (b. 1960), *White House press secy.;* Americans need to watch what they say, 79:4
Fleming, Thomas (b. 1929), *novelist, historian;* the past, 498:11
Flint, Timothy (1780–1840), *missionary, early biographer of Daniel Boone;* heaven & Kentuck, 355:2
Folsom, James [Elisha] ["Big Jim"] (1908–1987),

gov. of Ala.; as long as the Negroes are held down, 568:9

Fonda, Jane [Seymour] (b. 1937), *actor, political activist, exercise guru;* [right of] man & woman, 11:3

Forbes, Malcolm [Stevenson] (1919–1990), *magazine publisher;* difference between men and boys, 668:9

Ford, Eileen (b. 1922), *founder and head of Ford modeling agency;* slender people, 309:1

Ford, Gerald R[udolph] [born Leslie Lynch King, Jr.] **(b. 1931),** *U.S. rep. from Mich., 40th vice pres., 38th pres.;* the Granite State, 478:6; impeachable offence, 375:5; nightmare, long national, 713:4

Ford, Harrison (b. 1942), *actor;* lucky breaks, 397:1

Ford, Henry (1863–1947), *pioneer automobile manufacturer, political isolationist, anti-Semite, philanthropist;* as long as it's black, 606:5; history is bunk, 316:6; money, 441:3; out of the trenches by Christmas, 742:4; peace, I wanted to see (note), 742:4; present, we want to live in the, 540:6; spirit of progress, 555:5; work, 738:3

Ford, Henry, II (1917–1987), *automobile manufacturer;* never complain [or] explain, 242:4

Forgy, Howell M[aurice] (1908–1972), *WWII navy chaplain;* pass the ammunition, 745:5

Forrest, Nathan Bedford (1821–1877), *Confederate cavalry gen.; 1st Grand Wizard, Ku Klux Klan Empire;* first with the most, 423:3

Foster, Stephen [Collins] (1826–1864), *songwriter, composer;* I came from Alabama, 11:7; Kentucky Home, the old, 356:1,2; Swanee River, 636:2

Foster, Vincent W., Jr. ["Vince"] (1945–1993), *White House deputy counsel, whose suicide helped fuel attacks on the Clinton administration;* deathbed & office (note), 95:3

Fountain, Paul (fl. 1905), *English travel writer;* [Mount] Rainier, 709:3

F.P.A. See under Adams, Franklin Pierce

Frank, Thomas (b. 1965), *nonfiction writer;* Kansas (note), 353:8

Frankel, Max (b. 1930), *German-born reporter, editor, columnist;* journalists, 551:5

Frankenthaler, Helen (b. 1928) , *abstract expressionist painter;* light & scale, 73:6

Frankfurter, Felix (1882–1965), *Austrian-born lawyer, teacher, pres. adviser; assoc. just., U.S. Supreme* Court; all deliberate speed (note), 169:5; freedom to speak foolishly, 277:6; history of procedure, 374:9; if facts are changing, 373:4; morals & manners, 404:12; wisdom, 242:2

Franklin, Benjamin (1706–1790), *polymath: printer, inventor, scientist, philosopher, writer, editor, autobiographer, diplomat; public official before, during, and after the Revolution: member Pa. assembly, delegate to the 2nd Cont. Congress, 1st U.S. postmaster gen., delegate to Constitutional Convention;* Adam was never called Master Adam, 216:1; anger, 52:4; baby, what good is a newborn, 686:9; best, strive to be, 240:3; better guilty persons should escape, 371:2; body of B. Franklin, 228:1; brother & friend, 278:7; cat in gloves, 595:4; cause, our, 49:5; [chess:] wretched game, 283:6; children, two, 622:2; Christ's birthday, 109:6; conscience, 163:6; Constitution, our new, 165:3; creditors, 90:5; death and taxes, 165:3; desire many things, 192:4; digressions & growing older, 484:5; the doctor takes the fee, 201:3; early to bed, early to rise, 307:9; eat, 260:3, 4; employed, when men are, 735:7; enemy, no little, 220:6; enemy, you are now my, 337:1; experience, 244:6; faith, 248:5; fat kitchen & lean will, 719:2; fault, to confess a, 257:1; felicity, 301:8; a fool, 263:1,2; forewarned, forearmed, 357:6; foxes grow gray, 172:2; freedom of thought & speech, 273:1; gains & pains, 194:1; God governs, 288:2; God helps them that help themselves, 614:6; hope, 321:7 & note; infallibility (note), 164:9; laws, 370:5,6; laziness, 378:10; liberty, 273:3, 274:1 & note; life & time, 380:2; a little neglect, 629:3; live well, 380:3; loved, if you would be, 388:2; man: a tool-making animal, 323:4; mankind are very odd, 327:7; marriage, 405:3; marriage without love & love without marriage, 622:1; meals, lessen thy, 307:8; men & melons, 323:3; mine is better, 556:7; money, 438:5–7; necessity, 475:1; a new child among the immortals, 181:4; [New Jersey:] a beer barrel, 479:1; an office, 735:6; the older I grow, 485:4; one hundred guilty persons, 371:2; the orator, 658:2; pain & pleasure, 512:5; passion, 496:4,5; peace, never was a bad, 504:8; a penny saved, 438:9; Philadelphia has taken Howe (note), 139:4; pride, 551:8,9; private property, 557:1; purse, light, 532:5; quoted by other learned authors, 560:9; a reason for everything one has a mind to do, 575:2; a republic if you can keep it, 21:3; secure is not safe, 611:4; secret, three may keep, 610:6; sense, 156:9; single man, 405:4; Skugg, here lies, 228:3; sluggard, up, 205:1; stones, don't throw, 177:5; strokes, little, 194:2; success, 651:8; suicides, nine of ten men are, 307:10; sun, a rising, 164:9; talkers & doers, 658:1 & note; they are so grateful, 616:1; time, 669:1,2; time & life, 380:2; trade, 90:6; the turkey, 456:6; the used key, 735:5; the value of water, 688:2; the value of things, 688:4; war, never was a good, 702:8; Washington, General, 709:6; we are soon to follow (note), 181:4; we must all hang together, 187:1; word to the wise, 658:3; work/pray, 725:2

Fraser, Kennedy, *fashion writer, essayist;* fashion, 255:1

Frederick [II] the Great (1712–1786), *King of Prussia;* the whites of their eyes (note), 48:3; would you live forever (note), 744:5

Freed, Ralph [born Ralph Grossman] **(1907–1973),** *Canadian-born songwriter;* New York, 134:4

Freeman, Cliff (b. 1941), *advertising copy writer, agency head;* where's the beef, 9:4

Free Soil Party, free soil, free speech (note), 515:5

Frémont, John C[harles] ["The Pathfinder"] (1813–1890), *explorer, U.S. sen. from Cal., 1st candidate of Rep. party for pres., Union Army maj. gen., gov. of Ariz. Terr.;* a melancholy country, 328:4

Frick, Henry Clay (1849–1919), *industrialist;* s.o.b. didn't stay bought, 440:6 (note)

Guthrie, Woody (given forenames, Woodrow Wilson) **(1912–1967),** *folksinger, songwriter;* Pampa, a boom town, 137:3; some will rob you, 175:8; this land is your land, 30:5

Gwenn, Edmund (1875–1915), *actor;* comedy, 71:2

Hackett, Albert See under Goodrich, Frances

Hagen, Uta [Thyra] (1919–2004), *German-born actor, teacher;* ideals, 330:2; teach, who should, 215:4

Hagen, Walter [Charles] (1892–1969), *professional golfer;* smell the flowers, 384:2

Hague, Frank (1876–1956), *mayor, Jersey City, N.J. and longtime state Dem. Boss;* I am the law, 374:3

Hakluyt, Richard (c. 1552–1616), *English geographer;* likelihood of gold or silver, 96:1

Halberstam, David (b. 1934), *journalist, author;* best & brightest, 218:4; power, 535:13

Hale, Edward Everett (1822–1909), *minister, short-story writer;* senators & the people, 160:8; the something that I can do, 2:7; lend a hand, 106:8

Hale, Nathan (1755–1776), *spy, caught and hanged by the British;* one life to lose for my country, 49:2

Haley, Alex [Palmer] (1921–1992), *writer;* being a Southerner, 638:5

Hall, Basil (1788–1844), *British naval capt., travel writer;* streets starting up of their own accord, 141:5

Hall, Francis (d. 1833), *British army lt., travel writer;* Charleston, 118:4 cliffs [Palisades], 479:2

Halleck, Fitz-Greene (1790–1867), *poet, banker;* [Connecticut:] a rough land, 162:8

Halleck, Henry Wager (1815–1872), *general-in-chief of Union forces;* call no council of war, 423:7

Halsey, William F[rederick], Jr. ("Bull") (1882–1959), *U.S. navy adm.;* ships have been salvaged, 747:7

Hamburger, Philip [Paul] (1914–2004), *nonfiction writer;* Des Moines, 122:7

Hamer, Fannie Lou (1917–1977), *civil rights activist;* down so long, 533:11; sick and tired (note), 396:4

Hamill, Pete (b. 1935), *reporter, columnist, editor, author;* sport of the poor, 649:7

Hamilton, Alexander (1712–1756), *physician, traveler, diarist;* Boston, 115:6; Connecticut, 162:5; the country people in this island, 588:6; here lies John Purcell, 169:7

Hamilton, Alexander (1755–1804), *British West Indian-born soldier, lawyer, politician: Continental Army lt. col., delegate from N.Y. to Constitutional Convention, principal author of the* Federalist *papers, 1st secy. of treasury, maj. gen., killed in duel with Aaron Burr;* debt, national, 206:1; debt & taxes (& note), 206:3; democracy, 188:9; the few and the many, 589:7; judges, independence of, 166:1; laws are a dead letter, 371:3; overscrupulous, to be, 243:6; people, the voice of (note), 508:4; popular opinion, 558:2; power over a man's subsistence, 534:6; president, who will be the next, 541:2; unpolished and rude, 588:6; we suppose mankind more honest than they are,320:3; why government?, 293:6

Hamilton, Andrew (1676?-1741), *Scottish-born lawyer, politician, colonial official;* evidence, 237:1

Hamilton, Charles Vernon. See under Carmichael, Stokeley

Hamilton, Edith (1867–1963), *classicist, writer, translator;* the Greeks, 449:2

Hammerstein, Oscar [I] (1846–1919) , *German-born opera impresario, producer, composer, lyricist;* man in the theater business, 70:6; opera, 64:8

Hammerstein, Oscar [II] (1895–1960), *lyricist, librettist, producer;* beautiful morning, 470:8; Kansas City, 124:7; nothing like a dame, 731:5; Oklahoma, 485:1,2; Paris, the last time I saw, 138:1

Hammett, [Samuel] Dashiell (1894–1961), *detective turned hard-boiled detective-story writer and screenwriter, political radical;* do something about it, 585:5; style, 69:8; talking, 659:2

Hand, Learned [Billings] (1872–1961), *federal district judge;* jury, trial by, 350:4; justice, thou shalt not ration, 352:2; liberty, 276:4;, 5, 6 no surer way, 374:7; press, the hand that rules the, 412:2; publicity, the art of, 8:1; reputation, 581:9; short of sickness and death, 373:9; taxes, 661:2; words, 364:3

Hanna, Mark [given forenames, Marcus Alonzo] **(1837–1904),** *Rep. party power-broker;* [T. Roosevelt] damned cowboy is president, 594:3; two things important in politics, 526:2; we'll stand pat, 517:7

Hannay, [Sir] David (fl. 2000), *British diplomat;* Washington [D.C.], 147:8

Hansberry, Lorraine (1930–1965), *playwright;* Africa, 445:5

Harburg, Edgar Y. ("Yip"[sel]) [born Isidore Hochberg] **(1898–1981),** *lyricist, librettist;* brother, can you spare a dime, 192:1; listen to [a nation's] songs, 66:2; love, 391:4; over the rainbow, 302:8

Harding, George T., *physician, farmer;* thankful you're a boy, 303:7

Harding, Warren Gamaliel (1865–1923), *editor and publisher, U.S. sen. from Ohio, 29th pres.;* Founding Fathers (note), 303:9; normalcy, 38:3;, 519:1; when people are out of work (note), 303:9

Harfield, Henry (1913–2003), *Wall St. lawyer;* bankers, 94:8

Harkness, Richard (1907–1977), *radio and TV newscaster;* a committee, 156:4

Harlan, John Marshall (1833–1911), *Union Army col.; Ky. atty. gen.; assoc. just., U.S. Supreme Court;* segregation as badge of slavery (note), 42: civil freedom & equality, 565:8; Constitution is color blind, 167:2; right rather than consistent, 164:5; separate but equal (note), 167:2

Harlan, John Marshall (1899–1971), *assoc. just., U.S. Supreme Court;* vulgarity v. lyric, 278:5;

Harper, Robert Goodloe (1765–1825), *U.S. rep. from S.C., gen. in War of 1812, U.S. sen. from Md.;* not one cent for tribute, 34:1

Harper's Monthly, New York, 131:1

Harrell, Tom (b. 1946), *jazz musician, composer;* form & rhythm, 66:6

tions & concrete cases, 373:1; history, a page of, 316:9; if my fellow citizens want to go to hell, 275:9; imbeciles, three generations of (note), 553:5; the law, 372:2,3,5,8; 373:1; a less evil that some criminals escape, 237:4; life, 381:10; life is painting a picture, 382:7; riders in a race, 487:3; a river, 224:3; seventy again, O to be, 487:4; taxes & power to tax, 660:9,11; to act is to affirm, 3:6; truth accepted in competition, 277:5; war, 703:2; what we do and think, 300:8

Holzer, Jenny (b. 1950), *conceptual artist;* a relaxed man, 98:6; protect me from what I want, 192:8

Hone, Philip (1780–1851), *businessman, mayor of N.Y.C., diarist;* [J. Q. Adams] breathing his last, 229:4

Hoover, Herbert [Clark] (1874–1964), *dir. of Amer. relief efforts during and after WWI in Europe, secy. of commerce, 31st pres.;* apples, selling (note), 339:8; capitalism & greedy capitalists, 101:2; credit, 207:3; excessive fortunes (note), 101:2; government & honor, 296:8; grass will grow in the streets, 208:4; hair shirts, mental, 544:8; a noble experiment, 15:4; poverty, triumph over, 38:5; prosperity around the corner, 191:3; rugged individualism, 27:10; things that go around in the dark, 179:6; the trouble with this philosophy (note), 676:3; war & youth, 706:6

Horne, Lena (b. 1917), *singer, actor;* don't grow old, 488:3

House Un-American Activities Committee, member of the Communist party? (note), 158:2

Houston, Sam[uel] (1793–1863), *U.S. rep. from Tenn., gov. of Tenn, cmdr. of Texan army, 1st and 3rd pres. of Rep. of Tex., 1st U.S. sen. from Tex, gov. of Tex;* Texas, 367:3; Texas, Texas, 664:5

Houston Press, the 49th star twinkles, 13:3

Howard, James H. (d. 1995), *China-born American WWII fighter pilot;* I seen my duty, 747:2

Howard, Joseph Kinsey (1906–1951), *journalist, editor, historian;* Montana, 443:6

Howard, Sidney [Coe] (1891–1939), *playwright; screenwriter;* frankly I don't give a damn (note), 340:3

Howe, Edgar Watson ["the Sage of Potato Hill"] (1853–1937), *newspaper editor and publisher, novelist;* advice, 10:3; common sense, 157:2; credit v. money, 93:8; enemy, your, 220:10; guest, an ideal, 299:7; hope, 322:4; music, good, 64:9; neighbor, my, 475:6; scare, a good, 10:3; what people say behind your back, 581:8; a woman, 730:2

Howe, Irving (1920–1994), *social and literary critic, editor;* critics, 63:1

Howe, Julia Ward (1819–1910), *poet, novelist, social reformer;* disarm, disarm, 492:5; glory of the coming of the Lord (Battle Hymn of the Republic), 289:2; in the beauty of the lilies, 289:3; the sword, 694:7

Howe, Louis McHenry (1871–1936), *journalist, adviser to Franklin D. Roosevelt;* politics, 528:8

Howells, William Dean (1837–1920), *editor, poet, novelist, playwright, critic, U.S. consul in Venice;* books, mortality of, 88:9; human beings, 324:3; the novel, 74:7; prose, simple, 69:5; slavery, the wrecks of, 637:3; stay longer in an hour, 299:6

Howland, Bob [Robert M.] **(fl. 1860s),** *frontier marshal, prison warden;* all quiet in Aurora, 114:7

Hruska, Roman L[ee] (1904–1999), *U.S. rep. and sen. from Nebr.;* even if he is mediocre, 415:1

Hubbard, Elbert [Green] (1859–1915), *printer, editor, writer, publisher, lecturer;* Albany, 113:6; conformists & heretics, 197:7; a dangerous business, 382:4; [editor sees] that the chaff is printed, 550:2; explain, never, 242:1; failure, 247:5,6; Garcia, a message to, 3:1; God, 290:4; lawyer, 377:7; life is one damn thing after another, 382:6; love, 389:6; loyalty, 395:5; Missouri but, be from (note), 435:7; monkeys & monks, 622:9; nature, 455:4; one who thought he was above me, 551:12; a pessimist & optimist, 491:4; public opinion, 558:9; scars & God, 655:7; sins, 622:10; success, 653:2,3,4; temptations, 662:4; tyrants, 682:5; unsaid, leave a few things, 620:3; wisdom, 724:9; wise man, 724:8

Hubbard, Frank McKinney ("Kin") (1868–1930), *cartoonist and columnist;* classic music, 65:1; legislature, 161:3; poor, to be, 532:11

Hubbard, L[afayette] Ron[ald] (1913–1986), *science-fiction writer; founder, Church of Scientology;* start your own religion, 580:4

Hubbell, Webster L[ee] (b. 1949), *lawyer; mayor, Little Rock, Ark.; ch. just., Ark. State supreme court; U.S. assoc. atty. gen.;* the office of the independent counsel, 583:6

Huffington, Ariana [Stassinopoulos] (b. 1950), *Greek-born writer, columnist, pundit;* immortality, 332:9

Hughes, Charles Evans (1862–1948), *gov. of N.Y.; assoc. just., U.S. Supreme Court; Rep. candidate for pres.; secy. of state; chief just., U.S. Supreme Court;* the Constitution, 167:6; the judiciary (note), 167:6

Hughes, Charles Evans, Jr. (1889–1950), *lawyer, U.S. sol. gen.;* president, cannot be disturbed, 544:3

Hughes, Emmet John (1920–1982), *journalist, pres. speechwriter and adviser;* he [the President] must summon his people to be with him, 546:5

Hughes, [James Mercer] Langston (1902–1967), *poet, playwright, editor, essayist; a leader of Harlem Renaissance;* Alabama, daybreak in, 12:2; America, 28:8; a crumb from the tables of joy, 396:3; democracy, 190:3, 568:7; a dream deferred, 204:3; Harlem, 133:8 & note; I am a Negro (note), 571:2; railroad bridges's, 607:1; a raisin in the sun, 587:5; soul, my, 634:2; the War, 706:9; yesterday, 498:2;

Hugo, [Vicomte] Victor [Marie] (1802–1885), *French novelist, poet, playwright;* an idea (note), 330:3

Hume, David (1711–1776), *Scottish philosopher, historian;* testimony (note), 238:1

Humphrey, Hubert H[oratio] (1911–1978), *mayor, Minneapolis; U.S. sen. from Minn.; 38th vice pres.; Dem. pres. candidate;* Democratic party & states' rights

Hunter, [James Augustus] **Jim ("Catfish")**

(1946–1999), *baseball pitcher, baseball's 1st free agent;* thank you, God, 648:6
Hunter, Robert (b. 1941), *songwriter, singer, poet, lyricist for Grateful Dead;* strange trip, 675:6
Hupfield, Herman (1894–1951), *songwriter;* time goes by, 610:2
Hurston, Zora Neale (1901–1960), *folklorist, novelist, leading figure of Harlem Renaissance, then a domestic worker;* Ah ain't dead, 487:8; he was a glance from God, 394:5; I am a dark rock surged upon, 568:2; magic, 483:8; poverty, 533:5; ships at a distance, 619:11; world, the, 741:5
Huston, John (1906–1987) & Maddow, Ben (1909–1992), *screenwriters; Huston also acted and directed* crime, 176:6
Hutchins, Robert Maynard (1899–1977), *pres. and chancellor, U. of Chicago; foundation exec.; founder and chm., Center for Study of Democratic Institutions;* exercise, the urge to, 512:1
Huxley, Aldous [Leonard] (1894–1963), *English novelist, short-story writer, essayist;* City of Dreadful Joy, 126:5; nineteen suburbs, 126:4
Huxtable, Ada Louise (b. 1921), *architectural critic;* New York, 136:2
Hyde, Henry (b. 1924), *U.S. rep. from Ill.;* new is always better? (note), 264:5; stupid is forever, 264:5

Iacocca, Lee [given forename, Lidi Anthony] **(b. 1924),** *automobile company exec;* decisions, 183:10; safety & business, 612:1
Ice-T [born Tracy Morrow] **(b. 1959),** *gangsta rapper, actor, writer;* passion, 497:2
Ickes, Harold L[éclair] (1874–1952), *lawyer, secy. of interior, head of public works admin.;* government by crony, 296:4; cleaned his bureau drawers (note), 340:8; thrown his diaper into the ring (note), 340:8
Ignatieff, Michael (b. 1947), *Canadian-born novelist, historian, biographer,* words to keep us human, 326:2
Illinois Legislature, official language of Illinois, 244:1
Ingalls, John James (1833–1900), *U.S. sen. from Kans.;* [Delaware] has 3 counties, 187:3; government is force (note), 526:1; the purification of politics, 526:1
Inge, William (1913–1973), *playwright, critic, teacher;* success, 653:11
Ingersoll, Robert G[reen] ["the Great Agnostic"] (1833–1899), *lawyer, politician, orator, writer, noted opponent of religion;* devils v. gods, 196:2; god, an honest, 289:9; hope, 322:3; injustice, 336:2; laughing, 369:7; life, 381:9; a plumed knight, 311:5; progress & infidels (note), 555:11; property owns them, 557:8; religion, 579:2; rights, 593:2; a truth, 679:8; useful work, 737:6
Irving, John (b. 1942), *novelist;* loving as a parent, 495:4
Irving, Washington (1783–1859), *essayist, short-story writer, travel writer, biographer, historian; amb. to Spain;* compliment[s] about looking young, 486:2; dollar, the almighty, 439:1; Gotham, 130:7; history, 315:5; Italy, 449:7; a sharp tongue, 658:4; Switzerland, 454:4; woman's heart, 727:8; woman's life, 727:7
Isherwood, Christopher (1904–1986), *English-born playwright, novelist, short-story writer;* California, 97:8; landscape, prehistoric (note), 611:6; security, 611:6
Ivins, Molly [Tyler] (b. 1944), *reporter, columnist, nonfiction writer;* the Texas legislature, 666:2

Jackson, Andrew ["Old Hickory"] (1767–1845), *U.S. rep. and sen. from Tenn.; member, Tenn. Supreme Court; maj. gen. in War of 1812, defeating British at New Orleans; military gov. of Fla.; U.S. sen. from Tenn.; losing candidate for pres.; 7th pres.;* debt, national, 206:8; John Marshall, 656:5; law, arm & shield of the, 371:6; monopoly & privileges, 91:4; one man with courage, 171:6; the president, 541:9; a situation of dignified slavery, 541:8; spell a word, ways to, 212:3; taxation, 660:2; they shall not sleep on our soil, 709:1; Union, our Federal, 683:9 & note; we will all meet in heaven, 366:5
Jackson, Helen [Maria Fiske] Hunt (1830–1885), *poet, novelist, essayist, travel writer; spec. comm. to study needs of Mission Indians in Cal.;* A Century of Dishonor, 565:3
Jackson, Jesse [Louis] (b. 1941), *minister, civil rights activist;* America, the genius of, 31:3; America is like a quilt (note), 31:2; common sense, 157:4; I am somebody, 573:1; rainbow, our nation is a, 31:2; we can't just say no (note), 700:10
Jackson, Joseph Henry (1894–1955), *newspaper editor, writer;* that work had better be banned?, 103:3
Jackson, Phil[ip] [Douglas] (b. 1945), *pro basketball player and coach;* inner knowledge, 614:5
Jackson, Rachel [Donelson Robards] (1767–1828), *wife of Andrew Jackson;* New Orleans, 129:7
Jackson, Reggie [given forenames, Reginald Martinez] **(b. 1946),** *baseball outfielder;* straw that stirs the drink, 552:4
Jackson, Robert H[oughwout] (1892–1954), *U.S. sol. gen.; atty. gen.; assoc. just., U.S. Supreme Court; chief prosecutor at Nuremberg war-crimes trials;* bribed by loyalties & ambitions, 17:12; dissenting opinions, 348:6; fixed star in our constitutional constellation, 168:8; infallible, 348:5; irreligion & freedom, 77:3; odious of all oppressions, 352:1; security, 611:8; thought [to fanatics], 222:9; Supreme Court, whatever its defects, 657:4; [Supreme] Court & suicide pact, 169:2
Jackson, Thomas Jonathan ["Stonewall"] (1824–1863), *Confederate army corps commander;* death, my (note), 367:4; kill the brave ones, 152:1; let us cross over the river, 367:4; surprise the enemy, 423:5
Jackson, Wes (b. 1936), *environmental historian; pres., Land Institute;* farmers & companies, 253:4
Jacobs, Harriet [Ann] (1813–1897), *escaped slave, memoirist;* marriage, 406:2

politics, 528:9; share our wealth, 520:2; Washington [D.C.], 146:9; your tears have lasted for generations, 387:4

Long, James, *editor, writer;* time, 671:6

Long, Russell B. (1918–2003), *U.S. sen. from La.;* campaign contribution and a bribe, 531:2; congressman's first obligation, 161:6;

Long, Stephen H[arriman] (1784–1864), *surveyor, explorer;* [Nebraska:] unfit for cultivation, 473:7

Longfellow, Henry Wadsworth (1807–1882), *poet, translator;* age is opportunity, 486:5; ambitions, 17:6; anvil or hammer, 323:5; Arabs, fold their tents like the, 63:10; arrow in the air (note), 279:1; art, 57:8, 58:1–2; books, 88:3; Boston, a solid man of, 116:1; a boy's will, 750:7; the cares that infest the day, 676:1; children's hour, 108:6; Christmas day, 110:5; [Cincinnati:] Queen of the West, 120:9 & note; dawn, 490:8; day is done & darkness falls, 469:7; the dead remain, 229:5; death, exodus of, 181:9; death on reef of Norman's woe, 619:1; delay, do not, 188:5; fate of a nation was riding, 52:3; footprints in the sands of time, 298:6; the forest primeval, 717:7; friend, in the heart of a, 279:1; gift to each, 197:3; Gitche Gumee, 563:6; giver's loving thought, 106:9; God, the mills of, 289:8; girl who had a little curl, 108:7; hard words & a child, 108:4; the heart, 106:9, 219:2, 309:6; 8 holidays, the holiest of, 318:1; John Brown (note), 35:5; king, once more a, 627:1; learn to labor, 1:6; a lady with a lamp, 728:7; life, real and earnest, 380:5; life some rain must fall, 675:9; love, 388:8; manners, stately, 404:8; May, 463:5; men that women marry, 406:6; midnight ride of Paul Revere, 52:1; morning, 490:7; music, night shall be filled with, 63:10; music & poetry, 63:9; night, sleepless watches of, 470:4; nothing holier in this life, 388:5; one if by land, 52:2; ourselves, 613:4; past & present & future, 669:4; patient endurance, 220:4; patter of little feet, 108:6; Paul Revere, 52:1; Plymouth Rock, 409:8; [Portland, Me.:] the beautiful town, 140:6; Queen of the West [Cincinnati], 120:9; rain, how beautiful is the, 472:5; sail on, O ship of state, 23:1; ships & the sea, 619:6; ships that pass in the night, 381:6; silences, three, 620:1; singers, God sent his, 64:1; smithy, the village, 736:4; smoothly the ploughshare runs, 387:2; something attempted & done, 2:1; sorrow & silence, 220:4; sorrow & suffering, 220:7; sorrows, secret, 632:10; the soul, 380:5; so unto the man is woman, 732:8; spring, 463:1, 463:7; stars, the lovely, 467:11; suffer and be strong, 655:2; things are not what they seem, 380:5; time, 670:2; to suffer and be strong, 655:2; truth, 679:4; Union, O, 684:1; union, 685:4; up and doing, 1:6; useless is, nothing, 687:3; [Venice:] white swan of cities, 145:7; vessel, a goodly, 619:3; why don't you speak for yourself?, 393:3; the winds, 472:4; womanhood, heroic, 728:7; worth the wooing (note), 393:3; youth, the thoughts of, 750:7

Longworth, Alice Roosevelt (1884–1979), *grande dame of Washington, D.C., society;* Harding, 304:6; you can't make a souffle rise twice (note), 340:8; if you can't say anything good, 170:6; man on the wedding cake, 340:8; never trust a man who, 726:5; two-thirds mush, 593:10; weaned on a pickle (note), 659:1; youth, eternal, 751:9

Louis, Joe [born Joseph Louis Barrow] **["the Brown Bomber"] (1914–1981),** *world heavyweight boxing champion;* can run/can't hide, 645:7

Lovecraft, H[oward] P[hillips] (1890–1937), *short-story writer, novelist;* Providence [R. I.], 141:3

Lovell, James A., Jr. (b. 1928), *astronaut, commander of Apollo 13;* we've had a problem, 45:4

Lowell, Amy (1874–1925), *poet, critic, biographer;* war & patterns, 704:7; youth & maturity, 10:10

Lowell, James Russell (1819–1891), *poet, editor, critic, essayist; amb. to Spain and Great Britain;* airly [early], git up, 470:2; the birch, 471:3; charity, 106:10; dunce, well-meaning, 263:3; each day the world is born anew, 540:4; endurance & patience, 220:3 experience, 244:7, 561:6; facts, 245:9; fallen and the weak, speak for the, 532:6; forgive, yet, 272:1; Italy, 449:8; June, a day in, 463:2 & note; nobleness, 699:6 & note; no good arguing, 582:7; the pine, 471:4; princerple & interest, 92:3; review, can surely, 61:7; right, in the, 591:5; rights, 593:1; say nothin', 658:5; slaves who fear to speak, 584:2; summer, lavish (note), 463:2; taxed for a corner, 660:4; toil, horny hands of, 736:5; truth forever on the scaffold, 682:1; a weed & a flower, 460:8; who says it best, 561:2

Lowell, Robert [Trail Spence, Jr.] (1917–1977), *poet;* cured, 604:3; light at the end of the tunnel (note), 693:2; my mind's not right, 398:9; spiders marching through air, 171:4; this pioneer democracy [Venezuela], 454:1

Lowenstein, Allard K[enneth] (1929–81), *lawyer, civil rights activist;* [what's] worth trying, 156:8

Lucas, George (b. 1945), *movie director, producer, screenwriter;* may the force be with you, 483:10

Luce, Clare Boothe (1903–1987), *editor, playwright, U.S. rep from Conn., amb. to Italy;* home, a man's, 319:8; no good deed, 700:6; a woman's best protection, 731:6

Luciano, Charles ("Lucky") [born Salvatore Lucania] **(1897–1962),** *Italian-born gangster, freed from prison for helping U.S. gain cooperation of Sicilian mafia and deported to Italy;* to be a crumb, 552:1

Luhan, Mabel Dodge See Dodge, Mabel

Lumet, Sidney (b. 1924), *movie director, producer, screenwriter;* style, 70:4

Luttwak, Edward N[icolae] (b. 1942), *Romanian-born economist, historian;* war fought by so few, 300:4

Lynd, Robert S. (1892–1970) & Helen Merrell (1896–1982), *sociologists;* Middletown, 129:2,3,4

Lytle, Andrew [Nelson] (1902–1995), *novelist, editor, teacher;* family, 251:4

MacArthur, Charles (1895–1956), *journalist, playwright, screenwriter;* emeralds, 394:2

MacArthur, Douglas (1880–1964), *U.S. army gen.; West Point supt.; chief of staff; commander in*

Pacific in WWII; oversaw Allied occupation of Japan; commander, U.N. forces in Korea; I have returned, 748:2; I shall return, 746:4; old soldiers, 41:3; opportunity, 490:2; so much with so little, 746:5; victory, no substitute for, 359:5; war, 707:2,4,8

Macaulay, Lord [Thomas Babington, 1st Baron Macaulay] (1800–1859), *English historian, essayist, statesman;* your Constitution, 166:9

MacDonald, Dwight (1906–1982), *political, social, and movie critic; essayist;* the poor, 533:9

MacDonald, John D. (1916–1986), *mystery writer;* life is the process, 384:3; yesterday & tomorrow & todays, 671:3

MacDonald, [John] Ross [born Kenneth Millar] **(1915–1983),** *mystery writer;* California, 97:10; whose troubles are worse than your own (note), 727:2

MacKay, Charles (1814–1889), *Scottish journalist, editor, poet, travel writer;* [Columbia, S.C.] an air of neatness, 121:5; [Memphis:] a dreary town, 128:2

MacLaine, Shirley [born Shirley MacLean Beaty] **(b. 1934),** *actor, writer;* the way we see the world, 702:1

MacLean, Norman (1902–1990), *writer;* fly fishing, 648:3

MacLeish, Archibald (1892–1982), *poet, playwright, teacher, Librarian of Congress;* a poem, 67:9

Macmillan, [Maurice] Harold [1st Earl of Stockton] ["Supermac"] (1894–1986), *English book publisher, politician; M.P., P.M;* determination of an American mother, 495:5

Macon, Nathaniel (1758–1837), *U.S. rep. and sen. from N.C.;* where he can hear his neighbor's dog bark, 631:4

Maddow, Ben. See under Huston, John

Madison, James (1751–1836), *delegate from Va. to Continental Congress and Constitutional Convention, author, U.S. rep. from Va., secy. of state, 4th pres.;* a benefactor of human kind, 347:4; Constitution & Bill of Rights (note), 164:9; Constitution is a miracle, 21:7; different leaders, 523:5; different opinions, 197:1; government, 293:7; laws & rights, 233:9; liberty & power, 165:4; noxious branches [of the press], 547:6; property, 159:1; Russia, 451:6; safety and happiness, 336:5; states, union of these, 21:7

Mad Magazine, me worry?, 54:2

Madonna [born Madonna Louise Veronica Ciccone] **(b. 1958),** *singer, actor, writer, celebrity;* brushstroke, 615:2; goal . . . to rule world, 18:3

Mahan, Alfred T[hayer] (1840–1914), *U.S. navy capt., historian, biographer; pres., Naval War College;* Americans must begin to look outward, 25:1; beating, a good, 720:2; defeat & success, 720:3

Maibaum, Richard (1909–1991), *screenwriter, producer;* Kansas, 354:8

Maier, Charles S[teven] (b. 1939), *historian, teacher, writer;* [America] an empire (note), 32:3

Mailer, Norman (b. 1923), *novelist, essayist, journalist, short-story writer, social critic;* Chicago, 112:9, 120:5; Chicago [& other cities], 112:9; a hero, 313:8; hip or square, 335:6; horror of 20th cent., 82:2; Miami Beach, 128:5; most men, 417:5; a newspaper & a story, 550:9; sentimentality, 220:1; television, 413:6; the working class, 739:6

Makinson, Larry, *dpty. dir., Center for Responsive Politics;* money follows power, 443:1

Malcolm X [birth name, Malcolm Little; after 1964, El-Hajj Malik El-Shabazz] **(1925–1965),** *black nationalist leader; converted to separatist Nation of Islam, founded Organization of Afro-American Unity, assassinated;* be peaceful, 695:2; born in America with a black skin, 570:1; by any means necessary, 570:6; change according to circumstances, 164:6; education, 214:10; New York & Harlem, 136:1; patriotism, 504:1; power, 535:8; Plymouth Rock, 570:5; revolution, 587:8;,9 send him to the cemetery, 695:2

Mamet, David [Alam] (b. 1947), *playwright, director;* the actor, 73:3; the court doesn't exist, 352:7

Manchester, William (1922–2004), *historian, biographer, editor, novelist;* life, 385:1

Mankiewicz, Herman J[acob] (1897–1953), *journalist, drama critic, screenwriter;* disease you don't look forward to being cured of, 488:5; its going to be a bumpy night, 676:7; millions to be made out here, 126:6; Rosebud, 368:4, 576:5; there but for the grace of God goes God, 340:7

Mankiewicz, Joseph L[eo] (1909–1993), *screenwriter, producer, director;* ants to a picnic, 62:4; fasten your seat belts, 676:7

Mann, Horace (1796–1859), *secy., Mass. Board of ed.; U.S. rep. from Mass.; 1st pres., Antioch College;* education, 212:5; some victory for humanity, 324:2

Mannes, Marya [born Maria von Heimburg Mannes] **(1904–1990),** *journalist, critic, poet, novelist;* people on horses, 459:9

Mantle, Mickey [Charles] (1931–1995), *baseball centerfielder;* if I knew I was going to live this long (note), 308:9

Marcy, William Learned (1786–1857), *U.S. sen. from N.Y., gov. of N.Y., secy. of war, secy. of state;* victors & spoils. 524:2

Marion, Frances (1887–1973) and de Grésac, Fred [born Fréderique Rosine De Grésac] **(c. 1867–1943),** *screenwriters; Marion also actor, director, producer, novelist;* San Juan Capistrano, 97:9

Markham, Edwin [given forenames, Charles Edward Anson] **(1852–1940),** *poet, farmer, teacher, lecturer;* defeat may serve, 720:4; the sea, 462:2; when he [Lincoln] fell, 386:5

Marquis, Don[ald Robert Perry] (1878–1937), *journalist, poet, short-story writer;* civilization, 149:3 dance mehitabel dance, 487:1 each generation wastes more of the future, 284:7; the earth, 224:5,6; honesty is a good thing, 320:7; the hypocrite, 328:1; an idea, 329:5; integrity, 700:4; jocosity, coarse, 326:8; kittens, all these, 494:2; middle age, 420:7; old age, disorderly, 487:2; an optimist, 491:3; a pessimist (note), 491:4; poetry, publishing a volume of, 67:5; procrastination, 188:6; rich through hard work, 440:8; time when a man is, 420:7; think, really make them, 431:5; toujours gai, archy, 302:7 unlucky, so, 396:4

Marryat, Frederick (1792–1848), *English navy capt., novelist, editor, travel writer;* Americans & drink, 13:8; language in America, 361:2; "leg" & "limb" (note), 361:2

Marsh, George Perkins (1801–1882), *lawyer, philologist, conservationist; U.S. rep. from Vt., amb. to Turkey and Italy;* man & nature. 324:1

Marshall, John (1755–1835), *Continental Army officer; lawyer; U.S. rep. from Va.; secy. of state; 3rd chief just., U.S. Supreme Court;* constitution, 166:2,3; corn & colonels (note), 355:5; judicial distinction, the acme of, 348:2; tax, the power to, 660:1

Marshall, Thomas Riley (1854–1925), *gov. of Ind., vice pres.;* a good five-cent cigar, 672:7; Indiana, 334:5; the Vice President, 691:7

Marshall, Thurgood (1908–1993), *NAACP legal counsel; judge, U.S. Court of Appeals; U.S. sol. gen., assoc. just. (and 1st African-America member), U.S. Supreme Court;* divided society, 572:5; First Amendment, 169:6; I'm getting old, 489:7; judges & the people, 349:1; principles of democracy, 374:5; a white snake or a black snake, 573:4

Marshalov, Boris (1902–1967), *Russian-born American actor;* Congress, 161:8

Marshman, D.M., Jr. See under Brackett, Charles

Martin, Abe See under Hubbard, Frank McKinney

Martin, Billy [given forenames, Alfred Manuel] **(1928–1989),** *baseball manager;* a good loser (note), 644:1

Martin, Dean [born Dino Crocetti] **(1917–1995),** *singer, actor, TV show host;* not drunk if, 16:5

Martin, Jeff, *TV scriptwriter producer;* if you lose, 723:2

Martin, Graham A[nderson] (1912–1990), *amb. to Thailand, Italy, South Vietnam;* we simply cut and run, 694:5

Martineau, Harriet (1802–1876), *English author, travel writer;* Albany, 113:4; Michigan, 419:2; Vermont, 689:8

Marx, Chico [given first name, Leonard] **(1886–1961),** *comedian;* whispering in her mouth, 242:3

Marx, Groucho [Julius Henry] **(1895–1977),** *comedian;* bigamy, 407:5; club that would accept me, 218:1; marriage interferes, 408:6; money, 441:13; posterity, 285:3; a poultry matter, 440:9

Marx, Harpo [Adolph] **(1888–1964),** *comedian;* like the other side of the moon, 128:10

Marx, Karl (1818–1883), *German socialist philosopher;* classes struggle (note), 99:2

Mason, Bobbie Ann (b. 1940), *short-story writer, novelist, critic;* Southern behavior, 638:7

Mason, Donald F[rancis] (b. 1913), *WWII navy pilot;* sighted sub, 746:1

Mason, George (1725–1792), *author of the Va. Bill of Rights, the Va. Constitution, and the federal Bill of Rights; delegate from Va. to Constitutional Convention;* press, freedom of the, 547:1

Masters, Edgar Lee (1869–1950), *lawyer, poet, novelist, biographer;* immortality, 332:4

Mather, Cotton (1663–1728), *Puritan cleric, theologian, writer;* the devil, 195:9; New Englanders, 476:8; quarrels & prayers, 55:1; stoop, 725:1

Mather, Increase (1639–1723), *Puritan cleric, historian; pres., Harvard College;* thunder, 472:2

Matlovich, Leonard P., Jr. ["Lenny"] (1943–1988), *U.S. air force sgt., gay activist;* the military, 429:5

Matson, Vera. See under Elvis Presley

Matthews, Chris[topher] (b. 1945), *speechwriter, congressional aide, journalist, columnist, TV talk-show host;* don't get mad (note), 52:8; only talk when, 620:7; unanswered shot, 178:2

Mauldin, Bill [given forenames, William Henry] **(1921–2003),** *G.I. cartoonist in WWII;* an infantryman, 427:8

Maxwell, Elsa (1883–1963) ["the hostess with the mostest"], *songwriter; columnist; lecturer; radio show host; Washington, D.C., party-thrower;* cocktail parties, 323:1; mediocrity, 414:8

Maxwell, William [Keepers] (1908–2000), *short-story writer, novelist, editor;* your reader is bright, 76:5

Mays, Benjamin E[lijah] (1894–1984), *minister; pres., Morehouse Coll.;* dream, calamity not to, 204:6

McAdoo, William G[ibbs] (1863–1941), *lawyer, businessman, secy. of treasury, U.S. sen. from Calif.;* [Harding's] speeches, 304:2

McAllister, [Samuel] Ward (1827–1895), *lawyer, arbiter of society in N.Y.C. and Newport, R.I.;* a dinner invitation, 299:5; 400 people in New York society, 216:8

McAuliffe, Anthony C. (1898–1975), *acting cmdr., 101st Airborne Div., during Battle of the Bulge; c-in-c U.S. Army in Europe;* Nuts!, 748:4

McBride, Mary Margaret (1899–1976), *radio show host, columnist;* young girls in New York, 135:6

McCain, John S[idney], Jr. (1911–1981), *WWII submarine commander; c-in-c Pacific;* fleets, 429:3

McCain, John S[idney], III (b. 1936), *navy pilot, POW; U.S. rep. and sen. from Ariz.;* Washington & Hollywood (note), 147:9

McCall, Bruce, *Canadian-born American humorous writer, painter;* Canada, 446:8

McCarthy, Joseph [Raymond] (1908–1957), *Communist-hunting U.S. sen. from Wisc., censured by the senate;* list of 205 members of the Communist Party, 41:1

McCarthy, Mary [Therese] (1912–1989), *novelist and nonfiction author, critic;* "and" and "the," 342:3; decision, 183:6; happy ending, 81:3; madmen, 604:4; sex & love, 617:7; Venice, 146:1; violence, 695:1

McClellan, George B[rinton] (1826–1885), *gen. in chief of Union Army, pres. candidate;* all quiet, 150:3

McCloy, Helen (1904–1993), *mystery writer, literary agent;* habit, 301:4

from N.Y. to Continental Congress and from Pa. to Constitutional Convention; amb. to France; U.S. sen. from N.Y.; chm., Erie Canal Commission; he means well, 337:2; [Lafayette] unable to hold the helm (note), 337:2; sixty-four years ago, 366:2

Morris, Wright (1910–1998), *novelist, photographer;* withered towns, 423:1

Morrison, Robert F. (fl. 1900), *journalist;* he ain't no brother of mine (note), 640:2

Morrison, Toni [born Chloe Anthony Wofford] **(b. 1931),** *novelist, editor, teacher, playwright;* book you really want to read, 76:4

Morrow, Dwight W. (1873–1931), *banker, amb. to Mexico, U.S. sen. from N.J.;* any party which takes credit for the rain, 528:4

Morse, Samuel F[inley] B[reese] (1791–1872), *inventor of the telegraph;* what hath God wrought!, 605:2

Morton, Oliver Perry (1823–1877), *gov. of and U.S. sen. from Ind.;* waving the bloody shirt, 525:5

Mosby, John S[ingleton] (1833–1916), *Confederate partisan cavalry col., lawyer, U.S. consul at Hong Kong, memoirist;* the solid South, 637:4; war, 704:1

Moses, Robert (1888–1981), *N.Y. and N.Y.C. public agency official;* ends & means, 244:5

Moses, [Robert] Bob Parris (fl. 1961), *math teacher, civil rights organizer;* Mississippi, 435:4

Motion Pictures Producers and Distributors of America, Inc., marriage, 407:4; scenes of passion, 103:1; sex perversion, 103:2

Mosk, Stanley (1912–2001), *Calif. atty. gen., judge;* little old ladies, 530:3 & note

Moulter, Lawrence C. ["Larry"] (fl. 1993), *businessman;* politics, sports & revenge, 117:1

Mourning, Alonzo (b. 1970), *pro basketball center;* adversity, 677:6

Moyers, Bill [D.], [Jr.] (b. 1934), *Baptist minister; presidential asst. and press secy.; newspaper publisher; TV journalist, editor, producer; writer;* the delusional, 79:5; God & coincidence, 292:3

Moynihan, Daniel Patrick (1927–2003), *amb. to India and the U.N., U.S. sen. from N.Y., teacher, author* benign neglect, 571:8; Irish, being, 449:6

Muir, John (1838–1914), *Scottish-born naturalist, conservationist, author;* hitched to everything else in the universe, 686:5; in God's wildness, 718:5; the universe & a forest wilderness, 717:7

Mulligan, James H[ilary] ["Jim"] (1844–1916), *poet, journalist, judge, politician;* Kentucky, 356:3

Mullins, Edgar Young (1860–1928), *minister, teacher, seminary pres.;* unless man is immortal, 332:5

Mumford, Lewis (1895–1990), *social and architectural critic, teacher, writer;* the clock, 607:2; the concrete cloverleaf, 30:8; generation, every, 284:10; the notion for progress, 555:7; Society for the Prevention of Change, 336:9

Murdoch, [Keith] Rupert (b. 1931), *Australian-born newspaper publisher;* The Third World, 551:3

Murphy, Edward A., Jr. (b. 1917), *aeronautical engineer;* if anything can go wrong, 676:6

Murphy, Gerald [Clery] (1888–1964) and Sara [Sherman] (1883–1975), *expatriates of "the lost generation";* living well is the best revenge, 585:4

Murphy, Thomas S. ["Tom"] (b. 1925), *media exec.;* mediocre people, 415:3

Murrow, Edward R[oscoe] (1908–1965), *radio and television journalist; dir., U.S. Information Agency;* Berlin, 747:1; London, this is, 745:1; must not confuse dissent with disloyalty, 42:4; prejudices, 539:7; television, 412:7; we are not descended from fearful men (note), 42:2

Muste, A[braham] J[ohannes] (1885–1967), *Dutch-born minister, pacifist, political organizer, essayist;* peace is the way, 506:9

Myers, Norman (b. 1934), *English conservationist, Cornell U. prof.;* war against nature, 456:3

Myhrvold, Nathan P. (b. 1959), *physicist, computer scientist; chief tech. off., Microsoft;* decisions, 184:2

Nabokov, Vladimir (1899–1977), *Russian-born novelist, short-story writer, poet, translator, critic, teacher, memoirist, lepidopterist;* art, work of, 58:11; book, essence of, 70:3; college people, aging, 214:4; genius, 286:3; life, 383:12 & note; life & death, 183:1; material of the world, 741:9; nature, 455:9; my sin. my soul., 394:8; reading, 89:4; one of my favorite states [Wyoming], 750:4; solitude, 632:5; style & structure, 70:3

Nader, Ralph (b. 1934), *consumer advocate, minor party pres. candidate;* indentured to corporations, 94:7; Reagan & Harding (note), 303:9; unsafe at any speed, 611:11

Namath, Joseph [William] "Broadway Joe"] (b. 1943), *pro football quarterback;* half time, 421:2

National Aeronautics and Space Administration, first set foot on the moon [the moon plaque], 608:6

Nash, [Frederick] Ogden (1902–1971), *humorous poet, author of children's books;* billboard lovely as a tree, 7:5; the Bronx, 133:3; canaries, 459:2; candy is dandy, 15:7; Central Park, 135:10; dogs, 459:3; a door & a dog, 201:1; duty, 584:3; Englishman, to be an, 447:8; a heap o' payin' (note), 319:4; kin and kith, 250:6; a kitten, 459:1; liquor is quicker, 15:7; Lubbock [Tex.], 127:10; a Martini, 16:1; middle age, 420:10; New Year, 480:5; orgies, 623:7; progress, 555:8; Scandinavia, 452:8; sin & a grin, 623:8; troubles of the rich, 591:1; the turtle, 458:6; women would rather be right, 731:9

National Geographic, comets, 468:10

National Security Council, preemptive actions, 271:4

Naylor, Gloria (b. 1950), *novelist;* man, a handsome, 417:4

Nathan, George Jean (1882–1958), *drama critic, editor, author;* love, 389:11 & note; no such thing as a dirty theme (note), 60:5; songs, 65:2

NBC News, war, 707:10

Neff, Pat[rick Morris] (1871–1952), *gov. of Tex.; pres., Baylor U.;* Texas & Rhode Island, 589:2

Nelson, W[illiam] R[ockhill] (1841–1915), *founding publisher,* Kansas City Star; newspaper, 548:5

Nemerov, Howard (1920–1991), *poet, novelist,*

short-story writer; black hole, a small, 603:1; football, 647:1; history, 317:2 & note

Netanyahu, Benjamin [Binyamin] **["Bibi"] (b. 1949),** *Israeli politician; P.M.;* mistakes (note), 436:2

Neuberger, Richard L[ewis] (1912–1960), *U.S. sen. from Ore.;* Pocatello, 140:5

The New England Primer, Job blesses God, 576:10; life is but a span, 380:1; Xerxes the Great did die, 181:1

Newman, Aubrey S. (1904–1994), *U.S. army infantry colonel;* follow me!, 748:1

Newman, Paul (b. 1925), *actor, food manufacturer, philanthropist;* enemies & character, 221:6

Newman, Wallace (fl. c. 1930), *Whittier College football coach;* a good loser (note), 644:5

New York Daily News. See Daily News

The New York Times, depression, 604:9; Japanese surrender, 749:5; [New York:] livability, civility & affordability a room of one's own, 204:9; television, 412:1; to be mad, 399:7

New York Tribune, [slavery] a peculiar institution, 627:4

Nicklin, Philip Houlbrooke (1786–1842), *lawyer, bookseller, writer;* Philadelphia, 139:2

Niebuhr, Reinhold (1892–1971), *theologian, minister, teacher;* God give us grace to accept with serenity [the Serenity Prayer], 538:5; ignorance of the past, 497:10; limits & despair, 438:1

Nietzsche, Friedrich Wilhelm (1844–1900), *German philosopher;* better knowing nothing (note), 357:9

Nikolais, Alwin (1910–1993), *avant-garde choreographer;* dance, 63:4

Niles, Hezekiah (1777–1839), *printer, journalist, editor, publisher;* society seems unhinged, 78:1

Nimitz, Chester [William] (1885–1966), *U.S. adm.; c-in-c, Pacific fleet;* uncommon valor, 748:5

Nin, Anaïs (1903–1977), *French-born memoirist, novelist, short-story writer;* women, all elegant, 730:12

Nixon, Richard M[ilhouse] ["Tricky Dick"] (1913–1994), *navy officer in WWII, U.S. rep. and sen. from Calif., 36th vice pres, Rep. pres. candidate, 37th pres., 1st pres. to resign;* Checkers, 42:4; defeated, when he's, 722:5; game, how you play the (note), 644:5; hate, 306:3; honesty, 320:9; I brought myself down, 713:6; I have never been a quitter, 713:3; I'm not a crook, 713:2 & note; individual's right to privacy, 554:2; I screwed up terribly, 713:5; Keynesians, all now, 210:1; leader, unattractive habits of, 172:8; leaders make own rules, 315:1; majority, the great silent, 402:6 & note; pitiful, helpless giant, 693:7; president, rather be a one-term (note), 693:7; the press, 551:1 & note; a respectable Republican cloth coat, 41:4; the Soviets, 452:6; stonewall it, 712:4; Turkey, 453:9; the Vice President, 692:2; we can't stand pat (note), 517:7; when the president does it, 546:7; you won't have Nixon to kick around any more, 43:4

Nizer, Louis (1902–1994), *lawyer, memoirist;* beautiful old lady, 488:4

Noonan, Peggy (b. 1950), *political speechwriter, columnist, author;* a thousand points of light (note), 31:4; a kinder & gentler nation (note), 522:6; humor is the shock absorber, 327:6

Norris, Kathleen [Thompson] (1880–1966), *columnist, short-story writer;* [what] a girl needs, 11:1 (note)

Norquist, Grover (b. 1956), *anti-tax lobbyist;* government, 297:7; they want to tax you, 532:3

North, Edmund H. See under Francis Ford Coppola

Norton, Charles Eliot (1827–1908), *art historian, teacher, writer;* voice of protest, 704:5

Norworth, Jack (1879–1959), *songwriter, vaudeville entertainer;* take me out to the ballgame, 642:3

Novak, Michael (b. 1933), *theologian; amb. to U.N. human rts. comm.;* [president] a king (note), 543:1

Nye, Bill [pseudonym of Edgar Wilson] **(1850–1896),** *humorist, journalist;* Wagner's music, 64:6

Oates, Joyce Carol (b. 1938), *novelist, short-story writer, poet, critic;* despairing soul, 193:9; famous, 654:9; house is made of glass, 554:1; language, 364:9; snapshots, 74:2; spectacle [boxing], 648:7

O'Brien, [William] Tim[othy] (b. 1946), *novelist, short-story writer;* stories, 650:4

Ochs, Adolph S[imon] (1858–1935), *newspaper publisher;* all the news that's fit to print, 548:6 & note

O'Connor, Sandra Day (b. 1930), *Ariz. state senator; 1st woman appointed to U.S. Supreme Court as assoc. just.;* state of war, 375:7; money & water, 443:3

Odell, Allan G. (1904–1994), *businessman;* Burma-Shave, 7:6

Odets, Clifford (1906–1963) and Ernest Lehman (1920–2005), *screenwriters; Odets also actor, playwright, director; Lehman also novelist, short-story writer, producer, director;* buried, get yourself, 248:1; sweet smell of success, 693:9

Ogilvy, David [MacKenzie] (1911–1999), *English-born advertising man;* consumer not a moron, 9:1

Oglethorpe, [Gen.] James Edward (1696–1785), *English soldier, politician; founder of colony of Georgia;* [Savannah:] sheltered from winds, 143:9

O'Hara, Frank (1926–1966), *poet, art critic and editor, playwright;* boundless love, 391:6

O'Hara, John [Henry] (1905–1970), *novelist, short-story writer;* spenders & drinkers & socially secure, 217:4

O'Hara, Theodore (1820–1867), *poet, lawyer, U.S. Army maj. and Confederate Army col.;* bivouac of the dead, 229:3; dark and bloody ground, 355:3

O'Keeffe, Georgia (1887–1986), *painter;* nobody sees a flower, 702:3

Olmsted, Frederick Law (1822–1903), *landscape architect, writer;* [Austin:] Washington en petit, 114:8; Texas, 664:4

O'Neill, Buck [given forenames, John Jordan] **(b. 1911),** *pro baseball first-baseman and manager in Negro Leagues;* anger v. hatred. 306:5

O'Neill, Eugene (1888–1953), *playwright;* the

damned, 193:7; the dead, 182:9; doctors, 202:2; dreams, always one left, 204:2; fairy tale, obsessed by a, 574:9; God, 290:7; life, 383:1; no farther [down] they can go, 247:7; the past, 498:3,4; the present—strange interlude, 540:7; the sea, 462:4; strange interlude, 383:2; whiskey, gimme a, 15:3

O'Neill, Paul H. (b. 1935), *business exec., secy of treasury;* companies come & go, 102:1

O'Neill, Thomas P[hilip] Jr. ["Tip"] (1912–1994), *U.S. rep. from Mass., House speaker;* all politics is local, 529:1

Ono, Yoko (b. 1933), *Japanese-born artist, musician;* love, 392:3

Oppenheimer, J[ulius] Robert (1905–1967), *physicist; dir., atomic bomb development at Los Alamos; chm., Atomic Energy Commission's general advisory committee; dir., Institute of Advanced Study at Princeton;* I am become Death, 597:8; the optimist & pessimist (note), 491:2; they physicists, 597:9

Osgood, Charles (b. 1933), *radio & TV journalist;* television, 414:2

Ostrander, Gilman M. (1923–1986), *historian, teacher, versifier;* Massachusetts, settlers of, 410:3

O'Sullivan, John L[ouis] (1813–1895), *lawyer, editor, writer; charge d'affaires, then amb. to Portugal;* freedom of conscience etc. (note), 276:2; government is evil, 294:6; manifest destiny, 22:6 & note; nation of human progress, 22:5

O'Sullivan, Maureen. See under Weissmuller, Johnny

Otis, James (1725–1783), *lawyer, pamphleteer, politician;* libertas (note), 274:1; man's house is his castle, 552:6; taxation without representation, 659:6 & note

Owen, David (b. 1955), *writer, golfer, enthusiastic tennis-player;* no man a hero, 313:9

Page, William Tyler (1868–1924), *clerk, House of Reps.;* government of the people, 26:6

Paige, [Leroy Robert] "Satchel" (c. 1906–1982), *baseball pitcher; legendary star of the Negro leagues, barred by segregation from major-league baseball until age 42;* avoid fried meats, 726:6; don't look back, 726:6; how old would you be?, 489:6; vices, go light on, 726:6

Paine, Albert Bigelow (1861–1937), *friend and biographer of Mark Twain, editor, novelist, writer of children's books;* Great White Way, 131:8; Western humor, 715:8

Paine, Ralph D. (1906–1991) , *journalist, adventure-story writer;* New Hampshire, 478:4

Paine, Thomas ["Tom"] (1737–1809), *English-born editor and political pamphleteer; returned to England, fled to France, moved back to U.S.;* America, the cause of, 20:3; arms must decide the contest, 48:5; God, I believe in one, 577:4; government, 293:2,3; honest man, 319:9; moderation (note), 45:2; my country & religion, 235:2 & note; mystery, 444:1; prejudiced, 539:1; priests and conjurors, 577:5; religion, any system of, 577:6; revolutions, a share in two, 586:3; science, 596:1; society & government, 293:2; sublime, 652:1; summer soldier & the sunshine patriot, 49:3; these are the times that try men's souls, 49:3; time, 669:3; truth, 678:3; tyranny, 681:7; war, 602:6,7; Washington, George, 710:1,3; what we obtain too cheap, 688:3; world, to begin over, 20:4

Paley, Barbara ["Babe"] (1915–1978), *socialite;* too skinny or too rich, 442:5

Panetta, Leon [Edward] (b. 1938), *lawyer; dir., U.S. civil rts. office; U.S. rep. from Calif.; dir., U.S. mgt. and budget office; White House chief of staff;* govern through leadership or crisis, 297:8

Papagiannis, Michael (b. 1932), *astronomer, teacher;* absence of evidence, 238:3

Parker, Dorothy (1893–1967), *poet, critic, short-story writer, playwright, wit;* authors and actors and artists, 58:9; drink, one more, 623:4; dust, excuse my, 233:2; eighteen languages, 339:6; for tomorrow we shall die, 512:9; gamut of emotions, 340:1; the girls attending [the Yale prom], 623:5; glasses, girls who wear, 616:5; highballs, 15:6; horticulture, 213:7; House Beautiful, 340:2; how do they know? (note), 339:7; knit, if you don't (note), 340:2; life &love, 390:3; lingerie & brevity, 254:7; a lover and a foe, 733:8; not a novel to be thrown aside lightly (note), 339:5; passion undying, 390:2; rose, one perfect, 394:3; a satin gown, 254:6; seventy-two suburbs (note), 126:4; Tonstant Weader fwowed up, 339:5 & note; tragedy, 677:2; worm, to tread upon a, 182:6; you might as well live, 656:1

Parker, John (1729–1775), *capt. of militia at Lexington, Mass.;* if they mean to have a war, 48:1

Parker, Theodore (1810–1860), *clergyman, abolitionist;* government of all the people (note), 287:1

Parker, Trey (b. 1969) and Shaiman, Marc (b. 1959), *songwriters; both also act, write, direct, produce* Canada, 446:9

Parkinson, C[yril] Northcote (1909–1993), *English historian, novelist, satirist;* work (note), 739:10

Parkman, Francis (1823–1893), *historian, horticulturist;* buffalo, 457:2; change [out West], 715:5

Parks, Rosa ["the mother of the civil rights movement"] (b. 1913), *civil-rights activist, congressional aide;* my only concern was to get home, 572:3; tired of giving in (note), 572:3

Parrish, [Frederick] Maxfield (1870–1966), *illustrator, muralist;* New Hampshire & Vermont, 690:6

Parton, Dolly [Rebecca] (b. 1946), *country music singer, songwriter, actor;* don't lose your temper, 53:5

Parton, James (1822–1891), *English-born biographer;* England (note), 709:6; Pittsburgh, 140:3

Patterson, Floyd (b. 1935), *boxer; two-time world heavyweight champion;* defeat, 722:6

Patton, George S[mith], Jr. ["Old Blood and Guts"] (1885–1945), *U.S. army gen.; leader of Allied landings in North Africa and Sicily; 3rd Army commander on drive from Normandy;* command, the art of, 428:1; commander who fails to obtain his objective, 427:11; commanders are prima donnas, 314:10 discipline, 427:10 dying for his country, 706:3; fatigue, 258:5; fog of war, 424:1; I

Pitkin, Walter B[roughton] (1878–1953), *writer, editor, teacher;* life begins at 40, 420:5

Pitt, William [1st Earl of Chatham] ["the Great Commoner," "the Elder Pitt"] (1708–1778), *British politician; leading cabinet member, P.M.;* America, you cannot conquer, 50:2

Plath, Sylvia (1932–1963), *poet, novelist, memoirist;* dying is an art, 656:3

Plunket, Robert (fl. 1991–2000), *novelist, columnist, critic, actor;* planning a crime, 177:2

Plunkitt, George Washington ["the sage of Tammany Hall"] (1842–1924), *N.Y.C. Dem. political boss; member, state assembly and sen.;* [graft] & opportunities, 175:1; reformers, 526:5

Poe, Edgar Allan (1809–1849), *short-story writer, poet, critic;* Annabel Lee, 393:2; brute, love of a, 457:1; childhood, 107:8; a dream within a dream, 573:8; fever called "living," 181:7; Greece, the glory that was, 328:2; hide anything, best place to, 172:3; I have not been as others were, 16:7; The Imp of the Perverse, 612:8; "nevermore," quoth the Raven, 229:2; once upon a midnight dreary, 483:6; the poetry of words, 67:1; profound, being too, 397:9; Samarcand, 142:7; thou wast that all to me, 392:9

Polk, James K[nox] (1795–1849), *U.S. rep. from Tenn., house speaker, gov. of Tenn., 11th pres.;* I am the hardest working man in the country (note), 542:2; no president can have leisure, 542:2

Pollan, Michael [Kevin] (b. 1955), *editor, writer, teacher;* a lawn, 227:4; nature abhors, 461:9

Polykoff, Shirley (1908–1998), *advertising copywriter;* does she or doesn't she?, 8:4

Pope, Alexander (1688–1744), *English poet;* the people's voice (note), 508:4

Porter, Cole [Albert] (1891–1964), *composer and lyricist;* don't fence me in, 716:2; love for sale, 394:4

Porter, Horace (1837–1921), *Union army gen., aide-de-camp and exec. secy. to U.S. Grant, businessman, amb. to France;* a mugwump, 516:5

Porter, Katherine Anne (1890–1980), *short-story writer and novelist;* love, 392:1

Porter, William Sydney. See Henry, O.

Post, Emily [Price] (1873–1960), *authority on etiquette, columnist;* do as your neighbors do, 404:10

Post Office Motto, neither snow nor rain stays these couriers, 295:8

Pot, Pol [born Saloth Sar] **(1928–1998),** *Cambodian Khmer Rouge leader, P.M.;* mistakes (note), 436:2

Pound, Ezra [Loomis] (1885–1972), *poet, critic, translator;* autumn, 465:1; dreams, old, 203:4; emotion, 219:8; faces in the crowd, 508:8; grimace, accelerated, 437:3; literature, 74:9; lovest well, what thou, 389:9; poetry, 67:11; there died a myriad, 744:7; winter is icumen in, 464:11; word, no superfluous, 69:6

Pound, Roscoe (1870–1964), *legal writer; dean, Harvard Law School;* the law, 373:10

Powell, Adam Clayton, Jr. (1908–1972), *Baptist minister, U.S. rep. from N.Y.;* black power (note), 571:3; keep the faith, 395:7

Powell, Colin L[uther] (b. 1937), *U.S. gen.; 1st African-American chm. of joint chiefs of staff and secy. of state;* decisions, 184:1; first we are going to cut it off, 300:2; it can be done! 4:6; occupiers, 346:1; optimism, perpetual, 491:10; you break it, 344:9 & note

Powers, Thomas [Moore] (b. 1940), *journalist, novelist and nonfiction writer, essayist;* the truth, 681:4

Pozen, Robert C. See under Phelan, James

Pradt, Dominique Dufour de (1759–1837), *French cleric;* nation destined to exert its influence, 21:4

Prentice, George Dennison (1802–1870), *journalist, editor, poet, biographer;* tobacco, 672:2

Prescott, William (1726–1795), *Continental Army col.;* until you see the whites of their eyes, 48:3

Presley, Elvis [Aron] ["Elvis the Pelvis," "the King"] (1935–1977), *rock singer, actor,* **and Matson, Vera,** *songwriter;* love me tender, 395:2

Preston, James E. (b. 1933), *business exec.; C.E.O., Avon;* bad reputation, 582:4

Preston, Margaret Junkin (1820–1897), *poet, memoirist;* doing, `tis the, 2:9; Thanksgiving, 667:2

Preuss, Charles (1803–1854), *cartographer, memoirist;* a paradise, 96:3

Priestley, J[ohn] B[oynton] (1894–1984), *English novelist, critic, playwright, historian;* Nevada, 476:3; a society dominated by the masculine principle, 665:6

Proctor, Harley (fl. 1900), *soap and candle maker;* 99/44/100 per cent pure, 6:5

Proskauer, Joseph [Meyer] (1877–1971), *judge, N.Y. supreme ct.;* happy warrior (note), 311:7

Prouty, Olive [Higgins] (1882–1974), *novelist;* don't let's ask for the moon, 302:9

Pryor, Richard (b. 1940), *comedian, actor, screenwriter;* lookin' for justice, 352:8

Puzo, Mario (1920–1999), *novelist, screenwriter;* enemy, never hate, 221:9; friends & enemies, 221:2; lawyer with a briefcase, 378:5 politics, 531:7; refuse, 94:6; revenge, 585 :7

Pyle, Ernie (given forenames, Ernest Taylor) **(1900–1945),** *journalist, war correspondent;* Eskimos, 568:8

Quayle, Dan [given forenames, James Danforth] **(b. 1947),** *U.S. rep. and sen. from Ind., 44th vice pres., losing vice pres. candidate;* waste to lose one's mind (note), 432:7

Quayle, Marilyn [Tucker] (b. 1949), *lawyer;* golf v. sex (note), 342:6

Quincy, Josiah (1772–1864), *lawyer, jurist, Mass. state legislator; U.S. rep from Mass.; pres., Harvard U.;* Massachusetts, 409:4

Quindlen, Anna (b. 1953), *columnist, novelist, children's book writer;* school prayer, 538:1

Rademacher, Mary Anne (b. 1957), *inspirational writer;* courage, 172:1

Rado, James [born James Radomski] **(b. 1939) and Ragni, Gerome [Bernard] ["Gerry"] (1942–1991),** *songwriters, lyricists, actors;* age of Aquarius, 293:1

Ragovoy, Jerry (b. 1935) and Shuman, Mort (1936–1991), *lyricists & producers; Shuman also a singer;* get it while you can (note), 490:5

Rand, Ayn (1905–1982), *Russian-born novelist;* civilization & privacy, 149:4; great men, 299:2

Randall, James Ryder (1839–1908), *poet, journalist, teacher;* Maryland, 409:1

Randolph, A[sa] Philip (1889–1979), *founder and pres. of all-black Brotherhood of Sleeping Car Porters, pacifist, civil rights activist;* freedom, 276:1; nothing little counts, 82:1

Randolph, [James] Innes [Jr.] (1837–1887), *lawyer, poet, satirical writer;* a good old rebel, 637:2

Randolph, John ("John Randolph of Roanoke") (1773–1833), *U.S. rep. and sen. from Va.;* abilities so much below mediocrity, 337:4; he shines and stinks like rotten mackerel, 337:3; I am an aristocrat, 216:2; muffled oars (note), 337:3

Rankin, Jeanette (1880–1973), *U.S. rep. from Mont. (1st woman elected to Congress), suffragist, pacifist;* war, 705:12, 706:1

Rantoul, Robert, Jr. (1805–1852), *U.S. sen. and rep. from Mass.;* cheap land, 280:5

Raposo, Joe (1937–1989), *composer for film and TV;* not easy being green, 460:1

Rauch, John K., Jr. (b. 1930), *architect,* an expert, 245:3

Rawson, Clayton [Ashley] (1906–1971), *mystery writer and editor, magician;* crime does not pay, 176:3

Rayburn, Sam [Taliaferro] (1882–1961), *U.S. rep. from Tex.; House speaker;* a leader, 314:11; to get along, go along, 161:7; a wiser man this morning, 242:5

Read, Thomas B[uchanan] (1822–1872), *poet, painter, Union army major;* Sheridan, 153:5

Reagan, Nancy (b. 1923), *actor;* kinder and gentler than who? (note), 522:6; just say no, 700:10

Reagan, Ronald (1911–2004), *actor; gov., Calif.; 40th pres.; memoirist;* America, a promised land, 30:3; being shot at, 180:4; character & jelly beans, 106:4; evil empire, 452:7; facts (note), 245:5; Gipper, win just for the (note), 643:2; Gorbachev & wall, 45:6; government is like a baby, 297:1; government not the solution, 297:4; a nation that has a government, 31:1; once you've seen a redwood, 471:11; opponent's youth & inexperience, 11:2; politics is supposed to be, 531:1; struggle between good and evil, 270:3; sunset of my life, 369:2; tax increasers, 661:7; a tree is a tree, 226:3; trust but verify, 270:4; where people can still get rich, 531:5; where's the rest of me, 560:6

Red Cloud (1822–1909), *Oglala Sioux chief;* we were very many, and you were few, 564:6

Reddy, Helen (b. 1941), *Australian-born singer, songwriter;* woman, I am, 731:12

Redford, Robert [Charles], [Jr.] (b. 1937), *actor, director, producer;* cynics, 491:9

Reed, Ishmael (b. 1938), *poet, novelist, essayist, teacher;* the universe, 686:8

Reed, Rex (b. 1938), *movie critic;* Hollywood, 127:5

Reed, Thomas B[racket] ["Czar Reed"] (1839–1902), *U.S. rep. from Me.; House speaker;* a billion-dollar country, 25:2; friends & enemies, 220:9; habit, 301:2 he will never be either (note), 541:3; made light of his remarks (note), 339:1; Maine, 400:5; rather be wrong than president (note), 542:3; a statesman, 526:7; subtracting from the sum of human knowledge, 339:1 & note

Reid, Christian (1846–1920), *novelist;* the land of the sky, 482:2

Reich, Robert [Bernard] (b. 1946), *secy. of labor, economist, writer;* forecasters & astrologers, 210:3

Rense, Paige (b. 1929), *magazine editor, novelist;* good taste, 651:6

Republican Party, a chicken in every pot, 519:7; a choice not an echo (note), 522:1; Coolidge, 519:5,6; dinner pail, the full, 517:4; don't swap horses, 514:2; free soil—Fre-mont, 515:5; had enough?, 520:8; I like Ike, 521:2; in your heart you know he's right, 522:1; I still like Ike (note), 521:2; life, liberty, and Landon, 520:5; Nixon's the one, 522:2; public school system, 212:7; Roosevelt for ex-President, 520:6; school, the free, 212:8; stand pat (note), 520:6; Taft, get on the raft with, 518:2

Reston, James [Barrett] (1909–1965), *Scottish-born journalist;* instincts, [Nixon's], 343:2; politics, 402:5

Reuter, Babara, *R.J. Reynolds Co. marketing exec.;* nicotine delivery device, 672:8

Reuther, Walter [Philip] (1907–1970), *pres. United Automobile Workers, Congress of Industrial Organizations, and combined AFL-CIO;* if it walks like a duck, 237:5

Revere, Paul (1736–1818), *patriot leader and messenger, silversmith, engraver;* two lanterns, 47:6

Reynolds, Burt (b. 1936), *actor;* middle age, 421:1

Rhode Island Colonial Assembly, Ile of Rhods, 588:5

Ribaut, Jean (b. c. 1520–1565), *French mariner, colonizer;* greatest & fayrest havens, 634:6

Rice, Constance ["Connie"], *lawyer, social and civil rights activist;* Los Angeles, 127:9

Rice, Grantland (1880–1954), *sportswriter, poet, author;* the Four Horsemen, 643:5; game, how you played the, 642:5; a gray ghost [Red Grange], 644:1; how you played the game, 644:5; lies at rest by the nineteenth tee, 642:5; wars are planned by old men, 705:4

Rich, Adrienne (b. 1929), *poet, radical feminist;* every journey into the past, 498:8; language, 364:8

Richards, [Dorothy] Ann [Willis] (b. 1933), *teacher; state treas. and gov. of Tex.;* born on third base (note), 342:5; forgotten people (note), 421:8; politics a contact sport (note), 666:3

Richardson, Robert (1850–1901), *Australian poet;* good night, dear heart (note), 230:1

Richman, Murray, *N.Y.C. criminal defense lawyer;* I love murder, 177:3

Rickey, [Wesley] Branch ["the Mahatma"] (1881–1965), *baseball catcher and executive; integrated major league baseball as pres., Brooklyn Dodgers, by signing Jackie Robinson;* luck, 396:6 & note

infamy, 745:6; enemies, judge me by [my], 221:1; Fala, dog my (note), 42:1; fear, the only thing we have to, 39:3; the first 12 years, 545:1; fight, a good, 159:3; freedom & human rights, 276:3; freedoms, four essential, 276:2; generation of Americans, this, 285:2; good neighbor policy, 268:2; governments can err, 296:3; hand that held the dagger, 745:2; happiness, 302:6; happy warrior, 38:6, 311:7; ill-housed, ill-clad, ill-nourished, 192:3; indispensable man, no, 299:1; institutions & changing times, 336:7; lawlessness, world, 78:9; lead them straight, 747:5; man, the forgotten, 533:3; method, take a, 3:7; minds, prisoners of their own, 431:9; minorities, rights of, 568:3; neighbor, policy of the good, 268:2; new deal, 39:2; pain in my head, 368:5; peace & charity, 506:2; physical strength & spiritual force, 650:11; place of moral leadership, 544:9; pocketbook, a full, 441:10; private v. free enterprise, 101:4; progress, test of our, 590:5; prosperity [will] trickle down, 208:2; public opinion, arouses, 559:1; a radical, 529:4; a rattlesnake, 595:6; a reactionary, 529:6; rendezvous with destiny, 285:2; soil, the nation that destroys its, 224:7; son of a bitch, our, 268:3; taxes, 661:1,3; tough, to be, 650:10; vast fortunes, 590:4; war, 705:8,10; war, a new kind of, 746:2; war, we are going to win the, 745:8; war, we are now in this, 745:7

Roosevelt, Nicholas (1893–1982), *amb. to Hungary, writer, conservationist;* bride at every wedding, 594:8

Roosevelt, Theodore ["Teddy," "T.R."] (1858–1919), *writer, hunter; U.S. civil service commissioner; pres., N.Y.C. police board; asst. secy. of navy; col. in Spanish-American War; gov. of N.Y.; 25th vice pres.; 26th pres.; Progressive Party candidate for pres;* action, get, 3:2; Americanism, 50–50, 26:7; American, hyphenated, 503:4; Americanism, hyphenated, 265:2; arena, man who is in the, 3:3; Armageddon, we stand at, 37:5; the bear business, 594:1; big business & a square deal, 518:1 & note; black care & a fast pace, 640:5; bull moose, I am as strong as a, 526:4; bully pulpit, 544:2 & note; character is decisive factor, 105:11; a chocolate eclair & McKinley's backbone, 338:5; [Colorado:] Switzerland of America, 155:2; conservation & development, 223:8; the critic, 3:3; democracy, triumph of, 26:4; devil & Dark House, 193:6; diplomacy, 198:7; evil & expediency, 239:1; the fight is on (note), 543:7; heart & minds (note), 51:3; [Jefferson:] incapable executive, 347:5; justice, the peace of, 267:1; law, no man is above the, 372:7; the lunatic fringe, 527:10 & note; manhood, 416:3; mistakes, 463:3; muckrakes, men with the, 549:5; my hat is in the ring, 543:7 & note; Nationalism, A New, 518:3; natural resources, 223:6,7; navy, a great (note), 704:4; no criticism of the president, 544:4; North Dakota, 483:1; opportunity, 26:4; Panama, I took (note), 266:6; put out the light, 367:9; rather a cheap character, 338:6; righteousness, 592:3; speak softly and carry a big stick, 266:6; a square deal, 384:8; the strenuous life, 511:8; war-country needs one, 638:8; war, preparation for, 704:4 & note; wealth, malefactors of great, 324:4; we turn our rivers into sewers, 223:9; a wilderness called peace (note), 267:1; wilderness, hidden spirit, 718:6; wisdom, 724:7; word, shorter and more ugly, 362:5 & note; words, weasel, 363:1 & note; work, 737:7

Root, George Frederick (1820–1895), *composer, teacher;* rally 'round the flag, 152:3

Roper, Jack (1904–1966), *heavyweight boxer, actor;* I zigged, 645:5

Rose, Billy [born William Samuel Rosenberg] **(1899–1966),** *theatrical impresario, financial investor, art collector, philanthropist;* eats or needs painting, 442:1

Rosenblatt, Roger (b. 1940), *journalist, essayist;* the past, 498:10

Rosenthal, Jack (b. 1935), *Palestinian-born newspaper journalist and editor;* spin pays, 532:4

Ross, Alex [given forenames, Nelson Alexander] **(b. 1970),** *comic-book artist;* the devil, 196:10

Ross, Harold [Wallace] (1892–1951), *founder and editor of* The New Yorker; The New Yorker, 411:5; who he?, 559:7

Rosten, Leo C[alvin] (pen name, Leonard Q. Ross) (1908–1997), *Polish-born political scientist, novelist, lexicographer, humorist;* hates babies & dogs, 434:9; most men, 417:2

Rostropovich, Mstislav [Leopoldvich] (b. 1927), *Russian cellist, conductor;* more is more (note), 60:6

Rotary. See Sheldon, A.F.

Roth, Philip (b. 1933), *novelist;* a Jewish man with parents alive, 495:1; if world is a show, 72:3

Rough Riders, rough-tough, we're the stuff, 639:4

Rousseau, Jean Jacques (1712–1778), *Swiss-French philosopher, political theorist, composer, essayist* what does it matter to me, 614:4

Rove, Karl (b. 1950), *political consultant,* politics a full-contact sport (note), 666:3

Rowan, Carl [Thomas] (1925–2000), *journalist, author; amb. to Finland; dir., U.S. Information Agency;* questions & answers, 560:5

Rowland, Helen (1876–1950), *journalist, columnist, humorous writer, lecturer*; follies which a man regrets most, 576:2; how to say goodbye, 495:10; love, 407:3

Rowland, John G. (b. 1957), *U.S. rep. from, gov. of Conn. (resigned, imprisoned);* mistakes (note), 436:2

Rowlandson, Mary (ca. 1636–1711), *memoirist;* a stinking tobacco pipe, 671:7

Royal, Darrell [K.] (b. 1924), *U. of Texas football coach;* luck, 396:8

Rubin, Jerry C. (1938–94), *anti-war activist; Youth International Party co-founder;* weaker sex, 417:3

Rubinstein, Artur (1887–1982), *Polish-born pianist, memoirist;* the seasons, 467:8; talent v. work, 156:6

Rubinstein, Helena ["Madame"] (1882–1965], *Polish-born cosmetic business exec.;* women, 80:10

Rudd, Irving (1917–2000), *sports, press agent;* a

Scalpone, Al, *adv. copywriter, TV exec.;* prays together, 537:7
Schary, Dore. See Griffin, Eleanore
Schieffer, Bob [given forenames, Robert Lloyd] **(b. 1937),** *TV reporter and news-show anchor;* temporary assignment, 331:7
Schiffer, R. Michael and Rinzler, Michael P., *writers;* war, 708:1
Schlesinger, Arthur M[eier], Jr. (b. 1917), *historian, biographer, spec. asst. to presidents Kennedy and Johnson, teacher;* a dietary quest, 262:3; fatalism & responsibility, 256:8; liberalism & capitalism, 101:6; progress, conflict & stagnation, 159:4
Schlosser, Eric, *journalist, author, playwright;* farmers, 253:6
Schoepf, Johann David (1752–1899), *German surgeon (with Hessians in Amer. Rev.) and travel writer;* [Charleston has] a finer manner of life, 118:3
Schorr, Dan[iel] (b. 1916), *radio and TV journalist;* sincerity, 320:10
Schulberg, Budd (b. 1914), *novelist, screenwriter;* Florida, 259:9; good & bad for Sammy Glick, 244:3; I could've been a contender, 576:4; television, 412:6; What Makes Sammy Run?, 17:11
Schulz, Charles M[onroe] ["Sparky"] (1922–2000) , *cartoonist;* big sisters, 251:1; Charlie Brown, 313:1; Happiness, 302:11
Schumacher, E[rnst] F[riedrich] (1911–1977), *German-born English economist, conservationist; chief economic advisor, British Coal Board;* Small Is Beautiful (note), 630:8
Schurz, Carl (1829–1906), *German-born lawyer, amb. to Spain, U.S. sen. from Mo., secy. of interior, journalist, editor, biographer;* country, right or wrong [note], 500:1; full measure of liberty, 673:2
Schwartz, Delmore (1913–1966), *poet, short-story writer, teacher;* dreams, 204:1; paranoids, 398:6; poets' wives, 68:6; time, 670:8
Schwarzenegger, Arnold [Alois] (b. 1947), *Austrian-born body-builder; actor; gov., Calif.;* girlie-men, 343:3 & note
Schwed, Frederick R., Jr. ["Fred"] (c. 1901–1966), *stockbroker, writer;* customers' yachts? (note), 94:1
Scorsese, Martin (b. 1942), *film director, writer, actor, producer;* nonviolence, 493:5
Scott, Dred (c. 1795–1858), *African-American slave;* your petitioner, 35:3
Scott, Willard [Herman] (b. 1934), *TV weatherman;* it could be rain, 473:6
Scott, Winfield ["Old Fuss and Feathers"] (1786–1866), *U.S. army commander, Whig pres. candidate;* the greatest mistake of your life (note), 684:4; wayward sisters, depart in peace, 149:9
Scripps, E[dward] W[yllis] (1854–1926), *newspaper publisher, organizer of nation's 1st newspaper chain; philanthropist;* we shall tell no lies (note), 548:6
Sears, Edmund Hamilton (1810–1876), *minister, hymn writer;* it came upon the midnight clear, 110:4
Seattle [born Sealth] **(1786–1866),** *chief of Suquamish and Dewamish tribes;* death, 181:8; regret is useless, 680:5; white man will never be alone, 563:5
Seeger, Alan (1888–1916), *poet; killed in WWI;* a rendezvous with death, 742:6
Segal, Erich (b. 1937), *novelist, teacher;* love, 391:11 & note
Segar, Elzie [Crisler] (1894–1938), *cartoonist; creator of Popeye;* I yam what I yam, 613:6
Seinfeld, Jerry [given name, Jerome] **(b. 1954),** *comedian, actor, writer;* everybody lies about sex, 618:3
Seldes, George (1890–1996), *journalist, author;* tell the truth and run (note), 680:5
Seldes, Gilbert [Vivian] (1893–1970), *journalist, critic, novelist;* comedy, 327:1
Selzer, Richard [Alan] (b. 1928), *surgeon, essayist, short-story writer;* cities & oases of the spirit, 113:3
Selznick, David O[liver] (1902–1965), *movie producer;* El Paso and Amarillo, 113:8
Sendak, Maurice [Bernard] (b. 1928), *writer-illustrator of children's books;* having everything, 384:8
Serling, [Edwin] Rod[man] (1924–1975), *TV and film writer, producer;* [in Willoughby] a man can slow down, 688:1
Service, Robert William (1874–1958), *English-born Canadian poet, novelist;* later than you think, 670:3; God was tired when he made it [Alaska], 12:8; Yukon, the law of, 12:7
Sesame Street. See Joe Raposo
Seton, Julia M[oss] (1889–1975), *writer, lecturer, historian;* life has taught me, 504:7
Seuss, Dr. [Theodor Seuss Geisel] (1904–1991), *writer-illustrator of children's books;* an elephant's faithful, 395:6; quick, Henry the Flit, 7:1; the trees, I speak for, 226:7
Sevareid, Eric (1912–1992), *radio and TV journalist, memoirist;* Truman, 546:8
Seward, William Henry (1801–1872), *gov. of N.Y., U.S. sen. from N.Y., secy. of state;* conflict, an irrepressible, 149:7; the Constitution, 166:8; revolutions (note), 586:10; we elect a king, 543:1
Sexton, Anne (1928–1974), *poet, essayist;* a dream, 205:8; a possessed witch, 483:9; the sea, 462:9
Shakers, hands to work, 698:6; love is little, 388:3
Shakespeare, William (1564–1616), *English playwright, poet, actor, part owner of Globe theater;* blood will have blood (note), 173:1; greatness (note), 414:10; many strokes (note), 194:2; misery & bedfellows (note), 525:4; what a goodly outside falsehood hath (note), 7:4
Sharlet, Jeff, *editor, writer;* Colorado Springs, 121:4
Sharp, William [pseudonym: Fiona Macleod] **(1855–1905),** *Scottish poet, novelist;* heart, a lonely hunter (note), 309:10
Sharpton, [Jr.] Al[fred Charles] (b. 1954), *Pentecostal minister, civil rights activist, politician;* clothes, 255:4; justice, 352:9
Shaw, Artie [born Arthur Jacob Arshawsky] **(1910–2005),** *jazz clarinetist, bandleader;* more would have been less (note), 60:6; American Constitution, 127:6

Shaw, George Bernard (1856–1950), *Irish playwright, music critic, novelist, social reformer;* the Constitution, 167:7; who can & who teaches (note), 215:4
Shaw, Henry Wheeler. See Billings, Josh
Shaw, Irwin [born Irwin Gilbert Shamforoff] **(1913–1984),** *novelist, playwright, screenwriter, short-story writer;* New York & girls in summer dresses, 134:1
Shaw, Richmond, *U.S. army enlisted man in Iraq;* we live in this movie, 346:6
Shawn, Ted [given name, Edwin Myers Shawn] **(1891–1972),** *dancer, choreographer, teacher;* twirl, 63:3
Shawn, William (1907–1992), *editor,* The New Yorker*;* it takes as long as it takes (note), 257:5; falling short of perfection, 257:5
Sheed, Wilfrid [John Joseph] (b. 1930), *novelist, biographer, critic, essayist;* sanity, 399:8
Sheehan, George (1918–1983), *cardiologist, runner;* healthy way to be ill, 331:4
Sheen, Fulton J[ohn] (1895–1979), *R.C. bishop, evangelist, columnist, author;* an atheist, 77:4
Sheldon, A[rthur] F[rederick] ("Fred") (1868–1935), *business-school operator and teacher;* who serves best (Rotary motto), 700:9 (note)
Shelley, Percy Bysshe (1792–1822), *English poet;* best and brightest (note), 218:4
Shelton, Ron[ald] (b. 1945), *screenwriter, director, producer;* poor people of Louisiana, 387:5
Shepard, Odell (1884–1967), *biographer, writer, teacher, editor, poet;* Connecticut Yankee, 163:4
Sheridan, Philip H[enry] (1831–1888), *Union army general; commanding gen., U.S. Army;* Indians, the only good, 564:5; Texas, 664:3
Sherman, Sidney (1805–1873), *maj. gen. of Tex. militia, entrepreneur;* remember the Alamo!, 35:2
Sherman, William Tecumseh (1820–1891), *Union army general; commanding gen., U.S. Army;* hold out, 153:4; I will not accept if nominated, 543:3; make Georgia howl (note), 154:1; paid spies, 548:1; the penitentiary v. the White House, 541:4; press, a free (note), 548:1; Savannah (note), 154:1; South Carolina, vengeance on (note), 634:8; vox populi, 508:4; war, 702:4,5,7
Sherwood, [Mrs. John] M[ary] E[lizabeth] W[ilson] (1826–1903), *writer, poet;* beauty, 80:2
Shields, Ren (1868–1913), *lyricist;* Good Old Summertime, 464:8
Shriver, R[obert] Sargent ["Sarge"], [Jr.] (b. 1915), *dir., Peace Corps and Office of Econ. Opportunity; amb. to France, losing Dem. vice pres. candidate;* self-absorbed, 614:3
Sibert or **Siebert, Tallifero Lawrence (1877–1917),** *songwriter, vaudevillian;* Casey Jones (note), 737:8
Siegel, Jerry (1914–1996), and Shuster, Joe (1914–1992), *cartoonists, creators of Superman; Siegel wrote, Shuster illustrated;* It's Superman!, 312:4
Sigourney, Lydia Howard Huntley ["the Sweet Singer of Hartford"] (1791–1865), *poet;* their name is on your waters, 563:1
Silver, Nicky (b. c. 1961), *playwright;* I'm still your mother, 495:6
Silverman, Sime (1873–1933), *founding editor-publisher of* Variety; Wall St. Lays an Egg, 191:2
Simmons, Paul B[arrett] (c. 1942–1994), *journalist, speechwriter;* are you better off today?, 522:4
Simon, Paul (b. 1942), *singer, guitarist, songwriter, actor;* New Jersey Turnpike, 479:4
Simon, William [Edward] (b. 1927), *bond dealer, secy. of treasury, businessman;* tax structure, 661:6
Simpson, Louis [Aston Marantz] (b. 1923), *Jamaican-born poet, novelist, critic;* where are you, Walt? (note), 674:5
Sinclair, Upton [Beall] (1878–1968), *novelist, socialist, muckraker, editor;* Chicago, 119:5; fascism & capitalism, 682:6; a vision of power, 119:5
Singer, Isaac Bashevis (1904–1991), *Polish-born Yiddish-language novelist, short-story writer;* God, 292:1; free will, 719:7; love, 392:2
Siodmak, Curt [given name, Kurt] **(1902–2000),** *Austrian-born novelist, essayist, short-story writer, screenwriter;* when wolfbane blooms, 180:1
Sitting Bull [born Tatanka Iyotake] **(c. 1831–1890),** *head chief and holy man of Teton Sioux;* do you know who I am?, 565:4; white men, 565:5
Skelton, "Red" [given name, Richard] **(1913–1997),** *comedian;* cat's tail, I'm not pulling, 242:6; give the public something they want to see, 232:7; hell, people in, 311:1
Skinner, B[urrhus] F[rederic] (1904–1990), *behavioral psychologist, writer;* education, 214:9; life, satisfying, 437:8; reading, love of, 89:6; whether machines think & whether men do, 608:7
Skinner, Cornelia Otis (1901–1979), *actor, dramatist, writer, biographer;* women's virtue, 731:8
Slosson, Edwin E[mery] (1865–1929), *science writer and editor;* American crowd, 27:2
Slovik, Eddie [Edward] D[onald] (1920–1945), *pvt., U.S. Army,WWII;* I'll run away again, 748:3
Smith, [Gov.] Al[fred Emanuel] (1883–1944), *gov. of N.Y., 1st Roman Catholic to run for pres., businessman;* baloney, 261:6; kiss of death, 676:4; record, look at the, 246:4; statistics (note), 600:7
Smith, Bessie ["the Empress of the Blues"] (1894–1937), *blues singer;* I'm a young woman, 751:5
Smith, Betty [Wehner] (1904–1972), *novelist, playwright, teacher;* tree that grows in Brooklyn, 471:9
Smith, Edgar (1857–1938), *composer, lyricist, librettist;* the working girl, 738:2
Smith, Hedrick [Laurence] (b. 1933), *Scottish-born American journalist, writer, lecturer, TV producer and commentator;* Moscow, 129:1; nation [with] 11 time zones, 452:3; Russians, 452:4
Smith, John (1580–1631), *English soldier of fortune; Jamestown, Va., colonist;* a fair bay (note), 696:4; a place for man's habitation, 696:4 & note; pleasant hills and fertile valleys, 696:5
Smith, Joseph (1805–1844), *Mormon prophet;*

nist, founding editor of Ms. *magazine;* becoming the men, 732:1; the goddess is in the questions, 560:8; microcosm, 631:1; morally, art of acting, 236:9; mother & father, 495:2; suffering, worst thing, 655:10; woman, a liberated, 731:7; woman without a man, 735:3

Stengel, "Casey" [Charles Dillon] (1890–1975), *baseball outfielder and manager;* can't anyone play this here game?, 647:3; if you don't get it by midnight, 625:1; made up my mind both ways, 333:6; mistake of being 70, 488:10; most people my age are dead, 489:2; a time in every man's life, 610:4

Sterling, Andrew B. (1874–1955), *lyricist;* meet me in St. Louis, 145:1

Stern, Philip Van Doren (1900–1984), *historian, novelist, editor;* an angel gets his wings (note), 182:10

Stevens, Christine (1918–2002), *founder and pres., Animal Welfare Inst.;* animals, 460:4

Stevens, John Paul (b. 1920), *assoc. just., U.S. Supreme Court;* money & water, 443:3

Stevens, Wallace (1879–1955), *poet, essayist;* actual world & fantastic world, 574:6; beauty, 80:7; become an ignorant man again (note), 67:13; bee, booming of the new-come, 459:7; birds are gone, when the, 224:2; blue guitar, 65:5; body's beauty, 80:7; emperor of ice-cream, 314:5; God, 290:6, 291:1; the hero, 311:5; history, 316:10; the house was quiet, 467:1; insures all people against all happenings, 94:3; let be be, 54:7; the moon, 468:8; moonlight, book of, 468:4; pigeons, casual flocks of, 458:4; the plum, 261:3; a poem, 68:12; the poet, 68:3; poetry, 67:13 & note, 68:2; Satan, death of, 196:8; the world, 741:11

Stevenson, Adlai E[wing], [II] (1900–1965), *member, mission to U.N.; gov. of Ill.; Dem. pres. candidate; amb. to U.N.;* a new America (note), 521:3; Americans are suckers for good news, 30:6; candles, [E. Roosevelt] would rather light, 700:8; careless, 611:9; communism, 158:4; diplomacy, 199:2; eggheads unite, 217:8; flattery, 259:5; gains & pains (note), 194:1; God bless, 538:8; a hungry man, 533:6; an independent, 529:11; Kansas, 354:7; laws & habits, 301:5; a lie (note), 200:2; the mind, 432:3; New Dealers & car dealers (note), 341:5; patriotism, 503:7; Paul v. Peale, 432:3; politics [definition of], 529:10; prejudice, 539:9; president, any boy, 545:3; president, pick a & pick on, 545:3 (note); principles, 700:7 progress & unpopular positions, 555:11 too big to cry (note), 720:1; words, 364:4

Stevenson, Robert Louis (1850–1894), *Scottish novelist, short-story writer, poet, essayist;* a bleak climate [in Saranac], 481:1; catchwords (note), 364:4; Nebraska, the plains of, 474:2; paradise, it was a sort of, 422:6; plain, the green, 474:3; sagebrush (note), 750:1; sameness, this huge, 474:4

Stewart (fl. 1861), *journalist;* a strip of land (note), 482:3

Stewart, Potter (1915–1985), *judge, appeals ct.; assoc. just, U.S. Supreme Court;* fourth institution, 551:2; I know it when I see it, 103:4; official religion, 537:9; publishing business, 169:4; swift justice, 352:4

Stieglitz, Alfred (1864–1946), *photographer, exhibitor, editor;* truth & art, 58:5;

Stimson, Henry L[ewis] (1867–1950), *secy. of war, secy of state, lawyer;* gentlemen & others' mail, 553:2

Stinson, Joseph C. (b. 1947), *screenwriter;* make my day, 189:5

Stockman, David [Alan] (b. 1946), *U.S. rep. from Mich.; dir., U.S. mgt. and budget office, investment banker;* all these numbers (note), 210:1; starve the beast, 210:2; trickle down (note), 208:2

Stockton, Frank R. (Francis Richard) (1834–1902), *journalist, editor, novelist, short-story writer;* the lady or the tiger?, 559:5

Stoddert, Benjamin (1751–1831), *1st secy. of navy; real estate speculator;* bravery in officers, 425:4

Stone, Irving (1903–1989), *novelist, short-story writer;* [Bryan's] mind was like a soup dish, 342:1

Stone, I[sidor] F[Einstein] (1907–1989), *journalist, author;* burlesque & newspapers, 550:6

Stone, Oliver (b. 1930), *film director, screenwriter, producer;* greed (note), 442:8

Stong, Phil[ip Duffield] (1899–1957), *journalist, novelist, teacher;* Iowa, 344:3;-**4**

Storrs, Lucinda Howe (1758–1839), *homemaker, diarist;* prosperity, 725:3

Stout, Rex [Todhunter] (1886–1975), *mystery writer;* any spoke will lead an ant, 256:6

Stowe, Harriet Beecher (1811–1896), *novelist, social reformer;* age where nations are convulsed, 336:1; conscience & business, 91:9; the honorable, the just, 698:10; injustice, great and unredressed, 336:1; I 'spect I growed, 108:2; I's wicked, 238:6; is America safe?, 336:1; Kentuckians, 355:4; a mighty influence is abroad, 336:1; soul, my, 633:7; very stylish, 254:3

Stravinsky, Igor [Fyodorvich] (1882–1971), *Russian-born composer, memoirist;* music, 65:7

Strong, George A[ugustus] (1832–1912), *minister, versifier;* the Mudjokivis (note), 563:6

Strong, George Templeton (1820–1875), *lawyer, diarist;* a barbarian, 385:4; Dan Sickles' character, 338:1

Strout, Richard L[ee] (1898–1992), *reporter, columnist;* eight millionaires & a plumber (note), 341:5

Strunk, William, Jr. (1869–1946), *prof., Cornell U.;* words, omit needless, 69:7; writing, vigorous, 69:7

Strunsky, Simeon (1879–1948), *Russian-born journalist, essayist;* remark seldom quoted correctly, 561:9

Stryker, Fran [Francis Hamilton] (d. 1962), *radio scriptwriter;* Hi-yo, Silver! 312:3

Sturges, Preston (1898–1959), *playwright, screenwriter, director;* I've laid me down to die, 233:1; making people laugh, 370:3

Stutz, Geraldine (1924–2005), *editor, fashion merchandiser, publisher;* "dog-whistle" clothes, 254:10

Styron, [Jr.] William [Clark] (b. 1925), *novelist,*

looks like a singed cat, 476:1; courage, 235:7; customs, 301:3; a dark side, 610:7; death, the report of my, 548:7; difference of opinion, 197:4; a dog & a man, 324:4; education, 212:9, (note) 214:9; eggs in one basket, 725:5; exercise is loathsome, 511:9; an experience, 244:8; facts, get your, 246:2; fame is a vapor, 652:7; familiarity, 343:5; faith, 249:5; first half of life & the last half, 10:9; Florence, 123:6; fools, 263:6, 402:1; forbidden, the, 622:8; foreigners, 264:7; forty-eight, before & after, 490:9; France, 448:7; freedom of speech, freedom of conscience, 25:8; friendship, 279:6; German, the literary, 449:1; girls, 729:9; golf, 641:6; good, be, 699:9; a good example, 699:8; good night, dear heart, 231:1; habits, other people's, 300:7; Hartford, 124:2; [Hawaiian] islands (note), 306:6; [Hawaii:] that peaceful land, 306:6; health, your, 308:4; Heavenly Father invented man, 290:1; he is useless, 338:3; he telegraphed back for his blankets (note), 55:8; history, 316:2; humor, 326:5; idea, new, 480:3; illusions, 203:3; Italy, 441:9; a jay & a Congressman, 457:9; June bug, a young, 10:8; jury system, 350:1; justice, 351:6; justice system, 349:8; kings is mostly rapscallions, 314:3; [Kipling:] a remarkable man (note), 246:2; laugh and laugh, we, 369:9; laughter, 369:8; law, in the, 376:9; legislatures (note), 160:5; life, 10:9, 382:3, 431:4; lie v. cat, 200:3; lie, can get halfway around world, 200:1; lied, never seen anybody but, 199:10; lies [in Bible], 76:9; lies & statistics, 601:1; mad, we are all, 398:3; majority, 402:2; man is the only animal that blushes, 324:6; a mob, 508:6; modern inconveniences, 437:2; modify before we print, we, 102:6; moon, everyone is, 610:7; morals, 235:5,8; morals of America, 25:9; New England weather, 477:4; New Orleans, 129:9; Newport, 130:3; old age & broken health, 193:4; partialities and prejudices, our, 539:3; patriot & change, 502:7; persons attempting to find a motive in this narrative, 61:9; a pessimist & an optimist, 490:9; pray a lie, you can't, 537:2; profanity (note), 52:6; opinion, petrified, 329:3; the public [as] critic, 61:8; race, the most marvelous, 566:1; a raft, 619:9; remember anything, I could, 415:5; remember, things I can (note), 415:5; right, always do, 591:9; Salt Lake City, 142:6; Satan, 196:5,6; school boards, 213:2; sense, moral & immoral, 622:7; smoking, 672:5; a southerner talks music, 637:5; speculate, he should not, 92:10; speculate in stocks (note), 92:10; speech, 411:2; statesmanship, 198:5; success, 652:6; take the lies out of him, 338:2; tax collector & taxidermist, 660:8; temptation & cowardice, 662:3; thoughts, the storm of, 431:4; through a glass eye darkly, 338:4; training is everything, 212:10; truth, 679:9,10,11,12; the war [Civil War], 154:5; watermelon, 260:10; "we," the word, 362:2; weather, talks about the, 472:6 & note; we have ground the manhood out of them, 565:9; whiskey into the committee rooms, 160:3; woman, a thoroughly beautiful, 729:10; word, the right, 362:1; Yankee, I am a, 163:1; young June bug & old bird of paradise, 10:8

Tyson, Neil de Grasse, *astrophysicist, planetarium director, author;* natural selection, 599:3

Udall, Morris K[ing] (1922–1988), *U.S. rep. from Ariz.;* the people have spoken, 509:7

Udall, Stewart L[ee} (b. 1920), *U.S. rep. from Ariz., secy. of interior, writer;* conservation, 226:1; inner peace, 613:9; long waves, 410:4; The Quiet Crisis, 226:1; we have confused power with greatness, 535:9; science & the excellent, 443:5

Ullman, Harlan K. & Wade, James P. [Jr.], *military strategists, businessmen, writers; Wade also an asst. secy. of defense (c. 1984);* one man's vulgarity, 364:10; shock and awe, 345:1 & note

United Negro College Fund, a mind, 432:7

United States. See under U.S.

Unruh, Jesse M[arvin] (1922–1987), *Calif. Dem. political boss; state treas.;* money & politics, 530:1

Updike, John (b. 1932), *novelist, critic, essayist, short-story-writer, poet;* America is a conspiracy, 30:12; bore, healthy male adult, 90:3; gods & letters, 291:3; ghosts of Hawthorne and Melville, 477:9; memory, 415:9; neutrinos, 602:4; religion, 581:5; schools, 214:7; silence, 251:6; writing great, 76:3; yearning for an afterlife, 581:4

U.S. Army, Office of the Chief Signal Officer, Spartan simplicity must be observed, 427:7

U.S. Army Service Forces, the difficult & the impossible, 4:2

U.S. Census, Superintendent of, a frontier line (note), 281:4

U.S. Coast Guard, always ready/semper paratus, 426:7

U.S. Marines, first in the fight, 427:1

U.S. Motto, in God we trust, 288:3

U.S. Navy, praise in public, 403:1

U.S. Postal Service. See General Post Office, New York City

U.S. President's Science Advisory Committee, science & the excellent, 598:8

Valenti, [Joseph] Jack (b. 1921), *ad agency exec.; spec. asst. to pres.; pres., Motion Picture Assn. of Amer.* bury me in Texas, 666:5

Van Buren, Abigail [born Pauline Esther Friedman] **(b. 1918),** *advice columnist;* good marriage, 408:7

Vandenberg, Arthur [Hendrik] (1884–1951), *newspaper editor, publisher; U.S. sen. from Mich.;* expediency & justice, 244:4

Vanderbilt, Cornelius (1794–1877), *shipping & railroad magnate;* I will ruin you, 585:3

Vanderbilt, William H[enry] (1821–1885), *railroad magnate, financier;* public be damned, 92:5

Vandiver, Willard D[uncan] (1821–1885), *U.S. rep. from Mo.;* I am from Missouri, 320:8

Van Doren, Mark (1894–1972), *poet, editor, critic, novelist, short-story writer;* wit, 326:9

Van Duyn, Mona (1921–2004), *poet, 1st woman U.S. poet laureate;* a story, 650:6; the world, 742:1

Van Dyke, Henry (1852–1933), *preacher, teacher, writer, amb. to Netherlands and Luxembourg;* America for me!, 503:2

Van Loon, Hendrik Willem (1882–1944), *Dutch-born journalist, historian, children's book author;* history, 316:8; life & progress, 555:6

Work, Henry Clay (1831–1884), *songwriter;* father, dear father, 14:4; marching through Georgia, 154:1
Worth, Cedric R. (1900–1983), *writer, screenwriter, producer, asst. to undersecy. of navy;* hates dogs and children (note), 434:9
Wright, Frank Lloyd (1869–1959), *architect;* architecture, 61:5; the floo floo bird, 58:10; home in Japan, 450:6; Los Angeles, 127:1; luxuries, 397:5; plant vines, 61:3
Wright, Orville (1871–1948), *co-inventor of the airplane;* success, 606:2
Wright, Richard [Nathaniel] (1908–1960), *novelist, short-story writer, essayist;* jail, it's just like livin in, 568:4; self-realization, 613:7
Wright, Wilbur (1867–1912), *co-inventor of the airplane;* success, 606:2; talk, the only bird that can, 658:8
Wylie, Elinor [Hoyt] (1885–1928), *poet, novelist, short-story writer, essayist;* avoid the reeking herd, 632:1; hater, a good, 305:8; silence, 620:2; stone to throw, 177:10; woman, being, 739:5; words, 363:4,5

X, Malcolm. See Malcolm X

Yankwich, Léon R[ené] (1888–1975), *judge, fed. dist. ct.;* illegitimate parents, 494:4
Yeats, John Butler (1865–1939), *Irish poet, dramatist;* talk in America, 170:3
Yellen, Jack (1892–1991), *Polish-born lyricist, composer* happy days are here again, 292:6; Last of the Red Hot Mamas (note), 11:1
Yordan, Philip (1914–2003) and Wyler, Robert (1900–1971), *screenwriters;* a lawyer (note), 377:8
Young, Brigham (1801–1877), *Mormon leader; pres., Church of Latter-Day Saints; gov. of Utah terr.;* this is the place, 687:4
Young, Joe. See under Lewis, Sam M.
Young, Neil (b. 1945), *Canadian-born singer, songwriter;* burn out, better to, 241:6
Youngman, Henny [given name, Henry] **["King of the One-Liners"] (1906–1998),** *English-born comedian;* how's your wife (note), 408:3; take my wife, 408:3
Yzquierdo, Pedro (fl. c. 1492), *Spanish sailor;* light! land!, 32:4

Zadeh, Lotfi Asker [born Lotfi Aliaskerzadeh] **(b. 1921),** *Azerbaijan-born mathematician, teacher; proposed theory of "fuzzy logic";* nature writes, 456:1
Zangwill, Israel (1864–1926), *English journalist, novelist, nonfiction author;* America is God's ... melting pot, 26:3; New York, 132:3
Zanuck, Darryl [Francis] (1902–1979), *movie studio executive, producer, director;* yes, don't say until I've finished, 259:4
Zappa, Frank (1940–1993), *rock and jazz-rock guitarist, composer, singer;* deviation from the norm, 198:2
Ziegler, Ron[ald Louis] (1939–2003) , *press secy. to Pres. Nixon, lobbyist;* third-rate burglary, 711:5; the operative statement, 712:5
Zion, Sidney, *federal D.A., reporter, columnist, author;* failure, 248:4; flops (note), 248:4;

Keyword Index

Beaches
being killed on the b., 747:4
Beans
to know b., 460:11
Bear
dancing with a b., 180:6
my name & the b. business, 594:1
Beast
starve the b., 210:2
Beautiful
America the B., 24:7
a b. woman is practical poet, 80:3
if not moral, 137:7
it's b. over there, 368:2
young lady & old lady, 488:4
BEAUTY, 79
Beauty
a b. woman
a silent, lonely b., 145:2
appreciation of b., 489:1
around us, 80:2
being only skin-deep, 80:11
body's beauty lives, 86:5
I died for b., 329:1
is everlasting, 80:9
is indescribable, 80:4
is momentary in the mind, 80:7
is now underfoot, 8012
killed the beast, 80:8
perception of b., 80:1
simple b., 171:3
with b. before me I walk, 454:3
Bed
I should've stood in b., 645:2
& solution to habitual accidents, 611:7
Bedfellows
strange b., 525:4 & note
Bedrooms
sacred precincts of marital b. (note), 553:5
Bee
the new-come b., 459:7
Beef
where's the b.?, 9:4
Beer
barrel, tapped at both ends, 479:1
got between the people and its b., 15:1
Bees
buccaneers of buzz, 457:6
Beginning
in my. b, is my end, 256:7
is often the end, 81:2
that will be the b., 81:6
Behaviorism
of course b. "works", 604:6
Beings of an inferior order (note), 35:3
Belief
& a habit, 249:3
must mean more than desire, 332:6
without evidence, 249:4
Believe
each has to b. by himself, 249:10
I b. in the forest, 454:10
if I didn't b. it with my own mind, 701:10
what is it that men cannot be made to b.!, 248:7
you gotta b., 250:1
Bell,
every time a b. rings, 182:5
Belly
little round b., 110:2
Benefactor of human kind, 347:4
Beneficence
private b., 107:2
Berlin
was orchestrated hell, 747:1
Berliner
Ich bin ein B., 43:5
Best
and the Brightest, 218:4
strive to be the b., 240:3
way of doing everything, 417:8
Bethlehem, 110:7
Better
are you b. off today?, 522:4
dead than Red (note), 158:5
Red than dead, 158:5
Bible
[has] a thousand lies, 76:9
an unexpurgated b., 102:7
is literature, 579:6
things that you're liable to read in the B., 579:11
Bibliobibuli, 89:3
Big
apple, 132:7
I am b., pictures got small (note) 412:3
pray b.!, believe b.! act b.! (note), 432:3
Rock Candy Mountains, 687:11
Bigamy, 407:5
Bigger
they come, the harder
they fall, 642:1
Biggest
little place in America, 122:1
electric train set, 81:10
BIGNESS, 81
Bikini, the, 255:2
BILL OF RIGHTS, 82
Bill of Rights
a b. of rights, 165:2
[not] a suicide pact, 169:2
& the publishing business, 169:7-179
Billboard lovely as a tree, 7:5
Billion
here and a b. there, 442:4
Billionaires, 219:1
Billion-dollar country, 25:2
Biotic community, 225:5
BIOLOGY. See under SCIENCE.
Birch
bringing back the b., 624:8
most ladylike of trees, 471:3
Birches
swinger of b., 471:8
Bird
why the caged b. sings, 629:1
Birds
caged b., 275:8
days when the b. come back, 463:3
echelon of b. (note), 459:8
when the b. are gone, 224:2
BIRMINGHAM (ALA.), 115
Birth
copulation, and death, 383:4
Bitch-goddess success, 652:11
Bites off more than he can chaw, 257:3

Bury
me not on the lone prairie, 714:6
my heart at Wounded Knee, 363:3
BUSINESS, 90
Business
chief b. of the American people is b., 93:7
& conscience, 91:9
do b. [in Charleston], 118:5
sagacity, 93:5
was meant for the big fellows, 93:4
wish I had spent more time on b., 95:3
Businessman
& an offer, 94:6
Businessmen
farm the farmers, 252:3
Busted
by gosh (note), 135:1
Butte [Mont.], 117:5
Butter
wouldn't melt, 340:6
Button
collar b., 668:4
you press the b., 6:3
Buy
don't b. it, 93:10
Buying
and selling, 92:2, 92:7
By and by
God caught his eye, 232:2
[Washington state motto], 709:5
Bystander(s)
innocent b., 133:4 & 435:1

Cabbage
with college education, 212:10
Cabbages
inspiring the c., 338:23
Caesar and Christ, 580:1
Caesars
pity all the mighty C. (note), 7:6
Cage
can c. singer but not song, 278:6
Caged
birds, 276:8
why the c. bird sings, 629:1
Cages
[marriage] happens
as with c. (note), 406:1
Cairo [Ill.], 117:6
Cake
& debt, 397:2
Calculators
nature hates c., 575:4
Calamity, 676:2
CALIFORNIA, 96
California
annexes the U.S., 96:6
climate of C., 97:5
furnish[es] the best bad things, 96:5
& gunshot wounds, 96:10
has better days, 96:7
Here I come, 97:6
I have walked in C., 97:4
is a tragic country, 97:8
[is] a wonderful place to live, 97:7
kingdom of C., 96:4
scenery in C., 96:9
southern C., 97:10
state so blessed, 97:5
tree in C., 97:1
whatever starts in C., 98:1
& your I.Q., 97:12
Californian scoundrels, 96:8
Californians, 97:2
Caligula's horse, 337:4
Call me Ishmael, 16:8
Called
back, 230:4
CALMNESS, 98
Calmness is godlike, 98:3
Cambridge ladies, 116:8
Camelot, 546:1
Camera v. eye, 702:4
Camerado
this is no book, 88:6
Camp (note), 59:4
Campaign
contribution, 531:2
in poetry, govern in prose, 531:4
Campus
problems on c., 214:5
CANADA, 446
Canada
a kind of hunting preserve, 446:6
blame C., 446:9
don't know what street C. is on, 446:3
[is a] good neighbor, 446:2
Heaven was the word for C., 446:7
is a bore, 446:8
to talk about C., 446:4
Canal
the c. is ours, 270:2
Canaries, 459:2
Cancer
close to the presidency, 712:2
is the subversive sea, 331:5
Candle
better to light one c., 2:10
burns at both ends, 241:4
Candles
rather light c., 700:8
Candy is dandy, 15:7
Canoe
paddle your own c., 614:9
Capital
better to lose opportunity than c., 95:5
has its rights, 99:6
is a result of labor, 100:1
Capitalism
& communism, 158:3
& political power, 78:7
CAPITALISM & CAPITAL V. LABOR, 99
Capitalist
and laborer, 99:1
Capitalists, 99:3
Captain
O C.!, my C.!, 386:1
Car
you get there in a c., 607:6
Card
game is war, 284:2
Cards
cut the c., 677:10
game iv [sic] c., 284:3
Care
to c. and not to c., 582:8

Carelessness
& security & freedom, 611:9
Cares
that infest the day, 63:10
Cars
drive themselves to death in huge c., 608:8
people in c. (note), 459:9
Carson City, 118:1 & 2
Casbah, 674:4
Cases
concrete c., 373:1
great c. & bad law, 372:8
hard c. & bad law (note), 372:8
Casey
at the Bat, 641:23
Jones, 737:8, 738:1
Cash
they create it here!, 122:4
Castle
man's house is his c., 552:6
Cat
as the c. climbed, 458:7
if man could be crossed with the c., 458:1
in gloves catches no mice, 595:4
pulling the c.'s tail, 242:6
Catastrophic success, 346:4
Catch-22, 429:1 & 2
Catchwords (note), 364:4
Cater to the nation's whims, 413:1
Catholics believe in forgiveness, 581:2
Cats
and monkeys, 457:8
Cause
of all mankind, 49:5
C average, 214:6
Celebrity, 654:1 & 2
CENSORSHIP, 103
Censor's alert (note), 103:4
Censorship
is social control, 103:6
Vietnam, war without c., 694:4
Censure
pain of c., 177:6
Central Park, 135:10
Century
of Dishonor, 565:3
of the common man, 437:6
the coming c., 283:4
Certain
nothing c. except death and taxes, 165:3
Certainty is an illusion, 574:2
Chairs
three c. in my house, 621:1
Chameleons
we are c., 539:3
Championship playing for the national c., 722:4
CHANGE, 104
Change
don't c. horses (note), 104:4
& enemies, 105:2
if we don't c. directions, 105:9
in society today, 105:6
is not always p., 555:4
is the law of life, 105:5
people c., 105:3
power to c., 105:7
things do not c., 104:2
to c. the world, 105:8
why are we afraid to c.?, 30:9
Changeth
old order c. (note), 104:5
Changin'
times they are a- c., 105:4
Chaos
is a friend of mine, 418:3
is wrong in every appearance, 597:7
material of world is c., 741:9
material wants to return to its most stable form, c., 603:4
often breeds life, 417:9
CHARACTER, 105
Character
a rather cheap c., 338:6
& happiness, 106:1
is always known, 173:1
is like a tree, 699:4
is the decisive factor, 105:11
is what you are in the dark, 106:3
& jelly beans, 106:4
just c., 546:8
judged by the content of their c., 44:5
makes the man, 699:7
makes the person, 105:10
& other people, 106:2
rules cannot substitute for c., 106:6
will out, 173:1
Characters [in Arkansas], 56
Charity, 106:10
CHARITY & PHILANTHROPY, 106
Charlatan
of the highest skill, 594:6
Charleston, 118:4
Charlestonian, 118:6
Charlie Brown, 313:1
Charming
everything is c., 448:7
Chaws more than he bites off, 257:3
Cheated,
never c. an honest man, 176:7
Checkers
named it C., 41:1
Cheer
don't c., men, 469:1
Cheers
who only stands and c., 642:2
Chemical
barrage, 225:9
Chewing gum for the eyes, 412:4
Chicago
is the great American city, 120:4
is the product of capitalism, 119:6
they call it C., 119:1
where nobody could forget how the money was made, 120:5
we're going to C., 120:3
will give you a chance, 120:2
you C. people, 119:2
Chicken in every pot, 519:7 & note 519-520
Child
as soon c. has left the room (note), 107:9
hard words bruise a c., 108:4
make me c. again just for tonight, 669:9
no c. left behind, 214:7

it is the people's C., 294:5
one country, one C., 166:5
& right to be let alone, 168:2
& the courts, 167:5
the people made the c., 166:3
there is a higher law than the C., 166:8
was made for posterity, 166:7
what's the C. between friends?, 167:1 & note
your C. is all sail, 166:9
Constitutional
fixed star in our c. constellation, 168:8
right to be wrong, 509:8
this C. shield, 657:3
Consumer, is not a moron, 9:1
Consumption
conspicuous c., 439:8
Containment
policy (note), 268:4
Contender
I could have been a c., 576:4
Content
is a glimpse of something, 73 :10
j am c., 366:5
Contentment
squalid c., 414:5
Contest was inevitable, 150:1
Continent
ages quickly, 28:6
the end of a c., 97:11
Continental, a. 206:4
Continental Congress
great Jehovah and the C.C., 47:5
Contract, verbal, 374:6
Contradict
do I c. myself?, 164:3
Contribution
when you cease to make a c., 739:1
CONVERSATION, 170
Conversation,
art of 170:8
Conversations, 170:5
Converse
not many c., 170:2
Convict
No. 9653 for President, 519:4
Convictions
[that] change with the weather (note), 163:8
Convicts
a band of, 174:6
Coolidge
keep cool with C., 519:5
or chaos, 519:6
weaned on a pickle (note), 659:1
Corn
Colonels full of c., 355:5
raise less c. and more hell, 353:7
Corn Belt, the, 422:9
Cornbread, 260:8
Corn-pone
whar a man gits his c., 324:7
Corporation
is device for profit, 93:2
Corporations
can love each other, 92:9
have neither bodies nor souls, 91:3 & note
indentured to c., 94:7
most men are servants of c., 93:3
will do what individuals would not, 91:8
Correlative
objective-c., 60:1
Corrupt bargain, 513:5
Corruption
Era of C. (note), 292:4
hard to get people interested in c., 175:5
COSMOLOGY. See under SCIENCE.
Costume
of woman, 254:2
Cotton
is King, 636:3
Kingdom, 286:7
land of c., 636:4
Councils
of war, 423:7
Country
a closed c. 265:3
all for our c., 476:6
ask not what your c. can do for you, 615:4
what we can do for our country (note), 615:4
a tough country, 56:3
a very great c., 25:3
belongs to the people, 23:7
billion-dollar c., 25:2
brand-new c., 400:1
duty, honor, c.!, 504:3
is turned into a city, 223:2,
in this c. you can look farther and see less, 422:3
is not mountainous nor yet low, 696:5
I tremble for my c., 274:2
I want to stand by my c., 706:1
I would go to hell for my c., 499:79
it's a tough c., 56:3
looks like a singed cat, 476:1
love for his c., 503:6
melancholy strange-looking c., 328:4
my c. 'tis of thee, 501:2
my c. is the world, 235:2
my whole c. and nothing but my c., 516:1
not a c. at all, 281:6
Our C., our whole C, 500:3
our c. & democracy, 26:4
our c. right or wrong, 500:1
roads take me home, 717:3
say not, "My c. right or wrong", 501:4
served his c. faithfully, 229:1
shame to take this c. away from the rattlesnakes, 97:3
this hog-stomping c., 76:6
this is a beautiful c., 367:1
this is my c. (note), 274:1
vast c., 421:9
we are born for the c. (note), 406:4
what a happy c. this will be, if the whites will listen, 562:5
what we can do for our c. (note), 615:4
where none but malefactors will ever live, 12:5
COUNTRY LIFE & PEOPLE, 171
COURAGE, 171
Courage
doesn't always roar, 172:1
is resistance to fear, 171:7
is the price that life exacts, 171:8
moral c., 235:7
one man with c. makes a majority, 171:6
Couriers
these c. & their appointed rounds, 472:7

Court
doesn't exist to give justice, 352:7
foreign, c. (note), 165:4
honorable c's now in session, 372:4
Courts
& the Constitution, 167:5
stand against any winds, 657:3
Covenant with death, 166:6
Cover-up (note), 711:6
Cow, purple c., 197:5
Coward
dirty little c., 174:2
Cowards
fatigue makes c., 258:5
Cowardice, 258:4
Cowboy
Americans admire the c., 716:4
that damned c. is president, 594:3
wrapped up in white linen, 125:1
Cows
I never saw so many c., 114:6
Cox
and cocktails, 519:3
Crab
we were like a c. that could run either way (note), 50:6
Crackers
live off yams, 259:8
Cradle
hand that rocks the c., 728:10
of toleration and freedom, 507:3
CRAFTINESS, 172
Cranes
beyond the reach of words, 459:8
Crazy
all of us go a little c. at times, 399:1
Creativity
obsession with c., 332:9
Credit
buy it on c. (note), 207:5
cherish public c,, 206:5
coin, c., and circulation, 206:2
is [not] as good as money, 93:10
is lifeblood of business, 208:3
is the vital air, 91:6
strangulation of c. (note), 208:3
who gets the c., 95:2 & note
Creditors, 90:5
Cried all the way to bank, 62:9
Crime
commit a c., 173:2
does not pay, 176:3
don't do the c., 177:1
is contagious, 296:1
is [an] endeavor, 176:6
of 1873 (note), 207:3
planning a c., 177:2
CRIME, CRIMINALS & DETECTIVES, 173
Crimes
of this guilty land, 149:8
world teems with c., 77:6
Criminals
less evil that some c. escape, 237:4
Crises
great c. produce great men, 677:1
Crisis
in Chinese the word c., 677:4
Quiet C., The, 226:1
Critic
not the c. who counts, 3:3
the public is the only c., 61:8
CRITICISM. See under ART.
Criticism
be kind with your c., 62:5
CRITICISM, ART: 61
Criticize
right to c., 277:6
to c. is to appreciate (note), 62:1
Criticizes,
out of passion, 177:4
Critics
ought to hesitate, 63:1
Crockett, David, 83:6
Crook
I'm not a c., 713:2
Cross
No C., No Crown, 654:10
of gold, 207:3
no c. of gold, 517:5
over the river, 367:4
Crossroads
of America, 334:6
Crow
shook down dust of snow, 465:6
Crowded
it's too c. (note), 647:7
Cruel
nation does not have to be c. to be tough, 650:10
Crumb
to be a c., 552:1
Cry
too big to c., 720:1
Cultivators
of the earth, 251:1
Culture
ladies who pursue C., 58:7
no better than its woods, 225:6
of a nation, 59:2
Cup of endurance runs over, 583:4
Cure,
to c., relieve, comfort, 202:6
Cured
disease you don't [want] to be c. of, 488:5
I am frizzled, stale, and small, 604:3
if pain. could have c. us, 480:1
Curtain
behind the [stage] c's mystic fold, 70:5
CUSTOM. See HABIT & CUSTOM, 300
Custom
law v. c., 300:9 & 301:3
one good c., 104:5-105
Customer
is always right, 93:9
Customs
are rock, 301:3
& the experience of mankind, 300:5
Cut
must c. our way out, 151:2
Cynic
a blackguard whose faulty vision, 701:4
Cynical
no matter how c. we become, 79:3
Cynics,
low regard for c., 491

do not d., 188:5
is a decision, 188:7
Deliberate
speed 169:5 & note
Delight, 303:6
Demagogues, 160:3
DeMille, Mr., 412:3
Democratic party
& states' rights, 40:5
is like a mule, 525:1
DEMOCRACY, 188
Democracy
a d. half rich and half poor, 190:10
a gravity point for American d., 354:5
arsenal of d., 39:6
born of free land, 189:9
& criticism, 190:6
cure for evils of d., 190:1
is the recurrent suspicion, 190:5
is the theory that, 189:10
laboratories of d., 190:2
means everybody but me, 190:3
& mediocrity, 189:3
never lasts, 189:2
real disease is d., 188:9
& sacrifice, 189:4
& the frontier, 189:8
this pioneer d., 454:1
to practice d. as we do, 190:9
& trust, 190:11
Democrat
a D. is a fellow who, 528:10
I am a D., 528:11
I am a D. still, 526:3
to be a D. (note), 528:11
Democrats
never said all D. were saloon-keepers, 524:7
want to tax you, 532:3
Demonology, 196:3
Departure
a time for d., 496:12
DEPRESSION, THE, 191
Depression,
came on, 192:2
common cold of mental illness, 604:9
is a wimp of a word, 399:5
Depressions,
are farm led, 191:5
Deserts
asked to blossom, 227:5
Desire
if you d, many things, 192:4
DESIRES, 192
Desires
a thousand d., 192:6
to gratify d., 192:5
Des Moines, 122:6 & 7
DESPAIR, 193
Despair,
never d., 194:3
safe d., 193:3
white sustenance d., 193:2
Despairing
soul, 193:9 & note
Desperation
lives of quiet d., 381:3
Despotism, 682:4
DESTINY. See FATE & DESTINY, 255
Destiny
is not a matter of chance, 256:4
rendezvous with d., 285:2
the current of d., 256:2
to be a Jew is d. 567:7
to escape our d., 234:6
Destruction
if d. be our lot, 22:4
Detail
life is frittered away by d., 620:9
think in generalities but live in d. 630:4
DETAILS. See SMALLNESS, DETAILS, & LITTLE THINGS, 629
Details
& favorable impression, 630:7
God is in the d., 630:9
& reading, 89:4
DETERMINATION, EFFORT, PERSISTENCE, & PERSEVERANCE, 194
DETROIT, 122
Detroit,
capital of the new planet is D., 122:8
is hell on wheels, 122:9
say nice things about D., 123:1
Deus, ditat, 56:4
Deviation
& progress, 198:2
DEVIL, THE, 195
Devil
gets best lines, 196:10
there is a d., 195:9
made me do it, 196:9
object of reverence is d., 196:1
the D. and me, 196:4
Devils
have been better friends, 196:2
Dewey defeats Truman, 41:1
Diamonds
Are A Girl's Best Friend, 689:2
Diary, a, 74:11
Die
a duty to d., 489:8
I d. hard, 181:5
not that I'm afraid to d., 183:3
pity we can d. but once (note), 49:2
something to d. for, 330:1
wonder how I'm going to d., 183:4
you asked this man to d., 749:6
Died
as he must have wished to d., 229:4
there d. a myriad, 744:7
Dietary
quest, 262:3
Differ
to think is to d., 197:8
Difference
between one man and another 197:6
of opinion, 197:2, 683:7
DIFFERENCES, 197
Differences
the real d. today, 506:10
Different
doing something d., 198:3
drummer, 335:3
opinions, 197:1

Difficult
the d. we do immediately, 4:2
Difficulties, 676:6
Dime,
can you spare a d., 192:1
Dinners,
soirées, poets, 137:1
DIPLOMACY, 198
Diplomacy
dollar d., 267:2
[is] art of lying, 198:6
at the conference table, 199:3
& force, 198:7
[is] recognition of actuality, 199:2
is to do and say, 198:9
not backed by p., , 199:5
politics drives d., 199:6
shall proceed frankly, 267:5
Diplomats
don't mind starting a w., 199:1
Direction
you won't have to search for d. D. will come to you., 614:5
Dirigo, 401:2
Dirtiest
place in the world, 115:2
Disarm,
d., d., 492:5
Discipline, 424:7 & 427:11
Discontent, 682:10
Discrimination
the sorry history of d., 572:5
met more d. as a woman (note), 522:3
Disease
you don't [want] to be cured of, 488:5
what person the d. has, 331:6
DISHONESTY & LIES, 199
Disorderliness
careful d., 417:7
Dispute
to d. everything that is disputable, 55:2
Dissent
[is not] disloyalty, 42:4
must have d., 190:6
Dissenting opinions, 348:6
Distinguished
the d. thing, 182:5
Dispute
to d. upon everything, 55:2
Disputants, 55:3
Distrust
is very expensive, 677:8
Diversity, human, 198:1
Divided
every kingdom d. against itself (note), 684:3
man has d. his domain, 557:4
we fall, 47:4
Divine Soul (note), 614:7
DIVISIONS & BARRIERS, 200
Dixie Land, 636:24
D.N.A., 599:8
Do
a girl in, 175:6
exactly as your neighbors, 404:10
how d. you know what you're going to d.?, 4:4
I can d. something, 2:7
never d. anything I should be afraid to d., 698:3
some say she d., 582:2
the hardest thing in the world for you, 3:6
watch what we do, 4:5
we d. what we must, 243:7
your own work, 1:7
your thing, 1:7
Doctor
bills, 201:9
deference paid to a d.'s opinion, 201:5
kind of d. I want, 202:4
takes the fee, 201:3
that doctors on your throat, 202:1
when a d. kant see no money in me, 201:8
Doctors
I hate d.!, 202:2
DOCTORS & MEDICINE, 201
Doctrine, 248:11
Does
she or doesn't she?, 8:4
Dog. *See also Dawg*
& a door, 201:2
and your little d. too, 179:8
bites a man is not news, 548:4
died a gentleman, 457:7
if a d. jumps in your lap, 459:4
that caught the car, 345:4
was created for children, 457:11
Dogies
git along, little d., 749:7
Dogmas
of the quiet past, 540:3
Dogs
display reluctance, 459:3
hates d. and babies, 434:9
terrible thing to out live her d., 488:7
DOING. See ACTION & DOING, 1
Doing
always d., 1:2
'tis the d., 2:9
be up and d., 1:6
Dollar
almighty d., 439:1
diplomacy, 268:2
never owned a d. he could not take up to [heaven], 230:13
tear up everything to get a d., 225:2
Dollars
two d. a day and roast beef, 514:2
what's a thousand d.?, 440:9
Domestic bliss, 406:7
Dominion
good Old D., 697:5
Domino principle, 692:4
Don't
give up the ship, 708:6
Done
a thing well d., 2:2
it can be d.!, 4:6
nothing is d. as it was d. 20 years ago, 104:5
something attempted, something d., 2:1
Door
& a dog, 201:2
open d., 266:5
we never opened, 576:3
Dooth
with youre owene thynge (note), 1:7
Doubt
freedom of thought without d., 625:8

Eat
never e. more than you can lift, 262:10
not to dullness, 260:4
to live, 260:3
Eaten
never repent having e. little, 260:4
EATING. See FOOD, WINE, & EATING, 260
Ecological
an e. education, 224:8
Economic forecasters, 210:3
ECONOMICS, 208
Economics
as If People Mattered
(note), 630:8
in e. majority is always wrong, 209:7
& our culture, 211:2
voodoo e., 210:1 & note
Economist
one-armed e., 209:4
Economy
global, 211:1
it's the e., stupid, 523:1
Eden
is that old-fashioned house, 318:9
Editor
[definition of], 550:2
first duty of an e., 549:3
human cash-register
e. (note), 548:6
might begin a reformation (note), 547:7
Educated
and enlightened, 212:2
EDUCATION, 211
Education
[definition of], 213:3
enables you to earn, 214:3
if you think e. is expensive, 214:5
is a great equalizer, 212:5
is what survives, 214:9
of females, 211:5
makes a straight-cut ditch, 212:6
soap and e, 212:9
& tolerance, 673:3
& what we have unlearned (note), 214:9
without e., 214:10
Educational system, 214:2
Effectiveness, 403:4
Effete
corps of snobs, 218:5
Efficiency, 403:4
EFFORT. See DETERMINATION & EFFORT, 195.
Effort
conscious e., 195:1
Efforts
one's own, 738:8
Egg
try to spoil a rotten e., 338:1
Eggheads unite!, 217:8
Eggs
put all your e. in one basket, 725:5
Egypt
wa'n't goin' to keep nothin' of E. (note), 628:7
Elderly, the, 489:8
Eleanor
two-thirds mush and one-third E., 493:10
Election
this e. & a war, 531:8
Electric train set, 81:9
Electricity
by means of e. the world of matter has become a great nerve, 605:3
Elegance, 651:4
Elephant
an e.'s faithful 100 percent, 395:6
ELITE, THE, 216
El Paso, 113:8
Embattled
farmers stood, 51:4
Emergency,
more serious than war, 209:1
Emeralds
I wish they were e., 394:2
Emotion
endures, 219:8
heart so full of e., 219:2
is about nothing, 219:7
lives governed by e., 219:8
no e. can retain form, 219:5
remembered in tranquillity (note), 327:4
EMOTIONS, 219
Emotions, 220:1
Emperor of ice-cream, 314:5
Empire
dared not speak name, 32 :3 (note)
evil e., 452:7
we don't do e., 271:5
we're an e. now, 271:2
Empires
Mounting military campaigns, 708:1
we don't seek e. (note), 271:5
Employed
when men are e., 735:7
Employee
every e. & level of incompetence, 739:7
End
& a beginning, 81:2
in my beginning is my e., 256:7
keeps the e. from being hard, 487:7
Endeavor
set upon a mighty e., 747:5
that is worthwhile, 621:9
Ending, the happy, 81:2
ENDINGS. See BEGINNINGS & ENDINGS, 81
Ends
& means, 244:5
tell me how this e., 346:3
ENDURANCE, 220
Endurance
is the crowning quality, 220:3
patient e., 220:4
Endure
may she e. forever, 328:8
ENEMIES, 220
Enemies
accumulate, 221:7
bring j. to our e., 352:11
if you don't have e., 221:6
judge me by [my] e., 221:1
keep your e. closer, 221:2
know your e., 221:8
list, 712:7
love him for the e. he has made, 220:8
secret history of our e., 220:7
we must not be e., 504:10
your e. never [sleep], 220:9

just the f., ma'am, 246:8
of physical science have all been discovered, 601:8
person giving you f., 247:2
to front only the essential f., 381:4
your opinion v. your f., 247:3
Fail
freedom to f., 248:2
FAILINGS. See FAULTS & FAILINGS, 257
FAILURE, 247
Failure
is not an option, 248:5
line between f. and success, 247:6
[is] no success, 248:3
the loneliness of f., 247:8
no f. except in [not] trying, 247:5
nothing succeeds like f., 248:4
to communicate, 118:7
Faint
heart never filled a flush, 725:4
Fair
meet me at the f., 145:1
Fairy tale
obsessed by a f. t., 574:9
Faith
absolute f. corrupts, 249:11
an illogical belief, 249:7
belief without evidence, 249:4
feeds among tombs, 248:9
implies disbelief, 248:12
in a holy cause, 249:8
is a fine invention, 596:3
is believing what you know ain't so, 249:5
is sight and knowledge, 701:2
is the pierless bridge, 248:13
keeps the world alive, 249:6
keep the f., 395:7 & note
truth & death to f. are vain, 249:2
way to see by f., 248:6
Faithful
always f., 427:1
Fala (note), 42:1
Fall
in f., country goes to glory, 462:11
of an ocean, 136:8
Falsehood
what a goodly outside f. hath! (note), 7:4
FAME. See SUCCESS & FAME, 651
Fame
always brings loneliness, 653:6
common f. (note), 240:4
is a bee, 652:4
is a vapor, 652:7
love of f., 652:11
FAMILIARITY. See INTIMACY & FAMILIARITY, 343
Familiarity
breeds attempt, 343:7
breeds contempt and children, 343:5
breeds contentment, 343:6
Families
& hints, 251:3
FAMILY, 250
Family
in another city, 251:5
no f. is older, 251:4
love within a f., 251:2
that prays together, 537:7
Famous
they first make famous, 654:9
world-f. for 15 minutes, 654:3
Fanatic
does what he thinks th' Lord wud do, 222:3
Fanaticism, 222:4
Fanatics, 222:7
Farm
depressions are f. led. 191:5
is an infinite form, 253:3
Farmer
buys at retail & sells at wholesale, 253:2
is the fundamental citizen, 252:10
no one hates his job as [does} a f., 252:6
Farmers
are a vanishing breed, 253:6
are founders of civilization, 252:1
are totally dependent, 253:4
business men farm the f., 252:3
embattled f. stood, 51:4
smart enough to organize (note), 191:5
would not be enough f., 253:5
Farming
looks mighty easy, 252:8
FARMS & FARMERS, 251
Farms
leave our f., 252:4
Farther
no f. they can go, 247:7
Fascism
is capitalism plus murder, 682:6
FASHION & CLOTHES, 253
Fashion
defines the self-concept, 255:4
is in ceaseless pursuit, 255:1
means moment, 255:6
Fashionable
very f., 254:3
Fast
whose pace is f. enough, 640:5
Fasten
your seat belts, 676:7
Fat
the f. lady sings, 81:4 & note
Fatalism, 256:8
FATE & DESTINY, 255
Fate
can be shaped, 256:9
if f. means you to lose, 256:5
is a name for facts, 255:7
of a nation was riding that night, 52:3
superiority to f., 332:1
tangled skein of will and f., 381:7
whatever limits us we call f., 255:8
Fates
we are spinning our own f., 256:3
Father
Abraham, 151:7
dear f. come home, 14:4
moved through dooms of love, 494:7
of his country, 710:5
of Waters, 152:5
talks from our great f., 562:4
too little f., 495:2
Fatigue
makes cowards, 258:5
Fattening
immoral, illegal, or f., 623:6

our house is made of g., 554:1
own windows are made of g., 177:5
Glasses
girls who wear g., 616:5
Glick, Sammy. See under Sammy.
Global economy, 211:1
Glory
enough for all (note), 639:5
of everything, 253:1
of the coming of the Lord, 289:2
Old G.!, 501:1
over everything, 275:3
that was G., 213:8
What Price G.?, 705:2
Gluttony, 262:5
Go
ahead, make my day, 180:5
directly to jail, 373:12
west, young man, 714:4
where no man has gone before, 5:3
Goal
[is] to rule, 18:3
GOD, 288
God
act as if there were a G., 235:6
a . complex, 399:6
a G. so quickly, 290:9
an athlete of G., 298:3
and imagination, 291:1
as God now is, 289:10
belief in G., 77:1
both [North & South] pray to the same G., 536:8
builds his temple in the heart, 578:5
caught his eye, 232:2
coincidence is G.'s way, 292:3
does not play dice with the universe, 602:1
does not speak prose, 289:1
does not take sides in American politics, 531:6
do take care of yourself, 538:8
enriches, 56:4
enters by a private door, 288:6
evidence for G., 290:2
final proof of G's omnipotence, 291:2
gave him [Woodrow Wilson] a great vision, 231:6
gave us liberty, 273:5
gets an A (note), 65:3
git up airly ef you want to take in G., 470:2
give us grace to accept with serenity, 538:5
G's way of, 292:3 434:8
G.'s work must be our own, 739:2
governs in the affairs of men, 288:2
help me, I love it, 706:4
helps them that help themselves, 614:6
honest G. is noblest work of man, 289:9
honor thy g., 538:2
I can lay my finger on thy heart, 290:3
I believe in one G., 577:4
I never spoke with G., 249:1
if G: talks to you, 399:4
if you talk to G., 399:4
in G. we trust, 288:3
is a mother, 290:7
is an exalted man (note), 289:10-290
is a verb, 291:5
is and all is well, 289:5
is in me, 290:6
is in the details, 630:9
is love, 289:6
is our name for, 288:4
is slick (note), 290:10
is subtle but [not] malicious, 290:10
is the Celebrity Author, 291:4
[is] John Doe of philosophy, 290:4
know that I am G. (note), 444:8
love G. without a mediator, 288:5
mills of G. grind slowly, 289:8
nature of G., 290:5
of frolic, 457:11
of war, 7079
one on G.'s side is majority, 288:7
only G. can make a tree, 471:7
only money of G. is G., 288:8
our Father-Mother-G., 289:7
people see G. every day, 292:2
smile at puny fences, 557:4
spanked the town, 143:4
thank you God for this amazing day, 538:7
there but for the grace of G., goes G., 340:7
time & space & G., 292:1
to daydream about G., 581:3
to prescribe to G. (note), 602:1
under G. people rule, 635:8
union with G., 445:2
use of G.'s name on one's behalf, 291:8
what hath G. wrought?, 605:2
whether G. could have created world differently, 290:1
will not help, 290:28
with G. all things are possible, 484:4
world without G., 580:9
would reveal his will, 578:7
Goddess
is in the questions, 560:8
Godhead, the, 291:7
Godless
are the dull, 89:14
Gods
do not answer letters, 291:3
twenty g. or no God, 577:2
Going
if you don't know where you are g. (note), 647:7
it keeps g., and g., 9:6
Gold
almighty g. (note), 439:1
and silver, 443:10
cross of g., 207:3
or silver [in California], 96:1
Golden
age of poetry and power, 292:7
yesteryear, 326:1
Golf
links lie so near the mill, 590:3
Good
and the brave ever a majority?, 699:2
annoyance of a g. example, 699:8
any g. thing that I can do, 356:6
be g. and be lonesome, 699:9
be g. for something, 687:2
breeding consists in, 404:9
distinguishing between g. and evil, 235:11
doing g., 699:1
Era of G. Feelings, 292:4
famous g. time had by all, 340:5
men & laws, 371:8
no g. deed goes unpunished, 700:6
policy of the g. neighbor, 268:2

time that was had by all, 340:5
times women & Irish whiskey, 513:3
you never had it so good, 521:3
Goodbye
how to say g., 495:10
Good night
dear heart, 231:1
Goodness
best kind of g., 699:5
had nothing to do with it, 623:1
tainted, 257:2
GOOD TIMES, 292
Gorbachev, 45:6
Gospels
moral precepts [in] the g., 579:10
Gotham, city of, 130:7
Gott
Herr G., 290:10
Govern
through leadership or crisis, 297:8
to g. another, 295:3
Governed
world is too much g., 294:4
GOVERNMENT, 293
Government
all g. is evil, 294:6
all the g, we pay for, 297:5
art of g. is being honest, 293:9
belongs to the p., 296:5
best g. governs least, 294:6
big enough to give all you want, 296:9
by crony, 296:4
can err, 296:3
chair of government, 541:3
& citizenship [in Cleveland], 121:3
duty to obey established g., 293:10
era of big g., 297:6
& happiness of society, 293:4
how to behave toward this American g.?, 418:8
if g. becomes the lawbreaker, 296:1
in Washington still lives, 36:6
I don't want to abolish g., 297:7
is a rainbow, 31:2
is a trust (note), 295:5
is best which governs least (note), 294:6
is best which provides most, 295:7
is but a necessary evil, 293:2
is force, 295:6
is funnier than we are, 327:5
is involved in our lives, 296:10
is like a big baby, 297:1
is right to lie (note), 358:8
is the badge of lost innocence, 293:3
is the problem, 297:4
is the teacher, 296:1
lack of honor in g., 296:8
legitimate object of good g., 294:3
legitimate powers of g., 293:5
less g., the better, 295:1
nation that has a g., 31:1
natural [for] g. to gain ground, 293:8
no g. ought to be without censors, 547:5
of all the people (note), 287:1
of laws, 371:1
of the people, by the people, 26: 6 & 287:1
of the U.S. is lawyer's g., 377:1
people's g., 190:8 & 294:5
& power to control minds. 169:6
should not foster crimes (note), 237:4
subsidizes problems (note), 297:4
take g. off the backs of people, 297:2
that lives in spirit of charity, 296:3
trusted with the g. of others?, 294:2
what is g. itself?, 293:7
why has g. been instituted?, 293:6
& will of the people, 507:8
wise and frugal g., 294:1
worst g. is the most moral, 296:7
your g. failed you, 47:2
Governments
burdens [imposed] by their g., 499:5
Governors
if the people be the g., 188 :8
Gown
a satin g., 254:6
GRACE, 298
Grace
in presence of danger of death, 646:4
under pressure, 298:2
sign of grace, 298:4
Graces
never less than the g., 323:2
Graft
honest g. (note), 175:1
Graham, Katie, 711:6
Grammar
& morals and manners, 360:4
Grammatical
sentence with seven g. errors, 304:4
Grand Canyon, 55:9
Grand jury,125
(Amendment 5), 82:7
Grandfather
to G.'s house we go, 250:4
Granite State, 478:6
Grant
whiskey G. uses, 14:3
Ulysses S. G. ? (note), 257:8
Grape
peel me a g., 261:5
Grapes
of wrath, 289:2
Grass
was the country, 422:7
will grow in the streets, 191:4 & note
world of g. and flowers, 422:5
Grateful
they are so g.!, 616:1
Grave
down into the g., 182:8
Graves
sleep sweetly in your humble g., 230:1
GRAVESTONES, see EPITAPHS & GRAVESTONES, 227
Gravity
—it's not just a good idea, 603:6
point for American democracy, 354:5
Gray
flat, and spooky, 128:10
yon g. head (note), 501:6
Great
nations should keep their word, 269:3
good and a g. man, 711:2
lives of g. men, 298:6
man is willing to be little, 298:8
men can't be ruled, 299:2

she did it the h. way, 233:5
work, 195:6
Hardihood
our ideals of b., 426:6
HARDING, WARREN G., 303
Harding
he-harlot was H., 304:4
was just a slob, 304:6
you're the man for us, 518:6
Harlem
of honey (note), 133:8
[is] precious fruit, the big apple, 132:7
stars over H. , 133:8
was Seventh Heaven!, 136:1
where anything can happen, 135:8
Harm
I intend to go in h.'s way, 50:3
Hartford, 124
Harry
given em hell, H.!, 521:1
Harvard
football against H., 643:4
man, 217:2
Harvard Square, 213:11
Harvests
all greater than you wish, 696:3
Haste
nothing more vulgar than h., 404:4
HASTE V. GOING SLOW, 305
Hat
my h. is in the ring, 543:7
HATE, 305
Hate
cannot drive out h., 306:1
creative h., 305:6
everyone equally, 434:10
fear & h., 305:9
I don't hate it!, 638:2
is too great a burden, 306:4
those who h. you don't win unless, 306:3
to get up in the morning, 470:1
Hated
to be h. is [a] distinction, 305:5
Hater
I'm a good h., 305:8
Hates
dogs and babies, 434:9
Hating
the price of h., 306:2
Hatred
anger but not h., 306:5
paralyzes life, 391:10
Hatreds
systematic organization of h., 527:6
Haughty
never be h. to the humble, 404:5
Havens
one of the greatest h., 634:6
Haves
and have-mores, 443:2
Having
everything, 384:7
HAWAII, 306
Hawaii
is a paradise, 307:4
spiritual destiny of H., 307:6
we need H., 307:1
where they lay flowers on you, 307:5
Hawaiian
people are lovers of poetry, 307:2
He
belongs to the ages, 386:1
can run but, 645:7 & note
died as he must have wished, 229:4
done her wrong, 173:4
fell in whirlwind, 386:5
kept us out of war, 518:5
lived usefully v. died rich, 438:7
must summon his people, 546:5
was a gallant soldier, 229:7
was a glance from God, 394:5
was my North, my South, my East and West, 394:7
who accepts e., 239:8
who transplanted, 163:5
who is not with me (note), 239:8
He-harlot, 304:4
Head
if you can keep your h., 677:3
Headache
I have a terrific h. (note), 368:5
Healing, 202:3
HEALTH, 307
Health
v. disease, 308:10
first wealth is h., 308:2
less you think about your h. , 308:3
measure your h., 308:1
only way to keep your h., 308:4
Heard
ain't h. nothin' yet, 282:8
HEART, 309
Heart
bury my h. at, 363:3
desires of the h., 309:11
dungeon so dark as one's own h., 612:9
faint h. never filled a flush, 725:4
has its sabbaths and jubilees, 309:3
hath memory, 106:9
have a h. for every fate, 310:2
his h. was as great, 386:4
if I ever need a h. transplant, 343:1
Is a Lonely Hunter, 309:10
is a resilient muscle, 310:3
is forever inexperienced, 309:5
is so full of emotion, 219:2
is like a viper, 309:2
is slow to learn, 310:1
my h. is like a feather, 301:7
obey thy h., 388:9
of America is felt less here, 146:9
secret anniversaries of the h., 309:8
that is slow to learn, 310:1
to the highest doth attain, 309:6
up again old h.!, 309:4
Heartland
here in the h., 419:5
Heartless,
Godless, 132:8
Hearts
and minds (note), 693:7
and minds of the people, 51:3
men's h. and minds, 269:2
were touched with f., 496:8
Heat
if you can't stand the h., 650:12

must be impartial referees, 349:4
sometimes progress, 348:4
& the Constitution, 166:1
& the respect of the people, 349:1
Judgment
he was a walking day of j., 594:7
let j. run down as waters (note), 44:2
Rush to J., 352:6
Judicial
acme of j. distinction, 348:2
decrees, 375:2
independence, 349:3
political question & j. question, 371:7
restraint, 348:9
Judiciary
is the safeguard (note), 167:6
June
old sophistries of J., 463:3
rare as a day in J?, 463:2
June-bug, young, 10:8
JURIES, 349
Juries, 349:6
Jury
[definition of], 350:2
court is only as sound as its j., 350:6
every j. trial, 350:5
member ready to hang the panel, 349:7
persons appointed by a judge, 350:2
the j. system, 350:1
trial by j. (Amendment 7), 83:2, 349:5
trial by j. is a rough scales, 350:4
Just
say no, 700:10
JUSTICE, 351
Justice
and Right, and the Law!, 351:5
bring j. to our enemies, 352:11
compassion v. j, 352:12
court doesn't exist to give j., 352:7
expediency and j., 244:4
if we should deal out j. only, 351:6
is always in jeopardy, 351:3
is not to be taken by storm, 351:9
& Just-Us, 352:9
laws of changeless j. , 351:4
no j., no peace, 352:9
no such thing as j., 351:10
oppressions that mask as j., 352:1
peace of j., 267:1
procedure & justice, 375:6
swift j., 352:4
thou shalt not ration j., 352:2
until j. rolls down like waters, 43:2
what stings is j., 351:8
where j. is denied, 174:3
without j. courage is weak, 351:1
your j. would freeze beer!, 352:3

KANSAS, 353
Kansas
Bleeding K., 353:1
citizen & bootlegger in K., 354:2
Crime against K., 353:2
farmers ought to raise more hell, 353:7
happens first in K, 354:1
if we blow up K., 354:8
in K. we busted, 353:4
is a kind of barometer, 354:57
is one of our finest states, 354:9
is the child of Plymouth Rock, 354:4
roosters lay eggs in K., 353:5
they chew tobacco in K., 353:6
to make a city in K., 353:3
we're not in K. any more, 354:3
What's the Matter with K.?, 353:8 & note
Kansas City
Ev'rythin's up to date in K. C., 124:7
Keep
on truckin', 195:5
the faith, 395:7
Kelly
Slide, K., Slide, 641:5
Kentuck
heaven is a K. of a place, 355:2
Kentuckians, 355:4
KENTUCKY, 355
Kentucky,
hurrah for old K.!, 418:6
is garden spot of the world, 356:4
old K. home, 356:1&2
politics the damndest in K., 356:3
to hell or K., 355:1
Keynesians
we are all K., 209:8
Kickin'
never gets you nowhere, 725:4
Kid
here's looking at you, k., 394:6
Kidder, a, 326 :10
Kill
the brave, 152:1
Killed
being k. on the beaches, 747:4
Kilroy, 748:7
Kin
and kith, 250:6
Kind
be, 617:5
nobler to be k., 351:6
Kinder
gentler nation, 522:6
KINDNESS, 356
Kindness
little deeds of k., 302:1
nothing has happened except k., 357:4
of strangers, 357:2
King
can stand people's fighting, 314:6
every man a k.!, 520:1
good to be the k., 535:11
Naturalist is better than a k., 596:6
once more a k., 627:1
we elect a k. every four years, 543:1
when you strike at a k., 595:5
Kings
is mostly rapscallions, 314:3
Kiss
a k. is just a k., 610:2
of death, 676:4
K. K. Bang Bang, 72:5
Kisses, 390:1
Kissing
they go to k. one another, 448:6
Kitchen
get out of the k., 650:12
you are alone in the k., 262:13

Kitten
trouble with a k. is, 459:1
Kittens
wot have I done to deserve these k.?, 494:2
Knees
they fell upon their k., 32:6
Knight
like a plumed k., 311:5
Knights
It wasn't a game for k., 176:1
Knit
if you don't k. (note), 340:2
Know
better to k. nothing, 357:9 & note
how did they k.? 339:7
I k. nothing, 242:7 & note
it when see it, 103: 4
nothing but my Country, 516:1
one never k., do one?, 625:7
whence you came (note), 498:6
Know-Nothings (note), 516:1
Knowing
die k. something, 358:2
KNOWLEDGE & INFORMATION, 357
Knowledge
as k. expands, 359:1
between us we cover all k. (note), 246:2
& emotion and purpose, 358:3
& ignorance, 358:9
is the great sun, 357:7
is the knowing we cannot know, 357:8
is the recognition of something absent, 358:2
stored full of unused k., 358:1
trust your inner k., 614:5
Kodaks (note), 6:3
Korea
attack upon K., 359:2
I shall go to K., 360:2
what we are doing in K., 359:4
KOREAN WAR, 359
Kosmis
in my K. no feeva of discord, 687:10
Kuwait, 299:9 & 300:2

L.A.
to die in L.A., 127:4
LABOR. See CAPITALISM & CAPITAL v. LABOR, 99
Labor
[definition of], 100:2
& love, 736:2
all that serves l. (note to reader), 385:3
& capital, 99:6
disgraces no man, 99:8
in New England, 99:5
is true standard of value, 688:5
learn to l and to wait, 1:6
life of l., 736:3
love l., 735:4
omnia vincit, 485:3
those who l. in the earth, 251:7
Laboratories,
of democracy, 190:2
Ladies
little old l. in tennis shoes, 530:3
Lady
ain't no l.; she's my wife, 406:7
is serene, 404:1
no l. is ever a gentle man, 730:6
or the tiger?, 559:5
with a Lamp shall stand, 728:7
Lafayette we are here, 744:2
Laid end to end, 623:5
Lake Wobegon, 433:2
Lamarckian
& the growth of human culture, 599:3
Lambs
we are poor little l., 622:6
Land
abundance of vacant l., 280:4
area of free l., 281:2
a rough land, 162:8
as a community, 225:3
cheap l. & wages of labor, 280:5
convenient for building, 140:1
could not be far distant, 696:1
existence of free l., 281:2
fine l. to shun, 12:8
inherit the l. from our fathers, 557:3
life of the l. & righteousness, 307:7
my l., my home, 55:7
nothing but l., 281:5
of extremes & contrasts, 56:1
of steady habits, 162:3
of the Bad People, 399:9
of the Sky, 482:12
promised l., 291:6
seems forlorn (note), 286:7
stewardship of the l., 227:2
that peaceful l., 306:6
the l. we belong to is grand, 485:2
this l. is your l., 30:5
was ours, 29:3
we abuse the l., 225:3
where my fathers died, 501:2
Landon
life, liberty, and L., 520:5
Lands
and goods go to the strong, 557:6
determined to defend our l., 583:1
pleasant, with grass and flowers, 480:7
these l. are ours, 562:2
Landscape
this prehistoric l. (note), 611:6
LANGUAGE & WORDS, 360
Language
drawing on my fine command of l., 620:4
v. death and silence, 364:9
faults of American l., 361:1
has become debased in America, 361:2
is a virus from outer space, 365:1
is fossil poetry, 361:6
is the archives of history, 361:4
no l. for love within a family, 251:2
nothing in common with America except l., 447:
of the country he visits, 673:7
& world, 364:8
Lanterns
in the North Church steeple, 47:6
Laredo
the streets of L., 125:1
Lark
& music, 457:5
Las Vegas,
& a fortune, 125:2

Liberalism
& capitalism, 529:8
Liberated
the hell out of this place, 747:6
Liberators
we'll be greeted as l., 345:2
LIBERIA, 451:3
Libertas
ubi l. ibi patria (note), 274:1
Liberties
are gifts of God, 274:2
our l. we prize, 344:8
would give up essential l., 273:3
Liberty
and independence, 188:2
and independence forever, 274:6
and prosperity, 479:5
and union, 483:5
cost of l. v. cost of repression, 275:7
& eternal vigilance, 275:1 & note
give me l. or death, 273:7
God gave life & l., 273:5
inspire our souls, 273:6
is so much as powerful [give] weak, 275:5
lies in the hearts, 276:4
love of l. (note), 274:1
natural for l. to yield, 293:8
& order, 169:2
peace only under l., 410:5
power granted by l., 165:1
proclaim l., 273:2
& property, 556:10
right to l. and death, 275:4
security in this world, not l., 611:10
spirit of l., 275:6
& the powerful & weak, 276:5
tree of l. must be refreshed, 274:3
where l. dwells, 274:1
Libraries, 89:8 & 9
Lie
about the future, 200:6
a cat and a lie, 200:3
can get halfway around world, 200:1
can't tell a l., 199:7
don't l. if, 200:5
every word she writes is a l., 342:3
is an abomination & help, 200:2
is the handle, 199:9
they [skeletons] never l., 238:2
to tell a l. once, 199:28
Lied
one time or another, 199:10
Lies
no one ever l., 200:7
take the l. out of him, 338:2
LIFE, 380
Life
a broad margin to my l., 381:5
all the days of my life (note), 384:7
but one l. to lose, 49:2
consists in what a man is thinking, 380:8
consists of storm of thoughts, 431:4
& danger, 179:3
daily l., is the game, 384:4
dost thou love l.?, 380:2
events of life, 382:3
first half [versus] last half, 10:9
& having everything, 384:8
highest business is daily l., 384:4
is action and passion, 381:10
is a circle, 504:4
is a dangerous business, 382:4
is an offensive, 383:5
is a shadowy road, 381:9
is a solitary cell, 383:1
is but a span, 380:1
is like a pathless wood, 382:8
is mainly wasted time, 384:1
is marble and mud, 381:2
is not a business, 384:6
is one damn thing after another, 382:6
is one damn thing over and over, 383:3
is one long postponement, 383:9
is painting a picture, 382:7
is real, l. is earnest, 380:5
is second bests, 383:6
is series of footnotes (note), 383:12
is process of finding out too late, 384:3
is short, 384:12
is something to do when, 384:10
is the game, 382:1
is unfair, 384:5
is worth living, 382:2, 382:5
my life has been the poem, 381:1
& surprises, 380:6
liberty, and pursuit of happiness, 184:4
measured out my l. in coffee spoons, 382:10
realize l. while they live it?, 383:7
tends to go too long, 385:2
the terrors of l., 298:9
this thing called l., 445:3
tides of l., 380:7
what is l.?, 381:11
what makes l. so sweet, 381:8
Light
at end of tunnel, 693:2
& brother named Bright, 602:3
fantastic, 131:7 & note
Light! Land!, 32:4
put out the l., 367:9
& scale, 73:7
thousand points of, 31:4 & note
world is but thickened l., 601:7
Lightning
difference between l. bug and l., 362:1
he too l. from the sky, 272:7
Like
I know what I l., 62:2
Liked
but not well i., 257:4
Lilacs
when l. last in the dooryard bloomed, 633:1
Limousine
one perfect l., 394:3
LINCOLN (Kan.), 125
LINCOLN, ABRAHAM, 386
Lincoln
carrying L. home again, 386:8
memory of Abraham L. , 386:7
Line
in the sand, 300:2
on this l. if it takes all summer, 152:7
when I had crossed that l., 275:3
Lines,
know your l., 71:7

Lips
loose l. sink ships, 659:3
read my l., 661:9
Liquor
and love, 513:1
is quicker, 15:7
Listen
my children, 52:2
Literally
to read l., 374:7
Literary
genius, 75:9
man's reputation (note), 321:4
Literature
American l., 76:6
is my utopia, 88:8
is news, 74:9
loose popular l., 411:1
Little
deeds of kindness, 302:1
group of willful men, 161:2
make no l. plans, 630:5
nothing l. counts, 82:1
strokes & oaks, 194:2
things, 219:6
think l., 630:8
Live
all you can, 725:6
always getting ready to l., 380:4
as though Christ were coming, 250:1
can now only l. so long, 369:3
clean, think clean, 308:6
free or die, 478:7
he had decided to l. forever, 332:8
I wished to l. deliberately, 381:4
if I'd known I was going to l. this long, 308:9
I may l. too long, 486:1
to l., not to exist, 382:9
two can l. cheaper, 407:2
well, 380:3
you might as well l., 656:1
Lives
days of our l., 384:7
mysteries in l., 390 :7
of quiet desperation, 381:3
our l. carry us along, 384:11
Livin'
it takes a heap o' l., 319:4
Living
fever called "l.", 181:7
from the sweat of his brow, 736:7
gets his l. by such depressing devices, 738:4
getting a l., 736:6
fight like hell for the l., 382:11
is the trick, 384:9
less than two months old and tired of l., 17:3
on the edge, 87:3
tired of l., 17:3
well is the best revenge, 585:4
Living Room
the L. R. War, 693:6
Livingstone, Dr., 36:8
Lizzie Borden, see under Borden.
Loaf
I l. and invite my soul, 379:4
Loafer, 379:1
Lolita, 394:8
London
is epitome of our times, 125:6
it's still 1938 in L., 126:2
this is L., 745:1
LONELINESS. See SOLITUDE & LONELINESS, 631
Lonely
a silent, l. beauty, 145:2
Heart Is a L. Hunter, 309:10
I was born to be l., 631:9
things get l. in Washington, 146:7
Lonelyhearts
Miss L. are priests, 10:4
Lone Ranger (note), 312:3
Long
it takes as l. as it t. (note), 257:5
l. trail a-winding, 203:5
Longer
everything takes l. than you think (note), 676:6
Look
better to l. good, 54:10
don't l. back, 498:2
you could l. it up, 246:7
Looked
better to be l. over, 617:1
LOOKS. See BODY & LOOKS, 86
Loose
lips sink ships, 659:3
Lord
forgive O L. my little jokes, 538:9
grant that I may always be right, 538:3
has more truth and light, 288:1
I'll make a L. of him (note), 50:4
servant in the house of the L., 368:8
LOS ANGELES, 126
Los Angeles
a constellation of plastic, 112:9
a first-rate third world county, 127:1
the place where everything will fall, 127:1
Lose
as if you like it, 720:8
if you lose, 723:2
to have friends, l., 723:3
Loser
part of me suspects I'm a l., 614:2
good l., 644:5 (note), 720:6, 721:2
Losing
is the only American sin, 723:1
LOSING. See WINNING & LOSING, VICTORY & DEFEAT, 719
Lost
generation, 284:6
never have so few l. so much, 721:3
LOUISIANA, 387
Louisiana
in L. live-oak is the king, 387:3
poor people of L., 387:5
Lourdes
& fifteen years of therapy, 604:10
LOVE, 388
Love
all I want is boundless l., 391:6
& a poodle dog (note), 389:11
and marriage, 408:4
as rain falls so does your l., 390 :5
at the lips was touch as sweet, 389:10
breeds l., 392:3

good manners, 404:7
make the fortune, 404:3
morals & m., 404:12
require time, 404:4
stately m. of the old school, 404:8
Manunkind, 555:9
Many,
few v m., 564:6
out of, 20:5
so m. & so few, 300:4 & note
Maples, 464:7
March
a M. morning (note), 467:3
Marching
through Georgia, 154:1
Margaret
M's concert, 62:3
Marie of Roumania
I am M. of R., 390:3
Marine
another M. reporting, 746:6
Marines, 427:4 & 430:2
Marketplace
the truth of the m. (note), 277:5
MARRIAGE, 405
Marriage
[definition of], 406:9
a good m., 407:9, 408:7
a new m., 407:10
every m. is a battle, 408:8
heart of m. is memories, 408:9
is a romance, 408:10
is not m. an open question?, 406:1
keep eyes wide open before m., 405:3
love and m., 408:4
love-making & m., 407:8
love v. marriage, 406:10
must be a luxury, 406:5
must be protected, 407:4
& romance, 408:6
story ends with m., 406:2
the inquest, 407:3
without love, 622:1
Married
life & the fights, 408:2
climbs into their graves m., 407:7
I m. beneath me, 408:1
the m. & intimacy, 408:5
women are kept women, 407:6
Marries
who m. who is a small matter, 407:1
Marry
the men that women m., 406:6
Marrying
never again to think of m., 405:7
Mars
v. Venus, 271:3 & note
Marshall
John M. has made his decision, 656:5
Martini
dry m., 16:2 (and note)
something about a M., 16:1
MARYLAND, 408
Maryland
My Maryland!, 409:1
our summer in M., 408:12
was a raggedness, 409:12
Masculine
society dominated entirely by the m. principle, 665:7
tone is passing out of the world, 733:4
Mask
strike through the m.!, 54:6
MASSACHUSETTS, 409
Massachusetts
& the enterprise of its inhabitants, 409:5
has a good climate but, 409:9
have faith in M.!, 410:1
love of my heart is M., 409:4
settlers of M., 410:3
State of M., 409:5
Masses
action of m. of men, 507:9
huddled m., 37:1
sacrifice for the m., 189:4
Massive
retaliatory power, 268:7
Master
I would not be a m., 628:1
Matador, 646:4
Materialism, heroic, 101:7
Mathematical
the m. faculty, 450:4
Mathematician
union of the m. with poet, 600:6
MATHEMATICS. See under SCIENCE.
Mathematics
creation of the human spirit, 601:2
I don't believe in m., 601:4
In m. you don't understand things, you get used to them, 601:5
Maturity
condones, 10:17
May
all things possible in M., 467:4
the word M., 463:5
Mayflower
descendants, 217:5
my forefathers met the boat, 567:3
McClellan
Is not using the army, 151:3
McKinley v. Bryan, 517:6
Me
& you (note), 613:2
Meals
[the American] has no m., 260:7
lessen thy m., 307:8
Mean streets, 313:3
Means
by any m. that are necessary, 570:6 & note
ends & m., 244:5
discreditable m. & great results, 243:8
[he] m. well, 337:2
perfection of m., confusion of goals 437:9
Measure
you are what you m., 211:2
You Get What You M., 609:8
Meat
red m. and gin, 489:9
MEDIA, 411
Media
& privacy, 554:1
Medical
tyros, 201:4
in m. school, 202:5

MEDICINE. See DOCTORS & MEDICINE, 201
Mediocre
even if he is m., 415:1
if you hire m. people, 415:3
women want m. men, 414:9
MEDIOCRITY, 414
Mediocrity
intolerance of m., 414:8
of everything, 414:7
only sin is m., 415:2
smooth m., 414:5
some men have m. thrust upon them, 414:10
Medium
so called because, 412:4
which permits millions to listen to the same joke, 413:2
Meek
shall inherit the earth but, 591:2
Meet
me in St. Louis, 145:1
Mehitabel
dance, M., 487:1
Melancholy
days are come, 462:1
Melted
into a new race of men, 20:10
Melting pot
America Is the great m.p., 26:3
America not a m.p., 265:6
New City [not a] m.p., 134:8
Memorandum, 403:2
Memories
some m. are realities, 415:6
Members [of the House of Representatives], 162:2
MEMORY, 415
Memory
Americans are impatient with m., 415:8
life is all m., 540:9
& music, 415:7
nobody belongs to us except in m., 415:9
MEMPHIS (Tenn.), 128
MEN, 416
See also WOMEN & MEN.
Men
all m. would be tyrants, 732:3
and melons, 323:3
and women [are] different species, 734:8
a new race of m., 20:10
are from Mars, 735:2
are the weaker sex, 417:3
are what their mothers made them, 493:6
become m. at the cost of, 417:5
becoming the m. we wanted to marry, 732:1
build bridges, 416:5
difference between m. and boys, 668:9
first and subjects afterward, 274:7
have a much better time of it than women, 734:5
if m. & women suit each other, 734:7
if m. could get pregnant, 734:6
know so little of m., 324:8
lead lives of quiet desperation, 381:3
like peaches grow sweet, 420:1
little group of willful m., 161:2
many m., little time (note), 416:6
never mature, 417:2
not the m. in my life that counts, 308:5
taunted the lofty land with little m., 478:2
that women marry, 406:6
there lie many fighting m., 744:3
these m., cannot live in regular society, 690:2
two kinds of m. (note), 416:6
we are the hollow m., 264:1
who carry nations with them, 314:2
who will never lay down their arms (note), 34:7
& women [of California], 96:1
& women & talk, 170:10
Mendacity, 200:4
Merchants, 90:8
Merit
& baseball, 648:8
Mesa
plain of great antiquity, 479:7
Message to Garcia, 3:1
Metaphysics, 511:3
METHOD, 417
Method
disorderliness & m., 417:7
in business, 90:
take a m. and try it, 3:7
MEXICAN WAR, 418
MEXICO, 451
Mexico
Napoleon has no right to M., 451:4
poor M.!, 419:1
wasn't crazy about us (note), 418:8
Miami
is of unimaginable awfulness, 128:3
is more American, 128:6
Miami Beach
& air conditioning, 128:5
where neon goes to die, 128:4
Michelangelo, 170:4
MICHIGAN, 419:1
Michigan
& the machine & the North Country, 419:4
Milton must have traveled in M., 419:2
Michiganders
& Ford, 419:3
Middle
human nature to stand in the m., 333:4
way is none at all, 523:4
MIDDLE AGE & MIDLIFE, 419
Middle age
is when you've met so many people, 420:10
one of the pleasures of m. a., 420:6
the dead center of m. a., 420:9
they call that m. a., but, 421:1
Middle-aged, the, 420:8
MIDDLE CLASS, 421
Middle class
& equality, 421:4
melded into one m. c. 421:3
us m. c., 421:7
Middle West
& a great mail order company, 422:10
here the M. W. merges with the West, 474:7
Middletown, 129:3 & 4
Midnight
a m. dreary, 483:6
the m. clear, 110:4
MIDWEST, THE, 421
Midwest
puritanism and rich soil, 422:11
Mile
wide, an inch deep, 474:8

Modify
we "m." before we print, 102:6
Moider (sic)
I'll m. der bum, 645:6
Mom
a place called M's, 727:2
Moment
exhaust the little m., 540:18
I live only in the m., 5:2
seize the m., 3:2
the one present m., 540:9
the present m. of time, 540:5
Momentum
is fragile, 723:4
MONEY & THE RICH, 438
Money
a blessing when we part with it, 440:5
and morality, 235:3
as beautiful as roses, 439:3
dealers in m., 92:4
& differences, 438:10
don't grow old without m., 488:3
& experience, 95:4
follow the m., 442:6
follows power, 443:1
if you can count your m., 442:2
if you would know the value of m., 438:8
is always fashionable, 440:1
is power, freedom, 441:6
is sweeter than honey, 438:35
is the mother's milk of politics, 530:1
is the root of all evil (note), 441:6
love of m., 22:1
power to make m., 440:2
pretty soon you're talking about real m., 442:4
previntion of croolty to m. (note), 440:2
ready m., 438:6
ready m. of human experience, 561:6
should circulate like rainwater, 441:12
take half my m. from me, 661:4
that's where the m., 176:4
they say m. doesn't stink, 441:9
& toilet paper, 448:9
use it or lose it, 441:13
was like sex, 442:3
when m. talks, 441:8
will find a way, 443:4
will not make you happy, 441:13
Monkey
disappointed in the m., 290:1
Monkeys, 457:8 & 622:9
Monogamous
higgamus, hoggamus, woman's m., 616:4
Monopoly
every m., 91:4
is business, 92:8
Monroe Doctrine, 266:4
Monsters
to destroy, 21:6
MONTANA, 443
Montana
graveyards aren't big enough, 443:5
High, Wide, and Handsome, 443:6
I am in love with M., 443:7
Is a splash of grandeur, 443:8
Montani
semper liberi, 717:5
Montezuma
from the halls of M., 426:2
Moon
ascending, 468:2
blessed m., 340:4
don't let's ask for the m., 302:9
here men first set foot on the m., 608:6
if the m.'s a balloon, 468:6
is a desert (note), 608:5
is a different thing to each of us, 469:1
is a friend, 468:9
is a griffin's egg, 468:3
is the mother of pathos, 468:8
like the m. had fallen on me (note), 40:3
rising m., 467:9
& star-spangled banner, 605:7
Moonlight, 468:4
Moose
as strong as a bull m., 526:4
Moral
courage, 235:7
crisis & neutrality, 236:4
equivalent of war, 492:6
is what you feel good after, 235:10
questions, 235:9
sense, 622:7
victories, 236:8
MORALITY. See ETHICS & MORALITY, 235
Morality
basis of m., 236:3
money and m., 235:3
cannot be legislated, 375:2
Morally
acting m., 236:9
Morals
& manners, 404:12
not exact in his m., 235:1
three-quarters manners, 404:12
two sets of m., 235:8
use our m. on weekdays, 235:5
Mordre
wol out (note), 173:1
More
Is Different, 602:6
is more (note), 60:6
less is m., 60:6
we want m., 100:5 & note
would have been less (note), 60:6
Mormons
let the M. have the territory to themselves, 687:5
Mornin'
oh what a beautiful m., 470:8
Morning
air is awash with angels, 470:9
always m. somewhere, 490:7
get up the m. and laugh, 470:11
glorious m. for America, 48:2
I hate to get up in the m., 470:5
It's m. in America, 522:5
let me with the m. rise, 469:6
sympathy with m., 308:1
MOSCOW (Russia), 128
Moscow
is downhill, 129:1
Mother
a boy's best friend is his m., 494:11
American m., 495:5

earth is the m. of all people, 565:1
I'm still your m., 495:6
Knows Best, 494:3
m's advice is safest, 494:1
my m,, drunk or sober (note), 500:1
no such slave as a m., 493:8
socially ambitious m., 494:6
too much m., 495:2
what is home without a m., 493:7
what the m. sings to the cradle, 493:9
Mothers
free race cannot be born of slave m., 730:3
men are what their m. made them, 493:6
speak the same tongue, 494:5
Motivation
what's my m.?, 71:5
Motorcycle
are of m. maintenance, 609:1
& art of rationality, 575:8
Mountaineers
are always free, 717:4
Mountains
are earth's monuments, 455:1
I'll scrape the m. clean, 223:3
Mourned
I m. and yet shall mourn, 386:2
Mousetrap
better m., 240:4
Mouth
his mouth & his foot, 343:4
the bigger the m., 725:4
shut, 620:6
Movement
never lies, 63:8
Moves
if it m., salute it, 426:4
MOVIES. See under ART.
Moving
In what direction we are m., 2:5
Much
too much of a good thing, 241:5
Muckrake
with a m. in his hand (note), 549:5
Muckrakes
men with the m., 549:5
Mugwump, 361:9 & 516:5
MUNCIE (Ind.), 129
Munitions, 427:4
Murder
I love m., 177:3
never m. a man who is committing suicide, 241:3
shrieks out (note), 173:1
will speak out of stone walls, 173:1
Murdered
by a Traitor (note), 174:2
I m. my father, 174:4
Murderers
first-class m., 118:2
Mushroom hunters, 262:11
MUSIC. See ART: MUSIC, 63
Music
and art and poetry, 59:1
classic m., 65:1
heard so deeply, 65:8
I heard with you, 394:1
if m. appears to express something 65:7
memory & m., 415:7
is the universal language, 63:9
night shall be filled with m., 63:10
talking/writing about m., 66:5 & note
Van Gogh's ear for m., 342:4
when people hear good m., 64:9
Must
a man does what he m., 236:3
we do what we m., 243:7
My
country, 'tis of thee, 501:2
Myself
am hell (note), 398:9
I sing m., 613:2
I dote on m., 613:3
I should not talk so much about m., 613:1
Mysteries
talk of m. (note), 559:4
three great m., 390 :7
Mysterious
[is the] most beautiful thing, 444:7
MYSTERY. See MYSTICISM & MYSTERY, 444
Mystery
is antagonist of truth, 444:1
ultimate m. of things, 444:3
now comes the m., 367:6
the greatest m., 445:3
Mystic
can live happily, 444:5
is invulnerable, 444:4
MYSTICISM & MYSTERY, 444
Mysticism
& knowledge of God, 445:2
Mystics
& science , 444:6
Mystify
mislead and surprise, 423:5
Myth
bigger than the m., 550:10

NAFTA, 210:4
Nail
for want of a n., 629:3
Naked City, the, 134:9
Name
as long as they spell my n. right, 549:4
their n. is on your water, 563:1
what kind of n. he had, 582:3
Names
American n., 363:3
slang n., 24: 6
ugly n., 365:2
Nantucket, 409:7
Napalm
in the morning, 694:3
Narcissist, new, 54:5
NASHVILLE (TENN.), 129
Nation
[with] eleven time zones, 452:3
fate of a n. was riding, 52:3
favors from n. to n., 265:10
if we're an arrogant n., 270:6
kinder, gentler n., 522:6
march of a n., 21:4
n.'s finances, 206:6
n.'s honor, 321:4
no n. was ever ruined by trade, 90:6
of human progress, 22:5

Nominated
    I will not accept if n., 543:3
Nonviolence
    is a just weapon, 493:2
    is organized love, 493:4
    is the greatest thing, 493:4
NONVIOLENCE. See PACIFISM & NONVIOLENCE, 492
Normalcy
    return to n., 519:1
    strive for n. 38:3 & note
Norman's Woe, 619:1
North
    to the future, 13:7
    traveling n., 674:5
NORTH CAROLINA, 481
North Carolina
    Garden of Eden in N. C., 482:5
    is a valley of humility, 482:3
    less labor [needed] in N. C., 481:4
NORTH DAKOTA, 482
North Dakota
    experiences in N. D., 483:1
    is a doomed state, 482:7
Not a penny! (note), 34:1
Nothing
    a lot we don't know about n. 601:6
    between grief and n., 633:3
    people on whom n. is lost, 701:3
    progress yet n. has changed, 556:6
    to look forward to, 193:5
Novel
    de-furnished, (note) 60:2
    the business of the n., 74:7
November, 464:1 & 464:4
Now
    Dasher! n. Dancer! 110:1
    I live n., 540:1
    is the time to make real the promises, 43:6
    I've laid me down to die, 233:1
    plan executed now! 418:2
    word "n." is like a bomb, 540:10
Nuclear giants, 236:1
Nuisance, a, 373:11
Numbers
    all these n. (note), 210:1
    constitute the only universal language, 601:3
    no safety in n., 611:5
Nutriment
    gnaw the earth for n., 282:4
Nuts!, 748:4

OAKLAND (CAL.), 137:2
Oaks
    & little strokes, 194:2 & note
Oars
    with muffled o. (note), 337:3
Objective
    correlative, 60:1
    sources, 546:9
Objects
    inanimate o., 668:7
Obligations
    & privileges, 584:7
Obscenity, 278:2
Obvious
    analysis of the o., 597:1
OCCULT, THE, 483
Occupiers, we are not o., 346:1
Ocean
    I went into the o., 32:5
OCEANS. See under NATURE.
Oceanus, 462:6
Ocian [Ocean]
    in view!, 34:5
October
    point home in old 0., 466:5
Offense
    is best defense, 86:9
Offer
    he can't refuse, 94:6
Office
    Man who makes the o., 692:1
    more time at the o. (note), 95:3
    most insignificant o. that ever man contrived, 691:4
    never ask, never refuse an o., 735:6
    second o. of the land, 691:5
    See also under Public office
Offices
    as public trusts (note), 295:5
Oh say, can you see, 499:11
OHIO, 484
Ohio
    is farthest west of the east, 484:1
    why did I ever leave O.?, 484:3
Ohio River
    & [Cincinnati], 121:2
O.K. (note), 514:4-515
    I'm O.K.—You're O.K., 604:7
Okie
    use' ta mean you was from Oklahoma, 484:7
OKLAHOMA, 484
Oklahoma
    they swarmed on O., 484:6
    throw out anything in O., 484:5
    where the wind comes sweepin' down the plain, 485:1
Old
    age and broken health, 193:4
    age is 15 years older than I am, 488:8
    age is like an opium dream, 486:7
    age is not for sissies (note), 489:4
    age is unexpected thing (note), 486:4
    beautiful o. lady, 488:4
    called an o. man, 486:4
    disorderly o. age, 487:2
    don't grow o. without money, 488:3
    Folks at Home, 636:2
    forlorn rags of growing old, 488:9
    getting o. ain't for sissies, 489:4
    growing o., 486:2
    how o. would you be if, 489:6
    I grow o., I grow o., 486:8
    I'm getting o. and coming apart, 489:7
    it is time to be o., 486:3
    man in a dry month, 486:9
    Man of the Mountain (note), 478:1
    man who will not laugh, 10:11
    man is not o. until, 488:6
    no such thing as o. age, 487:6
    no time like the o. time, 497:6
    one advantage of getting o., 489:5
    reverence [for] what is o. (note) 438:10

Paved
they p. paradise, 226:6
Pay-as-you-go, 209:5
Pays
who p. us, 442:10
PEACE, 504
Peace
America & world peace, 506:6
and harmony with all, 266:1
best hope for p. is freedom, 277:3
better to live in p., 505:3
between equals, 505:5
by the sword he seeks p., 410:5
cannot be kept by force, 506:1
declare p.. upon the world, 506:4
hath higher tests of manhood, 504:9
I am willing to fight for p., 493:1
inner, 54:3
is a process, 506:8
is the way, 506:9
it isn't enough to talk about p., 506:5
I wanted to see p., 742:4 (note)
just and lasting p., 154:2
let us have p., 36:6 & 505:2
like charity, begins at home, 506:2
make a desert call it p. (note), 267:1
made wilderness called it p. (note), 267:1
must be kept by men, 506:7
never was a bad p., 504:8
no justice no p., 352:9
of justice, 267:1
on earth, 110:4 & 100:5
open covenants of p., 505:6
price too great to pay for p., 505:4
separate p., 505:7
take chances for p., 269:1
who desires p. should prepare for war (note), 702:9
without victory & between equals, 37:6
world p. or world destruction, 506:3
Peaceful
be p., be courteous, 695:2
coexistence, 270:1
Peach, ripest, 17:9
Peale
Paul appealing and P.. appalling, 432:3
Pecos
Law West of the P. (note), 372:4
no law west of the P., 664:6
Peculiar
institution, 627:4
Pecuniary interest, 439:6
Pedigree
of honey, 216:7
Pelican, 458:2
Peninsula
a pleasant p., 419:16
PENNSYLVANIA, 507
Pennsylvania
in P. this morning!, 507:5
is heaven for farmers, 507:1
is the Keystone, 507:2
mind was not complex, 507:3
Penny
saved is a p. earned, 438:9
PEOPLE, THE, 507
People
about one-fifth of the p. are against everything, 509:5
a humorless soldierly p., 453:8
are capable of anything, 176:7
are turbulent (note), 508:4
are universally kind, 663:8
change, 105:3
civilization & progress of the p., 508:1
common-looking p., 86:1
consensus of the p., 509:9
government belongs to the p., 296:5
government of the p., by the p., 26:6 & 287:1 l am the p., 508:7
if the p. be the governors, 188 :8
in the island are unpolished, 588:6
let my p. go, 626:4
most interesting p. in world, 28:1
& preservation of liberty, 507:7
slender p., 309:1
sober 2nd thought of the p., 188:10
some p. stay longer in an hour, 299:6
superior p. & long visits, 299:8
the great hero was The P. (note), 385:3
the p. come first, 336:10
the p. have spoken, 509:7
the p. rule, 57:7, 635:8
the p.'s Constitution & government, 294:4
the p.'s government & the p.'s business, 190:8
the p.'s government, made by the p., 294:4
these p. must die out, 564:2
ultimate justice of the p., 508:2
underestimating the intelligence of the p. (note), 509:1 & note
voice of the p. (note), 508:4
we first crush p. to the earth, 562:6
welfare of the p., 436:1
we the p., 165:1
when you meet p. (note), 232:1
where the p. possess no authority, 535:1
who know how to run the country, 245:14
who want to feel important, 552:2
will live on, 509:3
will of the p. & foundation of government, 507:8
you can fool too many of the p. (note), 508:3
you may fool all the p. some of the time, 508:3
PEOPLES,
see RACES & PEOPLES, 562
PEORIA (Ill.), 138
Peoria
will it play in P.?, 138:6 & note
PERCEPTION. See VISION & PERCEPTION, 701
Perdicaris
alive, 37:4
Perdition
hottest corner of p. (note), 55:8
Perfect
Thirty-six, 662:2
Storm, 677:5
Perfection
falling short of p., 257:5
Perform
over-p., 85:6
Permission slip, 271:6
PERSEVERANCE. See DETERMINATION, EFFORT, PERSISTENCE, & PERSEVERANCE, 194
Perseverance, 195:6
Persian messengers (note), 472:7

for man's habitation, 696:4
great, uninteresting p., 118:7
I pitched upon this p., 143:9
in the procession, 589:8
it was the best p. to be, 253:1
last best p. on earth, 443:9
most typically Amencan p., 118:8
my God, what is there in this p.?, 543:2
of moral leadership, 544:9
this cursed, p.!, 48:4
this is the p.!, 687:4
with most cows and least milk, 665:2
Plagiarism, 74:8
Plain
ran till it touched heaven, 474:3
Plains
of Kansas and Nebraska, 422:8
of Nebraska, 474:2
Plan
good p. executed now!, 418:2
Plans
make no little p. 630:5
Plane
if that p. leaves and you're not with him, 496:1
Planet
one look at this p., 227:1
vulnerability of our p., 225:10
Plant
I'm not a potted p., 378:7
PLANTS. See under NATURE.
Plastics
just one word p., 94:5
Platform
party p., 527:2
Plato, 511:1
Play
it, Sam , p. "As Time Goes By", 65:9
"Precious Lord" (note), 368:9-369
PLEASURE & HEDONISM, 512
Pleasure
an age of p., 512:6
[as a] guide, 62:6
left out of the p., 513:2
& life [in Paris], 137:4
& understanding, 512:5
Pleasures
high and serious, 59:4
man is richest whose p. are the cheapest, 512:7
Ploughshare
smoothly the p. runs, 387:2
Plum
survives its poems, 261:3
Plums, 261:2 & note
Pluribus Unum, 20:5
PLYMOUTH (MASS.), 140
Plymouth Rock
cornerstone of a nation, 409:8
landed on us, 570:5
Pnin, 214:4
POCATELLO (IDAHO), 140:2
Pocketbook
full p. often groans, 441:10
Poem
and a musical voice (note), 68:12-69
as lovely as a tree, 471:6
figure a p. makes, 68:4
is a meteor, 68:1
is a nature created by poet (note), 67:13-68
should not mean but be, 67:9
ways to ruin a p., 68:7
Poems
news from p., 68:8
Poet
courage of the p., 67:7
priest of the invisible, 68:3
with a p. in your pocket, 66:7
world waiting for its p., 67:2
POETRY. See ART: POETRY, 66
Poetry
& music, 67:11
can communicate before understood, 67:10
cleanses, 68:9
[is] emotion remembered in (note), 327 :4
golden age of p. and power, 292:7
is way of taking life by the throat, 68:5
is always unexpected, 68:11
is a phantom script (note), 67:8
is opening and closing of a door, 67:8
political, 68:12
is the subject of the poem, 67:13
[is] the rhythmical creation of beauty, 67:1
[is] the supreme fiction (note), 67:13-68
must be new as foam, 67:3
of words, 67:1
publishing p., 67:5
serves great ends (note), 67:13
& the inexplicable, 68:2
their pastime and delight, 63:9
what p. does, 68:10
v. power (note), 535:10
Poets
great p. & audiences, 67:4
immature p. imitate, 67 :6
'S wives, 68:6
Pointy-headed (note), 217:8-218
Police action
a limited war, 360:2 & note
Policeman's nightstick, 372:1
Politeness
& flattery, 405:2
Political
action is highest responsibility, 530:2
campaign & prosperity, 527:9
education & knowledge of human nature, 527:7
p. institutions, 336:5
p. question & judicial question, 371 :7
slavery, 38:4
POLITICAL SLOGANS, 513
Politician
best p.'s money can buy, 589:3
honest p. stays bought, 524:7
is an arse, 529:8
never forgets a favor, 527:4
tin-horn p., 303:8
who is given a job abroad, 198:10
Politicians, 528:6
are doing the best they can (note), 528:6
not over a year behind public opinion, 528:6
Politics
all p. is applesauce, 528:3
all p. is local, 529:1
are based on indifference of the majority, 402:5
are impossible without spoils, 525:8
as a profession, 528:2
expediency and morality in p., 530:7
fashion to despise "p.", 524:6

nothing that makes more cowardly men than p.o., 558:7
& politicians, 559:2
polls, 509:4
& power, 558:3
we are ruled by p.o., 558:9
world of p.o., bullhorn is king, 559:3
Publishers
are demons, 411:3
Publishing business,
& constitutional protection, 169:7-170
Puddle-wonderful, 465:7
Pulpit
bully p., 544:2
Pumpkin pie
hurrah for the p. p.!, 666:10
rich p.p., 666:9
Punishments
cruel and unusual p. (Amendment 8), 83:3
Puppy
happiness is a warm p., 302:11
Purcell
here lies John P., 228:2
Pure
and good like us, 268:1
as the driven slush, 624:1
Puritanism, 236:2
Puritans
'twas founded be th' P. to give thanks, 667:5
gave the world action, 2:4
Purple cow, 197:5
Purse
light p., heavy heart, 532:5
Put
on something more comfortable, 254:9
out the light, 367:9

Quaker
instincts from his Q. forebears, 343:2
Quakerism
meekness of Q., 523:6
Quantum
if q. mechanics is right, 603:3
if you aren't confused by q. physics (note), 602:1
Quarreled
did not know we had ever q. (note), 367:2
Quarrels
spoil our prayers, 55:1
Quarter
I never took a q., 528:2
Quayle, Dan, 342:6
Queen of the West, 120:9 & note
Queens
in history compare favorably, 729:5
Queensboro Bridge, 133:1
Question
to ask the hard q., 559:8
what is the q?, 368:6
QUESTIONS & ANSWERS, 559
Questions
& research, 559:6
better to ask some of the q., 560:1
goddess is in the q., 560:8
critical q. that are insoluble, 511:4
soluble q. that are trivial, 511:4
some q. don't have answers, 560:7
there aren't any embarrassing q., 560:5
which one asks oneself, 560:3
Qui Transtulit, 163:5
Quiet
all q., 150:3
Crisis, 226:1
hog (note), 98:5
Quitters, 195:3
Quits
man [is] finished when he q., 722:5
Quitter
I have never been a q., 713:3
Quitters
never win, 643:3
Quotation
I hate q., 560:10
should come unsought, 561:11
the act of repeating erroneously the words of another, 561:7
QUOTATIONS & PROVERBS, 560
Quote
monkey of a man is to q. him, 561:8
we all q., 561:5
Quoted
by other learned authors, 560:9
Quoter
& originator, 561:4

Race
benefit from benign neglect, 571:8
is not always to the swift, 645:4
take account of r., 572:4
these are the faults of an oppressed r., 563:3
RACES & PEOPLES, 562
Racism
& America, 569:5
beyond r., 572:4
& integrated community, 572:2
is not an excuse, 573:5
Radical
is a man with, 529:4
Raft
no home like a r., 619:9
Railroad
iron is a magician's rod, 604:11
rides upon us (note), 605:4
Rain
beautiful is the r!, 472:5
into each life some r. must fall, 674:9
it raineth all around (note), 661:2
Rainbow
our nation is a r., 31:2
sign, 586:7
somewhere over the r., 302:8
Rainier, Mt., 709:3
Raisin
in the sun, 204:3
Rally
'round the flag, 152:3
Range
home on the r., 714:6
Rangers
lead the way (note), 747:4
Rape
ruin and run, 226:10
Rascals
turn the r. out, 516:3
would you live for ever? (note), 744:5
Rattlesnake
bites and scorpion stings, 664:7

hisses a tune at my head (note), 474:1
poised to strike, 595:6
Rattlesnakes
to take this country away from the r., 97:3
Raven
quoth the R., 229:2
Razors
pain you, 656:1
Reactionary
is a somnambulist, 529:6
Read
every man able to r., 211:6
my lips, 661:9
the best books, 87:7
Reader, your, 76:5
READING. See BOOKS & READING, 87
Reading
a love of r., 89:5
creative r., 87:6
& details, 89:4
I prefer r., 88:12
Read
every man able to r., 211:6
my lips, 661:9
Rebellion
to tyrants, 48:6
Ready
always R., 426:7
Real
washed in the speechless r., 574:7
Realistic
decision, 183:6
Reality
& pigments of the past, 574:11
has strangled invention, 75:3
humankind cannot bear very much r., 574:4
in [America] r. is always material r., 574:5
is our ally, 575:1
minds are not here simply to copy a r. (note), 74:7
must take precedence over public relations, 609:3
we crave only r., 573:10
REALITY ILLUSIONS, & IMAGES, 573
REASONS & REASONABLE PEOPLE, 575
Reason
every man's own r. his oracle, 575:3
human form with r. fled, 397:8
if we would guide by the light of r., 373:13
let us r. together, 575:7 & note
Reasonable
convenience to be a r. creature, 575:2
Reasons
man always has two r. for what he does, 575:6
yours v theirs, 575:9
Rebel
I'm a good old r., 637:2
Rebels
Are our countrymen, 154:3
Rebellion
little r. now and then, 586:1
to tyrants, 681:5
Recession
v. depression, 209:3
Record
let's look at the r., 246:4
Red
better dead than R. (note) 158:5
better R. than dead, 158:5
when the last r. man shall have vanished, 563:5
Redeeming social importance, 278:2
Red River, 697:8
Red Sox, 47:3
Redwood,
once you've seen one r., 471:11
Redwoods, 471:10
Reform
has no gratitude, 524:4
is affirmative, 524:3
Reformer
can't last (note), 526:5
Reformers
Only Morning Glories, 526:5
Region
of shacks and hovels, 717:2
REGRET, 575
Regret
is useless, 575:11
never waste a moment on r., 576:7
one r. in life is that I am not someone else, 576:8
to r. deeply, 575:10
Regrets
hope to end up with the right r., 576:9
& opportunity, 576:2
take the place of dreams, 488:6
Reign
of error, 598:1
Relationship
discussing if r. existed, 734:9
Relaxed
Man, 98:6
RELIGION, 576
Religion
an establishment of r. (Amendment 1), 82:3
country that has the least r., 579:2
& egotism, 579:4
enables us to ignore nothingness, 581:5
is a man's total reaction, 579:3
is the love of life, 579:7
my r. is to do good, 235:2
respect the other fellow's r., 580:2
start your own r., 580:4
test of a r. or philosophy, 510:1
that shocks the mind of a child, 577:6
that old-time r., 579:8
science without r. & r. without science, 579:12
Religious
cosmic r. experience, 579:9
duties, 577:4
factions, 21:8
deeply r. nonbeliever, 580:8
we are a r. people, 580:6
Remarkable, wish to be, 17:7
Remarks
famous r., 561:9
REMEDIES. See ILLNESS & REMEDIES, 330
Remember
the Alamo!, 35:2
the Maine, 468:4
things I can r. that aren't so (note), 415:5
when I was young I could r. anything, 415:5
Rendezvous
with death, 742:6
with destiny, 285:2
RENO (NEV.), 141
Rented
never washed a r. car, 211:3

in your heart you know he's r., 522:1
is more precious than peace, 592:4 & (note) 743:2
is not what someone gives you, 593:8
makes might, 699:3
man more r. than his neighbors, 401:5
not wrong but r., 35:5
of privacy, 553:5 & 553:6
people who think they are r., 592:2
rather be r. than be president, 542:3
rather than consistent, 164:5
respect for the r., 371:9
rise above principle and do r., 592:8
"r.-thinking men", 592:7
struggle between r. and wrong, 270:3
the r. [is] expedient, 244:22
time is always ripe to do r., 592:5
to be let alone, 168:2 & 553:1
to criticize, 277:6
to go to hell, 593:6
to his property, 592:11
to liberty and death, 275:4
wing conspiracy, 531:9

Right-of-way
died defending his r.o.w, 475:7

Righteous
armor of a r. cause, 591:8

Righteousness,
between r. and peace, I choose r., 592:3
like a mighty stream, 43:2

RIGHTS, 592

Rights
animal r., 460:4
bill of r., 165:2
equal r., 750:5
human r. v property r., 593:3
& independent of government, 593:9
no such thing as r., 593:4
of every man diminished, r. of one are threatened, 593:7
of minorities, 568:3
of nation's citizens, 375:7
property in his r. 592:11
states' rights, see under States
they have r. who dare maintain them, 593:1
they will sacrifice the most for, 593:5
unalienable r., 184:4
we dare defend our r., 12:3
whose r. I trample under foot, 593:2

Risked
I r. much, 439:10

Risks
take calculated r., 87:1

River
cross over the r., 367:4
is more than an amenity, 224:3
red r., red r., 697:8
seems a magic thing, 455:10

Rivers
drain the r. dry, 223:3
we turn our r. into sewers, 223:9

Road
I take to the open r., 674:5
is paved with yellow brick, 674:6

Roads
country r., take me home, 717:3
two r, diverged in a wood, 576:1

Rob
the poor, 173:3
some will r. you with a pen, 175:7
why do you r. banks?, 176:4

Robbed
we wuz r.!, 645:1

Robotics
three fundamental Rules of R. 607:5

ROCHESTER (N.Y.), 141

Rock
a speck of r., 259:1

Rock Candy Mountains, 687:11

Roll
let's r.!, 46:6

Rolling Stone
Like a, 319:7

Romance
marriage interferes with r., 408:6
marriage is a romance, 408:10

ROME (ITALY), 142

Rome
dark cloud coming from R. (note), 385:3
grandeur that was R., 445:5
I've seen R., 142:2
more imagination wanted at R., 142:1
was a poem, 142:3

Room
at the top, 652:2
enough [in America], 280:3
in a smoke-filled r., 527:11
of one's own, 204:9

ROOSEVELT, FRANKLIN DELANO, 593

ROOSEVELT, THEODORE, 594

Roosevelt
for ex-President, 520:6
is dead (note), 368:5
let's re-re-elect R., 520:7
Niagara Falls and Theodore R. (note), 594:4
was like your first bottle of champagne, 593:11
was pure act, 594:5 & note

Root hog, or die, 514:1

Rose
is a r. is a r., 461:6
lives its little hour, 460:6
one perfect r., 394:3

Rosebud, 368:4, 576:5

Rough and Ready, 514:3

Rough-tough
we're the stuff!, 639:4

Round up the usual suspects, 176:2

Rowing,
[is] obscure sport, 649:5

Rugged
individualism, 27:10

Ruin
I will r. you, 585:3
the r. in things, 450:1

Rule
may none but honest men r., 541:5
some men are born to r., 295:2

RULERS. See HIGH P0SITION: RULERS & LEADERS, 314

Rules
There are no r., 612:3

Rum
demon r., 14:2
Romanism, and rebellion, 516:4

RUMOR, 595

Rumor travels faster, 595:1

Rumors are always true, 595:2

Sin
all s. addictive, 624:7
fashions in s., 239:4
only people who should really s., 623:8
physicists have know s., 597:9
travels faster than, 622:4
Sincerity, 320:10 & note
Sing
Lift Ev'ry Voice and S., 647
Singers
God sent his s.64:1
Single
a s. man, 405:4
Sins
of the cold-blooded, 296:3
punished by our s., 622:10
Si quaeris peninsulam amoenam, 419:6
Sisters
big s., 251:1
wayward s., 149:9
Sixteen
to one, 517:3
Size
no virtue goes with s., 81:7
of a dime & heart of a dollar, 125:5
SKEPTICISM, 625
Skepticism
is the chastity of the intellect, 625:6
Skies
blue s. smiling, 468:7
spacious, 24:7
scale the walls of people's s., 625:11
Skinny
can never be too s. or too rich, 442:5
Skugg
here S. lies snug, 228:3
Skunk
approach too close to a s. (note), 545:2
SKY. See under NATURE.
Sky
is daily bread of the eyes, 467:10
preoccupation with the sky. 469:2
the Land of the S., 482:2
Slang
rolls up its sleeves, 364:5
Slave
as I would not be a s., 628:1
death is a s.'s freedom, 571:5
half s. and half free, 627:6
in giving freedom to the s., 628:4
in this s. country (note), 35:5
see how a s. was made a man, 627:5
system on our place, 629:2
SLAVERY, 626
Slavery
badge of s. (note), 42:3
mine is a situation of dignified s., 541:8
object is not either to save or destroy s. 628:2
'our peculiar institutions' (note), 627:4
political s., 38:4
& selfishness, 627:3
& shocks & convulsions (note), 627:3
where s. is, there liberty cannot be, 628:5
wrecks of s., 637:3
Slaves
persons held as s. shall be free (note), 628:3
persons held as s. shall be free, 152:2
SLEEP. See DREAMS & SLEEP, 204
Sleep
in s. we all lie naked, 205:5
they shall not s. on our soil, 709:1
we never s., 173:6
Sleeps
every idle knave, 204:10
Slender people, 309:1
Slide
Kelly, S., 641:5
SLOGANS, POLITICAL. See POLITICAL SLOGANS, 513
Slowly
worth doing s., 305:1
SLOWNESS. See HASTE V. GOING SLOW. 305
Sluggard
up s., 205:1
Slum
if you've seen one s., 113:2
Small
is beautiful (note), 630:8
SMALLNESS, DETAILS & OTHER SMALL THINGS, 629
Smile
torn animals removed from that s. (note), 342:3
when you call me that, s., 179:4
Smith, Alfred, 38:6
Smithy
village s., 736:4
Smoke
-filled room, 527:11
man of no conversation should s., 672:3
never to s. more than one cigar, 672:5
Smoking
pistol (note), 712:1
Snake
stood up for evil, 196:7
white s. or black s., 573:3
Snapshots, 74:2
Snare
for the truth, 72:1
Snobs
effete corps of s., 218:5
Snow
I used to be S. White, 683:3
neither s., nor rain, 472:7
one s. a winter, 467:7
Snug
as a bug, 228:3
Soap
and education, 212:9
Social leveling, 234:5
SOCIALISM, 631
Socialism
paternalism and s. (note), 27:10
I am for s. 631:2
Socialist
before he is forty, 631:3
Socially
secure, the, 217:4
Society
dominated by the masculine principle, 665:7
Great S., 45:1 & 521:6
high s., 217:3
is spiritually a desert, 78:2
our s. is neither scientific nor splendid, 697:4
property is a creature of s., 557:1

are planned by old men, 705:4
are won by men, 705:5
& bombing, 424:3
not going to be sent into any foreign w., 745:3
WASHINGTON, D.C., 146
WASHINGTON, GEORGE, 709
Washington
central star of the constellation, 146:3
character of W. is a fixed star, 711:3 commanded the sun and the moon to stand still, 709:6
crazy in W., 146:8
fought on-and won (note), 720:5
friend of mankind (note), 709:6-710 goes around in circles, 147:5
if you want a friend in W., 147:2
is a city of Southern efficiency, 147:6
is a company town, 147:8
is Hollywood for [the] ugly, 147:9
is a puzzling state, 709:4
is full of famous men, 146:6
isn't a city, 147:4
look to the city of W., 146:4
never slopt over!, 711:4
stand with W., 513:4
things get lonely in W., 146:7
things wrong with W., 147:3
thou hero, patriot sage, 710:1
W. en petit, 114 :8
was created for a purpose, 147:1
what posterity will say of W. (note), 709:6-710
Waste
national vice is w., 29:7
Wasteland
vast w., 412:8
Watch what we do, 4:5
Watches of the night, 470:4
Watchful waiting, 267:3
Watching
observe a lot by w. (note), 647:7
Water
sweet w. from a foul well?, 60:5
little drops of w., 629:5
WATERGATE, 711
Watermelon, 260:10 & note
Waters, Father of, 152:5
Watson
Mr. W., come here, 605:8
Waving the bloody shirt, 525:5
Way
best w: of doing everything, 417:8
out or way in?, 655:12
to do it better, 417:10
We
are all Republicans/all Federalists, 683:7
are coming Father Abraham, 151:7
we are descended not only from monkeys, 622:9
don't have to be what you want us to be, 572:7
fight and fight again, 50:6
hold these truths to be self-evident, 184:4 (paragraph 2)
know we belong to the land, 485:2
we must cut our way out, 151:2
never sleep, 173:6
raise de wheat, 626 :2
shall meet the enemy (note), 325:8
shall overcome, 569:4
talked between the rooms (note), 329:1
the people, 165:1
the word "w.", 362:2
want more, 100:5
we'll stand pat, 517:7
we're history's actors, 4:7
were very tired very merry, 302:4
wuz robbed!, 645:1
were very many, and you were few, 626 :2
we will speak our own minds, 614:7
Weak
speak for the fallen and w., 532:6
WEALTH. See RICH & POOR, WEALTH & POVERTY, 589
Wealth
an aristocracy of w., 216:6
& inheritance, 590:4
conventional standard of w., 439:9
Impunity [same as] W., 440:4
malefactors of great w., 440:6
mere w., 439:2
production of w., 439:7
proper administration of w., 207:2
share our w., 520:2
those who produce all w., 99:2
Wealthy
never take a w. man on a jury (note), 350:3
Weasel words, 268:5 & note 363:1
WEATHER. See under NATURE.
Weather
everybody talks about the w. but, 472:6
in New England (note), 472:6
Weatherman
You don't need a w., 692:7
Weathermen
never know, 473:6
Weed
is a flower, 460:8
what is a w.?, 461:4
WEEHAWKEN (N.J.), 148
Welfare of the people, 436:1
Well
'tis w., 366:1
when the well's dry, 688:2
Well done
a thing w. d., 2:2
Well-dressed, 254:4
Wernher von Braun. See Von Braun.
WEST, THE, 714
West
ain't no law w. of St. Louis, 714:3
definition of term "W.", 714:1
everything in the W. is on a grander scale, 716 :1
go w., young man, 714:4
history of the colonization of the Great W., 715 :6
is hope's native home, 716:6
new states of the W., 422:2
no law w. of St. Louis, 714:3
that's where the W. begins, 715 :7
there is no more W., 716 :8
the true W., 716:5
to the W., to the W., 715 :3
Western
folk of the w. prairies (note), 474:6
humor, 715 :8
inventions, 716:6
settlements & democracy, 422:1
thronged to the w. wilds, 715 :5